Financial
Statement
Analysis

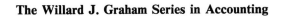

The Willard J. Graham Series in Accounting

FINANCIAL STATEMENT ANALYSIS

Theory, Application, and Interpretation

LEOPOLD A. BERNSTEIN, Ph.D., C.P.A.

Professor of Accounting
Bernard M. Baruch College
The City University of New York

 1983 • Third Edition

RICHARD D. IRWIN, INC.
Homewood, Illinois 60430

Material from Uniform CPA Examination Questions and Unofficial Answers,
copyright © 1958, 1966, 1973, 1974, 1975, 1976, 1978, 1979, 1980, 1981,
1982 by the American Institute of Certified Public Accountants, Inc.,
is reprinted (or adapted) with permission.

ISBN 0-256-02586-X

Library of Congress Catalog Card No. 82–84392

Printed in the United States of America

5 6 7 8 9 0 K 0 9 8 7 6 5

To
University Distinguished Professor Emeritus

EMANUEL SAXE

Teacher, Colleague, Friend

Preface

The major objective of this third edition, as was that of preceding editions, is to present a comprehensive and up-to-date treatment of the analysis of financial statements as an aid to decision making. While financial statement analysis serves many and varied purposes, its major usefulness is in making investing and lending decisions. Such decisions, and the actions to which they lead, are, of course, at the heart of the free market system.

Investing and lending decisions require the application of thorough analysis to carefully evaluated data. They require, moreover, the ability to forecast— to foresee. Sound information is obtained by an *understanding* of the data from which it is derived as well as by the application of tools of analysis to aid in its extraction and evaluation. Foresight, which is essential to the assessment of opportunity and risk, is also rooted in understanding: understanding of the elements comprising the data and of the factors that can change them. The common denominator is understanding. Alfred North Whitehead assured us that foresight can be taught when he wrote: "Foresight depends upon understanding. In practical affairs it is a habit. But the habit of foreseeing is elicited by the habit of understanding. To a large extent, understanding can now be acquired by a conscious effort and it can be taught. Thus the training of foresight is by the medium of understanding."

Organization of this work

The keynote of this work, thus, is understanding. It focuses on understanding the data which are analyzed as well as the methods by which they are analyzed and interpreted.

Part I is concerned with the relationship between the disciplines of financial analysis and accounting. First it examines the objectives of the users of financial statements. It then explores the objectives of accounting and the conventions accountants have adopted for their achievement. It concludes with an overview of analytical tools and techniques in common use.

Part II is devoted to an in-depth analysis of financial statements, and of the bases which underlie their preparation. A thorough understanding of the processes of income determination and of asset and liability measurement, as well as the distortions to which these may be subject, is an essential prerequisite to the intelligent analysis of financial data. These and other topics, such as the effects of price-level changes and the significance of the audit function, are examined here from the point of view of their implications to the user of financial statements. Analytical tools designed to shed light on the impact of alternative accounting methods are also emphasized.

Part III examines the processes and the methodology of financial statement analysis. The focus here is on the major objectives of users of financial statements and on the analytical tools and techniques applied by them in reaching significant conclusions and decisions. The analysis and evaluation of financial data are time-consuming and demanding tasks. Considering the importance of the decisions based thereon, however, and the magnitude of the resources that may be committed as a result, a painstaking job of analysis and evaluation is essential. Thorough analysis not only removes, to some degree, the great uncertainties inherent in investing and lending decisions, but also imparts to the decision maker a degree of confidence which is an essential precondition to timely and decisive action.

Since the ultimate decisions here must be quantified—that is, expressed, for example, in terms of the price of a stock or the amount of a loan— Part III emphasizes the need to link qualitative judgments to as many factors that lend themselves to quantification as is possible.

Major users of this work

This book should prove of value to all those who need a thorough understanding of the uses to which financial statements are put as well as to those who must know how to use them intelligently and effectively. This encompasses *accountants, security analysts, lending officers, credit analysts, managers,* and all others who must make decisions on the basis of financial data. Teachers in this area should likewise benefit greatly from its use.

Accountants should benefit from this book in two major ways:

1.   The primary justification of the accounting function is decision usefulness. By obtaining a full appreciation of the uses to which the end product of their work is put, accountants will be in a better position to improve upon it and to make it more responsive to the needs of users of financial statements.

2.   Primarily because the analysis of financial statements demands a thorough understanding of how and on what bases financial statements are constructed, accountants have often been called upon to aid in their analysis and interpretation. The study of the tools and techniques of financial statement analysis will open to the accountant important opportunities for the creative extension of his or her basic services into areas which are often as intellectually satisfying as they are financially rewarding.

Security analysts, lending officers, credit analysts, and investors, as well as others with financial responsibilities will find in this work a discussion of accounting concepts and measurements undertaken from their point of view as users of such data. The essential tools of the ingenious double-entry accounting system, such as the journal entry and the T-account, here are converted into primary useful tools for the analyst by means of which he or she can recapture the reality imbedded in published financial statements. Following this, in Part III, analysts will learn how knowledge of the accounting framework is integrated with the best tools and techniques available for the analysis and interpretation of financial statements.

Teachers of financial statement analysis will find that the organization and coverage of this work treats the subject matter of the field comprehensively and in depth and goes far beyond the superficial treatment often accorded to it. The constant link to published financial statements imparts a sense of reality that promotes understanding and learning. The book offers the instructor in this subject enough challenging material of substance to form the basis for courses in this area on both the undergraduate and the graduate levels of study. The instructor's manual provided with the book contains further specific suggestions on the organization of different course levels by chapter and subject matter.

THE THIRD EDITION

This edition brings into sharper focus the knowledge and skills required for the intelligent analysis of financial statements.

The first requirement clearly is the ability to read and understand a modern set of published financial statements and to comprehend complex financial communications. Part II covers the conceptual knowledge as well as analytical techniques needed for this task. Practical illustrations which draw on a comprehensive set of financial statements found in Appendix 4B have been expanded considerably. Extensive experience has shown that the use of published financial statements as principal teaching cases greatly heightens students' interest and participation while contributing to learning, to intellectual challenge, and to satisfaction.

The second major requirement is the ability to apply appropriate tools and techniques to the analysis and interpretation of financial statements. Here again numerous illustrations refer to and draw on the central set of financial statements presented in Appendix 4B.

Appendixes which follow the various chapters are designed to increase the flexibility of instructors in adding or deleting course material as well as varying its complexity. Generally, undergraduate courses will proceed from an assumption of a certain minimum background knowledge of accounting and then concentrate on the principal tools and techniques of financial statement analysis. Graduate courses should generally spend more time on an in-depth understanding of financial statements and communications as a step preceding the application of analytical tools and techniques. The instructor's manual contains additional suggestions for the organization of courses in financial statement analysis.

A major objective of this revision is to preserve and enhance those features of this work which have proved to be most valuable to its users and to update and improve that which experience indicates needed improvement. The valuable feedback provided by students, colleagues, and other users of the previous editions have greatly aided in this task. Also of considerable help was my continuing experience in using these materials to teach graduate and undergraduate accounting students, professional security analysts, bank loan officers, bond rating agency analysts, and others. Valuable feedback of other users ranged from those using this work in finance and investment courses or for purposes of CPA examination review, to those using it in the training of Chartered Life Underwriters and the teaching of Ph.D. candidates. Use of this work as a basis for expert testimony has also led to important improvements.

This revision reflects a comprehensive updating of all authoritative pronouncements on accounting and auditing standards and practices as well as the valuable suggestions of practicing financial analysts, credit analysts, and other users of financial data.

Numerous useful comments and suggestions by fellow educators have resulted in many modifications which are motivated by pedagogical considerations. The chapters on objectives of users of financial statements, objectives of accounting, the statement of changes in funds or cash, accounting for price changes, the analysis of capital structure and long-term solvency, and the analysis of results of operations have undergone considerable change. Many modifications and new illustrations have been provided throughout, new problems have been added, and existing problem material has been revised, enhanced, and expanded. An important feature is the use of comprehensive annual reports as the basis of questions and problems for most chapters. Also included are a significant number of problems taken from past examinations given by the Institute of Chartered Financial Analysts and by the American Institute of Certified Public Accountants whose permission to use these materials is hereby gratefully acknowledged.

ACKNOWLEDGMENTS

In performing the research for and the writing of this and the prior editions I was fortunate to benefit from the encouragement, help, and suggestions of many colleagues, professional associates, and students. University Distinguished Professor Emeritus Emanuel Saxe, a teacher, an esteemed colleague, and friend to whom this book is affectionately dedicated, has read the entire original manuscript as well as many revised parts of it and has made numerous valuable suggestions. To me the thoroughness of his review served as a shining example of the kind of dedicated effort a professional approach to financial statement analysis demands.

Deserving special mention for extensive and especially valuable comments are the following: My friend and coauthor on another work, Professor Calvin Engler, whose thoroughly professional review of this edition has provided many valuable comments. My associate for many years, Professor Jon A. Stroble, a skillful and outstanding trainer of bank loan officers from which association this book has benefited in many ways. Where possible I have given him specific credit, but many other areas—far too numerous to mention—have also benefited from his constructive suggestions and contributions. William C. Norby, an outstanding and leading financial analyst, who has read important portions of this revision and provided many insights as well as very valuable comments and suggestions.

Many other professionals have read portions of this work in its various editions. Professional debt or equity security analysts who have read portions of this work and made valuable suggestions include Gerald White of Grace & White, Inc.; Kenneth Alterman, Hyman C. Grossman, Richard Huff, and Robert J. Mebus of Standard & Poor's Corporation; Clyde Bartter, Portfolio Advisory Company; Michael A. Hyland, First Boston Corporation; David Norr, First Manhattan Corporation; Thornton L. O'Glove, the *Quality of Earnings Report;* Frances Stone, Merrill Lynch, Pierce, Fenner & Smith, Inc.; Jack L. Treynor, lately of Treynor-Arbit Associates; and Dr. Neil Weiss of Jon Stroble & Associates, Ltd.

Appreciation is also due to Fred Spindel, partner of Coopers & Lybrand; Robert Mednick, partner of Arthur Andersen; and Paul Rosenfield of the American Institute of Certified Public Accountants, for valuable comments on specific chapters.

My present and past colleagues at the City University of New York— Abraham J. Briloff, Martin Mellman, William T. Baxter, Douglas Carmichael, Peter M. Gutman, Peter Lloyd Davis, Hugo Nurnberg, Stanley C. W. Salvary, and Reed Storey—have read portions of this work and contributed valuable comments and suggestions; while Martin Benis, John Liapakis, Steven Lillien, and Harold Witner have contributed valuable comments as a result of class use of the book. Especially valuable assistance was provided by my former graduate assistant and present colleague Mostafa Maksy.

Other colleagues in academe who provided valuable comments and suggestions include Robert N. Anthony, Harvard University; Hector R. Anton, New York University; Rashad Abdel-Khalik of The University of Alberta; Terry Arndt and John Gentis, Ball State University; Shyam Bhandari of Bradley University; Fred Bien and Vince Brenner, Louisiana State University; Garry Bulmash, American University; Philip Chuey, Youngstown State University; Philip Gerdin, University of New Haven; Edwin Grossnickle, Western Michigan University; Eric S. Emory, Sacred Heart University; J. Larry Hagler, Mississippi State University; Yong-Ha Hyon, Temple University;

Henry Jaenicke, Drexel University; Homer Kripke, New York University; Russ Langer, San Francisco State University; Burton T. Lefkowitz, C. W. Post College; Jerrold Weiss, Lehman College; Richard F. Williams, Wright State University; Philip Wolitzer, Long Island University; and Stephen Zeff, Rice University.

Graduate assistants who provided valuable assistance include Ahmed El-zayaty, Tae-Whan Cho, Barbara Loveman, and Anne Kaplan. Outstanding typing service was performed by Mrs. Dorothy Conklin.

Finally, I wish to express appreciation to my wife Cynthia for valuable editorial help, to my daughter Debbie and to my son Jeffrey for earlier assistance with indexing, and to my mother Jeanette, as well as to Cynthia, for their patience and understanding over the many years during which the successive editions of this work were being written and revised, and for having provided me with the inspiration that helped bring them to a successful completion.

I earnestly solicit comments, suggestions, and constructive criticism from interested educators, professional financial and credit analysts, accountants, and other users in the hope that I shall be able to continue the unending task of improving this work.

Leopold A. Bernstein

Contents

PART II

FINANCIAL STATEMENTS—THE RAW MATERIAL OF ANALYSIS

on income. *Capital versus operating lease—the effect on funds. Implications for analysis.* "Off balance sheet" financing. Liabilities under the pension plans: *Implications for analysis.* Liabilities at the "edge" of equity. Deferred credits (income): *Deferred taxes. Deferred investment tax credit.* Minority interest: *Implications for analysis.* Reserves and provisions. Accounting for contingencies: *Implications for analysis.* Commitments. Contingent liabilities. Implications for analysis—assessing uncertainties.

Classification of capital stock: *Disclosure regarding capital stock. Additional capital. Treasury stock.* Retained earnings: *Dividends. Prior period adjustments. Appropriations of retained earnings. Restrictions on retained earnings.* Book value per share: *Significance of book value.* Implications for analysis.

Intercorporate investments: *Consolidated financial statements. The equity method. The cost method. Example of difference in income recognition—equity versus cost method. Intercorporate investments—less than majority ownership. Implications for analysis. Unconsolidated subsidiaries.* Accounting for business combinations: *Reasons for mergers. Distortions in accounting for mergers. Accounting for business combinations: Two methods.* Revised opinions on accounting for business combinations: *Pooling of interests and purchase accounting compared. Illustration of accounting mechanics: Purchase versus pooling of interest accounting. Pooling accounting. Purchase accounting. Implications for analysis. Pooling versus purchase accounting. Purchase accounting.* Accounting for foreign operations: *Foreign accounting practices and auditing standards. Translation of foreign currencies. Evolution of the accounting for foreign exchange translation. Major provisions of SFAS 52. Illustration of the translation procedure. Accounting for investment by parent company. Accounting where an investment in subsidiary is sold or liquidated. Disclosure requirements.* Implications for analysis.

A simple illustration. A variety of concepts of income. The accrual of revenue: *Conditions for revenue recognition. Uncertainty as to collection of receivables. Revenue recognition when right of return exists. Accounting for franchise fee revenue. Product financing arrangements. Transfers of receivables with recourse. Timing of revenue recognition. Contract accounting. Finance company accounting. When should the recording of interest income be discontinued. Accounting for lease income. "Sales" to leasing subsidiaries. Additional examples of income recognition problems. Income of subsidiaries and affiliates. Implications for analysis.* Cost and expense accrual: *Depreciation and depletion. Factors influencing the rate of depreciation. Implication for analysis.* Analytical measures of plant age. Misconceptions regarding the nature of depreciation.

Pension costs and other supplementary employee benefits: *Pension costs. Other supplementary employee benefits. Implications for analysis.* Research, exploration, and development outlays: *Types of research and development. The accounting problem. FASB Statement 2. Implications for analysis. Exploration and development in extractive industries.* Implications for analysis. Goodwill: *Implications for analysis.* Other intangible asset write-offs. Interest costs: *Interest capitalization. Implications for analysis.* Income taxes: *Permanent income tax differences. Timing differences. Treatment of tax loss carry-backs and carry-forwards. Accounting for income taxes by oil and gas producers. SEC disclosure requirements. Investment tax credit. Implications for analysis. Analytical significance of the SEC disclosure requirements.* Extraordinary gains and losses: *Cross currents of theory—the case of debt retirements. Discontinued operations. Implications for analysis.* Accounting changes: *Change in accounting principle. Change in accounting estimate. Change in reporting entity. Correction of an error. Materiality. Historical summaries of financial information. Implications for analysis.* The income statement—implications for analysis, an overview.

constant-dollar accounting. General versus specific price changes: *Monetary gains and losses. Effects of inflation.* Analytical considerations in the use of current cost accounting. Efforts to integrate CDA with CCA. **Appendix 14A:** The roll-forward procedure. **Appendix 14B:** Illustration of the minimum disclosure requirements of SFAS 33. **Appendix 14C:** Illustration of accounting for a transaction using four reporting frameworks.

What the analyst needs to know: *Knowing the auditor. What the auditor's opinion means.* The auditor's report: *The scope of the audit. The opinion section. "Fair presentation." Modification of the opinion.* Circumstances giving rise to qualifications, disclaimers, or adverse opinions. Qualifications—"except for" and "subject to." Adverse opinions. Disclaimer of opinion: *Adverse opinions versus disclaimers of opinion.* The form of the report. Limitations in the scope of the audit. Failure of financial statements to conform to generally accepted accounting principles. Financial statements subject to unresolved known uncertainties. Exceptions as to consistency. Special reports. Reports on "compiled" and "reviewed" financial statements. The SEC's important role. Implications for analysis: *Implications inherent in the audit process. Audit risk and its implications. Implications stemming from the standards that govern the auditor's opinion. Qualification, disclaimers, and adverse opinions.*

PART III

FINANCIAL STATEMENT ANALYSIS—THE MAIN AREAS OF EMPHASIS

Significance of short-term liquidity. Working capital: *Current assets. Current liabilities. Other problem areas in definition of current assets and liabilities. Working capital as a measure of liquidity.* Current ratio: *Limitations of the current ratio. Implications of the limitations to which the current ratio is subject. The current ratio as a valid tool of analysis. Measures that supplement the current ratio. Measures of accounts receivable liquidity.* Average accounts receivable turnover ratio: *Collection period for accounts receivable. Evaluation.* Measures of inventory turnover: *Inventory turnover ratio. Days to sell inventory. The effect of alternative methods of inventory management.* Current liabilities: *Differences in the "nature" of current liabilities. Days purchases in accounts payable ratio.* Interpretation of the current ratio: *Examination of trend. Interpretation of changes over time. Possibilities of manipulation. The use of "rules of thumb" standards. The net trade cycle. Valid working capital standards. The importance of sales. Common-size anaylsis of current asset composition. The liquidity index.* Acid-test ratio. Other measures of short-term liquidity: *Funds flow ratios. Cash flow related measures.* The concept of financial flexibility. Management's discussion and analysis: *Projecting changes in conditions or policies.*

Overview of cash flow and funds flow patterns. Short-term cash forecasts: *Importance of sales estimates. Pro forma financial statements as an aid to forecasting.*

Techniques of short-term cash forecasting. Differences between short-term and long-term forecasts. Analysis of statements of changes in financial position. Illustration of the analysis of statements of changes in financial position. The analytically recast statement of changes in financial position. Evaluation of the statement of changes in financial position. Projection of statements of changes in financial position. Illustration of a projection of statements of changes in financial position: *The impact of adversity. The funds flow adequacy ratio. Funds reinvestment ratio.*

Key elements in the evaluation of long-term solvency. Importance of capital structure. Accounting principles: *Deferred taxes. Long-term leases. Off-balance sheet financing. Liabilities for pensions. Unconsolidated subsidiaries. Provisions, reserves, and contingent liabilities. Minority interests. Convertible debt. Preferred stock.* Adjustments to the book value of assets: *Inventories. Marketable securities. Intangible assets.* The significance of capital structure. Reasons for the employment of debt: *The concept of financial leverage. The effect of tax deductibility of interest. Other advantages of leverage. Measuring the effect of financial leverage.* Measuring the effect of capital structure on long-term solvency. Long-term projections—usefulness and limitations. Capital structure analysis—common-size statements. Capital structure ratios. Total debt to total capital (debt and equity): *Ratio of total debt to total equity capital. Long-term debt/equity capital. Confusion in terminology. Short-term debt. Equity capital at market value.* Preferred stock within the capital structure. The analytically adjusted ratio of debt to equity. Interpretation of capital structure measures. Measures of assets distribution. Critical importance of "earning power." Measures of earnings coverage: *Earnings available to meet fixed charges. Fixed charges to be included. Income tax adjustment of fixed charges. Other elements to be included in fixed charges.* Ratio of earnings to fixed charges: *Illustration of earnings-coverage ratio calculations. Ratio of earnings to fixed charges—expanded concept of fixed charges.* Pro forma computations of coverage ratios. Funds flow coverage of fixed charges: *Other useful tests of funds flow relationships.* Stability of "flow of funds from operations." Earnings coverage of preferred dividends. Evaluation of earnings-coverage ratios: *Importance of earnings variability. Importance of method of computation and of underlying assumptions.* **Appendix 18A:** The rating of debt obligations. **Appendix 18B:** Ratios as predictors of business failure. **Appendix 18C:** Illustration of the computation of the analytically adjusted debt-to-equity ratio.

Diverse views of performance. Criteria of performance evaluation. Importance of return on investment (ROI). Major objectives in the use of ROI: *An indicator of managerial effectiveness. A measure of enterprise ability to earn a satisfactory ROI. A method of projecting earnings. Internal decision and control tool.* Basic elements of ROI: *Defining the investment base.* Book versus market values in the investment base: *Difference between investor's cost and enterprise investment base. Averaging the investment base. Relating income to the investment base.* Adjusting the components of the ROI formula: *Analysis and interpretation of ROI.* Analysis of asset utilization: *Evaluation of individual turnover ratios. Use of averages. Other factors to be considered in return on asset evaluation. Return on shareholders' equity.* Analysis of return on common stockholders' equity (ROCSE): *Equity growth rate. Analysis of financial leverage effects.*

The significance of income statement analysis. The major objectives of income analysis: *What is the relevant net income of the enterprise?* Analysis of components of the income statement: *Accounting standards used and their implication. Tools of income statement analysis.* The analysis of sales and revenues: *Major sources of revenue.* Financial reporting by diversified enterprises: *Reasons for the need for data by significant enterprise segments. Disclosure of "line of business" data. Income statement data. Balance sheet data. Research studies. Statement of Financial Accounting Standards 14. SEC reporting requirements. Implications for analysis.* Stability and trend of revenues. Management's discussion and analysis of financial condition and results of operations. Implications for analysis: Methods of revenue recognition and measurement.

Analysis of cost of sales. Gross profit: *Factors in the analysis of gross profit.* Analysis of changes in gross margin. Example of analysis of change in gross margin: *Interpretation of changes in gross margin.* Break-even analysis: *Concepts underlying break-even analysis. Equation approach. Graphic presentation. Contribution margin approach. Pocket calculator problem—additional considerations. Break-even technique—problem areas and limitations. Break-even analysis—uses and their implications. Analytical implications of break-even analysis. The significance of the variable-cost percentage. The significance of the fixed-cost level. First break-even situation. Second break-even situation—20 percent increase in fixed costs. The importance of the contribution margin.* Additional considerations in the analysis of cost of sales. Depreciation. Amortization of special tools and similar costs. Maintenance and repairs costs. Other costs and expenses—general: *Selling expenses.* Bad debt expenses: *Future directed marketing costs.* General, administration, financial, and other expenses: *Financial costs. "Other" expenses.* Other income. Income taxes. Analysis of income tax disclosures: *Objectives of the analysis. Analytical steps and techniques. Illustrations of income tax analysis of Alfa, Inc. Focus on pretax earnings.* The operating ratio. Net income ratio: *Statement accounting for variation in net income.*

Objectives of earnings evaluation. Evaluation of the quality of earnings: *The concept of earnings quality. Balance sheet analysis as a check on the validity and quality of reported earnings.* Evaluation of the earnings level and trend: *Factors affecting the level of earnings. The analytical recasting and adjustment of income statements. The recasting and adjusting procedure. The adjustment process. Determining the trend of income over the years. Income smoothing and income distortion. Income smoothing and income distortion—some implications for analysis. Extraordinary gains and losses.* The forecasting of earnings: *Can earnings be forecast? SEC disclosure requirements—aid to forecasting. Elements in earnings forecasts. Publication of financial forecasts.* The concept of earnings power: *Earning power time horizon. Adjustment of reported earnings per share.*

Monitoring performance and results: *Interim financial statements. APB Opinion 28. SEC interim reporting requirements. Implications for analysis.*

The methodology of financial statement analysis. Significance of the "building block" approach to financial analysis. The earmarks of good financial analysis. Special industry or environmental characteristics. Illustration of a comprehensive analysis of financial statements—Marine Supply Corporation: *Introduction. Financial statements. Additional information. Analysis of short-term liquidity. Cash from operations. Analysis of funds flow. Analysis of capital structure and long-term solvency. Analysis of return on investment. Analysis of asset utilization. Analysis of operating performance. Summary and conclusions.* Uses of financial statement analysis.

PART I

Financial statement
analysis and the
accounting framework

1

Objectives of financial statement analysis

THE NATURE OF FINANCIAL ANALYSIS

The process of financial statement analysis consists of the application of analytical tools and techniques to financial statements and data in order to derive from them measurements and relationships that are significant and useful for decision making. Thus, financial statement analysis, first and foremost, serves the essential function of converting *data,* of which, in this age of the computer, there are a bewildering quantity and variety, into useful information, which is always in scarce supply.

The processes of financial analysis can be described in various ways, depending on the objectives to be attained. Thus, financial analysis can be used as a preliminary *screening* tool in the selection of investments or merger candidates. It can be used as a *forecasting* tool of future financial conditions and results. It may be used as a process of *diagnosis* of managerial, operating, or other problem areas. It can serve as a tool in the *evaluation* of management. Above all, financial analysis reduces reliance on pure hunches, guesses, and intuition, and this reduces and narrows the inevitable areas of uncertainty that attend all decision-making processes. Financial analysis does not lessen the need for judgment but rather establishes a sound and systematic basis for its rational application.

APPROACHES TO THE SUBJECT

There are a number of possible approaches to a discussion of the tools and techniques of financial analysis. One way, popularly employed in most books on the subject, is to describe the analysis of specific financial statements, such as balance sheets, without a concurrent emphasis of objectives to be attained. The approach employed here will be to examine the processes of

3

financial statement analysis with emphasis on the major objectives (see Chapter 4, "Building blocks of financial statement analysis") that they are designed to achieve. In order to do this, we turn first to an examination of the information needs and the specific analytical objectives of the most important categories of users of financial data, namely:

Credit grantors.
Equity investors.
Management.
Acquisition and merger analysts.
Auditors.
Other interested groups.

Objectives of credit grantors

Credit grantors are lenders of funds to an enterprise. Funds are lent in many forms and for a variety of purposes.

Trade creditors usually extend very short-term credit. They ship goods or provide services and expect payment within the customary period that forms the terms of trade in their industry. Most trade credit ranges from 30 to 60 days, with cash discounts occasionally allowed for specified earlier payment. The trade creditor does not usually receive interest for an extension of credit. The trade creditor's reward takes the form of the business acquired and the possible profit that flows from it.

An enterprise receives other short-term and longer-term credit or loans from a variety of sources. Short-term credit is often provided by various sources but mainly by banks. Longer-term credit is provided by banks in the form of term loans and by financial institutions, such as insurance companies, through their purchase of bonds or notes or through private placements. Companies also obtain longer-term funds through the public sale of notes or bonds in the securities markets. Leasing and conditional sales are other forms of long-term financing. The sale of convertible, and generally subordinated, bonds combines the borrowing of money with the added feature of an option to the lender to exchange his or her claim for an equity interest should the lender find it profitable to do so. Similarly, the issuance of preferred stock, which is senior to the common equity but junior to debt, combines the fixed reward features of a loan with the absence of definite principal repayment requirements that characterize equity securities.

One outstanding characteristic of all pure credit extension relationships is the fixed nature of the rewards accruing to the credit grantor. Thus, should the enterprise prosper, the credit grantor will still be limited to his or her contractually fixed rate of interest, or to the profit on the goods supplied. However, should the enterprise incur losses or meet other adversities, the credit grantor's principal may be placed in jeopardy. This uneven nature of the lender's risk-reward ratio has a major effect on the lender's point of view and on the manner in which he or she analyzes the possibilities of credit extension.

The difference in the point of view of the lenders as compared to that of the equity investor results in differences in the way they analyze future prospects and in the objectives they seek. The equity investor looks for reward primarily to future prospects of earnings and to changes in those earnings. The credit grantor, on the other hand, is concerned primarily with specific security provisions of his or her loan, such as the fair market value of assets pledged; and for repayment of principal and interest, the credit grantor looks to the existence of resources and the projections of future flows of funds and the reliability and stability of such flows. Lenders differ in their abilities to obtain supplementary financial information from borrowers. Equity investors, as a result of the theoretically unlimited nature of their rewards, may be receptive to highly abstract descriptions of "concepts," potentials, and future probabilities. Lenders, on the other hand, require a more definite link between the projections of the future and the resources already at hand as well as the demonstrated ability to achieve operating results. Thus, credit grantors generally are more conservative in their outlook and approach and rely on financial statement analysis to an even greater extent than do equity investors, for it serves to reassure them regarding the borrower's demonstrated ability to control the flow of funds and to maintain a sound financial condition under a variety of economic and operating circumstances. The more speculative the loan, the more similar are the lender's analytical approaches to those of the equity investor.

The techniques of financial statement analysis used by lenders as well as the criteria of evaluation used by them vary with the term, the security, and the purpose of the loan.

In the case of short-term credit extension, the credit grantor is concerned primarily with the current financial condition, the liquidity of the current assets, and the rate of their turnover. These considerations are covered in Chapter 16.

The evaluation of longer-term loans, which includes the valuation of bonds, requires a far more detailed and forward-looking inquiry and analysis. Such an analysis includes projections of cash flows and fund flows and the evaluation of the longer-term earning power of the enterprise as the ultimate source of assurance of an enterprise's ability to meet the fixed charges arising from its debt as well as from its other commitments under a variety of economic conditions. This subject is examined in Chapter 18.

Since the profitability of an enterprise is a major element in the lender's security, the analysis of profitability is an important criterion to the credit grantor. Profit is viewed as the primary source for interest payments and as a desirable source of principal repayment.

Credit analysis, whether long term or short term, is concerned with capital structure because it has a bearing on risk and on the creditor's margin of safety. The relationship of equity capital to debt is an indicator of the adequacy of equity capital and of the cushion against loss that it provides. This relationship also reflects on the attitude of management toward risk and influences the income coverage of fixed charges.

Lenders, and bankers among them, generally look at asset values in the context of the going-concern assumption. Clearly, the assumption of liquidation would often lead to realizable values of assets that would generally be lower than those stated in accordance with generally accepted accounting principles (GAAP). For this reason, bankers tend to attach very conservative values to fixed and other assets, and to make allowance for all possible future contingencies.

Objectives of equity investors

The equity interest in an enterprise is the supplier of its basic risk capital. The capital is exposed to all the risks of ownership and provides a cushion or shield for the preferred or loan capital that is senior to it. This is why the equity interest is referred to as the *residual* interest. In the course of normal operations as a going concern, this residual interest may receive distributions (dividends) only after the prior claims of senior security holders for bond interest and/or preferred dividends have been satisfied. In liquidation, it has a claim only to what remains *after* the prior claims of creditors and preferred stockholders have been met. Thus, when an enterprise prospers, the equity owners stand to reap all the gains above the fixed amount of senior capital contributors' claims and, conversely, the equity owners will be the first ones to absorb losses should the enterprise flounder.

From the above it is clear that the information needs of equity investors are among the most demanding and comprehensive of all users of financial data. Their interests in an enterprise, of which they own a share, are the broadest because their interest is affected by all aspects and phases of operations, profitability, financial condition, and capital structure.

Common stock valuation. The valuation of common stock is a complex procedure involving, in addition to financial statement analysis, an assessment of such factors as the general state of the economy, industry position, competitive stance, and the quality of management. Since the most thorough and sophisticated analysis and evaluation of equity securities, for the purpose of deciding whether to buy, sell, or hold, is performed by professional security analysts, their point of view will be examined here.

A common stockholder, having no legal claim to a definite dividend or to a capital distribution, looks for three principal rewards from his or her holdings: current dividends, special distributions such as rights, and a market value of the security at a given time in the future that will, hopefully, result in a capital gain. The most important determinant of both dividends and market values is earnings. Current earnings, which are the basic source of dividends and the accumulation of undistributed earnings, as well as the earnings record, current and prospective, are major elements in the determination of the market price of the common stock.

Approaches to common stock valuation. The basis of most modern stock valuation techniques and models is present value theory. This approach, first set forth in detail by John B. Williams,[1] maintains that the present value of a share of stock is equal to the sum of all dividends expected to be received from it, discounted to the present at an appropriate rate of interest. The difficulty here, of course, as in all other approaches based on this theory, is the estimation of such future distributions.[2] What is clear, however, is the fact that all expected distributions, be they of a current dividend or of a liquidation residual nature, are based largely on earnings and the earning power of assets.

Security valuation models used by security analysts bear out the proposition that earnings, and particularly estimated future earnings, are the most important determinant of the value of common shares.

Graham, Dodd, and Cottle emphasized the importance of earnings as follows:

> The standard method of valuation of individual enterprises consists of capitalizing the expected future earnings and/or dividends at an appropriate rate of return. The average earnings will be estimated for a period running ordinarily between five and ten years.[3]

Most common stock valuation models incorporate earnings growth and earnings payout ratios as factors of prime importance.

The normal procedure in dynamic models is to state the price of a stock as the present value of a growing stream of dividends with each component of this stream discounted at the rate k. One of the best-known dynamic stock valuation models presented in recent years is that by Gordon and Shapiro. Assume that $E(t)$ are the earnings of an enterprise at time t, b is the dividend payout ratio, k is the market discount rate (the cost of capital), and g is the projected annual growth rate in earnings. The valuation formula for the company's justified market price V (intrinsic value) is:

$$V = \frac{bE(t)}{k - g}$$

---

[1] *The Theory of Investment Value* (Cambridge, Mass: Harvard University Press, 1938).

[2] The importance of expected distributions is largely responsible for the focus on cash (or funds) flow. However, so far, most valuation models have not concerned themselves with the purchasing power equivalent of such cash flows, a consideration that looms large in times of price-level changes. Thus, a security represents a contingent claim not only because of the uncertain outcome of future events but also (including here a "riskless" bond) because of an uncertain command over future goods and services. For a further discussion of these issues, see Chapter 14.

[3] *Security Analysis* (New York: McGraw-Hill, 1962), p. 435.

The above formula reduces long and awkward statements to more manageable but nevertheless mathematically equivalent terms. It states in effect that the market value V is equal to the current dividend discounted at a rate $k - g$, i.e.,

$$V = \frac{\text{Current dividend rate}}{\text{Discount rate} - \text{Growth rate}}$$

The elegance and the simplicity of the above formula should not obscure the fact that the most critical element in this or similar approaches to equity valuation is the valid quantification of the variables or inputs themselves. The more conventional approach by practitioners in the field of security analysis is to value a security by multiplying its earnings, which are really a surrogate for present and future dividends, by a *price-earnings ratio*[4] that is usually an imprecise expression of their assessment of external economic factors as well as of the growth prospects, financial strengths, capital structure, and other risk factors associated with the enterprise.

The similarity of the present value models of common stock valuation to the conventional method of bond valuation is quite obvious. In the case of bonds, the value, or proper purchase price, is calculated by discounting each coupon and the ultimate principal repayment to present value at a discount rate equal to the desired yield. In the case of growth stock valuations, the expected dividend corresponds to the bond coupon and the assumed market price of the stock at the model target date corresponds to the repayment of bond principal at maturity date.

The similarity of the bond and stock valuation models under these theories has led Molodovsky and others to construct stock valuation tables that can be used in a fashion similar to the use of bond tables.[5] The formula used by them for the value *(V)* of a stock is:

$$V = D_0 + \frac{D_1}{1+k} + \frac{D_2}{(1+k)^2} + \cdots + \frac{D_n}{(1+k)^n} + \cdots$$

where:

D_0 is the dividend initially.
D_n is the dividend in the nth year.
k is the discount rate, or the desired rate of return.

The model does not include a residual market value of the stock (similar to bond principal to be repaid) because it assumes dividend projections taken out to infinity. With regard to the latter, the authors assure us that because the discount factor becomes so large in the distant future, these increments

---

[4] Expressed in terms of the foregoing Gordon-Shapiro formula, the price-earnings ratio (P/E) can be stated as follows:

$$\text{P/E} = \frac{b}{k-g}$$

Thus, for example, if the dividend payout ratio *(b)* changes, so would the P/E ratio.

[5] N. Molodovsky, C. May, and S. Chottiner, "Common Stock Valuation—Principles, Tables, and Application," *Financial Analysts Journal,* March–April 1965.

to value become negligible. It is easy to bring the model closer in form to a bond model by assuming a specified sales price (realization of principal) at a specified date, but that price will itself depend on the application of the foregoing formula.

While we can readily understand why the stock valuation model builders have been attracted by the logic as well as the mathematical elegance of the bond valuation model, we must recognize the important differences that exist between the inputs required by the bond model as opposed to those required by the stock model. The focus on these differences is all the more important since the basic purpose of our discussion in this chapter is to relate the scope and the techniques of financial statement analysis to the purposes that they are designed to serve—in this instance, the valuation of equity securities.

In the case of bond valuation, the bond coupon is known and so is the amount of principal to be repaid at the maturity of the bond. Thus, as we saw in the section dealing with the objectives of credit grantors, the major questions to be considered are the *availability* of funds for the payment of interest and the repayment of principal. While the assessment of the probabilities of such availability of funds does involve the totality of enterprise prospects, the process of estimation is nevertheless less complex than the one involved in arriving at the proper parameters for the stock valuation model.

It should also be noted that there is a basic and important difference in the certainty of results that can be expected from an analysis of debt instruments (such as bonds) and those that can be expected from the analysis of equity securities. In the case of debt instruments, the results of the analysis depend almost entirely on a valid assessment of the borrower's ability to make timely payments of interest and principal. The relationship between analysis and the results achieved are far more complex in the case of equity securities. Thus, no matter how "right" the analyst is in assumptions and forecasts, a major part of the reward of that analysis, i.e., future capital values, depends on the perceptions of others. That is, on buyers agreeing with the analyst's conclusions and seeing things his or her way. No such dependence on validation by the marketplace exists in the case of results to be achieved from the analysis of debt instruments.

This difference, as well as the enormous complexities to which the analysis and evaluation of equity securities are subject, is in large part behind the skepticism with which many practicing security analysts treat those who attempt to compress the market reality into neat, streamlined, and elegant mathematical formulations.

Data required for stock valuation. Let us now consider the data that are required in order to quantify the factors present in most of the stock valuation models discussed above.

The expected dividend stream in the future is dependent on earnings and dividend payout policy. The latter depends on the company's financial condition, capital structure, and its need for funds both in the present and in the future.

The projection of future earnings (see Chapter 22) is always a complex process subject to varying degrees of uncertainty. The reported earnings must be evaluated and adjusted and, in turn, form the basis for projection. Unlike the bond coupon, which remains constant, the further into the future that earnings are projected, the more conjectural the estimates become.

The size of the discount factor that may properly be used in computing the present value of a future stream of dividends and residual interests depends to a significant extent on the risk involved. The risk reflects such factors as the stability of the industry, the past variability in earnings, and the leverage inherent in its capital structure.

No stock valuation formula has yet been devised and published that has proved to be an accurate forecaster of security market values under all conditions. Perhaps, the factors that bear on the determination of security values are too numerous and too complex for inclusion in a workable formula, and possibly not all such factors can be adequately measured, particularly because of the simplifying assumptions that are introduced in many such models.

Whatever method of stock valuation is used by the security analyst, be it either a simple short-term projection of earnings to be capitalized at a predetermined rate or a complex and sophisticated formula involving elegant mathematical techniques, the results can never reach a higher level of accuracy or be more reliable than the inputs used in such calculations. The reliability and the validity of these inputs, be they earnings projections, expected payout ratios, or various risk factors such as those inherent in capital structure, depend on the quality of the financial statement analysis performed.

The above view was best expressed by Douglas A. Hayes:

> Although the concept that investment results are likely to be heavily related to corporate performance in a long-term sense is generally accepted, some recent contributions to the field have alleged that the implementation methodology should be completely revolutionized. For example, Lerner and Carleton (*A Theory of Financial Analysis,* Harcourt, Brace, and World, Inc. New York: 1966, pp. 3–4) allege that a critical investigation of the past financial statements to reveal potential problems of consistency and comparability of reported income and balance sheet data can be largely discarded because accounting and disclosure standards have improved to the point where the underlying data require no critical review. Moreover, they allege that financial risk factors no longer require appraisal because of the greatly improved stability features of the economy; in lieu thereof, they suggest elegant mathematical techniques to develop the theoretical effects of assumed patterns of various management decisions and economic data on security values.
>
> However, the empirical evidence would suggest that these allegations are seriously in error.[6]

[6] "The Dimensions of Analysis: A Critical Review," *Financial Analysts Journal,* September–October 1966.

In short, while the goal of the analyst may be to go forward *from* the figures, a thorough job of the financial analysis requires that he also go *behind* the figures.[7] No present or prospective developments in the field of accountancy justify the assumption that this can be significantly changed in the near future (see also discussion at end of Chapter 3).

RECENT DEVELOPMENTS IN INVESTMENT THEORY

In recent years, the methods and approaches of practicing security analysts have come under repeated challenge by their academic counterparts who have developed a number of theories designed to provide insight into the overall investment process.

Portfolio theory

A pioneering contribution was that of Markowitz who addressed the problem of portfolio construction given analysts' estimates of possible future returns from securities.[8] He demonstrated that both risk and return must be considered, provided a formal framework for quantifying both and showed how the relationship among security risks and returns could be taken into account in portfolio construction.

He begins with the observation that the future return on a security can be estimated, and he equates risk with the variance of the distribution of returns. Markowitz demonstrated that under certain assumptions there is a linear relationship between risk and return. Using these variables, he provided a framework for deciding how much of each security to hold in constructing a portfolio. The two-dimensional risk-return approach offers the investor an ability to choose in the trade-off between risk and return.

Evaluation of risk and return

The relationship between the risk that must be accepted and the return that may be expected is central to all modern investing and lending decisions. It may seem obvious that the greater the perceived degree of risk of an investment or of a loan, the greater is the required rate of return to compensate for such risk.

Categories of risk

Risk is commonly associated with the uncertainty surrounding the outcome of future events. While many investors and lenders make subjective evalua-

---

[7] Author's note: Women have been analysts and auditors for years, and their numbers are growing. However, in this book, masculine pronouns are often being used for succinctness and are intended to refer to both males and females.

[8] H. Markowitz, "Portfolio Selection," *Journal of Finance,* March 1952, pp. 77–91.

tions of risk, academicians have developed statistical measures of risk that belong to the overall concept known as beta coefficient theory.

Under this theory, the total risk associated with an investment is composed of two elements:

1. *Systematic risk,* which is that portion of total risk attributable to the movement of the market as a whole.
2. *Unsystematic risk,* which is the residual risk that is unique to a specific security.

In the application of the theory, a quantitative expression of systematic risk (known as beta)[9] of one is attributed to the volatility of the market as a whole. The higher a security's beta, the greater will be its expected return. Treasury bills have a beta of zero because they are essentially riskless, i.e., they do not fluctuate with the market. A stock having a beta of 1.20 could rise or fall 20 percent faster than the market, while one having a beta of .90 would on average register market value changes 10 percent less in amplitude than those of the market as a whole. Thus, high beta stocks can expect high returns in a "bull market" and also larger than average declines during a "bear market."

Since by definition, unsystematic risk[10] is the *residual risk* that is unexplained by market movements, no unsystematic risk exists for the market as a whole and almost none exists in a highly diversified portfolio of stocks. Consequently, as portfolios become larger and more diversified, their unsystematic risk will approach zero.

Adherents to this theory hold that the market will not reward those exposing themselves to unsystematic risk that can be removed by proper diversification. They believe that the implication of the theory for common stock investors is to diversify, and if they expect the market to rise, to increase the beta of their portfolios and vice versa. Some experimental studies have indicated that between 30 and 50 percent of an individual stock's price is due to market (systematic) risk and that such influence reaches 85 to 90 percent in a well-diversified portfolio of 30 or more stocks.[11]

It follows that the portfolio manager who does not wish to rely only on market action for returns or who cannot forecast overall market action should

---

[9] Beta indexes are computed by use of regression analysis to relate the historical price movements of a stock to the movements of a general market price index such as the S&P 500 stock index. Alas, because of the ever-changing environment, capital structure, and operations of an enterprise, beta coefficients have exhibited a high degree of instability over time.

[10] A measure of unsystematic risk is alpha, which measures a stock's expected rate of return when the expected market rate of return is zero. Many academicians maintain that the expected alpha for a well-diversified portfolio is zero because the specific business circumstances that give rise to positive and negative alphas tend to cancel out in a portfolio of stocks. Practicing security analysts strive, however, to construct portfolios having positive alphas. In essence, alpha is derived from virtues in a stock that are not recognized by the market, thus resulting in returns above what beta would suggest.

[11] J. B. Cohen, E. D. Zinbarg, and A. Zeikel, *Investment Analysis and Portfolio Management,* 3d ed. (Homewood, Ill.: Richard D. Irwin, 1977), pp. 769–71.

seek nondiversification, i.e., exposure to the amount of unsystematic risk required for achieving the desired rate of return. Such a strategy would emphasize the analysis of individual securities, as discussed in this work, as opposed to overall portfolio risk balancing. Thus, reaping the rewards of exposure to nonsystematic risk is dependent on an ability to identify undervalued securities and on the proper assessment of their risk. (See discussion of efficient market hypothesis later in this chapter.)

Components of unsystematic risk

Those who want to obtain their rewards from exposure to unsystematic or nonmarket risk through the rigorous analysis of individual securities must focus on the various components of such risk. While those components are undoubtedly interrelated and subject to the influence of such elements of systematic risk as overall political, economic, and social factors, they can nevertheless be usefully classified as follows:

Economic risk reflects risks of the overall economic environment in which the enterprise operates including general economic risk (fluctuations in business activity), capital market risk (including changes in interest rates), and purchasing power risk—some aspects of which are discussed in Chapter 14.

Business risk is concerned with the ever-present uncertainty regarding a business enterprise's ability to earn a satisfactory return on its investments as well as with the multitude of cost and revenue factors that enter into the determination of such a return. It includes the factors of competition, product mix, and management ability (see Chapters 19–22).

Financial risk is basically concerned with capital structure and with the ability of an enterprise to meet fixed and senior charges and claims. These factors of short-term liquidity and long-term solvency are discussed in detail in Chapters 16, 17, and 18.

For a discussion of the concept of *accounting risk,* see Chapter 3.

Those who assume, as do beta theorists, that all investors are averse to risk and that they seek to diversify away the specific or unsystematic risks[12] of a security thus exposing themselves only to market risk, must also realize that the historical betas for individual securities have proven quite unstable over time and that consequently such betas seem to be poor predictors of future betas for the same security.[13] Thus, while overall concepts and theories

---

[12] What is often overlooked is that those who seek to diversify away unsystematic risk are also diversifying out a great deal of the rewards that equity investing holds for more aggressive investors.

[13] W. H. Beaver, P. Kettler, and M. Scholes have found that a high degree of association exists between accounting risk measures (such as average payout, asset growth, coverage, etc.) and beta. Thus, these accounting measures of risk may be used in a way that can lead to better forecasts of market determined risk measures (betas) than would be possible using past observed betas. (*The Accounting Review,* October 1970, pp. 654–82.) See also B. Rosenberg and J. Guy, "Prediction of Beta from Investment Fundamentals," *Financial Analysts Journal,* July–August, 1976.

are easier to apply to stock aggregates than to the evaluation of individual stocks, they are at the same time far less reliable and accurate instruments for the achievement of investment results.

Another, and perhaps even more troublesome, question is the assumption of beta theorists that past volatility alone is an acceptable measure of risk without reference to the current price of a security. Is a security that sells significantly *above* its value, as determined by some method of fundamental analysis, no more risky than a security of equal volatility (beta) that sells significantly *below* such fundamentally determined value? We know that paying an excessive price for a stable quality security can amount to as rank a speculation as investing in the most unseasoned of speculative securities.

While market theorists have not yet addressed the above troublesome question, they have addressed the problem of how securities are valued by the market.

The capital asset pricing model

Sharpe[14] and Lintner[15] have extended portfolio theory to a capital asset pricing model (CAPM) that is intended to explain how prices of assets are determined in such a way as to provide greater return for greater risk. This model is based on the assumption that investors desire to hold securities in portfolios that are efficient in the sense that they provide a maximum return for *a given level* of risk. Moreover, the model was derived under the following simplifying assumptions:

1. That there exists a riskless security.
2. That investors are able to borrow or lend unlimited amounts at the riskless rate.
3. That all investors have identical investment horizons and act on the basis of identical expectations and predictions.

Based on these assumptions, it can be shown that when capital markets are in a state of equilibrium, the expected return on an individual security, $E(\tilde{R}_i)$, is related to its systematic risk β_i in the following linear form:

$$E(\tilde{R}_i) = E(\tilde{R}_0) + [E(\tilde{R}_M) - E(\tilde{R}_0)]\beta_i$$

The above formulation states in essence that under conditions of equilibrium, a security's expected return equals the expected return of a riskless security, $E(\tilde{R}_0)$, plus a premium for risk taking. This risk premium consists of a constant, $[E(\tilde{R}_M - E(\tilde{R}_0)]$, which is the difference between the return expected by the market and the return on a riskless security (such as a

---

[14] W. F. Sharpe, "Capital Asset Prices: A Theory of Market Equilibrium under Conditions of Risk," *Journal of Finance,* September 1964, pp. 425–42.

[15] Lintner, "The Valuation of Risky Assets and the Selection of Risky Investments in Stock Portfolios and Capital Budgets," *Review of Economics and Statistics,* February 1965, pp. 13–37.

short-term government bond) multiplied by the systematic risk of the security β_i (its beta) as discussed earlier.

The CAPM thus indicates that the expected return on any particular capital asset consists of two components: (1) the return on a riskless security and (2) a premium for the riskiness of the particular asset computed as outlined above. Thus, under the CAPM, each security has an expected return that is related to its risk. This risk is measured by the security's systematic movements with the overall market, and it cannot be eliminated by portfolio diversification.

It remains for us to consider a related hypothesis that attempts to describe a different property of security prices, i.e., the efficient market hypothesis.

The efficient market hypothesis

Efficient market hypothesis (EMH) deals with the reaction of market prices to financial and other data. The EMH has its origins in the random walk hypothesis that basically states that at any given point in time the size and direction of the next price change is random relative to what is known about an investment at that given time. A derivative of this hypothesis is what is known as the *weak form* of the EMH, which states that current prices reflect fully the information implied by historical price time series. In its *semistrong form,* the EMH holds that prices fully reflect all publicly available information.[16] Moreover, in its *strong form,* the theory asserts that prices reflect *all* information including that which is considered "inside information."

The EMH, in all its terms, has undergone extensive empirical testing with much of the evidence apparently supportive of the weak and semistrong forms of the theory. Lorie and Hamilton[17] for example, present three studies in support of the semistrong form of the hypothesis indicating that:

1. Stock splits do not assure unusual profit for investors.
2. Secondary offerings depress the market price of a stock because such offerings imply that knowledgeable people are selling.
3. Unusual earnings increases are anticipated in the price of the stock before the company's earnings for the year are reported.[18]

None of these findings would, incidentally, clash with the intuition of experienced analysts or seasoned market participants.

---

[16] For one good discussion of this hypothesis, see E. F. Fama, "Efficient Capital Markets: A Review of Theory and Empirical Work," *Journal of Finance,* May 1970, pp. 383–417.

[17] J. H. Lorie and M. T. Hamilton, *The Stock Market: Theories and Evidence* (Homewood, Ill.: Richard D. Irwin, 1973).

[18] See, for example, R. Ball and P. Brown, "An Empirical Evaluation of Accounting Numbers," *Journal of Accounting Research* (Autumn 1968), pp. 159–78; and W. Beaver, "The Informational Content of Annual Earnings Announcements," *Empirical Research in Accounting: Selected Studies,* 1968, University of Chicago, Graduate School of Business 1969, pp. 48–53.

Research supportive of the EMH by accounting scholars on the effect of accounting changes on security prices has found that changes from accelerated to straight-line depreciation for accounting purposes only had no significant effect on stock prices.[19] Another study found that the stock market ignored the effects on income of changes in accounting procedures such as those relating to inventories, depreciation, revenue recognition, and so forth.[20]

Implications for financial statement analysis

The EMH is almost completely dependent on the assumption that competent and well-informed analysts, using tools of analysis such as those described in this book, will constantly strive to evaluate and act upon the ever-changing stream of new information entering the marketplace. And yet the theory's proponents claim that since all that is known is already instantly reflected in market prices, any attempt to gain consistently an advantage by rigorous financial statement analysis is not possible. As H. Lorie and M. T. Hamilton put it, "The most general implication of the efficient market hypothesis is that most security analysis is logically incomplete and valueless."[21]

This position presents an unexplained and unresolved paradox. The thousands of intelligent analysts are assumed to be capable enough to keep our security market efficient through their efforts, but they are not intelligent enough to realize that their efforts can yield no individual advantage. Moreover, should they suddenly realize that their efforts are unrewarded, the market would cease to be efficient.

There are a number of factors that may explain this paradox. Foremost among them is the fact that the entire EMH is built on evidence based on an evaluation of *aggregate*[22] rather than individual investor behavior. The focusing on macro or aggregate behavior results not only in the highlighting of average performance and results but also ignores and masks the results achieved by individual ability, hard work, and ingenuity, as well as by superior timing in acting on information as it becomes available.[23]

---

[19] T. R. Archibald, "Stock Market Reaction to the Depreciation Switch-Back," *The Accounting Review*, January 1972, pp. 22–30.

[20] R. Kaplan and R. Roll, "Accounting Changes and Stock Prices," *The Financial Analysts Journal* (January–February 1973), pp. 48–53; also R. Ball, "Changes in Accounting Techniques and Stock Prices," *Empirical Research in Accounting: Selected Studies*, 1972 (Chicago: Institute of Professional Accounting, Graduate School of Business, University of Chicago, 1974), pp. 1–38.

[21] Lorie and Hamilton, *The Stock Market*, p. 100.

[22] R. J. Chambers put it most effectively: "It is very difficult to escape the conclusion that the whole enterprise of aggregate market analysis with the object of resolving questions about the quality of accounting information is misguided. Men have never advanced their finite knowledge of any subject by attention only to what occurs in the aggregate or on average" (in "Stock Market Prices and Accounting Research," *Abacus*, June 1974, pp. 39–54).

[23] Evidence about superior investment performance by *individuals* is not a matter of public record and is consequently not readily available. But evidence of superior investment performance by portfolio managers is available, one example being *Forbes* magazine's annual "Honor Roll" of consistent long-term superior investment results in both up and down markets.

Few would doubt that important information travels fast. After all, enough is at stake to make it travel fast. Nor is it surprising that the securities markets are rapid processors of information. In fact, using the same type of deductive reasoning as used by the efficient market proponents, we could conclude that the speed and the hardworking efficiency of the market must be evidence that the market participants who make it happen are motivated by substantial rewards.

The reasoning behind the EMH's alleged implication for the usefulness of security analysis fails to recognize the essential difference between information and its proper interpretation. Even if all the information available on a security at a given point in time is impounded in its price, that price may not reflect *value*. It may be under- or overvalued depending on the degree to which an incorrect interpretation or evaluation of the available information has been made by those whose actions determine the market price at a given time.

The work of financial statement analysis is complex and demanding. The spectrum of users of financial statements varies all the way from the institutional analyst who concentrates on only a few companies in one industry to "Aunt Jane" who merely looks at the pictures of an annual report.[24] All act on financial information but surely not with the same insights and competence.

The competent evaluation of "new information" entering the marketplace requires the possession of a prior fund of knowledge, of an information mosaic into which the new information can be fitted, as part of a link in a chain of analytical information, before it can be evaluated and interpreted. Only few have the ability and are prepared to expend the efforts and resources needed to produce such information mosaics, and it is only natural that they would reap the rewards by being able to act both competently and confidently on the new information received. This advantage in timing is all-important in the marketplace.

The vast resources that must be brought to bear on the competent analysis of equity securities have caused some segments of the securities markets to be more efficient than others. Thus, the market for shares of the largest companies is more efficient because many more analysts follow such securities in comparison to those who follow small and lesser-known companies.

The function and purpose of the analysis of equity securities is construed much too narrowly by those who judge its usefulness in an efficient market.[25] While the search for overvalued and undervalued securities is an important function of security analysis, the importance of risk assessment and loss avoidance, in the total framework of investment decision making, cannot be overemphasized. Thus, the prevention of serious investment errors is at least as

---

[24] Comment by G. I. White, CFA, in *Journal of Accountancy,* August 1978, p. 44.

[25] For a more comprehensive discussion of these issues, see the author's article "In Defense of Fundamental Investment Analysis," *Financial Analysts Journal,* January–February 1975, pp. 57–61.

important as the discovery of undervalued securities. Yet, our review of the CAPM and of beta theory earlier in this discussion tends to explain why this important function of analysis is neglected by adherents to these macro models of the security markets. For to some it is a basic premise of these theories that the analysis of unsystematic risk is not worthwhile because that kind of risk taking is not rewarded by the market. They maintain that such risks should be diversified away and that the portfolio manager should look only to systematic or market risk for rewards.[26]

Our basic premise here is that investment results are achieved through the careful study and analysis of *individual* enterprises rather than by an exclusive focus on market aggregates. Our approach in this area is to emphasize the value of fundamental investment analysis not only as a means of keeping our securities markets efficient and our capital markets rational and strong but also as the means by which those investors who, having obtained information, are willing and able to apply knowledge, effort, and ingenuity to its analysis.[27] For those investors, the fruits of fundamental analysis and research, long before being converted to a "public good," will provide adequate rewards. These rewards will not be discernible, however, in the performance of investors aggregated to comprise major market segments, such as mutual funds. Instead, they will remain as individual as the efforts needed to bring them about.

The role of financial statement analysis in the professional decision process leading to the buying, selling, or holding of equity securities has always been the subject of controversy and debate. In times of high speculative market activity, fundamental factors inevitably give way in relative importance to the psychological or technical ones in the overall security appraisal and "valuation" process. The fact that these fundamental factors, based as they are on a concrete analysis of measurable elements, can lead to sounder decisions and to the avoidance of serious judgmental errors will not always prevent their abandonment in favor of the snap decisions that occur in times of speculative frenzy. Nevertheless, the ultimate return of more sober times after periods of speculation and the inevitable corrections of speculative excesses recurringly bring along with them a rediscovery of the virtues of thorough financial analysis as a sound and necessary procedure. In the aftermath of the 1969–70 bear market, David L. Babson urged such a return by stating:

> What we all should do now is to roll up our sleeves and go back to doing what we are paid for—to follow company and industry trends closely, to really dissect balance sheets and to dig into accounting practices—and maybe some

---

[26] A current investment vogue, based on the efficient market adherents' disenchantment with investment results, is the index fund. An index portfolio is merely designed to copy the composition of a market index to such an extent that it will replicate its market performance. Like other schemes that represent mechanical substitutes for analysis and judgment, this too is not likely to satisfy its adherents for too long.

[27] The value of such analysis for other purposes, such as credit evaluation, is not even at issue here.

future Jim Lings, Delbert Colemans and Cortes Randells won't make monkeys out of many of the prestigious firms in our industry again.[28]

The collapse in security values in the early 1970s was, of course, not the first such occurrence that was preceded by a widespread and reckless disregard for fundamentals. It is noteworthy that each generation of analysts has to relearn the lessons so heavily paid for by its predecessors. A. P. Richardson, in an editorial on "The 1929 Stock Market Collapse" published in the *Journal of Accountancy* of December 1929, emphasized this recurring phenomenon of the flight from facts and reason into the world of fancy and wishful thinking:

> The astounding feature of the decline and fall of the stock market in late October and early November was not the fact of descent itself, but the altogether unreasoning consternation which the public in and out of Wall Street displayed. There was nothing at all in the course of events which distinguished the break from its many predecessors. Month after month, even year after year, market prices of securities had climbed to even dizzier heights. Now and then a Jeremiah uttered warning and lament, but the people gave no heed. They thought and consequently dealt in far futures. What a company might earn when the next generation would come to maturity was made the measure of the current value of its stock. In many cases companies whose operations had never yet produced a penny of profit were selected, fortuitously or under artificial stimulation, as a sort of Golconda of the next voyage; and otherwise sane men and women eagerly bought rights of ownership in adventures whose safe return was on the knees of the sea gods. It was not considered enough to look ahead to what was visible. The unseen was the chief commodity. Good stocks, bad stocks and stocks neither good nor bad but wholly of the future rose with almost equal facility, until at last they were sold at prices which seemed to be entirely uninfluenced by the rates of dividend or even by the earnings of the issuing companies. Government bonds and other "gilt-edged" securities were sold at prices nearer the actual interest yield than were the prices of highly speculative stocks to the dividend return or even to the net earnings, past or soon expected, of the companies concerned. Anything was possible when vision was so blurred by success.

Financial statement analysis, while certainly not providing answers to all the problems of security analysis, at least keeps the decision maker in touch with the underlying realities of the enterprise that is investigated. It imposes the discipline of comparing the results already attained with the wide-ranging promises made for the future. As a very minimum, it represents a safeguard against the repetition of the grievous mistakes of judgment recurringly made by investors in time of speculative euphoria.

We have, in this section, examined the needs for information by equity investors. Not all such information can be obtained by means of financial statement analysis nor is the information so obtainable always the most critical

---

[28] "The Stock Market's Collapse and Constructive Aftermath," *The Commercial and Financial Chronicle,* June 4, 1970.

in the determination of security values. However, it should by now be clear to the reader that any rational and systematic approach to the valuation of common stocks must involve the use of quantified data that are mostly the end product of financial statement analysis, evaluation, and interpretation.

Objectives of management

Management's interest in an enterprise's financial condition, profitability, and progress is pervasive and all-encompassing. Management has a number of methods, tools, and techniques available to it in monitoring and keeping up with the ever-changing condition of the enterprise. Financial data analysis is one important type of such methods.

Financial data analysis can be undertaken by management on a continuous basis because it has unlimited access to internal accounting and other records. Such analysis encompasses changes in ratios, trends, and other significant relationships. Ratio, change, and trend analysis is based on an intelligent, alert, and systematic surveillance of significant relationships in a business situation and the timely detection and interpretation of problem areas by an analysis of changes taking place.

Management's primary objective in utilizing the tools of analysis described in this book is to exercise control over and to view the enterprise in the way important outsiders, such as creditors and investors, view it.

Ratio change and trend analysis make use of the numerous and inevitable relationships and interrelationships among the variables occurring in any business situation. Constant surveillance over the size and amplitude of change in these interrelationships provides valuable clues to important changes in underlying financial and operating conditions. Recognition of such changes and timely action to check adverse trends is the essence of control.

Management derives a number of important advantages from a systematic monitoring of financial data and the basic relationships that they display:

1. There is recognition that no event in a business situation is isolated and that it represents a cause or the effect of a chain of which it is but a link. This approach aims at discovering whether a given event or relationship is the cause or the effect of an underlying situation.
2. There is a recognition that one should not act on an isolated event, but rather by an examination of related changes, one should determine the basic causes of the event. Thus, an event cannot be judged as positive or negative until it has been properly related to other factors that have a bearing on it.
3. Such monitoring prevents management from getting submerged in a maze of facts and figures that in the typical business situation consist of a great variety of factors of varying sizes, velocities of change, and degrees of impact. Instead, it organizes the data and relates them to a pattern of prior experience and external standards.

4. Such monitoring calls for prompt and effective action as the situation unfolds, rather than for *"post mortem"* analyses of causes and effects.

Objectives of acquisition and merger analysts

The valuation of an enterprise in its entirety, for the purpose of purchasing a going concern or for the purpose of assessing the merger of two or more enterprises, represents an attempt to determine economic values, the relative worth of the merging entities, and the relative bargaining strengths and weaknesses of the parties involved. Financial statement analysis is a valuable technique in the determination of economic value and in an assessment of the financial and operating compatibility of potential merger candidates.

The objectives of the acquisition and merger analyst are in many respects similar to those of the equity investor except that the analysis of the acquisition of an entire enterprise must go further and stress the valuation of assets, including intangible assets such as goodwill, and liabilities included in the acquisition or merger plan.

Objectives of auditors

The end product of the financial audit is an expression of opinion on the fairness of presentation of financial statements setting forth the financial conditions and the results of operations of an enterprise. One of the basic objectives of the audit process is to obtain the greatest possible degree of assurance about the absence of errors and irregularities, intentional or otherwise, that if undetected could materially affect the fairness of presentation of financial summarizations or their conformity with generally accepted accounting principles (GAAP).

Financial statement analysis and ratio change and trend analysis represent an important group of audit tools that can significantly supplement other audit techniques such as procedural and validation tests.[29] This is so because errors and irregularities, whatever their source, can, if significant, affect the various financial operating and structural relationships; and the detection and analysis of such changes can lead to the detection of errors and irregularities. Moreover, the process of financial analysis requires of the auditor, and imparts to him, the kind of understanding and grasp of the audited enterprise that indicates the most relevant type of supportive evidence required in his audit work.

The application of financial statement analysis as part of the audit program is best undertaken at the very beginning of the audit because such analysis will often reveal the areas of greatest change and vulnerability, areas to which the auditor will want to direct most of his attention. At the end of the

---

[29] In 1978, the accounting profession formally recognized the importance of analytical audit approaches through issuance of *Statement of Auditing Standards No. 23,* "Analytical Review Procedures."

audit, these tools represent an overall check on the reasonableness of the financial statements taken as a whole.[30]

Objectives of other interested groups

Financial statement analysis can serve the needs of many other user groups. Thus, the Internal Revenue Service can apply tools and techniques of financial statement analysis to the audit of tax returns and the checking of the reasonableness of reported amounts.[31] Various governmental regulatory agencies can use such techniques in the exercise of their supervisory and rate-determination functions.

Labor unions can use the techniques of financial statement analysis to evaluate the financial statements of enterprises with which they engage in collective bargaining. Lawyers can employ these techniques in the furtherance of their investigative and legal work, while economic researchers will find them of great usefulness in their work.

Similarly customers can use such approaches to determine the profitability (staying power) of their suppliers, the returns they earn on capital, and other factors of consequence to them.

CONCLUSION

This chapter has examined the points of view and the objectives of a variety of important users of financial statements. These various objectives determine what aspects of financial statement analysis are relevant to the decision-making process of a particular user. In the chapters that follow, we shall first examine the relationship between financial statement analysis and the accounting framework as well as the tools and techniques of financial statement analysis in general. This will be followed in Part III by an examination of the major missions or objectives of financial analysis and the means by which they are accomplished.

QUESTIONS

1. Describe some of the analytical uses to which financial statement analysis can be put.
2. Why are the information needs of equity investors among the most demanding of all users of financial statements?

---

[30] For a more detailed discussion of this subject, see L. A. Bernstein, "Ratio Change and Trend Analysis," *Handbook for Auditors* (New York: McGraw Hill, 1971).

[31] Among the areas that can be analyzed are questions such as whether (1) the income reported is enough to support exemptions or expenses claimed, (2) the profit margin reported is out of line with that normal for that type of business, (3) the return reported is less than that which can be earned by banking the money, and (4) the changes in net worth support the amounts of reported income.

3. Why is the measurement and evaluation of earning power the key element in the valuation of equity securities?

4. What is the essential difference between a bond valuation model based on the present value of future inflows and a stock valuation model based on the same principles?

5. Differentiate between systematic risk and unsystematic risk and discuss the various components of the latter.

6. Discuss the capital asset pricing model (CAPM) and explain how it deals with the problem of securities valuation by the market.

7. Explain how the efficient market hypothesis (EMH) deals with the reaction of market prices to financial and other data.

8. Explain the concept of the trade-off between risk and return as well as its significance to portfolio construction.

9. Discuss the implications that the CAPM and the EMH present for financial statement analysis.

10. Why is the reliability and the validity of any method of stock valuation, no matter how complete and sophisticated, dependent on the prior performance of a quality analysis of financial statements?

11. Identify clearly three separate factors which have a significant influence on a stock's price-earnings ratio. (CFA)

12. What are the differences in point of view between lenders and equity investors? How do these differences express themselves in the way these two groups analyze financial statements and in the objectives that they seek?

13. *a.* Outline the principal risks inherent in a preferred stock as an investment instrument, relative to a bond or other credit obligation of the same company.
    b. Discuss the various influences of U.S. (or Canadian) income taxation trends on the inherent risks and yields of preferred stocks.
    c. What terms can be included in a preferred stock issue to compensate for its subordination to debt and its relationship to common stock? (CFA)

14. What uses can the management of an enterprise make of financial statement analysis?

15. Of what use can financial statement analysis be to the audit of an enterprise?

Financial statement analysis and accounting

THE FUNCTION OF FINANCIAL STATEMENT ANALYSIS

Financial statement analysis is the judgmental process that aims to evaluate the current and past financial positions and the results of operations of an enterprise, with the primary objective of determining the best possible estimates and predictions about future conditions and performance.

Financial statement analysis may be undertaken for many purposes. The security analyst is interested in future earnings estimates and in financial strength as an important element in the determination of security values. The credit analyst wants to determine future funds flows and the resulting financial condition as a means of assessing the risks inherent in a particular credit extension. Present owners of securities analyze current financial statements to decide on whether to hold, enlarge, or sell their positions. Merger and acquisition analysts study and analyze financial statements as an essential part of their decision processes leading to recommendations regarding the merger and acquisition of business enterprises. These are examples of situations involving outsiders—external analysts—trying to reach conclusions principally on the basis of published financial data.

Internal financial analysts, on the other hand, utilize an even larger and more detailed pool of financial data to assess, for internal management and control purposes, the current financial condition and results of an enterprise.

Two major foundations

The discipline of financial statement analysis rests on two major foundations of knowledge:

The *first* foundation involves a thorough understanding of the accounting model as well as the language, the meaning, the significance, and the limitations of financial communications, as most commonly reflected in published statements.

A prerequisite to effective decision making is to "get the facts." The facts about an enterprise's financial condition and results of operations are not available in plain English. They are first assembled and subsequently summarized and reported in a special-purpose language—the language of accounting. Thus, the first essential step in "getting the facts" is to understand this language and to translate the meaning of "the facts" from that special-purpose language.

A thorough understanding of financial statements is the condition precedent to the valid and intelligent computation and use of tools of analysis. In many cases, the amounts, as shown on the financial statements cannot be used without adjustments. Moreover, some of the amounts that need to be included in the computation of ratios and relationships are found in or must be computed from data provided in footnotes or elsewhere.

The *second* foundation, which inevitably builds on the first, consists of the mastery of the tools of financial analysis by means of which the most significant financial and operating factors and relationships can be identified and analyzed for purposes of reaching informed conclusions.

Design of this book

The *first* part of this book (Chapters 1 through 4) examines the objectives of financial statement analysis and the objectives of financial accounting, as well as the relationship of one to the other. Chapter 4 provides an early overview of some of the major tools and techniques used in the analysis of financial statements.

The *second* part deals with the accounting model with particular emphasis on the implications that the variety of accounting standards and procedures have on financial statement analysis. Also examined are tools and techniques that can be used by the analyst to reconstruct, from the highly summarized financial statements and related disclosures, the transactions and events that represent the underlying reality of the enterprise.

The *third* part examines in depth the major areas of concern in the analysis of financial statements, the analytical adjustments to be applied, and the major tools and techniques in use. Chapter 23 concludes with an example of a comprehensive analysis of financial statements.

THE RAW MATERIAL OF ANALYSIS

The analytical processes that underlie the conclusions of security analysts, credit analysts, and other external analysts, as well as internal analysts, make use of a vast array of facts, information, and data—economic, social, political, and other. However, the most important quantitative data utilized by these analysts are the financial data that are the output of an enterprise's accounting system. Presented for external use, principally in the form of formal financial

statements, these data are among the most important quantified elements
in the entire mix of inputs utilized by the decision maker. Since financial
accounting data are the product of a whole range of conventions, measurements, and judgments, their apparent precision and exactness can be misleading. Such data cannot be intelligently used in financial analysis without a
thorough understanding of the accounting framework of which they are the
end product, as well as of the conventions that govern the measurement of
resources, liabilities, equities, and operating results of an enterprise. This
book examines the accounting framework that underlies financial accounting
data as well as the tools of analysis that have been found useful in the analysis
and interpretation of such data.

IMPORTANCE OF ACCOUNTING DATA

Decision processes, such as those relating to the choice of equity investments or the extension of credit, require a great variety of data possessing
a wide range of reliability and relevance to the decision at hand. The information used includes data on general economic conditions and on industry
trends, as well as data on intangibles such as the character and motivation
of the management group. Financial statements and other data emanating
from the accounting process represent measurable indicia of performance
already achieved and of financial conditions presently prevailing.

In any given decision situation, the relative importance of unquantifiable
intangibles, as against quantified actual experience reflected in financial statements, will, of course, vary. Nevertheless, in most cases, no intelligent, well-
grounded decision can be made without an analysis of the quantifiable data
found in financial accounting reports.

In the realm of data available for meaningful analysis, financial statements
are important because they are objective in that they portray actual events
that already happened; they are concrete in that they can be quantified;
and being quantifiable they can, perhaps most importantly, be measured.
This attribute of measurability endows financial statement data with another
important characteristic: since they are expressed in the common denominator
of money, this enables us to add and combine the data, to relate them to
other data, and to otherwise manipulate them arithmetically. The above attributes contribute to the great importance of financial accounting data, both
historical or projected, to the decision-making process.

The indispensability of accounting statements

As this book will discuss and illustrate, financial accounting as a social
science is subject to many shortcomings, imperfections, and limitations. It
is also an evolving discipline subject to continuous change and improvement,
based mostly on experience.

Some users of accounting data, particularly those from other disciplines, become at times so impatient with these shortcomings, imperfections, and limitations as to suggest that some substitute be used instead. There is no such substitute. Double-entry bookkeeping, an ingenious recording and accounting system spawned in the middle ages[1] and perfected ever since into the modern discipline of accounting, is and remains the only viable system for the systematic recording, classification, and summarization of myriads of business activities. The only realistic hope for improvement lies in the improvement of this time-tested system rather than in its substitution by some other method which, while possessing theoretical elegance, cannot be implemented in practice.

It is thus incumbent on anyone who desires to analyze intelligently the financial position and the results of operations of an enterprise, to study the accounting framework, its terminology, and its conventions, as well as the imperfections and limitations to which it is subject.

While the improvement of accounting statements and presentations is a continuing process, these statements cannot be improved to the point where users will be able to utilize them without a need for a prior rigorous study and mastery of the intricacies of the accounting framework.

LIMITATIONS OF ACCOUNTING DATA

Recognition of the importance of financial accounting data should be tempered by a realization of the limitations to which they are subject. The following sections discuss some of the more important limitations.

Monetary expression

The first and most obvious limitation is that financial statements can only present information that lends itself to quantification in terms of the monetary unit; some significant facts about the enterprise do not lend themselves to such measurement. For example, the financial statements, as such, contain very little direct information about the character, motivation, experience, or age of the human resources. They do not contain, except in terms of aggregate final results, information about the quality of the research and development effort or the breadth of the marketing organization. Nor can we expect to find in the financial statements any detailed information on product lines, machinery efficiency, or advance planning. Equally absent will be information on organization structure and on such behavioral problems as the fact that the marketing manager is not on speaking terms with the controller, or that the entire success of the enterprise hinges on the talents

---

[1] By Luca Pacioli in *Summa de Arithmetica* published in Venice in 1494.

of a single person. Nevertheless, without a uniform unit of measurement, financial statements, as we know them, would not be possible.

Simplifications and rigidities inherent in the accounting framework

The portrayal by means of accounting statements of highly complex and diverse economic activities involves the need for simplification, summarization, and the use of judgments and estimates.

The simplification process is necessary in order to classify the great variety of economic events into a manageable number of categories. Inevitably, this simplification can be achieved only at the expense of clarity and detail, which, in some instances, may be useful to the user of financial data.

The need to keep the size of and detail in the financial statements within reasonable bounds, as well as cost versus benefit considerations, requires a high degree of summarization of economic events both in the initial recording of these events in the accounting records and subsequently in the preparation of the financial statements. Inevitably, in the process of such summarization, financial statements lose, perhaps more often than they should, comprehensiveness of description and clarity.

The simplifications and the rigidities inherent in the accounting framework as well as the high degree of summarization present in the financial statements make it imperative that the analyst be able to analyze and to reconstruct the events and the business transactions that they reflect. Indeed, it is an essential skill of the analyst to be able to recover from the financial presentations the realities imbedded in them and to recognize that which cannot be recovered and thus have a basis for asking meaningful questions of those able to provide additional information.

Use of individual judgment

The use of individual judgment in the preparation of financial statements is inevitable. The limitation to be recognized here is the resulting variety in the quality and reliability of financial statement presentations. Financial statements may not be of uniform quality and reliability because of differences in the character and the quality of judgments exercised by accountants in their preparation. Moreover, financial statements are general-purpose presentations; the extent of detail reflected therein is determined by the accounting profession's current view of the "average reader's" requirements and expectations. Such envisioned requirements do not necessarily coincide with those of a user with a specific purpose in mind.

Interim nature and the need for estimation

A further limitation of financial statements stems from the need to report for relatively short periods of the total life span of an enterprise. To be useful, accounting information must be timely; and therefore determinations of financial condition and results of operations must be made frequently. But such frequency of reporting, particularly on the results of operations, requires a great deal of estimation; and the greater the degree of such estimation required, the greater the amount of uncertainty that is inevitably introduced into the financial statements. Examples of estimates are:

- Amount and timing of cash collections on receivables.
- Future sales price and sales volume of inventory items.
- Life and salvage value of fixed assets.
- Future warranty claims.
- Percentage completion and costs to complete for long-term contracts.
- Tax expense.
- Loss reserves.

It is important to clarify the connection between the length of a period reported on and the degree of accounting uncertainty introduced. Many business transactions and operations require a long period of time for final completion and determination of results. For example, fixed assets are acquired for a long period of usefulness. The longer such period of use, the more tentative must be the estimates of their ultimate useful life span. Similarly, the value, if any, of investments in mining or exploration venturing may not become apparent until many accounting periods after the one in which they are incurred. Long-term contracts are another example in which the greater the length of time involved, the more tentative the estimation process must be.

Cost balances

As will be seen in Chapter 3, it still is a basic convention of accounting in the United States that accounting determinations be subject to objective ascertainment.[2] Since the cost of an asset arrived at by arm's-length bargaining may generally be objectively determined by inspection, it is claimed that the cost figure enjoys an objectivity surpassing any subsequent unrealized appraisal of value. Primarily for this reason, accounting adheres, with few exceptions, to the cost concept. The price we pay for this objectivity in accounting adds up to yet another important limitation upon the usefulness of accounting statements. Cost balances do not, in most cases, represent current market values. Yet the users of financial statements usually look for an assessment of value, and to them, historical-cost balances are of very

---

[2] There is slow movement in this country and more determined movement abroad towards some forms of current value accounting. These moves are prompted particularly by a desire to give recognition to the effects of inflation on accounting determinations (see also Chapter 14).

limited usefulness. Moreover, the analyst must be aware of valuation bases other than cost that are used in financial statements.

Unstable monetary unit

The first accounting limitation that we discussed above identified accounting expressions as being limited to those that could be expressed in monetary terms. The advantage of the monetary expression is, of course, that it provides a common denominator and enables us to add up the cost aggregates of such diverse assets as, say, shares of stock, tons of lead, and store furniture.

Over the years, however, the value of money in terms of general purchasing power has undergone significant fluctuations and generally has had a pronounced downward trend. The monetary unit has not retained its quality as a "standard of value," and, consequently, adding up the money cost of goods purchased in year 19x1 with those bought in 19x8 may result in serious distortions.

The accounting profession has recognized that "the assumption that fluctuations in the value of money can be ignored is unrealistic" and, as discussed in Chapter 14, *Statement of Financial Accounting Standards (SFAS) 33* requires certain large companies to issue supplementary statements that reflect the effect of price-level changes on conventional financial statements. However, no framework for relating the supplementary statements to the primary ones has yet evolved, and thus, present-day financial statements remain subject to serious limitations.

THE RELATIVE IMPORTANCE OF FINANCIAL STATEMENT ANALYSIS IN THE TOTAL DECISION EFFORT

The analysis of financial statements and data is an indispensable component of most lending, investing, and other related decisions. It is, however, important to understand that its relative importance in the total decision context can vary significantly.

In the lending decision, the lender looks mainly to the enterprise for his rewards, which come in the form of interest and principal repayment. We are not concerned here with interim changes in interest rates that depend on factors outside the scope of our discussion in this book. Since almost all the rewards (returns) that the lender expects come directly from the enterprise, financial statement analysis is a relatively large and important part of the total decision process. It is, in fact, the most important element in the entire decision set with which the lending officer or bond investor is concerned.[3]

---

[3] A decision set consists of the totality of all factors that enter into the making of a decision. The lending decision set includes many other important factors such as management ability and integrity, industry as well as broad economic conditions.

This is why most banks regard the ability to understand and analyze financial statements as one of the most critical skills to be possessed by the lending officer.

The role that financial statement analysis plays in the equity investing decision is quite different. One important reason for this is that the equity investor looks for his reward to two different sources: dividends and capital appreciation.

Dividends depend in the long run directly on profitability, growth, and liquidity—elements that lend themselves to evaluation by means of an analysis of the financial statements of the paying enterprise. But dividends, which come from and are subject to enterprise discretion, are only one part, and often the smaller element, of the total sought-for reward (return). In fact, many growing and successful enterprises pay minimal or no dividends.

The other, and often major portion, of the expected rewards comes not from the company directly but rather from other investors who it is expected will be willing, at some future time, to pay more for the equity investment than did our decision-making investor. While the willingness of investors to pay higher prices for an equity security depends importantly on earnings power and earnings growth, it often depends even more so on the state of the marketplace as well as on factors such as the rates of return available from other investments.

Thus, the investor's decision set must include considerations of market psychology and confidence that are factors of great importance not subject to analysis by use of the enterprise's financial statements. Consequently, investors in many successful and growing companies often do not obtain the expected returns when the marketplace, in its collective wisdom, refuses to capitalize the earnings they bought at prior or even higher multiples.

For these reasons, the relationship between the rates of return realized by the enterprise and those that the investor in it actually realizes in the marketplace is far from direct. This is often puzzling to those who do not fully appreciate the great importance of the marketplace as the final validator of value. Equity security markets are both logical and psychological, and the relative importance of these two factors is ever changing. Since the analysis of financial statements relates to the logical processes, the relative importance of financial statement analysis in the equity investing decision set varies with circumstances and the time on the market clock. Its importance is relatively greater when market valuations are low than when these valuations are determined by general market euphoria. Its relative importance is always greater when it is directed to the assessment of risk and to the detection of areas of vulnerability or of potential problems. The value of financial statement analysis in defensive investing and in the avoidance of loss is far clearer and direct than is its value in the detection of investment opportunity.

Having explored the relationship of financial statement analysis to the decision-making process and to the accounting framework on which it relies, we turn next to a more comprehensive consideration of the accounting process.

THE FUNCTION OF ACCOUNTING

Accounting is concerned with the quantitative expression of economic phenomena. As a discipline, it evolved from a need for a framework for recording, classifying, and communicating economic data. In the basic form existing today, it reflects the constant change and modification that it has undergone since its inception, in response to changing social and economic needs.

One of the best and most succinct definitions of the functions of accounting is found in *Accounting Research Study (ARS) 1,* entitled "The Basic Postulate of Accounting," which had as its aim the identification of the postulates or conventions of the discipline. According to this study, the function of accounting is:

1. To measure the resources held by specific entities.
2. To reflect the claims against and the interests in those entities.
3. To measure the changes in those resources, claims and interests.
4. To assign the changes to specifiable period of time.
5. To express the foregoing in terms of money as a common denominator.[4]

The function and purposes of accounting are accomplished at two levels. One is the recording function which is that part of the discipline that governs the mechanics of recording and summarizing the multitude of transactions and economic events that occur in an enterprise and that can be quantified in terms of money. The other level, a more complex one and more subject to individual judgment and opinion, governs the methods, procedures, and principles by which accounting data are measured and presented. This chapter will concern itself with an examination of the recording level of the accounting discipline, while subsequent chapters will take up the conventions and principles that govern accounting measurements and their presentation.

The recording function

The recording function in accounting is governed by the principle of double-entry bookkeeping, an ingenious system of accounting that has stood the test of time since its description by an Italian mathematician in 1494.

The study of the theory of double-entry bookkeeping is an integral part of the study of accountancy. Users of accounting statements will find that a general understanding of the double-entry system will aid them significantly in the analysis of financial statements as well as in the reconstruction of business transactions.

The basic concept of the double-entry system is based on the duality of every business transaction. For example, if a business borrows $1,000, it acquires an asset (cash), and counterbalancing this is a claim against the

---

[4] Maurice Moonitz, "The Basic Postulate of Accounting," *Accounting Research Study No. 1* (New York: American Institute of Certified Public Accountants, 1961).

enterprise (a liability) in an equal amount. Regardless of how many transactions an enterprise engages in, this duality and balance prevails at all times and provides the advantages of order, consistency, and control.

Continuing with a more generalized example, when an entity acquires an asset the counterbalancing effect results in one or a number of the following:

1. The incurrence of a liability.
2. The enlargement of the ownership's claim (capital funds).
3. The disposal of another asset.

Similarly, a liability is extinguished by:

1. The disposal of an asset, or
2. The enlargement of the ownership claim, or
3. Incurrence of another liability.

At all times, the assets of an enterprise equal the outsider's claims against these assets (i.e., liabilities) and the equity of the ownership (i.e., capital). Thus, the basic equation prevailing under the double-entry system is:

$$\text{Assets} = \text{Liabilities} + \text{Capital}$$

An expense or a cost incurred in the operations of the enterprise is accompanied by one, or a combination of, the following:

1. Reduction of assets.
2. Increase in liabilities.
3. Increase in the ownership's claim.

Conversely, revenue received by the enterprise—

1. Increases assets, or
2. Decreases liabilities, or
3. Decreases the ownership's claim or affects a combination of the above.

Under the double-entry system, all transactions are recorded and classified and then summarized under appropriate account designations. Financial statements are formal, condensed presentations of the data derived from these accounts.

One of the best ways of visualizing the basic system of record-keeping and the principal interrelationships within it is by means of a diagram that portrays the major classes of accounts as well as the typical relationships among them.

Exhibit 2–1 is a graphic portrayal of the accounting cycle. A careful study of the illustration and the main movements reflected therein will enable the reader to follow the principal basic financial relationships and flows within a manufacturing enterprise. For the sake of clarity, infrequent or unusual flows and relationships have not been included.

The arrows connecting the principal asset, liability, capital, income, cost, and expense accounts indicate the direction of the usual flows. They do not,

Exhibit 2–1: The accounting cycle

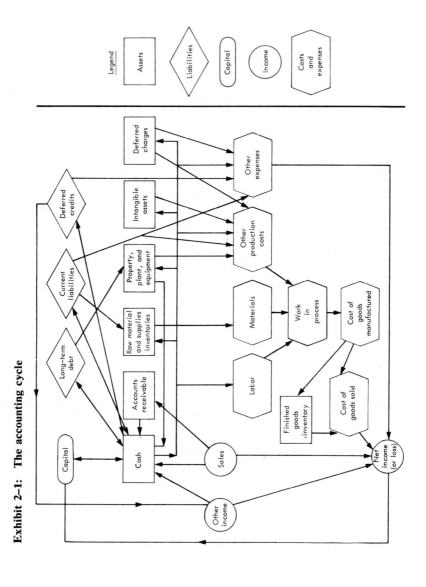

of course, indicate the relative size of the flows, which vary considerably from business to business and from one set of circumstances to another. The reader will notice that no account is dead-ended, that is, there are flows in and out of all accounts. This simply emphasizes the dynamic aspects of business and the accounting system that portrays its financial flows. As management invests, buys, makes, incurs costs, and sells, the quantity of money represented in each account is changing while the system as a whole remains in balance, its debit accounts (generally assets, costs, and expenses) always equaling its credit accounts (generally capital, liabilities, and income).

The flows into and out of each account shown in Exhibit 2–1 can be clearly traced in the diagram, and the chapters that follow—on the measurement of assets, liabilities, capital, and income—should increase and sharpen the reader's understanding of these flows as well as the principles governing their measurement.

The flows shown in the diagram of Exhibit 2–1, while always expressed in dollars, can be in many forms, such as cash, costs, and so forth. Thus, for example, if we trace the inflows and outflows affecting the Property, Plant, and Equipment account in Exhibit 2–1, we can learn a great deal about the interrelationships among the various accounts. The reader can, of course, focus in similar fashion on any account or constellation of accounts. Exhibit 2–2 presents those accounts appearing in the accounting cycle diagram (Exhibit 2–1) that relate to the Property, Plant, and Equipment account and the flows into and out of it.

Three distinct phases can be discerned here:

1. The accounting for the acquisition and disposition of property, plant, and equipment (PPE).
2. The accounting for the use of PPE (depreciation).
3. Accounting for the recovery, out of revenue, of amounts invested in PPE.

Acquisition and disposition of PPE.   The acquisition of PPE can be made by payment of cash or the incurrence of debt or both. Hence, the arrows in Exhibit 2–2 point to a flow from cash and/or long-term debt. Ultimately, the debt is paid back by cash, and this accounts for the flow from cash toward long-term debt. The flow from PPE to cash represents instances where PPE is sold for cash at any stage of its use. In all cases, the flows are equal; for example, an increase in PPE will result in an equal decrease in cash or a commensurate increase in long-term debt.

Use of PPE.   PPE is acquired mostly for productive use. Consequently, its cost is allocated by means of the depreciation process (see Chapter 11) to "cost of goods manufactured." The flows shown in Exhibit 2–2 are from PPE to the Other Production Costs account from where they are charged to the Costs of Goods Manufactured account. The cost of goods manufactured

Exhibit 2–2:   Typical flows to and from the Property, Plant, and Equipment account

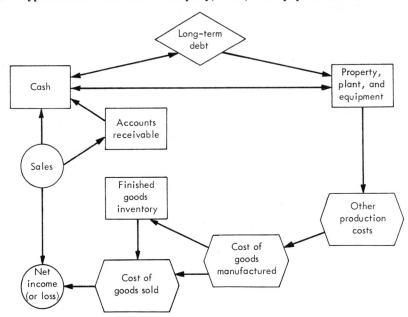

that are sold is charged to the Cost of Goods Sold account, which, in turn, flows into the Net Income (or Profit and Loss) account, where all cost and revenues of the period are accumulated. The unsold goods manufactured remain in the Finished Goods Inventory, which is an asset account to be carried over to the next period. Ultimately, when the finished goods are sold, they find their way into the Costs of Goods Sold account.

Recovery of cost of PPE.   To complete the cycle, we observe in Exhibit 2–2 that the sales of finished goods, which normally are made at amounts designed to recover all costs and earn a profit, generate sales that are either for cash or result in claims, such as accounts receivable, which are subsequently collected in cash. It is through these sales that the outlay for PPE is ultimately recovered by the enterprise.

This completes our tracing of the Exhibit 2–2 subcycle of the accounting system where cash was used to buy PPE and was finally collected from the sale of the products in whose production the PPE was used. Examination of Exhibit 2–1 will reveal the existence of numerous other subcycles that make up the integrated whole.

Financial statements

The accounting system that we examined above continually collects, summarizes, and updates data on assets, liabilities, capital, revenues, costs, and expenses. Periodically, it is necessary to take stock in order to ascertain the financial condition and the results of operations of the enterprise. This is done by presenting in summary form the details contained in the accounts. Based on the accounts included in the diagram of the accounting cycle (Exhibit 2–1), we can illustrate the composition of two major financial statements as follows:

Balance sheet (statement of financial condition).   Exhibit 2–3 shows all assets, liabilities, and capital accounts extracted from Exhibit 2–1 and presented in conventional balance sheet format. This presentation reveals a number of basic relationships worth noting. On the left side are all the assets and unexpired costs in which the resources of the enterprise are invested at a specific point in time. On the right side of the statement are the sources from which these invested funds were financed, that is, the liabilities and

Exhibit 2–3:   Statement of financial condition (balance sheet)

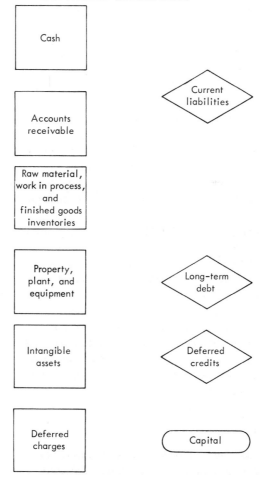

Exhibit 2–4: Income statement

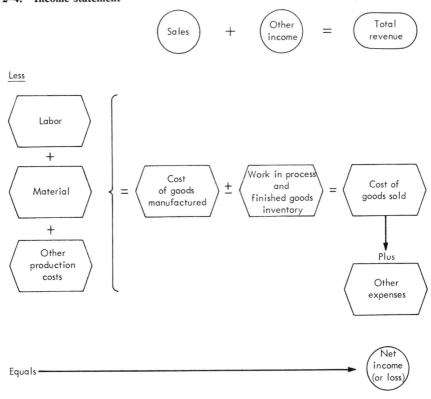

the equity (capital) accounts. Since the *current liabilities* represent a short-term claim against the enterprise, the balance sheet shows the *current assets* generally available to meet these claims, principally cash, accounts receivable, and inventories. The difference between current assets and current liabilities is the working capital.

Income statement (results of operations).   The second major financial statement differs in some important respects from the balance sheet. The income statement format shown in Exhibit 2–4 does not show the account balances as of a certain date, as is the case with the balance sheet, but rather shows the cumulative activity in the revenue, cost, and expense accounts for the period reported open. This is a report on the dynamic aspects of the enterprise—its results of operations. The final net income (or loss) is added to or deducted from capital through the Retained Earnings account. Thus, the net results of operations are incorporated in the balance sheet through their inclusion in the capital accounts.

Statement of changes in financial position.   This third major financial statement is designed to explain the changes in financial position that occur from one balance sheet date to another. As will be seen from our discussion in Chapter 13, this statement is of major importance and interest to the financial analyst.

Ingenious as the recording framework of accounting is, it represents only the mechanical aspects of the discipline. Controlling the method of recording of assets, liabilities, and capital, as well as the size and the timing of cost and revenue flows, is an elaborate and pervasive set of standards. These standards in turn reflect the application of the basic objectives and conventions of accountancy. Since this body of conventions and standards determines the methodology involved in the basic measurements in financial statements, as well as their form and the degree of disclosure therein, the intelligent analysis of these statements requires a thorough familiarity with, and an understanding of, these conventions and standards.

QUESTIONS

1. What is financial statement analysis?
2. Describe the major foundations of the financial statement analysis discipline.
3. Why are financial statements important to the decision process in financial analysis?
4. List some of the more important limitations to which accounting data are subject.
5. What are some of the simplifications and the rigidities inherent in the accounting framework?
6. Discuss the relative importance of financial statement analysis in the total decision effort.
7. Define briefly the function of accounting.
8. The functions and purposes of accounting are accomplished at two levels; describe them.
9. What is the basic equation prevailing under the double-entry system of bookkeeping?

3 Accounting objectives, conventions, and standards

THE OBJECTIVES OF ACCOUNTING

While accountants have enjoyed some degree of success in agreeing upon the proper accounting in specific areas of practice, they have, so far, not been able to agree on the basic bedrock objectives of accounting. Not that there is a lack of broad generalizations on the subject—one firm suggested "fairness" as such basic underlying tenant—but there is no broad consensus on objectives in a way that would help accountants settle their differences of opinion by referring to them. Accounting is, after all, not an exact science. It is rather a social science—its concepts, rooted in the value system of the society in which it operates, are socially determined and socially expressed. Consequently, broad agreement on *useful* generalizations regarding its basic objectives may be as hard to achieve in the future as it was in the past. The fact that the setting of accounting standards is basically a political process involving many parties at interest makes such agreement all the more difficult to attain.

In 1973, The Objectives of Financial Statements Study Group (Trueblood Committee) reported its conclusions in the "Objectives of Financial Statements." After agreeing with the generally held conclusion[1] that "the basic objective of financial statements is to provide information useful for making economic decisions," the Study Group listed, among others, the following two significant objectives:

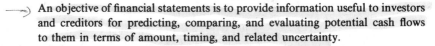 An objective of financial statements is to provide information useful to investors and creditors for predicting, comparing, and evaluating potential cash flows to them in terms of amount, timing, and related uncertainty.

---

[1] The Financial Accounting Standards Board (FASB) reports that only *37 percent* of respondents to its *First Discussion Memorandum* on the Conceptual Framework of Accounting could agree even with this basic conclusion. This provides an insight into the magnitude of the problem of reaching agreement on even the most basic accounting objectives.

> An objective of financial statements is to provide users with information for predicting, comparing, and evaluating enterprise earning power.

These objectives established a definite link between accounting and the basic decision functions that it serves, i.e., the investing and lending processes. The Study Group recognized however that the objectives it enunciated can be attained only in stages and over time.

THE FASB CONCEPTUAL FRAMEWORK

In the mid-1970s, the Financial Accounting Standards Board (FASB) embarked on its Conceptual Framework (CF) project whose purpose it described as the establishment of a coherent system of interrelated objectives and concepts that are expected to lead to consistent financial accounting and reporting. These concepts are expected to guide the selection of events to be accounted for, the measurement of those events as well as the means of their summarization and their communication to interested users.

It is expected that the CF should enable investors, creditors, and others to obtain increased understanding of and confidence in financial reporting. A CF centered on objectives can help narrow the range of acceptable accounting methods as well as promote increased comparability of financial information.

The FASB believes that without conceptual underpinnings, measures provided by accounting and financial reporting are essentially matters of judgment and personal opinion. Thus, the more precise definitions provided by the CF are expected to narrow subjectivity, circumscribe the areas for applying judgments as well as provide a frame of reference for those judgments.

ORGANIZATION OF THE CONCEPTUAL FRAMEWORK (CF)

To implement the development of the CF, the FASB established a program to issue *Statements of Financial Accounting Concepts (SFACs)*. The purpose of *SFACs* is to set forth fundamentals on which financial accounting and reporting standards should be based, and these should serve the Board in developing standards of financial accounting and reporting.[2]

To date, the FASB has issued four *SFACs*. In *SFAC 1* (1978), "Objectives of Financial Reporting by Business Enterprises," the Board establishes the objectives of general-purpose external financial reporting by business enterprises. In most respects, *SFAC 1* does not diverge from the above-mentioned Trueblood Report.[3] The *Statement* in essence states that financial reporting

---

[2] Unlike *Statements of Financial Accounting Standards* (SFASs), *SFACs* do not establish generally accepted accounting principles (GAAP) and therefore are not intended to invoke Rule 203 of the Code of Professional Ethics of the AICPA, which deals with adherence to professional pronouncements.

[3] Unlike the Trueblood Report, *SFAC 1* does not focus on forecasts or on accounting for social goals.

Exhibit 3–1:   A hierarchy of accounting qualities

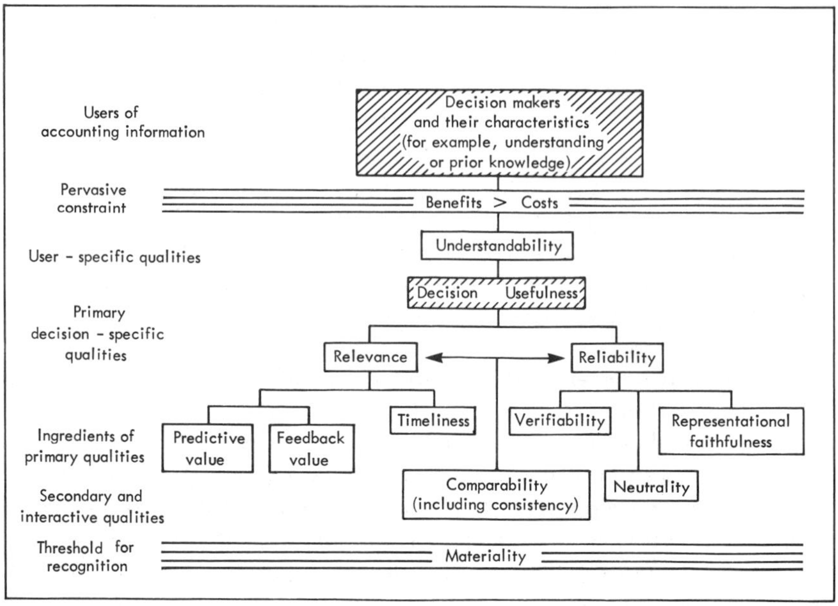

Source: FASB, *Statement of Financial Accounting Concepts No. 2,* "Qualitative Characteristics of Accounting Information" (Stamford, Conn., 1980).

can best serve investors and creditors to predict the amount, timing, and uncertainty of future cash flows *to them* by facilitating the prediction of the amount, timing, and uncertainty of future cash flows *to the business entity.* Moreover, financial reporting should provide information about the economic resources of an enterprise, the claims to those resources, and the effects of transactions, events, and circumstances that change its resources and claims to those resources.

A primary focus of financial reporting is information about earnings and its components. Financial reporting is also expected to provide information about an enterprise's financial performance during a period and about how management has discharged its stewardship responsibility to owners.[4]

SFAC 2 (1980), "Qualitative Characteristics of Accounting Information," is designed to examine the characteristics of accounting information that make it useful. These characteristics are viewed as a hierarchy of qualities (see Exhibit 3–1) among which usefulness for decision making is first in importance.

The hierarchy of accounting qualities separates user specific qualities (e.g., understandability) from qualities inherent in the information. Information

---

[4] While stewardship responsibilities are still mentioned, the shift in focus from stewardship accounting to user-oriented accounting is unmistakable. In earlier times, owners dissatisfied with the quality of stewardship moved to change managers. Modern investors, however, are more likely to change investments and thus need information on alternatives available to them.

cannot be useful to decision makers unless it is understood by them regardless of how relevant it may otherwise be.

Relevance and *reliability* are two primary qualities that make accounting information useful for decision making. Information is relevant if it has the capacity to confirm or change a decision maker's expectations.

If information is received by a user too late to have an effect on a decision, it cannot have an impact on that decision. Hence, *timeliness* is an important aspect of relevance. So are *predictive value*, i.e., value as an input into a predictive process, as well as *feedback value*, which is a characteristic of information that helps to confirm and to correct earlier predictions.

Information is *reliable* if it can be verified by agreement among a number of independent observers and if it represents what it purports to represent, i.e., it has *representational faithfulness.* Reliability also implies completeness and *neutrality* of information.[5]

Comparability, which includes consistency, interacts with relevance and reliability to contribute to the usefulness of information. Comparison is one of the most basic tools of analysis for decision making. Almost all evaluations and alternative-choice judgments involve comparisons of one sort or another. Thus, the ability to compare sets of accounting data of the same enterprise over time, or those of one enterprise with that of another, is very important to the decision-making process.

Overriding all these qualitative characteristics are *pervasive qualities* such as cost and benefits and materiality.

Information is costly to gather, process, interpret, and use. As with other services, information should be supplied only if its benefits exceed its costs.

Materiality is defined as "the magnitude of an omission or misstatement of accounting information that, in the light of surrounding circumstances, makes it possible that the judgment of a reasonable person relying on the information would be changed or influenced by the omission or misstatement."

---

[5] David Salomons in "The Politicization of Accounting," *Journal of Accountancy,* November, 1978 stated: "Information cannot be neutral—it cannot therefore be reliable—if it is selected or presented for the purpose of producing some chosen effect on human behavior. It is the quality of neutrality which makes a map reliable; and the essential nature of accounting, I believe it is cartographic. Accounting is financial map-making. The better the map, the more completely it represents the complex phenomena that are being mapped."

Oscar S. Gellein has provided us with an excellent and graphic description of neutrality: "Financial reporting is more like a barometer than a rainmaker. The barometer produces a reading for someone else to use in assessing the prospects of storm or clemency. The barometer has an impact if it causes someone to buy an umbrella, or not to buy an umbrella, or if someone invokes the power on high to prevent a storm, or sends a rainmaker up to seed the clouds. The barometer is useful to those with adverse interests if it describes what it purports to show and measures that accurately—that is, if it is neutral. But suppose those who designed the barometer decided that the public interest would be served better if forebodings of storm were minimized and, accordingly, a bias toward clemency was built into the calibrations of the barometer. Surely, it is reasoned, an improved expectation of sunshine would be for the public good. The difficulty is that some would get wet because they did not have umbrellas, others would beseech for rain not knowing that it was on its way, clouds would be seeded needlessly, and worst of all, some persons would not duck into storm cellars or batten down the hatches soon enough to protect against imminent storm. And so it is with financial reporting."

In accounting, the concept of materiality assumes special significance because by its nature accounting information is not comprehended easily by the reader. The introduction therein of redundancy can make the task of its absorption and analysis even more difficult. Hence, to keep the information from being misleading, trivia should be kept out of it.

If the issue were simply one of omitting trivia, where there is general agreement on what trivia are, materiality would not be the problem area it is. At its root, the problem of materiality rests on the claim by users that some preparers of financial statements and their auditors use the concept to avoid disclosing that which they do not wish disclosed. It is this aspect that makes this concept significant to users of accounting data who must realize that accountants do omit, reclassify, or ignore data and information on the basis of their materiality, but that there are, as of now, no set criteria that guide either the accountant or the user of information to distinguish between what is material and what is not.

This state of affairs has resulted in action on a number of fronts. Some professional pronouncements (such as those on earnings per share and intercorporate investments) contain quantitative materiality benchmarks, and some recent Securities and Exchange Commission (SEC) pronouncements also specify materiality boundaries. Moreover, the FASB has issued a voluminous *Discussion Memorandum* on the subject on which it accepted comments through early 1976. The subject will be considered as part of the overall conceptual framework.

SFAC 3 (1980), "Elements of Financial Statements of Business Enterprises," defines the following 10 elements of financial statements of business enterprises:

1. *Assets* are probable future economic benefits obtained or controlled by a particular entity as a result of past transactions or events.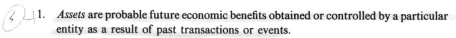
   - An asset has three essential characteristics:
     - It embodies a probable future benefit that involves a capacity, singly or in combination with other assets, to contribute directly or indirectly to future net cash inflows.
     - The enterprise can obtain the benefit and control others' access to it.
       - Legal enforceability of a claim to the benefit is not a prerequisite for a benefit to qualify as an asset if its receipt by the enterprise is otherwise probable.
     - The transaction or other event giving rise to the enterprise's right to or control of the benefit has already occurred.
   - Once acquired, an asset continues as an asset of the enterprise until the enterprise collects it, transfers it to another entity, or uses it, or some other event or circumstance destroys the future benefit or removes the enterprise's ability to obtain it.
   - Valuation accounts that reduce or increase the carrying amount of an asset are sometimes found in financial statements; these are part of the related assets and are neither assets in their own right nor liabilities.

2. *Liabilities* are probable future sacrifices of economic benefits arising from present obligations of a particular entity to transfer assets or provide services to other entities in the future as a result of past transactions or events.
   - A liability has three essential characteristics:
     - It embodies a present duty or responsibility to one or more other entities that entails settlement by probable future transfer or use of assets at a specified or determinable date, on occurrence of a specified event, or on demand.
     - The duty or responsibility obligates a particular enterprise, leaving it little or no discretion to avoid the future sacrifice.
       - The existence of a legally enforceable claim is not a prerequisite for an obligation to qualify as a liability if the future payment of cash or other transfer of assets to settle the obligation is otherwise probable.
     - The transaction or other event obligating the enterprise has already happened.
   - Once incurred, a liability continues as a liability of the enterprise until the enterprise settles it, or another event or circumstance discharges it or removes the enterprise's responsibility to settle it.

3. *Equity* is the residual interest in the assets of an entity that remains after deducting its liabilities.
   - In a business enterprise, the equity is the ownership interest (owners' equity).

4. *Investment by owners* are increases in net assets of a particular enterprise resulting from transfers to it from other entities of something valuable to obtain or increase equity (ownership interests).
   - That which is received includes most commonly assets, but may also include services or satisfaction or conversion of liabilities of the enterprise.
   - Investments by owners increase equity (ownership interests).

5. *Distributions to owners* are decreases in net assets of a particular enterprise resulting from transferring assets, rendering services, or incurring liabilities by the enterprise to owners.
   - Distributions to owners decrease equity (owners' interest).
     - When dividends are declared, the enterprise incurs a liability to transfer assets to owners in the future, resulting in equity being reduced and liabilities increased.
     - Reacquisition by an entity of its own equity securities by transferring assets or incurring liabilities to owners is a distribution to owners.

6. *Comprehensive income* is the change in equity (net assets) of an enterprise during a period from transactions and other events and circumstances from nonowner sources. It includes all changes in equity during a period except those resulting from investment by owners and distributions to owners.
   - Over the life of a business enterprise, its comprehensive income equals the net of its cash receipts and cash outlays (excluding cash investments by owners and cash distributions to owners).
   - Comprehensive income results from:
     - Exchange transactions and other transfers between the enterprise and other entities that are not its owners.
     - The enterprise's productive efforts.

- ○ Price changes, casualties, and other effects of interaction between the enterprise and its economic, legal, social, political, and physical environment.
- • Comprehensive income, as defined, is a return on financial capital as distinguished from a return on physical capital.
  - ○ The major difference between the two capital maintenance concepts is that "holding gains and losses" are included in return on capital under the financial capital concept, but these are called capital maintenance adjustments under the physical capital concept and are included directly in equity and are not included in return on capital (see also Chapter 14).
  - ○ The term *earnings* has not been used because it may be used to designate a different concept that is a component part of (narrower or less than) comprehensive income, and earnings, when defined, may be a return on physical capital or may be a return on financial capital.
- • The Board has not as yet chosen between the financial and physical capital maintenance concepts for deciding the meaning and appropriate display of "earnings."
- • Capital maintenance concepts are the subject of another project.
- • Comprehensive income comprises two related but distinguishable types of components:
  - ○ Revenues, expenses, gains, and losses.
  - ○ Intermediate components or measures that result from combining revenues, expenses, gains, and losses (in effect, subtotals); examples are gross margin, contribution margin, income from continuing operations (pretax and after tax), and operating income.

7. *Revenues* are inflows or other enhancements of assets of an entity or settlements of its liabilities (or a combination of both) during a period of delivering or producing goods, rendering services, or other activities that constitute the entity's ongoing major or central operations.
   - • Revenues represent actual or expected cash inflows (or the equivalent) that have occurred or will eventuate as a result of the enterprise's ongoing major or central operations during the period.

8. *Expenses* are outflows or other using up of assets or incurrences of liabilities (or a combination of both) during a period of delivering or producing goods, rendering services, or carrying out other activities that constitute the enterprise's ongoing major or central operations.
   - • Expenses represent actual or expected cash outflows (or the equivalent) that have occurred or will eventuate as a result of the enterprise's ongoing major or centeral operations during the period.

9. *Gains* are increases in equity (net assets) from peripheral or incidental transactions of an entity and from all other transactions and other events and circumstances affecting the entity during a period except those that result from revenues or investments by owners.

10. *Losses* are decreases in equity (net assets) from peripheral or incidental transactions of an entity and from all other transactions and other events and circumstances affecting the entity during a period except those that result from expenses or distributions to owners.

SFAC 3 also defines or describes certain other concepts that underlie the 10 elements listed above:

Items that qualify under the definitions of elements of financial statements and that meet the criteria for recognition and measurement are accounted for and included in financial statements by the use of accrual accounting procedures. Accrual accounting and related concepts include the following processes:

- Accrual accounting attempts to recognize noncash events and circumstances as they occur; specifically, accrual is the accounting process of recognizing assets, liabilities, and components of comprehensive income for amounts expected to be received or paid, usually in cash, in the future.
- Deferral is the accounting system process of recognizing a liability from a current cash receipt or an asset resulting from a current cash payment, with deferred recognition of components of comprehensive income.
- Allocation is the accounting process of reducing a liability recorded as a result of a cash receipt by recognizing revenues or reducing an asset recorded as a result of a cash payment recognizing expenses or cost production payment.
- Realization is the process of converting noncash resources and rights into money and is most precisely used in accounting and financial reporting to refer to sales of assets for cash or claims to cash. The related terms, realized and unrealized, therefore, identify revenues or gains or losses on assets sold and unsold, respectively.
- Recognition is the process of formally recording or incorporating an item in the financial statements of an entity. Thus, an asset, liability, revenue, expense, gain, or loss may be recognized (recorded) or unrecognized (unrecorded). "Realization" and "recognition" are not used as synonyms, as they sometimes are in accounting and financial literature.

The Board emphasizes that the definitions in this *Statement* neither require nor presage upheavals in present practice, although they may in time lead to some evolutionary changes in practice or in the ways certain items are viewed.

The Board expects most assets and liabilities in present practice to continue to qualify as assets or liabilities under the definitions in this *Statement.*

STATUS AND DIRECTION OF THE CONCEPTUAL FRAMEWORK

With the issuance of four *SFACs,* the FASB has made a significant start in its CF project. In the area of accounting measurement, *Statement of Financial Accounting Standards (SFAS) 33,* on price changes, represents an experiment that is to be evaluated around 1984 (see also Chapter 14). Still in various phases of deliberation are recognition criteria, financial statements versus financial reporting, and the reporting of income, cash flows, and financial position.

IMPLICATIONS FOR ANALYSIS

The CF project represents an earnest attempt by the FASB to establish a logical and coherent framework of interrelated objectives and concepts that are intended to enhance the conceptual foundations of accounting standards and to promote confidence in and acceptance of these standards.

The analyst must understand that contrary to what some would have us believe, accounting is *not* a science (concerned as science is with natural laws and predictions based on them) but rather a service activity[6] that in order to be useful to society draws for its execution and improvement on related fields of science and particularly, social science.

Being rooted in the social system of which it is part, accounting, whose issues affect different parties at interest in different ways, is always subject to political processes.[7] Thus, the setting of accounting concepts and standards is in itself a political process.[8]

As one astute observer put it, "Too often, accounting theory is invoked more as a tactic to buttress one's preconceived notions rather than as a genuine arbiter of contending views."[9] This problem was exemplified in the debate surrounding the replacement of *SFAS 8* by *SFAS 52* in which Board members for and against the change referred to identical portions of the CF as support for their respective positions.

Analysts should be understanding of the accounting profession's efforts in its attempts to establish a sound CF and should be supportive of its goals, which are, ultimately, in the analysts' best interests. At the same time, analysts must be aware of the fact that previous attempts at establishing conceptual frameworks have not yielded universally accepted concepts or "truths"— universal in the sense that men would settle differences of opinion by referring to them.[10]

Analysts must also realize that agreement on accounting objectives or standards is often obtained by couching such statements in language that is vague enough so as to allow room for various interest groups to adopt their

---

[6] K. S. Peasnell, in "Statement of Accounting Theory and Theory Acceptance: A Review Article," *Accounting and Business Research*, Summer 1978, pp. 220–21, stated it as follows: "Accounting, is not a science; it is a service activity. Accounting therefore should be equated not with the sciences, but with fields like medicine, technology, and law of which the principal raison d'etre is an external social need. Sure, service professions make use of scientific (i.e., empirical) knowledge—they often contribute to it—but their principal concern is with doing a particular job of work, fulfilling a social need."

[7] For example, in the United States, the investor is the primary focus of financial reporting. In other countries, the focus may be on different constituencies (e.g., labor) that have vital and legitimate interests in financial reporting.

[8] R. C. Watts and J. L. Zimmerman in "Towards a Positive Theory of the Determination of Accounting Standards," *The Accounting Review*, January 1978, demonstrate that accounting theories have been utilized in large measure to support a particular group's lobbying positions on existing or proposed standards.

[9] S. Zeff in R. Sterling, ed., *Institutional Issues in Public Accounting* (Lawrence, Kansas: Scholars Book Co., 1974), p. 177.

[10] Such views were expressed by this author on earlier attempts at establishing conceptual frameworks in "Whither Accounting Research?" *Journal of Accountancy*, December 1965. A pessimistic assessment of the potential value and effect of the FASB's statement of objectives and definitions is reached by Professors N. Dopuch and S. Sunder in an excellent analysis: "FASB's Statement on Objectives and Elements of Financial Accounting: A Review," *The Accounting Review*, January 1980.

own interpretations of the operational meaning. It follows that in using the accountant's product, analysts must be alert to the fact that in practice considerations of self-interest can govern accounting presentations just as much as can logic and rational objectives.

ACCOUNTING PRINCIPLES OR STANDARDS

Accounting principles are the rules and operative guides of accounting. These rules, which are now more accurately viewed as standards, determine such matters as how assets are measured, when liabilities are incurred, when income is recognized as earned, and when expenses and losses accrue. Thus, to the user of accounting data and statements, an understanding of these rules is essential. No intelligent and valid analysis of financial statements can be undertaken without ascertaining as fully as possible which accounting principles were used in the preparation of such statements and how they were applied.

How accounting standards are established

Accounting principles have been long in developing and are subject to continuous innovation, modification, and change. Thus, the principle of depreciation accounting, under which the cost of a productive fixed asset is allocated to revenue over the useful life of such asset, is well established today, but it was not fully accepted as recently as the turn of the century. The tremendous growth of leasing after World War II has moved the accounting profession to reconsider the accounting for leases and change it significantly. Over the years, accounting principles have thus changed in response to developments in, and the needs of, the business community and its requirements and expectations.

It is now generally accepted that the primary responsibility for the fair presentation of financial statements rests with the reporting management of an enterprise. However, the responsibility for the development of accounting principles, which govern this reporting, has been borne primarily by the organized accounting profession and by the Securities and Exchange Commission (SEC) and, to a lesser extent, by the American Accounting Association (AAA) and the New York Stock Exchange (NYSE).

The role of the accounting profession. The reasons for the accounting profession's assumption of early leadership in the development of accounting principles are not hard to find. One of the profession's major and unique functions is that of attesting to the fairness of presentation of financial statements. Yet, the term *fairness of presentation* requires a frame of reference by which it may be judged. Generally accepted accounting principles (GAAP) are intended to provide such a frame of reference, and the accounting profession is presumed to have both the independence and the technical capability required for their development. In pursuing the development of GAAP, the profession was not only performing a vital public service but was also catering to its own vital interests.

The earliest effort of the profession was a "Memorandum on Balance Sheet Audits" prepared by the American Institute of Certified Public Accountants (AICPA) at the request of the Federal Trade Commission. It was published in 1917 in the *Federal Reserve Bulletin* under the title "Uniform Accounting." A revision of this compendium of approved methods of preparing financial statements was prepared by the AICPA and published in 1929 by the Federal Reserve Board under the title "Verification of Financial Statements."

The winds of social and economic change that blew fast and furious starting with the 1929 financial collapse have exerted a strong and decisive influence on the pace of accounting change. While no knowledgeable source would place the major blame for the economic debacle at the door of poor accounting and inadequate reporting, there was, nevertheless, a general recognition of the fact that improvements in accounting principles and in disclosure were long overdue. The profession found a willing partner favoring change in the NYSE whose reputation was, to say the least, tarnished by the debacle that began in 1929. Propelled by strong and renewed incentives to lift the financial accountability of companies listed with it to higher standards, the NYSE cooperated with a Committee of the AICPA to spell them out. The result of a two-year correspondence between the AICPA Committee and the Committee on Stock List of the NYSE was published in 1934. It embodied a number of basic principles of accounting to be followed by listed companies—clarification on the limitations of financial statements and agreement with regard to the wording of the auditor's opinion. This was the first recorded instance where the phrase "accepted accounting principles" (later changed to "generally accepted accounting principles") was used.

With the establishment of a research department, the AICPA undertook in 1938 to put the effort of developing accounting principles on a permanent basis. To this end, a Committee on Accounting procedure was established whose purpose was to reduce the areas of difference in accounting and to narrow the choices available in the area of alternative accounting principles.

The Committee on Accounting Procedure at first endeavored to prepare a comprehensive statement on accounting principles but abandoned this goal for the more attainable one of dealing with individual areas of controversy and difficulty. During its tenure, the committee considered a great many accounting problems and issued pronouncements in the form of 51 *Accounting Research Bulletins (ARBs)*. Issued with the approval of at least two thirds of committee members, the authority of the *ARBs,* except in cases in which formal adoption by the Institute membership has been asked and secured, rested upon the general acceptability of opinions so reached.

By 1959, criticism from outside as well as from within the accounting profession led to the replacement of the Committee on Accounting Procedure by the Accounting Principles Board (APB). This body, vested with greater authority and supported by an enlarged research staff, was charged with narrowing the areas of differences in accounting principles and in promoting the written expression of what generally accepted accounting principles are. The APB, which was replaced by the Financial Accounting Standards Board (FASB) in 1973, issued 31 *Opinions,* some of which have improved the theory and the practice of significant areas (such as the area of pension accounting), some of which may have improved the theory but had an inadequate impact on practice (such as in the area of leasing), and some of which confused the areas of theory and practice (such as the areas of earnings per share.)

It is clear that in many cases the APB has attempted to change a principle adopted by its predecessor committee, not because the theory behind it was inherently deficient but rather because it had been ignored or abused in practice. The adoption of a new theory does not, however, remedy the original deficiency, which was a lack of voluntary observance of the old one by members of the profession. It does not, moreover, assure observance of the new theory introduced in place of the old one. The crux of the matter, especially as concerns the user of financial data, is, in short, that he must not only understand the theory behind the accounting principles promulgated by the accounting profession but he must also know:

1. To what extent the spirit as well as the letter of these principles is observed in practice.
2. What degree of latitude of implementation these principles, by their very nature, permit.

Generally, in determining the accounting standards applicable to a given situation, the auditor will first turn to official pronouncements of the FASB, which also incorporate pronouncements of its predecessors that are still in force, specialized sources such as AICPA Industry Guides, and, as applicable, to official pronouncements of the SEC, such as their regulations pertaining to disclosure in financial statements, the *Accounting Series Releases (ASRs), now codified as Financial Reporting Releases (FRRs), Staff Accounting Bulletins (SABs),* or administrative rulings.

In the absence of any authoritative pronouncement in the first category, the auditor will turn to books and articles written by eminent and well-known authors. He may also review published financial statements with a view to finding authority and precedent for various principles.

It appears that under the AICPA's directives, which required disclosure of departures from the pronouncements of the FASB and predecessors, the auditor will, for all practical purposes, have to follow the accounting principles laid down or adopted by the FASB. Use of alternative principles also enjoying authoritative support will shift the burden of their defense on to the auditor.

A departure from promulgated principles is, however, far from easy to identify. The criteria of many pronouncements and opinions are often so vague and broad and so much subject to a wide range of interpretation that at present definite departures from such pronouncements would be difficult to identify unequivocally. Consequently, the practical effect of the requirement to disclose departures from professional *Opinions* is more apparent than real.

Disclosure of accounting policies. In recognition of the fact that information about the accounting policies adopted and followed by both profit-oriented and not-for-profit entities is essential to users of financial statements, the APB issued *Opinion 22,* "Disclosure of Accounting Policies."

The *Opinion* requires disclosure of accounting policies either in a summary or a footnote that is an integral part of the financial statements. The disclosure would identify and describe accounting principles followed and the methods of applying those principles that materially affect the determination of financial position, changes in financial position, or results of operations. Emphasis should be placed on describing principles and methods where a selection had been made from existing acceptable alternatives and where unusual, innovative, or industry-oriented principles and methods had been followed. In addition, the *Opinion* provides examples, not necessarily all inclusive, of the other types of disclosures that would be common.

The *Financial Accounting Standards Board* (FASB), composed of seven full-time paid members, began to function as the accounting standards-setting body of the accounting profession in mid-1973. Board members are appointed by a group of trustees which in addition to AICPA members include representatives from private industry, security analysts, and others.

In spite of expected criticism from many quarters, the FASB represents a very significant improvement over its predecessors. Before issuing a Financial Accounting Standard on a subject, the Board issues, in most cases, a DISCUSSION MEMORANDUM that is exposed for public comment. Written comments can be filed with the Board, and oral comments can be voiced at public hearings that generally precede the issuance of an Exposure Draft of a *Statement of Financial Accounting Standards (SFAS).* After further exposure and comment, a final *SFAS* is usually issued. Interpretations of previously issued pronouncements are also issued from time to time.

Another significant improvement in procedure is the inclusion in most *SFAS* of careful and elaborate explanations of the rationale of the Board for the statements it issues, explanations of how comments to the Board were dealt with, as well as examples of actual applications.

In 1977, the Financial Accounting Foundation (the FASB's parent body) adopted a number of structural changes in the FASB's operations, including greater participation by financial statement users in the rule-making process.

The influence of the Securities and Exchange Commission. The SEC, which is an independent quasi-judicial agency of the U.S. government, administers, *inter alia,* the Securities Act of 1933 and the Securities Exchange Act of 1934.

The primary purpose of the 1933 act is to ensure that there be given to a potential investor in a security being offered for public sale all the material facts relating to the security that are needed in order to decide whether to buy it. Such facts are disclosed in a registration statement, which must be filed with the SEC and which must contain specified information.

The function of the SEC as regards a registration statement filed with it under the 1933 act is to examine it to see that a full and accurate disclosure is made of all pertinent information relating to the company's business, its securities, its financial position and earnings, and the underwriting arrangements relating to the particular security that is being marketed. The SEC can require such changes to be made in the original registration statements as are necessary to achieve this objective. Until the SEC approves the statement, amended as necessary, it can prevent the registration statement from becoming effective and the securities from being sold. The SEC is not, however, concerned with the merits of any security registered with it.

Since its inception, the SEC has encouraged the development and improvement of accounting and auditing practice. That encouragement has, in practice, taken on a number of forms. The Commission has issued specific rules and regulations concerning the preparation of financial statements that have to be filed with it and the degree of detail that they should contain. The Commission's prosecution of numerous accounting and auditing infractions of its rules has resulted in a form of "case law" that provides important clues and precedents in the area of accounting principles and auditing procedure. Some of the most important decisions on accounting and auditing, as well as other important pronouncements on these subjects, are incorporated in *Accounting Series Releases (ASRs)* which numbered 307 when the commission codified them in 1982 into *Financial Reporting Release (FRR)* No. 1 and for enforcement related releases into *Accounting and Auditing Enforcement Releases (AAERs)*. Less formal *Staff Accounting Bulletins (SABs)* are also issued.

While many of the aforementioned sources on the SEC's position on accounting and auditing matters deal with specific instances and applications, the Commission has recognized the impossibility of issuing rules to cover all possible situations. Thus, an important part of the SEC's influence on matters of accounting takes the form of conferences between companies and their accountants and the SEC staff and the numerous unpublished rulings and guidelines that are a result thereof.

The importance of the SEC position can be understood best in the light of the statutory authority vested in it. It has the ability to enforce the adherence to its rules over an ever-increasing number of companies that have come under its jurisdiction.

In over 50 years of its existence, the SEC has grown in competence and experience. It has wide regulatory authority over accounting and has the ability to enforce it. Moreover, it has assembled a fine and most experienced pool of accounting talent. It seems to have understood better than most the great difficulties and complexities involved in finding universally valid and acceptable accounting principles. As a result, it has recognized the superiority of a system of widely diffused research efforts to mere promulgation by central edict. The SEC has recognized that the requirement for certification of financial statements to be filed with the Commission has placed a heavy responsibility upon the accounting profession and has encouraged it to exercise leadership in accounting and auditing matters. "At the same time the Commission has not hesitated to criticize and prod, to take exception to accounting presentations, and to discipline members of the profession when circumstances warranted."[11] In short, the Commission has so far exemplified not a rigid and arbitrary exercise of governmental authority but the sparing use of this authority in a helpful way.

The SEC approach toward accounting practice is, in large measure, determined by current public attitudes toward, and confidence in, financial reporting and to some extent by the personality and the temperament of its chief accountant. These have changed over the years and so we have seen from time to time the application of novel approaches to the enforcement of auditing standards. Thus, in recent years, audit firms were forced to consent to quality reviews of their practice by committees of peers, and the FASB was confronted with a flood of new SEC requirements in areas it considered as being under its jurisdiction. Moreover, the SEC has become increasingly aggressive in modifying FASB standards as, for example, by its modification of the effective date of *SFAS 13* on leases, and its intervention in price-level accounting and in oil and gas accounting.

In 1973, the SEC reiterated in *FRR,* Section 101,[12] its policy of "looking to the private sector for leadership in establishing and improving accounting principles and standards."[13]

In its desire to submit its major policies to periodic reevaluation, the SEC appointed in early 1976 an Advisory Committee on Corporate Disclosure whose task is to examine the entire corporate disclosure system. The committee has recommended a number of changes including improvements in interim and segmental reporting, and its final conclusions do not appear to be far reaching.

The constructive influence that the SEC has been exercising over the development of accounting principles should, however, not mislead the financial

---

[11] Excerpts from testimony before the Subcommittee on Commerce and Finance of the Committee on Interstate and Foreign Commerce, House of Representatives, February 19, 1964, as reported in the *Journal of Accountancy,* June 1964, p. 58.

[12] In 1982, the *ASRs* were codified into *Financial Reporting Release (FRRs)* No. 1 and will be referred to by section number.

[13] This delegation of authority has been challenged in court by one large accounting firm. Even more importantly, in late 1976 and in 1977, congressional committees have taken a critical interest in the workings and the regulation of the accounting profession and have called for its stricter regulation and supervision. They also called for an even more active role by the SEC in the setting of accounting standards. In the early 1980s, however, the winds of political change have resulted in a far less aggressive regulatory stance by Congress and hence the SEC.

analyst into believing that the financial statements included in documents filed with the Commission are more reliable than others from the point of view of the accounting used in their preparation. They are unfortunately not much more reliable because they rarely reflect a higher-than-average level of the "state of the art" and also because the staff of the SEC is far too limited in number and in capabilities to enable it to review thoroughly all the documents submitted to it.

The influence of other organizations.   Two other bodies whose influence on the formation of accounting principles must be considered are the American Accounting Association (AAA) and the Stock Exchanges, particularly the New York Stock Exchange (NYSE).

The AAA has a membership composed primarily of accounting educators. Being one step removed from the practice of the profession, they have a more detached point of view and, by the very nature of their calling, a more scholarly and theoretical one. The AAA has long considered the inconsistencies in accounting theory as calling for a broad effort to establish an integrated framework of accounting theory. To this they have contributed significantly with a series of monographs (starting in 1937) and with statements on accounting principles and theory, the first one published in 1936 and the most recent in 1977. While the AAA statements on accounting theory have been influential in shaping accounting thought, they have no official standing in the accounting profession on which they are in no way binding.

The role of the NYSE in the formulation of accounting theory has never been an active one. As already shown, the Exchange had in the early 1930s taken an interest in financial reporting and in correspondence with the AICPA has promoted the setting down of accounting and auditing standards.

Like the SEC, the NYSE has the ability to enforce adherence to standards. The basic instrument by which the Exchange secures compliance to its standards is the listing agreement. This agreement defines, among other things, the minimum accounting disclosure required in the financial statements of the listed company.

One important way in which the New York and American Stock Exchanges have lent support to the efforts of the AICPA in the area of accounting improvements is by urging listed companies to comply with specific professional pronouncements.

Improvements in accounting principles—implications for financial analysis

In recent years, substantial progress has been made by professional bodies and by the SEC in their endeavor to narrow the range of acceptable alternatives in accounting principles, to increase the amount of meaningful disclosure, and to improve the overall level of financial accounting. This progress notwithstanding, the serious user of published financial reports knows that the room for further necessary improvements is great indeed and that much remains to be done in these areas.

It would be naive and unrealistic to hope that the time is anywhere near when the financial analyst will no longer need to concern himself with the accounting principles that underlie the financial statements that he uses and "go forward from the figures" with his analysis rather than spending time and energy to first "go behind those figures." The critical examination, analysis, and evaluation of the accounting behind the financial statements will, for the foreseeable future, remain an important part of the totality of the analyst's task. Among the more important reasons for this conclusion are the following:

1.   The vital interest of management in the results of operations and the financial position that it reports has in the past, and will continue in the future, to exert a strong influence on the manner in which it accounts for and presents these results. While the attesting auditor may, over the years, have increased his ability and his resolve to withstand management pressure, at the present time both his ability and his willingness to do so are limited. In addition to problems related to professional and financial independence, there are problems inherent in the accounting conventions and principles themselves:

   a.   There is the difference between theory and practice. Rarely are accounting theory pronouncements so well and so comprehensively spelled out as to prevent practice from deviating from their spirit and intent.[14] Moreover, most accounting principles apply only to factors that are considered "material," and yet, so far the profession has failed to provide guidelines and a working definition of what is to be considered "material." (See also discussion earlier in this chapter.)

   b.   A number of important areas of accounting theory, such as, for example, business combinations and product cost accounting and allocations, are not adequately covered by professional pronouncements. This contributes to even greater leeway and variety of practice.

   c.   New industries, changing business practices, and the ingenuity of "financial architects" result in an inevitable lag of accounting theory behind accounting practice. In general, accounting theory is developed to cope with existing problems rather than to anticipate new and emerging ones such as those recently found in the real estate development, real estate investment trust, and franchising industries.

2.   Progress toward the development of uniform and fair accounting principles has been and continues to be hampered by powerful interest groups. These exert pressure to have their interests represented in the formulation of accounting requirements that affect reporting practices in their particular

---

[14] For an informative analysis of abuses in financial reporting, see A. J. Briloff *Unaccountable Accounting* (New York: Harper & Row, 1972); and by the same author, *More Debits than Credits* (New York: Harper & Row, 1976) and *The Truth about Corporate Accounting* (New York: Harper & Row, 1981).

industries. Recent examples of such lobbying are the efforts of bankers, of the insurance industry, the extractive industries, and the real estate industry to have their reporting interests reflected in the formulation of accounting principles.

A particularly ominous development in 1975 was the intervention of congressional legislation in the establishment of accounting principles.[15] In its apparent desire to allow reflection of the maximum improvement in corporate reported earnings from the investment tax credit, Congress has stated that no taxpayer shall be required to use any particular method of accounting for the investment credit in reports subject to the jurisdiction of any federal agency. This legislation thwarted the second attempt by the APB to develop a single uniform method of accounting for the investment credit.

3. Even if progress towards the establishment of sound and uniform principles of accounting were to proceed at a much more rapid pace than can now be envisaged, the analyst cannot safely abdicate the job of scrutinizing and evaluating the accounting assumptions and principles that underlie the financial statements that he analyses. As a prerequisite to a thorough and intelligent analysis, he needs a firm understanding of the data being analyzed. Experience has shown that improvements in accounting principles are accompanied by a significant increase in the complexity of accounting data and determinations. Financial analysis bears on decisions of such importance that under no circumstance can the analyst place undue reliance on the data with which he works without examining it and adjusting it to conform it to his own objectives.

4. Regardless of how well covered by sound and accepted theory accounting procedures may be, the analyst must realize that much of the data presented in financial statements is of the "soft" variety. This is true in spite of the appearance of precision conveyed by neatly balanced presentations. "Soft" information is information based on subjective evaluation, on heavy reliance on forecasts of future conditions, and on assumptions regarding the integrity, competence, intent or motives of managements that are generally expressed by means of unquantifiable adjectives. Such information must always be evaluated as part of a complete analysis.

5. Finally, a firm overall understanding of the accounting model is of fundamental importance to the analyst. Thus, at present the basic orientation of financial statements is towards the income statement with balance sheet amounts representing mostly residuals rather than amounts derived from a valuation process. Income statements are, for example, not based on current cash flows but are designed instead to measure long-run average net cash flows at a *current or assumed level of activity*. These orientations have significant implications for those who make decisions on the basis of financial communications.

---

[15] That legislation obligated the SEC to prescribe accounting practices for the oil and gas industry in the United States. This specialized accounting topic was in recent years the subject of policy declarations and reversal by both the SEC and the FASB (see Chapter 11).

THE PERVASIVE HUMAN FACTOR

As we observed earlier in this chapter, accounting is a social science, and consequently no assessment of the value or the reliability of accounting concepts or standards or of the financial statements that are based on them can be complete without a consideration of the pervasive influence of human nature on them.

While formally the objective of accounting is to supply information useful for making economic decisions, we must recognize that in fact many interested parties engaged in the accounting function have more specific (and more narrow or selfish) objectives in mind. For example:

- Management or individual executives of an enterprise may want accounting presentations to help them with individual and specific objectives such as:

    a. Obtaining credit in order to ensure the survival of an enterprise in financial difficulties.

    b. The ability to sell securities in the open market in order to ensure survival, growth, the preservation of jobs, or similar objectives.

    c. To enhance the compensation of executives or employees or to reflect favorably on their operating performance or their egos.[16]

    d. To help management fend off hostile takeover attempts.[17]

    e. To enhance the wealth of present owners of the enterprise.

- Governments may want accounting to promote objectives such as helping to control inflation, enhance labor peace, foster economic growth, aid in antitrust enforcement, enlarge tax revenues, or help industries in distress.[18]

- Public accountants may want accounting to increase the market for their services, help maintain positive relations with important clients, as well as help those clients attain their own objectives.

---

[16] Peter F. Drucker (in *Managing in Turbulent Times* [New York: Harper & Row, 1980], p. 12) observed: "The U.S. tax system greatly favors stock options and bonuses tied to reported earnings, making it very much to the executives' self-interest to report inflated earnings. But in countries where stock options or bonuses of this kind are unknown, such as Japan, executives resist just as strenuously attempts to any adjustment of their reported figures for inflation. The major reason is surely vanity: executives like to take credit for record earnings even when they know that the figures are mere delusion.

[17] Bendix Corporation's 1982 takeover attempt of Martin Marietta Corporation and the latter's countermeasures finally involving two other suitors, presents a graphic illustration, in a related field, that the objectives of managers may not coincide with those of the owners that they are supposed to represent. Commented one observer of this wasteful use of corporate assets, "You don't see these things in closely held companies when the president is spending his own money."

[18] An example of attempted tampering with accounting by a governmental agency with the motivation of "helping out" an industry in financial difficulty is the 1982 proposal by the Federal Deposit Insurance Corporation to permit savings banks to defer and amortize all gains and losses on disposition of financial assets acquired prior to January 1, 1983. What was intended was the deferral of losses so that nonregulatory users of financial statements would be led to believe that the savings banks have not incurred the losses which they in fact did incur.

Examples of the use of accounting for the attainment of such, often more narrow objectives, abound in practice and are illustrated in this book. For example, Chapter 6 refers to Datapoint Corporation's reversal of questionable sales booked in an attempt to improve operating results. Chapter 22 discusses the H. J. Heinz case of income smoothing by "second tier" executives and the J. W. T. Group case in which fictitious assets and revenues were created by divisional executives who desired to look good by meeting increasing performance goals. Moreover, Chapter 11 refers to Itel Corporation's philosophy of "programmed" earnings as a means of promoting the corporate image of growth. Chapter 10 refers to the Yale Express case of substantial underaccruals of costs and of auditor carelessness in detecting them. Finally, Chapter 15 describes the huge and protracted equity funding fraud that involved management greed and deception and (luckily as a rare exception) auditor collusion in management's deception for purposes of achieving its own accounting "goals."

Now, as we all know, these narrow interests are not, nor should they be, the objectives of accounting. The FASB, now a body independent of all parties at interest, including the accounting profession, is in fact society's representative charged with the unwritten mission of ensuring that, at least in theory, the objectives of accounting coincide with those of society at large.

Human nature being what it is,[19] analysts must be ever aware that those with strong personal interests at stake will continue to try to bend the theory so that the practice favors their own more narrow interests. Society's most powerful countermeasures include institutions such as the SEC, the courts, as well as the organized auditing profession. While significant progress has been made in improving the overall integrity and reliability of financial reporting in this country, the analyst must be aware that individual exceptions have occurred, are occurring, and are likely to recur in the future.

The concept of accounting risk

The reader and user of accounting determinations must recognize a variety of risks. There is first the all-pervading risk associated with profit-seeking business enterprises: the risk of losses, of adversities, contingencies, and so forth. There is also the risk associated with reliance on audited financial statements on which we will elaborate in Chapter 15.

The user of financial statements prepared "in accordance with generally accepted accounting principles" must recognize yet another type of risk, best termed accounting risk.[20] This risk results from the human nature factor

---

[19] Soichero Honda, founder of Honda Motor Company, expressed it as follows: "God seems to give humans good things, and proportionately, the same degree of bad things to go with it. We humans must develop means to eliminate those bad aspects."

[20] This risk is greatest in companies with a strong stock market orientation whose managements need to produce earnings growth and companies in dire need for borrowed funds where accounting methods are regarded by managements as means of achieving reported results.

discussed in the preceding section as well as from the imprecision inherent in the basic accounting process. It is also due to the existence of alternative accounting principles, the loose criteria that define them, and the consequent instances of loose standards of practice. This lack of assurance about the standards used or the method and rigor of their application may lead to a wide variety of results and hence to a great degree of uncertainty. In this concept of accounting risk, we may also include the degree of conservatism of accounting principles in use or the lack of it. As we shall see in the following chapters, assumptions play an important role in accounting determinations; and such assumptions may be conservative or cautious, or they may be optimistic, daring, or too anticipative of favorable outcomes of things subject to normal doubt. Thus, the degree of conservatism found in the accounting principles in use will determine the magnitude of the setback that may result from assumptions that time shows to be overly optimistic. This aspect of analysis will be explored further in Chapter 22.

QUESTIONS

1. What is the basic purpose of financial accounting?

2. What is the purpose of the FASB's conceptual framework?

3. What are the salient features of *SFAC 1*?

4. What is *SFAC 2* concerned with? What are the characteristics that make accounting information useful? Discuss.

5. Discuss the "pervasive qualities" mentioned by *SFAC 2*.

6. Discuss the elements of financial statements identified by *SFAC 3*.

7. What are some implications for analysis resulting from the conceptual framework project?

8. What are accounting standards?

9. How are accounting standards established?

10. Does the FASB represent a significant improvement over its predecessors? Why?

11. Trace briefly the accounting profession's endeavors to promulgate accounting principles.

12. Can the user of financial statements rely on the use of "generally accepted accounting principles (GAAP)" to produce reliable financial presentations? Of what implication to financial analysis is the rate of progress of improvement in accounting principles and practice?

13. Accounting concepts and standards and the financial statements that are based on them are subject to the pervasive influence of human nature. Discuss.

4

Tools and techniques of financial statement analysis—an overview

Basic approaches to financial statement analysis

In the first chapter, we examined the various objectives of financial statement analysis as viewed from the point of view of specific user groups. In the performance of an analysis, such objectives can, in turn, be translated into a number of specific questions to which the decision maker needs an answer. Thus, for example, the equity investor may want to know:

1. What has the company's operating performance been over the longer term and over the recent past? What does this record hold for future earnings prospects?
2. Has the company's earnings record been one of growth, stability, or decline? Does it display significant variability?
3. What is the company's current financial condition? What factors are likely to affect it in the near future?
4. What is the company's capital structure? What risks and rewards does it hold for the investor?
5. How does this company compare on the above counts with other companies in its industry?

The banker who is approached with a short-term loan request may look to the financial statements for answers to questions such as the following:

1. What are the underlying reasons for the company's needs for funds? Are these needs truly short term, and if so, will they be self-liquidating?
2. From what sources is the company likely to get funds for the payment of interest and the repayment of principal?
3. How has management handled its needs for short-term and long-term funds in the past? What does this portend for the future?

An important first step in any decision-making process is to identify the most significant, pertinent, and critical questions that have a bearing on the

61

decision. Financial statement analysis does not, of course, provide answers to all such questions. However, each of the questions exemplified above can, to a significant extent, be answered by such analysis.

RECONSTRUCTION OF BUSINESS ACTIVITIES AND TRANSACTIONS

Basic to the analyst's work is the ability to reconstruct the business transactions that are summarized in the financial statements. One can visualize this important skill as the ability to replicate the accountant's work but in reverse order. The flow of the accountant's work is as follows:

=============================== **FLOW OF ACCOUNTANT'S WORK** ===============================>

| Perception of the reality behind business transactions | GAAP—The framework of accounting for these transactions | Express the transaction in the form of a journal entry | Accumulate transactions in T-accounts | Summarize and classify in the form of financial statements |

<=============================== **FLOW OF THE ANALYST'S WORK** ===============================

The accountant's effort and skill is first directed to understanding the reality of the transactions or events to be recorded. Next, there must be brought to bear the knowledge of the accounting framework—the generally accepted accounting principals (GAAP) that govern the recording of the transaction, its expression in the form of a journal entry, and its accumulation in accounts. No matter what form data recording and accumulation takes in this electronic age, the basic concepts of the journal entry and the T-account prevail. These, as we shall see, are particularly useful in analytical work. Finally, continuing to be guided by accepted standards of the accounting framework, the accountant summarizes all accounts of a period in the format of financial statements.

The flow of the analyst's work is basically in reverse order. He or she starts with the financial statements made available by the enterprise. The basic task is to recapture, as far as possible, the reality that is imbedded and summarized in these financial statements—the degree to which this is done being dependent on the particular analytical objectives at hand. This analytical process requires that the analyst visualize the journal entries made and that he or she reconstruct, in summary fashion, all or selected accounts in the financial statements. It also requires an understanding of the reality underlying such business transactions as well as a knowledge of the *accounting standards* employed in recording it properly within the accounting framework.

By these means, the analyst will be able to understand the changes in specific balance sheet items, trace the effect of a given transaction or specific accounts, and answer questions such as the following:

- What was the reason for the increase or the decrease in the investment in X Company?
- What effect did the debt refunding have on working capital?
- How much long-term debt was repaid this year?
- What was the effect of income taxes on the financial statements and how much tax was actually paid this year?

The reconstruction of business transactions requires a knowledge of accounting, i.e., the ability to visualize what kind of activities or events will increase or decrease a specific account. It also requires the ability to read carefully and interpret financial statements and related footnotes. Thus, the knowledge of what information can be found in financial statements, where it is to be found, and how to reconstruct transactions, including the making of reasonable assumptions, are important skills in the analysis of financial statements. Generally, in reconstructing transactions, the analyst will work with known information before attempting to deduce unknown facts. The degree of accuracy that can be expected in such reconstructions and the resulting analysis cannot be expected to be nor need it approach the degree of accuracy required in the accounting and recording function.

Throughout this book the T-account will be used as an important analytical tool. The emphasis is not on bookkeeping mechanics but rather on the use of T-account analysis in the reconstruction of transactions. Use of T-account analysis depends on the analyst's ability to express transactions in the form of journal entries.

ILLUSTRATION 1. The analyst of the financial statements of Alfa, Inc., (see Appendix 4B to this chapter) wants to determine the actual amount of long-term debt paid off in 19x6. This involves the reconstruction and analysis of two accounts. To get all the pertinent information, the analyst must refer to the balances of the long-term debt account in the balance sheet, to details about the "current portion of long-term debt" found in Note 8, and to the statement of changes in financial position. Boldface number references in squares refer to those found in the financial statements of Alfa. Amounts are in thousands of dollars.

Long-Term Debt

(b)	8,080	194,690		Bal. 38
		58,344	*(a)*	
		244,954		Bal. 38

(a) Additions to long-term debt (per funds statement 46)
(b) Reduction of long-term debt (per funds statement 55) transferred to current portion of long-term debt.

Current Portion of Long-Term Debt (included in $\boxed{32}$)

Long-term debt paid		8,701	Bal. (Note 8)
off (balancing amount)	9,453	8,080	Transfer from long-term debt
		7,328	Bal. (Note 8)

Based on the information available, the best estimate of the long-term debt paid off is $9,453. It must be noted that we are dealing here with aggregate (not individual) transactions for 19x6. When there is inadequate information, the analyst may have to combine accounts and transactions and consider them together. Having pinpointed what type of information is lacking, the analyst can develop informed questions for management in order to obtain the desired information that was not disclosed in the financial statements.

The analyst must also know what information is not generally available in financial statements so that he may attempt to secure it. In addition to information such as commitments, lines of credit, and order backlogs, the analyst will also generally not find the details of changes in many important accounts. Thus, for example, a Notes Payable account or a Loan to Officers account may show little or no change in year-end balances but may, in fact, have had significant interim balances that were liquidated during the year.

The analysis and reconstruction of business transactions is an important analytical procedure and will be illustrated throughout this book. Illustrations will be based on the financial statements of Alfa, Inc. (Appendix 4B).

IMPORTANCE OF THE STATEMENT OF CHANGES IN FINANCIAL POSITION

The analytical steps involved in the reconstruction of business transactions often involve use of the statement of changes in financial position (SCFP). For this and other reasons, this statement is of key importance to the analyst. Consequently, the placement of a chapter dealing with this statement in this book involves difficult choices. It would be advantageous to consider this subject as early as possible. On the other hand, a thorough and detailed consideration of the statement can be undertaken only *after* a consideration of all elements of the financial statements. For this reason, it is recommended that at this point Chapter 13 be read in a cursory fashion. Later, after Chapters 5 to 11 have been studied, Chapter 13 can be delved into much more thoroughly.

Additional analytical functions

The following are some additional analytical processes in widespread use:

Direct measurements. Some factors and relationships can be measured directly. For example, the relationship between the debt and the equity of an entity is a direct measurement. Both the amount of debt and that of equity can be measured in absolute terms (i.e., in dollars) and their relationship computed therefrom.

Indirect evidence. Financial statement analysis can provide indirect evidence bearing on important questions. Thus, the analysis of past statements of changes in financial position can offer evidence as to the financial habits of a management team. Moreover, the analysis of operating statements will yield evidence regarding mangement's ability to cope with fluctuations in the level of the firm's business activity. While such indirect evidence and evaluation are often not precise or quantifiable, the data derived therefrom nevertheless possess importance because the effects of almost all managerial decisions, or the lack of them, are reflected in the entity's financial statements.

Predictive functions. Almost all decision questions are oriented towards the future. Thus, an important measure of the usefulness of financial statement analysis tools and techniques is their ability to assist in the prediction of expected future conditions and results.

Comparison. This is a very important analytical process. It is based on the elementary proposition that in financial analysis no number standing by itself can be meaningful, and that it gains meaning only when related to some other comparable quantity. By means of comparison, financial analysis is useful in performing important evaluative, as well as attention-directing and control, functions. Thus, it focuses on exceptions and variations, and saves the analyst the need to evaluate the normal and the expected. Moreover, by means of comparison, selection among alternative choices is accomplished.

Comparison may be performed by using:

1. A company's own experience over the years (i.e., internally derived data);
2. External data, such as industry statistics; or
3. Compiled yardsticks, including standards, budgets, and forecasts.

Historical company data can usually be readily obtained and most readily adjusted for inconsistencies.

Uses of external data. Useful comparison may also be made with external data. The advantages of external data are: (1) they are normally objective and independent; (2) they are derived from similar operations, thus performing the function of a standard of comparison; and (3) if current, they reflect events occurring during an identical period having as a consequence similar business and economic conditions in common.

External information must, however, be used with great care and discrimination. Knowledge of the basis and method of compilation, the period covered, and the source of the information will facilitate a decision of whether the information is at all comparable. At times, sufficient detail may be available to adjust data so as to render them comparable. In any event, a decision on a proper standard of comparison must be made by choosing from those available. Differences between situations compared must be noted. Such differences may be in accounting practices or specific company policies. It must also be borne in mind that the past is seldom an unqualified guide to the future.

SOURCES OF INFORMATION

For basic data on an enterprise and for comparative data of comparable entities in its industry, published financial statements provide the best and most readily available source.

Appendix 4A to this chapter presents a listing of sources of information on financial and operating ratios of various industries as well as sample presentations from these sources. These data, while representing valuable sources for comparison, must be used with care and with as complete a knowledge of the basis of their compilation as is possible to obtain. A realistic and sometimes superior alternative for the analyst is to use as a basis of comparison the financial statements of one or more comparable companies in the same industry. In this way, one can usually have a better command over and comprehension of the data entering into the comparison base.

Annual reports to shareholders contain an ever-expanding amount of information required by either GAAP or by specific SEC requirements.[1]

In addition, company filings with the SEC, such as Registration Statements[2] pursuant to the Securities Act of 1933, supplemental and periodic reports which are required to be filed (such as Forms 8-K, 10-K, 10-Q, 14-K, and 16-K), or proxy statements contain a wealth of information of interest to the analyst.

---

[1] For example, Rule 14c-3 of the Securities Exchange Act of 1934 specifies that annual reports furnished to stockholders in connection with the annual meeting of stockholders include the following financial information: (1) audited financial statements—balance sheets as of the two most recent fiscal years, and statements of income and changes in financial position for each of the three most recent fiscal years; (2) selected quarterly financial data for each quarterly period within the two most recent fiscal years; (3) summary of selected financial data for last five years; (4) management's discussion and analysis of financial condition and results of operations; (5) market price of company's common stock for each quarterly period within the two most recent fiscal years; and (6) segment information.

[2] SEC Regulation S-X, which specifies the form and content of financial statements filed with the Commission, contains numerous requirements for specific disclosures.

THE TOTAL INFORMATION SET

In Chapter 2, we discussed the relative importance of financial statement analysis to the total decision effort. The total information set on which the decision maker draws includes financial as well as other types of information, and the relative importance of each varies from decision to decision. Exhibit 4–1 presents the composition of this information set (or spectrum).

THE PRINCIPAL TOOLS OF ANALYSIS

In the analysis of financial statements, the analyst has available a variety of tools from which he can choose those best suited to his specific purpose. The following principal tools of analysis will be discussed in this chapter:

1. Comparative financial statements.
   a. Year-to-year changes.
2. Index-number trend series.
3. Common-size financial statements.
   a. Structural analysis.
4. Ratio analysis.
5. Specialized analyses.
   a. Cash forecasts.
   b. Analysis of changes in financial position.
   c. Statement of variation in gross margin.
   d. Break-even analysis.

The application of these tools as well as other aspects of analysis will be illustrated throughout by means of the financial statements of Alfa, Inc., presented in Appendix 4B. Further examples of tabulations of analytical measures can be found in Chapter 23.

Comparative financial statements

The comparison of financial statements is accomplished by setting up balance sheets, income statements, or statements of changes in financial position (SCFP), side by side, and reviewing the changes that have occurred in individual categories therein from year to year and over the years.

The most important factor revealed by comparative financial statements is *trend.* The comparison of financial statements over a number of years will also reveal the direction, velocity, and the amplitude of trend. Further analysis can be undertaken to compare the trends in related items. For example, a year-to-year increase in sales of 10 percent accompanied by an increase in freight-out costs of 20 percent requires an investigation and explanation of the reasons for the difference. Similarly, an increase of accounts receivable of 15 percent during the same period would also warrant an investigation

Exhibit 4–1: Information set (or spectrum)

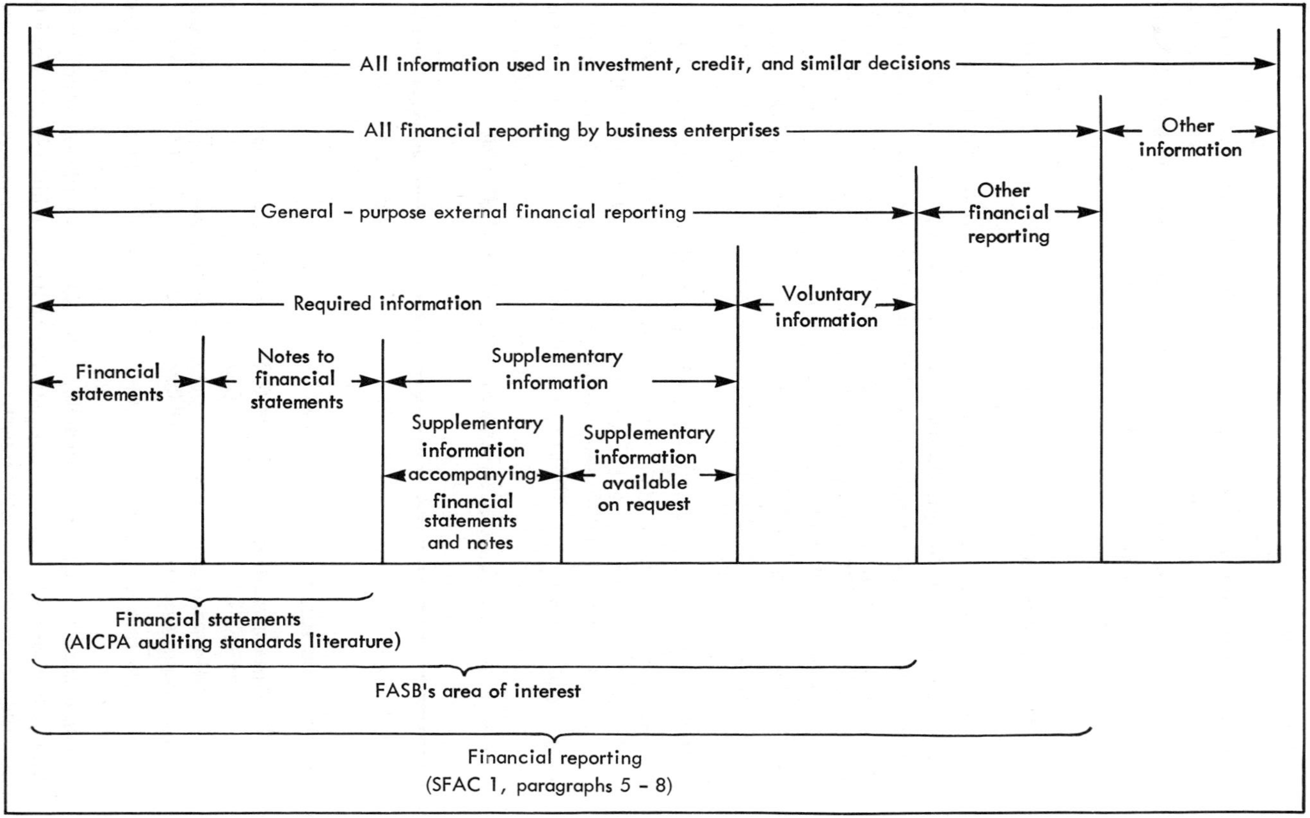

- All information used in investment, credit, and similar decisions
- All financial reporting by business enterprises
- General - purpose external financial reporting
- Required information
  - Financial statements
  - Notes to financial statements
- Supplementary information
  - Supplementary information accompanying financial statements and notes
  - Supplementary information available on request
- Voluntary information
- Other financial reporting
- Other information

Financial statements (AICPA auditing standards literature)

FASB's area of interest

Financial reporting (SFAC 1, paragraphs 5 - 8)

Source: FASB, *Invitation to Comment on Financial Statements and Other Means of Financial Reporting* (Stamford, Conn., 1980), p. 2.

into the reasons for the difference in the rate of increase of sales as against that of receivables.

Year-to-year change. A comparison of financial statements over two to three years can be undertaken by computing the *year-to-year change* in absolute amounts and in terms of percentage changes. Longer-term comparisons are best undertaken by means of *index-number trend series.*

Year-to-year comparisons of financial statements are illustrated in Appendix 4B. When a two- or three-year comparison is attempted, such presentations are manageable and can be understood by the reader. They have the advantage of presenting changes in terms of absolute dollar amounts as well as in percentages. Both have to be considered because the dollar size of the different bases on which percentage changes are computed may yield large percentage changes that are out of proportion to their real significance. For example, in the same financial statements, a 50 percent change from a base figure of $1,000 is far less significant than the same percentage change from a base of $100,000. Thus, reference to the dollar amounts involved is always necessary in order to retain the proper perspective and to reach valid conclusions regarding the relative significance of the changes disclosed by this type of analysis.

The computation of year-to-year changes is a simple matter. However, a few clarifying rules should be borne in mind. When a negative amount appears in the base year and a positive amount in the following year, or vice versa, no percentage change can be meaningfully computed. When an item has a value in a base year and none in the following period, the decrease is 100 percent. Where there is no figure for the base year, no percentage change can be computed. The following summary will illustrate this:

			Change increase (decrease)	
Item	*19x1*	*19x2*	*Amount*	*Per-cent*
Net income (loss).....	$ (4,500)	$ 1,500	$ 6,000	—
Tax expense	2,000	(1,000)	(3,000)	—
Notes payable	—	8,000	8,000	—
Notes receivable	10,000	—	(10,000)	(100)

Comparative financial statements can also be presented in such a way that the cumulative total for the period for each item under study and the average for that period are shown.

The value of comparing yearly amounts with an average covering a number of years is that unusual factors in any one year are highlighted. Averages smooth out erratic or unusual fluctuations in data.

Index-number trend series

When a comparison of financial statements covering more than three years is undertaken, the year-to-year method of comparison may become too cumbersome. The best way to effect such longer-term trend comparisons is by means of index numbers. Such a comparative statement for Alfa, Inc., is illustrated in Appendix 4B.

The computation of a series of index numbers requires the choice of a base year that will, for all items, have an index amount of 100. Since such a base year represents a frame of reference for all comparisons, it is best to choose a year that, in a business conditions sense, is as typical or normal as possible. If the earliest year in the series compared cannot fulfill this function, another year is chosen. In our example of the Alfa, Inc., comparative statements, the year 19x2 was chosen.

As is the case with the computation of year-to-year percentage changes, certain changes, such as those from negative to positive amounts, cannot be expressed by means of index numbers. All index numbers are computed by reference to the base year.

ILLUSTRATION 2. Assume that in the base year at 12/31/19xA, there is a cash balance of $12,000. Based on an index number of 100 for 19xA, if the cash balance in the following year (at 12/31/19xB) is $18,000, then the index number will be

$$\frac{\$18,000}{\$12,000} \times 100 = 150$$

On 12/31/19xC the cash balance is $9,000, the index will stand at 75 arrived at as follows:

$$\frac{\$9,000}{\$12,000} \times 100 \left(\frac{\text{Balance in current year}}{\text{Balance in base year}} \times 100 \right)$$

It should be noted that when using index numbers, percentage changes cannot be read off directly except by reference to the base year. Thus, the change of the cash balance between 19xA and 19xB is 50 percent (index 150 − index 100), and this can be read off directly from the index numbers. The change from 19xB to 19xC, however, is not 75 percent (150 − 75), as a direct comparison may suggest, but rather 50 percent (i,e., $9,000/$18,000), which involves computing the 19xB to 19xC change by reference to the amount at 19xB. The percentage change can, however, be computed by use of the index numbers only, for example, 75/150 = .5, or a change of 50 percent.

In planning an index-number trend comparison, it is not necessary to include in it all the items in the financial statements. Only the most significant items need be included in such a comparison.

Care should be exercised in the use of index-number trend comparisons because such comparisons have weaknesses as well as strengths. Thus, in trying to assess changes in the current financial condition, the analyst may use to advantage comparative statements of changes in financial position.

On the other hand, the index-number trend comparison is very well suited to a comparison of the changes in the *composition* of working capital items over the years.

The interpretation of percentage changes as well as those of index-number trend series must be made with a full awareness of the effect that the inconsistent application of accounting principles over the years can have on such comparisons. Thus, where possible, such inconsistencies must be adjusted. In addition, the longer the period covered by the comparison, the more distortive are the effects of price-level changes on such comparisons likely to be, and the analyst must be aware of such effects (see Chapter 14).

One important value of trend analysis is that it can convey to the analyst a better understanding of management's philosophies, policies, and motivations, conscious or otherwise, that have brought about the changes revealed over the years. The more diverse the economic environments covering the periods compared are, the better a picture can be obtained by the analyst of the ways in which the enterprise has weathered its adversities and taken advantage of its opportunities.

Common-size financial statements

In the analysis of financial statements, it is often instructuve to find out the proportion that a single item represents of a total group or subgroup. In a balance sheet, the assets as well as the liabilities and capital are each expressed as 100 percent, and each item in these categories is expressed as a percentage of the respective totals. Similarly, in the income statement, net sales are set at 100 percent and every other item in the statement is expressed as a percent of net sales. Since the totals always add up to 100 percent, this community of size has resulted in these statements being referred to as "common size." Similarly, following the eye as it reviews the common-size statement, this analysis is referred to as "vertical" for the same reason that the trend analysis is often referred to as "horizontal" analysis.

Selected common-size statements of Alfa, Inc., are presented in Appendix 4B.

Structural analysis. The analysis of common-size financial statements may best be described as an analysis of the internal structure of the financial statements. In the analysis of a balance sheet, this structural analysis focuses on two major aspects:

1. What are the sources of capital of the enterprise, that is, what is the distribution of equities as between current liabilities, long-term liabilities, and equity capital?
2. Given the amount of capital from all sources, what is the distribution of assets (current, fixed, and other) in which it is invested? Stated differently, what is the mix of assets with which the enterprise has chosen to conduct its operations.

The common-size balance sheet analysis can, of course, be carried further and extended to an examination of what proportion of a subgroup, rather than the total, an item is. Thus, in assessing the liquidity of current assets, it may be of interest to know not only what proportion of total assets is invested in inventories but also what proportion of current assets is represented by this asset.

In the case of the income statement, common-size statement analysis is a very useful tool transcending perhaps in importance the analysis of the balance sheet by such means. This is so because the income statement lends itself very well to an analysis whereby each item in it is related to a central quantum, that is, sales. With some exceptions, the level of each expense item is affected to some extent by the level of sales, and thus it is instructive to know what proportion of the sales dollar is absorbed by the various costs and expenses incurred by the enterprise.

Comparisons of common-size statements of a single enterprise over the years are valuable in that they show the changing proportions of components within groups of assets, liabilities, costs, and other financial statement categories. However, care must be exercised in interpreting such changes and the trend that they disclose. For example, the table below shows the amount of patents and total assets of an enterprise over three years:

	19x3	19x2	19x1
Patents	$ 50,000	$ 50,000	$ 50,000
Total assets	$1,000,000	$750,000	$500,000
Patents as a percentage of total assets	5%	6.67%	10%

While the amount of patents remained unchanged, the increase in total assets made this item a progressively smaller proportion of total assets. Since this proportion can change with either a change in the absolute amount of the item or a change in the total of the group of which it is a part, the interpretation of a common-size statement comparison requires an examination of the actual figures and the basis on which they are computed.

Common-size statements are very well suited to intercompany comparison because the financial statements of a variety of companies can be recast into the uniform common-size format regardless of the size of individual accounts. While common-size statements do not reflect the relative sizes of the individual companies that are compared, the problem of actual comparability between them is a matter to be resolved by the analyst's judgment.

Comparison of the common-size statements of companies within an industry or with common-size composite statistics of that industry can alert the analyst's attention to variations in account structure or distribution, the reasons for which should be explored and understood. A comparison of selected common-size statement items of the Marine Supply Company with similar industry statistics will be found in Chapter 23.

Ratio analysis

Ratios are among the best known and most widely used tools of financial analysis. At the same time, their function is often misunderstood, and consequently their significance may easily be overrated.

A ratio expresses the mathematical relationship between one quantity and another. The ratio of 200 to 100 is expressed as $2:1$, or as 2. While the computation of a ratio involves a simple arithmetical operation, its interpretation is a far more complex matter.

To begin with, to be significant, the ratio must express a relationship that has significance. Thus, there is a clear, direct, and understandable relationship between the sales price of an item, on one hand, and its cost, on the other. As a result, the ratio of cost of goods sold to sales is a significant one. On the other hand, there is no a priori or understandable relationship between freight costs incurred and the marketable securities held by an enterprise; and hence, a ratio of one to the other must be deemed to be of no significance.

Ratios are tools of analysis that in most cases provide the analyst with clues and symptoms of underlying conditions. Ratios, properly interpreted, can also point the way to areas requiring further investigation and inquiry. The analysis of a ratio can disclose relationships as well as bases of comparison that reveal conditions and trends that cannot be detected by an inspection of the individual components of the ratio.

Since ratios, like other tools of analysis, are future oriented, the analyst must be able to adjust the factors present in a relationship to their probable shape and size in the future. He must also understand the factors that will influence such ratios in the future. Thus, in the final analysis, the usefulness of ratios is wholly dependent on their intelligent and skillful interpretation. This is, by far, the most difficult aspect of ratio analysis. Let us, by way of example, consider the interpretation of a ratio derived from an area outside that of the business world: In comparing the ratio of gas consumption to mileage driven, A claims to have a superior performance, that is, 28 mpg compared to B's 20 mpg. Assuming that they drove identical cars, the following are factors that affect gas consumption and that will have to be considered before one can properly interpret the ratios and judge whose performance is better:

1. Weight of load driven.
2. Type of terrain (flat versus hilly).
3. City or country driving.
4. Kind of gasoline used.
5. Speed at which cars were driven.

Numerous as the factors that influence gas consumption are, the evaluation of the gas consumption ratio is, nevertheless, a simpler process than the evaluation of most ratios derived from business variables. The reason for this is that the interrelationships of business variables and the factors that affect them are multifaceted and very complex.

Factors affecting ratios

In addition to the internal operating conditions that affect the ratios of an enterprise, the analyst must be aware of the factors, such as general business conditions, industry position, management policies, as well as accounting principles, that can affect them. As far as the latter are concerned, the discussion of accounting principles in Part II of this book points up their influence on the measurements on which ratios are based.

Before ratios, or similar measures such as trend indexes or percentage relationships, are computed, the analyst must make sure that the figures entering into their computation are valid and consistent. For example, when inventories are valued on the LIFO basis (see Chapter 5), under conditions of increasing prices, the current ratio may be understated because LIFO basis inventories may be significantly understated in terms of current value. Similarly, some pension liabilities may be unrecorded and disclosed in footnotes only (see Chapter 7). Some analysts may wish to recognize these liabilities when computing the debt-to-equity ratio of an enterprise. Care must also be taken to recognize that when such adjustments are made in one ratio, consistency may also require that they be made in other ratios as well. Thus, the omission of the pension liability also means that pension expenses have been understated. As a result, the net income amount used in the computation of certain ratios may require adjustment.

The validity of ratios depends also on the validity of the numbers entering into their computation. Thus, when a company's internal controls are such that the accounting system cannot be relied upon to produce reliable figures, the ratios based on such figures are, of course, also unreliable. It is widely believed that such was the situation in the case of W. T. Grant Co. in the years immediately preceding the giant retailer's bankruptcy. (See also discussion in Chapter 13.)

Interpretation of ratios

Ratios should always be interpreted with great care since factors affecting the numerator may correlate with those affecting the denominator. Thus, for example, it is possible to improve the ratio of operating expenses to sales by reducing costs that act to stimulate sales. If the cost reduction consequently results in a loss of sales or share of market, such a seeming improvement in profitability may, in fact, have an overall detrimental effect on the future prospects of the enterprise and must be interpreted accordingly.

It should also be recognized that many ratios have important variables in common with other ratios, thus tending to make them vary and be influenced by the same factors. Consequently, there is no need to use all available ratios in order to diagnose a given condition.

Ratios, like most other relationships in financial analysis, are not significant in themselves and can be interpreted only by comparison with (1) past ratios of the same enterprise, or (2) some predetermined standard, or (3) ratios of other companies in the industry. The range of a ratio over time is also significant as is the trend of a given ratio over time.

ILLUSTRATION OF RATIO COMPUTATIONS

A great many ratios can be developed from the multitude of items included in an enterprise's financial statements. Some ratios have general application in financial analysis, while others have specific uses in certain circumstances or in specific industries. Listed below are some of the more significant ratios that have general applicability to most business situations. They are grouped by major objectives of financial analysis, and the data used to illustrate their computation are taken from the financial statements of Alfa, Inc. (see Appendix 4B):

Major categories of ratios	Method of computation	Alfa, Inc., ratio for 19x6

Short-term liquidity ratios:

Current ratio ....

$$\frac{\text{Current assets}}{\text{Current liabilities}} = \frac{406,784 \boxed{26}^{(a)}}{185,376 \boxed{35}} =$$

2.19

Acid test ratio ....

$$\frac{\text{Cash} + \text{Cash equivalents} + \text{Receivables}}{\text{Current liabilities}} = \frac{18,802 \boxed{22} + 179,652 \boxed{23}}{185,376 \boxed{35}} =$$

1.07

Days sales in receivables
(collection period) ....

$$\frac{\text{Accounts receivable}}{\text{Credit sales} \div 360} = \frac{179,652 \boxed{23}}{1,251,088 \boxed{1} \div 360} =$$

51 days

Inventory turnover ....

$$\frac{\text{Cost of goods sold}}{\text{Average inventory during period}} = \frac{840,043 \boxed{2}}{163,771 \boxed{24} + 192,543 \boxed{24} \div 2} =$$

4.72

Capital structure and long-term solvency ratios:

Total debt to total capital[b] ......

$$\frac{\text{Current liabilities} + \text{Long-term liabilities}}{\text{Equity capital} + \text{Total liabilities}} = \frac{185,376 \boxed{35} + 285,216 \boxed{36} + \boxed{37} + \boxed{38}}{331,080 \boxed{40} + 470,592 \text{ (Total numerator)}} =$$

.59

Long-term debt to equity capital ..

$$\frac{\text{Long-term debt}}{\text{Equity capital}} = \frac{35,404 \boxed{36} + 4,858 \boxed{37} + 244,954 \boxed{38}}{331,080} =$$

.86

Times interest earned[b] ....

$$\frac{\text{Income before interest and taxes}}{\text{Interest}} = \frac{25,368 \boxed{8} + 18,504 \boxed{5}}{18,504} =$$

2.37

Return-on-investment ratios:

Return on total assets ....

$$\frac{\text{Net income} + \text{Interest expense} (1 - \text{Tax rate})^{(c)}}{\text{Average total assets}} = \frac{19,139 \boxed{16} + 18,440 (\boxed{5} - \boxed{6})(1 - .48)}{(738,469 \boxed{31} + 801,672 \boxed{31}) \div 2} =$$

3.7%

Return on equity capital 5.9%

$$\frac{\text{Net income}}{\text{Average equity capital}} = \frac{19{,}139 \; \boxed{16}}{321{,}713 \; \boxed{40} + 331{,}080 \; \boxed{40} \div 2} =$$

Operating performance ratios:

Gross margin ratio 32.9%

$$\frac{\text{Gross profit (margin)}}{\text{Sales}} = \frac{411{,}045 \; (\boxed{1} - \boxed{2})}{1{,}251{,}088 \; \boxed{1}} =$$

Operating profits to sales 3.5%

$$\frac{\text{Operating profit}}{\text{Sales}} = \frac{43{,}808 \; (\boxed{1} - \boxed{2} - \boxed{3} - \boxed{4})}{1{,}251{,}088 \; \boxed{1}} =$$

Pretax income to sales 2.0%

$$\frac{\text{Pretax income}}{\text{Sales}} = \frac{25{,}368 \; \boxed{8}}{1{,}251{,}088 \; \boxed{1}} =$$

Net income to sales 1.5%

$$\frac{\text{Net income}}{\text{Sales}} = \frac{19{,}139 \; \boxed{16}}{1{,}251{,}088 \; \boxed{1}} =$$

Asset-utilization ratios:

Sales to cash 66.54

$$\frac{\text{Sales}}{\text{Cash}} = \frac{1{,}251{,}088 \; \boxed{1}}{18{,}802 \; \boxed{22}} =$$

Sales to accounts receivables 6.96

$$\frac{\text{Sales}}{\text{Accounts receivable}} = \frac{1{,}251{,}088 \; \boxed{1}}{179{,}652 \; \boxed{23}} =$$

Sales to inventories 6.50

$$\frac{\text{Sales}}{\text{Inventories}} = \frac{1{,}251{,}088 \; \boxed{1}}{192{,}543 \; \boxed{24}} =$$

Sales to working capital 5.65

$$\frac{\text{Sales}}{\text{Working capital}} = \frac{1{,}251{,}088 \; \boxed{1}}{221{,}408 \; (\boxed{26} - \boxed{35})} =$$

Sales to fixed assets 4.57

$$\frac{\text{Sales}}{\text{Fixed assets}} = \frac{1{,}251{,}088 \; \boxed{1}}{273{,}645 \; \boxed{29}} =$$

Sales to total assets 1.56

$$\frac{\text{Sales}}{\text{Total assets}} = \frac{1{,}251{,}088 \; \boxed{1}}{801{,}672 \; \boxed{31}} =$$

(concluded)

Major categories of ratios	Method of computation	Alfa, Inc., ratio for 19x6
Market measures:		
Price-earnings ratio	$\dfrac{\text{Market price}}{\text{Earnings per share}} = \dfrac{14^{[d]}}{1.50\;[18]} =$	9.3
Earnings yield	$\dfrac{\text{Earnings per share}}{\text{Market price}} = \dfrac{1.50\;[18]}{14^{[d]}} =$	10.7%
Dividend yield	$\dfrac{\text{Dividends per share}}{\text{Market price per share}} = \dfrac{1.00\;[19]}{14^{[d]}} =$	7.1%
Dividend payout ratio	$\dfrac{\text{Dividends per share}}{\text{Primary earnings per share}} = \dfrac{1.00\;[19]}{1.55\;[17]} =$	64%

[a] Key references are to financial statements of Alfa, Inc.
[b] These are simpler versions of more elaborate ratios discussed in Chapter 18.
[c] Using the marginal (corporate) tax rate.
[d] Average for last quarter of 19x6 [70].

Each of the above five major areas of objectives of financial statement analysis will be examined in Part III of this book; and therein the computation, use, and interpretation of the ratios listed under each category as well as other ratios will be examined in detail and thoroughly discussed.

MARKET MEASURES

Analysts and investors use a variety of measures to evaluate the price and yield behavior of securities. The *price-earnings ratio* measures the multiple at which the market is capitalizing the earnings per share of a company at any given time. The *earnings yield* is the inverse of the price-earnings ratio and represents the income-producing power of a share of common stock at the current price. The *dividend yield* is the return accruing to an investor on a share of stock based on the current dividend rate and current price. Thus, part of the earned yield may be distributed as dividends and the balance retained in the business. The *dividend payout ratio* measures the proportion of earnings that is currently paid out as common stock dividends.

TESTING THE UNDERSTANDING OF RELATIONSHIPS

The following is an example of an exercise designed to test the reader's understanding of various intra- and interstatement ratios and relationships.

ILLUSTRATION 3.   Given the following information, we are to complete the balance sheet below:

Cash	
Accounts receivable	
Inventory	$ 50
Building	
Land	
Current liabilities	
Common stock	
Retained earnings	100

Assets − Liabilities = $600.
Stockholders equity = 3 × debt.
The carrying amount of land is two thirds of that of the building.
Acid-test ratio = 1.25.
Inventory turnover based on cost of goods sold is 15.
Gross profit is 44 percent of the cost of goods sold.
There are 20 days sales in accounts receivable.
The determination of the balance sheet that follows is based on the steps described below:

Cash	$190	Current liabilities	$200
Accounts receivable.....	60	Common stock	500
Inventory	50	Retained earnings	100
Buildings	300		$800
Land	200		
	$800		

STEP 1:

Assets − Liabilities = $600
Stockholders equity = 600
Retained earnings   = 100 (as given)
Common stock   = 500

STEP 2:

Equity = 3 × debt
        3 × current liabilities (which are the total debt) = $600
        Add current liabilities 200
        So total assets equal $800

Step 3:

Acid test = 1.25

$$\frac{\text{Cash} + \text{Accounts receivable}}{\$200} = 1.25$$

Hence,
        Cash + Accounts receivable = $250

STEP 4:

Inventory + Buildings + Land = $550 [i.e., Total assets − (Cash + A/R)]
            Buildings + Land = $500 (since inventory is given at $50)
Land = ⅔ of building; thus, if x = carrying amount of building
    $x + ⅔ x = \$500$ $x = \$300$ (building)
        Land = $500 − $300 = $200

STEP 5:

$$\frac{\text{Cost of goods sold (CGS)}}{\text{Inventory}} = \text{Inventory turnover;} \quad \frac{\text{CGS}}{\$50} = 15$$

Cost of goods sold = $750   Gross profit, 44% of $750 = $330

STEP 6:

Cost of goods sold + Gross profit ($750 + $330) = Sales = $1,080

Amount of sales per day $\dfrac{\$1,080}{360} = \$3$

Accounts receivable = 20 days sales = 20 × $3 = $60
Cash = $250 − Accounts receivable ($60) = $190

Specialized tools of analysis

In addition to the multipurpose tools of financial statement analysis that
we discussed above, such as trend indexes, common-size statements, and

ratios, the analyst has at his or her disposal a variety of special-purpose tools. These tools focus on specific financial statements or segments of such statements, or they can address themselves specifically to the operating conditions of a particular industry, for example, occupancy-capacity analysis in the hotel, hospital, or airline industries. These special-purpose tools of analysis include cash forecasts, analyses of changes in financial position, statements of variation in gross margin, and break-even analyses.

BUILDING BLOCKS OF FINANCIAL STATEMENT ANALYSIS

Whatever approach to financial statement analysis the analyst takes and whatever methods are used, he or she will always have to examine one or more of the important aspects of an enterprise's financial condition and results of its operations. All such aspects, with perhaps the exception of the most specialized ones, can be found in one of the following six categories:

1. Short-term liquidity.
2. Funds flow.
3. Capital structure and long-term solvency.
4. Return on investment.
5. Operating performance.
6. Assets utilization.

Each of the above categories and the tools used in measuring them will be discussed in greater depth in Part III of this book. In this way, the financial analysis required by any conceivable set of objectives may be structured by examining any or all of the above areas in any sequence and with any degree of relative emphasis called for by circumstances. Thus, these six areas of inquiry and investigation can be considered as building blocks of financial statement analysis.

COMPUTER-ASSISTED FINANCIAL ANALYSIS

The major emphasis throughout this book is on the application of thoughtful and logical analysis upon carefully evaluated and verified data. Financial statement analysis does, however, involve a significant amount of work of a computational nature as well as numerous logical steps that can be preplanned and programmed. It is in these areas that the financial analyst can utilize computers to great advantage.

The modern electronic computer has a remarkable facility for performing complex computations with great speed. Moreover, it can perform these computations, comparisons, and other logical steps for long periods of time without exhaustion and once properly programmed will do them without error. In today's environment, when business complexity has outstripped our ability to grasp it and when our ability to generate information has outrun our ability to utilize it, the computer can render vital assistance.

The intelligent use of the computer's formidable capabilities in financial analysis depends, however, on thorough understanding of the limitations to which this powerful tool is subject. Thus, the computer lacks the ability to make intuitive judgments or to gain insights, capabilities that are essential to a competent and imaginative financial analysis.

There is nothing that the computer can do that a competent analyst armed with a calculator cannot do. On the other hand, the speed and the capabilities of modern computers are such that to accomplish what they can do would require so many hours of work as to render most such efforts uneconomical or unfeasible. Computers have thus automated some of the statistical and analytical steps that were previously done manually.

The stored data bases on which computer assisted security analysis often relies do not include all the information that, as discussed in Part II of this book, is needed to adjust accounting data in order to render it comparable or in order to make it conform to the analyst's specific needs. This is particularly true for the following reasons:

1. The data banks generally lack information on accounting policies and principles employed by a given enterprise. This information is essential to an interpretation of the data and to its comparison to other data.
2. Footnotes and other explanatory or restrictive information usually found in individual enterprise reports containing the financial statements are also generally not available in any meaningful detail.
3. Lack of retroactive adjustments because the necessary data are often not available.
4. Errors and omissions may occur when large masses of financial data are processed on a uniform basis for purposes of inclusion in the data base.
5. The aggregation of dissimilar or noncomparable data results in a loss of vital distinctions and thus reduces its meaning and its value for analysis.

Given an understanding of the capabilities as well as the limitations to which the computer is subject, the following are the more significant uses that can be made of this important tool in the broad area of financial analysis:

1. Data storage, retrieval, and computational ability

A machine-accessible comprehensive data base is essential to the use of the computer in most phases of security and credit analysis. The ability of the computer to store vast amounts of data and to afford access to them is one of its important capabilities. Another is the ability to sift these data, to manipulate them mathematically, and to select from among them in accordance with set criteria, as well as to constantly update and modify them. Moreover, the ability of computers to perform computations (of ratios etc.) is almost unlimited.

A large commercially available data base comprising financial information on many hundreds of corporations covering 20 or more years is available from COMPUSTAT, a service of Standard & Poor's Corporation. Another important data base is that provided by Value Line. Many other specialized data bases and time-sharing services are available from various sources and those include the AICPA time-sharing program library.

2. Screening large masses of data

The computer can be used to screen for specified criteria as a means of selecting investment opportunities and for other purposes. A variation of these techniques consists of "filtering" data in accordance with a set of preselected criteria (e.g., certain sales levels, returns, growth rates, financial characteristics, etc.)

3. A research tool

The computer can be used as a research tool for uncovering characteristics of and relationships between data on companies, industries, the market behavior, and the economy.

4. Specialized financial analyses

The computer can be an input tool for financial analysis in credit extension and security analysis.

  A. *Financial analysis in credit extension.*
1. Storage of facts for comparison and decision making.
2. Projection of enterprise cash requirements under a variety of assumptions.
3. Projection of financial statements under a variety of assumptions showing the impact of changes on key variables. Known as *sensitivity analysis,* this technique allows the user to explore the effect of systematically changing a given variable repeatedly by a predetermined amount.
4. The introduction of probabilistic inputs. The data can be inserted as probability distributions, either normally shaped or skewed, or random probability distributions otherwise known as Monte Carlo trials.

  B. *Security analysis.*
1. Calculations based on past data.
2. Trend computations.
   —Simple.
   —Regression analysis.
3. Predictive models.
4. Projections and forecasts.

5. Sensitivity analysis.
6. Complex probabilistic analysis.

Given an understanding of the capabilities of the modern electronic computer, as well as the limitations to which it is subject, the financial analyst will find in it an important tool that promises to grow in importance as new applications to which it can be put are perfected in the future.

ANALYTICAL REVIEW OF ACCOUNTING PRINCIPLES— PURPOSES AND FOCUS

In the chapters that follow, we shall present a review of accounting standards used in the preparation of financial statements. The purpose of this review is to examine the variety of standards that can be applied to similar transactions and circumstances, as well as the latitude that is possible in the interpretation and application of these standards in practice. Thus, the focus is on an understanding of accounting standards as well as on an appreciation of the impact that the application of these standards may have on the reported financial condition and results of operations of an enterprise. Such possible impact must be appreciated and understood before any intelligent analysis can be undertaken or any useful and meaningful comparison is made.

Example of importance of accounting assumptions, standards, and determinations: Illustration of a simple investment decision

The importance of standards and assumptions in accounting determinations can perhaps be best illustrated and understood within the framework of an exceedingly simple example of a business situation. Let us assume that the owner of an apartment building has found an interested buyer. How should the price be set? How should the buyer gain confidence in the soundness and profitability of such investment at a given price?

The first question is the method to be followed in arriving at a fair value of the building. While many approaches are possible, such as comparable current values, reproduction costs, and so forth, let us settle here on the most widely accepted method for the valuation of income-producing properties as well as other investments: the capitalization of earnings. If earning power is the major consideration, then the focus must be on the income statement. The prospective buyer is given the following income statement:

184 EAGLE STREET APARTMENT HOUSE

Income Statement

For the Year Ending December 31, 19x9

Revenue:

Rental revenue	$46,000
Garage rentals	2,440
Other income from washer and dryer concession	300
Total revenue	48,740

Expenses:

Real estate taxes	$4,900	
Mortgage interest	2,100	
Electricity and gas	840	
Water	720	
Superintendent's salary	1,600	
Insurance	680	
Repairs and maintenance	2,400	13,240
Income before depreciation		35,500
Depreciation		9,000
Net income*		$26,500

* Income taxes are excluded from consideration here because they depend on the owner's tax status.

The first questions the prospective buyer will want to ask himself about the foregoing income statement are these:

1. Can I rely on the fairness of presentation of the income statement?
2. What adjustments have to be made so as to obtain a net income figure that can be used with confidence in arriving at a proper purchase price?

In our society, the most common way of gaining assurance about the fairness of presentation of financial statements is to rely on the opinion of an independent certified public accountant. This professional is assumed to perform a skillful audit and to satisfy himself that the financial statements do accurately portray the results of operations and the financial position, in accordance with principles that are generally accepted as proper and useful in the particular context in which they are applied. Such an auditor is also presumed to understand that someone like our prospective buyer will rely on his opinion in reaching a decision on whether to buy and at what price. In Chapter 15, we will explore in more detail the function of the auditor and what his opinion means to the user of financial statements.

Our prospective buyer's second question is far more complex. The auditor's opinion relates to the income statement as representing fairly the net income for the year ended December 31, 19x9. That in no way means that this is *the* relevant figure to use in arriving at a valuation of the apartment building. Nor would an auditor ever claim that his opinion is directed at the relevance of financial statement figures to any particular decision. Let us then examine what information our buyer will need and what assumptions will have to be made in order to arrive at a figure of net income that can be used in setting the value of the apartment building.

Rental income.   Does the $46,000 figure represent 100 percent occupancy during the year? If so, should an allowance be made for possible vacancies? What are rental trends in the area? What would rents be in five years? In 10 years? Are demand factors for apartments in the area going to stay stable, improve, or deteriorate? The aim, of course, is to come nearest to that figure of yearly rental income that approximates a level that, on the average, can be expected to prevail over the forseeable future. Prior years' data will be useful in judging this.

Real estate taxes.   Here the trend of taxes over the years is an important factor. That in turn depends on the character of the taxing community and revenue and expense trends within it.

Mortgage interest.   This expense is relevant to the buyer only if he or she assumes the existing mortgage. Otherwise the interest cost that will be incurred as a result of new financing will have to be substituted.

Utilities.   These expenses must be scrutinized with a view to ascertaining whether they are at a representative level of what can be expected to prevail.

Superintendent's salary.   Is the pay adequate to secure acceptable services? Can the services of superintendent be retained?

Insurance.   Are all forseeable risks insured for? Is the coverage adequate?

Repairs and maintenance.   These expenses must be examined over a number of years in order to determine an average or representative level. Is the level of expenses such that it affords proper maintenance of the property or is the expense account "starved" so as to show a higher net income?

Depreciation.   This figure is not likely to be relevant to the buyer's decision unless his cost approximates that of the seller. If the cost to the buyer differs, then depreciation will have to be computed on that cost using a proper method of depreciation over the useful life of the building, so as to recover the buyer's original cost.

The buyer must also ascertain whether any expenses that he will be properly expected to incur are omitted from the above income statement. Additional considerations concern the method of financing this acquisition and other costs related thereto.

It should be understood that most of the above questions will have to be asked and properly answered even if the auditor issues an unqualified opinion on the financial statements. Thus, for example, while generally accepted accounting principles (GAAP) require that insurance expense include accruals for the full year, they are not concerned with the adequacy of insurance coverage or of the maintenance policy, or the superintendent's pay, or with expected, as opposed to actual, revenues or expense levels.

If one views the many complex questions and problems that arise in the attempt to analyze this very simple income statement for decision-making purposes, one can begin to grasp the complexities involved in the analysis of the financial statements of a sizable, modern business enterprise.

It is clear that essential to an intelligent analysis of such statements is an appreciation of what financial statements do portray as well as what they do not or cannot portray. As we have seen, there are items that properly belong in such statements and there are items that, because of an inability to quantify them or to determine them objectively, cannot be included.

Those items that properly belong in the financial statements should be presented therein in accordance with principles of accounting that enjoy general acceptance. The wide variety of standards that are "acceptable" as well as the even greater variety in the ways in which they can be applied in practice make it imperative that the user of financial statements be fully aware of these possibilities and their implications. The following chapters will explore this important area.

The example of the apartment house buyer illustrates the obvious fact that despite their limitations, financial statements and presentations are indispensible to the decision-making process. While the potential buyer could not use the income statement without obtaining more information and making further assumptions and adjustments, he would not have had any basis for his decision without it. Had he not received one, he would have had to make one up without utilization of the objectivity and the benefit of the experience of actual transactions over a period of time. Thus, in most cases, the interpretation of historical financial statements represents the essential first step in the decision-making process.

APPENDIX 4A

SOURCES OF INFORMATION ON FINANCIAL AND OPERATING RATIOS

A good way to achieve familiarity with the wide variety of published financial and operating ratios available is to classify them by the type of source that collects or compiles them. The specific sources given under each category are intended to exemplify the type of material available. These are by no means complete lists:

Professional and commercial organizations

Dun & Bradstreet, Inc., Business Economics Division, New York, N.Y.
Key Business Ratios. Important operating and financial ratios in 190 lines.
Selected operating expense figures for many retailing, wholesaling, manufacturing lines, as well as for contract construction; service/transportation/communication; finance/insurance/real estate; agriculture/forestry/fishing; mining.
Cost-of-Doing Business Series. Typical operating ratios for 185 lines of business, showing national averages. They represent a percentage of business receipts reported by a representative sample of the total of all federal tax returns.

Moody's Investor Service, New York, N.Y.

Moody's Manuals contain financial and operating ratios on individual companies covered.

National Cash Register Company. *Expenses in Retail Businesses.* Biennial.

Operating ratios for 35 lines of retail business, as taken from trade associations and other sources including many from *Barometer of Small Business.*

Robert Morris Associates. *Annual Statement Studies.*

Financial and operating ratios for about 300 lines of business—manufacturers, wholesalers, retailers, services, and contractors—based on information obtained from member banks of RMA. Data is broken down by company size.

Standard & Poor's Corporation

Industry Surveys in two parts: (1) Basic Analysis and (2) Current Analysis contains many industry and individual company ratios.

Analysts Handbook. "Composite corporate per share data—by industries," for over 90 industries. Statistics and percentages cover 13 components, including sales, operating profits, depreciation, earnings dividends, and the like.

Industry Surveys. Basic data on 36 important industries, with financial comparisons of the leading companies in each industry. Includes a "Basic Analysis" for each, revised annually. A "Current Analysis" is published quarterly for each industry. A monthly "Trends and Projections" includes tables of economic and industry indicators.

Almanac of Business and Industrial Financial Ratios by Leo Troy. Prentice-Hall, Englewood Cliffs, N.J.

A compilation of corporate performance ratios (operating and financial). The significance of these ratios is explained. All industries are covered in the study, each industry is subdivided by asset size.

The federal government

Small Business Administration

Publications containing industry statistics:
Small Marketers Aid.
Small Business Management Series.
Business Service Bulletins.

U.S. Department of Commerce

Census of Business—Wholesale Trade—Summary Statistics. Monthly Wholesale Trade Report. Ratio of operating expenses to sales.

Department of the Treasury

Statistics of Income, Corporation Income Tax Returns. Operating Statistics based on income tax returns.

Federal Trade Commission—Securities and Exchange Commission.

Quarterly Financial Report for Manufacturing, Mining and Trade Corporations. Contains operating ratios and balance sheet ratios as well as the balance sheet in ratio format.

U.S. Internal Revenue Service

Source Book: Statistics of Income: Corporation Income Tax Returns. Washington, D.C. Annual. "Balance sheet, income statement, tax and investment credit items by major and minor industries, broken down by size of total assets."

Statistics of Income: Corporation Income Tax Returns. Washington, D.C.: U.S. Government Printing Office. Annual. Balance sheet and income statement statistics from a sample of corporate returns. Includes tables by major industry, by asset size, and so on. Includes historical summaries.

Sources of specific industry ratios

Many retail and wholesale trade associations compile and publish periodic ratio statistics. Very few manufacturing associations compile ratios they make available to the public; and so for most manufacturing industries one must rely on general sources.

American Meat Institute. *Annual Financial Review of the Meat Packing Industry.* Washington, D.C. Includes operating ratios.

Bank Operating Statistics. Federal Deposit Insurance Corporation. Annual.

Institute of Real Estate Management. Experience Exchange Committee. *A Statistical Compilation and Analysis of Actual (year) Income and Expenses Experienced in Apartment, Condominium and Cooperative Building Operation.* Annual.

Discount Merchandiser. *The True Look of the Discount Industry.* June issue each year. Includes operating ratios.

National Electrical Contractors Association. *Operation Overhead.* Annual.

National Farm & Power Equipment Dealers Association. *Cost of Doing Business Study.* Annual.

National Retail Hardware Association. *Lumber/Building Material Financial Report.* Indianapolis. Annual.

Journal of Commercial Bank Lending. "Analysis of Year End Composite Ratios of Installment Sales Finance and Small Loan Companies."

Harris, Kerr, Forster & Company. *Trends in the Hotel-Motel Business.* Annual.

National Association of Music Merchants. *Merchandising and Operating Statistics.* New York. Annual.

National Decorating Products Association. *NDPA'S Annual Cost of Doing Business Survey.* St. Louis. Taken from *Decorating Retailer,* e.g., September 1980 issue.

National Office Products Association. *NOPA Dealers Operating Results.* Alexandria, Va. Annual.

Restaurant Industry Operations Report for the United States. Washington, D.C.: National Restaurant Association in cooperation with Laventhol & Horwath. Annual.

Bibliographies

Robert Morris Associates. *Sources of Composite Financial Data—A Bibliography.* 4th ed. N.Y., 1976, 29 pp.

An annotated list of sources, with an index by specific industry at front.

Sanzo, Richard. *Ratio Analysis for Small Business.* 4th ed. Washington, D.C., 1977. 66 pp. (U.S. Small Business Administration, Small Business Management Series, No. 20).

"Sources of Ratio Studies," pp. 22–35, lists the industries covered by basic sources such as D & B, Robert Morris Associates; also the names of trade associations that have published ratio studies.

APPENDIX 4B

This appendix contains the financial statements of Alfa, Inc., which are adapted from the published financial statements of a large company engaged in the processing of food products, production of raw cane sugar, merchandising, hospitality, and financial and asset management services.

The purpose of this appendix is to provide an illustration of the contents of a modern and comprehensive set of financial statements which will be referred to throughout the text for purposes of illustration and as a basis for problems. For ease of reference, the most important captions have been identified by key numbers.

Exhibit 4B–1

ALFA, INC., AND CONSOLIDATED SUBSIDIARIES
Statement of Income
Year Ended December 31

(All Dollars Reported in Thousands)

		19x6	19x5	19x4	19x3	19x2
1	**Revenues** (Notes, 2, 3, 4 and 6)	$1,251,088	$1,133,817	$1,147,288	$880,396	$694,958
	Costs And Expenses:					
2	Cost of sales	840,043	730,280	691,077	569,348	441,858
3	Selling, general and administrative	343,023	296,893	285,310	238,957	196,671
4	Depreciation and amortization	24,214	21,158	22,008	16,973	14,398
5	Interest (Note 6)	18,504	16,319	25,054	18,859	11,092
6	Interest capitalized	(64)	—	(3,267)	(1,287)	(463)
7	Total	1,225,720	1,064,650	1,020,182	842,850	663,556
8	**Income Before Income Taxes**	25,368	69,167	127,106	37,546	31,402
9	Income Taxes (Note 7)	7,600	33,000	65,006	13,640	10,858
10	Income From Consolidated Continuing Operations	17,768	36,167	62,100	23,906	20,544
11	Net Income Of Nonconsolidated Finance Subsidiaries	1,371	2,329	2,068	3,609	3,095
12	**Income From Continuing Operations**	19,139	38,496	64,168	27,515	23,639
13	Income (Loss) From Discontinued Operations (Note 3)	—	(1,000)	(7,325)	(957)	657
14	Income Before Cumulative Effect On Prior Years of Accounting Changes	19,139	37,496	56,843	26,558	24,296
15	Cumulative Effect On Prior Years Of Accounting Changes ($36,647 less income taxes of $19,240) (Note 2)	—	(17,407)	—	—	—
16	**Net Income** (Notes 2, 3 and 4)	$ 19,139	$ 20,089	$ 56,843	$ 26,558	$ 24,296

17 Primary Earnings Per Share (Note 10):					
Income from continuing operations	$ 1.55	$ 3.25	$ 5.57	$ 2.40	$ 2.06
Income (loss) from discontinued operations	—	(.08)	(.63)	(.08)	.06
Cumulative effect on prior years of accounting changes	—	(1.47)	—	—	—
Net income	$ 1.55	$ 1.70	$ 4.94	$ 2.32	$ 2.12
18 Fully Diluted Earnings Per Share (Note 10):					
Income from continuing operations	$ 1.50	$ 3.04	$ 5.14	$ 2.28	$ 1.97
Income (loss) from discontinued operations	—	(.07)	(.58)	(.08)	.05
Cumulative effect on prior years of accounting changes	—	(1.33)	—	—	—
Net income	$ 1.50	$ 1.64	$ 4.56	$ 2.20	$ 2.02
19 Cash Dividends Per Common Share	$ 1.00	$ 1.00	$ .70	$ .64	$ .60
20 Pro Forma Amounts (giving retroactive effect to accounting changes; Note 2):					
Revenues	—	$1,133,817	$1,114,937	$877,831	—
Income from continuing operations	—	38,496	48,801	25,475	—
Net income	—	37,496	41,476	24,518	—
Primary earnings per share:					
Income from continuing operations	—	3.25	4.24	2.29	—
Net income	—	3.17	3.61	2.21	—

21

ALFA, INC., AND CONSOLIDATED SUBSIDIARIES
Management's Analysis of the Statement of Income (Note 2)
(Unaudited)

(All Dollars Reported in Thousands)

	Increase (decrease) over prior year	
	19x6	19x5
Revenues		
Food	$ 76,928	$ 9,670
Agriculture	(51,248)	(81,467)
Retail	25,959	26,183
Distribution	42,558	34,404
Hospitality	22,743	9,062
Asset Management	98	(11,355)
Corporate investments	233	32
Total increase (decrease) in revenues	117,271	(13,471)
Cost Of Sales		
Food	55,664	(1,876)
Agriculture	264	8,277
Retail	13,766	12,800
Distribution	37,193	28,745
Hospitality	2,704	(299)
Asset Management	172	(8,444)
Total increase in cost of sales	109,763	39,203

For 19x6, revenues increased 10% and both cost of sales and expenses increased 15% over 19x5. Food Group revenues for 19x6 were up 56% over the prior year, including 34% relating to businesses acquired during the year. Volume increases accounted for the other 22% as selling prices remained relatively unchanged. Cost of food product sales increased 62% and expenses increased 44% over 19x5. Sugar prices for 19x6 were 31% lower than the prior year. Sugar sold was down 8% because fewer acres were harvested and yields were lower than 19x5. As a result of increased volume and prices, retail sales and cost of sales for 19x6 were 8% higher than 19x5 and expenses were 9% higher. Distribution sales were 10% ahead of the prior year primarily as a result of businesses acquired and new branches opened. Cost of sales was up 11% and expenses were up 14%, which resulted in lower contribution to earnings for the Distribution Group in 19x6 compared to 19x5. Hospitality revenues for 19x6 increased 19% over the prior year primarily as a result of new hotels, increased rates and occupancy. Hospitality costs and expenses increased 17% over 19x5. Interest costs for 19x6 were 13% higher than 19x5, principally because of increased borrowings.

For 19x5, revenues decreased 1%, cost of sales increased 6% and expenses increased 2% over 19x4. Food Group revenues for 19x5 were 8% over the prior year primarily as a result of increased selling prices. Cost of food product sales was slightly lower and expenses were 6% higher than 19x4. Sugar prices for 19x5 were 35% lower than the prior year. Sugar sold increased 18% primarily because more acres were harvested. Agriculture Group costs and expenses for 19x5 were up 6% over the prior year. Retail sales for 19x5 were 9% higher than 19x4, including 3% for new stores (net of closed stores). Cost of retail sales for 19x5 increased 8% as gross margins improved over 19x4 and expenses increased 9%. Distribution sales for 19x5 were 9% ahead of the prior year primarily because of businesses acquired and new branches opened. Cost of sales was up 9% and expenses were up 12% over 19x4. Hospitality revenues for 19x5 increased 8% over the prior year primarily as a result of new hotels and restaurants. Hospitality costs and expenses increased 7% over 19x4. Interest expense was 25% lower than 19x4, primarily as a result of lower borrowings during 19x5.

Expenses		
Food	14,524	2,018
Agriculture	723	(2,558)
Retail	10,764	9,647
Distribution	7,282	5,509
Hospitality	15,632	7,898
Asset Management	(283)	(9,598)
Accounting change for deferred preopening expenses (Note 2)		(3,205)
Corporate	544	1,022
Interest	2,121	(5,468)
Total increase in expenses	51,307	5,265
Decrease In Income Before Income Taxes	(43,799)	(57,939)
Decrease In Income Taxes (Note 7)	(25,400)	(32,006)
Decrease In Income From Consolidated Continuing Operations	(18,399)	(25,933)
Increase (Decrease) In Net Income Of Nonconsolidated Finance Subsidiaries	(958)	261
Decrease In Income From Continuing Operations	(19,357)	(25,672)
Discontinued Operations (Note 3)	1,000	6,325
Cumulative Effect On Prior Years Of Accounting Changes (Note 2)	17,407	(17,407)
Total Decrease in Net Income	(950)	(36,754)
Net Income Prior Year	20,089	56,843
Net Income Current Year	$ 19,139	$ 20,089

Exhibit 4B–2

ALFA, INC., AND CONSOLIDATED SUBSIDIARIES
Balance Sheet

(All Dollars Reported in Thousands)

ASSETS

		December 31	
		19x6	*19x5*
	Current Assets:		
22	Cash (Note 8)	$ 18,802	$ 20,677
23	Receivables—less allowance for doubtful receivables of $5,010 and $4,465 (Note 5)	179,652	158,056
24	Inventories (Notes 2 and 5)	192,543	163,771
25	Prepaid expenses	15,787	17,543
26	Total current assets	406,784	360,047
	Investments:		
27	Nonconsolidated finance subsidiaries (Note 13)	32,443	31,072
28	Other (Note 5)	23,053	22,377
29	**Property, Plant And Equipment**—less accumulated depreciation and amortization of $174,932 and $156,959 (Note 5)	273,645	253,580
30	**Other Assets** (Note 5)	65,747	71,393
31	Total	$801,672	$738,469

LIABILITIES

Current Liabilities:

32	Notes payable and current portion of long-term debt (Note 8)	$ 34,028	$ 38,951
33	Accounts payable and accrued expenses (Note 8)	127,144	118,868
34	Income taxes—including deferred taxes of $21,556 and $19,155	24,204	27,993
35	Total current liabilities	185,376	185,812
36	**Deferred Income Taxes**	35,404	31,883
37	**Other Deferred Credits**	4,858	4,371
38	**Long-Term Debt** (Note 8)	244,954	194,690
39	**Commitments and Contingent Liabilities** (Notes 11, 12 and 14)		
40	**Stockholders' Equity** (Note 9)	331,080	321,713
	Total	$801,672	$738,469

STOCKHOLDERS' EQUITY

Preferred Stock—authorized 5,000,000 shares of no par value:		
$2.50 cumulative convertible (involuntary liquidation value, $1,523) shares issued and outstanding, 38,076	$ 610	$ 610
Series B $1.00 cumulative convertible (involuntary liquidation value, $23,183) shares outstanding, 927,308 and 927,322	14,330	14,330
40 Common Stock—authorized 20,000,000 shares of no par value; shares outstanding, 11,723,774 and 11,243,734	90,138	90,088
Excess of Equity Over Cost Of Subsidiary Companies At Dates Of Acquisitions (no change during the five years ended December 31, 19x6)	11,171	11,171
Earnings Reinvested—$31,000 available for cash dividends under most restrictive terms of indebtedness agreements	214,954	205,637
Cost of Treasury Shares (6,667 Series B preferred shares)	(123)	(123)
Total	$331,080	$321,713

97

Exhibit 4B–3

ALFA, INC., AND CONSOLIDATED SUBSIDIARIES
Statement of Changes in Financial Position
Year Ended December 31

		19x6	19x5	19x4	19x3	19x2
	(All Dollars Reported in Thousands)					
	Sources:					
	Internally generated funds:					
41	Net income	$ 19,139	$ 20,089	$ 56,843	$ 26,558	$ 24,296
42	Depreciation and amortization	24,383	21,579	22,508	17,423	14,766
43	Deferred income taxes—noncurrent portion	3,521	207	223	5,983	5,962
44	Less undistributed income of non-consolidated domestic subsidiaries	(1,439)	(2,042)	(3,994)	(2,637)	(2,153)
45	Total from operations	45,604	39,833	75,580	47,327	42,871
46	Additions to long-term debt	58,344	16,323	31,698	73,476	51,563
47	Decrease in noncurrent receivables	7,886	—	—	—	—
48	Issuance of capital stock for businesses acquired	2,494	2,228	871	46	10,725
49	Property sales and retirements:					
	Sale—leaseback financing	—	853	9,827	25,272	8,580
	Other	3,409	7,824	9,616	8,866	8,986
50	Decrease in deferred charges	—	—	8,086	—	—
51	Other—net	—	618	—	181	24
	Total	117,737	67,679	135,678	155,168	122,749

Applications:

Property additions:

		Col 1	Col 2	Col 3	Col 4	Col 5
52	Businesses acquired	6,683	1,620	57	436	7,757
53	Existing businesses	41,174	41,094	56,661	59,628	63,165
54	Increase in noncurrent receivables	—	3,380	3,343	5,935	1,298
55	Reduction of long-term debt	8,080	24,092	26,633	31,789	26,080
56	Cash dividends on capital stock	12,266	11,989	8,664	7,971	7,448
57	Increase in investment in nonconsolidated finance subsidiaries	—	—	—	1,303	8,638
58	Increase in deferred charges	1,972	1,070	—	1,861	5,036
59	Other—net	389	—	189	—	—
60	Total	70,564	83,245	95,547	108,923	119,422
60	**Increase (Decrease) In Working Capital**	**$ 47,173**	**$(15,566)**	**$ 40,131**	**$ 46,245**	**$ 3,327**

Represented By:

Current assets—increase (decrease):

		Col 1	Col 2	Col 3	Col 4	Col 5
61	Cash and marketable securities	$ (1,875)	$ 645	$ 12,967	$ 3,646	$ (1,806)
62	Receivables	21,596	(51,453)	49,721	36,783	34,530
63	Inventories	28,772	3,953	14,332	37,139	16,887
64	Prepaid expenses	(1,756)	6,414	1,670	691	1,473
	Change in current assets	46,737	(40,441)	78,690	78,259	51,084

Current liabilities—increase (decrease):

		Col 1	Col 2	Col 3	Col 4	Col 5
65	Notes payable and current portion of long-term debt	(4,923)	13,298	(26,446)	15,535	20,134
66	Accounts payable and accrued expenses	8,276	(5,676)	12,432	17,325	31,087

Current income taxes:

		Col 1	Col 2	Col 3	Col 4	Col 5
67	Currently payable	(6,190)	(12,832)	21,670	(87)	(4,614)
68	Deferred	2,401	(19,665)	30,903	(759)	1,150
	Change in current liabilities	(436)	(24,875)	38,559	32,014	47,757
60	**Increase (Decrease) In Working Capital**	**$ 47,173**	**$(15,566)**	**$ 40,131**	**$ 46,245**	**$ 3,327**

Exhibit 4B–4

69

ALFA, INC., AND CONSOLIDATED SUBSIDIARIES
Statement of Earnings Reinvested
Year Ended December 31

	19x6	19x5	19x4	19x3	19x2
(All Dollars Reported in Thousands)					
Balance, Beginning of Year	**$205,637**	$196,582	$147,613	$129,043	$106,801
Minor Businesses Pooled (prior years not restated)	**2,444**	955	790	(17)	5,394
Net Income	**19,139**	20,089	56,843	26,558	24,296
Cash Dividends Declared:					
$2.50 Preferred	**(95)**	(95)	(95)	(95)	(124)
$1.00 Series B Preferred	**(927)**	(927)	(926)	(933)	(934)
Common (per share: $1.00, $1.00, 70¢, 64¢ and 60¢)	**(11,244)**	(10,967)	(7,643)	(6,943)	(6,390)
Balance, End of Year	**$214,954**	$205,637	$196,582	$147,613	$129,043

100

Exhibit 4B–5

70

ALFA, INC., AND CONSOLIDATED SUBSIDIARIES
Quarterly Financial Data
(Unaudited)

	Common (1)	$2.50 preferred (1)	$1.00 Series B preferred (1)	Revenues (2)	Net income (2)	Earnings per share (2)
19x6				$1,251,088	$19,139	$1.55
1st Quarter	$19⅞-14⅞	$ 25	$14¼-11¾	264,769	4,554	.37
2nd Quarter	18½-15⅛	28-25	13 -11½	312,276	6,970	.57
3rd Quarter	16⅝-14⅝	No Trades	12½-11	330,558	3,589	.29
4th Quarter	15 -13	No Trades	12 -11⅛	343,485	4,026	.32
19x5				$1,133,817	$20,089	$1.70
1st Quarter	$22 -15⅝	No Trades	$13⅞-10⅞	246,748	(7,159)	(.61)
2nd Quarter	21 -16⅝	No Trades	14 -11½	278,024	9,217	.78
3rd Quarter	18⅝-15¼	$ 26	12⅞-11⅛	302,184	9,606	.81
4th Quarter	15¾-13¾	No Trades	11⅞-11	306,861	8,425	.72

(1) Quarterly high and low stock price ranges. Alfa's common stock is registered on the New York, Pacific and Honolulu Stock Exchanges, the $2.50 preferred stock is registered on the Honolulu Stock Exchange and the $1.00 Series B preferred stock is registered on the Pacific Stock Exchange.

(2) 19x6 restated for December pooling of interests. First Quarter 19x5 includes cumulative effect on prior years of accounting changes which reduced net income $17,407 or $1.47 per share. Fourth Quarter 19x5 includes discontinued operations which reduced net income $1,000 or $.08 per share.

ALFA, INC., AND CONSOLIDATED SUBSIDIARIES
Notes to Financial Statements
(All Dollars Reported in Thousands)

1. **Accounting Policies:** The accounting policies of Alfa, Inc., considered significant to understanding its financial statements are:

Consolidation: Alfa's consolidated financial statements include the accounts of all domestic subsidaries except Alfa Financial, Inc., and its subsidiaries, Alfa Credit Corporation and its subsidiaries and an insurance company organized in 19x3 to provide Alfa and its subsidiaries with certain insurance. Significant intercompany transactions and balances are eliminated. Investments in common stock of nonconsolidated subsidiaries are accounted for by the equity method.

Sugar revenues: Alfa sells its sugar to California and Hawaiian Sugar Company (C and H), a nonprofit agricultural cooperative. Sugar revenues are accrued at the time of sale to C and H based on C and H's estimated net return (sales proceeds less costs and expenses including estimates for unsold sugar held by C and H). Estimated profits from Alfa's share of C and H's unsold sugar are deferred until sales are ultimately made by C and H to its customers; estimated losses based on current sales prices and estimated expenses are charged against income currently. Amounts withheld by and added to the capital of C and H are accounted for as an additional investment in C and H (see Note 2).

Leased department sales: In accordance with industry practice, revenues of retail operations include leased department sales.

Real property sales: Income from sales of real property is recognized when cash received as a percentage of total sales price is at least 10% for residences, 25% for raw land and 20% for other real property, collection of the balance of the sales price is reasonably assured and risks of ownership have passed to the buyer.

Pension plans: Alfa and its subsidiaries have pension plans covering substantially all full-time employees. Substantially all pension costs, including prior service costs amortized over 30 years or less, are funded as accrued.

Research, development and preopening costs: Such costs are charged to expense as incurred. Prior to 19x4, preopening costs, including initial operating losses, were deferred and amortized over three years (see Note 2).

Excess of cost over equity of subsidiary companies at dates of acquisition: Such excess relates principally to businesses acquired prior to 1970 which will not be amortized until, in the opinion of management, diminution in value is expected.

Income taxes: Federal income tax returns are filed on a consolidated basis. Income taxes are reduced by investment tax credits using the flow-through method. Deferred income taxes are provided on items (principally depreciation, installment sales and uncollected sugar revenues) recorded in different periods for tax than for financial reporting purposes.

Earnings per share: Primary earnings per share are based on the average number of outstanding shares of common stock and common stock equivalents (preferred stock and dilutive stock options). Fully diluted earnings per share also assume the conversion of the Company's convertible debentures and elimination of related interest expense (after applicable income taxes).

Inventories: All inventories are stated at the lower of cost or market. The cost of certain processed food, raw material and supply inventories is determined using the last-in, first-out (LIFO) inventory method. The costs of other inventories are determined princi-

71

102

pally by the first-in, first-out or average methods. Merchandise inventories in retail stores are determined by the retail method, which involves pricing individual items at current selling prices and reducing such amounts by the application of departmental mark-up ratios to the lower of average cost or market.

Growing crops: In accordance with Hawaii sugar industry practice, all costs of growing sugarcane (which has a growing cycle of approximately two years) are charged to expense in the year incurred.

Investments: Investments in partnerships, joint ventures and common stock of nonconsolidated affiliates over which Alfa exercises significant influence are accounted for by the equity method. Other investments are stated at cost or estimated realizable value if less than cost.

Property, plant and equipment: Property is stated at cost. In order to include all applicable costs, interest on funds borrowed for construction of buildings costing over $1,000 is capitalized during the construction period. Depreciation is provided using the straight-line method over the estimated economic lives for financial reporting purposes and accelerated methods as permitted for income tax purposes. The principal lives used for financial reporting purposes are 20–40 years for land improvements, 25–40 years for buildings, 3–18 years for machinery and equipment, and the term of the lease if less than the aforementioned lives for leasehold improvements. Maintenance and repairs are charged to operations. Renewals and betterments are capitalized. When properties are retired or otherwise disposed of in the normal course of business, the original cost, reduced by any salvage realized, is charged to accumulated depreciation, with no gain or loss reflected in income. Gains or losses on specifically identified abnormal retirements are reflected in income.

Excess of equity over cost of subsidiary companies at dates of acquisition: The excess of equity over cost of businesses acquired prior

to 19w9, which is not being amortized to income, is presented separately in stockholders' equity. Similar excesses arising since 19w9 have not been significant.

Stock options: No accounting entries are made when stock options are granted. When options are exercised, proceeds are credited to common stock.

2. Accounting Changes: Under new accounting methods adopted in 19x5, (a) estimated sugar profits are deferred until sales are ultimately made by C and H to its customers, (b) investment in C and H is stated at equity and (c) retail purchase discounts are deferred until sales are made to customers. Consistent with the change to the equity method, Alfa's net income of prior years has been restated to include its share of operating profits and losses reported by C and H. Such amounts include C and H's antitrust litigation settlement which C and H charged to the years covered by the litigation, 19w9–19x4 (see Note 12).

As shown in the following tabulation, net income for 19x5 would have been $1,140 or $.10 per share higher if (a) Alfa had not adopted the new accounting methods which it considers preferable and (b) its share of estimated future withholdings by C and H had been charged to 19x5 expenses instead of to the years covered by the litigation (see Note 12):

| | Increased (Decreased) | |
	Amount	*Per Share*
Sugar profits deferred at year-end	$ 1,603	$ .14
C and H litigation charge	(1,285)	(.11)
Retail purchase discounts deferred	822	.07
Total	$ 1,140	$ .10

72

103

Alfa's five sugar companies sell their sugar to C and H. Prior to 19x5, Alfa's investment in C and H was carried at cost and sugar revenues ($55,000, $68,000, $209,000 and $130,000 for the four years ended December 31, 19x5) were accrued at the time of sale to C and H based on C and H's estimated net return (sales proceeds, including estimates for unsold sugar of C and H less costs, expenses and withholdings for capital reserves). Since 1951, C and H has increased its capital principally through retaining in certain years a small portion of members' revenues from the sale of sugar. Alfa's interest in such capital reserves was not completely identified until September 19x5 when it was advised by C and H of its allocation.

Prior to 19x4, sugar prices remained relatively stable primarily because the domestic sugar industry was covered by the Sugar Act of 1948, as amended. This Act expired on December 31, 19x4 and no substitute legislation has been enacted to date. In 19x4, sugar prices increased to historic highs and have since declined substantially. The change in method of accounting for sugar profits was made because proceeds from the sale of C and H unsold sugar cannot be estimated accurately during periods of severely fluctuating sugar prices. The equity method for Alfa's investment in C and H is more consistent with its new method of accounting for sugar profits.

Prior period financial statements have been restated for the change to the equity method of accounting for the investment in C and H. Such restatement increased (decreased) previously reported net income as follows: 19x4 $920, 19x3 $(464), 19x2 $(448) and years prior $4,562.

Alfa also changed its method of accounting for retail purchase discounts. Previously, purchase discounts were treated as revenue when received. Such discounts are now included in income when the related merchandise is sold.

The cumulative effect on earnings reinvested at the beginning of 19x5 resulting from the changes in accounting for sugar revenues ($16,585 or $1.40 per share) and retail purchase discounts ($822 or $.07 per share) has been included in the accompanying financial statements as a charge against 19x5 net income. Pro forma amounts in the statements of income for 19x5, 19x4 and 19x3 include the effect of applying the new accounting methods retroactively. The effect on periods prior to 19x3 is not material.

Alfa's 19x4 net income was reduced $7,634 ($.66 per share) as a result of changes made in 19x4 to preferable accounting methods as set forth below:

In 19x4, Alfa adopted the last-in, first-out (LIFO) method for pricing Lamb-Weston's processed food, raw material and supply inventories. Previously, average, first-in, first-out (FIFO) or identified cost methods were used for pricing these inventories. The effect of the change was to reduce 19x4 net income by $6,112 ($.53 per share). There is no effect on prior years since the ending inventory previously reported for 19x3 is the beginning inventory in 19x4 for LIFO purposes.

Prior to September 30, 19x4, preopening expenses and initial operating losses incurred during the first six months after opening new department stores and hotels were deferred and amortized over three years. As of September 30, 19x4, the unamortized balances were charged to expense. This change in estimate effected by a change in accounting principle reduced 19x4 net income $1,522 ($.13 per share). Since September 30, 19x4, such costs have been charged to operations as incurred.

3. Unusual Items: On November 15, 19x4, Alfa decided to discontinue operations of its Wilhelm Foods division and since that date has been in the process of disposing of the division's assets. Wilhelm's remaining assets, totaling $4,123 at December 31, 19x6 and consisting principally of receivables and property, are expected to be sold in 19x7. During 19x5 and 19x4 provisions of $2,083 and $1,700, respectively, before income taxes were made for anticipated losses on sale of assets and from operations during phaseout periods. Such losses aggregated $427 in 19x6 and $2,713 in 19x5. Wilhelm's revenues were $5,952 in 19x6, $30,499 in 19x5, $67,741 in 19x4, $68,755 in 19x3 and $54,264 in 19x2. Operating results of Wilhelm are included as discontinued operations in the statement of income and are after income taxes (credits) of $1,448, $(1,048), $(7,722) and $(1,083) for the four years ended December 31, 19x5.

In 19x5, regulatory authorities disapproved the 19x3 sale of Alfa Credit Corporation to a bank. Primarily as a result of operating losses since the sale in 19x3, Alfa charged 19x6, 19x5 and 19x4 net income $260 ($.02 per share), $674 ($.06 per share) and $2,168 ($.19 per share), respectively. Alfa expects to sell Alfa Credit Corporation in 19x7.

In 19x4, Alfa charged net income $1,853 ($.16 per share) for losses expected to be incurred in connection with the planned liquidation of mobile home parks and disposal of certain other property in California.

In 19x3, net income was reduced $703 ($.06 per share) for costs incurred in connection with the final closing of the Rhodes-WAY mass merchandising stores in that year. 19x2 net income was reduced $3,221 ($.28 per share) by store operating losses and inventory write-downs in anticipation of such closings.

Alfa's 19x3 net income also included gains of $2,100 ($.18 per share) from the sale of one of Alfa's food processing plants. Net income also included gains of $1,824 ($.16 per share) in 19x3 and $1,573 ($.14 per share) in 19x2 from the sale of surplus property formerly used by Construction Materials Hawaii, Inc. (CMH), a subsidiary of Alfa.

4. Business Acquisitions: As of April 1, 19x3, Alfa acquired a 20-branch drug wholesaling business. The acquisition was accounted for as a purchase and, accordingly, its operations are included only from date of acquisition. Had its operations been included for the entire 19x3 fiscal year, Alfa's revenues and net income for that year would have been $900,521 and $26,734 ($2.33 per share), respectively.

On April 1, 19x2, Alfa Mortgage Corporation, a subsidiary of Alfa Financial, Inc. (a wholly-owned nonconsolidated finance subsidiary of Alfa, Inc.), acquired Commonwealth, Inc., a mortgage banking company, for $11,500 in cash.

Alfa acquired CMH under a Plan of Arrangement approved by the Federal District Court of Honolulu on August 9, 19x2. CMH, Alfa's former Construction Materials Division, was sold to Telecheck International, Inc. in 19x0.

Alfa has had additional acquisitions each of the years from 19x2 through 19x6, none of which has been material.

75 **5. Supplemental Assets Information:**

	December 31	
	19x6	19x5
Receivables:		
Trade accounts	$154,659	$140,900
California and Hawaiian Sugar Company—estimated market value for Alfa's share of unsold sugar held by C and H, less cash advances and deferred sugar profits of $3,375 in 19x5 ($6,622 less than cost in 19x6)	17,648	13,875
Trade notes	12,355	7,746
Allowance for doubtful receivables	(5,010)	(4,465)
Total	$179,652	$158,056
Inventories:		
Retail	$ 57,063	$ 53,735
Distribution	74,193	67,379
Food—net of LIFO reserves of $8,443 and $10,763	42,837	26,091
Real property development projects	8,598	6,383
Other	9,852	10,183
Total	$192,543	$163,771
Other investments:		
At equity:		
California and Hawaiian Sugar Company (Note 2)	$ 14,824	$ 14,824
Other nonconsolidated domestic subsidiaries	2,167	2,099
Other—principally joint ventures	4,957	4,604
At cost or less	1,105	850
Total	$ 23,053	$ 22,377

	December 31	
	19x6	19x5
Property, plant and equipment (about $77,000 and $71,000 pledged as collateral for mortgage and other loans):		
Land	$ 20,471	$ 20,858
Real estate improvements	85,875	82,223
Buildings	91,081	81,258
Machinery and equipment	234,418	215,359
Construction in progress	16,732	10,841
Total	448,577	410,539
Less accumulated depreciation and amortization	174,932	156,959
Total	$273,645	$253,580
Other assets:		
Excess of cost over equity of subsidiary companies at dates of acquisition prior to 1970	$ 22,010	$ 22,010
Noncurrent notes receivable	31,792	39,678
Land held for future property development	2,694	2,426
Deferred charges	9,251	7,279
Total	$ 65,747	$ 71,393
Growing crops not included in the balance sheet—estimated	$ 50,000	$ 46,000
Less applicable income taxes	26,000	24,000
Net addition to stockholders' equity if growing crop costs were deferred until harvest rather than expensed in the year incurred	$ 24,000	$ 22,000

6. Supplemental Income and Expense Information:

Year ended December 31

	19x6	19x5	19x4	19x3	19x2
Leased department sales	$ 44,897	$ 39,246	$ 33,975	$ 31,621	$ 33,532
Inventories entering into cost of sales (Note 2):					
Beginning of year	163,771	159,818	145,486	108,347	91,460
End of year	192,543	163,771	159,818	145,486	108,347
[77] Maintenance and repairs*	19,602	17,630	13,412	8,120	6,770
Taxes, other than income taxes	26,983	23,484	19,486	18,793	13,288
[78] Advertising	16,006	14,055	12,413	9,611	8,668
[79] Research and development costs	1,442	1,892	1,291	1,317	1,261
[80] Net deferral (amortization) of preopening expense and initial operating losses of new department stores and hotels (Note 2)	—	—	(3,149)	(808)	1,800
[81] Interest expense:					
Long-term debt	14,883	12,727	16,437	13,627	7,675
Short-term borrowings	3,621	3,592	8,617	5,232	3,417
Total charged to income	18,504	16,319	25,054	18,859	11,092
[82] Increase (decrease) in net income resulting from capitalizing interest	(47)	(75)	1,482	603	218

* Excluding maintenance and repairs of Agriculture Group subsidiaries which are not practicable to segregate.

7. Supplemental Income Tax Information:

Year ended December 31

	19x6	19x5	19x4	19x3	19x2
[83] Income taxes:					
Computed Federal tax at statutory rate	$11,437	$30,176	$55,592	$17,356	$14,441
%	48	48	48	48	48
[84] Benefit for income taxable at capital gains rate	(782)	(818)	(1,610)	(3,115)	(2,670)
%	(3.3)	(1.3)	(1.4)	(8.7)	(8.9)
[85] Investment tax credits	(4,311)	(2,734)	(1,618)	(1,483)	(1,898)
%	(18.1)	(4.3)	(1.4)	(4.1)	(6.3)
[86] Other—net	(284)	76	1,352	(508)	(334)
%	(1.2)	.1	1.2	(1.4)	(1.1)
[87] Reported Federal income tax	6,060	26,700	53,716	12,250	9,539
%	25.4	42.5	46.4	33.8	31.7
[88] State income taxes	1,540	6,300	11,290	1,390	1,319
Total	$ 7,600	$33,000	$65,006	$13,640	$10,858

Notes to Financial Statements (continued)

	Year ended December 31				
	19x6	19x5	19x4	19x3	19x2
Current					
Federal .... **[89]**	$ 5,139	$45,392	$28,870	$ 8,063	$ 6,367
Less investment tax credits .... **[90]**	(4,311)	(2,734)	(1,618)	(1,483)	(1,898)
State .... **[91]**	850	9,800	5,739	788	725
Total .... **[92]**	1,678	52,458	32,991	7,368	5,194
Deferred Federal and State:					
Excess tax depreciation	3,818	2,447	1,922	1,733	2,488
Net deferral of profits on installment sales ...	(192)	257	1,931	4,939	2,691
Uncollected sugar revenues	1,965	(22,682)	29,642	—	—
Net deferral (amortization) of preopening expenses and initial operating losses ...		—	(1,636)	(404)	900
Other—net	331	520	156	4	(415)
Total .... **[93]**	5,922	(19,458)	32,015	6,272	5,664
Total .... **[94]**	$ 7,600	$33,000	$65,006	$13,640	$10,858

8. Supplemental Liabilities and Debt Information:

	December 31	
	19x6	19x5
Accounts Payable and Accrued Expenses:		
Accounts payable—trade	$ 77,143	$ 71,754
Accrued compensation	17,663	16,142
Accrued interest	5,445	4,894
Alfa Financial, Inc.	656	2,208
Other	26,237	23,870
Total	$127,144	$118,868
Notes Payable and Current Portion of Long-Term Debt:		
Banks—average rate 6¼% and 8½%	$ 26,200	$ 25,250
Commercial paper—average rate 5% and 6¼% ...	35,500	30,000
Current portion of long-term debt	7,328	8,701
Less interim borrowings included in long-term debt ...	(35,000)	(25,000)
Total	$ 34,028	$ 38,951

	December 31	
	19x6	19x5
Notes Payable, Including Interim Borrowing in Long-Term Debt:		
Highest month-end borrowings	$ 72,250	$ 71,850
Average borrowings outstanding during the year ...	42,000	38,250
Weighted average interest on borrowings outstanding during the year ...	6⅛%	7⅜%
Unused bank credit at December 31 (also available for commercial paper support):		
Bank lines	11,800	37,750
Revolving credit	60,000	35,000
Standby credit at December 31 (available for commercial paper support)	—	20,000

Alfa utilizes commercial paper and bank lines of credit for its daily cash requirements. The Company intends to refinance certain short-term borrowings by issuance of the additional $35,000 of long-term notes described below. Accordingly, this amount has been classified as long-term.

In connection with its bank lines of credit Alfa has informally agreed to maintain average compensating balances based on available lines of credit. Such balances averaged about $6,000 during 19x6 and $7,000 during 19x5.

	December 31	
	19x6	19x5
Long-Term Debt—Less Current Portion Notes and mortgage loans:		
5% Notes due 19x8–19y2	$ 11,803	$ 13,503
7½% Notes due 19x8–19z2	22,500	22,500
8⅜% Notes due 19x8–19z3	48,750	48,750
8¾% Notes due 19x9–19y4	10,000	10,000
9½% Notes due 19y1–19z6	40,000	—
Mortgage loans average rate 7½% and 7%, due 19x8–2004	13,860	15,884
Interim borrowings to be refinanced by long-term loan	35,000	25,000
Other, average rate 8%, due 19x8–19z7	12,955	8,967
Total	194,868	144,604
Convertible subordinated debentures		
5% due 19y9	15,086	15,086
5¼% due 19z4	35,000	35,000
Total	50,086	50,086
Total	$244,954	$194,690

Annual maturities of long-term debt in the next five years are as follows:

19x7	$ 7,328
19x8	7,380
19x9	10,571
19y0	10,211
19y1	15,298

Under the revolving credit agreement with certain banks, Alfa may borrow up to $60,000 and may convert any such loans outstanding prior to September 3, 19x7 into five-year term loans with interest at ½% above prime rate.

On June 22, 19x6, Alfa issued $40,000 of its 9½% notes and agreed to issue an additional $35,000 on or about February 1, 19x7. These notes are due on July 1, 19z6, with annual installments of $4,690 required from July 1, 19y1.

95 **9. Capital Stock:** Changes in outstanding capital stock during 19x6 and 19x5 are summarized as follows:

| | Increase (Decrease) | | | |
| | 19x6 | | 19x5 | |
	Shares	Amount	Shares	Amount
Preferred Series B				
Conversions to common	(14)	$ —	—	$ —
Common:				
Acquisition of businesses	480,000	$ 50	283,841	$ 1,273
Stock options exercised:				
Previously unissued shares	—	—	1,876	25
Treasury shares (option price lower than cost)	—	—	1,999	(48)
Stock performance unit plan	32	—	21	—
Preferred stock conversions	8	—	—	—
Total	480,040	$ 50	287,737	$ 1,250

Shares of common stock were reserved as follows:

| | December 31 | |
	19x6	19x5
Outstanding stock options	98,721	133,835
Future stock option grants	113,879	138,129
Conversion of 19y9 debentures (initial conversion price $35.7143)	422,698	422,698
Conversion of 19z4 debentures (initial conversion price $43.67)	801,465	801,465
Conversion of $2.50 cumulative convertible preferred stock (1.2 for 1) (redeemable at $40 per share)	45,691	45,691
Conversion of Series B $1.00 cumulative convertible preferred stock (.5897 for 1) (redeemable at $25 per share)	546,834	546,842
Total	2,029,288	2,088,660

10. Earnings Per Share: The calculation of primary and fully diluted earnings per share follows (shares in thousands):

Year ended December 31

	19x6	19x5	19x4	19x3	19x2
Primary earnings per share:					
Average number of common shares outstanding during year	**11,724**	11,240	10,914	10,850	10,785
Average number of preferred shares outstanding during year converted into equivalent common shares:					
$2.50 series	—	46	46	49	66
Series B	—	547	547	548	551
Average number of dilutive stock options outstanding during year, less common shares which could be purchased from proceeds on exercise	**2**	4	4	13	70
Total average number of primary shares	11,726	11,837	11,511	11,460	11,472
Net income (19x6 after preferred dividends)	$18,117	$20,089	$56,843	$26,558	$24,296
Primary earnings per share	$ 1.55	$ 1.70	$ 4.94	$ 2.32	$ 2.12
Fully diluted earnings per share:					
Total average number of primary shares	11,726	11,837	11,511	11,460	11,472
Average debentures outstanding during the year converted into equivalent common shares	1,224	1,224	1,224	1,224	1,224
Additional dilutive stock options	—	—	2	—	2
Total average number of fully diluted shares	12,950	13,061	12,737	12,684	12,698
Net income (19x6 after preferred dividends)	$18,117	$20,089	$56,843	$26,558	$24,296
Interest expense on debentures for year, less applicable income taxes	1,284	1,245	1,265	1,297	1,296
Adjusted net income	$19,401	$21,334	$58,108	$27,855	$25,592
Fully diluted earnings per share	$ 1.50	$ 1.64	$ 4.56	$ 2.20	$ 2.02

11. Leased Properties: Alfa operates in various leased facilities which are not included in its balance sheet. Most of the major leases provide for renewal options and some provide for minimum rentals plus additional payments based on revenues or profits. Rent expense is summarized as follows:

Notes to Financial Statements (continued)

	Year ended December 31				
	19x6	19x5	19x4	19x3	19x2
Financing leases:					
Minimum and fixed	$16,050	$14,116	$11,489	$ 9,359	$ 7,628
Additional	2,716	2,170	1,754	2,179	1,479
Other leases over one year:					
Minimum and fixed	11,866	10,120	10,850	9,407	8,261
Additional	9,128	9,680	12,622*	5,699	4,120
Property taxes, insurance and other charges on above leases	3,986	3,455	3,110	2,772	3,772
Short-term leases	3,529	2,992	3,758	2,450	3,439
Total	$47,275	$42,533	$43,583	$31,866	$28,699

* Increase principally due to percentage rental on land leased for sugar operations

Financing leases include those which cover 75% or more of the economic life of the property or have terms which assure the lessor full recovery of the fair market value of the property plus a reasonable return. If financing leases had been capitalized and expenses included interest and depreciation over the lease terms instead of fixed rents, Alfa's consolidated net income would have been reduced by $1,900 for 19x6, $1,600 for 19x5, $1,210 for 19x4, $882 for 19x3 and $766 for 19x2.

98 Minimum rental commitments and the present value of lease obligations with remaining terms of one year or more at December 31, 19x6 follow:

	Financing	Other	Total
Minimum rental commitments:			
Year ending December 31:			
19x7	$ 16,361	$ 11,762	$ 28,123
19x8	16,159	11,521	27,680
19x9	16,349	10,875	27,224
19y0	16,098	10,324	26,422
19y1	15,918	9,537	25,455
Five years ending December 31:			
19y6	76,819	40,393	117,212
19z1	71,691	29,115	100,846
19z6	67,673	16,024	83,697
19z7 and thereafter (in total)	137,025	10,358	147,383
Total	$434,093	$149,949	$584,042

	Financing	Other	Total
By major categories of properties:			
Land	$ 18,867	$ 52,602	$ 71,469
Buildings	408,475	97,112	505,587
Machinery and equipment	6,751	235	6,986
Total	$434,093	$149,949	$584,042
Present value of minimum rental commitments:			
Land	$ 5,038	$ 23,920	$ 28,958
Buildings	157,213	55,916	213,129
Machinery and equipment	4,959	41	5,000
Total	$167,210	$ 79,877	$247,087
Discount rates:			
Range	3.1-12.0%	3.4-10.4%	3.1-12.0%
Average	8.0%	7.9%	8.0%

99

12. Contingent Liabilities: Contingent liabilities of the Company at December 31, 19x6 included a guaranty of a $8,960 mortgage loan of the Waikiki Beachcomber, a 50% joint venture which owns a 500-room hotel operated by Alfa (this loan is also guaranteed by UAL, Inc., a corporation with substantial net worth) and guarantees of loans totaling $38,450 including nonconsolidated subsidiaries of $25,640.

In December 19x4, C and H was named as one of several defendants, including five other sugar refiners, for alleged participation in regional conspiracies to fix refined sugar prices and to restrain the sale of refined sugar in violation of the Sherman Anti-

trust Act. A proposed settlement of the above litigation made in 19x5 is expected to be approved by most of the private claimants. In providing for the settlement, C and H charged each member's allocated capital in C and H in proportion to their respective sugar production during the years covered by the litigation. Alfa's portion of the settlement, net of applicable income taxes, was $429 for 19x4, $462 for 19x3, $447 for 19x2 and $1,232 for prior years.

Alfa is involved in various matters of litigation and other claims. Based on opinions of legal counsel, management is of the opinion that Alfa's liability, if any, when ultimately determined will not have a material adverse effect on Alfa's financial statements.

13. Nonconsolidated Finance Subsidiaries: A condensed balance sheet and related condensed statement of income of Alfa Financial, Inc., and subsidiaries follow:

CONDENSED BALANCE SHEET

	December 31	
	19x6	19x5
Assets:		
Cash	$ 6,880	$ 10,759
Receivables, less unearned finance charges and allowance for losses	223,937	219,635
Real property developments	20,590	23,578
Other assets	23,698	27,987
Total	$275,105	$281,959
Liabilities:		
Notes payable banks*—average rate 6¼% and 7¼%	$ 97,809	$109,269
Notes payable other—average rate 6½% and 8¼%	22,440	15,646
Investment certificates—average rate 7% and 8%	81,609	92,083
Accounts payable, income taxes and other liabilities	10,175	12,579
Long-term debt—average rate 8¾% and 8¼%	30,629	21,310
Stockholder's Equity (including undistributed earnings of $19,263 and $17,892; $12,561 available for dividends*)	32,443	31,072
Total	$275,105	$281,959

CONDENSED STATEMENT OF INCOME

Revenues	$ 43,860	$ 41,284
Costs and Expenses:		
Interest	15,917	17,990
Other costs and expenses	25,526	18,843
Income taxes	1,046	2,122
Net Income	$ 1,371	$ 2,329

* In connection with certain borrowings, Alfa, Inc., has agreed to maintain Alfa Financial, Inc.'s net worth and working capital at certain minimum levels. During 19x6 and 19x5, these levels were adequate by a reasonable margin.

	December 31	
	19x6	19x5
Bank borrowing arrangements of Alfa Financial, Inc.:		
Highest month-end borrowings	$116,400	$127,000
Average borrowings outstanding during the year	97,000	108,600
Weighted average interest rate on borrowings outstanding during the year	7%	8%
Unused short-term bank credit lines at December 31	6,200	50,700

Note. The above does not include Alfa, Inc.'s investment in Alfa Credit Corporation (see Note 3).

113

In connection with its bank lines of credit Alfa, Financial Inc., has informally agreed to maintain average compensating balances based on available lines of credit. Such balances averaged about $20,000 during 19x6 and $22,000 during 19x5.

During 19x6, subsidiaries of Alfa Financial, Inc., made construction loans totaling $13,100 to affiliated real property development joint ventures. Interest and loan fees are charged consistent with market conditions at the time such loans are originated.

14. Pension and Compensation Plans: Alfa has various formal pension plans which cover most full-time employees and provide benefits based on length of service and compensation levels. Pension expense, including amortization of prior service costs, totaled $7,500, $7,000, $6,600, $5,100, and $3,300 for the years ended December 31, 19x6 through 19x2, respectively. Based on most recent actuarial valuations (December 31, 19x5) vested benefits exceeded the fair value of plan assets by $19,300 and unfunded prior service costs totaled $32,500. Alfa's pension plans substantially meet the requirements of the Employee Retirement Income Security Act of 1974 and compliance with the Act is not expected to have a substantial effect on future pension expense.

Under Alfa's stock option plans, options to purchase up to 113,879 shares of common stock at December 31, 19x6 were available for future grants at not less than market prices. Options become exercisable in increments during periods from one to five years subsequent to date of grant. No stock options were granted during 19x6 and 19x5. Other stock option information is summarized as follows:

	Number of shares	Option price			Market price at date of transaction		
		Per share			Per share		
		From	To	Total	From	To	Total
Options outstanding December 31:							
19x6	98,721	$12.63	$41.00	$2,742			
19x5	133,835	12.63	41.00	3,628			
Options exercisable December 31:							
19x6	66,921	12.63	41.00	1,802	$13.25	$25.75	$1,194
19x5	66,334	12.63	41.00	1,737	13.25	38.75	1,218
Options which became exercisable:							
19x6	30,124	12.63	41.00	806	13.25	19.38	465
19x5	35,182	12.63	41.00	931	13.88	20.50	604
Options exercised:							
19x6	—	—	—	—	—	—	—
19x5	3,875	12.63	16.25	50	18.13	20.25	71

105

Alfa has granted certain officers and key employees units under its stock performance unit plan. Each unit has an assigned value equal to the market value of one share of Alfa's common stock on the award date. The benefits are payable (in cash, common stock or a combination of both) in 25% annual increments based on the excess (if any) of the market price of Alfa's common stock on the payment date over the market price on the award date, adjusted for cash dividends between the award and payment dates.

At December 31, 19x6, units outstanding totaled 105,606 at an average value per unit of $16.44. Expenses under this plan totaled $15 for 19x6, $19 for 19x5, $75 for 19x4 and $191 for 19x2 (there was no expense in 19x3).

Prior to 19x5, certain officers participated in an executive bonus plan which was discontinued when base salaries were increased to include the bonus. Such bonuses totaled $397 for 19x4, $342 for 19x3 and $348 for 19x2.

ALFA, INC., AND CONSOLIDATED SUBSIDIARIES
Five-Year Summary of Revenues and Contributions of Operating Groups

(All Dollars Reported in Thousands)

	19x6		19x5		19x4		19x3		19x2	
	Amount	%	Amount	%	Amount	%	Amount	%	Amount	%
Revenues:										
Food processing	$ 304,249	24%	$ 278,569	25%	$ 350,366	30%	$172,845	20%	$134,934	20%
Food²	215,118	17	138,190	12	128,520	11	95,674	11	72,139	11
Agriculture²	89,131	7	140,379	13	221,846	19	77,171	9	62,795	9
Merchandising	786,354	63	717,837	63	657,250	57	573,449	65	430,409	62
Retail²	335,296	27	309,337	27	283,154	25	276,857	31	241,389	35
Distribution	451,058	36	408,500	36	374,096	32	296,592	34	189,020	27
Hospitality	141,865	11	119,122	10	110,060	10	94,690	11	85,681	12
Asset Management³	17,770	2	17,672	2	29,027	3	34,045	4	20,055	3
Corporate	850	—	617	—	585	—	636	—	505	—
Other⁴	—	—	—	—	—	—	4,731	—	23,374	3
Total	$1,251,088	100%	$1,133,817	100%	$1,147,288	100%	$880,396	100%	$694,958	100%
Contribution:¹										
Food processing	$ 12,393	23%	$ 57,888	60%	$ 135,546	85%	$ 27,555	41%	$ 11,847	22%
Food²	22,017	40	15,277	16	5,749	4	14,323	21	8,403	16
Agriculture²	(9,624)	(17)	42,611	44	129,797	81	13,232	20	3,444	6
Merchandising	20,592	38	21,080	21	17,194	11	10,234	15	23,714	44
Retail²	8,453	16	7,024	7	3,288	2	129	—	15,992	30
Distribution	12,139	22	14,056	14	13,906	9	10,105	15	7,722	14
Hospitality	13,961	25	9,554	10	8,091	5	6,852	10	6,877	13
Asset Management²&³	7,749	14	8,580	9	2,425	1	21,535	32	15,280	29
Other⁴	—	—	—	—	(3,205)	(2)	1,277	2	(4,129)	(8)
Total	54,695	100%	97,102	100%	160,051	100%	67,453	100%	53,589	100%

Less Unallocated Expenses:

Corporate—net	8,420	8,109	5,531	7,119	5,799
Interest expense	18,440	16,319	17,572	21,787	10,629
Income taxes[1]	8,696	34,178	16,835	66,977	13,522
Income From Continuing Operations	19,139	38,496	27,515	64,168	23,639
Income (Loss) From Discontinued Operations	—	(1,000)	(957)	(7,325)	657
Income Before Cumulative Effect Of Accounting Changes	19,139	37,496	26,558	56,843	24,296
Cumulative Effect Of Accounting Changes ($36,647, less income taxes of $19,240)	—	(17,407)	—	—	—
Net Income	$ 19,139	$ 20,089	$ 26,558	$ 56,843	$ 24,296
Average Net Assets Employed[5]	$ 625,845	$ 592,934	$524,983	$ 592,520	$438,977

Market Data:

Common stock price range	19⅞-13	22-13¾	31⅜-11	21⅜-12⅝	39¾-25
Price-earnings ratio range[6]	13-8	13-8	14-5	4-3	19-12
Book value per share at year-end	$ 26.13	$ 26.42	$ 21.96	$ 26.16	$ 20.36

Pro Forma Amounts Assuming The New Accounting Method For Sugar Profits Is Applied Retroactively:

Agriculture: Revenues	$ —	$ 140,379		$ 189,495	$ 74,606
Contribution	$ —	$ 42,611		$ 97,446	$ 10,667

[1] Income before unallocated corporate expenses, interest expense and income taxes. Income taxes include those of nonconsolidated finance subsidiaries and $50 in 19x6 and $944 credit in 19x5 for Alfa Credit Corporation.

[2] See Notes 2 and 3 to Financial Statements for accounting changes and unusual items.

[3] Asset Management includes financial service operations which are conducted through nonconsolidated subsidiaries and, for such operations, contribution is after interest expense but before unallocated corporate expenses and income taxes. Revenues of these subsidiaries are not included because equity and net income is reported separately in Alfa's financial statements. Includes Alfa, Inc.'s temporary investment in Alfa Credit Corporation which had losses of $210 in 19x6, $1,420 in 19x5 and $4,565 in 19x4. See Notes 3 and 13 to Financial Statements.

[4] Includes RhodesWAY, gain on sale of Construction Materials Hawaii, Inc., surplus property and accounting change for deferred preopening expenses. (See Notes 2 and 3 to Financial Statements.)

[5] 13-month average of total assets (excluding cash) less accounts payable, accrued expenses and other deferred credits.

[6] Common stock price range divided by primary earnings per share.

Exhibit 4B-7

ALFA, INC., AND CONSOLIDATED SUBSIDIARIES
Ten-Year Financial Summary

(All Dollars and Shares Reported in Thousands)

	19x6	19x5	19x4	19x3	19x2	19x1	19x0	19w9	19w8	19w7
Revenues originally reported*	$1,251,088	$1,133,817	$1,147,288	$949,151	$749,222	$574,116	$406,725	$303,326	$205,321	$145,881
Add pooled businesses	—	—	—	—	—	—	50,317	45,586	50,008	80,960
Less discontinued operations	—	—	—	(68,755)	(54,264)	—	—	—	—	—
Revenues as restated	1,251,088	1,133,817	1,147,288	880,396	694,958	574,116	457,042	348,912	255,329	226,841
Income from continuing operations	19,139	38,496	64,168	27,515	23,639	19,134	16,550	13,781	10,873	6,906
Extraordinary items and discontinued operations	—	(18,407)	(7,325)	(957)	657	—	—	213	—	1,835
Net income	19,139	20,089	56,843	26,558	24,296	19,134	16,550	13,994	10,873	8,741
Earnings per share:										
Primary**										
Income from continuing operations	1.55	3.25	5.57	2.40	2.06	1.88	1.74	1.59	1.28	.83
Net income	1.55	1.70	4.94	2.32	2.12	1.88	1.74	1.62	1.28	1.05
Fully diluted**—Net income	1.50	1.64	4.56	2.20	2.02	1.79	1.65	1.55	1.28	1.05
Cash dividends per common share**	1.00	1.00	.70	.64	.60	.58	.53	.53	.49	.47

Financial position—as originally reported:										
Working capital	221,408	174,235	189,801	149,670	103,425	101,098	69,165	72,722	43,842	38,443
Property—net	273,645	253,580	241,122	226,355	217,852	179,262	148,436	112,270	78,195	74,332
Total assets	801,672	738,469	749,824	659,246	559,940	451,925	347,171	290,506	176,464	160,564
Long-term debt	244,954	194,690	202,459	197,394	155,707	130,224	128,246	96,871	35,974	40,145
Stockholders' equity	331,080	321,713	306,765	259,354	240,308	212,457	144,486	127,632	102,108	82,052
Return on year-end stockholders' equity	5.8%	6.2%	18.2%	10.4%	10.3%	9.2%	9.8%	9.0%	8.1%	7.6%
Common shares outstanding at end of year	11,724	11,244	10,956	10,852	10,837	10,308	5,071	4,777	4,276	2,466

* Includes changes in Alfa's equity in California and Hawaiian Sugar Co. and excludes equity in net income of nonconsolidated finance subsidiaries.
** Adjusted for stock dividends and splits.

Auditors' Opinion

To the Stockholders and Directors of Alfa, Inc.:

We have examined the balance sheet of Alfa, Inc. and its consolidated subsidiaries as of December 31, 19x6 and 19x5 and the related statements of income, earnings reinvested, and changes in financial position for the five years ended December 31, 19x6. Our examination was made in accordance with generally accepted auditing standards, and accordingly included such tests of the accounting records and such other auditing procedures as we considered necessary in the circumstances.

In our opinion, such financial statements present fairly the financial position of Alfa, Inc., and its consolidated subsidiaries at December 31, 19x6 and 19x5 and the results of their operations and the changes in their financial position for the five years ended December 31, 19x6, in conformity with generally accepted accounting principles consistently applied during the period except for the changes in accounting methods in 19x5 and 19x4, with which we concur, described in Note 2 to the financial statements.

Simon, Pure & Co.
Honolulu, Hawaii
January 19, 19x7

Exhibit 4B–8

ALFA, INC., AND CONSOLIDATED SUBSIDIARIES
Five-Year Summary of Revenues
and Contributions of Operating Groups

110

(All Dollars Reported in Thousands)

	19x6 Amount	19x6 %	19x5 Amount	19x5 %	19x4 Amount	19x4 %	19x3 Amount	19x3 %	19x2 Amount	19x2 %
Revenues:										
Food processing	$ 304,249	24%	$ 278,569	25%	$ 350,366	30%	$172,845	20%	$134,934	20%
Food	215,118	17	138,190	12	128,520	11	95,674	11	72,139	11
Agriculture	89,131	7	140,379	13	221,846	19	77,171	9	62,795	9
Merchandising	786,354	63	717,837	63	657,250	57	573,449	65	430,409	62
Retail	335,296	27	309,337	27	283,154	25	276,857	31	241,389	35
Distribution	451,058	36	408,500	36	374,096	32	296,592	34	189,020	27
Hospitality	141,865	11	119,122	10	110,060	10	94,690	11	85,681	12
Asset Management	17,770	2	17,672	2	29,027	3	34,045	4	20,055	3
Corporate	850	—	617	—	585	—	636	—	505	—
Other	—	—	—	—	—	—	4,731	—	23,374	3
Total	$1,251,088	100%	$1,133,817	100%	$1,147,288	100%	$880,396	100%	$694,958	100%
Contribution:[1]										
Food processing	$ 12,393	23%	$ 57,888	60%	$ 135,546	85%	$ 27,555	41%	$ 11,847	22%
Food	22,017	40	15,277	16	5,749	4	14,323	21	8,403	16
Agriculture	(9,624)	(17)	42,611	44	129,797	81	13,232	20	3,444	6
Merchandising	20,592	38	21,080	21	17,194	11	10,234	15	23,714	44
Retail	8,453	16	7,024	7	3,288	2	129	—	15,992	30
Distribution	12,139	22	14,056	14	13,906	9	10,105	15	7,722	14
Hospitality	13,961	25	9,554	10	8,091	5	6,852	10	6,877	13
Asset Management	7,749	14	8,580	9	2,425	1	21,535	32	15,280	29
Other	—	—	—	—	(3,205)	(2)	1,277	2	(4,129)	(8)
Total	54,695	100%	97,102	100%	160,051	100%	67,453	100%	53,589	100%

Less Unallocated

Expenses:

Corporate—net	**8,420**	8,109	7,119	5,531	5,799
Interest expense	**18,440**	16,319	21,787	17,572	10,629
Income taxes	**8,696**	34,178	66,977	16,835	13,522
Income From Continuing Operations	**19,139**	38,496	64,168	27,515	23,639
Income (Loss) From Discontinued Operations	**—**	(1,000)	(7,325)	(957)	657
Income Before Cumulative Effect Of Accounting Changes	**19,139**	37,496	56,843	26,558	24,296
Cumulative Effect Of Accounting Change ($36,647, less income taxes of $19,240)	**—**	(17,407)	—	—	—
Net Income	**$ 19,139**	$ 20,089	$ 56,843	$ 26,558	$ 24,296

Pro Forma Amounts Assuming The New Accounting Method For Sugar Profits Is Applied Retroactively:

Agriculture: Revenues	**$ —**	$ 140,379	$ 189,495	$ 72,875	$ —
Contribution	**$ —**	$ 42,611	$ 97,446	$ 8,936	$ —

121

Exhibit 4B–9

ALFA, INC.
Analysis of the Results of Operations
Common-Size Income Statement

	19x6	19x5	19x4	19x3	19x2
Revenues	100.00%	100.00%	100.00%	100.00%	100.00%
Costs and expenses:					
Cost of sales	67.14%	64.40%	60.23%	64.68%	63.58%
Selling, general, and administrative	27.42	26.19	24.87	27.14	28.30
Depreciation and amortization..............	1.94	1.87	1.92	1.93	2.07
Interest	1.48	1.44	2.18	2.14	1.60
Interest capitalized	(.01)	—	(.28)	(.15)	(.07)
Total	97.97%	93.90%	88.92%	95.74%	95.48%
Income before taxes	2.03%	6.10%	11.08%	4.26%	4.52%
Income taxes	(.61)	(2.91)	(5.67)	(1.54)	(1.56)
Income from consolidated continuing operations	1.42%	3.19%	5.41%	2.72%	2.96%
Net income of nonconsolidated finance subsidiaries	.11	.21	.18	.41	.45
Income from continuing operations	1.53%	3.40%	5.59%	3.13%	3.41%
Income (loss) from discontinued operations............	—	(.09)	(.64)	(.11)	.09
Income before cumulative effect on prior years of accounting changes........	1.53%	3.31%	4.95%	3.02%	3.50%
Cumulative effect on prior years of accounting changes....................	—	(1.54)	—	—	—
Net income	1.53%	1.77%	4.95%	3.02%	3.5%

Exhibit 4B–10

ALFA, INC.
Analysis of the Results of Operations
Trend Analysis (assuming 19x2 base year)

	19x6	19x5	19x4	19x3	19x2
Revenues	180	163	165	127	100
Costs and expenses:					
Cost of sales	190	165	156	129	100
Selling, general, and administrative	174	151	145	122	100
Depreciation and amortization	168	147	153	118	100
Interest	167	147	226	170	100
Interest capitalized	14	—	706	278	100
Total	185	160	154	127	100
Income before income taxes	81	220	405	120	100
Income taxes	70	304	599	126	100
Income from consolidated continuing operations	86	176	302	116	100
Net income of nonconsolidated subsidiaries	44	75	67	117	100
Income from continuing operations	81	163	271	116	100
Income (loss) from discontinued operations	—	—	—	—	—
Income before cumulative effect on prior years of accounting changes	79	154	234	109	100
Cumulative effect on prior years of accounting changes	—	—	—	—	—
Net income	79	82	234	109	100

QUESTIONS

1. Compare the flow of the analyst's work in reconstructing business transactions to that of the accountant's work. How does such reconstruction of accounts contribute to the analysis of financial statements?

2. As a potential investor in a common stock, what information would you seek? How do you get such information?

3. The president of your client company approached you, the financial officer of a local bank, for a substantial loan. What could you do?

4. What, in broad categories, are some of the approaches utilized by the financial analyst in diagnosing the financial health of a business?

5. How useful is a comparative financial analysis? How do you make useful comparison?

6. What are some of the precautions required of a financial analyst in his comparative analytical work?

7. Give four broad categories of analysis tools.

8. Is the trend of the past a good predictor of the future? Give reasons for your argument.

9. Which is the better indicator of significant change—the absolute amount of change or the change in percentage? Why?

10. What conditions would prevent the computation of a valid percentage change? Give an example.

11. What are some of the criteria to be used in picking out a base year in an index number comparative analysis?

12. What information can be obtained from trend analysis?

13. What is a common-size financial statement? How do you prepare one?

14. What does a common-size financial statement tell about an enterprise?

15. Do all ratios have significance? Explain.

16. What are some of the limitations of ratio analysis?

17. Give five ratios that can be prepared by use of balance sheet figures only.

18. Give five ratios that can be prepared by use of income statement data only.

19. Give seven ratios that require data from both the balance sheet and the income statement.

20. Give four examples of special-purpose analytical tools commonly utilized by the financial analyst.

21. What are the steps generally taken by the financial analyst in his work? What do these steps achieve?

22. Identify and explain two significant limitations associated with ratio analysis of financial statements. (CFA)

23. What are some of the principal uses of computers in investment analysis? (CFA)

24. What are the most important limitations or disadvantages to the application of computers to security analysis? (CFA)

PART II

Financial statements—the
raw material of analysis

Analysis of current assets

In considering the variety of standards that govern accounting transactions, determinations, and financial presentations, we shall be primarily concerned here with an examination of their significance to the intelligent user and analyst of financial statements. In this chapter, we shall deal with the principles that underly the measurement and presentation of current assets.

CASH

Cash is considered the most liquid of assets. In fact, it represents the starting point, as well as the finish line, of what is known as the accounting cycle. This cycle encompasses the purchase and manufacture of goods and services as well as their sale and the collection of the proceeds. The realization of a transaction is measured by sale and later by the ultimate conversion of the consideration received into cash. Excepting fixed commitments to the satisfaction of which cash must be applied, cash represents that point in the accounting cycle at which management has the maximum discretion with regard to the deployment and use of the resources.

By the very nature of its inherent liquidity, cash does not present serious valuation problems even though this characteristic requires special precautions against theft and defalcation. Care should be taken in the classification of cash items when restrictions have been placed on its disposition. For example, in the case of a segregation for plant expansion or for some other type of specific restriction, the cash balance involved should be separately shown. It may not, of course, be properly includable among current assets, which heading denotes liquidity and availability for the payment of current obligations. Cash set aside for "debt service" or "maintenance" under bond indenture is usually segregated on the balance sheet.

Accountants do not regard compensating balances maintained under a loan agreement as a restriction on cash because banks would generally honor checks drawn against such a balance. However, in accordance with guidelines promulgated by SEC *Financial Reporting Release (FRR),* No. 1 Section 203, compensating balances must be segregated on the balance sheet if they are legally restricted. Otherwise such balances must be disclosed in notes to the financial statements.

Compensating balances constitute that part of a demand deposit that is maintained to support existing borrowing arrangements and to assure future credit availability. Even though informal, such arrangements have considerable practical significance. Thus, in assessing the current ratio, the analyst must consider the repercussions that may follow from the breaking of a tacit agreement with the bank. This may involve the loss of a credit source, and thus have an effect on a company's liquidity and its future access to funds. Vulnerability in this area can be measured by computing the ratio of restricted cash to total cash.

Note 8 of the financial statements of Alfa, Inc. (see Appendix 4B), contains an example of disclosure of an agreement to maintain compensating balances.

Ordinarily, in reporting the cash balance, companies deduct checks issued but not yet paid by the bank, e.g., the float. Analysts should be aware of the practice of a few companies of including the float in the cash balance and including outstanding checks in accounts payable.

MARKETABLE SECURITIES

Marketable securities represent in most instances temporary repositories of excess cash. Alternatively, they may represent funds awaiting investment in plant and equipment, etc. They are usually shown among current assets. However, marketable securities that are temporary investments of cash designated for special purposes such as plant expansion or the meeting of requirements under sinking fund provisions should be shown among long-term investments.

Certain marketable equity securities carried as current assets must now be accounted for in accordance with *SFAS 12* entitled "Accounting for Certain Marketable Securities." The following are some of the salient provisions of this *Statement,* some of which apply also to marketable securities carried as noncurrent assets or carried in unclassified balance sheets and which are discussed under the appropriate heading in Chapter 6:

An equity security encompasses any instrument representing ownership shares or the right to acquire or dispose of ownership shares in an enterprise. This definition specifically excludes convertible bonds, treasury stock, and redeemable preferred stock.

The *Statement* basically requires that marketable equity securities held by enterprises in industries that do not have specialized accounting practices (e.g., investment companies, security brokers and dealers, stock life insurance companies, and fire and casualty insurance companies) shall be stated at the lower of cost or market.

For those securities classified as current assets by the enterprise, market value changes recognized in applying the lower-of-cost-or-market rule are to be included in the determination of net income. This will be accomplished by use of a "valuation allowance" that will generally represent the net unrealized loss in the portfolio. Marketable securities classified as current are treated as one portfolio, and those shown as noncurrent are considered a separate portfolio.

The lower-of-cost-or-market approach is based on the aggregate value of the portfolio of marketable equity securities rather than on the values of individual securities. A parent must group its securities with those of its consolidated subsidiaries (other than those in industries with specialized accounting practices) for the current and noncurrent classification.

Companies in certain industries where specialized accounting practices are applied for marketable securities generally are not required to change their reporting practices for gains or losses on marketable securities. However, those that carry their marketable equity securities on the basis of cost would be required to change to the lower of cost or market for those securities, except that they could adopt the market basis of accounting where that basis is an accepted alternative.

When a subsidiary follows accepted accounting practices that differ from those of the parent company, those practices must be retained in the consolidated financial statements in which the subsidiaries are included. However, when the parent company does include realized gains and losses in net income, the accounting by the subsidiary must be adjusted in consolidation to conform to that of the parent company.

If there is a change in classification of a marketable security between current or noncurrent or vice versa, the security must be transferred at the lower of cost or market at the date of transfer. If the market value is less than cost, it becomes the new cost basis, and the write-down must be charged to income as if it were a realized loss.

The following disclosures are required:

1. Aggregate cost and market value of the separate portfolios as of the balance sheet date, with identification as to which is the carrying amount.
2. Gross unrealized gains or losses related to market value over cost or cost over market value for all marketable equity securities in the portfolio.
3. Net realized gain or loss included in income determination, the basis on which cost was determined and the change in the valuation allowance that has been included in the equity section of the balance sheet during the period and, when a classified balance sheet is presented, the amount of such change included in the determination of net income.

Post balance sheet changes in market prices or realized gains and losses shall not be cause for adjusting the financial statements, although the effect of significant post balance sheet realized and unrealized gains and losses should be disclosed.

An exception to the general practice of valuing marketable securities at cost can be found in the stock brokerage industry where traditional thinking of necessity gave way to operating realities and needs. In this industry, it was agreed that it was appropriate to carry marketable securities, including those held as investments, at market quotations and that it was also appropriate in this industry to carry securities that are not readily marketable at fair values.

The 1975 Annual Report of Reynolds Securities states:

> Securities owned and securities sold—not yet purchased are carried at market value and the unrealized gains and losses on these securities are reflected in revenues.

"Specialized" industries, such as insurance, that have evolved their own methods of dealing with marketable securities are similarly unaffected by *SFAS 12.*

Implications for analysis

While *SFAS 12* has, in general, improved the accounting for "certain" marketable securities, there remain many gaps and inconsistencies in that accounting of which the analyst must be aware.

The definition of equity securities in the *Statement* is somewhat arbitrary and inconsistent. Often convertible bonds derive all or most of their value from their conversion feature (as has, indeed, been recognized by *APB Opinion 15,* "Earnings per Share") and are much more akin to equity securities than to debt instruments. Thus, the exclusion of these securities from the equity classification is not logical. Nor, for that matter, is there a sound reason for excluding from the valuation process debt securities and marketable mortgages that can fluctuate in value significantly either due to interest rate changes or to changes in credit standing. The continued carrying at cost and above market of debt obligations of issuers in default is particularly unwarranted.

SFAS 12 does not define when marketable securities should be carried as current and when as noncurrent, thus introducing a degree of arbitrariness in the decisions of how change in the market value of such securities should be accounted for. It is by no means self-evident that the manner of classifying securities in the balance sheet should determine whether changes in their value are reflected in income or not. While the *Statement* requires the transfer of a marketable security from one category to the next at the lower of cost or market, category switching could still allow a company some leeway in the determination of future results. In recent years (1969–71), for example, Signal Companies switched the classification of marketable securities four times. In 1975, Home Oil Company reduced its holdings in Atlantic Richfield Company substantially, and the reclassification of its remaining holdings to marketable securities from long-term investment resulted in a write-down of $1.7 million.

While the *Statement* does not address the question of how "cost" is determined, the analyst must be aware that a number of methods of determining the "cost" of marketable securities exists (e.g., specific identification, average, first-in, first-out) and that they can affect reported results.

It should be noted that under this *Statement,* the valuation concept accorded to marketable securities is analogous to that of accounts receivable valuation, and inconsistent with the concept of valuation applied to inventories—where once they are written down, subsequent write-ups are not allowed. The *Statement* also introduces an inconsistent treatment of anticipating gains, whereby it is acceptable to anticipate gains except when that would result in a valuation higher than original cost.

The aggregation of unrealized gains and losses can have an inconsistent effect on income recognition as is demonstrated by the following examples:

	End of year 1	
	Cost	Market
Security A	$10	$15
Security B	20	30
Security C	10	5
Security D	40	10
	$80	$60

Example 1. According to the *Statement,* a valuation allowance of $20 would be provided in year 1. If security D were sold in year 2 (assuming no change in market prices), an additional loss of $10 would be recorded (actual loss of $30 less elimination of $20 allowance). Thus, the $30 loss will have been recognized over two years rather than one.

Example 2. If security C is sold for a realized loss of $5, in year 2 (assuming no change in other market prices) the loss would be completely offset by a decrease in the allowance for unrealized losses and there would be no impact on net income.

Example 3. Assume that at the end of year 2, the portfolio of marketable securities is as follows:

	End of year 2	
	Cost	Market
Security A	$10	$20
Security B	20	30
Security C	10	25
	$40	$75

Any security or combination of securities can now drop a total of $35 in value before any loss will be recognized. Thus, security B could drop to $5 and security A to $10 (with C remaining unchanged) without any need for recognition of the loss. This is so because as long as the aggregate market value of the portfolio remains above cost, no individual gains or losses are recorded.

Additional considerations and analytical implications that relate to the accounting for marketable securities not carried as current assets will be considered in Chapter 6.

The current market value of investments is always relevant to an assessment of management performance. The argument that unrealized gains are only "paper profits" that could melt away before the investments are actually sold or otherwise disposed of does not recognize the fact that management makes the decision to hold or sell. Thus, a reduction in unrealized appreciation of an investment is as much a loss as would be a similar size loss on inventories or on equipment that became prematurely obsolete.

The analyst should treat with suspicion the amortization of bond discount (i.e., write-up of bond by crediting income) of an issue that from all available evidence sells at a discount because of doubt as to the ultimate collectibility of the principal amount.

The analyst, aware of accounting principles governing the presentation of investments, must pay particular attention to their valuation. On the one hand, they can be grossly undervalued on the balance sheet because of the convention prohibiting their write-up to market value no matter how obvious and soundly based such value may be.

On the other hand, the analyst must be alert to impairment of market value which because of loose standards in practice may not be fully reflected on the financial statements. If separately disclosed, the income generated by the investment may, at times, provide a clue to its fair value.

While the recognition of profits in nonequity securities must, according to present theory, await realization (i.e., in most cases sale), losses must be taken when they are deemed to be permanent in nature. However, the criteria for determining when a loss is "permanent" in nature are indefinite and allow for much leeway. With hope springing eternal, such write-downs occur in practice only when the evidence of loss in value is overwhelming. Since proper disclosure requires that the market value of securities be indicated, the alert analyst will be on the lookout for this information so that he can exercise his own judgment regarding the proper value to assign to these securities for the purpose of his analysis.

RECEIVABLES

Receivables are amounts due arising generally from the sale of goods or services. They may also represent accrued amounts due, such as rents, interest,

Exhibit 5–1: Operating cycle

and so forth. Notes receivable represent a more formal evidence of indebtedness due, but this characteristic does not make them more readily collectible than accounts receivable. Generally speaking, notes receivable are more easily negotiable and pledged for loans than are accounts receivable and, consequently, are considered the more liquid of the two. As a practical matter, this is, however, a superficial distinction.

Receivables classified as current assets should be reasonably expected to be realized or collected within a year or within the normal operating cycle of a business. *The normal operating cycle* is a concept that is important in the classification of items as current or noncurrent. The operating cycle generally encompasses the full circle of time from the commitment of cash for purchases until the collection of receivables resulting from the sale of goods or services. Exhibit 5–1 illustrates the concept.

ILLUSTRATION 1.   Great Lakes Dredge & Dock Company 1977 Annual Report, contains the following note: "Certain contracts entered into by the Company vary up to five years in length. For these contracts the Company classifies its contracting assets and liabilities as current."

If the normal collection interval of receivables is longer than a year (e.g., longer-term installment receivables), then their inclusion as current assets is proper provided the collection interval is normal and expected for the type of business the enterprise is engaged in. Because of their nature, certain types of receivables require separate disclosure. Examples are receivables from affiliated companies, officers, or employees.

Certain types of receivables are established without formal billing of the debtor. Thus, costs accumulated under a cost-plus-fixed-fee contract or some other types of government contracts are recorded as receivables as they accumulate.[1] Similarly, claims for tax refunds from the government are usually classified as receivables if no substantial question of technical compliance is involved.

---

[1] SEC FRR No. 1 Sec. 206 requires disclosure of amounts relating to long-term contracts included in receivables applicable to items billed but not paid under retainage provisions, items not yet billed or billable, and items representing claims subject to uncertainty as to their ultimate realization. Amounts expected to be collected after one year must also be disclosed.

To the financial analyst, the valuation of receivables is important from two main points of view:

1. The realization value of the assets.
2. The impact on income.

These two aspects are, of course, interrelated. It is a fact supported by experience that not all receivables will be collected nor will they all necessarily be collected in their entirety.

While a judgment about the collectibility of any one account can be made at any appropriate time, the collectibility of receivables as a group is best estimated on the basis of past experience with due allowance for current conditions. The "accounting risk" here is that the past experience may not be an adequate measure of future loss or that current developments may not have been fully taken into account. The resulting loss can be substantial and will affect both the current asset position as well as the net income for the period under review.

ILLUSTRATION 2.   In 1963, Brunswick Corporation made a "special provision for possible losses on receivables" of $15,000,000 *after* taxes. The assumption is that factors that became clear in 1963 were not "visible" or obvious to the auditor at the end of 1962 when a substantial amount of the receivables provided for was outstanding. Management explained the write-off as follows:

"Delinquencies in bowling installment payments, primarily related to some of the large chain accounts, *continued* at an unsatisfactory level. Nonchain accounts, which comprise about 80 percent of installment receivables, are generally better paying accounts.

"In the last quarter of 1963, average bowling lineage per establishment fell short of the relatively low lineage of the comparable period of 1962, resulting in an aggravation of collection problems on certain accounts. The bowling business may have felt the competition of outdoor activities associated with the unseasonably warm weather during the latter part of 1963. Some improvement in bowling lineage was noted in the early months of 1964 which tends to confirm this view. However, the fact that collections were lower in late 1963 contributed to management's decision to increase reserves. After the additional provision of $15,000,000, total reserves for possible future losses on all receivables amounted to $66,197,000, including $30,000,000 *transferred from deferred income taxes.*" [Author's emphasis.]

While it may be impossible to define the precise moment when the collection of a receivable is doubtful enough to require provision, the question may be properly asked whether the analyst could not, in 1962, have made an independent judgment on the adequacy of the bad debt provision in the light of developments in the bowling industry with which he should have been thoroughly familiar. It should be noted that Brunswick's earnings peaked out in early 1962.

Another aspect of receivable valuation relates to long-term receivables that are noninterest bearing or that bear unrealistically low rates of interest.

APB Opinion 21, "Interest on Receivables and Payables"

Objective. The primary objective of this *Opinion* is to refine the manner of applying existing accounting principles when the face amount of a note (as defined below) does not reasonably represent the present value of the consideration given or received in an exchange.

The *Opinion* covers receivables and payables that represent contractual rights to receive or pay money on fixed or determinable dates. These are collectively referred to as "notes."

The *Opinion* does not apply to trade receivables and payables due within one year, progress payments, deposits, retainages, customary activities of lending institutions, notes that bear interest at rates prescribed by governmental agencies, or intercompany transactions.

Significant provisions. A note may be issued for cash or for property, goods, or services.

When issued for cash, a note is presumed to have a present value at issuance measured by the cash proceeds exchanged, unless other rights or privileges (stated or unstated) are included (such as the issuance of a noninterest-bearing loan to a supplier who, in turn, charges less than the prevailing market price for products purchased by the lender under a contractual agreement).

When issued in a noncash transaction, the stated face amount of the note is generally presumed to represent the fair value of the consideration exchanged unless:

1. Interest is not stated,
2. The stated interest rate is unreasonable, or
3. The stated face amount of the note is materially different from the current sales price for the same or similar items or from the market value of the note at the date of the transaction.

When the stated face amount of the note does not represent the fair value of the consideration exchanged, the present value of the note must be established, taking into consideration:

1. The fair value of the consideration exchanged,
2. The market value of the note, or
3. The present value of all future payments.

The imputed rate of interest used for valuation purposes will normally be at least equal to the rate at which the debtor can obtain financing of a similar nature from other sources at the date of the transaction and may be influenced by:

1. An approximation of the prevailing market rates for the sources of credit that would provide a market for sale or assignment of the note;

2. The prime or higher rate for notes that are discounted with banks, giving due weight to the credit standing of the maker;
3. Published market rates for similar quality bonds;
4. Current rates for debentures with substantially identical terms and risks that are traded in open markets; or
5. The current rate charged by investors for first or second mortgage loans on similar property.

The difference between the present value and the face amount of the note should be treated as discount or premium and amortized as interest expense or income over the life of the note in such a way as to result in a constant rate of interest when applied to the amount outstanding at the beginning of any period (interest method).

The discount or premium should be reported in the balance sheet as a direct deduction from or addition to the face amount of the note.

Example of application of imputation of interest. The XYZ Corporation issued a noninterest-bearing note (face amount $5,180) to Toro Machinery Company for purchase of machinery on August 17, 19x1. The face amount of the note is to be paid on July 31, 19x8. It is felt that for a similar type note an interest rate of 8 percent is applicable.

Toro Machinery Company will record as sales and as the receivable from XYZ, $3,032, representing the present value of $5,180 to be received on July 31, 19x8. Over the intervening periods, Toro Machinery will pick up as interest income the increases in the present value of the receivable from XYZ. If we assume that Toro's fiscal year-end is September 30, the pattern of interest income pickup on a yearly basis and the carrying amounts of the receivable will be as follows:

Year	Month-end	Face amount	Imputed interest income	Unamortized discount	Discounted value of receivable (rounded)
19x1	8	$5,180.00	—	$2,147.54	$3,032.00
19x1	9	5,180.00	$ 29.65	2,117.89	3,062.00
19x2	9	5,180.00	245.69	1,872.20	3,307.00
19x3	9	5,180.00	264.62	1,607.58	3,572.00
19x4	9	5,180.00	285.79	1,321.79	3,858.00
19x5	9	5,180.00	308.66	1,013.13	4,166.00
19x6	9	5,180.00	333.35	679.78	4,500.00
19x7	9	5,180.00	360.02	319.76	4,860.00
19x8	7	—	319.76	—	—
Total			2,147.54		

Implications for analysis

The two most important questions facing the financial analyst with respect to receivables are:

1. Is the receivable genuine, due, and enforceable?
2. Has the probability of collection been properly assessed?

While the unqualified opinion of an independent auditor should lend assurance with regard to an affirmative answer to these questions, the financial analyst must recognize the possibility of an error of judgment as well as the lack of it.

1. The description of the receivables or the notes to the financial statement will usually not contain sufficient clues to permit an informed judgment as to whether a receivable is genuine, due, and enforceable. Consequently, a knowledge of industry practices and supplementary sources of information must be used for additional assurance.

In some industries, such as the phonograph record, toy, or bakery business, customers enjoy a substantial right of merchandise return, and allowance must be made for this.

ILLUSTRATION 3.   The case of Topper Corporation, a manufacturer and marketer of toys, is quite instructive and should serve as a significant lesson and warning to financial analysts about the dangers inherent in the evaluation of accounts receivable.

In mid-1970, Topper issued a prospectus for the public sale of common stock. The 1970 calendar-year financial statements indicated sales of $64 million, and a terse footnote related to the accounts receivable of $31 million at December 31, 1970, stated that "approximately $14 million of sales made in December 1970 carried extended credit terms of five to eight months. The comparable amount for the prior year was $2 million."

While the credit terms granted under the December sales program were by no means unusual or excessively extended, this "casual" footnote proved in retrospect to be an extraordinarily important piece of information for the analysts. For not only did the company, in its desire to report higher sales and earnings as a means to obtaining loans, grant its customers extended credit terms, free storage, and substantial discounts, it also granted them substantial rights of merchandise return and exchange to the point where the risk of ownership did in effect not pass from Topper to its customers.

The auditors, who gave Topper a clean opinion for 1970, claimed that they first learned about letters giving Topper's customers the right of merchandise return only in early 1972 and a full year later withdrew their opinion on the 1970 financial statements.

In May 1972, Topper incurred huge write-downs of receivables and inventory, and a year later Topper was adjudged bankrupt. Losses to shareholders and to some large pension funds that extended credit on the basis of information contained in the 1971 prospectus were very substantial.

The analyst must be ever alert to the possibility that either "loose" agreements with customers by suppliers anxious to sell or swiftly changing demand conditions can seriously impair the collectibility of accounts receivable.

ILLUSTRATION 4. Early in 1982, Dayco Corporation announced that it incurred an aftertax write-off of $11.7 million in its 1971 fiscal year because a foreign agent placed invalid orders. The company had to write off $20 million in accounts receivable, inventories, and prepaid expenses.

The following note to the financial statements appearing in the 1964 annual report of the O. M. Scott & Sons Company exemplifies the type of disclosure that does shed additional light on the contingencies to which receivables are subject:

> *Accounts receivable:* Accounts receivable are stated net after allowances for returns, allowances, and doubtful accounts of $472,000 at September 30, 1964 ($640,000 at September 30, 1963).
>
> Accounts receivable at September 30, 1964, include approximately $4,785,000 ($7,090,000 at September 30, 1963) for shipments made under a deferred payment plan whereby title to the merchandise is transferred to the dealer when shipped; however, the Company retains a security interest in such merchandise until sold by the dealer. Payment to the Company is due from the dealer as the merchandise is sold at retail. The amount of receivables of this type shall at no time exceed $11,000,000 under terms of the loan and security agreement.

In some instances, a receivable may not represent a true sale but rather a merchandise or service advance; these receivables cannot be considered in the same light as regular receivables.

A sale of receivables with recourse does not effectively transfer the risk of ownership of the receivables. The analyst must be alert to accounting treatments that consider the risk as having passed to the buyer and that mention such sales as creating merely contingent liabilities for the seller.

Some companies sell portions of their receivables to financial institutions, sometimes captive, unconsolidated finance subsidiaries. Since the risk of carrying the receivable is still with the company until the ultimate customer pays, the analyst can make the following *analytical* adjustment to reflect this:

Receivables .... $ of receivables sold

Short Term Debt .... $ of receivables sold

2. Most provisions for uncollectible accounts are based on past experience, although they should also make allowance for current and emerging industry conditions. In actual practice, the accountant is likely to attach more importance to the former than to the latter. The analyst must bear in mind that while a formula approach to the calculation of the provision for bad debts is convenient and practical for the accountant, it represents a type of mechanical judgment that can easily overlook changing or emerging conditions. The analyst must use his or her own judgment and knowledge of industry conditions to assess the adequacy of the provision for uncollectible accounts (see example of the Brunswick Corporation earlier in this chapter).

Unfortunately, information that would be helpful in assessing the general level of collection risks in the receivables is not usually found in published financial statements. Such information can, of course, be sought from other sources or from the company directly. Examples of such information are:

1. What is the customer concentration? What percentage of total receivables is due from one or a few major customers? Would failure of any one customer have a material impact on the company's financial condition?
2. What is the age pattern of the receivables?
3. What proportion of notes receivable represent renewals of old notes?
4. Have allowances been made for trade discounts, returns, or other credits to which customers are entitled?

The financial analyst, in assessing the current financial position and a company's ability to meet its obligations currently, as expressed by such measures as the current ratio (discussed in Chapter 16), must recognize the full import of those accounting conventions that relate to the classification of receivables as "current." Thus, the operating cycle theory allows the inclusion of installment receivables that may not be fully collectible for years. In balancing these against current obligations, allowance for these differences in timing should be made.

INVENTORIES

With the possible exception of some service organizations, in most businesses inventories represent assets of great importance. From the point of view of the analyst of financial statements, inventories are significant for two main reasons:

1. They represent a significant, major component of the assets devoted to the conduct of the business.
2. They enter importantly in the determination of net income.

Asset valuation

Inventories are goods that are acquired for resale or that enter into goods produced for resale. In nonmanufacturing enterprises, such as retail establishments, purchased merchandise requires little or no additional work before resale. In manufacturing organizations, we classify three main types of inventories:

1. Raw materials,
2. Goods in process, and
3. Finished goods,

depending on their stage of completion in the production process.

The importance attached to methods of inventory valuation and the controversies surrounding them is due primarily to the fact that they enter into the determination of the cost of goods sold and thus into the determination of net income. It is easy to understand why this is so. All material or goods purchased by an enterprise for resale are either sold or carried in inventory for use and sale at some future time. Thus, excluding material written off as worthless or missing, whatever is not on hand in the ending inventory must have been disposed of and, therefore, be part of the cost of goods sold and vice versa.

A most important factor to be recognized about accounting principles that govern the valuation of inventories is that they are primarily aimed at obtaining the best matching of cost and revenues. As a result of this orientation towards the income statement, the resulting, or residual, balance sheet inventory figure may be rendered inaccurate or even meaningless. This, as we shall see, can often be the case.

The basic principle of inventory valuation is that it be valued at "the lower of cost or market." This simple phrase belies the complexities and the variety of alternatives to which it is subject. This variety can, in turn, lead to significantly different figures of periodic income all "in accordance with generally accepted accounting principles."

What is cost?   The complexities of cost determination are caused by a diversity of assumptions and of practice in two main areas:

1. What is includable cost?
2. What assumptions do we make about the flow of inventory costs through an enterprise?

What is includable cost?   Let us start with a simple example. An office supply store buys a desk for resale. The invoice cost of the desk is obviously the basic cost. To that may properly be added the cost of freight-in as well as the costs of assembling the desk if that is the form in which it is kept in inventory. If the desk was imported, duty and other direct costs of clearing the desk through customs may properly be added. Suppose the president and others expend a great deal of time and effort in purchasing the desks. Should any part of the cost of their time be allocated to it, that is, inventoried if the desk is unsold at year-end? Here the answer is not so clear. Accounting principles would sanction allocation of such costs to inventories, but they would also sanction the current expensing of such costs. This will, of course, make a difference in the reported results for the year. Should expenses incurred in selling desks be added to their cost? Here there is more unanimity of view that such costs do not belong in inventory.

In spite of its importance, the matter of what costs are included in inventory or, conversely, excluded therefrom, is only rarely discussed or disclosed in published financial statements. The following example of disclosure, appearing in the 1967 annual report of the Eckmar Corporation, is an exception:

Note: Inventories. The carrying amounts of inventories as of December 31, 1967, include estimated amounts of costs, aggregating approximately $270,000, incurred for purchasing, freight, receiving, material handling, and warehousing applicable to materials and merchandise and for certain administrative functions considered to relate to manufacturing operations. Such costs previously had been charged to income when incurred. Inventories at December 31, 1967, also include certain items of supplies, amounting to approximately $30,000, not previously inventoried. The inclusion of these amounts in inventories as of December 31, 1967, had the effect of reducing cost of products and merchandise sold by approximately $150,000 and selling, administrative, and general expenses by approximately $150,000, and the net loss of the Corporation and subsidiaries for the year by approximately $300,000.

The need for this disclosure becomes clearer when we find that the auditor's opinion includes the following statement: "As explained in Note B to the financial statements, the Corporation revised as of December 31, 1967, its inventory policies to include in inventory additional amounts of overhead and supplies; our approval of these changes is conditioned upon the ability of the Corporation to recover such amounts in subsequent operations. In our opinion, subject (1) realization of the carrying amounts of inventories."

Notes 2 and 5 to the financial statements of Alfa, Inc. (see Appendix 4B), disclose that company's inventory policies and reveal the excess of FIFO over LIFO amounts by means of disclosure of "LIFO reserves" (Note 5).

It is important to understand the difference between the current expensing of a cost and its inclusion in inventory. The current expensing of a cost converts it into what is known as a period cost, that is, a cost deemed to expire during the fiscal period in which it is incurred, rather than its continuance by virtue of its conversion into an asset. Conversely, a cost that is inventoried is a product cost and does not become a charge against current income and remains, instead as an asset to be charged against future operations that are presumed to benefit from it. It can be readily seen that a decision to inventory a cost rather than expense it *shifts* a charge to income from the present to the future.

Cost accounting

The foregoing desk inventory example was relatively simple because the inventory problem was that of a retailer. If we consider the cost problem of the desk manufacturer, additional complexities are introduced.

In producing the desk from its basic components, the manufacturer will incur three main types of cost:

1. Raw materials going into the desk.
2. Labor to produce and assemble the desk.
3. Indirect expenses such as wear and tear of machinery, auxiliary supplies, heat, light and power, various factory occupancy costs, supervisory costs, etc.

While the first two categories of expense may present some problems of classification, it is in the third group that we will find the greatest variety of treatments and the most problems. This category is also known as indirect expenses or overhead costs.

Overhead costs. While it may be reasonably feasible to maintain control over the direct material and direct labor costs that go into the making of a desk, it is not practicable, if not impossible, to trace the specific overhead costs to the desk. This requires *allocation* of an entire pool of costs to the many products (e.g., desks, chairs, shelves, bookcases, etc.) that the manufacturer produces. This allocation requires a number of assumptions and decisions such as:

1.   What items should be includable in overhead costs?
2.   Over how many units (e.g., desks) do we allocate the overhead costs?

Includable costs in overhead. When we examine the costs that the retailer could include in the "cost per desk," we see that certain costs were generally accepted as includable while others were not clearly includable. In the area of manufacturing overheads, differences between theory and practice are even more prevalent because of the far greater variety of expenses involved and because of the wide variety of acceptable methods or because of practice that is not subject to meaningful restraints. In the matter of includable expenses, consider, for example, the following questions:

a.   Should costs of testing new designs and materials of a desk be charged to inventories? If so, on what basis and over how many units?
b.   Should general and administrative costs be included in inventory?

As of now there may be general acceptance of a number of ways in which to answer these questions. But there is by no means a single answer that is accepted more than all others.

Assumptions of activity. The allocation of overhead costs to all the desks, chairs, and other items produced must, of course, be done on a rational basis designed to get the best approximation of actual cost. However, this is far from an easy matter. The greatest difficulty stems from the fact that a good part of overhead represents "fixed costs," that is, costs that do not vary with production but vary mostly with the passage of time. Examples are rent payments and the factory manager's salary. Thus, assuming for a moment that only desks are produced, if the fixed costs are $100,000 and 10,000 desks are produced, each desk will absorb $10 of fixed costs. However, if only 5,000 desks are produced, each desk will have to absorb $20 of fixed costs. Clearly, then, the level of activity itself is an important determinant of unit cost. In other words, wide fluctuations in output can result in wide fluctuations in unit cost.

Since the allocation of overhead depends also on an accurate estimate of total overhead costs that will be incurred during the period, variations between estimated and actual costs can also result in overabsorbed or underabsorbed overhead.

In order to allocate fixed costs over output, an assumption must be made at the outset of the fiscal period as to how many units (desks) the company expects to produce, and that in turn will determine over how many units the overhead costs will be allocated. This procedure entails estimates of sales and related production. To the extent that the actual production differs from estimated production, the overhead will be either overabsorbed or underabsorbed. That means that production and inventory are charged with more than total overhead costs or with an insufficient amount of overhead costs.

A cost system that charges cost of goods sold and inventories with predetermined estimated costs is called a *standard cost* system. Variations between the estimates or standards and actual costs are called cost accounting variances. Generally speaking, when an inventory is described as being valued at standard cost, that should mean that variances are insignificant or have been allocated or otherwise adjusted; in other words, standard costs would approximate actual costs. Under generally accepted accounting standards, it is not permissible to carry inventories at only direct costs with the current expensing of all fixed overheads.

The next area of inventory cost determination that we will examine relates to assumptions regarding the *flow* of goods and their costs. While the methods used in this connection (LIFO, FIFO, average cost) are the most controversial methods associated with inventory accounting, it should be clear from the foregoing discussion that the problems of cost accounting and overhead allocations may produce even more variation in reported results than can the assumptions about cost flows.

Inventory cost flows

In order to keep the discussion simple, let us return to our example of the office furniture retailer and assume that in the fiscal year ended December 31, 19x2, the inventory record of desks showed the following details:

Inventory on January 1, 19x2	100 desks @ $40	$ 4,000
First purchase in 19x2	200 desks @ $50	10,000
Second purchase in 19x2	100 desks @ $50	5,000
Third purchase in 19x2	200 desks @ $60	12,000
Total available for sale	600 desks	$31,000

Assuming that 50 desks are in inventory as at December 31, 19x2, how should they be valued?

There are a number of methods, all enjoying the "generally accepted" label, of which the three most common are discussed in the sections that follow.

First-in, first-out (FIFO). This method assumes what is probably the most common and justified assumption about the flow of goods in a business, that is, that those units bought first are sold (or used) first. This comforms also to the best inventory management practice. Under this method, the 50 desks will be valued at $60 each, the unit cost of the last purchase, or $3,000. The resulting cost of goods sold is $28,000 ($31,000 representing the cost of all goods available for sale less $3,000 the value assigned to the ending inventory) based on the formula:

$$\underbrace{\frac{\text{Beginning}}{\text{inventory}} + \text{Purchases}}_{\text{Goods available for sale}} - \frac{\text{Ending}}{\text{inventory}} = \frac{\text{Cost of goods}}{\text{sold}}$$

Last-in, first-out (LIFO). The assumption that the earliest purchases are the ones in inventory has been likened to the pile "flow" of inventory. If an inventory consists of a pile of salt or coal, then the last quantity bought is likely to be the first removed and sold. But this concern with a parallel to physical movement of inventories misses the real intention in inventory valuation. That relates primarily to an assumption about the flow of *costs* rather than of physical units, and the flow of costs is chosen not because it parallels the physical goods movement but rather because it achieves certain objectives of inventory valuation. The major objective of the LIFO method is to charge cost of goods sold with the most recent costs incurred. Quite obviously where the price level remains stable, the results under either the FIFO or the LIFO method will be much the same; but under a changing price level, as the advancing one in our example, the results in the use of these methods will differ significantly. The use of the LIFO method has increased greatly due to its acceptance for tax purposes. Our tax law stipulates that its use for tax purposes makes mandatory its adoption for financial reporting, although in 1981 some *reporting* requirements were related.

The basic aim of LIFO accounting is to obtain a better matching of current revenues with current costs in times of inflation. As will be seen in the discussion of the effects of price-level changes, this objective is not always achieved. Nevertheless, in *ASR 293* (1981), the SEC exhorts preparers of financial reports to make sure that LIFO accounting is justified, based on the LIFO *accounting* concept of matching current costs with current revenues.

In our example, the inventory of 50 desks under the LIFO method will be valued at $40 each, or $2,000. The cost of goods sold is $29,000 ($31,000 − $2,000). The inventory figure of $2,000 on the balance sheet will be one third below current market (or at least one third below the latest cost), but the income statement will be more realistically presented in terms of matching current costs with current revenues.

Average cost. The average-cost method smoothes out cost fluctuation by using a weighted-average cost in valuing inventories and in pricing out the cost of goods sold. While the weighted-average cost of goods sold will depend on the timing of sales, we can, in this example, consider the average cost of all purchases during the year and the opening inventory. On that basis, the average price per desk is $51.67 ($31,000 ÷ 600), and the 50 desks will be valued at $2,583.50. The cost of goods sold would be $28,416.50 ($31,000 − $2,583.50).

To summarize, under the three methods, the following results are obtained:

	FIFO	LIFO	Average
Ending inventory	$ 3,000.00	$ 2,000.00	$ 2,583.50
Cost of goods sold	28,000.00	29,000.00	28,416.50

Assuming that the sales of desks for the period amounted to $35,000, the gross profit under each method would be as follows:

	FIFO	LIFO	Average
Sales	$35,000.00	$35,000.00	$35,000.00
Cost of goods sold	28,000.00	29,000.00	28,416.50
Gross profit	$ 7,000.00	$ 6,000.00	$ 6,583.50

It is clear that the choice of method (i.e., the assumption about cost flows) can make a significant difference in the determination of cost of goods sold and the valuation of inventories. Generally, the FIFO method provides a "good" inventory figure because it reflects the latest costs. The LIFO method, on the other hand, produces a better matching of costs and revenues. In times of changing prices, both virtues cannot be achieved simultaneously under the historical-cost method.

A method of inventory valuation in use especially for interim statement results is the gross profit method. This method derives the inventory figure by estimating the cost of goods sold on the basis of a normal gross profit ratio experienced in practice. This method is accurate only if the gross profit ratio has in fact not changed and if there are no unusual inventory shortages or spoilage.

The retail method of inventory estimation is an extension of the gross profit method. It uses sophisticated techniques that involve physical inventory taking, priced first at retail, and the reduction of this inventory to cost by means of gross profit ratios.

LIFO and changing price levels

The accelerated inflation rate of recent years renewed the business community's interest in the LIFO method. The rationale advanced for the flight to LIFO was that this method adjusts the financial statements for inflation. In fact, it merely postpones the recognition of the effects of inflation, although such postponement can be long term if prices continue to rise and the LIFO inventory base is not liquidated. The major reason for the method's popularity is, of course, the long-term postponement of taxes under such conditions, which is a very real and tangible benefit.

A good way to understand the concept of inventory profits as well as the effect of changing price levels is to trace the operating results recorded under different inventory methods. The following examples and analysis are designed to accomplish this.

ILLUSTRATION 5. *The effects of price-level changes on reported earnings under different inventory costing methods.*

Following are inventory purchase costs and selling prices for quarterly periods starting with the fourth quarter of 19x2. It is assumed that prices rise steadily in the first, second, and third quarter of 19x3, that they level off in the fourth quarter, and decline in the first quarter of 19x4. It is also assumed—for simplicity's sake—that the company's markup on cost is given as a constant $200 and that the company holds three units in inventory at all times and buys and sells one unit each quarter.

	4th Q 19x2	1st Q 19x3	2d Q 19x3	3d Q 19x3	4th Q 19x3	1st Q 19x4
Selling price	$1,300	$1,400	$1,500	$1,600	$1,600	$1,500
Inventory purchase cost ..	1,100	1,200	1,300	1,400	1,400	1,300

The following tables show the results under the three inventory costing methods, FIFO, LIFO, and weighted average. The tables show cost of inventory on hand at the start of each quarter and also the gross profit recorded under the three methods.

Table 1:   FIFO inventories on hand

Start of	Purchased 4th Q 19x2	1st Q 19x3	2d Q 19x3	3d Q 19x3	4th Q 19x3	1st Q 19x4	Balance sheet amount of inventory
2d Q 19x3 ...	$1,100	$1,200	$1,300				= $3,600
3d Q 19x3 ...		1,200	1,300	$1,400			= 3,900
4th Q 19x3 ..			1,300	1,400	$1,400		= 4,100
1st Q 19x4 ..				1,400	1,400	$1,300	= 4,100

Table 2: FIFO gross profit recorded

	2d Q 19x3	3d Q 19x3	4th Q 19x3	1st Q 19x4
Sales	$1,500	$1,600	$1,600	$1,500
Cost	1,100	1,200	1,300	1,400
(Purchased)	*(4th Q-x2)*	*(1st Q-x3)*	*(2d Q-x3)*	*(3d Q-x3)*
Gross profit	$ 400	$ 400	$ 300	$ 100

Table 3: LIFO inventories on hand

		Purchased					Balance sheet amount of inventory
Start of	*4th Q 19x2*	*1st Q 19x3*	*2d Q 19x3*	*3d Q 19x3*	*4th Q 19x3*	*1st Q 19x4*	
2d Q 19x3 .	$1,100	$1,200	$1,300				= $3,600
3d Q 19x3 .	1,100	1,200		$1,400			= 3,700
4th Q 19x3 .	1,100	1,200			$1,400		= 3,700
1st Q 19x4 .	1,100	1,200				$1,300	= 3,600

Table 4: LIFO gross profit recorded

	2d Q 19x3	3d Q 19x3	4th Q 19x3	1st Q 19x4
Sales	$1,500	$1,600	$1,600	$1,500
Cost	1,300	1,400	1,400	1,300
(Purchased)	*(2d Q-x3)*	*(3d Q-x3)*	*(4th Q-x3)*	*(1st Q-x4)*
Gross profit	$ 200	$ 200	$ 200	$ 200

Table 5: Average-cost inventories on hand

	Opening average cost[a]	Purchased						*Balance sheet amount of inventory*
		4th Q 19x2	*1st Q 19x3*	*2d Q 19x3*	*3d Q 19x3*	*4th Q 19x3*	*1st Q 19x4*	
2d Q 19x3 ...	—	$1,100	$1,200	$1,300				= $3,600
3d Q 19x3 ...	$2,400 [b]				$1,400			= 3,800
4th Q 19x3 ...	2,533.3 [c]					$1,400		= 3,933.3
1st Q 19x4 ...	2,622.2 [d]						$1,300	= 3,922.2

[a] Balance sheet value of inventory − Average cost of goods sold (B/S value ÷ 3).
[b] $3,600 − ($3,600 ÷ 3) = $3,600 − $1,200 = $2,400.
[c] $3,800 − ($3,800 ÷ 3) = $3,800 − $1,266.7 = $2,533.3.
[d] $3,933.3 − (3,933.3 ÷ 3) = $3,933.3 − $1,311.1 = $2,622.2.

Average cost gross profits recorded

	2d Q 19x3	3d Q 19x3	4th Q 19x3	1st Q 19x4
Sales	$1,500	$1,600	$1,600	$1,500
Cost (average)...................	1,200	1,266.7	1,311.1	1,307.4*
Gross profit.....................	$ 300	$ 333.3	$ 288.9	$ 192.6

* Balance sheet value of inventory ÷ 3 = $3,922.2 ÷ 3 = $1,307.4.

Analysis. *Under FIFO,* we note that the oldest cost in inventory at the start of the second quarter of 19x3, $1,100, is the first to be sold in that quarter. Compared with a sale price of $1,500, this produces a gross profit of $400.

This $400 is really composed of two elements. There is the normal $200 markup on cost and an additional $200 resulting from the matching of an older, lower inventory cost with a current selling price. This $200 is the "inflation profit" so often referred to recently.

As long as the inflation rate remains unchanged, reported profits will include both the normal markup of $200 and the inflation profit of $200. In the third quarter of 19x3, as the inflation continues, the gross profit remains at $400.

However, in the fourth quarter of 19x3, the price level remains unchanged from the third quarter. Following the established pattern, a higher priced FIFO inventory cost layer flows into cost of goods sold, but with the steady price level, the sales price does not rise and this results in a drop of 25 percent in gross profit to $300. In the first quarter of 19x4, there is a drop in price level, and both cost of new purchases and the sales price move down $100. The FIFO inventory system, however, continues as usual, to place the oldest unit (the item purchased for $1,400 in the third quarter of 19x3) into cost of goods sold to be matched against the reduced sale price of $1,500 with the gross profit dropping to $100.

Here, then, is the vulnerability of FIFO. Inventory costs flow into cost of goods sold after a delay equal to the inventory turnover period. In periods of continuing inflation, this matching produces a continuous inflation of profit. When the rate of inflation declines, revenues should immediately reflect the change; costs will not. For the length of one inventory turnover period, costs will continue to reflect the earlier rate of inflation and will constantly increase. *Thus, any reduction in the rate of inflation will affect the profits of FIFO companies adversely.*

Under LIFO, we note that the gross profits reported are the same for all quarters and they equal the normal markup of $200. This is so because under the LIFO system, the most recent purchase is the first deemed to be sold. Thus, LIFO cost is close to current cost, and the effects of inflation—both as the prices rise and as they fall—are largely eliminated from the income statement. Note, however, that in the real world, the correspondence between current cost and LIFO cost may not be quite as exact as in this illustration. However, there will rarely be any significant difference, unless there is a reduction in inventory *quantities.*

Thus, the LIFO inventory method will provide at least a temporary correction for the distorting effects of changing inflation rates, if purchases and sales are both made frequently and continually. In most cases, the price level at the time of the "last-in" purchase should be about the same as the price level at time of sale.

However, when purchases and sales are not closely linked, such as is the case with companies making seasonal purchases, the LIFO correction will not work. In this case, a time lag exists between purchase and sale. Reported income will tend to behave as if the company is on FIFO, even though it uses LIFO.

Under the average cost, we note that gross profits do vary with the price level, but not with as wide swings as under FIFO. This results because the time length of the time lag—in matching older costs with current revenues—is shorter under average cost than under FIFO, but longer than under LIFO. Thus, the inflation accounting problems of companies using average cost will be similar to those using FIFO, but the effects will be more moderate.

Inventory valuation at "market"

The inventory at cost must be compared with inventory at market and the lower of the two used.[2]

"Market value" is defined as current replacement cost except that market shall not be higher than net realizable value nor should it be less than net realizable value reduced by the normal profit margin.

The upper limit of market value in effect considers the costs associated with sale or other disposition costs. The lower limit means that if the inventory is written down from cost to market, it be written down to a figure that will ensure the realization of a "normal" gross profit on its sale in a subsequent period.

Inventories under long-term contracts

The accumulation of costs under long-term contracts, reduced by progress billings, are in the nature of inventories. Two methods of accounting are acceptable here, but it is intended that their use should be dictated by surrounding circumstances (see also Chapter 10).

1. Where estimates of the final outcome or results of the contracts are difficult or impossible to make and are too speculative to be reliable, the *completed-contract* method should be used. Under this method all costs of the contract, including related general and administrative costs, are accumulated and carried as assets (inventories) until completion of the contract when final net profit or loss is determined.

2. Where estimates of cost and related incomes at each stage of completion of the contract can be made, the *percentage-of-completion* method of long-term contract accounting should be used. Under this method, the estimated proportionate profit earned up to any particular point in time

---

[2] The use of the lower of cost on market for LIFO inventories, while not permitted for tax purposes, can be used in the financial statements and would not violate the Internal Revenue Code requirement that if the tax return is on LIFO, reports to outsiders must also be on this basis. Some modifications in the "LIFO conformity rule" have occurred in recent years.

may be credited to income and correspondingly included in accumulated costs (inventories).

Under either method, losses that are ascertainable at any point in time should be recognized and accounted for when first determined.

SEC *ASR 164* requires separate disclosure of inventoried costs related to long-term contracts, methods of determining cost, methods of determining market, and description of method by which amounts are removed from inventory.

Classification of inventories

Generally, inventories are classified as current assets. Indeed, they represent in most cases a very important part of the current asset group, although, ordinarily, they are considered less liquid than cash or receivables.

Under the "normal operating cycle" concept, inventories that would be kept beyond a year because of the requirements typical of an industry would nevertheless be classified as current. Thus, inventories in the tobacco industry or the liquor industry, which go through prolonged aging cycles, are nevertheless classified as current.

Inventories in excess of current requirements should not be classified as current.

ILLUSTRATION 6.   General Hobbies Corporation had the following footnote: Future operations (not covered by auditors' report):

Inventory quantities at July 31, 1975, are considerably in excess of the Company's estimated requirements for the next fiscal year. In its continuing effort to reduce inventories and the related carrying costs, the Company is continuing its inventory reduction programs at prices which may result in a gross profit lower than that realized in prior years. These efforts may have a materially adverse effect on the Company's operations in the July 31, 1976, fiscal year.

IMPLICATIONS FOR ANALYSIS

It is obvious that to the extent to which alternative choices of accounting standards, and the methods of their application, proliferate, the wider is management's flexibility in reporting results and in presenting the enterprise's financial condition. In the area of inventory accounting, where the impact of differing methods on income can be substantial, this flexibility is all the more likely to be availed of by management.

The auditor's opinion should provide assurance that certain minimum standards were upheld in the exercise of discretion with which such principles are applied. However, in some areas of inventory accounting, the permitted leeway is so considerable that management can exercise a great deal of discretion in its choices. Thus, as a minimum, the financial analyst must understand what these choices are, and they must be judged in the light of conditions that apply to each specific situation.

With regard to inventories, the financial analyst will expect information and assurance as to the following:

1. Is the inventory physically in existence and is it fairly valued?
2. Has the accounting for inventories been consistent?
3. Can the effect of the different accounting methods used be measured?

Audit procedures designed to give assurance about the physical existence of inventories have been improving over the years and have been especially tightened up since the 1938 SEC hearings in the matter of McKesson & Robbins, Inc. In this case, large-scale fraud that resulted in a substantial overstatement of inventories was not uncovered by the audit primarily because no attempt was made by the auditors to establish physical contact with the inventories. The SEC stated:

> In our opinion, the time has come when auditors must, as part of their examination whenever reasonable and practicable, make physical contact with the inventory and assume reasonable responsibility therefore as had already become the practice in many cases before the present hearings. By this we do not mean that auditors should be, or by making such tests become, the guarantors of inventories any more than of any of the other items in the financial statements but we do mean that they should make all reasonable tests and inquiries, and not merely those limited to the books, in order to state their professional opinion, as auditors, as to the truthfulness of that item in the same way as they do for the other items in the statements.

The accounting profession responded by adopting the requirement that auditors observe the taking of physical inventories whenever it was reasonable and practicable to do so. This requirement, as well as the refinement of audit techniques, has brought about great improvements in the reliability of inventory audits. Nevertheless, exceptional cases still arise.

Thus, in the 1970s, Patterson Parchment Company incurred a large inventory write-down because accountants in a key division counted the same inventory twice; Whittaker Corporation was forced to buy back two subsidiaries it sold because of multimillion inventory shortages discovered after their sale; and Cenco, Inc., was almost driven to insolvency because of a systematic inventory inflation scheme carried on over a number of years in a major division.

The fair statement of inventories is, of course, dependent not merely on a proper accounting for physical quantities but also on their proper pricing and summarization.

The analyst must be alert to the types of cost that are included in inventory. For example, under Internal Revenue Regulations adopted in 1975, marketing, sales, advertising and distribution expenses, interest costs, past service pension costs, and general and administrative costs pertaining to overall, rather than only to manufacturing activities, must be excluded from the overhead included in inventory under a full-absorption cost system. A reading of footnotes can reveal the inclusion of unusual costs. Sperry Rand, for example, included "learning curve" costs in inventories under a concept that involves deferral of costs early in a production cycle in the expectation that with experience, subsequent costs will be reduced. However, should such expectations not materialize, future write-offs will occur:

> At September 30 and March 31, 1975, gross inventories included approximately $136,900,000 and $127,500,000, respectively, of costs related to long-term contracts or programs. The aggregate of deferred or other costs under long-term contracts which exceeded the estimated average costs of all the units expected to be produced (learning curve concept) and included in inventories at September 30, 1975, and March 31, 1975, was not material.

While under the going-concern convention accountants are not concerned with the sale of inventories other than in the normal course of business, the analyst, and especially the credit analyst concerned with current values, may be interested in the composition of inventories. Thus, raw material may be much more readily salable than work in process since once raw material is converted into parts of certain specifications, it rapidly loses its value in case it then has to be liquidated.

The composition of total inventory between raw materials, work in process and finished goods can hold important analytical clues[3] as to future production plans or as to the existence of a divergence between actual as against expected sales. Thus, a decline in raw materials against an increase in work in process and finished goods may indicate a production slowdown, while an *inventory divergence* in the opposite direction may indicate actual or expected increases in orders booked.

ILLUSTRATION 7.   The quarterly and year-end comparison of inventory components of Digital Equipment Corporation indicate a relative decline in raw materials in contrast to an increase in both finished goods and work in process that should alert the analyst to the possibility of an expected future production slowdown:

	Inventories (in millions)			
	Quarter ended		*Year ended*	
	Sept. 81	*Sept. 80*	*June 81*	*June 80*
Inventory components:				
Raw materials	$ 221.3	$230.2	$ 221.3	$199.2
Work in process	352.5	315.4	346.8	271.3
Finished goods	567.0	418.1	534.1	349.4
Total inventories	1,140.8	963.7	1,102.2	819.9

---

[3] Credit for the development of these analytical tools belongs to Thornton L. O'Glove of Reporting Research Corporation.

The rate of change in inventories as against that in sales can also be of analytical significance.

ILLUSTRATION 8. The year-to-year rate of change in net sales and inventories of AMP, Inc., suggests that a continuing increase in the rate of inventory buildup as against a slower growth in sales may be a precursor of inventory liquidation or write-off with possible detrimental effects on profits (in millions):

9 months ended Sept. 30	Net sales	Year-to-year percent increase	Inventories	Year-to-year percent increase
1980	$864.9	17	$298.4	33
1979	741.3	29	224.6	34
1978	575.7	24	168.0	24
1977	462.8	22	136.0	23
1976	378.4		110.8	

Accepted reporting standards (which are part of generally accepted auditing standards) require that changes in the application of accounting principles be noted and the impact of the change reported. Thus, in audited financial statements, the analyst will expect to be alerted to changes in principles of inventory accounting, such as, for example, from LIFO to FIFO. However, the analyst must be aware of the fact that changes in accounting principles call for a consistency exception, whereas other changes affecting comparability do not necessarily call for disclosure in the auditor's report.

Of the various inventory methods in use, LIFO is the most complex and in addition has not only bookkeeping implications for management but behavioral ones as well. Thus, for example, in the case of LIFO, the year-end inventory level makes a definite difference in results, and management must plan and act accordingly.

The analyst must realize that the LIFO method of inventory accounting is not unitary but has rather many variations that can produce different results. It can be applied to all inventory components or to only a few.[4] It can be applied to material costs while other inventory methods are used for labor and overhead costs. Footnotes that merely disclose the variety of methods in use without giving breakdowns of respective inventory amounts lack analytical value.

The LIFO method permits income manipulation, and analysts must be ever alert to this possibility. For example, changing purchasing policy at the end of the year can affect reported results. This is not possible under FIFO.

---

[4] Some meat packers, for example, have used LIFO for pork but not for beef and lamb.

ILLUSTRATION 9.   The following purchases occurred in 19x1:

> January to June ..... 7,000 widgets at $1 per unit
> July to November.... 5,000 widgets at $1.20 per unit
> December .... 2,000 widgets at $1.30 per unit

The ending inventory consisted of 1,000 units. Under LIFO these would be reported at a cost of $1 per widget. Now, assume the enterprise had purchased 3,000 widgets in December—an additional 1,000. The additional purchase would have cost $1,300, but the additional ending inventory would have been only $1,000, thus decreasing profits by $300. Under different conditions, the act of buying more widgets could have increased profits.

When a reduction in the LIFO inventory quantities (base) takes place, old LIFO costs are matched with current revenues, thus resulting in increased profit margins.

ILLUSTRATION 10.   Assume that the widget company shows the results below for 19x2:

Sales (2,000 @ $1,375)		$2,750
Cost of sales:		
Beginning LIFO inventory (1,000 @ $1).....	$1,000	
Purchases (2,000 @ $1.10)	2,200	
Ending LIFO inventory (1,000 @ $1)	(1,000)	2,200
Gross profit..............................		$ 550
Gross profit percentage		20%

Assume that in 19x3 the company continues the policy of marking up widgets by 25 percent and that purchase and selling prices increase by 10 percent. However, a strike during the year prevents replacement of widget inventory, and this part of the LIFO base is liquidated. As can be seen below, this will increase profit margins as follows:

Sales (2,000 @ $1.5125)		$3,025
Cost of sales:		
Beginning LIFO inventory (1,000 @ $1).....	$1,000	
Purchases (1,500 @ $1.21)	1,815	
Ending LIFO inventory (500 @ $1)	(500)	2,315
Gross profit..............................		$ 710
Gross profit percentage		23.5%

In the same fashion, managements can by deliberate action manipulate profit levels by dipping into LIFO inventory pools. Analysts must watch for disclosure of such charges. An example is the following disclosure by Interlake, Inc.:

> **Inventories.**   Inventories are stated at the lower of cost or market value. Cost of domestic inventories is determined principally by the last-in first-out

method, which is less than current costs by $111,028,000, and $113,398,000 at December 28, 1980 and December 30, 1979, respectively. Cost of inventories of foreign subsidiaries is determined principally by the first-in first-out method.

During 1980, inventory quantities were reduced, resulting in a liquidation of LIFO inventory quantities carried at lower costs prevailing in prior years as compared with the cost of 1980 production. As a result, income before taxes was increased by $23,200,000, equivalent to $2.08 per share after applicable income taxes, of which $15,400,000, equivalent to $1.38 per share after applicable income taxes, was reflected in cost of products sold and the balance was included as a reduction of the shutdown/disposal provision.

While spotting an undisclosed LIFO inventory chargeout is not always easy, a crude check that the analyst can apply is to see whether the dollar value of the LIFO inventory has declined on a year-to-year basis. Moreover, information about such changes can also be found in the "Management's Discussion and Analysis of Financial Condition and Results of Operations" section of published financial reports.

The analyst must be particularly wary about the reliability of quarterly results published by companies using LIFO. By definition of the tax laws, LIFO is an *annual* calculation. Thus, at interim periods, the preparation of quarterly statements requires forecasts of costs of inventory items purchased or produced as well as projections of future changes in inventory quantities and mix within the entire year. These estimates are bound to be subjective and thus subject to managerial manipulation. Chapter 22 contains a more extensive discussion of problems associated with interim reports.

ANALYTICAL RESTATEMENT OF LIFO INVENTORIES TO FIFO

As is clear from the discussion above and the example that will follow, the LIFO inventory method understates inventories significantly in times of rising price levels thus understating a company's debt-paying ability (as measured, for example, by the current ratio). It overstates inventory turnover and in addition contains the means of income manipulation. An analytical technique available to the analyst is to adjust LIFO statements to the approximate pro forma situation that would exist had they been prepared on a FIFO basis. This is possible when the current cost of LIFO inventories is disclosed, a disclosure now generally available.

ILLUSTRATION 11.   To illustrate the restatement of financial statements from a LIFO to a FIFO basis, we will use data from the financial statements of Alfa, Inc. (see Appendix 4B):

Note 5 tells us that food inventories are net of LIFO reserves of (all amounts in thousands) $8,443 in 19x6 and $10,763 in 19x5. That means that the current cost of inventories (on FIFO basis) is higher by these amounts in the respective years over the carrying amount of inventories at LIFO. Thus, to restate the 19x6 *balance sheet* to the FIFO basis requires an entry as follows:

Inventories (A)	8,443	
Deferred Taxes Payable (B)		4,053
Retained Earnings (C)		4,390

(A) Inventories increased to approximately current replacement cost. (A slow turnover can result in inventories at FIFO not being stated at the most current cost.)

(B) Since inventories are increased, a provision for taxes payable in the future on this increase must be made—here at a tax rate of 48 percent. The reason for the tax deferral is that the pro forma balance sheet entry reflects an accounting method that differs from that used on the tax return (see also Chapter 11).

(C) Higher ending inventories mean lower cost of goods sold and a corresponding increase in cumulative net income to date that in the balance sheet flows into retained earnings (net of tax, of course).

In order to calculate the effect on 19x6 income of a restatement of inventories to FIFO, we must know the adjustment not only to the ending inventories but also to the beginning inventories as well. A good way to visualize this is by means of the following tabulation:

Computation of cost of goods sold

	19x6 (in thousands)		
	Under LIFO	Difference	Under FIFO
Beginning inventory ...	$163,771 [a]	$10,763 [b]	$174,534
+ Purchases (P) [c]	P	—	P
− Ending inventory	(192,543) [a]	(8,443) [b]	(200,986)
≐ Cost of goods sold	P − 28,772	2,320 [d]	P − 26,452

[a] As reported per balance sheet.

[b] Per Note 5 in the financial statements.

[c] Since purchases are the same under either the LIFO or FIFO basis, the amount of purchases need not be inserted to arrive at the effect on cost of goods sold or net income. If desired, the amount of purchases for 19x6 can be computed as follows:

$840,043 (CGS per income statement) + $192,543 (ending inventory)
— $163,771 (beginning inventory) = $868,815

[d] The effect of the restatement to FIFO is to *increase* cost of goods sold by $2,320. The resulting effect on net income is a decrease by $2,320(1 − .48), or *$1,207,* under a 48 percent tax rate assumption. Thus the effect of the restatement to the FIFO basis on 19x6 income is to decrease it by $1,207. It should be noted that under conditions of rising prices, LIFO net income is usually lower than FIFO net income. However, the net effect of the restatement in any given year depends, as in this case, on the combined effect of the change in beginning and ending inventories.

The adjustment of the 19x5 balance sheet to the FIFO basis will require the following adjusting entry:

Inventories (D)	10,763	
Deferred Taxes Payable (E)		5,166
Retained Earnings (F)		5,597

(D) Per Note 5.
(E) At 48 percent tax rate.
(F) Residual.

The earlier calculated effect of restatement to FIFO on the 19x6 income of $1,207 can now be reconciled with the credits to retained earnings in the foregoing two journal entries restating the 19x6 and 19x5 balance sheet inventories to the FIFO basis. Thus,

$$\frac{\text{19x5 credit to Retained Earnings}}{\$5,597^*} - \frac{\text{19x6 credit to Retained Earnings}}{\$4,390^*} = \frac{\text{Decline in 19x6 net income}}{\$1,207\dagger}$$

* Per above journal entries.
† See preceding computation.

The above illustration exemplifies the general methodology of the analytical restatement of LIFO based statements to FIFO.

Analytical adjustment required if the LIFO method is preferred

When the financial statements are already prepared using the LIFO inventory method, and that is the method preferred by the analyst, the income statement requires no adjustment because the cost of goods sold is already stated at current cost. The adjustment of LIFO inventories to FIFO has been illustrated above and may also approximate current cost.[5]

Under the historical-cost model, it is characteristic of the LIFO method that it introduces current costs *only* into the income statement while leaving inventories on the balance sheet at older, often understated costs. This can render meaningless measures such as the current ratio or the inventory turnover ratio. To correct for this and to establish current costs for inventories on the balance sheet, the analyst can make the following pro forma analytical entry to adjust Alfa's 19x6 balance sheet:

Inventories	8,443	
Deferred Taxes Payable		4,053
Revaluation Surplus		4,390

See Illustration above for an explanation of the derivation of these amounts.

It should be noted that the above is strictly an *analytical* adjustment because under present generally accepted accounting standards in the United States, the establishment of a Revaluation Surplus account in the primary financial statements, as part of shareholder's equity is not sanctioned.

As noted in the discussion earlier in this section, under the LIFO method, a reduction in inventories that are not replaced by year-end may result in the costing out of lower-cost inventory layers, a result also known as LIFO

---

[5] Under *SFAS 33*, large companies now disclose the current cost of inventories (see Chapter 14).

liquidation. Analytically, the amount of the LIFO liquidation gain, which is usually disclosed along with the tax effect, can be considered separately as an unusual nonrecurring item by removing it from the cost of goods sold amount in a recast income statement (see Chapter 22).

OTHER ANALYTICAL CONSIDERATIONS

Analysts, such as lending officers or investors with clout, who have access to managements can ask additional questions about LIFO inventories as follows:

1. How are LIFO inventories calculated—on an item-by-item basis or by use of dollar value pools (in which different items are grouped)?
2. Was income affected by changes in inventory pools and if so by how much? Was it affected by year-end purchasing decisions?
3. Did the company record extra expenses or losses in order to offset income arising from the involuntary liquidation of LIFO inventories?
4. What assumptions concerning LIFO inventories underlie the quarterly reported results?

The "lower-of-cost-or-market" principle of inventory accounting has additional implications for the analyst. In times of rising prices it tends to undervalue inventories regardless of the cost method used. This in turn will depress the current ratio below its real level since the other current assets (as well as the current liabilities) are not valued on a consistent basis with the methods used in valuing inventories. Under *SFAS 33*, certain companies must now disclose the current cost of inventories (see Chapter 14).

It is a fact that most published reports contain insufficient information to allow the analyst to convert inventories accounted for under one method to a figure reflecting a different method of inventory accounting. Most analysts would want such information in order to be able to better compare the financial statements of companies that use different inventory accounting methods.

To illustrate the effect that the use of a variety of inventory methods can have on reported net income or financial ratios, let us examine the case of a retailer who deals in only one product. We assume here no opening inventory, operating expenses of $5 million, and 2 million shares outstanding. The following purchases are made during the year:

	Units	Per unit	
January	100,000	$10	$ 1,000,000
March	300,000	11	3,300,000
June	600,000	12	7,200,000
October	300,000	14	4,200,000
December.....	500,000	15	7,500,000
Total ...	1,800,000		$23,200,000

Ending inventory at December 31 was 800,000 units. Assets, excluding inventories, amounted to $75 million, of which $50 million were current. Current liabilities amounted to $25 million, and long-term liabilities came to $10 million.

The tabulation which follows shows the net income arrived at by applying the FIFO, LIFO, and average-cost method, respectively. Sales are at $25 per unit, and taxes are ignored.

Computation of net income

	FIFO method	*LIFO method*	*Average costs*
Sales:			
1 million units @ $25	$25,000,000	$25,000,000	$25,000,000
Cost of sales:			
Beginning inventory	—	—	—
Purchases	23,200,000	23,200,000	23,200,000
Cost of goods available for sale	23,200,000	23,200,000	23,200,000
Less: Ending inventory	11,700,000	9,100,000	10,312,000
Cost of sales	11,500,000	14,100,000	12,888,000
Gross profit	13,500,000	10,900,000	12,112,000
Operating expenses	5,000,000	5,000,000	5,000,000
Net income	$ 8,500,000	$ 5,900,000	$ 7,112,000
Net income per share	$4.25	$2.95	$3.56

The FIFO inventory computation was based upon 500,000 units at $15 and 300,000 at $14 which yields a total of $11,700,000. The LIFO inventory cost was obtained following the assumption that the units purchased last were the first sold. Therefore, the 800,000 units are priced as 100,000 units at $10,300,000 units at $11, and 400,000 units at $12, totaling $9,100,000. The average cost was obtained by dividing $23,200,000 by 1,800,000 units purchased, yielding an average unit price of $12.89. The $12.89 unit price multiplied by 800,000 ending inventory units gives a total inventory cost of $10,312,000.

The table below shows the effect of the three inventory methods on a number of selected ratios:

	FIFO method	*LIFO method*	*Average costs*
Current ratio	2.47:1	2.36:1	2.41:1
Debt-to-equity ratio	1:5.17	1:4.91	1:5.03
Inventory turnover	2:1	3:1	2.5:1
Return on total assets	9.8%	7.0%	8.3%
Gross margin	54%	44%	49%
Net profit as percent of sales	34%	24%	29%

As the above discussion and examples clearly show, the analysis of financial statements where inventories are important requires that the analyst bring to bear a full understanding of inventory accounting methods and their impact on results.

QUESTIONS

1. Under presently accepted but changing practice, compensating balances under a bank loan agreement are considered as unrestricted cash and are classified as current assets.
   a. From the point of view of the analyst of financial statements, is this a useful classification?
   b. Give reasons for your conclusion and state how you would evaluate such balances.

2. a. What are some of salient provisions of *SFAS 12?*
   b. What are the disclosures required by *SFAS 12?*

3. What are some of the gaps and inconsistencies in *SFAS 12* of which the analyst must be aware?

4. a. What is meant by the "operating cycle"?
   b. What is the significance of the operating cycle concept to the classification of current versus noncurrent items in the balance sheet?
   c. Is this concept useful to those concerned with measuring the current debt-paying ability of an enterprise and the liquidity of its working capital components?
   d. Give the effect of the operating cycle concept on the classification of selected current assets in the following industries:
      (1) Tobacco.
      (2) Liquor.
      (3) Retailing.

5. a. What are the financial analyst's primary concerns when it comes to the evaluation of accounts receivable?
   b. What information, not usually found in published financial statements, should the analyst obtain in order to assess the overall risk of noncollectibility of the receivables?

6. Why do financial analysts generally attach such great importance to inventories?

7. Comment on the effect that the variety of accounting methods for determining the cost of inventories have on the determination of an enterprise income. As to the inclusion of which costs in inventories, is there considerable variation in practice? Give examples of three types of such cost elements.

8. Of what significance is the *level* of activity on the unit cost of goods produced by a manufacturer? The allocation of overhead costs requires the making of certain assumptions. Explain and illustrate by means of an example.

9. What is the major objective of LIFO inventory accounting? What are the effects of this method on the measurement of income and of inventories particularly from the point of view of the user of the financial statements?

10. Comment on the disclosure with respect to inventory valuation methods which

is practiced today. In what way is such disclosure useful to the analyst? What type of disclosure is relatively useful to the reader?

11. Accountants generally follow the lower-of-cost-or-market basis of inventory valuations.
    a. Define *cost* as applied to the valuation of inventories.
    b. Define *market* as applied to the valuation of inventories.
    c. Why are inventories valued at the lower of cost or market? Discuss.
    d. List the arguments against the use of the lower-of-cost-or-market method of valuing inventories. (AICPA)

12. Compare and contrast effects of the LIFO and FIFO inventory cost methods on earnings during a period of inflation. (CFA)

13. Discuss the ways and conditions under which the FIFO and LIFO inventory costing methods produce different inventory valuations. Do not discuss procedures for computing inventory cost.

14. What are some of the important questions about LIFO inventories that lending officers and investors with clout can ask?

Analysis of noncurrent assets

In this chapter, we conclude our examination of the measurement of assets by a discussion of the analysis of noncurrent assets.

LONG-TERM INVESTMENTS

Long-term investments are usually investments in assets such as debt instruments, equity securities, real estate, mineral deposits, or joint ventures acquired with longer-term objectives in mind. Such objectives may include the ultimate acquisition of control or affiliation with other companies, investment in suppliers, securing of assured sources of supply, and so forth.

Marketable securities

With the exception of the accounting for investments in common stock of certain sizes, which is discussed below, and of convertible bonds, preferred shares with a stated redemption value and nonequity securities, marketable equity securities classified as noncurrent assets or shown in balance sheets of enterprises that issue unclassified balance sheets (e.g., finance or real estate companies), are now accounted for in accordance with the provision of *SFAS 12*, the salient points of which are covered in the "Marketable securities" section of Chapter 5.

The following provisions of *SFAS 12* apply to the equity securities not classified as current:

Market value changes are to be reflected directly in the equity section of the balance sheet and are not to enter the determination of net income except where the change is other than temporary. Marketable equity securities held by enterprises that issue unclassified balance sheets are to be regarded as noncurrent.

For those marketable equity securities not classified as current assets (including marketable securities in unclassified balance sheets), a determination must be made as to whether a decline in market value as of the balance sheet date for each individual security is other than temporary. If the decline is other than temporary, the cost basis is to be written down, as a realized loss, to a new cost basis. The new cost basis is not to be changed for subsequent recoveries in market value.

Accumulated changes in the valuation allowance of noncurrent marketable securities shall be included in the equity section of the balance sheet and presented separately.

The valuation allowance, which may be called "net unrealized loss on noncurrent marketable equity securities," can be reduced for subsequent recoveries in market value, but at no time should the aggregate of marketable securities be carried on the balance sheet at an amount in excess of original cost.

Investments in common stock

Investments in common stock representing less than 20 percent of the equity securities of the investee must be accounted for in accordance with *SFAS 12* as detailed above and in the preceding chapter.

Companies 20 percent to 50 percent owned. *APB Opinion 18* concluded that even a position of less than 50 percent of the voting stock may give the investor the ability to exercise significant influence over the operating and financial policies of the investee. When such an ability to exercise influence is evident, the investment should be acccounted for under the equity method. Basically, this means at cost plus the equity in the undistributed earnings or losses of the investee since acquisition, with the addition of certain other adjustments. The mechanics of the equity method are discussed in Chapter 9.

Evidence of the investor's ability to exercise significant influence over operating and financial policies of the investee may be indicated in several ways, such as management representation and participation; but in the interest of uniformity of application, the APB concluded that in the absence of evidence to the contrary, an investment (direct or indirect) of 20 percent or more in the voting stock of an investee should lead to the presumption of an ability to exercise significant influence over the investee.[1] Conversely, an investment

---

[1] *SFAS Interpretation 35* finds the following factors as weighing against a finding of "significant influence": the company files a lawsuit against the investor or complains to a government agency; the investor tries and fails to become a member of the board of directors; the investor agrees to refrain from increasing its holding; the company is operated by a small group that ignores the investor's wishes and the investor tries and fails to obtain more financial information from the company.

in less than 20 percent of the voting stock of the investee leads to the presumption of a lack of such influence unless the ability to influence can be demonstrated.

It should be noted that while the eligibility to use the equity method is based on the percentage of voting stock outstanding, which may include, for example, convertible preferred stock, the percentage of earnings that may be picked up under the equity method depends on ownership of *common stock* only.

ILLUSTRATION 1.   Company A owns 15 percent of the common stock of Company B. By virtue of additional holdings of convertible preferred stock, the total percentage of voting power held is 20 percent. While the total holdings entitle Company A to account for its investment in Company B at equity, it can only pick up 15 percent of Company B residual income because that is the percentage of ownership of *common* stock that it holds.

The above principle of picking up income under the equity method is not consistent with the concept of "common stock equivalents" used in the computation of earnings per share (see Chapter 12). The effect of possible conversions, etc., must, however, be disclosed.

Corporate joint ventures.   Joint ventures represent investments by two or more entities in an enterprise with the objective of sharing sources of supply, the development of markets, or other types of risk. A common form of joint venture is a 50–50 percent sharing of ownership, although other divisions of interest are also found. An investment in a *corporate* joint venture should, according to *APB Opinion 18,* be accounted for by the equity method. An investment in a joint venture not evidenced by common stock ownership may presumably be accounted for at cost.

Overview of how investments in common stock are accounted for.   Exhibit 6–1 presents a summary indicating how investments in common stock of different sizes are accounted for under *APB Opinion 18* and other pronouncements governing the principles of consolidation accounting.

Implications for analysis

The analyst, aware of accounting principles governing the presentation of investments, must pay particular attention to their valuation. On the one hand, they can be grossly undervalued on the balance sheet because of the convention prohibiting their write-up market value (except in certain industries), no matter how obvious and soundly based such value may be.

On the other hand, the analyst must be alert to impairment of market value that, because of loose standards in practice, may not be fully reflected on the financial statements. If separately disclosed, the income generated by the investment may, at times, provide a clue to its fair value.

Exhibit 6–1:   Summary of accounting treatments by investor for investments in common stock

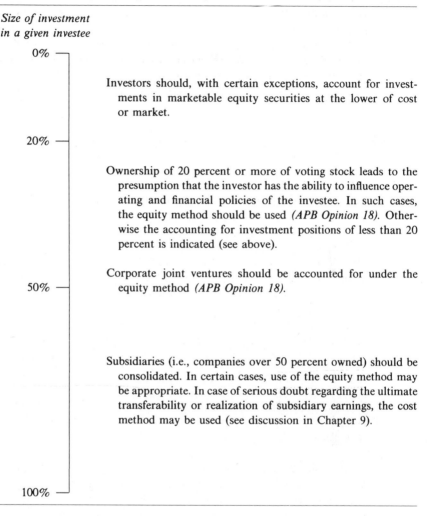

Size of investment
in a given investee

0% —

Investors should, with certain exceptions, account for investments in marketable equity securities at the lower of cost
or market.

20% —

Ownership of 20 percent or more of voting stock leads to the
presumption that the investor has the ability to influence operating and financial policies of the investee. In such cases,
the equity method should be used *(APB Opinion 18)*. Otherwise the accounting for investment positions of less than 20
percent is indicated (see above).

Corporate joint ventures should be accounted for under the
50% — equity method *(APB Opinion 18)*.

Subsidiaries (i.e., companies over 50 percent owned) should be
consolidated. In certain cases, use of the equity method may
be appropriate. In case of serious doubt regarding the ultimate
transferability or realization of subsidiary earnings, the cost
method may be used (see discussion in Chapter 9).

100% —

In Chapter 5, we considered some of the overall flaws and inconsistencies
in the accounting for marketable securities brought on by *SFAS 12*. Considered hereunder are some further considerations pertaining to the accounting
for marketable securities not carried as current assets that the analyst must
be aware of.

SFAS 12 does require the write-down of marketable securities classified
as noncurrent to market with a charge to income in cases where the change
in value is deemed to be other than temporary. However, there is no agreement
as to what constitutes "temporary" in this context. While the accounting
profession has issued some guidelines of how to audit the carrying amounts

of marketable securities (*Journal of Accountancy,* April 1975, p. 69), they by no means ensure logical and consistent procedures in this regard. Thus, practice will in all probability reflect arbitrary determinations that will make the carrying of marketable securities by one company not comparable to that of another. The analyst must also bear in mind that equity securities of companies in which the enterprise has a 20 percent or larger interest, and in some instances an even smaller interest than 20 percent, need not be adjusted to market but must instead be carried at equity that may at times be significantly below, and at other times above, market. Thus, with regard to such relatively substantial blocks of securities, the values at which they are carried on the balance sheet may be substantially in excess of their realizable value.

The creation of a new category in the equity section of the balance sheet where the "net unrealized loss on noncurrent marketable securities" is lodged must be regarded as a somewhat regressive step. One of the achievements of *APB Opinion 9* was the elimination, except in cases of prior year adjustments, of direct charges of losses to equity accounts. *SFAS 12,* brings us back, even if under different circumstances, to an area we were glad to leave in 1966.[2]

The accounting for investments in substantial blocks of *common stock* has undergone significant improvement. The carrying of investments representing control of 20 percent or over at equity is an improvement over the practice that prevailed prior to the issuance of *APB Opinion 18*—that of carrying such investments at cost. While the equity method is more realistic than cost, it must be borne in mind that it is not the equivalent of fair market value that, depending on circumstances, may be significantly larger or lower than the carrying amount at equity.

The analyst must remember that the assumption that an investment in 20 percent or more of the voting securities of an investee results in significant influence over that investee is an arbitrary one that had to be made in the interest of accounting uniformity.[3] If such influence is indeed absent, then there may be some question regarding the investor's ability to realize the amount stated at equity. The marketplace does not necessarily pay close attention to book values, and "equity" is book value. An improvement brought about by *APB Opinion 18* is the requirement that where available, the market value of investments in common stock (other than in subsidiaries) be disclosed.

APB Opinion 18 states that "a loss in value of an investment which is other than a temporary decline should be recognized the same as a loss in value of other long-term assets." This leaves a great deal to judgment and interpretation, and in the past this approach has resulted in companies being

---

[2] See also Chapter 9 for similar provisions of *SFAS 52.*

[3] As an example of an exception to this rule, Curtis Wright recently carried its 14 percent investment in Kennecot Copper at equity.

very slow to recognize losses in their investments. Since the *Opinion* does not consider a decline in market value to be conclusive evidence of such a loss, the analyst must be alert to detect situations where hope rather than reason supports the carrying amount of an investment. It must be recognized that the equity method reflects only current operating losses rather than the capital losses that occur when the earning power of an investment deteriorates or disappears.

Another area where assumptions and management discretion influence accounting is that regarding the provision for taxes to be paid at some future time when earnings recognized under the equity method are distributed in the form of dividends by the investee to the investor. *APB Opinion 23,* "Accounting for Income Taxes—Special Areas," held that the nature of an investor's influence over an investee is significantly different from the influence exercised by a parent over a subsidiary and, consequently, the investor should provide for taxes that will be payable when the earnings of the investee are received or otherwise realized by the investor. Thus, whether taxes at regular or capital-gains rates are provided for remains a matter of judgment by management and the independent auditors.

In the case of joint ventures, *APB Opinion 23* held that unless there are indications of a limited life for the joint venture, the same tax treatment as is applicable to subsidiaries should apply, that is, provision or nonprovision of taxes on unremitted earnings depends basically on management's judgment of whether these earnings are, or are not, to be permanently invested in the subsidiary or joint venture. Since the *Opinion* calls for disclosure of the tax provision that would have been made had permanent investment of earnings not been assumed, the analyst is not only able to form his own opinion regarding such probabilities but is also in a position to adjust for such taxes should his views of future probabilities differ from those of the reporting entity.

The accounting for other long-term investments (such as regular or convertible bonds) is presently not helpful to the analyst since historical cost is in most cases not relevant to decisions affecting the evaluation of profitability or of managerial performance. Moreover, the analyst must be alert to the overvaluation of longer-term investments under the still persisting theory of lack of "permanent" impairment in value. Managements, as is well known, often take a very optimistic view of the final workout of their investments that have temporarily fallen in market value.

ILLUSTRATION 2.   Centran, a bankholding company, which reported a profit of $9.5 million for the year ending June 30, 1980, did not include in its computation losses of over $120 million in its bond portfolio that was carried at cost, and far above market. This is acceptable accounting that seems to have fooled even its own management and directors who *increased* the dividend payout. When a *hoped-for* increase in interest rates failed to materialize, the subsequent quarters' reported results began to portray the company's operating realities.

ACCOUNTING BY DEBTORS AND CREDITORS FOR
TROUBLED DEBT RESTRUCTURINGS

SFAS 15 specifies the accounting in situations where a creditor for economic or legal reasons related to a debtor's financial difficulties grants a concession to the debtor.

The statement divides troubled debt restructurings into two broad categories: (1) those in which the debtor transfers receivables, real estate, or other assets to the creditor or issues its stock or otherwise grants an equity interest to the creditor to satisfy the creditor's claim; and (2) those in which the debt is continued but the terms are modified to defer or reduce cash payments the debtor is required to make to the creditor.

In cases falling under the first category, both debtor and creditor are required to account for the fair value of assets transferred and equity interests granted in a troubled debt restructuring. The statement requires debtors to recognize a gain and creditors a loss for a difference between those fair values and the recorded amount of the debt satisfied. Debtors must also recognize a gain or loss on assets transferred if their fair values differ from their recorded amounts.

The statement specifies that both debtor and creditor must account prospectively for the effects of modifications of terms of continuing debt as reduced interest expense or interest income for periods between the restructuring and maturity and should record no gain or loss at the time of restructuring. The one exception occurs when the total future cash payments specified by the new terms of the debt are less than the recorded amount of the debt at the time of restructuring. In that case, the debtor records a gain and the creditor records a loss to the extent of the differences.

Troubled debt restructurings that involve partial settlement by transfer of assets or grant of equity interests as well as modification of terms of the debt remaining outstanding after the restructuring are accounted for by combining the accounting for the two broad categories.

Implications for analysis

SFAS 15 raises serious questions for financial analysts regarding the realism and the validity of the accounting recommended therein.

The existing framework of accounting for most receivables and payables, governed by *APB Opinions 21* and *26*, is based on the present value, at inception, of the cash flows embodied in them. *SFAS 15*, in stressing form over substance, considers a modification of terms of debt to result in loss to the creditor (and gain to the debtor) only when the total future cash payments specified by the new terms of the debt (without regard to present value considerations) are less than the recorded amount of the debt. Thus, as shown in the following example, under *SFAS 15*, a loan that has been carried at $10,000,000 before a modification of terms will be carried as an asset of an identical amount after modification, even though its present value is 43 percent less.

	Before modification	After modification
Loan maturity	3 years	10 years
Effective interest rate	10%	3%
Total interest over life of loan	$ 3,000,000	$ 3,000,000
Principal amount of loan	10,000,000	10,000,000
Total cash receipts	13,000,000	13,000,000
Present value of total cash flow at market rate of interest (10%)	$10,000,000	$ 5,703,000

It is hard to understand how such disregard of reality can result in financial presentations that are useful to the analyst. In evaluating the carrying amounts of restructured loans, analysts, and particularly bank analysts, must be careful to question closely the basis of the computation.

TANGIBLE FIXED ASSETS

Assets that have an expected useful life of over a year and are used in operations and not acquired for sale in the ordinary course of business comprise this category. Property, plant, and equipment is the most important asset group included in it. They consist of those tangible assets used by business enterprises for the purpose of producing and distributing its goods and services.

Asset valuation

Currently, the only permissible basis of accounting for fixed assets in this country is historical cost. Historical cost means the amount of dollars paid for the asset at the date of acquisition plus any other costs properly includable, such as freight, installation, setup costs, and so forth.

The primary reasons advanced for retention of the historical-cost basis are that it is conservative in that it does not anticipate replacement costs; it is the amount for which management is accountable; and, above all, it is the best objectively determinable cost available. Moreover, after many years of acceptance as the basis at which fixed assets are stated, historical costs are recognized as not representing value but rather original costs that have not yet been charged to operations. Some even question the usefulness of costs based on some concept of current value that would change from year to year.

To the analyst of financial statements, the concept of fixed assets at (historical) cost is not a complicated one. The distinction between a current expenditure and an outlay that results in an asset that will be allocated to future operations is a well-established one that depends primarily on the purpose of the outlay, the expected life of the asset, and for internal accounting expediency, on the amount involved. Accounting principles in this area, if consistently applied, do not lend themselves to serious distortion. Such, of course, is not the case with the determination of depreciation, which is another matter to be discussed later.

One type of expense, sometimes included in the cost of fixed assets and which is subject to some debate, is interest cost during construction. This represents the cost of funds tied up while the property is being constructed and before it becomes productively utilized. This cost of funds committed to construction becomes part of the cost of the plant and equipment and is allocated to future operations along with all other costs. The inclusion of this cost in the cost of fixed assets was customary for public utilities and other companies until in 1979 *SFAS 34* required the capitalization of interest and defined the circumstances under which this is to be done (see also Chapter 11).

An area of some variety of practice relates to costs to be included in fixed assets constructed in a company's own facilities. While most direct costs are includable without question, one problem area is the allocation of variable overhead and particularly fixed overhead cost to such assets. Where idle capacity has been utilized to construct capital assets, the inclusion of fixed overhead may be debatable. However, if usable production was foregone to build such assets, there is full justification for the inclusion of all proportionate overhead in the cost of the fixed assets.

One serious problem that confronts the analyst of financial statements that include fixed assets stated at historical cost is that these long-lived assets are not expressed in terms of a stable measuring unit. The accumulation of costs of assets purchased in different years represents the aggregation of units of differing purchasing power. Since depreciation—that is, the currently expired portion of the cost of these assets—is based on this original cost, the distortion is carried into the income statement. Thus, repeatedly the case has been made for adjusting original cost for changes in the price level—not as an attempt to arrive at some kind of current market value but rather to adjust the original cost for changes in the purchasing power of the dollar. Others have argued for computing depreciation on the basis of the current replacement cost of the fixed assets. Under either model, it is argued, such more realistic measures will not only result in more valid income statements and in a proper distinction between income and "real" capital but will also present a fairer measure of how responsibly management has dealt with invested capital in terms of the purchasing power or the physical capital that has been entrusted to it.

The above discussion has pointed out the possible distortions to which historical-cost accounting for long-lived assets may be subject. *SFAS 33* mandates both constant-dollar and current-cost supplementary disclosures for certain companies. Further discussion of this broad subject will be found in Chapter 14 dealing with the problem of accounting under changing price levels.

The Property, Plant, and Equipment account is assumed to include assets in active or productive use. If such assets are temporarily idle, disclosure of this fact will usually be made in notes or comments in order to explain the resulting excess cost and lower profit margins.

The SEC in FRR No. 1 Sec. 209 points out the need for disclosure of significant idle facilities and changes in current year idle facilities that have a material impact on results of operations.

Should a substantial segment of assets be idle for a longer period of time and without definite prospects of use, they should no longer be included in the property, plant, and equipment designation where their inclusion would distort such relationships as that of sales to plant or the return on fixed assets. Instead, they should be segregated from other assets pending their reactivation, sale, or other disposition. Such idle assets represent not only an investment on which no return is earned but they often involve expenses of upkeep and maintenance.

Zenith Radio Corporation has the following footnote in its 1974 report:

> The company has approximately $40 million invested in plant and equipment representing facilities not now being utilized and that may not be utilized in 1975. Depreciation expense of $4 million on these assets will be charged to expense in 1975 whether or not these facilities are utilized.

While the write-up of assets to current market or appraised values is not an accepted accounting procedure in the United States, the convention of conservatism requires that a permanent impairment of value and/or loss of utility of fixed assets be reflected in the accounts by a write-down. This is needed not only to reflect a loss of value and utility but also in order to relieve future periods of charges that the usefulness and productivity of the assets can no longer support and justify. Thus, for example, Cudahy Packing Company, after many years of unsatisfactory operating results, decided in 1965 to write down some of its facilities and had the following explanation in its annual report:

> Operating income at the Company's four midwestern meat packing plants (Omaha, Wichita, Denver and Salt Lake City) has been generally unsatisfactory in recent years, and management studies give no assurance that significant long-term improvement can be expected. Earnings of these plants have not been sufficient to cover applicable depreciation, general office, administrative, and interest costs. In recognition of the loss in value of these plants as measured by their demonstrated lack of earning power, the Board of Directors determined that a special reserve should be provided equal to the net book value of the property and equipment at the four plants. No salvage values were reflected

in view of the substantial contingent liabilities under the labor contract covering employees at these plants.

The significance of Cudahy Packing Company's action should not be lost to the financial analyst. The cost of plant and equipment is an outlay of capital that must be recovered through revenues generated by operations before net income can be recognized. The process by means of which the cost of productive assets is allocated to operations is called depreciation. Depreciation covers not only deterioration due to physical wear and tear but also loss of value due to obsolescence that is caused by technical innovation and other economic factors. Prior to 1960, Cudahy reported net income, and in retrospect it appears that the depreciation provision was inadequate in that it did not allow for the obsolescence of the company's plant. Losses in the years 1960 to 1965 convinced the management of the need to relieve future operations of heavy depreciation charges, and the write-off has achieved just that.

It is interesting to note that in 1967, after what management described as further "study and analysis" of the situation, management reversed itself and reestablished part of the 1965 write-down of plant and equipment. Thus, depreciation on the book values was resumed and retroactively restated. Possibly some of the impetus for this action may have had its origin outside the company.

The following example of write-offs due to reduced economic value appears in the 1974 Airco annual report:

> Capital expenditures during 1974 aggregated $45,900,000 up from $28,-800,000 spent in 1973. Depreciation and amortization amounted to $45,386,000 in 1974 and $27,530,000 in 1973, of which $4,281,000 and $1,470,000, respectively, was for depreciation provided for idle plant facilities and equipment. Also included in 1974 was additional depreciation of $11,515,000 in recognition of the reduced economic value of certain production facilities and equipment of the Vacuum Metals and Electronics Division.

The issue of fixed-asset write-offs is still basically unresolved. In an issues paper submitted by the AICPA's Accounting Standards Executive Committee to the FASB in 1980 entitled "Accounting for the Inability to Fully Recover the Carrying Amounts of Long Lived Assets," the following "advisory conclusions" were advanced:

1. The inability to fully recover the carrying amounts of long lived assets should be reported in financial statements.
2. The concept of "permanent decline" is unsatisfactory and an alternate concept should be sought.
3. The probability test in *SFAS 5* is a workable alternative to the concept of permanent decline.
4. Judgment is necessary in selecting the asset measurement that best predicts future economic benefits, as it is difficult to select one measurement that would be appropriate in all circumstances.

5. If the inability to fully recover the carrying amounts of long lived assets is recorded in the accounts, future upward adjustment (not to exceed carrying amounts before the writedowns) should be permitted if evidence indicates a recovery.

The subject of depreciation, an important cost factor in most companies, is complex and subject to controversy. Its importance to the analyst cannot be overrated. It will be considered in Chapter 10 dealing with income determination.

Wasting assets

A category of assets that requires separate treatment is natural resources. With the exception of resources such as timber, which can be replenished by planned cutting and reseeding, most of such assets once exhausted cannot be used and lose most of their value. Examples of such resources are oil, gas, coal, iron ore, and sulphur.

Generally accepted accounting principles (GAAP) require that such assets be stated at original cost plus costs of discovery, exploration, and development. That means that the very significant value increment that occurs following the discovery of natural resources is not given immediate accounting recognition but shows up through the income stream when and as the resource is exploited.

The total cost of a wasting asset is generally allocated over the total units of estimated reserves available. This allocation process is known as depletion. Some companies in the mining field do not charge depletion to the income statement primarily because they believe the related assets to be grossly understated in terms of current and potential value. The subject of depletion will be discussed in Chapter 10.

Method of acquisition

Generally speaking, the method of acquiring assets or the use of assets should have no bearing on the basis on which they are carried in the accounting records. One method of acquisition that deserves separate mention, however, is leasing. Where leasing is short term, where it covers a period shorter than the asset's useful life, and where no property rights are acquired, no asset accounting is called for. In recent years, the practice of acquiring assets by means of leases that are in essence a financing method of purchases has grown and proliferated. Such leases should be accounted for as purchases, thus calling for the setting up of an asset at an amount equal to the present value of future rental payments, and this is essentially required by *SFAS 13*. Since the outstanding characteristic of this transaction is the *method* of financing, this topic will be considered in the chapter devoted to the measurement of liabilities.

Implication for analysis

In measuring property, plant, and equipment and in presenting it in conventional financial statements, accountants are concerned with a number of the objectives and conventions discussed in Chapter 3. They are concerned with the objectivity of original cost and the conservatism implicit therein, and with an accounting for the number of dollars originally invested in such assets. Judging from the resulting figures, they are quite clearly not overly concerned with the objectives of those who analyze financial statements. They are content to proclaim that "a balance sheet does not purport to reflect and could not usefully reflect the value of the enterprise." Not that the accountant is necessarily unmindful of the interests of those who use his statements; it is rather that his overwhelming concern lies in the real or imagined problems of his own art.

Only by sheer coincidence can historical costs be useful to analysts. They are not relevant to questions of current replacement or of future needs. They are not directly comparable to similar data in other companies' reports. They do not enable us to measure the opportunity cost of disposal and alternative use of funds, nor do they provide a valid yardstick against which to measure return. Moreover, in times of changing price levels, they represent an odd conglomeration of a variety of purchasing power disbursements.

It may be claimed that the value of assets is derived from their ability to earn a return and that consequently the key to their value lies in the income statement. While this is true in a significant number of cases, it does not provide the only avenue to an evaluation of an asset's worth. Thus, the earning of a return on an investment is dependent on managerial skill, and assets have a value tied to their capacity to produce. But in recognizing the importance of net income in the assessment of an asset's worth, the analyst must be aware of the problem which the method of depreciation has on the determination of net income. This aspect of the valuation of fixed assets and its effect on income is discussed fully in Chapter 10 on the analysis of income.

Supplementary data on the current cost of fixed assets and on depreciation computed on this basis are now provided by certain companies pursuant to the requirements of *SFAS 33* (see Chapter 14). In using such data, the analyst must be aware that they are not audited and that the method of their derivation can vary significantly from company to company.

INTANGIBLE ASSETS

Intangible assets represent rights to future benefits. One distinguishing characteristic of these assets, which is not, however, unique to them, is that they have no physical existence and depend on such expected future benefits for most of their value. In many cases, the value of these benefits is inextricably tied to the continuity of the enterprise.

Some important categories of intangibles are:

1. Goodwill.
2. Patents, copyrights, and trademarks.
3. Leases, leaseholds, and leasehold improvements.
4. Exploration rights and cost of development of natural resources.
5. Formulas, processes, and designs.
6. Licenses, franchises, memberships, and customer lists.

The basic rule in accounting for purchased intangibles is that they be carried at cost. If property other than cash is given in exchange for the intangible, it must be recorded at the fair market value of the consideration given. If liabilities are assumed, the intangible is valued by taking into consideration the present value of the future obligations.

There are some paradoxes in the valuation of intangibles that should be understood by the analyst. If a company spends material and labor in the construction of a "tangible" asset, such as a machine, these costs are capitalized and recorded as an asset that is depreciated over its estimated useful life. On the other hand, a company that spends a great amount of resources advertising a product or training a sales force to sell and service it, which, as we shall see, is a process of creating internally developed "goodwill," cannot usually capitalize such costs even though they may be as, or more, beneficial to the company's future operations than is the "tangible" machine. The reason for this inconsistency in accounting for the two assets is steeped in such basic accounting conventions (discussed in Chapter 3) as conservatism, which casts greater doubt on the future realization of unidentifiable intangible costs (such as advertising or training which create "goodwill") than costs sunk into tangible "hard" and visible goods.

APB Opinion 17 distinguishes between identifiable and unidentifiable intangible assets.

Identifiable intangibles

Identifiable intangibles can be separately identified and given reasonably descriptive names such as patents, trademarks, franchises, and the like. Identifiable intangibles can be developed internally, acquired singly or as part of a group of assets. In either case, they should be recorded at cost and amortized over their useful lives. Write-down or complete write-off at date of acquisition is not permitted.

Unidentifiable intangibles

Unidentifiable intangibles can be developed internally or purchased from others. They cannot, however, be acquired singly but form part of a group of assets or part of an entire enterprise. The excess of cost of an acquired company over the sum total of identifiable net assets is the most common unidentifiable intangible asset. *APB Opinion 17* refers to this unidentifiable mass of assets as "goodwill," and this is actually a residual amount in an acquisition after the amount of tangible and identifiable intangibles have been determined. It represents an expansion of the goodwill concept from what has obtained before this *Opinion* was issued.

The costs of developing, maintaining, or restoring intangibles that are unidentifiable, have indeterminate lives, or are inherent in a continuing enterprise should be expensed as incurred. By contrast, such intangible assets that are purchased must be carried at cost and amortized over their useful lives and cannot be written down or written off at date of acquisition.

Amortization of intangibles

Both types of intangibles, those identifiable as well as those unidentifiable, are believed to have limited useful lives and must be amortized accordingly. Depending on the type of intangible asset, its useful life may be limited by such factors as legal, contractual, or regulatory provisions; demand and competition; life expectancies of employees; and economic factors.

The cost of each intangible should be amortized over its individual useful life taking into account all factors that determine its length. The period of amortization cannot, however, exceed 40 years. Goodwill arising before 1970 (when *APB Opinion 17* was promulgated) need not be amortized. Thus, Alfa, Inc. (Appendix 4B), shows in Note 5, "excess of cost over equity of subsidiary companies at dates of acquisition prior to 1970" at unamortized amounts.

Other considerations regarding the accounting for intangibles

Goodwill is often a sizable asset. Since it can only be recorded on acquisition from a third party, it can be recorded only upon the purchase of an on-going business enterprise. The description of what is being paid for varies greatly, and the variety of views add to the confusion surrounding this subject. Some refer to the ability to attract and keep satisfied customers, while others point to qualities inherent in an enterprise that is well organized and is efficient in production, service, and sales. This distinction can also be seen in the difference that obviously exists between a business that is just starting and one that is successful and well established in its industry and that has spent a great deal on training and research to get there. Thus, what is obviously being paid for here is earning power, and since any given amount of invested capital should expect a minimum return adjusted for risk, most accountants agree that goodwill is associated with a level of earnings over and above that minimum. These are otherwise referred to as "super-earnings." Thus, goodwill implies exceptional profitability, and that should normally be evident when goodwill is being purchased, except in those cases where there is obvious mismanagement and the potential is evident and awaits to be tapped by good management.

United States Tobacco Company describes its goodwill accounting policy as follows:

> It is the Company's policy to carry goodwill, acquired prior to November 1, 1970, at cost until such time as there may be evidence of diminution in value. During 1980 the Company began amortizing the goodwill associated with two of its subsidiaries. Amortization (no tax benefit) for 1980 was approximately $1,920,000 (21 cents per share). This goodwill is being amortized over a three-year period ending December 1982. The remaining goodwill is not being amortized because, in the opinion of management, there has been no diminution in value.

When a business is being acquired, the book values, that is, the amounts at which its net assets are carried in accordance with accounting principles discussed in this book, are quite obviously not relevant in arriving at a purchase price, if only because they represent unamortized cost balances rather than values. Thus, the first requirement in purchase accounting is that the amount paid for the entity as a whole be allocated to all identifiable assets in accordance with their fair market values. If an excess remains after such allocation is made, it may be ascribed to the intangible "goodwill." If the fair market value of assets acquired exceeds the purchase price, a "bargain purchase credit" results, and it can, after adjustments, be amortized to income over a reasonable number of years. A detailed examination of the accounting for business combinations will be found in Chapter 9.

Most other intangible assets have a useful life that is limited by law, regulation, or agreement. Thus, *patents* are rights conveyed by government authority to the inventor granting the exclusive right to the invention for a term of years. Registered copyrights and trademarks also convey exclusive rights for specified periods of time. The cost of these assets should be written off against the revenues they help create over the maximum period coinciding with their legal life or over the minimum period of their estimated economic life.

The cost of franchises, licenses, or other such benefits must be written off over the period during which they are deemed to be economically productive. The cost of leaseholds and leasehold improvements are benefits of occupancy that are contractually limited. Thus, their cost must be amortized over the period of the lease contract.

As is true with all assets, accounting principles require that if it is evident that an intangible has lost all or most of its value or utility, it should be written down to its net realizable value measured by either future estimated utility or selling price, whichever is more appropriate in the circumstances.

Implication for analysis

Because of their very nature, intangibles have often been treated with suspicion by financial analysts. In fact, many analysts associate "intangibility" with riskiness. Quite obviously, caution and clear understanding of the nature of these assets is required in the evaluation of their worth to the enterprise. However, since these assets may, in many instances, be the most valuable asset an enterprise owns and since they can be undervalued as well as, as is often the case, carried at inflated amounts, it is inadvisable to remove them from all consideration in financial analysis.

Goodwill is a case in point. Having understood the accounting conventions governing the recording of goodwill, the analyst realizes that only purchased goodwill will be found among the recorded assets and that more "goodwill" may exist off the balance sheet than on it.

Another key point here is that if there is value in goodwill it must be reflected in earnings. True, if a mismanaged situation with great potential was purchased, the profits may not become visible immediately; but if there is value to goodwill, then such an asset should give rise to superior earnings within a reasonably short time after acquisition. If those earnings are not in evidence, it is a fair assumption that the investment in goodwill is of no value regardless of whether it is or is not found on the balance sheet. Goodwill represents an advantage that must evidence itself in superior earnings or else it does not exist.

Another important factor of which the analyst must be aware is that in practice, the accounting for goodwill is far from faithful to the theory. Due to the beneficial effect that an absence of write-off of assets has on the results of operations, particularly since goodwill amortization is *not* deductible for tax purposes, goodwill and other intangibles may not be written off as speedily as a realistic assessment of their useful life may require. While the overall limitation of 40 years on the assumed useful life of intangibles is arbitrary and may, in some instances, result in excessive amortization, it is safe to assume that in most cases the bias will be in the direction of too slow a rate of amortization. The analyst must be alert to this possibility.

Regardless of the amount of outlays incurred in the acquisition or in the internal development of an intangible, the rule applicable to the carrying amount of any asset is that it be carried at an amount not in excess of realizable value in terms of sales price or future utility. That, at least, is the intention and the theory. But, as in most other categories of accounting theory, actual implementation in practice is another matter, and the analyst must be prepared to form his own judgment on the amounts at which intangible assets are carried. The analyst must also bear in mind that goodwill recorded as a result of business combinations initiated before November 1, 1970, does not have to be amortized at all and that at the cutoff date there were billions of dollars of unamortized goodwill on corporate balance sheets in this country. Only in extreme situations will the auditors qualify their opinion with respect to the continuing value of unamortized goodwill as was the case in the 1974 report of United Brands Company.

The analyst must also be alert to the consideration with which the enterprise has parted in the acquisition of goodwill, for this may affect the amount of the intangible recorded. Payments in promoter stock should be thoroughly scrutinized. Also of concern to the analyst is the rate at which goodwill is amortized. The 40-year maximum, after all, is a long period exceeding a generation. The assumption of useful life should be realistic and should reflect the proper allocation of costs to revenues. A lump-sum write-off of an intangible may bring the asset down to its proper realizable value but by no means does it make up for the implicit overstatement of earnings of prior years.

PREPAID EXPENSES AND DEFERRED CHARGES

Prepaid expenses and deferred charges distinguished

Prepaid expenses represent advance payments for services yet to be received. Examples are advance payments for rent or prepaid insurance on a longer-term policy. Small supplies of stationery or stamps are often included in prepaid expenses. Prepaid expenses are generally classified among current assets because the services due that they represent would otherwise require the use of current resources during the following operating cycle. For reasons of expediency and lack of materiality, services due beyond one year are usually included among prepaid expenses classified as current.

Unlike prepaid expenses that represent advance payments for services yet to be received, *deferred charges* represent charges already incurred that are deferred to the future either because they are expected to benefit future revenues or because they represent a proper allocation of costs to future operations.

Over the years, the complexities of business operations as well as custom have sanctioned an ever-increasing number and types of deferred charges.

Why costs are deferred

The basic theory behind the deferral of expenses and costs is relatively simple. If a cost incurred in one period is going to benefit a future period or periods by a contribution to revenues or reduction in costs, then such a cost should be deferred to such future period. The basic accounting convention involved here is that of matching costs and revenues. Thus, if an enterprise incurs substantial start-up costs in placing into operation new, better, or more efficient, facilities, it may defer such costs and charge (amortize) them to the periods that are expected to benefit from them.

Research and development costs

Under FASB *SFAS* 2, almost all research and development (R&D) costs are required to be charged to expense when incurred. That requirement applies to a tangible or intangible asset that is purchased for use in a single R&D

project, although a purchased asset that has alternative future uses should be capitalized and amortized as such.[4]

Some public utility regulatory commissions require the deferral and amortization of significant R&D expenditures, and where they affect the rate-making process, they can be accounted for in this manner.

The costs of R&D activities conducted for others under a contractual arrangement, including indirect costs that are specifically reimbursable, can be treated as work in progress or receivables under contracts and are not covered by the expensing requirement. A further discussion of the implications of the accounting for R&D outlays will be found in found in Chapter 11.

Other types of deferred charges

Another category of deferred charges that borders on a deferral of costs of dubious future benefit is that of moving expenses and to a lesser degree, start-up costs. Thus, Willcox & Gibbs, Inc., had the following note in its annual report:

> The Company has deferred approximately $782,000 related to moving expenses and start-up costs associated with new facilities placed into operation during 1968. It is the Company's intention to amortize these costs over a five year period beginning in 1969.

Neptune International describes the deferral of start-up costs as follows:

> *Other assets.* The Corporation has incurred costs prior to attaining normal levels of production in connection with the start-up of two new manufacturing facilities during 1973 and 1972, and the start-up of a new foundry during 1974. These costs are being amortized over three-year periods.

As indicated before, the variety of deferred costs has been growing because of new complexities in both technology and in business practice. Since deferred charges represent future intangible benefits, they are sometimes very close in nature to intangible assets. Regardless of terminology, the following list should give the reader an indication of the variety of deferred charges now found in financial statements:

1. Business development, expansion, merger, and relocation costs.
   a. Preoperating expenses, initial start-up costs, and tooling costs.
   b. Initial operating losses or preoperating expenses of subsidiaries.
   c. Moving, plant rearrangement, and reinstallation costs.
   d. Merger or acquisition expenses.
   e. Purchased customer accounts.
   f. Noncompete agreements.

---

[4] The fair value of the R&D of an acquired enterprise must be determined and a suitable allocation of the purchase price made so that those costs that will not be used in R&D activities can be capitalized—those that will be used in such activities must be written off.

   2.   Deferred expenses.
        a.   Advertising and promotional expenses.
        b.   Imputed interest.
        c.   Selling, general, and administrative expenses.
        d.   Pension plan costs.
        e.   Property and other taxes.
        f.   Rental and leasing costs.
        g.   Vacation pay.
        h.   Seasonal growing and packing expenses.
   3.   Intangible costs.
        a.   Intangible drilling and development costs.
        b.   Contracts, films, copyright materials, art rights, etc.
   4.   Debt issue expenses.
   5.   Future income tax benefits.
   6.   Organization costs.
   7.   Advance royalties.

While we are here focusing on the validity of the assets represented by deferred charges, we must always bear in mind that each of these assets has "another side of the coin," that is, the deferral of a cost that would otherwise have been charged to results from operations. The impact of this aspect will be more fully discussed in Chapter 11, which is devoted to principles of income measurement.

Implications for analysis

While prepaid expenses are usually neither of the size or the significance sufficient to be of real concern to the analyst, deferred charges can be both sizable and significant and, hence, can present real challenges of understanding and interpretation.

Certain types of deferred charges, such as start-up costs or debt issue expenses, can be easily understood and defended on the basis of accounting theory. Moreover, the period of their amortization is clearly dictated by the circumstances that gave rise to them. Deferred charges, such as organization costs, on the other hand, while clearly designated to benefit an organization in the future, cannot be amortized on a logical or obvious basis. Thus, while an indefinite life may be inferred from the going-concern or continuity convention of accounting, organization costs are nevertheless usually amortized over an arbitrarily determined period of time.

However, the validity of deferring many other charges, such as moving costs, promotional costs, or initial operating losses of, say, loan offices, is subject to many imponderables and estimates. Similarly, the period over which they should properly be amortized is often subject to serious doubt. The analyst must be alert to the situation where the deferred charge is not really an asset representing a future benefit but is rather a deferred loss that is being carried forward for no better reason than the desire of management not to burden current operating results. While the auditor's opinion or mention of such assets can be helpful to the analyst, he must be prepared to evaluate on his own the evidence and information regarding such deferrals. In any event, deferred charges represent mostly assets that are incapable of satisfying claims of creditors. The other and perhaps even more significant implication that deferred charges carry is their effect on proper income determination, and this aspect will be examined in Chapter 11, which is devoted to this subject.

The analyst must, in general, treat with suspicion the propensity of managements to defer into the future the costs and problems of today. For example, following severe price increases of fuel beginning late in 1973, some electric utilities refused to face reality and deferred the absorption of these costs to future periods in the hope that these would be recouped through subsequent rate increases. This practice is symptomatic of the illusory accounting of which some companies are capable. The following is an additional illustration:

ILLUSTRATION 3.   Throughout the 1970s, Lockheed Corporation stuck with its unprofitable TriStar Jetliner program. Management's repeated forecasts about future favorable developments and new orders proved time and again to be overoptimistic. Management deferred "initial planning and tooling and unrecovered production start-up costs," and in 1975 adopted a policy of amortizing these deferred charges over a period planned at that time to end in 1985.[5] By the 1980 year-end, these deferred TriStar costs amounted to $281 million. Finally in 1981, the company had to abandon the program, recognize the inevitable, and write off the deferred charges that had overstated operating results over so many years. Inventory write-downs added substantially to the overall losses on this program.

UNRECORDED INTANGIBLE OR CONTINGENT ASSETS

A discussion of principles of asset measurement would not be complete without an examination of that category of assets that under GAAP would not be recorded in a statement of financial condition.

One category of assets that are not recordable has already been mentioned in the discussion of goodwill. In this case, if the intangible is internally developed rather than purchased from an outside party, it cannot normally be capitalized and results instead in a charge to current operations. Thus, to the extent that a valuable asset has been created, one that can be either sold or which generates superior earning power, the income charged with

---

[5] Deferrals are also made under the so-called program method in which each plane is assigned an estimated average cost (over the entire program period). Early in the program, actual costs exceed the estimated average costs and the excess is deferred on the assumption that when benefits from the learning curve are realized, subsequent actual costs will be below estimated costs thus permitting the absorbtion of previously deferred costs.

the expense of its development has been understated. This the analyst must realize and, if significant, take into consideration.

Another type of unrecorded asset is a tax loss carry-forward benefit that has a high probability of being realized in future years. Present accounting theory sanctions the recording of such a benefit only in those rare cases where its realization is "assured beyond any reasonable doubt." Thus, the analyst must look for evidence of such assets in the footnotes to the financial statements and other material containing comments about the company's financial condition.

Phoenix Steel Corporation presents the following disclosure of net operating loss carry-overs as well as the dates of expiration of such benefits:

> At December 31, 1980 loss carryforwards of approximately $48 million are available to offset future taxable income for financial reporting purposes. Such carryforwards for income tax purposes are approximately $43 million and expire $15 million in 1983, $23 million in 1984, $4 million in 1985 and $1 million in 1987.

A contingent asset is disclosed by Allegheny Ludlum Industries, Inc., as follows:

> In January 1980, a Federal District Court in Houston, Texas, following a jury trial completed earlier, entered judgment of approximately $18,900,000 in favor of Chemetron Corporation, a wholly-owned subsidiary of Allegheny, against Marathon Manufacturing Corporation and two individual defendants in a suit brought for securities law violations. That judgment has been appealed by the defendants and, since the outcome cannot be predicted at this time, no portion of the judgment has been reflected in the accompanying financial statements.

QUESTIONS

1. What are the provisions of *SFAS 12* that apply to the equity securities not classified as current assets?

2. What accounting principles govern the valuation and presentation of long-term investments? Distinguish between the accounting for investments in the common stock in an investee of *(a)* less than 20 percent of the shares outstanding and *(b)* 20 percent or more of the shares outstanding.

3. *a.* Evaluate the accounting for investments in between 20 percent to 50 percent of the common stock of an investee from the point of view of an analyst of the financial statements.

   b. When are losses in long-term investments recognized? Evaluate the accounting that governs the recognition of such losses.

4. What are some of the flaws and inconsistencies of *SFAS 12*, with regard to accounting for marketable securities not carried as current assets, of which the analyst must be aware?

5. How should idle plant and equipment be presented in the balance sheet? Explain the reasons for the presentation you describe.

6. The income of an enterprise from the exploration of wasting assets often bears no logical relation to the amount at which such investment is shown on the balance sheet.

   a. Why is this so?

   b. Under what circumstances would a more logical relationship be more likely to exist?

7. From the point of view of the user of financial statements, what are the objections to the use of original cost as the basis of carrying fixed assets?

8. a. What are the basic principles governing the valuation of intangible assets?

   b. Distinguish between the accounting for internally developed versus purchased intangibles.

   c. Of what significance is the distinction between (1) identifiable intangibles and (2) unidentifiable intangibles?

   d. What principles and guidelines underlie the amortization of intangible assets?

9. What are the implications for analysis of the accounting for goodwill?

10. List five categories of deferred charges and describe the rationale that is usually given for this deferral.

11. a. Give examples of two or more types of assets that are not recorded on the balance sheet.

    b. How should such assets be evaluated by the analyst?

7

Analysis of liabilities

Liabilities are obligations to pay money, render future services, or convey specified assets. They are claims against the company's present and future assets and resources. Such claims are usually senior to those of the ownership as evidenced by equity securities. This discussion will be broadly construed to include current liabilities, long-term liabilities, capital leases, and deferred credits which, as shall be seen, can vary significantly from conventional liabilities.

CURRENT LIABILITIES

Current liabilities are usually obligations for goods and services acquired, taxes owed, and any other accruals of expenses. They include deposits received, advance payments, trade acceptances, notes payable, short-term bank loans, as well as the current portion of long-term debt.

To be properly classified as current, a liability should require the use of current resources (assets) or the incurrence of another current liability for its discharge. As in the case of current assets, the period over which such liabilities are expected to be retired is one year or, for operating liabilities, the current operating cycle, whichever is longer.

As a general principle, the offsetting of assets against liabilities is permissible only where such a right specifically exists. Thus, the availability of cash for the payment of a liability does not justify the offset of one against the other. In practice, the only instances where offset is permissible is where government securities specifically designated as acceptable for the payment of taxes are acquired for that purpose.

The SEC in *Financial Reporting Releases (FRR)*, No. 1, Section 203, has significantly expanded the disclosure requirements in SEC filings (not necessarily in annual reports) regarding the terms of short-term debt:

1. Footnote disclosure of compensating balance arrangements including those not reduced to writing.
2. Balance sheet segregation of *(a)* legally restricted compensating balances and *(b)* unrestricted compensating balances relating to long-term borrowing arrangements if the compensating balance can be computed at a fixed amount at the balance sheet date.
3. Disclosure of short-term bank and commercial paper borrowings:
   a. Commercial paper borrowings separately stated in the balance sheet.
   b. Average interest rate and terms separately stated for short-term bank and commercial paper borrowings at the balance sheet date.
   c. Average interest rate, average outstanding borrowings, and maximum month-end outstanding borrowings for short-term bank debt and commercial paper combined for the period.
4. Disclosure of amounts and terms of unused lines of credit for short-term borrowing arrangements (with amounts supporting commercial paper separately stated) and of unused commitments for long-term financing arrangements.

SFAS 6 (1975) superseded some provisions of the above by establishing criteria for the balance sheet classification of short-term obligations that are expected to be refinanced.

Certain short-term obligations such as trade accounts payable and normal accrued liabilities always should be classified as current and included in a total of current liabilities of a company balance sheet. Other short-term obligations also should be classified as current liabilities unless the company intends to refinance them on a long-term basis and can demonstrate its ability to do so. Short-term obligations are those scheduled to mature in less than a year.

Refinancing on a long-term basis is defined to mean either replacing the short-term obligation with a long-term obligation or with equity securities; or renewing, extending, or replacing it with other short-term obligations for an uninterrupted period extending beyond one year from the balance sheet date.

Ability to refinance on a long-term basis should be demonstrated either (1) by actually having issued a long-term obligation or equity securities to replace the short-term obligation after the date of the company's balance sheet but before it is released, or (2) by having entered into an agreement with a bank or other source of capital that clearly permits the company to refinance the short-term obligation when it becomes due. Financing agreements that are cancelable for violation of a provision that can be evaluated differently by the parties to the agreement (such as "a material adverse change" or "failure to maintain satisfactory operations") do not meet this condition.[1] Also, an "operative" violation of the agreement should not have occurred.

---

[1] The FASB has proposed that where a company violates an objective provision (e.g., maintenance of specified amount of working capital) of a long-term debt agreement, the debt should be classified as a current liability unless a waver in writing is obtained.

Long-term debt may have to be classified as current when certain covenants are in default. Alfa, Inc. (see Appendix 4B), shows in note 8 "Interim borrowings included in long-term debt" of $35,000,000 for 19x6. The company's intention to convert this to a long-term indebtedness is clear; that it had secured a commitment by a financing source to achieve this objective is not so clear from the disclosure provided. Note also the disclosure concerning unused lines of credit and of compensating balances.

LONG-TERM LIABILITIES

Long-term liabilities may either represent bank term loans or more formal issuances of bonds, debentures, or notes. They represent obligations payable beyond the period of one year or beyond that encompassed by the operating cycle. Debt obligations may assume many and varied forms, and their full assessment and measurement requires disclosure of all significant conditions and covenants attached to them. Such information should include the interest rate, maturities, conversion privileges, call features, subordination provisions, and restrictions under the indenture. In addition, disclosure of collateral pledged (with indication of book and possible market values), sinking fund provisions subordination, revolving credit provisions, and sinking fund commitments should be disclosed. Any defaults in adherence to loan provisions, including defaults of interest and principal repayments, must also be disclosed.

Since the exact interest rate that will prevail in the bond market at the time of issuance of bonds can never be predetermined, bonds are sold in excess of par, or at a premium, or below par, that is, at a discount. The premium or discount represents in effect an adjustment of the effective interest rate. The premium received is amortized over the life of the issue, thus reducing the coupon rate of interest to the effective interest rate incurred. Conversely, the discount allowed is similarly amortized, thus increasing the effective interest rate paid by the borrower.

A variety of incentives are offered in order to promote the sale of bonds and to reduce the interest rates that would otherwise be required. They may take the form of convertibility features, attachments of warrants to purchase the issuer's common stock, or even warrants to purchase the stock of another company. It requires no great persuasion to understand that to the extent that these incentives are valuable they carry a cost to the issuing company. Whether the cost represents dilution of the equity or a fixed price call on an investment, these costs should be recognized. Although slow in doing so, accountants have recognized such costs and given expression to them as follows:

1. In the case of convertible features—through their effect on the computation of earnings per share (see Chapter 12).

2. In the case of warrants—by assigning a discount factor at the time of debt issuance which charge is amortized to income. In addition, the dilutive effects of warrants are given recognition in earnings per share (EPS) computations. (See also Chapter 12.)

Generally, the prohibitions against offsetting of assets against liabilities apply to the offsetting of debt against related assets. However, if a real estate company buys property subject to a mortgage that it does not assume, it may properly deduct the amount of the mortgage from the asset, thus showing it net.

When debt is not interest bearing, it is appropriate to show it at the present value of the amount that will be payable in the future discounted at the rate at which the company would otherwise borrow money. This not only shows debt as a proper amount, comparable to other interest-bearing debt obligations, but it also provides for the computation of the interest charge that reflects the use of these funds. Moreover, if the debt is the result of the acquisition of an asset, this treatment ensures that its cost is not overstated through the overstatement of the amount of debt incurred.

Reference to the discussion on the imputation of interest in the "Receivables" section of Chapter 5 will show that under the provisions of *APB Opinion 21*, noninterest-bearing obligations, or those bearing unreasonable rates of interest, must, under certain conditions, be shown at an amount that reflects the imputation of a reasonable discount rate.

Valuable disclosure, from the analyst's point of view, is the yearly loan payment requirement for a significant number of future years.

SFAS 47 requires footnote disclosure of commitments under unconditional purchase obligations that provide financing to suppliers. It also requires disclosure of future payments on long-term borrowings and redeemable stock. Among required disclosures are:

For purchase obligations not recognized on purchasers' balance sheet:
1. Description and term of obligation.
2. Total fixed and determinable obligation. If determinable, also show these amounts for each of the next five years.
3. Description of any variable obligation.
4. Amounts purchased under obligation for each period covered by an income statement.

For purchase obligations recognized on purchaser's balance sheet payments for each of the next five years.

For long-term borrowings and redeemable stock:
1. Maturities and sinking fund requirements for each of the next five years.
2. Redemption requirements for each of the next five years.

An example of the disclosure of both short- and long-term debt can be found in Note 8 of Alfa, Inc. (see Appendix 4B).

IMPLICATIONS FOR ANALYSIS

Liabilities are prior claims against a company's assets and resources; and the analyst needs assurance that they are fully stated with proper descriptions as to their amount, due dates, and the conditions, encumbrances, and limitations to which they subject the company.

The means by which auditors satisfy themselves that all liabilities have been properly recorded are such procedures as direct confirmation, scrutiny of board of director meeting minutes, the reading of contracts and agreements, and inquiry of those who may have knowledge of company obligations and liabilities. Since the nature of double-entry bookkeeping requires that for every asset, resource, or cost, a counterbalancing obligation, or investment, must be booked, the areas subject to considerable difficulty are those relating to commitments and contingent liabilities because they do not involve the commensurate recording of assets or costs. Here, the analyst must rely on the information that is provided in the notes to financial statements and in the general management commentary found in the text of the annual report and elsewhere.

The analyst must be aware of the possibility that understatement of liabilities can occur, and when it does, income will most likely be adversely affected. Thus, for example, Rocor International reported early in 1976 that the accounts payable balance on its books may be understated by as much as $1 million. In another example, the SEC found in 1976 that Ampex Corporation in its 1971 10-K and 1972 10-Qs did not disclose that it was obligated to pay royalty guarantees to record companies totaling in excess of $80 million, that it did not disclose that it was selling substantial amounts of prerecorded tapes that were improperly accounted for as "degaussed" or erased tapes to avoid payment of royalty fees, and that it understated by several millions of dollars the allowances for doubtful accounts receivable and provisions for losses arising from royalty contracts and overstated income due to inadequate credit allowances for returned tapes.

If short-term bank debt is included in the current liability section, it may mean that the company does not plan to refinance or the company cannot get a refinancing agreement with a lender that meets the requirements of *SFAS 6.* The analyst should attempt to determine the reason for the current liability classification of bank debt since an inability to secure a satisfactory refinancing agreement could indicate the company has problems beyond those revealed in its financial statements.

The analyst should realize that some companies are constantly on the lookout for ways to reduce the amount of liabilities in their financial statements.

An illustration of creativity in accounting and of "novel practices" of debt reduction is found in the practice of "in substance defeasance" of debt used by companies such as Exxon Corporation and Kellogg in 1982. In one variation of this practice, the enterprise buys government securities at a discount and places them in a trust that is devoted to paying off interest and principal on its own debt as it matures. This practice is used as justification for removing the debt from the balance sheet and for recording currently a profit on the constructive retirement of debt at a discount.

Maintaining that in the case of bankruptcy the assets of the government securities trust may be claimed by other creditors, the SEC ordered the practice discontinued pending a review of it by the FASB. The FASB, which has the matter under consideration, has tentatively concluded that companies should not consider debt as extinguished by this technique unless the debtor has no further legal obligation.

Evaluation of terms of indebtedness

The disclosure of the terms and conditions of regular recorded indebtedness and liabilities is another area deserving the analyst's careful attention. Here, the analyst must examine critically the description of debt, its terms, conditions, and encumbrances with a view to satisfying himself as to the term's feasibility and completeness. Important in the evaluation of a liability's total impact are such features as:

1. The terms of the debt.
2. Restrictions on deployment of resources and freedom of action.
3. Ability to engage in further financing.
4. Requirements such as those relating to maintenance of ratios of working capital, debt to equity, and so forth.
5. Dilutive conversion features to which the debt is subject.

Minimum disclosure requirements as to debt provisions vary somewhat, but auditors are bound by reporting standards to disclose any breaches in loan provisions that may restrict a company's freedom of action or set it on the road to insolvency. Thus, the analyst should be alert to any explanations or qualifications in the notes or in the auditor's opinion such as the following which appeared in the annual report of Lionel Corporation:

> Reference is made to Note G to the financial statements relating to a provision of the indenture covering the 5½% Convertible Subordinated Debentures due in 1980 and to information contained therein as to the failure of the Company to maintain the net working capital required thereunder and to the possible failure to observe other indenture covenants. The management has represented to us that it is actively negotiating certain arrangements and planning certain actions, which, it believes, will have the ultimate effect of remedying any breaches of covenants that may exist under the indentures as referred to in Note G.
>
> In view of the possible material effect which the final resolution of the matters referred to above could have on the consolidated financial position of the companies, and in view of the lack of knowledge at this time of the ultimate effect which the aforementioned negotiations and plans may have in finally disposing of the matters, we are precluded from expressing an opinion as to

the fair presentation of the consolidated balance sheet and related consolidated statement of earned surplus of the companies.

Naturally, an analyst would like to be able to foresee developments such as those described in the Lionel situation. One of the most effective ways of doing this is by means of financial analysis that compares the terms of debt with the margin of safety by which existing compliance exceeds the requirements under those terms.

OBLIGATIONS UNDER LEASES

Leasing, as a means of acquiring assets and the services and use of assets, has been known for a long time, but in recent decades its use has grown considerably. Our consideration of lease obligations at this point is due to their similarity to debt. Lease terms usually obligate entities to make a series of payments over a future period of time, and it is well known that in many cases such payments may contain, among others, elements of interest and principal amortization. The debate over which features of a lease agreement clinch it as a purchase (i.e., as a financing method) and which characteristics cause it to retain the nature of a rental contract has been going on for a long time.

When the accounting profession first recognized the problem of accounting for leases in 1949, it recommended in *ARB 38* that long-term leases be disclosed. It was reasoned that if a lease arrangement was in substance an installment purchase of property, it should be reflected as an asset and as a liability of the lessee. The spirit and intent of this pronouncement were largely ignored in practice.

As the attraction of leasing as a means of "off balance sheet financing" grew, so did the clamor for a more realistic accounting. While *Accounting Research Study (ARS) 4,* published by the AICPA in 1962, concluded that leases that give rise to property rights be so reported in the financial statements, the *APB Opinion* that followed (*5* of 1964) focused principally on the creation of a material equity in the property as a determining criterion requiring capitalization. This concept as well as the "soft" criteria that accompanied this *Opinion* was no match to the countervailing forces against capitalization that were motivated by considerations of the most favorable financial structure presentation and income pattern determination. Thus, only relatively few of the most obvious financing leases were capitalized in the financial statements in accordance with the provisions of *APB Opinion 5.*

In its last *Opinion* (*31*—1973), the outgoing APB called merely for improved lease disclosure. In an apparent reaction to slow progress, the SEC issued in the same year *ASR 147,* which called for footnote *disclosure* that went beyond those specified in *APB Opinion 31.* These included disclosure of details on the present value of financing leases, as defined, and of the impact on net income of the capitalization of such leases.

It was, however, not until November 1976 that a real tightening up of the accounting for leases occurred with the issuance of the more rigorous *SFAS 13* that superseded most prior pronouncements. The provisions of the *Statement* derive from the view that a lease that transfers substantially all of the benefits and risks incident to the ownership of property should be accounted for as the acquisition of an asset and the incurrence of an obligation by the lessee and as a sale or financing by the lessor. All other leases should be accounted for as operating leases. The *Statement* does not apply to leases relating to rights to explore natural resources or to licensing agreements. In 1977, the SEC moved to conform its lease accounting requirements to those of *SFAS 13*.

Accounting by lessees

In the case of the lessee, the *Statement* requires that a lease be classified and accounted for as a capital lease (shown as an asset and an obligation on the balance sheet) if at the inception of the lease it meets one of four criteria: (1) the lease transfers ownership of the property to the lessee by the end of the lease term, (2) the lease contains an option to purchase the property at a bargain price, (3) the lease term is equal to 75 percent or more of the estimated economic life of the property, or (4) the present value[2] of the rentals and other minimum lease payments, at the beginning of the lease term equal 90 percent of the fair value of the leased property less any related investment tax credit retained by the lessor. If the lease does not meet any of those criteria, it is to be classified and accounted for as an operating lease.

With regard to the last two of the above four criteria, if the beginning of the lease term falls within the last 25 percent of the total estimated economic life of the leased property, neither the 75 percent of economic life criterion nor the 90 percent recovery criterion is to be applied for purposes of classifying the lease. As a consequence, such leases will be classifed as operating leases.

The lessee shall record a capital lease as an asset and an obligation at an amount equal to the present value of minimum lease payments[3] during the lease term, excluding executory costs (if determinable) such as insurance, maintenance, and taxes to be paid by the lessor together with any profit

---

[2] A lessor shall compute the present value of the minimum lease payments using the interest rate implicit in the lease. A lessee shall compute the present value of the minimum lease payments using its incremental borrowing rate unless (a) it knows the lessor's computation of the implicit rate and (b) the implicit rate computed by the lessor is less than the lessee's incremental borrowing rate. If both of those conditions are met, the lessee shall use the implicit rate. The incremental borrowing rate is defined as the rate that at the inception of the lease, the lessee would have incurred to borrow the funds necessary to buy the leased asset on a secured loan basis with repayment terms similar to the payment schedule called for in the lease.

[3] These include the following: (a) minimum rental payments, (b) any guarantee by the lessee of the residual value at the expiration of the lease term, (c) any payment the lessee must make upon failure to renew or extend the lease at its expiration, and (d) the payment called for by a bargain purchase price.

thereon. However, the amount so determined should not exceed the fair value of the leased property at the inception of the lease. If executory costs are not determinable from the provisions of the lease, an estimate of the amount shall be made.

Amortization, in a manner consistent with the lessee's normal depreciation policy, is called for over the term of the lease except where the lease transfers title or contains a bargain purchase option; in the latter cases, amortization should follow the estimated economic life.

In accounting for an operating lease, the lessee will charge rentals to expense as they become payable except when rentals do not become payable on a straight-line basis, in which case they should be expensed on such a basis or on any other systematic or rational basis that reflects the time pattern of benefits derived from the leased property.

Accounting by lessors

In the case of the lessor, except for leveraged leases, if a lease meets any one of the preceding four criteria plus two additional criteria, it is to be classified and accounted for as a sales-type lease (if manufacturing or dealer profit is involved) or as a direct financing lease. The additional criteria are: (1) collectibility of the minimum lease payments is reasonably predictable, and (2) no important uncertainties surround the amount of unreimbursable costs yet to be incurred by the lessor under the lease. A lease not meeting those tests is to be classified and accounted for as an operating lease.

Sales-type leases

1. The minimum lease payments plus the unguaranteed residual value accruing to the benefit of the lessor shall be recorded as the *gross investment* in the lease.
2. The difference between gross investment and the sum of the present values of its two components shall be recorded as unearned income. The net investment equals gross investment less unearned income. Unearned income shall be amortized to income over the lease term so as to produce a constant periodic rate of return on the net investment in the lease. Contingent rentals shall be credited to income when they become receivable.
3. At the termination of the existing lease term of a lease being renewed, the net investment in the lease shall be adjusted to the fair value of the leased property to the lessor at that date, and the difference, if any, recognized as gain or loss. (The same procedure applies to direct financing leases—see below.)
4. The present value of the minimum lease payments discounted at the interest rate implicit in the lease shall be recorded as the *sales price*. The cost, or carrying amount, if different, of the leased property, plus

any initial direct costs (of negotiating and consummating the lease) less the present value of the unguaranteed residual value shall be charged against income in the same period.

5. The estimated residual value shall be periodically reviewed. If it is determined to be excessive, the accounting for the transaction shall be revised using the changed estimate. The resulting reduction in net investment shall be recognized as a loss in the period in which the estimate is changed. No upward adjustment of the estimated residual value shall be made. (A similar provision applies to direct-financing leases.)

Direct-financing leases

1. The minimum lease payments (net of executory costs) plus the unguaranteed residual value plus the initial direct costs shall be recorded as the *gross investment.*

2. The difference between the gross investment and the cost, or carrying amount, if different, of the leased property, shall be recorded as *unearned income. Net investment* equals gross investment less unearned income. The unearned income shall be amortized to income over the lease term. The initial direct costs shall be amortized in the same portion as the unearned income. Contingent rentals shall be credited to income when they become receivable.

Operating leases

The lessor will include property accounted for as an operating lease in the balance sheet and will depreciate it in accordance with his normal depreciation policy. Rent should be taken into income over the lease term as it becomes a receivable, except that if it departs from a straight-line basis, income should be recognized on such basis or on some other systematic or rational basis. Initial costs should be deferred and allocated over the lease term.

Principal disclosures

The principal items of information required to be disclosed by lessees are (1) future minimum lease payments, separately for capital leases and operating leases, in total and for each of the five succeeding years; and (2) rental expense for each period for which an income statement is presented. Information required to be disclosed by lessors includes (1) future minimum lease payments to be received, separately for sales-type and direct-financing leases and for operating leases; and (2) the other components of the investment in sales-type and direct-financing leases—estimated residual values and unearned income.

Leases involving real estate

These can involve (1) land only, (2) land and buildings, (3) equipment as well as real estate, or (4) only part of a building or building complex.

Generally, the above discussed accounting procedures will apply here with the following exceptions:

a. Where land only is involved, the lessee should account for it as a capital lease if either criterion (1) or (2) on page 192 is met. Land is not usually amortized.

b. In a lease involving both land and building(s), if the capitalization criteria applicable to land (see above) are met, the lease will retain the capital lease classification and the lessor will account for it as a single unit. The lessee will have to capitalize the land and buildings separately, the allocation between the two being in proportion to their respective fair values at the inception of the lease.

c. If the capitalization criteria applicable to land are not met, and at the inception of the lease the fair value of the land is less than 25 percent of total fair value of the leased property, both lessor and lessee shall consider the property as a single unit. The estimated economic life of the building is to be attributed to the whole unit. In this case, if either criteria (3) or (4) (see page 192) is met, the lessee should capitalize the land and building as a single unit and amortize it.

d. If the conditions in *(c)* above prevail *but* the fair value of land is 25 percent or more of the total fair value of the leased property, both the lessee and the lessor should consider the land and the building *separately* for purposes of applying capitalization criteria (3) and (4) (see page 192). If either of the criteria is met by the building element of the lease, it should be accounted for as a capital lease by the lessee and amortized. The land element of the lease is to be accounted for as an operating lease. If the building element meets neither capitalization criteria, both land and buildings should be accounted for as a single operating lease.

e. Equipment that is part of a real estate lease should be considered separately, and the minimum lease payments applicable to it should be estimated by whatever means are appropriate in the circumstances.

f. Leases of certain facilities such as airport, bus terminal, or port facilities from governmental units or authorities are to be classified as *operating leases.*

Sale—leaseback

When the lease meets the criteria for treatment as a capital lease, any gain on the sale should be deferred and amortized over the lease term in proportion to the amortization of the leased asset. When a capital lease is not present, any gain should be recognized at the time of the sale if the fair rental for the lease term is equal to or greater than the rental called for by the lease. If the lease rental exceeds the fair rental, any gain on the sale should be reduced by the amount of such excess.

When the leaseback is for only a portion of the property sold, an assessment should be made as to whether the leaseback of the portion of property sold at a profit represents a continued involvement in the property sufficient to require deferral of all or part of the profit on the sale.

Leveraged leases

Leveraged leasing, in which a lessor borrows heavily in order to finance a leasing transaction with a small, or even negative, equity in the leased property is a highly specialized topic.

Basically, the accounting method prescribed for use by lessors for leveraged leases, as they are defined in the statement, is called the separate phases method. This method recognizes the separate investment phases of a leveraged lease in which the lessor's net investment declines during the early years of the lease and rises during the later years. In the case of lessees, leveraged leases are to be classified and accounted for in the same manner as nonleveraged leases.

ACCOUNTING FOR CAPITAL LEASES

ILLUSTRATION 1

I. Lease terms and assumptions.
   A. Lessor acquires equipment to be leased for $10,000
   B. Fair value of the leased property at inception of the
        lease, January 1, 19x1 . . . . $10,000
   C. Estimated economic life of the leased property . . . .   8 years
   D. The lease has a fixed noncancelable term of five years with a rental of $2,400 payable at the end of each year. The lessee guarantees the residual value at the end of the five-year lease term in the amount of $2,000. The lessee is to receive any excess of the sales price of property over the guaranteed amount at the end of the lease term. The lessee pays executory costs.
   E. The rentals specified are determined to be fair, and the guarantees of residual value are expected to approximate realizable value. No investment tax credit is available.

II. Additional information.
   A. The lessee depreciates its owned equipment on a straight-line basis.
   B. The lessee's incremental borrowing rate is 10 percent per year.
   C. At the end of the lease term, the equipment is sold for $2,100.

   1. *Determination of minimum lease payments.*
        Minimum lease payments for both the lessee and the lessor are computed as follows:

Minimum rental payments over the lease
term = ($2,400 × 5 years) $12,000
Lessee guarantee of the residual value at
the end of the lease term.................. 2,000
Total minimum lease payments $14,000

2. *Determination of lessor's rate of interest implicit in the lease.*
This is the rate that equates the recovery of the fair value of the property
at the inception of the lease ($10,000) with the present value of both the
minimum lease payments ($2,400 × 5) plus the lessee's guarantee of the
residual value at the end of the lease ($2,000). This rate can be arrived at
on a trial and error basis. At 10 percent, the two discounted amounts add
up to $10,340; at 11 percent, to $10,057; while at 12 percent, they equal
$9,786. Through interpolation, we arrive at an implicit interest rate of 11.21
percent.

3. *Classification of the lease.*
The *lessee* will classify this as a capital lease because the present value
of the minimum lease payments at $10,340 (using its incremental borrowing
rate of 10 percent) exceeds 90 percent of the fair value of the property at
the inception of the lease ($10,000). The lessee will use its incremental borrow-
ing rate (10 percent) in discounting because it is less than the implicit interest
rate in the lease. The *lessor* will classify the lease as a direct financing lease
because the present value of the minimum lease payments using the implicit
rate of 11.21 percent ($10,000) exceeds 90 percent of the fair value of the
property, cost and fair value of the amount are equal at inception of lease,
and all other conditions of capitalization have been met.

III. Accounting on the lessee's books.

January 1, 19x1:

Leased property under Capital Leases 10,000
Obligations under Capital Leases 10,000*
To record the capital lease at the fair value of
the property.
* Obligation due within one year will be classified as current.

December 31, 19x1:

Obligations under Capital Leases 1,279
Interest Expense .... 1,121 [a]
Cash 2,400
To record first year rental payments.
[a] Obligation balance outstanding × Implicit interest
rate = $10,000 × 11.21% = $1,121.

Depreciation Expense .... 1,600 [b]
Accumulated Depreciation of Leased Property
under Capital Leases 1,600
To record first year depreciation.

[b] $\frac{\text{Cost-residual value}}{\text{Term of lease}} = \frac{\$10,000 - \$2,000}{5} = \$1,600.$

December 31, 19x5 (selected journal entry):

Cash	100	
Obligations under Capital Leases	2,000	
Accumulated Depreciation, Leased Property under Capital Leases	8,000	
Leased Property under Capital Leases		10,000
Gain on Disposition of Leased Property		100

To record liquidation of obligations under capital leases
and receipt of cash in excess of guaranteed residual value.

IV. Accounting on the lessor's books.

January 1, 19x1:

Equipment	10,000	
Cash		10,000

To record purchase of equipment for purpose of
financing lease.

Minimum Lease Payments Receivable	14,000	
Equipment		10,000
Unearned Income		4,000

To record investment in direct financing lease.

December 21, 19x1:

Unearned Income	1,121 [c]	
Earned Income		1,121

To recognize the portion of unearned income that
is earned during first year of investment.

[c] Net investment × implicit interest rate = 10,000
× 11.21% = $1,121

Cash	2,400	
Minimum Lease Payments Receivable		2,400

To record receipt of first year's rental.

December 31, 19x5 (selected journal entry):

Cash	2,000	
Minimum Lease Payments Receivable		2,000

To record the receipt of the lessee's guarantee.

Capital versus operating lease—the effect on income

As can be seen from the tabulation that follows, the interest expense pattern
of the capital lease follows that of a fixed payment mortgage with interest
expense decreasing over time as the principal balance decreases. The attraction
of operating lease accounting to the lessee is also clear because under the
capitalization procedure expenses incident to the lease, i.e., interest plus depreciation ($1,121 + $1,600), exceed the rental expense by $321. In later years,
this excess reverses, as over the least period total expense under either method
is equal, but the pattern of expense recognition is an important consideration

to many enterprises, and the higher beginning charge under capitalization is viewed as a distinct disadvantage of that method.

The tabulation also indicates the pattern of finance income recognition by the lessor that is proportional to the investment at risk.

Year	Rental	Interest: Income (lessor) expense (lessee)	Principal: Receipts (Lessor) payment (lessee)	Balance of obligations
19x0	—	—	—	$10,000
19x1	$ 2,400	$1,121	$1,279	8,721
19x2	2,400	977	1,423	7,298
19x3	2,400	818	1,582	5,716
19x4	2,400	641	1,759	3,957
19x5	2,400	443	1,957	2,200
Total	$12.000	$4,000	$8,000	$ 2,000

Capital versus operating lease—the effect on funds

It should be noted that as far as the flow of funds is concerned, there is only one reality, i.e., the yearly outflow of the $2,400 rental.

Under capital lease accounting, "funds from operations" are reduced yearly by declining interest charges (i.e., $1,121, $977 . . .), while the payment of lease obligations represents an "other" (nonoperating) use of funds that increases yearly (i.e., $1,279, $1,423 . . .). The two always equal the rental payment of $2,400. The amortization (depreciation) of the property right of $1,600 annually has no effect on funds because it is a nonfund-using expense.

Example of disclosure:

General Cinema Corporation's 1981 annual report contains the following lease disclosure (included with long-term debt):

	Interest rate	Maturity	1981	1980
Capitalized lease obligations[e]	6.25–15.46%	1982–2003	50,938	54,179

[e] Capitalized lease obligations relate to beverage plants and facilities, vending machines, vehicles, and theatres.

The minimum payment obligations arising from the above leases at October 31, 1981 are as follows: 1982—$16,578,000; 1983—$13,119,000; 1984—$10,021,000; 1985—$8,678,000; 1986—$8,407,000; all years thereafter—$34,970,000. Amounts representing interest and executory costs aggregate $29,869,000. The present value of the future minimum lease payments is $61,922,000.

Implications for analysis

Leasing as a means of financing is an area deserving the analyst's particular scrutiny. The major objective here is to make sure that accounting form is not permitted to mask the economic substance of debt[4] and its effect on capital structure, as well as exposure to fixed charges and the effects of leverage.

It is quite obvious that many long-term leases have all or most of the earmarks of debt. They create an obligation for payments under an agreement that is not cancelable. This represents a commitment to fixed payments that is what a debt obligation amounts to. The adverse effects of debt are also present in the case of a lease, that is, an inability to pay may result in insolvency. The fact that statutory limitations on lease obligations in case of bankruptcy limit the obligation to pay rent to one or a number of years is not a mitigating factor of substance because the process of financial analysis is usually designed to evaluate the probability of insolvency and the attendant adverse effects on asset values and credit standing, rather than an evaluation of the amount and standing of the obligations after insolvency proceedings have been started. The importance of the leased property to company operations is also a factor, since it may be so vital as to preclude the company's abandonment of the lease in reorganization proceedings.

It is very difficult, if not impossible, to compare the financial position of companies that use different methods of financing, including installment purchase in the form of a lease, for the financing of different assets. This is also true of comparisons of income, since when accounted as an operating lease, rentals are usually less than interest expense and depreciation expenses in the early stages of ownership in the form of a lease.

SFAS 13 represents a major step in the direction of providing the analyst with the information required for the proper reflection of leases in the financial statements and the evaluation of their impact on the financial position and results of operations of an enterprise. The criteria as well as the disclosure requirements embodied in this *Statement* are much more comprehensive and explicit than those contained in any former pronouncements, and this should assure that the abuses and distortions of the past will not inhibit the process of analysis. Nevertheless, the analyst, mindful of the historical tendencies and developments in areas of accounting that are affected by strong special interests, should be ever alert to the possibility that managements, aided by the seemingly inexhaustible ingenuity of their accountants, lawyers, and other financial advisers will often attempt to devise ways to circumvent this *Statement*. Accounting standards may, in time, be changed to meet these challenges, and so it is the interim period that presents the time of greatest risk exposure for the analyst. Many interpretations of *SFAS 13* have been

---

[4] Under Section 502(7) of the Bankruptcy Act of 1978, the damages allowable to the landlord of a debtor are limited to the greater of one year or 15 percent of the remaining portion of the lease not to exceed three years after the date of filing or surrender whichever is earler.

issued since the original promulgation of this standard. While, under the standards which preceded *SFAS 13,* only relatively few leases were capitalized, the new rules require the capitalization of most leases where there is an effective transfer of substantially all of the benefits and risks of ownership from lessor to lessee.

A research report[5] published by the FASB in 1981 concluded that it has not become more expensive for lessee companies to raise money or obtain waivers of restrictive covenants as a result of the issuance of *SFAS 13.* Nevertheless, a majority of respondents to an extensive mail survey indicated that new lease contracts were drafted to avoid capitalization, many indicated an increase in buying or constructing of assets instead of leasing them, and almost half of users and auditors surveyed indicated that existing lease contracts were renegotiated to avoid capitalization. In addition, the study revealed that more than 40 percent of the trained analysts surveyed considered a company that did not capitalize a lease as being more profitable than its identical counterpart that did capitalize. Thus, the need for a more informed approaches to the reading of financial statements by analysts is an ever-present need.

The provisions of *SFAS 13* that entail assumptions of fair values, selling prices, salvage or residual values, implicit rates of interest, and incremental borrowing rates are not so tight as to preclude substantive changes in accounting through manipulations of these relatively "soft" factors. Thus, as in the past, the analyst will have to be alert and vigilant when analyzing the impact of leases on financial statements.

"OFF BALANCE SHEET" FINANCING

In addition to leases, there are other "off balance sheet" financing methods that range from the simple to the highly complex. Moreover, this is an ever-changing field where as one standard is brought out to limit their use, new and innovative methods are devised to take their place. Thus, the analyst must be always on the lookout for methods by which debt is kept off the balance sheet.

Property, plant, and equipment can be financed by having an outside party acquire the facilities while the company agrees to do enough business with the facility to provide funds sufficient to service the debt. Examples of these kinds of arrangements are through-put agreement, in which the company agrees to run a specified amount of goods through a processing facility, or "take-or-pay" arrangements in which the company guarantees to pay for a specified quantity of goods whether needed or not. A variation of these arrangements involves the creation of separate entities for ownership and the

---

[5] A. Rashad Abdel-Khalik, "The Economic Effects on Leases of FASB Statement No. 13, Accounting for Leases."

financing of the facilities (such as joint ventures or limited partnerships) that are not consolidated with the company's financial statements and are, thus, excluded from its liabilities.

In recent years, companies have been financing inventory without reporting on their balance sheets the inventory or the related liability. These are generally product financing arrangements in which an enterprise sells and agrees to repurchase inventory with the repurchase price equal to the original sales price plus carrying and financing costs or other similar transactions such as a guarantee of resale prices to third parties.

SFAS 49 specifies criteria for determining when an arrangement involving the sale of inventory is in substance a financing arrangement that should be accounted for as a borrowing, with excess repurchase costs treated as financing or holding costs.

Seagram Company's 1978 annual report contains an example of an inventory financing agreement:

> The Company entered into a five-year contract in December 1973 whereunder it agreed to purchase Scotch whiskey from a subsidiary of a British bank. The amount of the commitment was $28,279,000 at July 31, 1978.

Another means of financing is to sell accounts receivable either with or without recourse. Under an FASB proposal, a sale of receivables need not be reported as a liability when the seller "surrenders its right to the future benefits relating to the receivables." Only when the seller "retains both the benefits and the risks associated with the receivables" must he report it as a liability. This position may not be sufficiently conservative and is controversial, but the analyst must at all times focus on the risks and realities of each separate arrangement.

Finally, there is the question of many captive finance subsidiaries that have little economic substance apart from that bestowed upon them by the parent. The parent sells receivables to these finance subsidiaries, thus keeping them and the related debt off its own balance sheet because these are presently not required to be consolidated. Here the analyst must again look to substance rather than to form. Should a receivable be considered as collected by an economic entity before payment from the ultimate customer has been received? Or, as is often the case, if such captive finance subsidiary finances the carrying of dealer inventory, should such inventory be considered to have been effectively sold by the enterprise?

LIABILITIES UNDER THE PENSION PLANS

Like the accounting for most obligations, that for pensions also has a dual aspect. Their impact on results of operations will be considered in Chapter 11, while the liability aspect will be discussed here.

SFAS 35 (1980) established standards of financial accounting and reporting for annual financial statements of defined benefit pension plans.

SFAS 36 (1980) amended *APB Opinion 8* by requiring revised disclosures about defined benefit pension plans in employers' financial statements. This standard requires disclosure, among other items, of the following data determined in accordance with *SFAS 35:*

    a. The actuarial present value of vested accumulated plan benefits;
    b. The actuarial present value of nonvested accumulated plan benefits;
    c. The plan's net assets available for benefits;
    d. The assumed rates of return used in determining the actuarial present value of vested and nonvested accumulated plan benefits; and
    e. The date as of which the benefit information was determined.

The data may be reported in total for all plans, separately for each plan, or in subaggregations. For plans for which the above data is not available or not applicable, the employer should continue to comply with the disclosure requirements of *APB Opinion 8* by disclosing the excess, if any, of the actuarially computed value of vested benefits over the total of the pension fund and any balance sheet pension accruals, less any pension prepayments or deferred charges; and the reasons why the information required by *(a)* above is not provided.

SFAS 36 represents a temporary approach to the overall problem of accounting for defined benefit pension plans pending completion of an FASB project to consider all aspects of accounting by employers for pensions and related benefits.

Two basic cost categories are associated with pensions: the *current cost,* which is the actuarially determined obligation incurred for pension benefits bestowed upon employees during a given period of time; and *prior service* costs representing pension credit given to employees for work performed before the inception of the pension plan or incident to a retroactive revision of plan terms.[6]

It is important to understand the difference between the *accrual* of the proper pension cost, which is a bookkeeping entry, and the *funding* of that cost, which involves the transfer of funds from the entity to the pension trustee.

Liabilities for current costs represent accruals that, for whatever reason, the company has not funded. However, pension legislation as well as tax considerations require that current service costs be funded promptly.

On the assumption that the payment of past period benefits obligations can be delayed and avoided indefinitely, *APB Opinion 8* states that "unfunded prior service cost is not a liability which should be shown in the balance sheet."

---

[6] *Past* service costs arise generally incident to new plans, whereas *prior* service costs refer to retroactive improvements in existing plans.

Implications for analysis

The analyst must be aware that both the shortcomings of present accounting and disclosure rules for pension liabilities as well as developments such as the Employee Retirement Income Security Act of 1974 (ERISA) can cause financial statements to understate significantly the actual and potential corporate liabilities for pensions.

Neither *APB Opinion 8* nor *SFAS 36* requires the disclosure of unfunded past service benefits, and the SEC deleted such a disclosure requirement. Consequently, the analyst will depend on voluntary disclosure or the ability to obtain such information by other means. The disclosures required by *SFAS 36* should aid in the analysis of pension liabilities.

Whenever vested benefits (those belonging to an employee in any event) exceed the net pension fund assets, the analyst is faced with a kind of "off balance sheet liability" that must be recognized and taken into account.

The relationship between *unfunded past service obligations* and *unfunded vested benefits* is not a direct one and will vary with circumstances. Generally, the latter will include some (but not necessarily all) of the former. Should the analyst desire to include in liabilities only the amount by which vested benefits exceed pension plan assets, the following analytical adjustment could be made:

Retained earnings = (1 − Tax Rate) (Unfunded Vested Benefits) X
Deferred Income Taxes = (Tax Rate) (Unfunded Vested Benefits) . . . . . . Y
     Pension Liability . . . .   Z

The charge to Retained Earnings reflects the cumulative expenses (less tax effect) charged to establish the pension liability. The charge to Deferred Income Taxes reflects the fact that pension expenses are not deductible for tax purposes until they are funded—hence recognition of a future tax benefit.

Implementation of such an adjustment will affect the debt-to-equity ratio and can be extended to affect earnings and the resulting return-on-investment measures as well. The fixed-charge coverage ratio can also be modified by inclusion in the denominator of the interest equivalent of the added pension liability (see Chapter 18).

ERISA has added weight to the argument that unfunded past service costs represent real liabilities because of requirements of the law that they be funded (i.e., paid) generally over a 40-year period.

There are additional serious problems with the computation of pension costs and related liabilities. The FASB mandated the use of an accrued benefit method that in economic terms understates pension liabilities by recording smaller amounts of liabilities in earlier years of the pension plan. Moreover, there is a lack of symmetry in the approach taken to calculate defined benefits and expected rates of return. Thus, because most pension plans are based on "final pay," inflation should be taken into account in computing the pay on which retirement benefits are to be based. In most cases, it is in fact not taken into account. Inflationary expectations are, on the other hand, incorporated in the rates of return that pension assets are expected to earn. Consistency of approach would require that the return assumed be at the riskless rate of interest of about 3 percent, rather than the much higher rates presently assumed which do, of course, include a premium for inflationary expectations.

Recently, General Motors cut its unfunded vested pension liability by over \$2 billion by raising its assumed rate of return from 7 percent to 8¼ percent, certainly not an excessive rate at the time.[7] Moreover, Value Line reports that similar increases in assumed rates of return caused the total of pension liabilities for 950 companies in its Industrial Composite to drop 40 percent from \$37 billion in 1979 to \$22.2 billion in 1980.

Comparisons between unfunded liabilities of companies are difficult because of variations due to:

1. Methods of evaluating assets and liabilities of the fund.
2. Methods of recognizing realized and unrealized gains and losses.
3. Discrepancies between actuarial assumptions and actual performance.
4. Different dates of actuarial valuations.

The potential seriousness of the size of unfunded vested benefits liabilities can be appreciated from the fact that recently Lockheed's unfunded pension liabilities came to over 160 percent of its net worth, Bethlehem Steel's amounted to over 50 percent, and Trans World Corporation's came to about 70 percent of net worth.

ERISA provides that on liquidation of an enterprise or the termination of a pension plan, up to 30 percent of the enterprise net worth (which may be greater or less than book value net worth) may be attached to make good pension fund deficiencies. This potential liability for "guaranteed unfunded benefits," which ranks in priority with a tax lien, is an additional element that may affect the debt-to-equity ratio of many enterprises.

The FASB has stated that it does not believe that ERISA creates a legal obligation for unfunded pension costs that warrants recognition as a liability on the balance sheet except generally for that unpaid portion currently required to be funded and where a legal liability is created as a result of the termination of the pension plan. The entire subject is, however, under active study now. As we have seen, the obligations may be very real and even the exception may become important. The analyst must be careful to assess pension liabilities fully and thoroughly.

---

[7] A 1982 study shows that in 1981 more than one third of major companies increased the interest rate used to compute the actuarial present value of accumulated plan benefits. Increases in the interest rate assumption serves to decrease the present value of plan benefits. Only changes in interest rate assumptions used for *funding* purposes affect pension expense and reported earnings.

LIABILITIES AT THE "EDGE" OF EQUITY

The analyst must be alert to the existence of equity securities (typically preferred stock) that because of mandatory redemption provisions are more akin to debt than they are to equity. Whatever their name, these securities impose upon the issuing companies obligations to lay out funds at specified dates, which is precisely a burden that a true equity security is not supposed to impose. Such preferred issues exist, for example, at Lockheed Corporation and Koppers Company, Inc., and are described in LTV Corporation's 1980 annual report as follows:

NOTE H—Preferred Stock with Mandatory Redemption

LTV is required to redeem the remaining shares outstanding in 1991 (86,737) and 1992 (119,227). The holders of the $5 Series A preferred stock are entitled to one vote per share.

In *FRR* No. 1, section 211, the SEC concluded that redeemable preferred stocks are significantly different from conventional equity capital and that they should not be included in the general caption of stockholders equity or combined in a total with nonredeemable equity securities. The release also requires disclosure of redemption terms and five-year maturity data.

SFAS 47 requires disclosure of redemption requirements of redeemable capital stock for each of the five years following the date of the latest balance sheet.

DEFERRED CREDITS (INCOME)

An ever-increasing variety of items and descriptions is included in this group of accounts. In many cases, these items are akin to liabilities; in others, they represent deferred income yet to be earned, while in a number of cases, they serve as income-smoothing devices. The confusion confronting the analyst is compounded by a lack of agreement among accountants as to the exact nature of these items or the proper manner of their presentation. Thus, regardless of category or presentation, the key to their analysis lies in an understanding of the circumstances and the financial transactions that brought them about.

At one end of this group's spectrum, we find those items that have the characteristics of liabilities. Here, we may find included such items as advances or billings on uncompleted contracts, unearned royalties and deposits, and customer service prepayments. Quite clearly, the outstanding characteristic of these items is their liability aspects, even though, as in the case of advances of royalties, they may, after certain conditions are fulfilled, find their way into the company's income stream. Advances on uncompleted contracts represent primarily methods of financing the work in process while deposits of rent received represent, as do customer service prepayments, security for performance of an agreement. Even though found sometimes among "deferred credits," such items are more properly classified as liabilities, or current liabilities if due within the company's operating cycle.

Next, we consider deferred income items that represent income or revenue received in advance and that will be earned over future periods through the passage of time, the performance of services, or the delivery of goods. Examples of deferred income items are magazine subscription income, representing the receipts by magazine publishers of advance payment for long-term subscriptions; and unearned rental income, which represents receipt of advance payment for rent. Other examples are unearned finance charges, deferred profit on installment sales, deferred gain on sales-and-leaseback arrangements, and unrealized profit on layaway sales.

It should be noted that this category includes a liability for future performance as well as a possible profit component in such income items received but not yet earned as, for example, subscription income, the future earning of which is dependent on the delivery of magazines. It also includes unearned finance charges that have already been deducted but that are allocated to the future on the assumption that they are earned with the mere passage of time. Still further along the "earned" scale are profits on installment sales that are deferred, not because they have not been earned but rather because the collection of the receivable resulting from such sales is going to occur over a period of time in the future. The preferred accounting treatment is not to defer such gains on installment sales but rather to give expression to any doubts about future collectibility of receivables by establishing a provision for doubtful accounts for that purpose.

Further on the other extreme of the deferred credit spectrum are so-called bargain purchase credits that arise in cases where the fair value of certain assets of an acquired company exceeds the consideration given. (Purchase accounting, which is governed by *APB Opinion 16,* is discussed in Chapter 9). In such cases, the resulting credit is amortized to income over what is usually an arbitrarily determined number of years. What we have here is a benefit derived from what is presumably an advantageous acquisition. The reason for the deferral of this benefit and its taking up in income over a number of years is not necessarily that this benefit has not been realized, but because of a desire to spread out, or smooth its effect, over a number of years.

One of the most complicated and controversial, as well as most substantial, of deferred credits is deferred income taxes.

Deferred taxes

Tax allocation, which is the accounting process giving rise to deferred tax credits (or debits in reverse circumstances), is primarily a device for matching the applicable tax expense with corresponding pretax income. A more comprehensive analysis of this accounting technique and its implications will be undertaken in Chapter 11 on the measurement of income. Here, we will examine primarily the nature of the deferred credit to which it gives rise.

For purposes of understanding how this deferred tax credit arises, let us consider the example of the depreciation deducted under circumstances where a company may elect an accelerated-depreciation method for tax purposes while using the straight-line method for book purposes. Since more depreciation is deducted for tax purposes in the early years, two things are evident: (1) there is a tax deferral in the early years and (2) that will have to be made up in the later years since in no event can depreciation for tax purposes exceed the total original cost. Thus, in theory, the tax savings are temporary; and under tax allocation, these savings are not used to reduce the tax expense but are rather accumulated as a deferred tax credit.

In practice, as a study by the firm of Price Waterhouse and Company, as well as other studies, shows this "deferred tax liability" is rarely paid in full.[8] The reason for this is that most companies keep expanding their plant, with inflation swelling the nominal dollar amounts further, so that every year there is new accelerated depreciation on new facilities to balance—and usually outweigh—the reduced depreciation on facilities that got the accelerated treatment earlier.[9]

The accounting profession, which in *APB Opinion 11* adopted the concept of comprehensive tax allocation, states that it does not regard deferred taxes as a liability but considers them rather a deferred credit account that must be established for the proper matching of costs and revenues. Be that as it may, the analyst must understand what this account represents when he finds it included within the deferred credits category. While we used depreciation as an example here, deferred taxes may arise in any instance where expense or income items are treated one way for tax purposes and another for book purposes. The entire subject of tax allocation is on the FASB's agenda for reexamination.

Deferred investment tax credit

Frequently included among deferred income taxes is the deferred investment credit. While also a tax benefit, the similarity between deferred income taxes, discussed above, and the deferred investment credit is more apparent than real.

Under various revenue acts, as amended, up to 10 percent of the cost of certain depreciable assets purchased and put into service during the year has been allowed as a credit against federal income taxes. Unlike deferred income taxes, which represent a postponement of tax liability, the investment

---

[8] It is interesting to note that in Britain, deferred tax accounting is now used only on a partial basis.

[9] Enterprises whose plant is shrinking are generally not likely to remain profitable for very long. Under such circumstances, they will not pay income taxes in any event.

credit results in a partial reduction of taxes in the years in which it is earned.[10] Under one alternative treatment, it is taken into income by means of a reduction of tax expenses in the year in which it is taken on the tax return, while under another alternative, it is taken into income over the productive lives of the assets whose acquisition gave rise to it. It is in the latter case that the deferred investment credit account is found on the balance sheet; and what it represents is, in essence, a device for spreading a benefit already earned over a number of years in order to achieve a more even determination of income. The income aspect of the investment credit will be considered more fully in Chapter 11.

Now that we have covered the entire spectrum of that family of accounts designated as deferred credits, we can clearly see that each must be examined and understood on its own merits if its significance to the analyst is to be properly assessed.

MINORITY INTEREST

Found among liabilities, and sometimes in the equity section, but not really representing an immediate claim on company resources, are the minority interests in consolidated entities. These represent the proportionate interest of minority stockholders in a majority-owned subsidiary that is consolidated. Since all the net assets (i.e., assets less liabilities) of the subsidiary are included in the consolidated statements, the minority's portion is shown on the credit, or financing, side of the consolidated balance sheet.

Implications for analysis

The key to the proper analysis of deferred credits is a clear understanding of what has brought them about. In the discussion concerning the accounting principles involved, we have pointed out that they encompass a wide variety of dissimilar items.

Those items that represent prepayments on services yet to be performed or goods yet to be delivered must be regarded as temporary sources of funds. In fact, often advances on contracts yet to be executed serve exactly the purpose of affording temporary financing to the supplier.

Deferred revenues may be viewed by the analyst as items that are on their way to the income stream of a company. What should not be lost sight of is the fact that many such items do not represent pure income elements as may be the case with interest or deferred installment sale profit that are deemed to be earned by the mere passage of time without the incurrence of additional expense. Thus, deferred subscription income represents the amount received in advance for magazines yet to be delivered. In spite of the fact that the earning of such subscription revenue will require paper,

---

[10] Under the Tax Equity and Fiscal Responsibility Act of 1982, the basis of assets will be reduced by half of the investment tax credit.

printing, editorial, and postage expense, such costs are usually not provided for when the revenue is deferred. Thus, while such items do represent temporary sources of funds, they are not sources of net profit and may, in fact, ultimately result in a net loss.

Certain deferred income items are clearly created, not for the purposes of fair presentation of financial positions but rather for purposes of income smoothing or equalization. Thus, the "bargain purchase credit" discussed earlier has as its main purpose and justification the smoothing of income over a period of years and must be regarded as such. Similarly the ratable taking up of installment sales profit is designed to provide for the contingency of possible noncollection of the sales price.

Perhaps the most confusing deferred credit to many analysts is the deferred tax credit. Because of its size, it is, by far, the most important item in this category. Its location in the twilight zone between liabilities and equity indicates that it is neither, but that in itself does not shed light on its true nature.

The reason that the deferred tax credit is not a liability is that it lacks some of the more important characteristics of debt. The government has no present claim for taxes nor is there a timetable for repayment. While the deferred tax account represents the loss of future deductibility of assets for tax purposes, the drawing down of this account to reduce tax expenses depends on future developments, such as asset acquisition and depreciation policies that are not predictable with certainty.

This kind of uncertainty attests to the fact that the deferred tax credit is also not in the nature of equity capital because it represents a tax benefit in the nature of a postponement of taxes rather than a savings of taxes.

The most meaningful thing that can be said about this account from the point of view of financial analysis is that it represents an often important source of funds derived from the postponement of taxes and that the duration of the overall postponement depends on factors such as the future growth or stability of the company's depreciable assets pool. It is the assessment of such factors and their future likelihood that will be helpful to the analysis of the deferred tax account.

The analyst who concludes that all or part of the deferred income taxes should be eliminated would make the following analytical adjusting entry:

Deferred Income Taxes (current and noncurrent credits) X
    Deferred Income Taxes (current and noncurrent debits) . . . . . .   Y
    Retained Earnings . . . .   Z

Elimination of the annual provision for deferred taxes can be effected by the following adjusting entry:

Deferred Income Taxes X
    Income Tax Expense   X

In some cases, the debits and credits of the above entry may be reversed.

RESERVES AND PROVISIONS

Another group of accounts, found between long-term liabilities and the stockholders' equity section, is that of reserves and provisions. These accounts are often lumped together or even found among current liabilities or as deductions from related asset accounts; consequently, it is most useful to classify them broadly so as to facilitate an understanding of their true nature.

The first category is most correctly described as comprising provisions for liabilities and obligations that have a high probability of occurrence, but which are in dispute or are uncertain in amount. As is the case with many financial statement descriptions, neither the title nor the location in the financial statement can be relied upon as a rule of thumb guide to the nature of an account. Thus, the best key to analysis is a thorough understanding of the business and financial transactions that give rise to the account. The following are representative items in this group: provisions for product guarantees, service guarantees, and warranties, which are established in recognition of the fact that these undertakings involve future costs that are certain to arise though presently impossible to measure exactly and whose timing is uncertain. Consequently, the provision is established by a charge to income at the time products covered by guarantees are sold, in an amount estimated on the basis of experience or on the basis of any other reliable factor.

Another type of obligation that must be provided for on the best basis available is the liability for unredeemed trading stamps issued. To the company issuing the trading stamps, there is no doubt about the liability to redeem the stamps for merchandise. The only uncertainty concerns the number of stamps that will be presented for redemption.

An important group of future costs that must be provided for is that of employee compensation. These, in turn, give rise to provisions for vacation pay, deferred compensation, incentive compensation, supplemental unemployment benefits, bonus plans, welfare plans, and severance pay.

Finally, the category of estimated liabilities includes provisions for claims arising out of pending or existing litigation.

The second category comprises reserves for expenses and losses, which by experience or estimate are very likely to occur in the future and which should properly be provided for by current charges to operations.

One group within this category comprises reserves for operating costs such as maintenace, repairs, painting, or furnace relining. Thus, for example, since furnace relining jobs may be expected to be required at regularly recurring intervals, they are provided for rateably by charges to operations in order to avoid charging the entire cost to the year in which the actual relining takes place.

Another group comprises provisions for future losses stemming from decisions or actions already taken. Included in this group are reserves for relocation, replacement, modernization, and discontinued operations.

ACCOUNTING FOR CONTINGENCIES

SFAS 5 sets definitive criteria for the accrual and disclosure of loss contingencies.

A loss contingency is defined in the *Statement* as an existing condition, situation, or set of circumstances involving uncertainty as to possible loss that will be resolved when one or more future events occur or fail to occur. Examples provided of loss contingencies are litigation, threat of expropriation, collectibility of receivables, claims arising from product warranties or product defects, self-insured risks, and possible catastrophe losses of property and casualty insurance companies.

The *Statement* specifies two conditions, both of which must be met before a provision for a loss contingency should be charged to income. First, it must be probable that an asset had been impaired or a liability incurred at the date of a company's financial statements. Implicit in that condition is that it must be probable that a future event or events will occur confirming the fact of the loss. The second condition is that the amount of loss can be reasonably estimated. The effect of applying these criteria is that a loss will be accrued only when it is reasonably estimable and relates to the current or a prior period.

In the Board's opinion, losses from uncollectible receivables and obligations related to product warranties and product defects would normally meet the conditions for accrual at the time a sale is made. On the other hand, accrual for loss or damage of a company's property and loss from injury to others, damage to the property of others, and business interruption—sometimes referred to as self-insurance risks—would not be appropriate until the actual event of loss has taken place. Catastrophe losses of property and casualty insurance companies and reinsurance companies would not be accruable until the catastrophe has occurred. According to the *Statement,* catastrophe losses do not meet the conditions for accrual because predictions of losses over relatively short periods of time are subject to substantial deviations. Accruals for losses from such matters as expropriation, litigation, claims, and assessments would depend on the facts in each case.

The *Statement* permits appropriations of retained earnings for specified risks provided these are kept in the equity section of the balance sheet and are not used to relieve the income statement of actual losses (see also Chapter 8).

The *Statement* requires that if no accrual is made for a loss contingency because one or both of the conditions for accrual are not met, disclosure of the contingency shall be made when there is at least a reasonable possibility that a loss may have been incurred. The disclosure shall indicate the nature of the contingency and shall give an estimate of the possible loss or range of loss, or state that such an estimate cannot be made.

Implications for analysis

Provisions, such as for service guarantees and warranties, represent, in effect, revenue received for services yet to be performed. Of importance to the analyst is the adequacy of the provision that is often established on the basis of prior experience or, absent that, on the basis of other estimates. Concern with adequacy of amount is a prime factor in the analysis of all other reserves, whatever their purpose. Reserves and provisions appearing above the equity section should almost invariably be created by means of charges to income. They are designed to assign charges to the income statement based on when they are incurred rather then when they are paid.

Reserves for future losses represent a category of accounts that require particular scrutiny. While conservatism in accounting calls for recognition of losses as they can be determined or clearly foreseen, companies tend, particularly in loss years, to overprovide for losses yet to be incurred such as on disposal of assets, relocation, or plant closings. Overprovision does, of course, shift expected future losses to a present period that already shows adverse results. (A more extended discussion of such practices will be found in Chapter 11). The problem with such reserves is that once established there is no further accounting for the expenses and losses that are charged against them. Only in certain financial statements required to be filed with the SEC (such as Form 10-K) are details of changes in reserves required, and even here there is no requirement for detailed disclosure of the nature of the changes. Normally, no information is given, and the analyst must adopt a critical attitude towards the establishment of such reserves and the means of their disposition.

Reserves have traditionally been a popular management device for earnings manipulation and smoothing. Overprovision of loss reserves were recorded in years when results of operations were richer than management wanted to report, or when they were so poor that the creation of a cushion for the future did not matter to reported results.

SFAS 5 has gone a long way towards removing or at least reducing this management option. The much stricter criteria that must now be met means that greater earnings volatility will be experienced by companies subject to foreign risks, casualty insurers, self-insurers, and companies in certain industries such as oil (e.g., risks affecting offshore rigs and tankers).

The *Statement* also recognized that "accounting reserves" do not protect against risk, have no "cash flow" significance, and do not provide an alternative to insurance.

The analyst cannot, however, safely assume that overprovisions or, for that matter, underprovisions for losses are a thing of the past. Analysts should always attempt to obtain the full details of reserves by category and amount. Under the Internal Revenue Code, the only anticipated losses that are specifically tax deductible are provisions for bad debts and inventory write-downs to the lower of cost or market (for companies not on LIFO). Thus, one method by which the analyst can detect undisclosed provisions for future expenses or losses is by an analysis of deferred taxes. The book expense not currently allowable for tax purposes should have its effect on the deferred (prepaid) tax account.

It is interesting to note that the disclosure requirements of *SFAS 5* with respect to contingency losses charged to income appears weaker than those concerning unbooked amounts. The analyst needs as much disclosure as possible because it is important to assess the adequacy of provisions for future losses particularly in such areas as claims and litigation where existing guidelines and standards are far from clear or rigorous.

COMMITMENTS

Commitments are claims that may occur upon the future performance under a contract. They are not given expression in accounting records, since the mere signing of an executory contract or the issuance of a purchase order does not result in a completed transaction.

Examples of commitments are long-term noncancelable contracts to purchase goods or services at specified prices or purchase contracts for fixed assets that call for payments during construction. In a sense, a lease agreement is also regarded by some as a form of commitment.

Commitments call for disclosure of all the factors surrounding the obligation, including amount, conditions, timing, and other facts of importance.

For example, Storer Broadcasting Company revealed the following commitment in its annual report:

> The Company has entered into contracts, covering rentals of television films, under which it is obligated to make payments totaling approximately $7 million during the next six years. Payments under these contracts are recorded as deferred film rentals which are charged to expense as the films are used by the Company.

A. G. Edwards & Sons Inc., disclosed the following in its annual report:

> In the normal course of business the Company enters into when-issued and underwriting commitments. Transactions relating to open commitments at February 28, 1981, and subsequently settled, had no material effect on the consolidated financial statements as of that date.

Professor Yuji Ijiri[11] has defined "firm commitments" as those whose performance cannot be avoided without incurring severe penalty and recommends their recording as assets and liabilities.

---

[11] FASB "Recognition of Contractual Rights and Obligations" (Stamford, Conn., 1981).

CONTINGENT LIABILITIES

Business enterprise is subject to constant and all-pervading uncertainty. It is assumed that the informed reader of the financial statements is aware of this. However, certain events may point to specific probabilities and contingencies in the future and should be disclosed as such. *Accounting Research Bulletin (ARB) 50* states that "in accounting, a contingency is an existing condition, situation, or set of circumstances, involving a considerable degree of uncertainty, which may, through a related future event, result in the acquisition or loss of an asset, or the incurrence or avoidance of a liability, usually with the concurrence of gain or loss."

The basic nature of a contingency is its dependence on a future development or intervening factor or decision by an outside factor. Usually the contingency is uncertain as to probability of occurrence, timing, and amount. The financial statements must disclose the degree of probability of occurrence and, if possible, the best estimate of financial impact.

Examples of contingent liabilities are those that could arise from litigation, from guarantees of performance, from agreements and contracts, such as purchase or repurchase agreements, and from tax assessments or renegotiation claims.

Concord Fabrics, Inc., makes the following disclosure:

> *Note L: Contingent liability.* In connection with certain warehouse space previously leased by the Company, the Company is contingently liable for the landlord's losses up to approximately $350,000 a year if the current tenant fails to fulfill its lease obligations. The contingency could extend to 1996, or expire by 1988 if certain lease renewal conditions are met.

FASB *Interpretation 34* requires that indirect guarantees of indebtedness (such as to advance funds or to cover fixed charges of another entity) be disclosed as contingencies.

Alfa, Inc's, Note 12 (see Appendix 4B, item ⌐100⌐) contains a disclosure of the company's contingent liabilities.

IMPLICATIONS FOR ANALYSIS—ASSESSING UNCERTAINTIES

Due to the uncertainties involved, the descriptions of commitments and especially of contingent liabilities in footnotes are often vague and indeterminate. In effect, that means that the burden of assessing the possible impact of the contingencies as well as the probabilities of their occurrence is passed on to the reader. The analyst should always determine whether the auditors feel that a contingency is serious enough and material enough to call for a qualification in their report. This was the case in the financial statements of Waldbaum, Inc., where the opinion was made subject to the effect on the financial statements of the determination of the company's liability incident to a disastrous fire which involved loss of life of six firemen as well as injuries.

The auditors opinion stated in part:

> As described in Note G (1), the Company, together with certain other parties, is a defendant in a number of lawsuits involving very significant sums arising from a fire in one of the Company's supermarkets. The damages claimed are substantially in excess of the Company's insurance coverage. Special counsel has advised that these cases are still in their preliminary stages and that they cannot express their opinion as to the ultimate outcome of the litigation.
>
> In our opinion, subject to the effect of such adjustments, if any, as might have been required had the outcome of the matter mentioned in the preceding paragraph been known, the financial statements referred to above present fairly.

A situation such as Waldbaum's poses difficult problems of analysis. However, the auditors, have at least unequivocally declared that not only are they unable to assess the ultimate impact of the contingency upon the company's financial position, but that the impact could be material enough to require them to qualify their opinion on the financial statement as a whole.

The analyst must also be alert to *potential* liabilities. Managements may be reluctant to divulge "unasserted claims" and so may their lawyers. In some cases, they may at the time be unknown even to the potential plaintiffs. However, as the case of Westinghouse Electric's uranium supply contracts commitment has shown, potential liabilities have a way of becoming actual liabilities.

While utilizing all the information available, the analyst must bring his own critical evaluation to bear on the assessment of all the contingencies to which the company may be subject. This process must draw not only on available disclosures and information but also on an understanding of industry conditions and practices.

QUESTIONS

1. What are the major disclosure requirements in SEC *FRR,* No. 1, Section 203, regarding the terms of short-term debt?
2. What are the conditions required by *SFAS 6* that will demonstrate the ability of a company to refinance its short-term debt on a long-term basis?
3. How do bond discounts and premiums usually arise? How are they accounted for?
4. Both the conversion feature of debt as well as warrants attached to debt instruments aim at increasing the attractiveness of debt securities and at lowering their interest cost. Describe how the costs of these two similar features are accounted for.
5. Describe the nature of *SFAS 47* and its major disclosure requirements.

6. What should the analyst be aware of if a company includes short-term bank debt in its current liabilities?

7. How does the analyst of financial statements evaluate an enterprise's liabilities—both present and contingent?

8. *a.* What are the criteria, stipulated by *SFAS 13,* for classifying leases by the lessee?

   b. Provide a summary of accounting for leases by lessee according to *SFAS 13.*

9. *a.* What are the different classifications of leases—according to *SFAS 13*—by lessors? What are the criteria for classifying each type?

   b. What are the accounting procedures for leases by lessors according to *SFAS 13?*

10. What are the provisions of *SFAS 13* concerning leases involving real estate?

11. What are the principal disclosures required by lessees and lessors according to *SFAS 13?*

12. What are the implications of *SFAS 13* for the financial analyst?

13. Companies use various financing methods to avoid reporting debt on the balance sheet. What are some of these methods?

14. What liabilities or potential liabilities must the financial analyst recognize with regard to pension plans?

15. Comparisons between unfunded pension liabilities of different companies are difficult for various reasons. Discuss.

16. What types of equity securities are akin to debt? Discuss.

17. Distinguish between different kinds of deferred credits appearing on a balance sheet. How should those be analyzed?

18. Describe the nature of deferred tax credits. How should the analyst interpret this account.

19. Into what types should reserves and provisions be subdivided for purposes of financial statement analysis?

20. Why must the analyst be particularly alert to the accounting for reserves for future costs and losses?

21. *a.* What is a loss contingency? Give some examples.

    b. What two conditions (as specified by *SFAS 5*) must be met before a provision for a loss contingency can be charged to income?

8

Analysis of stockholders' equity

The stockholders' equity section of the balance sheet represents the investment of the ownership in the assets of a business entity. While the claims of the ownership are junior to those in the current and long-term liability sections of the balance sheet, they represent, on the other hand, residual claims to all assets, once the claims of creditors have been satisfied. Thus, while being exposed to the maximum risk associated with the enterprise, the ownership is entitled to all the residual rewards that are associated with it.

The accounting for the equity section as well as the presentation, classification, and footnote disclosure associated therewith have certain basic objectives, the most important among which are:

1. To classify and distinguish the major sources of capital contributed to the entity.
2. To set forth the rights and priorities of the various classes of stockholders and the manner in which they rank in partial or final liquidation.
3. To set forth the legal restrictions to which the distribution of capital funds may be subject for whatever reason.
4. To disclose the contractual, legal, managerial, or financial restrictions to which the distribution of current or retained earnings may be subject.
5. To disclose the terms and provisions of convertible securities, of stock options, and of other arrangements involving the future issuance of stock, contingent and otherwise.

CLASSIFICATION OF CAPITAL STOCK

There are two basic kinds of capital stock—preferred and common. There are a number of different varieties within each category, and these, too, have basic differences worth noting.

218

The preferred stock is usually preferred in liquidation and preferred as to dividends. It may be entitled to par value in liquidation or it may be entitled to a premium. On the other hand, its rights to dividends are generally fixed, although they may be cumulative, which means that preferred shareholders are entitled to arrearages of dividends before the common stockholders may receive any dividends. The preferred features, as well as the fixed nature of the dividend, give the preferred stock some of the earmarks of debt with the important difference that preferred stockholders are not generally entitled to demand redemption of their shares. Nevertheless, there are preferred stock issues that have set redemption dates and that may require sinking funds to be established for that purpose. These are more akin to debt than to equity and are discussed in Chapter 7.

Characteristics of preferred stock that may make them more akin to common stock are dividend participation rights, voting rights, and rights of conversion into common stock.

Within the preferred stock classes we may find a variety of orders of priority and preference relating to dividends and liquidation rights.

The common stock is the basic ownership equity of a compnay having no preference but reaping all residual rewards as well as being subject to all losses. Occasionally, there is more than one class of common stock. In such cases, the distinctions between one class and the other express themselves in dividend, voting, or other rights.

The preferred stock generally has a par value that may or may not be the amount at which it was originally sold. Common stock may have a par value, and if not, it is usually assigned a stated value. The par value of the common stock has no substantive significance for analytical purposes.

Disclosure regarding capital stock

Proper disclosure requires that an analysis and explanation of changes in the number of shares of capital stock be given in the financial statements or in the notes related thereto. Such changes may be due to a variety of reasons including the following:

1. *Increases in capital stock outstanding:*
   a. Sale of stock.
   b. Conversion of debentures or preferred stock.
   c. Issuance pursuant to stock dividends or stock splits.
   d. Issuance of stock in acquisitions or mergers.
   e. Issuance of stock pursuant to stock options granted or warrants exercised.
2. *Decreases in capital stock outstanding:*
   a. Purchase and retirement of stock.
   b. Purchase of treasury stock.
   c. Reverse stock splits.

Another important aspect of disclosure with regard to the various classes of capital stock is the various options held by others which, when exercised, would cause the number of shares outstanding to be increased. Such options include:

1. Conversion rights of debenture or preferred stock into common.
2. Warrants outstanding for a specified period entitling the holder to exchange them for stock under specified conditions.
3. Stock options under supplementary compensation and bonus plans that call for the issuance of capital stock over a period of time at prices fixed in advance, such as qualified stock option plans and "employee stock purchase plans."
4. Commitments to issue capital stock, such as under merger agreements that call for additional consideration contingent on the happening of an event such as the reaching of certain earning levels by the acquired company, etc.

The importance of such disclosures lies in the need to alert all interested parties to the potential increase in the number of shares outstanding. The degree of the resultant dilution in earnings and book value per share depends, of course, on such factors as the amount to be paid in per share and other rights given up when conversions of securities are effected.

Up to the mid-1960s, the accounting profession has almost completely ignored the effect that potential dilution has on such basic valuation yardsticks as earnings per share (EPS) and, to a lesser extent, book value per share. More recently, alerted by the use of even more complex securities, the profession has finally recognized that dilution represents a very real cost to a company, a cost that had been given little if any formal recognition in financial statements. The impact of dilution on EPS will be examined in Chapter 12. Problems in the computation of book value are examined at the end of this chapter.

Disclosure must be made of a variety of terms to which preferred stock may be subject, including:

1. *Dividend rights,* including participating and cumulative features.
2. *Liquidation rights.* In *APB Opinion 10* the board stated:

> Companies at times issue preferred (or other senior) stock which has a preference in involuntary liquidation considerably in excess of the par or stated value of the shares. The relationship between this preference in liquidation and the par or stated value of the shares may be of major significance to the users of the financial statements of those companies and the Board believes it highly desirable that it be prominently disclosed. Accordingly, the Board recommends that in these cases, the liquidation preference of the stock be disclosed in the equity section of the balance sheet in the aggregate, either parenthetically or "in short" rather than on a per share basis or by disclosure in notes.

Such disclosure is particularly important since the discrepancy between the par and liquidation value of preferred stock can be very significant as is the case, for example, in General Aniline & Film Corporation where at one point in time the par value was $3.9 million as against a liquidation value of $85.7 million!

3. *Redemption rights. SFAS 47* requires disclosure of mandatory redemption requirements of redeemable preferred stock. In FRR No. 1 Sec. 211, the SEC requires separate balance sheet presentation of such shares. Because such shares have the characteristics of liabilities, they are considered in Chapter 7.

4. *Voting rights,* which may change with conditions such as arrearages in dividends.

5. *Conversion rights.*

6. *Sinking fund provisions,* which are not too common.

7. *Call provisions,* which usually protect the preferred stockholder against premature redemption. Call premiums often decrease over time.

In addition to a description of terms, disclosure must be made of any conditions affecting the relative standing of the various classes of stock such as, for example, dividend arrearages on preferred stock, which must generally be paid before the common stock can get any distribution at all.

Alfa, Inc. (see Appendix 4B), discloses the involuntary liquidation value of its two preferred stock issues in the equity section of the balance sheet. Note 9 discloses changes in capital stock accounts as well as shares of common stock reserved for various purposes.

Additional capital

Amounts paid in for capital stock are usually divided into two parts. One part is assigned to the par or stated value of capital shares, and the rest is shown in the capital surplus section. The term *surplus* is actually falling into disuse so that the additional capital section contains accounts having such descriptive titles as Capital in Excess of Par or Stated Value, Additional Capital, Additional Paid-In Capital, and Paid-In Capital. No matter what the title, these accounts signify the amounts paid in for capital stock in excess of par or stated value.

The additional accounts in the "capital" group do not result only from amounts paid in excess of par but include also charges or credits from a variety of other capital transactions, examples of which are:

1. Gains or losses from sale of treasury stock.
2. Capital changes arising from business combinations.
3. Capital donations, usually shown separately as donated capital.
4. Capital stock expenses, merger expenses, and other costs of a capital nature.
5. Capitalization of retained earnings by means of stock dividends.

Informative financial statements must contain a reconciliation of all capital surplus accounts so as to explain the changes which have occurred therein.

Treasury stock

Treasury stock is stock that has once been issued and was outstanding and that has been subsequently reacquired by the company. Treasury stock is generally carried at cost, and the most common method of presentation is to deduct such cost from the total equity section. Some companies that reserve their own treasury stock for such purposes as profit sharing, contingent compensation, deferred compensation, or other compensation plans, or for purposes of acquisitions of other companies do sometimes present such stock among assets which, while not a very logical procedure, is nevertheless acceptable.

RETAINED EARNINGS

While the capital stock and capital surplus accounts show primarily the capital contribution by various classes of stock, the Retained Earnings account represents generally the accumulation of undistributed earnings since inception. Conversely, a deficit account represents the accumulated net losses of the corporation.

Although some states permit distributions to shareholders from capital surplus accounts, such distributions represent, in effect, capital distributions. Thus, the Retained Earnings account is the prime source of dividend distributions to shareholders, and amounts distributed by charge to other accounts do not, strictly speaking, deserve the label *dividend.*

Dividends

The most common form of dividend is the cash dividend that once declared becomes a liability of the company. Another form of dividend is the dividend in kind, such as dividends in goods (e.g., cases of liquor) or dividends in the stock of another corporation. Such dividends should be valued at the fair market value of the assets distributed.

American Express provides an example of questionable accounting treatment for dividends in kind. In prior years, the company acquired shares in a brokerage firm. At the time, it distributed these shares to stockholders in 1975 as a dividend; it carried them at a cost of $26.8 million. However, the market value of the shares at the time of distribution was only $6.2 million; and by calling it a $26.8 million dividend (the amount charged to retained earnings), the company avoided charging a $20 million dollar loss to income.

Yet another form of dividend is the stock dividend that, in effect, represents the permanent capitalization of company earnings. As evidence of such a shift from retained earnings to the permanent capital accounts, shareholders receive additional shares. GAAP require that the stock dividends be valued at the fair market value of the shares to be issued as determined at the date of declaration. This principle is designed to put a realistic limit to the number of shares that can be issued as stock dividends. A stock distribution exceeding 20–25 percent is no longer to be accounted as a stock dividend and should instead be accounted for as a stock split. The latter represents, in essence, the subdivision of the net corporate pie into smaller shares.

Prior period adjustments

SFAS 16 requires that except for corrections of errors in the financial statements of a prior period and adjustments that result from realization of income tax benefits of preacquisition operating loss carry-forwards of purchased subsidiaries, all items of profit and loss recognized during a period, including accruals of estimated losses from loss contingencies, be included in the determination of net income for that period. The *Statement* permits limited restatements in interim periods of an enterprise's current fiscal year.

In addition to dividends and prior year adjustments, changes in retained earnings may include adjustments due to business combinations and other capital adjustments such as premiums on redemption of preferred stock, losses on sales of treasury stock, and so forth.

Appropriations of retained earnings

By managerial action, or in compliance with legal requirements, retained earnings are often appropriated or reserved.

Appropriated retained earnings, also known as reserves, established by managerial action include reserves for general contingencies, plant expansion, self-insurance, and other business contingencies. The basic idea here is to preserve a specific amount of capital that is available for absorption of possible losses or is frozen to provide permanent funds, such as for expansion. Thus, such appropriations should never be used to relieve the income statement of charges that are properly chargeable against it. After having served their purpose, such appropriations should be restored to unappropriated retained earnings.

Appropriations of retained earnings in an amount equal to the cost of treasury stock purchased is an example of appropriations established under the legal requirements of certain states. Such appropriations are restored to retained earnings after the treasury stock is sold, retired, or otherwise disposed of.

Restrictions on retained earnings

An important aspect of disclosure relating to retained earnings involves restrictions imposed on its distribution as dividends. This is, obviously, information of importance to potential investors and others. Examples of such restrictions which stem from debt indentures are:

Interlake

Note 5: Retained earnings. Under the most restrictive terms of the Company's various loan agreements, the Company could not as of December 28, 1980 pay cash dividends or repurchase the Company's capital stock in amounts aggregating more than $60,450,000.

Amax, Inc.

Note 19: Retained earnings. At December 31, 1980, under the most restrictive of the agreements entered into in connection with the notes and debentures payable (which also impose restrictions based on earnings and working capital), approximately $786 million of retained earnings was available for the payment of cash dividends. Retained earnings at December 31, 1980, included $169 million of undistributed earnings of affiliates accounted for by the equity method.

Alfa, Inc. (see Appendix 4B), discloses in the equity section of the balance sheet that of $215 million in retained earnings only $31 million is available for dividends.

BOOK VALUE PER SHARE

The term *book value* is conventional terminology referring to net asset value, that is, total assets reduced by the senior claims against them. Thus, the book value of the common stock equity is equal to the total assets less liabilities and claims of securities senior to the common stock, such as preferred stock, mostly at amounts at which they are carried on the financial statements but also unbooked claims of the senior securities. A simple way of computing book value is to add up the common stock equity accounts and reduce the total by any senior claims not reflected in the financial statements such as preferred stock dividend arrearages, liquidation premiums, or other asset preferences to which the preferred shares are entitled.

Book value is almost always presented on a per share basis (the significance of this figure will be considered later in the chapter). Once the underlying principles of computation are understood, the calculation of book value is relatively simple.

ILLUSTRATION 1. The following is the equity section of the Zero Corporation for years ended in 19x4 and 19x5:

	19x5	19x4
Preferred stock, 7% cumulative, par value $100 (authorized 4,000,000 shares; outstanding 3,602,811 shares)	$ 360,281,100	$ 360,281,100

Common stock (authorized
   90,000,000 shares; outstanding
   54,138,137 shares at December
   31, 19x5, and 54,129,987 shares
   at December 31, 19x4)...........   3,264,581,527   3,122,464,738

Common stock (authorized 90,000,000 shares; outstanding 54,138,137 shares at December 31, 19x5, and 54,129,987 shares at December 31, 19x4)		3,264,581,527	3,122,464,738
Par value $16⅔ per share	$ 902,302,283		
Income reinvested in business	2,362,279,244		
Total		3,624,862,627	3,482,745,838

The preferred shares are nonparticipating but are callable at 105. Dividends for 19x5 are in arrears.

Required:

Calculate the book value per share of both the common and preferred stock as of December 31, 19x5.

Computations

	Preferred	+	Common	=	Total
Preferred stock* (@ $100)	$360,281,100				$ 360,281,100
Dividends in arrears (7%)	25,219,677				25,219,677
Common stock			$ 902,302,283		902,302,283
Reatined earnings (net of amount attributed to dividend in arrears).........			2,337,059,567		2,337,059,567
Total	385,500,777		3,239,361,850		$3,624,862,627
Divided by number of shares outstanding..........	3,602,811		54,138,137		
Book value per share	$107.00		$59.84		

* The call premium does not normally enter into the computation of book value per share because the call provision is at the option of company.

ILLUSTRATION 2. The following is the stockholders' equity section of the balance sheet of the XYZ Company on June 30, 19x1:

Preferred stock—authorized 200,000 shares, issued and out- standing 100,000 shares, par value $100, 6% cumulative, nonparticipating	$10,000,000
Common stock—authorized 375,000 shares, issued and out- standing 200,000 shares, par value $100	20,000,000
Capital contributed in excess of par value	5,000,000
Retained earnings (deficit)	(7,000,000)
Total stockholders' equity	$28,000,000

The preferred shares have a liquidation value of $105 and are callable at $110. No dividends have been declared or paid by the company for either the preferred or common shares for two years. Assume that the preferred stock has a preference on assets in liquidation.

Required:

Compute the book value (equity) per share of all classes of stock as of June 30, 19x1.

Computations

	Preferred	*Common*
Par value	$10,500,000	$20,000,000
Dividends in arrears	1,200,000	
Net deficit (all applicable to common stock)		(3,700,000)
Total	11,700,000	16,300,000
Divided by number of shares outstanding	100,000	200,000
Book value (equity) per share	$117.00	$81.50

Explanations:
1. Liquidation value for preferred shares ($105) is used; call value does not enter into the computation of book value per share.
2. Preferred shares are entitled to two years' dividends (12% of $10,000,000 = $1,200,000).
3. Preference of assets for preferred shares means that the deficit is wholly applicable to the common.
4. Computation of net deficit:

Retained earnings (deficit)	$(7,000,000)
Paid-in capital	5,000,000
Dividends in arrears	(1,200,000)
Preferred liquidation premium	(500,000)
Net deficit	$(3,700,000)

As can be seen from the above illustrations, the major adjustments in book value per share computations arise from rights and priorities of securities that are senior to the common. In most cases, these are premiums and liquidation priority rights of a variety of classes of preferred stock.

Care must be taken to determine the liquidation value of preferred stock. Some companies have preferred stock issues outstanding that give the right to very substantial liquidation premiums that are far above the par value of such shares. The effect of such liquidation premiums on the book value of the common and other junior equities can be substantial.

ILLUSTRATION 3. In a listing application (A-25189) of Glen Alden Corporation appear the following details of book value computation:

Equity per share:
Equity per share of Glen Alden, Warner, and the Surviving Corporation, based on the initial redemption values of the preferred stocks and on the consolidated balance sheets of Glen Alden and Warner at December 31 and August 27, 1966, respectively, and the pro forma combined balance sheet follows:

Initial redemption per share values	Preferred stocks	Glen Alden December 31, 1966	Warner, August 27, 1966	Pro forma surviving corporation
$ 52.50	Senior stock	$52.50		$ 52.50
$107.00	Class B senior stock			$100.70
$110.00	Preferred stock	$88.89		None
$90.00	Class stock	$72.73		None
None	Common stock	None	$19.51	None

Based on the pro forma combined balance sheet, there would be no book value attributable to the preferred stock, class C stock, and common stock of the Surviving Corporation when the equity applicable to the senior stock and the class B senior stock is considered at aggregate initial redemption value. The aggregate initial redemption value of the senior stock and class B senior stock exceeds total pro forma stockholders' equity by approximately $141,816,000.

The pro forma initial redemption and liquidation prices of the preferred stocks in the aggregate ($343.821,848) exceed their stated values by $296,179,211, and such excess exceeds the aggregate amount of common stock and surplus by approximately $141,816,000. Upon liquidation, the senior stock is first in order of preference, followed by the class B senior stock. The preferred stock and class C stock are junior to the class B senior stock, but rank on a parity with each other. There are no restrictions upon surplus arising out of such excess.

As the above example shows, the liquidation premium of the senior stocks is of such magnitude as to wipe out the entire residual book value of the junior preferred and common stock issues.

The accounting profession has, in *APB Opinion 10,* recognized the problem posed by preference rights in involuntary liquidation that are substantially in excess of stated par values. Thus, the *Opinion* recommends that the aggregate liquidation preference be prominently disclosed in the equity section of the balance sheet. The *Opinion* also calls for disclosure of call prices and dividend arrearages.

Judging by actual practice, the rules involving "common stock equivalents" that govern the computation of EPS (see Chapter 12) do not seem to apply to the computation of book value per share. Nevertheless, a case can be made for extending the EPS rules to book value computations. The recent merger movement has given rise to increasingly complex securities, and there is not much justification for ignoring these in book value computations.

ILLUSTRATION 4. Company A has the following simplified balance sheet:

Assets less current liabilities	$1,000,000
Convertible debentures	100,000
Net assets	$ 900,000
Common shares	100,000

The debentures are convertible into 20,000 shares of common stock.

The company also has warrants outstanding entitling the holder to buy 10,000 shares at $6 per share. Stock options to buy 10,000 shares at an average price of $8 per share are also outstanding.

The conventional method of book value calculations would yield a book value per share of $9 (net assets/common shares = $900,000/100,000).

Giving effect to posssible conversions, the book value computation will look as follows:

Net assets (as above)	$ 900,000
Add convertible debentures	100,000
Proceeds from exercise of warrants (10,000 × $6)	60,000
Proceeds from exercise of stock options (10,000 × $8)	80,000
Adjusted net asset value	$1,140,000
Common shares outstanding	100,000
Add:	
Conversion of debentures	20,000
Exercise of warrants	10,000
Exercise of options	10,000
Adjusted number of common shares	140,000
Book value per share ($1,140,000/140,000)	$8.14

Clearly, the effect of conversions of debentures, options, and so forth, on book value depends on the conversion terms. If stock is converted at prices below conventional book value per share, the effect is, as in the above example, dilutive. Conversely, if the conversion is at prices above conventional book value, the effect will be antidilutive. Applying the conservative principles that have been devised by the accounting profession for the computation of EPS (see Chapter 12), antidilutive effects (i.e., those which enhance book value per share) would not be allowed to enter the computations.

Significance of book value

Once an important variable in investment decision making, book value has gradually dwindled in importance. The basic reason for this is that investment analysis generally emphasizes earning power and not asset size. Thus, the value of a company's securities is based primarily on the earning capacity of its asset base rather than on its size.

There are, of course, exceptions to this generalization, and they account for the continued use of the book value per share statistic:

1. Book value, properly adjusted, is often used in an assessment of merger terms.
2. Due to the fact that the rate base of public utilities often approximates its book value, this measure is important in this industry.
3. The analysis of companies that have mostly liquid assets such as those

in the finance, investment, insurance, and banking fields, rightfully affords greater than usual importance to book values.

4. The analyst of high-grade bonds and preferred stock usually attaches considerable importance to asset coverage in addition to earning capacity.

There are, of course, other factors that make net assets a measure of some importance in financial analysis. A company's earnings growth is sooner or later dependent on growth in assets and, consequently, on a choice of how to finance them. A large asset base has, depending on its composition, a certain potential of profitable utilization.

The accounting considerations that enter into computation of book value should be thoroughly understood by any user of this statistic:

1. The carrying values of assets, particularly long-lived assets such as plant and equipment, long-term investments, and some inventories, is usually at cost and may differ significantly from current market values.[1] Moreover, such carrying values will, as was seen in the preceding chapters, vary according to the accounting principles selected. Thus, for instance, in times of rising prices, the carrying value of inventories under the LIFO method of inventory accounting will be lower than under the FIFO method.

2. Intangible assets of great value may not be reflected in book value nor are contingent liabilities, which may have a high probability of occurrence, usually so reflected.

The decline in the use of book value may be due to a lack of usefulness of this measure. It is, undoubtedly also due to the very crude approaches taken in its reporting and application. Thus, for example, the blanket exclusion from book value of goodwill, patents, franchises, and other intangibles cannot make up for the lack of the analysis required to adopt this measure to the particular objective it is designed to meet. Either book value is computed on a "current value" basis or on a cost basis. In the latter case, the arbitrary exclusion of intangible assets makes no sense. If, for example, book value is to be used in comparing the relative value of two companies engaged in merger negotiations, adjustments, such as the following, may be required so that an intelligent comparison can be made:

1. The carrying value of assets should be adjusted to current market values.
2. Differences in the application of accounting principles should be adjusted for.
3. Unrecorded intangibles should be given recognition.
4. Contingent liabilities should be assessed and given appropriate recognition.
5. Accounting and other errors should be adjusted on the books of both companies.

---

[1] The disclosure requirements of *SFAS 33* of the current cost of certain assets of specified companies (see Chapter 14) may be helpful in arriving at more realistic book value figures.

Other adjustments may also be called for. Thus, if the preferred stock has the characteristics of debt, it may be appropriate to capitalize it at the prevailing interest rate, thus reflecting the benefit or disadvantage of it to the company.

The emphasis of earning power has, as was discussed above, resulted in a deemphasis of asset size. Sterile or unproductive assets are worse than worthless. They are often a drag on earnings because they require a minimum of upkeep and management expenses. Like any other analytical tools, book value is a measure that can be useful for certain purposes provided it is used with discrimination and understanding.

IMPLICATIONS FOR ANALYSIS

The accounting principles that apply to the equity section do not have a marked effect on income determination and, as a consequence, do not hold many pitfalls for the analyst. From an analytical point of view, the most significant information here relates to the composition of the capital accounts and to the restrictions to which they may be subject. It is important that the analyst know how to reconstruct and to explain changes in the capital accounts.

The composition of the equity capital is important because of provisions affecting the residual rights of the common equity. Such provisions include dividend participation rights, conversion rights, and the great variety of options and conditions that are characteristic of the complex securities frequently issued under merger agreements, most of which tend to dilute the common equity.

An analysis of restrictions imposed on the distribution of retained earnings by loan or other agreements will usually shed light on a company's freedom of action in such areas as dividend distributions, required levels of working capital. Such restrictions also shed light on the company's bargaining strength and standing in credit markets. Moreover, a careful reading of restrictive covenants will also enable the analyst to assess how far a company is from being in default of these provisions.

QUESTIONS

1. What are the objectives of the classifications and the footnote disclosure associated with the equity section of the corporate balance sheet? Of what significance are such disclosures to readers of financial statements?

2. What features of a preferred stock issue make it akin to debt? What features make it more like common stock?

3. Why is it important from the point of view of the analyst of financial statements that the liquidation value of preferred stock, if different from par or stated value, be clearly disclosed?

4. Presidential Realty Corporation reported as follows on distributions paid on common stock:

   "The cash distributions on common stock were charged to paid-in surplus because the parent company has accumulated no earnings (other than its equity in undistributed earnings of certain subsidiaries) since its formation.

   a. Are these cash distributions dividends?

   b. Why do you suppose did this realty company make such distributions?

5. Why does the proper accounting for stock dividends require that the fair market value, rather than the par value, of the shares distributed be charged against retained earnings?

6. What items of gain or loss may be treated as prior period adjustments?

7. Some companies present "minority interests in subsidiary companies" between the long-term debt and the equity sections of the consolidated balance sheet; others present them as part of equity capital.

   a. What is a "minority interest"? (Refer to Chapter 9).

   b. Where on the consolidated balance sheet does it belong? What different points of view do these differing presentations represent?

8. What is book value per share? How is it computed? What is its significance? (CFA)

9. Why has the use of the book value per share declined in relative importance over the past decades? What valid uses of book value are still made today?

10. What are some of the accounting considerations that enter into the computation of book value and about which the analyst should be aware?

11. What adjustments may be necessary to render the book value per share measure comparable as between two enterprises?

9
Intercorporate investments, business combinations, and foreign operations

In this chapter, we shall examine the analytical implications of a number of specialized topics in accounting, most of which straddle the areas of asset, liability, and income measurements and are thus discussed best in their entirety and in a separate and distinct fashion.

INTERCORPORATE INVESTMENTS

When one corporation owns all or a majority of the voting equity securities of another corporation, a parent-subsidiary relationship is said to exist. The reasons why one compnay may form or buy control of another entity are many and include sources of supply, enlargement of market coverage, entrance into new lines of business, taxes, reduction of risk because of limited liability, and the requirements of government regulation.

There are three basic methods by which a parent company can account for its ownership in a subsidiary. These are:

1. Consolidated financial statements.
2. Equity method.
3. Cost method.

We shall examine these hereunder in this order, which is the order of their preference from an accounting theory standpoint. This order of preference coincides also with that from the point of view of the financial analyst since, as we will see from the discussion that follows, the methods differ significantly in the amount of information they provide the analyst about the financial condition and results of operations of the combined parent-subsidiary entity.

Consolidated financial statements

On the parent company's financial statements, the ownership of stock in a subsidiary is evidenced by an investment account. From a legal point of view, the parent company owns the stock of its subsidiary; it does not own the subsidiary's assets nor is it normally responsible for the subsidiary's debts, although it frequently guarantees them. Consolidated financial statements disregard the legality of this situation in favor of its business substance and reflect the economic reality of a business entity under centralized control. There is a presumption that in most cases, consolidated financial statements are more meaningful than separate financial statements and that they are required for fair presentation of financial conditions and results of operations.

Basic technique of consolidation. Consolidated financial statements combine the assets, liabilities, revenues, and expenses of subsidiaries with the corresponding items in the financial statements of the parent company. To the extent that the parent does not own 100 percent of a subsidiary's equity securities, the minority interest of outsiders is recognized in the consolidation. Intercompany items are eliminated in order to avoid double counting and the premature recognition of income.

ILLUSTRATION 1.   Exhibit 9–1 presents the simplified balance sheet of Company P (the parent) at the time of its acquisition of Company S (the subsidiary). The assets and liabilities included in the balance sheet of Company S are already stated in terms of their fair market values at the time of acquisition. Company P paid $78,000 for 90 percent of Company S's common stock. Accounts receivable of Company P include $4,000 owed it by Company S.

The adjustments in the worksheet that combine the two companies are as follows:

a.   The investment at acquisition is eliminated against 90 percent of the equity (capital stock plus retained earnings) of Company S. The remaining 10 percent of Company S's equity belongs to outside stockholders and is shown as "minority interest" in the consolidated balance sheet. The amount of $6,000 that Company P paid in excess of the fair value of 90 percent of the tangible net assets of Company S is carried as "goodwill" in the consolidated balance sheet. The method of determination of goodwill will be discussed later in this chapter under "Purchase accounting."

b.   The accounts receivable of Company P and the corresponding payable of company S are eliminated in consolidation.

Under the consolidation method, the income statement of Company S will be combined with that of Company P, and the 10 percent share of the minority interest in the net income or loss of Company S for the period will be deducted from the consolidated income (or loss) and added to the minority's interest in order to show the consolidated net results of operations of the group.

Exhibit 9–1

COMPANY P AND COMPANY S
Consolidated Balance Sheet Worksheet
Date of Acquisition

	Company P	Company S	Adjustments and Eliminations Dr. (Cr.)	Minority Interest	Con-soli-dated
Assets					
Cash	16,000	11,000			27,000
Accounts receivable	32,000	19,000	*(b)* (4,000)		47,000
Inventories	42,000	18,000			60,000
Fixed assets	64,000	42,000			106,000
Investment in Company S: Fair value at acquisition	72,000	—	*(a)* (72,000)		—
Excess of cost over fair value (good will)	6,000	—			6,000
Total assets	232,000	90,000			246,000
Liabilities and Equity					
Accounts payable	12,000	10,000	*(b)* 4,000		18,000
Capital stock: Company P	120,000				120,000
Company S		50,000	*(a)* 45,000	5,000	
Retained earnings: Company P	100,000				100,000
Company S		30,000	*(a)* 27,000	3,000	
Minority interest					8,000
Total liabilities and equity	232,000	90,000			246,000

In consolidating the income statement of subsidiary Company S with parent Company P, intercompany profits on sales of inventories that remain within the consolidated group at year-end and intercompany profits on other assets, such as fixed assets, must be eliminated. This is so because the equity interest in the earnings of a consolidated entity relate to earnings with parties *outside* the group. Transactions among members within the group result in the profit being considered as unrealized.

Principles governing consolidation policy. There is a general presumption that consolidated statements are more meaningful than separate parent and subsidiary statements. Consequently, consolidation is the preferred method of presenting the financial statements of a parent and its subsidiaries. There are, however, a number of reasons why a subsidiary should not be consolidated. They are:

1. *Incomplete or temporary control.*   In general, in order to consolidate a subsidiary, a parent should have ownership or effective management control over the subsidiary. Thus, ownership of over 50 percent of the voting stock is generally required for consolidation, and consolidation is inappropriate where the control is temporary or where it will be disposed of or otherwise lost in the near future.

2. *Lack of homogeneity.*   The concept of what constitutes a homogenous unit has undergone considerable change over the years. More recently, corporate diversification has led to the creation of conglomerates that have interests in many different types of industries and activities. Generally speaking, a mere difference in the nature of business is not sufficient reason to bar consolidation. Nevertheless, certain businesses are so different in nature that consolidation is considered by some as misleading. Thus, credit or financial subsidiaries of industrial parents are mostly omitted from consolidation.

In amendments to its regulations, the SEC increased the number of situations where seprate financial statements must be submitted for consolidated subsidiaries engaged in financial activities (e.g., life, casualty and fire insurance, securities broker dealers, finance savings and loan, or banking).

3. *Uncertainty as to income.*   Where there is reason for serious doubt whether an increase in equity in a subsidiary has really accrued to the parent, consolidation is not appropriate. Such doubt can occur particularly in the case of foreign subsidiaries when there are restrictions on the conversion of foreign currencies or on the remittance of foreign earnings.

The need to consolidate leasing subsidiaries.   *APB Opinion 18* and *SFAS 13* reaffirm the requirement that subsidiaries whose principal business activity consists of leasing property or facilities to their parents or other affiliates be consolidated with such parents. The reason for this requirement is the significance of the assets and liabilities of such subsidiaries to the consolidated financial position of the entire group.

The equity method

The equity method should be used in consolidated financial statements for investments in common stock of all unconsolidated subsidiaries (foreign or domestic) where for reasons, such as those discussed above, consolidation is not appropriate. Under *APB Opinion 18,* the equity method is not a valid substitute for consolidation and should not be used to justify exclusion of a subsidiary when consolidation is otherwise appropriate.

The difference between consolidation and the equity method lies in the details reported in the financial statements. Under the equity method, the parent's share of the subsidiary results are presented in its income statement as a line item, and this has resulted in the equity method being also referred to as "one line consolidation."

As we saw in the discussion of the accounting for intercorporate investments in Chapter 6, the equity method of accounting should, generally, be used for investments in common stock that represent interests 20 percent or over in the voting stock of a company's equity securities, and it may be appropriate in some cases even for investments representing an interest of less than 20 percent.

Recognizing the wide application of the equity method to investments in subsidiaries, to investments in corporate joint ventures, as well as to investments in less than majority owned investees, *APB Opinion 18* listed a number of procedures that should be followed in applying this method:

1. Intercompany profits and losses should be eliminated until realized by the investor or investee as if a subsidiary, corporate joint venture, or investee company were consolidated.
2. A difference between the cost of an investment and the amount of underlying equity in net assets of an investee should be accounted for as if the investee were a consolidated subsidiary. (*APB Opinion 17* requires amortization of goodwill over a term not exceeding 40 years.)
3. The investment(s) in common stock should be shown in the balance sheet of an investor as a single amount, and the investor's share of earnings or losses of an investee(s) should ordinarily be shown in the income statement as a single amount except for the extraordinary items and prior period adjustments that should be separately classified in the income statement of the investor.
4. A transaction of an investee of a capital nature that affects the investor's share of stockholders' equity of the investee should be accounted for as if the investee were a consolidated subsidiary.
5. Sales of stock of an investee by an investor should be accounted for as gains or losses equal to the difference at the time of sale between selling price and carrying amount of the stock sold.
6. If financial statements of an investee are not sufficiently timely for an investor to apply the equity method currently, the investor ordinarily should record its share of the earnings or losses of an investee from the most recent available financial statements. A lag in reporting should be consistent from period to period.
7. A loss in value of an investment that is other than a temporary decline should be recognized the same as a loss in value of other long-term assets. Evidence of a loss in value might include inability to recover the carrying amount of investment, decline in market value, etc. All relevant factors must be evaluated.
8. The investor ordinarily should discontinue applying the equity method when the investment (and net advances) is reduced to zero and should not provide for additional losses unless the investor has guaranteed

obligations of the investee or is otherwise committed to provide further financial support for the investee. If the investee subsequently reports net income, the investor should resume applying the equity method only after its share of that net income equals the share of net losses not recognized during the period the equity method was suspended.

9. When an investee has outstanding cumulative preferred stock, an investor should compute its share of earnings (losses) after deducting the investee's preferred dividends, whether or not such dividends are declared.

10. The carrying amount of an investment in common stock of an investee that qualifies for the equity method of accounting as described above may differ from the underlying equity in net assets of the investee. The difference should affect the determination of the amount of the investor's share of earnings or losses of an investee as if the investee were a consolidated subsidiary. However, if the investor is unable to relate the difference to specific accounts of the investee, the difference should be considered to be goodwill and amortized over a period not to exceed 40 years, in accordance with *APB Opinion 17.*

The cost method

Under the prevailing system of accrual accounting, the cost method is the method least preferred among the three alternative ways of presenting investments in subsidiaries. Under this method, the investment in a subsidiary is recorded at cost and income is recognized only as it is received in the form of dividend distributions. A permanent impairment in the value of the investment, due to losses or other causes, should be recognized by a write-down of the investment.

The use of the cost method is now restricted to cases where there is considerable doubt that the equity in the earning of a subsidiary is effectively accruing to the benefit of the parent. Such cases include foreign subsidiaries that operate under conditions of exchange restrictions, controls, or other uncertainties of a type that casts doubt on the parent's ability to achieve an ultimate realization of these earnings.

Example of difference in income recognition—equity versus cost method

On January 1, 19x1, Company P acquired 80 percent of Company S for $900,000. The net assets of Company S at date of acquisition were $1,000,000.

During 19x1, Company S earned $100,000 and paid $40,000 in dividends, while in 19x2 it lost $20,000 and paid a dividend of $30,000. Exhibit 9–2 contrasts the accounting by Company P for the investment in Company S and the income derived from it under (1) the cost method and (2) the equity method:

Exhibit 9–2: Cost and equity methods of accounting for investment in subsidiary

	Cost method		Equity method	
	Invest- ment	Income (loss)	Invest- ment	Income (loss)
Cost acquisition	$900,000		$900,000	
Earnings for 19x1			80,000	$ 80,000 [a]
Amortization of goodwill			(2,500)	(2,500) [b]
Dividends—19x1		$32,000 [c]	(32,000)	
Earnings pickup— 19x1		$32,000		$ 77,500
Loss for 19x2			(16,000)	$(16,000) [d]
Amortization of goodwill			(2,500)	(2,500) [b]
Dividends—19x2		$24,000 [e]	(24,000)	
Earnings (loss) pickup—19x2		$24,000		$(18,500)
Investment at December 31, 19x2	$900,000		$903,000	

[a] 80% equity in earnings of $100,000.
[b] Cost of 80% interest in Company S $900,000
   80% of net assets ($1,000,000—assumed to represent fair market value)   800,000
   Excess of cost over net assets (goodwill)   100,000
   Yearly amortization (40-year basis) . . . . $ 2,500
[c] 80% of $40,000.
[d] 80% of $20,000.
[e] 80% of $30,000.

The disparity in the amount of income reported by the parent under the two methods is readily apparent. Under the cost method, the income pickup bears no relationship to actual results achieved during the period but is, instead, dependent on the amount of dividend distributions, a factor over which the parent has control.

The amount at which the investment is carried on the books of the parent company also varies considerably among these two methods. Under the cost method, the investment account remains unchanged (except in the case of losses that lead to a permanent impairment in value), while under the equity method the investment account reflects the parent company's equity in the underlying net assets of the subsidiary. Goodwill should, however, be amortized also under the cost method.[1]

---

[1] The goodwill element can, of course, also be present in an investment account of an unconsolidated subsidiary.

Intercorporate investments—less than majority ownership

Investments by one company in less than the majority of the voting security of another enterprise and investments in joint ventures are discussed in Chapter 6.

Implications for analysis

From the analyst's point of view, the financial reporting of intercorporate investments has undergone consistent improvement. This improvement is due in large measure to the sharp restrictions that are now placed on the use of the cost method of accounting.

Under the cost method, dividends remitted, rather than income earned, are the basis on which a parent company recognizes the earnings accruing from an investment in a subsidiary. The obvious disadvantage of the cost method is that the cost basis does not reflect the results of operations of the subsidiary and lends itself to income manipulation. Thus, dividends included in the parent company's income may be unrelated to the subsidiary's earnings, and losses of the subsidiary may go unreported for a number of periods. The trend in earnings can be completely distorted by use of the cost method.

Validity of taking up earnings. Consolidation and the equity method are based on the assumption that a dollar earned by a subsidiary is equal to a dollar's worth of parent company earnings. Even disregarding the possible tax liability that the parent company may incur on the remittance of earnings by the subsidiary, this dollar-for-dollar equivalence in earnings cannot be taken for granted. The following are some possible reasons for this:

1. The subsidiary may be under the supervision of a regulatory authority that can intervene in dividend policy.
2. The subsidiary may operate in a foreign country where there exist restrictions on the remittance of earnings abroad and/or where the value of the currency can deteriorate rapidly. Furthermore, changes in political climate may result in hampering the subsidiary's operations.
3. Dividend restrictions in loan agreements may become effective.
4. The presence of a stable or powerful minority interest may reduce the parent's discretion in setting dividend and other policy.

While considerations such as the above should govern the independent accountant's decision on whether or not to use the cost method, the analyst should, as a check on that judgment, form his own opinion in each given situation on whether a dollar earned by a subsidiary can indeed be considered the equivalent of a dollar earned by the parent company.

There are other problems in the analysis of consolidated financial statements or investments in subsidiaries carried at equity that the financial analyst must consider carefully.

Provision for taxes on undistributed earnings of subsidiaries. *APB Opinion 23,* "Accounting for Income Taxes—Special Areas," concluded that including undistributed earnings of a subsidiary in the pretax accounting income of a parent company, either through consolidation or accounting for the investment by the equity method, may or may not require a concurrent provision for taxes depending on the actions and intent of the parent company.

The Board believes that it should be presumed that all undistributed earnings will be transferred to the parent and that a provision for taxes should be made by assuming that the unremitted earnings were distributed to the parent in the current period and that the taxes provision is based on a computation benefiting from all the tax-planning alternatives to which the company may be entitled.

The foregoing presumption can be overcome if persuasive evidence exists that the subsidiary has or will invest the undistributed earnings permanently or that the earnings will be remitted in a tax-free liquidation.

The analyst should be aware that the decision of whether taxes on undistributed earnings should or should not be provided is, in effect, left largely to management. However, the amount of earnings on which no income taxes were provided by the parent must be disclosed.

In contrast, ownership in an investee (20 percent to 50 percent owned) calls for provision of taxes on equity in earnings because a presumption of an ability to reinvest earnings is assumed not to exist.

Debt shown in consolidated financial statements. Liabilities shown in the consolidated financial statements do not operate as a lien upon a common pool of assets. The creditors, be they secured or unsecured, have recourse in the event of default only to assets owned by the individual corporation that incurred this liability. If, on the other hand, a parent company guarantees a specific liability of a subsidiary, then the creditor would, of course, have the guarantee as additional security.

The consolidated balance sheet obscures rather than clarifies the margin of safety enjoyed by specific creditors. To gain full comprehension of the financial position of each part of the consolidated group, the analyst needs also examine the individual financial statements of each subsidiary. Legal constraints are not always effective limits to liability. Thus, American Express made good on obligations of a warehousing subsidiary not because it was legally obliged to do so but because of concern for its own financial reputation.

Additional limitations of consolidated financial statements. Consolidated financial statements generally represent the most meaningful presentation of the financial condition and the results of operations of a group. However, they do have limitations in addition to those discussed above:

1. The financial statements of the individual companies in the group may not be prepared on a comparable basis. Accounting principles applied and valuation bases and amortization rates used may differ, thus destroy-

ing homogeneity and the validity of ratios, trends, and relationships. Year-end dates of individual members of a group can vary by as much as 90 days.

2. Consolidated financial statements do not show the restrictions on the use of cash of individual companies. Nor do they show intercompany cash flows or the restrictions placed on such flows, thus obscuring the relationship between the liquidity of assets and the liabilities that they may be available to meet.

3. Companies in relatively poor financial condition may be combined with sound companies, thus obscuring information necessary for analysis.

4. The extent of intercompany transactions is unknown unless *consolidating* financial statements are presented. The latter generally reveal the adjustments involved in the consolidation process.

5. Unless specifically disclosed, it may be difficult to establish how much of the consolidated Retained Earnings account is actually available for payment of dividends.

6. The composition of the minority interest, for example, as between common and preferred, cannot be determined because the minority interest is generally shown as a combined amount in the consolidated balance sheet.

Unconsolidated subsidiaries

Presently "captive" finance companies and other types of nonhomogeneous subsidiaries are not consolidated. The analyst is interested in the legal control over fund flow that the parent has over the nonconsolidated entity Alfa, Inc. (see Appendix 4B), disclosed in Note 13 (items 101 to 104), the condensed financial statements of its nonconsolidated finance subsidiaries.

The analyst is also interested in the operating (economic) reality that is portrayed by a consolidation of the subsidiary (including its assets and substantial debt) with the parent company. Analytically, for a wholly owned subsidiary, this can be accomplished as follows:

As to the balance sheet:
Dr. Individual Assets of the Unconsolidated
Subsidiary X
    Cr. Individual Liabilities of the Unconsolidated
    Subsidiary .... Y
    Cr. Investment in Unconsolidated Subsidiary .... Z

As to the income statement:
Dr. Equity in Earnings of Unconsolidated
Subsidiary (if profitable) .... U
Dr. Individual Expense Accounts of the
Unconsolidated Subsidiary V
    Cr. Individual Revenue Accounts of the
    Unconsolidated Subsidiary .... W

Such consolidation is particularly appropriate where the parent funnels significant sales (by sale of receivables or otherwise) through finance subsidiaries. The consolidation will affect the current ratio (through inclusion of current assets such as receivables), the debt-to-equity ratio (through inclusion of long-term debt), and the rate of return on total assets. If, as is mostly the case, the finance company was accounted for by the equity method, the return on shareholders' equity will not be affected.

ACCOUNTING FOR BUSINESS COMBINATIONS

The combination of business entities by merger or acquisition is not a new phenomenon on the business scene. What is a relatively more recent development is the utilization of the merger technique as an instrument for the creation of "glamour" or of an image of growth, and as a means of increasing reported earnings.

Reasons for mergers

There are, of course, many legitimate reasons for *external* business expansion, that is, expansion by means of business combinations under which two or more entities are brought under common control. These reasons include: (1) acquisition of sources of new materials, productive facilities, production know-how, marketing organizations, and established shares of a market; (2) the acquisition of financial resources; (3) the acquisition of competent management; (4) savings of time in entering new markets; and (5) achieving economies of scale and acquiring tax advantages such as those relating to tax-loss carryovers.

Distortions in accounting for mergers

In addition to the above legitimate reasons for entering into business combinations, financial "architects" and operators of the 1960s have utilized merger techniques and loose merger accounting to serve up to a stock market obsessed with "earnings growth" a picture of growth that was, in large part, illusory.

The means by which such illusions of earnings growth were achieved were many. Briefly, some were as follows:

1. A great variety of convertible securities were issued without any recognition being given to their future potential dilutive effects on the common stockholder's equity. This phenomenon reached such heights of abuse that it was finally remedied by the issuance of *APB Opinion 15*. Chapter 12 contains a more extended discussion of this subject.

2. The merger of growing companies that have earned a high price-earnings ratio in the marketplace with companies of lesser growth prospects was achieved by payment in high price-earnings ratio stock. This contributed

to further earnings per share growth, thus reinforcing and even increasing the acquiring company's high price-earnings ratio. However, in many cases, the market failed to take into account the lower quality of the *acquired* earnings. This is mostly a transitory problem inherent in the market evaluation mechanism and is not readily subject to remedy by external factors.

3. The utilization of loose accounting rules governing merger accounting in order to create the illusion of earnings growth where, in fact, there is none. This is to be distinguished from the genuine economies and advantages that can accrue from business combinations. This problem area will be discussed below in our consideration of alternative accounting methods for business combinations.

Accounting for business combinations: Two methods

Prior to World War II, the accounting for business combinations was governed by the legal form that it assumed and that resulted in a majority of acquisitions by one company of another being treated as purchases. To businessmen, the one immediate disadvantage of purchase accounting was the creation of "goodwill" as an asset representing usually the excess of cost of acquisition over the amounts at which the acquired company's net assets were recorded on the acquiring company's books. Not only was goodwill a nontax deductible item which, if amortized, would have resulted in a reduction of earnings, but it was also an asset that bankers and other lenders considered of dubious value.

Pooling of interests. For this and other reasons, the search for an alternative method of accounting for business combinations led to the pooling of interests method. The rationale behind this method is that instead of an acquisition of one company by another, a pooling of interests reflects the merging of two stockholder groups that share in future risks and opportunities.

This accounting convention, which has gained wide acceptance in the post-1945 period, is based on the following assumptions about the two corporations combining—

1. That they would exchange voting securities; essentially, ownership would be continuing.
2. That the two corporations would be roughly comparable in size.
3. That management personnel would continue with the merged corporation.

The great attraction of the pooling method along with the vague criteria that were promulgated to govern its accounting led to a significant deterioration in actual practice. The criterion of relative size eroded, all manner of equity securities became acceptable, various means of circumventing the continuity of ownership provisions were devised, and where it was clearly impossible to justify the use of a full pooling, a part-pooling part-purchase method was devised. In short, we had here a classic illustration of the operation of Gresham's law in accounting.

With the growth in these abuses, the chorus of criticism grew, and this resulted in a call by many for the abolition of pooling of interests accounting. Instead, members of the APB compromised and issued *Opinion 16* which, as we shall see, established stricter and more specific conditions for use of this method of accounting in the future.

Purchase accounting. In the permissive atmosphere of the 1960s, accounting under the "purchase" convention also deteriorated in relation to its original intent. Abuses occurred in two major areas:

1. Assets and liabilities of purchased entities were not revalued at fair value before being included in the accounts of the acquiring company.
2. The resulting "goodwill" represented merely the excess of amounts paid over the carrying amounts of assets and liabilities assumed without even the pretense that such assets and liabilities were fairly valued. This resulting "goodwill" was very rarely amortized. It thus became a repository for all kinds of costs incurred in acquiring the company, costs that were thus kept out of present and future income statements. The curt note found in the Gould, Inc., prospectus dated February 17, 1970, was characteristic of this kind of treatment: "The cost of acquired businesses in excess of recorded net assets at dates of acquisition are considered to be attributable to intangible assets which will not be amortized."

While in theory a purchase is in substance quite a different business combination from a pooling of interests, by the late 1960s, the accounting for them became *in effect* quite similar. Under the pooling method, the understatement of assets took the form of carrying forward the merged company's assets at book value, while under the "polluted purchase"[2] method, the assets were similarly understated and the excess of cost over these understated assets was merely carried as a nondescript composite intangible that was rarely amortized. Thus, under either method, substantial costs were kept out of the income statement.

REVISED OPINIONS ON ACCOUNTING FOR BUSINESS COMBINATIONS

In an attempt to improve the accounting for business combinations, the APB issued in 1970 *Opinions 16* and *17.* However, in late 1976, the FASB

---

[2] This term was coined by Professor Abraham J. Briloff who has done more than anyone else to expose the abuses under both pooling and purchase accounting. Starting in 1967, his incisive and analytical articles, appearing mostly in the *Financial Analysts Journal* and *Barron's,* contributed greatly to a wider understanding of the distortions for which this type of accounting was responsible.

issued a voluminous *Discussion Memorandum* on the subject which was designed to lead to public hearings in 1977 and to a reconsideration of the entire subject. In 1982, the reconsideration of the subject was postponed pending completion of the Board's "conceptual framework."

We shall first consider the accounting required under these two *Opinions*. Following this consideration, we shall consider the implications that the present accounting holds for the analyst.

Pooling of interests and purchase accounting compared

Pooling of interests accounting is based on the assumption that the combination is a uniting of ownership interests achieved by means of an exchange of equity securities. Under this method, the former ownership interests continue and the recorded assets and liabilities of the constituents are carried forward to the combined entity at their recorded amounts. Since this is a combining of interests, income of the combined corporation includes income of the constituents for the entire fiscal period in which the combination occurs. Prior periods are also restated to show the combined companies as merged since their respective inceptions.

The purchase method of accounting views the business combination as the acquisition of one entity by another. The acquiring entity records the acquired assets, including goodwill, and liabilities at its cost which is based on fair values at date of acquisition. The acquiring entity picks up the income of the acquired entity, based on its cost, only from date of acquisition.

APB Opinion 16 concluded that if a business combination meets the 12 specific criteria enumerated in it, it must be accounted for as a pooling of interests. Otherwise, it must be accounted for as a purchase.

Conditions for the pooling of interests method. There are 12 conditions that must be met under the provision of *APB Opinion 16* before a business combination may be accounted for as a pooling of interests. These can be grouped under three main categories:

  I.   Attributes of the combining companies.
 II.   Manner of combining interests.
III.   Absence of planned transactions.

  I.   Attributes of the combining companies.
       A. Each of the combining companies should be autonomous and not
           have operated as a subsidiary or division of another company
           within two years before the plan of combination is initiated. An
           exception to this condition concerns the divestiture of assets that
           was ordered by a governmental or judicial body. A subsidiary
           that is divested under an order or a new company that acquires
           assets disposed of under such an order is considered autonomous
           for this condition.
       B. Each of the combining companies must be independent of each

other. That means that no combining company or group of combining companies can hold as an intercompany investment more than 10 percent of the outstanding voting common stock of any other combining company. To illustrate the 10 percent requirement, let's assume that Company A plans to issue its voting common stock to acquire the voting common stock of Companies B and C. If Companies A and B each own 7 percent of Company C's outstanding common stock, A can pool with B, but the combined entity cannot subsequently pool with C since more than 10 percent of Company C's outstanding stock would have been held by the other combining companies.

II. Manner of combining interests.

    C. The combination should be effected in a single transaction or should be completed in accordance with a specific plan within one year after the plan is initiated. The *Opinion* provides an exception to this one-year rule when the delay is beyond the control of the combining companies because of proceedings of a governmental authority or pending litigation.

    D. The combination should involve the issuance of voting common stock only in exchange for substantially all of the voting common stock interest of the company being combined. "Substantially all" in this context means at least 90 percent of the voting common stock interest of the company being combined. Thus, the issuer may purchase for cash or other nonvoting common stock consideration up to 10 percent of the voting common shares of the company to be pooled. Such a cash outlay may be necessary to eliminate fractional shares or to pay dissenting stockholders. The rationale of this criterion is that substantially all of the voting common stock interest in each party to a pooling should be carried forward as a voting common stock interest in the issuer in the pooling. The payment of cash, debt, or an equity instrument that does not satisfy this test destroys the most fundamental basis of a pooling. If the company being combined has securities other than voting stock, such securities may be exchanged for common stock of the issuing corporation or may be exchanged for substantially identical securities of the issuing corporation.

    E. None of the combining companies should change the equity interest of their voting common stock in contemplation of effecting the combination. This restriction applies during the period from two years preceding the date the plan is initiated through the date the plan is consummated. Changes in the equity interest of the voting common stock that may violate this condition include distributions to shareholders, additional issuance or exchange of securities, and the retirement of securities. The purpose of this rule is to disallow changes in equity interests prior to a combination because such changes indicate a sale rather than a combining and sharing of risks.

F. Each combining company may reacquire shares of voting common stock only for purposes other than business combinations, and no company may reacquire more than a normal number of shares between the date the plan of combination is initiated and consummated.

G. The ratio of the interest of an individual common stockholder to those of other common shareholders in a combining company should remain the same as a result of the exchange of stock to effect the combination. This condition ensures that no common stockholder is denied his potential share of a voting common stock interest in a combined corporation.

H. The stockholders of the resulting combined corporation cannot be deprived of, nor restricted in, their ability to exercise their voting rights on common stock of the combined corporation. For example, establishing a voting trust to hold some of the shares issued in the combination disqualifies the combination as a pooling of interests.

I. The combination must be resolved at the date the plan is consummated, and there must be no contingent arrangements for the issuance of additional securities or other consideration. All consideration to be given to effect the combination of the companies, must be determinable as of the date the plan of combination is consummated. The only exception to this would be a provision to adjust the exchange ratio as a result of a subsequent settlement of a contingency such as an existing lawsuit.

III. Absence of planned transactions.

J. The combined corporation should not agree directly or indirectly to retire or reacquire any of the common stock issued to effect the combination.

K. The combined corporation cannot enter into other financial arrangements for the benefit of the former stockholders of a combining company, such as a guarantee of loans secured by stock issued in the combination. This financial arrangement may require the payment of cash in the future that would negate the exchange of equity securities, and thus the combination would not qualify for pooling of interests treatment.

L. The combined corporation may not intend to plan to dispose of a significant part of the assets of the combining companies within two years after the combination. Some disposal of assets may be effected within the two-year period provided the disposals would have been in the ordinary course of business of the formerly separate companies or if the disposals were to eliminate duplicate facilities or excess capacity.

If a combining company remains a subsidiary of the issuing corporation after the combination is consummated, the combination could still be accounted for as a pooling of interests, as long as all the conditions for a pooling are met. Any business combination that meets all of the above conditions *must* be accounted for under the pooling of interests method.

Application of the purchase method. As we have seen in the foregoing discussion, under purchase accounting the business combination is viewed as the acquisition of one entity by another.

Problem of valuation of the consideration. One of the major problems in accounting for a purchase is to determine the total cost of an acquired entity. The same accounting principles apply whether determining the cost of assets acquired individually, in a group, or in a business combination. It is the nature of the transaction that determines which accounting principles apply in arriving at the total cost of assets acquired.

There usually is no problem in determining the total cost of assets acquired for cash, since the amount of cash disbursed is the total cost of the acquired assets. The difficulty is, however, in the proper allocation of the total cost to the individual assets acquired.

If assets are acquired by incurring liabilities, total cost of the assets is the present value of the amounts to be paid in the future. The present value of a debt security is the fair value of the liability. If the debt security has been issued at an interest rate that is substantially above or below the present effective rate for a similar security, the appropriate amount of premium or discount should be recorded. In some cases, the characteristics of a preferred stock may be so similar to a debt security that it should be valued in the same manner.

If assets are acquired in exchange for stock, the general rule for determining the total cost of the assets acquired would be that it is the fair value of the stock given or the fair value of the assets received, whichever is more clearly evident.

The fair value of securities traded in the market is normally more clearly evident than is the fair value of the acquired company. Quoted market price should serve as a guide in determining total cost of an acquired company after considering market fluctuations, the quantities traded, issue costs, and so forth.

If the quoted market price is not a reliable indicator of the value of stock issued, it is still necessary to determine the fair value of the assets received, including goodwill, even though this valuation is difficult.

In these cases, the best means of estimation should be used, including a detailed review of the negotiations leading up to the purchase and the use of independent appraisals.

Contingent additional consideration. The amount of any additional contingent consideration payable in accordance with the purchase agreement is usually recorded when the contingency is resolved and the consideration is to be issued or becomes issuable. Two of the most common types of contingencies are based on either earnings or security prices.

The following guides to the accounting for such contingent additional consideration are contained in *APB Opinion 16:*

1. A contingent issuance of additional consideration should be disclosed but should not be recorded as a liability or shown as outstanding securities unless the outcome of the contingency is determinable beyond a reasonable doubt.
2. A contingent issuance of additional consideration based on future earnings should be recorded as an additional cost of the acquisition when the contingency is resolved. In this case the total amount of consideration representing cost was not determinable at the date of acquisition.
3. A contingent issuance of additional consideration which is based on future security prices should be considered as an adjustment of the amount originally recorded for the securities at the date of acquisition.

Allocation of total cost. Once the total cost of an acquired entity is determined, it is then necessary to allocate this total cost to the individual assets received. All identifiable assets acquired and liabilities assumed in a business combination should be assigned a portion of the total cost, normally equal to their fair value at date of acquisition. The excess of the total cost over the amounts assigned to identifiable assets acquired, less liabilities assumed, should be recorded as goodwill. Such goodwill must be amortized over a period not to exceed 40 years.

It may be possible in some cases that the market or appraisal values of identifiable assets acquired, less liabilities assumed, exceeds the cost of the acquired company. In those cases, the values otherwise assignable to noncurrent assets acquired (except long-term investments in marketable securities) should be reduced by a proportionate part of the excess. Negative goodwill should not be recorded unless the value assigned to such long-term assets is first reduced to zero. If such allocation results in an excess of net assets over cost, it should be classified as a deferred credit and should be amortized systematically to income over the period estimated to be benefited but not in excess of 40 years.

North American Philips Corporation provides the following example of a "bargain purchase" acquisition:

> *Note 2: Acquisitions.* Effective October 1, 1974, a subsidiary of NAPC acquired approximately 84 percent of the common stock of The Maganvox Company (Magnavox) for an aggregate cash purchase cost of approximately $142 million. The transaction has been accounted for as a purchase and accordingly the operations of Magnavox are included in the consolidated statement of income from October 1, 1974. The equity in the net assets of Magnavox exceeded acquisition cost by $18,977,000. Of such amount, $12,552,000 was assigned to specific assets and liabilities and $6,425,000 was allocated to remaining noncurrent assets acquired on a pro rata basis in accordance with the provisions of *Accounting Principles Board Opinion No. 16.*

Guidelines for valuation of assets and liabilities. *APB Opinion 16* estab-lished general guides for assigning amounts to individual assets and liabilities assumed, except goodwill, as follows:

1. Marketable securities should be recorded at current net realizable values.
2. Receivables should be recorded at the present values of amounts to be received, determined at appropriate current interest rates, less allowances for uncollectibility and collection costs, if necessary.
3. Inventories:
   a. Finished goods should be recorded at selling prices less cost of disposal and reasonable profit allowance.
   b. Work in process inventories should be stated at estimated selling prices of finished goods less the sum of the costs to complete, costs of disposal, and a reasonable profit allowance for the completing and selling effort of the acquired corporation.
   c. Raw materials should be recorded at current replacement costs.
4. Plant and equipment to be used in the business should be stated at current replacement costs for similar capacity unless the expected future use of the assets indicates a lower value to the acquirer. Replacement cost may be determined directly if a used asset market exists for the assets acquired. Otherwise, replacement cost should be approximated from replacement cost new, less estimated accumulated depreciation.
5. Identifiable intangible assets should be valued at appraised values.
6. Other assets, such as land, natural resources, and nonmarketable securi-ties, should be recorded at appraised values.
7. Accounts and notes payable, long-term debt, and other claims payable should be stated at present values of amounts to be paid, determined at appropriate current interest rates.

An acquiring corporation should not record as a separate asset goodwill previously recorded by an acquired company, and it should not record de-ferred income taxes previously recorded by an acquired company. Amounts assigned to identifiable assets and liabilities should recognize that their value may be less, if part or all of the assigned value is not deductible for income taxes. However, the acquiring corporation should not record deferred tax accounts for the tax effect of these differences at the date of acquisition.

Treatment of goodwill. *APB Opinion 17* provides that for the intangible assets acquired in a business combination, the method of allocating the total cost of the acquired company depends on whether or not the asset is identifia-ble, such as a patent, or unidentifiable, such as goodwill. The cost of an identifiable intangible asset should be based on the fair value of the asset. The cost of an unidentifiable intangible asset is measured by the difference between total cost and the amount assigned to other assets acquired and liabilities assumed.

The cost of an intangible asset should not be written off in the period of acquisition but instead should be amortized based on the estimated life of that specific asset; the period of amortization, however, should not exceed

40 years. The straight-line method of amortization should be used unless the company can demonstrate that another systematic method is more appropriate. The method and period of amortization should be disclosed in the financial statements.

Pro forma supplementary disclosure. Under the purchase method, notes to the financial statements of the acquiring corporation for the period in which a business combination occurs should include as supplemental information the following results of operations on a pro forma basis:

1. Combined results of operations for the current period as though the companies had combined at the beginning of the period unless the acquisition was at or near the beginning of the period.
2. If comparative financial statements are presented, combined results of operations for the immediately preceding period should be reported as though the companies had combined at the beginning of that period.

This supplemental pro forma information should, as a minimum, show revenue, income before extraordinary items, net income, and earnings per share (EPS).

Illustration of accounting mechanics: Purchase versus pooling of interest accounting

Company Buy has agreed to acquire Company Sell in a transaction under which it will issue 1,200,000 of $1 par value common shares for all the common shares of Company Sell. The transaction qualifies as a pooling of interests, and consequently the fair market value of Sell's assets and liabilities at date of the merger do not enter into the accounting for it. Exhibit 9–3 presents in columnar fashion the balance sheets of Company Buy and Company Sell as well as the adjustments needed to effect the combination under pooling of interests accounting.

Pooling accounting

Briefly, the pooling method requires taking up Sell's assets and liabilities at recorded amounts and carrying forward the equity account balances, subject to adjustments required by differences in the par values of the securities exchanged.

Since the amount of the par value of the common stock of Company Buy ($1,200,000) is smaller than the amount of the par value of the stock of Company Sell, which is exchanged ($1,285,000), the difference is credited to Additional Paid-In Capital. In a pooling where the reverse to the above situation prevails, additional par value is taken out first of the existing paid-in capital accounts of the constituents and, if sufficient, from retained earnings. The balance in the retained earnings accounts is carried forward.

Exhibit 9–3: Merger of Company Sell into Company Buy

Summary of Pro Forma Condensed Combining Balance Sheet
(in thousands)

	Company Buy	Company Sell	Combining adjustments		Com-bined
			Debit	Credit	
Assets	$157,934	$28,013	—	—	$185,947
Liabilities	$ 42,591	$11,218	—	—	$ 53,809
Stockholders' equity:					
Company Buy:					
Preferred stock	810	—	—	—	810
Common stock	7,572	—	—	$1,200	8,772
Company Sell:					
Common stock	—	1,285	$1,285	—	—
Additional paid-in					
capital	31,146	137	—	85	31,368
Retained earnings	75,815	15,373	—	—	91,188
Total stockholders'					
equity	115,343	16,795	1,285	1,285	132,138
	$157,934	$28,013	$1,285	$1,285	$185,947

The entry on Company Buy's books of the pooling with Company Sell
will be as follows (in thousands of dollars):

	Debit	Credit
Assets	28,013	
Liabilities		11,218
Common Stock		1,200
Additional Paid-In Capital		222
Retained Earnings		15,373

To record the issuance of 1,200,000 shares of $1 par value
common stock for the merged net assets of Sell and to
credit to Retained Earnings the balance of retained earnings of Sell at date of acquisition.

Exhibit 9–3 reflected the pooling as a "statutory merger," that is, the
assets and liabilities of the two companies were combined and Company
Sell ceased its separate existence. If we assume that Company Sell was to
continue as a wholly owned subsidiary of Company Buy, the pooling would
be recorded as shown in Exhibit 9–4.

The accounting entries made on the parent company's books are as follows
(in thousands of dollars):

	Debit	Credit
Investment in Company Sell.........................	16,795	
Common Stock.................................		1,200
Additional Paid-In Capital		222
Retained Earnings from Pooled Company		15,373

To record the issuance of 1,200,000 shares of $1 par value common stock for the common stock of Sell and to credit to Retained Earnings the balance of retained earnings of Sell at date of acquisition.

The investment in Company Sell will continue to be carried on an equity basis by Company Buy, the parent. In consolidation, the investment account in Company Sell will be eliminated against subsidiary Company Sell's common stock, additional paid-in capital, and the parent company's retained earnings from the pooled company, all in accordance with normal consolidation procedure.

Purchase accounting

Let us now assume that instead of acquiring Company sell in an exchange of common stock, Company Buy acquires Company Sell for $25,000,000 in

Exhibit 9–4: Merger of Company Buy and Company Sell (Company Sell remains as a fully owned subsidiary of Company Buy)

Summary of Pro Forma Condensed Balance Sheet
(in thousands)

| | Company Buy | Parent company only | | |
| | Before pooling | Adjustments | | After pooling |
		Debit	Credit	
Assets	$157,934	—	—	$157,934
Investment in Sell		$16,795	—	16,795
	$157,934	16,795	—	$174,729
Liabilities	$ 42,591	—	—	$ 42,591
Stockholders' equity:				
Company Buy:				
Preferred stock	810	—	—	810
Common stock	7,572	—	$ 1,200	8,772
Company Sell: Common stock	—	—	—	—
Additional paid-in capital	31,146	—	222	31,368
Retained earnings	75,815	—	—	75,815
Retained earnings from pooled company	—	—	15,373	15,373
Total stockholders' equity	115,343	—	16,795	132,138
	$157,934	—	$16,795	$174,729

cash. Since this acquisition must be accounted for as a purchase, it is necessary to determine the fair values of Company Sell's assets and liabilities. The following tabulation compares Company Sell's recorded asset and liability amounts with indicated fair values at date of acquisition (in thousands):

	Amounts on Company Sell books	Fair values determined at date of acquisition
Assets	$28,013	$34,000
Liabilities	11,218	13,000
Net assets	$16,795	21,000
Cost to Company Buy	—	25,000
Amount assigned to goodwill	—	4,000

Exhibit 9–5: Purchase of Company Sell by Company Buy

Summary of Pro Forma Condensed Balance Sheet Consolidated
(in thousands)

	Company Buy	Company Sell (at fair values on date of acquisition)	Combining and consolidating adjustments		After purchase
			Debit	Credit	
Assets					
Assets (exclusive of goodwill)	$157,934	$34,000		$25,000	$166,934
Goodwill			$ 4,000		4,000
Total assets	$157,934	$34,000			$170,934
Liabilities and Stockholders' Equity					
Liabilities	$ 42,591	$13,000			$ 55,591
Stockholders' equity:					
Company Buy:					
Preferred stock	810				810
Common stock	7,572				7,572
Additional paid-in capital	31,146				31,146
Retained earnings	75,815				75,815
Net assets at fair value of company sell		21,000	21,000		
Total stockholders' equity	115,343	21,000			115,343
Total liabilities and stockholders' equity	$157,934	$34,000	$25,000	$25,000	$170,934

Assets and liabilities are valued in accordance with the valuation principles outlined in *APB Opinion 16.* The excess of purchase price over the fair value of net assets acquired assigned to goodwill must be amortized over its useful life not to exceed 40 years.

Exhibit 9–5 presents the consolidated balance sheet of Company Buy right after the purchase of Company Sell so as to enable a contrast with the balance sheet obtained right after the pooling accounting presented in Exhibit 9–3 on page 252.

A cash acquisition is, of course, not the only method requiring purchase accounting. As described earlier, under a great number of conditions involving an acquisition for stock purchase accounting would be required.

The following difference between the pooling and the purchase accounting should be noted. In the purchase—

1. The assets and liabilities are recorded at fair value. Goodwill is recognized. These will result in higher charges to income reflecting the higher net asset values acquired.
2. The total stockholder equity remains unchanged. There has been an exchange of resources, that is, Company Sell's net assets of $25,000,000 for Company Buy's cash.
3. Company Buy will record the acquisition on its books as follows:

Investment in Company Sell 25,000,000
    Cash   25,000,000

Alfa, Inc. (see Appendix 4B), discloses business acquisitions in Note 4 (item 74) including details of a purchase and pro forma information on revenues and net income.

Implications for analysis

An examination of the revised guidelines and principles governing the accounting for mergers and acquisitions reveals a serious attempt by the accounting profession to improve the accounting in this area and to prevent some of the glaring distortions and abuses of the past, as they perceived them, from recurring.

The new rules that govern the accounting for pooling of interests and for purchases are the result of a lengthy process of compromise; another important objective was the elimination of *specific* abuses of practice. The analyst must recognize this as well as the fact that the rationale that accountants use in distinguishing pooling of interests from purchases combinations is not necessarily relevant to his attempt to measure and analyze the economic consequences of business combinations.

Thus, in determining the implications that the new accounting rules on business combinations hold for the analyst of financial statements, we must examine the impact that these rules have on the realistic portrayal of the results of mergers and acquisitions.

Pooling versus purchase accounting

Before we examine the effect of pooling accounting on the financial statements of a combined entity, let us summarize the main arguments that have been advanced in defense of this method.

1. If cash is given as consideration in a business acquisition, the acquirer parts with a resource. But if a company's own unissued stock is given in exchange, no resource is given; instead, the equity is increased.
2. In exchange of common stock, the "seller" is getting back a part of itself as well as part of the buyer. Since he does not part with ownership in his own company, there is no valid basis for establishing new values.
3. In a combination of equals, which results from an exchange of stock, it is hard to determine who acquired whom.

It is not at all clear that cash is a resource while unissued stock is not. After all, if stock is an acceptable consideration to a seller, it should also command a price on the market. Some regard the ability to issue stock as equivalent to "a license to print money." The valuation of noncash consideration is a problem that accountants have to face frequently. Moreover, if a combination fails as a pooling on any one of the technical conditions enumerated in *APB Opinion 16,* a valuation of the stock issued will become necessary in order to account for the combination as a purchase.

There is some validity to the second argument above, but in most business combinations the relative size of the pooled-in company to the surviving entity is small indeed.

The third argument is rarely relevant today because the size test of poolings has been abandoned and consequently a large company can acquire a very small enterprise and still account for the combination as a pooling.

Aside from the above considerations, from the point of view of the analyst it is the results of pooling accounting that really matter. These can be best illustrated by means of a simplified example.

Assume that Company B, which wants to acquire Company S, earns $1,000 of net income and has 500 shares outstanding. Company S's condensed balance sheet is as follows:

Fixed assets*	$ 400	Liabilities	$ 200
Other assets	600	Capital accounts	800
	$1,000		$1,000
* Current value	600		

Company S has a net income of $200 after deduction of $20 for depreciation (10 percent of $400 in fixed assets less 50 percent tax effect).

Let us now consider the operating results of Company B one year after the acquisition of Company S for a price of $1,400 paid in (1) cash or (2) stock. Let us assume that the earnings of both companies remain unchanged and that the $1,400 purchase price (of Company S) is arrived at as follows:

Fixed assets (current value)	$ 600
Other assets	600
Goodwill	400
	1,600
Less liabilities assumed	200
Purchase consideration	$1,400

Payment in cash.   If the purchase price was in cash, the combined company's income statement would be accounted for on a purchase basis as follows:

Income of B			$1,000
Income of S (before depreciation		$220	
Depreciation (10% of $600)	$30*		
Goodwill amortization (2½% of 400†)	10	40	180
Net income of the combined enterprise			$1,180

* Aftertax effect.
† Assuming amortization over 40 years, no tax deduction.

Payment in stock.   If, however, the purchase price was in stock, under the pooling method of accounting the income statement of the enterprise would be as follows:

Income of B	$1,000
Income of S	200
Net income of the combined enterprise	$1,200

The difference in the net income is due to the inclusion, under the pooling method, of fixed assets at $400, the original cost on the books of Company S, and the complete omission of the goodwill that Company B paid in the acquisition of Company S.

Whether the reported income of the combined company is $1,200 or $1,180 depends in this case on how the purchase price was paid. Moreover, if the purchase price is paid in common stock and *any* of the other 11 conditions of a pooling are not met, the acquisition would have to be accounted for as a purchase and the reported income would be $1,180 instead of $1,200.

This, then, is the basic difference between pooling and purchase accounting. The nonrecording or suppression of asset values for which the acquiring company paid generally results in an understatement of assets and an overstatement of income. This is the primary reason why earnings that are the result of pooling combinations are viewed as being overstated in comparison with similar earnings resulting from purchase accounting.

As an astute financial analyst put it, "Dow Chemical with a market value of near $6 billion, offered stock worth $419 million for General Crude. The basis of accounting in a pooling will remain book value of General Crude which is about $82 million. Suppose instead International Paper had been successful and offered $419 in cash in a purchase. Then the new basis of General Crude's assets could have been $419 million. It seems that form prevails over substance in permitting pooling."[3]

APB Opinion 16 has done nothing to remove this problem which is inherent in the pooling of interests method. It has removed some of the abuses of the original criteria of the pooling of interests concept such as part pooling-part purchase, issuance of complex securities other than common stock in a pooling, retroactive pooling, and contingent additional consideration. But these features, while enabling the application of pooling accounting to many mergers, are not in themselves responsible for the suppression of asset values. This suppression is *inherent* in the pooling of interests concept, and all that *APB Opinion 16* achieved in this regard is to limit significantly the application of the concept by making it more difficult for companies to meet the criteria of a pooling. But once having met these criteria, many of the old problems and distortions remain.

ILLUSTRATION 2. Two examples taken from a study[4] by Professors A. J. Briloff and C. Engler highlight some significant effects of the pooling method of accounting (in millions):

Name of acquiring and pooled company and (year of acquisition)	Market value of shares issued in acquisition	Book value of acquired company	Unrecorded value of assets
Pepsico, Inc., and Taco Bell (1978)	$ 139	$ 36	$ 103
General Electric Company and Utah International, Inc. (1976)	2,130	640	1,490[5]

Clearly then, had these acquisitions been recorded on the purchase basis of accounting, the acquiring companies' books would have had to reflect substantially higher values for the assets they acquired with the result, among others, that the return on investment, operating performance, and other measures, such as liquidity, would have been significantly affected.

---

[3] D. Norr, *Accounting Theory Illustrated,* First Manhattan Co., 1974, p. 4.

[4] "Accountancy and the Merger Movement: A Symbiotic Relationship," *The Journal of Corporation Law,* Fall 1979.

[5] In 1983 General Electric sold Utah International's Australian division for $2.4 billion. Substantial amounts of these unrecorded assets should now surface as gains in G.E.'s income statement.

Let us now summarize the most important features of pooling of interests accounting which, from the point of view of the analyst, differentiate it from purchase accounting:

1. Assets acquired are carried at "book value" rather than at the current fair values reflected in the consideration given. To the extent that "goodwill" is paid for, the amount is not shown on the acquiring company's balance sheet.
2. The understatement of assets leads to an understatement of capital employed by the enterprise.
3. The understatement of assets such as inventory, property, plant, and equipment, as well as goodwill and other intangibles, will lead to an understatement of expenses such as cost of goods sold, depreciation, and amortization of goodwill and intangibles. In turn, this will lead to an overstatement of income.
4. The understatement of assets can lead not only to an understatement of expenses but can also result in an overstatement of gains realized on their disposition. Thus, the acquiring corporation can claim as part of its results of operations gains on the sale of assets that at the time of their acquisition were carried forward at unrealistically low amounts, amounts that are actually far below the amount that in the negotiations preceding the merger was the agreed fair value of these assets. In these cases, income is overstated and management performance is overrated. What we have here is clearly a recovery of cost rather than a profit.
5. Both the understatement of invested capital and the overstatement of income will lead to an overstatement of the return on investment.
6. The retained earnings of the acquired enterprise can be carried forward to the surviving company.
7. The income statements and the balance sheets of the combined enterprise are restated for all periods presented. Under purchase accounting, they are combined only since the date of acquisition, although pro forma statements showing preacquisition combined results are also furnished.

A crude way of adjusting for omitted values in a pooling is to determine the difference between the fair or market value of assets acquired. This difference can then be amortized against reported income on some reasonable basis in order to arrive at results that would be comparable to those achieved under purchase accounting.

Purchase accounting

Since purchase accounting is designed to recognize the acquisition values on which the buyer and seller of a business entity bargained, it is a more meaningful method of accounting from the analyst's point of view. Purchase accounting is more relevant to the analyst's needs because he is interested in values that were exchanged in a business combination rather than in amounts that represent original costs to the seller.

As we have noted earlier in this chapter, the abuses in purchase accounting that preceded the issuance of *APB Opinions 16* and *17* centered on attempts by acquiring companies to suppress the fair values of net assets acquired and paid for and to transplant the values paid for to a nondescript intangible asset account that was not amortized.

The effect of APB Opinions 16 and 17.   *APB Opinions 16* and *17* have directly and forthrightly addressed themselves to the problem and have as their primary objective the elimination of these abuses. However, the analyst must not confuse theory with practice: It must be realized that the objectives of many merger and acquisition-minded managements with respect to the accounting for these business combinations were in the past and are now likely to remain—

1.   To reduce as much as possible the impact on present and future income of charges arising from assets acquired in the purchase.
2.   To increase the post-acquisition income by understating assets acquired or by overproviding for future costs and contingencies.

Remaining room for distortions.   While *APB Opinion 16* contains specific provisions on the valuation of assets and liabilities, room for abuses and loose interpretations remains. In addition to the leeway that inevitably exists when broad rules of valuation and appraisal are applied, the analyst must also be alert to understatements of assets and overstatement of liabilities that result from provisions for future costs and losses.

ILLUSTRATION 3.   The acquisition by Gulf United of Southwestern Drug Company as analyzed by Professor C. Engler[6] points up some remaining opportunities for income management in purchase accounting.

Originally, pro forma financial statements indicated that the approximately one million shares of southwestern to be exchanged and purchased for cash were to be valued at $16 million (or $16 per share), and this would have resulted in a bargain purchase of Southwestern Drug that could not be explained by its financial statements or justified by its recent earnings history. In a supplement to its prospectus, Gulf United indeed increased the per share valuation to a more realistic $22.50 (when Gulf United's stock was trading at $23.50). However, a review of the final accounting by Gulf United of its acquisition of Southwestern revealed that only 116,000 shares of Southwestern that were purchased for cash were recorded at $22.50 per share while the balance of 900,000 shares exchanged on a one-for-one basis were valued at only $16 per share. The result of this accounting was that Southwestern's equipment was reduced to zero value and negative goodwill was booked that was to increase Gulf United's income for the following 20 years. So eager was Gulf United to use the purchase method for this acquisition that it made its ability to use this method of accounting a contractual condition for consummating the acquisition.

---

[6] Paper presented at the Annual Meeting of the American Accounting Association in Chicago, Illinois, on August 7, 1981.

Thus, in assessing the effect of a business combination accounted for as a purchase, the analyst must evaluate in detail the disclosures found regarding the process of valuation applied by the acquiring company. On the basis of such information, he or she must reach his own conclusions regarding the fairness of presentation of the acquired companies assets and liabilities. Particular attention must be paid to the possible overprovision for future costs and losses.

Acquisitions for equity securities. When an acquisition accounted for as a purchase is effected for stock or other equity securities, the analyst must be alert to the valuation of the net assets acquired in the combination. In periods of high market price levels, purchase accounting may tend to introduce inflated values when net assets, and particularly the intangible assets, of acquired companies are valued on the basis of market prices of the stock issued and where such inflated prices are not otherwise adjusted for. Such values, while determined on the basis of temporarily inflated stock prices, remain on a company's balance sheet and affect its operating results on a long-term basis.

Goodwill and its amortization. *APB Opinion 17* recognized that a payment made in anticipation of future earnings should be recovered from those earnings over the period of those excess earnings. The mandatory amortization of goodwill is, from the point of view of realistic income determination, a step in the right direction. The analyst must, however, remain alert to the possibility that many companies will use the maximum period of 40 years for amortization purposes rather than the "reasonable" estimate of useful life that *APB Opinion 17* calls for.

Moreover, the amount at which goodwill is often carried on the acquirer's books bears little relationship to its real value which must be based on the demonstrated superior earning power of the acquired enterprise.

ILLUSTRATION 4.   When Dow Jones & Company bought *Book Digest* in 1974, it paid over $13 million for the "goodwill" of an enterprise that reportedly never showed a profit. That goodwill was retained (except for amortization) in the face of losses that in 1980 alone amounted to about $2 million. Only in 1981 did Dow Jones write off $9.4 million of goodwill still leaving $3.3 million on the books at a time when losses in the millions were anticipated for the following year and beyond.

While management still considers *Book Digest* "a solid and sound concept," analysts may wonder what the concept of "goodwill" really means in practice.

ACCOUNTING FOR FOREIGN OPERATIONS

When the user of financial statements attempts to analyze an entity that has investments and operations in a foreign country,[7] he or she must add

---

[7] *SFAS 14* now requires information about foreign operations and export sales (see also Chapter 20).

to the problems that are discussed throughout this book those that are peculiar to foreign operations. These subdivide, broadly speaking, into two major categories:

1. Problems related to differences in accounting standards and practices that are peculiar to the foreign country in which the operations are conducted.[8]
2. Problems that arise from the translation of foreign assets, liabilities, equities, and results of operations into the U.S. dollar.

Foreign accounting practices and auditing standards

Accounting practices can vary significantly among countries. There are a variety of reasons for this including a lack of agreement on objectives of financial statements, the requirements of national company laws, the influence of tax laws, and differences in the strength and the development patterns of local professional bodies.

In recent years, serious attempts have begun to bring more conformity into international accounting practices. The most ambitious program for the establishment of international accounting standards was the establishment in 1973 of the International Accounting Standards Committee (IASC) by the professional institutes of nine countries. Its objective is to "formulate and publish in the public interest, basic standards to be observed in the presentation of audited accounts and financial statements and to promote their worldwide acceptance and observance." The IASC has published a number of standards covering a variety of areas such as accounting for changing prices, for income taxes, for contingencies, and other topics.

These are modest, if important, beginnings, and much remains to be done if the significant differences between the accounting practices of various countries are to be narrowed.

Differences in auditing standards. In the area of auditing, which is discussed in Chapter 15 and is concerned with the function of attesting to the reliability of financial statements, a wide variety of standards exist in international practice. In some countries, such as the United Kingdom and Canada, for example, the auditing profession is strong and well regarded, while in others its standing may be weak and, consequently, the reliability of financial statements may be subject to considerable doubt. Nevertheless, an auditing firm of international repute can enhance the credibility of a company's financial statements regardless of the location of the company's home base. Thus, the analyst must assess the reliability of the financial statements that are used on the basis of the individual circumstances surrounding their preparation and attestation.

---

[8] Foreign companies raising capital in the United States or listed on U.S. stock exchanges must conform substantially to U.S. GAAP in filing registration statements.

Peculiarities of foreign accounting practices. One of the central theses of this text is that no intelligent analysis of financial statements is possible without a thorough understanding of the assumptions and of the standards on the basis of which such statements were prepared. It follows that in the case of foreign companies, the analyst must at least obtain a working familiarity with such assumptions and principles.

While the differences in accounting practice between those obtaining in the United States and those in other countries vary significantly from country to country, they can be substantial. The following are merely indicative of the nature and extent of such differences. Thus, in some countries—

1. Inventory reserves and other secret reserves may be sanctioned.
2. Excessive depreciation may be recorded.
3. Because of substantial price-level changes, restatements of property accounts may be effected based on coefficients established by, and frequently revised by, the local government.
4. "Legal reserves" amounting to a fixed percentage of net income may be established.
5. Tax allocation may not be practiced.
6. Stock dividends may be recorded only on the basis of the par value of the stock issued.
7. Pooling of interests accounting may not be sanctioned.
8. Consolidation of parent and subsidiary financial statements may not be required.
9. The recognition of pension liabilities can vary widely.
10. General provisions (reserves) and subsequent reversals of such reserves may be used to shift income between periods.
11. Certain assets may be omitted from the financial statements.
12. No significance may be attached to consistency of application of accounting policies, and no disclosure of changes therein may be required.

A recitation of the differences in accounting as practiced in the United States and in other countries is beyond the scope of this book. The analyst must consult up-to-date sources of information that are relevant to the proper understanding and analysis of financial statements.[9]

In consolidating their foreign subsidiaries, U.S.–based multinational companies will usually conform their subsidiaries' accounting to the principles generally accepted in this country.

Translation of foreign currencies

In the discussion of intercorporate investments earlier in this chapter, it was emphasized that the consolidation of majority-owned subsidiaries is now

---

[9] See, for example, the most recent survey by Price Waterhouse such as "A survey in 46 countries" or "International Accounting Standards and Guidelines," Deloitte, Haskins & Sells, 1981.

a generally accepted procedure, and the reasons for nonconsolidation are few and well defined. With respect to subsidiaries of U.S.–based multinational companies, the most common reasons for nonconsolidation would be substantial uncertainty regarding the ultimate realization or transferability of foreign earnings.

In addition to the above provisions, *APB Opinion 18* requires a parent company to recognize in its financial statements the equity in earnings or losses of (1) unconsolidated foreign subsidiaries; (2) corporate joint ventures; and (3) other companies, less than 50 percent owned, over which the investor company exerts a significant influence.

The consolidation of, as well as equity accounting for, foreign subsidiaries and affiliates requires that their financial statements be translated into U.S.– dollar equivalents. This is, of course, necessary before the accounts of such foreign subsidiaries or affiliates can be combined with those of the U.S.– based company.

Evolution of the accounting for foreign exchange translation

Chapter 12 of *ARB 43* as modified by paragraph 18 of *APB Opinion 6* was the basic authoritative pronouncement on the subject before the FASB undertook to reconsider it. Chapter 12 of *ARB 43* called for the use of the *current-noncurrent* method of translation, i.e., the translation of current assets and liabilities at current rates and the translation of noncurrent assets and liabilities at historical rates.

The pronouncement contained some exceptions to the current-noncurrent rule; and in 1965, paragraph 18 of *APB Opinion 6* sanctioned further changes such as the translation of all payables and receivables at the current rate. This, in effect, was a move to permit another method of translation known as the *monetary-nonmonetary method*. Under this method, monetary assets and liabilities are translated at the current rate while nonmonetary assets and liabilities are translated at applicable historical rates. Assets and liabilities are regarded as monetary if they are expressed in terms of a fixed number of foreign currency units, e.g., cash, receivables, liabilities expressed in the foreign currency; all other assets and liabilities are regarded as nonmonetary.

Two other methods of foreign currency translation were also advanced during protracted discussions that preceded and continued during the FASB's consideration of the subject.[10]

The *current rate method* provides for the translation of all assets and liabilities at the current rate.

Under the *temporal method*, cash, receivables, and payables, as well as assets and liabilities carried at present or future prices, are translated at current rates while assets and liabilities carried at past prices (historical costs) are translated at applicable historical rates.

---

[10] In fact, nine distinct methods of foreign currency translations are illustrated in the FASB's *Financial Statement Model on Accounting for Foreign Currency Translation* (Stamford, Conn., 1974).

The following table summarizes the salient features of the four translation methods discussed above:

	Monetary-nonmonetary method	Current-noncurrent method	Current rate method	Temporal method
Cash, current receivables, current payables	Current	Current	Current	Current
Inventories, current prepaids, current unearned revenue ..	Historical	Current	Current	Historical*
Noncurrent receivable, long-term liabilities	Current	Historical	Current	Current
Fixed assets, deferred charges, noncurrent unearned revenue	Historical	Historical	Current	Historical

* With some exceptions.

In 1975, the FASB adopted *SFAS 8* which basically follows the temporal method of translation.

Since its issuance, *SFAS 8* has been one of the most controversial of all the standards promulgated by the FASB. In response to repeated criticism of this standard, the Board decided in 1979 to reconsider this *Statement* and in 1981 issued *SFAS 52,* which is effective for fiscal years beginning on or after December 15, 1982, with earlier application encouraged.

SFAS 52, "Foreign Currency Translation," represents a clear shift away from the philosophy of *SFAS 8.* The latter was based on the parent company perspective, which is consistent with the temporal method, and which required all transactions to be measured as if the transactions occurred in U.S. dollars. The shift is to a "local" perspective, i.e., that of the foreign entity itself and the economic relationships expressed within its operations as a separate business unit whose factual financial statements are those prepared in the currency of its own environment.

Thus, *SFAS 52* has as its major objectives to (1) provide information that is generally compatible with the expected economic effects of a change in exchange rates on an enterprise's cash flows and equity; and (2) to reflect in consolidated statements the financial results and relationships as measured in the primary currency of the economic environment in which the entity operates, which is referred to as its *functional currency.*[11] The *Statement*

---

[11] For an entity with operations that are relatively self-contained and integrated within a country, the functional currency will generally be the currency of that country. However, for example, if the foreign operations are a direct component or extension of a parent company's operations, then the parent's currency would be the functional currency. In this case, the translation principles of *SFAS 8* would generally hold, including the requirement for current inclusion in income of all gains and losses. Under *SFAS 52,* all deferred income taxes are to be translated at current exchange rates.

places reliance on management's judgment in determining what the functional currency of a foreign subsidiary is.

A major feature of the functional currency approach is the current rate translation method. A foreign entity's assets, liabilities, and operations exist basically in the economic environment of its functional currency. Its costs are incurred in its functional currency, and its revenues are produced in its functional currency. Use of a current exchange rate retains those historical costs and other measurements but restates them in terms of the reporting currency, thereby preserving the relationships established in the entity's economic environment. Accordingly, use of the current exchange rate reflects in the consolidated financial statements the inherent relationships appearing in the functional currency financial statements.

The functional currency approach entails:

a.   Identifying the functional currency of the entity's economic environment.
b.   Measuring all elements of the financial statements in the functional currency.
c.   Using the current exchange rate for translation from the functional currency to the reporting currency, if they are different.
d.   Distinguishing the economic impact of changes in exchange rates on a net investment from the impact of such changes on individual assets and liabilities that are receivable or payable in currencies other than the functional currency.

In adopting the functional currency approach, the Board had the following overall objectives of foreign currency translation in mind:

a.   To provide information that is generally compatible with the expected economic effects of a rate change on an enterprise's cash flows and equity.
b.   To present the consolidated financial statements of an enterprise in conformity with U.S. GAAP.
c.   To reflect in consolidated financial statements the financial results and relationships of the individual consolidated entities as measured in their functional currencies.

Another major change in the Board's approach is to report the adjustment resulting from translation of foreign financial statements not as a gain or loss in the income of the period but as a separate accumulation as part of equity that, in accordance with FASB *SFAC 3*, can be viewed as part of "comprehensive income."[12] This must be clearly distinguished from gains or losses on foreign currency *transactions* with specific exceptions,[13] must

---

[12] See Chapter 3 for a definition of *comprehensive income*.

[13] These exceptions are:

a.   Gains and losses attributable to a foreign currency transaction that is designated as, and is effective as, an economic hedge of a net investment in a foreign entity.
b.   Gains or losses attributable to intercompany foreign currency transactions that are of a long-term investment nature when the entities to the transaction are consolidated, combined, or accounted for by the equity method in the reporting enterprise's financial statements.

be currently included in *income*. These include gains and losses on settled as well as *unsettled* transactions, such as may occur when, for example, a U.S. company takes out a 20-year debt denominated in Swiss francs.

A change in the exchange rate between the U.S. dollar and the other currency produces a change in the U.S. dollar equivalent of the net investment, although there is no change in the net assets of the other entity measured in its functional currency. A strengthening of the foreign currency against the dollar enhances the U.S. dollar equivalent; a weakening reduces the U.S. dollar equivalent. Accordingly, the translation adjustment reflects an economic effect of exchange rate changes. However, that change in the U.S. dollar equivalent of the net investment is an unrealized enhancement or reduction, having no effect on the functional currency net cash flows generated by the foreign entity that may be currently reinvested or distributed to the parent. It is for this reason that the translation adjustment is reported separately from the determination of net income.

Major provisions of *SFAS 52:*

Based on the objectives and the considerations outlined above, the following are the major provisions of *SFAS 52:*

1. The translation process requires that the functional currency of the entity be identified first. Ordinarily it will be the currency of the country in which the entity is located or the U.S. dollar. All financial statement elements of the foreign entity must then be measured in terms of the functional currency in conformity with U.S. GAAP.

2. Translation from the functional currency into the reporting currency, if they are different, is to be at the *current* exchange rate[14] except that revenues and expenses are to be translated at the *average* exchange rates prevailing during the period.[15] The functional currency translation approach generally considers the effect of exchange rate changes to be on the net investment in a foreign entity rather than on its individual assets and liabilities which was the focus of *SFAS 8.*

3. Translation adjustments are not to be included in net income but are to be disclosed and accumulated as a separate component of stockholders' equity until such time that the net investment in the foreign entity is sold or completely or substantially liquidated. To the extent that the

---

[14] Usually the year-end rate that can be used for purposes of dividend remittances.

[15] A foreign entity's revenues, expenses, gains, and losses should be translated in a manner that produces amounts approximately as if the underlying elements had been translated on the dates they were recognized (sometimes referred to as the weighted-average exchange rate). This also applies to accounting allocations (e.g., depreciation, cost of sales, and amortization of deferred revenues and expenses) and requires translation at the current exchange rates applicable to the dates those allocations are included in revenues and expenses (i.e, not the rates on the dates the related items originated). In most cases, the average exchange rate prevailing during the year would be used.

sale or liquidation represents realization, the relevant amounts should be removed from the separate equity component and included as a gain or loss in the determination of the net income of the period during which the sale or liquidation occurs.

4. The statement of changes in financial position (SCFP) is to be translated by applying the current exchange rate as of the balance sheet date, except that those changes that result from revenues, expenses, gains, and losses are to be translated at the rates at which these items are translated in the income statement.

5. Exchange gains and losses attributable to intercompany foreign currency transactions and balances that are of a trading nature are to be included in income, while those that are of a long-term financing or capital nature for which settlement is not contemplated in the foreseeable future are to be reported in the separate component of shareholder's equity where adjustments arising from the translation of foreign currency financial statements are accumulated.

Using the current rate method to translate the nonmonetary assets of foreign subsidiaries located in highly inflationary economies can produce distorted results. The Board concluded that if a foreign entity's functional currency has been effected by cumulative inflation of 100 percent or more over a three-uear period, it is to be considered not stable enough to serve as a functional currency, and consequently, the financial statements of the entity shall be remeasured into the reporting (i.e. parent) currency. This remeasurement process, in effect, results in translation by the temporal method (i.e., the method of *SFAS 8*). Under *SFAS 52*, when the functional currency of a foreign subsidiary is that of the parent company, translation will follow the principles of *SFAS 8*, except that the translation of deferred taxes is to be at the current rate of exchange.

Illustration of the translation procedure

Forco is a wholly owned foreign subsidiary of Dollarco and has been since its incorporation in 19v8. On July 1, 19x6, the dollar was devalued in relation to the foreign currency (FC) from FC 1 = U.S. $1.20 to FC 1 = $1.40. This was the only significant change in the exchange rate since 19x0. A summary trial balance of Forco in FC at December 31, 19x6, is given below:

Cash	FC	100,000
Accounts receivable		300,000
Inventories, at cost		500,000
Prepaid expenses		25,000
Property, plant, and equipment (net)		1,000,000
Long-term note receivable		75,000
	FC	2,000,000

Accounts payable	FC	500,000
Current portion of long-term debt		100,000
Long-term debt		900,000
Capital stock		300,000
Retained earnings, January 1, 19x6		50,000
Sales		5,000,000
Cost of sales		(4,000,000)
Depreciation		(300,000)
Other expense		(550,000)
	FC	2,000,000

Additional information:

1. Fixed assets were purchased prior to July 1, 19x6.
2. The long-term note receivable was executed on January 31, 19x6.
3. FC 100,000 of the inventory on hand at year-end was purchased prior to July 1, 19x6.
4. Prepaid expenses represent unexpired insurance premiums that were paid on March 31, 19x6.
5. Long-term debt was incurred prior to July 1, 19x6.
6. All of the common stock was issued on the date of incorporation.
7. All accounts receivable and payable and long-term debt amounts are denominated in the local currency.
8. Sales, purchases, and all operating expenses are assumed to have occurred evenly throughout the year so that the application of the average exchange rate produced results as if each individual month's revenues and expenses were translated using the rate in effect during each month. It is appropriate to convert the cost of goods sold by use of the average rate.
9. The balance at the beginning of the year of the "equity adjustment from translation of foreign currency statements" is assumed to be $45,000 (debit). Income tax consequences, if any, relating to this account are to be ignored* in this illustration.

   * Generally interperiod tax allocation is required in accordance with *APB Opinion 11*, "Accounting for Income Taxes," if taxable exchange gains or tax-deductible exchange losses resulting from an entity's foreign currency transactions are included in net income in a different period for financial statement purposes than for tax purposes. Translation adjustments shall be accounted for in the same way as timing differences under the provisions of *APB Opinions 11, 23*, and *24. APB Opinion 23*, "Accounting for Income Taxes—Special Areas," provides that deferred taxes shall not be provided for unremitted earnings of a subsidiary in certain instances; in those instances, deferred taxes shall not be provided on translation adjustments.

Exhibit 9–6 presents the translation working paper for Forco Company.

A review of the translation working paper of the FORCO Company reveals the following noteworthy elements:

1. All items in the simplified income statement are converted at the average rate of exchange prevailing during the year.
2. All assets and liabilities are translated at the current rate of exchange. The Capital Stock account is translated at the historical rate. If all of a foreign entity's assets and liabilities are measured in its functional cur-

Exhibit 9–6

FORCO COMPANY
Translation Working Paper
Year Ended December 31, 19x6

	FC	Exchange rate	Translation code or explanation	U.S. dollars
Balance Sheet				
Cash	100,000	1.4	C	140,000
Accounts receivable	300,000	1.4	C	420,000
Inventories, at cost	500,000	1.4	C	700,000
Prepaid expenses	25,000	1.4	C	35,000
Property, plant, and equipment (net)	1,000,000	1.4	C	1,400,000
Long-term note receivable	75,000	1.4	C	105,000
Total Assets	2,000,000			2,800,000
Accounts payable	500,000	1.4	C	700,000
Current portion of long-term debt	100,000	1.4	C	140,000
Long-term debt	900,000	1.4	C	1,260,000
Total liabilities	1,500,000			2,100,000
Capital stock	300,000	1.2	H	360,000
Retained earnings:				
Balance, 1/1/x6	50,000		E	60,000
Current year net income	150,000		F	195,000
Balance, 12/31/x6	200,000			255,000
Equity adjustment from translation of foreign currency statements:				
Balance, 1/1/x6			E	(45,000)
Current year translation adjustment			G	130,000
Balance, 12/31/x6				85,000
Total stockholders' equity	500,000			700,000
Total liabilities and equity	2,000,000			2,800,000
Income Statement				
Sales	5,000,000	1.3	A	6,500,000
Cost of sales	(4,000,000)	1.3	A	(5,200,000)
Depreciation	(300,000)	1.3	A	(390,000)
Other expenses	(550,000)	1.3	A	(715,000)
Net income	150,000			195,000

Translation code or explanation:
C = current rate.
H = historical rate.
A = average rate.
E = balance in U.S. dollars at the beginning of the period.
F = per income statement.
G = amount needed to balance the financial statements.

rency and are translated at the current exchange rate, the net accounting effect of a change in the exchange rate is the effect on the net assets of the entity. That accounting result is compatible with the broad concept of economic hedging on which the net investment view is based. No gains or losses arise from hedged assets and liabilities, and the dollar equivalent of the unhedged net investment increases or decreases when the functional currency strengthens or weakens.

3. It will be noted that after the translated net income for 19x6 of $195,000 is added to the retained earnings section of the balance sheet, a translation adjustment of $130,000 must be inserted in order to balance the balance sheet. When this current year translation adjustment (credit) of $130,000 is added to the $45,000 opening debit balance of the Equity Adjustment from Translation of Foreign Currency Statements account, the resulting ending balance for this account is a credit of $85,000. This will be the opening balance of this equity account as of January 1, 19x7.

4. In this illustration, the translation is done in balance sheet and income statement (versus the trial balance)[16] format so as to highlight the FASB's treatment of classifying translation adjustments as a separate component of stockholders' equity.

5. In this particular example, the Equity Adjustment from Translation of Foreign Currency Statements account was affected only by the translation adjustment that was required in order to balance the translated balance sheet. In different circumstances, this account could also be debited or credited for:

    a. Gains and losses attributable to a foreign currency transaction that is designed as, and is effective as, an economic hedge of a net investment in a foreign entity.

    b. Gains or losses attributable to intercompany foreign currency transactions and balances that are of a long-term financing or capital nature when the entities to the transaction are consolidated, combined, or accounted for by the equity method in the reporting entity's financial statements.

---

[16] In the trial balance format where instead of a "cost of goods sold" figure, the opening inventory, purchases, as well as ending inventory are given, the translated dollar amount of the opening inventory will represent a forced figure computed as in the following example:

	FC	Exchange rate	U.S. dollars
Opening inventory	400,000	*	570,000
Add: Purchases	4,100,000	(A) 1.3	5,330,000
	4,500,000		5,900,000
Less: Ending inventory........	500,000	(C) 1.4	700,000
Equals cost of goods sold......	4,000,000	(A) 1.3	5,200,000

    * U.S. amount needed to allow cost of goods sold figure to be translated at average rate.

    A = Average rate.

    C = Current rate.

Accounting for investment by parent company

When the investment in the foreign subsidiary is accounted for by the parent company on the equity method, the parent will have to pick up *its* share of the translation adjustment.[17] Thus, in the case and our illustration for the year 19x6, Dollarco will make the following entries (figures in U.S. dollars):

Investment in Forco 195,000
    Equity in Earnings of Subsidiary   195,000
  To pick up earnings of Forco.

Investment in Forco 130,000
    Translation Adjustment   130,000
  To pick up the year translation adjustment.

Accounting where an investment in subsidiary is sold or liquidated

Continuing with our illustration, should Dollarco sell its investment in Forco on January 1, 19x7, then, *in addition* to recording a gain or loss on the difference between the proceeds of the sale and the carrying (book) value of the investment, Dollarco will close out the Equity Adjustment from Translation of Foreign Currency Statements account with a credit balance of $85,000 into income as part of this completed and realized sales transaction.

Disclosure requirements

SFAS 52 requires disclosure of the aggregate transaction gain or loss included in net income for the period as well as presentation of an analysis of the changes during the period in the separate component of equity for cumulative translation adjustments.

IMPLICATIONS FOR ANALYSIS

The fact that *SFAS 8* was one of the most criticized and controversial statements issued by the Board so far, as well as the fact that its replacement, *SFAS 52*, was issued by the narrow margin of 4 to 3, attests to the difficult and complex nature of the accounting for foreign exchange translation. In order for the analyst to be able to evaluate that accounting as well as to forecast the effect of currency rate changes on the results that it produces, the analyst must have a thorough understanding of both the philosophy underlying the new accounting standard as well as the mechanics which flow from it.

---

[17] Thus, if a parent owns only 80 percent of a subsidiary, it will pick up 80 percent of the translation adjustment.

The temporal method of translation under *SFAS 8* was the method most faithful to and consistent with the historical cost accounting model in present use. Under this method, and under the focus on the dollar that it embraced, nonmonetary items such as property, plant, and equipment and inventories are stated at the translated dollar amounts at date of acquisition. Similarly depreciation and cost of goods sold are reflected on the basis of such historical-dollar costs.

Since fluctuations in exchange rates did not affect the carrying amounts of these nonmonetary assets, it is clear that the real exposure to balance sheet translation gains and losses was measured by the excess of *monetary* assets over *monetary* liabilities (which were translated at *current* rates), or vice versa. Thus, under *SFAS 8* if a foreign subsidiary has an excess of monetary liabilities over monetary assets (i.e., heavy debt), then if:

As against local currency	Balance sheet translation effect is a—
Dollar strengthens	Gain
Dollar weakens	Loss

Conversely, if the foreign subsidiary has an excess of monetary assets over monetary liabilities (e.g., substantial equity capital), then if:

As against local currency	Balance sheet translation effect is a—
Dollar strengthens	Loss
Dollar weakens	Gain

It is clear that the impact of balance sheet translation under *SFAS 8* depended on circumstances, but the real complaint was that all these unpredictable gains and losses were included immediately in income thus resulting in earning volatility. As can be expected, company criticism was not as vocal when the translation process resulted in gains as when it resulted in losses. For that reason, not all companies were or are opposed to the methodology of *SFAS 8*. Some, in fact, are delaying the switch to *SFAS 52* until 1983.

SFAS 52 changed the accounting significantly except in two circumstances when the methodology of *SFAS 8* must continue to be employed:

1. When by virtue of its nature the foreign operation is merely an extension of the parent and consequently the dollar is its functional currency.
2. When hyper inflation (as defined) would cause the translation of nonmonetary assets at the current rate to result in unrealistically low carrying values. In such cases, in effect, the foreign currency has lost its usefulness

as a measure of performance and a more stable unit (i.e. the dollar) is used.

SFAS 52 introduced two radical departures. By moving away from the temporal method to the current exchange rate basis, it, in effect, selectively introduced current value accounting into this one area. Moreover, in allowing gains and losses to bypass the income statement, it reintroduced, in somewhat modified form, the long discredited "charge to surplus" approach (see Chapter 11). That, in effect, removed from current operations the effects of the risk of operating in a foreign environment along with the risks of changes in exchange rates.

While unquestionably insulating income from balance sheet *translation* gains and losses, as opposed to transaction gains and losses and income statement translation effects, *SFAS 52* introduced a translation exposure that differs from that of *SFAS 8.*

While under *SFAS 8* the translation exposure was measured by the excess of monetary assets over monetary liabilities (or vice versa), under *SFAS 52, all* balance sheet items, except the net equity, are translated at the current rate, and thus, the exposure is measured by the size of the net equity or net investment. This can be illustrated as follows:

ILLUSTRATION 5. Assume that Swissco, a subsidiary of Amerco, started operations on January 1, 19x1, with a balance sheet in Swiss Francs (SF) as follows:

	SF		SF
Cash	100	Accounts payable....	90
Receivables	120	Capital stock	360
Inventory	90		
Fixed assets	140		
	450		450

The income statement for the year ending January 31, 19x1, was:

	SF
Sales	3,000
Cost of sales (including depreciation of SF 20)....	(1,600)
Other expenses	(800)
Net income	600

The year-end balance sheet was as follows:

	SF		SF
Cash	420	Accounts payable	180
Receivables	330	Capital stock........	360
Inventories	270	Retained earnings	600
Fixed assets (net)	120		
	1,140		1,140

For ease of computation, the above changes were kept simple and we assume the following exchange rates:

$$
\begin{array}{ll}
\text{January 1, 19x1} \ldots\ldots & 1\$ = \text{SF } 2 \\
\text{December 12, 19x1} \ldots\ldots & 1\$ = \text{SF } 3 \\
\text{19x1 average} \ldots\ldots\ldots\ldots & 1\$ = \text{SF } 2.50
\end{array}
$$

The opening and closing balance sheets would be translated into dollars as follows:

	January 1, 19x1			December 31, 19x1		
	SF	Conversion	$	SF	Conversion	$
Cash	100	÷ 2	50	420	÷ 3	140
Receivables	120	÷ 2	60	330	÷ 3	110
Inventory	90	÷ 2	45	270	÷ 3	90
Fixed assets	140	÷ 2	70	120	÷ 3	40
	450		225	1,140		380
Accounts payable	90	÷ 2	45	180	÷ 3	60
Capital stock	360	÷ 2	180	360	÷ 2	180
Retained earnings				600	*	240
Translation adjustment						(100)
	450		225	1,140		380

* Per income statement—since *each* individual income statement item is translated at the average rate, net income in dollars is SF 600 ÷ 2.50 = $240.

The translation adjustment account (which is part of equity) can be independently calculated as follows:

		$
Total equity (which equals net assets):		
In SF at December 31, 19x1	SF 960	
Converted into dollars at year-end rate ÷ 3		$ 320
Less:		
Capital stock at December 31, 19x1 per		
convered balance sheet (in dollars)..............	$180	
Retained earnings balance at December 31, 19x1,		
per converted balance sheet (in dollars)..........	240	420
Translation adjustment—loss		$(100)

A number of analytical insights can be derived from this illustration:

1. The translation adjustment (in this case, a loss of $100 for the year 19x1) is a function of the net investment in Swissco at end of 19x1 (SF

960) times the change in the exchange rates. Since the exchange rate had declined from SF 2 to the dollar for the capital stock and from SF 2.50 to the dollar for retained earnings to the year-end rate of SF 3 to the dollar, the SF investment expressed in dollars has sufered a loss of $100. That makes sense—when you have an investment expressed in a foreign currency and that currency weakens in relation to the dollar then the value of your investment, in terms of dollars, declines.

2. While under *SFAS 52*, net income is not affected by *balance sheet* translation, the equity capital is. That will affect the debt-to-equity ratio (the level of which may be specified by certain debt covenants) and book value per share of the translated balance sheet but not of the foreign currency balance sheet. Since the entire equity capital is the measure of exposure to balance sheet translation gain or loss, that exposure may be even more substantial than that under *SFAS 8* particularly with regard to a subsidiary financed with low debt and high equity. The analyst can estimate the translation adjustment impact by multiplying year-end equity by the estimated change in the period to period rate of exchange.

3. The effect of a change in exchange rates on the translation of the income statement is another matter. If for simplicity we assume that in 19x2 Swissco will have exactly the same net income but that the SF has weakened further to SF 3.50 (average for year) to the dollar then the translated net income will total SF $600 \div 3.50 = \$171$, or a decline of $69 from the 19x1 level of $240. This loss will, of course, be reflected in the translated income statement.

Conversely, should the SF strengthen to SF 2 to the dollar (average for year), the translated net income will total SF $600 \div 2 = \$300$, or a gain of $60 from the 19x1 level of $240. Here again this is a gain that will be reflected in net income since the income earned in SF is worth more dollars. Note that under *SFAS 52*, translated reported earnings will vary directly with changes in exchange rates and that this makes estimation by the analyst of the "income statement translation effect" easier. Estimation of earnings under *SFAS 8* was more difficult.

The analyst must also be aware that in addition to the above, income will also include the results of completed foreign exchange transactions. Also, any gain or loss on the translation of a current payable by the subsidiary to parent (which is not of a long-term capital nature) will pass through consolidated net income.

In FRR 6, the SEC notes its concern about the adequacy of financial statement disclosure about the effects of translating foreign operations. The Release suggests that management's discussion and analysis should provide more information to supplement what's in the financial statements, such as:

> Information about how rate changes affect reported operating results—e.g., the depressing effect of weakening foreign currencies on reported sales.
> Identification of functional currencies used for significant foreign operations, and the extent of exchange rate risk involved.

Availability of cash flows from foreign operations to meet the company's overall needs.

Finally, analysts should realize that financial statements prepared in accordance with *SFAS 52* are not comparable to those prepared under the guides of *SFAS 8.*

QUESTIONS

1. *a.* List and explain three main reasons why a parent company may not choose to include certain subsidiaries in its consolidated financial statements.

   b. What significant information may be disclosed by inspection of individual parent company and subsidiary statements in addition to the consolidated statements? (CFA)

2. "A parent company is not responsible for the liabilities of its subsidiaries nor does it own the assets of the subsidiaries. Therefore, consolidated financial statements distort legal realities." Evaluate this statement from the financial analyst's viewpoint.

3. Which of the following cases would require consolidated financial statements?

   a. The parent company has a two-fifths ownership of the subsidiary.

   b. The parent company has temporary but absolute control over the subsidiary.

   c. The parent company has a controlling interest in the subsidiary but plans to dispose of it.

   d. Control of the subsidiary is to be relinquished in the near future as a result of a minority shareholder's derivative suit.

   e. A conglomerate parent company has a majority interest in diversified subsidiaries.

   f. The parent company has a 100 percent interest in a foreign subsidiary in a country where the conversion of currencies and the transfer of funds is severely restricted by the governmental authorities.

   g. The parent company has a 100 percent interest in a subsidiary whose principal business is the leasing of properties to the parent company and its affiliates.

4. Why is the cost method of accounting for investments in subsidiaries regarded as the least desirable?

5. Give some examples of situations in which the use of the cost method, rather than the equity method, is more appropriate.

6. What are some of the important limitations to which consolidated financial statements are subject?

7. The following note appeared in the financial statements of the Best Company for the period ending December 31, 19x1:

   "*Event subsequent to December 31, 19x1:* In January 19x2, the Company acquired Good Products, Inc., and its affiliates by the issuance of 48,063 shares of common stock. Net assets of the combined companies amounted to $1,016,198, and net income for 19x1 approximated $150,000. To the extent that the acquired companies earn in excess of $1,000,000 over the next five years, the Company will be required to issue additional shares not exceeding 151,500, limited, however, to a market value of $2,000,000."

a. Is the disclosure necessary and adequate?

b. If the Good Products, Inc., was acquired in December 19x1, at what price should the Best Company have recorded the acquisition, assuming the Best Company's shares are traded at $22 on that day?

c. On what is the additional consideration contingent?

d. If the contingency materializes to the maximum limit, how should Best Company record the investment?

8. How would you determine the valuation of assets acquired in a purchase in the following cases?

a. Assets acquired by incurring liabilities.

b. Assets acquired in exchange of common stock.

9. Assuming the total cost of a purchased entity is appropriately determined, how should the total cost be allocated to the following assets?

a. Goodwill.

b. Negative goodwill (bargain purchase).

c. Marketable securities.

d. Receivables.

e. Finished goods.

f. Work in process.

g. Raw materials.

h. Plant and equipment.

i. Land and mineral reserves.

j. Payables.

k. Goodwill recorded in the book of the acquired company.

10. One of the arguments for pooling of interests is that in pooling no resource is given in exchange for the acquisition: since the acquiring company gives its unissued stock, the acquisition cannot be regarded as purchase. Do you agree?

11. Company A accounts as a pooling of interests the acquisition of Company B, the market value of whose net assets is much higher than their book value. What will be the effect of the pooling of interests method on Company A's income statement? On its balance sheet? What significance does *APB Opinion 16* have on such effects?

12. How is "goodwill" treated in an acquisition accounted for as a pooling of interests?

13. If assets are understated as a result of a pooling of interests, what effect(s) would be the understatement having on the following:

a. Capital account.

b. Various expenses.

c. Disposition of assets acquired.

14. Is there any way an analyst can adjust the income statement under the pooling of interests method so that it can be comparable to a purchase method income statement?

15. From the anlyst's point of view, which method of accounting for a business combination is preferable and why?

16. When an acquisition accounted for as a purchase is effected for stock or other equity securities, what should the analyst be alerted to?

17. When the balance sheet shows a substantial amount of goodwill, to what should the analyst be alert?

18. A current accounting controversy concerns the widespread use of pooling in mergers. Opponents of the use of pooling believe that the surviving company often uses pooling (rather than purchase) to hide the "true" effects of the merger. What may be "hidden," and how is the analysis of a company's securities affected by pooling practices? (CFA)

19. Company X has engaged in an aggressive program of acquiring other companies through exchange of common stock.
    a. Explain briefly how an acquisition program might contribute to the rate of growth in earnings per share of Company X.
    b. Explain briefly how the income statements of prior years might be adjusted to reflect the potential future earnings trend of the combined companies. (CFA)

20. What are some factors that could change management's original estimates of the useful life of intangible assets?

21. What are some significant problem areas in accounting for foreign operations?

22. When a consolidated financial statement includes foreign operations, to what must the financial analyst be particularly alert?

23. What are the major objectives of *SFAS 52?*

24. What are the major provisions of *SFAS 52?*

25. Discuss the major changes that were introduced by *SFAS 52* on translation of foreign currency.

26. Under what circumstances must the provisions of *SFAS 8* continue to be employed?

27. What radical departures from the provisions of *SFAS 8* did *SFAS 52* introduce?

28. What are the implications for analysis resulting from *SFAS 52?*

10

Analysis of the income statement—I

The income statement portrays the net results of operations of an enterprise. Since results are what enterprises are supposed to achieve and since their value is, in large measure, determined by the size and quality of these results, it follows quite logically that the analyst attaches great importance to the income statement.

This chapter and the one that follows will examine the principles that underlie the preparation and presentation of the income statement. The analysis and interpretation of this important financial statement are discussed in Chapters 20 and 21. Such analysis can be undertaken intelligently only after the principles outlined in these chapters are fully understood.

What is income? An examination of this subject will reveal that significant differences of opinion exist among thoughtful and competent accountants, economists, and financial analysts on what income is and on how the net income of an enterprise for a given period should be measured.

A simple illustration

Take, for example, the very simple case of a business unit that has only $1,000 in cash, with which it buys at the beginning of the year a bond priced at par and carrying a 6 percent coupon. While we may readily agree that the gross income is $60 (the interest), the determination of net income depends, among other factors, on the value of the bond at year-end. Thus, if the market price at year-end is $950, the $50 loss would be recognized by the economist while the accountant may or may not recognize it, depending on a judgment of whether there has been a permanent impairment in the value of the bond and, also, on whether the loss must be recognized if it is the present intention of the enterprise to hold it to a not too distant maturity date. The economist would claim that it is not right to recognize the income of $60 without the offsetting shrinkage in capital in the amount of $50.

The essence of this argument is that the enterprise was not as well off at the end of the period as it was at the beginning if the $60 is all recognized as income and so distributed.

If, instead, the bond had a market quotation at year-end of $1,100, then some economists would consider the $100 accretion as a gain to be added to the $60 in interest earned. This most accountants would not do because the gain is not realized and the market value of the bond could fluctuate in either direction before it is finally sold. Other theoreticians would not rely on the current market price of the bond but, taking the going interest rate into account, would value the bond at the present value of future interest receipts ($60 a year) plus the present value of the bond principal at maturity discounted at the appropriate rate and would use such value in the determination of net income for the period. There again, accountants have, so far, shied away from such approaches mostly because the variables that make up the bond value can change very frequently before final realization through sale or redemption of the bond. They consider such realization as the necessary objective evidence needed to warrant recording of the gain.

Price-level changes complicate matters even further, and their effect as well as significant proposed accounting modifications are considered in Chapter 14.

If such a simple income-producing asset as a bond, which involves no complexities on the expense side, can give rise to so many possible interpretations of what the amount of the net income it produced is, it is obvious that the determination of the amount of net income of a full-fledged business enterprise is far more complex. It is in this light that one can, at least, understand, even if not fully agree with, the principles of income determination that accountants have established over the years.

A variety of concepts of income

Going from our simple specific example to generalizations, we see that the economist's concept of income is the amount that could be consumed or distributed by an entity during a period and still leave it as "well-off" at the end of the period as it was at the beginning.

It is in the area of measuring the degree of "well-offness" of an enterprise that the gap between the economist's view and that of the accountant is widest. The economist maintains that capital value can be measured by the present value of future net receipts. But such receipts are based on highly subjective and constantly shifting estimates of future probabilities applying to both the *size* of the net receipts and the discount factors to be applied to them. The degree of uncertainty present here dwarfs that involved in estimating, for example, the future useful life of plant and equipment or the probability of debt collection, which are estimates of a kind that accountants now make. Thus, while the economist, cognizant of the uncertainty pervading all of business life, is impatient with the accountant's great concern for objectivity, verifiability, and conservatism, the latter believes that the very utility of his professional service to the community is dependent upon his upholding these qualities and characteristics.

Because of the divergencies in viewpoint such as those discussed above, the differences in the concepts of income of economists and accountants have not been appreciably narrowed. This is, in large measure, also due to difficulties that a practicing profession found in implementing in practice the theoretical concepts of economic thought.

One way in which income can be measured is by comparing the capital balances at the beginning and end of a period.[1] Since capital is the excess of assets over liabilities, the problem of income determination is thus inseparable from the problem of asset and liability measurement. While, as we have seen, the economist focuses on a comparison of capital balances at successive points in time, in modern accounting, the income determination process centers around the relating of current costs and revenues within a specific span of time. To the analyst who is interested in using the income statement as a means of predicting future streams of income and expense, this is a much more useful approach, because he is very much interested in all the elements that make up the final net income figure.

The process of income determination thus involves two basic steps: (1) identification of the revenues properly attributable to the period reported upon and (2) relating of the corresponding costs with the revenues of this period either through direct association with the cost of the products sold therein or by assignment as expenses properly applicable as period costs.

THE ACCRUAL OF REVENUE

For every profit-seeking enterprise, the first step in the process of profit recognition is the accrual of revenue. Thus, the very important question arises when, that is, at what point in the entire sequence of revenue-earning activities in which an enterprise is engaged, is it proper to recognize revenue as earned? The improper accrual of revenue can have one of two undesirable effects:

1. Revenue may be recorded prematurely or belatedly, that is, it may be assigned to the wrong fiscal period.
2. Revenue may be recorded before there is a reasonable certainty that it will actually be realized. This in turn can lead to reporting of gain derived from such revenue in one period and the cancellation or reversal of such profit, with a resultant loss, in a subsequent period. The effect of

---

[1] FASB *SFAC 3*, "Comprehensive Income," best fits this concept of measurement and is defined as the overall return on financial capital (i.e., the change in net assets other than from transactions with owners).

this is to overstate net income in one period and to understate it in a subsequent period.

Conditions for revenue recognition

These two effects are, of course, highly undesirable and misleading; and in order to minimize such possibilities, accountants have adopted strict and conservative rules regarding the recognition of revenues.[2] The following criteria exemplify the rules that have been established to prevent the premature anticipation of revenues. Thus, recognition is deemed to take place only after the following conditions have been met:

1. The earning activities undertaken to create revenue have been substantially completed, for example, no significant effort is necessary to complete the transaction.
2. In case of sale, the risk of ownership has been effectively passed on to the buyer.
3. The revenue, as well as the associated expenses, can be measured or estimated with substantial accuracy.
4. The revenue recognized should normally result in an increase in cash, receivables, or marketable securities, under certain conditions in an increase in inventories or other assets, or a decrease in a liability.
5. The business transactions giving rise to the income should be at arm's length with independent parties (i.e., not with controlled parties).
6. The transactions should not be subject to revocation, for example, carrying the right of return of merchandise sold.

While the above criteria may appear to be pretty straightforward, they are, in fact, subject to a number of exceptions and have, in practice, been interpreted in a variety of ways. The best way to understand these variations is to examine the application of these concepts in a variety of circumstances.

Uncertainty as to collection of receivables

In normal circumstances, doubts about the collectibility of receivables resulting from a sale should be reflected in a provision for doubtful accounts. *APB Opinion 10* affirms this when it states that "profit is deemed to be realized when a sale in the ordinary course of business is effected, unless the circumstances are such that the collection of the sales price is not reasonably assured." At what point the collection of a receivable is no longer reasonably assured is, of course, a matter of judgment based on all the surrounding circumstances. Moreover, such judgment may be conservative or it may be based on liberal or optimistic assumptions.

---

[2] For an excellent summary of rules as well as the rationale behind them, see H. R. Jaenicke, *Survey of Present Practices in Recognizing Revenues, Expenses, Gains, and Losses* (Stamford, Conn.: FASB, 1981).

Installment sales. Installment sales normally result in a receivable that is collectible over a period of many months or even many years. Time is an important dimension in the assessment of risk, for the more distant the time of the collection of the proceeds of the sale, the more uncertain the final collection of the receivable. Conceivably, then, the length of time of collection is an important factor in assessing the probability of ultimate collection. Except in situations where the doubt about the collection of installment receivables is such as to make a reasonable estimate impossible, profit on installment sales is properly recognized at the time of sales.

Cost recovery method. When an entity has no reasonable basis for estimating the degree of collectability of receivables, it may use the cost recovery method under which no profit is recognized until the cost of the item sold has been recovered from actual collections.

Real estate accounting. The sale of real estate is often characterized by payment terms stretching over long time periods. A long-delayed collection period increases uncertainty, and thus the recognition of profit on such sales is dependent on an ability to assess the probability of collection of the full sales price.

SFAS 66, "Accounting for Sales of Real Estate," stipulates that for retail land sales, the full accrual method can be used only if the real estate seller's receivables from land sales are collectible and if the seller does not have any significant remaining construction or development obligations. In cases where these conditions are not met, the sales are to be reported under the percentage-of-completion or the installment method of accounting.

For sales of real estate other than retail land sales, *SFAS 66* requires the sale to be consummated, the buyer's down payment and committment for continuing investment in the property sold to be adequate, and the seller not to have a substantial continuing involvement with the property after the sale.

SFAS 67, "Accounting for Costs and Initial Rental Operations of Real Estate Projects," stipulates that when a rental project is being developed, the project changes from nonoperating to operating when it is substantially completed and held available for occupancy—that is, a completion of tenant improvements, but no later than one year from the cessation of major construction activities. From that time, only development and construction costs should be capitalized, and all capitalized costs should begin to be amortized. Costs that should be capitalized and those that should not are also identified.

Revenue recognition when right of return exists

SFAS 48, "Revenue Recognition When Right of Return Exists," specifies that revenue from sales transactions in which the buyer has a right to return the product should be recognized at the time of sale only if *all* of the following conditions are met:

- At the date of sale, the price is substantially fixed or determinable.
- The buyer has paid the seller, or is obligated to pay the seller (not contingent on resale of the product).
- In the event of theft or physical damage to the product, the buyer's obligation to the seller would not be changed.
- The buyer acquiring the product for resale has economic substance apart from that provided by the seller.
- The seller does not have significant obligations for future performance to directly bring about resale of the product.
- Product returns can be reasonably estimated.

If these conditions are not met, revenue recognition is postponed; if they are met, sales revenue and cost of sales should be reduced to reflect estimated returns and expected costs or losses should be accrued.

The *Statement* does not apply to accounting for revenue in service industries if part or all of the service revenue may be returned under cancellation privileges granted to the buyer, transactions involving real estate or leases, or sales transactions in which a customer may return defective goods, such as under warranty provisions.

Right of return problems vary from industry to industry. In the newspaper or perishable foods industry, returns follow sales relatively quickly. On the other hand, in book or record publishing, returns may occur after a longer period.

Warner Communications, Inc., made the following disclosure in its 1980 annual report:

> In accordance with industry practice, records, tapes, magazines and books are usually sold to customers with the right to return unsold items. Revenues from these and other sales represent gross sales less a provision for future returns. It is WCI's general policy to value returned goods included in inventory at estimated realizable value but not in excess of cost.

The ability to estimate future returns is an important consideration. Items that would appear to impair the ability to reasonably predict returns include:

Susceptibility to significant external factors, such as technological obsolescence or swings in market demand.

Long return privilege periods.

Absence of appropriate historical return experience.

Accounting for franchise fee revenue

SFAS 45, "Accounting for Franchise Fee Revenue," establishes accounting and reporting standards for franchisors. It requires that franchise fee revenue from individual and area franchise sales be recognized only when all material services or conditions relating to the sale have been substantially performed or satisfied by the franchisor. This *Statement* also establishes accounting standards for continuing franchise fees, continuing product sales, agency sales, repossessed franchises, franchising costs, commingled revenue, and relationships between a franchisor and a franchisee.

Church Fried Chicken makes the following disclosure:

> **Application, License and Royalty Fees.**   All fees from licensed operations are included in revenue as earned. In 1980, management accelerated the revenue recognition for application fees from the time the site is approved or construction begun to the time cash is received. Management believes this method will more accurately relate the income recognition to performance of the related service. As a result of this change, $515,000 was recognized as revenue in 1980 which was collected in prior years.
>
> License fees are earned when the related store opens. Unearned license fees which have been collected are included in current liabilities. Royalty fees are based on licensee revenues and are recognized in the period the related revenues are earned.

Product financing arrangements

Unlike the two *SFASs* discussed above, which deal with the *timing* of revenue recognition, *SFAS 49,* "Accounting for Product Financing Arrangements," is concerned with the issue of whether revenue has been earned.

A product financing arrangement is an agreement involving the transfer or sponsored acquisition of inventory which, although it sometimes resembles a sale of inventory, is in substance a means of financing inventory through a second part. For example, if a company transfers inventory to another company in an apparent sale, and in a related transaction agrees to repurchase the inventory at a later date, the arrangement may be a product financing arrangement rather than a sale and subsequent purchase of inventory.

In essence, if the party bearing the risks and rewards of ownership transfers inventory to a purchaser, and in a related transaction agrees to repurchase the product at a specified price, or guarantees some specified resale price for sales of the product to outside parties, the arrangement is a product financing arrangement and should be accounted as such (see also Chapter 7).

Transfers of receivables with recourse

Another important revenue recognition issue is the question of the circumstances under which transfers of receivables with recourse are to be accounted for as sales.

The FASB has concluded that a transfer of receivables with recourse would be reported as a sale, and gain or loss would be recognized if all of the following conditions are met:

1.   The transferor surrenders control of the future economic benefits of the receivables.

2.   Thé transferor's recourse obligation can be reasonably estimated.
3.   The transferee cannot require the transferor to repurchase the receivables, except under the recourse provisions.

Otherwise, the proceeds from the transfer would be reported as a liability. A transfer to a wholly owned finance subsidiary would not prohibit recognition as a sale.

Timing of revenue recognition

A major problem area in revenue recognition is the matter of *timing*. It is a basic principle of accounting that gains accrue only at the time of sale and that gains may not be anticipated by reflecting assets at their current sales prices. There are some exceptions to the rule, primarily in the case of smaller agricultural producers who, facing difficult cost determination problems, often use "the farm price method" (in which revenue is measured by the current market price less estimated costs of disposition) to value inventory. This method in essence recognizes revenue when production is complete. A variation of this method is the recording of a farmer's "sale" to a cooperative as the basis for revenue recognition. This practice is often of doubtful validity because the cooperative is not sufficiently independent for the "sale" to constitute an effective transfer of risk. An example of such revenue recognition method can be seen in Note 1 (item 71) of Alfa, Inc. (Appendix 4B), a method from which the company switched per Note 2 (item 72) in 19x5.

Another area of *seeming* exception to the principle that gains accrue only at the time of sale is contract accounting where, in effect, the contract to sell normally precedes production or construction and where profit may, under certain conditions, be taken up in proportion to activity.

Contract accounting

The basis of recording income on short-term construction or production contracts poses no special problems. Profit is ordinarily recognized when the end product is completed and has been accepted by the owner.

Long-term construction contracts, be they for buildings, battleships, or complex machinery, present a more difficult accounting problem. Here the construction cycle may extend over a number of accounting periods while substantial costs accumulate, financed in part by progress billings. Two generally accepted methods of accounting are in use:[3]

1.   The *percentage-of completion* method is preferred when estimates of costs to complete and estimates of progress towards completion of the contract

---

[3] ACSEC's *Statement of Position No. 81–1*, "Accounting for Performance of Construction-Type and Certain Production-Type Contracts," emphasizes that these two methods should not be used as acceptable alternatives for the same circumstances.

can be made with reasonable dependability. A common basis of profit estimation is to record that part of the estimated total profit that corresponds to the ratio that costs incurred to date bear to expected total costs.[4] Other methods of estimation of completion can be based on units completed, on qualified engineering estimates, or on units delivered.

2.   The *completed-contract* method of accounting is preferable where the conditions inherent in the contracts present risks and uncertainties that result in an inability to make reasonable estimates of costs and completion time. Problems under this method concern the point at which completion of the contract is deemed to have occurred as well as the kind of expenses to be deferred. Thus, some companies defer all costs to the completion date, including general and administrative overhead, while others consider such costs as period costs to be expensed as they are incurred.

Under either of the two contract accounting methods, losses, present or anticipated, must be fully provided for in the period in which the loss first becomes apparent.

Finance company accounting

Generally, the accrual of interest is a function of time. The income on a bond or a loan to others depends on principal outstanding, time elapsed, and rate.

Finance companies, such as in the consumer or sales finance fields, make loans under which a finance charge is added on to the face amount of the rate, that is, discount and add-on loans.

A number of alternative methods of taking up this discount exist. Thus, if the face of the note is $2,400 and the cash advanced is $2,160, the $240 unearned finance charge can be taken up over, say, 12 months, in a number of ways:

1.   Under the *straight-line method*, one twelfth or $20 would be taken up each month as an installment is collected.

2.   Under the *sum-of-the-months'-digits* method, larger amounts of income are recognized in the early part of the loan contract than in its latter period. In the case of a 12-month loan, the sum of the digits is 78. In the first month of the contract, 12/78th of the finance charge ($36.92) is taken into income; and in the last month, 1/78th ($3.14) is taken up. Under this method, the interest earned bears a closer relationship to funds out at risk than it does under the straight-line method. That is also true of other methods that take up income in proportion to the decreasing balance of the loan outstanding.

---

[4] Under this method the current year contract revenues equals

$$\left[\frac{\text{Total costs incurred to date}}{\text{Estimated total costs}} \times \frac{\text{Contract}}{\text{price}}\right] \text{less} \left[\begin{array}{c}\text{Contract revenue recognized}\\ \text{in prior years}\end{array}\right]$$

3. A variation of either of the above methods involves taking into income, immediately on granting of the loan, an amount, also called acquisition factor, which is designed to offset the initial loan acquisition expenses incurred by the company. The balance of the unearned finance charge is then taken into income by means of one of alternative methods.

When should the recording of interest income be discontinued

An AICPA *Statement of Position* on "Accounting Practices of Real Estate Investment Trusts" states that the recognition of interest revenue should be discontinued when it is not reasonable to expect that it will be received. The following conditions should be regarded as establishing such a presumption:

1. Payments of principal or interest are past due.
2. The borrower is in default under the terms of the loan agreement.
3. Foreclosure proceedings have been or are expected to be initiated.
4. The credit-worthiness of the borrower is in doubt because of pending or actual bankruptcy proceedings, the filing of liens against his assets, etc.
5. Cost overruns and/or delays in construction cast doubt on the economic viability of the project.
6. The loan has been renegotiated.

Accounting for lease income

Another special branch of revenue accounting is found in the case of companies leasing property to others. Their methods of revenue recognition are discussed in Chapter 7.

"Sales" to leasing subsidiaries

Before revenue under a sale can be considered as realized, there must be a genuine transfer of risk from seller to buyer. An interesting example of the importance of this principle is provided by the furor caused by the attempt by Memorex Corporation to treat as an immediate sale the transfer of equipment to the company's unconsolidated leasing subsidiary.

The basic flaw in the proposed accounting was (1) that the subsidiary had not been capitalized by the influsion of third-party capital and could, as a consequence, not pay Memorex for the equipment; and (2) that memorex had agreed to protect the subsidiary against losses. In short, these conditions clearly demonstrated that there was no transfer of the risk of ownership from Memorex to third parties, and consequently there was no genuine sale. Thus, the company had to agree to treat the transfer of the leased equipment as a lease rather than as an outright sale.

Additional examples of income recognition problems

Additional examples of problems regarding the timing of revenue recognition can be found in a number of industries.

Thus, Dow Jones & Company reports as follows on the accounting for unearned subscriptions that are carried as current liabilities:

> *Subscription revenue* is recorded as earned, pro rata on a monthly basis, over the life of the subscriptions. Costs in connection with the procurement of subscriptions are charged to expense as incurred.

In the liquor industry, Schenley Industries, Inc., reported on a timing aspect of income recognition as follows:

> The company sells certain whiskey in barrels in bond under agreements which provide for future bottling. In prior years, profits on such transactions were reflected as of the date of sale. The present company policy is to treat such profits as deferred income until the whiskey is bottled and shipped.

Income of subsidiaries and affiliates

When a company owns a part or the whole of another entity, the interest of the company in the subsidiary's income may be accounted for in a number of ways (see also Chapter 9).

1. Consolidated financial statements may be prepared, thus including the subsidiary's income in the consolidated income statement while excluding any minority interest in that income. It is generally recognized that such financial statements do in most cases represent the most meaningful presentation of the financial position and the results of operations.

2. If a subsidiary is not consolidated, two methods of reporting the parent company's investment in it are possible:

a. The cost method under which only dividends received are recorded as income by the parent. Because the latter has the power to control the amount and timing of dividend declarations by the subsidiary, the dividends may not reflect the actual earnings performance of the subsidiary and thus may lead to income distortion or manipulation.

Because of the above-mentioned possible distortions, *APB Opinion 18* now requires that if consolidation is not appropriate, for whatever reason, the investments in subsidiaries be carried "at equity."

b. The equity method takes up the parent company's proportionate part of a subsidiary's profits and losses, thus reflecting best the parent company's share of the subsidiary's results. The equity method is, thus, appropriate in all cases except those where there are serious limitations or restrictions on remittance of dividends, or where control is likely to be temporary or where it is not adequate.

When the parent company and its subsidiary are consolidated or when the parent picks up the equity in the earnings of the subsidiary, intercompany sales and profits must be eliminated from the consolidated statements and intercompany profits must be eliminated from the amounts the parent picks up as equity in the subsidiary's earnings.

Jointly owned companies. Frequently, two corporations join in forming a new corporation which, in effect, represents a joint venture in which each owns a 50 percent interest and has a voice in management. *APB Opinion 18* concluded that the equity method reflects best the underlying nature of investments in such ventures and calls for accounting for the investment at equity, thus recording a proportionate share of the results as they are earned. This method should be used regardless of the percentage of ownership, provided the corporate joint venture is operated by a small group of businesses for their mutual benefit and encompasses a pooling of resources and a sharing of risks and rewards as well as participation in the overall management of the investee.

Implications for analysis

The income statement, presenting as it does, the results achieved by an enterprise and the return achieved on invested capital is of great importance to the analyst in the valuation of an enterprise. For exactly this reason and for such reasons as pride, pressure to achieve results, compensation based on income, and the value of stock options, management is greatly interested in the results it reports. Consequently, the analyst can expect managements to choose those accounting principles and procedures that come closest to achieving their purposes.

The objectives of income reporting that management is desirous of achieving do not always result in the fairest or most proper measurement of results, and consequently the analyst must be ever alert to management's propensities as well as the choices available to it.

THE DATAPOINT CORPORATION CASE.   In 1982, it was discovered that Datapoint Corporation would have to reverse a significant amount of sales that hardpressed sales representatives booked by asking customers to order millions of dollars of computer equipment months in advance with payment to be made much later. On this basis, Datapoint recorded sales as revenue even though in many cases the equipment had not even been manufactured. It was reported that these sales representatives were under corporate pressure to achieve unreasonable or unattainable goals.

For additional cases, see the "Revenue Smoothing and Revenue Distortion" Section of Chapter 22.

Since the recording of revenue is the first step in the process of income recognition and on which the recognition of any and all profit depends, the analyst should be particularly inquisitive about the accounting methods chosen so as to ascertain whether they reflect economic reality. Thus, for example, if a manufacturer records profits on sale to the dealer, the analyst must inquire about dealer inventories because the real earning activity consists in selling to the ultimate consumer. Similarly, when a membership fee to a golf club is recorded at the time a contract is signed, the analyst must determine whether the crucial earning activity consists of selling memberships or in delivering the services of the golf club.

Problem of collectibility.   One element that casts doubt on the recording of revenue is *uncertainty about the collectibility* of the resulting receivable. We have examined the special problems relating to installment sales, real estate sales, and franchise sales. Problems of collection exist, however, in the case of all sales, and the analyst must be alert to them. Sales with right of return can often turn out not be be sales at all, and the analyst should be alert to these.

Let us conclude the consideration of the collection problem by an example from the bowling equipment manufacturing industry. The early 1960s witnessed a bowling boom that was attended by the building of a large number of bowling alleys that competed for a limited amount of business in restricted territories. The two major manufacturers of bowling equipment sold it to inexperienced and poorly financed operators against notes and receivables, mostly secured by the equipment itself. The full profit on this equipment was immediately taken up while the provision for bad debts concurrently established underestimated by a wide mark the special risks involved. Brunswick Corporation wrote off very substantial amounts of accounts receivable in 1963, while American Machine & Foundry made similarly substantial writeoffs of receivables only five years later. Long before the write-offs were announced, the alert analyst could have taken his cue from the deteriorating business conditions in the bowling industry. There was, however, little in the financial statements of the bowling manufacturers to forewarn of the losses yet to come.

Timing of revenue.   The emphasis on transactions rather than performance has resulted often in the anticipation of earnings ahead of completion of the earnings process. The analyst must be alert to the problems related to the *timing of revenue recognition*. We have examined the accounting concept of realization and the reasons for the accountant's great preoccupation with objective and verifiable evidence in this area. While the justification for this position is the subject of much debate both within and outside the accounting profession, it behooves the analyst to understand the implications of present accounting in this area on his work.

The present rules of realization generally do not allow for recognition of profit in advance of sale. Thus, increases in market value of property such as land, equipment, or securities, the accretion of values in growing timber, or the increase in the value of inventories are not recognized in the accounts (see, however, Chapter 14). As a consequence, income will not be recorded before sale, and the timing of sales is in turn a matter that lies importantly within the discretion of management. That, in turn, gives management a certain degree of discretion in the timing of profit recognition.

Contract accounting.   In the area of contract accounting, the analyst should recognize that the use of the completed-contract method is justified only in cases where reasonable estimates of costs and the degree of completion are not possible. In fact, from the statement user's point of view it is a poor method because results can be unpredictable and very erratic.

The percentage-of-completion method of accounting is, however, not free of problems and pitfalls. This can be seen from the following examples:

ILLUSTRATION 1.   Stirling Homex, a company that built modular houses, had strong incentives to show earnings growth because it was a "glamour company" and needed financing as well. Invoking percentage-of-completion contract accounting principles, it recognized the earnings process as completed when housing modules were "manufactured and assigned to specific contracts." In fact, this method was nothing but an earning-by-producing process, and the spurious "sales" were reversed in 1972—a process which triggered loan defaults and ultimately led to bankruptcy.

ILLUSTRATION 2.   The case of Four Seasons Nursing Centers, which collapsed around the early 1970s, presents a particularly vivid example of the dangers and the pitfalls of percentage-of-completion contract accounting *in actual application.* When, during their 1969 audit, the auditors, for whatever reasons, found physical engineering estimates of job completion to be unacceptable, the company was forced to base the degree of contract completion on the percentage that the costs incurred to date bore to total estimated costs. The company, which was at the time on the "glamour treadmill" of Wall Street with strong incentives to produce increasing earnings, proceeded to supply the auditors with cost invoices that later proved fictitious or inapplicable to the situation at hand.[5] These formed the basis for a higher percentage of completion with the resultant increased profit pickup. That was the road to the company's ultimate collapse.

Cost incurrence is at best a convenient rather than a precise method of estimating the degree of contract completion. Auditors are supposed to satisfy themselves that the cost method is a reliable substitute for more precise methods such as engineering estimates, etc.

In addition to the basic choice of method, the matter of which costs are to be considered contract costs and which period costs remains, to a significant degree, an area of management discretion.

Other problem areas of revenue recognition.   In finance company accounting, the analyst must be aware of the variety of methods, as outlined earlier

---

[5] ACSEC's *Statement of Position No. 81–1* now specifies that materials bought for a contract but not yet used be treated as inventory rather than as a cost.

in this chapter, available in the recognition of income as well as the option of taking into income at the inception of loan agreements of amounts designed to offset loans acquisition costs.

Other alternative methods of taking up revenue, as in the case of lessors, must be fully understood by the analyst before he attempts an evaluation of a company's earnings or a comparison among companies in the same industry.

Concept of materiality in income determination. The analyst must be aware of the fact that the concept of materiality remains undefined in accounting and is consequently subject to abuse and uncertainty. It is all too often employed by auditors in defense of the omission of disclosure when their clients are adamant in their resistance to certain disclosures. The analyst must also realize that the accountant's concept of materiality is presently a very narrow one indeed. It does not attempt to take into account the future implications of an emerging situation. All too often, what looks like a small problem area may be the beginning of a serious future problem. Recent examples of this were provided by Celanese Corporation, which lost heavily from what was initially a relatively small foreign venture, and American Express Company, which had to make good the losses of its relatively insignificant warehousing subsidiary when large-scale defalcations in the famous "salad oil swindle" were discovered. The FASB has the entire subject under study, but no early resolution appears likely.

COST AND EXPENSE ACCRUAL

Costs and expenses are resources and service potentials consumed, spent, or lost in the pursuit or production of revenues. The major problems of accounting for costs concern the measurement (size) of costs and the timing of their allocation to production time periods.

A basic objective of income accounting is to relate costs to the revenues recognized during a period. This is far from easy to do. There are many kinds of costs, and they behave in a variety of ways. Some costs can be specifically identified with a given item of revenue. At the other end of the spectrum are costs that bear no identifiable relationship to specific elements of revenue at all and can be identified only with the time period during which they are incurred. This variation in behavior of costs has given rise to certain useful classifications that are helpful in understanding the matching and allocation problems.

Variable costs are those that vary in direct proportion to activity, whether the latter is measured by means of sales, production, or other gauges of activity. Thus, for example, in the manufacture of electric cable, the consumption of copper wire may be said to vary in direct proportion to the sales volume of wire. The higher the cable sales figure, the higher the copper wire cost. In practice, many costs contain both fixed and variable elements and are usually referred to as semivariable costs.

Fixed costs are those that remain relatively constant over a considerable range of activity. Rent, property taxes, and insurance are examples of fixed costs. No category of cost can remain fixed indefinitely. For example, after reaching a certain level of activity, an enterprise will have to rent additional space thus bringing the rent expense to a new and higher level.

Costs can be classified in many additional ways depending on the purpose. Focusing on the problem of matching costs with revenues, we have *product costs* that attach to a specified good or service from which revenue is derived. Costs that cannot be identified with a product or service are called *period costs* because they can be identified only with the period in which they occur. We have already touched on this distinction of costs in our examination of inventory and related cost of goods sold accounting in Chapter 5. The allocation of costs to products sold and particularly manufactured products gives rise to a distinction among three major classes of cost:

1. *Direct product costs* represent charges that can be identified specifically with a product. Thus, for example, in a retailing business it is the cost of the item sold as well as the direct freight and other acquisition cost incurred in obtaining it. In a manufacturing enterprise, it represents the specific or direct cost of material and labor entering the production of the item. Direct product costs generally vary in amount in direct proportion to revenues, a characteristic that results in their being classified as variable costs. Direct product costs are among the easiest costs to match with specific revenue flows.

2. The cost of materials acquired for resale or manufacture should logically include in addition to invoice costs such additional costs as receiving, inspecting, purchasing, and storing. In reality, most enterprises find it impractical to allocate such costs or costs such as indirect labor directly to specific products. Consequently, such *indirect costs* are allocated to products on some reasonable bases. Most fixed costs, such as depreciation or supervision, are treated as indirect overhead costs and are allocated to products or services on bases that attempt to reflect consumption or benefits derived.

3. *Joint product costs* are costs that cannot be identified with any of a number of products that they jointly benefit as for example is the case in the meat-processing industry. Such costs are usually allocated on some reasonable basis which may include that based on the selling prices of end products, relative sales volume, or net realizable value.

Having outlined some basic aspects of cost behavior and the methods of cost allocation have been devised in response to it, we shall now proceed to examine the accounting problems that are encountered in the measurement and allocation of major categories of costs and expenses. Generally, a cost is a measure of service potential or utility that may be utilized in one accounting period or another. Those costs that relate to the revenue of future periods may be viewed as deferred costs and are shown as assets on the balance sheet. Major examples of such assets are inventories; property, plant, and equipment; intangibles; and deferred charges. The accounting problems of inventories are examined in Chapter 5. Property, plant, and equipment gives rise to allocations of costs in the form of depreciation and depletion, and they will be considered in this chapter. The allocation and amortization of intangibles and deferred charges have been examined in the chapter on asset measurement, and the income measurement aspects of these costs will be further considered in this chapter.

Generally, expenses are costs that are immediately chargeable to income. Most period costs become current expenses; and some categories of expense, such as selling and administrative,[6] are not usually deferred to the future. The measurement of costs and expenses is complicated whenever a significant lapse of time occurs between the time of payment for or incurrence of the cost and the time of its utilization in the earning of revenues. The longer such lapse of time, the more complicated and speculative such allocations and measurements become.

Let us now consider some important categories of costs and the principles governing their allocation to revenue.

Depreciation and depletion

The cost of assets that are in productive use, or otherwise income producing, must be allocated or assigned to the time periods that comprise their useful life. It is a basic principle of income determination that income that benefits from the use of long-lived assets must bear a proportionate share of their cost. Thus, the cost of the long-lived assets should, at the end of their useful lives, have been charged to operations.

Depreciation is the process whereby the cost of property, plant, and equipment is allocated over its useful life. The purpose of depreciation is to recover from operations, by means of this allocation, the original cost of the asset. Consequently, if operations are not profitable, the depreciation becomes an unrecovered cost, that is, a loss. This is as true of depreciation as it is of any other cost that cannot be recovered because of inadequate revenues. The depreciation process in itself is not designed to provide funds for the replacement of an asset. That objective can only be achieved by means of a financial policy that accumulates funds for a specific purpose to be available at a given time.

---

[6] The controversy surrounding the growing deferrals of marketing costs by SafeCard Services, Inc., (reaching about $25 million early in 1981) highlights the unsettled status of the proper accounting for these costs. In an article in *Barron's* of 7/6/1981 entitled "Lost and Found" Professor A. J. Briloff took issue with the escalating deferrals of marketing costs, maintaining that the deferrals were based on excessively optimistic expectations about future contract renewals and resulting revenues. Those trying to rebuff his arguments pointed primarily to *present* cash flow patterns and to the high discounted present value of those optimistic future expectations.

The above principles of depreciation accounting are now so firmly established that there are no significant differences of opinion about them. Nevertheless, depreciation remains an expense item that is the subject of confusion and controversy among users of financial statements. The controversy and confusion stems from the methods and the assumptions on the basis of which the cost of assets is allocated to operations over their useful life.

Factors influencing the rate of depreciation

1. Useful life

Almost all assets are subject to physical deterioration. A major exception is land that is consequently not subject to depreciation. While the "indestructible powers of the earth" have an unlimited life span, this quality does not ensure a similar resistance to loss of economic value. Such loss is, however, not provided for by means of depreciation but is instead recognized as and when it occurs. The exhaustion of natural resources lodged in or above the earth is recognized by means of depletion accounting, which will be discussed later.

Useful lives of assets can vary greatly. *Depreciation Guidelines and Rules,* published by the Internal Revenue Service, list the useful lives of assets and are based in part on policies influenced by economic and fiscal considerations. The accounting assumption as to the useful lives of assets should be based on economic and engineering studies, on experience, and on any other available information about an asset's physical and economic properties.

Physical deterioration is one important factor that limits the useful life of an asset. The frequency and quality of maintenance has a bearing on it. Maintenance can extend the useful life but cannot, of course, prolong it indefinitely.

Another limiting factor is obsolescence. Obsolescence is the impairment of the useful life of an asset due to progress or changes in technology, consumption patterns, and similar economic forces. Ordinary obsolescence occurs when technological improvements make an asset inefficient or uneconomical before its physical life is fully exhausted. Extraordinary obsolescence occurs when inventions of a revolutionary nature are developed or radical shifts in demand take place. Electronic data processing equipment and propeller driven aircraft were subject to rapid obsolence. The development of Xerography brought about extraordinary obsolescence in equipment using alternative methods of reproduction.

The integrity of the depreciation charge, and with it that of income determination, is dependent on a reasonably accurate estimate of useful life. That estimate should be determined solely by projections relating to physical life and economic usefulness and should not be influenced by management's desires with regard to the timing of income reporting.

2. Methods of allocation

Once the useful life of an asset has been determined, the amount of the periodic depreciation cost depends on the method used to allocate the asset's

cost over its useful life. As will be seen hereunder, that cost can vary significantly, depending on which method is chosen from the array of acceptable
alternatives available:

Straight-line method. This method of depreciation assigns the cost of
the asset over its useful life on the basis of equal periodic charges. Thus, in
Table 10–1, we can see how an asset that cost $110,000, has an estimated
useful life of 10 years, and an estimated salvage value of $10,000 at the
end of that period is depreciated. Every one of the 10 years is charged with
an allocation of one tenth of the asset's cost less the estimated salvage value.

The basic rationale of the straight-line depreciation method is that the
process of physical deterioration occurs uniformly over time. This is a more
valid assumption with regard to fixed structures than with regard to, say,
machinery where utilization or running time is a more important factor.
Moreover, the other element of depreciation, that is, obsolescence, does not
necessarily occur at a uniform rate over time. However, in the absence of
concrete information on the probable rate of actual depreciation in the future,
the straight-line method has the advantage of simplicity. This faculty, perhaps
more than any other, accounts for the method's popularity and widespread
adoption in practice.

There are other theoretical flaws in the straight-line depreciation method.
If the service value of an asset is to be charged evenly over its useful life,
then the loss of productivity and the increased maintenance costs should
not be ignored. Under the straight-line method, however, the depreciation
charges in the first years is the same as in the last years when the asset
can be expected to be less efficient and to require higher cost of repairs
and maintenance.

Another objection to the straight-line method, one which is of particular
interest to the financial analyst, is that it results in a distortion in the rate
of return on capital by introducing a built-in increase in this return over
the years. Assuming that the asset depreciated in Table 10–1 is a heavy
crane that yields a uniform return of $20,000 per year *before* depreciation,
we can see that the return on investment will be as follows:

Table 10–1: Straight-line method of depreciation

Year	Depreciation	Accumulated depreciation	Undepreciated asset balance
			$110,000
1	$10,000	$ 10,000	100,000
2	10,000	20,000	90,000
.			
.			
.			
9	10,000	90,000	20,000
10	10,000	100,000	10,000

Year	Book value	Income before depreciation	Depreciation	Net income	Return on book value
1 ...	$110,000	$20,000	$10,000	$10,000	9.1%
2 ...	100,000	20,000	10,000	10,000	10.0
3 ...	90,000	20,000	10,000	10,000	11.1
10 ...	10,000	20,000	10,000	10,000	100.0

Increasing maintenance costs may render the constant "income before depreciation" assumption a bit too high but will not negate the overall effect of a constantly increasing return on investment. Obviously, this increasing return on the investment in an aging asset is not an entirely realistic portrayal of the economic realities of investments. Under accelerated methods of depreciation, this kind of distortion in the return on book value of the asset can be even more marked.

Decreasing-charge method. The decreasing-charge method of depreciation, also known as declining-balance or accelerated depreciation, is a method whereby charges for depreciation decrease over the useful life of an asset.

The strongest support for this method arose from its approval by the Internal Revenue Code in 1954. Its value for tax purposes is obvious and relatively simple to understand. The earlier an asset is written off for tax purposes, the larger amount of tax deferred to the future and the more funds are available for current operations.

The theoretical justification of the decreasing charge method of depreciation for financial accounting is not clear-cut. Arguments in its favor are that over the years an asset declines in operating efficiency and service value and that lower depreciation charges would offset the higher repair and maintenance costs that come with the older age of assets. Moreover, it is claimed that to compensate for the increasing uncertainty regarding the incidence of obsolescence in the future, the earlier years should bear a larger depreciation charge.

There are two principal methods of computing the decreasing charge to depreciation. One, the declining-balance method, applies a constant percentage to the declining asset balance. Given the salvage value *(S)*, the original cost *(C)*, and the number of periods over which the asset is to be depreciated *(N)*, the rate (percentage) to be applied to the asset can be found by the following formula:

$$\text{Rate }(\%) = 1 - \sqrt[N]{\frac{S}{C}}$$

In practice, an approximation of the proper rate of declining-charge depreciation is to take it at twice the straight-line rate. Thus, an asset with an assumed 10-year useful life would be depreciated at a declining-balance rate of 20 percent. This is referred to as the double-declining-balance method.

The other method, involving simpler computations, is known as the sum-of-the-year's-digits method. Thus, the cost of an asset to be depreciated over a five-year period is written off by applying a fraction whose denominator is the sum-of-the-years digits $(1 + 2 + 3 + 4 + 5)$, that is, 15 and whose numerator is the remaining life from the beginning of the period, that is, $\frac{5}{15}$ in the first year and $\frac{1}{15}$ in the last year of assumed useful life.

Table 10–2 illustrates the depreciation of an asset having a cost of $110,000, a salvage value of $10,000, and an assumed useful life of 10 years under the double-declining-balance method and the sum-of-the-years'-digits method. Since under the first method an asset can never be depreciated to a zero balance, salvage value is not deducted before applying the yearly rate (20 percent) to the original cost.

The main theoretical justification for the decreasing-charge method are that charges for depreciation should decrease over time so as to compensate for (1) increasing repair and maintenance charges, (2) decreasing revenues and operating efficiency, and, in addition, to give recognition to the uncertainty of revenues in the later years of assumed useful life.

Other methods of depreciation. A method of depreciation found in some industries, such as steel and heavy machinery, relates depreciation charges to activity or intensity of use. Thus, if a machine is assumed to have a useful life of 10,000 running hours, then the depreciation charge will vary with number of hours of running time rather than the lapse of time. In order to retain its validity, it is particularly important that the initial assumption about useful life in terms of utilization be periodically reviewed in order to check its validity under changing conditions.

Another method of depreciation once advocated by some utilities but not now in general use is the compound interest method of depreciation. This

Table 10–2: Accelerated depreciation methods

	Depreciation		Cumulative amount	
Year	Double declining	Sum-of-the-years' digits	Double declining	Sum-of-the-years' digits
1	$22,000	$18,182	$22,000	$ 18,182
2	17,600	16,364	39,600	34,546
3	14,080	14,545	53,680	49,091
4	11,264	12,727	64,944	61,818
5	9,011	10,909	73,955	72,727
6	7,209	9,091	81,164	81,818
7	5,767	7,273	86,931	89,091
8	4,614	5,455	91,545	94,546
9	3,691	3,636	95,236	98,182
10	2,953	1,818	98,189	100,000

method views an investment in property as the present value of anticipated earnings. Thus, the depreciation charge is the amount that, invested yearly at a capital cost rate, will equal the cost of the asset, less any salvage value, at the end of its useful life. The addition of this interest factor causes this method to result in systematically increasing depreciation over the years. One advantage claimed for it is that it will result in a more uniform rate of return on investment than is the case with other methods.

Depletion. Depletion is the process by means of which the cost of natural resources is allocated on the basis of the rate of extraction and production. The essential difference between depreciation and depletion is that the former represents an allocation of the cost of a productive asset over time, and the latter represents the exploitation of valuable stocks such as coal deposits, oil pools, or stands of timber. Thus, in the case of depletion, the proportionate allocation of cost is entirely dependent on production; that is, no production, no depletion.

The computation of depletion is easy to understand. If the cost of an ore body containing an estimated 10,000,000 recoverable tons is $5,000,000, then the depletion rate per ton of ore mined is $.50. A yearly production of 100,000 tons would result in a depletion charge of $50,000 and a cost balance in the asset account at the end of the year of $4,950,000. The analyst must be aware of the fact that here, as in the case of depreciation, a simple concept may nevertheless result in a multitude of complications. One is the reliability of the estimate of recoverable resources, and it should be periodically adjusted in accordance with experience and new information. Another is the definition of "cost," particularly in case of a property still in process of development. Also, in the case of oil fields, for example, the depletion expense will vary with the definition of what constitutes an "oil field," since the depletion computation may not be based on individual wells but rather on entire fields. The depletion expense can vary with the definition of the boundaries of the field.

The argument, sometimes advanced, that the discovery value of a natural resource deposit is so great in relation to its cost that no depletion need be allowed for, is not a valid one nor is the argument that depletion should be ignored because of the very tenuous nature of the estimate of reserves.

Implication for analysis

From the point of view of the analyst, a very important dimension of cost and expense accounting is their proper accrual—that means that the income of a given period has been charged with all expenses properly assignable to it. Accountants refer to the procedure that ensures this as expense cutoff, i.e., properly cutting off at the point where expenses for a period end and those of the following period begin.

ILLUSTRATION 3. In 1963, Yale Express acquired Republic Carloading and Distributing Company (twice its own size) in a merger that resulted in substantial operating problems that contributed to the ultimate downfall of the combined enterprise. Yale (a short-haul trucker) used a fast cutoff method, i.e., it assumed (generally with validity) that most of its unpaid bills reached it shortly after its freight was trucked. Thus, it assumed that all bills due arrived within 20 days of year-end. Trouble arose when Yale extended this method of accrual to Republic where freight-handling bills came in months after performance of its service. This led to a substantial underaccrual of costs, and by the time this was discovered it led to the restatement of 1963's net income of $1 million to a loss of almost $2 million. In the resulting litigation, facts emerged that pointed to both auditor carelessness as well as management collusion to withhold all facts.

Most companies utilize long-lived productive assets in their operations, and whenever this is the case, depreciation tends to become a significant cost of operations. If we add to this the fact, as we have seen in the foregoing discussion, that many subjective assumptions enter into the determination of the depreciable basis, and of useful lives of assets and that alternative methods of depreciation coexist and that these factors can result in widely differing depreciation charges, all "in accordance with generally accepted accounting principles," it is obvious that the financial analyst needs a thorough understanding of all the factors entering into the depreciation computation before he can assess a reported earnings figure or before he attempts to compare it with that reported by another company.[7]

The information on depreciation methods presently available in corporate reports varies, and generally speaking, more is available in documents filed with the SEC than is available in annual reports. Thus, typically the more detailed information will contain the method or methods of depreciation in use as well as the range of useful lives assumptions that are applied to various categories of assets. Two things are obvious to the intelligent reader of information. One is that it is practically useless for purposes of deriving any conclusion from it. After all, what can one conclude from a statement that talks about this or that method being used without a quantitative specification of the extent of its use and the assets to which it applies. The second is that this information is supplied because it is required and not because of the supplying company's conviction about its usefulness.

Giving the ranges of useful lives or depreciation rates looks more informative than it is. It actually contributes very little to the basic objectives of the analyst, that is, the ability to predict future depreciation charges or the ability to compare the depreciation charges of a number of companies in the same industry.

The typical information supplied appears something like this:

---

[7] For a discussion of possible variations in practice, see AICPA, "Accounting for Depreciable Assets," *Accounting Research Monograph No. 1* (New York, 1975).

The estimated useful lives vary but generally fall within the following ranges: buildings and special-purpose structures . . . 10 to 25 years; leasehold improvements . . . estimated useful life or remaining term of lease, whichever is shorter; machinery and equipment . . . 3 to 5 years; special-purpose equipment . . . expensed or over the life of the initial related contract. Tooling costs are expensed as incurred.

There is usually no identification of the relationship between the depreciation rates disclosed and the size of the asset pool to which such rates apply. Moreover, there is normally no identification between the rate used and the depreciation method applied; that is, which rates are used in conjunction with straight-line methods of depreciation and which with accelerated methods.

There are, of course, additional complications. While the straight-line method of depreciation enables the analyst to approximate future depreciation charges with some degree of accuracy, accelerated methods of depreciation make this task much more difficult unless the analyst is able to obtain from the company additional data not now disclosed in public reports.

Another problem area in depreciation accounting arises from differences in the methods used for book purposes and those used for tax purposes. Three possibilities exist here:

1. The use of straight-line depreciation methods for both book and tax purposes.
2. The use of straight-line depreciation for book purposes and accelerated methods for tax purposes. The favorable tax effect that results from the higher depreciation for tax purposes compared to that for book purposes is offset by the use of tax allocation that will be discussed in the next chapter. The advantage to the reporting company is the postponement of tax payments, that is, the cost-free use of funds.
3. The use of accelerated methods for both book and tax purposes. This method gives a higher depreciation charge than does method 1 in early years, and for an expanding company, even in subsequent years.

Unfortunately, the amount of disclosure about the impact of these differing methods is not always adequate. The best type of disclosure is the one that gives the amount of depreciation that would have been charged under a number of alternatives, such as, for example, what the difference in depreciation would have been under an accelerated method as opposed to a straight-line method. If a company gives the amount of deferred taxes that arose from accelerated depreciation for tax purposes, the analyst can get the approximate amount of extra depreciation due to acceleration by dividing the deferred tax amount by the current tax rate. See the information yielded by expanded requirements of the composition of deferred taxes, discussed in the next chapter.

ANALYTICAL MEASURES OF PLANT AGE

There are a number of measures relating to plant age that are useful in comparing depreciation policies over time as well as for intercompany comparisons.

The average total life span of plant and equipment can be approximated as follows:

$$\frac{\text{Gross plant and equipment}}{\text{Current year depreciation expense}}$$

For Alfa, Inc. (see Appendix 4B), for 19x6 this can be computed as follows:

$$\frac{\$411,374^{(a)}}{\$24,214^{(b)}} = 17 \text{ years}$$

[a] Per Note 5, total plant and equipment ($448,577) less land ($20,471) and construction in progress ($16,732).
[b] From statement of income item [4].

The average age of plant and equipment can be computed as follows:

$$\frac{\text{Accumulated depreciation (reserve)}}{\text{Current year depreciation expense}}$$

For Alfa, Inc., it is computed as follows for 19x6:

$$\frac{\$174,932^{(c)}}{\$24,214} = 7.2 \text{ years}$$

[c] From balance sheet item [29].

The average remaining life of plant and equipment is computed as follows:

$$\frac{\text{Net depreciated plant and equipment}}{\text{Current year depreciation expense}}$$

Again, for Alfa, Inc., it is computed as follows for 19x6:

$$\frac{\$411,374 - \$174,932^{(d)}}{\$24,214} = 9.8 \text{ years}$$

[d] Gross plant and equipment per *(a)* above minus accumulated depreciation per *(c)* above.

As can be seen from the computations above, and as is logical:

$$\frac{\text{Average total}}{\text{life span}} = \text{Average age} + \text{Average remaining life}$$

The above ratios are helpful in assessing an enterprise's depreciation policies and assumptions over time. The ratios can be computed on a historical-cost basis as well as on a current-cost basis.

When these ratios are used as bases of comparison with other companies in the same industry, care must be exercised because depreciation expense will vary according to the method of depreciation used as well as the assumptions of useful life and salvage values. The average age of plant and equipment can be used in the evaluation of a number of factors including profit margins and financing requirements.

Thus, capital intensive companies with relatively old facilities may have profit margins that do not reflect the higher costs of replacing the aging plant. Similarly, the capital structure of such companies may not yet reflect the financing necessary for the replacement of the aging plant.

MISCONCEPTIONS REGARDING THE NATURE OF DEPRECIATION

Analysts who have despaired of making meaning out of depreciation information have tended to ignore it altogether by looking at income before depreciation in comparing company results. As will be more thoroughly discussed in the chapter on fund flows, depreciation is an expense that derives from funds spent in the past and thus does not require the outlay of current funds. For this reason, income before depreciation has also been called cash flow, an oversimplification for what is meant to be described as funds inflow from operations. This is, at best, a limited and superficial concept since it involves only selected inflows without considering a company's commitment to such outflows as plant replacement, investments, or dividends. Nor is this inflow strictly of a cash nature because funds provided by the recovery of depreciation charges from revenue are not necessarily kept as cash but may be invested in receivables, inventories, or other assets.

Another and even more dangerous misconception that derives from the cash flow concept, and against which the analyst must guard, is that depreciation is a kind of bookkeeping expense somehow different from such expenses as labor or material and that it can be ignored or at least accorded less importance than is accorded to other expenses.

One reason for this thinking is the cash outlay aspect already mentioned above. This represents, of course, entirely fallacious thinking. The purchase of a machine with a useful life of, say, five years is, in effect, a prepayment for five years of services. Let us assume that the machine is a bottle-filling machine and that its task can be performed normally by a worker working eight hours a day. If, as is not common but quite feasible, we contract with the worker for his services for a five-year period and pay him for it in advance, we would obviously have to spread this payment over the five years of his work. Thus, at the end of the first year, one fifth of the payment would be an expense and the remaining four-fifths prepayment would represent an asset in the form of a claim for future services. It requires little elaboration to see the essential similarity between the labor contract and the machine. In year 2 of the labor contract, no cash is spent, but can there be any doubt about the validity of the bottle-filling labor cost? The depreciation of the machine is a cost of an essentially identical nature.

Another reason for doubts about the genuine nature of depreciation expense is related to doubts about the loss of value of the asset subject to depreciation. On further examination, we can break these doubts into two major categories:

1.   Doubts about the rate of loss in utility of productive equipment.
2.   Doubts about loss in market value of assets such as real estate.

1.   When we see one airline depreciating a jet plane over eight years and another airline spreading the depreciation of an identical aircraft over, say, 12 years, we realize that depreciation rates are matters of opinion. What is not a matter of opinion is that the effect on income of such differing assumptions can be significant and can distort comparisons. Thus, the effect must be assessed by the analyst as best as he can in the light of industry practice as well as the apparent reasonableness of the useful life assumption. While there may be some guidelines about useful lives of assets for tax purposes, there are practically none for financial accounting purposes. Auditors are not specialists in the longevity or useful life of equipment, and they will challenge management's estimates only when they are way out of line with industry practice or recorded experience. Where recorded experience is nonexistent, as in the case of a new industry such as computer leasing, the auditor's willingness to question management's estimate is further reduced. All this leaves a great deal of room for interpretation and income manipulation. While it does nothing to render depreciation as less of a genuine expense than any other, it does raise questions about the proper allocation of a productive asset's cost over time. Moreover, as between two estimates of useful life on similar equipment in an industry, there is obviously more risk to the longer life assumption than to the lower.

The rate of write-off is another aspect of depreciation the analyst must be alert to. When the tax laws first permitted a variety of accelerations in the computation of depreciation, many companies adopted the method for both book and tax purposes. Later, however, a number of companies, such as those in the steel and paper industries, wanted to soften the impact of depreciation on reported income and switched back to the straight-line method while retaining accelerated methods for tax purposes. Such switching back and forth can usually not be said to be made in the interest of better reporting. Thus, though mostly unjustified and contributing to a discontinuity in comparability, it is nevertheless accepted by the accounting profession whose limited self-imposed responsibility it is to highlight the change and report its effect in the year in which it occurs. This practice along with the leeway allowed in setting useful lives has contributed in good measure to the skepticism regarding the measurement of depreciation expenses. *APB Opinion 20,* "Accounting Changes," which is more fully considered in the next chapter, is designed to remedy this obvious reporting deficiency by insisting that changes be made only in the direction of "preferable" accounting principles.

Since the concept of "preferable" in relation to accounting principles remains undefined, the analyst must retain a vigilant and critical attitude towards this area of accounting practice.[8]

2. In the case of assets such as real estate, the problem of depreciation is somewhat different. For one thing, constant maintenance can prolong its useful life considerably more than can maintenance of, say, machinery or automobiles. Moreover, those who look at loss of market value as a true index of depreciation claim that in times of rising price levels buildings gain rather than lose in value.

These are, however, not arguments against depreciation as such but rather questions of useful economic life and the proper time period over which an asset's cost should be written off. There is not more justification to a depreciation rate that is excessive than there is to one that is insufficient. Possibly, those companies that depreciate buildings at a rate exceeding their physical and economic decline do so in order to justify the rates they use for tax purposes. This procedure does not, however, result in proper income determination and must be understood as such by the analyst.

Rising real estate values are, of course, no reason to discontinue providing for depreciation. The adequacy of depreciation is dependent on many factors both physical and economic. The process of depreciation can be retarded but never abolished or reversed. The following note to the financial statements of Louis Lesser Enterprises, Inc., covering a period of generally rising prices, makes this clear:

> As a result of the general decline in certain aspects of the real estate industry, accentuated by conditions in the money market and continuing vacancy factors in certain of the Company's rental properties, management is of the opinion that the full cost of certain properties and investments in and advances to companies not majority owned will not be recovered in the normal course of operations or through sale. Accordingly, the carrying values of such properties and investments and advances have been reduced to the amount of expected recovery.

The losses above provided for exceeded $4 million in a year when the company's total revenues were only about $6 million. In retrospect, it is clear that management and its auditors underestimated the process of depreciation and value erosion of the company's income-producing properties. The values of such properties depend more on their income-generating capacity under a variety of economic conditions than on physical characteristics and maintenance levels.

As the above case illustrates, it is not prudent to rely on temporary economic conditions or market quotations to redress overoptimism that results in the willful underestimation of depreciation. After all, the depreciation concept encompasses a number of factors such as physical life, economic

---

[8] See, however, Chapter 15 for a discussion of new SEC requirements that the auditor take a position on the preferability of a switch in accounting methods.

usefulness, and technological and economic factors which affect obsolescence. The difficulties of such real estate operators as Zeckendorf, Kratter, and Glickman attest to the fact that real estate values move in a two-way street.

Changing price levels also introduce many complexities to the depreciation problem. Particularly in industries that are based on holdings of real estate, the argument is often advanced that rising prices (due in great measure to the decline in the purchasing power of money) obviate or reduce the need for depreciation charges. These arguments confuse the problems resulting from price-level changes, which affect all accounts rather than only the fixed assets, with the function of depreciation that is designed to allocate the cost of an asset over its useful life. Price-level changes in themselves do not, of course, prolong the useful life of an asset. The problem of price-level changes must be dealt with fully and apart from that of depreciation. Price-level problems will be examined in Chapter 14.

The analyst should realize that the variety of depreciation methods in use will cause not only problems of comparisons with other companies but internal measurement problems as well. This is particularly true with regard to the rate of return earned on the carrying value (book value) of an asset subject to different methods of depreciation. As the following example shows, only the "annuity" method of depreciation provides a level return on investment over the useful life of an asset. This method is, however, rarely found in practice.

ILLUSTRATION 4. Assume that a machine costing $300,000 and having a useful life of five years with no salvage value generates a yearly income before taxes of $100,000. According to the annuity method of depreciation, the cost of depreciable assets is the present value of an anticipated stream of future services, determined at some rate of discount. In our illustration, the assumed rate of discount is 19.86 percent. The following are the rates of return realized annually under *(a)* straight-line, *(b)* sum-of-the-years' digits, and *(c)* annuity depreciation methods (which is identical to the sinking fund depreciation method):

Year	Income before depreciation	Depreciation	Income after depreciation	Asset book value at beginning of year	Rate of return
		a. Straight-line depreciation			
1	$100,000	$ 60,000	$ 40,000	$300,000	13.3%
2	100,000	60,000	40,000	240,000	16.7
3	100,000	60,000	40,000	180,000	22.2
4	100,000	60,000	40,000	120,000	33.3
5	100,000	60,000	40,000	60,000	66.7
	$500,000	$300,000	$200,000		

Year	Income before depreciation	Depreciation	Income after depreciation	Asset book value at beginning of year	Rate of return
		b. Accelerated depreciation (sum-of-years' digits)			
1	$100,000	$100,000	$ —	$300,000	0.0
2	100,000	80,000	20,000	200,000	10.0
3	100,000	60,000	40,000	120,000	33.3
4	100,000	40,000	60,000	60,000	100.0
5	100,000	20,000	80,000	20,000	400.0
	$500,000	$300,000	$200,000		
		c. Annuity depreciation			
1	$100,000	$ 40,421	$ 59,579	$300,000	19.86
2	100,000	48,450	51,550	259,579	19.86
3	100,000	58,076	41,924	211,129	19.86
4	100,000	69,612	30,388	153,053	19.86
5	100,000	83,441	16,559	83,441	19.86
	$500,000	$300,000	$200,000		

From the foregoing discussion it is clear that the accounting for depreciation, which is a very real and significant cost of operation, contains many pitfalls for the analyst. Moreover, the information frequently supplied in published reports is mostly useless from the point of view of meaningful analysis. Thus, the analyst has to approach the evaluation of this cost with an understanding of the factors discussed above and with an attitude of questioning independence. In assessing the depreciation provision, he may have to evaluate its adequacy by such measures as the ratio of depreciation expense to total asset cost as well as its relationship to other factors which affect its size.

QUESTIONS

1. Why does the financial analyst attach great importance to the analysis of the income statement?
2. What conditions should usually be met before revenue is considered realized?
3. What conditions should usually be present before a sale with "right of return" can be recognized as. a sale and the resulting receivable can be recognized as an asset?
4. The ability to estimate future returns (when right of return exists) is an important consideration. What are some of the factors that might impair such ability to predict returns?

5. What is the main difference between *SFASs 48* and *45* and *SFAS 49?* How does *SFAS 49* define a product financing arrangement?

6. Distinguish between the two major methods used to account for revenue under long-term contracts.

7. According to the AICPA Statement of Position on "Accounting Practices of Real Estate Investment Trusts," the recognition of interest income should be discontinued when it is not reasonable to expect that it will be received. What are some of the conditions that would be regarded as establishing such a presumption?

8. How is income in a jointly owned company accounted for?

9. To what aspects of revenue recognition must the financial analyst be particularly alert?

10. Can the analyst place reliance on the auditor's judgment of what constitutes a "material" item in the income statement?

11. Distinguish between *(a)* variable, *(b)* semivariable, and *(c)* fixed costs.

12. Depreciation accounting leaves a lot to be desired; and no real progress, from the analyst's point of view, is imminent. Comment on the following observation:

    "The analyst of course cannot accept the depreciation figure unquestioningly. He must try to find out something about the age and efficiency of the plant. He can obtain some help by comparing depreciation, current and accrued, with gross plant, and by comparisons among similar companies. Obviously, he still cannot adjust earnings with the precision that the accountant needs to balance his books, but the security analyst doesn't need that much precision."

13. What are some of the analytical tools used in evaluating depreciation expense? Why are they helpful?

14. What means of adjusting for inconsistencies in depreciation methods are sometimes employed by analysts? Comment on their validity.

15. Which method of depreciation would result in a level return on asset book values? Why?

11

Analysis of the income statement—II

This chapter continues and concludes the discussion of the analysis of the income statement that was begun in Chapter 10.

PENSION COSTS AND OTHER SUPPLEMENTARY EMPLOYEE BENEFITS

Pension costs

Pensions are a major employee-benefit cost designed to contribute to security after retirement. Pension commitments by companies are formalized in a variety of ways by means of pension plans. As pensions grew in importance and in size as a significant cost of operations, so did the accounting for such costs become a matter of great significance.

APB Opinion 8 is presently the authoritative guide to the accounting for pension costs by employers. However, much has changed since issuance of this pronouncement, including promulgation of the Employee Retirement Income Security Act (ERISA) of 1974 as well as changes in the social, economic, and demographic forces that impinge on a vastly expanded private pension system. The FASB has, as a temporary measure, issued *SFAS 36* in order to improve defined benefit pension plan disclosures pending a reconsideration of the entire subject which is now under way. A discussion of *SFAS 35* that deals with the accounting of and reporting by defined benefit pension plans as well as *SFAS 36* is found in the "pension liabilities" section of Chapter 7.

APB Opinion 8 views pension costs basically as covering the longer term because they encompass the entire workspan of a group or groups of employees. Thus, such costs must be provided for on an accrual basis based on the actuarial assumptions that govern the pension plan. Limitations of legal

311

liability to pay pensions should not normally affect accruals that are based on an assumption of indefinite continuance of benefits. Nor should the method used to fund the pension obligation affect the accrual of proper cost. Funding of pension obligations is essentially a matter of financial management, and it may or may not coincide with proper accrual for accounting purposes, which is a decision as to the appropriate charge of pension costs against the operations of a given period.

APB Opinion 8 establishes both a floor and a ceiling for the annual accrual of pension costs. Under *either* the minimum or the maximum pension cost provision, the *normal accrual cost* must be provided for. This must be arrived at by use of an actuarial cost method that is rational, systematic, and consistently applied and relates to years after adoption of the pension plan.

The minimum and maximum cost provision is as follows:[1]

Minimum pension cost provision:

1. The normal cost.
2. A provision of interest on unfunded prior service cost.
3. A supplementary provision called for in cases where the value of vested benefits at the beginning of the year are not reduced by at least 5 percent in relation to the comparable amounts at the end of the year. Such comparison should be made exclusive of any net increase of vested benefits occurring during the year. If a supplementary provision for vested benefits is required, the total pension provision may be the lesser of the amount computed above or an amount sufficient to make the aggregate annual pension provision equal to:
   a. The normal cost.
   b. Amortization of prior service cost on 40-year basis (including interest).
   c. Interest equivalents on the difference between the provisions for pension costs accrued and the amount of such costs actually funded.

Maximum pension cost provision:

1. The normal cost.
2. Ten percent of past service cost at inception of plan and of increases and decreases in prior service cost arising from plan amendments. Since the 10 percent includes an interest factor, it will require, depending on interest rate assumed, more than 10 years for full amortization.
3. Interest equivalents on the difference between provision for pension costs and the amount of such costs actually funded.

---

[1] In the light of the pension legislation (ERISA), the AICPA Accounting Standards Executive Committee concluded that the minimum expensing level should be revised to require amortization of unfunded past and prior service costs in conformity with the minimum funding requirements of the law and that the maximum expensing level should be revised to permit amortization of such cost over 10 years.

In the above context, "past service cost" refers to the portion of the total pension cost that under the actuarial cost method in use is identified with periods prior to the adoption of the pension plan, while "prior service costs" refers to costs including past service costs, resulting from plan improvements. "Vested benefits" refers to benefits accrued that are not contingent on the employee's continuing in the service of the employer.

APB Opinion 8 generally aims at avoiding wide year-to-year fluctuations in pension costs. Consequently, it prescribed the averaging of actuarial gains and losses as well as of unrealized appreciation or depreciation of fund investments.

To the extent that actual experiences subsequent to an actuarial valuation differs from the actuarial assumptions (e.g., those relating to employee turnover, mortality or income yield of investments), actuarial gains or losses will arise. Under the *Opinion,* such losses or gains should be spread or averaged over a period from 10 to 20 years, or alternatively, the gains may be offset as a reduction of prior service costs.

The *Opinion* calls for recognition of unrealized appreciation or depreciation of fund assets in the determination of pension cost on a rational and systematic basis that avoids giving undue weight to short-term market fluctuations. Thus, the *Opinion* recommends the averaging of such appreciation or depreciation or its recognition on the basis of expected long-term performance.

The following is designed to illustrate the actual workings of the minimum-maximum pension cost provision approach. For purposes of this illustration, we assume the following:

Normal pension cost for the year (i.e., the cost arrived by an acceptable actuarial method)	$ 400,000
Prior service cost:	
Unfunded at beginning of year	3,000,000
Funded in prior years	2,000,000
Amortization of actuarial gains	7,000
Amortization of unrealized appreciation	3,000
Unfunded pension accruals (beginning and end of year)	100,000
Actuarial value of vested benefits:	
Beginning of year	10,000,000
End of year	10,600,000
Fund assets:	
Beginning of year	4,000,000
End of year	4,800,000
Assumed rate of interest	8%

Under the above assumptions, the computation of minimum and maximum allowable provisions for current pension costs would be as follows:

		Minimum		
		A	B	Maximum
1.	Normal cost	$400,000	$400,000	$400,000
2.	Interest on unfunded prior service cost	240,000		
3.	Provision for vested benefits (Note 1)	95,000		
4.	Amortization of prior service cost:			
	I on a 40-year basis, interest included (Note 2)		252,500	
	II at 10% per year			500,000
5.	Interest on excess of prior years' accounting provisions over amounts actually funded		8,000	8,000
6.	Amortization of actuarial gains	(7,000)	(7,000)	(7,000)
7.	Amortization of unrealized asset appreciation	(3,000)	(3,000)	(3,000)
	Total	$725,000	$650,500	$898,000

The pension expense for the year may not exceed the maximum amount and may not be less than the lesser of columns A or B under the minimum provision caption.

Note 1: The provision for vested benefits is arrived as follows:

		This year's valuation	Preceding valuation
1.	Actuarial value of vested benefits	$10,600,000	$10,000,000
2.	Amount of pension fund	4,800,000	4,000,000
3.	Unfunded amount (1 − 2)...........................	5,800,000	6,000,000
4.	Net amount of balance sheet pension accruals	100,000	100,000
5.	Actuarial value of unfunded (unprovided for) vested benefits (3 − 4)...................................	5,700,000	5,900,000
6.	Five percent of item 5 for prior year	295,000	
7.	Year-to-year change in item 5	200,000	
8.	Excess of item 6 over item 7 which represents provision for vested benefits..................................	$ 95,000	

Note 2: Level annual charge that will amortize total prior service cost of $5,000,000 (with interest) on a 40-year basis; amortization will cease when the unfunded component of $3,000,000 has been amortized.

The following disclosure by Waste Management, Inc., complies with disclosure requirements as amended by *SFAS 36:*

The Company has a qualified pension plan for all non-union domestic employees. Warner Company, a subsidiary of the Company, has several pension plans covering substantially all employees not covered separately by various union-administered pension plans. The total pension expense accrued for all of the above plans was $2,433,000 for 1979, $3,189,000 for 1980, and $4,070,000 for 1981, which includes amortization of past service liability over periods ranging from 25 to 40 years. The Company's policy is to fund pension costs accrued. A comparison of total accumulated plan benefits and plan net assets for the Company's plan as of January 1, 1980, and 1981 and for Warner's pension plans as of July 1, 1980, and 1981 is presented below (Unaudited):

	(in thousands)	
	1980	*1981*
Actuarial present value of accumulated plan benefits:		
Vested	$ 9,803	$10,486
Nonvested	2,124	2,726
	$11,927	$13,212
Net assets available for benefits	$14,481	$17,620

The weighted average assumed rate of return used in determining the actuarial present value of accumulated plan benefits was seven per cent in both years for the Company's plan and six per cent in both years for the Warner plans.

Other supplementary employee benefits

Social pressures, competition, and the scarcity of executive talent have led to the proliferation of employee benefits that are supplementary to wages and salaries. Some fringe benefits, such as vacation pay, bonuses, current profit sharing, and paid health or life insurance are clearly identifiable with the period in which they are earned or granted and thus do not pose problems of accounting recognition and accrual.

Other supplementary compensation plans, because of the tentative or contingent nature of their benefits, have not been accorded full or timely accounting recognition, but accounting pronouncements have recently resulted in improvements in this area.

SFAS 43, "Accounting for Compensated Absences," requires employers to accrue the costs of compensated absences on a current basis when all of the following conditions are met:

a. The employer's obligation relating to employee's rights to receive compensation for future absences is attributable to that employee's services already rendered.

b. The obligation relates to rights that vest or accumulate.

c. Payment of the compensation is probable.

d. The amount can be reasonably estimated.

Such absences include vacation, holidays, illness, or other personal activities for which it is expected that an employee will be paid. Not included are severance or termination pay, post-retirement benefits, deferred compensation, stock or stock options issued to employees, or other long-term fringe benefits (e.g., group insurance, long-term disability pay), or absences due to an employee's illness.

Deferred compensation contracts are usually awarded to executives with whom the company wants to develop lasting ties and who are interested in deferring income to their post retirement and lower taxbracket years. Generally, provisions in such contracts that specify an employee's undertaking not to compete or that specify his availability for consulting services are not significant enough to justify deferring the current recognition of such costs. Thus, *APB Opinion 12* requires that at least the present value of deferred compensation to be paid in the future "be accrued in a systematic and rational manner over the period of active employment from the time the contract is entered into, unless it is evident that future services expected to be received by the employer are commensurate with the payments or a portion of the payments to be made." Similar accruals are called for in cases of contracts that guarantee minimum payments to the employee or his beneficiaries in case of death.

Stock options are incentive compensation devices under which an executive receives the right to buy a number of shares at a certain price over a number of years and subject to conditions designed to identify him with the employer's interests.

The usual rationale advanced in defense of stock options is that business will be run better by managers who are important share owners. Options allow executives to build an estate and offer significant tax advantages.

In theory, the accounting for stock options defines the compensation to be recognized as the excess of the fair value of the optioned shares, at the dates the options are granted, over the option price. In practice, since the spread, if any, between the market price and the option price at the date of grant is negligible, the compensation inherent in stock options were generally not recorded on the basis of lack of materiality.

APB Opinion 25, "Accounting for Stock Issued to Employees," specifies that when stock options are granted, the excess of the market price of the stock over the option price should be accounted for as compensation over the periods benefited. In this computation, the discounting of market value to allow for restrictions placed on the use or disposition of the stock by the employee is not permitted.

Implications for analysis

By providing for full and systematic accrual of all pension costs, *APB Opinion 8* has narrowed the areas of differences in pension accounting and improved the underlying theory. The financial analyst is, however, not yet entitled to assume that the intent of the *APB Opinions* will be adhered to in all cases. There remains a great deal of room for maneuvering in this area.

Changes in actuarial methods and assumptions can have a significant effect on earnings as the following note in General Motors' 1981 annual report indicates.

> Total pension expense of the Corporation and its consolidated subsidiaries amounted to $1,493.8 million in 1981, $1,922.1 million in 1980 and $1,571.5 million in 1979. For purposes of determining pension expense, the Corporation uses a variety of assumed rates of return on pension funds in accordance with local practice and regulations, which rates approximated 6% in 1980 and 1979. In 1981, the assumed rate of return used in determining retirement plan costs in the United States and Canada was increased to 7%. The Corporation's independent actuary recommended this change, and other changes in actuarial assumptions, after taking into account the experience of the plans and reasonable expectations. The total effect of these changes was to reduce retirement plan costs for 1981 by $411.1 million and accordingly increase net income by $205.6 million ($0.69 per share).

It is clear that existing standards permit the use of any of several different methods for measuring pension expense, resulting in a lack of comparability among companies. These and similar conditions have led to a reconsideration of this subject by the FASB. Preliminary thinking by the Board is that un-funded pension benefits attributed to employee service to date should be reported as a net pension liability in a company's balance sheet rather than only being disclosed in a footnote as presently done. The balance sheet also would include an intangible asset equivalent to the past service credits granted when a pension plan is initiated or amended. A single measurement approach would be used by all companies to compute pension liability and expense.

The accounting problem regarding stock options is serious. Basically there is a failure to reflect in operating costs compensation granted to employees. No serious student of accounting and finance can deny the real cost to a company of selling its shares at prices below what it could get on the open market. The justification of the lack of accounting for the cost of stock options is a sort of "coin-clipping" operation whereby the small annual dilu-tion of stockholder equity is overlooked without an assessment of its more significant cumulative effect.

The plain fact is that the compensation inherent in stock options is unre-corded under present GAAP. The improvements brought about by *APB Opin-ion 25* are more apparent than real. This *Opinion* continues the accounting profession's long-standing reluctance to face up to the fact that an option to buy a share of stock for a number of months or years at the current market price is a valuable privilege. The prices at which call options as well as longer-term warrants sell in the marketplace is adequate testimony to this.

In 1972, the United States Pay Board faced the problem of valuing stock options and decided that their value is equivalent to 25 percent of the fair market value of the stock at the date of grant plus the excess of fair market value of the shares over the option price at the time of grant (Regulation

201.76). This rule is somewhat arbitrary in that it may fail to take into account restrictions to which a stock option is subject or the length of its duration. Nevertheless, it proves that stock options can be valued, and this valuation is a far more realistic approach than that adopted by the accounting profession in this matter. Financial analysts may well use the Pay Board's valuation rule as a rough guide whenever they want to estimate the unbooked compensation inherent in stock option plans.

One saving feature in the stock option accounting problem is a development brought about through "the back door" by *APB Opinion 15,* "Earnings per Share." Under this *Opinion,* stock options that have a dilutive effect on earnings per share (EPS) must enter into the computation of that figure, thus showing in this statistic some of the effect which is missing in the reported "net income" figure. The computation and evaluation of EPS is discussed in Chapter 12.

RESEARCH, EXPLORATION, AND DEVELOPMENT OUTLAYS

Research, exploration, and development efforts are undertaken by business enterprises for a variety of reasons, all aiming at either short-term improvements or longer-term profit and improved market position. Some research efforts are directed towards maintaining existing product markets, while others aim at the development of new products and processes.

Types of research and development

One type of research is *basic* or *pure research,* that is, directed towards the discovery of new facts, natural laws, or phenomena without regard to the immediate commercial application to which the results may be put. Benefits from such research programs are very uncertain, but if successful, they may be among the most rewarding of all.

Unlike pure research, *applied research* is directed towards more specific goals such as product improvement or the perfection and improvement of processes or techniques of production.

Exploration is the search for natural resources of all kinds. Exploration is always an "applied" kind of activity in that it has a definite and known objective.

Development begins where research and exploration end. It is the activity devoted to bringing the fruits of research or the resources discovered by exploration to a commercially useful and marketable stage. Thus, development may involve efforts to exploit a new product invention or it may involve the exploitation of an oil well, a mineral deposit, or a tract of timber.

Research and development (R&D) may be one part of many activities of an ongoing enterprise, or it may be the almost sole activity of an enterprise in its formative stages.

The accounting problem

The problem of accounting for R&D costs is difficult and defies easy solutions. There are a number of reasons for this, among which the most important are:

1. The great uncertainty of ultimate results that pervades most research efforts. Generally, the outcome of a research project is more uncertain than that of an immediately productive operation.
2. In most cases, there is a significant lapse of time between the initiation of a research project and the determination of its ultimate success or failure. This, in effect, is another dimension of uncertainty.
3. Often the results of research are intangible in form, a fact that contributes to the difficulty of evaluation.

It is this all-pervading uncertainty of ultimate results that causes the difficulty in accounting for R&D costs rather than the absence of logical reasoning or a lack of clear objectives of accounting. Such objectives are clear and well known:

1. Costs should be related to the revenues with which they are associated.
2. Costs should not be deferred unless there is a reasonably warranted expectation that they will be recovered out of future revenues or will benefit future operations.

FASB *Statement 2*

After a great deal of discussion and deliberation, the FASB has arrived in its *SFAS 2* at a rather simple solution to the complex problem of accounting for R&D costs: They should be charged to expense when incurred.

FASB *SFAS 2* has expanded considerably the definition of what is to be included in R&D costs. It maintains that only a very small percentage of R&D projects are successful (recognizing the difficulty in defining what constitutes a successful project) and that even if the rate of success could be predicted with reasonable accuracy, it still would be difficult to forecast the period of future benefit.

The Board concluded, therefore, that subject to exceptions indicated below, all R&D costs should be charged to expense as incurred.

Definition of research and development activities

Research activities are aimed at discovery of new knowledge for the development of a new product or process or in bringing about a significant improvement to an existing product or process.

Development activities translate the research findings into a plan or design for a new product or process or a significant improvement to an existing product or process.

R&D specifically excludes routine or periodic alterations to ongoing operations and market research and testing activities.

Accounting for research and development costs

The majority of expenditures incurred in R&D activities as defined above constitutes the costs of that activity and should be charged to expense when incurred.

Costs of materials, equipment, and facilities that have alternative future uses (in R&D projects or otherwise) should be capitalized as tangible assets.

Intangibles purchased from others for R&D use that have alternative future uses should also be capitalized.

Elements of costs that should be identified with R&D activities are:

 a. Costs of materials, equipment, and facilities that are acquired or constructed for a particular R&D project and purchased intangibles, that have no alternative future uses (in R&D projects or otherwise).
 b. Costs of materials consumed in R&D activities, the depreciation of equipment or facilities, and the amortization of intangible assets used in research and development activities that have alternative future uses.
 c. Salaries and other related costs of personnel engaged in R&D activities.
 d. Costs of services performed by others.
 e. A reasonable allocation of indirect costs. General and administrative costs that are not clearly related to R&D activities should be excluded.

Disclosure requirements

For each income statement presented, the total R&D costs charged to expense shall be disclosed.

Government regulated companies that defer R&D costs in accordance with the addendum to *SFAS 2* must make certain additional disclosures.

While it is difficult to estimate the future benefits from R&D outlays, it is even more difficult and speculative to estimate the future benefits to be derived from costs of training programs, product promotions, and advertising. Consequently, deferral of such costs is very difficult to justify.

Implications for analysis

The evaluation of R&D outlays presents a serious problem in the analysis of financial statements. Often the size of these outlays is such that they must be taken into account in any analysis of current income and of future prospects.

The FASB's simplistic solution to the accounting for R&D outlays has been described as "really a way of avoiding responsibility" and as arriving at "too easy a solution to an extremely difficult problem."[2] Professors Bierman and Dukes, in questioning the basic reasoning that led the FASB to arrive at the expensing solution, maintain that it is "incorrect to conclude that, because it has been difficult to observe a significant correlation between expenditures and subsequent benefits, future benefits are not generated by research and development expenditures." The professors conclude that "from the point of view of accounting theory, the expenditures for R&D, which are made in the expectation of benefiting future periods, should not be written off against the revenues of the present period. Justification for such practice must be found elsewhere, if it is to be found."

The analyst should realize that while *SFAS 2* assures that there will be no overstated R&D deferrals on the balance sheet, it does so at the expense of any reasonable attempt to match the expenditure of the resources against the revenues that it helps produce. Thus, this new accounting is safe rather than more useful; it overlooks the history of productivity of many ongoing research efforts as opposed to the uncertainty involved in one-shot research projects.

It is possible that the FASB's pragmatic solution that requires the current expensing of practically all R&D outlays will help accountants achieve a uniformity of approach in this area and at the same time avoid the difficult choices and judgments that a policy of capitalization and deferral imposes. It is, however, doubtful that such a policy of, in effect, nonaccounting for R&D costs along with the very limited disclosure requirements it requires will really serve the needs and interests of serious analysts of financial statements.

Granting the difficulty of measuring and estimating the future benefits to be derived from R&D outlays, it is nonetheless reasonable to assume that managements enter into such projects with firm expectations of returns on these investments. Moreover, in many cases, they have specific expectations about such potential returns that the realization or nonrealization of which can be monitored and estimated as a research project progresses. In the past, a policy of deferral R&D costs afforded managements and their independent accountants, who normally judge uncertainties and estimate results in most of their work, an opportunity to carry to the reader their estimate of the future potential promise of such outlays at a given point in time. Under the new rules, all R&D is treated as if it has no future value, and the analyst will no longer have the benefit of the estimates of those in the best position to offer them.

Recognizing the limitations of such accounting, the Institute of Chartered Accountants of Scotland took the position that pure and applied research

---

[2] Harold Bierman Jr. and Ronald E. Dukes, "Accounting for Research and Development Costs," *Journal of Accountancy,* April 1975.

are akin to maintenance expenses essential to preserving a company's business and its competitive position and should consequently be written off as incurred. However, expenditures for new and improved products that are made with a reasonable expectation of specific commercial success may, if they satisfy stringent criteria established for their evaluation, be carried forward and amortized over the period that they are expected to benefit.

SFAS 2 requires only disclosure of total R&D outlays charged to expense in a given period. In order to form an opinion on the quality and the future potential value of research outlays, the analyst needs to know, of course, a great deal more than the totals of periodic R&D outlays. Information is needed on the types of research performed, the outlays by category, as well as the technical feasibility, commercial viability, and future potential of each project assessed and reevaluated anew at the time of each periodic report. He or she also needs information on a company's success-failure experience in its several areas of research activity to date. Of course, present disclosure requirements will not give the analyst such information, and it appears that, except in cases of voluntary disclosures, only an investor or lender with the necessary clout will be able to obtain such information.

In general, one can assume that the outright expensing of all R&D outlays will result in more conservative balance sheets and fewer painful surprises stemming from the wholesale write-offs of previously capitalized R&D outlays. However, the analyst must realize that along with a lack of knowledge about future potential, he or she will—unless the analyst probes widely and deeply—also be unaware of the potential disasters that can befall an enterprise tempted or forced to sink ever greater amounts of funds in R&D projects whose promise was great but whose failure is nevertheless inevitable.

Exploration and development in extractive industries

The search for new deposits of natural resources is the function of a very important industry segment encompassing the oil, natural gas, metals, coal, and nonmetallic minerals industries. While the unique accounting problems of these industries deserve separate consideration, it should be borne in mind that no new accounting principles are involved here but rather the application of such principles and concepts to special circumstances. Thus, while the search for and development of natural resources is characterized by exposure to high degrees of risk, so is, as we have seen, the search for new knowledge, new processes, and new products. Risk involves uncertainty; and within a framework of periodic income determinations, uncertainty always presents very serious problems of income and expense determination.

In extractive industries, under the historical-cost model, the major problems lie on the cost and expense side. Essentially, the problem is one of whether exploration and development costs that may reasonably be expected to be recovered out of the future lifting of the natural resources should be charged in the period incurred or should be capitalized and amortized over future recovery and production.

While many companies charge off all exploration costs currently, some charge off only a portion and capitalize another portion. A few companies capitalize almost all development costs and amortize them over future periods.

The accounting profession has recognized that the divergent practices create a need for reforms in this area. As a first step, *Accounting Research Study (ARS) 11,* "Financial Reporting in the Extractive Industries," recommends, among others, that:

> Expenditures for prospecting costs, indirect acquisition costs and most carrying costs should be charged to expense when incurred as part of the current cost of exploration.
>
> Direct acquisition costs of unproved properties should be capitalized and the estimated loss portion should be amortized to expense on a systematic and rational basis as part of the current cost of exploration.
>
> Unsuccessful exploration and development expenditures should be charged to operations even though incurred on property units where commercially recoverable reserves exist.

In mid-1973, the Committee on Extractive Industries of the APB rendered its final report with the purpose of providing the FASB with a summary of the committee's research in accounting for the oil and gas industry. The committee stated:

> Throughout the committee's deliberations it became increasingly clear that there exists in practice two basic concepts or philosophies regarding accounting in the oil and gas industry; namely, full-cost accounting and successful efforts accounting. The basic concept of the full-cost method is that all costs, productive and non-productive, incurred in the search for oil and gas reserves should be capitalized and amortized to income as the total oil and gas reserves are produced and sold. The basic concept of the successful efforts method is that all costs which of themselves do not result directly in the discovery of oil and gas reserves have no future benefit in terms of future revenues and should be expensed as incurred. It was equally clear that the application of the two concepts in practice varies to such an extent that there are in fact numerous different methods of accounting.

In recent years, the standard setting process for oil and gas producing companies was marked by disagreements, indecision, and changes in direction.

SFAS 19 prescribed the "successful efforts" method of cost accounting for all oil and gas producing companies. That is, all exploration costs except the costs of drilling exploratory wells are to be charged to expense when incurred; the costs of drilling exploratory wells are capitalized as "construction in progress" when incurred, to be expensed later if the well is unsuccessful or to be reclassified as an amortizable asset if proved oil or gas reserves are discovered.

The SEC disagreed with *SFAS 19* and focused instead on Reserve Recognition Accounting (RRA—a current value accounting method), while allowing either successful efforts or full cost accounting in the interim. That led the FASB to issue *SFAS 25* which suspended the effective date of *SFAS 19* for requiring successful efforts accounting, in effect allowing the existing alternative to continue.

In early 1981, the SEC abandoned its attempt to substitute RRA for the two historical accounting methods and returned jurisdiction on the issue to the FASB with the request that it develop supplementary disclosures, including value-based disclosures.

SFAS 69, "Disclosures about Oil and Gas Producing Activities," supersedes the disclosure requirements of previous board statements in this area and requires that the following supplementary information be disclosed by publicly owned oil and gas producers:

- Proved oil and gas reserve quantities.
- Capitalized costs relating to oil and gas producing activities.
- Costs incurred in acquisition, exploration and development activities.
- Results of operations for oil and gas producing activities.
- Standardized measures of discounted future net cash flows related to proved reserves.

Both publicly traded and other companies will continue to be required to disclose the method of accounting for costs incurred in oil and gas producing activities and the manner of disposing of related capitalized costs.

The statement also allows companies to use historical cost/constant dollar measures in presenting current cost information about oil and gas mineral interests.

The SEC has adopted final rules requiring compliance with *SFAS 69* with minor modifications.

IMPLICATIONS FOR ANALYSIS

With regard to exploration and development costs in the extractive industries, the analyst faces at present the problem of a variety of acceptable methods of treating such costs. This in turn hampers the comparison of results among companies in the same industry.

In the aftermath of the SEC's espousal and subsequent abandonment of RRA, it will take additional time for the accounting in this industry to be brought to some degree of standardization. The two methods in current use, and the many variations within these methods, can yield significantly differing results, and the analyst must be aware of this. An earlier survey found that a large majority of financial analysts favor successful efforts accounting over the full cost method because it improves matching of costs with related revenues and is more consistent with the accounting model in present use.[3] This method does, in fact, require that a direct relationship be established between costs incurred and specific oil and gas reserves discovered before such costs are identified as assets.

GOODWILL

Finally, in a consideration of intangible costs, we should add here to the discussion of goodwill that was begun in Chapter 6.

Goodwill is usually the measure of value assigned to a rate of earnings above the ordinary. It is, in some respects, similar to the premium paid for a bond because its coupon rate exceeds the going interest rate. That goodwill has value at the time it is purchased cannot be disputed. Otherwise corporations would be spending billions for assets devoid of value. The real problem with the accounting for purchased goodwill is that of measuring its expiration. There is no need to write off against earnings an asset whose values does not expire. Land is a prominent example of this. However, the superior earning power of an enterprise is not indestructible or everlasting. Goodwill can, at times, be the major part of the consideration paid for a going business. Thus, Standard & Poor's Corporation reported as follows:

> Standard & Poor's purchased all the stock of Trendline Corp. and O.T.C. Publications, Inc., for a price of approximately $2,425,000, which exceeded the net tangible assets of the acquired companies by $2,154,061. That amount was charged to goodwill.

As can be seen in the more comprehensive discussion of the subject in Chapters 6 and 9, *APB Opinion 17* requires that the excess paid over fair market value of net assets acquired in a purchase, that is, goodwill, be amortized to income over a period not to exceed 40 years.

Implications for analysis

One of the most common solutions applied by analysts to the complex problems of the analysis of goodwill is to simply ignore it. That is, they ignore the asset shown on the balance sheet. And yet by ignoring goodwill, analysts ignore investments of very substantial resources in what may often be a company's most important asset.

Ignoring the impact of goodwill on reported periodic income is, of course, also no solution to the analysis of this complex cost. Thus, even considering the limited amount of information available to the analyst, it is far better that he or she understand the effects of accounting practices in this area on reported income rather than dismiss them altogether.

---

[3] A. Naggar, "Oil and Gas Accounting: Where Wall Street Stands," *Journal of Accountancy,* September 1978.

Goodwill is measured by the excess of cost over the *fair market value* of tangible net assets acquired in a transaction accounted for as a purchase. It is the excess of the purchase price over the fair value of all the tangible assets acquired, arrived at by carefully ascertaining the value of such assets. That is the theory of it. At least up to 1970 when *APB Opinion 17* took effect, companies have failed to assign the full fair market value to tangible assets acquired and have, instead, preferred to relegate as much of the purchase price as possible to an account bearing the rather literally descriptive, but meaningless, title of "excess of cost over book value of assets acquired." The reasons for this tendency are simple to understand. Costs assigned to such assets as inventories, plant and equipment, patents, or future tax benefits must all ultimately be charged to income. Goodwill, prior to *APB Opinion 17,* had to be amortized only when its value was impaired or was expiring, and such a judgment was difficult to prove let alone to audit or second-guess. Thus, many companies have included much of the cost of acquisition over the book value on the *seller's* books in the "excess of cost . . ." account and thereafter proceeded to claim that the amount is not amortized because its value to the enterprise is undiminished. We may add here that since the amortization of goodwill is not a tax-deductible expense, its deduction for financial reporting purposes has a magnified adverse impact that managements desire to avoid. The change in accounting requirements toward mandatory amortization will change the effects of the aforementioned practices over time. Financial analysts should, however, be aware of the large stagnant "pools" of goodwill that will remain on the books of many corporations. American Medical International, Inc., reports this as follows:

> Goodwill acquired prior to November 1, 1970, was $10,000,000 and is not being amortized since, in management's opinion, there has been no diminution in the value of these purchased businesses. Similar costs relating to subsequent acquisitions are being amortized on a straight line basis over 40 years.

The financial analyst must be alert to the makeup and the method of valuation of the Goodwill account as well as to the method of its ultimate disposition. One way of disposing of the Goodwill account, frequently chosen by management, is to write it off at a time when it would have the least serious impact on the market's judgment of the company's earnings, for example, a time of loss or reduced earnings. Goodwill should be written off when the superior earning power originally justifying its existence is no longer present. Dow Jones & Company did this in 1981 as follows:

> As a result of *Book Digest Magazine's* continuing losses, management concluded that there had been a substantial reduction in the value of the magazine's net assets. Accordingly, in September 1981, Excess of Cost over Net Assets of Businesses Acquired was reduced by $9,400,000.

Under normal circumstances, goodwill is not indestructible but is rather an asset with a limited useful life. Whatever the advantages of location, of market dominance and competitive stance, of sales skill or product acceptance, or other benefits are, they cannot be unaffected by the passing of time and by changes in the business environment. Thus, the amortization of goodwill gives recognition to the expiration of a resource in which capital has been invested, a process which is similar to the depreciation of fixed assets. The analyst must recognize that a 40-year amortization period, while adhering to the minimum accounting requirement, which represents a compromise position, may not be realistic in terms of the time expiration of economic values. Thus, he or she must assess the propriety of the amortization period by reference to such evidence of continuing value as the profitability of units for which the goodwill consideration was originally paid.

OTHER INTANGIBLE ASSET WRITE-OFFS

The Motor Carrier Act of 1980 which deregulated interstate trucking eliminated the value of exclusive franchises of truckers. This was dealt with by *SFAS 44* as explained by Purolator, Inc.:

> Enactment of the Motor Carrier Act of 1980 and recent actions of the Interstate Commerce Commission and various states which regulate the motor carrier industry simplified entry by new carriers and eliminated many route, territory and commodity restrictions for existing carriers. As a result, the Financial Accounting Standards Board issued Statement No. 44 requiring the write-off in 1980 of costs assigned to operating rights which resulted in an extraordinary charge of $12,363,000.

INTEREST COSTS

The interest cost to an entity is the nominal rate paid including, in the case of bonds, the amortization of bond discount or premium. A complication arises when companies issue convertible debt or debt with warrants, thus achieving a nominal debt coupon cost that is below the cost of similar debt not enjoying these added features.

After trial pronouncements on the subject and much controversy, *APB Opinion 14* has concluded that in the case of *convertible debt,* the inseparability of the debt and equity features is such that no portion of the proceeds from the issuance should be accounted for as attributable to the conversion feature.

In the case of debt issued with stock warrants attached, the proceeds of the debt attributable to the value of the warrants should be accounted for as paid-in capital. The corresponding charge is to a debt discount account that must be amortized over the life of the debt issue, thus increasing the effective interest cost.

Interest capitalization

Interest, being an expense that accrues with the lapse of time, was generally considered a period cost except in the case of public utilities and industries such as real estate. Over the years, the practice of interest capitalization spread, and the resulting uneven practice led the SEC to impose a moratorium on new switches to capitalization of interest pending a resolution of this entire matter by the FASB.

The FASB acted by issuing *SFAS 34,* "Capitalization of Interest Cost," which requires capitalization of interest cost as part of the historical cost of "assets that are constructed or otherwise produced for an enterprise's own use (including assets constructed or produced for the enterprise by others for which deposits or progress payments have been made)." Inventory items that are routinely manufactured or produced in large quantities on a repetitive basis do not qualify for interest capitalization.

The objectives of interest capitalization according to the FASB are (1) to measure more accurately the acquisition cost of an asset and (2) to amortize that acquisition cost against revenues generated by the asset.

The amount of interest to be capitalized is based on the entity's actual borrowings and interest payments. The rate to be used for capitalization may be ascertained in this order: (1) the rate of specific borrowings associated with the assets; and (2) if borrowings are not specific for the asset, or the cost of the asset exceeds specific borrowings therefor, a weighted average of rates applicable to other appropriate borrowings may be used. Alternatively, a company may use a weighted average of rates of all appropriate borrowings regardless of specific borrowings incurred to finance the asset. Interest capitalization may not exceed total interest costs for any period, nor is imputing interest cost to equity funds permitted. A company without debt will have no interest to capitalize.

The capitalization period begins when three conditions are present: expenditures for the asset have been made by the entity, work on the asset is in progress, and interest cost is being incurred. Interest capitalization ceases when the asset is ready for its intended use.

SFAS 34 requires disclosure of: (1) for an accounting period in which no interest cost is capitalized, the amount of interest charged to expense during the period; and (2) for an accounting period in which interest is capitalized, the total amount of interest incurred during the period, and the amount that has been capitalized.

The Pittston Company reported interest capitalization as follows:

> As required by FASB Statement No. 34, which became effective for fiscal years beginning after December 15, 1979, the Company capitalized $5,831,000 of interest cost in 1980. The effect was to increase 1980 net income by $3,099,000 or $.08 per share.

Implications for analysis

Financial analysts should realize that in spite of the position taken in *APB Opinion 14,* there are many who disagree with the *Opinion's* position on convertible debt. The dissenters, which included members of the APB, contend that by ignoring the value of the conversion privilege and instead using as a sole measure of interest cost the coupon rate of interest, the *Opinion* specifies an accounting treatment that ignores the true interest cost to the corporation.

It should be noted, however, that *APB Opinion 15*, "Earnings per Share," by requiring in specified circumstances the inclusion in the computation of earnings per share (EPS) of the number of shares issuable in the event of conversion of convertible debt, in effect creates a charge additional to the coupon interest cost by way of diluting the reported EPS figure.

The capitalization of interest is a controversial subject. The concept passed the FASB by only a four to three margin. The Financial Analysts Federation's position was that interest is basically a period cost.

For companies starting to capitalize interest in 1980, the initial effect on income will be positive. Depending on the rate at which capitalized interest is amortized, that beneficial effect should be gradually offset by the increasing amounts of amortized interest (mostly as part of depreciation expense). On a longer-term basis, the net effect of this process will depend on factors such as interest rate level, interest currently capitalized, and rates of amortization of capitalized interest.

The analyst must also realize that many of the definitions and criteria in *SFAS 34* are loose enough to lead to significant variations in their application. This is also true of materiality thresholds. Moreover, the criteria for capitalization are arbitrary with, for example, some inventories qualifying while others do not.

In order to assess the impact of the capitalization of interest on the net income of a period, the analyst needs to know the amount of capitalized interest that is currently charged to income via the depreciation and amortization process. This amount is also needed in order to compute correctly the fixed-charge coverage ratio (see Chapter 18). Unfortunately *SFAS 34* does not require disclosure of these amounts so that the analyst will often not be able to obtain it from published financial statements. One possible source may be Schedule VI of SEC Form 10-K. Alfa, Inc. (see Appendix 4B), is an example where enough disclosure is provided to enable the analyst to compute the amount of capitalized interest that has been amortized:

ILLUSTRATION 1.   Alfa's income statement for 19x6 shows (item $\boxed{6}$) interest capitalized of $64,000. Note 6 (item $\boxed{82}$) shows a 19x6 *decrease* in net income of $47,000 resulting from the capitalization of interest. Given these data and assuming a 48 percent tax rate, we can compute the amortization of previously capitalized interest in 19x6 as follows:

Let X be the amount of previously capitalized interest amortized in 19x6, then (in thousands):

$$\$47 = (X - \$64)(1 - .48) \text{ solving for } X = \$154$$

The net income effect can be proved as follows:

	Dr. or (Cr.) effect
Interest capitalized	$ (64)
Amortization of previously capitalized interest	154
Before-tax net effect	90
Income tax at 48%	(43)
Effect on net income as given	$ 47

Since *SFAS 34* did not allow retroactive restatements, the impact of interest capitalization may be especially large in the years immediately after adoption until the future amortization of capitalized interest begins to have its offsetting effect. Thus, particularly in this interim period, analysts must be alert to "gains" in earnings that arise from the capitalization of interest.

INCOME TAXES

Income taxes are a very substantial cost of doing business. In many cases, they amount to roughly half a corporation's pretax income. It follows that the accounting for income taxes is an important matter that should be clearly understood. This discussion is not primarily concerned with matters of tax law but rather with the accounting principles that govern the proper computation of the periodic tax expense. *APB Opinion 11* is the accounting profession's authoritative pronouncement on this subject. The SEC has additional important requirements.

The current provision for taxes is governed by any number of tax regulations that may apply in a given situation. Regulations such as those concerning the depletion allowance or capital gains treatment can reduce the effective tax rate of a corporation below statutory levels. Proper disclosure requires that information be given regarding the reasons for deviations from normal tax incidence.

Permanent Income Tax Differences

The net income computed on the basis of GAAP (also known as book income) is often not identical to the "taxable income" computed on the entity's tax return. This is due to two types of differences: permanent differences, which are discussed here, and timing differences, which are covered in the section that follows.

Permanent differences result from provisions of the tax law under which:

		Examples
A.	Certain items may be nontaxable.	Income on tax-exempt obligations; proceeds of life insurance on officer.
B.	Certain deductions are not allowed.	Amortization of goodwill; penalties for filing certain returns; fines; officer life insurance premiums.

C. Special deductions granted by law.   Dividend exclusion on dividends from un-consolidated subsidiaries and from dividends received from other domestic corporations.

In addition, the effective tax rate paid by a corporation on its income will vary from the statutory rate (e.g., 46 percent) because:

D. The basis of carrying property for accounting purposes may differ from that for tax purposes as a result of reorganizations, business combinations, etc.
E. Nonqualified as well as qualified stock-option plans may result in tax-book differences.
F. Certain industries, such as savings and loan associations, shipping lines, and insurance companies enjoy special tax privileges.
G. Certain gains (e.g., capital gains) are taxed at lower tax rates (the first $100,000 of income is also taxed at a lower rate)
H. Certain credits apply—e.g., investment tax credits, foreign tax credits.
I. Foreign income taxed at different rates.
J. State and local income taxes, net of federal tax benefit, are included in total tax expense.

What makes these differences and factors permanent is the fact that they do not have any future repercussions on a company's taxable income. Thus, as we shall see, they must be taken into account when reconciling a company's actual (effective) tax rate to the statutory rate of, say, 46 percent.

Timing differences

It is well known that financial accounting, which is governed by considerations of fair presentation of financial position and results of operations, does not share in all respects the principles that govern the computation of taxable income, the latter being governed by economic or revenue raising objectives. Consequently, there are a great many cases of differences between tax and "book" accounting.

Unlike permanent differences, these are known as *timing* differences because they are expected to affect taxable income at some future time, i.e., they are expected to reverse.

ILLUSTRATION 2.   For financial accounting purposes, a company depreciates a $1,000 asset over 10 years on a straight-line basis. To conserve its cash, the company elects for tax purposes to use the double-declining-balance method of depreciation. In the first year, the book depreciation is $100 while the tax depreciation is $200. In later years, the book depreciation will exceed the tax depreciation because under either method the total depreciation cannot exceed $1,000. Thus, the difference is one of timing.

There are a variety of timing differences between tax and financial accounting. They subdivide into four categories as follows:

1. Revenue or gain is deferred for tax-reporting purposes but is recognized in the current period for financial reporting purposes.
   a. The installment method is used for tax purposes; the accrual method is used for financial reporting purposes.
   b. The completed-contract method is used for tax purposes; the percentage-of-completion method is used for financial reporting purposes.
2. Expenses deducted for tax purposes in the current period exceed expenses deducted for financial reporting purposes.
   a. Accelerated depreciation is taken for tax purposes; straight-line depreciation is used for financial reporting purposes.
   b. Land reclamation and similar costs are deducted for tax purposes; capitalization and amortization are utilized for financial reporting purposes.
3. Revenue or gain is recognized for tax purposes in the current period, but all or part of the amount is deferred for financial reporting purposes.
   a. Rent income or other income received in advance is recognized for tax purposes.
   b. Unearned finance charges and other deferred credits are recognized for tax purposes but are taken into income over a number of years for financial reporting purposes.
4. Expenses deducted for financial reporting purposes in the current period exceed expenses deducted for tax purposes.
   a. Estimated expenses (repair and maintenance, warranty servicing costs, and vacation wages) are accrued for financial reporting purposes but not deducted for tax purposes.
   b. Estimated refunds due the government for price redetermination and renegotiation are accrued for financial reporting purposes.

These four categories may be summarized as follows:

	Reported on		Initial income tax journal entries	
Category of transaction	Income statement	Tax return	Income tax expense	Balance sheet deferred tax accounts
1. Revenue or gain	Earlier	Later	Debit	Credit
2. Expenses	Later	Earlier	Debit	Credit
3. Revenue or gain	Later	Earlier	Credit	Debit
4. Expenses	Earlier	Later	Credit	Debit

* These may reverse later. Some reversals may occur in the normal course of business, while some may occur due to a switch in policy, e.g., deferred installment profits reverse when receivables are sold to a bank and deferred tax must be paid; or tax deferrals due to accelerated depreciation reverse because company switches from owning assets to leasing them.

While all four categories are found in practice, the desirable timing differences that companies that owe income taxes strive to have are those that result in initial credits to the balance sheet deferred tax account—thus resulting in a postponement of taxes. Categories 3 and 4 are undesirable in that they result in the prepayment of taxes.

Revenues or expenses that relate to current accounts (e.g., receivables or inventories) result in current deferred balance sheet accounts while those that relate to noncurrent accounts result in noncurrent deferred balance sheet accounts. Current deferred balance sheet accounts must be netted into one account (debit or credit, as the case may be) and the same procedure applies to noncurrent deferred accounts.

The basic problem with these timing differences, from the accounting point of view, is that there will be differences between the income before tax shown in the income statement and the taxable income shown in the tax return. Thus, if the actual tax paid is considered as the period expense, it will not match the pretax income shown in the income statement. This would violate the basic accounting principle that there should be a matching of income and related costs and expenses. Interperiod tax allocation is designed to assure that in any one period, income shown in the financial statements is charged with the tax applicable to it regardless of how such income is reported for tax purposes.

ILLUSTRATION 3.   Application of the principle of tax allocation:

A retailer sells air conditioners on the installment basis. On January 1, 19x1, he sells a unit for $720 payable at the rate of $20 a month for 36 months. For purposes of this illustration, we ignore finance charges and assume a gross profit to the retailer of 20 percent and a tax rate of 50 percent.

In accordance with proper accrual accounting, the retailer will recognize in the year of sale (19x1) a gross profit of $144 (20 percent of $720). For tax purposes, he can recognize profit based on actual cash collections as follows:

	Cash collection	Taxable gross profit (20%)	Actual tax payable
19x1	$240	$ 48	$24
19x2	240	48	24
19x3	240	48	24
Total	$720	$144	$72

In the absence of tax allocation, the results shown by the retailer on this transaction would be as follows:

	Pretax profit	Tax payable	Profit (loss)
19x1	$144	$24	$120
19x2	—	24	(24)
19x3	—	24	(24)
Total	$144	$72	$ 72

The flaws in this presentation are readily apparent. The book profit of 19x1 does not bear its proper share of tax, thus resulting in a profit overstatement of $48, which distortion is carried over to 19x2 and 19x3, whose profits will be understated by $24 each because they will bear a tax in the absence of the revenues that give rise to it. Moreover, this kind of accounting would appear to suggest that in 19x1, our retailer is more profitable than his competitor who may have sold the air conditioner for cash ($720), realized a gross profit of $144, and paid a tax of $72, thus realizing an aftertax profit of $72 (versus $120 on the installment sale).

Tax allocation is designed to remedy the above distortions by means of a deferred tax account, which results in the matching of tax with the corresponding revenue as follows:

Year	Pretax profit	Taxes			Aftertax profit	Deferred tax account
		Actually payable	Deferred	Total		
19x1	$144	$24	$ 48	$72	$72	$48
19x2	—	24	(24)	—	—	24
19x3	—	24	(24)	—	—	—

APB Opinion 11 has adopted the position that the deferred tax account (e.g., the $48 in 19x1) is not a liability but rather a deferred credit meaning an equalization account that is used to achieve a matching of income and expense. Such an equalization account would appear on the asset side as a deferred charge when, due to timing differences, the taxable income is higher than the book income. The present-day emphasis on the importance of the income statement has resulted in balance sheet items designed specifically to serve such expense and revenue allocation purposes.

As will be seen in Chapter 13, the provision for noncurrent deferred taxes does not require funds, and the tax credit arising from the reversal of noncurrent deferred taxes is not a source of funds.

The above installment sale example is a simplification of a complex process. While the tax deferral pertaining to the *specific* air conditioner is, as shown in the example, completely extinguished at the end of the third year, the aggregate tax deferral account will usually not behave this way. Thus, if another air conditioner is sold in 19x2, the aggregate deferred tax account will stay the same; and if a growing number of air conditioners are sold, the deferred tax account will also grow. In the case of tax-book differences attributed to depreciation, where the assets are long lived, the deferred tax account may grow over the years or at least stabilize. A study by Price Waterhouse & Company of 100 major corporations concluded that the bulk of the deferred tax accounts were not likely to be "paid off" or drawn down. There are also those who claim that only taxes actually due should be accrued. While the matter of accepted accounting practice for taxes has been settled by *APB Opinion 11,* the controversy surrounding it has not ended, and the subject is under reconsideration by the FASB.

Should the FASB ultimately restrict the application of deferred tax accounting, the foregoing accounting is likely to apply to a much more limited number of cases where the likelihood of future reversal of the tax deferrals would be high.

Another form of tax allocation concerns the distribution of the tax effect within the various segments of the income statement. The basic principle here is that each major category should be shown net of its tax effect. Thus, for example, an extraordinary item should be shown net of its appropriate tax effect so that the tax related to operating results is properly stated. This is known as *intra*period allocation.

Treatment of tax loss carry-backs and carry-forwards

A corporation incurring an operating loss may carry such loss *back;* and if it cannot be fully utilized in the preceding 3 years, it may be carried *forward* for 15 years. The status of a tax loss *carry-back* is usually simple to determine: either it is available or it is not. The value of a tax loss *carry-forward* depends on a company's ability to earn taxable income in the future, and that, in most cases, is not a certainty.

Thus, the tax effects of a tax loss carry-back should be recognized in the determination of the results of the loss period. The benefits of a tax loss carry-forward should not normally be recognized until they are actually realized. The only exception to this rule occurs in unusual circumstances when realization of the tax loss carry-forward is assured "beyond any reasonable doubt."

The SEC has insisted on strict adherence to both requirements that must exist before tax loss carry-forward benefits can be booked as assets, to wit: *(a)* the loss results from an identifiable, isolated, and nonrecurring cause and the company either has been continuously profitable over a long period or has suffered occasional losses that were more than offset by taxable income in subsequent years; and *(b)* future taxable income is virtually certain to be large enough to offset the loss carry-forward and will occur soon enough to provide realization during the carry-forward period.

In its 1975 Annual Report, Kaufman and Broad disclosed that on SEC

ILLUSTRATION 4. *Accounting for tax loss carry-backs and carry-forwards.*

The Erratic Corporation had income (loss) and taxes as follows (for simplicity assume a 50 percent tax rate throughout):

Tax return data (in thousands)

	19x1	19x2	19x3	19x4	19x5	19x6	19x7
Taxable income (loss)	$120	$80	$160	$100	$(600)	$100	$220
Tax loss carry-back [a]		80	160	100			
Tax loss carry-forward [b]						100	160
Refund of prior year taxes (carry-back) [c]...............					(170)		
Carry-forward benefits (which reduce current year taxes) [d]						50	80

[a] Taxable income of preceding three years—here $340, which is all usable being less than the 19x5 loss of $600.

[b] Having used up $340 of the $600 loss in carry-backs, the tax loss carry-forward available at the end of 19x5 stood at $260 ($600 − $340) and can be carried forward to reduce taxes of the following 15 years.

[c] The tax refund amounts to 50 percent of $340 (i.e., $80 + $160 + 100). Regardless of tax rate prevailing at any given time, only taxes actually paid are recoverable.

[d] In 19x6, $100 in tax loss carry-forwards are used up resulting in a $50 tax benefit. In 19x7, the remaining $160 tax loss carry-forward is used up which results in a $80 tax benefit.

Income statement presentation (in thousands)

	19x1	19x2	19x3	19x4	19x5	19x6	19x7
Income (loss) before taxes and extraordinary gain (assumed were same as taxable income)	$120	$80	$160	$100	$(600)	$100	$220
Less: Tax expense (refund) [e]..................	60	40	80	50	(170)	50	110
Income (loss) before extraordinary gain	60	40	80	50	(430)	50	110
Extraordinary gain— benefit of tax loss carry-forward [f]	—	—	—	—	—	50	80
Net income (loss)	$ 60	$40	$ 80	$ 50	$(430)	$100	$190

[e] In all years except 19x5—50 percent of income; for 19x5, see tax return data above.

[f] The following entries are recorded:

	19x6	19x7
Tax Expense	50	110
Taxes Payable	50	110
To record taxes related to pretax income.		
Taxes Payable	50	80
Extraordinary gain—Benefit		
of tax loss carry-forward	50	80
To record reduction in taxes payable because of tax loss carry-forward benefit.		

Should Erratic Corporation have been able to establish in 19x5 that its prospects of earning taxable income of $260 over the following 15 years were "beyond any reasonable doubt," it could have reduced the 19x5 loss by a further $130 as follows:[4]

Future Tax Benefit (Asset)	130	
Carry-Forward Tax Benefit		130

In such a case, the $50 tax loss carry-forward benefit in 19x6 and $80 in 19x7 would have been credited to the Future Tax Benefit account while in the income statement no extraordinary carry-forward benefits would have been booked.

insistence it reversed a $12 million future tax benefit booked in an earlier period.

Tax reductions resulting from tax loss carry-forwards are, if material, shown as extraordinary credits so as not to distort the normal reltionship prevailing between a company's income and the tax to which it is subject. Analytically, these tax loss carry-forward benefits are best related to the loss year(s) that gave rise to them.

Accounting for income taxes by oil and gas producers

FASB *SFAS* 9 requires the allocation of income taxes for timing differences arising from intangible drilling and development costs and other costs associated with the exploration for and development of oil and gas reserves that are charged to expense in income statements in one period but deducted for income tax purposes in a different period.

SEC disclosure requirements

To enable users of financial statements to understand better the tax components of an enterprise, its tax accounting, its effective tax rate, and the current and prospective cash drains associated with tax payments, the SEC has called in FRR No.1 Sec. 204, as well in subsequent 1980 amendments, for disclosure of:

The components of income tax expense (e.g., current and deferred taxes, net operating tax carry-forwards, and investment credits.)

A reconciliation between the effective income tax rate and the statutory federal income tax rate.

---

[4] Computed as follows:

19x5 loss	$600
Loss used up in carry-back	340
Carry-forward available	260
Tax benefit of loss carry-forward......	$130

Components of deferred tax expense.

Domestic and foreign components of income before income tax expense.

Investment tax credit

The investment tax credit has been used as an instrument of economic policy for the stimulation of capital investment when this is deemed a desirable objective. Thus, for example, a 10 percent investment credit was allowed in the year of an asset's acquisition. An industrial company acquiring an asset of $100,000 would have its tax bill for the year reduced by $10,000.

In its time, the APB has repeatedly tried to obtain acceptance of an accounting treatment whereby the investment credit benefit would be spread over the useful life of the asset acquired. The basic argument in favor of this method is that one does not enhance earnings by the act of buying assets but rather by using them. Under the deferral method, if the above-mentioned asset has a useful life of 10 years, the $10,000 investment credit would be taken into income (as a reduction of taxes) at the rate of $1,000 per year.

The APB has not been successful in obtaining acceptance of this view. The position of those who favor the immediate reflection of the investment credit in income (also known as the flow-through method) is that the investment credit is a selective reduction in taxes unrelated to the use of the asset. The flow-through method of taking the investment credit into income in the year of the asset purchase is in more widespread use than the deferral method, which calls for taxing in the credit as a reduction of taxes over the years of useful life of the asset. Both methods enjoy the label of "generally accepted accounting principles" The effect of the investment tax credit on the effective tax rate was discussed in the section dealing with "Permanent income tax differences."

Implications for analysis

Taxes are almost always substantial expense items, and the analyst must be sure that he or she understands the relationship between pretax income and the income tax expense.

The analyst should note that the procedures applied to loss carry-forwards differ from those applied to carry-backs. While the tax loss carry-back results in a tax refund in the loss year and is recognized as such, a loss carry-forward that should have a similar impact is not so recognized because its realization is not usually "assured beyond any reasonable doubt." Thus, in this situation the "realization convention" in accounting takes precedence over the "matching concept." The subsequent actual realization of a tax loss carry-forward is designated as an extraordinary item so as to indicate that it has really nothing to do with the normal tax for the year. In the analysis of a loss year, the analyst should consider a tax loss carry-forward as a contingent benefit, especially since it can now be utilized over a span of 15 years.

In spite of all the heated arguments surrounding tax allocation,[5] it is obvious that this accounting principle makes an important contribution to proper tax accrual and, hence, income reporting. It separates tax strategy from the reporting of results of operations, thus removing one possiblity of management determining the size of results by means of bookkeeping techniques alone.

Another good argument for tax allocation, from an analytical point of view, is the fact that assets whose future tax deductibility is reduced cannot be worth as much as those that have a higher tax deductibility. Thus, for example, if two companies depreciate an identical asset costing $100,000 under different tax methods of depreciation that result in a first-year depreciation of $10,000 and $20,000, respectively, then it is obvious that at the end of that year, one company has an asset that it can still depreciate for tax purposes to the tune of $90,000 while the other can depreciate it only to the extent of $80,000. Obviously the two assets are not equally valuable, and the tax deferral adjustment recognizes this fact.

One of the flaws remaining in tax allocation procedures is that no recognition is given to the fact that the present value of a future obligation, or loss of benefits, should be discounted rather than shown at par as today's tax deferred accounts actually are. This was a question that was also debated within the APB, but the Board decided to postpone a decision on this matter.

The failure of the accounting profession to face the issue of discounting squarely should cause the analyst to be even more aware of the serious objections many in industry continue to have to the tax deferral concept in general and to the relentless buildup of deferred tax credits which, while reducing income, do not represent a legal obligation to an outsider. When forced to adopt deferred tax accounting Exxon's management expressed its objection as follows:

> It is the opinion of Management that the total of these deferred tax credits, which do not represent liabilities, will continue to grow rather than be restored to income. Management believes that its former method of accounting for income taxes was more realistic than the new method it was required to adopt in 1968.

So far its prediction has proved correct.

An error sometimes committed by analysts is to assume that deferred tax accounting acts as a complete offset to differences between tax and financial accounting methods. Actually, if we assume that the accelerated depreciation method used for tax purposes is more realistic than the straight-line method used in reporting income, then the effect of deferred taxes is to remove only

---

[5] Tax allocation is now being reconsidered by the FASB.

approximately *half* of the overstatement of income that results from the use, for book purposes, of the slower depreciation method.

FASB *SFAS 9* on tax allocation by petroleum companies represents more of a compromise with a divided industry than a creditable attempt to provide similar accounting for similar circumstances. Given the highly technical and complex provisions that provide for alternative ways of deferred tax computations, the analyst must now be aware that the use of these different methods by the oil companies can affect comparability among their reported results.

Accounting for the investment credit is subject to two very different acceptable alternatives. In our example of the company that buys a 10-year life asset for $100,000, one allowable method is to take the $10,000 investment credit into income in the first year while under the alternative and preferred method, only $1,000 is so taken into the first year income. It is obvious that the $9,000 tax difference on a $100,000 asset purchase may have a significant impact on results and on intercompany comparability. The fact is that the flow-through method enjoys substantial acceptance and the analyst must be aware of this in his evaluation of relative results.

Analytical significance of the SEC disclosure requirements

The SEC disclosure requirements (FRR No.1 Sec. 204) and 1980 integrated disclosure system amendments provide the analyst with significant income tax information beyond that required by *APB Opinion 11.*

The requirements for an explanation of why the effective tax expense percentage differs from the current statutory rate (e.g., 46 percent), if it does, gives the analyst important means of judging whether the present tax benefits or extra costs that an enterprise enjoys or fears, can be expected to continue in the future. This can improve predictions of cash flow and earnings. Thus, such benefits as the Investment Tax Credit, DISCS, foreign tax shelter (e.g., Puerto Rico), depletion allowances, and capital gains treatment depend on legislative sanction and are always subject to change, repeal, or expiration. Other differences, such as those arising from foreign tax differentials, depend on conditions that must be carefully monitored. Some tax benefits may or may not remain part of the tax laws. Other benefits depend on the company's ability to take advantage of them, e.g., capital expenditures in order to earn investment tax credits.

The continuation of accounting related differentials, such as those relating to the use of the equity method income pickup or the amortization of goodwill, can be evaluated by the analysis of underlying transactions. In the same way that a low effective tax rate will lead the analyst to investigate the livelihood of the recurrence of tax benefits, so will a higher than normal tax rate be reason for further inquiry. Thus, for example, a higher than normal effective tax rate may be due to subsidiary losses that for one reason or another the company may not be able to be offset on the tax return.

New information can also be obtained by an analysis of the effective tax rate reconciliation. Thus, for example, if the analysis indicates that tax-free interest reduced taxes by $144,000, one can determine the amount of tax-free income by dividing $144,000 by .46 (the statutory tax rate) which equals $313,043.

A reconciliation of the tax rate of Alfa, Inc. (see Appendix 4B), can be found in Note 7.

The analysis of components of the deferred income tax expense can lead to significant analytical insights. The analyst may through this medium find out about the capitalization of costs, the early recognition of revenues, or about other book accounting methods of which he would otherwise not have been aware. Alfa, Inc.'s analysis of the principal items giving rise to deferred income taxes is found in Note 7 (item 93).

ILLUSTRATION 5.   Alfa changed its accounting for sugar revenues in 19x5, but (per Note 7) the company shows deferred taxes of $29,642 in *19x4* (a year earlier) for "uncollected sugar revenues." The analyst may wonder what this figure represents. Further, analysis will reveal that this amount must have originated as a result of a timing difference between the recognition of revenue for accounting purposes and for tax purposes. Obviously, the cause of the timing difference is these uncollected revenues, and therefore the only reasonable conclusion one could make from this treatment is that the company's tax return must show revenues at the time of collection.

Information about expected "substantial" future reductions in deferred income taxes, which do, of course, spell higher tax expense cash outlays, is valuable for the liquidity implications that it carries. Whenever a deferred tax credit "reverses," it means that the book-tax *expense* is reduced by the amount of the reversal but that the *actual* tax bill is higher than the net expense appearing in the income statement. The implication is a cash drain.

Puerto Rican Cement described such a projected situation as follows:

> Based upon currently anticipated expenditures and operations, it is expected that the deferred income tax balance will be reduced in 1975, 1976, and 1977 and the cash outlay for taxes associated with those years will exceed tax expense by approximately $1,550,000, $1,640,000 and $1,640,000, respectively, primarily due to the reversal of flexible depreciation taken in prior years for tax purposes over depreciation for book purposes.

In its 1980 amendments, the SEC unforunately deleted the requirement for disclosing expected future outlays for income taxes. The SEC encourages use of this type of information, where appropriate, in the liquidity section of "management's discussion and analysis."

EXTRAORDINARY GAINS AND LOSSES

Most items of revenue and cost discussed so far in this chapter are of the ordinary operating and recurring variety. Thus, it can be assumed that their inclusion in the income statement results in a figure that is a fair reflection of the period's operating results. Such reported results are a very important element in the valuation of securities, in the evaluation of managements, and in many other respects; and they are used as indicators of a company's earning power (see Chapter 22). Consequently, ever since the income statement became the important financial statement it is today, the treatment of unusual and extraordinary gains and losses and prior period adjustments has been a major problem area of income measurement and reporting.

Extraordinary items are distinguished by their unusual nature *and* by the infrequency of their occurrence. Examples of extraordinary items include substantial uninsured losses from a major casualty (such as an earthquake) or a loss from an expropriation.

Items affecting results of prior years are now limited by *SFAS 16* to correction of errors in prior period financial statements and to adjustments resulting from realization of income tax benefits of preacquisition operating loss carry-forwards of purchased subsidiaries.

There are two main schools of thought on how to handle extraordinary gains and losses. One is the "all-inclusive" concept, which gives recognition in determining net income to all items affecting the change in equity interests during the period except dividend payments and capital transactions. The other is the so-called "current-operating-performance" concept. This concept would exclude from net income any items that, if included, would impair the significance of the net income as a measure of current earning power. Under this latter concept, prior to 1966, actual income reporting practice had deteriorated to such an extent that a complete reversal in philosophy and approach became necessary.[6] The change came in stages, first with *APB Opinion 9* (1966) and in 1973 with *APB Opinion 30* which restricted still further the use of the extraordinary category by requiring that in order to qualify for this designation an item be *both* unusual in nature and infrequent of occurrence. It defined these terms thus:

    a.   *Unusual nature*—the underlying event or transaction should possess a high degree of abnormality and be of a type clearly unrelated to, or only incidentally related to, the ordinary and typical activities of the entity, taking into account the environment in which the entity operates.

    b.   *Infrequency of occurrence*—the underlying event or transaction should be of a type that would not reasonably be expected to recur in the foreseeable future, taking into account the environment in which the entity operates.

APB Opinion 30 held that certain gains and losses should not be reported as extraordinary items because they are usual in nature and may be expected to recur as a consequence of customary and continuing business activity. Examples include:

---

[6] For a comprehensive discussion of all aspects of this issue see the author's book *Accounting for Extraordinary Gains and Losses* (New York: Ronald Press, 1967).

1. Write-down or write-off of receivables, inventories, equipment leased to others, deferred R & D costs, or other intangible assets.
2. Gains or losses on disposal of a segment of a business.
3. Other gains or losses from sale or abandonment of property, plant, or equipment used in the business.
4. Effects of a strike, including those against competitors and major suppliers.
5. Adjustment of accruals on long-term contracts.

The *Opinion* also calls for the separate disclosure in income before extraordinary items of unusual *or* nonrecurring events or transactions that are material but that do not meet both conditions for classification as extraordinary.

Cross currents of theory—the case of debt retirements

When the APB considered in 1972 the question of gains and losses on debt retirement, its desire to limit further the items qualifying for the "extraordinary" label led it to the conclusion that these should be shown as ordinary items of gain and loss. Gains and losses on debt retirement arise when, due to changes in interest rates and/or credit standing, a debt can be satisfied by repurchase in the open market or otherwise at an amount below (gain) or above (loss) par.

Thus, when in 1974, soaring interest rates reduced the price of older, low coupon bonds, companies rushed to exchange high coupon bonds of lower aggregate par values for outstanding low coupon bonds. The resulting "profits" were substantial, as was the case of General Host which included in ordinary income $16 million of such gains which in turn represented 9 percent of net income.

Cases such as that of General Host prompted the SEC to induce the FASB to issue *SFAS 4* (1975) which requires material debt retirements of all kinds, except for sinking fund purchases, to be separately disclosed as extraordinary items. Material sinking fund gains and losses must, however, be aggregated and separately identified in the income statement.

These shifting theories reflect an ambivalence, i.e., a desire to do away with the label "extraordinary," on the one hand, and, on the other, an attempt to counter the ever-present propensity of some managements to augment income with a variety of "profits."

Discontinued operations

APB Opinion 30 also deals with the accounting for and the presentation of discontinued operations and the disposal of a segment of a business. These are not extraordinary items but should be presented separately as in the model of the lower part of an income statement on page 344.

The analyst will recognize that in the estimation of *future* earning power, results from discontinued operations can be omitted. The losses on disposal must be treated analytically in a way similar to that accorded to extraordinary items, i.e., while not entering the computation of the results of a single year, they must be included in the longer-term earnings record of the enterprise.

Alfa, Inc. (see Appendix 4B), describes in detail in Note 3 (item $\boxed{73}$) the results, losses, and provisions made in the discontinuance of a division. The income statement presentation can be seen in item $\boxed{13}$ in Alfa's statement of income.

Model of lower part of an income statement

Income from continuing operations before income taxes		$xxx
Provision for income taxes		xxx
Income from continuing operations		xxx
Discontinued operations (described in a note):		
Income (loss) from discontinued operations (less applicable income taxes of $xxx)[a]	$xxx	
Loss on disposal of discontinued operations including provision of $xxx for operating losses during phaseout period (less applicable income taxes of $xxx)[b]	xxx	xxx
Extraordinary item less income taxes of $xxx		xxx
Cumulative effect on prior years of change in accounting principle (less tax effect of $xxx)		xxx
Net income		$xxx

[a] Includes operating losses to date of commitment to formal disposition of a segment, i.e., a separately identifiable entity—physically, operationally, and financially.

[b] Includes estimated operating losses from date of decision to discontinue to expected disposal date. (Expected net gains on disposals can be recorded only *when realized.*)

Implications for analysis

To the intelligent analyst, the single most desirable characteristic in the income statement is that of adequate disclosure. Most analyses of the income statement, except possibly for evaluation of the quality of management, are predictive in nature. Analysts rely on factors whose stability of relationship and recurrence facilitate the extrapolation and forecasting function. Similarly, adjustments must be made for the erratic, sporadic, and nonrecurring elements of reported income. For all this, the analyst needs, above all, sufficient information about the nature of all the material elements entering the determination of the results of operations of a period. He needs such information presented in adequate detail so as to enable him to form an opinion as to its impact on his conclusions and projections, and he needs it presented without bias so that he can use it with confidence. This, then, is the reason for the need for the largest possible measure of fair and adequate disclosure.

While there is need for full details of all normal operating elements of revenue and expense, the need for information regarding the nature of extraordinary gains and losses is even more essential. This is true because of the material nature of such items as well as the need to form judgments and conclusions regarding how they should be treated in an assessment of the overall results of operations and what probability of recurrence should be assigned to them. It is this special nature of extraordinary items that has caused so much debate and controversy within the accounting profession as to their treatment.

The financial analyst should realize that one important aspect of that controversy is of no real concern to him. It focuses on the one figure of net income that many superficial users of financial data rely upon almost to the exclusion of all other factors. In such a context, the matter of whether an extraordinary item is or is not included in the determination of net income is of great importance. To the analyst who most carefully analyzes all elements of the income statement, the exact positioning of the extraordinary item within the income statement is not of great import. He is much more concerned with the adequate description of the extraordinary item as well as the circumstances that gave rise to it, so that he can classify it properly in the context of long run as well as short-term analysis.

APB Opinion 9 represented the start of a reversal of attitude on the part of the accounting profession with regard to its responsibilities towards income reporting. Apparently discouraged by the abuses that resulted under the former approach, the profession has all but abandoned its professed intention to arrive at a meaningful or reliable measure of current operating performance. Instead, in order to insulate itself from the pressures of managements, the profession decided that with the exception of "rare" prior year adjustments, *all* items of income and expense shall be included in the determination of a "net income" figure which thus assumed a new and altogether different meaning.[7]

While one may wonder whether those who rely on the sole "net income" statistic will be helped by this new approach, the analyst must clearly understand the implications that the reporting under *APB Opinion 30* and *SFAS 16* holds for him.

To begin with, the analyst should not assume that the accountant's designation of an item as "extraordinary" even under the stricter criteria set forth by *Opinion 30* renders it automatically excludable from the measure of periodic operating results. The best that can be expected here is that under the requirements of the *Opinion,* full disclosure will be made of all *material* credits and charges in the income statement regardless of their designation. However, despite the fact that "materiality" is an important criterion in determining whether an item is "extraordinary" or not, the profession has, so far, not developed a meaningful standard that would guide it in distinguishing between items which are material and those which are not. Consequently, practice enjoys an undue amount of flexibility in this area.

An extraordinary item is now defined as being nonrecurring and outside an enterprise's normal operations. It is, sometimes, the result of a freak or of an unexpected or unpredictable occurrence. However, this concept of nor-

---

[7] *SFAS 52* departed from this "all inclusive" approach by allowing translation gains and losses to be accumulated in the equity section of the balance sheet.

malcy is one that must not be taken too seriously. Business is always subject
to contingencies and to the unexpected. This is the very essence of business
risk.[8] Moreover, variability is a fact of business life; and in spite of management's desire for stable growth trends, business results do not come in neat
uniform installments. Thus, the "bunching up" of positive and negative factors
that often causes items to become extraordinary should not lead to the conclusion that since they require adjustment of any one year's result, they should
be disregarded in an evaluation of an entity's long-term average performance.

Extraordinary items should never be completely disregarded. They often
bear the mark of the particular type of risks to which an enterprise is subject.
While they may not recur yearly, the fact of their occurrence attests to the
possibility of their recurrence. In their final impact on a business entity,
they are not different from operating items. After all, a loss from a flash
flood affects the entity's wealth every bit as much as does an equal loss on
the sale of merchandise below cost. Moreover, the cumulative importance
of extraordinary items can be considerable.

The analyst should always be aware of management's reporting propensities
and the fact that often it is in its power to decide both the size and the
timing of gains and losses. Thus, management can decide when to sell an
asset, when to discontinue a product line, or when, subject to the limiting
provisions of *SFAS 5* discussed in Chapter 7, to provide for a future loss;
and often the timing of such decisions is affected by its probable impact on
reported results. Since materiality is a consideration in the determination
of whether an item is "extraordinary" or not, losses that are small and considered "operating" can be permitted to accumulate to the point where they
are large enough to be labeled extraordinary. In assessing extraordinary items,
the analyst should be aware of the possibility that both their size and their
timing can be "managed."

Chapter 22 contains additional discussion of the significance of extraordinary and other unusual items to the financial analyst. What must be emphasized here is that regardless of the good intentions of those who promulgate
official accounting policies, the analyst can never assume that the intent and
spirit of these pronouncements will be implemented in practice. Instead, he
must pay close attention to actual practice. For example, the author has
documented the abuses of practice that have occurred after the promulgation
of *APB Opinion 9.*[9] The following examples will illustrate that in spite of a
considerable tightening up of the rules, opportunities for violating their spirit
or their letter still exist:

---

[8] See Chapter 1 for a discussion of unsystematic risk.

[9] See "Reserves for Future Costs and Losses—Threat to the Integrity of the Income Statement," *Financial Analysts Journal,* January–February 1970, pp. 45–48; and "Reporting the
Results of Operations—A Reassessment of *APB Opinion 9,*" *Journal of Accountancy,* July 1970,
pp. 57–61.

ILLUSTRATION 5.   In a 1975 refinancing, Reliance Group sold to banks for $53.4 million
        lease receivables with a book value of $57 million. It labeled the resulting $3.6
        million loss as extraordinary because it regarded it as resulting "from the early
        extinguishment of debt. . . ." In fact, the purchase agreements that led to the
        transfer of the leases to the banks indicate that this was a sale and not a debt
        swap.[10] We have here an example of management's use of accounting standards
        (i.e., *SFAS 4*) to further its particular interests which seem to be the exclusion
        of an ordinary loss from reported operating income.

ILLUSTRATION 6.   Norton Simon, Inc., in its 1976 annual report had the following note:
        In accordance with the provisions for the initial application of *Statement 12*
        of the Financial Accounting Standards Board, the marketable equity securities
        transferred from short-term to long-term investments at December 31, 1975, were
        transferred at cost, and a valuation allowance was established by a charge to
        shareholders' equity. The short-term valuation allowance of approximately $10
        million, established in prior years, was included in other income. Other income
        in 1976 was charged with provisions aggregating approximately $8 million against
        the realization of certain noncurrent receivables, investments other than marketable
        equity securities, and for certain other nonrecurring items. The net aftertax effect
        of the above items was to increase earnings by approximately $.01 a share.

In 1973, Western Union and United Brands, among others, used profits from debt retirements as the opportunity to absorb substantial unrelated write-offs. These are illustrations of the persisting technique of offset. The propensity of management to offset items of gains with provisions for present and future losses is not difficult to understand. It accomplishes two objectives: (1) it removes from the income stream an unusual profit boost that an earnings-trend conscious company may find difficult to match in the following year, and (2) it provides a discretionary "cushion" against which future losses and expenses can be charged so as to improve the earnings trend, or it provides for losses that up to now it did not find expedient to provide for. Thus, the timing of income and loss recognition can be "managed."[11]

In FRR No. 1 Sec. 305, the SEC reminds companies that full and timely disclosure of material charges or credits to income is expected irrespective of the absence of a requirement in a specific form.

From the above discussion it is clear that the financial analyst must adopt an independent and critical attitude towards items in the income statement be they classified as unusual, extraordinary or in any other fashion. Only on the basis of a full understanding of the nature of such items can a conclusion be reached regarding their impact on the earnings performance of a business entity.

---

[10] For further details, see A. J. Briloff, "Whose Deep Pocket," *Barron's*, July 19, 1976
[11] Chapter 11 of the first edition of this book contains additional examples in this area.

ACCOUNTING CHANGES

In an attempt to reduce the unwarranted switching by management from one accepted method of accounting to another, *APB Opinion 20* states that:

> in the preparation of financial statements there *is a presumption that an accounting principle once adopted should not be changed in accounting for events and transactions of a similar type.* Consistent use of accounting principles from one accounting period to another enhances the utility of financial statements to users by facilitating analysis and understanding of comparative accounting data.
>
> *   *   *   *   *
>
> The presumption that an entity should not change an accounting principle *may be overcome* only if the enterprise justifies the use of an alternative acceptable accounting principle on the basis that *it is preferable.*[12] (Emphasis supplied.)

The Board distinguishes in this *Opinion* among three types of accounting changes, that is, a change in (1) an accounting principle, (2) an accounting estimate, and (3) the reporting entity.

Change in accounting principle

As a general rule (see exceptions below), the cumulative effect of the change (net of taxes) on the amount of retained earnings at the beginning of the period in which the change is made should be included in net income and shown in the statement of income between "extraordinary items" and "net income." This is the so-called "catchup adjustment." Previously issued financial statements should *not* be adjusted.

A change in the method of allocating the cost of long-lived assets to various accounting periods, if adoped only for newly acquired assets, does not result in the "catchup adjustment" described above.

Under this general rule, the following disclosures are called for:

1. Nature of and justification for adopting the change.
2. Effect of the new principle on income before extraordinary items and net income for the period of change, including related earnings per share data.
3. Pro forma effects of retroactive application of the accounting change on income before extraordinary items and the net income (and related earnings per share data) should be shown on the face of the income statement for all periods presented.

When pro forma effects are not determinable, disclosure must be made as to why such effects are not shown.

---

[12] In FRR No. 1 Sec. 304, the SEC introduced the requirement that when an accounting change is made: "a letter from the registrant's independent accountants shall be filed as an exhibit indicating whether or not the change is to an alternative principle which in his judgment is *preferable* under the circumstances." (Emphasis added.)

There are three specific exceptions to the general rule that previously issued financial statements not be restated. In the case of the following accouting changes, previously issued statements should be restated:

1. Change *from* LIFO to another inventory pricing method.
2. Change in accounting method for long-term construction type contracts.
3. Change *to* or *from* the "full cost" method used in extractive industries.

These exceptions were included presumably because these adjustments normally result in large credits to income. The FASB has extended the exceptions to include changes resulting from the adoption of accounting standards required in *SFASs 2, 5, 8, 9,* and *52.*

Alfa, Inc. (see Appendix 4B), presents the "Cumulative Effect on Prior Years of Accounting Changes" in the statement of income (item $\boxed{15}$) and the "Pro Forma Amounts" giving retroactive effect to accounting changes (see item $\boxed{20}$). Note 2 (item $\boxed{72}$) explains the accounting changes and their effect.

Change in accounting estimate

In accounting, periodic income determination requires the estimation of future events such as inventory obsolescence, useful lives of property, warranty costs, or uncollectible receivables. These are known as accounting estimates. The following provisions in *APB Opinion 20* apply to changes in accounting estimates:

1. Retroactive restatement is prohibited.
2. The change should be accounted for in the period of change and, if applicable, future periods.
3. A change in accounting estimate that is recognized by a change in accounting principle should be reported as a change in estimate.
4. Disclosure is required of the effect on income before extraordinary items and net income (including related earnings per share data) of the current period when a change in estimate affects future periods as well.

Change in reporting entity

A change in the reporting entity can occur in the following ways:

1. Initial presentation of consolidated financial statements.
2. Changing the consolidation policy with respect to specific subsidiaries.
3. A pooling of interests.

APB Opinion 20 calls for restatement of all periods presented in the financial statements and for disclosure of the nature of the change and the reasons therefore.

Correction of an error

Errors in financial statements can arise from mistakes in arithmetic, mistakes in the application of accounting principles, or even the use of an unacceptable accounting principle.

APB Opinion 20 does not consider the correction of an error as being in the nature of an accounting change. Consequently, the correction of an error should be treated as a prior period adjustment, and disclosure should include:

1. The nature of the error.
2. The effect on previously reported income before extraordinary items and net income (and related earnings per share data).

Materiality

The materiality of an accounting change for reporting and disclosure purposes should be considered in relation to current income on the following bases:

1. Each change separately.
2. The combined effect of all changes.
3. The effect of a change on the trend of earnings.
4. The effect of a change on future periods.

The APB, in what appears to be a reaction to the increasing dissatisfaction of financial statement users with the failure of the profession to promulgate criteria for judging materiality, has narrowed its interpretation of this concept as applied to *Opinion 20.* Particularly noteworthy is the recognition by the Board of the importance that the analyst and other users of financial statements accord to earnings *trends.*

Historical summaries of financial information

APB Opinion 20 also applies to historical summaries of financial information that customarily appear in published financial statements or elsewhere. However, since these summaries are not normally covered by the auditor's opinion and their presentation is not mandatory, companies can avoid the need for restatement by merely shortening the period that they cover or by omitting them altogether.

Implications for analysis

The requirement that changes in accounting principles be undertaken only when the change is in the direction of preferable accounting is a significant development. Much depends on the judgment that independent accountants will use in deciding when a change is in the direction of preferable accounting

ILLUSTRATION 7.   The Changing Company's 19x5 annual report states: "Effective as of
January 1, 19x4, the Company adopted the last-in, first-out (LIFO) method of determining inventory cost. . . . LIFO inventories at December 31, 19x4, and 19x5
were $58,970,000 and $55,723,000, respectively. Under the average-cost method
of accounting, hitherto in use, inventories would have been $14,580,000 and
$19,311,000 higher than those reported at December 31, 19x4, and 19x5, respec-
tively."

The effect of the *change* from average cost to LIFO cost is as follows (in thousands):

	Debit (credit)		
	19x5	*19x4*	*19x3*
On balance sheet:			
△ Inventories	$(19,311)(a)	$(14,580)(a)	–0–
△ Taxes payable—current	8,883	6,709	
△ Retained earnings	10,428	7,871	
On retained earnings statement:			
△ Beginning balance	7,871	–0– (a)	
△ Net income	2,557	7,871	
△ Ending balance	10,428	7,871	
On income statement:			
△ Cost of sales	4,731	14,580	
△ Tax expense	(2,174)	6,709)	
△ Net income (net decrease)	2,557	7,871	
On changes in financial position (working capital):			
△ Net income	2,557	7,871	
Decrease in working capital from operations	2,557	7,871	

The following should be noted:

1. Items marked *(a)* are as given in the annual report. The reduction in inventories
    was offset by a reduction in taxes payable (i.e., a reduced cash drain) here
    calculated at 46 percent and a reduction in retained earnings.
2. Since the company switched to LIFO on January 1, 19x4, the January 1,
    19x4, inventories and retained earnings would be the *same* for both methods
    (i.e., zero effect shown above).
3. The effect on cost of sales was calculated as the difference in the inventory
    change. Thus, in 19x5, the inventory *reduction* was higher at year-end than
    at the beginning, resulting in an increase in cost of goods sold of $4,731
    ($19,311 − $14,580). Similarly, in 19x4 the change in ending inventory to a
    reduction of $14,580 (when comparing average cost to LIFO) resulted in a
    corresponding increase in cost of goods sold because opening inventory was
    unchanged.

4. All remaining amounts are derived. For example, in 19x4, we know that since inventories were reduced (credited) by $14,580 under the new method, taxes payable would be reduced (debited) by 46 percent of that amount. (Lower ending inventories [compared to beginning of period] result in higher costs and in lower profits.) That leaves a charge (debit) to retained earnings of $7,871. Since the total effect on retained earnings was $7,871 (debit) and the effect on the opening balance of that account is known to be zero, it follows that the entire 19x4 income effect had to be $7,871. That is corroborated by the change in the income statement as shown.
5. The decrease in working capital from operations (see Chapter 13) is due to a decrease in inventory offset by a decrease in taxes payable.

and when it is not. The potential for improvements in financial reporting that *APB Opinion 20* holds is undeniably great.

Similarly, the SEC's controversial rule on preferability is a favorable development from the analyst's point of view. To reduce an accountant's propensity for liberal interpretation of this rule, the Commission stated that it would expect accounting firms to be consistent between clients when making their preferability judgments.

The inclusion of the "catchup" adjustment, which results from accounting changes, in the determination of the net income of the period in which the change takes place strengthens the need to deemphasize the net income of any one year and to focus instead on the average earnings achieved over a number of years.

The analyst will often need to assess the effect on the financial statements of the use of different accounting principles or estimates. That may occur because the analyst may want to adjust the financial statements to reflect a different accounting principle for analytical purposes, or in order to compare financial statements of companies using different accounting policies, or because he may want to estimate the effect on the various components of the current or past financial statements of such a change. Alternatively, he may want to estimate the effect of such changes on past financial statements where restatements have not been provided.

The best technique of analysis in this case, as in so many others, is first to establish what journal entries are required by each alternative and then to compare these.

THE INCOME STATEMENT—IMPLICATIONS FOR ANALYSIS, AN OVERVIEW

The position of importance and predominance assumed by the income statement is due to a number of factors. For one, it is the financial statement that presents the dynamic aspects of an enterprise, the results of its operations, and the quality of its performance. Moreover, it is the basis on which extrapolations and projections of future performance are built. The income statement's importance is emphasized by the accounting process that favors it and focuses on it, often to the neglect of the balance sheet. The attempt to increase the significance of the income statement has often resulted in distortions in the balance sheet. Thus, for example, the use of the LIFO method of inventory accounting in times of rising price levels introduces current costs into the income statement but undermines the significance of the balance sheet where inventories are carried at unrealistically low amounts. The balance sheet is cast mostly in a supporting role, containing as it does residual balances of assets and deferred credits that will ultimately become costs and revenues, the investments and working funds necessary to conduct operations, and the various sources of funds such as the liability and capital accounts.

As we have seen throughout this and the preceding chapters, the accounting rules governing the determination and measurement of periodic income are far from uniform, and much leeway exists in their selection, interpretation, and application. It may be useful to conclude this discussion with an overview of the possibilities that exist in the distortion of reported income.

If we accept the proposition that there is such a thing as "true" or "real" income, that is, income that could be determined when all the facts are known and all the uncertainties are resolved, then it is obvious that most reported income must deviate somewhat from this ideal figure. We can never be sure about the useful life of an asset until it has actually come to an end; we cannot be certain about the ultimate profitability of a contract until it is fulfilled, nor can we be certain about the revenue received from a transaction until the sales price is actually collected. There is nothing one can do about these uncertainties except to estimate their ultimate disposition on the basis of the best information and judgment available. Periodic income reporting requires that we not wait for final disposition of uncertainties but that we estimate them as best we can. Such a system is subject to many errors: errors of estimation, errors of omission, and errors of commission. The better and the more conscientious a company's management and the better its internal controls, the less likely it is that such errors will substantially distort report results.

The more serious and frequent cases of income distortion arise when managements set out to "manage" reported results in such a way that instead of portraying economic results as they are, they are presented as nearly as possible as management wants them presented.

Thus, for example, *Forbes,*[13] in writing on the earnings reporting practices of Itel Corporation, a major equipment marketing and leasing company, had this to say:

> Itel's hard sell is aimed at its shareholders, too. Since the debacle of the early Seventies, the company's earnings-per-share curve has been rising steadily and magnificently, from $1.28 in 1974 to $3.86 in 1978—a fact which, former

---

[13] May 28, 1979, p. 40.

Itel officials say, is a big deal with Redfield. "Programmed earnings are a part of his philosophy," says a former Itel executive. By this he means that where there is a discretion as to when to take a profit, Itel will advance or retard the profit-taking in the interest of a smooth earnings curve. For example, management has great discretion as to when to cash in on residual values of leased equipment. If earnings are falling short of projections, Itel can simply cash in on some residuals. This practice is common in a corporate environment where security analysts award high P/Es on the basis of smooth upward earnings curves, and Redfield is sophisticated enough to play this corporate game with the best of managements.

We have seen that such distortions can be accomplished by means of the timing of transactions, the choice from a variety of generally accepted principles, the introduction of conservative or, alternatively, very optimistic estimates, and the arbitrary choice of methods by which elements of income and expenses are presented or their nature is disclosed. (See also the discussion on the evaluation of earnings quality in Chapter 22.)

Generally, an enterprise wishing to benefit current income at the expense of the future will engage in one or a number of practices such as the following:

1. It will choose inventory methods that allow for maximum inventory carrying values and minimum current charges to cost of goods or services sold.
2. It will choose depreciation methods and useful lives of property that will result in minimum current charges as depreciation expense.
3. It will defer all manner of costs to the future such as, for example:
   a. Preoperating, moving, rearrangement, and start-up costs.
   b. Marketing costs.
   Such costs would be carried as deferred charges or included with the costs of other assets such as property, plant, and equipment.
4. It will amortize assets and defer costs over the longest possible period. Such assets include:
   a. Goodwill.
   b. Leasehold improvements.
   c. Patents and copyrights.
5. It will elect the method requiring the lowest possible pension and other employment compensation cost accruals.
6. It will inventory rather than expense administrative costs, taxes, etc.
7. It will choose the most accelerated methods of income recognition such as in the areas of leasing, franchising, real estate sales, and contracting.[14]
8. It will take into income right away, rather than defer, such benefits as investment tax credits.

---

[14] The profession is, of course, continuously working on restricting the free choices available in the selection of accounting alternatives. Thus, in the "Introduction and Background Information" section of *SFAS 56,* we find the statement that "The percentage-of-completion and completed-contract methods are not intended to be free choice alternatives for the same circumstances. . . ."

Enterprises that wish to "manage" the size of reported income can still regulate to some extent the flow of income and expense by means of reserves for future costs and losses.

Exhibit 11–1 illustrates the possible impact on reported income of some of the alternative accounting principles available to managements.

Exhibit 11–1: Example of the effect of the variety of accounting principles on reported income

RIVAL MANUFACTURING COMPANY
Consolidated Statement of Income
For Year Ended 19xx

	Method A	Method B
Net sales	$ 365,800,000	$ 365,800,000
Cost of goods sold (1) (2) (3) (4) (5)	(276,976,200)	(274,350,000)
	88,823,800	91,450,000
Selling, general, and administrative expenses (5) (6)	(51,926,000)	(42,700,000)
	36,897,800	48,750,000
Other income (expenses):		
Interest expenses	(3,085,000)	(3,095,000)
Net income—subsidiaries	1,538,000	1,460,000
Amortization of goodwill (7)	(390,000)	(170,000)
Miscellaneous expenses	(269,000)	(229,000)
Income before taxes	34,691,800	46,715,800
Taxes:		
Income taxes—deferred (8)	(756,000)	(850,000)
Income taxes—current	(16,716,900)	(22,397,900)
Reductions from investment tax credits (9)	10,400	758,400
Net income	$ 17,229,300	$ 24,226,300
Earnings per share	$5.74	$8.08

Explanations:
  (1) Inventories:
        A uses last-in, first-out
        B uses first-in, first-out
             Difference—$1,780,000
  (2) Administrative costs:
        A includes some administrative costs as period costs
        B includes some administrative costs as inventory costs
             Difference—$88,000
  (3) Depreciation:
        A uses sum-of-the-years'-digits method
        B uses straight-line method
             Difference—$384,200
  (4) Useful lives of assets:
        A uses conservative assumption—8 years (average)
        B uses liberal assumption—14 years (average)
             Difference—$346,000
  (5) Pension costs:
        A uses "maximum provision" under *APB Opinion 8*
        B uses "minimum provision" under *APB Opinion 8*
             Difference—$78,000

Exhibit 11–1 *(concluded)*

> (6) Executive compensations:
>   A compensates executives with cash bonuses
>   B compensates executives with stock options
>   Difference—$840,000
> (7) Goodwill from acquisition:
>   A amortizes over 10 years
>   B amortizes over 40 years
>   Difference—$220,000
> (8) Taxes on subsidiary profits:
>   A makes provision as income earned
>   B makes no provision until dividends received
>   Difference—$67,000
> (9) Investment tax credits:
>   A amortizes over useful lives of equipment
>   B credits against current taxes
>   Difference—$748,000

The financial analyst, while welcoming improvements in the scope and quality of financial statements as well as in their integrity and reliability, must nevertheless be ever alert to the innumerable possibilities and avenues available for the distortion of reported results.

QUESTIONS

1. What are past service costs? Vested benefits?

2. How is compensation granted by means of stock options measured? Does *APB Opinion 25* call for a realistic recognition of the compensation cost inherent in stock options granted?
   a. Discuss the accounting standards that govern R&D costs as stipulated by *SFAS 2.*
   b. What are the disclosure requirements as stipulated by the same statement?

4. What information does the financial analyst need regarding R&D outlays, especially in light of the limited disclosure requirements stipulated by *SFAS 2?*

5. To what aspects of the valuation and the amortization of goodwill must the analyst be alert?

6. Contrast the computation of total interest costs of a bond issue with warrants attached with that of an issue of convertible debt.

7. *a.* What is the main provision of *SFAS 34* and what are its objectives?
   b. How is the amount to be capitalized computed and how is the rate to be used ascertained?
   c. What restrictions to capitalization are imposed by *SFAS 34* and when does the capitalization period begin?

8. The net income computed on the basis of book income will often differ from taxable income due to permanent differences. What are permanent differences and how do they arise?

9. What factors will cause the effective tax rate to differ from the statutory rate?

10. What are the requirements that must be met before tax-loss carry-forward benefits can be booked as assets?

11. List four circumstances giving rise to book-tax timing differences.

12. Describe "income tax normalizing." (CFA)

13. Discuss the accounting treatment of income taxes by oil and gas producers as stipulated by *SFAS 9.*

14. *a.* What are the major SEC disclosure requirements regarding income taxes?
    b. What is their significance to the financial analyst?

15. Name one flaw to which tax allocation procedures are still subject.

16. How has the accounting profession defined an extraordinary item? Give three examples of such items.

17. What conditions are necessary before an item qualifies as a prior period adjustment?

18. In the never-ending debate on the proper treatment of extraordinary items, what should be the financial analyst's main interest?

19. Describe some of the abuses in the area of extraordinary item reporting that are found in practice and that have not been dealt with by recent APB pronouncements on this subject.

20. Why do some companies try to offset items of gains with provisions for present and future losses?

21. Why is it impossible to arrive at an absolutely "precise" measure of periodic net income?

22. What are some of the types of methods by means of which income can be distorted?

23. For each of the items below (1–3), explain:
    a. Two acceptable accounting methods for corporate reporting purposes.
    b. How each of these two acceptable accounting methods will affect the earnings of the current period.
      (1) Depreciation.
      (2) Inventory.
      (3) Installment sales. (CFA)

24. What are the objectives of *APB Opinion 20?* It distinguishes among four types of accounting changes. Which are they?

12

Earnings per share— computation and evaluation

The determination of the earnings level of an enterprise that is relevant to the purposes of the analyst is a complex analytical process. This earnings figure can be converted into an earnings per share (EPS) amount that is useful in the evaluation of the price of the common stock, in the evaluation of dividend coverage and dividend paying ability, as well as for other purposes. The analyst must, consequently, have a thorough understanding of the principles that govern the computation of EPS.

The intelligent analyst will never overemphasize the importance of, or place exclusive reliance on, any one figure, be it the widely used and popular EPS figure or any other statistic. In using the EPS figure, he or she should always be alert to the composition of the "net income" figure used in its computation.

In the mid-1960s, when a wave of mergers brought with it the widespread use of convertible securities as financing devices, the attention of analysts and of accountants turned also to the denominator of the EPS computation, that is, the number of shares of common stock by which the earnings should be divided. It became obvious that the prior practice of considering only the common shares actually outstanding without a consideration of the future potential dilution that is inherent in convertible securities, had often led to an overstatement of EPS.

The managements of merger-minded companies had discovered that it was possible to buy the earnings of a company by compensating its owners with low-yield convertible securities that in effect represented a deferred equity interest. Since the acquired earnings were immediately included in the combined income of the merged enterprise while the dilutive effect of the issuance of convertible securities was ignored, an illusory increase in EPS was thus achieved. Such growth in EPS increased the value of the securities, thus enabling the merger-minded company to carry this value enhancing process

358

even further by using its attractive securities to effect business combination at increasingly advantageous terms of its existing stockholders.

ILLUSTRATION 1.   Merging Company A, which pays no dividend and whose stock sells at $35, issued to merged Company B, which is earning $3 per share, $1 convertible preferred, on a share-for-share basis that allows for conversion into Company A's common at $40 per share. Because of the dividend advantage, there is no prospect of an early conversion of the convertible preferred into common. Thus, prior to *APB Opinion 15,* Company A realized "instant earnings" by getting a $3 per share earnings boost in return for a $1 preferred dividend requirement. It is obvious that the $1 convertible preferred derives most of its value from the conversion feature rather than from its meager dividend provision.

MAJOR PROVISIONS OF *APB OPINION 15*

APB Opinion 15 put an end to this unrealistic disregard of the potential dilutive effect of securities convertible into common stock. The *Opinion* looks to the substance of a securities issue rather than merely to its legalistic form.

Simple capital structure

If a corporation has a simple capital structure that consists only of common stock and nonconvertible senior securities and does not include potentially dilutive securities, then most of the provisions of the *Opinion* do not apply. In that case, a single presentation of EPS is called for and is computed as follows:

$$\frac{\text{Net income less claims of senior equity securities}}{\substack{\text{Weighted-average number of common shares outstanding during} \\ \text{the period after adjustments for stock splits and dividends (including} \\ \text{those effected after balance sheet date but before completion of} \\ \text{financial statements)}}}$$

In the above computation, dividends of cumulative senior equity securities, whether earned or not, should be deducted from net income or added to net loss.

Computation of weighted average of common shares outstanding

The theoretically correct weighted-average number of shares is the sum of shares outstanding each day divided by the number of days in the period. Less precise averaging methods, such as on a monthly or quarterly basis, where there is little change in the number of shares outstanding, is also permissible.

In the computation:

1. Reacquired shares should be excluded from date of acquisition.
2. Shares sold or issued in a purchase of assets should be included from date of issuance.
3. Previously reported EPS data should be adjusted retroactively for changes in outstanding shares resulting from stock splits or stock dividends.

Example of computation or weighted-average number of shares outstanding

19x1	*Transactions in common stock*	*Number of shares*
January 1	Outstanding	1,200
February 2	Stock options exercised	200
April 15	Issued at 5% stock dividend	70
August 16	Issued in pooling of interests	400
September 2	Sale for cash	300
October 18	Repurchase of treasury shares	(100)
		2,070

Computation of weighted-average number of shares

		Shares outstanding		*Product:*
		Number	*Days*	*Share—days*
Date of change:				
January 1		1,200		
Retroactive adjustment:				
For stock dividend (5%)		60		
Issued in pooling		400		
January 1—adjusted		1,660	32	53,120
February 2—stock option ...	200			
+5% stock dividend	10	210		
		1,870	212	396,440
September 2—sale for cash ..		300		
		2,170	46	99,820
October 18—repurchase		(100)		
		2,070	75	155,250
			365	704,630

$$\text{19x1 weighted-average number of shares } \frac{704,630}{365} = 1,930 \text{ shares}$$

As can be seen in the illustrations above, shares issued in a pooling of interests are included in the computation of EPS as of the beginning of all periods presented. This is so because under the pooling of interests concept, the merged companies are assumed to have been combined since their respective inceptions. In the case of purchases, the EPS reflect new shares issued only from date of acquisition.

Stock dividends are also adjusted retroactively, thus applying to the computation of the entire year. Issuances of stock (as a result of stock options or sale) as well as repurchases of stock all involve changes in entity resources and thus enter the computation only from the date of the transaction.

The term *earnings per common share* should be used without qualifying language only when the company has in fact a simple capital structure and no agreements exist for contingent issuances of common stock. A company can also make such presentation of EPS if the total dilution from dilutive securities or other provisions does not exceed 3 percent (i.e., if the adjusted net income divided into total shares that include dilutive securities results in an EPS number not lower than 97 percent of that arrived at without considering such dilutive securities).

COMPLEX CAPITAL STRUCTURE

A company is deemed to have a complex capital structure if it has outstanding potentially dilutive securities such as convertible securities, options, warrants, or other stock issue agreements.

By dilution is meant a reduction in EPS (or increase in net loss per share) resulting from the assumption that convertible securities have been converted into common stock, or that options and warrants have been exercised, or that shares have been issued in compliance with certain contracts.

A company having a complex capital structure has to give a dual presentation of EPS if the aggregate dilutive effect of convertible and other securities is more than 3 percent. Such dual presentation is to be effected with equal prominence on the income statement and show (1) primary EPS and (2) fully diluted EPS.

Primary earnings per share

Primary EPS is the amount of earnings attributable to each share of common stock outstanding plus dilutive common stock equivalents.

Definition of common stock equivalents (CSE). The concept of CSE is basic to the approach adopted in the *APB Opinion 15*. It denotes a security that derives the major portion of its value from its common stock characteristics or conversion privileges. Thus, a CSE is a security that because of its terms or the circumstances under which it was issued is deemed to be in substance equivalent to common stock. The following are examples of CSE.

1. *Convertible debt and convertible preferred stocks* are CSE only if at the time of issuance they have a cash yield (based on market price) of less than 66⅔ percent of the then average Aa corporate bond yield.[1] If a convertible security is issued that is a CSE and that same security was previously issued when it was not a CSE at time of issuance, the earlier issued shares or debt should be considered a CSE *from the date of issuance of the later shares or debt.* Prior periods EPS should not be restated. Similarly, any subsequent issuance of shares or debt with the same terms as previously issued shares or debt classified as a CSE should be classified as a CSE at its time of issuance even though the later issue of shares or debt would not be a CSE under the yield test at the later date of issue. This requirement can be overcome by a change in a term or condition having economic significance that is expected to affect prices in the securities market.

2. *Stock options and warrants (including stock purchase contracts)* are always to be considered as CSE.

3. *Participating securities and two-class common stocks* are CSE if their participation features enable their holders to share in the earnings potential of the issuing corporation, on substantially the same basis as common stock, even though the securities may not give the holder the right to exchange his shares for common stock.

4. *Contingent shares*—if shares are to be issued in the future upon the mere passage of time, they should be considered as outstanding for purposes of computing EPS. If additional shares of stock are issuable for little or no consideration upon the satisfaction of certain conditions, they should be considered as outstanding when the conditions are met.

5. *Securities of subsidiaries* may be considered common stock equivalents and conversion or exercise assumed for computing consolidated or parent company EPS when—

    a. *As to the subsidiary.*
        (1) Certain of the subsidiaries' securities are CSE in relation to its own common stock.
        (2) Other of the subsidiary's convertible securities, although not CSE in relation to its own common stock, would enter into the computation of its fully diluted earnings per share.

    b. *As to the parent.*
        (1) The subsidiary's securities are convertible into the parent company's common stock.

---

[1] Modified by *SFAS 55*, which also stated that if the convertible securities are sold outside the United States, the most comparable long-term yield in the foreign country should be used for this test.

(2) The subsidiary issues options and warrants to purchase the parent company's common stock.

Computation of primary EPS. If CSE with a dilutive effect are present, then primary EPS should be based on the weighted-average number of shares of common stock and CSE. The computation is also based on the assumption that convertible securities that are CSE were converted at the beginning of the period (or at time of issuance, if later), and that requires adding back to net income any deductions for interest or dividends, net of tax effect, related to such securities, a procedure known as the "if converted" method.

It can be summarized as follows:

Numerator	*Denominator*
Net income for the period.	Average of shares outstanding.
(Less preferred dividends applicable to preferred stock not considered as CSE).	Add—number of common shares into which convertible preferred shares and convertible bonds (which are deemed to be CSE) are convertible adjusted for proportion of time outstanding.
Add back tax adjusted interest on convertible bonds considered as CSE	

Options and warrants

Options and warrants are instruments that entitle the holder to buy a given amount (or fraction) of common shares at a given price for a specified period of time (usually shorter in the case of options than in the case of warrants). The computation of the dilutive effects of options and warrants, which are always considered as CSE, must, in turn, recognize the benefits accruing from the cash, or "boot," which the converter of these instruments into common must pay to the issuing company. This has given rise to the *treasury stock* method.

The treasury stock method

The *treasury stock* method recognizes the use of proceeds that would be obtained upon exercise of options and warrants in computing EPS. It assumes that any proceeds would be used to purchase common stock at current market prices. For options and warrants, the treasury stock method of computing the dilution to be reflected in EPS should be used (except for two exceptions to be explained). Under the treasury stock method:

1. EPS data are computed as if the options and warrants were exercised at the beginning of the period (or at time of issuance, if later) and as if the funds obtained thereby were used to purchase common stock at the average market price during the period.
2. But the assumption of exercise is not reflected in EPS data until the

market price of the common stock obtainable has been in excess of the exercise price for substantially all of three consecutive months ending with the last month of the period to which EPS relate.[2]

Example of treasury stock method

Assumptions:
    1,000,000 common shares outstanding (no change during year)
       $80 average market price for the common stock for the year
       100,000 warrants outstanding exercisable at $48

Computation:
  Shares
   100,000 shares issuable on exercise of warrants (proceeds $4,800,000)
   (60,000) shares acquirable with $4,800,000 proceeds (at $80 per share)
    40,000 CSE
 1,000,000 common shares
 1,040,000 shares used for computing primary EPS

First exception to treasury stock method. Warrants or debt indentures may permit or require certain uses of funds with exercise of warrants. Examples:

1. Debt is permitted or required to be tendered towards exercise price.
2. Proceeds of exercise are required to retire debt.
3. Convertible securities require cash payments upon conversion.

In these cases, an "if converted" method, which assumes conversion on exercise at the beginning of the period should be applied as if retirement or conversion of the securities had occurred and as if the excess proceeds, if any, had been applied to the purchase of common stock under the treasury stock method.

Second exception to treasury stock method. If the number of shares of common stock obtainable upon exercise of outstanding options and warrants in the aggregate exceeds 20 percent of the number of common shares outstanding at the end of the period for which the computation is being made, the treasury stock method should be modified. In these circumstances, all the options and warrants should be assumed to have been exercised and the aggregate proceeds therefrom to have been applied in two steps:

---

[2] The following formula will yield the number of incremental shares that will result from applying the treasury stock method to options or warrants (Y);

$$Y = \frac{M - E}{M} \ (N)$$

where M is the market price per share, E is the exercise price of option or warrant per common share, and N is the total number of shares obtainable on exercise.

1. As if the funds obtained were first applied to the repurchase of outstanding common shares at the average market price during the period (treasury stock method) but not to exceed 20 percent of the outstanding shares; and then
2. As if the balance of the funds were applied first to reduce any short-term or long-term borrowings and any remaining funds were invested in U.S. government securities or commercial paper, with appropriate recognition of any income tax effect.
3. The results of steps 1 and 2 of the computation (whether dilutive or antidilutive) should be aggregated, and if the net effect is dilutive, it should enter into the EPS computation.

Example of second exception of treasury stock method

	Case 1	Case 2
Assumptions:		
Net income for year	$ 4,000,000	$ 3,000,000
Common shares outstanding (no change during year)	3,000,000	3,000,000
Options and warrants outstanding to purchase equivalent shares	1,000,000	1,000,000
20% limitation on assumed repurchase	600,000	600,000
Exercise price per share	$15	$15
Average market value per common share to be used	$20	$14*
Interest rate on borrowings	6%	6%
Computations:		
Application of assumed proceeds ($15 × 1,000,000 shares) toward repurchase of outstanding common shares at applicable market value (600,000 × $20) and (600,000 × $14)	$12,000,000	$ 8,400,000
Reduction of debt	3,000,000	6,600,000
	15,000,000	15,000,000
Adjustment of net income:		
Actual net income	4,000,000	3,000,000
Interest reduction on debt (6%) less 50% tax effect	90,000	198,000
Adjusted net income (A)	$ 4,090,000	$ 3,198,000
Adjustment of shares outstanding:		
Actual number outstanding	3,000,000	3,000,000
Net additional shares issuable (1,000,000 − 600,000)	400,000	400,000
Adjusted shares outstanding (B)	3,400,000	3,400,000
Primary EPS:		
Before adjustment	$1.33	$1.00
After adjustment (A ÷ B)	1.20	0.94

* The three consecutive months test has previously been met.

Provisions concerning antidilution. Antidilution is an increase in EPS resulting from the assumption that convertible securities have been converted or that options and warrants have been exercised or other shares have been issued upon the fulfillment of certain conditions. For example, although stock options and warrants (and their equivalents) and stock purchase contracts should always be considered CSE, they should not enter into EPS calculations until the average market price of the common stock exceeds the exercise price of the option or warrant for preferably three consecutive months before the reporting period.

Computations of primary EPS should not give effect to CSE or other contingent issuance for any period in which their inclusion would have the effect of increasing the EPS amount or decreasing the loss per share amount otherwise computed.

Fully diluted earnings per share

Definition of fully diluted EPS. Fully diluted EPS is designed to show the maximum potential dilution of current EPS on a prospective basis. Fully diluted EPS is the amount of current EPS reflecting the maximum dilution that would have resulted from conversions of all convertible securities whether they are CSEs or not, as long as they are dilutive. Fully diluted EPS are also intended to reflect dilution resulting from exercises and other contingent issuances that individually would have decreased EPS and in the aggregate would have had a dilutive effect. All such issuances are assumed to have taken place at the beginning of the period (or at the time the event or contingency arose, if later).

When required. Fully diluted EPS data are required for each period presented if shares of common stock (1) were issued during the period on conversions, exercise, etc.; or (2) were contingently issuable at the close of any period presented and if primary EPS for such period would have been affected (dilutively or incrementally) had such actual issuances taken place at the beginning of the period or would have been reduced had such contingent issuances taken place at the beginning of the period.

Computation of fully diluted EPS. The computation should be based on the assumption that all such issued and issuable shares were outstanding from the beginning of the period (or from the time the contingency arose, if after the beginning of the period). Interest charges applicable to convertible securities and nondiscretionary adjustments that would have been made to items based on net income or income before taxes—such as profit-sharing expense, certain royalties, and investment credit—or preferred dividends applicable to the convertible securities should be taken into account in determining the balance of income applicable to common stock.

Use ending market price for treasury stock method.   The treasury stock method (along with the two exceptions) should be used to compute fully diluted EPS if dilution results from outstanding options and warrants; however, in order to reflect maximum potential dilution, the market price at the close of the period reported upon should be used to determine the number of shares that would be assumed to be repurchased (under the treasury stock method) if such market price is higher than the average price used in computing primary EPS.

Example of computation of fully diluted EPS.   Assume that there are 1,000,000 shares of class A preferred stock and 1,500,000 shares of class B preferred stock outstanding, both issues convertible into common on a share-for-share basis. Two million shares of common are outstanding. Class A preferred is a CSE with a $1.80 dividend; class B is a nonCSE preferred with a $1 dividend. Net income before either preferred dividend was $7,300,000.

Computation

	Shares	Net income	EPS
Net income		$ 7,300,000	
Shares outstanding	2,000,000		
$1.80 preferred dividend		(1,800,000)	
$1.00 preferred dividend		(1,500,000)	
($2 per share)	2,000,000	4,000,000	
Assume conversion of CSE class A preferred ..	1,000,000	1,800,000	
	3,000,000	5,800,000	
Primary EPS			$1.93
Assume conversion of nonCSE class B			
preferred	1,500,000	1,500,000	
	4,500,000	$ 7,300,000	
Fully diluted EPS (beginning with primary			
EPS)			$1.62

Since the intention in presenting fully diluted EPS is to show the *maximum* dilution possible, an alternative computation is possible in this case that would yield a lower figure of fully diluted EPS. This computation has as a starting point the outstanding common shares and income after preferred dividends rather than the primary EPS.

Computation

	Shares	Net income	EPS
Shares outstanding and income after dividends	2,000,000	$4,000,000	
Assume conversion of nonCSE class B preferred	1,500,000	1,500,000	
	3,500,000	$5,500,000	
Fully diluted EPS—beginning with outstanding shares and income after preferred dividends			$1.57

The reason why the alternative computation yields a lower fully diluted EPS is that while the $1.80 preferred issue is dilutive for purposes of computing primary EPS, it is antidilutive for purposes of computing the fully diluted EPS.

Provisions regarding antidilution. As with primary EPS, no antidilution should be recognized. Consequently, computations should exclude those securities whose conversion, exercise, or other contingent issuance would have the effect of increasing the EPS amount or decreasing the loss per share amount for each period. Therefore, fully diluted EPS should be $1.57 rather than the $1.62 shown in the preceding computation.

ILLUSTRATION OF THE COMPUTATION OF PRIMARY AND FULLY DILUTED EARNINGS PER SHARE

The Complex Corporation had the following changes in its capital structure during 19x6:

	Number of shares
Common stock:	
Balance on January 1	500,000
April 1—issued in conversion of preferred stock	200,000
July 1—sold for cash	100,000
Balance on December 31	800,000

Number of shares

Preferred stock:

  $10 par 8 percent, each convertible into two common shares, issued
    in 19x3 at $12 per share when the average Aa corporate bond
    yield was 7½ percent (dividend requirement on outstanding
    shares is $80,000)

  Outstanding, January 1, 19x6   175,000
  Converted on April 1, 19x6 (into 200,000 common)   100,000
  Outstanding since April 1, 19x6 (and year-end)   75,000

Subordinated debentures:

  $800,000 of 4 percent debentures issued at par in 19x4 when the
    average Aa corporate bond yield was 9 percent. The debentures
    are convertible into 12,000 shares of common and are all
    outstanding.

Warrants:

  100,000 warrants issued in 19x4, each to purchase one common share
    at $80 per share until December 31, 19x9. So far none have been
    exercised.

Additional information:

  Market prices of common for 19x6 were as follows:

	Average for quarter	*End of quarter*
First quarter	$78	$79
Second quarter	80	85
Third quarter	90	89
Fourth quarter	88	86

Preferred dividends paid in 19x6:	
First quarter	$ 35,000
Second quarter	15,000
Third quarter . . . . :	15,000
Fourth quarter	15,000
Income before extraordinary item in 19x6	1,200,000
Extraordinary item—condemnation gain	
(net of tax effect)	300,000
Income tax rate	50%

The following are the steps in the computation of primary and fully diluted
EPS of the Complex Corporation for 19x6:

Primary earnings per share

*Step 1: Computation of weighted-average number of common shares outstand-
ing in 19x6:*

	Shares outstanding	No. of months	Product
January 1	500,000	3	1,500,000
April 1	700,000	3	2,100,000
July 1	800,000	6	4,800,000
		12	8,400,000

$$\text{Weighted-average:} \quad \frac{8{,}400{,}000}{12} = 700{,}000 \text{ shares}$$

Step 2: Identification of common stock equivalents (CSE):

Security	(A) Cash yield at issuance	(B) Two thirds of average Aa corporate bond rate at date of issuance	Classification and elaboration
8% convertible preferred	$\dfrac{\$0.80}{\$12} = 6.67\%$	⅔ of 7½% = 5%	Not a CSE because (A) exceeds (B)
4% subordinated debentures	4% (issued at par)	⅔ of 9% = 6%	A CSE because (B) exceeds (A)
Warrants	—	—	Warrants are always considered as CSE

Step 3: Computation of primary EPS:

	Shares	Earnings
Income before extraordinary item		$1,200,000
Dividends requirements of outstanding preferred stock (as also paid in 19x6)		80,000
Income available for common shares		1,120,000
Weighted average of common shares outstanding (see computation)	700,000	
Assumed conversion of 4% subordinated debentures	12,000	

Add back to income interest:
4% of $800,000 = $32,000
Less tax effect at 50%   16,000   16,000

Effect of assumed conversion of warrants:

1st quarter ⎧ Assumed exercise of warrants should not
⎪ be reflected until market price of common
⎨ has been in excess of exercise price for sub-
2d quarter ⎪ stantially all of three consecutive months
⎩ (a *one-time* test).

	Shares	*Earnings*

3d quarter In this quarter above condition was fulfilled.

Total shares issuable on conversion 100,000

$$\frac{\text{Proceeds}}{\text{Average price for quarter}} = \frac{\$8,000,000}{\$90} \quad . . . . \qquad 88,889$$

Incremental shares for quarter 11,111

4th quarter Total shares available

for conversion 100,000

$$\frac{\text{Proceeds}}{\text{Average price for quarter}} = \frac{\$8,000,000}{\$88} \quad . . . . \qquad 90,909$$

Incremental shares for quarter 9,091

Total incremental shares for all quarters . . 20,202

20,202 divided by 4 5,050

Totals 717,050 $1,136,000

Primary EPS—before extraordinary item . . . . $\dfrac{\$1,136,000}{717,050} = \$1.58$

Extraordinary item . . . . $\dfrac{\$300,000}{717,050} = \quad .42$

Net income per share . . . . $\dfrac{\$1,436,000}{717,050} = \$2.00$

Step 4: Computation of fully diluted EPS:

	Shares	*Earnings*

Income before extraordinary item $1,200,000

Weighted average of common shares (as above)   700,000

Add: Assumed conversion of 4% debentures [a]

Assumed conversion of 8% convertible

Preferred (175,000 × 2) 350,000

Less: Converted preferred already included in

700,000 weighted-average 200,000 × ¾ year . . . 150,000   200,000 [b]   —

Warrants: Assumed conversion:

Total shares available for conversion 100,000

$$\frac{\text{Proceeds}}{\text{Year-end market price}} = \frac{100,000 \times \$80 \, [c]}{\$86} = \quad . . . . \qquad 93,023$$

Incremental shares 6,977

906,977 $1,200,000

[a] These debentures are excluded from this computation because they are antidilutive (i.e., they result in an EPS increment of $1.33). Interest requirement is $32,000 (4 percent of 800,000) less 50% tax = $16,000. $16,000 ÷ 12,000 (shares) = $1.33. Thus, the inclusion of the debentures in the computation would *increase* EPS.

[b] *Alternative proof:*

	Months	*Product*
175,000 pfd × 2 outstanding 1st Q 350,000	3	1,050,000
75,000 pfd × 2 outstanding 3d Q 150,000	9	1,350,000
		2,400,000 ÷ 12 = 200,000

[c] Note that a computation using individual quarters would have resulted in *fewer* incremental shares.

Fully diluted EPS:

Income before extraordinary item: $\dfrac{\$1,200,000}{906,977} = \$1.32$

Extraordinary item: $\dfrac{\$300,000}{906,977} = \underline{\quad .33}$

Net income: $\dfrac{\$1,500,000}{906,977} = \$1.65$

EXAMPLES OF EPS COMPUTATIONS WHEN BUSINESS COMBINATIONS OCCUR

Pooling of interests

Assumptions: On July 1, 19x2, Company A and Company B merged to form Company C. The transaction was accounted for as a *pooling of interests.*

	Company A	Company B
Net income January 1 to June 30, 19x2	$100,000	$150,000
Outstanding shares of common stock at June 30, 19x2	20,000	8,000
Shares sold to public April 1, 19x2	10,000	

	Company C
Net income July 1 to December 31, 19x2	$325,000
Common shares issued for acquisition of:	
Company A	200,000
Company B	400,000

Computation:

Net income ($100,000 + $150,000 + $325,000)		575,000
Average shares outstanding during year, using equivalent shares for pooled companies:		
Company A:		
100,000 [a] × 3 months	300,000	
200,000 [b] × 3 months	600,000	
Company B:		
400,000 × 6	2,400,000	
Company C:		
600,000 × 6	3,600,000	
	6,900,000	
Weighted average (6,900,000 ÷ 12)	575,000	

Net income per weighted-average number of shares of common stock outstanding during the year (equivalent shares used for pooled companies) $1.00

[a] 10,000 × 10 (exchange ratio).
[b] 20,000 × 10 (exchange ratio).

Purchase

Assumptions: Company X has outstanding at December 31, 19x2, 120,000 shares of common stock. During the year (October 1), Company X issued 30,000 shares of its own common stock for another company. This transaction was accounted for as purchase. Net income for 19x2 was $292,500.

Computation:

9 months × 90,000 shares outstanding	810,000
3 months × 120,000 shares outstanding	360,000
	1,170,000

$$\text{Average shares } \frac{1,170,000}{12} = 97,500$$

Net income per weighted-average number of shares of common stock outstanding during the year $\dfrac{\$292,500}{97,500} = \$3.$

RESTATEMENT OF PRIOR PERIOD EARNINGS PER SHARE

Whenever comparative EPS figures are presented for a number of years, these must be restated to reflect changes in the number of common shares outstanding due to stock dividends, stock splits (and reverse stock splits), issuance of shares in an acquisition accounted under the pooling of interests method, and prior period adjustments of net income. On the other hand, issues of stock for cash or in an acquisition or the repurchase of stock do not require adjustment because the earnings generated are deemed to be affected by the new resources acquired or relinquished in exchange for the shares.

Illustration of prior period EPS restatement

The following are the reported EPS of the Taylor Company for the respective fiscal years shown:

	19x9	19x8	19x7	19x6	19x5	19x4
EPS	$5	$5	$9	$6	$3	$4

The following changes in capitalization took place at the beginning of each of the years shown:

19x5	100% stock dividend paid
19x6	500,000 shares of common stock issued for cash

19x7	200,000 shares of common issued on conversion of bonds
19x8	3-for-1 stock split
19x9	50% stock dividend paid

The table adjusting the reported EPS figures for the above changes follows. Note that since the change of the 50 percent stock dividend, for example, occurred in 19x9, it has already been allowed for in that year's EPS computation. All prior years, however, must be adjusted for that dividend by multiplying reported EPS figures by a factor of 100/150.

	Year	Reported EPS	Adjustments	Adjusted EPS
50% stock dividend accounted for:	19x9	$5.00	None	$5.00
3-for-1 stock split accounted for:	19x8	5.00	(100/150)	3.33
	19x7	9.00	(100/300)(100/150)	2.00
	19x6	6.00	(100/300)(100/150)	1.33
100% stock dividend	19x5	3.00	(100/300)(100/150)	.67
accounted for:	19x4	4.00	(100/200)(100/300)(100/150)	.44

Requirements for additional disclosures in conjunction with the presentation of earnings per share data

Complex capital structures require additional disclosures either on the balance sheet or in notes. Financial statements should include a description sufficient to explain the pertinent rights and privileges of the various securities outstanding.

With regard to EPS data, disclosure is required for—

1. The bases upon which both primary and fully diluted EPS are calculated, identifying the securities entering into computations.
2. All assumptions and any resulting adjustments used in computations.
3. The number of shares issued upon conversion, exercise, etc., during at least the most recent year.

Supplementary EPS data should be disclosed (preferably in a note) if—

1. Conversions during the period would have affected primary EPS (either dilutive *or* incremental effect) if they had taken place at the beginning of the period, or
2. Similar conversions occur after the close of the period but before completion of the financial report.

This supplementary information should show what primary EPS would have been if such conversions had taken place at the *beginning* of the period or date of issuance of security if within the period.

It should be understood that the designation of securities as CSE is done solely for the purpose of determining primary EPS. No changes from practices in the accounting for such securities or in their presentation within the financial statements are required.

Note 10 (item 96) of Alfa, Inc. (see Appendix 4B), contains disclosures and detail regarding the computation of EPS.

IMPLICATIONS FOR ANALYSIS

APB Opinion 15 has been criticized, particularly by accountants, because it covers areas outside the realm of accountancy, relies on pro forma presentations that are influenced in large measure by market fluctuations, and because it deals with areas properly belonging to financial analysis.

Whatever the merit of these criticisms, and they do have merit, the financial analyst must welcome this initiative by the accounting profession. It does provide specific and workable guidelines for a meaningful recognition of the dilutive effects, present and prospective, of securities that are the equivalents of common stock. The elements entering the consistent computation of primary EPS and fully diluted EPS are so many and varied and require so many internal data that it is best that the accounting profession has assumed the responsibility for their computation rather than choosing the alternative of disclosing the information and leaving it to outsiders to make their own computations. The financial analyst must, however, have a thorough understanding of the bases on which EPS are computed.

APB Opinion 15 has a number of flaws and inconsistencies that the analyst must consider in his interpretations of EPS data:

1. There is a basic inconsistency in treating certain securities as the equivalent of common stock for purposes of computing EPS while not considering them as part of the stockholders equity in the balance sheet. Consequently, the analyst will have difficulty in interrelating reported EPS with the debt-leverage position pertaining to the same earnings.

2. There are a number of arbitrary benchmarks in the *Opinion,* such as the 20 percent treasury stock repurchase assumption limitation and the 66⅔ percent of the average Aa corporate bond rate test.

3. Generally EPS are considered to be a factor influencing stock prices. The *Opinion* considers options and warrants to be CSE at all times, and whether they are dilutive or not depends on the price of the common stock. Thus, we can get a circular effect in that the reporting of EPS may influence the market price, which, in turn, influences EPS. Also, under these rules earnings may depend on market prices of the stock rather than only on economic factors within the enterprise.

Under these rules, the projection of future EPS requires not only the projection of earnings levels but also the projection of future market prices.

4. Since the determination of whether a security is a CSE or not is made only at the time of issuance, it is quite possible that a security that was not originally a CSE is later so recognized in the marketplace. Nevertheless, the status of the security in the computation of EPS cannot be changed to recognize the new reality.

Despite these limitations, primary EPS and fully diluted EPS computed under the provisions of *APB Opinion 15* are more valid measurements of EPS than those which were obtained under the rules which were previously in effect.

In analyzing the factors that cause changes in the EPS figure, the analyst must focus on changes in earnings as well as changes in the number of shares outstanding. Regarding the latter, the analyst will now find details in "management's discussion and analysis" section required by the SEC (see Chapter 20). In *Staff Accounting Bulletin 29,* the SEC staff concluded that an increase in EPS resulting from an improvement in earnings with an unchanged number of shares outstanding has significantly different implications from an increase in per share earnings achieved by a reduction of the company's capital base.

Regardless of the reasons for and method of a company's purchase of its own equity securities, the transaction can have a material effect on reported earnings and EPS amounts. In such cases, the following explanations should be made:

*   The effect of the transaction on the trend of reported earnings;
*   Any increased leveraging resulting from the transaction, such as a higher debt to total capitalization ratio;
*   The effect of the transaction on the trend of reported earnings per share amounts.

Also, any material issuer equity purchase transaction that occurs toward the end of the reporting period and does not significantly affect current EPS (because of the use of a weighted average) should be explained when such a transaction may have a significant effect on future reported results.

Statement accounting for changes in earnings per share

When analyzing or projecting EPS, the analyst can focus on changes in income on a per share basis. Table 12–1 presents an analysis of the changes in the EPS of a large chemical company for 19x4.

This published analysis is noteworthy particularly because it contains details such as those pertaining to changes due to sales volume and selling prices, which are normally available only to those with access to internal

Table 12–1: Analysis of changes in earnings per share

			EPS
Year 19x3 earnings			$2.77
Additional earnings resulting from:			
Higher sales volume		$1.20	
Manufacturing cost savings		0.37	
Lower raw material prices		0.06	
		1.63	
Reductions in earnings caused by:			
Lower selling prices.............................	$ .25		
Higher selling, administrative research, development, and other expenses	.49	0.74	
Increase in operating results			0.89
			3.66
Nonoperating items:			
Lower income taxes, due primarily to difference in tax rate		$0.12	
Higher investment tax credit on property additions		0.12	
Other income and charges—net		0.03	
Unusual write-offs:			
Obsolescence.................................	(.06)		
Self-insurance reserve	(.07)		
Other..	.03	(.10)	
Effect on earnings of shares issued during the year		(.11)	0.06
Year 19x4 earnings			$3.72
Increase in EPS			$0.95

management records. This information, whenever available, can be of significant help to the analyst in the evaluation and prediction of earnings and EPS.

QUESTIONS

1. Why is a thorough understanding of the principles governing the computation of EPS important to the financial analyst?

2. What developments caused the accounting profession to issue an *Opinion* on the computation of EPS?

3. Discuss uses of EPS and reasons or objectives of the method of reporting EPS under *APB Opinion 15*.

4. What is the purpose in presenting fully diluted EPS?

5. How do cumulative dividends on preferred stock affect the computation EPS for a company with a loss?

6. What is the two-class method and when is it used?

7. At the end of the year a company has a simple capital structure consisting only of common stock, as all its preferred stock was converted into common shares during the year. Is a computation of fully diluted EPS required?

8. If a warrant is not exercisable until seven years after the end of the period presented, should it be excluded from the computation of fully diluted EPS?

9. Under *APB Opinion 15* how should dividends per share be presented?

10. How does the payment of dividends on preferred stock affect the computation of EPS?

11. When and why would the following securities be considered CSE:
    a. Convertible debentures?
    b. Shares issuable in the future upon satisfaction of certain conditions?

12. EPS can affect market prices. Can market prices affect EPS?

13. Can CSE enter into the determination of EPS in one period and not in another?

14. What is meant by the term *antidilution?* Give an example of this condition.

15. How do we include stock options and warrants as CSE? What is the treasury stock method?

16. Is the treasury stock method always used? Which are the exceptions?

17. What are supplementary EPS? How are they disclosed?

18. *APB Opinion 15* has a number of flaws and inconsistencies that the analyst must consider in his interpretation of EPS data. Discuss these.

19. In estimating the value of common stock, the amount of EPS is considered to be a very important element in the determination of such value.
    a. Explain why EPS are important in the valuation of common stock.
    b. Are EPS equally important in valuing a preferred stock? Why or why not? (CFA)

Statements of changes in financial position—funds and cash

SIGNIFICANCE AND PURPOSE

The cash and working capital of a business entity represent important indicators of financial health. The ability of an enterprise to meet its obligations as they become due and its ability to expand and grow depend on adequate levels of liquid funds. The statement of changes in financial position (SCFP) provides information regarding the sources and uses of working capital or cash over a period of time as well as information about major financing and investment activities that do not involve sources and uses of working capital or cash.

While fragmentary information on sources and uses of funds can be obtained from comparative balance sheets and income statements, a comprehensive picture of this important area of activity can be gained only from a SCFP. This fact accounts for the growing importance and use of this statement that can provide information on such questions as:

1. What utilization was made of funds provided by operations?
2. What was the source of funds invested in new plant and equipment?
3. What use was made of funds derived from a new bond issue or the sale of common stock?
4. How was it possible to continue the regular dividend in the face of an operating loss?
5. How was the debt repayment achieved, or what was the source of the funds used to redeem the preferred stock?
6. How was the increase in working capital financed?
7. Why, despite record profits, is the working capital position lower than last year?

379

TWO MAJOR CONCEPTS OF LIQUIDITY

There are a number of recognized indicators of liquidity, but the two most common are working capital and cash (including cash equivalents such as marketable securities). In the present context, the term *funds* is equivalent to *working capital,* and these two terms are often used interchangeably in practice. A statement of sources and uses of working capital (funds) explains the change in the level of working capital between two dates by listing the factors that contributed to its increase and those that brought about its decrease. Similarly, a statement of sources and uses of cash explains the reasons for increases and decreases of this asset over a given period of time.

STATEMENT OF CHANGES IN FINANCIAL POSITION—A BROADER CONCEPT

Recognizing that the statement of sources and applications of working capital or of cash can omit important financing and investing transactions that do not involve either working capital or cash, *APB Opinion 19* called for a broadening of both statements to include such transactions and recommended that it be referred to as a statement of changes in financial position (SCFP). This statement is now a basic financial statement required to be furnished whenever a profit-oriented business entity issues financial statements that present *both* financial position (balance sheet) *and* results of operations (statement of income and retained earnings).

Items such as the following should be shown at the gross amount and not netted against each other unless one item is immaterial:

  a.   Acquisition and retirement of property, plant, and equipment.

  b.   New long-term borrowings and repayment of long-term debt. The effects of extraordinary items should be reported separately.

In general, the SCFP focuses on changes in working capital or on changes in cash and cash equivalents.[1] In addition, either statement includes major financing and investing transactions that do not involve funds or cash, such as the following:

1.   Issuance of securities to acquire property or other long-term assets.
2.   Conversion of long-term debt or preferred stock into common stock.
3.   Other nonmonetary exchanges.

The intelligent analysis and use of any financial statement requires a thorough understanding of the principles and methods that underlie its preparation. We shall examine below the principles underlying the preparation of

---

[1] While the focus on changes in working capital is more prevalent in practice, an FASB exposure draft recommended in 1981 adoption of the cash focus, a position that was endorsed by the Financial Executives Institute.

the SCFP. The principles governing the preparation of the SCFP—cash focus will be examined later in this chapter.

Basis of preparation

In order to focus on changes in working capital, let us visualize two highly condensed balance sheets that are divided into sections disclosing (1) current (or working capital) items and (2) all the other (noncurrent) accounts:

	End of year 1	End of year 2
Current items:		
Current assets.....................	$12,000	$16,000
Current liabilities	8,000	10,000
Net current items (working capital).....	4,000	6,000
Noncurrent items:		
Noncurrent assets	(6,000)	(8,000)
Long-term liabilities.................	3,000	5,000
Equity (capital) accounts	7,000	9,000
Net noncurrent items	$ 4,000	$ 6,000

While the above is certainly not a conventional form of balance sheet presentation, it provides a very useful framework for understanding the interaction between changes in the current (i.e., working capital) section and changes in the noncurrent section. Thus, we can readily observe that the change in working capital from year-end 1 to year-end 2 ($2,000) is matched exactly, both in amount and direction, by the change in the net noncurrent items between these two year-ends ($2,000). This is, of course, true because assets always equal liabilities plus capital; and consequently a change in one sector of the balance sheet must be matched by an equal change in the remaining accounts.

The above-described relationship between the current and noncurrent sectors of the balance sheet provides a useful means for understanding the basis underlying the preparation of the SCFP—working capital focus. Visualizing the two sections of the balance sheet as follows,

CURRENT SECTION	Current assets	Current liabilities
NONCURRENT SECTION	Fixed assets Other assets	Long-term liabilities Deferred credits Equity accounts

the following generalizations may be made:

1. Net changes in the current section can be explained in terms of changes in the accounts of the noncurrent section. These are the *only* changes with which the SCFP is concerned.
2. Internal changes *within* the current section are not relevant here because the statement indicates the *net* change in working capital without regard to individual changes in the composition of the working capital accounts. For example, the purchase of inventory for cash or the payment of a current liability, while affecting the composition of the working capital, leaves no effect on its net amount. *APB Opinion 19* requires, however, a separate statement explaining the net changes in working capital components.
3. Similarly, internal changes *within* the noncurrent section have no effect on working capital. However, changes caused by transactions such as the conversion of debt into equity or the acquisition of fixed assets with long-term debt are significant financial transactions, and consequently the SCFP would include these.

The best way for us to start the discussion of how the SCFP is prepared is to examine a very simple illustration of the principles involved. The following is a pair of simplified and condensed comparative balance sheets as at two consecutive year-ends:

Condensed Balance Sheets
(in thousands)

		December 31		Changes during 19x2	
		19x1	19x2	Use of funds	Source of funds
1.	Working capital	$320	$ 290		$ 30
2.	Fixed assets	660	874	$214	
3.	Accumulated depreciation	(200)	(244)		44
4.	Intangible assets	150	100		50
	Total assets	$930	$1,020		
5.	Long-term debt	$420	$ 400	20	
6.	Capital stock and paid-in capital	250	300		50
7.	Retained earnings	260	320		60
	Total equities	$930	$1,020		
	Total			$234	$234

The extension columns showing the year-end to year-end changes in account balances do not represent a comprehensive SCFP because they can hide a considerable amount of significant detail. The following analysis of each change will make this clear:

1. The $30,000 change in working capital should be viewed as the difference to be explained because it is the change in funds (i.e., working capital) on which the statement focuses.
2. The $214,000 increase in fixed assets is composed in this case of two elements: purchases of fixed assets of $314,000 and sale of fixed assets with a net book value of $80,000 (cost of $100,000 less accumulated depreciation of $20,000).
3. The net increase in accumulated depreciation of $44,000 is after a charge to that account of $20,000 for accumulated depreciation on the assets sold (see 2 above). Thus, the total addition to the accumulated depreciation account (with a contra charge to depreciation expense) was $64,000.
4. In the absence of further data, the decline of $50,000 in the intangible assets can represent a sale of an intangible or the amortization of the intangible by a charge to income. Let us assume here that the latter is true.
5. The net reduction of $20,000 in the long-term debt represents a repayment of $10,000, and the conversion of another $10,000 into common stock which while not affecting working capital is a significant transaction.
6. The increase in the capital stock and paid-in capital accounts is due to the sale of stock of $40,000 and the conversion of debt of $10,000.
7. The change in the retained earnings balance almost always requires further data for proper analysis. The data provided here are as follows:

Balance of retained earnings, January 1, 19x2	$260,000
Net income for 19x2	180,000
	440,000
Less cash dividends paid	120,000
Balance of retained earnings, December 31, 19x2..	$320,000

From the above it is clear that the cash dividend represented a use of funds of $120,000 and that the net income of $180,000 provides the basis for computing the sources of funds from operations. The reason why the $180,000 cannot be taken to be a source of funds arising from operations is that the income statement includes items of income and expense that do not provide or use funds (working capital items). The net income figure must be adjusted for such items. Let us now see how this is done.

Arriving at "sources of funds from operations"

Normally, a detailed income statement is provided. In the present example, the income statement is as follows:

Sales		$900,000
Cost of sales:		
Labor	$200,000	
Material	120,000	
Depreciation	64,000	
Other overhead	76,000	460,000
Gross margin		440,000
Selling, general, and administrative expenses (including		
$50,000 of intangible amortization)		85,000
Income before taxes		355,000
Income taxes—current		175,000
Net income		$180,000

An examination of this income statement reveals that the individual items have the following usual (normal) effect on other balance sheet items:

	Items affected	
	Working capital	*Other*
Sales	Cash, accounts receivable	
Labor	Cash, accounts payable	
Material	Cash, accounts payable, and inventories	
Depreciation		Fixed assets
Other overhead	Cash, accounts payable, and prepaid expenses	
Selling, general, and administrative expenses	Cash, accounts payable, and prepaid expenses	
Amortization of intangibles		Intangible assets
Income taxes (current)	Cash, accounts payable	

We see, thus, that in this example depreciation and amortization of intangibles are expenses that, unlike all others, do not require an outlay of current funds. In other words, they derive from the noncurrent section of the balance sheet, and since the income statement is included in the Retained Earnings account of the balance sheet, they are internal to the noncurrent section of the balance sheet and consequently do not affect funds.

The required adjustment in our case is to start with the net income (or income before extraordinary items which is to be shown separately) of $180,000 and add back charges that did not require funds.

Net income		$180,000
Depreciation	$64,000	
Amortization of intangibles	50,000	114,000
Funds provided by operations		$294,000

It is obvious that this figure of $294,000 could also have been obtained by reconstructing the income statement so as to include only those items that either provide or require funds (working capital).

The reason the net-income-adjustment method is almost always used in practice to arrive at the "funds provided by operations" figure is that it makes unnecessary the reciting of all the above detail that is to be found in the income statement anyway. Thus, the point to understand here is that the "net income" figure is a convenient starting point for arriving at the adjusted "funds provided by operations" figure. Moreover, doing it this way provides a verifiable and reassuring link to the income statement.

In addition to depreciation and amortization of intangibles, the following are further examples of items that may appear in the income statement and that have no effect on funds (working capital).

Income statement item	*Related to the following noncurrent balance sheet item*
Amortization of bond premium	Unamortized bond premium
Amortization of bond discount	Unamortized bond discount
Warranty expenses	Provision for warranty costs (noncurrent)
Deferred income tax expense	Deferred taxes (noncurrent)
Amortization of leasehold improvements	Leasehold improvements
Subscription income	Deferred subscription income (noncurrent portion)
Equity in earnings of an unconsolidated subsidiary or investee	Investment account
Minority interest in income (loss)	Minority interest

This concept can also be summarized as follows:

Income statement item	*Related to contra account*	*Effect on working capital from operations*
Dr. expense or loss	Cr. to current account	Use of working capital
	Cr. to noncurrent account	Add back—not using working capital
Cr. income, or gain, or expense	Dr. to current account	Source of working capital
	Dr. to noncurrent account	Deduct—not providing working capital

The statement of changes in financial position

Returning to our example, we can now construct a SCFP that is more detailed and more comprehensive than if based solely on the changes that we could have developed from the comparative balance sheets above.

Source of funds:

Funds provided by operations:			
Net income		$180,000	
Add back—charges not requiring funds in the current period:			
Depreciation	$64,000		
Amortization of intangibles	50,000	114,000	$294,000
Sale of fixed assets			80,000
Capital stock issued in conversion of debt			10,000
Sale of capital stock			40,000
Total sources of funds			424,000

Use of funds:

Purchases of fixed assets	314,000
Payment of dividends	120,000
Repayment of long-term debt	10,000
Debt converted into capital stock	10,000
Total uses of funds....................	454,000
Decrease in working capital	$ 30,000

Illustration of T-account technique

The simple illustration above indicated some of the more common problems involved in the preparation of the SCFP. These, and others found in more complex examples, are:

1. The analysis of net changes based on further detail provided.
2. The reversal or elimination of transactions internal to the noncurrent accounts.
3. Regrouping and reconstruction of transactions in the noncurrent group that affect, and hence explain, the changes in the working capital sector.

The methods used to implement these adjustments vary from elaborate multicolumn worksheets to highly summarized adjustments that are performed mentally. One of the most direct and most flexible methods utilizes the reconstruction of summarized T-accounts. This method, developed by Professor W. J. Vatter, will be illustrated here.

The basic objective of the T-account method is to reconstruct in summary fashion by means of T-accounts for the noncurrent accounts all the transactions that went through them during the period reported upon. If the reconstructed transaction reveals that it was a source or a use of funds, it is posted to the summary Working Capital T-account. If the transaction has no effect on funds, and is not of a significant investing or financing nature, it is reversed among the applicable noncurrent T-accounts. The following is a summary of the steps involved in this method.

1. A T-account is set up for each noncurrent account appearing in the change column of the comparative balance sheet. The opening and closing balance of the account is posted to the T-account as follows:

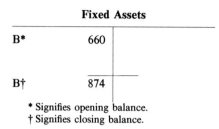

Fixed Assets

B*	660
B†	874

* Signifies opening balance.
† Signifies closing balance.

2. A Working Capital T-account, divided into an "Operations" and an "Other" section, as illustrated in the comprehensive example that follows, is also opened.
3. Based on information supplied and inferences drawn from the changes in the noncurrent account, the balance in the T-account is reconstructed by:
    a. Debiting or crediting all revenue and expense items to the "Operations" section of the Working Capital account.
    b. Debiting or crediting all other items affecting working capital (funds) to the "Other" section of the Working Capital account.
4. When the process is completed, the Working Capital T-account will contain the detail necessary for the preparation of the SCFP.

Illustration 1 which follows provides a more comprehensive example of the steps required in the preparation of the SCFP.

ILLUSTRATION 1.   The following are the comparative balance sheets of the Vatter Company, as at December 31, 19x1, and 19x2 and the changes during 19x2:

THE VATTER COMPANY
Comparative Balance Sheet
As of December 31

Assets	19x1	19x2	Increase (decrease)
Current assets:			
Cash	$ 240,000	$ 120,000	$ (120,000)
Receivables	360,000	450,000	90,000
Inventories	750,000	1,053,000	303,000
Total current assets	1,350,000	1,623,000	273,000
Fixed assets	4,500,000	6,438,000	1,938,000
Accumulated depreciation	(1,500,000)	(1,740,000)	(240,000)
Investment in subsidiary	1,000,000	1,050,000	50,000
Goodwill	950,000	980,000	30,000
Total assets	$6,300,000	$8,351,000	$2,051,000

ILLUSTRATION 1 (concluded)

Assets	19x1	19x2	Increase (decrease)
Liabilities and Capital			
Accounts payable	$ 360,000	$ 590,000	$ 230,000
Bonds payable	300,000	700,000	400,000
Deferred income taxes	240,000	260,000	20,000
Capital stock	2,400,000	3,200,000	800,000
Paid-in capital	900,000	1,300,000	400,000
Retained earnings	2,100,000	2,301,000	201,000
Total liabilities and capital	$6,300,000	$8,351,000	$2,051,000

The income statement for the year ending December 31, 19x2, of the Vatter Company is as follows:

Sales......................................		$19,950,000
Cost of goods sold (includes $360,000 depreciation) ...		11,101,000
Gross profit..................................		8,849,000
General, selling, and administrative expenses	$7,000,000	
Amortization of goodwill	30,000	7,030,000
		1,819,000
Equity in earnings of unconsolidated subsidiary		50,000
Gain on sale of fixed assets		2,000
Income before taxes		1,871,000
Income taxes:		
Current	900,000	
Deferred	20,000	920,000
Net income		$ 951,000

The following additional information is available:

1. On March 1, 19x2, the company bought for cash of $510,000 a going concern with fixed assets having a value of $450,000, with current assets equal to current liabilities, and the excess of $60,000 being considered as the cost of goodwill acquired.
2. Old machinery was sold for $18,000; it originally cost $36,000, and $20,000 of depreciation had been accumulated to date of sale.
3. In April, the company acquired $100,000 in fixed assets by issuing bonds with $100,000 par value.
4. In June, the company received $1,000,000 in cash for a new issue of capital stock with a par value of $600,000. $200,000 of convertible bonds were converted into capital stock, par value $200,000. Long-term bonds were also sold for $500,000 (at par).
5. Fully depreciated assets of $100,000 were written off.
6. Dividends paid amounted to $750,000.

Based on the above financial statements and the additional data, we are to prepare a SCFP, working capital focus, by means of the T-account method. The *first* step is to set up T-accounts for:

1. A Working Capital account subdivided into an "Operations" section and an "Other" section.
2. All noncurrent accounts in order to reconstruct the transactions affecting working capital (funds).

The *second* step is to enter the opening and closing balances in each T-account and designate these as "B" for balance. The upper amount is the opening balance and the amount below the bottom line is the closing balance.

The *third* step is to reconstruct all the transactions for the year in the T-accounts in summary fashion. It is best to start first with the supplementary information given.

T-accounts (in thousands of dollars)

Working Capital

B		990*			

Operations

Net income	*(m)*	951	2	*(b)*	Gain on sale of fixed assets
Depreciation expense	*(g)*	360	50	*(p)*	Equity in earnings of subsidiary
Deferred income taxes	*(k)*	20			
Goodwill amortization	*(o)*	30			

Other

Sale of fixed assets	*(b)*	18	450	*(a)*	Acquisition of fixed assets
			60	*(a)*	Acquisition of goodwill
Bonds issued to acquire fixed assets	*(d)*	100	100	*(c)*	Fixed assets acquired with bonds
			1,524	*(f)*	Purchase of fixed assets
Bonds sold	*(h)*	500			
Stock issued in bond conversion	*(j)*	200	200	*(i)*	Bond conversion into stock
Sale of capital stock	*(l)*	1,000	750	*(n)*	Dividends paid
B		1,033†			

* CA-CL = $1,350 − $360.
† $1,623 − $590.

Fixed Assets			
B	4,500		
(a)	450		
(c)	100	36	(b)
(f)	1,524	100	(e)
B	6,438		

Accumulated Depreciation			
		1,500	B
(b)	20	360	(g)
(e)	100		
		1,740	B

Investment in Subsidiary		
B	1,000	
(p)	50	
B	1,050	

Goodwill			
B	950		
(a)	60		
		30	(o)
B	980		

Bonds Payable			
		300	B
(i)	200	100	(d)
		500	(h)
		700	B

Deferred Income Taxes		
	240	B
	20	(k)
	260	B

Capital Stock			
		2,400	B
		200	(j)
		600	(l)
		3,200	B

Paid-In Capital		
	900	B
	400	(l)
	1,300	B

Retained Earnings			
		2,100	B
(n)	750	951	(m)
		2,301	B

Fixed assets and goodwill

The acquisition of the going concern can be reconstructed as follows:

(a)

Fixed assets	450,000	
Goodwill	60,000	
Working Capital—Other		450,000
Working Capital—Other		60,000

Since we are explaining here changes in working capital (a group of items that includes cash), we post the payment as a use of working capital.

We know that equipment costing $36,000 and having accumulated depreciation of $20,000 was sold for $18,000. Entry *(b)* reconstructs the transactions in summary fashion.

(b)

Working Capital—Other	18,000	
Accumulated Depreciation	20,000	
Fixed Assets		36,000
Working Capital—Operations		2,000

Working Capital—Other is debited for the cash received on the sale of the old machinery. By showing the entire proceeds of $18,000 as a source of working capital, we must remove from net income the $2,000 gain included therein. In effect, we are combining the recovery of the book value of the equipment of $16,000 ($36,000 − $20,000) with the $2,000 gain to show the entire proceeds as a source of Working Capital—Other. The removal of the $2,000 gain on sale of equipment is achieved by crediting Working Capital—Operations. That credit *reduces* the amount of working capital provided by operations.

We know that $100,000 of fixed assets were acquired through issuance of bonds. This transaction does not affect working capital but must be shown in the statement because it represents a significant investing and financing transaction. It can be reconstructed as follows:

(c)

Fixed Assets	100,000	
Resources Used (Working Capital account)		100,000

(d)

Resources Obtained (Working Capital account)	100,000	
Bonds payable		100,000

These types of transactions that do not affect working capital are self-balancing. For convenience of statement preparation, they are posted to the Working Capital account where their net effect cancels out, thus confirming that they have no effect on working capital.

We also know that fully depreciated assets with a cost of $100,000 were written off. This bookkeeping entry does not represent an important investing or financing transaction so the entry that reconstructs this transaction cancels out and bypasses the Working Capital account since it does not affect items appearing in the SCFP.

(e)

Accumulated Depreciation	100,000	
Fixed Assets		100,000

Now that we have posted all known entries to the Fixed Asset T-account, we know that we still need a debit of $1,524,000 in order to balance the account. In the absence of specific information, we assume, as we always do in this process, the most reasonable and plausible transaction, i.e., that this amount represents purchases of fixed assets during the year. The entry is as follows:

(f)

Fixed Assets	1,524,000	
Working Capital—Other		1,524,000

Accumulated depreciation

We now have two debits posted to the account totaling $120,000. In order to balance the account, we need a credit of $360,000 that we know coincides with the total depreciation expense shown in the income statement. The entry is:

(g)

Working Capital—Operations...................	360,000	
Accumulated Depreciation		360,000

The charge to Working Capital—Operations represents an add-back of an expense deducted in arriving at net income which does not require working capital.

Bonds payable

The sale of bonds resulted in a source of funds that is reflected as follows:

(h)

Working Capital—Other	500,000	
Bonds Payable		500,000

The conversion of bonds into capital stock is not a transaction affecting working capital. It is, nevertheless, a significant financing transaction resulting in a change in capital structure and as such should be reflected in the SCFP. This is done as follows:

(i)

Bonds Payable	200,000	
Resources Used (Working Capital account)		200,000

(j)

Resources Obtained (Working Capital account)	200,000	
Capital Stock		200,000

Deferred income taxes

The charge for deferred income taxes increases a noncurrent deferred credit account and, like that for depreciation and goodwill amortization, does not require current funds, and thus the adjustment is carried to Working Capital—Operations. It is an add-back to income for an expense not requiring working capital.

(k)

Working Capital—Operations....................	20,000	
Deferred Income Taxes		20,000

Capital stock and paid-in capital

The sale of stock is a source of funds and is reconstructed as follows:

(l)

Working Capital—Other	1,000,000	
Capital Stock		600,000
Paid-In Capital		400,000

Retained earnings

Reconstruction of the Retained Earnings account change usually relies on supplementary detail provided or, as in this case, the income statement. Thus, net income amounted to $951,000, and this source of funds (*before* adjustment for nonfund items) is transferred to Operations Summary.

(m)

Working Capital—Operations....................	951,000	
Retained Earnings		951,000

The cash dividends amounted to $750,000, and this is a use of funds.

(n)

Retained Earnings	750,000	
Working Capital—Other		750,000

Goodwill amortization

From the income statement we learn that $30,000 of goodwill was amortized in 19x2. Since this charge to income did not require funds (i.e., it drew a "noncurrent" account), we increase the operations summary by this amount, thus:

(o)

Working Capital—Operations....................	30,000	
Goodwill		30,000

Thus, the net change in the Goodwill account has been accounted for.

Investment in subsidiary

The income statement reveals another item that is the result of the adjustment of a noncurrent account and that consequently does not affect working

Exhibit 13–1

THE VATTER COMPANY
Statement of Changes in Financial Position
For the Year Ended December 31, 19x2

Financial resources were provided by:

Net income		$ 951,000
Add: Expenses not requiring outlay of working capital in the current period:		
Depreciation of fixed assets	$360,000	
Amortization of goodwill	30,000	
Deferred income taxes	20,000	410,000
Deduct: Income not providing working capital:		
Undistributed income of unconsolidated subsidiary		(50,000)
Deduct gain on sale of fixed assets (included in proceeds from sale)..............		(2,000)
Working capital provided by operations ...		$1,309,000
Sale of fixed assets	18,000	
Net proceeds of sale of bonds	500,000	
Issuance of bonds in exchange of fixed assets	100,000	
Issuance of stock for conversion of bonds	200,000	
Sale of capital stock	1,000,000	1,818,000
		$3,127,000

Financial resources were used for:

Purchase of fixed assets*	1,974,000	
Purchase of goodwill	60,000	
Fixed assets acquired for bonds	100,000	
Retirement of debentures on conversion into capital stock	200,000	
Payment of dividends	750,000	$3,084,000
Increase in working capital		43,000
		$3,127,000

Analysis of increase (decrease) in working capital:†

Cash	(120,000)	
Receivables	90,000	
Inventory	303,000	
Net increase in current assets		$ 273,000
Increase of accounts payable		(230,000)
Net increase in working capital		$ 43,000

* $450,000 + $1,524,000.
† *APB Opinion 19* requires such an analysis.

capital, i.e., Equity in Earnings[2] of Unconsolidated Subsidiary. The reconstructed entry is:

(p)

Investment in Subsidiary	50,000	
Working Capital—Operations		50,000

The credit to Working Capital—Operations reduces income by an item that does not provide working capital.

We have now accounted for the changes in all the noncurrent T-accounts. The changes internal to the noncurrent group of T-accounts do not affect working capital. However, most such changes, which represent significant financing and/or investing activities, must be included in the SCFP.

The Working Capital account now contains all the detail needed to prepare the SCFP shown in Exhibit 13-1.

STATEMENT OF CHANGES IN FINANCIAL POSITION— CASH FOCUS

While many published SCFP focus on explaining changes in working capital, in addition to other important investing and financing transactions, there are increasing demands for these statements to focus on cash instead.

Analytical importance of cash flow data

One such emphasis was expressed in *SFAC 1*[3] which concluded that the objectives of financial reporting indicate that users need information about cash inflows and outflows to help with assessments of future cash flows and to provide feedback about previous assessments.

Moreover, cash flow information is needed by many decision makers and particularly by lenders who are concerned with the inflows and outflows of the means of payment, i.e., cash. As we shall see, net income has never been a good surrogate for cash flow from operations in the short run, and this is particularly true in times of inflation when the gap between earnings and cash flow from operations tends to widen. That gap is particularly widened by an ever-increasing investment in receivables and inventories that is not fully offset by a corresponding increase in trade credit. Analysts also find cash flow figures to be free from the influence of accounting accruals and allocations and use them as a means of assessing the quality of earnings

---

[2] This entry is based on the assumption that none of these earnings have been distributed as dividends. Dividends received from unconsolidated subsidiaries or affiliates are considered sources of funds from operations.

[3] See also FASB, "Reporting Income, Cash Flows, and Financial Position of Business Enterprises," Exposure Draft, November 16, 1981.

(see Chapter 22). Moreover, many analysts believe that cash accounting facilitates comparison and is an antidote to complexity. Cash flows are also a good predictor of dividends.[4]

CASE STUDY.   A study of financial indicators of W. T. Grant Company[5] during the 1966–75 period preceding its bankruptcy, such as profitability, turnover, and liquidity ratios, as well as working capital provided by operations, while showing some downtrends provided no definitive clues to the company's impending financial collapse. However, a study of the company's cash flows from operations clearly revealed that with minor exceptions in 1968–70, the company's operations, instead of providing cash, were causing an increasing drain of cash that had to be made up with various kinds of external financing. Clearly then, in this case, an analysis of cash flows would have provided creditors and investors of W. T. Grant with a most valuable analytical tool.

Because of the increasing importance of cash flow analysis, we shall discuss here the technique of preparing the SCFP—cash focus. Since the analyst will often find statements prepared with a different focus (i.e., working capital) or in a format not useful for analysis, Appendix 13A presents methods of converting such statements to the analytically more useful cash flow statements.

Preparation of the statement of changes in financial position—cash focus

The technique of preparing the cash focus statement can be viewed as an extension of the T-account technique of preparing the working capital focus statement. Recall that in the latter case changes in current assets and liabilities as a group were explained by means of changes in the noncurrent accounts. Since we now focus only on the change in cash (and cash equivalents such as marketable securities), it follows that the preparation of the cash focus statement involves, *in addition* to the procedures followed in the preparation of the working capital statement, an explanation of changes in all current assets and liabilities with the exception of cash and cash equivalents. In the interest of clarity and economy of effort, we will now take up the preparation of the cash focus statement in this *incremental* fashion by continuing our illustration based on the financial statements of the Vatter Company on page 387.

---

[4] William C. Norby, "Interpretation of Inflation Accounting Information," Emanuel Saxe Distinguished Lecture, B. M. Baruch College, December 17, 1981.

[5] J. A. Largay III, and C. P. Stickney, "Cash Flows, Ratio Analysis and the W. T. Grant Company Bankruptcy," *Financial Analysts Journal,* July–August 1980, pp. 51–54.

Let us first consider the impact that changes in the working capital accounts have on operations as distinguished from "other" effects.

Considering operations as encompassing broadly the *earning related activities* of the enterprise, it is clear that changes in most working capital accounts would affect operations so defined. This is so because the focus is not only on income and expense items but also on the inflows and outflows of funds that operations impose on the enterprise, e.g., extension of credit to customers, investment in inventories, and conversely obtaining credit from suppliers.

Let us take the change in accounts receivable as an example. They increased by $90,000 during 19x2, and that means that on a net basis, the sales figure for the year is $90,000 higher than the collections of cash from sales. This can also be shown by a reconstruction of the *aggregate* entries in the Accounts Receivable account for 19x2.

Accounts Receivable (in thousands of dollars)

	B	360		
Sales		19,950	19,860	Cash collections*
	B	450		

* This amount would actually be lower by the amount of bad debts written off during the year and credited to this account. As is true in the case of most published financial statements, bad debt write-offs are not disclosed and so we must treat them as relatively insignificant. In certain cases, such an assumption may not be warranted.

Using a similar line of analytical reasoning, we can see that changes in the following working capital accounts would have effects as follows:

Account	*Change:* *Dr. (debit)* *Cr. (credit)*	*Effect on operations*
Accounts Receivable	Increase (Dr.)	Sales not collected in cash.
	Decrease (Cr.)	Collections exceed sales for the period, i.e., some prior period receivables collected.
Inventories	Increase (Dr.)	Purchases exceed cost of goods sold.
	Decrease (Cr.)	Some of the cost of goods sold represents a reduction in inventories, i.e., purchases are less than cost of goods sold.
Prepaid Expenses	Increases (Dr.)	Cash laid out for expenses that are to be charged to future periods.

Account	*Change:* *Dr. (debit)* *Cr. (credit)*	*Effect on operations*
	Decreases (Cr.)	Some expenses in the income statement were paid for in prior years and consequently did not require a current cash outlay.
Trade Accounts or Notes Payable	Increase (Cr.)	Some purchases were not yet paid for in cash.
	Decrease (Dr.)	Cash payments to suppliers exceed purchases for the period.

A study of the above chart reveals that the use of the debit and credit designation for changes in the current accounts is a useful check on the effects of changes on sources and uses of cash. Thus, a credit change adds to cash from operations while a debit change reduces cash from operations.

It should also be noted that the listed "effects on operations" involve the basic assumption that only *operating* items flow through the current accounts (e.g., that receivables do not include amounts receivable for sales of fixed assets and that accounts payable do not include amounts due for purchases of long-lived assets). This is a crucial and inevitable assumption that will in most cases be *substantially* (but not entirely) correct. The analyst must be aware, however, that in some cases additional information from management may be required to clarify substantial exceptions to this assumption.

It should also be noted that some current accounts have nothing to do with operations and must be classified as sources or uses of cash—other. For example:

Account	*Type of activity*
Loans Receivable (e.g., from officers)	Lending
Current portion of Long-Term Debt	Financing
Notes Payable to Bank	Financing
Dividends Payable	Payments to owners

In our illustration of Vatter Company, we do not happen to have such nonoperating current accounts.

Since we are extending our illustration on an incremental basis, we will now pick up where we left off in Illustration 1 where the focus was on changes in working capital. The master T-account will now be labeled Cash and we will record in it all the entries *(a)* through *(p)* which explained the changes in the noncurrent accounts. Next, we establish T-accounts for all the other current accounts.

In order to distinguish clearly the entries that explain the changes in the current accounts from those relating to the noncurrent accounts, we will identify them with double letters starting with *(aa):*

THE VATTER COMPANY
T-accounts for Preparation of SCFP–Cash Focus
(in thousands of dollars)
Cash

B	240				

Operations

Net income	*(m)*	951	2	*(b)*	Gain on sale of fixed assets
Depreciation expense	*(g)*	360	50	*(p)*	Equity in earnings of sub-sidiary
Deferred income taxes	*(k)*	20	90	*(aa)*	Increase in receivables
Goodwill amortization	*(o)*	30	303	*(bb)*	Increase in inventories
Increase in accounts payable	*(cc)*	230			

Other

Sale of fixed assets	*(b)*	18	450	*(a)*	Acquisition of fixed assets
			60	*(a)*	Acquisition of goodwill
Bonds issue to acquire fixed assets	*(d)*	100	100	*(c)*	Fixed assets acquired with bonds
Bonds sold	*(h)*	500	1,524	*(f)*	Purchase of fixed assets
Stock issued in bond conversion	*(j)*	200	200	*(i)*	Bond conversion into stock
Sale of capital stock	*(l)*	1,000	750	*(n)*	Dividends paid
B		120			

Receivables			**Inventories**		
B	360		B	750	
(aa)	90		*(bb)*	303	
B	450		B	1,053	

Accounts Payable

	360	B
	230	(cc)
	590	B

(aa)*

Receivables	90,000	
Cash—Operations		90,000

(bb)*

Inventories	303,000	
Cash—Operations		303,000

(cc)*

Cash—Operations	230,000	
Accounts Payable		230,000

* For an explanation of and the rationale for these entries see the preceding discussion.

With the posting of these additional entries, the change in the Cash T-account, from opening balance of $240,000 to ending balance of $120,000, is now fully explained and using the detail in it we can proceed to construct Exhibit 13–2 which shows the SCFP—cash focus.

DIFFERENT STATEMENTS—DIFFERENT OBJECTIVES

In the Vatter Company illustration, we have considered three statements (or portions of statements) that dealt with operations:

Income statement

Working capital from operations (WCFO)

Cash from operations (CFO)

There seems to be endless confusion, particularly among users of financial statements, about the concept of "operations" and about the different aspects of operations that these three statements are designed to portray.

A good way in which we can focus on the differences between these statements and on the different objectives they are designed to serve is to consider them side by side as is done for the Vatter Company in Exhibit 13–3.

The function of the *income statement* is to measure the *profitability* of the enterprise for a given period. This is presently done by relating, as well as is possible, expenses and revenues. While no other statement measures profitability as well as the income statement, it does not show the *timing* of cash flows and the effect of operations on liquidity and solvency. Conse-

Exhibit 13–2

THE VATTER COMPANY
Statement of Changes in Financial Position
For the Year Ended December 31, 19x2

Financial resources were provided by:

Net income			$ 951,000
Add: Expenses not requiring cash:			
Depreciation of fixed assets	$360,000		
Amortization of goodwill	30,000		
Deferred income taxes	20,000		
Increase in accounts payable	230,000	640,000	
		1,591,000	
Deduct: Undistributed income of unconsolidated subsidiary not providing cash	50,000		
Increase in receivables	90,000		
Increase in inventories	303,000		
Gain on sale of fixed assets (included in proceeds from sale)	2,000	445,000	
Cash provided by operations			$1,146,000
Sale of fixed assets		18,000	
Net proceeds of sale of bonds		500,000	
Issuance of bonds in exchange of fixed assets		100,000	
Issuance of stock for conversion of bonds		200,000	
Sale of capital stock		1,000,000	1,818,000
			2,964,000
Decrease in cash			120,000
			$3,084,000

Financial resources were used for:

Purchase of fixed assets*	1,974,000	
Purchase of goodwill	60,000	
Fixed assets acquired for bonds	100,000	
Retirement of debentures on conversion into capital stock	200,000	
Payment of dividends	750,000	$3,084,000

* $450,000 + $1,524,000.

quently, other specialized statements are needed to focus on the latter, which are different dimensions of earnings-related activities.

Working capital from operations (WCFO) is a specialized operations concept. It is first and foremost a *definitional* concept depending, as it does, on the accountant's definition of working capital.[6] Chapter 16 discusses the shortcomings and the weaknesses of the working capital concept.

[6] It is also subject to the weaknesses of the accounting model. Thus, working capital with inventories valued on the LIFO basis is different from working capital with inventories valued on the FIFO basis.

Exhibit 13–3

THE VATTER COMPANY
Comparison of Three Bases of Reporting

	Income statement	Working capital from operations	Operating cash receipts and disbursements (CFO)
Sales	19,950	$19,950	$19,860 [b] Collections from customers
Equity in earnings of unconsolidated subsidiary	50	—	—
Gain on sale of fixed assets	2	— [c]	— [c]
	20,002	19,950	19,860 Total collections
Cost of goods sold [a]	10,741	10,741	10,814 [d] Payments to suppliers and labor
Depreciation	360	—	—
General, selling, and administrative expenses	7,000	7,000	7,000 Payments for expenses
Amortization of goodwill	30	—	—
Income taxes: Current	900	900	900 Payments for taxes
deferred	20	–	–
	19,051	18,641	18,714 Total disbursements
Net income	$ 951		
Working capital from operations ..		$ 1,309	
Cash from operations			$ 1,146

[a] Exclusive of depreciation.

[b] $19,950 (sales)—$90 (increase in receivables).

[c] Omitted only because it is linked up with proceeds from sale assets.

[d] $10,741 (cost of goods sold) + $303 (increase in inventories)—$230 (increase in payables)

Note that the linkage of accounts payable to cost of goods sold is arbitrary because some may relate to other expense categories. However no further breakdown is possible.

As we can see from Exhibit 13–3, WCFO excludes from the measurement of operations those items of revenue and expense that do not affect current assets or current liabilities, as defined. Thus, it is a very specialized notion of operating results and certainly does not measure profitability. It does attempt to measure the amount of working capital provided by operations and as such is designed to supply significant information to those who view working capital as a significant measure of liquidity. In most cases, this amount will exceed net income because it excludes such important and substantial costs as depreciation, depletion, amortization of intangibles, and deferred income taxes. The financial community's frequent reference to this measure as "cash flow" is, as we shall see, both superficial and uninformed.

Cash from Operations (CFO) encompasses the broadest concept of operations of these three measures. Here we encompass all earning related activities of the enterprise. As the earlier discussion made clear, here we are not concerned only with costs and revenues but also with the cash demands of these activities, such as investments in customer receivables and in inventories as well as the financing provided by suppliers of goods and services. This can be clearly seen from Exhibit 13–3 where we arrive at operating cash receipts and disbursements by adjusting the items comprising WCFO for changes in operating current assets or current liabilities. In Vatter Company's case, the amount of CFO is smaller than WCFO because Vatter's added investment in receivables and inventories in 19x2 exceeds the additional credit extension received from suppliers during that period.

Like WCFO, CFO focuses on the liquidity aspect of operations and is *not* a measure of profitability because it does not include important items of cost such as the use of long-lived assets in operations or revenue items such as the equity in the earnings of nonconsolidated subsidiaries or affiliates.

Further analytical considerations

It must be born in mind that a *net* figure, as such, be it net income, WCFO, or CFO, is of very limited analytical value. Whether the purpose of the analyst is the evaluation of past performance or the prediction of future performance or conditions, the key to such analytical procedures is information about the *components* of such net measures.

As the discussion in Chapter 22 shows, the analyst, in the evaluation of operating performance and in the determination of present or future earning power, focuses not on net income but rather on the components that make up that number.

Because WCFO and CFO, as measures of performance, are less subject to distortion than is the net income figure, the analysis of the trend of the former, over time, can provide valuable analytical insights. Divergences in trends among these performance measures can also provide significant analytical clues.

As is further discussed in Chapter 17, one of the most valid analytical uses of the SCFP, or of its subset WCFO, is as a basis for the *longer-term* projection of sources and uses of funds. The emphasis here is on *long-term* because the distinction between cash and working capital diminishes over the longer term. Moreover, cash is, realistically speaking, much more difficult to project into the distant future than is the projection of working capital, which can be related to projected sales and which is a more encompassing concept of liquidity.

The same considerations apply to the SCFP—cash focus, or to its subset CFO, which has a financing rather than profit-measurement focus and which is consequently particularly suited to the evaluation of current liquidity and the projection of short-term cash position.

Here we must recognize that the analyst obtains details about the components of CFO in one of two formats.

1. The format shown in Exhibit 13–2 which, in arriving at CFO, merely lists the changes in operating current assets and liabilities without associat-

ing them with specific revenues or costs. This format, known as the net or indirect approach, concentrates on producing a correct net figure for CFO.

2.   The format shown in the last column of Exhibit 13–3 focuses on the revenue inflow and the cost outflow *components* of CFO, adjusted by the related current account changes (e.g., sales adjusted by the change in receivables, etc.). This format, known as the direct, or more descriptively, the inflow-outflow approach is analytically more significant and valuable because it gives the analyst a feel of actual cash flows through the enterprise. (This concept will be elaborated on in Appendix 13A.) Even though some inflows require related outflows, this format nevertheless enables the analyst to judge the degree of discretion that management has over the size and directions of its cash flows. Moreover, for purposes of short-term forecasting, this format is a more meaningful tool because it contains details about the financing options available to management.

Both the WCFO and the CFO concepts are subject to the limitation that they *exclude,* by definition, those elements of revenue and expense that do not affect current accounts. That, as we saw, means that they exclude from consideration such important costs as those associated with the operating use of long-lived assets. No comprehensive, longer-term analysis of operations can, of course, be undertaken without a consideration of all elements of costs and expenses.

Accounting is a complex measurement system governed by many conventions and specialized definitions. The special-purpose statements that we have examined here, the income statement and those that measure WCFO and CFO, have been developed to fill specialized needs by the use of specific and sometimes narrow perspectives. The valid analytical use of these statements requires that the analyst bear firmly in mind these specialized definitions as well as their inherent limitations.

IMPLICATIONS FOR ANALYSIS

The balance sheet portrays the variety of assets held by an entity at a given moment in time and the manner in which those assets are financed. The income statement portrays the results of operations for a specific fiscal period. Income results in increases of a variety of kinds of assets, some cash, some current, and some noncurrent. Expenses result in the consumption of different kinds of assets (or the incurrence of liabilities)—some cash, some of a current and some of a noncurrent nature. Thus, net income cannot be equated with an increment in liquid resources. It is quite conceivable that a very profitable enterprise may find it difficult to meet its current obligations and to lack funds for further expansion. The very fact that a business is successful in expanding sales may bring along with it a worsening of liquidity and the tying up of its funds in assets that cannot be liquidated in time to meet maturing obligations.

Clear thinking and analysis demands that we separate issues of operating performance and profitability from those concerned with the financing of the enterprise. Both are vital; they are interconnected; but they are not identical, and confusing the two can lead to fuzzy analysis.

The SCFP sheds light on the effects of earning activities on liquid resources and focuses on such matters as what became of net income during the period, and on what assets were acquired and how they were financed. It can highlight more clearly the distinction between net income and funds provided by operations.

The disparity between net income and WCFO, on one hand, and CFO, on the other, can also be very significant. Earlier in the chapter we discussed W. T. Grant Company's inability to generate any meaningful cash from operations even though it was, for many years prior to its bankruptcy, able to report relatively steady net income and WCFO amounts.

The ability of an enterprise to generate cash from operations on a consistent basis is an important indicator of financial health. Analysts must, however, guard against too simplistic an interpretation of CFO figures and trends.

Prosperous as well as failing entities may find themselves unable to generate cash from operations at any given time—but for different reasons. The entity caught in the "prosperity squeeze" of having to invest its cash in receivables and inventories in order to meet ever-increasing customer demand will often find that its profitability will facilitate financing by equity as well as by debt. That same profitability should ultimately turn CFO into a positive figure. The unsuccessful firm, on the other hand, will find its cash drained by slow-downs in receivable and inventory turnovers, by operating losses, or by a combination of these factors. These conditions usually contain the seeds of further losses and cash drains and may also lead to the drying up of trade credit. In such cases, a lack of CFO has different implications. Even if the unsuccessful firm manages to borrow, that will only magnify the ultimate drains of its cash. Thus, profitability is a key consideration, and while it does not insure CFO in the short run, it is essential to a healthy financial condition in the long run.

The unsuccessful or financially pressed firm can increase its CFO by reducing accounts receivable and inventories, but usually this is done at the expense of future profitability. It should be readily apparent that the evaluation of CFO must be done with great care and with a consideration of all surrounding circumstances.

The 1981 annual report of Digital Equipment Corporation illustrates not only the disparities that can exist between net income (reported as $343 million), WCFO ($456 million), and CFO ($182 million), but also the increasing confusion of what is meant by the term *operations*. This company deducts "Additions to property, plant, and equipment" of $398 million from CFO of $182 million to arrive at a "Net *decrease* in funds from operations" of

$216 million. The presentation of the entire new investment in property, plant, and equipment (leading to a 46 percent year-to-year increase in the Gross Property account) as a use of funds for "operations" would not only be considered as most conservative but indicates how loosely defined this term is in actual practice. It also points up the need for the analyst to adopt an independent attitude towards such definitions and presentations and to recast the SCFP to serve his or her own analytical purposes (see Appendix 13A).

The inflationary conditions of recent years have added to the financial burdens and challenges of enterprises. Most significant among these are the need to replace plant and equipment at costs far exceeding the related provision for depreciation, added investments in inventories and receivables, and a dividend distribution policy that is based on a profits calculus that does not provide fully for current costs of resources used up in operations (see also Chapter 14).

It is true to say that in times of inflation, a company's managerial decisions are not necessarily made on the basis of its published historical-cost statements. The analyst, however, looks to the SCFP for information on the fund effects, in *current* dollars, of how managements have actually coped under such conditions. This leads to a focus on how much cash the management had available after deducting from CFO capital expenditures and dividends. While this approach can lead to useful insights, the analyst must make sure that he can distinguish between *replacement* of facilities used up and *additions* to productive capacity. This information is often not readily available. To equate long-term investment in equipment with its current use for operations is a superficial treatment that can be very misleading.

The SCFP is also of great value to the analyst who wants to project operating results on the basis of productive capacity acquired and planned to be acquired, and who wants to assess a company's future capacity to expand, its capital needs, and the sources from which they may be met. The statement is, thus, an essential bridge between the income statement and the balance sheet.

The SCFP probably owes its inception to a desire to learn more about the flow of liquid resources of a business. However, the SCFP can provide more than information on the changes in liquid resources and their effect on a company's ability to meet current obligations. To the financial analyst, the statement provides clues to important matters such as:

1. Feasibility of financing capital expenditures and possible sources of such financing.
2. Sources of funds to finance an expansion in the volume of business.
3. Dependence of the enterprise on external sources of financing, e.g., borrowing or new equity.
4. Future dividend policies.
5. Ability to meet future debt service requirements.

6. An insight into the financial habits of management and resulting indications of future policies.
7. Indications regarding the quality of earnings.

Regarding the last-mentioned use, the SCFP is useful for identifying faulty or erroneous operating results. In the income statement true operating results may be masked for a time through the use of devices such as premature revenue recognition or unwarranted cost deferrals. A further discussion of earnings quality will be found in Chapter 22.

The SCFP as a summary of overall investment and financing activities of an enterprise is, of course, far more reliable and credible evidence of a company's actions and intentions than are the statements and speeches of its management.

The analyst must be careful to examine the form in which the SCFP is presented. Thus, some transactions are definitely related such as, for example, the purchase of certain assets and the issuance of debt. The analyst must, however, be careful not to impute relationships among items merely on the basis of their presentation lest he reach misleading conclusions.

The significance of a change in liquidity, whether positive or negative, cannot be judged by means of the statement of sources and applications of funds alone. It must, of course, be related to other variables in a company's financial structure and operating results. Thus, for example, an increase of funds may have been gained by selling off various assets whose earning power will be missed in the future; or the increase may have been financed by means of incurrence of debt which is subject to high costs and/or onerous repayment terms.

Cash is the most liquid of assets and is not only the most ready and acceptable means of discharging obligations but is also the ultimate measure of realization of sales transactions. Thus, in certain types of business where liquidity and cash flows are of paramount importance, a statement of sources and applications of cash is often presented. Here the analyst will find the effect of all transactions on the company's cash (or cash plus marketable securities) balance. Although the statement is also referred to as a "statement of cash flow," this term is subject to considerable confusion and requires clarification.

CASH FLOW

The term *cash flow* was probably first coined by financial analysts. Its most common meaning is net income adjusted for charges not involving funds such as, for example, depreciation and depletion. In this sense, the term *cash flow* can be equated with *sources of funds from operations* found in the SCFP, except that while the latter term includes adjustments of *all* nonfund items included in net income, the popular concept of "cash flow" is, all too often, merely one of net income with depreciation expense added back, and hence a much cruder concept. In any event, the mixup in terminology only leads to confusion.

The most valid analytical use made of cash flow is when security analysts, in an attempt to eliminate distortions that arise from the variety of depreciation methods in use and the loose standards that govern the assumptions of useful lives of assets, try to compare the earnings of companies before depreciation.

The following example points up the distortions in net income comparisons that can occur due to the use of different depreciation methods. The use of different useful-life assumptions for the same kind of fixed assets can, of course, introduce additional distortions.

Assume that two companies (A and B) each invest $50,000 in a machine that generates $45,000 per year from operations before provision for depreciation. Thus, for the five-year assumed useful life of the machine, the results are as follows:

	Five-year period
Funds provided by operations ($45,000 × 5 years)	$225,000
Cost of the machine	50,000
Income from operations of the machine	175,000
Average yearly net income	$ 35,000

However, the same $175,000 income over five years can be reported quite differently by using straight-line or sum-of-the years'-digits depreciation. Thus (ignoring taxes), we have:

Year	Income before depreciation*	COMPANY A: Straight-line depreciation		COMPANY B: Sum-of-the-years'-digits depreciation	
		Depreciation	Net income	Depreciation	Net income
1	$ 45,000	$10,000	$ 35,000	$16,667	$ 28,333
2	45,000	10,000	35,000	13,334	31,666
3	45,000	10,000	35,000	10,000	35,000
4	45,000	10,000	35,000	6,667	38,333
5	45,000	10,000	35,000	3,332	41,668
Total	$225,000	$50,000	$175,000	$50,000	$175,000

* Popularly termed *cash flow.*

As the above example shows, while the predepreciation "cash flow" of the two companies is identical, indicating as it should, identical earning power, the after-depreciation income, while identical for the entire five-year period, can be quite different on a year-to-year basis, depending on the depreciation method in use.

The use of *cash flow* or more properly labeled *income before depreciation* is thus a valid analytical tool so long as the user knows specifically what its significance is and what its limitations are.

The limitations of the cash flow concept are entirely due to the widespread confusion of the term's meaning and to its misuse.

One source of confusion stems from a lack of definition of what cash flow really is. It is, of course, strictly speaking neither *cash* nor *flow* (see earlier description of cash from operations). It is not cash because it is used within broader meaning of funds, that is, working capital. It is not flow because it represents net change and a very limited aspect of funds flow, that is, funds generated by operations. Moreover the flow focuses on an inflow and disregards mandatory or necessary outflows. Thus, there are many other flows, even among those identified with operations, that should be found in a complete SCFP.

The assertion sometimes made that cash flow represents a discretionary fund that management can use as it sees fit is also misleading. There are mandatory outflows such as debt service, required dividends, preferred stock redemptions, and essential capital asset replacements that cannot be avoided or postponed and that can sharply reduce or even eliminate the discretionary cash flow pool generated by operations.

Another and even more serious confusion arises from the assertion of some, and particularly those managements that are dissatisfied by the level of their reported net income, that cash flow is a measure of performance superior to or more valid than net income.[7] This is like saying that depreciation, or other costs not involving the use of current funds, are not genuine expenses. This misconception is also discussed in Chapter 11. Only net income can be properly regarded as a measure of performance and can be validly related to the equity investment as an indicator of operating success. If we add back depreciation to net income and compute the resulting return on investment, we are, in effect, confusing the return *on* investment with an element of return *of* investment in fixed assets. Moreover, it should also be born in mind that not only is depreciation a valid cost but that in times of inflation the depreciation funds recovered from sales may not be sufficient to replace the equipment because the charges are based on the lower historical costs (see also Chapter 14).

---

[7] In FRR No. 1 Sec. 202, the SEC concluded that certain approaches to cash flow reporting may be misleading to investors. Per share data other than that relating to net income, net assets, and dividends should be avoided in reporting financial results.

Closely linked with the doubts of laymen, and even of those who should know better, about the true nature of the depreciation cost is the confusion stemming from whether or not depreciation is a source of funds.

DEPRECIATION—A SOURCE OF FUNDS?

One major cause for the belief that depreciation is a source of funds is the manner in which it is presented in some SCFPs. Thus, the adding back of depreciation to net income is all too often not shown as an *adjustment* of net income in order to arrive at the desired figure of "funds provided by operations" but rather as if it is an independent source of funds similar to that stemming from borrowing of money or the sales of assets.

ILLUSTRATION 2

Misleading presentation

Sources of funds:

Net income	$ 75,000
Depreciation	25,000
Sale of bonds	60,000
Sale of machinery	40,000
Total	$200,000

Proper presentation

Sources of funds:

Net income	$75,000	
Add back* deprecia- tion charge	25,000	
Funds provided by operations		$100,000
Sale of bonds		60,000
Sale of machinery		40,000
Total		$200,000

* Expense not requiring current outlay of funds.

It is not hard to understand why the misleading presentation could lead laymen into believing that depreciation is a source of funds. Since it is shown in the same way as all sources of funds, it is a "source" like all others and would seem to suggest that the act of increasing the depreciation expense will increase the total sources of funds. This thinking overlooks, of course, the fact that depreciation acts to reduce net income, and thus the act of increasing depreciation can have no effect on funds. On the other hand, the act of increasing permitted depreciation charges for tax return purposes may temporarily conserve funds by reducing the current tax liability.

The thinking regarding depreciation as a source of funds is encouraged by loose discussion in some of our best financial publications. Thus, *Business Week*[8] commented, "Since then the company has improved cash flow further by depreciating existing planes." As readers of this book know, added depreciation (except that resulting in added tax write-offs) cannot be considered a source of cash.

---

[8] Dated May 19, 1980, in an article entitled "Trans World Corporation—The Strategy Squeeze on the Airline."

The proper presentation brings out the essential fact that the reason depreciation (or similar charges or credits that do not affect current funds) is shown in the SCFP is in order to show to the reader how the net income figure is converted to a "funds provided by operations" figure needed in the funds statement.[9]

The essential fact to be understood is that aside from miscellaneous sources of income, the *basic* source of funds from operations in any enterprise is sales to customers. It is out of sales that all expenses are recovered and a profit, if any, is earned. If the sales price is sufficient to cover *all* costs, that is, those requiring and those not requiring current funds, then the process of sales will recover the depreciation costs in addition to other costs. If the sales price is not sufficiently high to cover all costs, depreciation will not be recovered or will not be fully recovered. Thus, the importance of revenues as *the* source of funds from operations should never be lost sight of.

The above discussion clearly points out that the financial analyst must approach the funds statements as well as such concepts as "cash flow" and depreciation with understanding and with independence of viewpoint so as to avoid being trapped by the numerous cliches and useless generalizations which are all too often employed even by those who should know better.

APPENDIX 13A

STATEMENT CONVERSION FROM WORKING CAPITAL
FOCUS TO CASH FOCUS

In this chapter, we have examined the analytical importance of cash flows and particularly of cash from operations (CFO) as contrasted to working capital from operations (WCFO).

While the trend is in the direction of refocusing of the statement of changes in financial position (SCFP) from working capital to cash, many companies still focus on changes in working capital. Moreover, among the companies who focus on cash in preparing the SCFP, many present within such a statement the conventional funds provided by operations format which focuses on working capital. In addition, the format used in presenting WCFO or CFO is the net, or indirect, approach that starts with net income (which, of course is a net figure that represents neither a source nor a use of any

---

[9] One exception to the rule that the recording of depreciation does not provide working capital should be noted. Depreciation is a cost included in inventories, and thus the process of production converts a noncurrent asset (e.g., machinery) into a current one thus creating working capital.

type of funds) rather than the analytically more desirable inflow-outflow or direct format.[1]

For these reasons, this appendix presents two approaches to converting SCFP with a working capital focus to a cash focus:

I. The direct method of conversion (by inspection).

II. Conversion by the worksheet technique.

I. The direct method of conversion of working capital from operations to cash from operations

This method is most suitable when the financial statements are relatively simple so that the adjustments can be done by mental inspection or on a scrap of paper.

The inflow-outflow format

As was discussed in the chapter, analytically, the most useful way to compute CFO is to show the elements of revenue that generate cash and the expenses that use cash (the *inflow-outflow* format) rather than to adjust net income for noncash affecting items (the *net* format).

The first step is to identify and list all elements of income and expense *that affect* working capital. The second step is to adjust these for changes in *working capital items* (other than cash) that are *assumed* to affect operations. Thus:

From cash inflows:

> *Starting with sales*
>> + Decrease (− increase) in accounts receivable
>> _____
>> = Cash collections on sales
>> + Other revenues (+ or − adjustments for noncash items)
> = *Total cash collections from operations*

Deduct cash outflows:

> *Cost of goods sold** (e.g. *excluding* depreciation, amortization, *etc.*).
> Operating expenses*
> Other expenses (including interest)
>> + Increase (− decrease) in inventories
>> + Decrease (− increase) in trade payables
>> + Increase (− decrease) in prepaid expenses
>> + Decrease (− increase) in accrued liabilities

----

[1] AICPA's *Accounting Trends & Techniques* reported that in 1980, 517 of 600 companies surveyed used the net or indirect approach in presenting WCFO or CFO.

Income tax expense* (e.g. excluding deferred taxes—noncurrent).

+ Decrease (− increase) in accrued taxes

= *Total cash outflows for operations*

Result: Cash from or for operations (CFO)

  * Excluding items which don't affect cash.

Using the financial statements of Vatter Company (page 387) and the SCFP of that company prepared in Exhibit 13–1, we can illustrate in Exhibit 13A–1 this direct or mental form of preparation. The simplicity of these financial statements makes this approach particularly appropriate here.

It should be noted that for the sake of consistency with prior presentations, the $2,000 gain on sale of fixed assets was omitted from the CFO computation. The omission, as was noted before, has nothing to do with the operating nature of this item but is rather intended to link it with the proceeds from the sale of equipment as an "other" rather than "operating" source of cash.

The net format

The net format of converting WCFO to CFO, while analytically less useful, is easier to compute. The approach is:

I. Start with working capital provided by operations.

II. *Add* the amount of *change* in working capital accounts (other than cash) that experienced a net *credit* change for the period. That is, reductions in current assets* (other than cash) or increases in current liabilities,* all of which increases of cash available.

Exhibit 13A–1

VATTER COMPANY

Direct Conversion of WCFO to CFO for 19x2

(in thousands)

Sales	$19,950	
Less increase in receivables	90	
Cash collections		$19,860
Cash outflows:		
Cost of goods sold	11,101	
Less depreciation	360	
	10,741	
Add: Increase in inventories	303	
	11,044	
General, selling and administrative expenses	7,000	
Less: Increase in accounts payable	(230)	17,814
Income taxes—current		900
Total cash outflows		18,714
Cash from operations (CFO)		$ 1,146

III. *Deduct* the amount of *change* in working capital accounts (other than cash) that experienced a net *debit* change during the period. That is, increases in current assets* (other than cash) and decreases in current liabilities,* all of which decreases of cash available.

IV. The result is net cash flow from operations.

* Excluding nonoperating items such as changes in marketable securities, which are not cash equivalents, bank loans and dividends payable.

The application of the above approach to the Vatter Company figures is as follows (in thousands):

Working capital provided by operation (WCFO)		$1,309
Add: Increase in accounts payable (net credit)		230
		1,539
Deduct: Increase in receivables (net debit)	$ 90	
Increase in inventories (net debit)	303	393
Cash from operations (CFO)		$1,146

The "net format" should be used when only the CFO figure is desired, and the detail of how it is obtained is not important to the user. It can also be used as a quick check on the CFO computation under the inflow-outflow format.

It can readily be seen that the above techniques can be used to convert an entire SCFP from a working capital focus to a cash focus. In such a conversion, those accounts (other than cash) that do not affect operations (e.g., loans payable, dividends payable) are used to adjust nonoperating sources and uses in order to arrive at their net cash effect.

II. Conversion by the worksheet technique[2]

As already indicated, conversion by the worksheet technique is particularly useful when there is considerable complexity in the financial statements and in the notes thereto and the analyst desires an organized step-by-step approach to conversion, one that will leave a trail for rechecking of computations and steps and that will ensure accuracy and a consideration of all elements. Moreover, the worksheet technique leads to a better and more careful distinction between working capital and cash.

Let us now consider the steps involved in worksheet conversion procedure (refer to Exhibit 13A–2):

1. The *first* conversion step involves a rearrangement of income statement items into revenues (credits) and expenses (debits) so that the "inflows"

---

[2] Credit for the development and refinement of this technique belongs to Jon A. Stroble, a leading developer of bank loan officer training seminars.

and the "outflows" can be properly identified and measured. The use of the debit and credit format is very useful in avoiding computational errors. The *rearrangement* process is basically as follows:

Net format		Inflow-outflow format		
Net income as reported	$400	┌►Total revenues	$20,000	
Add: Depreciation	500-	┐ Less: Equity in earnings of		
	900	┆┼--►unconsolidated subsidiary ..	100	$19,900
Less: Equity in earnings		┆└►Total expenses	19,600	
of unconsolidated		┆ └Less: Depreciation	500	19,100
subsidiary	100┘	WCFO		$ 800
WCFO	$800			

After inserting the inflows and outflows of funds from operations onto the first worksheet column, copy the remaining items from the SCFP onto that same column. By including a net *increase* in working capital as a *source* or a net decrease in working capital as a *use*, total sources and uses will now be in balance.

2. The *second* step involves placing in the next column (the Conversion column) the net increase or decrease in working capital items besides the amount in the first column to which it relates.[3] Since this column redistributes the net change in working capital, it will always add up to zero. Amounts in this column must *carefully* be labeled as debit or credit. Changes in the current asset and current liability accounts are usually shown at the bottom of the SCFP or in a footnote. If the SCFP has a cash focus, they may be scattered in the body of the statement.[4]

3. Add across the amount in column 1 plus or minus the amount in column 2 and place total in column 3 (the Cash column), always paying careful attention to the debit or credit designation of the amount.

4. Use the figures in column 3 to prepare a formal cash statement.

---

[3] The analyst will need to separate the nonoperating current accounts from those that are of an operating nature (as was discussed in the chapter) thus:

Current account	*Relates to—*
• Cash	• Place on bottom line
• Receivables	• Total revenues
• Inventories	• ⎫
• Prepaid expenses	• ⎬ Total expenses
• Accounts and accruals payable	• ⎪
• Income taxes payable	• ⎭
• Short-term debt	• Place on a separate line as *net* source or use (nonoperating)
• Current portion of long-term debt	• Reduction in long-term debt (nonoperating)
• Dividends payable	• Dividends declared (nonoperating)

[4] In this case, the SCFP will have to be first rearranged into a working capital format.

Exhibit 13A-2

THE VATTER COMPANY
Conversion from Working Capital to Cash
for the Year 19x2
(in thousands)

	Working capital (1)	Conversion	Dr. (Cr.) (2)	Cash (3)
Sources (credits):				
From operations:				
Revenue providing	$19,950 (a)	Increase in receivables	$ 90	$19,860
Less: Expenses using (debits)	18,641 (b)	⌠Increase in inventories	303	18,714
		⌡Increase in payables	(230)	
Net from operations	1,309			1,146
Sale of fixed assets	18			18
Sale of bonds	500			500
Sale of capital stock	1,000			1,000
Total sources	2,827			2,664
Uses (debits):				
Purchase of fixed assets	1,974			1,974
Purchase of goodwill	60			60
Payment of dividends	750			750
Net increase in working capital	43	Remove (redistribute) working capital increase	(43)	—
Total uses	$ 2,827			2,784
		Decrease in cash	(120)	$ (120)
			-0-	

(a) Total revenues and gain* ... $20,002
Less: Equity in earnings
of unconsol. subsidiaries ... (50)
Gain on sale of fixed assets ... (2)
Revenues providing working capital ... $19,950

(b) Total expenses* ... $19,051
Less: Depreciation ... $360
Goodwill amortization ... 30
Deferred taxes ... 20 ... 410
Expenses using working capital ... $18,641

* See "single step" income statement format in Exhibit 13–3.

⇒ Please note carefully.

First illustration of the conversion process

Exhibit 13A–2 presents the worksheet in which the Vatter Company's SCFP (working capital focus) is converted to the cash basis. The following steps, additional to those discussed above, are noteworthy:

1. The first column of the worksheet presents the *rearranged* SCFP of Vatter Company in a balanced format, i.e., the net increase in working capital balances the sources and uses.

2. The Conversion column lists all *changes* in current assets and current liabilities that must always coincide with the net change in working capital (in this example an increase of $43,000). Since this net change is *redistributed* in this column it must always add up to zero. That ensures the accuracy of the redistribution of the net working capital change, and thus ensures the accuracy of the conversion process.

   In this example, we have only operations-related working capital changes, and these are used to adjust the relevant operating inflows and outflows in order to convert them to a cash basis.

3. The right-hand Cash column, while not representing a statement of sources and uses of cash, contains all the information needed for its preparation. In this case, that portion of the statement which relates to *operations* will be as shown in Exhibit 13A–1.

4. The conversion worksheet is an analytical statement. Consequently, it should include footnotes that explain the derivation of specific amounts, adjustments undertaken, and the assumptions underlying such adjustments, as well as any questions or uncertainties remaining due to lack of information or for other reasons.

IMPROVING AND ADJUSTING THE SCFP FORMAT

In some cases, the analyst may need to examine the format of the SCFP in order to determine whether the explanations of changes in balance sheet accounts in the statement are adequate to serve his purposes. To the extent that such explanations appear not to be adequate, the analyst should reconstruct all or selected accounts in order to determine the extent of missing information that needs to be obtained or taken into account. Only a complete reconstruction will assure that all aspects of transactions listed in the SCFP have been considered, but such a step may not be required too often. Appendix 13B illustrates such a reconstruction of transactions.

Information that is gleaned from such a reconstruction or from a further analysis of disclosures should be presented in footnotes to the cash statement so that the reader can fully understand the details as well as the limitations of the statement.

EXAMPLE 1. When a business is purchased during a period, information on working capital items acquired is often available only in the aggregate. Thus, part of the

Exhibit 13A–3

ALFA, INC.
Conversion of Working Capital to Cash—19x6

	Working capital			Conversion†	Dr. (Cr.)	Cash
	Reported	Adjustment	Revised			
Sources:						
From (for) operations revenues providing	$1,251,020(a)	Cr. $7,886(a)	$1,258,906	Increase in current receivables [62]	$ 21,596	$1,237,310
Costs and expenses:						
Cost of sales	839,874(b)		839,874			
Selling, general, and administrative [3]*	343,023		343,023	Increase in inventory [63]	28,772	
				Decrease in prepaid expenses [64]	(1,756)	
Interest [5]	18,504		18,504	Increase in accounts payable and accrued expenses [66]	(8,276)	
Interest capitalized [6]	(64)		(64)			
Income tax expense	4,079(c)		4,079	Decrease in accrued and current deferred income taxes [67] and [68]	3,789	
Total costs and expenses	1,205,416		1,205,416	Subtotal	22,529	1,227,945
Net from operations →	45,604		53,490		44,125	9,365
Additions to long-term debt [46]	58,344		58,344	Decrease in current portion of long-term debt(e)	1,373	56,971
Decrease in noncurrent receivables [47]	7,886	Dr. 7,886(a)	–0–			–0–
Issuance of capital stock for businesses acquired [48]	2,494		2,494			2,494
Property sales and retirements: Other [49]	3,409		3,409			3,409
Total sources	117,737		117,737			72,239

Uses:

Property additions:

Businesses acquired **52**	$ 6,683		6,683
Existing businesses **53**	41,174		41,174
Reduction of long-term			
debt **55**	8,080		8,080
Cash dividends **56**	12,266		12,266
Increase in deferred charges **58**	1,972		1,972
Other—net **59**	389		389
Increase in working capital **60**	47,173		–0–
Total uses	117,737	–0–	

Remove (redistribute) change in working capital .... (47,173)

Decrease in short-term notes payable[(e)] 3,550   3,550

Total .... (1,875)   74,114

Decrease in cash **61** .... $ –0– $ (1,875)

(a) $1,251,088 Total income **1**

1,251,020

(68) Net income of other unconsolidated subsidiaries **11**–**44**

(b) $840,043 Cost of goods sold **2** – **4**)

169 Depreciation incl. (**42**–**4**)

839,874

(c) $7,600 Tax expense **9**

3,521 Noncurrent deferred **43**

4,079

(d) To net noncurrent receivables against revenues **47**.

(e) Notes payable and current portion of long-term debt **65**

  decrease $4,923

Less: Decrease in current portion of long-term debt **94** 1,373

Decrease in short-term notes payable $3,550

---

* References in boldface square numbers are to Alfa's financial statements.

† Note that all items in the "increase (decrease) in working capital section" **61** to **68** are included in this column.

change in receivables, inventories, or payables may be due to the acquisition and should not be used to adjust sales and cost of sales for the period. The analyst, if unable to obtain additional information from management, must footnote his inability to make correct adjustments due to such circumstances.

EXAMPLE 2.   When operations are discontinued during a period, their effect on operations is often given only in net or aggregate form (e.g., if pro forma net income and sales are provided total expenses can be derived). Because the related changes in current assets and liabilities are usually not disclosed, discontinued operations can generally not be segregated from continuing operations.

The analyst must also consider whether income statement or SCFP items need to be adjusted or rearranged to make them responsive to the analyst's needs or assumptions. As is illustrated in the example that follows, such adjustments are made in the first column by changing to the following format:

Working capital

Reported	*Adjustments*	*Revised*

The following are examples of such adjustments:

EXAMPLE 3.   The operating-nonoperating distinction is merely one of definition or convenience. Thus, we consider an outlay for long-lived productive assets as nonoperating simply because their costs do not enter the income statement in the year of acquisition. The same is true of the acquisition of a patent that is amortized rather than immediately expensed or motion-picture films that are amortized as costs over a number of fiscal periods. The analyst must decide what a useful definition of operations is in any given situation. Thus, he will choose to consider changes in noncurrent receivables as relating to operations to the extent that they arose from the sale of operating assets such as inventories. Unfortunately, such information is often not found in published financial statements.

EXAMPLE 4.   When a company sells its receivables to a financial institution with recourse, the risk of ownership of these receivables remains with that company. Consequently, the analyst may choose not to consider the reduction in receivables occurring because of such sales as equivalent to collections from customers, but rather as short-term borrowing. Analytically this is accomplished by reducing cash receipts from operations and increasing short-term borrowing. The opposite adjustment is indicated when there is a decrease of receivables.

Second illustration of the conversion process

The conversion of the SCFP (working capital basis) of Alfa, Inc., (see Appendix 4B) to a cash basis is illustrated in Exhibit 13A–3. In the preceding illustration, the overall conversion sheet technique was already discussed. We shall now address ourselves to the additional considerations involved in the complete conversion of Alfa's SCFP, which represents a more elaborate published financial statement.

Note that all items of Alfa's SCFP are included in the first column but the "Net income" item |41|[5] is replaced by all the details of the income statement, adjusted for items not providing or using working capital.

In the process of eliminating nonworking capital items, a practical problem arose because of the unexplained difference between the depreciation and amortization amount in the income statement |4| $24,214 and the "add back" for depreciation and amortization |42| of $24,383 shown in the SCFP. The difference of $169 was deducted from cost of goods sold (see Note B to Exhibit 13A–3). This is an example of the inconsistencies that the analyst faces in actual practice and that must be dealt with.

In the Adjustment column, the analyst implements the assumption that noncurrent receivables relate to current (operating) items, e.g. sale of inventories, rather than to nonoperating items such as sales of fixed assets. The decrease in these receivables represents an increase in revenues which provide cash.

Note that "Notes payable and current portion of long-term debt" |32| and "Current income taxes payable" |34| are composite accounts that must be analysed and decomposed with the aid of information provided paranthetically in the captions or in footnotes.

In this example are changes in two current accounts, current portion of long-term debt and short-term notes payable, which are *financing* in nature and consequently do not relate to operations.

APPENDIX 13B

ANALYTICAL RECONSTRUCTION OF ALL TRANSACTIONS

As was indicated in Appendix 13A, a reconstruction, in the aggregate, of all transactions for a period can provide assurance that the SCFP satisfactorily explains all the changes in the balance sheet accounts, can provide additional information that is helpful in the conversion of working capital to cash, and generally can provide analytically useful insights into the aggregate transactions of a period and the relationships among them.

The process of *reconstruction* is basically the reverse of the process of preparing the SCFP as outlined in Chapter 13. The steps of reconstruction are as follows:

1. Establish T-accounts for all noncurrent balance sheet accounts and one T-account for all working capital items. (When a cash focus SCFP serves

---

[5] References are to keys in Alfa's financial statements—Appendix 4B.

as basis for reconstruction, the master T-account will be Cash and T-accounts will be established for all noncash accounts.)

2. Insert opening and closing balances in all accounts. Check to see that when added up, the debits and credits of all accounts are in balance.

3. Use all the items in the SCFP as well as additional information found in other financial statements, in footnotes, and elsewhere to reconstruct all the T-accounts.

Exhibit 13B–1 presents the reconstruction of the T-accounts of Alfa, Inc., for 19x6 (see Appendix 4B). Note that all items in the SCFP are listed in the Working Capital T-account. In order not to omit any items from consideration, the best way of doing this systematically is to list the items in the exact order in which they appear in the SCFP. Placing the corresponding debits or credits in the related T-accounts requires a basic knowledge of accounting as well as use of all available information found within the financial report.

Exhibit 13B–1

ALFA, INC.
T-account Reconstruction for Year Ended December 31, 19x6

Working Capital

B	174,235	1,439	**44** Undistributed income of
41 Net income	19,139		nonconsolidated subsi-
42 Depreciation	24,383		diaries
43 Deferred income		47,857	**52** & **53** Property additions (6,683
taxes (noncurrent)	3,521		**52** + 41,174 **53**)
46 Additions to long-		8,080	**55** Reduction of long-term
term debt	58,344		debt
47 Decrease in noncur-		12,266	**56** Cash dividends on capital
rent receivables	7,886		stock
48 Issuance of capital		1,972	**58** Increase in deferred
stock for busi-			charges
nesses acquired	2,494*	389	**59** Other (net)
49 Property sales and			
retirements	3,409		
B	221,408		

Investment in Nonconsol-idated Finance Subsidiaries		**Other Investments**	
B 31,072		B 22,377	
44 1,371		**44** 68	
		59 608	
B 32,443		B 23,053	

Property, Plant, and Equipment (Net)

B	253,580		
52	6,683	24,383	42
53	41,174	3,409	49
B	273,645		

Other Assets

B	71,393		
58	1,972	7,886	47
59	268		
B	65,747		

Deferred Income Tax

	31,883	B
	3,521	43
	35,404	B

Other Deferred Credits

	4,371	B
	487	59
	4,858	B

Long-Term Debt

		194,690	B
55	8,080	58,344	46
		244,954	B

Preferred Stock $2.50 Cumulative

610	B
610	B

Preferred Stock—$1.00 Cumulative

14,330	B
14,330	B

Common Stock

90,088		B
50	48	*
90,138		B

Excess of Equity Over Cost of Subsidiary

11,171	B
11,171	B

Earnings Reinvested

		205,637	
56	12,266	19,139	41
		2,444	48
		214,954	B

* The reconstruction of this entry was facilitated by referring to Note 9 (item 95) where we learn that 50,000 was credited to Common Stock and the balance (by inference) to Earning Reinvested.

Cost of Treasury Shares

B	123		
B	123		

The reconstruction of the entry representing the deduction from net income of "undistributed income of nonconsolidated domestic subsidiaries" presents us with an example of how supplemental information found in footnotes can help refine the accuracy of our reconstruction. We know the credit of $1,439 goes to the Working Capital account (entry *(d)*). From Note 13 (item ⃞103⃞) we learn that the equity in income of the "Investment in nonconsolidated finance subsidiaries" amounts to $1,371 which is properly debited to this account. The balance of $68 is debited to Other Investments, and this is corroborated in Note 5 where the composition of this account is shown in further detail. There we find that "Other nonconsolidated domestic subsidiaries" increased by exactly $68—presumably the equity in earnings of these subsidiaries.

Analytical uses and implications

Frequently, as is the case with Alfa, the SCFP will have an item, or even items, designated as "Other" sources or uses. It will also be frequently found that the "Other" item (item ⃞59⃞ in Alfa's SCFP) represents the net effect of a number of transactions that are not explained in the SCFP. These "Other" items can be summarized by listing the debits and credits needed to complete those T-accounts that have not been fully explained by the posting of transactions. Arithmetically, they *must* equal the amount or amounts designated as "Other."

In the Alfa example, we summarize the effects which explain the $389,000 "Other—net" item by listing the debits and credits needed to close out those T-accounts that are still open (that is, not fully explained by other entries[6]). Thus:

⃞59⃞ *(in thousands of dollars)*

Other Investments	608	
Other Assets	268	
Other Deferred Credits		487
Working Capital		389

---

[6] All entries in the T-accounts are keyed into Alfa's SCFP (see Appendix 4B).

FURTHER ANALYSIS OF THE COMPOSITE ENTRY
OF "OTHER" CHANGES

Having identified the items that comprise the "Other" changes category in the SCFP, the analyst can now proceed to obtain further clarifications regarding the nature of these items by referring to footnotes and other details given in the financial statements.

Generally, the only justification for lumping a number of items under the "Other"[7] designation is that these are either insignificant or immaterial. An example of insignificant transactions is the write-off of fully depreciated assets which is basically a bookkeeping entry. Lack of materiality generally refers to the relatively small size of the amount involved.

Examination of the "Other assets" section of Notes (item 75) reveals that the increase in "Other assets" relates to "Land held for future property development." We also are led to assume that the increases in Other Investments as well as the increases in Other Deferred Credits are of no significance. We have no basis for judging this and further inquiry of management depends on how important reassurance on these items is to the purposes of the analysis at hand. It must be emphasized that these unexplained changes are *net* in nature. That is, they can be the result of a number of significant debit and credit transactions which net out to a relatively small amount. Moreover, such transactions can have informational value about a company's activities (e.g., new or additional investments, losses, etc.) which can go far beyond the significance of the amounts involved. For example, the unexplained debit to "Other Investments" of $608,000 may be a significant investment in itself or may be the net of even larger debits and credits to this account. Going from the specific example of Alfa to a general conclusion, the analyst must be aware of the possibility that "Other—net" items in the SCFP may include items of significance to the analysis. As we saw, he can identify the composition of such items up to a certain point. Beyond that, however, he must, when necessary, use this information as the basis for further inquiries of management or as a basis for further analytical steps.

QUESTIONS

1. What information can the user of financial statements obtain from the SCFP?
2. Which are the two major concepts of liquidity commonly used in the preparation of the SCFP?
3. While the SCFP focuses normally on changes of working capital or cash, it also includes transactions that affect neither. Give two examples of such transactions.

---

[7] For example, Huges Tool Co.'s 1979 SCFP contains *three* items labeled "Other."

4. In addition to depreciation, what are some other examples of costs and expenses not requiring the outlay of cash or working capital? What are examples of income items not bringing in cash or working capital?

5. Could the form in which revenues are received affect the SCFP?

6. The book value of assets sold is often shown as a separate source of working capital or cash. What is the reason for this presentation?

7. *APB Opinion 19* states that stock dividends and split-ups are not required to be disclosed in the SCFP. What is the reason for this exception? Would the conversion of preferred stock into common be shown in the SCFP.

8. Why is there increasing interest in the cash focus in the preparation of the SCFP?

9. *a.* How can the technique of preparing the cash focus SCFP be viewed?
   b. What effect do changes in the working capital accounts have on operations?

10. Contrast the concept of income with those of working capital from operations and cash from operations.

11. Contrast the *inflow-outflow* format with the *net* format of CFO presentation.

12. What are some of the important clues that an analysis of the SCFP can provide for the analyst?

13. What is meant by the term *cash flow?* Why is this term subject to confusion and misrepresentation?

14. A member of the board of directors of a company that faces shortage of funds in the coming year is told that none of the sources of funds available in the preceding year can be increased. He thereupon suggests increasing the amount shown as "depreciation" in the "sources" section of the funds statement. Comment on his suggestion.

15. A prominent academician wrote some years ago:
   "just as in the first half of this century we saw the income statement displace the balance sheet in importance, so we may now be deemphasising the income statement in favour of a statement of fund flows or cash flows . . . my own guess is that, so far as the history of accounting is concerned, the next 25 years may subsequently be seen to have been the twilight of income measurement."
   Comment on this prediction.

Appendix 13A

16. *a.* What are the underlying principles and assumptions in the conversion of WCFO to CFO?
   b. Contrast the inflow-outflow approach of conversion to the net approach under the direct conversion method.

17. What are the steps involved in the worksheet conversion procedure?

Appendix 13B

18. What are the steps involved in a reconstruction of transactions?

19. How is the "Other" category reconstructed and of what significance is it to the analyst.

14

Effects of price changes on financial statements

The comparability over time of accounting measurements expressed in dollars can be fully valid only if the general purchasing power of the dollar remains unchanged. This has only rarely been the case; indeed, the value of the dollar in terms of purchasing power has changed over any length of time. In recent experience, such change has invariably been a decline in purchasing power, i.e., inflation.

In times of inflation, the monetary unit becomes increasingly distorted as a measure of the actual or physical dimensions of business activities. The distortive effect of general price-level changes on accounting measurements has long been recognized by leaders of industry and finance as well as by economists and accountants.[1] However, as long as the annual rate of inflation was moderate, accountants, as those best situated to move towards change, elected to rely on education and disclosure rather than on a restatement of the financial statements as the means of conveying such effects to the general reader.

In times of more severe inflation, there is always clamor for a more formalized and systematic approach designed to allow for the distortions arising from changes in the price level. There are businessmen who feel that recovery of depreciation based on original cost is not sufficient to provide for replacement of assets used up in production. They are, of course, except under certain imposed circumstances, not bound to historical-cost depreciation in setting their prices, and thus their arguments are often directed towards

---

[1] We must distinguish between specific price changes and general price-level changes affecting the purchasing power of the currency. For example, price changes in goods and services reflecting changes in quality do not affect the general purchasing power of the currency.

the goal of having the tax authorities accept price-level adjusted depreciation in computing taxable income. This quest has, so far, not born fruit.

Research and professional pronouncements

In the early 1960s, the accounting profession recognized that it could no longer ignore the effect of continuing inflation on the financial statements. Accordingly, it commissioned a research study which was published in 1963 as *Accounting Research Study (ARS) 6,* "Reporting the Financial Effects of Price-Level Changes."

Following a period of further significant inflation, the APB issued, in June 1969, its *Statement 3* entitled "Financial Statements Restated for General Price-Level Changes." This advisory pronouncement for the first time spelled out specific steps to be followed in the preparation of general price-level restated financial statements.

After public exposure and discussion, the FASB issued in 1974 an exposure draft of a *Statement* that would have required the inclusion with conventional financial statements, of certain specified financial information stated in terms of units of general purchasing power patterned after the concepts embodied in *APB Statement 3.* However, in 1976 the SEC took the initiative and required larger registrants to disclose the current replacement cost of inventories, depreciable and amortizable assets used in operations, cost of sales, and the provision for depreciation and amortization.

The SEC requirements were primarily designed to move from a debating phase to some actual experimentation with supplementary disclosure. The FASB, aware that it had the primary responsibility to come up with a satisfactory reporting framework undertook field tests in order to experiment with various reporting approaches. After considerable debate and continuing disagreements, the FASB chose in 1979 an experimental approach that is embodied in *SFAS 33,* "Financial Reporting and Changing Prices." The provisions of this *Statement,* which superseded the SEC disclosure requirements, are discussed later in this chapter.

Accounting and reporting alternatives

For hundreds of years, accounting has evolved around the concept of historical costs and measurements in terms of money whatever the purchasing power of that money was. In spite of their complexity, accounting presentations enjoyed a degree of acceptance and were understood by informed users. The accelerating erosion of the value of the currency has caused financial statements based on that framework to become less and less relevant to users of financial statements. Now that a departure from the comfort and the familiarity of present conventions appears inevitable, the debate among theorists concerns the best means of reflecting the effects of price changes and general price-level changes on financial statements.

TWO SCHOOLS OF THOUGHT

Let us examine the problem of accounting when prices change by using a simplified example that ignores taxes. A fuel dealer needs an inventory of 100,000 gallons of oil in order to conduct business. The present inventory of fuel was bought on January 1, 19x1, at $1 per gallon when the general price-level index (GPI) stood at 100. On March 1, 19x1, the dealer sold 10,000 gallons for $2 per gallon, at which time the oil would cost $1.50 per gallon to replace and the GPI was 110.

On an average basis, our conventional accounting model would show a profit of $10,000 on the sale (sales of $20,000 minus cost of sales $10,000), and most observers would agree that this accounting does not fully reflect reality. But there is disagreement on how to account for this transaction.

The financial capital maintenance concept

While most observers agree that income is earned only after a provision is made to keep capital intact, there is disagreement on the nature of that capital. Those who claim that investors are concerned with maintaining the general purchasing power of their invested capital adhere to the financial capital concept. Under this concept, the $10,000 cost of 10,000 gallons of oil on January 1, 19x1, is equivalent to $11,000 ($10,000 × 110/100) in constant dollars on March 1, 19x1. That is, since the *general* price level increased by 10 percent, it would take, on average, 10 percent more dollars or $11,000 to buy the same goods and services that cost $10,000 on January 1, 19x1. Since the receipts for the sale of oil are in March 1, 19x1, dollars, we must measure the cost in the same, or constant, dollars, i.e., $11,000. Under this concept, a charge of $11,000 as cost of oil sold will recover the financial capital invested in the 10,000 gallons sold and will result in a profit of $9,000 (i.e., sales of $20,000 less cost of $11,000). This accounting for profit is designed to prevent the distribution of the purchasing power residing in the financial capital of the enterprise.

The physical capital maintenance concept

Adherents to this concept claim that an enterprise cannot be said to earn income unless it has first provided for the maintenance of existing operating capability. In terms of our example, this means that the cost of sales of the 10,000 gallons of oil is computed as $15,000 (10,000 gallons × $1.50 current cost at time of sale) and that the profit is $5,000 ($20,000 − $15,000 cost). Any distribution of profit in excess of $5,000 would prevent the fuel dealer from fully replenishing the 10,000 gallons of oil sold and thus to carry the 100,000-gallon inventory of oil needed to conduct business.

TWO ACCOUNTING MODELS

The two schools of thought about the nature of capital as well as other considerations have given rise to two main models of accounting:

Constant-dollar (or general price-level) accounting (CDA) is advocated by those who want to deal with the effects of the decline in the purchasing power of the currency and who prefer the financial concept of capital.

Current-cost accounting (CCA) is advocated by those who want to focus on changes in specific prices affecting a firm's operations and who are concerned with the maintenance of the physical capital of the enterprise.

While constant-dollar accounting focuses on the *measuring unit,* current-cost accounting focuses on the *attribute being measured.* Consequently, though they are often discussed as alternative methods, they cannot truly be so regarded. Constant-dollar accounting retains the historical accounting model but changes the unit of measurement to a constant dollar. Current-cost accounting changes the historical accounting model because, it is felt, it does not deal satisfactorily with the problem of price changes.

Reflecting its inability to decide which model is better in dealing with financial reporting and price changes, the FASB, in *SFAS 33,* included both in its experimental approach. We first examine the methodology used under these two models in the comprehensive restatement or adjustment of financial statements. We subsequently examine the specific FASB reporting requirements.

FOUR REPORTING FRAMEWORKS

In our subsequent discussions, we refer to four reporting frameworks as follows:

Historical cost/nominal dollars (HC/ND)—the framework under which the conventional primary financial statements are now prepared.

Historical cost/constant dollars (HC/CD)—financial statements restated for general price-level changes and expressed in a constant dollar of a given date.

Current cost/nominal dollars (CC/ND)—financial statements restated for specific price changes.

Current cost/constant dollars (CC/CD)—financial statements restated for both specific and general price-level changes.

CONSTANT-DOLLAR ACCOUNTING (CDA)

A basic problem with HC/ND financial statements as presently prepared is that they include dollar amounts that represent a variety of purchasing power units. Thus, due to the decline in the purchasing power of the dollar, $100,000 spent on a plant in 1970 represents a far greater sacrifice in purchasing power than does $100,000 spent on a plant bought in 1983. Yet HC/ND financial statements do not recognize that difference and would, in fact, add up the dollar costs of the two assets even though they are not expressed in terms of a common unit of measure.

The basic purpose of financial statements restated for general price-level changes (HC/CD financial statements) is to present all elements of the financial statements in terms of units of the same general purchasing power restated by means of a general price-level index. General price-level financial statements differ from historical-dollar financial statements only in the unit of measure used in them. Consequently, they do not depart from the historical-cost principle. Moreover, they are subject to the same accounting standards as are used in the preparation of HC/ND financial statements with the exception that gains or losses in the purchasing power of the dollar are recognized in HC/CD statements.

A general price-level index measures the price behavior of a group or "basket" of representative items. While there are a number of indexes that measure general purchasing power, we will use here a widely used index selected for *SFAS 33*, i.e., the Consumer Price Index for All Urban Consumers (CPI-U).

The restatement of financial statements by the HC/CD basis requires a distinction between monetary and nonmonetary items.

Monetary items represent claims to fixed numbers of dollars such as cash, accounts and notes receivable, and investments in bonds, or those representing obligations to pay fixed numbers of dollars such as accounts and notes payable and bonds payable. *SFAS 33* classifies deferred taxes as monetary.

Conversely, *nonmonetary items* are those that represent claims other than to a fixed number of dollars, such as inventory, property plant and equipment, common stock, and equity accounts such as capital stock and retained earnings. If an item does not qualify as monetary, it is nonmonetary, as for example prepaid expenses, which represent claims to future services.

RESTATEMENT PROCEDURE

Monetary items, representing the general purchasing power of dollars at any given point in time, require no restatement. Because monetary items represent a claim or an obligation of a fixed number of dollars rather than a given amount of purchasing power, they give rise to purchasing power gains and losses. Thus, holding monetary assets in times of inflation results in a *loss* of purchasing power while owing monetary liabilities results in a gain of purchasing power. Because nonmonetary items do not represent a fixed number of dollars, they must be restated. Thus, if a piece of land is bought on January 1, 19x2, for $10,000, when the index was 100, it will be converted (restated) to December 31, 19x2, dollars (when the index is 120) by multiplying the January 1, 19x2, cost of $10,000 by a conversion factor expressed as

$$\frac{\text{Index at measurement date}}{\text{Index at date of acquisition}} : \frac{120}{100}, \text{ or } \$12,000$$

The $12,000 expresses the 10,000 January 1, 19x2, dollar acquisition in terms of December 31, 19x2, dollars. Put another way, when the inflation rate is 20 percent, it takes 20 percent more dollars to have the same amount of general purchasing power as is residing in this piece of land.

SIMPLE ILLUSTRATION 1. On January 1, 19x3, when the index was 100, Fred Inactive had assets and equities as follows. No transactions took place until December 31, 19x3, when the index was 110.

	January 1, 19x3, dollars	Restatement ratio	Purchasing power gain (loss)	In December 31, 19x3, c $ *
Monetary assets	$1,000	None—but holding results in	(100)	$1,000
Inventories	2,000	110/100		2,200
Land	4,000	110/100		4,400
	$7,000			$7,600
Liabilities (monetary)	$2,000	None—but owing results in	200	$2,000
Capital	5,000	110/100		5,500
Net general purchasing power gain		....	100	100
	$7,000			$7,600

* c $ signifies constant dollar of a particular date.

The loss on monetary assets (e.g., cash, receivables) is computed by taking what these assets would have been stated as had they maintained their purchasing power, i.e., $1,000 × 110/100 = $1,100 and comparing it with their actual purchasing power on December 31, 19x3, i.e., $1,000. Similarly, the monetary liabilities (e.g., payables, short- and long-term debt) cause a gain because had the purchasing power inherent in the obligation been maintained, it would have amounted to $2,000 × 110/100 or $2,200 on December 31, 19x3, while, in fact, it is only $2,000 on that date. The net monetary gain is added to capital as part of retained earnings. The restatement of the nonmonetary items completes the conversion and remeasures all items in terms of December 31, 19x3, dollars.

Extended illustration of CDA

The conventional (HC/ND) financial statements of Inflato Company, shown in Exhibits 14–1 and 14–2 are restated into financial statements expressed in terms of December 31, 19x6, dollars.

Exhibit 14–1

INFLATO COMPANY

Income Statement

For Year Ended December 31, 19x6

(In thousands)

Sales		$200,000
Beginning inventory	$ 20,000	
Purchases	110,000	
	130,000	
Less: Ending inventory	30,000	
Cost of goods sold		100,000
Gross profit..................		100,000
Depreciation expense	10,000	
Other operating expenses	40,000	50,000
Pretax income		50,000
Income tax expense		20,000
Net income		$ 30,000

Exhibit 14–2

INFLATO COMPANY

Balance Sheet

At December 31

Assets	*19x5*	*19x6*
Current assets:		
Cash	$ 5,000	$ 7,000
Accounts receivable.............................	15,000	20,000
Inventory	20,000	30,000
Total current assets	40,000	57,000
Equipment	100,000	100,000
Less: Accumulated depreciation	—	(10,000)
Total assets	$140,000	$147,000
Liabilities and Equity		
Current liabilities....................................	$ 10,000	$ 15,000
Long-term debt	40,000	22,000
Capital stock	60,000	60,000
Retained earnings	30,000	50,000
Total equity	90,000	110,000
Total liabilities and equity	$140,000	$147,000

Additional information:

1. The following CPI-U prevailed on the dates indicated:

January 1, 19x4 (date of issuance capital stock) 110

October 31, 19x4 (date of acquisition of December 31, 19x5,

inventory) 118

December 31, 19x5 (date of acquisition of equipment)   120
September 30, 19x6 (date of acquisition of December 31, 19x6,
    inventory)   127
Average for 19x6 (or midyear dollars)   125
December 31, 19x6   130

2. A dividend of $10,000 was paid in average of the year dollars.
3. The Retained Earnings balance at December 31, 19x5, expressed
   in December 31, 19x5, dollars was $24,884.*

    * In order to restate the Retained Earnings account (which is a composite of various elements)
into December 31, 19x6, dollars, it is necessary to know what the beginning balance (at December
31, 19x5) was expressed in constant dollars as of that date. This amount was obtained from a
restatement of the December 31, 19x5, balance sheet on a HC/CD basis.

    The first step in the preparation of HC/CD financial statements is to
compute the gain or loss on net monetary items which is demonstrated in
Exhibit 14–3:

Exhibit 14–3

INFLATO COMPANY
Computation of Gain or Loss on Net Monetary Items
For the Year Ended December 31, 19x6

	HC/ND	*Restatement ratio (RR)*	*HC/CD*
Net monetary items,* January 1, 19x6 . . .	$ (30,000)	130/120	c$ (32,500)†
+ Sales	200,000	130/125	208,000
	170,000		175,500
Less: *Items reducing monetary items*			
Purchases	110,000	130/125	114,400
Operating expenses (excluding deprecia-tion)	40,000	130/125	41,600
Income tax expense	20,000	130/125	20,800
Dividends paid	10,000	130/125	10,400
	180,000		187,200
Net monetary items,* December 31, 19x6, in ND	(10,000)		
Net monetary items, December 31, 19x6, in CD	(11,700)		(11,700)
Gain (loss) on net monetary items	$ 1,700		

Net monetary items Dr. (Cr.)	*January 1, 19x6*	*December 31, 19x6*
Cash	$ 5,000	$ 7,000
Accounts receivable	15,000	20,000
Current liabilities	(10,000)	(15,000)
Long-term debt	(40,000)	(22,000)
Net monetary liabilities	$(30,000)	$(10,000)

    † c$ signifies constant dollar of a particular date.

This is, in essence, a statement of sources and uses of monetary items, and as a first step, we must determine that on a HC/ND basis the statement explains the change in net monetary items from beginning balance to ending balance. The next step is to restate each item from its date of origination to the date of remeasurement which is the end of the period. For convenience, income statement items that are related to monetary items (e.g. sales are related to cash or accounts receivable) are assumed to occur evenly throughout the period, and hence the origination of the item is identified with the average index for the period.

The restated net monetary items at year-end (here net monetary liabilities) are compared with the HC/ND net monetary items, and on this basis the gain or loss is determined. Here, the HC/CD net monetary liability would be $11,700 had it maintained its general purchasing power, but since it did not, representing only c$10,000 at the end of the period, it yielded a gain on monetary items of $1,700. The explanation is that holding monetary liabilities in a period in which the price level rose (i.e., the value of money declined) results in purchasing power gains. Conversely, if Inflato Company would have held net monetary assets throughout this period, it would have incurred a purchasing power loss.

Having determined the gain or loss on net monetary items, we can now prepare the restated income statement shown in Exhibit 14–4.

Exhibit 14–4

INFLATO COMPANY
Restatement of Income Statement for 19x6 from HC/ND to HC/CD

	HC	ND	Restatement ratio	HC	CD
Sales		$200,000	A		c$208,000
Beginning inventory	$ 20,000		130/118	c$ 22,034	
+ Purchases	110,000		A	114,400	
	130,000			c$136,434	
Less: Ending inventory	30,000		130/127	30,709	
Cost of goods sold		100,000			105,725
Gross profit		100,000			102,275
Depreciation expense	10,000		130/120	c$10,833	
Other operating expenses	40,000		A	41,600	
		50,000			52,433
Pretax income		50,000			49,842
Income tax expense		20,000	A		20,800
Income before GPP gain (loss)		30,000			29,042
General purchasing power gain (Exhibit 14–3)		—			1,700
Net income		$ 30,000			c$ 30,742

A = Restated from average to yearend index: 130/125. Amounts from statement of gain or loss on net monetary items.

It should be noted that the amounts for income statement items to be restated from the average index for the period can be taken from Exhibit 14–3. The other items are related to nonmonetary items and are restated from the date they originated. Thus, the beginning inventory was acquired when the index was 118, and the equipment on which depreciation is computed was acquired when the index was 120.

Exhibit 14–5 presents the restatement of the HC/ND balance sheet of Inflato Company at December 31, 19x6, into HC/CD.

Exhibit 14–5

INFLATO COMPANY
Restatement of December 31, 19x6, Balance Sheet from HC/ND to HC/CD

Assets	HC/ND	Restatement ratio	HC/CD
Current assets:			
Cash	$ 7,000	M	c$ 7,000
Accounts receivable	20,000	M	20,000
Inventory	30,000	A	30,709
Total current assets	57,000		57,709
Equipment	100,000	130/120	108,333
Less: Accumulated depreciation	(10,000)	130/120	(10,833)
Total assets	$147,000		c$155,209

Liabilities and Equity			
Liabilities:			
Current liabilities	15,000	M	c$ 15,000
Long-term debt	22,000	M	22,000
Total liabilities	37,000		37,000
Equity:			
Capital stock	60,000	130/110	70,909
Retained earnings	50,000	B	47,300
Total equity	110,000		118,209
Total liabilities and equity	$147,000		c$155,209

M = Monetary items—no restatement.
A = From income statement.
B = Amount derived as follows:

Opening balance	$30,000	c$26,958*
Add: Net income..	30,000	30,742
	60,000	57,700
Less: Dividend paid	10,000	10,400
Ending balance	$50,000	c$47,300

* Retained earnings December 31, 19x5, c$24,884 × 130/120 = c$26,958. (To convert the opening retained earnings balance into December 31, 19x6, dollars.)

We now have a complete set of financial statements for Inflato Company for 19x6 on a HC/CD basis.

THE ROLL-FORWARD PROCEDURE

One of the important advantages claimed for HC/CD financial statements is that they are expressed in a uniform measuring yardstick—the constant dollar as of a given date. In order to validly compare two or more financial statements, it is necessary that they *all* be prepared in terms of constant dollars as of a given date. Thus, if we want to compare the December 31, 19x6, balance sheet of Inflato Company with that as of December 31, 19x5, we would first have to restate the December 31, 19x5, HC/CD balance sheet into one expressed in December 31, 19x6, dollars. This is accomplished by rolling forward the December 31, 19x5, balance sheet, i.e., multiplying *all* balance sheet items by the restatement ratio of 130/120. This procedure is illustrated in Appendix 14A.

CURRENT-COST ACCOUNTING (CCA)

Current-cost accounting (CCA), which in our present discussion uses the current cost/nominal dollar (CC/ND) framework, is advocated by those who believe that the more useful way to account for price changes is to depart from the historical-cost model. They argue that historical costs, even when restated for general price-level changes, are not fully relevant to decision making. Business enterprises are directly affected by *specific* price changes of the specific goods and services that they use rather than by general price-level changes. Consequently, specific price changes are the ones that are more useful to use in preparing financial statements.

There are a number of concepts of current cost (CC), but we shall use here the concept adopted by *SFAS 33*, which focuses on the current cost of replacing the service potential of specific existing assets[2] of a firm.

RESTATEMENT PROCEDURE

Assets such as cash or accounts receivable, as well as current liabilities, are usually stated at their cash equivalent value. The CC of investments can often be obtained from market quotations, while the CC of inventories and of plant and equipment can be obtained from price lists, standard manufacturing cost computations, or by use of specific price indexes. Debt may have to be adjusted to reflect current market rates of interest if they differ from those prevailing at the time the debt was issued.

---

[2] Other concepts of asset valuation include the current price at which assets could be sold also known as net realizable value or exit value and the present value of future cash flows, which equals the discounted net cash flows expected to be generated from an asset.

Revenues as well as most expenses (except cost of goods sold and depreciation) are likely to be stated at approximate current cost. Cost of goods sold must be restated to the current cost of goods at times of sale based on sources such as price lists or invoice prices. The computation of CC depreciation is subject to controversy, but the *SFAS 33* requirement is to measure as expense the CC of the service potential used up even when value changes in the remaining asset offset this expense.

Though some hold that the income tax provision should be based on pretax CC income, *SFAS 33* requires that it be recorded on the basis of pretax historical-cost income.

The concept of current cost income can be understood best through the following simple illustration:

SIMPLE ILLUSTRATION 2.   A holds for sale 10 widgets that were purchased at a cost of $20 each constituting a starting capital of $200. In a given week, three widgets are sold for $30 each and the inventory is replenished at a price of $25 each. As shown in Chapter 5, conventional accounting can provide three different profit figures for this transaction i.e., $30 under FIFO, $26.50 under average cost, and $15 under the LIFO assumption with the latter most closely approximating (but not necessarily equaling, as it does here by coincidence) current cost.

CCA departs from both historical cost and the concept of realization. Under the assumption that the units sold had a cost equal to the units that replaced[3] them, the operating profit of $15 is arrived at by deducting the current cost of sales $75 (3 × $25) from sales $90 (3 × $30), and this profit is represented by cash that can indeed be distributed without affecting the business's ability to carry its normal inventory of 10 widgets, i.e., 10 × $25 = $250. It is in fact, a basic principle of CCA that no profit should be reported as earned until the replacement of inventory (or of productive capacity) has been provided for. In addition, the increment in the current cost of the original seven widgets still in inventory $35 (7 × $5) is recognized as an unrealized holding gain. There is also a cost saving[4] or realized holding gain of $15 by having bought the three widgets that were sold at a cost of $20 each instead of the $25 current cost. Adding the $50 total holding gain to operating profit of $15, we get a net income of $65 (assuming no other expenses), and this separate classification of results is one of the advantages of CCA. A's CCA balance sheet is now as follows:

Cash	$ 15	Owner's equity at beginning	$200
Inventory (10 × $25)	250	Operating profit	15
		Holding gains:	
		Realized $15	
		Unrealized 35	50
	$265		$265

---

[3] Just as under historical-cost accounting we assume the flow of inventory, under current cost, we conveniently assume that sales occur on inventory purchase dates.

[4] This term appears in Edwards and Bell, *The Theory and Measurement of Business Income* (Berkeley: University of California Press, 1961), a seminal work in this area.

The income statement could have these captions:

Sales (3 × $30)	$90.00
Cost of sales (3 × $25)	75.00
Sustainable income*	15.00
Realized holding gains	15.00
Realized income† (equals conventional net income)	30.00
Unrealized holding gains	35.00
Net income	$65.00

* Income that would enable entity to sustain present level of operations were price changes to stop.
† Sustainable income plus realized holding gains (income realized in transactions with outsiders).
These concepts and terms were introduced by S. Davidson and R. L. Weil in "Inflation Accounting," *Financial Analysts Journal*, March–April 1976, pp. 57–66.

The illustration reflects two additional matters. One is that unlike CDA, CCA, in comparison with historical cost, changes only the *timing* but not the amount of the total profit recognized. Thus, when the 10 widgets are finally sold, the profit under both historical and CCA bases will be identical but the timing will not be, because under CCA we recognize both current costs and holding gains. The other is that some accountants believe that unrealized holding gains do not belong in income and should instead bypass it and be shown directly in stockholders' equity. In the extended illustration below, we include unrealized holding gains in net income and show cumulative unrealized holding gains or losses not as part of retained earnings but as a separate component of stockholders' equity.

Extended illustration of CCA

Restatement of the conventional (HC/ND) financial statements of Inflato Company, shown in Exhibits 14–1 and 14–2 above, into CC/ND financial statements is now illustrated. The following additional information is provided for the illustration.

Current cost estimates provided by management are:

	19x5	19x6
At December 31:		
Inventory	$ 22,000	$ 35,000
Equipment (gross)	100,000	120,000
For year ended December 31:		
Depreciation expense		12,000
Cost of goods sold		110,000

Exhibit 14–6 presents the worksheet that adjusts the HC/ND financial statements of Inflato Company to CC/ND financial statements.

Exhibit 14–6

INFLATO COMPANY
Worksheet to Restate the 19x6 HC/ND Financial Statements to the CC/ND Basis

	HC/ND $	HC/ND $	Adjustments Dr. $	Adjustments Cr. $	CC/ND $	CC/ND $
Income Statement for 19x6						
Sales		200,000				200,000
Cost of goods sold	100,000		(1) 10,000		110,000	
Depreciation expense	10,000		(2) 2,000		12,000	
Other expense (including taxes)	60,000	170,000			60,000	182,000
Current operating income						18,000
Realized holding gains:						
On goods sold				(1) 10,000	10,000	
On equipment used up				(2) 2,000	2,000	
Total						12,000
Realized income		30,000				30,000
Unrealized holding gains:						
On ending inventory			(3A) 2,000	(3) 5,000	3,000	
On ending equipment, net			(4A) 2,000	(4) 20,000	18,000	
Total						21,000
Net income						51,000

Balance Sheet at December 31, 19x6

Current assets:								
Cash	7,000						7,000	
Accounts receivable	20,000						20,000	
Inventory	30,000		(3)	5,000			35,000	
Total current assets		57,000						62,000
Equipment	100,000		(4)	20,000			120,000	
Less: Accumulated depreciation	10,000				(4A) 2,000		12,000	
Equipment, net		90,000						108,000
Total assets		147,000						170,000
Liabilities:								
Current liabilities	15,000						15,000	
Long-term debt	22,000						22,000	
Total liabilities		37,000						37,000
Capital stock		60,000						60,000
Retained Earnings: January 1, 19x6	30,000						30,000	
+ (Realized) income for year	30,000						30,000	
− Dividends paid December 31, 19x6	(10,000)						(10,000)	
		50,000						50,000
Unrealized holding gains:								
Balance, January 1, 19x6					(3A) 2,000		2,000	
Accrued for year							21,000	
Balance, December 31, 19x6								23,000
Total equity		110,000						133,000
Total liabilities and equity		147,000						170,000

The following are explanations of the keyed-in adjustment entries in Exhibit 14–6:

1. To adjust cost of goods sold to a current cost basis with credit going to realized holding gains (realized because goods were sold to outsiders) that are shown as a separate segment of income.

2. To adjust depreciation to a current-cost basis with credit going to realized holding gains on equipment used up (assumed to relate to production sold).

3. To adjust HC/ND inventory to current cost with credit going to the "unrealized holding gains" segment of the income statement.

3A. This important adjustment, usually the first to be made on the worksheet, should be thoroughly understood. Note that entry (3) above results in the entire difference between HC and CC inventory being credited to this year's unrealized gains. However, comparison of the December 31, 19x5, inventory of $20,000 (Exhibit 14–2) with current-cost data of the inventory provided as of the same date ($22,000) reveals that $2,000 of unrealized holding gains existed already at the end of 19x5. Thus, this entry debits unrealized holding gains with $2,000 and credits the *opening* balance of unrealized holding gains in the equity section. This prevents the double counting of the unrealized holding gains and establishes the proper unrealized holding gain on inventory for 19x6 (i.e., total unrealized holding gain $5,000 less attributable to prior years $2,000 = $3,000 attributable to 19x6). Examination of the data reveals that there was no unrealized holding gain or loss on equipment at December 31, 19x5.

4. To adjust HC/ND equipment to current cost with credit going to the "unrealized holding gains" segment of the income statement.

4A. This adjustment, adjusting the HC/ND accumulated depreciation to its CC/ND equivalent, is the reverse of entry (4) in that it results in a reduction of unrealized holding gains for 19x6.

Note that unrealized holding gains are shown separately in the equity section and are not combined with retained earnings.

The CC/ND column of the worksheet serves as the basis for preparing formal CC financial statements that are not illustrated here.

DISCLOSURE REQUIREMENTS OF *SFAS 33*

As we discussed earlier, the FASB, recognizing that each of the two frameworks discussed above, CDA and CCA, provides different kinds of information about price-level changes, decided to require, on an experimental basis, certain supplementary information from large companies[5] about the effects of changing prices. *SFAS 33* encourages but does not require the presentation

---

[5] Those whose total assets (net of accumulated depreciation) exceed $1 billion or those whose inventory and properties (before accumulated depreciation) exceed $125 million.

of a comprehensive set of financial statements based on the constant-dollar and current-cost frameworks as illustrated above. The minimum disclosure requirements of *SFAS 33* are illustrated in Appendix 14B and are based on the data of Inflato Company (Exhibits 14–1 through 14–6).

SFAS 70, "Financial Reporting and Changing Prices: Foreign Currency Translation," determined that an enterprise that measures a signficant part of its operations in functional currencies other than the U.S. dollar is exempted from *SFAS 33* requirements to present historical-cost information measured in units of constant purchasing power.

IMPLICATIONS FOR ANALYSIS

As can be seen from a review of this work, the accounting framework is a measurement system of considerable complexity. If we superimpose on this the problem of an unstable measurement unit (money), this complexity is compounded to a considerable degree. And yet, the greater the rate of price-level changes, the more necessary it becomes for the analyst to comprehend the factors that affect changes in financial statements and the manner in which such changes occur in real terms.

Price changes have many causes including changes in technology, product quality, or circumstances. Thus, even without changes in the purchasing power of money, accounting for historical costs only would not be fully relevant. However, the unquestionably major problem is purchasing power changes, or specifically *inflation.*

Earlier in the chapter we examined two major schools of thought on how accounting should deal with and reflect the effect of price changes. It is clear that the concerns that *both* constant-dollar accounting (CDA) and current-cost accounting (CCA) address and the objectives that they seek have considerable validity. That is reflected in the fact that the FASB has been, so far, unable to choose one model over the other with the result that the analyst in this country is presently faced with sketchy and partial disclosures which, depending on how they are used, can result in a variety of adjusted net income amounts. Thus, unless an enterprise chooses to report comprehensively restated financial statements on a basis with which the analyst happens to agree, he or she has no choice but to do his or her own adjusting or restating. To aid in this process, we now discuss the considerations entering into the use of CDA or CCA or possibly combinations of parts of both models.

ANALYTICAL CONSIDERATIONS IN THE USE
OF CONSTANT-DOLLAR ACCOUNTING

There are a few basic facts about the effect of price-level changes on the conventional financial statements that must be thoroughly understood. One is that money, whether expressed in dollars or any other currency, is worth only what it will buy. Thus, if the price level changes, the value of money changes along with it; and hence a dollar received or spent in one period may not be comparable with that received or spent in another period, the distortion being in proportion to the cumulative change in the general price level. It is part of the "money illusion" to consider a dollar a dollar and to forget the obvious fact that the 1983 dollar represents a much smaller unit of general purchasing power than did, say, the 1965 dollar.

In times of changing prices, the income statement, to single out one of the important measures of corporate performance, is composed of at least two distinct elements: (1) results of business activities expressed in terms of units of equal purchasing power and (2) changes resulting from price-level changes. An intelligent assessment and analysis of these results require a separation and an understanding of these two disparate effects.

ILLUSTRATION 3. In times of significant inflation, a small-loan company whose assets are mostly monetary must charge a rate of interest that will compensate it not only for the use of its funds but also for the loss of purchasing power of the funds lent. Thus, the proper interpretation of its interest income, which by conventional standards may seem unduly large, must include recognition of the offsetting general price level loss incurred on monetary assets.

A major objective of financial statements expressed in CD is thus to present them in terms of uniform units of purchasing power rather than in terms of units of money that distort interperiod and intercompany comparisons.

GENERAL VERSUS SPECIFIC PRICE CHANGES

A major objection to CDA is that it focuses on *general* price-level changes rather than on changes in the prices of the *specific* goods and services in which a given enterprise deals. Thus, for example, when prices of petroleum products skyrocketed, adjustment by a general price-level index failed by far to reflect the price increase in these specific commodities. Conversely, prices of small calculators experienced cost and price declines in recent years, and the restatement by a general price index of financial statement of companies in this field may lead to a distortion of real effects and trends.

Opponents of CDA object also to the abstract nature of the unit of measure. They claim that business is transacted with money, not with bundles of purchasing power. Moreover, they claim that statements expressed in CD are not useful in the prediction of cash flows, which is a central function of accounting.

Monetary gains and losses

A highly controversial product of CDA is monetary gains and losses. In theory, monetary losses represent the loss of holding on to items representing claims to a depreciating currency. Conversely, monetary gains represent the reduced economic significance of repayments of obligations in depreciating currency. Carried to an extreme, the example of the debtor in the Germany of 1923 can be cited. His obligation dwindled to nothing when the purchasing power of the mark virtually disappeared.[6]

One reason these gains and losses are poorly understood is that they produce no parallel cash inflows or outflows. Moreover, there is no identifiable change in accounts as a result of a change in the purchasing power of assets and liabilities. These gains and losses are basically arrived at by means of a retrospective calculation.

A further objection is that the advantage of borrowing differs from company to company depending on how profitably the assets acquired with debt are employed. Moreover, the largest monetary gains are likely to be shown by highly leveraged companies which may be near insolvency. Thus, the need for concurrent funds flow analysis is critical.

Any evaluation of purchasing power gains and losses requires an understanding of their relation to interest expense. The interest rate charged by lenders and agreed to by borrowers reflects their expectations of future inflation. Both recognize that the higher the expected inflation the higher the nominal interest rate must be to compensate the lender for being paid back in progressively "cheaper" dollars. Thus, the borrower's interest expense should be offset by the purchasing power gains recorded on the monetary liabilities.

ILLUSTRATION 4. In its commentary on its 1980 information reflecting the effects of inflation, McDonald's Corporation stated that "the effect of inflation on property and equipment is inseparable from its effect on debt used to finance such assets. The purchasing power gain on the debt is an economic benefit to the company since, with inflation, the debt is paid back in cheaper dollars. Accordingly, we believe that this gain should be viewed as an adjustment to interest and therefore have included it in arriving at constant dollar net income." Interestingly, in its comprehensively restated 1980 HC/CD financial statements, the company shows interest expense as c$95 million and at the same time credits income with c$146 million in "purchasing power gains on net amounts owed." As a result, reported HC/CD net income is considerably higher than its HC/ND counterpart.

Effects of inflation

Inflation acts as a tax on cash balances. It causes losses on monetary assets, gains on monetary liabilities, and significant changes in the values (expressed in terms of money) of other assets as well as changes in funds flows, the demand for funds, and in the uncertainties and risks affecting with differing impacts business enterprises of various kinds. In the words of Professor John Lintner, ". . . higher inflation rates would increase a firm's

---

[6] See P. Rosenfield, "A History of Inflation Accounting," *Journal of Accountancy,* September 1981, p. 108.

relative dependence on external funds *even if* there were no phantom inventory profits and depreciation could be charged on replacement costs and there were no added needs due to backups of unsold inventories, increased sales on credit, or delays in collections or credit losses, and so on. Any adverse change in any of these conditions of course merely compounds the adverse effects of increased inflation rates."[7]

The effect of price-level changes on an entity's financial statements depends on both the rate of price-level changes and the composition of assets, liabilities, and equities. Empirical studies have shown that inflation can cause very significant changes in reported operating and financial results.[8]

The composition of assets, liabilities, and equities is an important determinant of the effect of price-level changes on an entity and on its financial statements.

The following are some useful generalizations regarding such effects in times of significant inflation:

1. The larger the proportion of depreciable assets and the higher their age, the more unrestated income tends to be overstated. Thus, the income of capital intensive companies tends to be affected more than that of others by price-level restatements. Accelerated depreciation reduces this effect.

2. The rate of inventory turnover has a bearing on price-level effects. The slower the inventory turnover, the more operating income tends to be overstated, unless the LIFO method is used.

3. The mix of assets and liabilities as between monetary and nonmonetary is important. A net investment in monetary assets will, in times of rising price levels, lead to purchasing power losses, and purchasing power gains will result from a net monetary liability position.

4. The methods of financing also have an important bearing on results. The larger the amount of debt, at fixed and favorable rates relative to the inflation rate, and the longer its maturities, the better is the protection against purchasing power losses or the better is the exposure to purchasing power gains.

ANALYTICAL CONSIDERATIONS IN THE USE
OF CURRENT COST ACCOUNTING

CCA overcomes the criticism that businesses experience specific price changes rather than general inflation. Under CCA, profits are reported only

---

[7] John Lintner, "Inflation and Security Returns," *The Journal of Finance,* May 1975, pp. 273–74.

[8] W. C. Norby reported in the *Financial Analysts Journal* of November–December 1981 that a study of *SFAS 33* disclosures for 1979 and 1980 showed that the "inflation adjustments reduced aggregate earnings from continuing operations by 60 percent on a current cost basis and by 53 percent on a constant dollar basis."

when the sales price exceeds the current cost of the item sold. Thus, physical capital maintenance is at the heart of this system. The excess of CC over HC is considered as holding gains. While both realized and unrealized holding gains are often considered part of net income, their exact treatment is controversial. Because profit determination under CCA more closely parallels management decision processes, it provides a more consistent basis for the evaluation of management's actions and performance. As the rate of inflation increases, the separation of operating income from holding gains becomes more important in terms of capital maintenance.

Distributable earnings measured on the basis of CCA provide a sound basis for the evaluation of dividend policy.[9]

CC balance sheets present a more realistic indication of the current economic value of assets and liabilities than do either HC/ND or HC/CD balance sheets. Lower CC earnings in conjunction with higher CC equity generally reduces the return on equity. However, the inclusion of unrealized holding gains in income will generally result in returns on equity exceeding those calculated on a HC basis.

A CCA system is a form of current value accounting. Opponents of CCA worry that it will lead to income recognition on a pre-realization basis. That is not necessarily so because while unrealized holding gains can be considered as income, they can instead be considered as capital maintenance adjustments.

A CCA system will be most effective in reflecting the effect of price changes on nonmonetary items; however, it will not deal with the erosion in value of monetary assets or the declining economic significance of liabilities.

Not surprisingly the greatest strengths of CDA are most often cited as the weaknesses of CCA and vice versa. Thus, CCA in ND fails to recognize that the unit of measure used to calculate CC is not uniform. Thus, comparability is impaired when CC amounts of one period are compared with those of another. Moreover, CCA fails to recognize the effects of inflation on monetary items in the form of monetary gains and losses.

EFFORTS TO INTEGRATE CDA WITH CCA

A careful evaluation of the perceived strengths and weaknesses of both CDA and CCA reveals that a combination of the best features of both methods should best satisfy the needs of decision makers. The two methods can be combined because CDA deals with the measuring unit while CCA deals with the attribute being measured. Thus, there is no conceptual obstacle.

The combination of accounting methods can be best understood by means of a simple illustration, presented in Appendix 14C, which uses the four reporting frameworks described earlier in the chapter.

Appendix 14C, while illustrating the feasibility of combining different re-

---

[9] The study reported on by W. C. Norby, *Financial Analysts Journal,* revealed that dividends in 1980 exceeded earnings on a CC basis thus resulting in a disinvestment rate of 2.4 percent.

porting frameworks also leads to the inescapable conclusion that the process of combination greatly increases the complexity of the presentations.

The search for methods by which CD measurements can be incorporated into the CCA framework has taken a number of forms. Norby[10] would deflate important key figures taken from CC/ND financial statements, such as sustainable earnings, economic earnings, dividends, and book value, by a general price index in order to enable the investor to judge how well he has been protected from the ravages of inflation. He recommends further analysis of the effect of a net monetary position by means of cash flow analysis. As part of such an analysis part of the cash provided by operations is allocated to the replacement of inventories and fixed assets.

Fraser, Inc., a Canadian pulp and paper manufacturer presents such an allocation of funds in its 1979 annual report:

Effects of Inflation

The impact of inflation on the financial strength of the Corporation continues to concern management and should be considered in evaluating the financial results for the year.

The statement below which incorporates three adjustments (inventories, property and plant, and financing) has been prepared using the proposals suggested by the Ontario Committee on Inflation Accounting. This method describes how funds generated from operations should be allocated to ensure the maintenance of productive capacity during inflation

		$'000
During the year funds generated from operations totalled (from statement of changes in financial position)		$53 694
From this should be deducted the funds required to finance original cost of productive assets (historical-cost depreciation and lease amortization)		12 220
		41 474
To take account of increased cost of maintaining operating capacity in our inflationary environment requires the following allocation of funds:		
To replace inventories	2 900	
For plant, machinery and equipment	7 800	
	10 700	
Less additional funds which may be available from borrowing if present debt-equity ratio is maintained	3 050	7 650
Funds hypothetically available from the year's operations for distribution or expansion.		$33 824

---

[10] W. C. Norby, "A Conceptual Framework for Inflation Accounting," *Financial Analysts Journal,* July–August 1979.

This statement indicates that Fraser has continued to maintain the viability of the business but not to the degree that historical accounting would indicate.

The funds generated from operations totalled $53,694,000 in 1979, an increase of 38% from 1978; however, after provision for capital maintenance costs, funds available in "real" terms were 37% lower in 1979.

In the above, the additional allocation for the replacement of inventories and property, plant, and equipment will generally correspond to the difference between the current and the historical costs of the cost of goods sold and depreciation expense. This indicates the analytical use that can be made of such information. The adjustment described as "additional funds which may be available from borrowing if the present debt-equity ratio is maintained" is akin to the British "gearing adjustment" which is described below.

A British inflation accounting standard known as current-cost accounting—*SSAP 16* adopted in 1980, after years of controversy[11]—opted for the CCA model with two adjustments designed to recognize monetary working capital and financing effects.

> *A monetary working capital adjustment* recognizes that in maintaining operating capability, maintenance of monetary working capital is just as important as the maintenance of fixed capital. Thus the added investment in receivables, reduced by payables and other specified current borrowings, is considered an extension of the cost of goods sold adjustment and is debited or credited to it as circumstances require.
>
> Furthermore a *gearing adjustment* is introduced which is concerned with the effect of financing in a period of price changes. If for example an entity finances 40% of its assets with debt then 40% of current cost adjustments (i.e. those induced by price changes) could theoretically be financed by issuing new debt thus preserving the company's debt to equity ratio. Hence only 60% of the burden of current cost adjustments need be borne by the stockholders with the 40% being the gearing adjustment which is offset against interest expense. The benefit to stockholders of the gearing adjustment is obtained at the expense of lenders. Thus, from the point of view of the entity as a whole reported income generated by the gearing adjustment cannot be distributed without reducing operating capability.

---

[11] The process by which this standard was arrived at provides a vivid illustration of the political nature of the standard setting process (see also discussion in Chapter 3). The auditing profession, favoring the point of view of proprietors and taking ease of auditing into consideration backed the financial concept of capital maintenance. Dissension among the auditors and a realization by the government that national issues of great significance were at stake led to the establishment of a governmental commission on the subject of inflation accounting. There, the emphasis of management on the entity rather than on the proprietary point of view, along with the government's concerns led to a result where the maintenance of operating capacity emerged as the prime objective of accounting for inflation.

The above discussion illustrates the alternative approaches advocated or taken in order to deal with the problem of reflecting the impact of inflation on financial statements and at the same time keeping the complexity of needed adjustments within reasonable bounds.

The analyst in this country, faced with multiple presentations which, in most cases, do not result in "bottom-line" numbers must base his or her conclusions[12] on computations which take the above discussed considerations into account.

APPENDIX 14A

THE ROLL-FORWARD PROCEDURE

The HC/ND balance sheet of Inflato Company is shown in Exhibit 14–2 of this chapter. Exhibit 14A–1 presents the restatement of this balance sheet to a HC/CD basis stated in terms of December 31, 19x5, dollars. As a second step, this balance sheet is rolled forward so that it is expressed in terms of December 31, 19x6, dollars. It should be noted that unlike the restatement procedure, the roll-forward procedure applies a *uniform* restatement ratio

$$\frac{\text{Index at measurement date}}{\text{Index at financial statement date}} \left(\frac{130}{120}\right)$$

to *all* balance sheet items, monetary as well as nonmonetary. The resulting December 31, 19x5, balance sheet, now expressed in December 31, 19x6, dollars can be compared directly to the December 31, 19x6, HC/CD balance sheet shown on Exhibit 14–5.

---

[12] The SEC's mandated discussion of inflation effects as part of "Management's discussion and analysis of financial condition and results of operations" should also be helpful.

Exhibit 14A–1

INFLATO COMPANY

Restatement of HC/ND Balance Sheet at December 31, 19x5, to HC/CD Basis and
Roll Forward of Balance Sheet to Restate to December 31, 19x6, Dollars

	HC/ND	RR	HC/CD	Roll-forward ratio	In December 31, 19x6 CD
Assets					
Current assets:					
Cash	$ 5,000	M	c$ 5,000	130/120	c$ 5,416
Accounts receivable	15,000	M	15,000	130/120	16,250
Inventory	20,000	120/118	20,339	130/120	22,034
Total current assets	40,000		40,339	130/120	43,700
Equipment	100,000	120/120	100,000	130/120	108,333
Less: Accumulated depreciation	—		—		—
Total assets	$140,000		c$140,339	130/120	c$152,033
Liabilities and Equity					
Liabilities:					
Current liabilities	$ 10,000	M	c$ 10,000	130/120	c$ 10,833
Long-term debt	40,000	M	40,000	130/120	43,333
Total liabilities	50,000		50,000	130/120	54,166
Equity:					
Capital stock	60,000	120/110	65,455	130/120	70,909
Retained earnings	30,000	A	24,884	130/120	26,958
Total Equity	90,000		90,339	130/120	97,867
Total liabilities and equity	$140,000		c$140,339	130/120	c$152,033

M = Monetary items—need no restatement.
A = Given.

APPENDIX 14B

ILLUSTRATION OF THE MINIMUM DISCLOSURE
REQUIREMENTS OF *SFAS 33*

The illustration in Exhibit 14B–1 below is based on the various financial statements of Inflato Company, presented in Exhibit 14–1 through 14–6 of this chapter. These required supplementary disclosures are expressed in terms of average (midyear) current year dollars.[1] The advantage that led the FASB to require the use of this otherwise awkward measurement date is that most income statement items expressed in ND are already stated in terms of average-of-year purchasing power. Cost of goods sold and depreciation are the most important exceptions. Thus, use of the average or midyear measurement date saves many computations. The derivation of items that are not taken directly from the basic or restated financial statements of Inflato Company presented in the chapter is separately explained in footnotes to Exhibit 14B–1.

Exhibit 14B–1

INFLATO COMPANY
Statement of Income from Continuing Operations
Adjusted for Changing Prices
For Year Ended December 31, 19x6
(in average 19x6 dollars)

	As reported in primary statements	Adjusted for general inflation (CD)	Adjusted for changes in specific prices (CC)
Sales	$200,000	c$200,000	$200,000
Cost of goods sold	100,000	101,658 (A)	110,000 (B)
Depreciation expense	10,000	10,417 (C)	11,000 (D)
Other operating expenses	40,000	40,000	40,000
Income tax expense	20,000	20,000	20,000
	170,000	172,075	181,000
Income (loss) from continuing operations	$ 30,000	c$ 27,925	$ 19,000
Gain (loss) from decline in purchasing power of net amount owed		1,635 (E)	1,635 (E)

---

[1] As an alternative, companies may present comprehensively restated financial statements, as illustrated in this chapter, and use midyear or end-of-year dollars.

Exhibit 14B–1 *(continued)*

	As reported in primary statements	Adjusted for general inflation (CD)	Adjusted for changes in specific prices (CC)
Increase in specific prices (CC) of inventory and PPE held during the year* (F)			32,000
Effect of increase in general price level (F)			10,584
Excess of increase in specific prices over increase in general price level (F)			$ 21,416

* At December 31, 19x6, current cost of inventory was $35,000; and current cost of property, plant, and equipment, net of accumulated depreciation, was $108,000.

A. Cost of goods on HC/CD basis using *average* 19x6 dollars is computed as follows:

	HC/ND	RR	HC/CD
Beginning inventory	$ 20,000	125/118	$ 21,186
Purchases	110,000	*	110,000
	130,000		131,186
-Ending inventory	30,000	125/127†	29,528
Cost of goods sold	$100,000		$101,658

* Assumed to be in average 19x6 dollars.
 † The ending inventory was acquired on September 30, 19x6, when the index was 127. The restatement is to midyear dollars.

B. Given and assumed to be in average 19x6 dollars.

C. HC/CD depreciation expense for 19x6 in average 19x6 dollars is computed as follows:

$$\$10,000 \times \frac{125}{120} = \$10,417$$

D. CC depreciation expense in average 19x6 dollars is computed as follows:

Average CC of equipment × Depreciation rate
$$= [(100,000 + 120,000) \div 2] \times 10\% = \$11,000$$

E. Gain (loss) from decline in purchasing power of net amounts owed using average 19x6 dollars is computed as follows:

	Nominal dollars	RR	Average 19x6 dollars
Net monetary obligations, January 1, 19x6	$ 30,000	125/120	$31,250
Decrease in monetary obligations during the year	(20,000)	*	(20,000)
Net monetary obligations restated to average dollars			11,250
Net monetary obligations, December 31, 19x6	10,000	125/130	9,615
Gain (loss) from decline in GPP† of amounts owed			$ 1,635

* Assumed to be in average 19x6 dollars.
 † General purchasing power.

F. Increase in specific prices (CC) and related inflation component for inventory and equipment are computed as follows in average 19x6 dollars:

Exhibit 14B–1 (*concluded*)

	CC/ND	RR	CC average 19x6 dollars
Increase in CC of inventory			
Inventory balance January 1, 19x6	$ 22,000	125/120	c$ 22,917
Purchases during 19x6†	110,000	*	110,000
Cost of goods sold†	(110,000)	*	(110,000)
Inventory balance December 31, 19x6	(35,000)	125/130	(33,654)
(Increase) decrease in CC of inventory	$ (13,000)		c$ (10,737)

Inflation component of increase
  in CC of inventory = $13,000 − $10,737 = $2,263

Increase in CC of equipment, net			
Balance of net equipment, January 1, 19x6	$ 100,000	125/120	c$ 104,167
Depreciation expense for 19x6	(11,000)	*	(11,000)
Balance of net equipment December 31, 19x6	(108,000)	125/130	(103,846)
(Increase) decrease in CC of equipment	$ (19,000)		c$ (10,679)

Inflation component of increase
  in CC of equipment = $19,000 − $10,679 = $8,321

Summary	Increase in current cost	Inflation component	Increase in CC net of inflation components
Inventory	$13,000	$ 2,263	$10,737
Equipment	19,000	8,321	10,679
Totals	$32,000‡	$10,584‡	$21,416‡

* Assumed to be in average 19x6 dollars.
† Purchases and cost of goods sold are equal only by coincidence.
‡ Amounts disclosed in Exhibit 14B–1.

Further comments on Exhibit 14B–1

Sales and expenses related to monetary items are the same in all three columns because they are assumed to be stated in average 19x6 dollars.

Disclosure of the "effect of increase in general price level," also known as "the inflation component," requires an explanation.

In times of price-level changes (here inflation), current-cost measurements of an asset made at different times are not comparable in terms of the purchasing power of the dollar. For this reason, the FASB requires that unrealized (or realizable) holding gains or what are called "increases in specific prices (current cost)" be reported "both before and after eliminating the effects of general inflation."

The inflation component of the increase in current costs is that portion of this increase which is nullified by contemporary inflation. Note F to Exhibit 14B–1 computes the increases in current cost and the inflation components as follows:

The increase for 19x6 in the CC of inventory expressed in ND was
   (this embraces all effects including that of inflation) $13,000

The increase for 19x6 in the CC of inventory expressed in CD
(measured in average 19x6 dollars), i.e., without
reflecting the effect of inflation was 10,737

$ 2,263

Consequently, the difference between the two amounts is the
amount of the increase due to inflation, that is, the price-
level change for the year—also known as the *inflation
component.*

To keep pace with inflation, the current cost of inventory would have
had to increase in nominal dollars by $2,263. Thus, if the current cost of
inventory had increased by $2,263 during the year, then the general purchasing
power invested in inventory would be the same at the end of the period as
at the beginning. Since the current cost of inventory actually increased by
$13,000 during the year, the general purchasing power invested in the inven-
tory had increased by $10,737 ($13,000 − $2,263). This $10,737 amount is
sometimes referred to as the *real portion* of the increase in current costs
(or holding gain). The inflation component is sometimes called the *fictional
portion* of the holding gain.

A similar reasoning applies to the analysis of the change
(i.e., *increase*) in the current cost of equipment which
in ND increased by $19,000
While in CD it actually increased only by 10,679

Thus, making the *increase* due to inflation—or the
inflation component .... $ 8,321

The internal consistency of the amounts presented in the last two columns
of Exhibit 14B–1 can be proved by reconciling the stockholders equity (net
assets) as of December 31, 19x6, of the two presentations as follows:

	HC/CD[(a)]	CC/CD[(a)]
Equity at January 1, 19x6:		
Inventory	c$ 21,186 [(b)]	c$ 22,917 [(c)]
Equipment, net	104,167 [(c)]	104,167 [(c)]
Net monetary items	(31,250) [(d)]	(31,250) [(d)]
Balance at January 1, 19x6	94,103	95,834
Income (loss) from continuing operations	27,925 [(e)]	19,000 [(e)]
Purchasing power gains	1,635 [(d)]	1,635 [(d)]
Excess of increase in specific prices over increase in general price level	—	21,416 [(c)]
Dividends paid	(10,000) [(g)]	(10,000) [(g)]
Equity at December 31, 19x6	c$113,663	c$127,885

Equity at December 31, 19x6, represented by:

Inventory	c\$ 29,528 [b]	c\$ 33,654 [c]
Equipment, net	93,750 [f]	103,846 [c]
Net monetary items	(9,615) [d]	(9,615) [d]
Balance at December 31, 19x6	c\$113,663	c\$127,885

[a] In average 19x6 dollars.
[b] See Note A to Exhibit 14B–1.
[c] See Note F to Exhibit 14B–1.
[d] See Note E to Exhibit 14B–1.
[e] See Exhibit 14B–1.
[f] Equipment at January 1, 19x6, less 19x6 depreciation expense both stated in average 19x6 dollars, i.e., \$104,167 (Note F) − \$10,417 (Note C) = \$93,750.
[g] Dividend assumed paid in average of year dollars (see Exhibit 14–2 of chapter).

SFAS 33 specifies that neither the restated CD amounts nor the CC amounts may exceed the net "recoverable amount" defined as the net amount of cash expected to be recoverable through sale or use.

The supplementary reporting focus is income from continuing operations and thus excludes extraordinary items, cumulative effect of accounting principle changes, and gains or losses on discontinuance of operations.

SFASs 39, 40, and *41* establish requirements for the measurement and disclosure of information about mining and oil and gas, timberlands, and income-producing real estate, respectively.

Additional required disclosures

SFAS 33 also requires a Five-Year Comparison of Selected Supplementary Data[2] (not illustrated here) as follows:

- Historical cost information (from the primary financial statements adjusted to a constant-dollar basis).
- Net sales and other operating revenues.
- Income (loss) from continuing operations.
- Income (loss) per common share from continuing operations.
- Net assets at fiscal year-end.
- Purchasing power gain or loss on net monetary items.
- Current-cost information.
- Increases or decreases in the current-cost-amounts of inventory and property, plant, and equipment held during the fiscal period (holding gains or losses), net of general inflation.

---

[2] In a baffling reversal, the FASB voted four to three to issue *SFAS* 54 which in effect deprives shareholders of the largest investment companies of this useful information which would have allowed them to compare the performance and dividend record of investment companies on an inflation adjusted basis.

- Other information.
- Cash dividends declared per common share.
- Market price per common share at fiscal year-end.
- Average level of the Consumer Price Index for All Urban Consumers (CPI-U).
- Explanatory notes.

The five-year supplementary information must be reported in dollars having a purchasing power equal to either:

- that of dollars of the base period used by the Bureau of Labor Statistics for the CPI-U (presently 1967 = 100), or
- that represented by the average level of the CPI-U during the current fiscal year.

APPENDIX 14C

ILLUSTRATION OF ACCOUNTING FOR A TRANSACTION USING FOUR REPORTING FRAMEWORKS

Assume that Edwards, Inc., acquired a truck on January 1, 19x1, for $4,000 when the relevant CP Index was 120. On June 30, 19x8, when the truck was sold for $2,200, the accumulated depreciation on the truck was $3,000, the CPI stood at 198, and the CC of the truck was $2,100. Exhibit 14C–1 presents the computation of the gain on sale of the truck under four reporting frameworks, assuming that the transaction is reported as of December 31, 19x8, when the CPI stood at 203.

Column 1 presents the conventional HC/ND computation of gain on sale of the truck. Column 2 measures this transaction in terms of December 31, 19x8, dollars. Column 3 accounts for the transaction on a CC/ND basis and separates the gain on sale of equipment based on current cost on date of sale from the holding gain which occurred between the date of acquisition and the date of sale. Column 4 expresses both the gain on sale and the holding gain in terms of dollars of December 31, 19x8, purchasing power.

Exhibit 14C–1: Calculation of gain on sale of truck under four reporting frameworks

	HC/ND (1)	HC/CD (2)	CC/ND (3)	CC/CD (4)
Selling price:				
Nominal price	$2,200		$2,200	
CD price $= \$2,200 \times \dfrac{203 \text{ (year-end)}}{198 \text{ (time of sale)}}$		$2,256		$2,256
Less adjusted cost:				
HC/ND ($4,000 [a] − $3,000 [b])	1,000			
HC/CD $1,000 [d] $\times \dfrac{203 \text{(year-end)}}{120 \text{ (acquisition)}}$		1,692		
CC/ND (given)			2,100	
CC/CD $2,100 $\times \dfrac{203}{198}$				2,153
Gain on sale (before realized holding gain)	1,200	564	100	103
Plus realized holding gain:				
CC/ND $2,100 [c] − 1,000 [d]			1,100	
CC/CD $\left(\$2,100\,[c] \times \dfrac{203}{198} \right) - \left(\$1,000\,[d] \times \dfrac{203}{120} \right)$				461
Total gain	$1,200	$ 564	$1,200	$ 564

[a] Original cost.
[b] Accumulated depreciation on date of sale.
[c] CC on date of sale.
[d] Net book value on date of sale (HC/ND).

QUESTIONS

1. Briefly trace the evolution of research and professional pronouncements on the subject of "accounting for the effect of price-level changes" preceding issuance of *SFAS 33*.

2. Differentiate between the financial capital maintenance concept and the physical capital maintenance concept. You may use an example to illustrate the difference between the two.

3. Differentiate among the four reporting frameworks discussed in the chapter.

4. Differentiate between monetary and nonmonetary items. Give examples.

5. Summarize the restatement procedure from HC/ND to HC/CD.

6. Summarize the restatement procedure from HC/ND to CC/ND.

7. Why are monetary gains and losses so poorly understood?

8. List some useful generalizations regarding the effects of price-level changes on an entity and its financial statements in times of significant inflation.

9. Describe the meaning of—
   a. Monetary working capital adjustment.
   b. Gearing adjustment.

10. *SFAS 33* requires a five-year comparison of selected supplementary data. Summarize its disclosure requirements.

15

The auditor's opinion—meaning and significance

An entity's financial statements are the representations of its management. Management bears a primary responsibility for the fairness of presentation and the degree of informative disclosure in the financial statements it issues to interested parties, such as present and potential owners, creditors, and others. It has, however, become generally accepted that there is a need for an independent check on management's financial reporting.

The profession that serves society's need in this respect by performing the attest function is the public accounting profession. It may be readily observed that the more developed a country's economy and the more diverse, free, and mobile its capital and money markets, the stronger and the more important its public accounting profession is likely to be. Surely, the United States experience supports this conclusion, for the public accounting profession here is perhaps the world's largest and most vital.

Some states recognize and license "Public Accountants" and "Licensed Accountants," and the requirements for practice under these titles vary from strict to feeble. However, there is another title that has the most consistent significance—that of "Certified Public Accountant." It can be acquired only by those who have passed the CPA examination, a rigorous series of tests that are uniform in all states and that are graded centrally under the auspices of the American Institute of Certified Public Accountants (AICPA). While no profession can ensure uniformity of quality among its members, the successful completion of these examinations does ensure that the candidate has demonstrated a sufficiently acceptable knowledge of accounting and auditing principles and practices.

Since the CPAs represent by far the most important segment of public accounting practice in the United States, our consideration of the auditor's opinion will be confined to that issued by the CPA and governed by the various pronouncements issued by their professional association, the AICPA.

In spite of the many real and imagined shortcomings of the auditor's

459

work, and, as this book illustrates, there are many of both varieties, the auditor's function is of critical importance to the financial analyst. While improvements are needed in many areas of the auditor's work, his attestation to the fair presentation of the financial statements greatly increases their reliability to the analyst as well as the degree and quality of disclosure provided in them.

As in many areas of endeavor, so in the analysis of financial statements, partial or incomplete knowledge can be more damaging than a complete lack of it. This truth applies to the analyst's understanding and knowledge of the auditor's work and the significance of his opinion.

WHAT THE ANALYST NEEDS TO KNOW

In relying on the auditor's opinion, which covers the financial statements subject to review, the analyst must—

1. Learn as much as he can about the auditor upon whom he is relying.
2. Understand fully what the auditor's opinion means and the message it is designed to convey to the user.
3. Appreciate the limitations to which the opinion is subject, as well as the implications that such limitations hold for the analysis of financial statements covered by the opinion.

Knowing the auditor

The possession by the auditor of the CPA certificate does assure the analyst of a reasonable qualification for practice as an auditor. However, as is the case in other professions, differences in ability, competence, and qualifications can be considerable.

The relationship between the auditor and those who rely on his opinion differs markedly from that existing in other professional relationships. While the auditor has both an obligation and a concurrent responsibility to users of his opinion, he is in most cases neither appointed nor compensated by them. He must look mostly to management for both recommendation for his appointment and the determination of his fee. When management's desires with respect to financial reporting are in conflict with the best interests of the outside users of financial statements, the auditor's integrity and independence are put to a stern test. Thus, one criterion of the auditor's reliability is his reputation for integrity and independence in the community at large and among respected members of the financial community. Whatever else the auditor must have, and his qualifications and skill must be considerable, without these attributes nothing else counts for very much. The reputation of an auditor for competence and for knowledge of his work can be established in a variety of ways. The auditor's professional credentials, including the length, breadth, and quality of his experience, are one element, his membership and standing in state and national accounting associations another, and his participation in professional organizations yet another factor to be assessed by the analyst. An auditing firm's activities and past performance are usually well known in the community in which it operates.

Finally, the analyst, from his own experience is often able to form a judgment about the auditor's reputation for quality work. Since there exists considerable leeway in adherence to audit standards and in the application of accounting principles, an audit firm's "track record" of actual level of performances in these critical areas provides a firsthand guide to its reliability and integrity. The analyst would do well to note instances in which a CPA firm has accepted the least desirable acceptable accounting principle among the available alternatives, has equivocated unnecessarily in its opinion, or was found wanting in its application of auditing procedures.

Good sources of information on the capabilities of an audit firm include local bankers, investment bankers, and attorneys.

What the auditor's opinion means

The auditor's opinion is the culmination of a lengthy and complicated process of auditing and investigation. It is here, and only here, that the auditor reports on the nature of his work and on the degree of responsibility he assumes. While his influence may be indirectly felt throughout the financial statements by the presentation, description, and footnote disclosure that he may have suggested or insisted upon, the opinion, and the opinion alone, remains his exclusive domain. Thus, the opinion and the references to the financial statements which it contains should always be carefully read. To ignore the auditor's opinion, or to assume that it does not mean what it says, or that it means more than it says, is foolhardy and unwarranted.

The auditor's responsibility to outsiders whom he does not know and who rely on his representations is considerable, and his exposure to liability arising therefrom is growing. Thus, the obligations that the standards of his profession impose on him, while extensive, are at the same time defined and limited. Consequently, no analyst is justified in assuming that the association of the auditor's name with the financial statements goes beyond what the auditor's opinion says, or is a form of insurance on which the analyst can rely to bail him out of bad decisions.

What exactly does the auditor's opinion say? The best starting point for us is an examination of an auditor's "clean opinion," that is, an opinion that is not qualified in any way. This will give us an idea of the greatest degree of responsibility the auditor is willing to assume. The "clean opinion," which covers two annual examinations, reads as follows:

> To the Shareowners and Board of Directors
> (Name of Company)
> We have examined the balance sheet of (name of company) as of (date), and the related statements of income and retained earnings, and the statement

of changes in financial position for the year then ended. Our examination was made in accordance with generally accepted auditing standards, and accordingly included such tests of the accounting records and such other auditing procedures as we considered necessary in the circumstances. We previously examined and reported upon the financial statement of the Company for the year ended (date).

In our opinion, the aforementioned financial statements present fairly the financial position of (name of company) at (date) and (date), and the results of its operations and the changes in its financial position for the years then ended, in conformity with generally accepted accounting principles applied on a consistent basis.

(Name of accountants)

(City and date)

THE AUDITOR'S REPORT

The auditor's report is divided into two distinct parts: (1) the scope of the audit and (2) the auditor's opinion.

The scope of the audit

The scope paragraph of the auditor's report sets forth the financial statements examined, the period of time that they cover, and the scope of the audit to which they and the underlying records have been subjected.

The standard terminology refers to an examination made in accordance with "generally accepted auditing standards." This is "shorthand" for a very comprehensive meaning that is elaborated upon in the profession's literature and particularly in *Statements on Auditing Standards* and subsequent codifications. These auditing standards are broad generalizations classified under three headings: (1) general standards (2) standards of fieldwork, and (3) standards of reporting.

General standards define the personal qualities required of the independent CPA. They are:

- a. The examination is to be performed by a person or persons having adequate technical training and proficiency as an auditor.
- b. In all matters relating to the assignment an independence in mental attitude is to be maintained by the auditor or auditors.
- c. Due professional care is to be exercised in the performance of the examination and the preparation of the report.

Standards of fieldwork embrace the actual execution of the audit and cover the planning of the work, the evaluation of the client's system of internal control, and the quality and sufficiency of the audit evidence obtained. *SAS 1* enumerates them as follows:

1. The work is to be adequately planned and assistants, if any, are to be properly supervised.

2. There is to be a proper study and evaluation of the existing internal control as a basis for reliance thereon and for the determination of the resultant extent of the tests to which auditing procedures are to be restricted.
3. Sufficient competent evidential matter is to be obtained through inspection, observation, inquiries and confirmations to afford a reasonable basis for an opinion regarding the financial statements under examination.

Reporting standards govern the preparation and presentation of the auditor's report. They are intended to ensure that the auditor's position is clearly and unequivocally stated and that the degree of responsibility he assumes is made clear to the reader. These standards are four in number:

1. The report shall state whether the financial statements are presented in accordance with generally accepted accounting principles.
2. The report shall state whether such principles have been consistently observed in the current period in relation to the preceding period.
3. Informative disclosures in the financial statements are to be regarded as reasonably adequate unless otherwise stated in the report.
4. The report shall either contain an expression of opinion regarding the financial statements, taken as a whole, or an assertion to the effect that an opinion cannot be expressed. When an overall opinion cannot be expressed, the reasons therefore should be stated. In all cases where an auditor's name is associated with financial statements, the report should contain a clear-cut indication of the character of the auditor's examination, if any, and the degree of responsibility he is taking.

Audit standards are the yardsticks by which the quality of audit procedures are measured.

Auditing procedures.   The second phrase of the scope section states that the examination "included such tests of the accounting records and such other auditing procedures" as were considered necessary in the circumstances.

This statement encompasses the wide sweep of auditing theory brought to bear on the particular examination, as well as the professional discretion the auditor uses in the performance of his work.

The subject of auditing is, of course, a discipline in itself requiring for successful mastery a period of study and practical application. Thus, while we obviously cannot go with any degree of detail into what constitutes the process of auditing, it behooves all who use its end product to have a basic understanding of the process by which the auditor obtains assurance about the fair presentation of the financial statements as to which he expresses an opinion.

A basic objective of the financial audit is the detection of errors and irregularities, intentional or unintentional, which if undetected would materially affect the fairness of presentation of financial summarizations or their conformity with GAAP.

To be economically feasible and justifiable, auditing can aim only at a reasonable level of assurance in this respect about the data under review.

This means that under a testing system, assurance can never be complete, and that the final audit conclusions are subject to this inherent probability of error.

Briefly stated, the auditor's basic approach is as follows: to gain assurance about financial summarizations the auditor must examine the accounting system of which they are a final product. If the system of internal control is well conceived, properly maintained, and implemented, it is assumed that it should result in valid financial records and summarizations.

Thus, the need for and the extent of the testing of the records is dependent on the degree of proper operation of the system of internal control.

The importance of internal control. The importance of the review of the system of internal control in the total audit framework can be gauged from a reading of the scope paragraph of the original standard opinion (used from about 1939 to 1948) which read in part as follows:

> have reviewed the system of internal control and the accounting procedures of the company, and, without making a detailed audit of the transactions, have examined or tested accounting records of the company and other supporting evidence by methods, and to the extent we deemed appropriate.

Even though these specific words have been deleted from the form of the present opinion, the phrase still accurately describes the auditor's work.

After ascertaining, by means of investigation and inquiry, what management's plan and design for a system of internal control is, if any, the auditor proceeds to test the system in order to ascertain whether it is in existence and is, in fact, being implemented as intended. This testing is called compliance testing.

If after application of compliance testing, the system of internal control is found to be well conceived and in proper operation, the amount of testing to which income statement items or individual assets and liabilities will be subjected can be significantly restricted. The latter type of testing, which may be called substantive testing, will have to be increased significantly if compliance testing reveals the system of internal control to be deficient or not operational.

This method of checking out the system and then performing additional sample tests on the basis of its evaluation does, of course, leave room for a great deal of professional discretion, for "corner-cutting," and for a variety of qualities of judgment. Hence, it is subject to the risk of failure. Moreover, since the usual audit is based on a system of selective testing, it cannot be relied on to disclose defalcations, although their discovery may result.

From the above discussion it should be clear that reliance on an audit must be based on an understanding of the nature of the audit process and the limitations to which it is subject.

The opinion section

The first paragraph of the auditor's report, which we discussed above, deals with the scope of his examination and the limitations or restrictions, if any, to which it was subject. The second paragraph (in practice the order of these paragraphs may be reversed) sets forth the auditor's opinion on:

1. The fairness of presentation of the financial statements.
2. Their conformity with GAAP.
3. The consistent application of these principles in the financial statements.

"Fair presentation"

One of the great debates among auditors and between auditors and society in general, particularly the courts, concerns the meaning of the phrase "present fairly" which is found in the auditor's report. Most auditors maintain that financial statements are fairly presented when they conform to GAAP and that "fairness" is meaningful only in this context.

Yet, clearly, in quite a number of cases reaching the courts in recent years, financial statements that, according to expert testimony were prepared in accordance with GAAP, were nevertheless found to be misleading in an overall sense. This became particularly apparent in the landmark Continental Vending case where the lack of disclosure of certain highly dubious transactions was defended as not being, at that time, required by GAAP. In refusing to instruct the jury that conformity with GAAP was a complete defense to the charge of fraud, the trial judge maintained that the critical question was whether Continental's financial statements, taken as a whole, "fairly presented" its financial picture. He found that while conformity with GAAP might be very persuasive evidence of an auditor's good faith, it was not necessarily conclusive evidence of it.

The auditors, in an attempt to respond to a clear divergence between their and society's views of what is meant by "present fairly," issued a statement on the matter in 1975. While still maintaining that "fairness" must be applied within the framework of GAAP, they stated that "fair presentation" also requires that—

a. The accounting principles selected and applied must have general acceptance.[1]
b. The accounting principles must be appropriate in the circumstances.
c. The financial statements must be "informative of matters that may affect their use, understanding, and interpretation."
d. The information must be presented and summarized "in a reasonable manner, that is, neither too detailed nor too condensed."

---

[1] *SAS 43* (1982) details the hierarchy of sources of established accounting principles.

   e. The financial statements must reflect "the underlying events and transactions" in a way that states the results within "a range of acceptable limits that are reasonable and practicable."

As part of the accounting profession's periodic attempts at self-examination and assessment, especially in the face of congressional and public scrutiny and criticism, an AICPA appointed Commission on Auditor's Responsibilities issued its "Report, Conclusions, and Recommendations" in 1978. Only some of the commission's recommendations may ultimately be adopted in modified form.

Modification of the opinion

The standard short-form report presented earlier in the chapter contained a "clean opinion;" that is, the auditor had no qualifications to record as to any of the three criteria enumerated above. Any modifications of substance in the language of the auditor's opinion paragraph is, technically speaking, considered to be a qualification, a disclaimer, or an adverse opinion. Not all modifications are, of course, of equal significance to the user. Some deviations in language are explanatory in character reflecting matters that the auditor wishes to emphasize and may not affect the auditor's opinion significantly. References to the work of other auditors is not regarded as a qualification but rather an indication of divided responsibility for the financial statements. Other explanatory comments may not carry over to affect the auditor's opinion and, at times, one may wonder why mention of them is necessary. On the other hand, certain qualifications or disclaimers are so significant as to cast doubt on the reliability of the financial statements or their usefulness for decision-making purposes.

Let us then examine the major categories of the auditor's qualifications and disclaimers, the occasions on which they are properly used, and the significance which they hold to the user of financial statements.

CIRCUMSTANCES GIVING RISE TO QUALIFICATIONS, DISCLAIMERS, OR ADVERSE OPINIONS

There are four main categories of conditions that require qualifications, an adverse opinion, or a disclaimer of opinion:

1. Limitations in the scope of the auditor's examination affected by *(a)* conditions that preclude the application of auditing procedures considered necessary in the circumstances or *(b)* restrictions imposed by the client.
2. The financial statements do not present fairly the financial position and/or results of operations because *(a)* they fail to conform with GAAP or *(b)* they do not contain adequate disclosure.
3. There exist uncertainties about the future resolution of material matters,

the effect of which cannot presently be estimated or the outcome of which cannot reasonably be determined.

4. A change in comparability affects the consistency of presentation.

Before we consider the variety of conditions that call for qualified opinions, let us examine the major types of qualifications that the auditor may express.

QUALIFICATIONS—"EXCEPT FOR" AND "SUBJECT TO"

These qualifications express an opinion on the financial statements except for repercussions stemming from conditions that must be disclosed. They may arise from limitations in the scope of the audit which, because of circumstances beyond the auditor's control or because of restrictions imposed by the audited company, result in a failure to obtain reasonably objective and verifiable evidence in support of events which have taken place. They may arise from a lack of conformity of the financial statements to GAAP. When they arise because there are uncertainties about future events that cannot be resolved or the effect of which cannot be estimated or reasonably provided for at the time the opinion is rendered, the words *subject to* are substituted for *except for.*

An uncertainty, such as one due to operating losses or serious financial weakness that calls into question the fundamental assumption that an entity can continue to operate as a going concern, calls for a "subject to" qualification. In cases of pervasive uncertainty that cannot be adequately measured, an auditor may, but is not required to, issue a disclaimer of opinion rather than a "subject to" opinion.

ADVERSE OPINIONS

An adverse opinion should be rendered in cases when the financial statements are not prepared in accordance with GAAP, and this has a significant effect on the fair presentation of those statements. An adverse opinion results generally from a situation in which the auditor has been unable to convince his client to amend the financial statements so that they reflect the auditor's estimate about the outcome of future events or so that they otherwise adhere to GAAP. The issuance of an adverse opinion must always be accompanied by a statement of the reasons for such an opinion.

DISCLAIMER OF OPINION

A disclaimer of opinion is a statement of inability to express an opinion. It must be rendered when, for whatever reason, insufficient competent evidential matter is available to the auditor to enable him to form an opinion on the financial statements. It can arise from limitations in the scope of the audit as well as from the existence of uncertainties the ultimate impact of which cannot be estimated. Material departures from GAAP do not justify a disclaimer of opinion.

Adverse opinions versus disclaimers of opinion

The difference between adverse opinions and disclaimers of opinion can be best understood in terms of the difference that exists between exceptions that affect the quality of the financial statements, on one hand, and those that express uncertainties affecting the auditor's opinion, on the other. Thus, a situation that may call for an "except for" opinion may at some point result in such a degree of pervasive or material disagreements with management that it will require an adverse opinion. Similarly, pervasive and/or material uncertainties may, at some point, result in the conversion of a "subject to" opinion into a disclaimer of opinion.

THE FORM OF THE REPORT

Whenever the auditor expresses a qualified opinion, he must disclose in a middle paragraph, or in a footnote that is referred to in that paragraph, the substantive reasons for the qualification. The explanatory paragraph should disclose the principal effects of the subject matter of the qualification on financial position, results of operations, and changes in financial position, if reasonably determinable. The paragraph should also make it clear whether the qualification results because of a difference of opinion between the auditor and the client or whether it results because of an uncertainty not subject to present resolution.

All qualifications must be referred to in the opinion paragraph, and a qualification due to scope or lack of sufficient evidential matter must be also referred to in the scope paragraph. Thus, a mere explanatory statement should not be referred to in either the scope or the opinion paragraphs.

Having covered the various types of opinions an auditor can express, let us now turn to the various conditions that call for qualifications in such opinions.

LIMITATIONS IN THE SCOPE OF THE AUDIT

A limitation in the scope of the auditor's examination, that is, an inability to perform certain audit steps that he considers necessary, will, if material, result in a qualification or disclaimer of his opinion.

Some limitations in the scope of the auditor's examination arise from an inability to perform certain audit steps because of conditions beyond the auditor's and the client's control, for example, an inability to observe the opening inventory where the audit appointment was not made until the close of the year. Other limitations may result from a client-imposed restriction on the auditor's work. Whatever the reason for an incomplete examination, the auditor must report the inadequacy of the examination and the conclusions that flow from such an inadequacy.

The accounting profession has given special status to procedures with respect to observation of inventories and the confirmation of accounts receivable. If these steps cannot be reasonably or practically performed, the auditor must, in order to issue an unqualified opinion, satisfy himself about the inventories and accounts receivable by alternative means. He must, however, no longer indicate such an omission of regular procedures in his opinion.

FAILURE OF FINANCIAL STATEMENTS TO CONFORM TO GENERALLY ACCEPTED ACCOUNTING PRINCIPLES

The auditor brings to bear his expertise in the application of auditing techniques and procedures to satisfy himself about the existence, ownership, and validity of presentation of the assets, the liabilities, and net worth as well as the statement of results. As an expert accountant, the auditor judges the fairness of presentation of financial statements and their conformity with GAAP. The latter is one of the most important functions of the auditor's opinion.

Fair presentation is, to an important extent, dependent on the degree of informative disclosure provided. Adherence to GAAP, which is another prerequisite of fairness of presentation, depends on the employment, in the financial statements, of principles having authoritative support. *Opinions* of the APB and *Statements* of the FASB enjoy, by definition, authoritative support. If the accountant concurs in a company's use of an accounting principle which differs from that approved by an authoritative body but which he believes enjoys the support of other authoritative sources, he need not qualify his opinion, but he must disclose that the principle used differs from those approved by such authoritative body. This, of course, puts the onus on the auditor in justifying the departure from a principle which enjoys authoritative approval.

If, because of lack of adequate disclosure or the use of accounting principles that do not enjoy authoritative support, the auditor concludes that the financial statements are not fairly presented, he must qualify his opinion or render an adverse opinion. The decision of whether to make his opinion an "except-for" type, which is a qualified opinion, or to render an adverse opinion, which states that the "financial statements do not present fairly . . ." hinges on the materiality of the effect of such a deficiency on the financial statements taken as a whole. The concept of materiality in accounting and auditing is, however, very vague and remains so far undefined.

It is obvious that a qualification due to a lack of disclosure or a lack of adherence to GAAP is the result of the auditor's inability to persuade his client to modify the financial statements. Thus, an "except for" type of opinion is not proper, and an adverse opinion is called for together with a full description of the shortcomings in the financial statements as well as their total impact thereon.

The following are pertinent excerpts from an opinion qualified because of lack of adherence to GAAP:

> As explained in Note A, the 19x3 financial statements include interest expense that has not been capitalized as required by *SFAS 34.*
>
> In our opinion, except that in 19x3 interest expense has not been capitalized as described in the preceding paragraph . . .

FINANCIAL STATEMENTS SUBJECT TO UNRESOLVED KNOWN UNCERTAINTIES

Whenever uncertainties about the future exist that cannot be resolved, or whose effect cannot be estimated or reasonably provided for at the time of the issuance of the auditor's opinion, a qualified opinion or a disclaimer of opinion may be indicated. Such uncertainties may relate to lawsuits, tax matters, or other contingencies, the outcome of which is dependent upon decisions of parties other than management. Or the uncertainties may relate to the recovery of the investment in certain assets through future operations, or through their disposition.

The practical effect of an uncertainty qualification is to state the auditor's inability to assess the impact of the contingency, or the likelihood of its occurrence, and to pass on to the reader the burden of its evaluation.

One variety of qualification relates to the question of whether the going-concern assumption in accounting (see Chapter 3) is justified. This question arises when a company is incurring continued operating losses, deficits in the stockholder's equity, working capital insufficiencies, or defaults under loan agreements. In such cases, the auditor expresses his doubt about the propriety of applying practices implicit in the going-concern concept such as the valuation of fixed assets at cost.

The following are examples of pertinent portions of auditor reports relating to uncertainties:

> As discussed in Note 4, because of the uncertainty of mining plans it may be necessary at some indeterminate future date to write off a significant amount of net book investment in the Company's Questa mine and mill.
>
> In our opinion, subject to the realization of the Company's investment in Questa property referred to above.
>
> * * * * *
>
> The accompanying financial statements of the Company have been prepared on the basis of a going concern, although the ability of the Company to continue

as a going concern is dependent upon future earnings. In this connection, it should be noted that in the period from commencement of operations through June 30, 19x8, the Company accumulated a net loss of $150,340.

Except for the appropriateness of the going-concern concept and for the ability of the Company to realize its unamortized programming development costs through future profitable operations, in our opinion the accompanying financial statements present fairly.

EXCEPTIONS AS TO CONSISTENCY

The second standard of reporting requires that the auditor's report state whether the principles of accounting employed "have been consistently observed in the current period in relation to the preceding period."

The basic objective of the consistency standard is to assure the reader that comparability of financial statements as between periods has not been materially affected by changes in the accounting principles employed or in the method of their application. Thus, if a change has been made affecting the comparability of the financial statements, a statement of the nature of the changes and their effect on the financial statements is required.

There are three types of changes that must be considered here:

1. Changes in accounting principles employed; for example, a change in the method of depreciation.
2. Changes required by altered conditions; for example, a change in the estimated useful life of an asset.
3. Changed conditions unrelated to accounting that nevertheless have an effect on comparability; for example, the acquisition or disposition of a subsidiary.

Changes of type 1 involve the consistency standard and must be dealt with in the auditor's opinion. Changes of type 2 and 3 affect comparability, and while not requiring comment in the auditor's report, they do require footnote disclosure.

SPECIAL REPORTS

In certain cases the standard short-form report of the auditor is not appropriate because of special circumstances or because of the limited scope of the examination that the auditor is requested to undertake. It is particularly important that the analyst read such reports carefully so that he is not misled into believing that the auditor is assuming here his ordinary measure of responsibility. The following are some types of special reports that the reader may encounter:

1. Reports by companies on a cash or incomplete basis of accounting.
2. Reports by nonprofit organizations.
3. Reports prepared for limited purposes. Such reports usually deal with certain aspects of the financial statements (such as computations of royalties, rentals, profit-sharing arrangements, or compliance with provisions of bond indentures, etc.).

In *FRR* No. 1, Section 304 the SEC has called for the auditor's "association" with published interim reports based on performance of a limited review.

REPORTS ON "COMPILED" AND "REVIEWED" FINANCIAL STATEMENTS

In 1979, the AICPA made available to "nonpublic entities" compilation and review services that, while falling short of a full audit, provide the reader with lower defined levels of assurance.

Compiled financial statements are accompanied by a report that indicates that a compilation has been performed and that such a service is limited to presenting, in financial statement format, information that is the representation of management or owners. The report should also state that the financial statements have not been audited or reviewed; thus no opinion or any other form of assurance is expressed on them. No reference is made to any other procedures performed before or during the compilation engagement.

Reviewed financial statements are accompanied by a report that indicates that a review was performed in accordance with AICPA standards. The report describes a review engagement, states that the information in the financial statements is the representation of management (or owners), and disclaims an opinion on the financial statements taken as a whole. The report should state that: "The accountant is not aware of any material modifications that should be made to the financial statements in order for them to be in conformity with generally accepted accounting principles, other than those modifications, if any, indicated in his report." No reference is made to any other procedures performed before or during the review engagement.

THE SEC'S IMPORTANT ROLE

The SEC has in recent years moved particularly forcefully to monitor auditor performance as well as to strengthen the hands of auditors in their dealings with managements.

Disciplinary proceedings against auditors were expanded to include requirements for improvements in internal administration procedures, professional education, and a review of a firm's procedures by outside professionals.

SEC *FRR* No. 1, Section 603, in moving to strengthen the auditor's position, requires increased disclosure of the relationship between auditors and their clients, particularly in cases where changes in auditors take place. Disclosure must include details of past disagreements, including those resolved to the satisfaction of the replaced auditor, as well as footnote disclosure of the effects on the financial statements of methods of accounting advocated by a former auditor but not followed by the client.

IMPLICATIONS FOR ANALYSIS

Auditing as a function and the auditor's opinion as an instrument of assurance are widely misunderstood. The responsibility for this lack of communication cannot be all laid at the auditor's door, for the profession has published a number of pamphlets in which it has endeavored to explain its function. Nor should the readers of financial statements bear the full responsibility for this state of affairs, because the accounting profession's message in this area is often couched in technical and cautious language and requires a great deal of effort and background information for a full understanding.

A useful discussion of the implications of the current state of auditing to the user of audited financial statements may be presented in two parts:

1. Implications stemming from the nature of the audit process.
2. Implications arising from the professional standards which govern the auditor's opinion.

Implications inherent in the audit process

Auditing is based on a sampling approach to the data under audit. Statistical sampling uses a rigorous approach to this process, which lends itself to a quantification of conclusions. Nevertheless, many audit tests are based on "judgmental samples" of the data, that is, samples selected by the auditor's intuition, judgment, and evaluation of many factors. Often the size of the sample is necessarily limited by the economics of the accounting practice.[2]

The reader must realize that the auditor does not aim at, nor can he ever achieve, complete certainty. Even a review of every single transaction—a process that would be economically unjustifiable—would not achieve a complete assurance.

Auditing is a developing art. Even its very basic theoretical underpinnings are far from fully understood or resolved. There is, for instance, no clear

---

[2] This and other "inherent limitations of the auditing process," are emphasized in an SAS issued in 1977 on "The Independent Auditor's Responsibility for the Detection of Errors and Irregularities." The *Statement* declares that the auditor's examination is subject to the inherent risk that material errors or irregularities, if they exist, will not be detected.

relationship between the auditor's evaluation of the effectiveness of the system of internal controls, which is a major factor on which the auditor relies, and the extent of audit testing and the nature of audit procedures employed. If we add to that the fact that the qualities of judgment among auditors do vary greatly, we should not be surprised to find that the history of auditing contains many examples of spectacular failure. On the other hand, as is the case with the risk of accidental death in commercial aviation, the percentage of failure to the total number of audits performed is very small indeed. Thus, while the user of audited financial statements can, in general, be reassured about the overall results of the audit function, he must remember that there is substantial risk in reliance on its results in specific cases. Such risks are due to many factors, including the auditor's inability to detect fraud at the highest level and the application of proper audit tests to such an end (McKesson and Robbins case through the Cenco, Inc., case and all the way to the Equity Funding case), the auditor's inability to grasp the extent of a deteriorating situation (the Yale Express case), the auditor's conception of the range of his responsibilities to probe and disclose (the Continental Vending and National Student Marketing cases), and the quality of the audit (Bar Chris Construction, U.S. Financial, Whittaker Corporation, Mattel, and McCormick Company, cases).

Thus, while the audit function may generally justify the reliance that financial analysts place on audited financial statements, such a reliance cannot be a blind one. The analyst must be aware that the entire audit process is a probabilistic one subject to many risks. Even its flawless application may not necessarily result in complete assurance, and most certainly cannot ensure that the auditor has elicited all the facts, especially if there is high-level management collusion to withhold such facts from him. Finally, the heavy dependence of the auditing process on judgment will, of necessity, result in a wide range of quality of performance.

An insight into what can be missed, and why, in the internal and external audit of a large corporation can be obtained from a reading of the *Report of the Special Review Committee of the Board of Directors of Gulf Oil Corporation* (the McCloy report—December 1975). In searching for reasons why Gulf's internal financial controls, its internal auditors, and its external auditors failed to detect or curb the expenditure of large amounts of corporate funds through "off the books" bank accounts for unlawful purposes the review committee concluded that internal control committees chose not to control; that the corporate comptroller did not exercise the control powers vested in him, that the internal auditing department (reporting to the comptroller rather than to an audit committee of the board) lacked in independence and stature, and that while it is clear that the external auditors had some knowledge of certain unusual transactions, the extent of their knowledge could not be determined.

To provide the reader with insights into how wrong things can go in the "audit" of a major corporation, let us focus on the landmark Equity

Funding case.[3] This case includes expected elements such as human greed and shortcomings, the resulting fraud and deception and audit failure. It also includes the highly unusual in that never before have public accountants been charged with knowing complicity in a fraud extending over many years.

THE EQUITY FUNDING CASE. The Equity Funding Corporation of America (EFCA) was an organization which sold mutual fund shares and used these as security against which the investor could borrow moneys for the payment of life insurance premiums on his or her behalf (the "funding" concept). From its inception as a public company in 1964, the major holders of its stock were obsessed with a desire to keep aloft the market price of its stock by fraudulently inflating reported earnings. As the fraud progressed and grew, vanity, pride, and the fear of being discovered provided added incentives to keep the fraud going.

An amazing aspect of this case is the relatively crude and unsophisticated design and execution of the fraud which relied on fictitious manual accounting entries lacking any real support.

In its early stages, the fraud consisted of recording nonexistent commission income with the charge (debit) going to a greatly inflated "Funding Loans Receivable" asset, supposedly representing borrowings by customers for life insurance premiums, etc. Over the years, $85 million in such bogus income was recorded. As is true with most frauds, the fictitious entries involved do not, of course, create cash. Thus, to provide cash and at the same time keep the mushrooming "Funding Loans Receivable" in check, the conspirators borrowed money (on the basis of glowing earning results), and instead of booking the corresponding liabilities, credited the Funding Loans Receivable account. Other complicated shams involved foreign subsidiaries.

As the cash-hungry fraud monster grew, the expanding circle of fraud participants, now including senior as well as lower-management levels, had to invent new cash raising schemes. This led to the involvement of Equity Funding Life Insurance Company (EFLIC), a unit involved in reinsurance, i.e., in the sale to others of insurance risks in force. Starting with intermediate, less crass and ambitious steps, there ultimately evolved a practice of creating totally fictitious products (insurance policies) that were sold to unsuspecting reinsurers who provided significant cash inflows. The process involved the "creation" of all needed documentation and related fictitious records. But, it also created the need for EFLIC to remit increasing amounts of cash to these reinsurers representing the premium payments which the company presumably collected from the fictitious policyholders. This created monumental documentation problems as well as severe cash flow problems (in 1972 reaching $1.7 million in cash flow deficit). These ever-growing fictions and problems that fed on themselves created a "house of cards" that would have collapsed of its own weight even without the whistle blowing of a disgruntled dismissed employee in early 1973.

The sheer size of the deception as well as its duration should give pause to any analyst. From 1964 through 1972, at least $143 million in fictitious pretax

---

[3] Most of the public documents as well as commentaries on this case are contained in L. J. Seidler, F. Andrews, and M. J. Epstein, *The Equity Funding Papers: The Anatomy of a Fraud* (New York: Wiley, 1977).

income was reported in EFCA's financial statements. During the same period, the net income reported by the company amounted to about $76 million. Thus, this company whose reported success captured the imagination of Wall Street, in fact never earned a dime.

The bankruptcy proceedings and investigation which started in 1973 also revealed that:

> Latecomers to the fraud benefited from and were motivated by prestigious and well-paying positions. This in turn led to a climate of dishonesty which included theft, expense account padding, and other manifestations of a breakdown of restraint and morality.

> The small audit firm performed its audit during 1961–70 with such manifest incompetence that it could only be explained by a knowledge of the fraud. A larger successor audit firm that purchased the practice of the smaller firm changed practically nothing in the sloppy and uncoordinated audit approach.

> The "big 8" audit firm of EFLIC failed to review internal controls and based its audit conclusions almost solely on internal records, thus omitting the crucial audit steps of independent outside verification.

> The auditors had to settle for about $39 million in damages.

Rigorous financial analysis should have revealed the propensities of the defrauders if not the specific elements of the fraud. Thus, a comparison of quarterly reports in 1971 would have revealed that derived fourth-quarter income was inflated while the related expenses were understated in relation to the revenue amounts. The EFCA fraud holds many important lessons about the dynamics of a fraudulent process as well as the weak points that it can reveal to a trained and inquisitive eye.

In relying on audited financial statements, the analyst must be ever aware of the risks of failure inherent in an audit; he must pay attention to the identity of the auditors and to what their record has been; and armed with a knowledge of what auditors do and how they do it, he must himself assess the areas of possible vulnerability in the financial statements. This brings us to the concept of audit risk.

Audit risk and its implications

We have in Chapter 3 examined the concept of accounting risk. Audit risk, while related, is of a different dimension and represents, as a study of some of the above-mentioned cases will reveal, an equally clear and present danger to lenders and investors who rely on audited financial statements.

It is impossible for the analyst to substitute completely his judgment for that of the auditor. However, armed with an understanding of the audit process and its limitations, he can, through identification of special areas of vulnerability, make a better assessment of the degree of audit risk present in a given situation. The following are circumstances that can point to such areas of vulnerability:

Glamour industry and company with need for continuing earnings growth to justify high market price or to facilitate acquisitions.

Company in difficult financial condition requiring credit urgently and frequently.

Company with high market visibility issuing frequent progress reports and earnings estimates.

Managements dominated mostly by one or a few strong-willed individuals or consisting mostly of financial people including CPAs.

Management compensation or stock options importantly dependent on reported earnings.

Managements that have displayed a propensity for earnings maximization and manipulation by various means.

Indications of personal financial difficulties by members of the senior management team.

Deterioration in operating performance.

Deterioration in liquidity or long-term solvency.

A capital structure far too complex for company's operations or site.

Problem industry displaying weaknesses, in such areas as receivable collection, inventories, contract cost overruns, dependence on few products, and so forth.

Dealings with insiders or related parties, stockholder lawsuits, frequent turnover of key officers, legal counsel, or auditors.[4]

Audit conducted by a firm that has, for whatever reason, experienced a higher than normal incidence of audit failures.

While none of the above situations can be relied on to indicate situations of higher audit risk, they have been shown by experience to have appeared in a sufficient number of problem cases to warrant the analyst's close attention.

Implications stemming from the standards that govern the auditor's opinion

In relying on the auditor's opinion, the analyst must be aware of the limitations to which the audit process is subject, and this was the subject of the preceding discussion. Moreover, he must understand what the auditor's opinion means and particularly what the auditor himself thinks he conveys to the reader by means of his opinion.

Let us first consider the unqualified opinion or the so-called "clean" opinion. The auditor maintains that he expresses an opinion on *management's* statements. He is very insistent on this point and attaches considerable impor-

---

[4] The SEC in *FRR* No. 1, Section 603, required increased disclosure of relationships between registrants and their independent public accountants, including disputes, particularly in cases where changes in accountants occur.

tance to it. It means that normally he did not prepare the financial statements nor did he choose the accounting principles embodied in them. Instead, he reviews the financial statements presented to him by management and ascertains that they are in agreement with the books and records that he audited. He also determines that generally acceptable principles of accounting have been employed in the preparation of the financial statements, but that does not mean that they are the *best* principles that could have been used. It is a well-known fact that management will often rely on the auditor, as an expert in accounting, to help them pick the principle that, while still acceptable, will come nearest to meeting their reporting objectives. Finally, the auditor will determine that the minimum standards of disclosure have been met so that all matters essential to a fair presentation of the financial statements are included in them.

One might well ask what difference it makes whether the auditor prepared the statements or not so long as he expresses an unqualified opinion on them. The accounting profession has never clearly explained what the implications of this really are to the user of the financial statements. However, a number of such possible implications should be borne in mind by the analyst:

1. The auditor's knowledge about the financial statements is not as strong as that of the preparer who was in more intimate contact with all the factors which gave rise to the transactions. He knows only what he can discern on the basis of a sampling process and may not know all that he should know.

2. Since many items in the financial statements are not capable of exact measurement, he merely reviews such measurements for reasonableness. His are not the original determinations, and unless he can successfully prove otherwise (as for example in the case of estimates of useful lives of property), management's determination will prevail. Thus, the auditor's opinion contains no reference to "present exactly" or "present correctly" but rather states that the statements "present fairly."

3. While the auditor may be consulted on the use of accounting principles, he, as auditor rather than as preparer of such statements, does not select the principles to be used. Moreover, he cannot insist on the use of the *best* available principle any more than he is likely to *insist* on a degree of disclosure above the minimum considered as acceptable at the time.

4. The limitations to which the auditor's ability to audit are subject have never been spelled out by the accounting profession. Knowledgeable auditors do, of course, know about them; but there seems to be a tacit agreement, of doubtful value to the profession, not to discuss them. For example, is the auditor really equipped to audit the value of complex technical work in progress? Can he competently evaluate the adequacy of insurance reserves? Can he second-guess the client's estimate of the percentage of completion of a large contract? While such questions are rarely raised in public, let alone answered, they cannot be unequivocally answered in the affirmative.

5. While the preparer must, under the rules of double-entry bookkeeping, account for all items, large or small, the auditor is held to less exacting standards of accuracy in his work. Thus, the error tolerances are wider. He leans on the doctrine of materiality that in its basic concept simply means that the auditor need not concern himself, in either the auditing or the reporting phases of his work, with trivial or unimportant matters. What is important or significant is, of course, a matter of judgment, and so far the profession has neither defined the concept nor set limits or established criteria to govern the overall application of the concept of materiality. This has given it an unwarranted degree of reporting latitude.[5]

Of course, auditors even as a profession, in contra-distinction to a business, must pay attention to the economics of their function and to the limits of the responsibilities they can assume. Thus, whether the foregoing limitations on the auditor's function and responsibility are justified or not, the analyst must recognize them as standards applied by auditors and evaluate his reliance on audited financial statements with a full understanding of them.

The auditor's reference to "generally accepted accounting principles" in his opinion should be well understood by the user of the financial statements. Such reference means that the auditor is satisfied that such principles, or standards, have authoritative support and that they have been applied "in all material respects." Aside from understanding the operation of the concept of materiality, here the analyst must understand that the definition of what constitutes "generally accepted accounting principles" is often vague and subject to significant latitude in interpretation and application. For example, a *SAS* issued in 1975 states that "when criteria for selection among alternative accounting principles have not been established to relate accounting methods to circumstances (e.g., as in case of inventory and depreciation methods) the auditor may conclude that more than one accounting principle is appropriate in the circumstances."

Similarly indeterminate are present-day standards relating to disclosure. While minimum standards are increasingly established in professional and SEC pronouncements, accountants have not always adhered to them. The degree to which the lack of disclosure impairs the fair presentation of the financial statements remains subject to the auditor's judgment and discretion, and there are no definite standards that indicate at what point lack of disclosure is material enough to impair fairness of presentation thus requiring a qualification in the auditor's report.

When the auditor qualifies his opinion, the analyst is faced with an additional problem of interpretation, that is, what is the meaning and intent of

---

[5] See Leopold A. Bernstein, "The Concept of Materiality," *The Accounting Review,* January 1967; and Sam M. Woolsey, "Approach to Solving the Materiality Problem," *Journal of Accountancy,* March 1973. As of now the FASB has published a *Discussion Memorandum* on the subject and held public hearings on it.

the qualification and what effect should such qualifications have on his reliance on the financial statements? The usefulness of the qualification to the analyst depends, of course, on its clarity, its lack of equivocation, and on the degree to which supplementary information and data enable an assessment of its effect.

An additional dimension of confusion and difficulty of interpretation is introduced when the auditor includes explanatory information in his report, merely for emphasis, without a statement of conclusions or of a qualification. The analyst may in such situations be left wondering why the matter was emphasized in this way and whether the auditor is attempting to express an unstated qualification or reservation.

ILLUSTRATION 1. The U and I Incorporated auditor report contains the following explanatory middle paragraph:

> As discussed in Note B to the consolidated financial statements, in February 1979 the Company discontinued its sugar processing operations and is in the process of selling or otherwise disposing of the related assets.

In light of a full footnote explanation of the matter, the analyst is left wondering why the auditors chose to emphasize this particular matter.

Qualification, disclaimers, and adverse opinions

As discussed in an earlier part of this chapter, generally when an auditor is not satisfied with the fairness of presentation of items in the financial statements, he issues an "except-for" type of qualification, and when there are uncertainties that he cannot resolve, he issues a "subject to" qualification. At some point, the size and importance of items under qualification must result in *adverse opinions* or *disclaimers of opinion,* respectively. Where is this point? At what stage is a specific qualification no longer meaningful and an overall disclaimer of opinion necessary? Here again, the analyst won't find any guidelines by turning to the auditor's own professional pronouncements or literature. The boundaries are left entirely to the realm of judgment without the existence of even the broadest of criteria or guidelines.

ILLUSTRATION 2. Callahan Mining Corporation indicated in Note 5 of its 1980 annual report that at December 31, 1980, capitalized expenditures for exploration projects aggregated $4,612,000, the recovery of which is subject to the success of the project which cannot be forecast at this time.

The auditor report stated:

> As described in Note 5 to the consolidated financial statements, the recovery of the Company's investment in the Caladay Project, which is carried at cost, is subject to the success of the project and cannot be forecast at this time.

It was left to the reader to judge the significance of these disclosures.

Uncertainty qualifications.   When the auditor cannot assess the proper carrying amount of an asset or determine the extent of a possible liability or find other uncertainties or contingencies that cannot be determined or measured, he will issue a "subject to" opinion describing such uncertainties. The analyst using financial statements that contain such a qualification is, quite bluntly, faced with a situation where the auditor has passed on to him the uncertainty described and, consequently, the task of evaluating its possible impact. The analyst should recognize the situation for what it really is and not assume that he is dealing with a mere formality designed only for the auditor's self-protection. Moreover, the auditor's efforts to estimate future uncertainties cannot normally be expected to exceed those of management itself. As a *SAS* issued in 1974 put it, "The auditor's function in forming an opinion on financial statements does not include estimating the outcome of future events if management is unable to do so."

In those cases where the "subject to" opinion is given because of uncertainties that cannot be resolved, it is hard to blame the auditor for shifting the burden of evaluation on to the reader. At the same time, it must be remembered that as between the reader and the auditor, the latter, due to his firsthand knowledge of the company's affairs, is far better equipped to evaluate the nature of the contingencies as well as the probabilities of their occurrence. Thus, the analyst is entitled to expect, but will unfortunately not always get, a full explanation of all factors surrounding the uncertainty.

Lest the absence of an uncertainty qualification in the auditor's report lull the analyst into a false sense of security, it must be borne in mind that there are many contingencies and uncertainties that do not call for a qualification but that may nevertheless have very significant impact on the company's financial condition or results of operations. Examples of such contingencies or possibilities are:

1.   Obsolescence of a major product line.
2.   Loss of a significant customer.
3.   Overextension of a business in terms of management capabilities.
4.   Difficulty of getting large and complex production units on stream on time.

These matters must, however, be discussed by management in the SEC mandated "Management's Discussion and Analysis of Financial Condition and Results of Operations" (see Chapter 20).

From the above discussion it should be obvious that the analyst must read with great care the auditor's opinion as well as the supplementary information to which it refers. The analyst can place reliance on the auditor, but regardless of the latter's standing and reputation, the analyst must maintain an independent and open-minded attitude.

QUESTIONS

1. In relying on an auditor's opinion what should the financial analyst know about the auditor and his work?

2. What are "generally accepted auditing standards"?

3. What are auditing procedures? What are some of the basic objectives of a financial audit?

4. What does the opinion section of the auditor's report usually cover?

5. The auditors, in an attempt to respond to a clear divergence between their and the society's views of what is meant by "fair presentation," issued a statement on the matter in 1975. What are the major points of that statement?

6. Which are the three major categories of conditions that require the auditor to render qualifications, disclaimers, or adverse opinions?

7. What is an "except-for" type of audit report qualification?

8. What is a *(a)* disclaimer of opinion and *(b)* an adverse opinion? When are these properly rendered?

9. What is the practical effect of an uncertainty qualification in an auditor's report?

10. What types of changes may result in a consistency qualification in the auditor's report?

11. Give two examples of auditor reports that, while falling short of a full audit, provide the reader with lower-defined levels of assurance.

12. What are the major disclosures required by SEC's *FRR* No. 1, Section 603 on the relationship between auditors and clients?

13. What are some of the implications to financial analysis which stem from the audit process itself?

14. The auditor does not prepare the financial statements on which he expresses an opinion but instead he samples the data and examines them in order to render a professional opinion on them. List some of the possible implications of this to those who rely on the financial statements.

15. What does the auditor's reference to "generally accepted accounting principles" mean to the analyst of financial statements?

16. Of what significance are "uncertainty qualifications" to the financial analyst? What type of contingencies may not even be considered by the auditor in his report.

17. What are some of the circumstances which can point to areas of higher audit risk?

PART III

Financial statement analysis—the main areas of emphasis

16 Analysis of short-term liquidity

SIGNIFICANCE OF SHORT-TERM LIQUIDITY

The short-term liquidity of an enterprise is measured by the degree to which it can meet its short-term obligations. Liquidity implies the ready ability to convert assets into cash or to obtain cash. The short term is conventionally viewed as a time span up to a year, although it is sometimes also identified with the normal operating cycle of a business, that is, the time span encompassing the buying-producing-selling and collecting cycle of an enterprise.

The importance of short-term liquidity can best be gauged by examining the repercussions that stem from a lack of ability to meet short-term obligations.

Liquidity is a matter of degree. A lack of liquidity may mean that the enterprise is unable to avail itself of favorable discounts and is unable to take advantage of profitable business opportunities as they arise. At this stage, a lack of liquidity implies a lack of freedom of choice as well as constraints on management's freedom of movement.

A more serious lack of liquidity means that the enterprise is unable to pay its current debts and obligations. This can lead to the forced sale of long-term investments and assets and, in its most severe form, to insolvency and bankruptcy.

To the owners of an enterprise, a lack of liquidity can mean reduced profitability and opportunity or it may mean loss of control and partial or total loss of the capital investment. In the case of owners with unlimited liability, the loss can extend beyond the original investment.

To creditors of the enterprise, a lack of liquidity can mean delay in collection of interest and principal due them or it can mean the partial or total loss of the amounts due them.

Customers as well as suppliers of goods and services to an enterprise can also be affected by its short-term financial condition. Such effects may take the form of inability of the enterprise to perform under contracts and the loss of supplier relationships.

From the above description of the significance of short-term liquidity it can be readily appreciated why the measures of such liquidity have been accorded great importance. For, if an enterprise cannot meet its current obligations as they become due, its continued existence becomes doubtful and that relegates all other measures of performance to secondary importance if not to irrelevance. In terms of the framework of objectives discussed in Chapter 1, the evaluation of short-term liquidity is concerned with the assessment of the unsystematic risk of the enterprise.

While accounting determinations are made, as we have seen in Chapter 3, on the assumption of indefinite continuity of the enterprise, the financial analyst must always submit the validity of such assumption to the test of the enterprise's liquidity and solvency.

One of the most widely used measures of liquidity is working capital. In addition to its importance as a pool of liquid assets that provides a safety cushion to creditors, net working capital is also important because it provides a liquid reserve with which to meet contingencies and the ever-present uncertainty regarding an enterprise's ability to balance the outflow of funds with an adequate inflow of funds.

WORKING CAPITAL

The basic concept of working capital is relatively simple. It is the excess of current assets over current liabilities. That excess is sometimes referred to as *net working capital* because some businessmen consider current assets as working capital. A working capital deficiency exists when current liabilities exceed current assets.

The importance attached by credit grantors, investors, and others to working capital as a measure of liquidity and solvency has caused some enterprises, desiring to present their current condition in the most favorable light, to stretch to the limit the definition of what constitutes a current asset and a current liability. For this reason, the analyst must use his own judgment in evaluating the proper classification of items included in working capital.

Current assets

Current assets include cash and other assets that are reasonably expected to be realized in cash or sold or consumed during the normal operating cycle of the business or within one year if the operating cycle is shorter than one year. Current liabilities include those expected to be satisfied by either the use of assets classified as current in the same balance sheet or the creation of other current liabilities, or those expected to be satisfied within a relatively short period of time, usually one year. [APB *Statement 4,* par. 198.]

The general rule about the ability to convert current assets into cash within a year is subject to important qualifications. The most important qualification relates to the operating cycle. As more fully described in Chapter 5, the operating cycle comprises the average time span intervening between the acquisition of materials and services entering the production or trading process to the final realization in cash of the proceeds from the sale of the enterprise's products. This time span can be quite extended in industries that require a long inventory holding period (e.g., tobacco, distillery, and lumber) or those that sell on the installment plan. Whenever no clearly defined operating cycle is evident, the arbitrary one-year rule prevails.

The most common categories of current assets are:

1. Cash.
2. Cash equivalents (i.e., temporary investments).
3. Accounts and notes receivable.
4. Inventories.
5. Prepaid expenses.

Cash is, of course, the ultimate measure of a current asset since current liabilities are paid off in cash. However, earmarked cash held for specific purposes, such as plant expansion, should not be considered as current. Compensating balances under bank loan agreements cannot, in most cases, be regarded as "free" cash. SEC FRR No. 1 Sec. 203 requires the disclosure of compensating balance arrangements with the lending banks as well as the segregation of such balances (see also Chapter 5).

Cash equivalents represent temporary investments of cash in excess of current requirements made for the purpose of earning a return on these funds.

The analyst must be alert to the valuation of such investments. Equity investments are now accounted for in accordance with *SFAS 12* as detailed in Chapter 5. Debt securities may still be carried above market if management views a decline as merely "temporary" in nature. Similarly, the "cash equivalent" nature of securities investments may sometimes be stretched quite far.

The mere ability to convert an asset to cash is not the sole determinant of its current nature. It is the intention and normal practice that governs. Intention is, however, not always enough. Thus, the cost of fixed assets that are intended for sale should be included in current assets only if the enterprise has a contractual commitment from a buyer to purchase the asset at a given price within the following year or the following operating cycle.

An example where the above principle was not followed is found in the 1970 annual report of International Industries. In this report, the company carries as a current asset $37.8 million in "Real estate held for sale." A related footnote explains that "the company intends to sell this real estate during the ensuing operating cycle substantially at cost under sale-and-lease-back agreements, however, prevailing economic conditions may affect its ability to do so."

This is an obvious attempt to present a current position superior to the one the company can justifiably claim. Without the inclusion of real estate, the company's current ratio would have dropped to 1.1 (with working capital at about $3 million) as against a current ratio, based on reported figures, of 1.8 and a working capital of $40.3 million.

This reinforces the ever-recurring message in this text that the analyst cannot rely on adherence to rules or accepted principles of preparation of financial statements, but instead must exercise eternal vigilance in his use of ratios and all other analytical measures that are based on such statements. If anything, attempts by managements to stretch the rules in order to present a situation as better than it really is should serve as an added warning of potential trouble and risk.

Accounts receivable, net of provisions for uncollectible accounts, are current unless they represent receivables for sales, not in the ordinary course of business, which are due after one year. Installment receivables from customary sales usually fall within the operating cycle of the enterprise.

The analyst must, as the discussion in Chapter 5 indicates, be alert to the valuation as well as validity of receivables particularly in cases such as those where "sales" are made on consignment or subject to the right of return.

Receivables from affiliated companies or from officers and employees can be considered current only if they are collectible in the ordinary course of business within a year or, in the case of installment sales, within the operating cycle.

Inventories are considered current assets except in cases where they are in excess of current requirements. Such excess inventories, which should be shown as noncurrent, must be distinguished from inventories, such as tobacco, which require a long aging cycle. The variations in practice in this area are considerable, as the following illustrations will show, and should be carefully scrutinized by the analyst.

ILLUSTRATION 1. National Fuel Gas Company (prospectus dated July 23, 1969) shows a current as well as a noncurrent portion of gas stored underground and explains this as follows:

"Included in property, plant, and equipment as gas stored underground—noncurrent is $18,825,232 at April 30, 1969, the cost of the volume of gas required to maintain pressure levels for normal operating purposes at the low point of the storage cycle. The portion of gas in underground storage included in current assets does not exceed estimated withdrawals during the succeeding two years."

ILLUSTRATION 2. Some trucking concerns include the tires on their trucks as current assets, presumably on the theory that they will be used up during the normal operating cycle.

The analyst must pay particular attention to inventory valuation. Thus, for example, the inclusion of inventories at LIFO can result in a significant understatement of working capital.

Prepaid expenses are considered current, not because they can be converted into cash but rather because they represent advance payments for services and supplies that would otherwise require the current outlay of cash.

Current liabilities

Current liabilities are obligations that would, generally, require the use of current assets for their discharge or, alternatively, the creation of other current liabilities. The following are current liabilities most commonly found in practice:

1. Accounts payable.
2. Notes payable.
3. Short-term bank and other loans.
4. Tax and other expense accruals.
5. Current portion of long-term debt.

The foregoing current liability categories are usually clear and do not require further elaboration. However, as is the case with current assets, the analyst cannot assume that they will always be properly classified for his purposes. Thus, for example, current practice sanctions the presentation as noncurrent of current obligations that are expected to be refunded. The degree of assurance of the subsequent refunding is mostly an open question that in the case of adverse developments may well be resolved negatively as far as the enterprise is concerned.

SEC FRR No. 1 Sec. 203 has expanded significantly the disclosure requirements regarding short-term bank and commercial paper borrowing. *SFAS 6* established criteria for the balance sheet classification of short-term obligations that are expected to be refinanced (see Chapter 7).

The analyst must also be alert to the possibility of presentations designed to present the working capital in a better light than warranted by circumstances.

ILLUSTRATION 3. Penn Central Company excluded the current maturities of long-term debt from the current liability category and included it in the "long-term debt" section of the balance sheet. In 1969, this treatment resulted in an excess of current assets over current liabilities of $21 million, whereas the inclusion of current debt maturities among current liabilities would have resulted in a working capital *deficit* of $207 million. (The subsequent financial collapse of this enterprise is now a well-known event.)

The analyst must also ascertain whether all obligations, regarding which there is a reasonably high probability that they will have to be met, have been included as current liabilities in computing an effective working capital figure. Two examples of such obligations follow:

1. The obligation of an enterprise for notes discounted with a bank where the bank has full recourse in the event the note is not paid when due

is generally considered a contingent liability. However, the likelihood of the contingency materializing must be considered in the computation of working capital. The same principle applies in case of loan guarantees.

2.   A contract for the construction or acquisition of long-term assets may call for substantial progress payments. Such obligations for payments are, for accounting purposes, considered as commitments rather than liabilities, and hence are not found among the latter. Nevertheless, when computing the excess of liquid assets over short-term obligations such commitments may have to be recognized.

Other problem areas in the definition of current assets and liabilities

An area that presented a problem of classification but that has now been settled in favor of consistency is that of deferred tax accounting (see Chapter 11). Thus, if an asset (e.g., installment accounts receivable) is classified as current, the related deferred tax arising from differences in treatment between book and tax return must be similarly classified.

Current deferred tax debits are no more true current assets than current deferred tax credits are real current liabilities. While, as discussed in Chapter 11, these are the result of present generally accepted methods of accounting for taxes (now under review), the resulting debits do not represent expected means of payment nor do the resulting credits necessarily represent obligations currently due.

Many concerns that have fixed assets as the main "working assets," such as, for example, trucking concerns and some leasing companies, carry as current prospective receipts from billings out of which their current equipment purchase obligations must be met. Such treatments, or the absence of any distinction between current and noncurrent on the balance sheet, as is the case with real estate companies, some contractors, banks, and insurance companies, are attempts by such concerns to convey to the reader their "special" financing and operating conditions that, they claim, make the current versus noncurrent distinction inapplicable and that have no parallel in the regular trading or industrial concern.

Some of these "special" circumstances may indeed be present, but they do not necessarily change the relationship existing between current obligations and the liquid funds available, or reasonably expected to become available, to meet them. It is to this relationship that the analyst, faced with the task of evaluating liquidity, must train his attention.

Working capital as a measure of liquidity

The popularity of working capital as a measure of liquidity and of short-term financial health is so widespread that it hardly needs documentation. Credit grantors compute the relationship between current assets and current liabilities; financial analysts measure the size of the working capital of enterprises they analyze; government agencies compute aggregates of working capital of corporations; and most published balance sheets distinguish between current and noncurrent assets and liabilities. Moreover, loan agreements and bond indentures often contain stipulations regarding the maintenance of minimum working capital levels.

The absolute amount of working capital has significance only when related to other variables such as sales, total assets, and so forth. It is at best of limited value for comparison purposes and for judging the adequacy of working capital. This can be illustrated as follows:

	Company A	Company B
Current assets	$300,000	$1,200,000
Current liabilities	100,000	1,000,000
Working capital	200,000	200,000

While both companies have an equal amount of working capital, a cursory comparison of the relationship of current assets to current liabilities suggests that Company A's current condition is superior to that of Company B.

CURRENT RATIO

The above conclusion is based on the ratio of current assets to current liabilities. It is $3:1$ ($300,000/$100,000) for Company A and $1.2:1$ ($1,200,000/$1,000,000) for Company B. It is this ratio that is accorded substantial importance in the assessment of an enterprise's current liquidity.

Some of the basic reasons for the widespread use of the current ratio as a measure of liquidity are obvious:

1. It measures the degree to which current assets cover current liabilities. The higher the amount of current assets in relation to current liabilities, the greater the assurance that these liabilities can be paid out of such assets.

2. The excess of current assets over current liabilities provides a buffer against losses that may be incurred in the disposition or liquidation of the current assets other than cash. The more substantial such a buffer is, the better for creditors. Thus, the current ratio measures the margin of safety available to cover any possible shrinkage in the value of current assets.

3. It measures the reserve of liquid funds in excess of current obligations that is available as a margin of safety against uncertainty and the random shocks to which the flows of funds in an enterprise are subject. Random shocks, such as strikes, extraordinary losses, and other uncertainties, can temporarily and unexpectedly stop or reduce the inflow of funds.

What is not so obvious, however, is the fact that the current ratio, as a measure of liquidity and short-term solvency, is subject to serious theoretical as well as practical shortcomings and limitations. Consequently, before we embark on a discussion of the uses of the current ratio and related measures of liquidity, these limitations must be thoroughly understood.

Limitations of the current ratio

The first step in our examination of the current ratio as a tool of liqudity and short-term solvency analysis is to examine the components that are normally included in the ratio shown in Exhibit 16–1.

Exhibit 16–1

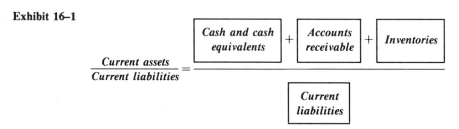

Disregarding, for purposes of this evaluation, prepaid expenses and similar unsubstantial items entering the computation of the current ratio, we are left with the above four major elements that comprise this ratio.

Now, if we define liquidity as the ability to balance required cash outflows with adequate inflows, including an allowance for unexpected interruptions of inflows or increases in outflows, we must ask: Does the relationship of these four elements at a given point in time—

1. Measure and predict the pattern of future fund flows?
2. Measure the adequacy of future fund inflows in relation to outflows?

Unfortunately, the answer to these questions is mostly negative. The current ratio is a static or "stock" concept of what resources are available at a given moment in time to meet the obligations at that moment. The existing reservoir of net funds does not have a logical or causative relationship to the future funds that will flow through it. And yet it is the future flows that are the subject of our greatest interest in the assessment of liquidity. These flows depend importantly on elements *not* included in the ratio itself, such as sales, profits, and changes in business conditions. To elaborate, let us examine more closely the four elements comprising the ratio.

| Cash and cash equivalents | The amount of cash held by a well-managed enterprise is in the nature of a precautionary reserve, intended to |

take care of short-term imbalances in cash flows. For example, in cases of a business downturn, sales may fall more rapidly than outlays for purchases and expenses. Since cash is a nonearning asset and cash equivalents are usually low-yielding securities, the investment in such assets is kept at a safe minimum. To conceive of this minimum balance as available for payment of current debts would require the dropping of the going-concern assumption underlying accounting statements. While the balance of cash has some relation to the existing level of activity, such a relationship is not very strong nor does it contain predictive implications regarding the future. In fact, some enterprises may use cash substitutes in the form of open lines of credit that, of course, do not enter at all into the computation of the current ratio.

The important link between cash and solvency in the minds of many is due to the well-known fact that a shortage of cash, more than any other factor, is the element that can clinch the insolvency of an enterprise.

| *Accounts receivable* | The major determinant of the level of accounts receivable is sales. The size of accounts receivable in relation to sales is |

governed by terms of trade and credit policy. Changes in receivables will correspond to changes in sales though not necessarily on a directly proportional basis.

When we look at accounts receivable as a source of cash, we must, except in the case of liquidation, recognize the revolving nature of the asset with the collection of one account replaced by the extension of fresh credit. Thus, the level of receivables per se is not an index to future net inflows of cash.

| *Inventories* | As is the case with accounts receivable, the main determinant of the size of inventories is the level of sales, or expected |

sales, rather than the level of current liabilities. Given that the level of sales is a measure of the level of demand then, scientific methods of inventory management (economic order quantities, safe stock levels, and reorder points) generally establish that inventory increments vary not in proportion to demand but vary rather with the *square root* of demand.

The relationship of inventories to sales is further accented by the fact that it is sales that is the one essential element that starts the conversion of inventories to cash. Moreover, the determination of future cash inflows through the sale of inventories is dependent on the profit margin that can be realized because inventories are generally stated at the lower of *cost* or *market*. The current ratio, while including inventories, gives no recognition to the sales level or to profit margin, both of which are important elements entering into the determination of future cash inflows.

| *Current liabilities* | The level of current liabilities, the safety of which the current ratio is intended to measure, is also largely determined by |

the level of sales.

Current liabilities are a source of funds in the same sense that receivables and inventories tie up funds. Since purchases, which give rise to accounts payable, are a function of the level of activity (i.e., sales), these payables vary with sales. As long as sales remain constant or are rising, the payment of current liabilities is essentially a refunding operation. There again the components of the current ratio give little, if any, recognition to these elements and their effects on the future flow of funds. Nor do the current liabilities that enter into the computation of the current ratio include prospective outlays, such as commitments under construction contracts, loans, leases, or pensions, all of which affect the future outflow of funds.

Implications of the limitations to which the current ratio is subject

There are a number of conclusions that can be reached on the basis of the foregoing discussion:

1. Liquidity depends to some extent on cash or cash equivalents balances and to a much more significant extent on prospective cash flows.
2. There is no direct or established relationship between balances of working capital items and the pattern that future cash flows are likely to assume.
3. Managerial policies directed at optimizing the levels of receivables and inventories are oriented primarily towards efficient and profitable assets utilization and only secondarily at liquidity.[1]

Given these conclusions, which obviously limit the value of the current ratio as an index of liquidity, and given the static nature of this ratio and the fact that it is composed of items that affect liquidity in different ways, we may ask why this ratio enjoys such widespread use and in what way, if any, it can be used intelligently by the analyst.

The most probable reasons for the popularity of the current ratio are evidently the simplicity of its basic concept, the ease with which it can be computed, and the readiness with which data for it can be obtained. It may also derive its popularity from the credit grantor's, and especially the banker's, propensity to view credit situations as conditions of last resort. They may ask themselves: "What if there were a complete cessation of funds inflow? Would the current assets then be adequate to pay off the current liabilities?" The assumption of such extreme conditions is, of course, not always a useful way of measuring liquidity.

To what use can the intelligent analyst put the current ratio?

Let it first be said that the analyst who wishes to measure short-term liquidity and solvency will find cash flow projections and pro forma financial statements to be the most relevant and reliable tools to use. This involves

---

[1] The nature of the business is also a factor. In the case of many electric utilities, current liabilities exceed current assets because the prompt payment by utility customers enables the utilities to pay off their obligations on time. In other words, utility current assets get converted into cash faster than current obligations must be met. As an added example from another field, Fair Lanes, a bowling lanes operator, obviously does not sell on credit and thus has no receivables. It also carries no inventories of any consequences. Consequently, it has during most of its 50-year existence operated with a working capital deficiency. With almost all of its current assets in cash, it has no problem meeting current obligations.

obtaining information that is not readily available in published financial statements and it also involves the need for a great deal of estimation. This area of analysis will be discussed in the next chapter.

The current ratio as a valid tool of analysis

Should the analyst want to use the current ratio as a static measure of the ability of current assets to satisfy the current liabilities, he will be employing a different concept of liquidity from the one discussed above. In this context, liquidity means the readiness and speed with which current assets can be converted to cash and the degree to which such conversion will result in shrinkage in the stated value of current assets.

It is not our purpose here to discredit the current ratio as a valid tool of analysis but rather to suggest that its legitimate area of application is far less wide than popularly believed.

Defenders of this, the oldest and best known of financial ratios, may say that they are aware of the multitude of limitations and inconsistencies of concept outlined above but that they will "allow" for them in the evaluation of the ratio. A careful examination of these limitations suggests that such process of "allowing" for such limitations is well nigh impossible.

The best and most valid way to use this ratio is to recognize its limitations and to restrict its use to the analytical job it can do, that is, measuring the ability of *present* current assets to discharge *existing* current liabilities and considering the excess, if any, as a liquid surplus available to meet imbalances in the flow of funds and other contingencies. This should be done with an awareness of the fact that the test envisages a situation of enterprise liquidation,[2] whereas in the normal, going-concern situation current assets are of a revolving nature, for example, the collected receivable being replaced with a newly created one, while the current liabilities are essentially of a refunding nature, that is, the repayment of one is followed by the creation of another.

Given the analytical function of the current ratio, as outlined above, there are two basic elements that must be measured before the current ratio can form the basis for valid conclusions:

1. The quality of the current assets and the nature of the current liabilities that enter the determination of the ratio.
2. The rate of turnover of these assets and liabilities, that is, the average time span needed to convert receivables and inventories into cash and the amount of time that can be taken for the payment of current liabilities.

---

[2] It should be realized that the circumstances leading to bankruptcy or liquidation will have an effect on how much the amounts realized on asset dispositions will shrink. They will, for example, be likely to shrink more severely if the liquidation is caused by overall adverse industry conditions than if caused by specific difficulties such as poor management or inadequate capitalization.

To measure the above, a number of ratios and other tools have been devised, and these can enhance the use of the current ratio as an analytic tool.

Measures that supplement the current ratio

The most liquid of current assets is, of course, cash, which is the standard of liquidity itself. A close second to cash is "temporary investments" that are usually highly marketable and relatively safe temporary repositories of cash. These are, in effect, considered as "cash equivalents" and usually earn a modest return.

Cash ratios. The proportion that cash and cash equivalents constitute of the total current assets group is a measure of the degree of liquidity of this group of assets. It is measured by the cash ratio that is computed as follows:

$$\frac{\text{Cash} + \text{Cash equivalents}}{\text{Total current assets}}$$

Evaluation. The higher the ratio, the more liquid is the current asset group. This, in turn, means that with respect to this cash and cash equivalents component there is a minimal danger of loss in value in case of liquidation and that there is practically no waiting period for conversion of these assets into usable cash.

APB Opinion 18 generally requires the carrying of investments, representing an interest of 20 percent or higher, at underlying equity. This is, of course, neither cost nor, necessarily, market value. While such substantial positions in the securities of another company are not usually considered cash equivalents, *should* they nevertheless be so considered, their market value would be the most appropriate figure to use in the computation of liquidity ratios. The equity method of accounting is discussed in Chapters 5 and 9.

As to the availability of cash, the analyst should bear in mind possible restrictions that may exist with respect to the use of cash balances. An example is so-called compensating balances that banks extending credit expect their customers to keep. While such balances can be used, the analyst must nevertheless assess the effect on a company's credit standing and credit availability, as well as on its banking connection, of a breach of the tacit agreement not to draw on the compensating cash balance.

Two additional factors bearing on the evaluation of cash ratios should be mentioned. One is that modern computerized cash management methods have led to more efficient uses of cash by corporations and this has led to lower levels of cash needed for ordinary operations. The other is that open lines of credit and other standby credit arrangements are effective substitutes for cash balances and should be so considered.

An additional ratio that measures cash adequacy should be mentioned. The cash to current liabilities ratio is computed as follows:

$$\frac{\text{Cash} + \text{Cash equivalents}}{\text{Current liabilities}}$$

It measures how much cash is available to pay current obligations. This is a severe test that ignores the refunding nature of current liabilities. It supplements the cash ratio discussed above in that it measures cash availability from a somewhat different point of view.

To view the cash ratio as a further extension of the acid-test ratio (see below) would, except in extreme cases, constitute a test of short-term liquidity too severe to be meaningful. Nevertheless, the importance of cash as the ultimate form of liquidity should never be underestimated. The record of business failures provides many examples of insolvent companies, possessing sizable noncash assets, current and noncurrent, and no cash to pay debts or to operate with.

Measures of accounts receivable liquidity

In most enterprises that sell on credit, accounts and notes receivable are a significant part of working capital. In assessing the quality of working capital and of the current ratio, it is important to get some measure of the quality and the liquidity of the receivables.

Both the quality[3] and liquidity of accounts receivable are affected by their rate of turnover. By quality is meant the likelihood of collection without loss. An indicator of this likelihood is the degree to which receivables are within the terms of payment set by the enterprise. Experience has shown that the longer receivables remain outstanding beyond the date on which they are due, the lower is the probability of their collection in full. Turnover is an indicator of the age of the receivables, particularly when it is compared with an expected turnover rate that is determined by credit terms granted.

The measure of liquidity is concerned with the speed with which accounts receivables will, on average, be converted into cash. Here again turnover is among the best measures to use.

AVERAGE ACCOUNTS RECEIVABLE TURNOVER RATIO

The receivable turnover ratio is computed as follows:

$$\frac{\text{Net sales on credit}}{\text{Average accounts receivable}}$$

---

[3] The validity of the collection claim is also one aspect of quality. Thus, the analyst must be alert to problems that can arise from "sales" on consignment or those with right of return that are more fully discussed in Chapters 5 and 10.

The quickest way for an external analyst to determine the average accounts receivable is to take the beginning receivables of the period, add the ending receivables, and divide the sum by two. The use of monthly or quarterly sales figures can lead to an even more accurate result. The more widely sales fluctuate, the more subject to distortion this ratio is, unless the receivables are properly averaged.

Notes receivable arising from normal sales should be included in the accounts receivable figure in computing the turnover ratio. Discounted notes receivable that are still outstanding should also be included in the accounts receivable total.

The sales figure used in computing the ratio should be that of credit sales only, because cash sales obviously do not generate receivables. Since published financial statements rarely disclose the division between cash and credit sales, the external analyst may have to compute the ratio under the assumption that cash sales are relatively insignificant. If they are not insignificant, then a degree of distortion may occur in the ratio. However, if the proportion of cash sales to total sales remains relatively constant, the year-to-year comparison of changes in the receivables turnover ratio may nevertheless be validly based.

The average receivables turnover figure indicates how many *times,* on average, the receivables revolve, that is, are generated and collected during the year.

For example, if sales are $1,200,000 and beginning receivables are $150,000 while year-end receivables are $250,000, then receivable turnover is computed as follows:

$$\frac{\$1,200,000}{(\$150,000 + \$250,000) \div 2} = \frac{\$1,200,000}{\$200,000} = 6 \text{ times}$$

While the turnover figure furnishes a sense of the speed of collections and is valuable for comparison purposes, it is not directly comparable to the terms of trade that the enterprise normally extends. Such comparison is best made by converting the turnover into days of sales tied up in receivables.

Collection period for accounts receivable

This measure, also known as *days sales in accounts receivable,* measures the number of days it takes, on average, to collect accounts (and notes) receivable. The number of days can be obtained by dividing the average accounts receivable turnover ratio discussed above into 360, the approximate round number of days in the year. Thus,

$$\text{Collection period} = \frac{360}{\text{Average accounts receivable turnover}}$$

Using the figures of the preceding example, the collection period is:

$$\frac{360}{6} = 60 \text{ days}$$

An alternative computation is to first obtain the average daily sale and then divide the *ending gross* receivable balance by it.

$$\text{Accounts receivable} \div \frac{\text{Sales}}{360}$$

The result will differ from the foregoing computation because the average accounts receivable turnover figure uses *average* accounts receivable, while this computation uses *ending* accounts receivable only; it thus focuses specifically on the latest accounts receivable balances. Using the figures from our example, the computation is:

$$\text{Average daily sales} = \frac{\text{Sales}}{360} = \frac{\$1,200,000}{360} = \$3,333$$

$$\frac{\text{Accounts receivable}}{\text{Average daily sales}} = \frac{\$250,000}{\$3,333} = 75 \text{ days}$$

Note that if the collection period computation would have used ending receivables rather than *average* receivables turnover, the identical collection period, that is, 75 could have been obtained as follows:

$$\frac{\text{Sales}}{\text{Accounts receivable (ending)}} = \frac{\$1,200,000}{\$250,000} = 4.8 \text{ times}$$

$$\frac{360}{\text{Receivables turnover}} = \frac{360}{4.8} = 75 \text{ days}$$

The use of 360 days is arbitrary because while receivables are outstanding 360 days (used for computational convenience instead of 365), the sales days of the year usually number less than 300. However, consistent computation of the ratio will make for valid period to period comparisons.

Evaluation

Accounts receivable turnover rates or collection periods can be compared to industry averages (see Chapter 4) or to the credit terms granted by the enterprise.

When the collection period is compared with the terms of sale allowed by the enterprise, the degree to which customers are paying on time can be assessed. Thus, if the average terms of sale in the illustration used above are 40 days, then an average collection period of 75 days reflects either some or all of the following conditions:

1. A poor collection job.
2. Difficulty in obtaining prompt payment from customers in spite of diligent collection efforts.
3. Customers in financial difficulty.

The first conclusion calls for remedial managerial action, while the last two reflect particularly on both the quality and the liquidity of the accounts receivable.

An essential analytical first step is to determine whether the accounts receivable are representative of company sales activity. Significant receivables may, for example, be lodged in the captive finance company of the enterprise. In that case, the bad debt provision may also relate to receivables not on company books.

It is always possible that an *average* figure is not representative of the receivables population it represents. Thus, it is possible that the 75-day average collection period does not represent an across-the-board payment tardiness on the part of customers but is rather caused by the excessive delinquency of one or two substantial customers.

The best way to investigate further an excessive collection period is to *age* the accounts receivable in such a way that the distribution of each account by the number of days past due is clearly apparent. An aging schedule in a format such as given below will show whether the problem is widespread or concentrated:

Accounts receivable aging schedule

		Days past due			
	Current	0–30	31–60	61–90	Over 90
Accounts receivable					

The age distribution of the receivables will, of course, lead to better informed conclusions regarding the quality and the liquidity of the receivables as well as the kind of action that is necessary to remedy the situation. Another dimension of receivables classification is by quality ratings of credit agencies such as Dun & Bradstreet.

Notes receivable deserve the particular scrutiny of the analyst because while they are normally regarded as more negotiable than open accounts, they may be of poorer quality than regular receivables if they originated as an extension device for an unpaid account rather than at the inception of the original sale.

In assessing the quality of receivables, the analyst should remember that a significant conversion of receivables into cash, except for their use as collateral for borrowing, cannot be achieved without a cutback in sales volume. The sales policy aspect of the collection period evaluation must also be kept in mind. An enterprise may be willing to accept slow-paying customers who provide business that is, on an overall basis, profitable; that is, the profit on sales compensates for the extra use by the customer of the enterprise funds. This circumstance may modify the analyst's conclusions regarding the *quality* of the receivables but not those regarding their *liquidity*.

In addition to the consideration of profitability, an enterprise may extend more liberal credit in cases such as (1) the introduction of a new product, (2) a desire to make sales in order to utilize available excess capacity, or (3) special competitive conditions in the industry. Thus, the relationship between the level of receivables and that of sales and profits must always be borne in mind when evaluating the collection period. The trend of the collection period over time is always important in an assessment of the quality and the liquidity of the receivables.

Another trend that may be instructive to watch is that of the relationship between the provision for doubtful accounts and gross accounts receivable. The ratio is computed as follows:

$$\frac{\text{Provision for doubtful accounts}}{\text{Gross accounts receivable}}$$

An increase in this ratio over time may indicate management's conclusion that the collectibility of receivables has deteriorated. Conversely, a decrease of this ratio over time may lead to the opposite conclusion or may cause the analyst to reevaluate the adequacy of the provision for doubtful accounts.

Measures of accounts receivable turnover are, as we have seen in this section, important in the evaluation of liquidity. They are also important as measures of asset utilization, a subject that will be covered in Chapter 19.

MEASURES OF INVENTORY TURNOVER

Inventories represent in many cases a very substantial proportion of the current asset group. This is so for reasons that have little to do with an enterprise's objective of maintaining adequate levels of liquid funds. Reserves of liquid funds are seldom kept in the form of inventories. Inventories represent investments made for the purpose of obtaining a return. The return is derived from the expected profits that may result from sales. In most businesses, a certain level of inventory must be kept in order to generate an adequate level of sales. If the inventory level is inadequate, the sales volume will fall to below the level otherwise attainable. Excessive inventories, on the other hand, expose the enterprise to expenses such as storage costs, insurance and taxes, as well as to risks of loss of value through obsolescence and physical deterioration. Moreover, excessive inventories tie up funds that can be used more profitably elsewhere.

Due to the risk involved in holding inventories as well as the fact that inventories are one step further removed from cash than receivables (they have to be sold before they are converted into receivables), inventories are normally considered the least liquid component of the current assets group. As is the case with most generalizations, this is not always true. Certain staple items, such as commodities, raw materials, standard sizes of structural steel, etc., enjoy broad and ready markets and can usually be sold with little effort, expense, or loss. On the other hand, fashion merchandise, specialized components, or perishable items can lose their value rapidly unless they are sold on a timely basis.

The evaluation of the current ratio, which includes inventories in its computation, must include a thorough evaluation of the quality as well as the liquidity of these assets. Here again, measures of turnover are the best overall tools available for this purpose.

Inventory turnover ratio

The inventory turnover ratio measures the average rate of speed with which inventories move through and out of the enterprise.

Computation. The computation of the average inventory turnover is as follows:

$$\frac{\text{Cost of goods sold}}{\text{Average inventory}}$$

Consistency of valuation requires that the cost of goods sold be used because, as is the case with inventories, it is stated principally at *cost*. Sales, on the other hand, normally include a profit. Although the cost of goods sold figure is now disclosed in most published income statements, the external analyst is still occasionally confronted with an unavailability of such a figure. In such a case, the sales figure must be substituted. While this results in a theoretically less valid turnover ratio, it can still be used for comparison and trend development purposes, especially if used consistently and when sharp changes in profit margins are not present.

The average inventory figure is most readily obtained as follows:

$$\frac{\text{Opening inventory} + \text{Closing inventory}}{2}$$

Further refinement in the averaging process can be achieved, where possible and necessary, by averaging quarterly or monthly inventory figures.

When an inventory turnover ratio is computed in order to evaluate the *level* of inventory at a certain date, such as the year-end inventory, the inventory figure in the denominator should be the figure as of that date rather than an average inventory figure.

Before a turnover ratio is computed, the analyst must carefully examine the composition of the inventory figure and make adjustments, such as those from LIFO to FIFO, etc.

Days to sell inventory

Another measure of inventory turnover that is also useful in assessing purchasing policy is the required number of *days to sell inventory*. The computation that follows, that is,

$$\frac{360 \text{ days}}{\text{Average inventory turnover}}$$

measures the number of days it takes to sell the average inventory in a given year, and an alternative computation

$$\frac{\text{Ending inventory}}{\text{Cost of average day's sales}}$$

measures the number of days that are required to sell off the ending inventory, assuming the given rate of sales where the

$$\text{Cost of an average day's sales} = \frac{\text{Cost of goods sold}}{360}$$

Example of computations

Sales	$1,800,000
Cost of goods sold	1,200,000
Beginning inventory	200,000
Ending inventory	400,000

$$\text{Inventory turnover} = \frac{\$1,200,000}{(\$200,000 + \$400,000) \div 2} = \frac{\$1,200,000}{\$300,000} = 4 \text{ times}$$

$$\text{Number of days to sell average inventory} = \frac{360}{4} = 90 \text{ days}$$

Alternatively the computation based on ending inventory is as follows:

Step 1:

$$\frac{\text{Cost of goods sold}}{360} = \frac{\$1,200,000}{360} = \$3,333 \text{ (cost of average day's sales)}$$

Step 2:

$$\frac{\text{Ending inventory}}{\text{Cost of average day's sales}} = \frac{\$400,000}{\$3,333} = 120 \text{ days}$$

Interpretation of inventory turnover ratios. The current ratio computation views its current asset components as sources of funds that can, as a means of last resort, be used to pay off the current liabilities. Viewed this way, the inventory turnover ratios give us a measure of the quality as well as of the liquidity of the inventory component of the current assets.

The quality of inventory is a measure of the enterprise's ability to use it and dispose of it without loss. When this is envisaged under conditions of forced liquidation, then recovery of cost is the objective. In the normal course of business, the inventory should, of course, be sold at a profit. Viewed from this point of view, the normal profit margin realized by the enterprise assumes importance because the funds that will be obtained, and that would theoretically be available for payment of current liabilities, will include the profit in addition to the recovery of cost. In both cases, costs of sale will reduce the net proceeds.

In practice, a going concern cannot use its investment in inventory for the payment of current liabilities because any drastic reduction in normal inventory levels will surely cut into the sales volume.

A rate of turnover that is slower than that experienced historically, or that is below that normal in the industry, would lead to the preliminary conclusion that it includes items that are slow moving because they are obsolete, in weak demand, or otherwise unsalable. Such conditions do, of course, cast doubt on the feasibility of recovering the cost of such items.

Further investigation may reveal that the slowdown in inventory turnover is due to a buildup of inventory in accordance with a future contractual commitment, in anticipation of a price rise, in anticipation of a strike or shortage, or for any number of other reasons that must be probed into further.

A better evaluation of inventory turnover can be obtained from the computation of separate turnover rates for the major components of inventory such as (1) raw materials, (2) work in process, and (3) finished goods. Departmental or divisional turnover rates can similarly lead to more useful conclusions regarding inventory quality. One should never lose sight of the fact that the total inventory turnover ratio is an aggregate of widely varying turnover rates of individual components.

The biggest problem facing the external analyst who tries to compute inventory turnover ratios by individual product components is obtaining the necessary detailed data. This is, at present, rarely provided in published financial statements.

The turnover ratio is, of course, also a gauge of liquidity in that it conveys a measure of the speed with which inventory can be converted into cash. In this connection, a useful additional measure is the conversion period of inventories.

Conversion period of inventories. This computation adds the collection period of receivables to the days needed to sell inventories in order to arrive at the time interval needed to convert inventories into cash.

Using figures developed in our examples of the respective ratios above, we get:

	Days
Days to sell inventory	90
Days to collect receivables	60
Total conversion period of inventories	150

It would thus normally take 150 days to sell inventory on credit and to collect the receivables. This is a period identical to the *operating cycle* that we discussed earlier in this chapter.

The effect of alternative methods of inventory management

In evaluating the inventory turnover ratio, the analyst must be alert to the influence that alternative accounting principles have on the determination of the ratio's components. The basic discussion on alternative accounting principles of inventory measurement is found in Chapter 5. It is obvious that the use of the LIFO method of inventory valuation may render both the turnover ratios as well as the current ratio practically meaningless. Information is usually found in published financial statements that enable the analyst to adjust the unrealistically low LIFO inventory valuation occurring in times of rising price levels so as to render it useful for inclusion in turnover ratio or the current ratio. Even if two companies employ LIFO cost methods for their inventory valuation computation of their ratios, using such inventory figures may nevertheless not be comparable because their respective LIFO inventory pools (bases) may have been acquired in years of significantly different price levels. The inventory figure enters the numerator of the current ratio and also the denominator because the inventory method utilized affects the income tax liability.

The analyst must also bear in mind that companies using the so-called natural year may have at their year-end an unrepresentatively low inventory level and that this may increase the turnover ratio to unrealistically high levels.

Prepaid expenses are expenditures made for benefits that are expected to be received in the future. Since most such benefits are receivable within a year or within an enterprise's operating cycle, they will conserve the outlay of current funds.

Usually, the amounts included in this category are relatively small compared to the size of the other current assets, and consequently no extensive discussion of their treatment is needed here. However, the analyst must be aware of the tendency of managements of enterprises with weak current positions to include in prepaid expenses deferred charges and other items of dubious liquidity. Such items must consequently be excluded from the computation of working capital and of the current ratio.

CURRENT LIABILITIES

In the computation of working capital and of the current ratio, current liabilities are important for two related reasons:

1. A basic objective of measuring the excess of current assets over current liabilities is to determine whether the latter are covered by current assets and what margin of safety is provided by the excess of such assets over current liabilities.
2. Current liabilities are deducted from current assets in arriving at the net working capital position.

In the computation of the current ratio, the point of view adopted towards current liabilities is *not* one of a continuing enterprise but rather of an enterprise in liquidation. This is so because in the normal course of operations, current liabilities are not paid off but are rather of a refunding nature. As long as the sales volume remains stable, purchases will also remain at a stable level, and that in turn will cause current liabilities to remain level. Increasing sales, in turn, will generally result in an increasing level of current liabilities. Thus, it can be generally stated that the trend and direction of sales is a good indication of the future level of current liabilities.

In assessing the quality of the current ratio, the nature of the current liabilities must be carefully examined.

Differences in the "nature" of current liabilities

Not all liabilities represent equally urgent and forceful calls for payment. At one extreme we find liabilities for taxes of all kinds that must be paid promptly regardless of current financial difficulties. The powers of collection of federal and local government authorities are as well known as they are powerful.

On the other hand, current liabilities to suppliers with whom the enterprise has a long-standing relationship and who depend on, and value, the enterprise's business are of a very different degree of urgency. Postponement and renegotiation of such debts in times of financial stringency are both possible and are commonly found.

The "nature" of current liabilities in terms of our present discussion must be judged in the light of the degree of urgency of payment that attaches to them. It should be understood that if fund inflows from current revenues are viewed as sources of funds available for the payment of current liabilities, then labor costs and other current fund-requiring costs and expenses have a first call on sales revenues and that trade bills and other liabilities can be paid only after such recurring outlays have been met. This dynamic aspect of funds flow will be examined more closely in the chapter that follows.

The analyst must also be aware of unrecorded liabilities that may have a claim to current funds. Examples of these are purchase commitments and obligations under pensions and leases. Moreover, under long-term loan acceleration clauses, a failure to meet current installments of long-term debt may render the entire debt due and payable, that is, cause it to become current.

Days purchases in accounts payable ratio

A measure of the degree to which accounts payable represent current rather than overdue obligations can be obtained by calculating the *days purchases in accounts payable ratio.* This ratio is computed as follows:

$$\frac{\text{Accounts payable}}{\text{Purchases per day*}} = \text{Days purchases in accounts payable}$$

* Computed: Purchases/360.

The difficulty that the external analyst will encounter in computing this ratio is that normally purchases are not separately disclosed in published financial statements. For retailers a rough approximation of the amount of purchases can be obtained by adjusting the cost of goods sold figure for depreciation and other nonfund requiring charges as well as for changes in inventories. However, the cost of goods sold figure may contain significant cash charges, and this may reduce the validity of a computation that contains such an approximation of purchases.

INTERPRETATION OF THE CURRENT RATIO

In the foregoing sections, we have examined the means by which the quality and the liquidity of the individual components of the current ratio is measured. This evaluation is, of course, essential to an overall interpretation of the current ratio as an indicator of short-term liquidity and financial strength.

The analyst must, however, exercise great care if he wants to carry the interpretation of the current ratio beyond the conclusion that it represents an excess of current resources over current obligations as of a given point in time.

Examination of trend

An examination of the trend of the current ratio over time can be very instructive. Two tools of analysis that were discussed in Chapter 4 are useful here. One is *trend analysis,* where the components of working capital as well as the current ratio would be converted into an index to be compared over time. The other is *common-size analysis,* by means of which the *composition* of the current asset group is examined over time. A historical trend and common-size comparison over time, as well as an intra-industry comparison of such trends, can also be instructive.

Interpretation of changes over time

Changes in the current ratio over time must, however, be interpreted with great care. They do not automatically imply changes in liquidity or operating results. Thus, for example, in a prosperous year an increased liability for taxes may result in a lowering of the current ratio. Conversely, during a business contraction, current liabilities may be paid off while there may be a concurrent involuntary accumulation of inventories and uncollected receivables causing the ratio to rise.

In times of business expansion, which may reflect operating successes, the enterprise may suffer from an expansion in working capital requirements, otherwise known as a prosperity squeeze with a resulting contraction of the current ratio. This can be seen in the following example:

	Year 1	Year 2
Current assets	$300,000	$600,000
Current liabilities.....	100,000	400,000
Working capital	$200,000	$200,000
Current ratio	3:1	1.5:1

As can be seen from the above example, a doubling of current assets, accompanied by a quadrupling of current liabilities and an unchanged amount of working capital will lead to a halving of the current ratio. This is the effect of business expansion unaccompanied by an added capital investment. Inflation can have a similar effect on a business enterprise in that it will lead to a substantial increase in all current items categories.

Possibilities of manipulation

The analyst must be aware of the possibilities of year-end manipulation of the current ratio, otherwise known as window dressing.

For example, towards the close of the fiscal year, the collection of receivables may be pressed more vigorously, advances to officers may be called in for temporary repayment, inventory may be reduced to below normal levels, and normal purchases may be delayed. Proceeds from these steps can then be used to pay off current liabilities. The effect on the current ratio of the reduction of current liabilities through the use of current assets can be seen in the following example:

	Payoff of $50,000 in liabilities	
	Before	*After*
Current assets	$200,000	$150,000
Current liabilities.....	100,000	50,000
Current ratio	2:1	3:1

The accounting profession, sensing the propensity of managements to offset liabilities against assets, has strengthened its prohibitions against offsets by restricting them strictly to situations where the legal right to offset exists.

To the extent possible, the analyst should go beyond year-end measures and should try to obtain as many interim readings of the current ratio as possible, not only in order to guard against the practice of window dressing described above but also in order to gauge the seasonal changes to which the ratio is exposed. The effect of a strong current ratio in December on an assessment of current financial condition may be considerably tempered if it is discovered that at its seasonal peak in July the enterprise is dangerously close to a serious credit squeeze.

The use of "rules of thumb" standards

A popular belief that has gained considerable currency is that the current ratio can be evaluated by means of *rules of thumb*. Thus, it is believed that if the current ratio is $2:1$ (or 200 percent), it is sound and anything below that norm is bad while the higher above that figure the current ratio is, the better.

This rule of thumb may reflect the lender's, and particularly the banker's, conservatism. The fact that it is down from the norm of $2.5:1$ prevailing at the turn of the century may mean that improved financial reporting has reduced this size of the "cushion" that the banker and other creditors would consider as the minimum protection they need.

What the $2:1$ standard means is that there are $2 of current assets available for each dollar of current liabilities or that the value of current assets can, on liquidation, shrink by 50 percent before it will be inadequate to cover the current liabilities. Of course, a current ratio much higher than $2:1$, while implying a superior coverage of current liabilities, may also mean a wasteful accumulation of liquid resources which do not "carry their weight" by earning an appropriate return for the enterprise.

It should be evident by now that the evaluation of the current ratio in terms of rules of thumb is a technique of dubious validity. This is so for two major reasons:

1. As we have learned in the preceding sections, the quality of the current assets, as well as the composition of the current liabilities that make up this ratio, are the most important determinants in an evaluation of the quality of the current ratio. Thus, two companies that have identical current ratios may nevertheless be in quite different current financial condition due to variations in the quality of the working capital components.

2. The need of an enterprise for working capital varies with industry conditions as well as with the length of its own particular *net trade cycle.*

The net trade cycle

An enterprise's need for working capital depends importantly on the relative size of its required inventory investment as well as on the relationship between the credit terms it receives from its suppliers as against those it must extend to its customers.

ILLUSTRATION 4.   Assume a company shows the following data at the end of 19x1:

Sales for 19x1	$360,000
Receivables	40,000
Inventories	50,000
Accounts payable.....	20,000

The following tabulation measures the company's cash cycle in terms of days:

$$\text{Sales per day} \frac{\$360,000}{360} = \$1,000$$

Number of days sales in—	*Days*
Accounts receivable........	40
Inventories	50
Total trade cycle	90
Less: Accounts payable.....	20
Net trade cycle	70

From the above we can see that the company is keeping 50 days of sales in inventory and that it receives only 20 sales days of trade credit while it must extend 40 sales days of credit to its customers. Obviously, the higher the *net trade cycle* a company has the larger its investment in working capital is likely to be. Thus, in our above example, if the company could lower its investment in inventories by 10 sales days, it could lower its investment in working capital by $10,000. A similar result can be achieved by increasing the number of days sales in accounts payable by 10.

It should be noted that for the sake of simplicity and uniformity, the net trade cycle computation uses number of *days sales* as a common factor. This does introduce, however, a degree of distortion because while receivables can be related directly to sales, inventories are more logically related to cost of goods sold and accounts payable to purchases. This distortion will, however, not normally be large enough to invalidate the tool for analytical and comparison purposes and the degree of distortion will depend on factors such as the profit margin.

The working capital requirements of a supermarket with its high inventory turnover and low outstanding receivables are obviously lower than those of a tobacco company with its slow inventory turnover.

Valid working capital standards

Comparison with industry current ratios as well as analyses of working capital requirements such as the net trade cycle analysis described above can lead to far more valid conclusions regarding the adequacy of an enterprise's working capital than can a mechanical comparison of its current ratio to the 2:1 rule of thumb standard.

The amount of working capital needed by an enterprise is importantly determined by industry conditions and practices. In recent years, the average industrial company needed about 15 cents of working capital for every dollar of sales. But averages can be misleading, and therefore it is best to focus on specific industry conditions and standards as cases for comparison.

The importance of sales

In an assessment of the overall liquidity of current assets, the trend of sales is an important factor. Since it takes sales to convert inventory into receivables or cash, an uptrend in sales indicates that the conversion of inventories into more liquid assets will be easier to achieve than when sales remain constant. Declining sales, on the other hand, will retard the conversion of inventories into cash.

Common-size analysis of current assets composition

The composition of the current asset group, which can be analyzed by means of common-size statements, is another good indicator of relative working capital liquidity.

Consider, for example, the following comparative working capital composition:

	Year 1		Year 2	
Current assets:				
Cash	$ 30,000	30%	$ 20,000	20%
Accounts receivable	40,000	40	30,000	30
Inventories	30,000	30	50,000	50
Total current assets	$100,000	100%	$100,000	100%

From the simple illustration above it can be seen, even without the computation of common-size percentages, that the liquidity of the current asset group has deteriorated in year 2 by comparison with year 1. However, the use of common-size percentage comparisons will greatly facilitate the evaluation of comparative liquidity, regardless of the size of the dollar amounts involved.

The liquidity index

The measurement of the comparative liquidity of current assets can be further refined through the use of a *liquidity index*. The construction of this index (first suggested by A. H. Finney) can be illustrated as follows:

Using the working capital figures from the common-size computation above, and assuming that the conversion of inventories into accounts receivable takes 50 days on average and that the conversion of receivables into cash takes an average of 40 days, the index is computed as follows:

Year 1

	Amount ×	Days removed from cash	=	Product dollar-days
Cash	$ 30,000	—		—
Accounts receivable	40,000	40		1,600,000
Inventories	30,000	90		2,700,000
Total	$100,000 *(a)*			4,300,000 *(b)*

$$\text{Liquidity index} = \frac{b}{a} = \frac{4{,}300{,}000}{\$100{,}000} = \underline{\underline{43}}$$

Year 2

	Amount ×	Days removed from cash	=	Product dollar-days
Cash	$ 20,000	—		—
Accounts receivable	30,000	40		1,200,000
Inventories	50,000	90		4,500,000
Total	$100,000			5,700,000

$$\text{Liquidity index} = \frac{5{,}700{,}000}{\$100{,}000} = \underline{\underline{57}}$$

The computation of the respective liquidity indexes for the years 1 and 2 tells what we already knew instinctively in the case of this simple example, that is, that the liquidity has deteriorated in year 2 as compared to year 1.

The liquidity index must be interpreted with care. The index is in itself a figure without significance. It gains its significance only from a comparison between one index number and another as a gauge of the period to period change in liquidity or as a company to company comparison of relative liquidity. Increases in the index signify a deterioration in liquidity while decreases signify changes in the direction of improved liquidity. The index that is expressed in days is a weighing mechanism and its validity depends on the validity of the assumptions implicit in the weighing process.

An additional popular technique of current ratio interpretation is to submit it to a somewhat sterner test.

ACID-TEST RATIO

This test is the acid-test ratio, also known as the *quick ratio* because it is assumed to include the assets most quickly convertible into cash.

The acid-test ratio is computed as shown in Exhibit 16–2.

The omission of inventories from the acid-test ratio is based on the belief that they are the least liquid component of the current asset group. While this is generally so, we have seen in an earlier discussion in this chapter that this is not always true and that certain types of inventory can be more liquid than are slow-paying receivables. Another reason for the exclusion of inventories is the belief, quite often warranted, that the valuation of inventories normally requires a greater degree of judgment than is required for the valuation of the other current assets.

Exhibit 16–2

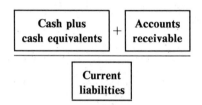

Since prepaid expenses are usually insignificant in relation to the other current assets, the acid-test ratio is sometimes computed simply by omitting the inventories from the current asset figure.

The interpretation of the acid-test ratio is subject to most of the same considerations which were discussed regarding the interpretation of the current ratio. Moreover, the acid-test ratio represents an even sterner test of an enterprise's liquidity than does the current ratio, and the analyst must judge by himself what significance to his conclusions the total omission of inventories, as a source of current funds, is.

OTHER MEASURES OF SHORT-TERM LIQUIDITY

The static nature of the current ratio that measures the relationship of current assets to current liabilities, at a given moment in time, as well as the fact that this measure of liquidity fails to accord recognition to the great importance that funds or cash flows play in an enterprise's ability to meet its maturing obligations has led to a search for more dynamic measures of liquidity.

Funds flow ratios

Funds flow ratios relate obligations to funds (working capital) generated by operations that are available to meet them. These resources do consequently not include funds from nonoperating sources such as borrowing or the sale of fixed assets.

One such ratio relates current liabilities to the funds from operations for the year:

$$\frac{\text{Funds provided by operations}}{\text{Current liabilities}}$$

This is a measure of how many times current liabilities are covered by the funds flow of the year just elapsed. It is, of course, backward looking while current liabilities as of a certain date must be paid out of *future*, rather than past, funds flow. Nevertheless, in the absence of drastic changes in conditions, the latest yearly funds flow represents at least a good basis for an estimate of the next period's funds flow.

Importance of nonfund items in net income. Since the conversion of income into funds flow depends on the size of the net *nonfund* items included in it, a useful comparison measure is the relationship between the net nonfund items in income and net income. The computation of this ratio is as follows:

$$\frac{\text{Net nonfund items in income}}{\text{Net income}}$$

The higher the relationship of net nonfund requiring items to net income, the greater the funds flow is in relation to reported net income and, thus, the higher the funds flow will be in relation to a given net income figure. An example of the computation of the *net nonfund items* follows:

Depreciation	$3,500,000
Depletion	1,200,000
Patent amortization	400,000
Deferred income taxes	2,800,000
Total nonfund charges	7,900,000
Less: Unremitted earnings of foreign subsidiaries	2,100,000
Net nonfund requiring items	$5,800,000

If net income is $58,000,000, the net nonfund items ratio is as follows:

$$\frac{\$5,800,000}{\$58,000,000} = .1, \text{ or } 10 \text{ percent}$$

This means that funds flow will normally be expected to approximate 110 percent of net income.

Cash flow related measures

Since liabilities are paid with cash rather than funds (i.e., working capital), the relationship of cash provided by operations to current liabilities is even more significant. Chapter 13 discusses the derivation of the "cash from operations" amount.

A ratio, which focuses on cash expense of the year and measures how many days of expenses the most liquid current assets could finance, assuming that all other cash inflows were to suddenly dry up, can be computed as follows:

$$\frac{\text{Cash} + \text{Cash equivalents} + \text{Receivables}}{\text{Year's cash expense}}$$

Like the acid-test ratio, the sternness of this test is such that its usefulness must be carefully weighed by the analyst.

THE CONCEPT OF FINANCIAL FLEXIBILITY

In addition to the tools of analysis of short-term liquidity with which we have dealt here and which lend themselves to quantification, there are important qualitative considerations that also have an important bearing on the short-term liquidity of an enterprise. These can be usefully characterized as depending on the financial flexibility of an enterprise.

Financial flexibility is characterized by the ability of an enterprise to take steps to counter unexpected interruptions in the flow of funds for reasons however unexpected. It means the ability to borrow from a variety of sources, to raise equity capital, to sell and redeploy assets, and to adjust the level and the direction of operations in order to meet changing circumstances.

The capacity to borrow depends on numerous factors and is subject to rapid change. It depends on profitability, stability, relative size, industry position, asset composition, and capital structure. It depends, moreover, on such external factors as credit market conditions and trends.

The capacity to borrow is important as a source of funds in time of need for funds and is also important when an enterprise must roll over its short-term debt. Prearranged financing or open lines of credit are more reliable sources of funds in time of need than is potential financing.

Other factors that bear on the assessment of the financial flexibility of an enterprise are the ratings of its commercial paper, bonds, and preferred stock; restrictions on the sale of its assets; the degree to which expenses are of a discretionary nature as well as the ability to respond quickly to changing conditions such as strikes, shrinking demand, or the cessation of sources of supply.

Financial flexibility is also important in the assessment of long-term solvency (see Chapter 18).

MANAGEMENT'S DISCUSSION AND ANALYSIS

Within the framework of its new Integrated Disclosure System, the SEC now requires an expanded management discussion and analysis of Financial

Condition and Results of Operations. The "Financial Condition" portion of that discussion requires a discussion of liquidity factors—including known trends, demands, commitments, or uncertainties likely to have a material impact on the enterprise's ability to generate adequate amounts of cash. If a material deficiency in liquidity is identified, management must discuss the course of action it has taken or proposes to take in order to remedy the deficiency. In addition, internal and external sources of liquidity as well as any material unused sources of liquid assets must be identified and described.

Excerpts from Rohr Industries 1981 management discussion will convey a notion of the types of areas covered:

> Working capital requirements are expected to increase substantially in future years, with the anticipated reduction of investments in the older programs in future years more than offset by requirements of the "new generation" programs which either are or will be entering the production stage. The sums required for working capital and other purposes have been, and will continue to be, difficult to determine, but the Corporation estimates that such additional requirements for funds cumulatively could approximate a range of $42 million to $98 million during the three fiscal years ending July 31, 1984. The actual amount will depend on a number of key factors, the most significant of which are: the ability to obtain significantly increased advances from customers by renegotiating existing contracts to help finance working capital needs; the amount of internally generated funds; the ability to reduce the continued heavy inflow of materials and to improve program inventory turnover ratios to historical levels; the level of deliveries on older programs and on "new generation" programs presently under contract; bank interest rates; various levels of participation in and payment terms of certain additional aircraft programs; continued improvement in production efficiencies; the ability to meet technical and production problems (particularly as may be encountered in new programs); and the level of capital facilities expenditures. In addition, this range assumes the Corporation is able to defer for two years the $18.7 million repayments of bank debt presently scheduled for fiscal 1983, and to defer subsequent scheduled payments. The actual amount of these future requirements for funds could change significantly as the various assumptions and estimates involved in analyzing these factors are changed over time. . . . The Corporation anticipates that it will require substantial additional financing to meet the above-described needs, as the Corporation does not expect to be able to generate sufficient funds from operations to provide all of the necessary working capital and other funds required by the introduction of the "new generation" programs currently under contract or to provide for further sums for future new programs in which the Corporation may participate.

Financial analysts should benefit significantly from a careful analysis and evaluation of such required management discussion and analysis (see also Chapter 20).

Projecting changes in conditions or policies

It is possible and often very useful to trace through the effects of changes in conditions and/or policies on the funds or cash resources of an enterprise.

ILLUSTRATION 5.   Assume that the Foresight Company has the following account balances at December 31, 19x1:

	Debit	Credit
Cash	$ 70,000	
Accounts receivable	150,000	
Inventory	65,000	
Accounts payable		$130,000
Notes payable		35,000
Accrued taxes		18,000
Fixed assets	200,000	
Accumulated depreciation		43,000
Capital stock		200,000

The following additional information is available for 19x1:

Sales	$750,000
Cost of sales	520,000
Purchases	350,000
Depreciation	25,000
Net income	20,000

The company anticipates a growth of 10 percent in sales for the coming year. All corresponding revenue and expense items are also expected to increase by 10 percent, except for depreciation which will remain the same. All expenses are paid in cash as they are incurred during the year. The 19x2 ending inventory will be $150,000. By the end of 19x2, the company expects to have a notes payable balance of $50,000 and no balance in the accrued taxes account. The company maintains a minimum cash balance of $50,000 as a managerial policy.

I.   Assume that the company is considering a change in credit policy so that the ending accounts receivable balance will represent 90 days of sales. What impact will this change have on the company's cash balance? Will it have to borrow?

   This can be computed as follows:

Cash, January 1, 19x2		$ 70,000
Accounts receivable, January 1, 19x2 ..	$150,000	
Sales	825,000	
	975,000	
Less: Accounts receivable,		
December 31, 19x2	206,250 [a]	768,750
Total cash available		838,750

Explanation:

[a] $\$750,000 \times \dfrac{90}{360} = \$206,250.$

Cash disbursements:

Accounts payable, January 1, 19x2 ..	$130,000		
Purchases	657,000 [b]		
	787,000		
Accounts payable, December 31, 19x2	244,000 [c]	543,000	
Notes payable, January 1, 19x2	35,000		
Notes payable, December 31, 19x2 ..	50,000	(15,000)	
Accrued taxes		18,000	
Cash expenses [d]		203,500	749,500
			89,250
Cash balance desired			50,000
Cash excess			$ 39,250

[b] 19x2 cost of sales*: $520,000 \times 1.1 = $572,000

Ending inventory (given)	150,000
Goods available for sale	722,000
Beginning inventory	65,000
Purchases	$657,000

* Which excludes depreciation.

[c] Purchases $\times \dfrac{\text{Old accounts payable}}{\text{Old purchases}} = \$657,000 \times \dfrac{\$130,000}{\$350,000}$

$$= \$244,000$$

[d] Gross profit ($825,000 − $572,000) $253,000

Less: Net income	$24,500*	
Depreciation	25,000	49,500
Other cash expenses		$203,500

* 110 percent of $20,000 (19x1 N.I.) + 10 percent of $25,000 (19x1 depreciation).

II. What would the effect be if the change, instead of as in I, is to an *average* accounts receivable turnover of 4?

We compute this as follows:

Excess cash balance as computed above		$39,250
Change from an *ending* to an *average* accounts receivable turnover will increase year-end accounts receivable balance to:		

$$\dfrac{\$825,000}{4} = \$206,250 \times 2$$

$= \$412,500 - \$150,000 =$	$262,500 [e]	
Less: Accounts receivable balance as above (I)	206,250	56,250 (cash decrease)
Cash required to borrow		$17,000

[e] $\dfrac{\text{Sales}}{\text{Average A/R turnover}} =$ Average A/R;

Ending A/R $= [(\text{Average A/R}) \times 2] -$ Beginning A/R

III. Assuming that in addition to the conditions prevailing in II above, suppliers require the company to pay within 60 days, what would be the effect on the cash balance?

The computation is as follows:

Cash required to borrow (from II above) .... $ 17,000

Ending accounts payable (I above) $244,000

Ending accounts payable under 60-day payment

$$= \text{Purchases} \times \frac{60}{360} = \$657,000 \times \frac{60}{360} = \qquad \qquad 109,500$$

Additional disbursements required 134,500

Cash to be borrowed $151,500

QUESTIONS

1. Why is short-term liquidity so significant? Explain from the viewpoint of various parties concerned.

2. The concept of working capital is simple, that is, the excess of current assets over current liabilities. What are some of the factors that make this simple computation complicated in practice?

3. What are cash equivalents? How should an analyst value them in his analysis?

4. Can fixed assets be included in current assets? If so, explain the situation under which the inclusion may be allowed.

5. Some installment receivables are not collectible within one year. Why are they included in current assets?

6. Are all inventories included in current assets? Why or why not?

7. What is the theoretical justification for including prepaid expenses in current assets?

8. The company under analysis has a very small amount of current liabilities, but the long-term liabilities section shows a significant balance. In the footnote to the audited statements, it is disclosed that the company has a "revolving loan agreement" with a local bank. Does this disclosure have any significance to you?

9. Some industries are subject to peculiar financing and operating conditions that call for special consideration in drawing the distinction between what is *current* and what is *noncurrent*. How should the analyst recognize this in his evaluation of working capital?

10. Your careful computation of the working capitals of Companies A and B reveals that both have the same amount of working capital. Are you ready to conclude that the liquidity position of both is the same?

11. What is the current ratio? What does it measure? What are the reasons for its widespread use?

12. The holding of cash generally does not yield a return. Why does an enterprise hold cash at all?

13. Is there a relationship between the level of inventories and that of sales? Are inventories a function of sales? If there is a functional relationship between the two, is it proportional?

14. What are the major objectives of management in determining the size of inventory and receivables investment?

15. What are the theoretical limitations of the current ratio as a measure of liquidity?

16. If there are significant limitations attached to the current ratio as a measure of liquidity, what is the proper use of this tool?

17. What are cash ratios? What do they measure?

18. How do we measure the "quality" of various current assets?

19. What does the average accounts receivable turnover measure?

20. What is the collection period for accounts receivable? What does it measure?

21. A company's collection period is 60 days this year as compared to 40 days last year. Give three or more possible reasons for this change.

22. What is an accounts receivable aging schedule? What is its use in the analysis of financial statements?

23. What are the repercussions to an enterprise of (a) overinvestment or (b) underinvestment in inventories?

24. What problems would you expect to encounter in an analysis of a company using the LIFO inventory method in an inflationary economy? What effects do the price changes have (a) on the inventory turnover ratio and (b) on the current ratio?

25. Why does the "nature" of the current liabilities have to be analyzed in assessing the quality of the current ratio?

26. An apparently successful company shows a poor current ratio. Explain the possible reasons for this.

27. What is *window dressing?* Is there any way to find out whether the financial statements are window dressed or not?

28. What is the rule of thumb governing the expected size of the current ratio? What dangers are there in using this rule of thumb mechanically?

29. Describe the importance which the sales level plays in the overall current financial condition and liquidity of the current assets of an enterprise.

30. What is the liquidity index? What significance do the liquidity index numbers have?

31. What do cash flow ratios attempt to measure?

32. In addition to the tools of analysis of short-term liquidity that lend themselves to quantification, there are important qualitative considerations that also have an important bearing on the short-term liquidity of an enterprise. What are such considerations? And what are the SEC disclosure requirements that would help financial analysts in this regard?

33. What is the importance of projecting the effects of changes in conditions or policies on the cash resources of an enterprise?

17

Funds flow analysis and financial forecasts

The preceding chapter examined the various measures that are derived from past financial statement data and that are useful in the assessment of short-term liquidity. The chapter that follows will focus on the use of similar data in an evaluation of longer-term solvency. The limitations to which these approaches are subject are due mainly to their static nature, that is, to their reliance on status reports, as of a given moment, of claims against an enterprise and the resources available to meet these claims.

An important and, in many cases, superior alternative to such static measures of conditions prevailing at a given point in time is the analysis and projection of more dynamic models of cash and funds flow. Such models use the present only as a starting point, and while building on reliable patterns of past experience, utilize the best available estimates of future plans and conditions in order to forecast the future availability and disposition of cash or working capital.

OVERVIEW OF CASH FLOW AND FUNDS FLOW PATTERNS

Before we examine the methods by means of which funds flow projections are made, it would be useful to get a thorough understanding of the nature of funds flow. Exhibit 17–1 presents a diagram of the flow of funds through an enterprise. This diagram parallels the accounting cycle diagram presented in Chapter 2 (Exhibit 2–1).

The flow of funds diagram focuses on two concepts of funds: cash and working capital (also known as funds).

Cash (including cash equivalents) is the ultimate liquid asset. Almost all decisions to invest in assets or to incur costs require the immediate or eventual use of cash. This is why managements focus, from an operational point of view, on *cash* rather than on working capital. The focus on the latter represents

521

Exhibit 17–1: Flow of funds through an enterprise

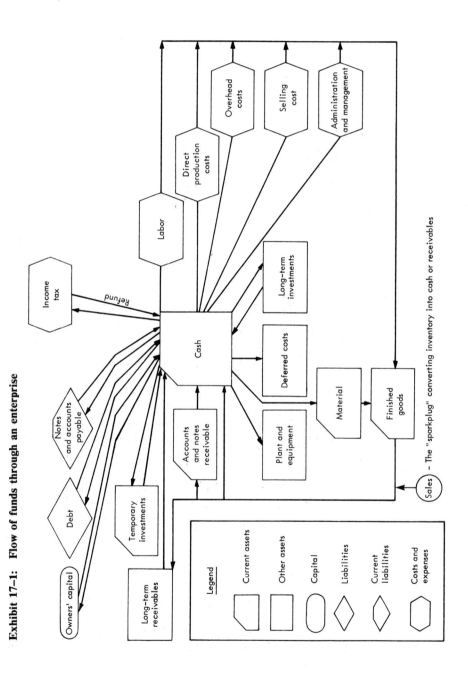

mainly the point of view of creditors who consider as part of the liquid assets pool other assets, such as receivables and inventories, which are normally converted into cash within a relatively short time span.

Careful examination of the flows depicted in Exhibit 17–1 should contribute greatly to the reader's understanding of the importance of liquid funds in an enterprise as well as the factors which cause them to be converted into assets and costs. The following factors and relationships are worthy of particular note:

Since the diagram focuses on cash and funds flows only, assets, liabilities, and other items that are not directly involved, such as prepayments and accruals, as well as the income account are not included in it. Some flows are presented in simplified fashion for an easier understanding of relationships. For example, accounts payable are presented as direct sources of cash, whereas in reality they represent a temporary postponement of cash payment for the acquisition of goods and services.

It is recognized that the holding of cash provides no return or a very low return and that in times of rising price levels, cash as a monetary asset is exposed to purchasing power loss. However, these considerations aside, the holding of this most liquid of assets represents, in a business sense, the lowest exposure to risk. Management must make the decision to invest cash in assets or costs, and such a conversion increases risk because the certainty of ultimate reconversion into cash is less than 100 percent. There are, of course, a variety of risks. Thus, the risk involved in a conversion of cash into temporary investments is lower than the risk involved in committing cash to long-term, long-payout assets such as plant, machinery, or research costs. Similarly, the investment of cash in a variety of assets and costs for the creation and marketing of a new product involves serious risk regarding the recovery in cash of amounts so committed. The short-term liquidity as well as the long-term solvency of an enterprise depends on the recovery and realizability of such outlays.

The inflow and outflow of cash (or funds) are highly interrelated. A failure of any part of the system to circulate can affect the entire system. A cessation of sales affects the vital conversion of finished goods into receivables or cash and leads, in turn, to a drop in the cash reservoir. Inability to replenish this reservoir from sources such as owners' capital, debt, or accounts payable (upper left-hand corner of diagram) can lead to a cessation of production activities that will result in a loss of future sales. Conversely, the cutting off of expenses, such as for advertising and marketing, will slow down the conversion of finished goods into receivables and cash. Longer-term blockages in the flows may lead to insolvency.

The diagram clarifies the interrelationship between profitability, income, and cash flow. The only real source of funds from operations is sales.

When finished goods, which for the sake of simplicity represent the accumulation of *all* costs and expenses in the diagram, are sold, the profit margin will enhance the inflow of liquid funds in the form of receivables and cash. The higher the profit margin, the greater the accretion of these funds.

Income, which is the difference between the cash and credit sales and the cost of goods sold, can have a wide variety of effects on cash flow. For example, the costs that flow from the utilization of plant and equipment or from deferred charges generally do not involve the use of current funds. Similarly, as in the case of land sales on long-term installment terms, the creation of long-term receivables through sales reduces the impact of net income on cash flow. It can be readily seen that adding back depreciation to net income creates a very crude measure of cash flow.

The limitation of the cash flow concept can be more clearly seen. As cash flows into its reservoir, management has a *degree* of discretion as to where to direct it. This discretion depends on the amount of cash already committed to such outlays as dividends, inventory accumulation, capital expenditures, or debt repayment. The total cash inflow also depends on management's ability to tap sources such as equity capital and debt. With respect to noncommitted cash, management has, at the point of return of the cash to the reservoir, the discretion of directing it to any purpose it deems most important. It is this noncommitted cash flow segment that is of particular interest and importance to financial analysts.

Under present accounting conventions, certain cash outlays, such as those for training or sales promotion, are considered as business (period) costs and are not shown as assets. These costs can, nevertheless, be of significant future value in either the increasing of sales or in the reduction of costs.

SHORT-TERM CASH FORECASTS

In the measurement of short-term liquidity, the short-term cash forecast is one of the most thorough and reliable tools available to the analyst.

Short-term liquidity analysis is of particular interest to management in the financial operations of an enterprise and to short-term credit grantors who are interested in an enterprise's ability to repay short-term loans. The security analyst will pay particular attention to the short-term cash forecast when an enterprise's ability to meet its current obligations is subject to substantial doubt.

Realistic cash forecasts can be made only for relatively short time spans. This is so because the factors influencing the inflows and outflows of cash are many and complex and cannot be reliably estimated beyond the short term.

Importance of sales estimates

The reliability of any cash forecast depends very importantly on the forecast of sales. In fact, a cash forecast can never reach a higher degree of reliability than the sales forecast on which it is based. Except for transactions involving the raising of money from external sources or the investment of money in long-term assets, almost all cash flows relate to and depend on sales.

The sales forecast involves considerations such as:

1. The past direction and trend of sales volume.
2. Enterprise share of the market.
3. Industry and general economic conditions.
4. Productive and financial capacity.
5. Competitive factors.

These factors must generally be assessed in terms of individual product lines that may be influenced by forces peculiar to their own markets.

Pro forma financial statements as an aid to forecasting

The reasonableness and feasibility of short-term cash forecasts can be checked by means of pro forma financial statements. This is done by utilizing the assumptions underlying the cash forecast and constructing, on this basis, a pro forma statement of income covering the period of the forecast and a pro forma balance sheet as at the end of that period. The ratios and other relationships derived from the pro forma financial statements should then be checked for feasibility against historical relationships that have prevailed in the past. Such relationships must be adjusted for factors that it is estimated will affect them during the period of the cash forecast.

Techniques of short-term cash forecasting

ILLUSTRATION 1. The Prudent Corporation has recently introduced an improved product that has enjoyed excellent market acceptance. As a result, management has budgeted sales for the six months ending June 30, 19x1, as follows:

	Estimated sales
January	100,000
February	125,000
March	150,000
April	175,000
May	200,000
June	250,000

The cash balance at January 1, 19x1, is $15,000, and the treasurer foresees a need for additional funds necessary to finance the sales expansion. He has obtained a commitment from an insurance company for the sale to them of long-term bonds as follows:

April ..... $50,000 (less $2,500 debt costs)
May 60,000

He also expects to sell real estate at cost: $8,000 in May and $50,000 in June. In addition, equipment with an original cost of $25,000 and a book value of zero was to be sold for $25,000 cash in June.

The treasurer considers that in the light of the expanded sales volume the following minimum cash balances will be desirable:

January $20,000
February 25,000
March 27,000
April, May, and June 30,000

He knows that during the next six months he will not be able to meet his cash requirements without resort to short-term financing. Consequently, he approaches his bank and finds it ready to consider his company's needs. The loan officer suggests that in order to determine the cash needs and the sources of funds for loan repayment, the treasurer prepare a cash forecast for the six months ending June 30, 19x1, and pro forma financial statements for that period.

The treasurer, recognizing the importance of such a forecast, proceeded to assemble the data necessary to prepare it.

The pattern of receivables collections based on experience was as follows:

Collections	Percent of total receivable
In month of sale	40
In the second month	30
In the third month	20
In the fourth month	5
Write-off bad debts	5
	100

On the basis of this pattern and the expected sales, the treasurer constructed Schedule A shown in Exhibit 17–2.

An analysis of past cost patterns resulted in the estimates of cost and expense relationships for the purpose of the cash forecast (Schedule B) shown in Exhibit 17–3.

It was estimated that all costs in Schedule B (exclusive of the $1,000 monthly depreciation charge) will be paid for in cash in the month incurred,

Exhibit 17–2

SCHEDULE A
Estimates of Cash Collections
For the Months January–June, 19x1

	January	February	March	April	May	June
Sales	$100,000	$125,000	$150,000	$175,000	$200,000	$250,000
Collections:						
1st month—40% . .	40,000	50,000	60,000	70,000	80,000	100,000
2d month—30% . .		30,000	37,500	45,000	52,500	60,000
3d month—20% . .			20,000	25,000	30,000	35,000
4th month—5% . .				5,000	6,250	7,500
Total cash collections . . .	40,000	80,000	117,500	145,000	168,750	202,500
Write-offs—5%				5,000	6,250	7,500

Exhibit 17–3

SCHEDULE B
Cost and Expense Estimates for Six Months
Ending June 30, 19x1

Materials	30% of sales
Labor	25% of sales
Manufacturing overhead:	
Variable	10% of sales
Fixed	$48,000 for six months (including $1,000 of depreciation per month)
Selling expenses	10% of sales
General and administrative expenses:	
Variable	8% of sales
Fixed	$7,000 per month

Exhibit 17–4

SCHEDULE C
Pro Forma Schedule of Cash Payments for Materials Purchases
For the Months January–June 19x1

	January	February	March	April	May	June
Materials purchased during month*	$40,000	$38,000	$43,000	$56,000	58,000	$79,000
Payments:						
1st month—50%	20,000	19,000	21,500	28,000	29,000	39,500
2d month—50%		20,000	19,000	21,500	28,000	29,000
Total payments	$20,000	$39,000	$40,500	$49,500	$57,000	$68,500

* These reconcile with material costs and changes in inventories.

except for material purchases that are to be paid 50 percent in the month of purchase and 50 percent in the following month. Since the product is manufactured to specific order, no finished goods inventories are expected to accumulate.

The raw materials inventory at the end of each month for the period January to June 19x1 is expected to be as follows: $67,000, $67,500, $65,500, $69,000, $67,000, and $71,000, respectively. Raw materials inventory on January 1, 19x1, was $57,000.

Schedule C (Exhibit 17–4) shows the pattern of payments of accounts payable (for materials).

Exhibit 17–5

THE PRUDENT CORPORATION
Cash Forecast
For the Months January–June 19x1

	January	February	March
Cash balance—beginning	$15,000	$20,000	$ 25,750
Add: Cash receipts:			
Collections of accounts receivable			
(Schedule A)...............	40,000	80,000	117,500
Proceeds from sale of real estate .			
Proceeds from additional			
long-term debt			
Proceeds from sale of			
equipment			
Total cash available	$ 55,000	$100,000	$143,250
Less: Disbursements:			
Payments for:			
Materials purchases			
(Schedule C)	20,000	39,000	40,500
Labor	25,000	31,250	37,500
Fixed factory overhead	7,000	7,000	7,000
Variable factory overhead	10,000	12,500	15,000
Selling expenses	10,000	12,500	15,000
General and administrative	15,000	17,000	19,000
Taxes.....................			
Purchase of fixed assets		1,000	1,000
Total disbursements	87,000	120,250	135,000
Tentative cash balance (negative)...	(32,000)	(20,250)	8,250
Minimum cash balance required ...	20,000	25,000	27,000
Additional borrowing required ...	52,000	46,000	19,000
Repayment of bank loan			
Interest paid on balance out-			
standing at rate of ½ per			
month*			
Ending cash balance	$ 20,000	$ 25,750	$ 27,250
Loan balance	$ 52,000	$ 98,000	$117,000

* Interest is computed at the rate of ½ percent per month and paid on date of repayment which occurs at month end. Loan is taken out at beginning of month.

Equipment costing $20,000 will be bought in February for notes payable that will be paid off, starting that month, at the rate of $1,000 per month. The new equipment will not be fully installed until sometime in August 19x1.

Exhibit 17–5 presents the cash forecast for the six months ending June 30, 19x1, based on the data given above. Exhibit 17–6 presents the pro forma income statement for the six months ending June 30, 19x1. Exhibit 17–7 presents the actual balance sheet of The Prudent Corporation as at January 1, 19x1, and the pro forma balance sheet as at June 30, 19x1.

The financial analyst should examine the pro forma statements critically and submit to feasibility tests the estimates on which the forecasts are based. The ratios and relationships revealed by the pro forma financial statements

April		May		June		Six-month totals	
$ 27,250		$ 30,580		$ 30,895		$ 15,000	
145,000		168,750		202,500		753,750	
		8,000		50,000		58,000	
47,500		60,000				107,500	
				25,000		25,000	
	$219,750		$267,330		$308,395		$959,250
49,500		57,000		68,500		274,500	
43,750		50,000		62,500		250,000	
7,000		7,000		7,000		42,000	
17,500		20,000		25,000		100,000	
17,500		20,000		25,000		100,000	
21,000		23,000		27,000		122,000	
				19,000		19,000	
1,000		1,000		1,000		5,000	
	157,250		178,000		235,000		912,500
	62,500		89,330		73,395		46,750
	30,000		30,000		30,000		
	—		—		—		117,000
	30,000		58,000		29,000		(117,000)
	1,920		435		145		2,500
	$ 30,580		$ 30,895		$ 44,250		$ 44,250
	$ 87,000		$ 29,000		—		—

Exhibit 17–6

THE PRUDENT CORPORATION
Pro Forma Income Statement
For the Six Months Ending June 30, 19x1

		Source of estimate
Sales	$1,000,000	Based on sales budget (page 525)
Cost of sales:		
Materials	300,000	Schedule B
Labor	250,000	Schedule B
Overhead	148,000	Schedule B
	.698,000	
Gross profit	302,000	
Selling expense	100,000	Schedule B
Bad debts expense	18,750	Schedule A
General and administrative		
expense	122,000	Schedule B
Total	240,750	
Operating income	61,250	
Gain on sale of equipment.....	25,000	
Interest expense	(2,500)	Exhibit 17–5, footnote
Income before taxes	83,750	
Income taxes	38,050	30% of first $25,000; 52% of balance. Pay ½ in June and accrue balance.
Net income	$ 45,700	

should be analyzed and compared to similar ratios of the past in order to determine whether they are reasonable and feasible of attainment. For example, the current ratio of The Prudent Corporation increased from 2.6 on January 1, 19x1, to 3.2 in the pro forma balance sheet as of June 30, 19x1. During the six months ended June 30, 19x1, a pro forma return on average equity of almost 16 percent was projected. Many other significant measures of turnover, common-size statements, and trends can be computed. The reasonableness of these comparisons and results must be assessed. They can help reveal serious errors and inconsistencies in the assumptions that underlie the projections and thus help strengthen confidence in their reliability.

Differences between short-term and long-term forecasts

The short-term cash forecast is, as we have seen, a very useful and reliable aid in projecting the state of short-term liquidity. Such a detailed approach is, however, only feasible for the short term, that is, up to about 12 months.

Exhibit 17–7

THE PRUDENT CORPORATION
Balance Sheets

	Actual *January 1, 19x1*		*Pro forma* *June 30, 19x1*	
Assets				
Current assets:				
Cash........................	$ 15,000		$ 44,250	
Accounts receivable (net)	6,500		234,000	
Inventories—raw materials	57,000		71,000	
Total current assets		$ 78,500		$349,250
Real estate....................	58,000		—	
Fixed assets...................	206,400		201,400	
Accumulated depreciation	(36,400)		(17,400)	
Net fixed assets		228,000		184,000
Other assets		3,000		3,000
Deferred debt expenses				2,500
Total assets		$309,500		$538,750
Liabilities and Equity Capital				
Current liabilities:				
Accounts payable	2,000		41,500	
Notes payable	28,500		43,500	
Accrued taxes	—		19,050	
Total current liabilities.....		$ 30,500		$104,050
Long-term debt................	15,000		125,000	
Common stock	168,000		168,000	
Retained earnings	96,000		141,700	
		279,000		434,700
Total liabilities and equity capital .		$309,500		$538,750

Beyond this time horizon the uncertainties become so great as to preclude detailed and accurate cash forecasts. Instead of focusing on collections of receivables and on payments for labor and materials, the longer-term estimates focus on projections of net income and on other sources and uses of funds. Over the longer term, the emphasis on cash becomes less important, and the estimation process centers on funds, that is, working capital. Over the short term, the difference between cash and other working capital assets is significant. Over the longer term, however, the distinction between cash, receivables, and inventories becomes less significant because the conversion period of these assets to cash is not significant relative to the period encompassed by the longer term. In other words, if the trade cycle is 90 days long, such a period is not as significant in a 3-year forecast as it is in relation to a 6 or 12 months' span. The further we peer into the future, the broader are the financial statement categories that we must estimate and the less detailed can the data behind the estimates be.

The projection of future statements of changes in financial position (SCFPs) is best begun with an analysis of prior year funds statements. To these data can then be added all available information and estimates about the future needs for funds and the most likely sources of funds needed to cover such requirements.

ANALYSIS OF STATEMENTS OF CHANGES IN FINANCIAL POSITION

In Chapter 13, we examined the principles underlying the preparation of the SCFP (funds statement) as well as the uses to which the statement may be put by the analyst. We shall now focus on the analysis of the SCFP paying particular attention to the value of such an analysis to a projection of future funds flows.

In any analysis of financial statements, the most recent years are the most important because they represent the most recent experience. Since there is an inherent continuity in business events, it is this latest experience that is likely to have the greatest relevance to the projection of future results. So it is with the SCFP.

It is important that the analyst obtain SCFPs for as many years as possible. This is particularly important in the case of an analysis of this statement since the planning and execution of plant expansions, of modernization schemes, of working capital increases as well as the financing of such activities by means of short-term and long-term debt and by means of equity funds is an activity that is likely to encompass many years. Thus, in order for the analyst to be able to assess management's plans and their execution, SCFPs covering a number of years must be analyzed. In this way, a more comprehensive picture of management's financial habits can be obtained and an assessment of them made.

Because conditions vary so greatly from enterprise to enterprise, only a few useful generalizations regarding the thrust of such analysis are possible.

The analyst must first establish which the major sources of funds over the years were and what the major uses were to which these funds were put. A common-size analysis of the funds statements will aid in this year-to-year comparison. Detailed funds statements often tend to obscure the major sources and uses of funds. In assessing overall trends and practices, it is best to cumulate the major sources and uses over a span of years, such as 5 or 10, because single fiscal periods are too short for purposes of reaching meaningful conclusions. Thus, for example, the financing of a major capital expansion may be accomplished years before it is in full swing.

In evaluating sources and uses of funds, the analyst should focus on questions such as these:

- Has the enterprise been able to finance fixed asset *replacements* from internally generated funds? Historical-cost as well as current-cost depreciation may be useful in this assessment. Many companies do not provide adequate information to enable the analyst to distinguish between replacement and capacity expansion.
- How have expansion and business acquisitions been financed?
- To what extent is the enterprise dependent on outside financing? How frequently is it required, and what form does it take?
- What does the company's need for funds and its access to funds suggest as implications for its dividend policy?

When funds are defined as working capital, further analysis is required in order to focus on cash. Thus, the changes in receivables, inventories, payables, and accruals will have to be analyzed and interpreted (see also Chapter 13).

ILLUSTRATION OF THE ANALYSIS OF STATEMENTS OF CHANGES IN FINANCIAL POSITION

In this illustration, we shall analyze the statements of changes in financial position of Alfa, Inc. (see Appendix 4B), covering the five-year period ending December 31, 19x6. Exhibit 17–8 presents these statements in common-size format.

During the five-year period the major sources of funds of Alfa were (dollars in millions): operations $\boxed{251}$, long-term debt ($\boxed{115}$ net of debt reductions), and property sales $\boxed{82}$. The major uses were property additions $\boxed{278}$ and cash dividends $\boxed{48}$ which resulted in a net addition to working capital of $\boxed{121}$. During this period, operations as a percentage of total sources fluctuated from a low of 30.5 percent in 19x3 to a high of 58.9 percent in 19x5. The preceding year, 19x4, was by far the most profitable year in this period. In 19x5, Alfa not only used up more than its funds from operations to invest in long-term assets but it also reduced its working capital by $15.5 million in order to repay debt and raise cash dividends to a new high level. That level of dividends required 17.7 percent of total sources compared to only 6.4 percent in the previous year. The higher absolute level of dividends was maintained in 19x6.

Over the five-year period, funds from operations did not cover property additions and thus dividends were in effect financed by either long-term debt or property sales.

Over the five-year period, Alfa's addition of $121 million to working capital was necessitated by the growth in the volume of its business. Cash increased by only $13.4 million over this period while receivables grew by $91.1 million and inventories by $100.5 million. Accounts payable and accrued expenses grew by $63.3 million. The reasons for the company's failure to use more

Exhibit 17–8

ALFA, INC.
Common-Size Statement of Changes in Financial Position
For the Five Years Ended December 31, 19x6

	19x6	19x5	19x4	19x3	19x2
Sources:					
Internally generated funds:					
Net income	16.2%	29.7%	41.9%	17.1%	19.8%
Depreciation and amortization	20.7	31.9	16.6	11.2	12.0
Deferred income taxes— noncurrent portion	3.0	.3	.1	3.9	4.9
Less undistributed income of unconsolidated domestic subsidiaries	(1.2)	(3.0)	(2.9)	(1.7)	(1.8)
Total from operations	38.7	58.9%	55.7%	30.5	34.9%
Additions to long-term debt	49.6	24.1	23.4	47.4	42.0
Decrease in noncurrent receivables	6.7	—	—	—	—
Issuance of capital stock for businesses acquired	2.1	3.3	.6	—	8.8
Property sales and retirements:					
Sale-and-leaseback financing	—	1.3	7.2	16.3	7.0
Other	2.9	11.5	7.1	5.7	7.3
Decrease on deferred charges			6.0		
Other net	—	.9		.1	—
Total	100.0%	100.0%	100.0%	100.0%	100.0%
Applications:					
Property additions:					
Businesses acquired	5.7%	2.4%	—	.3%	6.3%
Existing businesses	35.0	60.7	41.8%	38.4	51.4

Increase in noncurrent receivables	—	5.0	2.5	3.8	1.1
Reduction of long-term debt	6.8	35.6	19.6	20.5	21.2
Cash dividends on capital stock	10.4	17.7	6.4	5.1	6.1
Increase in investment in non-consolidated finance subsidiaries	—	—	—	.9	7.1
Increase in deferred charges	1.7	1.6	—	1.2	4.1
Other—net	.3	—	.1	—	—
Total	59.9	123.	70.4	70.2	97.3
Increase (decrease) in working capital	40.1%	(23.0)%	29.6%	29.8%	2.7%

Represented by:

Current assets—increase (decrease):					
Cash and marketable securities	(4.0)%	4.1%	32.3%	7.9%	(54.3)%
Receivables	45.8	(330.5)	123.9	79.5	1037.9
Inventories	61.0	25.4	35.7	80.3	507.5
Prepaid expenses	(3.7)	41.2	4.2	1.5	44.3
Change in current assets	99.1	(259.8)	196.1%	169.2%	1535.4
Current liabilities—increase (decrease):					
Notes payable and current portion of long-term debt	(10.4)	85.4	(65.9)	33.6	605.2
Accounts payable and accrued expenses	17.5	(36.5)	31.0	37.4	934.4
Current income taxes:					
Currently payable	(13.1)	(82.4)	54.0	(.2)	(138.7)
Deferred	5.1	(126.3)	77.0	(1.6)	34.5
Change in current liabilities	(.9)	(159.8)	96.1	69.2	435.4
Increase (decrease) in working capital	100.0%	(100.0)%	100.0%	100.0%	100.0%

trade credit are not clear. As discussed above, this net investment in working capital was financed mostly by debt. The company did not resort to equity financing during this period.

A forecast of future SCFPs would have to take into consideration all above discussed trends that the enterprise has exhibited, such as those relating to income, the elements that convert it to sources of funds from operations, fixed assets additions, the relationship of sales to growth in working capital and possibly to sources of funds provided by operations as well. The size of nonfund adjustments, such as depreciation, depends on future depreciation policies and equipment acquisitions. The latter as well as write-off methods to be used for tax purposes will in turn determine the size of the deferred tax adjustments. The more we know about factors such as these the more reliable the forecast will be.

THE ANALYTICALLY RECAST STATEMENT OF CHANGES IN FINANCIAL POSITION

The analysis of the SCFP can often be facilitated by recasting the statement to a form that differs from that in which it was presented by the company. Exhibit 17–9 illustrates such a recasting of Alfa, Inc.'s SCFP (see Appendix 4B) for two years. Often the analysis will require the recasting of the statements for a longer period.

The recasting of Alfa's SCFP is illustrative of the types of adjustments and rearrangements that can be effected—others are possible depending on circumstances and on analytical objectives. The major changes in this recasting are a switch to a cash focus and the deduction from "cash from operations" of the best available estimate of the current (replacement) cost of long-term assets used up in the profit-directed activities of the period. Thus, capital expenditures are subdivided into replacement of long-lived assets used in operations with the balance being designated as expansion and/or improvement.

A review of the analytically recast SCFP reveals that compared to 19x5, 19x6 had a substantial ($33.5 million) adjusted outflow of cash for operations. As a result, this outflow, the dividends, investments in long-lived assets as well as required debt repayments, all had to be financed in 19x6 by a substantial issuance ($58 million) of long-term debt as well as by depleting cash by almost $2 million.

EVALUATION OF THE STATEMENT OF CHANGES IN FINANCIAL POSITION

The foregoing example of an analysis of the SCFP illustrates the variety of information and insights that can be derived. Of course, the analysis of

Exhibit 17–9

ALFA, INC.
Analytically Recast SCFP (Cash Focus)
(in thousands)

	19x6	19x5
Sources:		
Cash from operations	$ 9,365 *(a)*	$42,746
Replacement of long-term assets used		
up in operations	42,860 *(b)*	37,450 *(b)*
Adjusted cash from operations	(33,495)	5,296
Dispositions of:		
Property, plant, and equipment	3,409 49 †	8,677
Debt sources of funds:		
Short term	— 65	13,298
Long term...........................	58,344 46	16,323
Equity sources of funds:		
Common	2,494 48	2,228
Preferred		
Miscellaneous other*	51	618
Total sources	30,752	46,440
Uses:		
Acquisition and/or improvement of:		
Property, plant, and equipment	4,997 *(c)*	5,264 *(d)*
Other assets	1,972 54 + 58	4,450
Repayment of debt (net):		
Short term	4,923 65	—
Long term...........................	8,080 55	24,092
Dividends paid:		
On common	11,244 69	10,967
On preferred	1,022 69	1,022
Miscellaneous other*	389 59	—
Total uses	32,627	45,795
Net change in cash and		
cash equivalents	$(1,875) 61	$ 645

* Nonmaterial items can be aggregated.
† Refers to key numbers in Alfa, Inc.'s financial statements (Appendix 4B).
(a) Assuming that decrease in noncurrent receivables 41 represents operating receipts. See Exhibit 13A–3 for computation.
(b) Current cost depreciation as reported by management. (Information available from *SFAS 33* data—see Chapter 14).
(c) Property additions: Items 52 + 53 = $47,857 minus *(b)* above or $42,860 = $4,997 which is assumed to represent capital improvements and/or expansion.
(d) Property additions: Items 52 + 53 = $42,714 minus *(b)* above or $37,450 = $5,264 which is assumed to represent capital improvement and/or expansion.

SCFPs is to be performed within the framework of an analysis of all the financial statements, and thus the conclusion reached from an analysis of one statement may be strengthened and corroborated by an analysis of the other financial statements.

There are some useful generalizations that can be made regarding the value of the analysis of the SCFP to the financial analyst.

This statement enables the analyst to appraise the quality of management decisions over time, as well as their impact on the results of operations and financial condition of the enterprise. When the analysis encompasses a longer period of time, the analyst can evaluate management's response to the changing economic conditions as well as to the opportunities and the adversities which invariably present themselves.

Evaluation of the SCFP analysis will indicate the purposes to which management chose to commit funds, where it reduced investment, the source from which it derived additional funds, and to what extent it reduced claims against the enterprise. Such an analysis will also show the disposition of earnings over the years, as well as how management has reinvested the internal fund inflow over which it had discretion. The analysis will also reveal the size and composition of funds from operations, as well as their pattern and degree of stability.

As depicted in Exhibit 17–1 earlier in this chapter, the circulation of funds in an enterprise involves a constant flow of funds and their periodic reinvestment. Thus, funds are invested in labor, material, and overhead costs as well as in long-term assets, such as inventories and plant and equipment, which join the product-cost stream at a slower rate. Eventually, by the process of sales, these costs are converted back into accounts receivable and into cash. If operations are profitable, the funds recovered will exceed the amounts invested, thus augmenting the funds inflow or cash flow. Losses have, of course, the opposite effect.

What constitutes funds inflow, or cash flow, as it is often more crudely referred to, is the subject of considerable confusion. Generally, the funds provided by operations, that is, net income adjusted for nonfund requiring or supplying items, is an index of management's ability to redirect funds away from areas of unfavorable profit opportunity into areas of greater profit potential. However, not all the funds provided by operations may be so available because of existing commitments for debt retirement, stock redemption, equipment replacement, and dividend payments. Nor are funds provided by operations the only potential cash inflows, since management can avail itself of external sources of capital in order to bolster its funds inflow. The components of the "sources of funds from operations" figure hold important clues to the stability of that source of funds. Thus, for example, depreciation is a more stable element in the total than net income itself in that it represents a recovery by the enterprise of the investment in fixed assets out of selling prices even before a profit is earned.

In evaluating the SCFP, the analyst will judge a company's quality of earnings by the impact that changes in economic and industry conditions have on its flow of funds. The statement will also reveal nonfunds generating income that may have a bearing on the evaluation of earnings quality.

If in his estimates of future earnings potential the analyst foresees a need for additional capital, his analysis of the funds statement will be directed towards a projection of the source from which these funds will be obtained, and what dilution of earnings per share, if any, this will involve.

The analysis and evaluation of the SCFP is, as the foregoing discussion suggests, an important early step in the projection of future SCFPs.

PROJECTION OF STATEMENTS OF CHANGES IN FINANCIAL POSITION

No thorough model of an enterprise's future results is complete without a concurrent forecast of the size of funds needed for the realization of the projections in the model as well as an assessment of the possible sources from which such funds can be derived.

If a future expansion of sales and profits is forecast, the analyst must know whether the enterprise has the "financial horsepower" to see such an expansion through by means of internally generated funds and, if not, where the required funds are going to come from.

The projection of the SCFP will start with a careful estimate of the expected changes in each individual category of assets and the funds that will be derived from or required by such changes. Some of the more important factors to be taken into consideration follow:

1. The net income expected to be generated by future results will be adjusted for nonfund items, such as depreciation, depletion, deferred income taxes, and nonremitted earnings of subsidiaries and investees, in order to arrive at estimates of funds provided by operations.
2. Sources of funds from disposals of assets, sales of investments, and the sale of stocks and bonds will be estimated.
3. The needs for working capital will be arrived at by estimating the required level of the individual working capital items such as cash, receivables, and inventories and reducing this by the expected levels of payables. There is usually a relationship between incremental sales and the corresponding increment in required working capital amounts.
4. Expected capital expenditures will be based on the present level of operations as compared with productive capacity, on an estimate of the future level of activity implied by the profit projections, as well as on current replacement cost data.
5. Mandatory debt retirement and desirable minimum levels of dividend payments will also be estimated.

ILLUSTRATION OF A PROJECTION OF STATEMENTS OF CHANGES IN FINANCIAL POSITION

Based on the financial statements of Alfa, Inc. (see Appendix 4B), and on the preceding analysis we will prepare a forecast of the SCFPs of Alfa for 19x7 and 19x8 based on the following assumptions:

Forecast (in thousands)	19x8	19x7
Sources of funds:		
Undistributed income of nonconsolidated domestic subsidiaries	$ (2,000)	$ (1,500)
Issuance of capital stock for businesses acquired	2,000	2,500
Property sales and retirements		
Sale-and-leaseback financing	9,000	8,000
Other	4,000	3,500
Other—net	—	300
Applications of funds:		
Property additions:		
Businesses acquired	5,000	7,000
Existing businesses	50,000	45,000
Increase in noncurrent receivables	3,300	3,000
Cash dividends on capital stock	14,000	13,000
Increase in deferred charges	2,500	2,000
Other—net	400	—
Increase in investments in nonconsolidated finance subsidiaries	7,400	7,300
Other projections:		
Revenues	1,500,000	1,350,000

Assumptions

The remaining sources and uses of funds will be estimated based on the following assumptions:

1. Net income in 19x7 and 19x8 will be at a level representing the average percentage of net income to revenues as prevailed in the five-year period ended December 31, 19x6.
2. Depreciation and amortization in 19x7 and 19x8 will bear the same relationship to net income as has the average depreciation and amortization over the five-year period 19x2–x6 borne to average net income over the same period.
3. Deferred income taxes—noncurrent portion—will be in 19x7 at a level that reflects the relationship of total five-year deferred taxes (noncurrent) to total five-year net income. It will change in 19x8 by the percentage change that 19x8 net income bears to 19x7 net income.

4.   Additions to long-term debt in 19x7 and 19x8 will be at the level needed
     to meet the needed year-end working capital. The assumed year-end
     working capital needs will be at a level that is measured by the ratio
     of working capital to revenues reflecting the working capital to revenue
     ratio that prevailed in 19x6.

     Exhibit 17–10 presents the projected SCFPs for Alfa, Inc., for 19x7
     and 19x8.

Some assumptions in the above projections may be considered as somewhat
mechanical. They are presented here merely for purposes of illustration. In
practice, more refined relationships may be calculated on the basis of detailed
studies of past relationships.

The impact of adversity

The projected SCFP is useful not only in estimating the funds implications
of future expansion and opportunity but also in assessing the impact on
the enterprise of sudden adversity.

A sudden adversity, from the point of view of its impact on the flow of
funds, will usually manifest itself in a serious interruption in the inflow of
funds. This can be brought about by such events as recessions, strikes, or
the loss of a major customer or market. In this context, a projection of
the SCFP would be a first step in the assessment of the defensive posture
of an enterprise. The basic question to which such an analysis is directed
is this: what can the enterprise do; and what resources, both internal and
external, can it marshal to cope with a sudden and serious reduction in the
inflow of funds?

The strategies and alternatives available to an enterprise faced with such
adversities are ably examined and discussed in a work by Professor Donaldson.
Dr. Donaldson defines financial mobility as the capacity to redirect the use
of financial resources in response to new information about the company
and its environment.[1] This concept is related to that of "financial flexibility"
discussed in the preceding chapter.

The projected sources and uses of funds statement is an important tool
in the assessment of the resources available to meet such "new information"
as well as in planning the changes in financial strategy which this may require.

To the prospective credit grantor such an approach represents an excellent
tool in the assessment of risk. In estimating the effects of, for example, a
recession, on the future flow of funds he can trace through not only the
potential shrinkage in cash inflows from operations but also the effects of
such shrinkage on the uses of funds and on the sources from which they
can be derived.

---

[1] Gordon Donaldson, *Strategy for Financial Mobility* (Boston: Graduate School of Business
Administration, Harvard University, 1969).

Exhibit 17–10

ALFA, INC.
Projected Statement of Changes in Financial Position
(in thousands)

	19x8	19x7
Sources:		
Internally generated funds:		
Net income [a]	$ 43,500	$ 39,150
Depreciation and amortization [b]	29,798	26,818
Deferred income taxes—noncurrent portion [c]	4,693	4,228
Less undistributed income of nonconsolidated domestic subsidiaries [d]	(2,000)	(1,500)
Total from operations	75,991	68,696
Additions to long-term debt—net [f]	18,159	11,846
Issuance of capital stock for businesses acquired [d]	2,000	2,500
Property sales and requirements:		
Sale-and-leaseback financing [d]	9,000	8,000
Other [d]	4,000	3,500
Other—net [d]		300
Total	109,150	94,842
Applications:		
Property additions:		
Businesses acquired [d]	5,000	7,000
Existing businesses [d]	50,000	45,000
Increase in noncurrent receivables [d]	3,300	3,000
Cash dividends on capital stock [d]	14,000	13,000
Increase in investment in nonconsolidated finance subsidiaries [d]	7,400	7,300
Increase in deferred charges [d]	2,500	2,000
Other—net [d]	400	
Total	82,600	77,300
Increase (decrease) in working capital [c]	$ 26,550	$ 17,542
Working capital at year-end [e]	$265,500	$238,950

[a] Average percent of net income to revenues in 19x2–x6 $= \dfrac{\text{Total net income}}{\text{Total revenues}} = \dfrac{\$146,925}{\$5,107,547} = 2.9$ percent.

Net income for 19x7 $= \$1,350,000 \times .029 = \$39,150$
Net income for 19x8 $= \$1,500,000 \times .029 = \$43,500$

[b] Average percent of depreciation and amortization to net income in 19x2–x6
$= \dfrac{\text{Total depreciation and amortization}}{\text{Total net income}} = \dfrac{\$100,659}{\$146,925} = 68.5$ percent.

Depreciation and amortization for 19x7 $= \$39,150 \times .685 = \$26,818$
Depreciation and amortization for 19x8 $= \$43,500 \times .685 = \$29,798$

[c] Average percent of deferred income taxes (noncurrent portion) to net income
in 19x2–19x6 $= \dfrac{\text{Total deferred taxes—noncurrent}}{\text{Total net income}} = \dfrac{\$15,896}{\$146,925} = 10.8$ percent.

Exhibit 17–10 (*concluded*)

$$\text{Deferred income taxes—noncurrent for } 19x7 = \$39,150 \times .108 = \$4,228$$

$$\text{Percent change of } 19x8 \text{ net income to } 19x7 \text{ net income } \frac{= \$43,500}{\$39,150} = 1.11$$

$$\text{Deferred taxes noncurrent for } 19x8 = \$4,228 \times 1.11 = \$4,693$$

[d] Given.

[e] Percentage of year-end working capital to revenues in

$$19x6 = \frac{\$221,408}{\$1,251,087} = .177.$$

$$\text{Yearend working capital in } 19x7 = \$1,350,000 \times .177 = \$238,950$$
$$\text{Yearend working capital in } 19x8 = \$1,500,000 \times .177 = \$265,500$$
$$\text{Increase in working capital in } 19x7 = \$238,950 - \$221,408 = \textit{\$17,542}$$
$$\text{Increase in working capital in } 19x8 = \$265,500 - \$238,950 = \textit{\$26,550}$$

[f] Amounts needed to balance the statements.

The funds flow adequacy ratio

The purpose of this ratio is to determine the degree to which an enterprise generated sufficient funds from operations to cover capital expenditures, net investment in inventories, and cash dividends. To remove cyclical and other erratic influences, a five-year total is used in the computation of the ratio, thus:

$$\frac{\text{Five-year sum of sources of funds from operations}}{\text{Five-year sum of capital expenditures, inventory}}$$
$$\text{additions, and cash dividends}$$

The investment in the other important working capital item, receivables, is omitted on the theory that it can be financed primarily by short-term credit, i.e., growth in payables, and so forth.

A ratio of 1 indicates that an enterprise has covered its needs based on attained levels of growth without the need for external financing. To the degree that the ratio falls below 1, internally generated funds may be inadequate to maintain dividends and current operating growth levels. This ratio may also reflect the effect of inflation on the fund requirements of an enterprise. The reading of this, like any other ratio, can provide no definitive answers and is only a pointer to further analysis and investigation. The ratio for Alfa, Inc., (see Appendix 4B) for the five years ending 19x6 is:

$$\frac{\$251,215^{(a)}}{\$278,275^{(b)} + \$101,083^{(c)} + 48,338^{(d)}} = .59$$

From statement of changes in financial position— five years sum of:

[a] Funds from operations—item 45.
[b] Property additions—items 52 and 53.
[c] Inventories—item 63.
[d] Cash dividends—item 56.

This ratio indicates that for the five years ending in 19x6 Alfa's funds from operations fell far short of covering the three items in the denominator of the ratio.

Funds reinvestment ratio

This ratio is useful in measuring the percentage of the investment in assets, which is being retained and reinvested in the enterprise for the replacement of assets and for growth in operations. The formula is:

$$\frac{\text{Funds provided by operations} - \text{Dividends}}{\text{Gross plant} + \text{Investment} + \text{Other assets} + \text{Working capital}}$$

A reinvestment rate of 8 to 10 percent is considered generally to be at a satisfactory level. The ratio for Alfa, Inc. (Appendix 4B), for 19x6 is:

$$\frac{\$45,604^{(e)} - \$12,266^{(f)}}{\$448,577^{(g)} + \$55,496^{(h)} + \$65,747^{(i)} + \$221,408^{(j)}} = 4.2 \text{ percent}$$

  (e) Funds from operations—item [45].
  (f) Cash dividends—item [56].
  (g) Gross property, plant, and equipment item [29].
  (h) Investments items [27] + [28].
  (i) Other assets—item [30].
  (j) Total current assets [26] − Total current liabilities [35].

Alfa's funds reinvestment ratio for 19x6 is a rather low 4.2 percent that compares to the corresponding ratio of 3.9 percent in 19x5.

CONCLUSION

In the assessment of future liquidity, the use of cash forecasts for the short term and of projected SCFPs for the longer term represent some of the most useful tools available to the financial analyst. In contrast to ratio measures of liquidity, these tools involve a detailed examination of sources and uses of cash or funds. Such examination and estimation processes can be subjected to feasibility tests by means of pro forma statements and to the discipline inherent in the double-entry accounting system.

QUESTIONS

1. What is the primary difference between funds flow analysis and ratio analysis? Which is superior and why?
2. "From an operational point of view, management focuses on cash rather than working capital." Do you agree with the statement? Why or why not?
3. What is the relationship between inflows and outflows of cash?
4. Why is the short-term cash forecast important to the financial analyst?

5. What is the first step to be taken in preparing a cash forecast, and what considerations are required in such a step?

6. What are pro forma financial statements? How are they utilized in conjunction with funds flow projections?

7. What are the limitations of short-term cash forecasts?

8. If the usefulness of a short-term cash forecast is limited, what analytical approach is available to the financial analyst who wants to analyze future flows of working capital?

9. What questions will the analyst focus on in evaluating sources and uses of funds?

10. What useful information do you, as a financial analyst, expect to get from the analysis of past SCFPs (funds statement)?

11. What would a forecast of future SCFPs have to take into consideration?

12. What are the differences between short-term and long-term financial forecasts?

13. What analytical function does the common-size SCFP serve?

14. Why is a projected SCFP necessary when you have historical data which are based on actual performance?

15. If actual operations are seriously affected by unforeseen adversities, would a projected SCFP still be useful?

16. "Cash flow per share" is sometimes used in common stock analysis in the same fashion as *earnings per share*. In financial analysis, shouldn't the former be used more often than the latter? Explain. (CFA)

18

Analysis of capital structure and long-term solvency

The financial strength and stability of a business entity and the probability surrounding its ability to weather random shocks and to maintain its solvency in the face of adversity are important measures of risk associated with it. This evaluation of risk is critical because, as discussed in Chapter 1, the equity investor as well as the lender require returns that are commensurate with the levels of risk that each assumes. This and the preceding two chapters deal with the evaluation of the financial strength and viability of enterprises within different time frames.

KEY ELEMENTS IN THE EVALUATION
OF LONG-TERM SOLVENCY

The process of evaluation of long-term solvency of an enterprise differs markedly from that of the assessment of short-term liquidity. In the latter, the time horizon is short and it is often possible to make a reasonable projection of funds flows. It is not possible to do this for the longer term, and thus the measures used in the evaluation of longer-term solvency are less specific but more all-encompassing.

There are a number of key elements involved in the evaluation of the long-term solvency of an enterprise. The analysis of capital structure is concerned with the types of capital funds used to finance the enterprise, ranging from "patient" and permanent equity capital to short-term funds that are a temporary, and, consequently, a much more risky source. There are different degrees of risk associated with the holding of different types of assets. Moreover, assets represent secondary[1] sources of security for lenders ranging from

---

[1] When lending to going concerns, lenders should regard the liquidation of assets for the purpose of recovery of principal and interest as a measure of last resort and as an undesirable source of funds to rely on at the time credit is granted.

loans secured by specific assets to assets available as general security to unsecured creditors.

On a long-term basis, earnings and earning power (which implies the recurring ability to generate cash in the future) are some of the most important and reliable indications of financial strength available. Earnings are the most desirable and reliable sources of funds for the longer-term payment of interest and repayment of principal. As a surrogate for funds generated by operations, earnings are the yardstick against which the coverage of interest and other fixed charges is measured. Moreover, a reliable and stable trend of earnings is one of the best assurances of an enterprise's ability to borrow in times of funds shortage and its consequent ability to extricate itself from the very conditions that lead to insolvency.

In addition to general measures of financial strength and long-term solvency, lenders rely on the protection afforded by loan covenants or the pledges of specific assets as security. All loan covenants define default and the legal remedies available when it occurs in order to give the lender the right to step in at an early stage. Most are designed to alert the lender to the deterioration in such key measures of financial health as the current ratio and the debt-to-equity ratio, against the issuance of further debt, or to ensure against the disbursement of resources through the payments of dividends above specified levels or through acquisitions. Of course, there can be no prohibition against operating losses, a core problem attending most cases of deterioration in financial condition. Thus, the existence of protective provisions cannot substitute for alertness and a continuous monitoring of the financial condition of an enterprise in which long-term funds are at risk.[2]

The vast amount of public and private debt outstanding has led to standardized approaches to its analysis and evaluation. By far the most important is the rating of debt securities by rating agencies that is discussed in Appendix 18A to this chapter. Appendix 18B examines the use of ratios as predictors of failure.

In this chapter, we shall examine in further detail the tools and the measures available for the analysis of long-term solvency.

IMPORTANCE OF CAPITAL STRUCTURE

The capital structure of an enterprise consists basically of equity funds and debt. It is measured in terms of the relative magnitude of the various

---

[2] Lenders have learned that senior positions in the debt hierarchy do not always afford in practice the security they seem to afford in theory. Thus, subordinated debt is not akin to capital stock because subordinated creditors have a voice in determining whether a debtor should be rescued or be thrown into bankruptcy. This interdependence between junior and senior lenders has led some to the belief that one might as well buy the highest yielding obligation of an enterprise since any situation serious enough to affect the value of the junior security is likely to affect the senior security as well.

Exhibit 18–1:   Asset distribution and capital structure of an enterprise

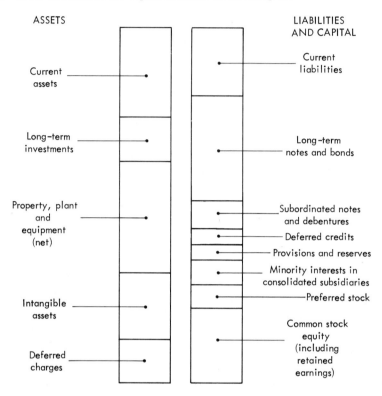

sources of funds of the enterprise. The inherent financial stability of an enterprise and the risk of insolvency to which it is exposed are importantly dependent on the sources of its funds as well as on the type of assets it holds and the relative magnitude of such asset categories. Exhibit 18–1 presents an example of the distribution of assets of an enterprise and the sources of funds used to finance their acquisition. It is evident from the diagram in Exhibit 18–1 that within the framework of equality prevailing between assets and liabilities plus capital, a large variety of combinations of assets and sources of funds used to finance them is possible.

ACCOUNTING PRINCIPLES

The amounts at which liabilities and equity accounts are shown on the financial statements are governed by the application of GAAP. The principles governing the measurement of liabilities are discussed in Chapter 7, and those governing the accounting for equities are covered in Chapter 8. The analyst must keep these principles in mind when analyzing the capital structure and its effect on long-term solvency. While it can be stated, as a broad

the total debt to which an entity is subject, the analyst must be aware that some managements will attempt to understate debt and that new methods of doing this are constantly tried. Chapter 7 contains a discussion of recent methods in use such as "take or pay contracts," "sales" of receivables, and inventory repurchase agreements. A careful reading of footnotes and of management comments along with inquiries of management can shed light on the existence of such practices.

Liabilities for pensions

As was discussed in Chapter 7, analysts should regard an excess of vested pension benefits over pension plan assets as an *unfunded vested pension liability* (UVPL), even though presently accepted accounting standards do not regard them as liabilities. While we favor focusing on this amount as the unrecorded liability, two other elements deserve consideration. If we take a liquidating point of view then, if 30 percent of shareholders' equity is lower than the UVPL, it should be substituted as the pension liability because in liquidation a company's liability for pensions is limited to 30 percent of net worth. The other element deserving consideration is the case when the unfunded past or prior service costs (UPSC) exceed the UVPL. If we adopt the going-concern point of view, then we can regard the larger of the two amounts as an unrecorded interest-bearing pension liability, and this is a reasonable point of view.[4] The amount of the unfunded prior service cost is not easily or readily obtainable.

The analyst will adjust for the unrecorded pension liability by reducing stockholders' equity to reflect the charges to income that would have been made all along in recording the obligation. However, recognition should be given to the fact that when pension costs will ultimately be funded, they will be tax deductible and that consequently a future tax benefit also arises. Thus, the *analytical* entry to record a pension liability of $1,000 is as follows:[5]

Stockholders' Equity	540	
Deferred Taxes* (balance sheet account for future tax benefits assuming a 46 percent tax rate)	460	
Long-Term Pension Liability*		1,000

* Since the future tax benefit will be realized at the same time that the pension liability will be discharged analytically, one can be netted against the other thus creating a net liability of $540.

---

[4] Two articles that ably discuss these issues are P. J. Regan, "Credit Ratings and Pension Costs," *Financial Analysts Journal*, March–April 1979; and D. A. Lasman and R. L. Weil, "Adjusting the Debt-Equity Ratio," *Financial Analysts Journal*, September–October, 1978.

[5] Another point of view in making this adjustment, one of doubtful validity in our opinion, is to debit an asset instead of stockholders' equity with $1,000 on the assumption that the pension obligation gives rise to substantial future benefits in the form of higher morale and increased productivity.

Unconsolidated subsidiaries

As we saw in Chapter 9, the preferred method of presenting the financial statements of a parent and its subsidiary is in consolidated format. This is also the preferred method from the analyst's point of view for most analytical purposes, although separate financial statements of the consolidated entities are necessary in some cases, such as when the utilization of assets of a subsidiary (e.g., an insurance company or a bank) is not subject to the full discretion of the parent.

Information on unconsolidated subsidiaries may also be important because bondholders of such subsidiaries can look only to the latter's assets as security for their bonds. Moreover, bondholders of the parent company (particularly holding companies) may derive a significant portion of their fixed-charge coverage from the dividends of the unconsolidated subsidiaries. Yet, in the event of the subsidiary's bankruptcy, the parent bondholders may be in a junior position to the bondholders of the subsidiary.

When the financial statements of a finance subsidiary are not consolidated with the parent, consolidation may be undertaken as an analytical adjustment as follows:

Subsidiary's Assets*		X
Subsidiary's Liabilities*		Y
Parent's Investment in Subsidiary		Z

* Using as much detail as is needed or is available.

If the subsidiary has unrecorded lease or pension liabilities, they too may be consolidated for purposes of analysis.

Provisions, reserves, and contingent liabilities

Provisions such as for guarantees and warranties represent obligations to offer future service and should be classified as such. Generally speaking, reserves created by charges to income may also be considered as liabilities. However, general contingency reserves or reserves for very indeterminate purposes (most of which are now prohibited by *SFAS 5*) should not be considered as genuine liabilities.

The analyst must make a judgment regarding the probability of commitments or contingencies becoming actual liabilities and should then treat these items accordingly. Thus, guarantees of indebtedness of subsidiaries or others that are likely to become liabilities should be treated as such.

Minority interests

Minority interests in consolidated financial statements represent the ownership interests of minority shareholders of the subsidiaries included in the consolidated group. These are not liabilities similar in nature to debt because they have neither mandatory dividend payment nor principal repayment requirements. Capital structure measurements concentrate on the mandatory payments aspects of liabilities. From this point of view, minority interests are more in the nature of outsider's claim to a portion of the equity or an offset representing their proportionate ownership of assets.[6]

Convertible debt

Convertible debt is generally classified among liabilities. However, if the conversion terms are such that the only reasonable assumption that can be made is that the debt will be converted into common stock, then it may be classified as equity for purposes of capital structure analysis.

Preferred stock

Most preferred stock entails no absolute obligation for payment of dividends or repayment of principal, possessing thus the characteristics of true equity. However, as was discussed in Chapter 7, preferred stock with a fixed maturity or subject to sinking fund requirements should, from an analytical point of view, be considered as debt.

As discussed in Chapter 7, preferred stock with mandatory redemption requirements is akin to debt and should be considered as such by the analyst.

ADJUSTMENTS TO THE BOOK VALUE OF ASSETS

Because the owners' equity of an enterprise is measured by the excess of total assets over total liabilities, any analytical revision of asset book values (i.e., amounts at which assets are shown in the financial statements) will also result in a change in the amount of the owners' equity. For this reason, in assessing capital structure, the analyst must decide whether or not the book value amounts of assets are realistically stated. The following are examples of the need for possible adjustments. Different or additional adjustments may be needed depending on circumstances.

Inventories

Inventories carried at LIFO are generally understated in times of rising prices. The amount by which inventories computed under FIFO (which are closer to replacement cost) exceed inventories computed under LIFO is now disclosed. So is the current cost of inventories under *SFAS 33* (see Chapter 14). These disclosures should enable the analyst to adjust inventory amounts

---

[6] Minority interests are shown at book value. Thus, if the analyst wants to assess what the parent company would have to pay in order to acquire the minority interest, market rather than book values will be the determining factor.

and the corresponding owners' equity amounts (after tax) to more realistic current costs or values.

Marketable securities

Marketable securities are generally stated at cost that may be below market value. Using parenthetical or footnote information, the analyst can make an analytical adjustment increasing this asset to market value and owners' equity (after tax) by an equal amount.

Intangible assets

Intangible assets and deferred items of dubious value that are included on the asset side of the balance sheet have an effect on the computation of the total equity of an enterprise. To the extent that the analyst cannot evaluate or form an opinion on the present value or future utility of such assets, they may be excluded from consideration thereby reducing the amount of equity capital (after tax) by the amounts at which such assets are carried. However, the arbitrary exclusion of all intangible assets from the capital base is an unjustified exercise in overconservatism.

The foregoing discussion related to the evaluation and the classification of debt and equity accounts. Let us now turn to an examination of the significance of capital structure in financial analysis.

THE SIGNIFICANCE OF CAPITAL STRUCTURE

The significance of capital structure is derived, first and foremost, from the essential difference between debt and equity.

The equity is the basic risk capital of an enterprise. Every enterprise must have some equity capital that bears the risk to which it is inevitably exposed. The outstanding characteristic of equity capital is that it has no guaranteed or mandatory return that must be paid out in any event and no definite timetable for repayment of the capital investment. Thus, capital that can be withdrawn at the contributor's option is not really equity capital and has, instead, the characteristics of debt.[7] From the point of view of an enterprise's stability and exposure to the risk of insolvency, the outstanding characteristic of equity capital is that it is permanent, can be counted on to remain invested in times of adversity, and has no mandatory requirement for dividends. It is such funds that an enterprise can most confidently invest in

---

[7] For example, during the financial crisis that befell many brokerage houses in the late 1960s, it was discovered that much "equity" capital that was thought to lend strength to the enterprise and additional security to customers and creditors was in effect subject to withdrawal by owners. At the sign of real trouble, these owners withdrew their capital, thus compounding the financial problems even more.

long-term assets and expose to the greatest risks. Their loss, for whatever reason, will not necessarily jeopardize the firm's ability to pay the fixed claims against it.

Both short-term and long-term debt, in contrast to equity capital, must be repaid. The longer the term of the debt and the less onerous its repayment provisions, the easier it will be for the enterprise to service it. Nevertheless, it must be repaid at certain specified times regardless of the enterprise's financial condition; and so must interest be paid in the case of most debt instruments. Generally, the failure to pay principal or interest will result in proceedings under which the common stockholders may lose control of the enterprise as well as part or all of their investment. Should the entire equity capital of the enterprise be wiped out by losses, the creditors may also stand to lose part or all of their principal and interest due.

It can be readily appreciated that the larger the proportion of debt in the total capital structure of an enterprise, the higher the resulting fixed charges and repayment commitments and the greater the probability of a chain of events leading to an inability to pay interest and principal when due.

To the investor in the common stock of an enterprise, the existence of debt represents a risk of loss of his investment, and this is balanced by the potential of high profits arising from financial leverage. Excessive debt may also mean that management's initiative and flexibility for profitable action will be stifled and inhibited.

The creditor prefers as large a capital base as possible as a cushion that will shield him against losses that can result from adversity. The smaller the relative capital base, or conversely, the larger the proportionate contribution of funds by creditors, the smaller is the creditors' cushion against loss and consequently the greater their risk of loss.

While there has been a considerable debate, particularly in academic circles, over whether the *cost of capital* of an enterprise varies with different capital structures, that is, with various mixes of debt and equity, the issue seems significantly clearer from the point of view of outsiders to the enterprise, such as creditors or investors, who must make decisions on the basis of conditions as they are. In the case of otherwise identical entities, the creditor exposes himself to greater risk if he lends to the company with 60 percent of its funds provided by debt (and 40 percent by equity capital) than if he lends to a similar company that derives, say, only 20 percent of its funds from debt.

Under the Modigliani-Miller thesis, the cost of capital of an enterprise in a perfect market is, except for the tax deductibility of interest, not affected by the debt-to-equity relationship.[8] This is so, they assert, because each individual stockholder can inject, by use of personally created leverage, his own

---

[8] F. Modigliani and M. Miller, "The Cost of Capital, Corporation Finance and the Theory of Investment," *American Economic Review*, June 1958, pp. 261–97.

blend of risk into the total investment position. Thus, under this theory, the advantage of debt will be offset by a markdown in a company's price-earnings ratio.

The degree of risk in an enterprise, as judged by the outside prospective investor is, however, a given; and our point of view, as well as our task here, is to measure the degree of risk residing in the capital structure of an enterprise.

REASONS FOR EMPLOYMENT OF DEBT

In addition to serving as an inflation hedge, a primary reason for the employment of debt by an enterprise is that up to a certain point, debt is, from the point of view of the ownership, a less expensive source of funds than equity capital. This is so for two main reasons:

1. The interest cost of debt is fixed,[9] and thus, as long as it is lower than the return that can be earned on the funds supplied by creditors, this excess return accrues to the benefit of the equity.
2. Unlike dividends, which are considered a distribution of profits, interest is considered an expense and is, consequently, tax deductible.

A further discussion of these two main reasons follows.

The concept of financial leverage

Financial leverage means the use in the capital structure of an enterprise of debt that pays a fixed return. Since no creditor or lender would be willing to put up loan funds without the cushion and safety provided by the owners' equity capital, this borrowing process is also referred to as "trading on the equity," that is, utilizing the existence of a given amount of equity capital as a borrowing base.

In Exhibit 18–2, a comparison is made of the returns achieved by two companies having identical assets and earnings before interest expense. Company X derives 40 percent of its funds from debt while Company Y has no debt. In year 1, when the average return on total assets is 10 percent, the return on the stockholders' equity of Company X is 13.3 percent. This higher return is due to the fact that the stockholders benefited from the excess return on total assets over the cost of debt. For Company Y, the return on equity always equals the return on total assets. In year 2, the return on total assets of Company X was equal to the interest cost of debt and, consequently, the effects of leverage were neutralized. The results of year 3 show that leverage is a double-edged sword. Thus, when the return on total assets

---

[9] Except for debt subject to variable interest rates.

Exhibit 18–2: Trading on the equity—results under different earning assumptions (dollars in thousands)

	Assets	Debt payable	Stock-holders' equity	Income before interest and taxes	10 percent debt interest	Taxes[a]	Net income	Net income + (Interest) × (1 − Tax rate)	Return on	
									Total assets[b]	Stock-holders' equity[c]
Year 1:										
Company X	$1,000,000	$400,000	$ 600,000	$200,000	$40,000	$ 80,000	$ 80,000	$100,000	10.0%	13.3%
Company Y	1,000,000	—	1,000,000	200,000	—	100,000	100,000	100,000	10.0	10.0
Year 2:										
Company X	1,000,000	400,000	600,000	100,000	40,000	30,000	30,000	50,000	5.0	5.0
Company Y	1,000,000	—	1,000,000	100,000	—	50,000	50,000	50,000	5.0	5.0
Year 3:										
Company X	1,000,000	400,000	600,000	50,000	40,000	5,000	5,000	25,000	2.5	.83
Company Y	1,000,000	—	1,000,000	50,000	—	25,000	25,000	25,000	2.5	2.5

[a] Assuming a 50 percent tax rate.

[b] $\dfrac{\text{Net income} + \text{Interest } (1 - .50)}{\text{Total assets}}$.

[c] $\dfrac{\text{Net income}}{\text{Stockholders' equity}}$.

falls below the cost of debt, Company X's return on the equity is lower than that of debt-free Company Y.

The effect of tax deductibility of interest

The second reason given for the advantageous position of debt is the tax deductibility of interest as opposed to the distribution of dividends. This can be illustrated as follows:

Assume the facts given in Exhibit 18–2 for year 2, and that the operating earnings of Company X and Company Y, $60,000 for each, are both of equal quality.[10] The results of the two companies can be summarized as follows:

	Company X	Company Y
Income before interest and taxes	$200,000	$200,000
Interest (10% of $400,000)	40,000	
Income before taxes	160,000	200,000
Taxes	80,000	100,000
Net Income	80,000	100,000
Add back interest paid to bondholder	40,000	
Total return to security holders (debt and equity)	$120,000	$100,000

Disregarding leverage effects that are neutral in the above example, even if the return on assets is equal to the interest rate, the total amount available for distribution to the bondholders and stockholders of Company X is $20,000 higher than the amount available for the stockholders of Company Y. This is due to the lower total tax liability to which the security holders of Company X are subject.

It should be borne in mind that the value of the tax deductibility of interest is dependent on the existence of sufficient earnings. However, unrecovered interest charges can be carried back and carried forward as part of tax loss carry-overs permitted by law.

Other advantages of leverage

In addition to the advantages accruing to equity stockholders from the successful employment of financial leverage and the tax deductibility of interest expenses, a sound longer-term debt position can result in other advantages to the equity owner. A rapidly growing company can avoid earnings dilution

---

[10] The concept of the quality of earnings is discussed in Chapter 22.

through the issuance of debt. Moreover, if interest rates are headed higher, all other things being equal, a leveraged company paying fixed interest rates will be more profitable than its nonleveraged competitor. There is, moreover, a financial benefit from advantageously placed debt because debt capital is not always available to an enterprise and the capacity to borrow may disappear should adverse operating results occur. Finally, in times of inflation, monetary liabilities will result in price-level gains (see Chapter 14).

Measuring the effect of financial leverage

The effect of leverage on operating results is positive when the return on the equity capital exceeds the return on total assets. This difference in return isolates the effect that the return on borrowed money has on the return on the owner's capital. As was seen in the example in Exhibit 18–2, leverage is positive when the return on assets is higher than the cost of debt. It is negative when the opposite conditions prevail. The terms *positive* and *negative* are not used here in the strict algebraic sense.

The effect of financial leverage can be measured by the following formula:

$$\text{Financial leverage index} = \frac{\text{Return on common equity}}{\text{Return on total assets}}$$

Using the data in Exhibit 18–2, we compute the financial leverage indexes of Company X for years 1, 2, and 3 as follows:

Financial leverage index

$$\text{Year 1:} \quad \frac{13.3}{10.0} = 1.33$$

$$\text{Year 2:} \quad \frac{5.0}{5.0} = 1$$

$$\text{Year 3:} \quad \frac{.83}{2.5} = .33$$

In year 1, when the return on equity exceeded that on total assets, the index at 1.4 was positive. In year 2, when the return on equity equaled that on total assets, the index stood at 1 reflecting a neutralization of financial leverage. In year 3, the index, at .07, was way below 1.0, thus indicating the very negative effect of financial leverage in that year. The subject of return on investment is discussed in Chapter 19.

The financial leverage index for Alfa, Inc. (Appendix 4B), for 19x6 is calculated as follows:

$$\frac{\text{Return on common equity}}{\text{Return on total assets}} = \frac{5.82\%}{3.73\%} = \underline{\underline{1.56}}$$

with both returns calculated as follows:

Return on common equity:

$$\frac{\$19,139^{(a)} - \$1,022^{(b)}}{(\$331,080^{(c)} - \$14,940^{(d)}) + (\$321,713^{(c)} - \$14,940^{(d)}) \div 2} = \underline{\underline{5.82}} \text{ percent}$$

Return on total assets:

$$\frac{\$19,139^{(a)} + \$18,440^{(e)}(1 - .48)^{(f)}}{(\$801,672 + \$738,469) \div 2^{(g)}} = \underline{\underline{3.73}} \text{ percent}$$

[a] Net income (item 16).
[b] Preferred dividends (from statement of earnings reinvested—item 69).
[c] Total stockholders' equity (item 40). We accept here the company's classification of "Excess of Equity Over Cost of Subsidiary Companies at Dates of Acquisition" as part of equity. After 1970, these amounts have to be amortized to income.
[d] Sum of two issues of preferred stock (item 40).
[e] Net interest expense = Item 5 − Item 6 .
[f] 1 − Marginal tax rate.
[g] Average total assets 31 .

MEASURING THE EFFECT OF CAPITAL STRUCTURE ON LONG-TERM SOLVENCY

From the foregoing discussion it is clear that the basic risk involved in a leveraged capital structure is the risk of running out of cash under conditions of adversity.

Debt involves a commitment to pay fixed charges in the form of interest and principal repayments. While certain fixed charges can be postponed in times of cash shortage, those associated with debt cannot be postponed without adverse repercussion to the ownership and also to the creditor groups.

Another important repercussion of excessive debt is a loss of financing flexibility, i.e., the ability to raise funds particularly in adverse capital markets.

LONG-TERM PROJECTIONS—USEFULNESS AND LIMITATIONS

If a shortage of cash required to service the debt is the most adverse possibility envisaged, then the most direct and most relevant measure of risk inherent in the leveraged capital structure of an enterprise would be a projection of future cash resources and flows that would be available to meet these cash requirements. These projections must assume the worst set of economic conditions that are likely to occur, since this is the most realistic and useful test of safety from the creditor's point of view. If only prosperous and normal times are to be assumed, then the creditor would not need his preferred position and would be better off with an equity position where the potential rewards are higher.

In Chapter 17, we concluded that detailed cash flow projections can be reliably made only for the short term. Consequently, they are useful only in the measurement of short-term liquidity.

The statement of changes in financial position (SCFP) can be projected over a relatively longer term because such a projection is far less detailed than a projection of cash flows. However, as we saw in the discussion of such projections in the preceding chapter, this lack of detail as well as the longer time horizon reduces the reliability of such projections.

The short term is understood to encompass, generally, a period of up to one year. The longer term, however, is a much wider ranging period. Thus, it may include a solvency analysis with respect to a three-year term loan, or it may encompass the evaluation of risk associated with a 30-year bond issue. Meaningful projections covering the period over which the interest and principal of the term loan will be paid can still reasonably be made. However, a 30-year projection of funds flow covering the bond issue would be an unrealistic exercise. For this reason, longer-term debt instruments often contain sinking fund provisions that act to reduce the uncertain time horizon, and stipulations of additional security in the form of specific assets pledged as collateral. Moreover, they often contain provisions requiring the maintenance of minimum working capital levels or restrictions on the payment of dividends, all of which are designed to ensure against a deterioration in the financial ratios prevailing at the time the bonds are issued. They cannot, of course, prohibit adverse operating results.

Desirable as funds flow projections may be, their use for the extended longer term is severely limited. For this reason, a number of measures of long-term solvency have evolved that are more static in nature and are based on measures of capital structure as well as on asset and earnings coverage tests. These measures will be considered below.

CAPITAL STRUCTURE ANALYSIS—COMMON-SIZE STATEMENTS

A simple measure of financial risk in an enterprise is the composition of its capital structure. This can be done best by constructing a common-size statement of the liabilities and equity section of the balance sheet as shown in Exhibit 18–3.

An alternative way of analyzing capital structure with common-size percentages would be to focus only on the longer-term capital funds by excluding the current liabilities from total funds.

The advantage of a common-size analysis of capital structure is that it presents clearly the relative magnitude of the sources of funds of the enterprise, a presentation that lends itself readily to a comparison with similar data of other enterprises.

Exhibit 18–3: Liabilities and equity section—with common-size percentages

Current liabilities	$ 428,000	19.0%
Long-term debt	500,000	22.2
Equity capital:		
Preferred stock	400,000	17.8
Common stock	800,000	35.6
Paid-in capital	20,000	.9
Retained earnings	102,000	4.5
Total equity capital	1,322,000	58.8
Total liabilities and equity capital	$2,250,000	100.0%

A variation of the approach of analyzing capital structure by means of common-size or component percentages is to analyze it by means of ratios.

CAPITAL STRUCTURE RATIOS

The basic ratio measurements of capital structure relate the various components of the capital structure to each other or to their total. Some of these ratios in common use are explained below.

TOTAL DEBT TO TOTAL CAPITAL (DEBT AND EQUITY)

The most comprehensive ratio in this area is that which measures the relationship between *total debt* (i.e., Current liabilities + Long-term debt + any other form of liability determined by the analyst to be debt, such as obligations under capitalized leases) to *total capital* that in addition to total debt includes the stockholders' equity (inclusive of preferred stock). The ratio can thus be expressed as

$$\frac{\text{Total debt}}{\text{Total capital}} \text{ as defined above}$$

and can also be expressed as debt as a percentage of total capitalization (rather than the ratio of one to the other).

The 19x6 debt to total capital ratio for Alfa, Inc. (Appendix 4B), is computed as follows (dollars in millions):

$$\frac{\$186^{(a)} + \$35^{(b)} + \$5^{(c)} + \$245^{(d)} + \$167^{(e)}}{\$331^{(f)} + \$638^{(g)}} = \frac{\$638}{\$969} = .66$$

[a] Total current liabilities (item $\boxed{35}$).
[b] Deferred income taxes (item $\boxed{36}$), assumed here to be liabilities.
[c] Other deferred credits (item $\boxed{37}$).
[d] Long-term debt (item $\boxed{38}$).
[e] Present value of long-term financing lease obligations (item $\boxed{99}$). *SFAS 13* requires capitalization and inclusion among balance sheet liabilities.
[f] Stockholder's equity (item $\boxed{40}$) including "negative goodwill" as classified by company.
[g] Total debt (total numerator).

The result can be expressed as a ratio of .66 or as debt being 66 percent of Alfa's total capital (Debt + Equity).

Ratio of total debt to total equity capital

An alternate measure of the relationship of debt to capital sources is the ratio of total debt (as defined above) to total equity capital only. Thus:

$$\frac{\text{Total debt}}{\text{Total stockholders' equity}}$$

This ratio for 19x6 for Alfa, Inc., is computed as follows:

$$\frac{\$638*}{\$331*} = 1.93$$

* See above
for derivation.

This ratio means that Alfa's total debt is 1.93 times its equity capital or that the company borrowed from all sources $1.93 for every dollar of equity capital it has.

A reciprocal measure of the above is:

$$\frac{\text{Total stockholders' equity}}{\text{Total debt}}$$

For Alfa, $\frac{\$331}{\$638} = .52$, and this can be interpreted from the creditor's point of view as meaning that every dollar of debt is backed by only 52 cents of equity capital. This also clarifies the fact that the owners have a smaller stake in the enterprise than do all creditors. The creditors have, conversely, $1.52 in assets (at book value) backing up each dollar claim. This relationship ignores, of course, prior, senior, or specific claims some creditors may have as compared to others.

Long-term debt/equity capital

This ratio measures the relationship of long-term debt to equity capital.[11] A ratio in excess of 1:1 indicates a higher long-term debt participation as compared to equity capital. This ratio is the familiar debt-to-equity ratio that is computed as follows:

$$\frac{\text{Long-term debt}}{\text{Equity capital}}$$

For Alfa, the 19x6 long-term debt to stockholders' equity ratio is computed as follows:

---

[11] The term *long-term debt* usually includes *all* liabilities that are not current.

$$\frac{\$638^{(a)} - \$186^{(b)}}{\$331^{(c)}} = \underline{\underline{1.37}}$$

(a) Total debt.
(b) Total current liabilities.
(c) Stockholders' equity.
(For derivation of amount,
see above.)

Confusion in terminology

Analysts must be aware that in this area, as in many others, the popular name of a ratio may not convey precisely its meaning and, hence, the method of its computation. Before any measure or ratio is used, care must be taken that the method of its computation is thoroughly understood.

Short-term debt

The ratio of debt that matures over the short term to total debt is an important indicator of the short-run funds and financing needs of an enterprise. Short-term debt, as opposed to maturing long-term debt or sinking fund requirements, is often an indicator of enterprise reliance on bank financing. Moreover, short-term debt is subject to frequent changes in interest rates.

Equity capital at market value

Accounting principles in current use place primary emphasis on historical costs rather than on current values. Since the shareholders' capital is the residual of assets minus liabilities, this accounting can result in equity capital book value figures that are far removed from realistic market values.

One method of correcting this flaw in the stated equity capital amounts, particularly when they enter importantly into the computation of many of the ratios that we have considered above, is to restate them by converting the assets from historical cost to current market values. This may be particularly important in the case of natural resource companies whose book values greatly understate the market value of their assets.

Although SEC disclosure requirements affecting certain companies will provide analysts with some replacement cost data (see Chapter 14), we are still far from having complete market values available.

One way of overcoming the problem of giving recognition to market values is to compute the equity capital at current (or some kind of average) market value of the stock issues that comprise it. On the assumption that the valuation placed by the market on the equity capital recognizes the current values of assets and their earning power, this amount can then be used in the computation of the various debt-to-equity ratios.

A serious objection to this method is that stock prices fluctuate widely and may, particularly in times of overspeculation, not be representative of "true" values at a given moment. However, this argument can be countered with considerable evidence that the judgment of the marketplace is most of the time superior to that of other judgmental processes and that use of average market prices would solve the problem of temporary aberrations. Thus, the use of equity capital figures computed at current, or at average, market values has much to commend it. Being more realistic, they can improve the ratio measurements in which they are used and can provide a more realistic measure of the asset cushion that bondholders can count on.[12]

A persistent trend of equity at book value that is in excess of equity at market value can be interpreted as a sign of financial weakness and of restricted financial capability, such as the capability to sell equity capital or even raise new debt capital.

One important advantage of earnings-coverage ratios, as will be seen in the subsequent discussion of this subject, is that they are based on the earning power of assets rather than on the amount at which they are carried in the financial statements. Market values do, of course, give recognition to such earning power of an entity's assets. In that sense, ratio measures, such as debt-to-equity ratios, that use equity capital amounts at market value, are more consistent with earnings-coverage ratios than are ratios using historical book values.

Using Alfa Inc.'s (see Appendix 4B) average common stock market price for 19X6 (item $\boxed{107}$ bottom) we can compute ($ millions):

$$\frac{\text{Total debt}}{\text{Common equity at market value} + \text{Preferred equity at book value}} =$$

$$\frac{638^*}{(11,723,774 \text{ shares} \times \$16.50) + .610 + 14.330} = \frac{638^*}{208} = 3.08$$

* See preceding derivation of amount.

Comparing the above ratio with the corresponding 1.93 ratio computed at book value we can conclude that due to the market's low evaluation of Alfa's stock (average $16.50 price vs. 26.13 of book value) the market value based Debt/Equity ratio is far worse than the book value computed ratio. This low market evaluation can be interpreted as a negative factor in Alfa's financial strength, and in its ability to sell equity shares.

---

[12] B. Graham, D. L. Dodd, and S. Cottle in their *Security Analysis,* 4th ed. (New York: McGraw-Hill, 1962), p. 361, suggest that the ratio of

$$\frac{\text{Market value of junior equity}}{\text{Par value of bonds}}$$

should not be less than .5 and can be used to corroborate earnings coverage measures. It would not be prudent to have to assume, they maintain, that the junior equity is undervalued by the market.

PREFERRED STOCK WITHIN THE CAPITAL STRUCTURE

Within the total stockholders' equity, preferred stock holds a preferential position with a prior claim on assets ahead of the common stock. Thus, it is instructive to compute the ratio of preferred stock to total stockholders' equity which is done as follows:

$$\frac{\text{Preferred stock at stated value (or liquidating value if higher)}}{\text{Total stockholders' equity}}$$

Alfa, Inc.'s (see Appendix 4B) 19x6 ratio is calculated as follows (dollars in millions):

$$\frac{\$1.5\,^{(a)} + \$23.2\,^{(b)}}{\$331.1\,^{(c)}} = 7.46 \text{ percent}$$

See item 40 .

$^{(a)}$ \$2.50 cumulative convertible preferred at liquidation value.
$^{(b)}$ Series B \$1 cumulative convertible preferred at liquidation value.
$^{(c)}$ Total stockholders' equity.

Analytically, the excess of liquidation over stated values (\$1.5 − \$.6) + (\$23.2 − \$14.3) that is added to the preferred equity should be charged to retained earnings, i.e., the common equity.

The above computation shows the preferred stock to constitute 7.46 percent of the total shareholders' equity.

The analyst must also consider how to treat preferred stock subject to mandatory redemption requirements. While, as discussed in Chapter 7, such stock is akin to a liability more than to equity, it must be recognized that a failure to meet the redemption requirements may not have as dire a result on the entity's status as would a failure to meet a sinking fund requirement of debt.

THE ANALYTICALLY ADJUSTED RATIO OF DEBT TO EQUITY

In our earlier discussion of the elements that enter into an entity's capital structure, we concluded that there are many types of analytical adjustments that the analyst may wish to make to the published financial data in computing debt-to-equity ratios.[13] An illustration of the computation of the analytically adjusted debt-to-equity ratio is given in Appendix 18C.

---

[13] For an excellent discussion of such adjustments, see Lasman and Weil, "Adjusting the Debt-Equity Ratio."

INTERPRETATION OF CAPITAL STRUCTURE MEASURES

The common-size and ratio analyses of capital structure, which have been examined above, are all measures of risk inherent in the capital structure of an enterprise. The higher the proportion of debt, the larger the fixed charges of interest and debt repayment, the greater the likelihood of insolvency during protracted periods of earnings decline or other adversities.

One obvious value of these measures is that they serve as screening devices. Thus, when the ratio of debt-to-equity capital is relatively small, say, 10 percent or less, there is normally no need to be concerned with this aspect of an enterprise's financial condition; and the analyst may well conclude that he can spend his time better by directing his attention to the more critical areas revealed by analysis.

Should an examination of the debt-to-equity ratios reveal that debt is indeed a significant factor in the total capitalization, then further analysis is necessary. Such an analysis will encompass many aspects of an enterprise's financial condition, results of operations, and future prospects.

An analysis of short-term liquidity is always important because before the analyst starts to assess long-term solvency he has to be satisfied about the short-term financial survival of the enterprise. Chapter 16 examines the analysis of short-term liquidity, and the analyst will use the tools discussed there to assess the situation and also to relate the size of working capital to the size of long-term debt. Loan and bond indenture covenants requiring the maintenance of minimum working capital ratios attest to the importance attached to current liquidity in ensuring the long-term solvency of an enterprise.

Additional analytical steps of importance will include an examination of debt maturities (as to size and spacing over time), interest costs, and other factors that have a bearing on the risk. Among those, the earnings stability of the enterprise and its industry as well as the kind of assets its resources are invested in are also important factors.

MEASURES OF ASSETS DISTRIBUTION

The type of assets an enterprise employs in its operations should determine to some extent the sources of funds used to finance them. Thus, for example, it is customarily held that fixed and other long-term assets should not be financed by means of short-term loans. In fact, the most appropriate source of funds for investment in such assets is equity capital, although debt also has a place in such financing especially in industries such as utilities that generally enjoy stable revenue sources. On the other hand, working capital, and particularly seasonal working capital needs, can be appropriately financed by means of short-term credit. The ratio of working capital to long-term debt should generally not fall below 1, and in most industries that are affected by the business cycle, a ratio below 1.5 to 2 may indicate weakness and vulnerability.

In judging the risk exposure of a given capital structure, the asset composition is one of the important factors to consider. This asset composition is best measured by means of common-size statements of the asset side of the balance sheet. For example, Exhibit 18–4 shows the common-size asset section of the balance sheet whose liabilities and equity section was presented in Exhibit 18–3.

Exhibit 18–4:   Assets section—with common-size percentages

Current assets:		
Cash	$ 376,000	16.7%
Accounts receivable (net)	425,000	18.9
Merchandise inventory	574,000	25.5
Total current assets	1,375,000	61.1
Investments	268,000	11.9
Land, property, and equipment (net).....	368,000	16.4
Intangibles	239,000	10.6
Total assets.......................	$2,250,000	100.0%

Judging *only* by the distribution of assets and the related capital structure, it would appear that since a relatively high proportion of assets is current (61 percent), a 41 percent debt and current liabilities position (see Exhibit 18–3) is not excessive. Other considerations and measurements may, however, change this conclusion.

Asset coverage is an important element in the evaluation of long-term solvency. Assets of value provide protection to holders of debt obligations both because of their earning power and because of their liquidation value. Additionally, they represent the bases on which an enterprise can obtain the financing that may be required to tide it over a period of financial stringency.

The relationship between asset groups and selected items of capital structure can also be expressed in terms of ratios.

Fixed assets equity capital is a ratio that measures the relationship between long-term assets and equity capital. A ratio in excess of 1:1 means that some of the fixed assets are financed by means of debt.

Net tangible assets as a percentage of long-term debt is a measure of asset coverage of long-term obligations. It excludes assets of doubtful realizability or value and represents a measure of safety of debt based on liquidation of assets.

Total obligations to total net tangible assets (including net working capital) is another useful measure of the relationship between debt and the entity's investment in operating assets. An analysis of the property backing enjoyed by creditors is likely to be most useful in the case of companies, such as those in the natural resource field, where book values may be significantly understated.

If the financial structure ratios are such that they require further analysis, one of the best means for further investigation are tests that measure an enterprise's ability to service its debt requirements out of earnings. This is the area we shall turn to next.

CRITICAL IMPORTANCE OF "EARNING POWER"

One conclusion of our discussion of debt-to-equity ratios was that a major usefulness of these measurements lies in their function as a screening device, that is, a means of deciding whether the apparent risk inherent in the capital structure of an enterprise requires further investigation and analysis. An important limitation of the measurements of debt-to-equity relationships is that they do not focus on the availability of funds or cash flows that are necessary to service the enterprise's debt. In fact, as a debt obligation is repaid, the debt-to-equity ratio tends to improve whereas the yearly amount of cash needed to pay interest and sinking fund requirements may remain the same or may even increase, as, for example, in the case of level payment debt or loans with "balloon" repayment provisions.

The long-term creditor must in the final analysis rely on the enterprise's earning power as the most reliable source of interest and principal repayments. While a highly profitable enterprise can in the short run be illiquid because of the composition of its assets, earning power is in the long run the only reliable source of liquidity and of borrowing capacity.

MEASURES OF EARNINGS COVERAGE

Earnings-coverage ratios measure directly the relationship between debt related fixed charges and the earnings available to meet these charges.[14] The concept of the basic earnings coverage of fixed-charges ratio is simple:

$$\frac{\text{Earnings available to meet fixed charges}}{\text{Fixed charges (as defined)}}$$

While the concept behind this measurement is simple and straightforward, its practical implementation is complicated by the problem of defining what should be included in "earnings" and in "fixed charges."

Earnings available to meet fixed charges

As was seen in Chapter 13, net income determined under the principles of accrual accounting is not the same thing as sources of funds provided

---

[14] Fixed-charges-coverage ratios represent important inputs in bond rating decisions. Bond indentures often specify that minimum levels of this ratio must be maintained before additional debt can be issued.

by operations. Specifically, certain items of income, such as undistributed earnings of subsidiaries and controlled companies or sales on extended credit terms, do not create funds, that is, working capital. Similarly, certain expenses such as depreciation, amortization, depletion, and deferred income tax charges do not require the outlay of current funds. On the other hand, it should be borne in mind that a parent company can determine the dividend policy of a controlled subsidiary.

Fixed-debt charges are paid out of current funds rather than out of net income. Thus, the analyst must realize that an unadjusted net income figure may not be a correct measure of funds available to meet fixed charges.

Since fixed charges are paid off with cash, a clarification is needed as to why we accept here working capital as a surrogate for cash. The reason is that over the longer term the conversion period of current assets into cash becomes relatively insignificant. Thus, even if the conversion period of inventories into receivables, and ultimately into cash, is 120 days, this period is not significant compared with the longer-term period over which the fixed charges of debt must be paid.

The use of net income as an approximation of funds provided by operations may, in some instances, be warranted while in others it may significantly overstate or understate the amount actually available for the servicing of debt. Thus, the soundest approach to this problem lies not in generalizations but rather in a careful analysis of the nonfund generating items included in income as well as the nonfund requiring expenses charged to that income. Thus, for example, in considering depreciation as a nonfund requiring expense, the analyst must realize that over the long run an enterprise must replace its plant and equipment.

The problem of determining the amount of income to be included in fixed-charges-coverage ratios requires consideration of a number of additional factors:

1. *The treatment of extraordinary gains and losses.* As pointed out in the more comprehensive discussion of this subject in Chapters 11 and 22, extraordinary gains and losses enter into the determination of longer-term average earnings power. As such they must be recognized as a factor that may, over the longer term, contribute to or reduce the funds available to pay fixed charges. Any computation of earnings-coverage ratios utilizing average earnings figures must recognize the existence of extraordinary gains and losses over the years. This is particularly true of earnings-coverage ratios where what we measure is the risk of loss of sources of funds for payment of fixed charges.

2. *Preferred dividends* need not be deducted from net income because the payment of such dividends is not mandatory. However, in consolidated financial statements, preferred dividends of a subsidiary whose income is consolidated must be deducted because they represent a charge that has priority over the distribution of earnings to the parent.

3. Earnings that are attributed to *minority interests* are usually deducted

from net income available for fixed charges even though minority shareholders can rarely enforce a cash claim under normal operating conditions. An exception arises where the consolidated subsidiary has fixed charges. In such instances, the coverage ratio should be computed on the basis of earnings before deducting minority interests.

If a subsidiary with a minority interest has a loss, the credit in the income statement that results from the minority's share in the loss should be excluded from consolidated earnings for purposes of the coverage ratio computation. The parent would, in most cases, meet fixed-charges obligations of its subsidiary to protect its own credit standing, whether or not legally obligated to do so.

4. *The impact of income taxes* on the computation of earnings-coverage ratios should always be carefully assessed. Since interest is a tax-deductible expense, it is met out of pretax income. Thus, the income out of which interest payments are met is pretax income. On the other hand, preferred dividends or sinking fund payments are not tax deductible and must be paid out of aftertax earnings.

5. *Add-back of fixed charges.* In order to determine the amount of pretax earnings available to meet specific fixed charges, those fixed charges that were deducted in arriving at pretax earnings must be added back to pretax income in the numerator of the ratio.

6. *The level of income* used in the computation of earnings-coverage ratios deserves serious consideration. The most important consideration here is: what level of income will be most representative of the amount that will actually be available in the *future* for the payment of debt-related fixed charges. An average figure of earnings from continuing operations encompassing the entire range of the business cycle, and adjusted for any known factors that may change it in the future, is most likely to be the best approximation of the average source of funds from future operations that can be expected to become available for the payment of fixed charges. Moreover, if the objective of the earnings-coverage ratio is to measure the creditor's maximum exposure to risk, then the proper earnings figure to use is that achieved at the low point of the enterprise's business cycle.

Fixed charges to be included

Having considered the amount of earnings that should be included in the earnings coverage, we shall now turn to an examination of the types of fixed charges that are generally includable in the computation of this ratio.

1. Interest incurred

Interest incurred is the most direct and most obvious fixed charge that arises from the incurrence of indebtedness. Interest expense includes the amortization of deferred bond discount and premium. The bond discount and issue expenses represent the amount by which the par value of the bond indebtedness exceeded the proceeds from the bond issue. As such, the discount amortization represents an addition to the stated interest expense. The amortization of bond issue premium represents the reverse situation, and thus results in a reduction of interest expense over the period of amortization.[15]

If low coupon bonds have only a short period to run before maturity and it is likely that they will have to be refinanced with higher coupon bonds, it may be appropriate to incorporate in fixed charges the expected higher interest costs.

Interest on income bonds must, at best, be paid only as earned. Consequently, it is not a fixed charge from the point of view of the holder of fixed-interest securities. It must, however, be regarded as a fixed charge from the point of view of the income bond issuer.

2. Capitalized interest

SFAS 34 requiring the capitalization of certain interest costs (see Chapter 11) has greatly increased the practice of interest capitalization. Care must be taken to arrive at proper amounts in both the numerator and the denominator of the fixed-charges-coverage ratio.

Let us clarify where interest can be found in the income statement and the terminology that relates to it. Interest that the enterprise pays or is obligated to pay during a period is referred to as *interest incurred*. This is the amount we focus on as being covered by earnings. Interest incurred that is not expensed but rather charged to some asset account is *interest capitalized*. Interest incurred less interest capitalized equals *interest expensed*. Since interest that is expensed is that which enters into the determination of pretax income, it should be added back to the pretax income found in the numerator of the ratio. The denominator of the ratio will, however, include as a fixed-charge interest incurred whether capitalized or not.

Interest capitalized in one period will find its way into the income statement in the form of costs such as depreciation or amortization. Such amortized interest that was previously capitalized must be added back to pretax income.[16] In effect, failure to add back such interest results in including earnings in the numerator *after* some interest costs rather than *before* interest, with a resulting understatement of the fixed-charges-coverage ratio. Since the FASB has not required the disclosure of the amount of previously capitalized interest that is amortized in a given period, analysts can obtain these amounts through voluntary disclosure by companies or they can sometimes derive them from other disclosures such as those relating to deferred taxes.

---

[15] Bond discount and premium amortization, which are usually relatively insignificant in amount, do not, strictly speaking, require a current outlay of funds. They represent cost or income item allocations over the term of the loan.

[16] SEC regulations require that different methods of computation apply to rate regulated public utilities. In their case, the allowance for funds used during construction shall be added to gross income but not deducted from interest expense. Utilities may not add to earnings the amount of previously capitalized interest amortized during the period.

3. Interest implicit in lease obligations

Chapter 7 on the analysis of liabilities discusses the present status of accounting recognition of leases as financing devices. *SFAS 13* requires the capitalization of most financing leases.

When a lease is capitalized, the interest portion of the lease payment is designated as such on the income statement while most of the balance is usually considered as repayment of the principal obligation. A problem arises, however, when the analyst feels that certain leases that should have been capitalized are not so treated in the financial statements. The issue here actually goes beyond the pure accounting question of whether capitalization is, or is not, appropriate. It stems rather from the fact that a long-term lease represents a fixed obligation that must be given recognition in the computation of the earnings-coverage ratio. Thus, even long-term leases that, from an accounting theory point of view, need not be capitalized may be considered as including fixed charges that have to be included in the coverage ratio computation.[17]

The problem of extracting the interest portion of long-term lease payments is not a simple one. The external analysts can possibly obtain the implicit interest rate of financing leasing from an examination of the more extensive disclosure now available on the subject. Otherwise a rough rule of thumb, such as that interest represents one third of rentals, originally suggested by Graham and Dodd, may have to be used.[18] The SEC, which had used this rule, no longer accepts it automatically and insists on a more reliable estimate of the portion of rentals that represent interest.[19] "Delay rentals" in the extractive industries represent payment for the privilege of deferring the development of properties and, being in the nature of not regularly recurring compensation to owners, are not considered as rentals includable in the earnings-coverage ratio.

As with the offsetting of interest income against interest expense, the general rule is that rental income should not be offset against rental expense when determining fixed charges. An exception is made, however, where the rental income represents a direct reduction in rental expense.

4. Preferred stock dividend requirements of majority owned subsidiaries

These are considered fixed charges because they have priority over the distribution of earnings to the parent. Items that would be or are eliminated in consolidation should not be considered fixed charges.

---

[17] In the discussion preceding the release of its 1982 revised regulations concerning the computation of the fixed-charges-coverage ratio, the SEC has reemphasized that "some long-term leases may narrowly miss the criteria for a capital lease but still have the characteristics of a financing transaction. The Commission does not believe that the presence of an interest factor is dependent upon the rental contract extending over any given period of time."

[18] Graham, Dodd, and Cottle, *Security Analysis,* p. 344. (This rule was developed in a previous edition of this book.)

[19] SEC *Accounting Series Release 155* (now superseded), as well as discussion preceding the SEC's release of revised rules concerning the computation of the ratio in 1982.

Income tax adjustment of fixed charges

Fixed charges that are not tax deductible must be tax adjusted. This is done by increasing them by an amount equivalent to the income tax that would be required to obtain an aftertax income sufficient to cover such fixed charges. The above preferred stock dividend requirement is one example of such nontax-deductible fixed charge. The following adjustment is made to compute the "grossed-up" amount:

$$\frac{\text{Preferred stock dividend requirements}}{1 - \text{Income tax rate}}$$

The tax rate to be used should be based on the relationship of the provision for income tax expense applicable to income from continuing operations to the amount of pretax income from continuing operations, i.e., the company's normal effective tax rate.

Other elements to be included in fixed charges

The foregoing discussions concerned the determination of fixed financing charges, that is, interest and the interest portion of lease rentals. These are the most widely used measures of "fixed charges" included in conventional fixed-charges-coverage ratios such as that required by the SEC which we adopt as the standard required computation.

However, if the purpose of this ratio is to measure an enterprise's ability to meet fixed commitments that if unpaid could result in repercussions ranging all the way from financial embarrassment to insolvency, there are other fixed charges to be considered. The most important categories of such additional fixed charges that we shall consider here are an interest equivalent on unrecorded pension obligations, principal repayment obligations such as sinking fund requirements, serial repayment provisions, and the principal repayment component of lease rentals. These items are not usually included as fixed charges, and the inclusion of some may be quite controversial. The inclusion of these fixed charges will not be illustrated here.

5.   Interest equivalent on unrecorded pension obligations

Earlier in this chapter we concluded that an analyst may regard as unrecorded pension obligations the larger of unfunded vested pension liability (UVPL) or unfunded past service costs (UPSC). Since such unrecorded obligation is interest bearing, we can regard the interest on the unrecorded pension obligation as a fixed charge. While one could argue for use of the actuarial interest rate assumption, we are inclined to accept the suggestion[20] that an interest rate reflecting the cost of new debt capital be used. An approximation of that rate could also be the most recent interest rate incurred. Thus, if

---

[20] By Moody's Investor Service.

the unrecorded pension obligation is found to be $100 million and the appropriate interest rate is 9 percent, then the "interest equivalent" fixed charge is $9 million. It can be argued that the imputed interest number is an approximation of what *may* become an obligation which is, however, subordinated to debt requirements.

6. Principal repayment requirements

Principal repayment obligations are, from a cash-drain point of view, just as onerous as obligations to pay interest. In the case of rentals, the obligations to pay principal and interest must be met simultaneously.

A number of reasons have been advanced to indicate why the requirements for principal repayments are not given recognition in earnings-coverage ratio calculations:

1. The coverage of fixed-charges ratio is based on income. It is assumed that if the ratio is at a satisfactory level, it will be possible to refinance obligations as they become due or mature. Consequently, they may not have to be met from funds provided by earnings.
2. If the company has an acceptable debt to equity ratio it should be able to reborrow amounts equal to the debt repayments.
3. Another objection to the inclusion of sinking fund or other periodic principal repayment provisions in the calculation of the earnings-coverage ratio is that this may result in double counting, that is, the funds recovered by depreciation already provide for debt repayment. Thus, if earnings reflect a deduction for depreciation, then fixed charges should not include provisions for principal repayments.

    There is some merit to this argument if the debt was used to acquire depreciable fixed assets and if there is some correspondence between the pattern of depreciation charges and that of principal repayments. It must, moreover, be borne in mind that depreciation funds are recovered generally only out of profitable, or at least break-even, operations, and consequently this argument is valid only under an assumption of such operations.

    Our discussion of the definition of "earnings" to be included in the coverage-ratio calculations emphasized the importance of funds provided by operations as the measure of resources available to meet fixed charges. The use of this concept would, of course, eliminate the double-counting problem since nonfund-requiring charges such as depreciation would be added back to net income for the purpose of the coverage computations.

A more serious problem regarding the inclusion of debt repayment provisions among "fixed charges" arises from the fact that not all debt agreements provide for sinking fund payments or similar repayment obligations. Any arbitrary allocation of indebtedness over time would be an unrealistic theoretical exercise and would ignore the fact that to the extent that such payments are not required in earlier years, the immediate pressure on the cash resources of the enterprise is reduced. In the longer run, however, larger maturities as well as "balloon" payments will have to be met.

The most useful solution to this problem lies in a careful analysis and assessment of the yearly debt repayment requirements that will serve as the basis on which to judge the effect of these obligations on the long-term solvency of the enterprise. The assumption that debt can always be refinanced, rolled over, or otherwise paid off from current operations is not the most useful approach to the problem of risk evaluation. On the contrary, the existence of debt repayment obligations as well as the timing of their maturity must be recognized and included in an overall assessment of the long-term ability of the enterprise to meet its fixed obligations. The inclusion of sinking fund or other early repayment requirements in fixed charges is one way of recognizing the impact of such requirements on fund adequacy. Another method would, as a minimum, call for scheduling total debt repayment requirements over a period of 5 to 10 years into the future and relating these to aftertax funds expected to be available from operations.

7. Other fixed charges

While interest payments and debt repayment requirements are the fixed charges most directly related to the incurrence of debt, there is no logical justification to restrict the evaluation of long-term solvency only to these charges and commitments. Thus, a complete analysis of fixed charges that an enterprise is obliged to meet must include all long-term rental payment obligations[21] (not only the interest portion thereof) and particularly those rentals that must be met under any and all circumstances under noncancelable leases, otherwise known as "hell-and-high-water" leases.

The reason why short-term leases can be excluded from consideration as fixed charges is that they represent an obligation of limited duration, usually less than three years, and can consequently be discontinued in a period of severe financial stringency. Here, the analyst must, however, evaluate how essential the rented items are to the continuation of the enterprise as a going concern.

Other charges that are not directly related to debt but that may nevertheless be considered as long-term commitments of a fixed nature are long-term purchase contracts in excess of normal requirements not subject to cancellation and other similar obligations.

8. Guarantees to pay fixed charges

Guarantees to pay fixed charges of unconsolidated subsidiaries or of unaffiliated persons (such as suppliers) should result in additions to fixed charges if the requirement to honor the guarantee appears imminent.

---

[21] Capitalized long-term leases affect income by the interest charge implicit in them as well as by the amortization of the property right. Thus, to consider the "principal" component of such leases as fixed charges (after income was reduced by amortization of the property right) may amount to double counting.

RATIO OF EARNINGS TO FIXED CHARGES

In its 1982 revised regulations concerning the "Ratio of Earnings to Fixed Charges," the SEC's concept of computing this ratio moved so close to our own that we present it here as the standard conventional[22] way of computing the ratio:

The SEC's formula for computing the ratio is:

(Numerator)

(A) Pretax income from continuing operations *plus* (B) Interest expensed *plus* (C) Amortization of debt expense and discount or premium *plus* (D) Interest portion of operating rental expenses *plus* (E) Tax adjusted preferred stock dividend requirements of majority-owned subsidiaries *plus* (F) Amount of previously capitalized interest amortized during the period *minus* (G) Undistributed income of less than 50% owned persons (affiliates)

(Denominator)

(H) Total interest incurred *plus* (C) Amortization of debt expense and discount or premium *plus* (D) Interest portion of operating rental expenses *plus* (E) Tax adjusted preferred stock dividend requirements of majority-owned subsidiaries

The key letters above will serve for later reference to computations as well as for the summary amplifying notes below:

A   Income before discontinued operations, extraordinary items, and cumulative effects of accounting changes.

B   Interest incurred *less* interest capitalized.

C   Whether expensed or capitalized.

D   Since all financing leases are capitalized, the interest implicit in these is already included in interest expense—the interest portion of long-term operating leases is included on the theory that many long-term operating leases narrowly miss the criteria for a capital lease under *SFAS 13* but still have the characteristic of a financing transaction.

E   Excluding in all cases items eliminated in consolidation. The dividend has to be increased to pretax earnings that would be required to cover such dividend requirements, that is:

$$\frac{\text{Preferred stock dividend requirements}}{100 \text{ percent} - \text{Income tax rate*}}$$

* Based on relationship between applicable actual income tax provision to income *before* income taxes, extraordinary items, and cumulative effect of accounting changes.

---

[22] Still in some use but too simplistic to be considered here is the times interest earned ratio which considers only interest as a fixed charge to be covered, thus:

$$\frac{\text{Pretax income} + \text{Interest expense}}{\text{Interest expense}}$$

Exhibit 18–5

THE LEVERED CORPORATION
Abbreviated Income Statement

Net sales		$13,400,000
Undistributed income of less than 50% owned affiliates		600,000
		14,000,000
Cost of goods sold	$7,400,000	
Selling, general, and administrative expenses	1,900,000	
Depreciation (excluded from above costs) (3)	800,000	
Interest expense (1)—net	700,000	
Rental expense (2)	800,000	
Share of minority interests in consolidated income*	200,000	11,800,000
Income before taxes		2,200,000
Income taxes:		
Current	800,000	
Deferred	300,000	1,100,000
Income before extraordinary items		1,100,000
Gain on sale of investment in land (net of $67,000 tax)		200,000
Net income		$ 1,300,000
Dividends:		
On common stock	200,000	
On preferred stock	400,000	600,000
Earnings retained for the year		$ 700,000

* These subsidiaries have fixed charges.

Selected notes to the financial statements:

1. The interest expense is composed of the following:

Interest incurred (except items below)	$740,000
Amortization of bond discount	60,000
Interest portion of capitalized leases	100,000
Interest capitalized	(200,000)
Interest expense	$700,000

2. Interest implicit in noncapitalized leases amounts to $300,000.
3. Depreciation includes amortization of previously capitalized interest of $80,000.

F Applies to nonutility companies only. In most cases, disclosure of this amount is not made.

G Minority interest in income of majority-owned subsidiaries that have fixed charges may be included in income.

H Whether expensed or capitalized.

General

To reduce the complexity of the formula, two items (provisions) were left out:

1. In computing earnings, the *full* amount of losses of majority-owned subsidiaries should be considered.
2. Losses on investments in less than 50 percent owned companies accounted for by the equity method should not be included in earnings *unless* the company has guaranteed the debt of the affiliate.

If the ratio of earnings to fixed charges is less than one, the amount of insufficiency of earnings to cover the fixed charges should be given (rather than a ratio).

Illustration of earnings-coverage ratio calculations

Having discussed the various considerations that enter into the decision of what factors to include in the earnings-coverage ratio computation, we will address ourselves now to the question of how the ratio is computed. The computation of the various coverage ratios will be based on the illustration in Exhibit 18–5.

Using the data in Exhibit 18–5 and letter references to the above formula, we compute the ratio of earnings to fixed charges as follows (dollars in thousands):

$$\frac{\$2,200\,(A) + \$700\,(B\text{ and }C) + \$300\,(D) + \$80\,(F) - \$600\,(G) + \$200^*}{\$840\,(H) + \$60\,(C) + \$300\,(D)} = \underline{\underline{2.4}}\text{ times}$$

* The SEC permits the inclusion in income of the minority interest in the income of majority-owned subsidiaries that have fixed charges. This amount is added in order to reverse a similar deduction from income.

The ratio of earnings to fixed charges of Alfa, Inc. (see Appendix 4B), can be computed as follows (letter references are to the formula above—dollars in thousands):

$$\frac{\$25,368^{(1)}\,(A) + \$18,440^{(2)}\,(B) + \$19,767^{(3)}\,(D) + \$154^{(4)}\,(F)}{\$18,504^{(5)}\,(H) + \$19,767^{(3)}\,(D)} = \underline{\underline{1.67}}\text{ times}$$

(1) Item $\boxed{8}$.
(2) Item $\boxed{5}$ — Item $\boxed{6}$.
(3) Interest component of *all* leases per Note 11 (item $\boxed{99}$) — present value of leases ($247,087) × .08 (average interest rate).
(4) Note 6 (item $\boxed{82}$) discloses that income decreased in 19x6 because of interest capitalization. Based on this and other information given, we can reconstruct the effect on income of interest capitalization and derive the amount of amortization of previously capitalized interest:

	Dr. (Cr.)
Interest capitalized (given) item $\boxed{6}$	$ (64)
Amortization of previously capitalized interest	154 ←derived
	90
Income tax effect at 48%	(43)
Effect on net income (given)—item $\boxed{82}$	$ 47

(5) Item $\boxed{5}$.

At 1.67 times, Alfa's ratio of earnings to fixed charges is relatively low.

Ratio of earnings to fixed charges—expanded concept of fixed charges

If we adopt the point of view that failure to meet any fixed obligations can lead to trouble or to a chain of events leading to insolvency, then we want to establish how well such fixed obligations are covered by earnings. Thus, in addition to the fixed charges included in the computation in the preceding example based on Exhibit 18–5, the following must now be considered for inclusion:

Interest equivalent on unrecorded pension obligations. This represents, as discussed earlier in the chapter, interest that must be currently provided for by the enterprise. In the case of the Levered Corporation, the interest factor is 10 percent of a $400,000 unfunded vested pension liability, or $40,000.

Annual sinking fund requirements. The question of whether principal repayment requirements should be considered fixed charges has been discussed above. Their consideration as fixed charges is more valid when pre-depreciation earnings are used. See "Funds flow coverage of fixed charges" below.

PRO FORMA COMPUTATIONS OF COVERAGE RATIOS

In cases where fixed charges yet to be incurred are to be recognized in the computation of the coverage ratio, as, for example, interest costs under a prospective incurrence of debt, it is quite proper to estimate the offsetting benefits that will ensue from such future inflows of funds and to include these estimated benefits in the pro forma income. Benefits to be derived from a prospective loan can be measured in terms of interest savings obtainable from a planned refunding operation, income from short-term investments in which the proceeds may be invested, or similarly reasonable estimates of future benefits.

The SEC will usually insist on the presentation of a pro forma computation of the ratio of earnings to fixed charges that reflects changes to be effected under prospective financing plans when the effect of the refinancing changes the historical ratio by 10 percent or more.

FUNDS FLOW COVERAGE OF FIXED CHARGES

The discussion earlier in this chapter pointed out that net income is generally not a reliable measure of funds provided by operations that are available to meet fixed charges. The reason is, of course, that fixed charges are paid with cash or, from the longer-term point of view, with funds (working capital), while net income includes items of revenue that do not generate funds as well as expense items which do not require the current use of funds. Thus, a better measure of fixed-charges coverage may be obtained by using in the numerator funds obtained by operations rather than net income. This figure can be obtained from the SCFP.

Under this concept, the coverage ratio would be computed as follows:

$$\frac{\text{Funds provided by operations} + \text{Fixed charges}}{\text{Fixed charges}}$$

Using the data in Exhibit 18–5 we compute the coverage ratio as follows:

Funds provided by operations (pretax):

Income before extraordinary items		$1,100,000
Add-back—income taxes		1,100,000
Pretax income		2,200,000
Less: Nonfund generating income:		
Undistributed income of less than 50%		
owned affiliates		600,000
		1,600,000
Add: Expenses not requiring funds:		
Depreciation	$800,000	
Share of minority interests in consolidated income	200,000	
Amortization of bond discount	60,000	
Deferred income taxes (already added above)		1,060,000
Funds provided by operations (before taxes)		$2,660,000

The fixed charges to be added back to pretax funds provided by operations of

		$2,660,000
Interest expensed (less bond discount added		
back above)		640,000
Interest portion of operating rental expense		300,000
Amount of previously capitalized interest		
amortized during period*		—
Total numerator		$3,600,000

* Assumed here to be included in depreciation (already added back).

Note that the numerator does not reflect a deduction of $600 (undistributed income of affiliates) because that figure, being a nonfund providing item, was already deducted at arriving at pretax funds provided by operations. Similarly, the "share of minority interests in consolidated income" has already been added back in arriving at the pretax funds provided by operations figure.

The fixed charges in the denominator are computed as follows:

Interest incurred	$ 900,000
Interest portion of operating rentals	300,000
	$1,200,000

Thus, the ratio of pretax funds provided by operations to fixed charges is:

$$\frac{\$3,600,000}{\$1,200,000} = \underline{\underline{3.0}}$$

Should the analyst wish to base the computation on "cash flow" or, more accurately, cash provided by operations the "funds from operations" figure must be appropriately adjusted for changes in such operations related current items as accounts receivable, inventories, prepayments, accounts payable, and accruals (see Appendix 13A of Chapter 13).

As discussed earlier, the inclusion of principal repayment requirements, (tax adjusted) as fixed charges in this computation is justifiable because use of a pre-depreciation income figure here avoids the issue of double counting.

Other useful tests of funds flow relationships

A comprehensive study[23] found the ratio

$$\frac{\text{Working capital provided by operations}}{\text{Total debt and preferred stock}}$$

to be the best single predictor of financial failure. A deterioration in this ratio indicates that a firm is generating decreasing levels of funds from its operations in relation to the burden of debt it is carrying. This ratio is similar to the popular cash flow/debt ratio where "cash flow" is simply a crude measure of "funds from operations."

Net funds (or cash) flows as a percentage of capital expenditures relates funds provided by operations *after* dividends to needed capital plant and equipment replacements and additions. This is a measure of fund commitments to outlays that do not enter the fixed charges total but that may nevertheless be vital or important to the continuing operation of an enterprise.

STABILITY OF "FLOW OF FUNDS FROM OPERATIONS"

Since the relationship between the "flow of funds from operations" to the fixed charges of an enterprise is so important to an evaluation of long-term solvency, it is important to assess the stability of that flow. This is done by a careful evaluation of the elements that comprise the sources of funds from operations. For example, the depreciation add-back to net income is a more stable element than is net income itself because the recovery of the depreciation cost from selling prices precedes the earning of any net income, and has thus a higher degree of probability of happening. Even in very competitive industries selling prices must, in the long run, reflect the cost of plant and equipment used up in production.

---

[23] William H. Beaver, "Financial Ratios as Predictors of Failure," *Empirical Research in Accounting: Selected Studies 1966* (Chicago: The Institute of Professional Accounting, School of Business, University of Chicago, 1967), pp. 71–111.

EARNINGS COVERAGE OF PREFERRED DIVIDENDS

In the evaluation of preferred stock issues, it is often instructive to calculate the earnings coverage of preferred dividends, much in the same way the interest or fixed-charges coverage of debt issues is computed. The computation of the earnings coverage of preferred dividends must include as charges to be covered by earnings all fixed charges that take precedence over the payment of preferred dividends.[24] As is the case with all fixed-charges-coverage computations, the final ratio depends on a definition of "fixed charges."

Since preferred dividends are not tax deductible, aftertax income must be used to cover them. Consequently, the basic formula for computing preferred dividend coverage is:

$$\frac{\text{Income before tax} + \text{Fixed charges*}}{\text{Fixed charges*} + \text{Preferred dividends} \times \left(\dfrac{1}{1 - \text{Tax rate}}\right)}$$

* Which *are* tax deductible.

To the formula we used earlier (see page 579) to compute the ratio of earnings to fixed charges for The Levered Corporation based on data in Exhibit 18–5, we now add the tax-adjusted preferred dividend requirement in order to derive the preferred dividend coverage ratio as follows (dollars in thousands):

$$\frac{\$2,200 \text{ (A)} + \$700 \text{ (B and C)} + \$300 \text{ (D)} + \$80 \text{ (F)} - \$600 \text{ (G)} + \$200*}{\$840 \text{ (H)} + \$60 \text{ (C)} + \$300 \text{ (D)} + \$400 \left(\dfrac{1}{1 - .50}\right)^{\dagger}} = \underline{\underline{1.44}}$$

* Minority interest in income of majority-owned subsidiaries (see prior discussion).
† Tax-adjusted preferred dividend requirement.

If there are two or more preferred issues outstanding, a by-class coverage ratio can be computed by omitting the dividend requirements of the junior issue but always including all prior fixed charges and preferred dividends.

EVALUATION OF EARNINGS-COVERAGE RATIOS

The earnings-coverage ratio test is a test of the ability of an enterprise to meet its fixed charges out of current earnings.[25] The orientation towards

---

[24] This is also the position of the SEC. Care must be exercised in comparing these coverage ratios because some analysts and financial services include only the preferred dividend requirements in the computation.

[25] W. B. Hickman, *Corporate Bond Quality and Investor Experience* (Princeton, N.J.: Princeton University Press, 1958), p. 11, found, for example, that bonds with poor earnings coverage had a probability of default 17 times greater than those with good coverage.

earnings is a logical one because the bondholder or other long-term creditor, while interested in asset coverage or what he can salvage in times of trouble, relies even more on the ability of the enterprise to stay out of trouble by meeting its obligations currently and as a going concern. Given the limited returns obtainable from debt instruments, an increase in the interest rate can rarely compensate the creditor for a serious risk of loss of principal. Thus, if the probability of the enterprise meeting its obligations as a going concern is not strong, then a creditor relationship can hardly be advantageous.

The coverage ratio is influenced by the level of earnings and by the level of fixed charges, which in turn depend importantly on the debt-to-equity relationship within the capitalization.

Importance of earnings variability

One very important factor in the evaluation of the coverage ratio is the pattern of behavior of cash flows over time, or the behavior of its surrogate—earnings. The more stable the earnings pattern of an enterprise or industry, the lower the relative earnings-coverage ratio that will be acceptable. Thus, a utility, which in times of economic downturn is likely to experience only a mild fall off in demand, can justify a lower earnings-coverage ratio than can a cyclical company such as a machinery manufacturer that may experience a sharp drop in sales in times of recession. Variability of earnings is, then, an important factor in the determination of the coverage standard. In addition, the durability and the trend of earnings are important factors that must be considered apart from their variability.[26]

Importance of method of computation and of underlying assumptions

The coverage standard will also depend on the method of computation of the coverage ratio. As we saw above, varying methods of computing the coverage ratio assume different definitions of "income" and of "fixed charges." It is reasonable to expect lower standards of coverage for the ratios that employ the most demanding and stringent definitions of these terms.

The SEC formula for computing the fixed-charges-coverage ratio that we have adopted here is based on income *before* discontinued operations, extraordinary items, and cumulative effects of accounting changes. While these exclusions impart a degree of stability to the earnings, they also remove from them important elements that must be considered as part of the operating experience of the entity. These elements should always be included in computing the *average* coverage ratio over a number of years.

---

[26] Most factors that will affect an entity's equity securities will also affect its bonds. For example, when Consolidated Edison Company passed its dividend in 1974, its bonds plunged along with its common stock which was the security directly affected. The market, aside from taking its cue from this action, may also have concluded that the company's ability to sell equity securities as well as its overall financing flexibility had been impaired.

The standards will also vary with the kind of earnings that are utilized in the coverage computation, that is, average earnings, the earnings of the poorest year, etc. Moreover, the quality of earnings is an important consideration (see Chapter 22).

It is not advisable to compute earnings-coverage ratios under methods that are not theoretically sound and whose only merit is that they are conservative. Thus, using aftertax income in the computation of the coverage ratio of fixed charges that are properly deductible for tax purposes is not logical and introduces conservatism in the wrong place. Any standard of coverage adequacy must, in the final analysis, be related to the willingness and ability of the lender to incur risk.

Appendix 18A includes references to standards of fixed-charges-coverage ratios used by rating agencies in determining the ratings of individual debt securities.

APPENDIX 18A

THE RATING OF DEBT OBLIGATIONS

Since the turn of the century, there has become established in the United States a comprehensive and sophisticated system for rating debt securities. Most ratings are performed by two highly regarded investment research firms, Moody's and Standard & Poor's (S&P).[1]

A bond credit rating is a composite expression of judgment about the credit worthiness of the bond issuer as well as the quality of the specific security being rated. A rating measure credit risk, that is, the probability of occurrence of developments adverse to the interests of the creditor.

This judgment of credit worthiness is expressed in a series of symbols that express degrees of credit risk. Thus, the top four rating grades of Standard & Poor's are:

AAA. Bonds rated AAA are highest-grade obligations. They possess the ultimate degree of protection as to principal and interest. Marketwise they move with interest rates, and hence provide the maximum safety on all counts.

AA. Bonds rated AA also qualify as high-grade obligations, and in the majority of instances differ from AAA issues only in small degree. Here, too, prices move with the long-term money market.

A. Bonds rated A are regarded as upper medium grade. They have considerable investment strength but are not entirely free from adverse effects of changes in economic and trade conditions. Interest and principal

---

[1] In recent years, the ratings performed by Duff and Phelps have gained increasing acceptance in the marketplace. Many institutions also develop their own "in house" ratings.

are regarded as safe. They predominantly reflect money rates in their market behavior, but to some extent, also economic conditions.

BBB. The BBB, or medium-grade category is borderline between definitely sound obligations and those where the speculative element begins to predominate. These bonds have adequate asset coverage and normally are protected by satisfactory earnings. Their susceptibility to changing conditions, particularly to depressions, necessitates constant watching. Marketwise, the bonds are more responsive to business and trade conditions than to interest rates. This group is the lowest that qualifies for commercial bank investment.

The major reason why debt securities are widely rated while equity securities are not lies in the fact that there is a far greater uniformity of approach and homogeneity of analytical measures used in the evaluation of credit worthiness than there can be in the evaluation of the future market performance of equity securities. Thus, the wide agreement on what is being measured in credit risk analysis has resulted in a widespread acceptance of and reliance on published credit ratings.

The criteria that enter into the determination of a rating have never been precisely defined, and they involve both quantitative measures (e.g., ratio analysis) as well as qualitative factors such as market position and management quality. The major rating agencies refuse to be pinned down on what precise mix of factors enter into their rating process (which is a committee decision) because it is both art and science and also because to do so would cause endless arguments about the validity of the many judgmental factors that enter into a rating decision.

We can then see that in arriving at ratings these agencies must undertake analyses along the lines discussed throughout this book, the differences being mainly in the vast number of debt issues covered and the standardization of approaches which this entails. The following description of factors entering the rating process is based on published sources as well as on discussions with officials of the rating agencies.

THE RATING OF CORPORATE BONDS

In rating an industrial bond issue, the rating agency will focus on the issuing company's asset protection, financial resources, earning power, management, and the specific provisions of the debt security.

Also of great importance are size of firm, market share, industry position, susceptibility to cyclical influences,[2] and other broad economic factors.

Asset protection is concerned with measuring the degree to which a company's debt is covered by the value of its assets. One measure is net tangible

---

[2] There are, for example, no AAA rated companies in the steel or paper industries.

assets to long-term debt. At S&P, an industrial needs a ratio of 5 to 1 to get an AAA rating, a ratio of over 4 to 1 to qualify for an AA rating, 3 to 3.5 to 1 for an A, and about 2.5 to 1 for a BBB rating.

Understated assets, such as those of companies in the natural resource or real estate fields, are generally accorded recognition in the rating process.

The long-term debt as a percentage of total capitalization calls for a ratio of under 25 percent for an AAA, around 30 percent for a AA, 35 percent for an A, and about 40 percent for a BBB rating.

Other factors entering the consideration of asset protection include the determination of book value, the makeup of working capital, the quality and age of property, plant, and equipment as well as questions of off-balance sheet financing and unrecorded liabilities.

Financial resources encompass, in particular, such liquid resources as cash and other working capital items. Quality measures here include the collection period of receivables and inventory turnover. These are judged by means of industry standards. The use of debt, both short term and long term, as well as the mix between the two is also investigated.

Future earning power and the resulting cash generating ability is a factor of great importance in the rating of debt securities because the level and the quality of future earnings determine importantly an enterprise's ability to meet its obligations. Earning power is generally a more reliable source of security than is asset protection.

A prime measure of the degree of protection afforded by earning power is the fixed-charges-coverage ratio. To qualify for consideration for an AAA rating, an industrial company's earnings should cover its interest and rental charges after taxes above five to seven times, for an AA rating above four times, for an A rating over three times, and a BBB over two times.

Another measure of debt service paying ability is cash flow (crudely net income plus depreciation) to total funded debt. It should be 65 percent or more for an AAA, 45 to 60 percent for an AA, 35 to 45 percent for an A, and 25 to 30 percent for a BBB rating.

Management abilities, philosophy, depth, and experience always loom importantly in any final rating judgment. Through interviews, field trips, and other analyses, the raters probe into the depth and breadth of management, as well as into its goals, the planning process, and strategies in such areas as research and development, product promotion, new product planning, and acquisitions.

The specific provisions of the debt security are usually spelled out in the bond indenture. What is analyzed here are the specific provisions in the indenture that are designed to protect the interests of bondholders under a variety of future conditions. Included in consideration here are, among others, conditions for issuance of future debt issues, specific security provisions such as mortgaging, sinking fund and redemption provisions, and restrictive covenants.

As can be seen, debt rating is a complex process involving quantitative as well as qualitative factors all of which culminate in the issuance of a single quality rating. The weights that may be assigned to each factor will vary among analysts, but the final conclusion will generally represent the composite judgment of several experienced raters.

THE RATING OF MUNICIPAL SECURITIES

Buyers of municipal bonds depend for their security of principal and interest on factors that are quite different from those that determine the quality of corporate debt. Hence, the processes of analysis differ.

Municipal securities, those issued by state and local governmental authorities, comprise a number of varieties. Many are general obligation bonds backed by the full faith and credit of the governmental unit that issues them. Others are special tax bonds that are limited in security to a particular tax that will be used to service and retire them. Then there are revenue bonds secured only by revenues of municipal enterprises. Other categories comprise housing authority bonds, tax anticipation notes, and so forth. Although the amount of information provided to buyers of municipal bonds is of very uneven quality moves are afoot to correct this, primarily by way of legislation.

Raters require a great variety of information from issuers of municipal debt. In case of general obligation bonds, the basic security rests on the issuer's ability and willingness to repay the debt from general revenues under a variety of economic conditions.[3] The fundamental revenue source is the taxing power of the local municipality. Thus, the information they require includes current population and the trend and composition of population, the largest 10 taxpayers, the current market value of taxable properties, the gross indebtedness, and the net indebtedness (i.e., after deducting self-sustaining obligations, sinking fund, etc.), recent annual reports, budgets, and estimates of capital improvement and future borrowing programs, as well as an overall description of the area's economy.

While rating techniques have the same objectives as in the case of corporate bonds, the ratios used are adapted to the specific conditions that exist with respect to municipal debt obligations. Thus, debt as a percentage of market value of real estate is an important indicator: 10 percent is considered high while 3–5 percent is on the low side. Annual debt service of 10 percent of total revenue is considered comfortable while percentages in the high teens are considered as presenting a warning sign. Per capita debt of $400 or less is considered low while debt in the $900 to $1,000 area is considered

---

[3] The decision of New York State's highest court to overturn the New York City Moratorium on its notes strengthens the meaning of the concept of "full faith and credit." Said Chief Justice C. J. Breitel: "A pledge of the city's faith and credit is both a commitment to pay and a commitment of the city's revenue generating powers to produce the funds to pay . . . that is the way both words 'faith' and 'credit' are used and they are not tautological."

excessive and, hence, a negative factor. Tax delinquencies should generally not exceed 3–4 percent.

Other factors of interest include unfunded pension liabilities as well as the trend of indebtedness. A steady increase in indebtedness is usually a danger sign. As in all cases of debt rating, the factor of management, though largely intangible and subject to measurement only through ultimate results, is of critical importance.

LIMITATIONS OF THE RATING PROCESS

As valuable and essential as the rating process is to buyers of the thousands upon thousands of bond issues of every description, the limitations of this standardized procedure must also be understood. As is true in any phase of security analysis, the analyst who can, through superior analysis, improve on what is conventionally accepted stands to benefit accordingly. As was seen in Chapter 1, this is even more true in the case of debt securities than in the case of equity securities.

Bond ratings are very wide, and they consequently present opportunities for those who can identify these differences within a rating classification. Moreover, rating changes generally lag the market, and this presents additional opportunities to the analyst who with superior skill and alertness can identify important changes before they become generally recognized.

References

"The Rating Game." New York: The Twentieth Century Fund, 1974.

"Higher Stakes in the Bond-Rating Game." *Fortune,* April 1976.

H. C. Sherwood. *How Corporate and Municipal Debt Is Rated: An Inside Look at Standard & Poor's Rating System.* New York: John Wiley & Sons, 1976.

Corporate Bond Ratings: An Overview. New York: Standard & Poor's Corporation, 1978.

APPENDIX 18B

RATIOS AS PREDICTORS OF BUSINESS FAILURE

The most common use to which financial statement ratios are put is to use them as pointers in the direction of further investigation and analysis. Some investigation and experimentation has been undertaken to determine to what extent ratios can be used as predictors of failure. As such they could provide valuable additional tools in the analysis of long-term solvency.

The basic idea behind bankruptcy prediction models is that through observation of the trend and behavior of certain ratios of various firms before failure, those characteristics in ratios that predominate in failing firms can be identified and used for prediction purposes. The expectation is that signs of deterioration observed in ratio behavior can be detected early enough and clearly enough so that timely action can be taken to avoid substantial risk of default and failure.

Empirical studies

Among the earliest studies to focus on the behavior of ratios prior to the failure of firms were those of Winakor and Smith who studied a sample of 183 firms that experienced financial difficulties for as long as 10 years prior to 1931, the year when they failed.[1] Analyzing the 10-year trend of 21 ratios, they concluded that the ratio of net working capital to total assets was among the most accurate and reliable indicator of failure.

Fitzpatrick analyzed the three- to five-year trends of 13 ratios of 20 firms that had failed in the 1920–29 period.[2] By comparing them to the experience of a control group of 19 successful firms, he concluded that all of his ratios predicted failure to some extent. However, the best predictors were found to be the return on net worth and the net worth to total debt ratio.

Merwin studied the experience of a sample of 939 firms during the 1926–36 period.[3] Analyzing an unspecified number of ratios he found that three ratios were most sensitive in predicting "discontinuance" of a firm as early as four to five years before such discontinuance. The three ratios were the current ratio, net working capital to total assets, and net worth to total debt. They all exhibited declining trends before "discontinuance" and were at all times below estimated normal ratios.

Focusing on the experience of companies that experienced defaults on debt and bank credit difficulties, Hickman studied the experience of corporate bond issues during 1900–1943 and reached the conclusion that the times interest earned ratio and the net profit to sales ratio were useful predictors of bond issue defaults.[4]

In a study using more powerful statistical techniques than used in its predecessors, Beaver found that financial ratios proved useful in the prediction of bankruptcy and bond default at least five years prior to such failure. He determined that ratios could be used to distinguish correctly between failed

---

[1] Arthur Winakor and Raymond F. Smith, *Changes in Financial Structure of Unsuccessful Firms,* Bureau of Business Research (Urbana, Ill.: University of Illinois Press, 1935).

[2] Paul J. Fitzpatrick, *Symptoms of Industrial Failures* (Washington: Catholic University of America Press, 1931); and Paul J. Fitzpatrick, *A Comparison of the Ratios of Successful Industrial Enterprises with Those of Failed Companies* (Washington: The Accountants Publishing Co., 1932).

[3] Charles L. Merwin, *Financing Small Corporations: In Five Manufacturing Industries, 1926–36* (New York: National Bureau of Economic Research, 1942).

[4] W. Braddock Hickman, *Corporate Bond Quality and Investor Experience* (Princeton, N.J.: Princeton University Press, 1958), pp. 395–431.

and nonfailed firms to a much greater extent than would be possible by random prediction.[5]

Among his conclusions were that both in the short term and the long term, cash flow to total debt ratios were the best predictors, capital structure ratios ranked second, liquidity ratios third, while turnover ratios were the worst predictors.

In an investigation of the ability of ratios to predict bond rating changes and bond ratings of new issues, Horrigan found that the rating changes could be correctly predicted to a much greater extent by the use of ratios than would be possible through random prediction.[6]

Altman extended Beaver's univariate analysis to allow for multiple predictors of failure.[7] Altman used multiple discriminant analysis (MDA) that attempts to develop a linear function of a number of explanatory variables to classify or predict the value of a qualitative dependent variable; for example, bankrupt or nonbankrupt. Twenty-two financial ratios, based on data one period before bankruptcy, were examined, and Altman selected five of these to be included in his final discriminant function: working capital/total assets (liquidity), retained earnings/total assets (age of firm and cumulative profitability), earnings before interest and taxes/total assets (profitability), market value of equity/book value of debt (financial structure) and sales/total assets (capital turnover rate).

Altman was not able to use a cash flow variable, which Beaver found to be the most discriminating in his study since apart from other elements, Altman did not have depreciation figures.

Conclusions

The above research efforts, while pointing out the significant potential that ratios have as predictors of failure, nevertheless indicate that these tools and concepts are in an early stage of development.

The studies focused on experience with failed firms *after the fact.* While they presented evidence that firms that did not fail enjoyed stronger ratios than those that ultimately failed, the ability of ratios alone to predict failure has not been conclusively proved. Another important question yet to be resolved is whether the observation of certain types of behavior by certain ratios can be accepted as a better means of the analysis of long-term solvency than is the integrated use of the various tools described throughout this

---

[5] William H. Beaver, "Financial Ratios as Predictors of Failure," *Empirical Research in Accounting, Selected Studies, 1966,* Supplement to *Journal of Accounting Research 4,* pp. 71–127.

[6] James O. Horrigan, "The Determination of Long-Term Credit Standing with Financial Ratios," *Empirical Research in Accounting, Selected Studies, 1966,* Supplement to *Journal of Accounting Research 4,* pp. 44–62.

[7] Edward Altman, "Financial Ratios, Discriminant Analysis, and the Prediction of Corporate Bankruptcy," *Journal of Finance* 22 (September 1968), pp. 589–609.

work. Further research may show that the use of ratios as predictors of failure will best complement and precede, rather than supplement, the rigorous financial analysis approaches suggested in this work. However, as screening,[8] monitoring, and attention-directing devices they hold considerable promise.

APPENDIX 18C

ILLUSTRATION OF THE COMPUTATION OF THE ANALYTICALLY ADJUSTED DEBT-TO-EQUITY RATIO

The conventional long-term debt to long-term debt and equity ratio is expressed as

$$\frac{LTD}{LTD + OE}$$

The formula that follows incorporates other analytical adjustments which can be made:

$$\frac{LTD + NFL + UPO\,(1 - TR) + LTDU}{LTD + NFL + UPO\,(1 - TR) + LTDU + OE + CDT + NDT + FIFOA + MSA - UPO\,(1 - TR)}$$

where:

LTD   = Long-term debt (including capitalized leases but excluding minority interests).

CDT   = Current deferred taxes—which are judged as unlikely to reverse in the foreseeable future.

NDT   = Noncurrent deferred taxes—which are judged as unlikely to reverse in the foreseeable future.

OE   = Owners' equity (including minority interests).

FIFOA = Excess of disclosed FIFO value of ending inventory over reported LIFO amount.

MSA   = Excess of market value of marketable securities over cost.

NFL   = Present value of noncapitalized financial leases.

UPO   = Present value of unrecognized pension obligations (the larger of unfunded vested benefits or unfunded prior service costs).

LTDU = Long-term debt of unconsolidated subsidiaries.

TR   = Marginal or statutory corporate tax rate.

---

[8] Banks have for years been using credit scoring for personal loans, which gives weight to credit worthiness characteristics such as income, employment, homeownership, etc. But for loans above $10,000–$25,000, banks do no longer rely on the mass-production techniques of credit scoring.

This rationale behind these adjustments was discussed earlier in this chapter. The unrecognized pension obligation (UPO) adjustment that was discussed also in Chapter 7 merits further elaboration. Assuming a marginal tax rate of 48 percent, the analytical adjustment for a UPO of $100 is:

Retained Earnings ($100 × (1 − .48)) 52
Deferred Taxes (future tax benefit on balance sheet) 48
    Pension Obligation   100

Since the future tax benefit will be realized simultaneously with the payment of the UPO, it is proper to net the two and thus the analytical entry reduces to:

Retained Earnings (owners' equity) 52
    Pension Obligation   52

In the above formula we add UPO $(1 - TR)$ to debt in the numerator, add it to debt in the denominator, and reduce owners' equity by the same amount.

Using the 19x6 data of Alfa, Inc. (see Appendix 4B), we can now illustrate the adjustment of the conventional debt to debt + equity ratio (dollars in millions):

$$\text{Alfa's conventional ratio is } \frac{\$245^{(a)} + \$167^{(b)}}{\$245^{(a)} + \$167^{(b)} + \$331^{(c)}} = .55$$

Alfa's adjusted ratio is computed as follows:

$$\frac{\$245^{(a)} + \$167^{(b)} + \$22^{(d)} + \$32\,(1 - .48)^{(e)} + \$31^{(f)}}{\begin{array}{c}\$245^{(a)} + \$167^{(b)} + \$22^{(d)} + \$32(1 - .48)^{(e)} + \$31^{(f)} \\ + \$331^{(c)} + \$35^{(g)} + \$8^{(h)} - \$32(1 - .48)^{(e)}\end{array}} = .57$$

    [a] LTD (item 38).
    [b] Present value of long-term financing lease obligations (item 99)—these would normally be found recorded and in the balance sheet in accordance with *SFAS 13.**
    [c] Stockholders' equity (item 40) accepting the company's classification of "negative goodwill."
    [d] Current deferred tax (item 34) considered here as debt.
    [e] Present value of unfunded prior service pension costs (Note 14—item 105) times $(1 - \text{Tax rate})$.
    [f] Long-term debt of nonconsolidated finance subsidiaries (Note 13—item 102).
    [g] Noncurrent deferred taxes—considered here as equity.
    [h] LIFO reserve (equivalent to difference between LIFO and FIFO)—per Note 5 (item 75)—added to equity.
    * Thus leaving it for the analyst to decide which non-capitalized leases, or operating leases, should nevertheless be considered as long-term financing leases for purposes of analysis.

Two adjustments which are found in the model adjustment formula above were not made in Alfa's case. There were no marketable securities to adjust. Alfa discloses in Note 11 (item 99) "other" lease obligations with a present value of $80 million. The analyst has to make a judgment whether any of these should be capitalized as liabilities. In the above adjustment we omitted them on the assumption that they were all truly operating, rather than financing leases.

QUESTIONS

1. Generally speaking, what are the key elements in the evaluation of long-term solvency?

2. How should deferred income taxes be treated in the analysis of capital structure?

3. In the analysis of capital structure how should lease obligations that have not been capitalized be treated? Under what conditions should they be considered the equivalent of debt?

4. What is "off-balance sheet" financing? Name some examples.

5. What are liabilities for pensions? What factors should analysts assessing total pension obligations of the firm take into consideration?

6. When will information on unconsolidated subsidiaries be important to the analysis of long-term solvency?

7. How would you classify (i.e., equity or liability) the items that follow? State your assumptions and reasons.
   a. Minority interest in consolidated financial statement.
   b. General contingency reserve for indefinite purpose.
   c. Reserve for self-insurance.
   d. Guarantee for product performance on sale.
   e. Convertible debt.
   f. Preferred stock.

8. *a.* Why might the analyst need to adjust the book value of assets?
   b. Give three examples of the need for possible adjustments.

9. Why is the analysis of capital structure important?

10. What is meant by "financial leverage," and in what case(s) is such leverage most advantageous?

11. In the evaluation of long-term solvency why are long-term projections necessary in addition to a short-term analysis? What are some of the limitations of long-term projections?

12. What is the difference between common-size analysis and capital structure ratio analysis? Why is the latter useful?

13. The amount of equity capital shown on the balance sheets, which is based on historical cost, at times differs considerably from realizable market value. How should a financial analyst allow for this in the analysis of capital structure?

14. Why should the analyst compute the ratio of preferred stock to total stockholders' equity? How should preferred stock with mandatory redemption requirements be treated?

15. Why is the analysis of assets distribution necessary?

16. What does the earnings-coverage ratio measure and in what respects is it more useful than other tools of analysis?

17. For the purpose of earnings-coverage ratio computation, what are your criteria for inclusion of an item in "fixed charges"?

18. The company under analysis has a purchase commitment of raw materials under a noncancelable contract that is substantial in amount. Under what conditions would you include the purchase commitment in the computation of fixed charges?

19. Is net income generally a reliable measure of funds available to meet fixed charges? Why or why not?

20. What are some of the useful tests of funds flow relationships?

21. Company B is a wholly owned subsidiary of Company A. The latter is also Company B's principal customer. As potential lender to Company B, what particular facets of this relationship would concern you most? What safeguards, if any, would you require?

22. Comment on the statement: "Debt is a supplement to, not a substitute for, equity capital."

23. A company in need of additional equity capital decides to sell convertible debt thus postponing equity dilution and ultimately selling its shares at an effectively higher price. What are the advantages and disadvantages of such a course of action?

24. *a.* What is the basic function of restrictive covenants in long-term debt indentures (agreements)?
    b. What is the function of provisions regarding:
    (1) Maintenance of minimum working capital (or current ratio)?
    (2) Maintenance of minimum net worth?
    (3) Restrictions on the payment of dividends?
    (4) Ability of creditors to elect a majority of the board of directors of the debtor company in the event of default under the terms of the loan agreement?

25. What is your opinion on the use of ratios as predictors of failure? Your answer should recognize the empirical research that has been done recently in this area.

26. Dogwood Manufacturing, Inc., a successful and rapidly growing company, has always had a favorable difference between the rate of return on its assets and the interest rate paid on borrowed funds. Explain why the company should *not* increase its debt to the 90 percent level of total capitalization and thereby minimize any need for equity financing. (CFA)

27. Why are debt securities widely rated while equity securities are not?

28. On what aspects do the rating agencies focus in rating an industrial bond? Elaborate.

29. *a.* Municipal securities comprise a number of varieties. Discuss.
    b. What factors are considered in the rating of municipal securities?

30. Can the analyst improve on a rating judgment? Discuss.

19

Analysis of return on investment and of asset utilization

DIVERSE VIEWS OF PERFORMANCE

In this age of increasing social consciousness, there exist many views of what the basic objectives of business enterprises are or should be. There are those who will argue that the main objective of a business enterprise should be to make the maximum contribution to the welfare of society of which the enterprise is capable. That includes, aside from the profitable production of goods and services, consideration of such immeasurables as absence of environmental pollution and a contribution to the solution of social problems. Others, who adhere to the more traditional *laissez faire* school, maintain that the major objective of a business enterprise organized for profit is to increase the wealth of its owners and that this is possible only by delivering to society (consumers) that which it wants. Thus, the good of society will be served.

An extended discussion of these differing points of view on performance is beyond the purpose of this book. Since the analysis of financial statements is concerned with the application of analytical tools to that which can be measured, we shall concentrate here on those measures of performance that meet the objectives of financial analysis as outlined in Chapter 1. In that context, performance is the source of the rewards required to compensate investors and lenders for the risks that they are assuming.

CRITERIA OF PERFORMANCE EVALUATION

There are many criteria by which performance can be measured. Changes in sales, in profits, or in various measures of output are among the criteria frequently utilized.

No one of these measurements, standing by itself, is useful as a comprehensive measure of enterprise performance. The reasons for this are easy to grasp. Increases in sales are desirable only if they result in increased profits. The same is true of increases in volume of production. Increases in profits, on the other hand, must be related to the capital that is invested in order to attain these profits.

IMPORTANCE OF RETURN ON INVESTMENT (ROI)

The relationship between net income and the capital invested in the generation of that income is one of the most valid and most widely recognized measures of enterprise performance. In relating income to invested capital, the ROI measure allows the analyst to compare it to alternative uses of capital as well as to the return realized by enterprises subject to similar degrees of risk. The investment of capital can always yield some return. If capital is invested in government bonds, the return will be relatively low because of the small risk involved. Riskier investments require higher returns in order to make them worthwhile.[1] The ROI measure relates income (reward) to the size of the capital that was needed to generate it.

MAJOR OBJECTIVES IN THE USE OF ROI

Economic performance is the first and foremost purpose of business enterprise. It is, indeed, the reason for its existence. The effectiveness of operating performance determines the ability of the enterprise to survive financially, to attract suppliers of funds, and to reward them adequately. ROI is the prime measure of economic performance. The analyst uses it as a tool in three areas of great importance:

1.   An indicator of managerial effectiveness.
2.   A measure of an enterprise's ability to earn a satisfactory return on investment.
3.   A method of projecting earnings.

An indicator of managerial effectiveness

The earning of an adequate or superior return on funds invested in an enterprise depends first and foremost on the resourcefulness, skill, ingenuity, and motivation of management. Thus, the longer-term ROI is of great interest and importance to the financial analyst because it offers a prime means of evaluating this indispensible criterion of business success: the quality of management.

---

[1] See Chapter 1 for an examination of the importance of the evaluation of risk and return in investing and lending decisions.

A measure of enterprise ability to earn a satisfactory ROI

While related to managerial effectiveness, this measure is a far more reliable indicator of long-term financial health than is any measure of current financial strength based only on balance sheet relationships. For this reason, ROI is of great importance and interest to longer-term creditors as well as to equity investors.

A method of projecting earnings

A third important function served by the ROI measure is that of a means of earnings projection. The advantage of this method of earnings projection is that it links the amount of earnings that it is estimated an enterprise will earn to the total invested capital. This adds discipline and realism to the projection process, which applies to the present and expected capital investment the return that is expected to be realized on it. The latter will usually be based on the historical and incremental rates of return actually earned by the enterprise and adjusted by projected changes, as well as on expected returns on new projects.

The rate of ROI method of earnings projection can be used by the analyst as either the primary method of earnings projection or as a supplementary check on estimates derived from other projection methods.

Internal decision and control tool

While our focus here is on the work of the external financial analyst, mention should be made of the very important role that ROI measures play in the individual investment decisions of an enterprise as well as in the planning, budgeting, coordination, evaluation, and control of business operations and results.

It is obvious that the final return achieved in any one period on the total investment of an enterprise is composed of the returns (and losses) realized by the various segments and divisions of which it is composed. In turn, these returns are made up of the results achieved by individual product lines, projects, and so forth.

The well-managed enterprise exercises rigorous control over the returns achieved by each of its "profit centers" and rewards its managers on the basis of such results. Moreover, in evaluating the advisability of new investments of funds in assets or projects, management will compute the estimated returns it expects to achieve from them and use these estimates as a basis for its decision.[2]

---

[2] Managements' emphasis on these techniques has recently been challenged. In their article "Managing Our Way to Economic Decline" in the *Harvard Business Review* of July–August 1980, Professors R. Hayes and W. Abernathy argue that this preoccupation with ROI and the related discounted cash flow measures has led to an emphasis on short-term profits at the expense of long-term risk taking based on improved technology.

BASIC ELEMENTS OF ROI

The basic concept of ROI is relatively simple to understand. However, care must be used in determining the elements entering its computation because there exist a variety of views, which reflect different objectives, of how these elements should be defined.

The basic formula for computing ROI is as follows:

$$\frac{\text{Income}}{\text{Investment}}$$

We shall now examine the various definitions of *investment* and of the related *income.*

Defining the investment base

There is no one generally accepted measure of capital investment on which the rate of return is computed. The different concepts of investment reflect different objectives. Since the term *return on investment (ROI)* covers a multitude of concepts of investment base and income, there is need for more specific terms to describe the actual investment base used.

Total assets.   Return on total assets is perhaps the best measure of the *operating efficiency* of an enterprise. It measures the return obtained on *all* the assets entrusted to management. By removing from this computation the effect of the method used in financing the assets, the analyst can concentrate on the evaluation or projection of operating performance.

Modified asset bases.   For a variety of reasons, some ROI computations are based not on total assets but rather on an adjusted amount.

One important category of adjustments relates to "unproductive" assets. In this category, assets omitted from the investment base include idle plant, facilities under construction, surplus plant, surplus inventories and surplus cash, intangible assets, and deferred charges. The basic idea behind these exclusions is not to hold management responsible for earning a return on assets that apparently do not earn a return. While this theory may have validity in the use of ROI as an internal management and control tool, it lacks merit when applied as a tool designed to evaluate management effectiveness on an overall basis. Management is entrusted with funds by owners and creditors, and it has discretion as to where it wants to invest them. There is no reason for management to hold on to assets that bring no return. If there are reasons for keeping funds invested in such assets, then there is no reason to exclude them from the investment base. If the long-run profitability of an enterprise is benefited by keeping funds invested in assets that have no return or a low return in the interim, then the longer-term ROI should reflect such benefits. In conclusion, it can be said that from the point of view of an enterprise evaluation by the external analyst, there is rarely any justification to omit assets from the investment base merely because they are not productively employed or do not earn a current return.

The exclusion of intangible assets from the investment base is often due to skepticism regarding their value or their contribution to the earning power of the enterprise. Under generally accepted accounting principles (GAAP), intangibles are carried at cost. However, if the cost exceeds their future utility, they must be written down or else the analyst will at least find an uncertainty exception regarding their carrying value included in the auditor's opinion. Accounting for intangible assets was discussed in Chapter 6. The exclusion of intangible assets from the asset (investment) base must be justified on more substantial evidence than a mere lack of understanding of what these assets represent or an unsupported suspicion regarding their value.

Depreciable assets in the investment base. An important difference of opinion prevails with respect to the question of whether depreciable assets should be included in the investment base at original cost or at an amount net of the accumulated allowances for depreciation.

One of the most prominent advocates of the inclusion of fixed assets at gross amount in the investment base for purposes of computing the ROI is the management of E. I. du Pont de Nemours Company which pioneered the use of ROI as an internal management tool.

In a pamphlet describing the company's use of the ROI method in the appraisal of operating performance, this point of view is expressed as follows:

> *Calculation of return on investment.* Return on investment as presented in the chart series is based upon *gross* operating investment and earnings *net* of depreciation.
>
> Gross operating investment represents all the plant, tools, equipment and working capital made available to operating management for its use; no deduction is made for current or other liabilities or for the reserve for depreciation. Since plant facilities are maintained in virtually top productive order during their working life, the depreciation reserve being considered primarily to provide for obsolescence, it would be inappropriate to consider that operating management was responsible for earning a return on only the net operating investment. Furthermore, if depreciable assets were stated at net depreciated values, earnings in each succeeding period would be related to an ever-decreasing investment; even with stable earnings, Return on Investment would continually rise, so that comparative Return on Investment ratios would fail to reveal the extent of trend of management performance. Relating earnings to investment that is stable and uniformly compiled provides a sound basis for comparing the "profitability of assets employed" as between years and between investments.
>
> In the case of any commitment of capital—e.g., an investment in a security— it is the expectation that in addition to producing earnings while committed, the principal will eventually be recovered. Likewise, in the case of funds invested in a project, it is expected that in addition to the return earned while invested, the working capital will be recovered through liquidation at the end of the project's useful life and the plant investment will be recovered through deprecia-

tion accruals. Since earnings must allow for this recovery of plant investment, they are stated net of depreciation.[3]

It is not difficult to take issue with the above reasoning. It must, however, be borne in mind that the duPont system is designed for use in the internal control of separate productive units as well as for the control of operating management. Our point of view here is, however, that of evaluating the operating performance of an enterprise taken as a whole. While by an enterprise operating at a profit, the recovery of capital out of sales and revenues (via depreciation) can be disregarded in the evaluation of a *single* division or segment, it cannot be disregarded for an enterprise taken as a whole because such recovery is reinvested somewhere within that enterprise even if it is not reinvested in the particular segment that gave rise to the depreciation and that is evaluated for internal purposes. Thus, for an enterprise taken as a whole, the "net of depreciation" asset base is a more valid measure of investment on which a return is computed. This is so for the reasons given above and also because the income that is usually related to the investment base is net of the depreciation expense.

The tendency of the rate of return to rise as assets are depreciated (see also Chapter 10) is offset by the retention of capital recovered by means of depreciation, on which capital a return must also be earned. Moreover, maintenance and repair costs rise as equipment gets older, thus tending to offset the reduction, if any, in the asset base.

Among other reasons advanced in support of the use of fixed assets at their gross amount is the argument that the higher amounts are designed to compensate for the effects of inflation on assets expressed in terms of historical cost. In the discussion of the price-level problem in Chapter 14, it was pointed out that price-level adjustments can validly be made only within the framework of a complete restatement of all elements of the financial statements. Crude "adjustments," such as using the gross asset amount, are apt to be misleading and are generally worse than no adjustments at all.

Long-term liabilities plus equity capital.   The use of long-term liabilities plus equity capital as the investment base differs from the "total assets" base only in that current liabilities are excluded as suppliers of funds on which the return is computed. The focus here is on the two major suppliers of longer-term funds, that is, long-term creditors and equity shareholders.

Shareholders' equity.   The computation of return on shareholders' equity measures the return accruing to the owners' capital. As was seen in the discussion of financial leverage in Chapter 18, this return reflects the effect of the employment of debt capital on the owners' return. Since preferred stock, while in the equity category, is usually nevertheless entitled only to

---

[3] American Management Association, *Executive Committee Control Charts,* AMA Management Bulletin No. 6, 1960, p. 22.

a fixed return, it is also omitted from the calculation of the final return on
equity computation.

Book versus market values in the investment base

Return on asset calculations are most commonly based on book values
appearing in the financial statements rather than on market or fair values
that are, in most cases, analytically more significant and relevant. Also, quite
often, a return is earned by enterprises on assets that either do not appear
in the financial statements or are significantly understated therein. Examples
of such assets are intangibles such as patents, trademarks, expensed research
and development (R&D) costs, advertising and training costs, and so forth.
Other excluded assets may include leaseholds and the value of natural resources discovered.

As was discussed in Chapter 14, there exists a trend towards current
value accounting, and information on the current cost of assets of large corporations is already available. One alternative to the use of such data is to
rely on the valuation that the market places on the equity securities of the
enterprise in order to approximate fair values. Thus, we can substitute the
market value of equity securities and debt for the book value of total assets
in computing a proper investment base.

Difference between investor's cost and enterprise investment base

For purposes of computing the ROI, a distinction must be drawn between
the investment base of an enterprise and that of an investor. The investor's
investment base is, of course, the price he paid for his equity securities.
Except for those cases in which he acquired such securities at book value,
his investment base is going to differ from that of the company in which
he has invested. In general, the focus in ROI computations is on the return
realized by the enterprise rather than the return realized on the investment
cost of any one shareholder.

Averaging the investment base

Regardless of the method used in arriving at the investment base, the
return achieved over a period of time is always associated with the investment
base that was, on average, actually available to the enterprise over that period
of time. Thus, unless the investment base did not change significantly during
the period, it will be necessary to average it.

The most common method of averaging for the external analyst is that
of adding the investment base at the beginning of the year to that at the
end of the year and dividing their total by two. Care must, however, be
used in employing this method of averaging. Companies in some industries
choose a "natural" rather than the calendar business year. Thus, for example,
in retailing, the natural business year ends when inventories are at their
lowest (e.g., January 31 after the holiday selling season) and when it is easiest

to count them. In such case, averaging two year-ends may yield the *lowest* rather than the average amount of assets employed.

In such or similar cases, more accurate methods of averaging, where the data are available, are to average by month-end balances, that is, adding the month-end investment bases and dividing the total by 12, or to average on a quarterly basis.

Relating income to the investment base

In the computation of ROI, the definition of return (income) is dependent on the definition of the investment base.

If the investment base is defined as comprising total assets, then income *before* interest expense is used.[4] The exclusion of interest from income deductions is due to its being regarded as a payment for the use of money to the suppliers of debt capital in the same way that dividends are regarded as a reward to suppliers of equity capital. Before deductions for interest or dividends, income is used when it is related to total assets or to long-term debt plus equity capital (assuming most of the interest expense is on long-term obligations).

The income of a consolidated entity that includes a subsidiary that is partially owned by a minority interest usually reflects a deduction for the minority's share in that income. The consolidated balance sheet, however, includes all the assets of such a subsidiary, i.e., those belonging to the parent as well as those belonging to the minority (see also Chapter 9). Because the investment in the denominator includes all the assets of the consolidated entity, the income (in the numerator) should include all the income (or loss), not just the parent's share. For this reason, the minority's share of earnings (or loss) must be added back to income in computing return on total assets. When the denominator is the equity capital only, the minority share in income (or loss) need not be added back if equity capital excludes minority interest.

When the return on the equity capital is computed, net income *after* deductions for interest and preferred dividends is used. If the preferred dividends are cumulative, they are deducted in arriving at the balance of earnings accruing to the common stock, whether these dividends were declared or not.

The final ROI must always reflect all applicable costs and expenses and that includes income taxes. Some computations of ROI nevertheless omit deductions of income taxes. One reason for this practice is the desire to isolate the effects of tax management from those of operating performance. Another reason is that changes in tax rates affect comparability over the years. Moreover, companies that have tax loss carry-forwards find that the deduction of taxes from income adds confusion and complications to the ROI computations.

---

[4] Interest expense means interest incurred less interest capitalized. In theory, the amount of previously capitalized interest currently amortized and included in expenses should also be added back to income.

It must, however, be borne in mind that income taxes reduce the final return and that they must be taken into consideration particularly when the return on shareholders' equity is computed.

ADJUSTING THE COMPONENTS OF THE ROI FORMULA

In computing any measure or ratio, the analyst uses the amounts in the financial statements only as starting points. As was seen in the discussion in Chapter 18 on the adjustment of the debt-to-equity ratios, some amounts need analytical adjustment and some amounts not found in the financial statements need to be included in the adjusted computation. Reference to the discussion in Chapter 18 will reveal that some of the items discussed therein, such as adjustment of inventory amounts, may affect the ROI computation while others, such as reclassification of deferred taxes, may not. Moreover, some adjustments, such as those relating to inventory amounts, affect both the numerator and the denominator of the formula, thus moderating the net effect on the ratio.

The computation of ROI under the various concepts of "investment base" discussed above will now be illustrated by means of the data contained in Exhibits 19–1 and 19–2. The computations are for the year 19x9 and based on figures rounded to the nearest million dollars.

Exhibit 19–1

AMERICAN COMPANY
Statement of Income
For Years Ended December 31, 19x8, and 19x9
(in thousands)

	19x8	19x9
Net sales	$1,636,298	$1,723,729
Costs and expenses	1,473,293	1,579,401
Operating income	163,005	144,328
Other income net	2,971	1,784
	165,976	146,112
Interest expense*	16,310	20,382
Income before tax	149,666	125,730
Provision for federal and other taxes		
on income	71,770	61,161
Net income	77,896	64,569
Less dividends:		
Preferred stock	2,908	2,908
Common stock	39,209	38,898
	42,117	41,806
Net income reinvested in the business	$ 35,779	$ 22,763

* In 19x9, interest on long-term debt was $19,695.

Exhibit 19–2

AMERICAN COMPANY
Statements of Financial Position
As at December 31, 19x8, and 19x9
(in thousands)

	19x8	*19x9*
Assets		
Current assets:		
Cash	$ 25,425	$ 25,580
Eurodollar time deposits and temporary cash		
investments	38,008	28,910
Accounts and notes receivable—net	163,870	176,911
Inventories	264,882	277,795
Total current assets	492,185	509,196
Investments in and receivables from nonconsolidated		
subsidiaries	33,728	41,652
Miscellaneous investments and receivables	5,931	6,997
Funds held by trustee for construction	6,110	
Land, buildings, equipment, and timberlands—net	773,361	790,774
Deferred charges to future operations	16,117	16,452
Goodwill and other intangible assets	6,550	6,550
Total assets..................................	$1,333,982	$1,371,621
Liabilities		
Current liabilities:		
Notes payable to banks—principally Eurodollar	$ 7,850	$ 13,734
Accounts payable and accrued expenses	128,258	144,999
Dividends payable	10,404	10,483
Federal and other taxes on income	24,370	13,256
Long-term indebtedness payable within one year	9,853	11,606
Total current liabilities	180,735	194,078
Long-term indebtedness	350,565	335,945
Deferred taxes on income	86,781	101,143
Total liabilities	618,081	631,166
Capital		
Preferred, 7% cumulative and noncallable, par		
value $25 per share; authorized 1,760,000 shares ..	41,538	41,538
Common, par value $12.50 per share; authorized		
30,000,000 shares	222,245	222,796
Capital in excess of par value....................	19,208	20,448
Earnings reinvested in the business	436,752	459,515
Less: Common treasury stock	(3,842)	(3,842)
Total capital	715,901	740,455
Total liabilities and capital	$1,333,982	$1,371,621

Return on total assets

Applying the basic formula to the data of American Company for 19x9 we get:

$$\frac{\text{Net income} + \text{Interest expense} \times (1 - \text{Tax rate}) + \text{Minority interest in earnings}}{(\text{Beginning total assets} + \text{Ending total assets}) \div 2}$$

$$= \frac{\$65 + \$20\,(1 - .46) + 0^*}{(\$1,334 + \$1,372) \div 2} = .056, \text{ or } 5.6 \text{ percent}$$

* No minority interest in this case.

The tax adjustment of the interest expense recognizes that interest is a tax-deductible expense and that if the interest cost is excluded, the related tax benefit must also be excluded from income. The *tax rate* we use is the *marginal* or corporate tax rate of 46 percent because the tax incidence with respect to any one item (such as interest expense) can be measured by the marginal tax rate. In computing the fixed-charges-coverage ratio (see Chapter 18), we use the *effective* tax rate because we have adopted the SEC's computation which requires its use.

The assets have been averaged by using the year-end figures for total assets. As discussed earlier, this method of computing the average may yield misleading results in some cases.

Return on modified asset bases. Since our discussion earlier in the chapter came to the conclusion that in normal circumstances most of the modifications in the amount of total assets are not logically warranted, no illustrations of such computation will be given.

Return on long-term liabilities plus equity capital

$$\frac{\begin{array}{c}\text{Net income} + \text{Interest expense}^* \times (1 - \text{Tax rate}) \\ + \text{Minority interest in earnings}\end{array}}{\text{Average long-term liabilities} + \text{equity capital}}$$

Using the data in Exhibits 19–1 and 19–2 for 19x9:

$$\frac{\$65 + \$20^*\,(1 - .46) + 0}{(\$437 + \$716 + \$437 + \$740) \div 2} = .065, \text{ or } 6.5 \text{ percent}$$

* On long-term debt ($19,695 rounded).

Decisions of how to classify items such as deferred taxes as between debt and equity will have to be made by the analyst using the considerations already discussed in Chapter 18. It should be noted that deferred taxes on income are included here among the long-term liabilities. In the computation of return on long-term liabilities and equity capital, the question of how to classify deferred taxes does not really present a problem because in this computation both debt and equity are aggregated anyway. The problem of classification becomes more real in computing the return on shareholders' equity.

In the examples that follow, we assume circumstances where deferred taxes are considered to be more in the nature of long-term liability than equity. In many cases, the classification decision can have a significant effect on the return computation.

Return on stockholders' equity.   The basic computation of return on the equity excludes from the investment base all but the common stockholders' equity.

$$\frac{\text{Net income} - \text{Preferred dividends}}{\text{Average common stockholders' equity}}$$

Using data in Exhibits 19–1 and 19–2 for 19x9:

$$\frac{\$65 - \$3}{(\$674 + \$699) \div 2} = 9 \text{ percent}$$

The higher return on shareholders' equity as compared to the return on total assets reflects the positive workings of financial leverage.

Should it be desired, for whatever reason, to compute the return on total stockholders' equity, the investment base would include the preferred shareholders' equity, while net income would not reflect a deduction for preferred dividends. The formula[5] would then be:

$$\frac{\text{Net income}}{\text{Average total shareholders' equity (common and preferred)}}$$

Where convertible debt sells at a substantial premium above par and is clearly held by investors for its conversion feature, there is justification for treating it as the equivalent of equity capital. This is particularly true when the company can choose at any time to force conversion of the debt by calling it.

Analysis and interpretation of ROI

Earlier in the chapter we mentioned that ROI analysis is particularly useful to the analyst in the areas of evaluation of managerial effectiveness, enterprise profitability, and as an important tool of earnings projection.

The evaluation of ROI and the projection of earnings by means of ROI analysis are complex processes requiring thorough analysis. The reason for this is that the ROI computation usually includes components of considerable complexity.

---

[5] The return on common stockholders' equity may also be computed thus:

$$\frac{\text{Earnings per share}}{\text{Book value per share}}$$

But the results will often not be identical because the earnings per share computation includes adjustments for common stock equivalents, etc. (see Chapter 12).

Components of the ROI ratio. If we focus first on return on total assets, we know that the primary formula for computing this return is:

$$\frac{\text{Net income} + \text{Interest} \times (1 - \text{Tax rate})^*}{\text{Average total assets}}$$

> * Omitting the add-back of minority interest in earnings in order to simplify the discussion does not impair its validity.

For purposes of our discussion and analysis, let us look at this computation in a simplified form:

$$\frac{\text{Net income}}{\text{Total assets}}$$

Since sales are a most important yardstick in relation to which profitability is measured and are, as well, a major index of activity, we can recast the above formula as follows:

$$\frac{\text{Net income}}{\text{Sales}} \times \frac{\text{Sales}}{\text{Total assets}}$$

The relationship of net income to sales measures operating performance and profitability. The relationship of sales to total assets is a measure of asset utilization or turnover, a means of determining how effectively (in terms of sales generation) the assets are utilized. It can be readily seen that both factors, profitability as well as asset utilization, determine the return realized on a given investment in assets.

Profitability and asset utilization are, in turn, complex ratios that normally require thorough and detailed analysis before they can be used to reach conclusions regarding the reasons for changes in the return on total assets.

Exhibit 19–3 presents the major factors that influence the final return on total assets. In the next section, we shall be concerned with the interaction of profitability (net income/sales) and of asset utilization or turnover (sales/total assets) that in Exhibit 19–3 is regarded as the first level of analysis of the return on total assets. As can be seen from Exhibit 19–3, the many important and complex factors that, in turn, determine profitability and asset utilization represent a second level of analysis of the return on total assets. Chapters 20 and 21 will take up the analysis of results of operations, and Chapter 22 will deal with the evaluation and projection of earnings. The analysis of asset utilization will be discussed in subsequent sections of this chapter.

Relationship between profitability and asset turnover. The relationship between return on total assets, profitability, and capital turnover (utilization) is illustrated in Exhibit 19–4, which indicates that when we multiply profitability (expressed as a percentage) by asset utilization (expressed as a turnover) we obtain the return on total assets (expressed as a percentage relationship).

Exhibit 19–3

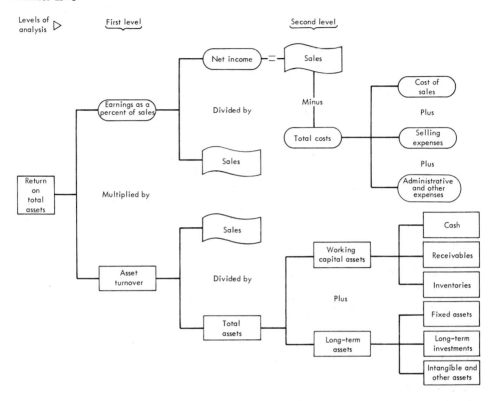

Exhibit 19–4: Analysis of return on total assets

	Company X	Company Y	Company Z
1. Sales	$5,000,000	$10,000,000	$10,000,000
2. Net income	500,000	500,000	100,000
3. Total assets	5,000,000	5,000,000	1,000,000
4. Profit as percent of sales $\left(\frac{2}{1}\right)$	10%	5%	1%
5. Asset turnover $\left(\frac{1}{3}\right)$	1	2	10
Return on total assets (4 × 5)	10%	10%	10%

Company X realizes its 10 percent return on total assets by means of a relatively high profit margin and a low turnover of assets. The opposite is true of Company Z, while Company Y achieves its 10 percent return by means of a profit margin half that of Company X and an asset turnover rate twice that of Company X. It is obvious from Exhibit 19–4 that there are many combinations of profit margins and turnover rates that can yield a return on assets of 10 percent.

In fact, as can be seen from Exhibit 19–5, there exist an infinite variety of combinations of profit margin and asset turnover rates that yield a 10 percent return on assets. The chart in the exhibit graphically relates asset turnover (vertical axis) to profitability (horizontal axis).

The curve, sloping from the upper left area of low profit margins and high asset turnover rates, traces out the endless combinations of profitability and asset turnover rates that yield a 10 percent return on total assets. The data of Companies X and Y (from Exhibit 19–4) are represented by dots on the graph, while the data of Company Z cannot be fitted on it since the full curve has not been shown. The other lettered dots represent the profit-turnover combination of other companies within a particular industry. This clustering of the results of various companies around the 10 percent return on assets slope is a useful way of comparing the returns of many enterprises within an industry and the major two elements that comprise them.

The chart in Exhibit 19–5 is also useful in assessing the relative courses of action open to different enterprises that want to improve their respective returns on investments.

Companies B and C must, of course, restore profitability before the turnover rate becomes a factor of importance. Assuming that all the companies represented in Exhibit 19–5 belong to the same industry and that there is an average representative level of profitability and turnover in it, Company P

Exhibit 19–5

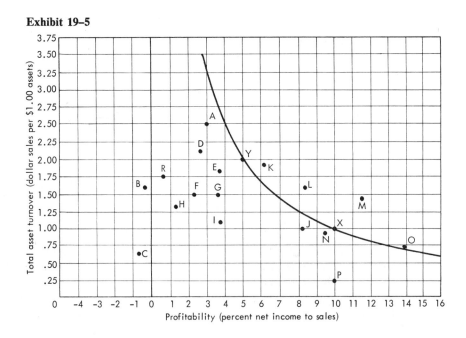

will be best advised to pay first and particular attention to improvement in its turnover ratio, while Company R should pay foremost attention to the improvement of its profit margin. Other companies, such as Company I, would best concentrate on both the turnover and the profit margin aspects of ROI improvement.

While the above analysis treats profitability and turnover as two independent variables, they are, in fact, interdependent. As will be seen from the discussion of break-even analysis in Chapter 21, when fixed expenses are substantial, a higher level of activity (turnover) will tend to increase the profit margin because within a certain range of activity, costs increase proportionally less than sales. In comparing two companies within an industry, the analyst, in evaluating the one having the lower asset turnover, will make allowance for the potential increase in profitability that can be associated with a projected increase in turnover that is based primarily on an expansion of sales.

Analysis of return on total assets can reveal the weaknesses as well as the potential strengths of an enterprise. Assume that two companies in the same industry have returns on total assets as follows:

	Company A	Company B
1. Sales	$ 1,000,000	$20,000,000
2. Net income	100,000	100,000
3. Total assets	10,000,000	10,000,000
4. Profitability $\left(\frac{2}{1}\right)$	10%	0.5%
5. Turnover of assets $\left(\frac{1}{3}\right)$	.1 times	2 times
Return on investment (4 × 5)	1%	1%

Both companies have poor returns on total assets. However, remedial action for them lies in different areas, and the analyst will concentrate on the evaluation of the feasibility of success of such improvement.

Company A has a 10 percent profit on sales that, let us assume, is about average for the industry. However, each dollar invested in assets supports only 10 cents in sales, whereas Company B gets $2 of sales for each dollar invested in its assets. The analyst's attention will naturally be focused on Company A's investment in assets. Why is its turnover so low? Are there excess assets that yield little or no return or are there idle assets that should be disposed of? Or, as often is the case, are the assets inefficiently or uneconomically utilized? Quite obviously, Company A can achieve more immediate and significant improvements by concentrating on improving turnover (by increasing sales, reducing investment, or both) than by striving to increase the profit margin beyond the industry average.

The opposite situation prevails with respect to Company B where attention should first be focused on the reasons for the low profit margin and to the improvement of it as the most likely avenue of success in increasing ROI. The reasons for low profitability can be many, including inefficient equipment and production methods, unprofitable product lines, excess capacity with attendant high fixed costs, excessive selling or administrative costs, etc.

The company with the low profitability may discover that changes in tastes and in technology have resulted in an increased investment in assets being needed to finance a dollar of sales. This means that in order to maintain its return on assets, the company must increase its profit margin or else production of the product is no longer worthwhile.

There is a tendency to regard a high profit margin as a sign of high earnings quality. This view was rebutted by W. M. Bennett who pointed out the importance of return on capital as the ultimate test of profitability.[6] He presented the following table comparing during a given year the similar profit margins of five companies with their respective returns on capital:

	Profit margin as percent of sales	Profit as percent of capital
Whirlpool	5.3	17.1
Corn Products	5.9	12.0
Goodyear	5.5	9.6
U.S. Plywood	5.5	8.0
Distillers Seagram	5.0	6.7

It is evident that in the case of these five companies, which have similar profit margins, the rate of capital turnover made the difference in the return on capital performance, and this must be taken into account by the analyst. Thus, a supermarket chain will be content with a net profit margin of 1 percent or less because it has a high rate of turnover due to a relatively low investment in assets and a high proportion of leased assets (such as stores and fixtures). Similarly, a discount store will accept a low profit margin in order to obtain a high rate of asset turnover (primarily of inventories). On the other hand, capital intensive industries such as steels, chemicals, and autos, which have heavy investments in assets and resulting low asset turnover rates, must achieve high net profit margins in order to offer investors a reasonable return on capital.

In most cases, the focus on single-year rates of return are apt to be misleading. The cyclical nature of many industries cause such swings in profitability

---

[6] William M. Bennett, "Capital Turnover vs. Profit Margins," *Financial Analysts Journal,* March–April 1966, pp. 88–95.

that some years' profits may appear exorbitant while others barely are sufficient to justify the related investment. Such enterprises can only be validly evaluated on the basis of average returns over a number of years covering a full economic cycle.

ANALYSIS OF ASSET UTILIZATION

As is graphically illustrated in Exhibit 19–3, the return on total assets depends on (1) getting the largest profit out of each dollar of sales and (2) obtaining the highest possible amount of sales per dollar of invested capital (net assets).

The intensity with which assets are utilized is measured by means of asset turnover ratios.[7] That utilization has as its ultimate measure the amount of sales generated since sales are in most enterprises the first and essential step to profits. In certain special cases, such as with enterprises in developmental stages, the meaning of turnover may have to be modified in recognition of the fact that most assets are committed to the development of future potential. Similarly, abnormal supply problems and strikes are conditions that will affect the state of capital utilization and, as such, will require separate evaluation and interpretation.

Evaluation of individual turnover ratios

Changes in the basic turnover ratio that enters the determination of the ROI calculation, that is,

$$\frac{\text{Sales}}{\text{Total assets}}$$

can be evaluated meaningfully only by an analysis of changes in the turnover rates of individual asset categories and groups that comprise the total assets.

Sales to cash. As was seen in the discussion in Chapter 16, cash and cash equivalents are held primarily for purposes of meeting the needs of day-to-day transactions as well as a liquidity reserve designed to prevent the shortages that may arise from an imbalance in cash inflows and outflows. In any type of business, there is a certain logical relationship between sales and cash level that must be maintained to support it.

Too high a rate of turnover may be due to a cash shortage that can

---

[7] P. F. Drucker in "Managing in Turbulent Times" (New York: Harper & Row, 1980) writes: "In the United States the General Electric Co., for example, does not owe its leadership position primarily to technological achievement. What sets it apart from Westinghouse, its closest competitor and the industry's number two, is above all productivity of capital. GE gets about twice as much work out of a dollar as Westinghouse does."

ultimately result in a liquidity crisis if the enterprise has no other ready sources of funds available to it.

Too low a rate of turnover may be due to the holding of idle and unnecessary cash balances. Cash accumulated for specific purposes or known contingencies may result in temporary decreases in the rate of turnover.

The basic trade-off here is between liquidity and the tying up of funds that yield no return or a very modest return.

Sales to receivables. Any organization that sells on credit will find that the level of its receivables is a function of sales. A relatively low rate of turnover here is, among other reasons, likely to be due to an overextension of credit, to an inability of customers to pay, or to a poor collection job.

A relatively high rate of turnover may indicate a strict credit extension policy or a reluctance or inability to extend credit. Determining the rate of turnover here is the trade-off between sales and the tying up of funds in receivables.

Sales to inventories. The maintenance of a given level of sales generally requires a given level of inventories. This relationship will vary from industry to industry depending on the variety of types, models, colors, sizes, and other classes of varieties of items that must be kept in order to attract and keep customers. The length of the production cycle as well as the type of item (e.g., luxury versus necessity; perishable versus durable) has a bearing on the rate of turnover.

A slow rate of turnover indicates the existence of problems such as overstocking, slow-moving or obsolete inventories, overestimating of sales, or a lack of balance in the inventory. Temporary problems such as strikes at important customers may also be responsible for such a condition.

A higher than normal rate of turnover may mean an underinvestment in inventory that can result in lack of proper customer service and in loss of sales.

In this case, the trade-off is between tying up funds in inventory, on one hand, and sacrificing customer service and sales, on the other.

Sales to fixed assets. While the relationship between property, plant, and equipment and sales is a logical one on a long-term basis, there are many short-term and temporary factors that may upset this relationship. Among these factors are conditions of excess capacity, inefficient or obsolete equipment, multishift operations, temporary changes in demand, and interruptions in the supply of raw materials and parts.

It must also be remembered that increases in plant capacity are not gradual but occur, instead, in lumps. This too can create temporary and medium-term changes in the turnover rates. Often, leased facilities and equipment, which do not appear on the balance sheet, will distort the relationship between sales and fixed assets (see, however, Chapter 7).

The trade-off here is between investment in fixed assets with a correspondingly higher break-even point, on one hand, and efficiency, productive capacity, and sales potential, on the other.

Sales to other assets.   In this category, we find, among others, such assets as patents and deferred charges or other costs. While the direct relationship between these individual categories of assets and current sales levels may not be evident, no assets are held or should be held by an enterprise unless they contribute to sales or to the generation of income. In the case of deferred R&D costs, the investment may represent the potential of future sales. In the evaluation of rates of asset utilization, the analyst must allow for such factors.

Sales to short-term liabilities.   The relationship between sales and short-term trade liabilities is a predictable one. The amount of short-term credit that an enterprise is able to obtain from suppliers depends on its needs for goods and services, that is, on the level of activity (e.g., sales). Thus, the degree to which it can obtain short-term credit depends also importantly on the level of sales. This short-term credit is relatively cost-free and, in turn, reduces the investment of enterprise funds in working capital.

Use of averages

Whenever the level of a given asset category changes significantly during the period for which the turnover is computed, it is necessary to use averages of asset levels in the computation. The computation then becomes

$$\frac{\text{Sales}}{(\text{Asset at beginning of period} + \text{Asset at end of period}) \div 2}$$

To the extent that data is available and the variation in asset levels during the period dictates it, the average can be computed on a monthly or quarterly basis.

Other factors to be considered in return on asset evaluation

The evaluation of the return on assets involves many factors of great complexity. As will be seen from the discussion in Chapter 22, the inclusion of extraordinary gains and losses in single period and average net income must be evaluated. Chapter 14 has examined the effects of price-level changes on ROI calculations, and these, too, must be taken into account by the analyst.

In analyzing the trend of return on assets over the years, the effect of acquisitions accounted for as poolings of interest (see Chapter 9) must be isolated and their chance of recurrence evaluated. The effect of discontinued operations must be similarly evaluated.

The external analyst will not usually be able to obtain data on ROI by segments, product lines, or divisions of an enterprise. However, where his bargaining power or position allows him to obtain such data, they can make a significant contribution to the accuracy and reliability of his analysis.

A consistently high return on assets is the earmark of an effective management and can distinguish a growth company from one experiencing merely a cyclical or seasonal pickup in business.

An examination of the factors that comprise the return on assets will usually reveal the limitations to which their expansion is subject. Neither the profit margin nor the asset turnover rate can expand indefinitely. Thus, an expanding asset base via external financing and/or internal earnings retention will be necessary for further earnings growth.

Return on shareholders' equity

Up to now we have examined the factors affecting the return on total assets. However, of great interest to the owner group of an enterprise is the return on the stockholders' equity. The rate of return on total assets and that on the stockholders' equity differ because a portion of the capital with which the assets are financed is usually supplied by creditors who receive a fixed return on their capital or, in some cases, no return at all. Similarly, the preferred stock usually receives a fixed dividend. These fixed returns differ from the rate earned on the assets (funds) that they provide, and this accounts for the difference in returns on assets and those on stockholders' equity. This is the concept of financial leverage that was already discussed in Chapter 18.

ANALYSIS OF RETURN ON COMMON STOCKHOLDERS' EQUITY (ROCSE)

The ROCSE can be disaggregated into the following elements that facilitate its analysis:

$$\frac{\text{Net income} - \text{Preferred dividends}}{\text{Average common stockholders' equity}} = \frac{\text{Net income} - \text{Preferred dividends}}{\text{Sales}} \times \frac{\text{Sales}}{\text{Average total assets}} \times \frac{\text{Average total assets}}{\text{Average common stockholders' equity}}$$

Descriptively, we can express this formula as follows:

$$\frac{\text{Rate of return}}{\text{on CSE}} = \frac{\text{Net income margin}}{\text{after preferred dividends}} \times \frac{\text{Assets turnover}}{\text{ratio}} \times \frac{\text{Common stockholders'}}{\text{leverage ratio}}$$

The net income margin represents the portion of the sales dollar that is left for the common shareholder after providing for all costs[8] and claims (e.g., those of the preferred shareholders). The asset turnover was discussed above. The common stockholders' leverage ratio measures the extent to which total assets are financed by common stockholders. The larger this ratio is the smaller the proportion of assets financed by common stockholders and the greater the extent of leverage. Leverage can also be measured by means of the financial leverage index as was illustrated in Chapter 18.

Using the data in Exhibits 19–1 and 19–2 of the American Company, we can compute the disaggregated ROCSE for 19x9 as follows (dollars in millions):

$$\frac{\$65 - \$3}{(\$674 + \$699) \div 2} = \frac{\$65 - \$3}{\$1,724} \times \frac{\$1,724}{\$1,334 + \$1,372) \div 2} \times \frac{(\$1,334 + \$1,372) \div 2}{(\$674 + \$699) \div 2} \text{ or}$$

	Net income margin		Common
Rate of return	after preferred	Assets turnover	stockholders'
on CSE	dividends	ratio	leverage ratio
9% =	3.6% ×	1.27 ×	1.97

Using the type of return on equity analysis that we have discussed above, here is how Tandy Corporation explained the growth in return on equity over a period of time:

June 30	Asset turnover	×	Return on sales	=	Return on assets	×	Financial leverage	=	Return on equity
1977	2.16	×	7.3%	=	15.7%	×	2.37	=	37.2%
1978	2.06	×	6.2	=	12.8	×	3.39	=	43.6
1979	2.09	×	6.9	=	14.3	×	3.35	=	47.9
1980	2.10	×	8.1	=	17.0	×	2.69	=	45.7
1981	2.06	×	10.0	=	20.6	×	1.93	=	39.7
1982	1.88	×	11.0	=	20.7	×	1.56	=	32.3

Equity growth rate

The equity growth rate by means of *earnings retention* can be calculated as follows:

$$\frac{\text{Net income* } - \text{ Dividend payout}}{\text{Average common shareholders' equity}} = \text{Percent increase in common equity}$$

  * Minus preferred dividend requirements.

---

  [8] A refinement can be introduced into this analysis by focusing first on the pretax profit margin and multiplying it by 1 − Marginal tax rate (referred to as tax retention rate) in order to arrive at the net income margin. This additional analysis focuses on the effect of tax management on the final return achieved by the CSE.

This is the growth rate due to the retention of earnings and assumes a constant dividend payout over time. It indicates the possibilities of earnings growth without resort to external financing. These increased funds, in turn, will earn the rate of return that the enterprise can obtain on its assets and thus contribute to growth in earnings.

For the American Company, the equity growth rate can be computed for 19x9 as follows:

$$\frac{\$65 - \$3 - \$39^*}{(\$674 + \$699) \div 2} = 3.4 \text{ percent}$$

* Common stock dividends.

Analysis of financial leverage effects

The effect that each noncommon equity capital source has on the return on the common equity can be analyzed in detail. Using the data of American Company that was included in Exhibits 19–1 and 19–2 earlier in this chapter, we can undertake such an analysis as follows:

An analysis of the American Company balance sheet as at December 31, 19x9[9] discloses the following major sources of funds (in thousands):

Current liabilities (exclusive of current portion of long-term debt)		$ 182,472
Long-term debt	$335,945	
Current portion	11,606	347,551
Deferred taxes		101,143
Preferred stock		41,538
Common stockholders' equity		698,917
Total investment or total assets		$1,371,621

The income statement for 19x9 includes (in thousands):

Income before taxes	$125,730
Income (and other) taxes	61,161
Net income	64,569
Preferred dividends	2,908
Income accruing to common shareholders	$ 61,661
Total interest expense	$ 20,382
Assumed interest on short-term notes (5%)	687
Balance of interest on long-term debt	$ 19,695

---

[9] A year-end based analysis (rather than one based on average for the year amounts) is used here in order to simplify the computations.

The return on total assets is computed as follows:

$$\frac{\text{Net income} + \text{Interest} \times (1 - \text{Tax rate})}{\text{Total assets (year-end)}}$$

$$= \frac{\$64,569 + \$20,382\,(1 - .46)}{\$1,371,621} = 5.51 \text{ percent}$$

The 5.51 percent return represents the average return on all assets employed by the company. To the extent that suppliers of capital other than the common stockholders get a lower reward than an average of 5.51 percent, the common equity benefits by the difference. The opposite is true when the suppliers of capital receive more than a 5.51 percent reward in 19x9.

Exhibit 19–6 presents an analysis showing the relative contribution and reward of each of the major suppliers of funds and their effect on the returns earned by the common stockholders.

Exhibit 19–6: Analysis of composition of return on shareholders' equity (approximate computations in thousands of dollars)

Category of fund supplier	Fund supplied	Earnings on fund supplied at rate of 5.51 percent	Payment to suppliers of funds	Accruing to (detracting from) return on common stock
Current liabilities	$ 182,472	$10,054	$ 371 (a)	$ 9,683
Long-term debt	347,551	19,150	10,635 (b)	8,515
Deferred taxes	101,143	5,573	none	5,573
Preferred stock	41,538	2,289	2,908 (c)	(619)
Earnings in excess of compensation to suppliers of funds				23,152
Add: Common stockholders' equity	698,917	38,510		38,510
Totals	$1,371,621	$75,576	$13,914	
Total income (return) on stockholders' equity				$61,662 (d)

(a) Interest cost of $687 less 46 percent tax.
(b) Interest cost of $19,695 less 46 percent tax.
(c) Preferred dividends—not tax deductible.
(d) Slight differences with statement figures are due to rounding.

As can be seen from Exhibit 19–6, the $9,683,000 accruing to the common equity from use of current liabilities is largely due to its being free of interest costs. The advantage of $8,515,000 accruing from the use of long-term debt is substantially due to the tax deductability of interest. Since the preferred dividends are not tax deductible, the unimpressive return on total assets of 5.51 percent resulted in a disadvantage to the common equity of $619,000. The value of tax deferrals can be clearly seen in this case where the use of cost-free funds amounted to an annual advantage of $5,573,000.

We can now carry this analysis further (dollars in thousands):

The return on the common stockholder equity is as follows:

$$\frac{\text{Net income less preferred dividends}}{\text{Common stockholders' equity}} = \frac{\$61,661^*}{\$698,917} = 8.8 \text{ percent}$$

> * Ties in (except for rounding difference) with total income accruing to common stockholders in Exhibit 19–6.

The net advantage that the common equity reaped from the working of financial leverage (Exhibit 19–6) is $23,152.

As a percentage of the common stockholders' equity, this advantage is computed as follows:

$$\frac{\begin{array}{c}\text{Earnings in excess of compensation}\\ \text{to outside suppliers of funds}\end{array}}{\text{Common stockholders' equity}} = \frac{\$23,152}{\$698,917} = 3.3 \text{ percent}$$

The return on common stockholders' equity can now be viewed as being composed as follows:

Return on assets	5.51%
Leverage advantage accruing to common equity	3.30
Return on common equity	8.81%

QUESTIONS

1. Why is return on investment (ROI) one of the most valid measures of enterprise performance? How is this measure used by the financial analyst?
2. How is ROI used as an internal management tool?
3. Discuss the validity of excluding "nonproductive" assets from the asset base used in the computation of ROI. Under what circumstances is the exclusion of intangible assets from the asset base warranted?
4. Why is interest added back to net income when the ROI is computed on total assets?
5. Under what circumstances may it be proper to consider convertible debt as equity capital in the computation of ROI?
6. Why must the minority interest's share in net income be added back when ROI is computed on total assets?
7. Why must the net income figure used in the computation of ROI be adjusted to reflect the asset base (denominator) used in the computation?
8. What is the relationship between ROI and sales?

9. Company A acquired Company B because the latter had a record of profitability (net income to sales ratio) exceeding that of its industry. After the acquisition took place, a major stockholder complained that the acquisition resulted in a low ROI. Discuss the possible reasons for his complaint.

10. Company X's profitability is 2 percent of sales. Company Y has a turnover of assets of 12. Both companies have ROIs of 6 percent that are considered unsatisfactory by industry standards. What is the asset turnover of Company X and what is the profitability ratio of Company Y? What action would you advise to the managements of the respective companies?

11. What is the purpose of measuring the asset utilization of different asset categories?

12. What factors enter into the evaluation of the ROI measures?

13. How is the equity growth rate computed? What does it signify?

14.   *a.*   How do the rate of return on total assets and that on stockholders' equity differ?

       b.   What are the components of the rate of return on common stockholders' equity and what do they represent?

15.   *a.*   What is *equity turnover* and how is it related to the rate of return on equity?

       b.   "Growth in per share earnings generated from an increase in equity turnover probably cannot be expected to continue indefinitely." Do you agree or disagree? Explain briefly, bringing out in your answer the alternative causes of an increase in equity turnover. (CFA)

20

Analysis of results of operations—I

THE SIGNIFICANCE OF INCOME STATEMENT ANALYSIS

The income statement presents in summarized fashion the results of operations of an enterprise. These results, in turn, represent the major reason for the existence of a profit-seeking entity, and they are important determinants of its value and its solvency.

As was brought out in the discussion of objectives of financial analysis in Chapter 3, some of the most important decisions in security analysis and credit evaluation are based on an evaluation of the income statements. To the security analyst, income is often the single most important determinant of security values, and hence the measurement and the projection of income are among his most important analytical objectives. Similarly, to the credit grantor, income and funds or cash provided by operations are the most natural as well as the most desirable source of interest and principal repayment. In almost all other aspects of financial analysis, the evaluation and projection of operating results assume great importance.

THE MAJOR OBJECTIVES OF INCOME ANALYSIS

In the evaluation of the income of an enterprise, the analyst is particularly interested in an answer to the following questions:

1. What is the relevant net income of the enterprise and what is its quality?
2. What elements in the income statement can be used and relied upon for purposes of earnings forecasting?
3. How stable are the major elements of income and expense and what is their trend?
4. What is the "earning power" of the enterprise?

These questions will be examined in this and in the two chapters that follow.

What is the relevant net income of the enterprise?

Based on the simple proposition that net income is the excess of revenues over costs and expenses during an accounting period, many people, including astute professional analysts, are exasperated at the difficulties they encounter in their search for the "true earnings" or the "real earnings" of an enterprise.

Why, they ask, should it be possible for so many different "acceptable" figures of "net income" to flow out of one set of circumstances? Given the economic events that the enterprise experienced during a given period, is there not only *one* "true" result, and is it not the function of accountancy to identify and measure such result?

Those who have studied Part II of this book will know why the answer to the last question must be "no." In this chapter, dealing with the analysis of income, it is appropriate to summarize *why* this is so.

Net income is not a specific quantity. Net income is not a specific flow awaiting the perfection of a flawless meter with which it can be precisely measured. There are a number of reasons for this:

1. The determination of income is dependent on estimates regarding the outcome of future events. This peering into the future is basically a matter of judgment involving the assessment of probabilities based on facts and estimates.

While the judgment of skilled and experienced professionals, working on the basis of identical data and information, can be expected to fall within a narrow range, it will nevertheless *vary* within such a range. The estimates involve the allocation of revenues and costs as between the present and the future. Put another way, they involve the determination of the future utility and usefulness of many categories of unexpired costs and of assets as well as the estimation of future liabilities and obligations.

2. The accounting standards governing the determination and measurement of income at any given time are the result of the cumulative experience of the accounting profession, of regulatory agencies, of businessmen, and others. They reflect a momentary equilibrium that is based partly on knowledge and experience and partly on the compromise of widely differing interests and views on methods of measurement. Chapter 10 indicates the great variety of these views. While the accounting profession has moved to narrow the range of acceptable alternative measurement principles, alternatives nevertheless remain; and their complete elimination in the near future is unlikely.

3. Beyond the problem of honest differences in estimation and other judgments, as well as of the variety of alternative acceptable principles, is also the problem arising from the diverse ways in which the judgments and principles are applied.

Theoretically, the independent professional accountant should be concerned first and foremost with the fair presentation of the financial statements. He should make accounting a "neutral" science that gives expression and effect to economic events but does not itself affect the results presented. To this end, he should choose from among alternative principles those most applicable to the circumstances and should disclose all facts, favorable and adverse, that may affect the user's decision.

In fact, the accounting profession as a whole has not yet reached such a level of independence and detachment of judgment. It is subject to the powerful pressures on the part of managements who have, or at least feel that they have, a vital interest in the way in which results of operations are presented. The auditors are most vulnerable to pressures in those areas of accounting where widely differing alternatives are equally acceptable and where accounting theory is still unsettled. Thus, they may choose the lowest level of acceptable practice rather than that which is most appropriate and fair in the circumstances. Although relatively less frequent, cases of malpractice and collusion in outright deception by independent accountants nevertheless still surface from time to time.

The analyst cannot ignore these possibilities, and must be aware of them and be ever alert to them. It calls for constant vigilance in the analysis of audited data, particularly when there is reason to suspect a lack of independence and objectivity in the application of accounting principles.

In addition to the above reasons that are inherent in the accounting process, there exists another reason why there cannot be such a thing as an absolute measure of "real earnings." It is that financial statements are general-purpose presentations designed to serve the diverse needs of many users. Consequently, a single figure of "net income" cannot be relevant to all users, and that means that the analyst must use this figure and the additional information disclosed in the financial statements and elsewhere as a starting point and adjust it so as to arrive at a "net income" figure that meets his particular interests and objectives.

ILLUSTRATION 1.   To the buyer of an income-producing property, the depreciation expense figure that is based on the seller's cost is not relevant. In order to estimate the net income he can derive from such property, depreciation based on the expected purchase price of the property must be substituted.

ILLUSTRATION 2.   To the analyst who exercises independent judgment and uses knowledge of the company he is analyzing and the industry of which it is a part, the reported net income marks the start of his analysis. He adjusts the net income figure for changes in income and expense items that he judges to be warranted. These may include, for example, estimates of bad debts, of depreciation, and of research costs as well as the treatment of gains and losses that are labeled extraordinary. Comparisons with other companies may call for similar adjustments so that the data can be rendered comparable.

From the above discussion it should be clear that the determination of *a* figure of net income is from the point of view of the analyst secondary to the objective of being able to find in the income statement all the disclosures needed in order to arrive at an income figure that is relevant for the purpose at hand.

The questions regarding the quality of earnings, of what elements in the income statement can be relied on for forecasting purposes, of what the stability and the trend of the earning elements are, and finally, of what the "earning power" of the enterprise is, will all be considered in Chapter 22.

We shall now proceed to examine the specific tools that are useful in the analysis of the various components of the income statement.

ANALYSIS OF COMPONENTS OF THE INCOME STATEMENT

The analysis of the income statements of an enterprise can be conceived as being undertaken at two levels: (1) obtaining an understanding of the accounting standards used and of their implication and (2) using the appropriate tools of income statement analysis.

Accounting standards used and their implication

The analyst must have a thorough understanding of the standards of income, cost, and expense accounting and measurement employed by the enterprise. Moreover, since most assets, with the exception of cash and receivables actually collectible, represent costs deferred to the future, the analyst must have a good understanding of the standards of asset and liability measurements employed by the enterprise so that he can relate them to the income accounting of the enterprise as a means of checking the validity of that accounting. Finally, he must understand and assess the implications that the use of one accounting principle, as opposed to another, has on the measurement of the income of an enterprise and its comparison to that of other enterprises.

Most chapters in Part II of this book deal with this important phase of financial statement analysis.

Tools of income statement analysis

The second level of analysis consists of applying the appropriate tools of analysis to the components of the income statement and the interpretation of the results shown by these analytical measures. The application of these tools is aimed at achieving the objectives of the analysis of results of operations mentioned earlier, such as the projection of income, the assessment of its stability and quality, and the estimation of earning power.

The remainder of this chapter will be devoted to an examination of these tools and to the interpretation of the results achieved through their use.

THE ANALYSIS OF SALES AND REVENUES

The analysis of sales and revenues is centered on answers to these basic questions:

1. What are the major sources of revenue?
2. How stable are these sources and what is their trend?
3. How is the earning of revenue determined and how is it measured?

Major sources of revenue

Knowledge of major sources of revenues (sales) is important in the analysis of the income statement particularly if the analysis is that of a multimarket enterprise. Each major market or product line may have its own separate and distinct growth pattern, profitability, and future potential.

The best way to analyze the composition of revenues is by means of a common-size statement that shows the percentage of each major class of revenue to the total. This information can also be portrayed graphically on an absolute dollar basis as shown in Exhibit 20–1.

Alfa, Inc. (see Appendix 4B), presents a five-year summary of segment revenues (item $\boxed{106}$) and segment contribution as well as other data (item $\boxed{107}$).

FINANCIAL REPORTING BY DIVERSIFIED ENTERPRISES

The user of the financial statements of diversified enterprises faces, in addition to the usual problems and pitfalls of financial analysis, the problem of sorting out and understanding the impact that the different individual segments of the business have on the sum total of reported results of operations and financial condition. The author of an important study in the reporting by diversified companies has defined a conglomerate company as follows:

> . . . one which is so managerially decentralized, so lacks operational integration, or has such diversified markets that it may experience rates of profitability, degrees of risk, and opportunities for growth which vary within the company to such an extent that an investor requires information about these variations in order to make informed decisions.[1]

Reasons for the need for data by significant enterprise segments

The above definition suggests some of the most significant reasons why financial analysts require as much information and detailed data as possible

---

[1] R. K. Mautz, "Identification of the Conglomerate Company," *Financial Executive,* July 1967, p. 26.

Exhibit 20–1:   Analysis of sales by product line over time

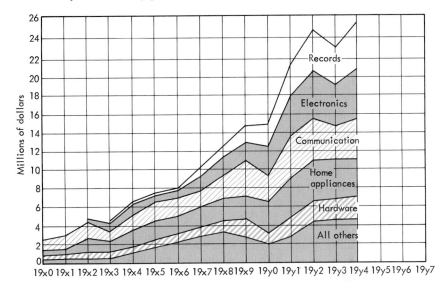

about the various segments of an enterprise. The analysis, evaluation, projection, and valuation of earnings requires that these be broken down into
categories that share similar characteristics of variability, growth potential,
and risk. Similarly, the asset structure and the financing requirements of
various segments of an enterprise can vary significantly and thus require
separate analysis and evaluation. Thus, the credit grantor may be interested
in knowing which segments of an enterprise provide funds and which are
net user of funds.

The composition of an enterprise, the relative size and profitability of its
various segments, the ability of management to make profitable acquisitions,
and the overall performance of management represents additional important
information that the analyst seeks from its segmented data.[2] As will be seen
from the discussion in Chapter 22, among the best ways to construct an
earnings forecast is to build the projections, to the extent possible, segment
by segment.

The evaluation of the growth potential of earnings requires that as much
information as possible be obtained about the different product lines or segments that make up the aggregate earnings. Rappaport and Lerner have
illustrated the use of a segmented earnings contribution matrix that may

---

[2] D. W. Collins in a study of 150 multisegment firms found that "SEC product-line revenue
and profit disclosures together with industry sales projections published in various government
sources provide significantly more accurate estimates of future total-entity sales and earnings
than do those procedures that rely totally on consolidated data." *Journal of Accounting Research,*
Spring 1976, pp. 163–77.

Table 20–1: Earnings contribution and growth rates by industry segments

Industry	Earnings contributions (in thousands)	Growth rate of earnings contribution over the past three years
Leisure time:		
1. Camp equipment	$100	11%
2. Fishing equipment	50	2
3. Boats	72	15
4. Sporting goods	12	3
	234	
Agribusiness:		
1. Milk processing	85	2
2. Canning........................	72	8
3. Chicken farming..................	12	15
	169	
Education:		
1. Text publishing	40	3
2. Papers and supplies	17	6
	57	
Total	$460	

Table 20–2: Segmented earnings contribution matrix

Industry	Growth rate (in percent) 0–5	5–10	10–15	Total
Leisure time	$ 62	$ 0	$172	$234
Agribusiness	85	72	12	169
Education	40	17	0	57
Total	$187	$89	$184	$460

prove useful in an assessment of earnings quality and growth potential, as well as in the valuation of aggregate earnings.[3] These are shown in Tables 20–1 and 20–2.

Disclosure of "line of business" data

The degree of informative disclosure about the results of operations and the asset base of segments of a business can vary widely. Full disclosure would call for providing detailed income statements, statements of financial position, and statements of changes in financial position (SCFPs) for each

---

[3] A. Rappaport and E. M. Lerner, *A Framework for Financial Reporting by Diversified Companies* (New York: National Association of Accountants, 1969), pp. 18–19.

significant segment. This is rarely found in practice because of the difficulty of obtaining such breakdowns internally, and also because of management's reluctance to divulge information that could harm the enterprise's competitive position. Short of the disclosure of complete financial statements by business segment, a great variety of partial detail has been suggested.

Income statement data

Revenues only.   In most enterprises, this should not present great difficulties.

Gross profit.   This involves complex problems of interdivisional transfer pricing as well as allocation of indirect overhead costs.

Contribution margin.   Contribution margin reporting (see also Chapter 21) is based on assigning to each segment the revenues, costs, and expenses for which that segment is solely responsible. It is a very useful concept in management accounting, but for purposes of public reporting of segment data, it presents problems because there are no generally accepted methods of cost allocation and, consequently, they can vary significantly from company to company and even within one enterprise. Disclosure of allocation methods, while helpful, will not remove all the problems facing the user of such data.

Net income (after full cost allocation).   The further down the income statement we report by segment, the more pervasive and the more complex the allocation procedures become. Reporting segment net income would require allocating all joint expenses to each specific business activity on some rational basis, even though they may not be directly related to any particular one.

Balance sheet data

A breakdown by segments of assets employed is needed in an assessment of the efficiency of operations by segment, in the evaluation of segmental management, as well as in the computation of divisional return on investment.

In most companies, only certain assets, such as, for example, plant and equipment, inventories, and certain intangibles, are identified directly with a specific segment. An allocation of all assets would have to be arbitrary since in many enterprises cash, temporary investments, and even receivables are centralized at the group or corporate headquarters level.

Research studies

Interest in the subject of reporting by diversified companies has sparked research efforts into the types of disclosures that are necessary and feasible and the problems related thereto.[4] The most extensive research effort was that undertaken by Professor R. K. Mautz,[5] and in 1974, the FASB published an extensive *Discussion Memorandum* on the subject.

Statement of Financial Accounting Standards 14

In 1976, the FASB issued *SFAS 14,* "Financial Reporting for Segments of a Business Enterprise." This *Statement* establishes requirements for disclosures to be made in company financial statements concerning information about operations in different industries, foreign operations, export sales, and major customers.

The *Statement* recognizes that evaluation of risk and return is the central element of investment and lending decisions. Since an enterprise operating in various industry segments or geographic areas may have different rates of profitability, degrees and types of risk, and opportunities for growth, disaggregated information will assist analysts in analyzing the uncertainties surrounding the timing and amount of expected cash flows—and hence the risks—related to an investment in or a loan to an enterprise that operates in different industries or areas of the world.

The *Statement* requires companies to report in their annual financial statements the revenues, operating profit (revenue less operating expenses), and identifiable assets of each significant industry segment of their operations. Certain other related disclosures are required. *SFAS 14* does not prescribe methods of accounting for transfer pricing or cost allocation. However, it does require that the methods in use be disclosed.

A segment is regarded as significant, therefore reportable, under the *Statement* if its sales, operating profit, or identifiable assets are 10 percent or more of the related combined amounts for all of a company's industry segments.[6] To ensure that the industry segments for which a company reports information represent a substantial portion of the company's overall operations, the *Statement* requires that the combined sales of all segments for

---

[4] See Morton Backer and Walter B. McFarland, *External Reporting for Segments of a Business* (New York: National Association of Accountants, 1968). Also see Robert T. Sprouse, "Diversified Views about Diversified Companies," *Journal of Accounting Research* 7, no. 1 (Spring 1969), pp. 137–59; and A. Rappaport and E. H. Lerner, *A Framework for Financial Reporting by Diversified Companies* (New York: National Association of Accountants, 1969).

[5] R. K. Mautz, *Financial Reporting by Diversified Companies* (New York: Financial Executives Research Foundation, 1968).

[6] Specifically, an industry segment is significant if in the latest period for which statements are presented:

1. Its revenue is 10 percent or more of the *combined* revenue of all industry segments; or
2. Its operating profit (loss) is 10 percent or more of the greater of *(a)* the combined operating profit of all segments that did not incur a loss, or *(b)* the combined operating loss of all segments that did incur a loss; or
3. Its identifiable assets are 10 percent or more of the combined identifiable assets of all industry segments.

which information is reported shall be at least 75 percent of the company's total sales. The *Statement* also suggests 10 as a practical limit to the number of industry segments for which a company reports information. If that limit is exceeded, it may be appropriate to combine certain segments into broader ones to meet the 75 percent test with a practical number of segments.

Under *SFAS 14*, if a company derives 10 percent or more of its revenue from sales to any single customer, that fact and the amount of revenue from each such customer also must be disclosed.

The *Statement* provides guidelines for determining a company's foreign operations and export sales and for grouping operations by geographic areas. Information similar to that required for industry segments also is required for a company's operations in different geographic areas of the world.

SEC reporting requirements

In 1969, the SEC took an early lead in requiring disclosure of sales and profit information by lines of business. Following promulgation of *SFAS 14*, the SEC, by means of *FRR* No. 1 Section 503, conformed SEC reporting requirements to those of the *Statement*. However, the SEC reporting requirements, incorporated in Regulation S-K, differ from *SFAS 14* in that it requires that segment revenue, operating profit, and asset information be presented for three years. Moreover, an additional narrative description is called for in Regulation S-K covering the registrant's business by reportable segments including information on competition, dependence on a few customers, principal products and services, backlog, sources and availability of raw materials, patents, research and development (R&D) costs, number of employees, and the seasonality of the business.

Implications for analysis

The increasing complexity of diversified business entities and the loss of identity that acquired companies suffer in the published financial statements of conglomerates have created serious problems for the financial analyst.

The disclosure requirements of *SFAS 14* as well as those of the SEC will increase the amount of segmental information available for analysis. However the analyst will have to be very careful in his assessment of the reliability of the data on which he bases his conclusions.

The more specific and detailed the information provided is, the more likely it is to be based on extensive allocations of costs and expenses. Allocation of common costs, as practiced for internal accounting purposes, are often based on such concepts as "equity," "reasonableness," and "acceptability to managers." These concepts have often little relevance to the objective of financial analysis.

Bases of allocating joint expenses are largely arbitrary and subject to differences of opinions as to their validity and precision. Some specific types of joint expenses that fall into this category are general and administrative expenses of central headquarters, R&D costs, certain selling costs, advertising, interest, pension costs, and federal and state income taxes.

There are, at present, no generally accepted principles of cost and expense allocation or any general agreement on the methods by which the costs of one segment should be transferred to another segment in the same enterprise. Moreover, the process of formulating such principles of reaching such agreement has barely begun. The analyst who uses segmented data must bear these limitations firmly in mind.

In *SFAS 14,* the Board has, in effect, recognized the above described limitations and realities. Consequently, the disclosure of profit contribution (revenue less only those operating expenses that are directly traceable to a segment), which was proposed in the exposure draft issued for public comment, was not required in the final *Statement.* Similarly, the Board concluded that revenue from intersegment sales or transfers shall be accounted for on whatever basis is used by the enterprise to price intersegment sales or transfers. No single basis was prescribed or proscribed.

Moreover, the Board concluded that certain items of revenue and expense either do not relate to segments or cannot always be allocated to segments on the basis of objective evidence, and consequently, there is no requirement in *SFAS 14* that net income be disclosed for reportable segments. The Board also noted in the *Statement* that "determination of an enterprise's industry segments must depend to a considerable extent on the judgment of the management of the enterprise."

The implication for analysts of this lack of firmer guidelines and definitions is that segmental disclosures are and must be treated as "soft" information that is subject to manipulation and preinterpretation by managements. Consequently, such data must be treated with a healthy degree of skepticism, and conclusions can be derived from them only through the exercise of great care as well as analytical skill.

STABILITY AND TREND OF REVENUES

The relative trend of sales of various product lines or revenues from services can best be measured by means of trend percentages as illustrated in Table 20–3.

Table 20–3:   Trend percentage of sales by product line (19x1 = 100)

	19x1	19x2	19x3	19x4	19x5
Product A	100	110	114	107	121
Product B	100	120	135	160	174
Product C	100	98	94	86	74
Service A	100	101	92	98	105

Sales indexes of various product lines can be correlated and compared to composite industry figures or to product sales trends of specific competitors.

Important considerations bearing on the quality and stability of the sales and revenues trend include:

1. The sensitivity of demand for the various products to general business conditions.
2. The ability of the enterprise to anticipate trends in demand by the introduction of new products and services as a means of furthering sales growth and as replacement of products for which demand is falling.
3. Degree of customer concentration (now required to be disclosed by *SFAS 14*), dependence on major customers, as well as demand stability of major customer groups.[7]
4. Degree of product concentration and dependence on a single industry.
5. Degree of dependence on relatively few star salesmen.
6. Degree of geographical diversification of markets.

MANAGEMENT'S DISCUSSION AND ANALYSIS OF FINANCIAL CONDITION AND RESULTS OF OPERATIONS

A significant new concept of disclosure from the analyst's point of view was instituted by the SEC in 1974 and further broadened in 1980 and is now codified in *FRR,* Section 501. The disclosures that are required are of an interpretative or explanatory nature that is necessary to enable investors to understand and evaluate significant period-to-period changes in the various items that report the enterprise's financial condition and results of operations.

Management's Discussion and Analysis of Financial Condition and Results of Operations (MDA) requirements, which were adopted as part of the SEC's new integrated disclosure system, now require three years of income statements and focus *in addition* to results of operations also on liquidity, capital resources, and the impact of inflation. These latter topics are discussed in Chapters 16, 17, 18, and 14.

In the area of results of operations, MDA must cover revenue and expense components that are needed for understanding of results by the reader, major unusual or infrequent events that materially affect reported income from continuing operations, trends or uncertainties that have affected or are likely to affect results, and impending changes in cost/revenue relationships such as increases in materials or labor costs. MDA must also include a discussion of the extent to which material increases in revenues are attributable to increases in prices or to increases in volume or amount of goods or services

---

[7] *Statement on Auditing Standards (SAS) 6* (AICPA) requires disclosure of the economic dependency of a company on one or more parties with which it transacts a significant volume of business, such as a sole or major customer, supplier, franchisor, franchisee, distributor, borrower, or lender.

being sold or to the introduction of new products or services as well as a discussion of the impact of inflation and changing prices on the registrant's revenues and on income from continuing operations.

Overall, the SEC desires that MDA's emphasis be redirected from operations to financial results; that forward-looking information should, if possible, be included; and the discussion should focus on trends and implications that are not evident from an examination of the financial statements.[8]

IMPLICATIONS FOR ANALYSIS

In its instructions to the revised MDA requirements, the SEC states that the purpose of the discussion and analysis is to provide investors and others with information relevant to an assessment of the financial condition and results of operations of the registrant as determined by evaluating the amounts and the certainty of cash flows from operations and from outside sources.

Even more so than under the previous requirements, the instructions for preparation of MDA make it clear that managements have a great deal of discretion on how to communicate to the reader and what to stress in such communications. The aim is meaningful disclosure in narrative form by those in charge of operations who are really in a position to know and who can supply significant additional details not usually found in the financial statements. The results will depend on management's attitudes and objectives.

While analysts must be aware that much information included in MDA is likely to be "soft" in nature, it must be borne in mind that in reporting in accordance with SEC requirements, managements cannot risk being careless or deceptive in their statements in such financial filings.

On balance, the analyst will have here much information that is valuable, that provides added insights, and that cannot readily be obtained in other ways. Thus, without having to take them at face value, the analyst can nevertheless use these disclosures as valuable analytical supplements for both the information that they provide and the insights into the thinking and the attitude of managements which they afford.

METHODS OF REVENUE RECOGNITION AND MEASUREMENT

Chapter 10 contains a discussion of the variety of methods of revenue recognition and measurement that coexist in various industries. Some of these

---

[8] In *FPR*, No. 1, Section 501, the SEC released the staff's assessment of disclosures contained in MDA in 1980 annual reports. Examples cited in the release cover areas such as impact on pretax income of closing unprofitable facilities; effect of LIFO inventory liquidation on pretax income; changes in revenues by segment; forward-looking information; cash flow from operations on a trend basis; available sources of liquidity; known or reasonably likely liquidity deficiencies; and impact of inflation on sales, cost of sales, assets, and liabilities.

methods are more conservative than others. The analyst must understand the income recognition methods used by the enterprise and their implications as well as the methods used by companies with which the results of the enterprise under analysis are being compared. A foremost consideration is whether the revenue recognition method in use accurately reflects an entity's economic performance and earnings activities.

QUESTIONS

1. What are the major objectives of income analysis?
2. Why can "net income" not be a single specific quantity?
3. Two levels can be identified in the analysis of the income statement. Name them.
4. Why is knowledge of major sources of revenue (sales) of an enterprise important in the analysis of the income statement?
5. Why are information and detailed data about the segments of diversified enterprises important to financial analysts?
6. Disclosure of various types of information by "line of business" has been proposed. Comment on the value of such information and the feasibility of providing it in published financial statements.
7. What are the major provisions of *SFAS 14?*
8. To what limitations of public segmental data must the analyst be alert?
9. Which important considerations have a bearing on the quality and the stability of a sales and revenue trend?
10. How were the requirements for additional disclosures of an interpretive or explanatory nature in the form of Management's Discussion and Analysis of Financial Condition and Results of Operations (MDA) changed in 1980?
11. Cite some of the examples of the types of subjects that should be covered in the MDA.
12. What are the objectives of discussions required by the revised MDA?

21

Analysis of results of operations—II

This chapter continues the discussion of the analysis of results of operations begun in the preceding chapter.

ANALYSIS OF COST OF SALES

In most enterprises,[1] the cost of goods or services sold is, as a percentage of sales, the single most significant cost category. As the discussion in Chapter 10 shows, the methods of determining cost of sales encompass a wide variety of alternatives. Moreover, there is, particularly in unregulated industries, no agreed-to uniform cost classification method that would result in a clear and generally accepted distinction among such basic cost and expense categories as cost of sales, administrative, general, sales, and financial expenses. This is particularly true in the classification of general and administrative expenses. Thus, in undertaking cost comparisons, the analyst must be ever alert to methods of classification and the effect they can have on the validity of comparisons within an enterprise or among enterprises.

GROSS PROFIT

The excess of sales over the cost of sales is the gross profit or gross margin. It is commonly expressed as a percentage:

Sales	$10,000,000	100%
Cost of sales	7,200,000	72
Gross profit	$ 2,800,000	28%

---

[1] Exceptions can be found, for example, in some land sales companies where selling and other costs may actually exceed the cost of land sold.

The gross profit percentage is a very important operating ratio. In the above example, the gross profit is $2,800,000, or 28 percent of sales. From this amount, all other costs and expenses must be recovered and any net income that is earned is the balance remaining after all expenses. Unless an enterprise has an adequate gross profit, it can be neither profitable nor does it have an adequate margin with which to finance such essential future-directed discretionary expenditures as research and development and advertising. Gross profit margins vary from industry to industry depending on such factors as competition, capital investment, the level of costs other than direct costs of sales that must be covered by the gross profit, and so forth.

Factors in the analysis of gross profit

In the analysis of gross profit, the analyst will pay particular attention to:

1. The factors that account for the variation in sales and costs of sales.
2. The relationship between sales and costs of sales and management's ability to control this relationship.

ANALYSIS OF CHANGES IN GROSS MARGIN[2]

A detailed analysis of changes in gross margin can usually be performed only by an internal analyst because it requires access to data such as the number of physical units sold, unit sales prices, as well as unit costs. Such data are usually not provided in published financial statements. Moreover, unless the enterprise sells a single product, this analysis requires detailed data by product line. The external analyst, unless he has special influence on the company analyzed, will usually not have access to the data required for the analysis of gross margin.

Despite the above limitations to which gross margin analysis is subject, it is instructive to examine its process so that the elements accounting for variations in gross margin can be more fully understood.

EXAMPLE OF ANALYSIS OF CHANGE IN GROSS MARGIN

Company A shows the following data for two years:

---

[2] In this discussion, the terms *gross profit* and *gross margin* are used interchangeably. Some writers reserve the term *gross margin* for situations where the cost of goods sold excludes overhead costs, that is, direct costing. This is not the intention here.

	Unit of measure	Year ended December 31		In- crease	De- crease
		19x1	19x2		
1. Net sales	Thousands of dollars	$657.6	$687.5	$29.9	
2. Cost of sales	Thousands of dollars	237.3	245.3	8.0	
3. Gross margin	Thousands of dollars	420.3	442.2	21.9	
4. Units of product sold	Thousands	215.6	231.5	15.9	
5. Selling price per unit (1 ÷ 4)	Dollars	$ 3.05	$ 2.97		$.08
6. Cost per unit (2 ÷ 4)	Dollars	1.10	1.06		.04

Based on the above data, Exhibit 21–1 presents an analysis of the changes in gross margin of $21,900 from 19x1 to 19x2.

Exhibit 21–1

COMPANY A
Statement Accounting for Variation in Gross Margin
Between Years 19x1 and 19x2 (in thousands)

I. *Analysis of variation in sales*
   1. Variation due to change in volume of products sold:
      Change in volume (15.9) × 19x1 unit selling price ($3.05) $48.5
   2. Variation due to change in selling price:
      Change in selling price (−$.08) × 19x1 sales
      volume (215.6) .... −17.2
      31.3
   3. Variation due to combined change in sales volume
      (15.9) and unit sales price (−$.08) .... − 1.3
   Increase in net sales 30.0*

II. *Analysis of variation in cost of sales*
   1. Variation due to change in volume of products sold:
      Change in volume (15.9) × 19x1 cost per unit ($1.10) 17.5
   2. Variation due to change in cost per unit sold:
      Change in cost per unit (−$.04) × 19x1
      sales volume (215.6) .... − 8.6
      8.9
   3. Variation due to combined change in volume (15.9)
      and cost per unit (−$.04) .... − .6
   Increase in cost of sales 8.3*
   Net variation in gross margin $21.7*

   * Differences are due to rounding.

This analysis is based on the principle of focusing on one element of change at a time. Thus, in Exhibit 21–1, the analysis of variation in sales involves the following steps:

Step 1: We focus on the year-to-year change in volume while *assuming* that the unit selling price remained unchanged at the former, 19x1, level. Since both the volume change (15.9) and the unit selling price ($3.05) are positive, the resulting product ($48.5) is positive.

Step 2. We focus next on the change in selling price that represents a year-to-year decrease (−$.08) and *assume* the volume (215.6) to be unchanged from the prior year level so as to single out the change due to price change. Algebraically, here the multiplication of a negative (price change) by a positive (volume) results in a negative product (−$17.2).

Step 3: We must now recognize that the *assumptions* used in steps 1 and 2 above, that is, that the volume remained unchanged while the unit price changed and vice versa, are temporary expedients used to single out major causes for change. To complete the computation, we must recognize that by making these assumptions we left out the *combined* change in volume and unit price. The change in volume of 15.9 represents an *increase* and, consequently, is *positive*. The unit selling price change represents a *decrease* (−$.08) and hence is *negative*. As a result, the product is negative (−$1.3).

Step 4: Adding up the—

Variation due to volume change	$48.5
Variation due to price change	−17.2
Combined change of volume and unit price	− 1.3
We account for the causes behind the sales increase	$30.0

The analysis of variation in the cost of sales follows the same principles.

Interpretation of changes in gross margin

The analysis of variation in gross margin is useful in identifying major causes of change in the gross margin. These changes can consist of one or a combination of the following factors:

1. Increase in sales volume.
2. Decrease in sales volume.
3. Increase in unit sales price.
4. Decrease in unit sales price.
5. Increase in cost per unit.
6. Decrease in cost per unit.

The presence of the "combined change of volume and unit sales price" and the "combined volume and unit cost" in the analysis presents no problem in interpretation since their amount is always minor in relation to the main causative factors of change.

The interpretation of the results of the analysis of gross margin involves the identification of the major factors responsible for change in the gross margin and an evaluation of the reasons for change in the factors. Such an analysis can also focus on the most feasible areas of improvement (i.e., volume, price, or cost) and the likelihood of realizing such improvements. For example, if it is determined that the major reasons for a decline in gross margin is a decline in unit sales prices and that it reflects a situation of overcapacity in the enterprise's industry with attendant price cutting, then the situation is a serious one because of the limited control management has on such a development. If, on the other hand, the deterioration in the gross margin is found to be due to increase in unit costs, then this may be a situation over which management can exercise a larger measure of control and, given its ability to do so, an improvement is a more likely possibility.

BREAK-EVEN ANALYSIS

The second level of cost analysis is importantly concerned with the relationship between sales and the cost of sales but goes beyond that segment of the income statement. This level encompasses break-even analysis and is concerned with the relationship of sales to most costs, including, but not limited to, the cost of sales.

Concepts underlying break-even analysis

The basic principle underlying break-even analysis is the behavior of costs. Some costs vary directly with sales while others remain essentially constant over a considerable range of sales. The first category of costs is classified as *variable* while the latter are known as *fixed* costs.

The distinction among costs according to their behavior can be best understood within the framework of an example. In order to focus first on the basic data involved and on the technique of break-even analysis, we shall examine it by means of a simple illustration:

An enterprising graduate student saw an opportunity to sell pocket calculators at a financial analysts' convention due to take place in his hometown. Upon inquiry, he learned that he would have to get a vendor's license from the convention organizing committee at a cost of $10 and that the rental of a room in which to sell would amount to $140. The cost of calculators was to be $3 each with the right to return any that were not sold. The student decided that $8 was the proper sales price per calculator and wondered whether the undertaking will be worthwhile. As a first step he decided to compute the number of calculators he will have to sell in order to break even.

Equation approach

We start from the elementary proposition that:

$$\text{Sales} = \text{Variable cost} + \text{Fixed costs} + \text{Profit (or} - \text{Loss)}$$

Since at break even there is neither gain nor loss, the equation is:

$$\text{Sales} = \text{Variable cost} + \text{Fixed costs}$$

If we designate the number of calculators that must be sold to break even as X, we have

$$\$8X = \$3X + \$150$$

where:

Sales = Unit sales price ($8) $\times X$
Variable costs = Variable cost per unit ($3) $\times X$
Fixed costs = License fee ($10) + Rental ($140)

These costs are fixed because they will be incurred regardless of the number of calculators sold.

Solving the equation we get:

$$\$5X = \$150$$
$$X = \ 30 \text{ units or calculators}$$
$$\text{to be sold to break even}$$

In this example, the number of calculators to be sold is important information because the student needs to assess the likelihood of obtaining the size of demand that will make his venture profitable. This approach is, however, limited to a single product enterprise.

If, as is common in business, an enterprise sells a mix of goods, the unit sales break-even computation becomes impracticable and the focus is on dollar sales. This would be the situation if our student sold stationery and books in addition to calculators.

This more prevalent break-even computation can be illustrated with the data already given.

If we designate the dollar sales at break even as Y, we get:

$$Y = \text{Variable-cost percentage } Y + \text{Fixed costs}$$
$$= .375\,Y + \$150$$
$$.625\,Y = \$150$$
$$Y = \$240 \text{ (sales at break even)}$$

Exhibit 21–2:   Calculator illustration—break-even chart

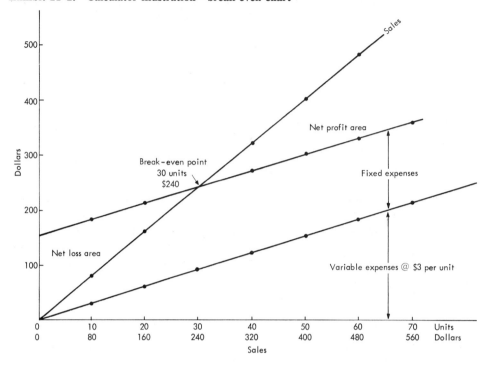

In this computation, the variable-cost percentage is the ratio of variable costs ($3) to sales price ($8). This means that each dollar of sales entails an incurrence of $.375 for variable costs, or 37.5 percent of the sales price.

Graphic presentation

Exhibit 21–2 portrays the results attained above in graphic form. A graph drawn to scale will yield a solution approximating in accuracy that obtained by the formula method. Moreover it portrays under one set of assumptions not only the break-even point but also a whole range of profitable operations above that point as well as the losses below it.

Contribution margin approach

Another technique of break-even analysis that can produce additional insights into the relationship of sales, costs, and profits is the contribution margin approach. It will be illustrated here by means of the foregoing pocket calculator example.

The contribution margin is what is left of the net sales price after deduction of the variable costs. It is from this margin that fixed costs must first be met and after that a profit earned.

$$
\begin{array}{lr}
\text{Sales price per calculator } \dots\dots\dots\dots\dots & \$8 \\
\text{Variable costs per calculator } \dots\dots\dots\dots & \underline{3} \\
\text{Unit contribution margin } \dots\dots\dots\dots\dots & \underline{\underline{\$5}}
\end{array}
$$

Since each unit (calculator) sold contributes $5 to overhead and for profit, the break-even point in units is

$$
\frac{\text{Fixed costs}}{\text{Unit contribution margin}} = \frac{\$150}{\$5} = 30 \text{ units}
$$

Thus, after 30 units are sold, the fixed costs are covered and each additional unit sale yields a profit equal to the unit contribution margin, that is, $5.

If, as is more usual, the break-even point is to be expressed in dollars of sales, the formula involves use of the contribution margin ratio rather than the unit contribution margin. The contribution margin ratio is a percentage relationship computed as follows:

$$
\frac{\text{Unit contribution margin}}{\text{Unit sales price}} = \frac{\$5}{\$8} = .625, \text{ or } 62.5 \text{ percent}
$$

The calculator problem dollar break-even point can now be calculated as follows:

$$
\frac{\text{Fixed costs}}{\text{Contribution margin ratio}} = \frac{\$150}{.625} = \$240
$$

The contribution margin is an important tool in break-even analysis, and its significance will be the subject of further discussion later in this section.

Pocket calculator problem—additional considerations

The break-even technique illustrated above lends itself to a variety of assumptions and requirements. The following are additional illustrations, all using the original data of our example, unless changed assumptions are introduced:

ILLUSTRATION 1.   Assume that our student decided that in order to make the venture worthwhile he requires a net profit of $400. How many calculators must be sold to achieve this objective?

$$
\begin{array}{l}
\text{Sales} = (\text{Variable cost percent})(\text{sales}) + \text{Fixed costs} + \text{Profit} \\
S = .375S + \$150 + \$400 \\
.625S = \$550 \\
S = \$880 \\
\dfrac{\$880}{\$8} = 110 \text{ units}
\end{array}
$$

ILLUSTRATION 2. Assume that the financial analysts convention committee offered to provide the student with a room free of charge if he agreed to imprint on the calculators the Financial Analysts Society's seal. However, this would increase the cost of calculators from $3 to $4 per unit. Under the original assumptions, the break-even point was 30 calculators. What should it be if the student accepts the committee's proposal?

Here we have a reduction of fixed costs by $140 and an increase in variable costs of $1 per unit.

If X be the number of calculators sold at break-even point, then:

$$\text{Sales} = \text{Variable costs} + \text{Fixed costs}$$
$$\$8X = \$4X + \$10$$
$$\$4X = \$10$$
$$X = 2.5 \text{ calculators (rounded to 3)}$$

This proposal obviously involves a much lower break-even point and hence reduced risk. However, the lower contribution margin will at higher sales levels reduce total profitability. We can determine at what level of unit sales the original assumption of a $3 per unit variable cost and $150 fixed cost will equal the results of the $4 per unit variable cost and $10 fixed costs.

Let X be the number of units (calculators) sold, then:

$$\$4X + \$10 = \$3X + \$150$$
$$\$1X = \$140$$
$$X = 140 \text{ calculators}$$

Thus, if more than 140 calculators are sold, the alternative that includes the $3 variable cost will be more profitable.

Having examined the break-even analysis technique and some types of decisions for which it is useful, we will now turn to a discussion of the practical difficulties and the theoretical limitations to which this approach is subject.

Break-even technique—problem areas and limitations

The intelligent use of the break-even technique and the drawing of reasonably valid conclusions therefrom depends on a resolution of practical difficulties and on an understanding of the limitations to which the techniques are subject.

Fixed, variable, and semivariable costs. In the foregoing simple examples of break-even analysis, costs were clearly either fixed or variable. In the more complex reality found in practice, many costs are not so clearly separable into fixed and variable categories. That is, they either do not stay constant over a considerable change in sales volume or respond in exact proportion to change in sales.

We can illustrate this problem by reference to the costs of a food supermarket. As was discussed above, some costs will remain fixed within a certain range of sales. Rent, depreciation, certain forms of maintenance, utilities, and supervisory labor are examples of such fixed costs. The level of fixed costs can, of course, be increased by simple management decision unrelated to the level of sales; for example, the grocery manager's salary may be increased.

Other costs, such as the cost of merchandise, trading stamps, supplies, and certain labor will vary closely with sales. These costs are truly variable. Certain other costs may, however, contain both fixed and variable elements in them. Examples of such *semivariable* costs are repairs, some materials, indirect labor, fuel, utilities, payroll taxes, and rents that contain a minimum payment provision and are also related to the level of sales. Break-even analysis requires that the variable component of such expenses be separated from the fixed component. This is often a difficult task for the management accountant and an almost impossible task for the outside analyst to perform without the availability of considerable internal data.

Simplifying assumptions in break-even analysis.   The estimation of a variety of possible results by means of break-even calculations or charts requires the use of simplifying assumptions. In most cases, these simplifying assumptions do not destroy the validity of the conclusions reached. Nevertheless, in reaching such conclusions, the analyst must be fully aware of these assumptions and of their possible effect.

The following are some of the more important assumptions implicit in break-even computations:

1. The factors comprising the model actually behave as assumed, that is:
   a. That the costs have been reasonably subdivided into their fixed and variable components.
   b. That variable costs fluctuate proportionally with volume.
   c. That fixed costs remain fixed over the range relevant to the situation examined.
   d. That unit selling prices will remain unchanged over the range encompassed by the analysis.
2. In addition, there are certain operating and environmental assumptions that emphasize the static nature of any one break-even computation. It is assumed:
   a. That the mix of sales will remain unchanged.
   b. That efficiency of operations will remain constant.
   c. That prices of costs factors will not change.
   d. That the only factor affecting costs is volume.
   e. That beginning and end-of-period inventory levels will remain substantially unchanged.
   f. That there is no substantial change in the general price level during the period.

The formidable array of assumptions enumerated above points out the susceptibility of break-even computations to significant error. Not all the assumptions are, however, equally important, or, if not justified, will have an equal impact on the validity of conclusions. For example, the assumption that the selling price will not change with volume is contrary to economic theory and often is contrary to reality. Thus, the sales line is a curved rather than a linear function. However, the degree of error will depend on the actual degree of deviation from a strict linear relationship. Another basic assumption is that volume is *the* major, if not the only, factor affecting costs. We know, however, that strikes, political developments, legislation, and competition, to name a few other important factors, have a decided influence on costs. The analyst must, consequently, keep these simplifying assumptions firmly in mind and be aware of the dynamic factors that may require modifications in his conclusions.

Break-even analysis—uses and their implications

The break-even approach can be a useful tool of analysis if its limitations are recognized and its applications are kept in proper perspective.

The emphasis on the break-even, that is, zero profit, point is an unfortunate distortion of the objective of this type of analysis. Instead, the break-even situation represents but one point in a flexible set of projections of revenues and of the costs that will be associated with them under a given set of future conditions.

The managerial applications of break-even analysis are many. It is useful, among others, in price determination, expense control, and in the projection of profits. Along with standard cost systems it gives management a basis for pricing decisions under differing levels of activity. In conjunction with flexible budgets, it represents a powerful tool of expense control. The break-even chart is also a useful device with which to measure the impact of specific managerial decisions, such as plant expansion and new product introduction or of external influences, on the profitability of operations over various levels of activity.

To financial analysts, the function of profit projections is one of major importance. Moreover, the ability to estimate the impact of profitability of various economic conditions or managerial courses of action is also an extremely important one. Both of these are importantly aided by break-even analysis. The intelligent use of this technique and a thorough understanding of its operation are the factors that account for its importance to the external financial analyst.

Illustration of break-even technique application. Exhibit 21–3 presents the break-even chart of the Multi-Products Company at a given point in time. It is subject to the various assumptions that were discussed above including that relating to the ability to separate costs into their fixed and variable components.

Exhibit 21–3: Multi-Products Company break-even-chart—all operations

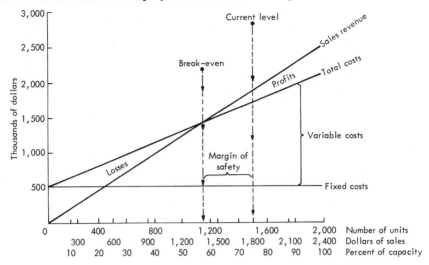

At break even, a very condensed income statement of Multi-Products Company will be as follows:

Sales		$1,387,000
Costs:		
Variable	$887,000	
Fixed..............	500,000	1,387,000
Net income		–0–

The variable-cost percentage is $887/$1,387, or about 64 percent. The contribution margin ratio is 36 percent (100 − Variable-cost percentage of 64). The variable-cost percentage means that on average, out of every dollar of sales 64 cents go to meet variable costs, that is, costs that would not be incurred if the sale did not occur. The contribution margin ratio is basically the complement of the variable-cost percentage.

Break-even point:	
Sales	$1,387,000
Units	1,156,000
Average selling price per unit.....	$1.20

This indicates that each dollar of sales generates a contribution of 36 cents toward meeting fixed expenses and the earning of a profit beyond the break-even point. The contribution margin earned on sales of $1,387,000 is just sufficient to cover the $500,000 in fixed costs. Quite obviously, the lower the fixed costs, the less sales it would take to cover them and the lower the resulting break-even point. In the most unlikely event that the Multi-Products Company would have no fixed costs, that is, all costs varied directly with sales, the company would have no break-even point, that is, it would start making a profit on the very first dollar of sales.

The break-even chart reflects the sale of a given mix of products. Since each product has different cost patterns and profit margins, any significant change in the product mix will result in a change in the break-even point and consequently in a change in the relationship between revenues, costs, and results. Although Exhibit 21-3 shows the number of units on the sales (volume) axis, this figure and the average selling price per unit are of limited significance because they represent averages prevailing as a result of a given mix of products.

The importance of a relatively stable sales mix to the successful application of break-even analysis suggests that this technique cannot be usefully employed in cases where the product mix varies greatly over the short term. Nor, for that matter, can break-even analysis be usefully applied in cases where there are sharp and frequent fluctuations in sales prices or in costs of production, such as raw materials.

Exhibit 21-3 indicates that given the existing mix of products, the present level of fixed costs of $500,000 can be expected to prevail up to a sales level of approximately $2,400,000. This is the point at which 100 percent of theoretical capacity will be reached. The break-even point is at 60 percent of capacity, while the current level of sales is at about 75 percent of capacity. This means that when the 100 percent capacity level is reached, the fixed costs may have to undergo an upward revision. If Multi-Products is reluctant to expand its capacity and thus increase its fixed costs and break-even point, assuming that variable costs do not decrease, it may have to consider other alternatives such as:

1. Foregoing an increase in sales.
2. Increasing the number of shifts, which could increase variable costs significantly.
3. Subcontracting some of its work to outsiders, thus foregoing some of the profit of increased activity.

Exhibit 21-3 also presents to the analyst at a glance the company's present position relative to the break-even point. The current level of sales of $1,800,000 is about $413,000 above the break-even point. This is also known as the *safety margin,* that is, the margin that separates the company from a no-profit condition. This concept can be expanded to indicate on the chart at what point the company will earn a desired return on investment (ROI), at what point the common dividend may be in jeopardy, and at what point the preferred dividend may no longer be covered by current earnings.

It is obvious that the data revealed by a reliably constructed break-even chart or by the application of break-even computations are valuable in profit projection, in the assessment of operating risk, as well as in an evaluation of profit levels under various assumptions regarding future conditions and managerial policies.

Analytical implications of break-even analysis

From the above discussion of a specific situation, such as that illustrated in Exhibit 21–3, we will now turn to a more general review of conclusions that can be derived from break-even analysis.

The concept of operating leverage. Leverage and fixed costs go together. As we have seen in Chapter 18, financial leverage is based on fixed costs of funds for a portion of the resources used by the enterprise. Thus, earnings above that fixed cost magnify the return on the residual funds and vice versa.

The fixed costs of a business enterprise, in the sense in which we have discussed them so far in this chapter, form the basis of the concept of operating leverage. Until an enterprise develops a volume of sales that is sufficient to cover its fixed costs, it will incur a loss. Once it has covered the fixed costs, further increments in volume will result in more than proportionate increases in profitability. The following will illustrate the nature of operating leverage:

Illustration of the working of operating leverage. In a given enterprise, the cost structure is as follows:

$$\text{Fixed costs} = \$100,000$$
$$\text{Variable-cost percentage} = 60 \text{ percent}$$

The following tabulation presents the profit or loss at successively higher levels of sales and a comparison of relative percentage changes in sales volume and in profitability:

| | | | | Percentage increase over preceding step | |
| | *Variable* | *Fixed* | *Profit* | | |
Sales	*costs*	*costs*	*(loss)*	*Sales*	*Profit*
$100,000	$ 60,000	$100,000	$(60,000)	—	—
200,000	120,000	100,000	(20,000)	100%	—
250,000	150,000	100,000	—	25	—
300,000	180,000	100,000	20,000	20	Infinite
360,000	216,000	100,000	44,000	20	120%
432,000	259,200	100,000	72,800	20	65%

The working of operating leverage is evident in the above tabulation. Starting at break even, the first 20 percent sales increase resulted in an infinite increase in profits because they started from a zero base. The next 20 percent increase in sales resulted in a 120 percent profit increase over the preceding level, while the sales increase that followed resulted in a 65 percent profit increase over the preceding level. The effects of leverage diminish as the sales increase above the break-even level because the bases to which increases in profits are compared get progressively larger.

Leverage, of course, works both ways. It will be noted that a drop in sales from $200,000 to $100,000, representing 50 percent decrease, resulted in a tripling of the loss.

One important conclusion from this to the analyst is that enterprises operating near their break-even point will have relatively larger percentage changes of profits or losses for a given change in volume. On the upside, the volatility will, of course, be desirable. On the downside, however, it can result in adverse results that are significantly worse than those indicated by changes in sales volume alone.

Another aspect is operating *potential,* sometimes erroneously referred to as leverage, which derives from a high level of sales accompanied by very low profit margins. The potential here, of course, is the room for improvements in profit margins. Even relatively slight improvements in profit margins, applied on a large sales level, can result in dramatic changes in profits. Thus, the popular reference to a semblance of leverage for what is really a potential for improvement.

Another aspect of the same *potential* occurs when the sales volume *per share* is large. Obviously an improvement in profitability will be translated into larger earnings per share improvements.

The significance of the variable-cost percentage

The volatility of profits is also dependent on the variable cost percentage. The low-cost enterprise will achieve higher profits for a given increment in volume once break-even operations are reached than will the high variable-cost enterprise.

ILLUSTRATION 3.   Company A has fixed costs of $70,000 and a variable cost equal to 30 percent of sales. Company B has fixed costs of $300,000 and variable costs equal to 70 percent of the sales. Assume that both companies have now reached sales of $1,000,000 and are, consequently, at break even. A $100,000 increment in sales will result in a profit of $70,000 for Company A and only in a profit of $30,000 for Company B. Company A has not only greater operating leverage but can, as a result, afford to incur greater risks in going after the extra $100,000 in sales than can Company B.

From the above example it is evident that the *level* of the break-even point is not the only criterion of risk assessment but that the analyst must also pay attention to the variable-cost ratio.

The significance of the fixed-cost level

Given a certain variable-cost percentage, the higher the fixed costs, the higher the break-even point of an enterprise. In the absence of change in other factors, a given percentage change in fixed costs will result in an equal percentage change in the break-even point. This can be illustrated as follows:

First break-even situation

Sales		$100,000
Variable expenses	$60,000	
Fixed costs	40,000	100,000
Profit		–0–

Second break-even situation—20 percent increase in fixed costs

Sales (increase of 20%)		$120,000
Variable expenses (60%)	$72,000	
Fixed costs ($40,000 + 20%)	48,000	120,000
		–0–

Thus, a fixed cost increase of 20 percent, with the variable-cost ratio remaining unchanged, resulted in a 20 percent increase in the break-even point.

An increase in the break-even point of an enterprise generally increases operational risk. It means that the enterprise is dependent on a higher volume of sales in order to break even. Looked at another way, it means that the enterprise is more vulnerable to economic downturns as compared to its situation with a lower break-even point. The substantial acquisition of the large capacity Boeing 747 aircraft by the airlines provides an example of the effects of high break-even points. While these large aircraft lowered the variable cost per passenger, they relied also on a projected increase in the number of passengers. When this failed to materialize, the airlines' profit margins deteriorated swiftly with many of them going into the red. There are other repercussions to high levels of fixed costs. Thus, for example, a higher break-even point may mean that the enterprise has less freedom of action in fields such as labor relations. A high level of fixed costs makes strikes more expensive and subjects the enterprise to added pressure to submit to higher wage demands.

Often, added fixed costs in the form of automatic machinery are incurred in order to save variable costs, such as labor, and to improve efficiency. That can be very profitable in times of reasonably good demand. In times of low demand, however, the higher level of fixed costs sets in motion the process of reverse operational leverage discussed above, with attendant rapidly shrinking profits or even growing losses. High fixed costs reduce an enterprise's ability to protect its profits in the face of shrinking sales volume.

Investments in fixed assets, particularly in sophisticated machinery, can bring about increases in fixed costs far beyond the cost of maintaining and replacing the equipment. The skills required to operate such equipment are quite specialized and require skilled personnel which the enterprise may be reluctant to dismiss for fear of not being able to replace them when business turns up again. This converts what should be variable costs into de facto fixed costs.

While fixed costs are incurred in order to increase capacity or to decrease variable costs, it is often advisable to cut fixed costs in order to reduce the risks associated with a high break-even point. Thus, a company may reduce fixed costs by switching from a salaried sales force to one compensated by commissions based on sales. It can avoid added fixed costs by adding work shifts, buying ready-made parts, subcontracting work, or discontinuing the least profitable product lines.

In evaluating profit performance, past and future, of an enterprise, the analyst must always keep in mind the effect that the level of fixed costs can have on operating results under a variety of business conditions. Moreover, in projecting future results, the analyst must bear in mind that any given level of fixed costs is valid only up to the limits of practical capacity within a range of product mixes. Beyond such a point, a profit projection must take into consideration not only the increased levels of fixed costs required but also the financial resources that an expansion will require as well as the cost and sources of the funds that will be needed.

The importance of the contribution margin

The analyst must be alert to the absolute size of an enterprise's contribution margin because operating leverage is importantly dependent on it. He must, moreover, be aware of the factors that can change this margin, that is, changes in variable costs as well as changes in selling prices.

While we have focused on the individual factors that affect costs, revenues, and profitability, in practice, changes result from a combination of factors. Projected increases in sales volume will increase profits only if costs, both fixed and variable, are controlled and kept within projected limits. Break-even analysis assumes that efficiency remains constant. However, experience teaches us that cost controls are more lax in times of prosperity than they are in times of recession. Thus, the analyst cannot assume constant efficiency any more than he can assume a constant product mix. The latter is also an important variable that must be watched by the analyst. Questions of why an enterprise realized lower profits on a higher volume of sales can often be explained, at least in part, by reference to changes in sales mix.

In spite of its important limitations, the break-even approach is an important tool of analysis to the financial analyst.

Its ability to aid the external analyst in performance evaluation and in profit projection makes its use worthwhile to him in spite of the laborious work that it often entails and the fragmentary and scarce amounts of information on which, of necessity, it must be based.

ADDITIONAL CONSIDERATIONS IN THE ANALYSIS
OF COST OF SALES

Gross margin analysis focuses on changes in costs, prices, and volume. Break-even analysis, in turn, focuses on the behavior of costs in relation to sales volume and on management's ability to control costs in the face of rising and falling revenues. The effectiveness of these and other methods of cost analysis depends on the degree of data availability as well as on an understanding of the accounting principles that have been applied.

The ability of the analyst to make the rough approximations that are necessary to separate costs into fixed and variable components depends on the amount of detail available. Disclosure of major cost components such as materials, labor, and various overhead cost categories can be helpful. The more detailed the breakdowns of expense categories, the more likely is the analyst to be able to construct meaningful break-even estimates.

In the evaluation of the cost of sales and the gross margin, and particularly in its comparison with those of other enterprises, the analyst must pay close attention to distortions that may arise from the utilization of a variety of accounting principles. While this is true of all items of cost, attention must be directed particularly to inventories and to depreciation accounting. These two areas, considered in detail in Chapters 6 and 10, merit special attention not only because they represent costs that are usually substantial in amount but also because of the proliferation of alternative principles that may be employed in accounting for them.

DEPRECIATION

Depreciation is an important cost element particularly in manufacturing and service enterprises. It is mostly fixed in nature because it is computed on the basis of elapsed time. However, if its computation is based on production activity, the result is a variable cost.

Because depreciation is computed in most cases on the basis of time elapsed, the ratio of depreciation expense to income is not a particularly meaningful or instructive relationship. In the evaluation of depreciation expense, the ratio of depreciation to gross plant and equipment is more meaningful. The ratio is computed as follows:

$$\frac{\text{Depreciation expense}}{\text{Assets subject to depreciation}}$$

This ratio can, of course, be computed by major categories of assets. The basic purpose is to enable the analyst to detect changes in the composite rate of depreciation used by an enterprise as a means of evaluating its adequacy and of detecting attempts at income smoothing. The computation of average age of assets in use is covered in Chapter 6.

AMORTIZATION OF SPECIAL TOOLS AND SIMILAR COSTS

The importance of the cost of special tools, dies, jigs, patterns, and molds varies from industry to industry. It is of considerable importance, for example, in the auto industry where special tool costs are associated with frequent style and design changes. The rate of amortization of such costs can have an important effect on reported income and is important to the analyst in an assessment of that income as well as in its comparison with that of other entities within an industry. The ratios that can be used to analyze changes in the deferral and amortization policies of such costs are varied and focus on their relationship to sales and other classes of assets.

The yearly expenditure for special tools can be related to and expressed as a percentage of (1) sales and (2) net property and equipment.

The yearly amortization of special tools can be related to (1) sales, (2) unamortized special tools, and (3) net property and equipment.

A comparison of the yearly trend in these relationships can be very helpful in an analysis of the consistency of income reporting of a single enterprise. The comparison can be extended further to an evaluation of the earnings of two or more enterprises within the same industry. This approach is indicative of the type of analysis which various elements of cost lend themselves to.

MAINTENANCE AND REPAIRS COSTS

Maintenance and repairs costs vary in significance with the amount invested in plant and equipment as well as with the level of productive activity. They have an effect on the cost of goods sold as well as on other elements of cost. Since maintenance and repairs contain elements of both fixed and variable costs, they cannot vary directly with sales. Thus, the ratio of repairs and maintenance costs to sales, while instructive to compare from year to year or among enterprises, must be interpreted with care. To the extent that the analyst can determine the fixed and the variable portions of maintenance and repairs costs, his interpretation of their relationship to periodic sales will be more valid.

Repairs and maintenance are, to a significant extent, discretionary costs. That is, the level of expense can, within limits, be regulated by management for a variety of reasons including those aimed at the improvement of reported income or at the preservation of liquid resources. Certain types of repairs cannot, of course, be postponed without resulting breakdowns in productive equipment. But many types of preventive repairs and particularly maintenance can be postponed or skimped on with results whose effects lie mainly in the future. Thus, the level of repairs and maintenance costs both in relation to sales and to plant and equipment is of interest to the analyst. It has, of course, a bearing on the quality of income, a subject that we shall consider in the next chapter.

The level of repairs and maintenance costs is also important in the evaluation of depreciation expense. Useful lives of assets are estimated by the use of many assumptions including those relating to the upkeep and maintenance of the assets. If, for instance, there is a deterioration in the usual or assumed level of repairs and maintenance, the useful life of the asset will, in all probability, be shortened. That may, in turn, require an upward revision in the depreciation expense or else income will be overstated.

OTHER COSTS AND EXPENSES—GENERAL

Most, although not all, cost and expense items found in the income statement have some identifiable or measurable relationship to sales or revenues. This is so because sales are the major measure of activity in an enterprise except in instances when production and sales are significantly out of phase.

Two analytical tools whose usefulness is based, in part, on the relationship that exists between sales and most costs and expenses should be noted here:

1. The *common-size income statement* expresses each cost and expense item in terms of its percentage relationship to net sales. This relationship of costs and expenses to sales can then be traced over a number of periods or compared with the experience of other enterprises in the same industry. Appendix 4B of Chapter 4 contained an illustration of a common-size income statement covering a number of years.

2. The *index number analysis of the income statement* expresses each item in the income statement in terms of an index number related to a base year. In this manner, relative changes of income statement items over time can be traced and their significance assessed. Expense item changes can thus be compared to changes in sales and to changes in related expense items. Moreover, by use of common-size balance sheets, percentage changes in income statement items can be related to changes in assets and liabilities. For example, a given change in sales would normally justify a commensurate change in inventories and in accounts receivable. Appendix 4B of Chapter 4 contained an illustration of an index number analysis.

Selling expenses

The analysis of selling costs has two main objectives:

1. The evaluation over time of the relationship between sales and the costs needed to bring them about.
2. An evaluation of the trend and the productivity of future-directed selling costs.

The importance of selling costs in relation to sales varies from industry to industry and from enterprise to enterprise. In some enterprises, selling costs take the form of commissions and are, consequently, highly variable in nature, while in others, they contain important elements of fixed costs.

After allowing for the fixed and variable components of the selling expenses, the best way to analyze them is to relate them to sales. The more detailed the breakdown of the selling expense components is—the more meaningful and penetrating can such analysis be. Exhibit 21–4 presents an example of such an analysis.

Analysis of Exhibit 21–4 indicates that for the entire period selling costs have been rising faster than sales and that in 19x3 they took 5.6 percent more of the sales dollar than they did in 19x0. In this period, salesmen's salaries increased by 1.0 percent of sales, advertising by 3.6 percent of sales, and branch expenses by 2.2 percent of sales. The drop in delivery expense may possibly be accounted for by the offsetting increase in freight costs.

A careful analysis should be made of advertising costs in order to determine to what extent the increase is due to the promotion of new products or the development of new territories that will benefit the future.

Exhibit 21–4

TRYON CORPORATION
Comparative Statement of Selling Expenses
(in thousands)

	19x3		19x2		19x1		19x0	
Sales	$1,269		$935		$833		$791	
Trend percentage		160.0%		118.0%		105.0%		100.0%
Selling expenses (percent are of sales):								
Advertising . .	$ 84	6.6	$ 34	3.6	28	3.4	24	3.0
District branch expenses* . .	80	6.3	41	4.4	38	4.6	32	4.1
Delivery expense (own trucks)	20	1.6	15	1.6	19	2.3	22	2.8
Freight-out . .	21	1.7	9	1.0	11	1.3	8	1.0
Salesmen's salary expense . . .	111	8.7	76	8.1	68	8.1	61	7.7
Salesmen's travel expense . . .	35	2.8	20	2.1	18	2.2	26	3.3
Miscellaneous selling expense	9	.7	9	1.0	8	.9	7	.9
Total . . .	$ 360	28.4%	$204	21.8%	$190	22.8%	$180	22.8%

* Includes rent, regional advertising, etc.

When selling expenses as a percentage of sales show an increase, it is instructive to focus on the selling expense increase that accompanies a given increase in sales. It can be expected that beyond a certain level, greater sales resistance is encountered in effecting additional sales. That sales resistance or the development of more remote territories may involve additional cost. Thus, it is important to know what the percentage of selling expense to sales is or to new sales as opposed to old ones. This may have, of course, implications on the projection of future profitability. If an enterprise can make additional sales only by increasing selling expenses, its profitability may suffer. Offsetting factors, such as those related to break-even operations or to economies of scale, must also be considered.

BAD DEBT EXPENSES

These expenses are often regarded as a cost of marketing. Since the size of the expense is importantly tied to the size of "allowance for doubtful accounts," it is best evaluated in terms of the relationship between that allowance and gross accounts receivable. The following analysis[3] of the allowance for doubtful accounts of Mattel, Inc., is an example of such an evaluation:

	Fiscal 1982—quarter ending		
	Aug. 1, 1981	May 2, 1981	Jan. 31, 1981
Allowance for doubtful accounts (in thousands)	$ 13,500	$ 15,600	$ 19,200
Gross receivables (in thousands)	343,319	223,585	179,791
Allowance as percent of gross receivables	3.93%	6.98%	10.68%

	Fiscal 1981—quarter ending		
	Aug. 2, 1980	May 3, 1980	Feb. 2, 1980
Allowance for doubtful accounts (in thousands)	$ 16,600	$ 15,000	$ 12,200
Gross receivables (in thousands)	331,295	215,660	172,427
Allowance as percent of gross receivables	5.01%	6.96%	7.07%

It is noteworthy that there was a significant decline in Mattel's allowance for doubtful accounts in relation to gross receivables in the fiscal 1982 quarters

[3] Source "Quality of Earnings Report, November 20, 1981," issued by Reporting Research Corporation, Englewood Cliffs, N.J.

as compared to similar quarters in the preceding year. The reasons can be varied including improvement in the collectibility of receivables or inadequate provisions that result in understated bad debt expense. This analysis certainly calls for further investigation by the analyst.

Future directed marketing costs

Certain categories of sales promotion costs, particularly advertising, result in benefits that extend beyond the period in which they were incurred. The measurement of such benefits is difficult if not impossible, but it is a reasonable assumption that there is a relationship between the level of expenditures for advertising and promotion and the sales level, present and future.

Since expenditures for advertising and other forms of promotion are discretionary in nature, the analyst must carefully follow the year-to-year trend in these expenditures. Not only does the level of such expenditures have a bearing on future sales estimates, but it also indicates whether management is attempting to "manage" reported earnings. The effect of discretionary costs on the "quality" of earnings reported will be the subject of further discussion in the chapter that follows.

GENERAL, ADMINISTRATION, FINANCIAL, AND OTHER EXPENSES

Most costs in this category tend to be fixed in nature. This is largely true of administrative costs because such costs include significant amounts of salaries and occupancy expenditures. However, there may be some "creep" or tendency for increases in this category, and this is particularly true in prosperous times. Thus, in analyzing this category of expense, the analyst should pay attention to both the trend of administrative costs as well as to the percentage of total sales that they consume.

Financial costs

Financial costs are, except for interest on short-term indebtedness, fixed in nature. Moreover, unless replaced by equity capital, most borrowed funds are usually refinanced. This is because of the long-term nature of most interest-bearing obligations. Included in these costs are the amortization of bond premium and discount as well as of debt issue expenses. A good check on an enterprise's cost of borrowed money as well as credit standing is the calculation of the average effective interest rate paid. This rate is computed as follows:

$$\frac{\text{Total interest cost}}{\text{Average total indebtedness subject to interest}}$$

Alfa, Inc.'s (see Appendix 4B) average interest rate on long-term debt can be computed for 19x6 as follows:

$$\frac{\$14,883\,^{(a)}}{(\$244,954 + \$194,690 + \$7,328 + \$8,701)\,^{(b)} \div 2} = 6.5 \text{ percent}$$

[a] Long-term debt interest expense (item $\boxed{81}$).
[b] Beginning + Ending balances of long-term debt (item $\boxed{38}$) + Beginning and ending current portion of long-term debt (note 8—item $\boxed{94}$) ÷ 2.

The average effective interest rate paid can be compared over the years or compared to that of other enterprises. It is also significant in that it sheds light on the credit standing of the enterprise.

A measure of sensitivity to interest changes is obtained by determining the portion of debt that is tied to the prime rate. In periods of rising interest rates, a significant amount of debt tied to the prime rate exposes an enterprise to sharply escalating interest costs. Conversely, falling interest rates are a beneficial factor to such an enterprise.

"Other" expenses

"Other" expenses are, of course, a nondescript category. The total amount in this category should normally be rather immaterial in relation to other costs. Otherwise, it can obscure substantial costs that, if revealed, may provide significant information about the enterprise's current and future operations. Nonrecurring elements may also be included in the "other expense" category, and this may add to the significance of this category to the analyst.

The analyst must also be alert to the tendency to offset "other" expenses against "other" income. Here too the major problem is one of concealment of important information and data. Here it is important that details of the major items comprising the offset amount be given.

OTHER INCOME

Miscellaneous income items that are small in amount are usually of no significance to the analyst. However, since "other income" may include returns from various investments, it may contain information about new ventures and data regarding investments that is not available elsewhere. Such investments may, of course, have future implications, positive or negative, that exceed by far in significance the amounts of current income that are involved.

INCOME TAXES

Income taxes represent basically a sharing of profits between an enterprise and the governmental authority by which they are imposed. Since most enterprises with which this book is concerned are organized in corporate form, we shall focus primarily on corporate income taxes.

Income taxes are almost always significant in amount and normally can amount to about half of a corporation's income before taxes. For this reason, the analyst must pay careful attention to the impact that income taxes have on net income.

Except for a lower rate on a first modest amount of income (e.g., $100,000), corporate income is normally taxed at the rate of about 50 percent (presently 46 percent). Differences in the timing of recognition of income or expense items as between taxable income and book income should not influence the effective tax rate because of the practice of interperiod income tax allocation that aims to match the tax expense with the book income regardless of when the tax is paid. Income tax allocation was discussed in Chapter 11.

The relationship between the tax accrual and the pretax income, otherwise known as the effective tax rate or tax ratio, will, however, be influenced by permanent tax differences.[4] The nature of and reasons for these differences were also discussed in Chapter 11.

The effective tax rate or tax ratio is computed as follows:

$$\frac{\text{Income tax expense for period}}{\text{Income before income taxes}}$$

For Alfa, Inc. (see Appendix 4B), the effective tax rate is:

$$\frac{\$7,600 \text{ (item } \boxed{9}\text{)}}{\$25,368 \text{ (item } \boxed{8}\text{)}} = 30 \text{ percent}$$

For purposes of evaluation of the level of earnings, the trend of earnings, as well as for net income projection, the analyst must know the reasons why the tax ratio deviates from the normal or the expected. Income taxes are such an important element of cost that even relatively small changes in the effective tax rate can explain important changes in net income. Moreover, without an understanding of the factors that cause changes in the effective tax rate of a company, the analyst is missing an important ingredient necessary in the forecasting of future net income.

FRR No. 1 Section 204 contains rules in which the SEC expanded significantly the required analytical disclosures concerning current and deferred income taxes. Chapter 11 included a description of these as well as a discussion of their significance to the analyst.

The analysis of these and other aspects of income tax disclosures are important to the analyst and will be discussed and illustrated in the section that follows.

---

[4] This term includes differences due to state and local taxes, foreign tax rate differentials, and investment tax credits.

ANALYSIS OF INCOME TAX DISCLOSURES

Objectives of the analysis

The analysis of income tax disclosures may be undertaken with specific or specialized objectives in mind. However, the more general objectives of such an analysis are:

- To understand the tax accounting of the enterprise and its impact on income, on related assets and liabilities, as well as on the sources and uses of funds or cash.
- To judge the adequacy of the enterprise's tax disclosure.
- To provide a basis for assessing the effect of taxes on future income and funds flows.
- To provide a basis for informed queries to be put to management in order to clear up questions arising during the analysis.
- To identify unusual gains or losses not otherwise disclosed but whose tax effect is highlighted.

Analytical steps and techniques

A. Establish a T-account for each tax-related account in the balance sheet and income statement.

   A current tax liability and/or a current receivable for overpayment or tax refunds will almost always be found. In addition, there will be one or two deferred tax accounts (one current and one noncurrent) in the balance sheet.

   Care must be taken to identify the income taxes (current and possibly deferred) that relate to each separate section of the income statement: (1) continuing operations, (2) discontinued operations, (3) extraordinary items, and (4) cumulative effect of change(s) in accounting principles.

   The analyst should be aware that information on income tax effects can be found in parenthetical notes to financial statement items, in sections containing management discussion, and in footnotes in general and particularly in those relating to income taxes.

B. A good next step is to attempt to reconstruct as best as is possible the summary entry by means of which the tax expense for the period was booked. It is easier to do this if the entry is divided into the current and the deferred portions of the tax expense.

C. After the opening and closing balances of all tax-related balance sheet T-accounts have been posted the tax expense entries and the relevant tax-related accounts and data should be used to aid in as complete a reconstruction of these accounts as is possible.

   The changes in the deferred tax accounts on the balance sheet should generally agree with the deferred tax expense for the period as shown in the income statement or in related footnotes. Nonfund adjustments to net income and other information in the statement of changes in financial position (SCFP) often can provide added insights. If all attempts at reconciliation fail, it is possible that a deferred tax account is buried or combined under some other caption in the balance sheet, or that the company made some undisclosed entries for purposes of correcting errors or for other reasons. In such a situation, the analyst can only identify the needed balancing amount and label it as such, realizing that the correctness of any conclusions regarding balancing (plugged) amounts in the reconciliation is subject to the validity of assumptions that have been made. The Taxes Currently Payable account should be credited, and the related income statement tax expense will consist of various debits and credits to items in the four income statement categories mentioned above as applicable. In case of a loss there may instead be a debit to a "Tax Refund Receivable account."

D.   The accounting for the investment tax credit (ITC) requires care. If the company uses the *flow-through method*, the ITC should be debited to Current Taxes Payable and credited to Income Tax Expense. In this case, the "current" income tax expense is also the amount payable. If the *deferral method* is used, the reconstruction involves debiting this year's amortization of the ITC to the Deferred ITC account with a credit to Tax Expense. The actual amount of the ITC earned (realized) in the current year is debited to Current Taxes Payable and credited to Deferred ITC account.

E.   After using knowledge of tax accounting and all the disclosures in the financial statements, as well as the assumptions required in the situation, the tax T-accounts should be fully reconstructed. At this point, the amount of taxes paid during the year is arrived at as a "plug" to the current Taxes Payable account.

It should be noted that the quality of the analysis will depend on the quality of disclosure found in the financial statements. A lack of good disclosure will require more analytical ingenuity such as the combining of certain accounts (such as current tax receivable and payable accounts). The analyst must also be aware that the acquisition or disposition of businesses during a period will result in related additions or deductions to balance sheet tax accounts.

Illustration of income tax analysis of Alfa, Inc.

Let us first analyze the changes in Alfa's 19x5 and 19x6 income tax accounts. The *first* step is to draw a T-account for each tax-related balance sheet account and one for each income tax expense and tax effect account in the 19x5 and 19x6 income statements. (All number references are to Alfa's financial statements in Appendix 4B.)

Income Tax Payable—Current

		21,670	(a)	(19x5) BB
		32,135	(d)	
Plug				
paid	44,967			
		8,838	(a)	(19x6) BB
		1,678	(k)	
Plug				
paid	7,868			
		2,648	(t)	EB

Deferred Tax (current liability)

		38,820	(b)	(19x5) BB
(e)	19,665			
		19,155	(b)	(19x6) BB
		2,401	(i)	
		21,556	(g)	

Deferred Tax (noncurrent liability)

		31,676	(c)	(19x5) BB
		207	(e)	
		31,883	(c)	(19x6) BB
		3,521	(i)	
		35,404	(h)	EB

Tax Expense*

19x5	(d)	52,458	19,458	(e)	
EB		33,000			
19x6	(i)	5,922			
	(k)	1,678			
EB		7,600			

* In certain cases, the analysis process can be simplified by subdividing the Tax Expense account into (1) Tax Expenses—Current, (2) Tax Expenses—Deferred (current portion) and (3) Tax Expenses—Deferred (noncurrent portion).

Tax Effect of Discontinued Operations

	1,083	*(d)*
	1,083	Total 19x5

**Tax Effect of Cumulative Effect of Accounting
Change**

	19,240	*(d)*
	19,240	Total 19x5

The *second* step is to enter the beginning balance (BB) and the ending balance (EB) of each balance sheet account. Note that since we are, for purposes of illustration, analyzing *two* years, the EB of 19x5 coincides with the BB of 19x6. Letter references in the notes that follow refer to various entries in the T-accounts.

(a) Since we do not have the 19x4 balance sheet, we do not have the BB of this account. We can, however, derive it by using the 19x5 EB of $8,838 (income taxes—including deferred $27,993 less $19,155 deferred portion—see item 34). To the $8,838 EB of 19x5, we *add the change in* currently payable taxes for 19x5 of $12,832 located in the funds statement (see item 67) to get the 19x5 BB of $21,670.

(b) Using a similar approach to the one in *(a)* above, we can derive the 19x5 BB of the Deferred Tax (current) account: 19x5 EB $19,155 (item 34) plus the change in 19x5 deferred taxes (current) account of $19,665 (item 68) equals 19x5 BB of $38,820.

(c) The 19x5 BB of this account can be derived only after the 19x5 activity has been posted. The 19x5 EB of this account is given as $31,883 (item 36).

The *third* step is to enter the activity during 19x5 based on all available information in the financial statements and notes.

(d) The current tax expense entry can be reconstructed as follows:

		Source—Alfa item
Tax Expense (current)	52,458	92
Tax Effect of Discontinued Operations	1,083*	13
Tax Effect Cumulative Accounting Change	19,240	15
Taxes Payable—Current	32,135	Plug

* $2,083 − $1,000 (source is Note 3)

This is accomplished by making sure that all tax expense (or credit) items are identified in the income statement.

(e) The deferred tax entry can be reconstructed as follows:

Deferred Taxes (current) 19,665		68 *
— Tax Expense	19,458	93
Deferred Taxes (noncurrent)	207	43 *

* In this case all amounts are fully corroborated in the financial statements. Sometimes one unknown amount may have to be derived in order to balance the entry.

Note that the Deferred Taxes (noncurrent) can *usually* be found in the "add-back" section of the funds statement. In this case, the entry is also validated by the fact that the changes in the tax expense of $33,000 (Alfa 9). Deferred Taxes—Current, and Deferred Taxes—Noncurrent accounts are now fully explained.

We can now *plug* the amount of taxes paid in 19x5 ($44,967) with a debit to the Taxes Payable account.

The analytical process can now be repeated for 19x6. This is somewhat simpler because of the absence of "below the line" tax items in the income statement. We have the beginning balances 19x6 already in place (from the 19x5 analysis), and we enter the ending balances as follows:

(f) $24,204 − $21,556 = $2,648 34 .

(g) Deferred taxes given in balance sheet, $21,556 34 .

(h) 36 .

Now we reconstruct the deferred tax portion of the 19x6 tax expense:

			Source
(i) Tax Expense—Deferred 5,922			93
Deferred Taxes (current)		2,401	68
Deferred Taxes (noncurrent)		3,521	43

This entry is further corroborated by the fact that it explains fully the changes in the deferred tax balance sheet accounts.

Next, we post the current tax expense:

(k) Tax Expense—Current 1,678			92
Taxes Payable		1,678	Derived

With this entry we have fully explained all changes in the tax accounts of Alfa for 19x5 and 19x6. The plugged figure of $7,868 in the Income Taxes Payable account represents taxes paid in 19x6.

In some instances, the analysis may not go as smoothly, in which case certain accounts may have to be combined or certain amounts may have to be plugged if the amounts are significant. Such cases provide the basis for informed questions to management concerning unexplained tax entries.

Explaining the tax rate

At another level of analysis, we can explain how Alfa with a pretax income of $25,368 in 19x6 could report only $828 (items $\boxed{89}$ − $\boxed{90}$) of current federal income tax.

		Source	
Expected federal income tax at 48% = $25,368 × .48 = ...		$\boxed{8}$	$12,176
Less 48% of State tax = $1,540 × .48*		$\boxed{88}$	739
Computed federal tax at statutory rate of 48%			
(per Note 7)		$\boxed{83}$	11,437
Less permanent differences:			
For income taxable at capital gains rate	$ 782	$\boxed{84}$	
For other items, net	284	$\boxed{86}$	1,066
Subtotal..			10,371
Less deferred tax:			
Total (per Note 7)	5,922	$\boxed{83}$	
Current portion = $1,540 − $850)	690	$\boxed{88}$ − $\boxed{91}$	
Deferred federal tax.............................			5,232
Reported current federal tax			
(before investment tax credit)		$\boxed{89}$	5,139
Less investment tax credit		$\boxed{90}$	4,311
Current federal income tax			$ 828

* The pretax income of $25,368 *excludes* the state tax of $1,540 which is, however, tax deductible. Thus, the related tax benefit reduces the total federal tax.

Focus on pretax earnings

While the focus on net income and on earnings per share requires a thorough analysis of changes in the effective tax rate, it must be borne in mind that many analysts attach great importance to pretax earnings. This is due to the greater importance that is assigned to pretax operating results, which require management skills of a higher order, as compared with changes due to variations in the effective tax rate over which, it is assumed, management has comparatively more limited control.

THE OPERATING RATIO

The operating ratio is yet another intermediate measure in the analysis of the income statement. It measures the relationship between all operating costs and net sales and is computed as follows:

$$\frac{\text{Cost of goods sold} + \text{Other operating expenses}}{\text{Net sales}}$$

The ratio is designed to enable a comparison within an enterprise or with enterprises of the proportion of the sales dollar absorbed by all operating

Exhibit 21–5

ALFA, INC.
Statement Accounting for Variations in Net Income
For the Year Ended December 31, 19x6

			Percentage increase (decrease)
Items tending to increase net income:			
Increase in gross margin on sales:			
Increase in net sales:			
Net sales, 19x6	$1,251,088		
Net sales, 19x5	1,133,817	$117,271	10.3
Deduct: Increase in cost of goods sold:			
Cost of goods sold, 19x6	840,043		
Cost of goods sold, 19x5	730,280	109,763	15.0
Net increase in gross margin:			
Gross margin, 19x6	411,045		
Gross margin, 19x5	403,537	7,508	1.9
Decrease in income taxes:			
Income taxes, 19x6	7,600		
Income taxes, 19x5	33,000	25,400	(77.0)
Decrease in loss from discontinued operations:			
Loss, 19x6	–0–		
Loss, 19x5	1,000	1,000	(100.0)
Decrease in negative cumulative effect, net:			
Effect, 19x6	–0–		
Effect, 19x5	17,407	17,407	(100.0)
Total of items tending to increase income		$51,315	
Items tending to decrease net income:			
Increase in selling, administrative, and general expenses (SAG):			
SAG, 19x6	343,023		
SAG, 19x5	296,893	46,130	15.5
Increase in depreciation and amortization (DA):			
DA, 19x6	24,214		
DA, 19x5	21,158	3,056	14.4
Increase in interest expensed:			
Interest expensed, 19x6	18,440		
Interest expensed, 19x5	16,319	2,121	13.0
Decrease in "equity on income" (19x5 – 19x6 = $2,329 – $1,371)		958	41.0
Total of items tending to decrease net income		52,265	
Net decrease in net income:			
Net income, 19x6	19,139		
Net income, 19x5	20,089	$ (950)	(4.7)

costs. Only other income and expense items as well as income taxes are excluded from the computation of this ratio.

In effect, this ratio represents but an intermediate step in the common-size analysis of the income statement. It is, in and of itself, not of great analytical significance because it is a composite of many factors that require separate analysis. These factors comprise the analysis of gross margin and of other major expense categories discussed earlier. Thus, the operating ratio cannot be properly interpreted without a thorough analysis of the reasons accounting for variations in gross margin and for changes in selling, general, administrative, and other costs.

NET INCOME RATIO

The net income ratio is the relationship between net income and total revenues and is computed as follows:

$$\frac{\text{Net income}}{\text{Total revenues}}$$

It represents the percentage of total revenue brought down to net income. In addition to its usefulness as an index of profitability, the net profit ratio represents, as was seen in Chapter 19, a main component of the computation of the return on investment (ROI).

Statement accounting for variation in net income

In the analysis of year-to-year changes in net income, it is useful to separate the elements that contributed to an increase in net income from those that contributed to a decrease. A statement that does this and also indicates the percentage increase or decrease in these factors is the "statement accounting for variations in net income." Exhibit 21–5 presents such a statement for Alfa, Inc., based on its income statements included in Appendix 4B.

QUESTIONS

1. What are the most important elements in the analysis of gross profit?
2. What is the basic principle underlying break-even analysis? What are fixed costs? Variable costs? Semivariable costs?
3. Certain assumptions that underlie break-even computations are often referred to as simplifying assumptions. Name as many of these as you can.
4. In break-even computation, what is the *variable-cost percentage?* What is its relationship to the *contribution margin ratio?*
5. What alternatives to an increase in fixed costs can an enterprise consider when it approaches 100 percent of theoretical capacity?

6. What is operating leverage? Why do leverage and fixed costs go together? What are the analytical implications of operating leverage?

7. Of what analytical significance are *(a)* the break-even point and *(b)* the variable-cost ratio?

8. What is a useful measure of the adequacy of current provisions for depreciation?

9. To what factors can maintenance and repairs costs be meaningfully related?

10. What are the main objectives of an analysis of selling expenses?

11. How can bad debt expense be evaluated most meaningfully? To what can a decline in the allowance to doubtful accounts be attributed?

12. *a.* What is the tax ratio and how is it computed?

    b. What are the objectives of an analysis of income tax disclosures?

The evaluation and projection of earnings

OBJECTIVES OF EARNINGS EVALUATION

In the preceding chapters, we examined the steps that have to be taken and the understanding that must be brought to bear on the analysis of the operating performance of an enterprise. This chapter will examine the additional considerations involved in the achievement of the major objectives of income statement analysis:

The evaluation of the quality of earnings.

Evaluation of the earnings level and trend.

The forecasting of earnings.

The estimation of earning power.

Monitoring performance and results.

EVALUATION OF THE QUALITY OF EARNINGS

The discussions through Part II of this book have pointed out that much of the accounting process of income determination involves a high degree of estimation. Chapters 10 and 11 on the analysis of the income statement have explained that the income of an enterprise, as measured by the accounting process, is not a specific amount but can vary depending on the assumptions used and the various principles applied. Complicating these measurements still further is the fact that numerous accounting periods can receive benefits from a single cash outlay and that it may take a number of periods before a transaction results in the collection of all amounts due. For that reason, creditors, in particular, are greatly interested in the cash equivalent of reported earnings (see also Chapter 13).

This distinction between accrual income and the related cash flows has led some of those uninitiated in the income determination process to doubt the validity of all accounting measurements. This, however, is an extreme and unwarranted position because, as any student of accounting should know, the concept of income is the result of a series of complex assumptions and conventions, and exists only as the creation and the approximation of this system of measurement. This system is always subject to reexamination and is, despite its shortcomings, still the most widely accepted method of income determination.

In examining the level of reported income of an enterprise, the analyst must determine the effect of the various assumptions and accounting principles used on that reported income. Beyond that he must be aware of the "accounting risk" as well as the "audit risk" to which these determinations are subject.

Over the years, and especially since the enactment of the Securities Acts of 1933 and 1934, and with improvement in the audit function in this country, the incidence of outright fraud and deliberate misrepresentation in financial statements has diminished markedly. But they have not been completely eliminated and probably never will. Nor can the analyst ever rule out the possibility of spectacular failures in the audit function. While each major audit failure tends to contribute to the improvement of regulation and of auditing, they have not prevented the recurrence of such failures as the security holders of McKesson & Robbins, of Seaboard Commercial Corporation, of H. L. Green, of Miami Window, of Yale Express, of BarChris Construction Company, of Continental Vending Company, of Mill Factors Corporation, of W. T. Grant, and Equity Funding Company, well know.

The analyst must always assess the vulnerability to failure and to irregularities of the company under analysis and the character and the propensities of its management, as a means of establishing the degree of risk that it will prove to be the exception of the general rule. (The audit process is discussed in Chapter 15.)

The evaluation of the earnings level and of the earnings trend is intimately tied in with the evaluation of management. The evaluation of the management group cannot be separated from the results that they have actually achieved. Whatever other factors may have to be considered, results over a period of time are the acid test of management's ability, and that ability is perhaps the most important intangible (i.e., unquantifiable) factor in the prediction of future results. The analyst must be alert to changes in the management group and must assess its depth, stability, and possible dependence on the talents of one or a few individuals.

The analyst must also realize that not only is it impossible to arrive at a single figure of "net income" but that identical earnings figures may possess different degrees of "quality."

The concept of earnings quality

The concept of earnings quality arose out of a need to provide a basis of comparison among the earnings of different entities as well as from the need to recognize such differences in "quality" for valuation purposes. There is almost no general agreement on definitions of or on assumptions underlying this concept. The elements that comprise the "quality of earnings" can be classified as follows:

a. One type of factor that affects the quality of earnings is the accounting and computational discretion of management and that of the attesting accountants in choosing from among accepted alternative accounting principles. These choices can be liberal, that is, they can assume the most optimistic view of the future, or they can be conservative. Generally, the quality of conservatively determined earnings is higher because they are less likely to prove overstated in the light of future developments than those determined in a "liberal" fashion. They also minimize the possibility of earnings overstatement and avoid retrospective changes. LIFO inventory accounting in rising markets and accelerated depreciation methods are examples of conservative accounting methods. On the other hand, unwarranted or excessive conservatism, while contributing to the temporary "quality" of earnings, actually results in a lack of reporting integrity over the long run and cannot be considered as a desirable factor. Quite apart from the impact that these accounting choices have on the financial statements, they also hold important clues to management's propensities and attitudes.

b. The second type of factor affecting the quality of earnings is related to the degree to which adequate provision has been made for the maintenance of assets and for the maintenance and enhancement of present and future earning power. In most enterprises, there exists considerable managerial discretion over the size of income streams, and particularly over the reported amounts of costs and expenses. Discretionary types of expenses, such as repairs and maintenance, advertising, and research and development (R&D) costs can be varied for the sole purpose of managing the level of reported net income (or loss) rather than for legitimate operating or business reasons. Here, too, the analyst's task is to identify the results of management practices and to judge its motivations.

c. The third major factor affecting the quality of earnings is not primarily a result of discretionary actions of managements, although skillful management can modify its effects. It is the effect of cyclical and other economic forces on earnings, on the stability of their sources, and particularly on their variability. Variability of earnings is generally an undesirable characteristic, and, consequently, the higher the variability the lower the quality of these earnings.

The fairly broad tolerances within which generally accepted accounting principles (GAAP) can be applied have been discussed throughout this book. A consideration of other aspects that affect earnings quality follows.

Evaluation of discretionary and future-directed costs.   Discretionary costs are outlays that managements can vary to some extent from period to period in order to conserve resources and/or to influence reported income. For this reason, they deserve the special attention of analysts who are particularly interested in knowing whether the level of expenses is in keeping with past trends and with present and future requirements.

Maintenance and repairs.   As was already discussed in the preceding chapter, management has considerable leeway in performing maintenance work and some discretion with respect to repairs. The analyst can relate these costs to the level of activity because they do logically vary with it. Two ratios are particularly useful in comparing the repair and maintenance levels from year to year:

$$\frac{\text{Repairs and maintenance}}{\text{Sales}}$$

This ratio relates the costs of repairs and maintenance to this most available measure of activity. In the absence of sharp inventory changes, sales are a good indicator of activity. If year-to-year inventory levels change appreciably, an adjustment may be needed whereby ending inventories at approximate selling prices are added to sales, and beginning inventories, similarly adjusted, are deducted from them.

ILLUSTRATION 1.   For the years 1976, 1977, 1978, 1979, and 1980, General Electric had maintenance and repairs expenses that amounted, as a percentage of sales, to 3.41 percent, 3.42 percent, 3.42 percent, 3.45 percent, and 3.14 percent, respectively. The significant decline in repair and maintenance costs as a percent of sales in 1980 deserved further analysis.

The other ratio is:

$$\frac{\text{Repairs and maintenance}}{\substack{\text{Property, plant, and equipment (exclusive of land)} \\ \text{net of accumulated depreciation}}}$$

It measures repair and maintenance costs in relation to the assets for which these costs are incurred. Depending on the amount of information available to the analyst, the ratio of repair and maintenance costs to specific categories of assets can be developed. It should be noted that substandard repairs and maintenance on assets may require revisions in the assumptions of useful lives for depreciation purposes.

The absolute trend in repair and maintenance costs from year to year can be expressed in terms of index numbers and compared to those of related accounts. The basic purpose of all these measurements is to determine whether the repair and maintenance programs of the enterprise have been kept at normal and necessary levels or whether they have been changed in a way that affects the quality of income and its projection into the future.

Advertising.   Since a significant portion of advertising outlays has effects beyond the period in which it is incurred, the relationship between advertising outlays and short-term results is a tenuous one. This also means that managements can, in certain cases, cut advertising costs with no commensurate immediate effects on sales, although it can be assumed that over the longer term sales will suffer. Here again, year-to-year variations in the level of advertising expenses must be examined by the analyst with the objective of assessing their impact on future sales and consequently on the quality of reported earnings.

There are a number of ways of assessing the trend in advertising outlays. One is to convert them into trend percentages using a "normal" year as a base. These trend percentages can then be compared to the trend of sales and of gross and net profits. An alternative measure would be the ratio of

$$\frac{\text{Advertising expenses}}{\text{Sales}}$$

which, when compared over the years, would also indicate shifts in management policy.

ILLUSTRATION 2. During 1978, 1979, and 1980, Ford Motor Company's percentages of advertising costs to sales were .8 percent, 1.0 percent, and 1.6 percent respectively. In this case, far from reducing earnings quality, these costs were intended to stem declining sales and profits as well as a significant loss in 1980.

The ratio of

$$\frac{\text{Advertising}}{\text{Total selling costs}}$$

must also be examined so as to detect shifts to and from advertising to other methods of sales promotion.

An analysis of advertising to sales ratios over several years will reveal the degree of dependence of an enterprise on this promotional strategy. Comparison of this ratio with that of other companies in the industry will reveal the degree of market acceptance of products and the relative promotional efforts needed to secure it.

Research and development costs. The significance and the potential value of R&D costs are among the most difficult elements of the financial statements to analyze and interpret. Yet they are important, not only because of their relative size but even more so because of their significance for the projection of future results.

R&D costs have gained an aura of glowing potential in security analysis far beyond that warranted by actual experience. Mentioned most frequently are some of the undeniably spectacular and successful commercial applications of industrial research in the post–World War II era in such fields as chemistry, electronics, photography, and biology. Not mentioned are the vast sums spent for endeavors labeled *research* which are expensed or written off while benefits from these fall far short of the original costs.

The analyst must pay careful attention to R&D costs and to the absence of such costs. In many enterprises, they represent substantial costs, much of them fixed in nature, and they can represent the key to future success or failure. We must first draw a careful distinction between what can be quantified in this area and, consequently, analyzed in the sense in which we consider analysis in this book, and what cannot be quantified and must, consequently, be evaluated in qualitative terms.

In the area of R&D costs, the qualitative element looms large and important. The definition of what constitutes "research" is subject to wide-ranging interpretations as well as to outright distortion. The label *research* is placed on activities ranging from those of a first-class scientific organization engaged in sophisticated pure and applied research down to superficial and routine product-and-market-testing activities.

Among the many factors to be considered in the evaluation of the quality of the research effort are the caliber of the research staff and organization, the eminence of its leadership, as well as the commercial results of their research efforts. This qualitative evaluation must accompany any other kinds of analysis. Finally, a distinction must be drawn between government or outsider sponsored research and company directed research that is most closely identified with its own objectives. From the foregoing discussion it is clear that research cannot be evaluated on the basis of the amounts spent alone. Research outlays represent an expense or an investment depending on how they are applied. Far from guaranteeing results, they represent highly speculative ventures that depend on the application of extraordinary scientific as well as managerial skills for their success. Thus, spending on research cannot guarantee results and should not be equated with them.

Having considered the all-important qualitative factors on which an evaluation of R&D outlays depends, the analyst should attempt to determine as best he can how much of the current R&D outlays that have been expensed have future utility and potential.

From the point of view of the analyst, the "future potential" of R&D costs is a most important consideration. Research cost productivity can be measured by relating R&D outlays to:

1. Sales growth.
2. New product introductions.
3. Acquisition of plant and equipment (to exploit the results of research).
4. Profitability.

Another important aspect of R&D outlays is their discretionary nature. It is true that those enterprises that have established R&D departments impart a fixed nature to a segment of these costs. Nevertheless, they can be increased or curtailed at the discretion of managements, often with no immediate adverse effects on sales. Thus, from the point of view of assessing the quality of reported income, the analyst must evaluate year-to-year changes in R&D

outlays. This he can do by means of trend percentage analysis as well as by years of analysis of ratios such as the ratio of

$$\frac{\text{R\&D outlays}}{\text{Sales}}$$

A careful comparison of outlays for R&D over the years will indicate to the analyst whether the effort is a sustained one or one that varies with the ups and downs of operating results. Moreover, "one shot" research efforts lack the predictability or quality of a sustained, well-organized longer-term research program.

Other future-directed costs. In addition to advertising and R&D, there are other types of future-directed outlays. An example of such outlays are the costs of training operating, sales, and managerial talent. Although these outlays for the development of human resources are usually expensed in the year in which they are incurred, they may have future utility, and the analyst may want to recognize this in his evaluation of current earnings and of future prospects.

Balance sheet analysis as a check on the validity and quality of reported earnings

The amounts at which the assets and liabilities of an enterprise are stated hold important clues to an assessment of both the validity as well as the quality of its earnings. Thus, the analysis of the balance sheet is an important complement to the other approaches of income analysis discussed in this chapter, and elsewhere in this book.

Importance of carrying amounts of assets. The importance that we attach to the amounts at which assets are carried on the balance sheet is due to the fact that, with few exceptions such as cash, some investments, and land, the cost of most assets enters ultimately the cost stream of the income statement. Thus, we can state the following as a general proposition: Whenever assets are overstated, the cumulative income[1] is overstated because it has been relieved of charges needed to bring such assets down to realizable values.

It would appear that the converse of this proposition should also hold true; that is, that to the extent to which assets are understated, cumulative income is also understated. Two accounting conventions qualify this statement importantly. One is the convention of conservatism, already discussed in Chapter 2, which calls for the recognition of gains only as they are actually realized. Although there has been some movement away from a strict interpretation of this convention, in general most assets are carried at original cost even though their current market or realizable value is far in excess of that cost.

---

[1] The effect on any one period cannot be the subject of generalization.

The other qualifying convention is that governing the accounting for business combinations. As was seen in the discussions in Chapter 9, the pooling of interests concept allows an acquiring company to carry forward the old book values of the assets of the acquired company even though such values may be far less than current market values or the consideration given for them. Thus, the analyst must be aware of the fact that such an accounting will allow the recording of profits, when the values of such understated assets are realized, which represents nothing more than the surfacing of such hitherto understated assets. Since such profits have, in effect, previously been bought and paid for, they cannot be considered as representing either the earning power of the enterprise or an index of the operating performance of its management.

Importance of provisions and liabilities. Continuing our analysis of the effect of balance sheet amounts on the measurement of income, we can enunciate the further proposition that an understatement of provisions and liabilities will result in an overstatement of cumulative income because the latter is relieved of charges required to bring the provision or the liabilities up to their proper amounts. Thus, for example, an understatement of the provision for taxes, for product warranties, or for pensions means that cumulative income is overstated.

Conversely, an overprovision for present and future liabilities or losses results in the understatement of income or in the overstatement of losses. As was seen in the discussion in Chapter 11, provisions for future costs and losses that are excessive in amount represent attempts to shift the burden of costs and expenses from future income statements to that of the present.

Bearing in mind the general propositions regarding the effect on income of the amounts at which assets and liabilities are carried in the balance sheet, the critical analysis and evaluation of such amounts represents an important check on the validity of reported income.

Balance sheet analysis and the quality of earnings. There is, however, a further dimension to this kind of analysis in that it also has a bearing on an evaluation of the quality of earnings. This approach is based on the fact that various degrees of risk attach to the probability of the future realization of different types of assets.

Thus, for example, the future realization of accounts receivable has generally a higher degree of probability than has the realization of, say, inventory or unrecovered tools and dies costs. Moreover, the future realization of inventory costs can, generally, be predicted with greater certainty than can the future realization of goodwill or of deferred start-up costs. The analysis of the assets carried in the balance sheet by risk class or risk category holds clues to and is an important measure of the quality of reported income. Stated another way, if the income determination process results in the deferral of outlays and costs which carry a high degree of risk that they may not prove realizable in the future, then that income is of a lower quality than income that does not involve the recording of such high-risk assets.

Effect of valuation of specific assets on the validity and quality of reported income. In order to illustrate the importance of balance sheet analysis to an evaluation of reported income, let us now examine the effect of the valuation of specific assets on the validity and quality of that income.

Accounts receivable. The validity of the sales figure depends on the proper valuation of the accounts receivable that result from it. This valuation must recognize the risk of default in payment as well as the time value of money. On the latter score, *APB Opinion 21* provides that if the receivable does not arise from transactions with customers or suppliers in the normal course of business under terms not exceeding a year, then, except for some other stated exceptions, it must be valued using the interest rate applicable to similar debt instruments. Thus, if the receivable bears an interest rate of 8 percent while similar receivables would, at the time, be expected to bear an interest rate of 12 percent, both the receivable and the sale from which it arose would be restated at the lower discounted amount.

The relative level of accounts receivable and its relationship to sales can hold clues to income quality. If an increase in accounts receivable represents merely a shifting of inventory from the company to its customers because of aggressive sales promotion or costly incentives, then these sales accomplish nothing more than "borrowing from the future" and thus reduce earnings quality.

Inventories. Overstated inventories lead to overstated profits. Overstatements can occur due to errors in quantities, errors in costing and pricing, or errors in the valuation of work in process. The more technical the product and the more dependent the valuation is on internally developed cost records, the more vulnerable are the cost estimates to error and misstatement. The basic problem here arises when costs that should have been written off to expense are retained in the inventory accounts.

An understatement of inventories results from a charge-off to income of costs that possess future utility and that should be inventoried. Such an understatement of inventories results in the understatement of current income and the overstatement of future income.

Deferred charges. Deferred charges such as deferred tooling or start-up and preoperating costs must be scrutinized carefully because their value depends, perhaps more than that of other assets, on estimates of future probabilities and developments. Experience has shown that often such estimates have proven overoptimistic or that they did not contain sufficient provisions for future contingencies. Thus, the risk of failure to attain expectations is relatively higher here than in the case of other assets.

The effect of external factors on the quality of earnings. The concept of earnings quality is so broad that it encompasses many additional factors that, in the eyes of analysts, can make earnings more reliable or more desirable.

The effect of changing price levels on the measurement of earnings was examined in Chapter 14. In times of rising price levels, the inclusion of "inventory profits" or the understatement of expenses such as depreciation lowers in effect the reliability of earnings and hence their quality.

The quality of foreign earnings is affected by factors such as difficulties and uncertainties regarding the repatriation of funds, currency fluctuations, the political and social climate as well as local customs and regulation. With regard to the latter, the inability to dismiss personnel in some countries in effect converts labor costs into fixed costs.

Regulation provides another example of external factors that can affect earnings quality. The "regulatory environment" of a public utility affects the "quality" of its earnings. Thus, an unsympathetic or even hostile regulatory environment that causes serious lags in the obtaining of rate relief will detract from earnings quality because of uncertainty about the adequacy of future revenues.

The stability and reliability of earnings sources affect earnings quality. Defense related revenues can be regarded as nonrecurring in time of war and affected by political uncertainties in peacetime.

Finally, some analysts regard complexity of operations and difficulties in their analysis (e.g., of conglomerates) as negative factors.

EVALUATION OF THE EARNINGS LEVEL AND TREND

The analyst will concentrate on identifying those elements in the income and cost streams that exhibit stability, proven relationships, and predictability, and will separate them from those elements that are random, erratic, or nonrecurring and that, consequently, do not possess the elements of stability required for a reasonably reliable forecast or for inclusion in an "earning power" computation.

The analyst must be on his guard against the well-known tendency of managements to practice income smoothing, thus trying to give to the income and expense streams a semblance of stability that in reality they do not possess. This is usually done in the name of "removing distortions" from the results of operations, whereas what is really achieved is the masking of the natural and cyclical irregularities that are part of the reality of the enterprise's experience and with which reality it is the analyst's primary task to come to grips.

Factors affecting the level of earnings

We have, so far, discussed the *qualitative* factors that may cause the analyst either to adjust the earnings number of a given period (generally, a year) or to adjust the valuation (e.g., the price-earnings multiple) accorded such earnings.

The next step in the determination of the *level* of earnings of a given period is to recast the published income statements in such a way that the stable, normal, and continuing elements in the income statement are separated and distinguished from random, erratic, unusual or nonrecurring elements that require separate analytical treatment or consideration. Moreover, such recasting also aims at identifying those elements included in the income statement of a given period that should more properly be included in the operating results of one or more prior periods.

The analytical, recasting and adjustment of income statements

The income statement along with all other financial statements and data contained in management's report represent the logical starting point of the analysis. It is clear that reported income is but the *starting point* of analysis and that from the point of view of the intelligent analyst, the most desirable income statement is the one containing a maximum of meaningful disclosure rather than one containing built-in interpretations that channel him to specific conclusions.

Over the years, notable shifts have occurred in the thinking of the accounting profession regarding the function of the income statement. An early position was that items of gain or loss should be included or excluded from income on the basis of the accountant's interpretation of what "normal operations" are. This position has resulted in much controversy and criticism to the point where the profession has adopted the "clean surplus" approach of including *all*[2] items of gain and loss in the income of the period in which they occur and, with few exceptions, such as corrections of errors, has also taken a position against the restatement of prior period results.

Major sources of information. As a consequence, the analyst will find data needed for the analysis of the results of operations and for their recasting and adjustment in:

1. The income statement which is generally subdivided into the following:

    Income from continuing operations.
    Income from discontinued operations (which includes gain or loss from disposal).
    Extraordinary gains and losses.
    Cumulative effect of changes in accounting principles.

2. The other financial statements and the footnotes thereto.

---

[2] It should be noted that a departure from this position occurred in *SFAS 52* where, with few exceptions, gains and losses on the translation of foreign currency financial statements of subsidiaries bypass income and are accumulated in a separate stockholders' equity account. To a more limited extent, *SFAS 12* also represented such a departure.

3. Management's comments found throughout its published report.
4. "Management's Discussion and Analysis of Financial Condition and Results of Operations" as required by the SEC's 1980 revised disclosure system (see also Chapter 20).

The analyst may also find "unusual" items segregated within the income statement (generally on a pretax basis), but their disclosure is optional. Such disclosure may not include items that the analyst may regard as significant, noteworthy, or unusual; and, consequently, the analyst will consult all the above-mentioned sources as well as management, if possible, in order to obtain the needed facts. These will include facts that affect the comparability and the interpretation of income statements, such as product-mix changes, production innovations, strikes, and raw material shortages that may or may not be included in management's mandatory discussion and analysis of the results of operations.

The recasting and adjusting procedure

Once the analyst has secured as much information as it is possible to obtain, the income statements of a number of years (generally at least five) should be recast and adjusted in such a way as to facilitate their further analysis to evaluate the trend of earnings as well as to aid in determining the average earning power of the enterprise for the period. While this procedure can be accomplished in one statement, it is simpler and clearer to subdivide it into two distinct steps: (1) recasting and (2) adjusting.

The recasting process. The recasting process aims at a rearranging of the items within the income statement in such a way so as to provide the most meaningful detail and the most relevant format needed by the analyst. At this stage, the individual items in the income statement may be rearranged, subdivided, or tax effected, but the total must reconcile to the net income of each period as reported.

The analytical reclassification of items *within* a period will help in the evaluation of the earnings level. Thus, discretionary and other noteworthy expenses should be segregated. The same applies to net items such as equity in income or loss of unconsolidated subsidiaries or associated companies, which are usually shown net of tax. Items shown in the pretax category must be removed *together* with their tax effect if they are to be shown below normal "income from continuing operations."

Expanded tax disclosure (see Chapter 11) enables the analyst to segregate factors that reduce taxes as well as those that increase them, thus enabling an analysis of the degree to which these factors are of a recurring nature. All material permanent differences and credits, such as the investment tax credit, should be included. The analytical procedure involves computing taxes at the statutory rate (currently 46 percent) and deducting tax benefits such

Exhibit 22–1

ALFA, INC.
Analytically Recast Income Statements for 19x2–19x6
(in thousands)

	Item reference no.	19x6	19x5	19x4	19x3	19x2
Revenues[a]	1	$1,251,020	$1,134,104	$1,145,362	$881,368	$695,900
Costs and expenses:						
Cost of sales[b]	2	820,441	712,650	677,665	561,228	435,088
Selling, general, and administrative expenses[c]	3	325,575	280,946	271,606	228,029	186,742
Depreciation and amortization[d]	4	24,214	21,158	25,157	17,781	12,598
Maintenance and repairs[b]	77	19,602	17,630	13,412	8,120	6,770
Advertising[c]	78	16,006	14,055	12,413	9,611	8,668
Research and development costs[c]	79	1,442	1,892	1,291	1,317	1,261
Net deferral (amortization) of pre-opening expense and initial losses of new department stores and hotels[d]	80			(3,149)	(808)	1,800
Interest expense	5	18,504	16,319	25,054	18,859	11,092
Interest capitalized	6	(64)	—	(3,267)	(1,287)	(463)
Total costs and expenses	7	1,225,720	1,064,650	1,020,182	842,850	663,556
Income before taxes		25,300	69,454	125,180	38,518	32,344
Taxes at 48% (before items marked (e) below)		12,144	33,338	60,086	18,489	15,525
Income from continuing operations		13,156	36,116	65,094	20,029	16,819
Benefit for income taxable at capital gains rate[e]	84	782	818	1,610	3,115	2,670
Investment tax credit[e]	90	4,311	2,734	1,618	1,483	1,898
State income taxes[e]	88	(1,540)	(6,300)	(11,290)	(1,390)	(1,319)
Tax benefit equal to 48% of state income taxes above*[e]		740	3,024	5,419	666	632

Other tax adjustments—net [e] $\boxed{86}$	284	(76)	(1,352)	508	334
Equity in earnings or (loss) of unconsolidated subsidiaries [a]†	35	(149)	1,001	(505)	(490)
Net income of nonconsolidated finance subsidiaries‡ $\boxed{11}$	1,371	2,329	2,068	3,609	3,095
Income (loss) from discontinued operations $\boxed{13}$	—	(1,000)	(7,325)	(957)	657
Cumulative effect on prior years of accounting changes $\boxed{15}$	—	(17,407)	—	—	—
Net income as reported $\boxed{16}$	$ 19,139	$ 20,089	$ 56,843	$ 26,558	$ 24,296

* Note 7 shows the computed federal tax at statutory rate net of tax benefit on state income tax expense—for example, the $11,437 (item $\boxed{83}$) federal tax at statutory rate for 19x6 is computed as follows: 48 percent of $25,368 (pretax income as per income statement) = $12,177 − $740 (48 percent of $1,540 state income tax expense) = $11,437.

† Net of tax of 48 percent (this rate may or may not be applicable). In 19x6, 52 percent of $68 = $35, and in 19x5, 52 percent of $287 loss or $149—see note (a) below. Note, however, that a good case can also be made for the assumption that the equity in earnings of other unconsolidated subsidiaries is stated after tax (e.g., $68 in 19x6) and consequently revenues include the pretax amount, i.e., 68 ÷ .52 or 131.

‡ Note that these are shown net of income taxes in the income statement.

(a) Equity in earnings of unconsolidated subsidiaries (item $\boxed{44}$) consists of net income of nonconsolidated finance subsidiaries (item $\boxed{11}$) shown separately net of tax and equity in income or loss of other nonconsolidated domestic subsidiaries (see also Note 5) which is assumed to be included in revenues (item $\boxed{1}$). In 19x6, for example, the latter was derived by deducting $1,371 (item $\boxed{11}$) from $1,439 (item $\boxed{44}$) to get $68 as equity in income of other nonconsolidated domestic subsidiaries, which figure is deducted from revenues (item $\boxed{1}$) and included, net of tax, in the lower part of the recast statement so as to be highlighted separately. A similar process of derivation for 19x5 determined that the equity in loss of other nonconsolidated subsidiaries was $287 ($2,329 − $2,042). Analysis revealed that no dividends were received from nonconsolidated subsidiaries in 19x6 and none were assumed to have been received in preceding years.

(b) Maintenance and repairs (item $\boxed{77}$) was deducted from cost of sales so that it can be shown separately for analytical purposes.

(c) Selling, general, and administrative expenses were reduced by advertising (item $\boxed{78}$) and research and development costs (item $\boxed{79}$) which are highlighted separately.

(d) Net deferral (amortization) of pre-opening expense and initial losses of new department stores and hotels (see Note 6) excluded from normal depreciation and amortization on continuing operations and shown separately.

(e) All items marked (e) below income from continuing operations modify the federal tax, at the statutory 48 percent rate, on pretax income from continuing operations and are shown separately for analytical purposes (they are disclosed in Note 7).

Other comments:

Per Note 2, Alfa's net income for 19x4 was reduced by $7,634 because of changes to preferable accounting methods in two areas: a switch to LIFO in the Lamb-Weston Division (reducing income by $6,112) and a switch from deferral to current expensing of preoperating expenses of new department stores and hotels (reducing income by $1,522). The specific income statement categories affected by these changes are not disclosed.

as arising from investment tax credits, capital gains rates, tax-free income, or lower foreign tax rates, and adding factors such as additional foreign taxes, nontax-deductible expenses, and state and local taxes (net of federal tax benefit). Immaterial items may be considered in one lump sum labeled "other."

Analytically recast income statements will contain as much detail as is needed for analysis and are supplemented by explanatory footnotes. Exhibit 22–1 presents the analytically recast income statements of Alfa, Inc., which are annotated with key numbers for ease of reference to the financial statements of Alfa found in Appendix 4B.

The adjustment process

Based on data developed in the recast income statements as well as on other available information, certain items of income or loss are to be assigned by the analyst to the period to which they most properly belong.

The reassignment of extraordinary items or unusual items (net of tax) to other years must be done with care. Thus, the income tax benefit of the carry-forward of operating losses should generally be moved to the year in which the loss occurred. The costs or benefits from the settlement of a lawsuit may relate to one or more preceding years. The gain or loss on disposal of discontinued operations will usually relate to the results of operations over a number of years.

If possible, all years under analysis should be placed on a comparable basis when a change in accounting principle or accounting estimate occurs. If, as is usually the case, the *new* accounting principle is the desirable one, prior years should, if possible, be restated to the new method, or a notation made regarding a lack of comparability in certain respects. This procedure will result in a redistribution of the "cumulative effect of change in accounting principle" to affected prior years. Changes in estimates can be accounted for only prospectively and GAAP prohibit prior year restatements except in specified cases (see Chapter 11). The analyst's ability to place all years on a comparable basis will depend on availability of information.

Before the trend in earnings can be evaluated it is necessary to obtain the best approximation possible of the adjusted earnings *level* of each year. All items in the income statement must be considered, and none can be excluded or "dropped by the wayside." Thus, if it is decided that an item in the income statement does not properly belong in the year in which it appears, it may be either:

1. Shifted (net of tax) to the result of another year or a number of other years, or
2. If it cannot be identified with another specific year or years, it should be included in the *average* earnings of the period under analysis. While the averaging process helps in the determination of average earning power, it is not helpful in the determination of earnings trend.

It must be realized that moving an item of gain or loss to another year or recording one's inability to assign an item to the proper year does not remedy the fact that the results of some prior year(s) have been misstated. For example, a damage award in one year for patent infringement means that prior years had suffered from lost sales or similar damage.

Exhibit 22–2 presents the analytically adjusted income statements of Alfa, Inc.

Determining the trend of income over the years

Having determined the size of a company's basic earnings as well as the factors that require adjustment before those earnings can be used as a basis for forecasts, the analyst will next determine the variability of these earnings, that is, changes in their size over the business cycle and over the longer term.

Evaluation of earnings variability. Earnings that fluctuate up and down with the business cycle are less desirable than earnings that display a larger degree of stability over such a cycle. The basic reason for this is that fluctuating earnings cause fluctuations in market prices. Earnings that display a steady growth trend are of the most desirable type. In the evaluation of earnings, the intelligent analyst realizes the limitations to which the earnings figure of any one year is subject. Therefore, depending on his specific purposes, he will consider the following earnings figures as improvements over the single-year figure:

1. *Average earnings* over periods, such as 5 to 10 years, smooth out erratic and even extraordinary factors as well as cyclical influences, thus presenting a better and more reliable measure of "earning power" of an enterprise.
2. *Minimum earnings* are useful in decisions, such as those bearing on credit extension, which are particularly sensitive to risk factors. They indicate the worst that could happen during a complete business cycle, based on recent experience.

The importance of earnings trends. In addition to the use of single, average, or minimum earnings figures, the analyst must be alert to earnings trends. These are best evaluated by means of trend statements such as those presented on page 123. The relevant earnings numbers to be included in the trend analysis will be derived from adjusted income statements as exemplified in Exhibit 21–2. The earnings trend contains important clues to the nature of the enterprise (i.e., cyclical, growth, defensive) and the quality of its management.

Distortions of trends. Analysts must be alert to accounting distortions that affect trends. Among the most important are changes in accounting principles and the effect of business combinations, particularly purchases. These must be adjusted for.

Exhibit 22–2

ALFA, INC.
Analytically Adjusted Income Statements for 19x2–19x6
(in thousands) (Dr.) Cr.[a]

	Total	19x6	19x5	19x4	19x3	19x2
Net income as reported	$146,925	$19,139	$20,089	$56,843	$26,558	$24,296
Assignment of cumulative effect of accounting change to prior years (Dr.) Cr.[b]			17,407	(15,367)	(2,040)	
Anticipated losses on phaseout of Wilhelm Foods Division[c]			1,083	884		
Losses expected in liquidation of mobile home parks, etc.[c] ...				1,853		
Gains from sale of food processing plant[d]					(2,100)	
Gains from sale of surplus property[e]					(1,824)	(1,573)
Adjusted net income for individual years[f]		$19,139	$38,579	$44,213	$20,594	$22,723
Total net income for period[g]	$146,925					
Average earnings for period[g]	$ 29,385					

[a] The Dr. and Cr. framework is very useful in keeping track of the direction of adjustments. Here we start with net income figures that are all credits. Since a debit adjustment will reduce the amount of net income, it is convenient to show the debit adjustments in parenthesis. For example, the gain from sale of food processing plant of $2,100 is removed from net income of 19x3 by a debit adjustment.

(b) This adjustment is based on information obtained from pro forma amounts (item [20]) which shows net income after giving *retroactive* effect to accounting changes:

	19x5	19x4	19x3
Pro forma net income [20]	$37,496	$ 41,476	$ 24,518
Net income as reported [16]	20,089	56,843	26,558
Difference	$17,407	$(15,367)	$ (2,040)

Thus, of the cumulative change of $17,407 made in 19x5, $15,367 belonged to 19x4 and $2,040 to 19x3.

(c) Note 3 (item [73]) contains information on various discontinued operations. Gains and losses on disposition of discontinued operations usually relate to operating performance over a number of years, but rarely does the analyst have enough information to assign these to specific periods. Thus, while we remove these losses from the results of the year in which they occurred, we cannot assign them to other specific periods. We distinguish gains or losses on *disposition* from the *operating* losses of discontinued divisions before and during the phaseout period, which while significant for purposes of estimating future results are not removed from the year in which they occur for purposes of trend analysis. The figures given in Alfa's income statement (item [13]) aggregate both kinds of losses.

Since the provisions for anticipated losses of Wilhelm Foods are stated before tax, we convert them to an aftertax basis by multiplying them by (1 − Tax rate). Thus, in 19x5, $2,083 × .52 = $1,083; and in 19x4, $1,700 × .52 = $884. Information on losses on mobile parks is provided net of tax. This, as well as the other two adjustments discussed in notes (d) and (e) below, while modifying the results of individual years for trend evaluation purposes are incorporated for purposes of computing average earnings for the five-year period which must include *all* gains and losses experienced by the enterprise.

(d) and (e) These gains reported in Note 3 are removed from (debited to) the net income of the respective years.

(f) Because adjustments (c), (d), and (e) have been made to individual years only, the adjusted net income figures, which are used for trend analysis, do not add up to the total income for the period. Analysts must also consider the effect of business acquisitions on earning trends. Acquisitions accounted for as poolings of interest are restated while those accounted for as purchases include results from date of acquisition (see Chapter 9).

(g) The average earnings for the period include all items of gain or loss incurred during the period, and except for most unusual circumstances, they represent the average earnings power experienced by the enterprise during this period.

Some of the most common and most pervasive manipulative practices in accounting are designed to affect the presentation of earnings trends. These manipulations are based on the assumptions, generally true, that the trend of income is more important than its absolute size; that retroactive revisions of income already reported in prior periods have little, if any, market effect on security prices;[3] and that once a company has incurred a loss, the size of the loss is not as significant as the fact that the loss has been incurred.

These assumptions and the propensities of some managements to use accounting as a means of improving the appearance of the earnings trend has led to techniques that can be broadly described as income smoothing.

Income smoothing and income distortion

A number of requirements must be met by the income-smoothing process so as to distinguish it from outright falsehoods and distortions.

The income-smoothing process is a rather sophisticated and insidious device. It does not rely on outright or patent falsehoods and distortions but rather uses the wide leeway existing in alternatively acceptable accounting principles and their interpretation in order to achieve its ends. Thus, income smoothing is performed within the framework of GAAP. It is a matter of form rather than one of substance. Consequently, it does not involve a real transaction (e.g., postponing an actual sale to another accounting period in order to shift revenue) but only a redistribution of credits or charges among periods. The general objective is to moderate income variability over the years by shifting income from good years to bad years, by shifting future income to the present (in most cases presently reported earnings are more valuable than those reported at some future date), or vice versa. Similarly, income variability can be moderated or modified by the shifting of costs, expenses, or losses from one period to another.

Income smoothing may take many forms. Hereunder are listed some forms of smoothing to which the analyst should be particularly alert:

1. Changing accounting methods or assumptions with the objective of improving or modifying reported results. For example, to offset the effect on earnings of slumping sales and of other difficulties. Chrysler Corporation revised upwards the assumed rate of return on its pension portfolio, thus increasing income significantly. Similarly, in 1980, Union Carbide improved results by switching to a number of more liberal accounting alternatives.

2. Misstatements, by various methods, of inventories as a means of redistributing income among the years. The Londontown Manufacturing Com-

---

[3] This was recognized by *APB Opinion 20* and later *SFAS 16*, which, with but two exceptions, forbids the retroactive restatement of prior year financial statements. For a discussion of this topic, see Chapter 11.

pany case provides a classic example of such practices.[4] Some of these practices are outside the framework allowed by GAAP.

3. The offsetting of extraordinary credits by identical or nearly identical extraordinary charges as a means of removing an unusual or sudden injection of income that may interfere with the display of a growing earnings trend. (For examples and further discussion see Chapter 11.)

4. The provision of reserves for future costs and losses as a means of increasing the adverse results of what is already a poor year and utilizing such reserves to relieve future years of charges against income that would otherwise be properly chargeable against it. (Abuses in this area have been curtailed by *SFAS 5*.)

5. The substantial write-downs of operating assets (such as plant and equipment) or of intangibles (such as goodwill) in times of economic slowdown when operating results are already poor. The reason usually given for such write-downs is that carrying the properties at book value cannot be economically justified. (For example, Cudahy Packing Company has effected such a write-down of plant but had to reverse it in a subsequent year.) Particularly unwarranted is the practice of writing down operating assets to the point at which a target return on investment (which management thinks it *should* earn) is realized.

6. Timing the inclusion of revenues and costs in periodic income in such a way as to influence the overall trend of income (or loss) over the years. (Examples are the timing of sales or other disposition of property, incurring and expensing of discretionary costs such as R&D, advertising, maintenance, etc.) This category, unlike most others, entails more than accounting choice in that it may involve the timing of actual business transactions. Thus, in recent years, Franklin Mint inflated sales and income by accelerating shipments to customers ahead of a schedule called for by customer subscription terms and booking these as sales immediately.

Income smoothing and income distortion—some implications for analysis

There are powerful factors and incentives at work that motivate companies and their employees to engage in income smoothing (see also discussion in Chapter 3).

Companies in financial difficulties may be motivated to engage in such practices for what they see and justify as their battle for survival. Successful companies will go to great lengths to uphold a hard-earned and well-rewarded image of earnings growth by smoothing those earnings artificially. Moreover, compensation plans or other incentives based on earnings will motivate man-

---

[4] Details can be found in an SEC decision issued October 31, 1963 (41 SEC 676–688).

agements to accelerate the recognition of income by anticipating revenues or deferring expenses.

THE H. J. HEINZ COMPANY CASE. The recent case of H. J. Heinz Company has shown that even second-tier divisional executives, motivated by self-interest in meeting earnings targets and in smoothing earnings, can without the knowledge of top management engage in income manipulation. In this case, "hidden reserves" were created during 1971 to 1978 by prepaying for services not yet received, such as advertising, and by the improper recording of sales.

THE J. W. T. GROUP, INC., CASE. This case, first brought to light in 1982, did not seem to involve a desire for personal gain but is rather a case of falsifying records in order to make the syndication department look good by meeting its goals.

The department purchased programming from independent producers and bartered the programs to television stations in return for future commercial time that was in turn used to build "time banks" for sale to agency clients. The accounting deception involved the creation of fictitious time banks, fictitious clients, and fictitious revenues over a period of four years. So successful was the computerized deception that for a time, management invested additional capital in the division lured by the substantial, if fictitious, returns it appeared to earn.

Analysts must appreciate the great variety of incentives and objectives that lead managements and, at times, second-tier management without the knowledge of top management, to engage in practices ranging from smoothing to the outright falsification of income.

The smoothing of earnings is often achieved by first understating reported earnings. Thus, in the 1970s, Firestone Tire and Rubber Company engaged in the practice of hiding income in secret accounts for the purpose of drawing on these during leaner years.

Some serious academicians have suggested that smoothing is justified if it can help a company report earnings closer to its true "earning power" level. Such is not the function of financial reporting. As we have repeatedly seen in this book, the analyst will be best served by a full disclosure of periodic results and the components that comprise them. It is up to the analyst to average, smooth, or otherwise adjust reported earnings in accordance with specific analytical purposes.

The accounting profession has earnestly tried to promulgate rules that discourage practices such as the smoothing of earnings. However, given the above mentioned powerful propensities of companies and of their owners and employees to engage in such practices, analysts must realize that where there is a will to smooth or even distort earnings, ways to do so are available and will be found. Consequently, particularly in the case of companies where incentives to smooth are likely to be present, analysts should analyze and scrutinize accounting practices in order to satisfy themselves to the extent possible, regarding the integrity of the income reporting process.

Extraordinary gains and losses

The evaluation of current earnings levels, the determination of earnings trends as well as the projection of future earnings rely importantly on the separation of the stable elements of income and expense from those that are random, nonrecurring, and erratic in nature.

Stability and sustainability are important characteristics that enter significantly into the determination of earning power. Moreover, in making earnings projections, the forecaster relies also on repetitiveness of occurrence. Thus, in order to separate the relatively stable elements of income and expense of an enterprise from those that are random or erratic in nature, it is important, as a first step, to identify those gains and losses that are nonrecurring and unusual as well as those that are truly extraordinary.

This separation is a first step that is mostly preparatory in nature. Following it is a process of judgment and analysis that aims at determining how such nonrecurring, unusual, or truly extraordinary items should be treated in the evaluation of present income, and of management performance as well as in the projection of future results.

Significance of accounting treatment and presentation. The value of any accounting treatment and presentation is largely dependent on its usefulness to those who make decisions on the basis of financial statements. Unfortunately, particularly in the area of the accounting for, and the presentation of, extraordinary gains and losses, the usefulness of this accounting has been impaired because of the great importance attached to it by those who report the results of operations and who are judged by them.

The accounting for, and the presentation of, extraordinary gains and losses has always been subject to controversy. Whatever the merits of the theoretical debate surrounding this issue, the fact remains that one of the basic reasons for the controversial nature of this topic is reporting management's great interest in it. Managements are almost always concerned with the amount of net results of the enterprise as well as with the manner in which these periodic results are reported. This concern is reinforced by a widespread belief that most investors and traders accept the reported net income figures, as well as the modifying explanations that accompany them, as true indexes of performance. Thus, extraordinary gains and losses often become the means by which managements attempt to modify the reported operating results and the means by which they try to explain these results. Quite often these explanations are subjective and are designed to achieve the impact and impression desired by management.

The accounting profession has tacitly, if not openly, recognized the role that the foregoing considerations play in the actual practice of reporting extraodinary gains and losses. Its last pronouncement on this subject, which was discussed in Chapter 11, has at least ensured a fuller measure of disclosure of extraordinary gains and losses and their inclusion in the income statement.

This represents an improvement over prior pronouncements that, in an attempt to arrive at a "true" index of operating performance, sanctioned the exclusion of certain extraordinary gains and losses from the income statement.

Analysis and evaluation. The basic objectives in the identification and evaluation of extraordinary items by the analyst are:

1. To determine whether a particular item is to be considered "extraordinary" for purposes of analysis, that is, whether it is so unusual, nonoperating, and nonrecurring in nature that it requires special adjustment in the evaluation of current earnings levels and of future earning possibilities.
2. To decide what form the adjustment for items that are considered as "extraordinary" in nature should take.

Determining whether an item of gain or loss is extraordinary. The infirmities and shortcomings of present practice as well as the considerations which motivate it, lead to the inescapable conclusion that the analyst must arrive at his own evaluation of whether a gain or loss should be considered as extraordinary, and if so, how to adjust for it.

In arriving at this decision, it is useful to subdivide items, commonly classified as unusual or extraordinary, into three basic categories:

a. Nonrecurring operating gains or losses. By "operating" we usually identify items connected with the normal and usual operations of the business. The concept of normal operations is more widely used than understood and is far from clear and well defined. Thus, in a company operating a machine shop, operating expenses would be considered as those associated with the work of the machine shop. The proceeds from a sale above cost of marketable securities held by the company as an investment of excess cash would be considered a nonoperating gain. So would the gain (or loss) on the sale of a lathe, even if it were disposed of in order to make room for one that would increase the productivity of the shop.

The concept of recurrence is one of frequency. There are no predetermined generally accepted boundaries separating the recurring event from the nonrecurring. An event (which in this context embraces a gain or loss) occurring once a year can be definitely classified as "recurring." An event, the occurrence of which is unpredictable and which in the past has either not occurred or occurred very infrequently, may be classified as nonrecurring. On the other hand, an event that occurs infrequently but whose occurrence is predictable raises some question as to its designation. An example of the latter would be the relining of blast furnaces. They last for many years; while their replacement is infrequent, the need for it is predictable. Some companies provide for their replacement by means of a reserve. Casualties do not, however, accrue in similar fashion.

Nonrecurring operating gains or losses are, then, gains or losses connected with or related to operations that recur infrequently and/or unpredictably.

In considering how to treat nonrecurring, operating gains and losses, the analyst would do best to recognize the fact of inherent abnormality and the lack of a recurring annual pattern in business and treat them as belonging to the results of the period in which they are reported.

We must also address ourselves to the question of what should be considered as "normal operations." Thus, it is a bakery's purpose to bake bread, rolls, and cakes, but it is presumably outside its normal purpose to buy and sell marketable securities for gain or loss, or even to sell baking machinery that is to be replaced for the purpose of more efficient baking.

This narrow interpretation of the objectives of a business has undergone considerable revision in modern financial theory. Thus, rather than the "baking bread" or any other specific objective, the main objective and task of management is viewed as that of increasing the capital of the owners, or expressed differently, the enhancing of the value of the common stock. This, according to modern financial theory, can be accomplished by means of the judicious combination of an optimal financing plan and any mix of operations opportunities that may be available to achieve the desired purpose.

The analyst should not be bound by the accountant's concept of "normal operations," and thus he can usefully treat a much wider range of gains and losses as being derived from "operations." This approach reinforces our conclusion that from the point of view of analysis, most nonrecurring, *operating* gains and losses should be considered part of the operating results of the year in which they occur.

This approach is offered as a general guideline rather than as a mechanical rule. After examination of all attendant circumstances, the analyst may conclude that some such items require separation from the results of a single year. The relative size of an item could conceivably be a factor requiring such treatment. In this case, the best approach is to emphasize *average earnings* experience over, say, five years rather than the result of a single year. This approach of emphasizing average earnings becomes almost imperative in the case of enterprises that have widely fluctuating amounts of nonrecurring and other extraordinary items included in their results. After all, a single year is too short and too arbitrary a period on the basis of which to evaluate the earnings power of an enterprise or the prospects for future results. Moreover, we are all familiar with enterprises that defer expenses and postpone losses and come up periodically with a loss year that cancels out much of the income reported in preceding years.

b. Recurring nonoperating gains or losses. This category includes items of a nonoperating nature that recur with some frequency. An example would be the recurring amortization of a "bargain purchase credit." Other possible examples are interest income and the rental received from employees who rent company-owned houses.

While items in this category may be classified as unusual in published financial statements, the narrow definition of *nonoperating* which they involve as well as their recurrent nature are good reasons why they should not be excluded from current results by the analyst. They are, after all, mostly the result of the conscious employment of capital by the enterprise, and their recurrence requires inclusion of these gains or losses in estimates designed to project future results.

c. Nonrecurring nonoperating gains or losses. Of the three categories, this one possesses the greatest degree of "abnormality." Not only are the events here nonrepetitive and unpredictable, but they do not fall within the sphere of normal operations. In most cases, these events are extraneous, unintended, and unplanned. However, they can rarely be said to be totally unexpected. Business is ever subject to the risk of sudden adverse events and to random shocks, be they natural or man-made. In the same manner, business transactions are also subject to unexpected windfalls. One good example in this category is the loss from damage done by the crash of an aircraft on a plant not located in the vicinity of an airport. Other, but less clear-cut, examples in this category may also include:

1. Substantial uninsured casualty losses that are not within the categories of risk to which the enterprise can reasonably be deemed to be subject.
2. The expropriation by a foreign government of an entire operation owned by the enterprise.
3. The seizure or destruction of property as a result of an act of war, insurrection, or civil disorders, in areas where this is totally unexpected.

It can be seen readily that while the above occurrences are, in most cases, of a nonrecurring nature, their relation to the operations of a business varies. All are occurrences in the regular course of business. Even the assets destroyed by acts of God were acquired for operating purposes and thus were subject to all possible risks.

Of the three categories, the third comes closest to meeting the criterion of being "extraordinary." Nevertheless, truly unique events are very rare. What looks at the time as unique may in the light of experience turn out to be the symptom of new sets of circumstances that affect and may continue to affect the earning power as well as the degree of risk to which an enterprise is subject.

The analyst must bear in mind such possibilities, but barring evidence to the contrary, items in this category can be regarded as extraordinary in nature and thus can be omitted from the results of operations of a *single* year. They are, nevertheless, part of the longer-term record of results of the enterprise. Thus, they enter the computation of *average earnings,* and the propensity of the enterprise to incur such gains or losses must be considered in the projection of future average earnings.

The foregoing discussion has tried to point out that the intelligent classification of extraordinary items provides a workable solution to their treatment by the analyst. There are, however, other aspects of the evaluation of extraordinary items that must be considered here. One is the effect of extraordinary items on the resources of an enterprise; the other is their effect on the evaluation of management performance.

Effect of extraordinary items on enterprise resources. Every extraordinary gain or loss has a dual aspect. In addition to recording a gain (whether extraordinary or not), a business records an increase in resources. Similarly, a loss results in a reduction of resources. Since return on investment (ROI) measures the relationship of net income to resources, the incurrence of extraordinary gains and losses will affect this important measure of profitability. The more material the extraordinary item, the more significant that influence will be. In other words, if earnings and events are to be used to make estimates about the future, then extraordinary items convey something more than past performance. Thus, if an extraordinary loss results in the destruction of capital on which a certain return is expected, that return may be lost to the future. Conversely, an extraordinary gain will result in an addition of resources on which a future return can be expected.

This means that in projecting profitability and return on investment, the analyst must take into account the effect of recorded "extraordinary" items as well as the likelihood of the occurrence of future events that may cause extraordinary items.

Effect on evaluation of management. One implication frequently associated with the reporting of extraordinary gains and losses is that they have not resulted from a "normal" or "planned" activity of management and that, consequently, they should not be used in the evaluation of management performance. The analyst should seriously question such a conclusion.

What is "normal activity" in relation to management's deliberate actions? Whether we talk about the purchase or sale of securities, of other assets not used in operations, or of divisions and subsidiaries that definitely relate to operations, we talk about actions deliberately taken by management with specific purposes in mind. Such actions require, if anything, more consideration or deliberation than do ordinary everyday operating decisions because they are most often unusual in nature and involve substantial amounts of money. They are true tests of management ability. The results of such activities always qualify or enhance the results of "normal" operations, thus yielding the final net results.

Similarly, management must be aware of the risk of natural or manmade disasters or impediments in the course of business. The decision to engage in foreign operations is made with the knowledge of the special risks that this involves and the decision to insure or not is a normal operating decision. Nothing can really be termed completely unexpected or unforeseeable. Management does not engage, or is at least not supposed to engage, in any activity unconsciously; hence, whatever it does is clearly within the expected activity of a business. Every type of enterprise is subject to specific risks that are inherent in it, and managements do not enter such ventures blindly.

When it comes to the assessment of results that count and results that build or destroy value, the distinction of what is normal and what is not fades almost into insignificance. Management's beliefs about the quality of its decisions are nearly always related to the normalcy, or lack thereof, of surrounding circumstances. This can be clearly seen in the management report section of many annual reports. Of course, management has to take more time to explain failure or shortcomings than to explain success. Success hardly needs an explanation, unless it involves circumstances not likely to be repeated. Failure often evokes long explanations, and more often than not, unusual or unforeseeable circumstances are blamed for it. If only normal conditions had prevailed, everything would have been much better. But in a competitive economy, normal conditions hardly ever prevail for any length of time. Management is paid to anticipate and expect the unusual. No alibis are permitted. Explanations are never a substitute for performance.

THE FORECASTING OF EARNINGS

A major objective of income analysis is the forecasting of income. From an analytical point of view, the evaluation of the level of earnings is closely related to their forecast. This is so because a valid forecast of earnings involves an analysis of each major component of income and a considered estimate of its probable future size. Thus, some of the considerations discussed above are also applicable to earnings forcasting.

Forecasting must be differentiated from extrapolation. The latter is based on an assumption of the continuation of an existing trend and involves, more or less, a mechanical extension of that trend into the uncharted territory of the future.

Forecasting, on the other hand, is based on a careful analysis of as many individual components of income and expense as is possible and a considered estimate of their future size taking into consideration interrelationships among the components as well as probable future conditions. Thus, forecasting requires as much detail as is possible to obtain. In addition, the "stability" of the individual components must be assessed in terms of the likelihood of their future recurrence. This lends particular importance to the analysis of nonrecurring factors and of extraordinary items. Some of the mechanics of earnings forecasting were considered in Chapter 17 as part of the process of projecting short-term fund flows.

A financial or earnings projection differs from a forecast in that the assumptions used may not necessarily be the most probable, but rather the assumptions represent a conditon that the projection desires to test.

Forecasting requires the use of an earnings record covering a number of periods. Repeated or recurring performance can be forecast with a better degree of confidence than can random events.

Forecasting also requires use of enterprise data by product line or segment wherever different segments of an enterprise are subject to different degrees of risk, possess different degrees of profitability, or have differing growth potentials.

For example, the following tabulation of divisional earnings results indicates the degree to which the results of a component of an enterprise can be masked by the aggregate results:

	Earnings in millions			
	19x1	*19x2*	*19x3*	*19x4*
Segment A	$1,800	$1,700	$1,500	$1,200
Segment B	600	800	1,100	1,400
Total net income	$2,400	$2,500	$2,600	$2,600

Judgment on the earnings potential of the enterprise depends, of course, importantly on the relative importance of, as well as the future prospects of, segment B. The subject of product line reporting is discussed in Chapter 20.

Can earnings be forecast?

Statistical studies by Little,[5] and Little and Rayner[6] in England, and by Brealey[7] in the United States documented the apparent random behavior of reported earnings. Since these studies showed that earnings growth occurs in an almost purely random fashion, the implication was drawn that earnings changes cannot be accurately forecasted. Here again we have the problem of deriving from the behavior of large aggregates conclusions about what can or cannot be done in individual cases. Operationally, such generalized conclusions are of very limited practical use.

Serious forecasting is not done by the naive extrapolation of past growth trends of earnings. It is done by a painstaking analysis of the *components* of earnings, the revenues, and the expenses, as well as of all factors that are known or are expected to alter these in the period of the forecast. No knowledgeable forecaster would work only with the earnings figure that is merely a net residual. Thus, it was reported[8] that Days Inns, a motel chain, has been including forecasts in its annual reports for years and that their accuracy was satisfactory to many users, including bankers. Nor is it hard to envisage highly accurate forecasts in such businesses as apartment buildings or hospitals. It is equally easy to find business categories where forecasting would be very difficult and unreliable.

---

[5] I. M. D. Little, "Higgledy Piggledy Growth" (Oxford, England: Oxford University Institute of Statistics, 1962).

[6] I. M. D. Little, "Higgledy Piggledy Growth Again" (Oxford, England: Basil Blackwell, 1966).

[7] Richard A. Brealey, *Introduction to Risk and Return from Commerce Stocks* (Boston: MIT Press, 1969), chap. 8.

[8] *Forbes,* October 26, 1981, p. 189.

A paper[9] that undertook a comprehensive review of the research on earnings forecasts concluded: "We feel that both the properties of earnings forecasts and the question of their value continues to be a fertile area of research." It is equally clear that those seriously interested in the earnings forecasting function will find the study of specific tools and conditions to be of considerably more value than the statistical study of large aggregates.

SEC disclosure requirments—aid to forecasting

The "Management's Discussion and Analysis of Financial Condition and Results of Operations" disclosure requirements of the SEC (see Chapter 20) contain a wealth of information on management's views and attitudes as well as on factors that can influence enterprise operating performance. Consequently, the analyst may find much information in these analyses to aid in the forecasting process. Moreover, while not requiring it, the SEC encourages the inclusion in these discussions of forward-looking information.

Elements in earnings forecasts

Granted that the decision maker is interested primarily in future prospects, his approach to assessing them must be based primarily on the present as well as on the past. While expected future changes in conditions must be given recognition, the experience of the present and the past form the base to which such adjustments are applied. In doing this, the analyst relies on the degree of continuity and perseverance of momentum that is the common experience of the enterprise and the industry of which it is part. Random shocks and sudden changes are always possible, but they can rarely be foreseen with any degree of accuracy.

The importance to the analyst of the underlying continuity of business affairs should not be overemphasized. One should not confuse the basis for the projection of future results, which the past record represents, with the forecast which is the end product. As a final objective, the analyst is interested in a projection of net income. Net income is the result of the offset of two big streams: (1) total revenues and (2) total costs.

Considering that net income represents most frequently but a relatively small portion of either stream, one can see how a relatively minor change in either of these large streams can cause a very significant change in net income.

A significant check on the reasonableness of an earnings projection is to test it against the return on invested capital which is implicit in the forecast. If the result is at variance with returns realized in the past, the underlying

---

[9] A. R. Abdel-Khalik and R. B. Thompson, "Research on Earnings Forecasts: The State of the Art," *The Accounting Journal,* Winter 1977–78.

assumptions must be thoroughly examined so that the reasons for such deviations can be pinpointed.

In terms of the framework examined in Chapter 19, the ROI depends on earnings that are a product of *management* and of *assets* that require funds for their acquisition.

1. Management. It is well known that it takes resourceful management to "breathe life" into assets by employing them profitably and causing their optimum utilization. The assumption of stability of relationships and trends implies that there has been no major change in the skill, the depth, and the continuity of the management group or a radical change in the type of business in which their skill has been proven by a record of successful performance.

2. Assets. The second essential ingredient to profitable operations is funds or resources with which the assets essential to the successful conduct of business are acquired. No management, no matter how ingenious, can expand operations and have an enterprise grow without an adequate asset base. Thus, continuity of success and the extrapolation of growth must be based on an investigation of the sources of additional funds that the enterprise will need and the effect of the method of financing on net income and earnings per share.

The financial condition of the enterprise, as was seen in Chapters 16 and 18, can have a bearing on the results of operations. A lack of liquidity may inhibit an otherwise skillful management, and a precarious or too risky capital structure may lead to limitations by others on its freedom of action.

The above factors, as well as other economic, industry, and competitive factors, must be taken into account by the analyst when forecasting the earnings of an enterprise. Ideally, in forecasting earnings, the analyst should add a lot of knowledge about the future to some knowledge of the past. Realistically the analyst must settle for a lot of knowledge about the past and present and only a limited knowledge of the future.

In evaluating earnings trends, the analyst relies also on such indicators of future conditions as capital expenditures, order backlogs, as well as demand trends in individual product lines.

It is important to realize that no degree of sophistication in the techniques used in earnings forecasting can eliminate the inevitable uncertainty to which all forecasts are subject. Even the best and most soundly based projections retain a significant probability of proving widely off the mark because of events and circumstances that cannot be foreseen.

The most effective means by which the analyst and decision maker can counter this irreducible uncertainty is to keep close and constant watch over how closely actual results conform to his forecasts. This requires a constant monitoring of results and the adjustment and updating of projections in the light of such results. The monitoring of earnings is considered later in this chapter.

Publication of financial forecasts

Recent years have witnessed intensified interest in publication by companies of forecasts of earnings and other financial data. The publication of forecasts in Britain in certain specialized situations as well as a belief that forecasts would be useful to investors were major factors behind this interest. This type of forecasting by insiders (i.e., management) is to be distinguished from forecasts made by financial analysts that are based on all the information that they can obtain.

In early 1977, an advisory committee to the SEC recommended that the agency design procedures to encourage companies to make forecasts of their economic performance. Following this, the SEC deleted in its regulations a reference to predictions of "earnings" as possibly misleading in certain situations. Thus the Commission will no longer object to disclosure in filings with it of projections that are made in good faith and have a reasonable basis, provided that they are presented in appropriate form and are accompanied by information adequate for investors to make their own judgments. In 1978 the SEC issued "Guides for Disclosure of Projections of Future Economic Performance."

Following this up, in 1979 the SEC issued a rule intended to encourage companies to make public their financial forecasts by protecting them from lawsuits in case their predictions did not come true, these "safe harbor" rules against fraud charges will protect companies as long as their projections have a "reasonable basis" and are made in good faith.

The interest in financial forecasts has resulted in a formal consideration of some of the issues by the AICPA which in 1975 issued two statements on the subject.[10]

These statements recommend, among others, that financial forecasts should be presented in a historical financial statement format and that they include regularly a comparison of the previous forecast with attained results.

Both statements recognize the primary importance that assumptions play in the reliability and creditability of a financial forecast. Consequently, those assumptions that management thinks most crucial or significant to the forecast—or are key factors upon which the financial results of the enterprise depends—should be disclosed to provide the greatest benefit to users of forecasts. There ordinarily should be some indication of the basis or rationale for these assumptions.

In 1980, the Financial Forecasts and Projections Task Force of the AICPA issued a *Guide for a Review of a Financial Forecast.* This publication set forth the scope as well as the procedures to be followed by an accountant in reviewing a financial forecast and the method of reporting on such a review.

---

[10] "Guidelines for Systems for the Preparation of Financial Forecasts" and "Presentation and Disclosure of Financial Forecasts," AICPA, 1975. (Auditing implications are also being considered.)

Speagle, Clark, and Elgers have categorized assumptions underlying forecasted financial statements as (1) "ongoing assumptions relating to the forecast methodology, company operating characteristics, and so on; (2) standard assumptions bearing upon the continuity in accounting policy, company management, supply sources, etc.; and (3) transitory assumptions covering events in a particular year such as recapitalizations, labor settlements, new product introductions, facilities expansion, etc."[11]

The validity of any forecasted financial data depends to a high degree on the assumptions, both implicit and explicit, upon which the forecasting technique is based. The financial analyst who uses a management forecast as input to his own projections should pay first and primary attention to the assumptions on which it is based.

THE CONCEPT OF EARNINGS POWER

The best possible estimate of the *average* earnings of an enterprise, which can be expected to be sustained and be repeated with some degree of regularity over a *span of future years,* is referred to as its earning power. Except in specialized cases, earning power is universally recognized as the single most important factor in the valuation of an enterprise. Most valuation approaches entail in one form or another the capitalization of earning power by a factor or multiplier that takes into account the cost of capital as well as future expected risks and rewards.

The importance of "earning power" is such that most analyses of the income and related financial statements have as one of their ultimate objectives the determination of its amount. Earning power is a concept of financial analysis, not of accounting. It focuses on stable and recurring elements and thus aims to arrive at the best possible estimate of repeatable average earnings over a span of future years. Accounting, as we have seen, can supply much of the essential information for the computation of earning power. However, the process is one involving knowledge, judgment, experience, and a time horizon, as well as a specialized investing or lending point of view, such as is described in Chapter 1.

Investors and lenders look ultimately to future cash flows as sources of rewards and safety. Accrual accounting, which underlies income determination, aims to relate sacrifices and benefits to the periods in which they occur. In spite of known shortcomings, this framework represents the most reliable and relevant indicator of longer-term future probabilities of *average* cash inflows and outflows presently known.

While in its objectives, valuation is *future* oriented, we must recognize that the only sound and realistic basis for estimating future conditions and

[11] R. E. Speagle, J. J. Clark, and P. Elgers, *Publishing Financial Forecasts: Benefits, Alternatives, Risk* (Laventhol Krekstein Horwath & Horwath, 1974).

probabilities is the actual track record of the enterprise's achievement in the most recent past. Not only does such an earning record over a representative span of years, usually encompassing an entire business cycle, represent what has in fact been achieved as the actual operating experience of the enterprise, but it also represents the operating model on the basis of which we can give effect to assumptions about future conditions that we expect to differ from those prevailing in the past.

In this context, it must be realized that valuation, whether it is performed for purposes of investment, taxation, or the adjudication of disputes as to value, is of such importance to the parties at interest that estimates, if they are made, must be most soundly based. Thus, any departure from actual experience must be most carefully verified and justified. Our ability to pierce the veil of the future is limited indeed. As Bennian[12] stated it:

> It is impossible to make an economic forecast in which full confidence can be placed. No matter what refinements of techniques are employed, there still remain at least some exogenous variables. It is thus not even possible to say with certainty how likely our forecast is to be right. We must be brash enough to label a forecast as "most probable," but this implies an ability on our part to pin an approximate probability co-efficient on a forecast: 1.0 if it is virtual certainty, 0.0 if it is next to an impossibility, or some other co-efficient between these extremes. But, again, since we have no precise way of measuring the probability of our exogenous variables behaving as we assume them to do, there is no assurance that the estimated probability co-efficient for our forecast is anything like 100 percent correct.

It is for this reason that the courts and others have been reluctant, except in the most persuasive of circumstances, to substitute guesses about the future for the experience of the past, and, for this reason, *average* past earnings enter very importantly into the determination of earning power.

Earning power time horizon

It can be readily recognized that one year represents too short and too arbitrary a time period for purposes of income measurement and evaluation. Because of the length of time required to assess the ultimate workout and the results of many investments and outlays, because of the ups and downs of the business cycle, and because of the presence of numerous nonrecurring and extraordinary factors, the earning power of an enterprise is best measured by means of average earnings realized over a number of years. Thus, while gains and losses may be unusual or extraordinary with respect to any one period, they are, nevertheless, still part of the enterprise's longer-term operating experience.

---

[12] Edward G. Bennian, "Capital Budgeting and Game Theory," *Harvard Business Review,* November–December 1956, pp. 115–23.

The period of time over which an earnings average should be calculated will vary with the industry of which the enterprise is part and with other special circumstances. However, in general, a from 5- to 10-year earnings average will smooth out many of the distortions and the irregularities that impair the significance of a single year's results. A five-year earnings average will, in most cases, be adequate to retain an emphasis on recent experience while avoiding the inclusion of years that may no longer be representative or relevant.

Our discussion of the analysis of the income statement has shown that the analysis must focus on the level of income for each year as well as on the *trend* of earnings over time. Trend is an important factor in valuation.

If the earnings are subject to a sustainable trend, the averaging process may have to be weighted so as to accord more weight to most recent earnings. Thus, in a five-year average computation, the last year may be given a weight of 5/15, the preceding year a weight of 4/15, and the first year a weight of 1/15.

The more representative the most recent enterprise experience and the nature of its operations are of what can be expected in the future, the more valid the averaging process is. Conversely, if there have been significant recent changes in the nature of the enterprise's operations, the averaging period may have to be shortened and/or greater emphasis may have to be placed on estimation of future conditions.

Adjustment of reported earnings per share

In our discussion of the adjustment of earnings, we concluded that in determining the earning power of an enterprise, no item of income and expense should be completely excluded. Since every item of income or expense is part of the enterprise's operating experience, the question is only to what year items should be assigned or into what period of time they should be included when an average of earnings is computed.

For purposes of analysis or comparison, analysts may, however, wish to focus on an adjusted level of earnings for a short period, for example, for two years. This can be done by adding to, or removing from, reported earnings per share selected items of income or expense that were included therein. If this is to be done on a per share basis, every item must be adjusted for tax effect (by using the enterprise's effective tax rate unless the tax rate is otherwise specified) and must be divided by the number of shares that are used in the basic computation of earnings per share (see Chapter 12).

The following example of such suggested analytical adjustments is based on a tabulation prepared by "The Quality of Earnings Report"[13] concerning the reported earnings of A. H. Robins Company.

---

[13] Published by Reporting Research Corporation, Englewood Cliffs, N.J., and dated April 15, 1981.

Per share earnings impact

Item	1980	1979
Effective tax rate change	+.02	
Settlement of Hartz litigation	+.07	+.57
Change to straight-line depreciation	+.02	
Reserves for losses on Iranian assets	+.02	−.15
Loss on sale of divisions	−.19	
Change to LIFO	−.07	
Litigation settlements and expense	−.09	−.12
Foreign exchange translation	−.03	−.04
Above trend R&D expenditures	−.11	
Higher percent allowance for doubtful accounts	−.02	
± Per share earnings impact	−$ .38	+$ .26
Per share earnings as reported	*$1.01*	*$1.71*
Add back negative (−) impact to 1980	.38	
Subtract positive (+) impact from 1979		(.26)
Adjusted earnings per share	*$1.39*	*$1.45*

(+) Positive.
(−) Negative.

In the above tabulation, items that increased earnings are listed as positive (+) and items that diminished earnings are listed as negative (−), Thus, in order to remove them from reported earnings, positive items are deducted while negative items are added back. The validity of each adjustment is, of course, a matter for the analyst's judgment.

MONITORING PERFORMANCE AND RESULTS

The judgments of what the proper financial forecast of an enterprise is or what its earning power is, are based on estimates that hinge on future developments that can never be fully forseen. Consequently, the best course of action is to monitor performance closely and frequently and to compare it with earlier estimates and assumptions. In this way, one can constantly revise one's estimates and judgments and incorporate the unfolding reality into earlier judgments and conclusions. One of the best ways of monitoring performance is to follow interim reports closely.

Interim financial statements

The need to follow closely the results achieved by an enterprise requires frequent updatings of such results. Interim financial statements, most frequently issued on a quarterly basis, are designed to fill this need. They are used by decision makers as means of updating current results as well as in the prediction of future results.

If, as we have seen, a year is a relatively short period of time in which to account for results of operations, then trying to confine the measurement of results to a three-month period involves all the more problems and imperfections. For this and other reasons the reporting of interim earnings is subject to serious limitations and distortions. The intelligent use of reported interim results requires that we have a full understanding of these possible problem areas and limitations. The following is a review of some of the basic causes of these problems and limitations, as well as their effect on the determination of reported interim results.

Year-end adjustments. The determination of the results of operations for a year requires a great many estimates, as well as procedures, such as accruals and the determination of inventory quantities and carrying values. These procedures can be complex, time-consuming, and costly. Examples of procedures requiring a great deal of data collection and estimation include estimation of the percentage of completion of contracts, determination of cost of work in process, the allocation of under- or over absorbed overhead for the period, and the estimation of year-end inventory levels under the LIFO method. The complex, time-consuming, and expensive nature of these procedures can mean that they are performed much more crudely during interim periods and are often based on records that are less complete than are their year-end counterparts. The result inevitably is a less accurate process of income determination which, in turn, may require year-end adjustments that can modify substantially the interim results already reported.

Seasonality. Many enterprises experience at least some degree of seasonality in their activities. Sales may be unevenly distributed over the year, and so it may be with production and other activities. This tends to distort comparisons among the quarterly results of a single year. It also presents problems in the allocation of many budgeted costs, such as advertising, R&D, and repairs and maintenance. If expenses vary with sales, they should be accrued on the basis of expected sales for the full year. Obviously, the preparer of yearly financial statements has the benefit of hindsight that the preparer of interim statements does not. There are also problems with the allocation of fixed costs among quarters.

ILLUSTRATION 3. A study of the affairs of Mattel, Inc., reveals how company executives came up with targeted earnings quarter by quarter in fiscal years ending January 31, 1971, and 1972 using misleading or blatantly false methods to increase recorded sales or to decrease recorded expenses to reach targets. Mattel used an accounting practice known as *annualization* to match incurred expenses against sales on a year-to-year basis and these were juggled to achieve preselected results.

ILLUSTRATION 4.   The tenuous nature of quarterly gross profit estimates is exemplified by this note by Bristol Products, Inc.: "Results of Fourth Quarter, 1974—As indicated in Note 1, the Company's interim financial statements for 1974 reflected results of operations using estimated gross profit percentages for its wholesale divisions. Physical inventories of these divisions at December 31, 1974, disclosed that the interim gross profit estimates and resultant net income were understated. If fourth quarter 1974 results were computed using the annual gross profit percentages determined for the wholesale divisions, fourth quarter net income would have amounted to approximately $114,000 or $.10 per share. This compares with fourth quarter net income of $228,645 or $.24 per share computed by substracting interim results reported for the first three quarters of 1974 from results for the year."

ILLUSTRATION 5.   The following is an example of adjustments that can result from seasonal variations: "Because of a seasonal production cycle, and in accordance with practices followed by the Company in reporting interim financial statements prior to 19x4, $435,000 of unabsorbed factory overhead has been deferred at July 4, 19x5. Due to uncertainties as to production and sales in 19x4, $487,000 of such unabsorbed overhead was expensed during the first 6 months of 19x4."

APB Opinion 28

In its *Opinion 28,* the APB concluded that interim reports should be prepared in accordance with GAAP used in the preparation of the latest financial statements. Adopting mostly the point of view that a quarterly report is an integral part of a full year rather than a discrete period, it calls for the accrual of revenues and for the spreading of certain costs among the quarters of a year. For example, it sanctions the accrual of such year-end adjustments as inventory shrinkages, quantity discounts, and uncollectible accounts; but it prohibits the accrual of advertising costs on the ground that benefits of such costs cannot be anticipated. Losses cannot, generally, be deferred beyond the interim period in which they occur. LIFO inventory liquidations should be considered on an annual basis. Only permanent declines in inventory values are to be recorded on an interim basis. Moreover, the *Opinion* calls for the inclusion of extraordinary items in the interim period in which they occur.[14] Income taxes should be accrued on the basis of the effective tax rate expected to apply to the full year.

SEC interim reporting requirements

The SEC took a relatively early and strong interest in interim reporting and as a result brought about very significant improvements in reporting

---

[14] *SFAS 3* specifies that "if a cumulative effect type accounting change is made in other than the first interim period of an enterprise's fiscal year, no cumulative effect of the change shall be included in net income of the period of change. Instead, financial information for the pre-change interim periods of the fiscal year in which the change is made shall be restated by applying the newly adopted accounting principle to those pre-change interim periods."

and disclosure in this area. In 1972, it required quarterly reports (on Form 10-Q) and reports on current developments (Form 8-K), disclosure of separate fourth quarter results and details of year-end adjustments.

In 1975, the SEC issued requirements (now in codification of *FRR,* Sections 301, 303, and 304) that served to expand substantially the content and the utility of interim reports filed with the Commission. The principal requirements include:

Comparative quarterly and year-to-date abbreviated income statement data—this information may be labeled *unaudited* and must also be included in annual reports to shareholders. (Small companies are exempted).

Year-to-date statements of changes in financial position.

Comparative balance sheets.

Increased pro forma information on business combinations accounted for as purchases.

Conformity with the principles of accounting measurement as set forth in professional pronouncements on interim financial reports. Increased disclosure of accounting changes with a letter from the registrant's independent public accountant stating whether or not he judges the changes to be preferable.

Management's narrative analysis of the results of operations, explaining the reasons for material changes in the amount of revenue and expense items from one quarter to the next. (See discussion in Chapter 20).

Indications as to whether a Form 8-K was filed during the quarter—reporting either unusual charges or credits to income or a change of auditors.

Signature of the registrant's chief financial officer or chief accounting officer.

In promulgating these expanded disclosure requirements, the Commission indicated that it believed that these disclosures will assist investors in understanding the pattern of corporate activities throughout a fiscal period. It maintained that presentation of such quarterly data will supply information about the trend of business operations over segments of time which are sufficiently short to reflect business turning points.

Implications for analysis

While there have been some notable recent improvements in the reporting of interim results, the analyst must remain constantly aware that accuracy of estimation and the objectivity of determinations are and remain problem areas that are inherent in the measurement of results of very short periods. Moreover, the limited association of auditors with interim data, while lending some unspecified degree of assurance, cannot be equated to the degree of assurance that is associated with fully audited financial statements. SEC insistence that the professional pronouncements on interim statements (such as *APB Opinion 28*) be adhered to should offer analysts some additional comfort. However, not all principles promulgated by the APB on the subject of interim financial statements result in presentations useful to the analyst. For example, the inclusion of extraordinary items in the results of the quarter in which they occur will require careful adjustment to render them meaningful for purposes of analysis.

While the normalization of expenses is a reasonable intraperiod accounting procedure, the analyst must be aware of the fact that there are no rigorous standards or rules governing its implementation and that it is consequently, subject to possible abuse. The shifting of costs between periods is generally easier than the shifting of sales; and, therefore, a close analysis of sales may yield a more realistic clue to a company's true state of affairs for an interim period.

Since the price of the common stock influences the computation of earnings per share (see Chapter 12), the analyst should in his evaluation of per share results be alert to the separation of these market effects from those related to the operating fundamentals of an enterprise.

Some problems of seasonality in interim results of operations can be overcome by considering in the analysis not merely the results of a single quarter, but also the year-to-date cumulative results which incorporate the results of the latest available quarter. This is the most effective way of monitoring the results of an enterprise and bringing to bear on its analysis the latest data on operations that are available.

QUESTIONS

1. Distinguish between income and cash flow. Why should there be a distinction between the two?
2. *a.* What is meant by *quality of earnings?* Why do analysts assess it?
   b. On what major elements does the quality of earnings depend?
3. *a.* What are discretionary costs?
   b. Of what significance are discretionary costs to an analysis of the quality of earnings?
4. *a.* Why is the evaluation of R&D costs important in the analysis and projection of income?
   b. What are some of the precautions required in analyzing R&D expenses?
5. *a.* What is the relationship between the carrying amounts of various assets and the earnings reported?
   b. What is the relationship between the amounts at which liabilities, including provisions, are carried and the earnings reported?
6. In what way is balance sheet analysis a check on the validity as well as the quality of earnings?

7. Comment on the effect which the "risk category" of an asset has on the quality of reported earnings.

8. Explain briefly the relationship between the quality of earnings and the following balance sheet items:
   a. Accounts receivable.
   b. Inventories.
   c. Deferred charges.

9. What is the effect of external factors on the quality of earnings?

10. What is the objective of recasting the income statement?

11. Where will the analyst find data needed for the analysis of the results of operations and for their recasting and adjustment?

12. What is the aim of the recasting process and how is the recasting accomplished?

13. Describe the income statement adjustment process.

14. What is income smoothing? How can it be distinguished from outright falsehoods?

15. Name and explain three forms of income smoothing.

16. a. What factors and incentives motivate companies to engage in income smoothing?
    b. What are the implications for analysis?

17. Why are managements so greatly interested in the reporting of extraordinary gains and losses?

18. What are the basic objectives of the analyst in the identification and the evaluation of extraordinary items?

19. a. Into what categories can items which are described as unusual or extraordinary in the financial statements be usefully subdivided for purposes of analysis?
    b. Give examples of each such category.
    c. How should the analyst treat items in each category? Is such a treatment indicated under all circumstances? Explain.

20. What are the effects of extraordinary items on—
    a. Enterprise resources?
    b. The evaluation of managements?

21. Comment on the following statement:
    "Extraordinary gains or losses have not resulted from a 'normal' or 'planned' activity of management and, consequently, they should not be used in the evaluation of managerial performance."
    Do you agree?

22. What is the difference between forecasting and extrapolation of earnings?

23. How can SEC disclosure requirements aid in forecasting?

24. What are the categories of assumptions underlying forecasted financial statements? Give examples of each category. What is the importance of these assumptions to the financial analyst?

25. What is earning power? Why is it important?

26. a. What are interim financial statements used for?
    b. What accounting problems which are peculiar to interim statements must the analyst be aware of?

27. Interim financial reporting can be subject to serious limitations and distortions. Discuss some of the reasons for this.

28. What are the major disclosure requirements by the SEC with regard to interim reports? What are the objectives behind them?

29. What implications do interim reports hold for the financial analyst?

23

Comprehensive analysis of financial statements

THE METHODOLOGY OF FINANCIAL STATEMENT ANALYSIS

The marshalling, arrangement, and presentation of data for purposes of financial statement analysis can be standardized to some extent in the interest of consistency and organizational efficiency. However, the actual process of analysis must be left to the judgment of the analyst so that he or she may allow for the great diversity of situations and circumstances that are likely to be encountered in practice, and thus give full reign to his or her own initiative, originality, and ingenuity. Nevertheless, there are some useful generalizations and guidelines that may be stated as to a general approach to the task of financial statement analysis.

To begin with, financial statement analysis is oriented towards the achievement of definite objectives. In order that the analysis best accomplish these objectives, the first step is to define them carefully. The thinking and clarification leading up to such a definition of objectives is a very important part of the analytical process, for it ensures a clear understanding of objectives, that is, of what is pertinent and relevant and what is not, and thus also leads to avoidance of unnecessary work. This clarification of objectives is indispensable to an *effective* as well as to an *efficient* analysis; *effective,* in that, given the specifications, it focuses on the most important and most relevant elements of the financial statements; *efficient,* in that it leads to an analysis with maximum economy of time and effort.

ILLUSTRATION 1. The bank loan officer, dealing with a request for a short-term loan to finance inventory, may define his objective as assessing the intention and the ability of the borrower to repay the loan on time. Thus, the analyst can concentrate on what is needed to achieve this objective and need not, for instance, address himself to industry conditions that can affect the borrowing entity only over the longer term.

Once the objective of the analysis has been defined, the next step is the formulation of specific questions the answers to which are needed in the achievement of such objectives.

ILLUSTRATION 2. The loan officer in Illustration 1 now needs to define the critical criteria that will affect his decision. For instance, the question of the borrower's *willingness* to repay the short-term loan bears on his character; and financial statement analysis can reveal only the history of past loans granted it. Thus, tools other than financial statement analysis will have to be employed to get complete information on the borrower's character.

Among the other questions on which the loan officer will need information are the following:

1. What is the enterprise's short-term liquidity?
2. What will its sources and uses of cash be during the duration of the loan agreement?

Financial statement analysis can go far towards providing answers to such questions.

Having defined the objective and having translated it into specific questions and criteria that must be resolved, the analyst is ready for the third step in the analysis process. This is to decide which tools and techniques of analysis are the most appropriate, effective, and efficient ones to use in working on the particular decision problem at hand.

ILLUSTRATION 3. Following the sequence developed in Illustrations 1 and 2, the loan officer will now decide which financial statement analysis tools are the most appropriate to use in this case. He may choose one or more of the following:

1. Short-term liquidity ratios.
2. Inventory turnover measures.
3. Cash flow projections.
4. Analyses of changes in financial position.

These analyses will have to include estimates and projections of future conditions toward which most, if not all, financial analysis is oriented.

The fourth and final step in analysis is the interpretation of the data and measures assembled as a basis for decision and action. This is the most critical and difficult of the steps, and the one requiring the application of a great deal of judgment, skill, and effort. Interpretation is a process of investigation and evaluation, and of envisaging the reality that lies behind the figures examined. There is, of course, no mechanical substitute for this process of judgment. However, the proper definition of the problem and of the critical questions that must be answered, as well as the skillful selection of the most appropriate tools of analysis available in the circumstances, will go a long way towards a meaningful interpretation of the results of analysis.

ILLUSTRATION 4. Following the sequence of the first three examples above, the collection, by the loan officer, of the data described in Illustration 3 is, of course, not the end result of his analysis. These data must be integrated, evaluated, and interpreted for the purposes of reaching the basic decision of whether to make the loan and, if so, in what amount.

By way of analogy, the weather forecasting function provides an example of the difference between the availability of analytical data and its successful interpretation. Thus, the average listener to weather information does not know how to interpret barometric pressure, relative humidity, or wind velocity. What one needs to know is the weather forecast that results from an interpretation of these data.

The intelligent analyst and interpreter of financial statement data must always bear in mind that a financial statement is at best an abstraction of an underlying reality. Further mathematical manipulation of financial data can result in second, third, and even further levels of abstractions; and the analyst must always keep in mind the business reality behind the figures. No map of the Rocky Mountains can fully convey the grandeur of the terrain. One has to see them in order to appreciate them because maps, like financial statements, are, at best abstractions. That is why security analysts must, at some point, leave the financial statements and visit the companies that they analyze in order to get a full understanding of the phenomena revealed by their analysis. This is particularly true because the static reality portrayed by the abstractions found in the financial statements cannot remain stable for very long. Reality is ever changing.

A recognition of the inherent limitations of financial data is needed for intelligent analysis. This does not detract from their importance because financial statements and data are the only means by which the financial realities of an enterprise can be reduced to a common denominator that is quantified and that can be mathematically manipulated and projected in a rational and disciplined way.

SIGNIFICANCE OF THE "BUILDING BLOCK" APPROACH TO FINANCIAL ANALYSIS

The six major building blocks of financial analysis that we have examined in this text are:

1. Short-term liquidity.
2. Funds flow.
3. Capital structure and long-term solvency.
4. Return on investment (ROI)
5. Asset utilization.
6. Operating performance.

The building block approach to financial statement analysis involves:

1. The determination of the major objectives that a particular financial analysis is to achieve.
2. Arriving at a judgment about which of the six major areas of analysis (i.e., our "building blocks") must be evaluated with what degree of emphasis and in what order of priority.

For example, the security analyst, in the evaluation of the investment merit of a particular issue of equity securities, may attach primary importance to the earning capacity and potential of the enterprise. Thus, the first building block of the analysis will be the evaluation of *operating performance* and the next, perhaps, *return on investment (ROI)*. A thorough analysis will, of course, require that attention be paid to the other four major areas of analysis, although with perhaps lesser degrees of emphasis, that is, depth. This attention to the other major areas of analysis is necessary in order to detect possible problem areas, that is, areas of potential risk. Thus, further analysis may reveal a liquidity problem arising from a "thin" working capital condition, or it may reveal a situation of inadequate capital funds that may stifle growth and flexibility. It is conceivable that these problem areas may reveal themselves to be so important as to overshadow the question of earning power, thus leading to a change in the relative emphasis that the analyst will accord to the main areas of his particular analysis.

While the subdivision of the analysis into six distinct aspects of a company's financial condition and performance is a useful approach, it must be borne in mind that these areas of analysis are highly interrelated. For example, the operating performance of an enterprise can be affected by the lack of adequate capital funds or by problems of short-term liquidity. Similarly, a credit evaluation cannot stop at the point where a satisfactory short-term liquidity position has been determined because existing or incipient problems in the "operating performance" area may result in serious drains of funds due to losses. Such drains can quickly reverse the satisfactory liquidity position that may prevail at a given point in time.

At the start of his analysis, the analyst will tentatively determine the relative importance of the areas that he will examine and the order in which they will be examined. This order of emphasis and priority may subsequently change in the light of his findings and as the analysis progresses.

THE EARMARKS OF GOOD FINANCIAL ANALYSIS

As we have noted, the foundation of any good analysis is a thorough understanding of the objectives to be achieved and the uses to which it is going to be put. Such understanding leads to economy of effort as well as to a useful and most relevant focus on the points that need to be clarified and the estimates and projections that are required.

In practice, rarely can all the facts surrounding a particular analysis be obtained, so that most analyses are undertaken on the basis of incomplete and inadequate facts and data. The process of financial analysis is basically one of reducing the areas of uncertainty—which can, however, never be completely eliminated.

A written analysis and report is not only a significant medium of communication to the reader but it also serves importantly to organize the thinking of the analyst as well as to allow him or her to check the flow and the logic of the presentation. The process of writing reinforces our thinking and vice versa. As we revise our words, we also refine our thoughts—and improvements in style lead, in turn, to the sharpening and improvement in the thinking process itself.

A good analysis separates clearly for the reader the interpretations and conclusions of the analysis from the facts and data upon which they are based. This not only separates fact from opinion and estimate but also enables the reader to follow the rationale of the analyst's conclusions and allows him to modify them as his judgment dictates. To this end, the analysis should contain distinct sections devoted to:

1. General background material on the enterprise analyzed, the industry of which it is a part, and the economic environment in which it operates.
2. Financial and other data used in the analysis as well as ratios, trends, and other analytical measures that have been developed from them.
3. Assumptions as to the general economic environment and as to other conditions on which estimates and projections are based.
4. A listing of positive and negative factors, quantitative and qualitative, by important areas of analysis.
5. Projections, estimates, interpretations, and conclusions based on the aforementioned data. (Some analyses list only the positive and negative factors developed by the analysis and leave further interpretations to the reader.)

A good analysis should start with a brief "Summary and Conclusion" section as well as a table of contents to help the busy reader decide how much of the report he wants to read and on which parts of it to concentrate.

The writer of an analytical report must guard against the all-too-common tendency to include irrelevant matter. For example, the reader need not know the century-old details of the humble beginnings of the enterprise under analysis nor should he be taken on a "journey" along all the fruitless byways and missteps that the analyst inevitably encountered in his process of ferreting out and separating the important from the insignificant. Irrelevant bulk or "roughage" can only serve to confuse and distract the reader of a report.

Ambiguities and equivocations that are employed to avoid responsibility or to hedge conclusions do not belong in a good analytical report. Finally, the writers of such reports must recognize that we are all judged on the basis of small details. Consequently, the presence of mistakes in grammar

or of obvious errors of fact in a report can plant doubt in the reader's mind
as to the competence of the author and the validity of the analysis.

SPECIAL INDUSTRY OR ENVIRONMENTAL CHARACTERISTICS

In this book, the analysis of the various segments of financial statements
was treated from the point of view of the ordinary commercial or industrial
enterprise. The financial analyst must, however, recognize that there are industries with distinct accounting treatments that arise either from their specialized
nature or from the special conditions, such as governmental regulation, to
which they are subject. The analysis of the financial statements of such enterprise requires a thorough understanding of the accounting peculiarities to
which they are subject, and the analyst must, accordingly, prepare himself
for his task by the study and the understanding of the specialized areas of
accounting that affect his particular analysis.

Thus, for example, the analysis of a company in the oil and gas industry
requires a thorough knowledge of such accounting concepts peculiar to that
industry such as the determination of "cost centers," prediscovery costs,
discovery costs, and the disposition of capitalized costs. There are particular
problems in the treatment of exploratory, development, and other expenditures as well as in amortization and depletion practices.

Life insurance accounting, to cite another example, also requires specialized
knowledge that arises from the peculiarities of this industry and from the
regulation to which it is subject. There are special problems in the area of
recognition of premium revenues, the accounting for acquisition costs of
new business, and the determination of policy reserves.

Public utility regulation has resulted in specialized accounting concepts
and problems of which even utility analyst must be aware. There are tax
allocation problems resulting in differences among companies that "normal-
ize" taxes versus those which "flow" them through. Then there are problems
related to the adequacy of provisions for depreciation, and problems concerning the utility's "rate base" and the method by which it is computed.

SFAS 71 "Accounting for the Effects of Certain Types of Regulation,"
gives guidance for public utilities and certain other rate-regulated companies,
and generally endorses the principal accounting practices that those entities
currently follow. It holds that if the rate-setting process for a regulated enterprise gives assurance that incurred costs will be eventually recovered, they
should be deferred until the corresponding revenues are recognized. Conversely, if rates are set to cover future costs, current receipts should be recorded as liabilities until the associated costs are incurred.

The Statement upholds the industry practice of capitalizing interest costs
of financing construction based on the amounts used for rate-setting purposes,
which could include an imputed interest cost on equity funds. Changes from
current industry practice include a requirement to capitalize leases if *SFAS*

13 tests are met, and a prohibition against prior period adjustments for refunds to customers.

The Statement applies primarily to public utilities that provide services or products subject to rate-setting by independent, third-party regulators. The rates must be set to recover the utility's specific costs, and be chargeable to and collectible from customers, not the regulator itself.

As in any field of endeavor, specialized areas of inquiry require that specialized knowledge be brought to bear upon them. Financial analysis is, of course, no exception.

ILLUSTRATION OF A COMPREHENSIVE ANALYSIS OF FINANCIAL STATEMENTS—MARINE SUPPLY CORPORATION

The following analysis of the financial statements and other data of the Marine Supply Corporation will serve as an illustration of this process.

Introduction

The Marine Supply Corporation, a leader in the outboard motor industry, was incorporated some 40 years ago. While outboard motor engines and related marine products still account for the bulk of the company's sales, other products are gaining in importance and growing at a rate much faster than the primary products (see Exhibit 23–1, sales breakdown).

Snow vehicle production was launched in fiscal year 19x4. Its growth rate looks dramatic because it starts from extremely low base. Outboard motors can be regarded as the primary base of the company's growth, and outboard engines contribute an even larger portion of corporate profits.

Exhibit 23–1

MARINE SUPPLY CORPORATION
Sales Breakdown
(in millions)

Product	19x5		19y0		Sales increase 19x5– y0 percent	Annual growth rates* percent
	Sales	Percent	Sales	Percent		
Marine products	$135.0	74.5	$217.3	71.0	+ 61	10
Lawn care equipment ..	16.2	9.0	30.5	10.0	+ 88	13
Vehicles	14.1	7.8	19.6	6.4	+ 39	7
Chain saws	9.4	5.2	9.5	3.1	+ 1	0
Snow vehicles	5.1	2.8	23.4	7.7	+359	36
Miscellaneous	.9	.7	4.2	1.8	+367	36
Total	$180.7	100.0	$304.5	100.0	+ 69	11.2

* Five-year period, compounded annually.

While most of Marine Supply Corporation's products have some commercial applications, they are sold primarily for recreation or leisure-time purposes. Being generally big-ticket items, the company's sales are greatly subject to swings in consumer buying cycles.

The use of outboard motors and the majority of the company's other products is largely confined to the warmer months of late spring, summer, and early fall. This means peak retail demand for these items is seasonal; dealer buying tends to be concentrated in this period as well. As a result, the first quarter of the company's fiscal year (ending December) frequently produces a nominal deficit while the June quarter generates 40 percent or more of annual profits.

Marine Supply is one of the world's largest manufacturers of outboard motors; its twin lines command something more than one half the U.S.–Canadian market (by far the most important), and the company estimates a similar proportion overseas. Competition in the industry is keen but is generally centered on performance (racing) results rather than price. Marine Supply's principal advantages are:

1. A highly efficient sales-distribution-repair network (currently about 8,000 dealers) in North America.
2. Exceptional brand loyalty.
3. Almost total domination of the lower horsepower ranges where the vast majority of engines are still sold.

Marine Supply's position in golf carts is also dominant, but its degree of domination is less pronounced. While an important factor in snow vehicles, lawn care, and chain saws, these are highly fragmented markets with many competitors. Still, the company's marketing strategy is the same as in outboards: build a quality product with a strong dealer organization, use intensive advertising, and maintain a premium price structure. This approach has been successful in lawn mowers where Lawn King is a strong competitor despite tremendous product similarity among all brands. In snow vehicles—a comparatively new product to which Marine Supply was a comparative late comer— the company has not yet been totally successful in building its market share.

Financial statements

The financial statements of Marine Supply Corporation are presented in Exhibits 23–2, 23–3, and 23–4 below.

The auditor's opinion on the financial statements has been unqualified for the past six years.

Additional information

Marine Supply has a good, if very cyclical, historic operating performance record. In 19w4, for example, sales were only $73 million as against $304.5

Exhibit 23–2

MARINE SUPPLY CORPORATION
Balance Sheets
As of September 30 for Years 19x5–19y0
(in millions)

	19x5	19x6	19x7	19x8	19x9	19y0
Assets						
Current assets:						
Cash and equivalents	$ 15.00	$ 24.30	$ 12.10	$ 17.40	$ 19.50	$ 17.48
Receivables	22.50	24.50	31.40	35.40	46.50	53.70
Inventories	49.50	57.60	64.70	78.90	100.80	97.32
Other current assets	—	.00	.00	.10	.00	.00
Total current assets	87.00	106.40	108.20	131.80	166.80	168.50
Gross plant	85.20	88.60	98.70	114.70	129.70	137.90
Accumulated depreciation	(45.20)	(48.70)	(52.50)	(56.10)	(60.80)	(65.88)
Net plant	40.00	39.90	46.20	58.60	68.90	72.02
Intangibles and other assets	7.00	6.40	10.70	11.90	12.70	15.45
Total assets	$134.00	$152.70	$165.10	$202.30	$248.40	$255.97
Liabilities and Capital						
Current liabilities:						
Accounts payable	$ 1.10	$ 1.10	$ 7.00	$ 15.20	$ 24.60	$ 24.53
Other current liabilities	15.80	24.90	23.50	26.90	35.00	36.75
Total current liabilities	16.90	26.00	30.50	42.10	59.60	61.28
Long-term debt	14.50	13.50	12.40	28.70	45.70	46.04
Deferred taxes and investment credits	1.94	2.19	2.57	4.58	5.38	7.14
Other liabilities	2.39	2.57	2.03	1.52	2.57	1.05
Total liabilities	35.73	44.26	47.50	76.90	113.25	115.51
Net worth	98.27	108.44	117.60	125.40	135.15	140.46
Total liabilities and capital	$134.00	$152.70	$165.10	$202.30	$248.40	$255.97

Exhibit 23–3

MARINE SUPPLY CORPORATION
Income Statements
For Years Ending September 30
(in millions)

	19x5	19x6	19x7	19x8	19x9	19y0
Net sales	$180.70	$212.50	$233.40	$280.20	$327.10	$304.48
Other income	—	—	—	—	—	.19
Total revenue	180.70	212.50	233.40	280.20	327.10	304.67
Cost of goods sold*						
(excluding depreciation)	113.35	130.95	145.03	180.16	209.52	190.58
Depreciation	4.28	4.26	4.40	4.75	5.59	6.25
Gross profit	63.07	77.29	83.97	95.29	111.99	107.84
Selling, general, and adminis-						
trative expense........	41.98	47.04	54.04	61.99	71.44	72.99
Operating income	21.09	30.25	29.93	33.30	40.55	34.85
Interest expense..........	.70	1.05	1.23	2.10	4.73	6.60
Other expenses	.62	.54	.62	1.05	1.54	—
Income before tax	19.77	28.66	28.08	30.15	34.28	28.25
Income taxes:						
Deferred..............	.47	.26	.38	.37	.80	1.75
Current	8.66	12.73	12.47	14.12	16.40	13.11
Net income	10.64	15.67	15.23	15.66	17.08	13.39
Common dividends.......	5.13	6.35	6.37	7.98	8.06	8.08
Retained earnings	$ 5.51	$ 9.32	$ 8.86	$ 7.68	$ 9.02	$ 5.31
* Includes:						
R&D costs	11.8	11.2	13.4	12.1	12.4	12.8
Maintenance and repairs .	10.3	10.4	11.6	12.4	12.7	11.5

million in 19y0, more than 300 percent increase. Over the same span net income grew from $5.5 million to $13.4 million, an increase of 144 percent. The slower gain in net income, reflecting sharply reduced operating margins due largely to Federal Trade Commission action in the mid 19w0s, has meant erosion of the company's ROI from an exceptional 25 percent (on net worth) in the 19w4–w6 period to just over 11 percent for the last three years.

Exhibit 23–5, 15-year growth rates—annually compounded, compares various growth rates, first using single years, then a 3-year span.

Note that with the exception of sales per share, the growth rates are still higher for the single-year comparisons. This is attributable to the very low 19w4 base and the tremendous gains from 19w4 through 19w6—a three-year span in which sales, net income, dividends, and book value each increased from 75 percent to 133 percent.

Exhibit 23–6, five-year growth rates—annually compounded indicates the most recent five-year performance, first on a single-year basis, then using three-year "smoothed" base. On either basis, the company's record looks better in recent years than over the long pull.

Exhibit 23–4

MARINE SUPPLY CORPORATION
Statement of Changes in Financial Position
For Years Ending September 30
(in thousands)

	19x5	19x6	19x7	19x8	19x9	19y0	Total Percent	Total Amount
Sources:								
From operations:								
Net earnings	$10,642	$15,666	$15,375	$15,662	$17,078	$13,390	46.5	$ 87,813
Depreciation	4,284	4,264	4,448	4,747	5,587	6,254	15.7	29,584
Amortization of tooling	—	3,360	2,755	4,595	6,484	6,637	12.6	23,831
Other—principally provision for deferred income taxes	755	527	493	372	800	1,753	2.5	4,700
Total from operations	15,681	23,817	23,071	25,376	29,949	28,034	77.3	145,928
Proceeds from sale of:								
Long-term borrowings	—	—	—	17,030	18,202	1,391	19.4	36,623
Plant and equipment (net)	174	662	326	146	347	112	.9	1,767
Common stock	52	859	294	317	732	—	1.2	2,254
Other items, net	—	—	45	1,808	413	—	1.2	2,266
	15,907	25,338	23,736	44,677	49,643	29,537	100.0	188,838
Applications:								
Additions to plant and equipment	2,964	4,739	11,177	16,639	16,109	9,461	32.3	61,089
Tooling expenditures	—	2,565	7,635	6,430	6,825	7,398	16.3	30,853
Long-term debt maturing currently	1,136	1,073	1,126	1,035	1,142	1,073	3.6	6,585
Dividends paid	5,128	6,351	6,369	7,981	8,060	8,080	22.2	41,969
Other items, net	408	355	—	1,199	—	3,526	2.9	5,488
Total applications	9,636	15,083	26,307	33,284	32,136	29,538	77.3	145,984
Working capital increase (decrease)	$ 6,271	$10,255	$(2,571)	$11,393	17,507	$ (1)	22.7	$ 42,854

Exhibit 23–5

MARINE SUPPLY CORPORATION
Fifteen-Year Growth Rates
(annually compounded)

Per share	19w4–y0	19w4–w6 to 19x8–y0
Sales	8.0%	8.0%
Net income	4.6	3.3
Dividends	10.0	7.4
Book value	11.0	7.4

Exhibit 23–6

MARINE SUPPLY CORPORATION
Five-Year Growth Rates
(annually compounded)

Per share	19x5–y0	19x5–x7 to 19x8–y0
Sales	10.5%	7.4%
Net income	4.2	1.9
Dividends	9.0	6.0
Book value	7.0	6.9

Two noteworthy points should be made about this record:

1. The gains represent almost solely internal growth. Acquisitions have been few, their relative size quite small, and their profit contributions have often been negative.
2. No adjustments need be made for dilution. The company has no convertible securities outstanding; stock options are also insignificant.

Exhibits 23–7 through 23–10 are based on the financial statements of Marine Supply Corporation.

While the economy in general was slow in 19y0, 19x8 and 19x9 were good years for boat sales; and responses at boat shows across the country were strong in those years. Compared to automobiles, revolutionary model changes are rare in the boating industry.

The company's contract with the union expired at the end of 19y0, and the company was not sure during 19y0 whether it could avoid a strike.

After careful analysis, we conclude that about one half of deferred taxes and investment credits account balances will be reversed in the future; however, the possibility of reversal in the foreseeable future for the remaining one half is very remote. "Other liabilities" represent various debts having the characteristic of long-term debt. "Other current liabilities" represent amounts owing to various banks under revolving credit agreement.

The company is nearing its production capacity limits, necessitating new

Exhibit 23–7

MARINE SUPPLY CORPORATION
Common-Size Balance Sheets

	19x5	19x6	19x7	19x8	19x9	19y0
Assets						
Cash assets:						
Cash and equivalents	11%	16%	7%	9%	8%	7%
Receivables	17	16	19	17	18	21
Inventories	37	38	39	39	41	38
Total current assets	65	70	65	65	67	66
Land, plant, and equipment, net	30	26	28	29	28	28
Intangibles and other assets	5	4	7	6	5	6
Total assets	100%	100%	100%	100%	100%	100%
Liabilities and Equity						
Current liabilities	13%	17%	18%	21%	24%	24%
Long-term debt	11	9	8	14	18	18
Deferred taxes and investment credits	1	1	2	2	2	3
Other liabilities	2	2	1	1	1	—
Total liabilities	27	29	29	38	45	45
Net worth	73	71	71	62	55	55
Total liabilities and equity	100%	100%	100%	100%	100%	100%

Exhibit 23–8

MARINE SUPPLY CORPORATION
Common-Size Income Statements

Item	19x5	19x6	19x7	19x8	19x9	19y0	Industry composite 19y0
Net sales	100.0%	100.0%	100.0%	100%	100.0	100.0%	100.0%
Cost of goods sold* (excluding depreciation)	62.7	61.6	62.1	64.3	64.1	62.6	64.6
Depreciation	2.4	2.0	1.9	1.7	1.7	2.0	2.8
Gross profit	34.9	36.4	36.0	34.0	34.2	35.4	32.6
Selling, general, and administrative expenses	23.2	22.2	23.2	22.1	21.8	24.0	21.0
Operating income	11.7	14.2	12.8	11.9	12.4	11.4	11.6
Interest expense	.4	.5	.5	.8	1.4	2.2	0.8
Other interest (expense)	(.3)	(.2)	(.3)	(.4)	(.5)	.1	0.2
Net income before tax	11.0	13.5	12.0	10.7	10.5	9.3	11.0
Deferred taxes	.3	.1	.2	.1	.3	.6	.3
Income taxes	4.8	6.0	5.3	5.0	5.0	4.3	4.9
Net income	5.9	7.4	6.5	5.6	5.2	4.4	5.8
*Including:							
R&D costs	6.5	5.2	5.7	4.3	3.8	4.2	5.4
Maintenance and repairs	5.7	4.9	5.0	4.4	3.9	3.9	6.2

Exhibit 23–9

MARINE SUPPLY CORPORATION
Trend Index of Selected Accounts
(19x5 = 100)

Account	19x6	19x7	19x8	19x9	19y0
Cash	162	81	116	130	117
Accounts receivable	109	140	157	207	239
Inventory	116	131	159	204	197
Total current assets	122	124	151	192	194
Total current liabilities	154	180	249	353	363
Working capital	115	111	128	153	153
Fixed assets	100	116	147	172	180
Other assets	94	157	175	187	227
Long-term debt	93	86	198	315	318
Total liabilities	124	133	215	317	323
Equity capital	110	120	128	138	143
Net sales	118	129	155	181	169
Cost of goods sold	116	128	159	185	168
Gross profit	123	133	151	178	171
Selling, general, and administrative expenses	112	132	148	170	174
Interest expense	150	176	300	676	945
Total expenses	114	128	155	182	172
Operating income	143	142	158	192	165
Profit before taxes	145	142	153	173	143
Net income	147	143	147	161	126

Exhibit 23–10

MARINE SUPPLY CORPORATION
Selected per Share Results

Item	19x5	19x6	19x7	19x8	19x9	19y0
Sales	$22.90	$26.71	$29.28	$34.85	$40.48	$37.68
Net income	1.35	1.97	1.91	1.95	2.11	1.66
Dividends	.65	.80	.80	1.00	1.00	1.00
Book value	12.43	13.63	14.76	15.60	16.73	17.38

construction. For example, in 19x8 and 19x9, the company was forced to utilize some aging facilities on a multishift basis.

The period 19x5–y0 has been by far the most prosperous in Marine Supply's history. Sales and earnings have each reached peak levels, although the last six years have not been as profitable as mid 19w0s.

Based on the foregoing data and information, we are to analyze the financial statements of Marine Supply Corporation with the following alternative points of view (objectives) in mind:

1. That of a bank to extend to the company a short-term loan of $15 million.

2. That of an insurance company to whom the company wants to sell privately $30 million of 25-year bonds.
3. That of an investor considering a substantial investment in the company.

These diverse and broad points of view require that we analyze all major aspects of the company's financial condition and results of operations, that is:

1. Short-term liquidity.
2. Funds flow.
3. Capital structure and long-term solvency.
4. Return on investment (ROI).
5. Asset utilization.
6. Operating performance.

The following assumptions will be used in the projection of operating results and of fund flows for 19y1:

It is expected that the annual growth rate by product line will continue except that snow vehicles and miscellaneous are expected to grow at a rate of 29 percent and 30 percent, respectively. Improvements in production facilities will lower the cost of goods (exclusive of depreciation) to 60 percent of sales. The composite depreciation rate (depreciation expense as a percent of ending net plant) is expected to be 10 percent. Amortization of tooling costs included in cost of goods sold will be 10 percent higher than in 19y0. Selling expenses, which amount to one fourth of the selling, general, and administrative group of expenses, are expected to go up by 10 percent in 19y1. The other three fourths of this category will remain unchanged. Taxes will average 53 percent of income before taxes, and the amount of deferred taxes will amount to the same proportion of the total tax accrual as in 19y0. Dividend payout is expected to amount to 50 percent of net income.

In order to retire $15 million in revolving credit notes (shown under current liabilities) and to finance a major plant expansion and modernization program just starting, the company expects to sell at par, early in 19y1, $30 million in 30-year, 7 percent sinking fund bonds. That will leave $20 million in revolving credit notes outstanding. Interest expenses in 19y1 are estimated at $5,810,000. The maturities and sinking fund requirements of long-term debt are as follows:

	(In millions)
19y1	$ 1.0
19y2	2.3
19y3	4.4
19y4	8.6
19y5	12.2

R&D outlays are expected to amount to $3 million in 19y1, and outlays for tooling are planned at $13 million.

The company plans to spend $30 million in 19y1 on plant and equipment. Sales of equipment are expected to bring in $200,000 after tax. The chainsaw division which has a book value of $5 million is expected to be disposed of for $2 million, net of tax.

The problem of obtaining a meaningful and valid standard of external comparison for this analysis has been a difficult one. Two major sources of such data are industry statistics, such as those compiled by Robert Morris Associates, Standard & Poor's, or Dun & Bradstreet, or comparative data derived from companies of similar size and in similar lines of business. In this case, comparative data was developed from the published reports of companies in lines of business similar to those of Marine Supply Company.

Analysis of short-term liquidity

Exhibit 23–11 presents some important liquidity measures of Marine Supply Corporation over the last six years. Both the current ratio and the acid-test ratio have been declining over this period. However, they are still at sound levels in 19y0 on an absolute basis and also when compared to industry averages. The downward trend in these measures must be interpreted in the light of management's possible policy and intent. It is quite conceivable, particularly in view of the lower levels of the comparable industry ratios, that the current position in earlier years was unnecessarily strong and represented a wasteful tying up of resources that did not earn an acceptable return for the company. A glance at the common-size analysis in Exhibit 23–7 reveals the changes that have occurred in the composition of working capital elements over the past six years; the proportion of cash and cash equivalents among the current assets has dropped by almost half even though the absolute amount of cash and equivalents has not diminished on average. There has been a significant increase in current liabilities; they now represent almost a quarter of the funds invested in the enterprise, whereas in 19x5 they represented 13 percent of the total. This is confirmed in the trend index analysis (Exhibit 23–9) that shows that since 19x5 current liabilities have increased 3.63 times while cash increased 1.17 times, receivables 2.39 times, and inventories only 1.97 times. That the increase in current liabilities was out of proportion to that of sales is seen by the fact that during the same period sales increased only 1.69 times. That means that Marine Supply Corporation was somehow able to secure short-term credit from suppliers and banks at a rate twice as fast as that warranted by growth in sales. This, in turn, is importantly responsible for the steady decline in the current and the acid-test ratios.

A more serious problem area is the quality of the two important elements of current assets: accounts receivable and inventories. The accounts receivable turnover has undergone constant decline over the past six years, reaching a low point of 5.67 in 19y0. In that year, it compared unfavorably as to 8.2 turnover in the industry. The alternative measure of "days' sales in accounts receivable" presents a similar picture with an increasing number of "days'

Exhibit 23–11

MARINE SUPPLY CORPORATION
Short-Term Liquidity Analysis

Units		19x5	19x6	19x7	19x8	19x9	19y0	Industry composite 19y0
Ratio	Current ratio	5.15	4.09	3.55	3.13	2.80	2.75	2.40
Ratio	Acid-test ratio	2.22	1.88	1.43	1.26	1.11	1.16	.90
Times	Accounts receivable turnover	8.03	8.67	7.43	7.92	7.03	5.67	8.20
Times	Inventory turnover	2.29	2.27	2.24	2.28	2.08	1.96	2.30
Days	Days sales in receivables	44.80	41.50	48.50	45.5	51.20	63.50	43.90
Days	Days to sell inventory	157.20	158.60	160.70	157.9	173.10	183.70	156.50
Days	Conversion period	202.00	200.10	209.20	203.4	224.30	247.20	200.40
%	Cash to current assets	17.24	22.84	11.18	13.20	11.69	10.37	9.80
%	Cash to current liabilities	88.76	93.46	39.67	41.33	32.72	28.52	29.60
$(MM)	Working capital	70.10	80.40	77.70	89.70	107.20	107.22	—
#	Liquidity index	127	118	139	134	150	163	—

sales" tied up in receivables. The 19y0 figure of 63.5 days compares to an industry experience of 44.0 days. It also compares unfavorably to the company's most common terms of sales of net 30 days. Thus, it is possible that the collectibility and the liquidity of accounts receivable have deteriorated.

Inventory turnover has also decreased over the past six years, although the deterioration has not been as marked as has been the case with receivables. A number of factors could account for this, including a larger number and variety of outboard motors, lawn mowers, and snow vehicles models that must be stocked, the larger variety of spare parts that these require, as well as a possible accumulation of raw materials in anticipation of a strike at suppliers. It is also possible that Marine Supply Corporation overestimated sales for 19y0, while sales dropped 7 percent from the 19x9 level, inventories dropped by only 3 percent, thus contributing to the turnover slowdown. The 19y0 turnover of Marine Supply Corporation of 1.96 compares unfavorably with the 2.3 industry average. In 19y0, it took 183.7 days to sell the average inventory compared to an industry average of 156.2 days. The comparable figure for the company in 19x5 was 157.2 days.

The deterioration in the liquidity of the principal operating assets of the current asset group, accounts receivable, and inventories is also seen in the period of days it takes to convert inventories into cash. It grew from 202 days in 19x5 to 247.2 days in 19y0 and compares to an industry average of only 200.2 days in the latter year.

The liquidity index at 163 in 19y0 up from 127 in 19x5 also corroborates the deterioration in the liquidity of the current assets that we have already determined in the analysis of individual components of working capital.

It is conceivable that further analysis and inquiry from management will reveal that the slowdown in the turnover of accounts receivable and inventories does not affect their ultimate realization even if that would take a longer time. In that case, the repercussions of such a slowdown lie in the area of liquidity and funds flow as well as in the area of asset utilization which will be examined later in this analysis.

Cash from operations

The amount of cash generated from operations is another important aspect of liquidity. Marine Supply generated cash from operations as follows (in millions):

	19x6	19x7	19x8	19x9	19y0	Total
Cash from operations	$22.8	$13.6	$18.8	$14.4	$26.0*	$95.6

* Cash from operations was computed, for example, for 19y0 as follows: working capital from operations (28.0) plus increase in current liabilities (1.7) plus decrease in inventories (3.5) less increase in accounts receivable (7.2). "Other current liabilities" are assumed to relate to operations.

While operations provided significant amounts of cash each year, it should be noted that the amounts of cash provided by operations were lower *each* year compared to the amounts of working capital provided by operations, the disparity being over $15 million in 19x9. Over the five-year span, cash from operations was lower than working capital from operations by about $35 million. The reasons for this disparity were significant increases in accounts receivable ($31.2 million) and inventories ($47.8 million) partially offset by increases in liabilities. A continuation of these trends suggests the need for a more permanent financing of working capital needs.

Analysis of funds flow

This analysis has two main objectives:

1. To supplement the static measures used to assess short-term liquidity by means of a short-term funds flow forecast.
2. To analyze the statement of changes in financial position (SCFP) in order to assess its implications on the longer-term flow of funds (i.e., long-term solvency).

Our first step will be to build a funds flow forecast for Marine Supply Corporation in 19y1. Since sources of funds from operations are an important element of funds and a projection of earnings will be necessary anyway, we start with such a projection for 19y1, using the data and the supplementary information provided (see Exhibit 23–12).

Having established the estimated net income for 19y1, we can now proceed, using the data and the additional information we now have, to construct an estimated statements of sources and uses of working capital (funds) for 19y1.

Exhibit 23–13 projects an increase in working capital of about $16 million. If this forecast proves reasonably accurate, the current ratio should improve to about 3:1. As is true of all forecasts, their reliability depends on the validity of the assumptions on which they are based.

The assumption that Marine Supply Corporation can sell $30 million in 7 percent sinking fund bonds appears reasonable in the light of the company's present capital structure. Its failure to do so would require either the abandonment or deferral of expansion and modernization plans or it will result in a deterioration of the current ratio to about 2.5.

The projected net income of $16.6 million for 19y1 appears reasonable because it is based on the assumption of a continuation of present sales trends and a reduction in the growth rate of two product line categories. However, it is more vulnerable on the expense side. The increase in the gross margin is predicated on increases in productivity that are envisaged but which are yet to be realized. Moreover, any program of expansion and modernization is subject to the risk of delays, misjudgments, and short falls that may delay, postpone, or completely undermine the realization of improvements and economies. On the other hand, the increases in fixed costs that such a program entails are a reality with which the enterprise must live for a long time.

Any degree of failure to realize savings and improvements will also affect the short-term flow of funds. Thus, for example, continuing the assumption

Exhibit 23–12

MARINE SUPPLY CORPORATION
Projected Income Statement for 19y1
(in millions)

	19y0 sales level	Incre-ment factor	19y1 esti-mated amount	Total	Percent
Net sales:					
Marine products	$217.3 ×	1.10	$239.03		
Lawn care equipment	30.5 ×	1.13	34.47		
Vehicles	19.6 ×	1.07	20.97		
Snow vehicles	23.4 ×	1.29	30.19		
Miscellaneous	4.2 ×	1.30	5.46	$330.12	100.0
Cost of goods sold (exclusive of depreciation)			198.07		60.0
Depreciation [a]			8.70		2.6
				206.77	62.6
Gross profit				123.35	37.4
Selling, general, and administrative expenses:					
General and administrative [b] . . .			54.74		
Selling [c]			20.08		
Amortization of deferred start-up costs			1.00	75.82	23.0
				47.53	14.4
Interest expenses				5.81	1.8
Income before taxes				41.72	12.6
Income taxes:					
Current			19.24		
Deferred [d]			2.88	22.12	6.7
				19.60	5.9
Loss on disposal of chain-saw division (net of tax)				3.00	.9
Net income				$ 16.60	5.0

[a] Beginning net plant plus half of 19y1 additions times 10 percent: (72.2 + 15.0) × 10%. It is assumed that the plant additions were in use, on average, half of the year.
[b] Three fourths of 72.99 (last year selling, general, and administrative).
[c] Selling expenses at 10 percent above the 19y0 level (72.99 − 54.74) × 1.10.
[d] Deferred taxes at 13 percent of the total provision for the year which amounts to 53 percent of pretax income.

Exhibit 23–13

MARINE SUPPLY CORPORATION
Projected Statement of Sources and Uses of Funds for 19y1
(in millions)

Sources of funds:

From operations:

Net income	$16.60	
Add: Items not requiring current funds:		
Depreciation	8.70	
Amortization of tooling costs	7.30	
Deferred income taxes	2.88	
Amortization of start-up costs.................	1.00	
Loss on sale of chain-saw division	3.00	
Total from operations.........................		$39.48
Proceeds from sale of 7% sinking fund bonds		30.00
Sale of chain-saw division		2.00
Sale of equipment		0.20
Total sources		71.68

Uses of funds:

Additions to plant and equipment	30.00	
Outlays for tooling	13.00	
Outlays for R&D	3.00	
Long-term debt maturities	1.00	
Dividends declared	8.30	
Total uses		55.30
Increase in working capital		$16.38

that 50 percent of the net income will be distributed as dividends, a 5 percent increase in cost of goods sold (exclusive of depreciation) will lower the inflow of funds as follows:

	In millions (approximately)
Increase in cost of goods sold (exclusive of depreciation)—5% of $198 million	$9.90
Less: Tax effect at 53%	5.25
	4.65
Less: Dividend reduction (50%)........................	2.32
	2.33
Less: Deferred taxes (13% of 5.25)	.68
Reduction in funds available from operations	$1.65

A similar computation can, of course, be made for any other change in assumptions. The likelihood of any of the above assumptions materializing and the probability attached to them is, ultimately, a matter of judgment.

The longer-range funds flow picture is subject to a great many uncertainties. Examination of the company's historical pattern of fund flows over the 19x5 to 19y0 period (see Exhibit 23–4) is revealing. Funds from operations provided 77 percent of all funds inflows while long-term borrowing provided most of the rest. Such borrowing occurred mostly in 19x8 and 19x9. Equity financing was negligible.

Additions to plant and equipment used about 32 percent of all funds available. These outlays were, however, twice as high as the provision for depreciation. With the company bumping against the ceiling of its practical capacity in many lines, this trend is likely to continue. Already in 19y1, capital expenditures are planned at three times the 19y0 level and long-term debt will be incurred to finance this as well as the working capital needs of an expanding business. As will be discussed further under "capital structure," there is, of course, a limit to the company's debt capacity, and equity financing will be required. This may explain the company's relatively generous dividend policy over the recent years.

In spite of relatively heavy long-term borrowing in 19x8 and 19x9, long-term debt maturities and sinking fund requirements are low. These will, however, increase sharply from $1 million in 19y1 to $12 million in 19y5. The proposed $30 million bond issue in 19y1 will undoubtedly add to these maturities.

The longer-term fund flow outlook of Marine Supply Corporation is one of increasing demand for funds due to accelerating outlays for plant equipment and tooling as well as sharply rising debt service outlays. While funds from operations have been significant and are growing, they will have to continue to do so to meet increasing demands. Since funds from operations represented 77 percent of all sources of funds in the past six years, the company's fund flow is particularly vulnerable to any reduction in net income. Working capital needs will also increase along with the expected increase in sales volume.

It should be borne in mind that focusing on *net* working capital does not tell the whole story of Marine Supply Corporation's borrowing. Included in current liabilities are $35 million in revolving credit notes. The company may well want to convert this short-term interest sensitive debt into a longer-term type of obligation. A beginning towards this goal is expected to be made in 19y1. That too will require using up some of the company's shrinking capacity to finance by means of long-term debt.

Analysis of capital structure and long-term solvency

Having just examined the funds aspect of Marine Supply Corporation's long-term solvency, we now turn to an examination of its capital structure and the risk inherent in it. The change in the company's capital structure can be gauged by means of a number of measurements and comparisons.

Looking at Exhibit 23–7, we see that the contribution of equity capital to the total funds invested in the enterprise has shrunk from 73 percent in 19x5 to 55 percent in 19y0. With the expected issuance of $30 million of additional bonds, this proportion can be expected to dip below 50 percent. The long-term debt portion of the total funds invested in the enterprise increased from 11 percent in 19x5 to 18 percent in 19y0 and is headed considerably higher in 19y1.

In Exhibit 23–9, we can see the relative change in debt, equity, and other related elements in the financial statements. On a basis of 19x5 = 100, long-term debt rose to 318 while equity capital increased only to 143. In the same period, net sales rose only to 169, net income to 126, while interest costs soared to 945. Quite clearly the company decided to finance its needs by means of debt, both short and long term. Reasons for this could be an unwillingness to dilute the equity or a desire to incur monetary liabilities in times of inflation. Whatever the reason, the leverage and hence the risk in the capital structure increased substantially. This is particularly true because Marine Supply Corporation is in a relatively cyclical industry and relies on a share of the consumer's discretionary dollar.

The capital structure and long-term solvency ratios in Exhibit 23–14 bear

Exhibit 23–14

MARINE SUPPLY CORPORATION

Capital Structure and Long-Term Solvency Ratios

	19x5	19x6	19x7	19x8	19x9	19y0	19y0 industry composite
Equity to total	99.24*	109.54	118.89	127.69	137.84	144.03	
debt	34.76	43.16	46.21	74.61	110.56	111.94	
	= 2.86	= 2.54	= 2.57	= 1.71	= 1.25	= 1.29	1.4
Equity to long-	99.24	109.54	118.89	127.69	137.84	144.03	
term debt	17.86*	17.16	15.71	32.51	50.96	50.66	
	= 5.56	= 6.38	= 7.57	= 3.93	= 2.70	= 2.84	3.1
Total debt to total capital ...	.259	.283	.280	.369	.445	.437	N.A.
Equity to net fixed assets	2.48	2.75	2.57	2.18	2.00	2.00	2.2
Ratio of earnings to fixed charges	29.24	28.30	23.83	15.36	8.25	5.28	8.6

Computed as following:

One half of deferred income taxes	.97
Net worth shown	98.27
Adjusted net worth	99.24
Total liabilities shown	35.73
Less: One half of deferred income taxes	.97
Adjusted total liabilities	34.76
Less: Total current liabilities	16.90
Adjusted long-term debt	17.86

out these conclusions. Equity to total debt stands at 1.29 in 19y0 compared to 2.86 in 19x5, and compares to an industry composite of 1.4. Similarly, equity to long-term debt stands at 2.84 in 19y0 compared to an industry composite of 3.1. Debt as a percentage of total capital has been increasing steadily from about 26 percent in 19x5 to almost 44 percent in 19y0—a significant increase in leverage.

The trend in the ratio of earnings to fixed charges bears out the deterioration in the margin of safety for creditors. This ratio plummeted from 29.24 in 19x5 to 5.28 in 19y0 and compares with an industry composite of 8.6. The income projections as well as the borrowing plans for 19y1 would result in an improved earnings to fixed charges ratio of 8.2 as a consequence of the refinancing of high-interest short-term debt and also because the 7 percent bonds will be outstanding for only part of the year. This improvement in the ratio may, however, prove to be only temporary in nature given the longer-term trend we observe here.

As we saw from the longer-term funds flow analysis, the company is now entering a period of increasing capital investment needs and of increasingly heavy debt service schedules. It does this at a time when its debt is high in relation to its equity capital and when shrinking ratios of earnings to fixed charges exert downward pressure on its credit rating. Moreover, the increasing fixed charges that stem from recent substantial additions to plant and equipment make operating results more vulnerable to cyclical downturn with the result that sources of funds from operations are similarly vulnerable.

Analysis of return on investment

The return that the company realizes on total assets, Exhibit 23–15, has been on the decline in recent years, having declined from 10.6 percent in 19x6 (which was the best year in this respect) to 6.4 percent in 19y0. Even if we regard 19x6 as an unusually good year, the decline from the prior year return levels is quite significant. In comparison with an industry return on total assets in 19y0 of 9.3 percent, the company's 6.4 percent return is also significantly worse. This negative trend over the past six years is reason for concern and requires further investigation. The two major elements which make up the return on total assets, that is, net profit margin and asset turnover, will be examined later in this analysis.

In comparison with the return on total assets, the decline in the return on equity has not been quite as significant. This is mainly due to the relatively advantageous use of short-term and long-term credit. The financial leverage index (Exhibit 23–15) that in 19y0 stands at 1.33 is practically unchanged from its 19x5 level. It must be noted, however, that the company cannot expand its debt much more from the present level since over the past six years debt has expanded very significantly. Thus, in the immediate future an adequate return on equity will be dependent primarily on improvements

Exhibit 23–15

MARINE SUPPLY CORPORATION
Return on Investment Ratios

	19x5		19x6	19x7	19x8	19x9	19y0	19y0 industry composite
Return on total assets	8.2%	(1)	10.6%	9.6%	8.3%	7.8%	6.4%	9.3%
Return on equity capital	10.8%	(2)	14.5%	13.0%	12.5%	12.6%	9.5%	12.8%
Return on long-term liabilities and equity	9.4%	(3)	12.8%	11.8%	10.5%	10.3%	8.5%	10.6%
Financial leverage index	1.32	(4)	1.37	1.23	1.27	1.32	1.33	1.38
Equity growth rate .	5.6	(5)	8.6	7.5	6.1	6.7	3.88	—

Notes:

1. $\dfrac{\text{Net income} + \text{Interest expense} \times (1 - \text{Tax rate})}{\text{Total assets}} = \dfrac{10.64 + .7(1 - .46)}{134}$

2. $\dfrac{\text{Net income}}{\text{Net worth}} = \dfrac{10.64}{98.27}$

3. $\dfrac{\text{Net income} + \text{Interest expense} \times (1 - \text{Tax rate})}{\text{Long-term liabilities} + \text{Equity}} = \dfrac{11.018}{134.0 - 16.90}$

4. $\dfrac{\text{Return on equity capital}}{\text{Return on total assets}} = \dfrac{10.8}{8.2}$

5. $\dfrac{\text{Net income} - \text{Payout}}{\text{Common shareholders equity}} = \dfrac{\text{Amount retained}}{\text{Common shareholders' equity}} = \dfrac{5.51}{98.27}$

in profitability and in asset utilization. Because of the significant increase in debt in recent years, growth in leverage cannot be expected to benefit that return in the future to the extent it did in these past years. As can be seen from Exhibit 23–15, the equity growth rate from earnings retention has shrunk in 19y0 to 3.8 percent from over 6 percent in the two years before that and from 8.6 percent in 19x6. This is largely due to the maintenance of a generous dividend policy in the face of shrinking earnings. This shrinkage in the internal equity growth rate comes at a time when the company is increasingly in need of additional equity capital. Conceivably, however, a liberal dividend record can facilitate the future raising of equity capital.

Analysis of asset utilization

Exhibit 23–16 indicates that in most categories the asset utilization ratios have been declining over the past six years. The sales to total assets ratio is down to 1.2 in 19y0 from the 1.4 level in 19x8 and compares to an industry average 1.5 times. The impact of this change can be assessed as follows:

Exhibit 23–16

MARINE SUPPLY CORPORATION
Asset Utilization Ratios

	19x5	19x6	19x7	19x8	19x9	19y0	19y0 industry composite
Sales to cash and equivalents	12.0	8.7	19.3	16.1	16.8	17.4	9.1
Sales to receivables	8.0	8.7	7.4	7.9	7.0	5.7	10.6
Sales to inventories	3.7	3.7	3.6	3.6	3.2	3.1	4.1
Sales to working capital	2.6	2.6	3.0	3.1	3.1	2.8	4.0
Sales to fixed assets	4.5	5.3	5.1	4.8	4.7	4.2	6.4
Sales to other assets	25.8	33.2	21.8	23.4	25.8	19.7	22.3
Sales to total assets	1.3	1.4	1.4	1.4	1.3	1.2	1.5
Sales to short-term liabilities	10.7	8.2	7.7	6.7	5.5	5.0	—

Given the company's net income to sales ratio in 19y0 of 4.4 percent and a net of tax interest expense of about 1.1 percent (Exhibit 23–8) a total asset turnover of 1.4 (the 19x8 rate) would have yielded a return on total assets of 7.7 percent [(4.4 + 1.1) × 1.4] rather than the 6.4 percent return actually realized in 19y0. At a rate of turnover of 1.5 (industry average), the present profit rate would yield a ROI of about 8.2 percent [(4.4 + 1.1) × 1.5].

The asset categories where the turnover rate has dropped most sharply over the six years are "other assets" and "receivables." Only cash showed an increase in turnover (utilization). Judging by the fact that there were significant fixed asset additions in 19x8 and 19x9 (see Exhibit 23–9), the drop in the fixed asset turnover rate was moderate. It must be borne in mind that it takes time before fixed asset additions become sufficiently productive to generate an expected volume of sales. In addition, certain types of fixed asset outlays represent improvements in production facilities which lead to efficiencies and savings rather than to expansion of productive capacity. Such outlays, consequently, do not lead to greater sales but rather to savings in variable costs and result in improvements in profit margins. Exhibit 23–8 indicates that while profit margins are below the 19x6–x7 levels, they have been in an improving trend in the last three years. The drop over the six-year span in the turnover of the "other assets" group reflects growth in deferred charges, particularly tooling.

Analysis of operating performance

Exhibit 23–8 presents common-size income statements of the company for the six years, 19x5–y0.

The gross profit of Marine Supply Corporation has held within a relatively narrow range over the last six years. In 19y0, at 35.3 percent, the gross profit margin is higher than in the preceding two years but is below the levels reached in 19x6 and 19x7. It does compare favorably to the industry gross margin of 32.6 percent. However, the R&D costs as well as the repair and maintenance costs included in the cost of goods sold figure are lower, as a percentage of sales than the industry composite. This aspect of the quality of earnings will be further discussed below.

In 19y0, the percentage relationship between depreciation expense and sales was 2.1 percent up from 1.7 percent the year before. The disparity between this percentage and the industry composite of 2.8 percent is noteworthy because it may affect the quality of Marine Supply Corporation's earnings. It would appear that an inadequate amount of depreciation is recorded by Marine Supply Corporation. Before a definite judgment can be made, additional information would be required. The company is now approaching the limit of practical capacity in many of its product lines. Competitors may have more reserve capacity available and that may express itself in a relatively higher composite depreciation rate. It is also possible that Marine Supply Corporation's equipment is, on average, of an older vintage, and hence lower cost, than the equipment of its competitors. On the other hand, a lower composite depreciation rate than necessary is a factor that lowers the quality of the company's earnings.

We have two more measures available to judge the size of the yearly depreciation charge:

	19x5	19x6	19x7	19x8	19x9	19y0
Accumulated depreciation as a percentage of gross plant	53	55	53	49	47	48
Annual depreciation expense as a percentage of gross plant	5.0	4.8	4.4	4.2	4.3	4.5

The decline in the percentage of accumulated depreciation in relation to gross plant most likely reflects the substantial additions of new equipment in recent years. The decline of depreciation expense as a percentage of gross plant is, however, indicative of a less conservative depreciation policy in the more recent years.

Selling, general, and administrative expenses as a percentage of sales have, generally, been on the rise. In 19y0, they stood at 24 percent which compares to an industry composite figure of only 21 percent. Thus, by the time we reach operating income, the advantage that the company held over the industry because of larger gross margin has now been neutralized. Operating income for Marine Supply Corporation represents 11.4 percent of sales, and that compares with 11.6 percent for the industry. Further inquiries should be made to determine whether the selling expense component or the general and administrative part are responsible for the increase in this category.

Interest expenses have shown by far the steepest increase over the past six years. On the basis of 19x5 = 100, they have grown to 945 (almost tenfold) by 19y0 (Exhibit 23–9). This is due, of course, primarily to the sharp expansion of debt. Moreover, the short-term revolving debt is interest sensitive and thus introduces a measure of uncertainty in the forecasting of future interest charges.

Two other aspects of the quality of Marine Supply Corporation's earnings should be noted.

R&D costs as a percentage of sales have been in a declining trend having reached 4.2 percent in 19y0 down from 6.5 percent in 19x5 (Exhibit 23–3). This raises a question about the effect on future sales and profits of the decline in the R&D cost outlays in relation to sales. Similarly, the percentage of sales devoted to repairs and maintenance has declined from 5.7 percent in 19x5 to 3.8 percent in 19y0, a matter of concern particularly in the light of the fact that Marine Supply Corporation's facilities are, on average, older now than in 19x5. In the latter year, the percentage of repair and maintenance expense in relation to gross plant was 12.1 percent. In 19y0, that relationship dropped to 8.3 percent. This *prima facie* evidence of a deterioration in the quality of Marine Supply Corporation's earnings merits further investigation.

The total effective tax rate of Marine Supply Corporation in 19y0 is 52 percent which compares to the industry composite effective rate of 47 percent. The net income to sales of Marine Supply Corporation is 4.4 percent for 19y0, significantly below the industry composite of 5.8 percent for that year. However, since 19y0 was a year of labor trouble for the company, the percentages of net income to sales prevailing in the prior years, which are closer to the industry average, may be taken as more representative of the company's earning power.

Exhibit 23–17 analyzes the change occurring in net income between the 19x5–x7 period and the 19x8–y0 period. Sales increased by 46 percent, but due largely to greater increases in the cost of goods sold (49 percent) and interest expenses (353 percent) the increase in net income was held to only 11 percent.

Summary and conclusions

This analysis has examined all facets of Marine Supply Corporation's record of results of operations and financial position and has estimated the projected results and fund flows for one year. An analysis such as this is an indispensable step in arriving at a decision on the three questions posed. Nevertheless, essential as the data and information developed by this analysis

Exhibit 23-17

MARINE SUPPLY CORPORATION
Statement Accounting for Variations in Net Income
Three-Year Period 19x5–19x7 (average) Compared to
Three-Year Period 19x8–19y0 (average)
(in millions)

Items tending to increase net income:			
Increase in net sales:			
Net sales, 19x8–y0	$303.93		
Net sales, 19x5–x7	208.87	$95.06	46%
Deduct increase in cost of goods sold:			
Cost of goods sold, 19x8–y0	193.42		
Cost of goods sold, 19x5–x7	129.78	63.64	49
Net increase in gross margin		$31.42	
Items tending to decrease in net income:			
Increase in depreciation:			
Depreciation, 19x8–y0	5.53		
Depreciation, 19x5–x7	4.31	1.22	28
Increase in selling, general, and administrative expenses:			
SGA, 19x8–y0	68.81		
SGA, 19x5–x7	47.69	21.12	44
Increase in interest expense:			
Interest expense, 19x8–y0	4.48		
Interest expense, 19x5–x7	.99	3.49	353
Increase in other income and expense:			
Other income and expense, 19x8–y0	.80		
Other income and expense, 19x5–x7	.59	.21	36
Net increase in expenses		26.04	
Net increase in profit before taxes ..		5.38	21
Increase in income taxes:			
Income taxes, 19x8–y0	15.52		
Income taxes, 19x5–x7	11.66	3.86	33
Net increase in net income		1.52	11

is, it is not sufficient in most cases to arrive at a final conclusion. This is so because qualitative and other factors can have an important bearing on the final conclusion. Only when all the factors, those developed by the analysis as well as the others, have been assembled can a decision be reached by the application of judgment.

For example, the *bank* that is asked to extend short-term credit must take into consideration the character of the management, past loan experience, as well as the ongoing relationship with the loan applicant.

In addition to the foregoing intangibles, the long-term lender will focus on such matters as security arrangements and provisions that safeguard the solvency of the recipient of the loan.

The *equity investor* is, of course, interested in earning power and in earnings per share, but many considerations and judgments must be joined with these data before an investment decision is made. Thus, for instance, what earnings are, and what they are likely to be, is the product of financial analysis. At what price-earnings ratio they should be capitalized is a question for investment judgment. Similarly, the risk inherent in an enterprise, the volatility of its earnings, and the breadth and quality of the market for its securities are factors which must also be considered. They determine whether an investment fits into the investor's portfolio and whether it is compatible with his investment objectives.

Since the ultimate conclusions regarding problems, such as the lending and investing decision that we consider in this case, is based on more than the data and facts brought out by financial analysis alone, it follows that the most useful way to present the results of financial analysis is to summarize them by listing the most relevant and salient points which were developed by the analysis and which the decision maker should consider. This we shall do in this case.

The following are the main points that have been developed by our analysis of Marine Supply Corporation.

Short-term liquidity. The current ratio is in a downtrend but still stands at a relatively sound level. The downtrend may, in part, represent a correction of former excessive levels in the ratio.

The current assets are, as a whole, less liquid than in former years. The slower turnover in accounts receivable indicates a possible deterioration in collectibility. The decline in inventory turnover may be due to diversity of product line rather than to unsalable or obsolete items in stock.

Current liabilities have risen sharply in recent years, and they now represent one fourth of all funds available to the enterprise.

The decline in liquidity is evidenced by a rise in the liquidity index.

Fund projections for 19y1 indicate a projected increase in working capital of $16 million by the end of that year. This assumes, however, the successful sale of $30 million in bonds and that expense projections which incorporate benefits of efficiencies will be realized. There is a moderate amount of risk that these projections may not be realized.

Capital structure and long-term solvency. In 19y0, equity capital represented 55 percent of total funds invested in the enterprise down from 73 percent in 19x5. In recent years (see Exhibit 23–9), long-term debt increased drastically (3.18 times), out of proportion to such measures as growth in sales (1.69 times) or in equity (1.43 times).

The reduction of equity capital relative to debt and all funds invested in the company is not a favorable development in view of the fact that Marine Supply Corporation is in a cyclical industry. The company may be nearing the limit of its debt capacity.

The ratio of earnings to fixed charges is down to 5.28 in 19y0 (from 29.24 to 19x5). If a portion of rentals would be included as fixed charges, the coverage ratio would drop lower still. Next year, assuming the $30 million in long-term bonds are sold, this ratio is slated to improve to 8.2 times.

Over the last six years 77 percent of all funds inflows were funds generated by operations. Thus, a very substantial source of funds is vulnerable to changes in operating results. Over the longer term, demand for funds is expected to increase significantly. Long-term debt maturities are slated to increase sharply even excluding those from the $30 million bond issue that is expected to be sold in 19y1. There will be a growing need of funds for plant and equipment. Provisions for depreciation were consistently below fixed-asset additions in recent years.

Return on investment and asset utilization.   The ROI is in a declining trend. In 19y0, the return on total assets was 6.4 percent compared with an industry composite of 9.3 percent. The return on equity capital was 9.5 percent in 19y0, making the disparity with the industry composite of 12.8 percent somewhat less marked.

The decline in return on total assets is due to the twin effects of declining asset utilization rates as well as a decline in profitability per dollar of sales. The effect of increasing leverage has slowed the decline of return on equity in comparison with the return on total assets.

Operating performance.   The company's gross profit percentage has held relatively steady over the past six years. Other costs have neutralized Marine Supply Corporation's higher gross margin compared to the industry. Interest expenses have risen sharply over recent years. Both R&D expenses and repair and maintenance outlays have declined as a percentage of sales in recent years.

The significant decline in net income as a percentage of sales to 4.4 percent in 19y0 (industry composite 5.8 percent) is due to the particularly adverse labor and economic conditions of that year. In prior years, the company's net as a percentage of sales compared more favorably to industry experience.

Projected income for 19y1, based on the assumptions stated in the analysis, is $16.6 million after a loss of $3 million on disposal of the chain-saw division. On a per share basis, the net income per share is expected to be $2.06 per share compared to earnings per share in 19y0 of $1.66 and in 19x9 of $2.11. In 19y0, income per share before the loss on the chain-saw division is projected at $2.43.

USES OF FINANCIAL STATEMENT ANALYSIS

The foregoing analysis of the financial statements of Marine Supply Corporation consists of two major parts: (1) the detailed analysis and (2) the summary and conclusions. As was mentioned earlier, in a formal analytical report the summary and conclusions section may precede the detailed analysis so that the reader is presented with material in the order of its importance to him.

The *bank* loan officer who has to decide on the short-term loan application by the company will normally give primary attention to short-term liquidity analysis and to the funds flow projection and secondarily to capital structure and operating results.

The investment committee of the *insurance company* may, in taking a longer-term point of view, pay attention first to capital structure and long-term solvency and then to operating performance, ROI, asset utilization, and short-term liquidity, and in that order of emphasis.

The *potential investor* in Marine Supply Corporation's shares will, of course, be interested in all the aspects of our analysis. His emphasis may, however, be different again and take the following order of priority: results of operations, ROI, capital structure, and long-term solvency and short-term liquidity.

An adequate financial statement analysis will, as the Marine Supply Corporation analysis illustrates, contain in addition to the analysis of the data, enough information and detail so as to allow the decision maker to follow the rationale behind the analyst's conclusions as well as to allow him to expand it into areas not covered by the analysis.

QUESTIONS

1. What kind of processes should normally precede an analysis of financial statements?

2. What are the analytical implications of the fact that financial statements are, at best, an abstraction of underlying reality?

3. Name the six major "building blocks" of financial analysis. What does the "building block" approach involve?

4. What are some of the earmarks of a good analysis? Into what distinct sections should a well-organized analysis be divided?

5. What additional knowledge and analytical skills must an analyst bring to bear upon the analysis of enterprises in specialized or regulated industries?

Problems

Chapter 3

3–1. FASB member David Moso expressed the following view:

"Are we going to set accounting standards in the private sector or not? . . . Part of the answer depends on how the business community views accounting standards. Are they *rules of conduct,* designed to restrain unsocial behavior and arbitrate conflicts of economic interest? Or are they *rules of measurement,* designed to generalize and communicate as accurately as possible the complex results of economic events? . . . Rules of conduct call for a political process. . . . Rules of measurement, on the other hand, call for a research process of observation and experimentation. . . . Intellectually, the case is compelling for viewing accounting as a measurement process. . . . But the history of accounting standard setting has been dominated by the other view—that accounting standards are rules of conduct. The FASB was created out of the ashes of predecessors burned up in the fires of the resulting political process."

Required:
a. How do you view the difference between "rules of conduct" and "rules of measurement"?
b. In what way is the standard-setting process a political process? What would be arguments for and against considering it as such?

3–2. FASB member Robert T. Sprouse commented as follows on the nature of accounting information:

"We of the FASB are as concerned as anyone else about the formation of capital. I am convinced that preparers, users, and auditors share with us a common objective with respect to the improvement of financial reporting. The ability of a capitalistic system to allocate capital efficiently is necessarily dependent upon informed intelligent decision makers and readily available reliable information. I believe financial reporting that conceals relevant information, or that is designed to produce a desired result, or that is based on a paternalistic perception of users' incompetence would be antithetical and counterproductive."

Please note: Problems marked with an * are of a more advanced or more challenging nature.

Required:
a. To what quality of accounting information is Dr. Sprouse alluding?
b. Explain why this quality is so important.

3–3. Russell J. Morrison wrote in the *Financial Analysts Journal:*

"Strictly speaking, the objectives of financial reporting are the objectives of society and not of accountants and auditors, as such. Similarly, society has objectives for law and medicine—namely, justice and health for the people—which are not necessarily the objectives of lawyers and doctors, as such, in the conduct of their respective 'businesses.'

"In a variety of ways, society exerts pressure on a profession to act more nearly *as if* it actively shared the objectives of society. Society's pressure is to be measured by the degree of accommodation on the part of the profession under pressure, and by the degree of counter-pressure applied by the profession. For example, doctors accommodate society by getting better educations than otherwise and reducing incompetence in their ranks. They apply counter-pressure and gain protection by forming medical associations."

Required:
a. In what way has society brought pressure on accountants to serve it better?
b. How has the accounting profession responded to these pressures? Are there better responses?

3–4. "Despite its intrinsic intellectual appeal, complete uniform accounting seems unworkable in a complex industrial society that relies, at least in part, on economic market forces."

Required:
a. Discuss briefly at least three disadvantages of national or international accounting uniformity.
b. Does uniformity in accounting necessarily mean comparability? Explain.

(CFA)†

3–5. A professor of finance wrote:

"An accountant's job is to conceal, not to reveal. An accountant is not asked to give outsiders an accurate picture of what's going on in a company. He is asked to transform the figures on a company's operations in such a way that it will be impossible to recreate the original figures.

"An income statement for a toy company doesn't tell how many toys of various kinds the company sold, or who the company's best customers are. The balance sheet doesn't tell how many of each kind of toy the company has in inventory, or how much is owed by each customer who is late in paying his bills.

"In general, anything that a manager uses to do his job will be of interest to some stockholders, customers, creditors, or government agencies. Managerial accounting differs from financial accounting only because the accountant has to hide some

---

† Material from the Chartered Financial Analyst Examinations published by The Institute of Chartered Financial Analysts. Reprinted by permission.

of the facts and figures managers find useful. The accountant simply has to throw out most of the facts and some of the figures that the managers use when he creates the financial statements for outsiders."

The rules of accounting reflect this tension. Even if the accountant thought of himself as working only for the good of society, he would conceal certain facts in the reports he helps write. Since the accountant is actually working for the company, or even for the management of the company, he conceals many facts that outsiders would like to have revealed.

Required:
a. Comment on the professor's view of the accountant's job.
b. What type of omitted information is the writer referring to?

3–6. In commenting on mergers as a strategy for rescuing struggling savings banks, *Forbes* (January 31, 1983) cited the FASB's reluctance to allow a method of purchase accounting and goodwill amortization that would have an unwarranted positive effect on the reported earnings of the acquiring bank.

This reluctance by the FASB elicited the following responses:

" 'This is plain silly accounting,' says Astoria Federal Savings' Executive Vice President George Engelke Jr. 'It will destroy all mergers.' Big Eight accounting firm Arthur Young is uncharacteristically vocal as it leads the charge against the FASB proposal. 'The Board has missed the mark, and observers will be questioning its credibility,' says Robert McLendon, national director of accounting standards at Arthur Young."

In its comments, *Forbes* admits that "there has been misuse of this kind of purchase accounting," and this accounting can deceive depositors into thinking that banks are on solid ground when actually they are no better off than before the merger.

Required:
What possible objectives of accounting do Messrs. Engelke and McLendon have in mind when making their respective comments? Discuss.

Chapter 4

4–1. Having just been hired by the First Fearless National Bank as a junior analyst, your supervisor hands you the financial statements of Alfa, Inc. (Appendix 4B), and the list of ratios for 19x6 (found on pages 76–78). "Please compute the identical ratios for 19x5," said he, and added, "Although it amounts to only a two-year comparison, please comment on the significance of the year-to-year changes."

(Hint: Using skills you will learn in Chapter 13, you determine that the 19x4 year-end inventory is $159,818. Total assets and total equity for 19x4 are disclosed elsewhere in Alfa's financial statements.)

Required:
Please comply with the supervisor's request.

4–2. Complete the following comparative operating statement of Forward Corporation:

FORWARD CORPORATION
Operating Statement
For Years Ending on December 31
(in thousands of dollars).

	19x4	19x3	19x2	Cumulative amount	Annual average amount
Net sales		2,280	1,998		
Cost of goods sold	1,910				1,920
Gross profit		300			357
Total operating expenses					280
Income before taxes	186	25	20		
Net income	93	13	10		

4–3. Compute the increases (decreases) from the preceding year in percentage and fill in the blanks in the following table:

	19x9		19x8		19x7
	Index no.	Change in percent	Index no.	Change in percent	Index no.
Net sales		50	100		80
Cost of goods sold	165		100		90
Gross profit	127		100		85
Total operating expenses		35	100		70
Income before tax		20	100		60
Net income	130		100		55

4–4. Use the given information for Rigid Company to complete the following balance sheet. These are the only items in the balance sheet. Show computations.

Cash
Accounts receivable
Inventory $40
Fixed assets (net)
Current liabilities
Common stock 50
Retained earnings

1. Total assets minus liabilities equals $110.
2. Stockholders' equity equals 2.75 times total debt.
3. Current ratio is 2.25 to 1.
4. Inventory turnover is 14.4 times (based on cost of goods sold and ending inventory).
5. Days sales in accounts receivable are 15 days (based on a 360-day year).
6. Gross profit is 25 percent of cost of goods sold.

4–5. The following data are available for the Disco Company for 19x1 and 19x2:

	19x2	19x1
Gross profit percentage	40%	35%
Ending accounts receivable	$150,000	$90,000
Number of days sales in ending accounts receivable	60	45
Income tax rate	50%	40%
Net income as a percent of sales	6%	9%
Maximum credit allowed to creditors	60 days	30 days

Required:
a. Prepare income statements in comparative form for the two years.
b. Comment on the trend in sales volume, gross profit percentage, and net income percentage.
c. Compute the ending accounts receivable turnover ratios and briefly comment on the trend in view of the changing credit terms. All sales are made on credit.

4–6. The Burnt Company had maintained its records in a safe place for many years. However, a fire has destroyed them just before its June 19x8 fiscal year-end, leaving only the following information:

Inventory	$ 40,000
Common stock, no par	50,000
Net assets	110,000
Current ratio	2.25 to 1
Inventory turnover	14.4
Accounts receivable turnover	24
Gross profit	20%
Ratio of debt (all current) to equity	1 to 2.75

Additional balance sheet accounts must be computed. There were no prepaid expenses or accumulated depreciation at June 30, 19x8.

Required:
Prepare a balance sheet in good form. Use a 360-day year in your computations.

4–7. The audit manager on your present job decided to undertake an analytical review of sales expenses of the Speedy Company, a manufacturer of garden tools, in order to determine which expense categories may require special audit emphasis. You have assembled the following data (dollar amounts in thousands):

	19x3		19x2		19x1		19x0	
	Dollars	*Percent*	*Dollars*	*Percent*	*Dollars*	*Percent*	*Dollars*	*Percent*
Sales	1,300		935		830		790	
Trend percentage ...		165		118		105		100
Selling expenses (percent are of sales):								
Advertising	90	6.9	34	3.6	28	3.4	24	3.0
District branch expenses*	80	6.2	41	4.4	38	4.6	32	4.1
Delivery expense (own trucks) ...	20	1.5	15	1.6	19	2.3	22	2.8
Freight-out	21	1.6	9	1.0	11	1.3	8	1.0
Salesmen's salary expense	120	9.2	76	8.1	68	8.2	61	7.7
Salesmen's travel expense	35	2.7	20	2.1	18	2.2	26	3.3
Miscellaneous selling expense .	24	1.9	9	1.0	8	.9	7	.9
Total	390	30.0	204	21.8	190	22.9	180	22.8
Trend percent of-total selling expenses		217.0		113.0		106.0		100.0

* Includes such fixed occupancy expenses as rent, advertising, etc.

Required:

a. What relationships need further investigation?

b. What are possible explanations or possible problem areas?

c. Where would we look for relevant information?

4–8. It is Sunday and you have just opened your briefcase in order to work with Elusive Company's December 31, 19x1, balance sheet. To your dismay you discover that the computer printouts that your assistant stuffed into your briefcase contained only the sketchy information below:

1. Accounts receivable and inventory were the same at the end of the year as at the beginning.
2. Net income, $600.
3. Times interest earned is 5 (ignore income taxes). The company has outstanding 5 percent bonds issued at par.
4. Net income to sales, 20 percent. Gross margin ratio, 40 percent. Inventory turnover, 6.
5. Accounts receivable turnover, 4.
6. Sales to working capital, 5. Current ratio, 1.6.
7. Acid-test ratio, 1.0 (exclude prepaid expenses).
8. Plant and equipment is one third depreciated.

9. Dividends paid on 8 percent nonparticipating preferred stock was $40. The effective yield in the current year was 10 percent. These shares were issued two years ago at par.
10. Earnings per common share, $2.80.
11. Common stock has a $10 par value and was issued at a 5 percent premium.
12. Retained earnings at January 1, 19x1, was $900.

Required:

Given the information available, complete the balance sheet as at December 31, 19x1. Also, determine the amount of dividends paid on the common stock in 19x1.

Cash	
Accounts receivable	
Inventory	
Prepaid expenses	
Plant and equipment (net)	$6,000
Total assets	
Current liabilities	
Bonds payable	
Stockholders' equity	
Total liabilities and equity	

4–9. Early one morning, even before your coffee break, a senior member of your institution's financial policy committee hurriedly walks into your office and hands you the data that follows. "This afternoon our committee will consider the relative merits of Re Company and Flex Company which are both in the flexible hose manufacturing business," said he and added: "Please prepare a preliminary ratio analysis and conclusions so as to enable me to give intelligent answers to expected questions."

Balance Sheets
As of December 31, 19x7
(in thousands)

	Re Company	Flex Company
Cash	$ 15	$ 10
Accounts receivable	50	90
Inventory	55	117
Plant and equipment, net ...	150	240
Total assets	$270	$457
Current liabilities	$ 57	$101
Bonds payable	75	100
Common stock, $10 par	50	70
Retained earnings	88	186
Total liabilities and equity	$270	$457

Data from Income Statements
For Year Ending December 31, 19x7
(in thousands)

Sales	$500	$700
Cost of goods sold	325	455
Interest expense	7	8
Income before taxes	60	88
Net income	24	35
Tax rate	60%	60%

Balances at January 1, 19x7
(in thousands)

Accounts receivable	$ 46	$ 86
Inventory	51	113
Total assets	250	425

Other Selected Data for 19x7

Dividends paid per share ...	$ 2.50	$ 2.50
Market price per share at year-end	72.00	85.00

Flexible Hose Manufacturing Industry
Averages for 19x7

Current ratio	2.1 to 1
Acid-test ratio	1.1 to 1
Accounts receivable turnover (average)	10 times
Inventory turnover (average)	5.7 times
Times interest earned	9 times
Debt-to-equity ratio	9 to 1
Dividend yield	4%
Price-earnings ratio	15
Dividend payout ratio	60%
Return on total assets (average)	9%
Return on common equity	15.5%

Required:
To satisfy the senior member's request—
1. Compute the following ratios for each company:
   (a) Current ratio.
   (b) Acid-test ratio.
   (c) Average accounts receivable turnover.
   (d) Average collection period for receivables.
   (e) Average inventory turnover.
2. Using the above ratios, as well as industry ratios, indicate which company is the better short-term credit risk and why.
3. Compute the following ratios for each company:

    (a) Times interest earned.
    (b) Total debt-to-equity ratio.
4. Using the above ratios and any other applicable ratios from *(a)* above, determine which company should be in a better position to take on *additional* long-term debt and why?
5. Compute the following ratios for each company:
    (a) Earnings per share.
    (b) Dividend yield.
    (c) Price-earnings ratio.
    (d) Dividend payout ratio.
    (e) Return on total assets.
    (f) Return on common equity.
6. Using the above ratios and any other applicable ratios from *(a)* and *(c)* above, present preliminary conclusions regarding the relative market standing and attractiveness of both companies.

    4–10. Based on the following data of Rex Corporation, compute the following:
a. Quick (acid-test) ratio as of December 31, 1980.
b. Receivable turnover for 1980.
c. Merchandise inventory turnover for 1980.
d. Current ratio at December 31, 1980.

REX CORPORATION
Selected Financial Data

	As of December 31	
	1980	*1979*
Cash	$ 10,000	$ 80,000
Accounts receivable (net)	50,000	150,000
Merchandise inventory	90,000	150,000
Short-term marketable securities	30,000	10,000
Land and buildings (net)	340,000	360,000
Mortgage payable (no current portion)	270,000	280,000
Accounts payable (trade)	70,000	110,000
Short-term notes payable	20,000	40,000

	Year ended December 31	
	1980	*1979*
Cash sales	$1,800,000	$1,600,000
Credit sales	500,000	800,000
Cost of goods sold	1,000,000	1,400,000

    4–11. The following balance sheet, income statement, and related information of the Bravo Company pertain to questions *(a)* through *(g).*

BRAVO COMPANY
Balance Sheet
As of December 31, 19x1

Assets

Cash	$ 100,000
Accounts receivable	572,000
Inventories	320,000
Plant and equipment, net of depreciation	740,000
Patents	25,000
Other intangible assets	15,000
Total assets	$1,772,000

Equities

Accounts payable	$ 170,000
Federal income tax payable	30,000
Miscellaneous accrued payables	40,000
Bonds payable (4%, due 19z2)	300,000
Preferred stock ($100 par, 7% cumulative nonparticipating and callable at $110)	200,000
Common stock (no par, 20,000 shares authorized, issued and outstanding)	400,000
Retained earnings	720,000
Treasury stock—800 shares of preferred	(88,000)
Total equities	$1,772,000

BRAVO COMPANY
Income Statement
For Year Ended December 31, 19x1

Net sales	$1,500,000
Cost of goods sold	900,000 -
Gross margin on sales	$ 600,000
Operating expenses (including bond interest expense)	500,000
Income before federal income taxes	100,000
Income tax expense	35,000
Net income	$ 65,000

Additional information:

There are no preferred dividends in arrears, and the balances in the Accounts Receivable and Inventory accounts are unchanged from January 1, 19x1, and there were no changes in the Bonds Payable, Preferred Stock, or Common Stock accounts during 19x1.

Required:

Compute the following:

a. The current ratio at December 31, 19x1.
b. The number of times bond interest was earned during 19x1 using the theoretically preferable method.

c. The number of times bond interest and preferred dividends were earned in 19x1.
d. The average number of days' sales in ending inventories during 19x1.
e. The December 31, 19x1, book value per share of common stock.
f. The rate of return for 19x1 based on the year-end common stockholders' equity.
g. The debt-to-equity ratio at December 31, 19x1, with debt defined as total liabilities.

(AICPA adapted)†

4–12. Comparative financial position and operating statements are commonly used tools of analysis and interpretation.

Required:
a. Discuss the inherent limitations of single-year statements for purposes of analysis and interpretation. Include in your discussion the extent to which these limitations are overcome by the use of comparative statements.
b. Comparative balance sheets and comparative income statements that show a firm's financial history for each of the last 10 years may be misleading. Discuss the factors or conditions that might contribute to misinterpretations. Include a discussion of the additional information and supplementary data that might be included in or provided with the statements to prevent misinterpretations.

(AICPA adapted)

Chapter 5

5–1. Please refer to the financial statements of Alfa, Inc., in Appendix 4B.

Required:
I. Alfa uses the LIFO cost flow assumption in determining its cost of goods sold and beginning and ending inventory amounts for some of its inventory items. Determine the *gross profit* of Alfa if FIFO had been used for all items of inventory. (See Notes 1,2 and 5 and use a 48 percent tax rate.)
    (1) For 19x6.
    (2) For 19x5.
II.* Alfa adopted the LIFO method for certain inventories in 19x4. What is the effect on net income for 19x4, 19x5, and 19x6 of using LIFO (instead of FIFO)? (See Notes 2 and 5 and use a 48 percent tax rate.)
III. Note 8 discloses that Alfa has "informally agreed to maintain "compensating balances." What are these and what is their significance?

5–2. Although cash generally is regarded as the simplest of all assets to account for, certain complexities can arise for both domestic and multinational companies.

Required:
a. What are the normal components of cash?
b. Under what circumstances, if any, do valuation problems arise in connection with cash?

---

* Designates problems of a more advanced or more challenging nature.

† Material from the Uniform CPA Examinations and Unofficial Answers, copyright © by the American Institute of Certified Public Accountants, Inc., is reprinted (or adapted) with permission.

5–3. Part a. At January 1, 1978, the credit balance in the allowance for doubtful accounts of the Master Company was $400,000. For 1978, the provision for doubtful accounts is based on a percentage of net sales. Net sales for 1978 were $50,000,000. Based on the latest available facts, the 1978 provision for doubtful accounts is estimated to be 0.7 percent of net sales. During 1978, uncollectible receivables amounting to $410,000 were written off against the allowance for doubtful accounts.

Required:
Prepare a schedule computing the balance in Master's allowance for doubtful accounts at December 31, 1978. Show supporting computations in good form.

Part b. The Guide Company requires additional cash for its business. Guide has decided to use its accounts receivable to raise the additional cash as follows:

1. On July 1, 1978, Guide assigned $200,000 of accounts receivable to the Cell Finance Company. Guide received an advance from Cell of 85 percent of the assigned accounts receivable less a commission on the advance of 3 percent. Prior to December 31, 1978, Guide collected $150,000 on the assigned accounts receivable, and remitted $160,000 to Cell, $10,000 of which represented interest on the advance from Cell.
2. On December 1, 1978, Guide sold $300,000 of net accounts receivable to the Factoring Company for $260,000. The receivables were sold outright on a non-recourse basis.
3. On December 31, 1978, an advance of $100,000 was received from the Domestic Bank by pledging $120,000 of Guide's accounts receivable. Guide's first payment to Domestic is due on January 30, 1979.

Required:
Prepare a schedule showing the income statement effect for the year ended December 31, 1978, as a result of the above facts. Show supporting computations in good form.

(AICPA adapted)

5–4. Layne Corporation, a manufacturer of small tools, provided the following information from its accounting records for the year ended December 31, 1980:

Inventory at December 31, 1980 (based on physical count of goods in Layne's plant at cost on December 31, 1980)	$1,750,000
Accounts payable at December 31, 1980	1,200,000
Net sales (sales less sales returns)	8,500,000

Additional information is as follows:

1. Included in the physical count were tools billed to a customer FOB shipping point on December 31, 1980. These tools had a cost of $28,000 and were billed at $35,000. The shipment was on Layne's loading dock waiting to be picked up by the common carrier.
2. Goods were in transit from a vendor to Layne on December 31, 1980. The invoice cost was $50,000, and the goods were shipped FOB shipping point on December 29, 1980.
3. Work in process inventory costing $20,000 was sent to an outside processor for plating on December 30, 1980.

4. Tools returned by customers and held pending inspection in the returned goods area on December 31, 1980, were not included in the physical count. On January 8, 1981, the tools costing $26,000 were inspected and returned to inventory. Credit memos totaling $40,000 were issued to the customers on the same date.

5. Tools shipped to a customer FOB destination on December 26, 1980, were in transit at December 31, 1980, and had a cost of $25,000. Upon notification of receipt by the customer on January 2, 1981, Layne issued a sales invoice for $42,000.

6. Goods, with an invoice cost of $30,000, received from a vendor at 5:00 P.M. on December 31, 1980, were recorded on a receiving report dated January 2, 1981. The goods were not included in the physical count, but the invoice was included in accounts payable at December 31, 1980.

7. Goods received from a vendor on December 26, 1980, were included in the physical count. However, the related $60,000 vendor invoice was not included in accounts payable at December 31, 1980, because the accounts payable copy of the receiving report was lost.

8. On January 3, 1981, a monthly freight bill in the amount of $4,000 was received. The bill specifically related to merchandise purchased in December 1980, one half of which was still in the inventory at December 31, 1980. The freight charges were not included in either the inventory or in accounts payable at December 31, 1980.

Required:

Using the format shown below, prepare a schedule of adjustments as of December 31, 1980, to the initial amounts per Layne's accounting records. Show separately the effect, if any, of each of the eight transactions on the December 31, 1980, amounts. If the transactions would have no effect on the initial amount shown, state NONE.

	Inventory	Accounts payable	Net sales
Initial amounts	$1,750,000	$1,200,000	$8,500,000
Adjustments—increase (decrease):			
1			
2			
3			
4			
5			
6			
7			
8			
Total adjustments			
Adjusted amounts	$	$	$

(AICPA adapted)

5–5. Part a. Inventory may be computed under one of various cost flow assumptions. Among these assumptions are FIFO and LIFO. In the past, some companies have changed from FIFO to LIFO for computing portions or all of their inventory.

Required:
(1) Ignoring income tax, what effect does a change from FIFO to LIFO have on net earnings and working capital? Explain.
(2) Explain the difference between the FIFO assumption of earnings and operating cycle and the LIFO assumption of earnings and operating cycle.

Part b. Companies using LIFO inventory sometimes establish a Reserve for the Replacement of LIFO Inventory account.

Required:
Explain why and how this "Reserve" account is established and where it should be shown on the statement of financial position.

(AICPA)

5–6. Inventories are described in the "Summary of Significant Accounting Policies" and in Note 3 below.

Summary of Significant Accounting Policies:
Inventories. Inventories at Modulus Corporation (a subsidiary purchased during October 1974) are primarily valued by the LIFO method. Inventories at other companies are generally valued at the lower of cost (determined on the FIFO basis) or market.

Note 3—Inventories:
The major components of inventory at December 31, 1974, and 1973 were as follows (in thousands):

	1974	1973
Raw materials and supplies	$ 7,593	$1,738
Work in process	10,294	759
Finished goods	4,234	1,023
	$22,121	$3,520

At December 31, 1974, $19,111,000 of the inventories is valued under the LIFO method. If the FIFO method of inventory accounting had been used by the company overall, inventories would have been $589,000 higher than reported at December 31, 1974.

The LIFO inventories were acquired in a taxable transaction requiring a different allocation of the total purchase price than that required for financial reporting purposes. The LIFO basis for financial purposes exceeds the tax basis by $9,381,000 at December 31, 1974. The different allocations to the inventories, however, did not result in a difference between income for federal income tax purposes and income for financial purposes for the year ended December 31, 1974.

Required:
(1) How much would "income from continuing operations" have been increased *or* decreased *if* the FIFO method had been used for all inventories.
(2) During a period of rapidly rising prices, why would the FIFO inventory valuation at December 31, 1974, be only $589,000 greater than under LIFO valuation?
(3) Note 3 indicated that the LIFO valuation for financial statement purposes exceeds the tax return valuation ("basis") by $9,381,000. There was *no* difference in

1974 net income for book versus tax. Under what circumstances would this LIFO valuation difference on the balance sheet cause a future difference between book income and tax income?

5–7. The following footnote from the 1973 annual report of ASARCO explains the inventories of $193,100,000 shown on the balance sheet.

Note 3. Inventories at smelters, refineries, and secondary metal plants include $45,800,000 (1972—$95,100,000) at LIFO cost; $60,700,000 (1972—$46,900,000) at privisional cost of metals purchased for which prices had not yet been fixed; and $71,700,000 (1972—$43,300,000) at sales prices for metals sold at firm contracts for future delivery. Inventories at mines aggregate $14,900,000 (1972—$20,300,000) at FIFO cost. Inventory values do not exceed market.

Required:
From the view point of a creditor analyzing the 1973 financial statements of ASARCO, discuss the *accounting* significance of the above note (what questions are raised; what portions of the note seem to raise no questions).

5–8. In 1974, many companies changed from the FIFO method to the LIFO method for valuing inventories and determining cost of goods sold. Important reasons for this change were the tax benefits of LIFO inventory accounting and the presentation of a more realistic earnings figure in a period of generally rising prices. *Even so, a number of companies have continued to use FIFO.*

Required:
Give *five* reasons why the management of a company might be *hesitant* to change from FIFO to LIFO.   (CFA)

5–9. (1) a. The following data are given:
Beginning inventory: 30 desks, $900 (at cost).

Purchases			*Sold*	
June 1	30 desks @ 30	$900	June 5	20 desks
10	40 desks @ 32	$1,280	15	30 desks
20	30 desks @ 31	$930	25	40 desks

Required:
a. Compute the cost of goods sold under the FIFO, LIFO, and moving-average cost inventory accounting for Company A.
b. Compute the costs of goods sold under the three methods of inventory for Company B which has exactly same beginning inventory, purchases, and sales as Company A above, except that it sold 20 more desks on June 30. Thus, on June 30, Company B has an ending inventory of 20 desks.

(2) b. Because of a fire, all the inventory and records of the Climax Company were burned. For insurance claim purposes, you are asked to estimate the inventory of desks burned. There was no inventory at the beginning of the period, and purchases during the period amounted to $3,000. The company usually makes 15 percent gross profit, and the sales during the period were $3,200.

Required:
What was the amount of the inventory burned by the fire?

5–10. A company uses the LIFO method (see the note below):
Inventories. Inventories are stated at the lower of cost or market value. Cost of domestic inventories is determined principally by the LIFO method, which is less than current costs by $69,460,000 and $53,962,000 at December 28, 19x5 and December 29, 19x4, respectively. Cost of inventories of foreign subsidiaries is determined principally by the FIFO method.

Required:
(1) What is the *dollar* effect of the use of LIFO *instead of* FIFO upon:
  (a) 19x5 balance sheet.
  (b) 19x5 net income.
  (c) Trend of net income from 19x4 to 19x5.
  (d) (Assume a 50 percent tax rate.) 19x5 working capital statement.
(2) Does the use of LIFO have any impact upon an analyst reviewing the financial statements (both qualitative and quantitative consideration)? Be specific.

Chapter 6

6–1. Please refer to the financial statements of Alfa, Inc., in Appendix 4B.

Required:
I.* By means of T-account analysis explain the changes in Property, Plant, and Equipment accounts for 19x5 and 19x6. Provide as much detail as the disclosure enables you to supply. (Hint: For 19x6 use also the "accumulated depreciation" account and reconstruct the aggregate entry made on the sale of equipment.)
II. (See Note 1, paragraph before last.) Alfa recognizes no gain or loss on normal retirements and disposals of plant and equipment.
  (1) What is the journal entry by which the company records the sale of such plant and equipment.
  (2) What justification is there for such practice?
III. (See Notes 1 and 5.) Refer first to Note 1 with regard to "Growing Crops":
  a. Discuss this accounting practice from the view point of an analyst.
  b. Why has management decided (and the accountants approved) to exclude $50 million of assets? (Refer to Note 5.)
  c. If Alfa had always shown growing crops as an asset, what amount would be shown for 19x6 net income.

6–2. Part A. *SFAS 12* was issued to clarify accounting methods and procedures with respect to certain marketable securities. An important part of the Statement concerns the distinction between noncurrent and current classification of marketable securities.

Required:
(1) Why does a company maintain an investment portfolio of current and noncurrent securities?

---

* Designates problems of a more advanced or more challenging nature.

(2) What factors should be considered in determining whether investments in marketable equity securities should be classified as current or noncurrent, and how do these factors affect the accounting treatment for unrealized losses?

Part B.   Presented below are four *unrelated* situations involving marketable equity securities:

Situation I.   A noncurrent portfolio with an aggregate market value in excess of cost includes one particular security whose market value has declined to less than one half of the original cost. The decline in value is considered to be other than temporary.

Situation II.   The statement of financial position of a company does not classify assets and liabilities as current and noncurrent. The portfolio of marketable equity securities includes securities normally considered current that have a net cost in excess of market value of $2,000. The remainder of the portfolio has a net market value in excess of cost of $5,000.

Situation III.   A marketable equity security, whose market value is currently less than cost, is classified as noncurrent but is to be reclassified as current.

Situation IV.   A company's noncurrent portfolio of marketable equity securities consists of the common stock of one company. At the end of the prior year, the market value of the security was 50 percent of original cost, and this effect was properly reflected in a valuation allowance account. However, at the end of the current year, the market value of the security had appreciated to twice the original cost. The security is still considered noncurrent at year-end.

Required:
What is the effect upon classification, carrying value, and earnings for each of the above situations. Complete your response to each situation before proceeding to the next situation.

6–3.   Among the principal topics related to the accounting for the property, plant, and equipment of a company are acquisition and retirement.

Required:
a. What expenditures should be capitalized when equipment is acquired for cash?
b. Assume that the market value of equipment acquired is not determinable by reference to a similar purchase for cash. Describe how the acquiring company should determine the capitalizable cost of equipment purchased by exchanging it for each of the following:
   (1) Bonds having an established market price.
   (2) Common stock not having an established market price.
   (3) Similar equipment having a determinable market value.
c. Describe the factors that determine whether expenditures relating to property, plant, and equipment already in use should be capitalized.
d. Describe how to account for the gain or loss on the sale of property, plant, and equipment for cash.

6–4.   An excerpt from the "Principal Accounting Policies" of Esmark, Inc., below states that "gains and losses resulting from normal dispositions of certain types of facilities are included in accumulated depreciation." How does this work mechanically *and* how can this treatment of gains and losses be justified?

"Gains and losses on property and operating facilities dispositions and closings are reflected in operating results in the year of disposition as to gains and in the year in which the decision is made to sell or close as to losses except that gains and losses resulting from normal dispositions of certain types of facilities are included in accumulated depreciation."

6–5. Jay Manufacturing, Inc., began operations five years ago producing probos, a new type of instrument it hoped to sell to doctors, dentists, and hospitals. The demand for probos far exceeded initial expectations, and the company was unable to produce enough probos to meet demand.

The company was manufacturing its product on equipment that it built at the start of its operations. To meet demand, more efficient equipment was needed. The company decided to design and build the equipment since that currently available on the market was unsuitable for producing probos.

In 1968, a section of the plant was devoted to development of the new equipment and a special staff of personnel was hired. Within six months, a machine was developed at a cost of $170,000 which successfully increased production and reduced labor costs substantially. Sparked by the success of the new machine, the company built three more machines of the same type at a cost of $80,000 each.

Required:
a. In addition to satisfying a need that outsiders cannot meet within the desired time, why might a firm construct fixed assets for its own use?
b. In general, what costs should be capitalized for a self-constructed fixed asset?
c. Discuss the propriety of including in the capitalized cost of self-constructed assets:
  (1) The increase in overhead caused by the self-construction of fixed assets.
  (2) A proportionate share of overhead on the same basis as that applied to goods manufactured for sale.
d. Discuss the proper accounting treatment of the $90,000 ($170,000 − $80,000) by which the cost of the first machine exceeded the cost of the subsequent machines.

(AICPA)

6–6. The following is a recent news item:
"GENOA, Italy—The twin luxury liners Michelangelo and Raffaello, once the proud representatives of Italy's passenger fleet, have been sold to Iran, it was announced by officials of the state-controlled shipping line.

"The price wasn't disclosed but reports put the figure at $35 million, compared with the 1963 construction cost of $145 million.

"The announcement said the two vessels will be transferred to Iran after being refurbished as floating hotels."

It was followed by another news item which stated:

"The greatest nonevent in the annals of the sea occurred last Thursday in Japan, when the world's biggest oil tanker, the 484,377-ton Nissei Maru, was completed— and went straight into lay-up. Between the time the keel of the monster vessel was laid and its delivery, its hypothetical market value plunged 90 percent. Moreover, it will cost a small fortune to maintain it in lay-up. Then there is the delicate problem of accepting a ship without putting it through its sea trials. What will be the validity of the shipyard's guarantees if it is put through its paces for the first time two or three years hence?"

Required:

a. What determines the value of assets?
b. Do present-day accounting principles give prompt recognition to changes in economic values? Discuss.

6–7. On June 30, 1970, your client, The Vandiver Corporation, was granted two patents covering plastic cartons that it has been producing and marketing profitably for the past three years. One patent covers the manufacturing process, and the other covers the related products.

Vandiver executives tell you that these patents represent the most significant breakthrough in the industry in the past 30 years. The products have been marketed under the registered trademarks Safetainer, Duratainer, and Sealrite. Licenses under the patents have already been granted by your client to other manufacturers in the United States and abroad and are producing substantial royalties.

On July 1, Vandiver commenced patent infringement actions against several companies whose names you recognize as those of substantial and prominent competitors. Vandiver's management is optimistic that these suits will result in a permanent injunction against the manufacture and sale of the infringing products and collection of damages for loss of profits caused by the alleged infringement.

The financial vice president has suggested that the patents be recorded at the discounted value of expected net royalty receipts.

Required:

a. What is an intangible asset? Explain.
b. (1) What is the meaning of "discounted value of expected net receipts"? Explain.
   (2) How would such a value be calculated for net royalty receipts?
c. What basis of valuation for Vandiver's patents would be generally accepted in accounting? Give supporting reasons for this basis.
d. (1) Assuming no practical problems of implementation and ignoring generally accepted accounting principles, what is the preferable basis of evaluation for patents? Explain.
   (2) What would be the preferable theoretical basis of amortization? Explain.
e. What recognition, if any, should be made of the infringement litigation in the financial statements for the year ending September 30, 1970? Discuss.

(AICPA)

6–8. Wells, Rich, Greene, Inc., an advertising agency, presented the following unamortized balances of deferred costs:

	April 30, 1968	September 30, 1968
Initial advertising service costs—new clients (including $46,400 at April 30, 1968, and $20,500 at September 30, 1968, attributed to initial campaigns	$ 495,745	$ 518,502
Development service costs—new products (including $181,700 at April 30, 1968, and $202,000 at September 30, 1968, relating to products with agreed initial media billing dates)	554,398	693,566
Total	$1,050,143	$1,212,068

A footnote explained this further:

"Because the costs which an advertising agency incurs shortly after its appointment and the costs incurred in connection with product development services are usually recoverable only against commissions from subsequent media billings, the company defers these costs and amortizes them principally over 36 months following the start of media billings. . . . Any unamortized deferred costs attributable to clients or client products for which advertising services are terminated will be written off against commissions received during the final months of media billing.

"Although the company is not aware of any other advertising agency following this accounting method, the management is of the opinion that this accounting method more fairly matches these costs with their related revenues than expensing such costs as they are incurred."

Required:

a. What is the basic justification for the deferral of—
    (1) Initial advertising service costs?
    (2) Development service costs?
b. Does a 36 months write-off period appear reasonable?
c. Do you agree with the contention that deferral procedures result in a more fair accounting? What additional information may you need before you can decide how to answer this question?

6–9. The Barb Company has provided information on intangible assets as follows:

1. A patent was purchased from the Lou Company for $1,500,000 on January 1, 1977. Barb estimated the remaining useful life of the patent to be 10 years. The patent was carried in Lou's accounting records at a net book value of $1,250,000 when Lou sold it to Barb.

2. During 1978, a franchise was purchased from the Rink Company for $500,000. In addition, 5 percent of revenue from the franchise must be paid to Rink. Revenue from the franchise for 1978 was $2,000,000. Barb estimates the useful life of the franchise to be 10 years and takes a full year's amortization in the year of purchase.

3. Barb incurred research and development costs in 1978 as follows:

Materials and equipment	$120,000
Personnel	140,000
Indirect costs	60,000
	$320,000

Barb estimates that these costs will be recouped by December 31, 1981.

4. On January 1, 1978, Barb, based on new events that have occurred in the field, estimates that the remaining life of the patent purchased on January 1, 1977, is only five years from January 1, 1978.

Required:

a. Prepare a schedule showing the intangibles section of Barb's balance sheet at December 31, 1978. Show supporting computations in good form.
b. Prepare a schedule showing the income statement effect for the year ended Decem-

ber 31, 1978, as a result of the above facts. Show supporting computations in good form.

6–10. During the examination of the financial statements of the Fendo Company, your assistant calls attention to significant costs incurred in the development of EDP programs (i.e., software) for major segments of the sales and production scheduling systems.

The EDP program development costs will benefit future periods to the extent that the systems change slowly and the program instructions are compatible with new equipment acquired at three to six-year intervals. The service value of the EDP programs is affected almost entirely by changes in the technology of systems and EDP equipment and does not decline with the number of times the program is used. Since many system changes are minor, program instructions frequently can be modified with only minor losses in program efficiency. The frequency of such changes tends to increase with the passage of time.

Required:
a. Discuss the propriety of classifying the unamortized EDP program development costs as—
 (1) A prepaid expense.
 (2) An intangible fixed asset with limited life.
 (3) A tangible fixed asset.
b. Numerous methods are available for amortizing assets that benefit future periods. Each method (like a model) presumes that certain conditions exist and, hence, is most appropriate under these conditions.

 Discuss the propriety of amortizing the EDP program development costs with—
 (1) The straight-line method.
 (2) An increasing-charge method (e.g., the annuity method).
 (3) A decreasing-charge method (e.g., the sum-of-the-years'-digits method).
 (4) A variable-charge method (e.g., the units-of-production method).

(AICPA)

6–11. Which of the following can be classified as assets on a balance sheet?
a. Depreciation.
b. President's salary.
c. Cash.
d. Deferred income taxes.
e. Installment receivable (to be collected in three years).
f. Capital withdrawal.
g. Inventories.
h. Prepaid expenses.
i. Deferred charges.
j. Work in process.
k. Allowance for depreciation.
l. Allowance for bad debt.
m. Loan to officers.
n. Loan from officers.
o. A fully trained sales force.

   p. Common stock of a subsidiary.
   q. Trade name purchased.
   r. Company developed goodwill.
   s. Valuable franchise agreements obtained at no cost.

6–12. The balance sheet, which is intended to present fairly the financial condition of a company, is frequently criticized for not reflecting many corporate liabilities. Similarly, the balance sheet is also faulted for not reflecting many corporate assets. Two examples are the excess of replacement value of plant and equipment over cost, and the LIFO inventory reserve.

Required:

List *five* other examples of *assets* that are not presently included on corporate balance sheets.

(CFA)

Chapter 7

7–1. Please refer to the financial statements of Alfa, Inc., in Appendix 4B.

Required:
  I. How much long-term debt was paid during
     (1) 19x6?
     (2) 19x5?
  II. (See Note 8.) The explanation of "Notes Payable and Current Portion of Long-Term Debt" shows a $35 million reduction in 19x6 for "interim borrowings included in long-term debt."
     (1) Explain the nature of this $35 million item.
     (2) How can the company's presentation be justified?
  III. (See Note 14.) Of what significance to the analyst are the $19,300 and $32,500 amounts disclosed in this note?

7–2. One way for a corporation to accomplish long-term financing is through the issuance of long-term debt instruments in the form of bonds.

Required:
  a. Describe how to account for the proceeds from bonds issued with detachable stock purchase warrants.
  b. Contrast a serial bond with a term (straight) bond.
  c. For a five-year term bond issued at a premium, why would the amortization in the first year of the life of the bond differ using the interest method of amortization instead of the straight-line method? Include in your discussion whether the amount of amortization in the first year of the life of the bond would be higher or lower using the interest method instead of the straight-line method.
  d. When a bond issue is sold between interest dates at a discount, what journal entry is made and how is the subsequent amortization of bond discount affected? Include in your discussion an explanation of how the amounts of each debit and credit are determined.

e. Describe how to account for and classify the gain or loss from the reacquisition of a long-term bond prior to its maturity.

(AICPA)

7–3. Financial publications frequently carry articles similar to the one from *Forbes,* from which excerpts are quoted below:

"The Supersolvent—No longer is it a mark of a fuddy-duddy to be free of debt. There are lots of advantages to it. One is that you always have plenty of collateral to borrow against if you do get into a jam. Another is that if a business investment goes bad, you don't have to pay interest on your mistake.

"Debt-free, you don't have to worry about what happens if the prime rate goes to 12 percent again. You might even welcome it. You could lend out your own surplus cash at those rates."

The article then went on to list 92 companies that reported on their balance sheets no more than 5 percent of total capitalization in noncurrent debt.

Required:
Give examples and explain why so-called debt-free companies in the sense used by this article may actually have long-term debt or other long-term liabilities.

(CFA)

7–4. The equityholders of a business entity usually are considered to include both creditors and owners. These two classes of equityholders have some characteristics in common, and sometimes it is difficult to make a clearcut distinction between them. Examples of this problem include (1) convertible debt and (2) debt issued with stock purchase warrants. While both examples represent debts of a corporation, there is a question as to whether there is an ownership interest in each case which requires accounting recognition.

Required:
a. Identify:
    (1) Convertible debt.
    (2) Debt issued with stock purchase warrants.
b. With respect to convertible debt and debt issued with stock purchase warrants, discuss:
    (1) The similarities.
    (2) The differences.
c. (1) What are the alternative accounting treatments for the proceeds from convertible debt? Explain.
    (2) Which treatment is preferable? Explain.
d. (1) What are the alternative accounting treatments for the proceeds from debt issued with stock purchase warrants? Explain.
    (2) Which treatment is preferable? Explain.

(AICPA)

7–5. Doherty Company leased equipment from Lambert Company. The classification of the lease makes a difference in the amounts reflected on the balance sheet and income statement of both Doherty Company and Lambert Company.

Required:
a. What criteria must be met by the lease in order that Doherty Company classify it as a capital lease?

b. What criteria must be met by the lease in order that Lambert Company classify it as a sales-type or direct financing lease?

c. Contrast a sales-type lease with a direct financing lease.

(AICPA)

7–6. The Hawk Company (the lessor) leased a machine to the Dove Corporation (the lessee) for five years, the life of the machine, at an annual rental, paid in advance, of $120,000. The machine cost Hawk $480,000, and it determined the rental based on a 10 percent rate of return. Dove uses the same rate. The present value of the lease payments amounts to $480,000. The machine has no salvage value and is depreciated under the straight-line method.

Required:

Please prepare all journal entries for the first and second years for both the lessor and lessee.

7–7. The Davids Corporation is a diversified company with nationwide interests in commercial real estate developments, banking, copper mining, and metal fabrication. The company has offices and operating locations in major cities throughout the United States. Corporate headquarters for Davids Corporation is located in a metropolitan area of a midwestern state, and executives connected with various phases of company operations travel extensively. Corporate management is presently evaluating the feasibility of acquiring a business aircraft that can be used by company executives to expedite business travel to areas not adequately served by commercial airlines. Proposals for either leasing or purchasing a suitable aircraft have been analyzed, and the leasing proposal was considered to be more desirable.

The proposed lease agreement involves a twin-engine turboprop Viking that has a fair market value of $900,000. This plane would be leased for a period of 10 years beginning January 1, 1979. The lease agreement is cancelable only upon accidental destruction of the plane. An annual lease payment of $127,600 is due on January 1 of each year; the first payment is to be made on January 1, 1979. Maintenance operations are strictly scheduled by the lessor, and Davids Coporation will pay for these services as they are performed. Estimated annual maintenance costs are $6,200. The lessor will pay all insurance premiums and local property taxes, which amount to a combined total of $3,600 annually and are included in the annual lease payment of $127,600. Upon expiration of the 10-year lease, Davids Corporation can purchase the Viking for $40,000. The estimated useful life of the plane is 15 years, and its salvage value in the used plane market is estimated to be $100,000 after 10 years. The salvage value probably will never be less than $75,000 if the engines are overhauled and maintained as prescribed by the manufacturer. If the purchase option is not exercised, possession of the plane will revert to the lessor, and there is no provision for renewing the lease agreement beyond its termination on December 31, 1988.

Davids Corporation can borrow $900,000 under a 10-year term loan agreement at an annual interest rate of 12 percent. The lessor's implicit interest rate is not expressly stated in the lease agreement, but this rate appears to be approximately 8 percent based on 10 net rental payments of $124,000 per year and the initial market value of $900,000 for the plane. On January 1, 1979, the present value of all net rental payments and the purchase option of $40,000 is $800,000 using the 12 percent interest rate. The present value of all net rental payments and the $40,000 purchase option on January 1, 1979, is $920,000 using the 8 percent interest rate implicit in the lease agreement. The financial vice president of Davids Corporation has established that this lease agreement is a capital lease as defined in Statement of Financial Accounting Standard No. 13, "Accounting for Leases."

Required:

A. What is the appropriate amount that Davids Corporation should recognize for the leased aircraft on its statement of financial position after the lease is signed?
B. Without prejudice to your answer in Requirement *(a)*, assume that the annual lease payment is $127,600 as stated in the question, that the appropriate capitalized amount for the leased aircraft is $1,000,000 on January 1, 1979, and that the interest rate is 9 percent. How will the lease be reported in the December 31, 1979, statement of financial position and related income statement. (Ignore any income tax implications.)
C. Identify and explain the four factors which differentiate a capital lease from an operating lease.

(CMA)

7–8. On January 1, 19x1, Burton Company leased equipment from Nelson Company at an annual lease rental of $10,000. The lease term was five years, and the lessor's interest rate implicit in the lease was 8 percent. The lessee's incremental borrowing rate was 8¼ percent.

The useful life of the equipment was five years, and it is estimated that its residual value will be equal to its removal cost.

The annuity tables indicate that the present value of annual rental of $1 (at 8 percent rate) is $3.993. The fair value of the leased equipment equals the present value of rentals.

Required:
Assuming that the lease is capitalized.

a. Show entries required in Burton Company's books for 19x1.
b. Show the effect on the income statement for the year ended December 31, 19x1, and on the balance sheet as at December 31, 19x1.
c. Construct a table to show payments of interest and of principal to be made every year for the five-year term of the lease.
d. Construct a table to show expenses to be charged to the income statement for five-year term of the lease (show a column for amortization, a column for interest and a third column for total) if the equipment is purchased.

7–9. Define or describe the following:
a. Prior service costs and past service costs.
b. Vested benefits.
c. Unfunded vested benefits relative to a company's assets or net worth.

(CFA adapted)

7–10. Loss contingencies may exist for companies.

Required:
1. What conditions should be met for an estimated loss from a loss contingency to be accrued by a charge to income?
2. When is disclosure required, and what disclosure should be made for an estimated loss from a loss contingency that need not be accrued by a charge to income?

Chapter 8

8–1. Please refer to the financial statements of Alfa, Inc., in Appendix 4B.

Required:
I. What caused the $9,367 million increase in stockholder's equity during 19x6 and the $14,948 increase in 19x5? (Hint: See item ⃞109 for the December 31, 19x4, balance of stockholder's equity.)
II. Compute the December 31, 19x6, book value of the common stock and the two issues of preferred stock.
III. Why does the per share amount in the common stock account differ from year to year?

8–2. The ownership interest in a corporation is customarily reported in the balance sheet as stockholders' equity.

Required:
a. List the principal transactions or items that reduce the amount of retained earnings. (Do not include appropriations of retained earnings.)
b. In the stockholders' equity section of the balance sheet, a distinction is made between contributed capital and earned capital. Why is this distinction made? Discuss.
c. There is frequently a difference between the purchase price and sale price of treasury stock, but accounting authorities agree that the purchase or sale of its own stock by a corporation cannot result in a profit or loss to the corporation. Why isn't the difference recognized as a profit or loss to the corporation? Discuss.
(AICPA)

8–3. On a given day, the stock of Superior Oil Corporation sold on the N.Y. Stock Exchange for $1,492, while Getty Oil Company was selling for $64.

Required:
a. How can you account for the fact that Superior Oil was selling for a much greater price? What can you conclude about the relative profitability of the two companies?
b. On the previous day, Superior Oil stock had sold for $1,471, while Getty Oil sold for $62. Which stock had the greater price rise?
c. If you had purchased Getty Oil at $62 and sold it the next day for $64, what effect would this have on the accounting records of the company?

8–4. The analyst is frequently interested in identifying all activities in a company's stockholders' equity section. Many companies present a statement of stockholders' equity showing changes in each stockholders' equity account (the analyst must deduce the offsetting effects to cash, debt, etc.). Other companies merely explain the changes in retained earnings and paid-in capital (the analyst must use the footnote and working capital disclosure to identify the various activities with stockholders). The following statement of shareholders' equity is from Martin Marietta Corporation's 1978 financial statements.

Statement of Shareowners' Equity

	Common stock $1 par value	Additional paid-in capital	Retained earnings	Treasury common stock	Total shareowners' equity
Net earnings for the year 1978	—	—	$136,003,000	—	$136,003,000
Cash dividends declared on common stock ($1.70 a share)	—	—	(42,128,000)	—	(42,128,000)
Stock options exercised (34,006 shares from treasury)	11,000	168,000	(89,000)	674,000	764,000
Conversion of 6% convertible subordinated debentures	1,739,000	43,879,000	—	—	45,618,000
Common stock purchased for treasury (66,700 shares)	—	—	—	(1,984,000)	(1,984,000)
Balance at December 31, 1978	$27,507,000	$219,646,000	$656,283,000	$(39,519,000)	$863,917,000

Required:

Analyze the changes in Martin Marietta's stockholders' equity accounts for 1978. (Hint: Draw T-accounts for each of the four categories above and explain the change from beginning to ending balance.) For each entry indicate which other account(s) (debit or credit) is (are) affected.

8–5. Part a. Capital stock is an important area of a corporation's equity section. Generally the term *capital stock* embraces common and preferred stock issued by a corporation.

Required:

(1) What are the basic rights inherent in ownership of common stock, and how are they exercised?
(2) What is preferred stock? Discuss the various preferences afforded preferred stock.

Part b. In dealing with the various equity securities of a corporate entity, it is important to understand certain terminology related thereto.

Required:

Define the following terms.
(1) Treasury stock.
(2) Legal capital.
(3) Stock right.
(4) Stock warrant.

Part C. Georgia, Inc., has an authorized capital of 1,000 shares of $100 par, 8 percent cumulative preferred stock and 100,000 shares of $10 par common stock. The equity account balances at December 31, 1981, are as follows:

Cumulative preferred stock	$ 50,000
Common stock	90,000
Additional paid-in capital	9,000
Retained earnings	13,000
Treasury stock, common—	
100 shares at cost	(2,000)
	$160,000

Dividends on preferred stock are in arrears for the year 1981.

Required:

Determine the book value of a share of common stock at December 31, 1981.

8–6. The Apex Corporation has paid its preferred dividends over the past two years. The preferred stock is of the nonparticipating variety. No dividends were paid on the common stock in 19x5.

APEX CORPORATION

	19x5	19x4
Stockholders' equity:		
Preferred stock—7% noncumulative—par value $25 per share: Authorized—93,200 shares Issued—93,200 shares—including shares in treasury 19x5, 38,548 shares and 19x4, 21,508 shares	$ 2,330,000	$ 2,330,000
Common stock—no par value: Authorized—2,400,000 shares Issued—1,831,400 shares—including shares in treasury 19x5, 34,380 shares and 19x4, 62,900 shares	14,943,700	14,943,700
Retained earnings	18,649,861	17,146,574
	35,923,561	34,420,274
Less: Cost of shares in treasury	2,616,583	2,707,499
Total stockholders' equity	33,306,978	31,712,775
	$47,216,729	$40,694,371

Required:
Compute the book value per share of both the common and preferred stock for 19x4 and 19x5.

8–7. The balance sheet of the Exeter Products Corporation discloses the following information:

1. 6,000 shares of common stock were issued and outstanding; par value $100.
2. 3,000 shares of preferred stock were issued and outstanding; par value $100, 5% cumulative, but nonparticipating. No dividends have been declared for three years. The stockholders' equity discloses the following balances: paid-in surplus, $90,000; appropriation for contingencies, $30,000; and unappropriated retained earnings, $90,000.

Required:
a. Compute equity per share of each class of stock. Also compute the equity per share of each class of stock under the following assumptions:
b. Use the same data as in *(a),* except that the preferred is given normal participation in dividends. By normal participation it is meant that the preferred will share proportionately with the common in the surplus, after the common receives an initial dividend equivalent to the preferred.
c. Use the same data as in *(a),* except that preferred is participating *after* one year's dividend at 10 percent is allowed.
d. Prepare work sheet as in *(a),* except that common stock has a par value of $50; shares outstanding are 12,000; participation of preferred is normal, but on a pro rata basis when computation for the per share is made; there is no appropriation for contingencies or unappropriated retained earnings.

e. Same as *(d)*, except the preferred shares have a liquidating value of $110 and a call value of $125.

f. Same as *(d)*, except there is a debit balance in Retained Earnings of $180,000. You may assume that there is no provision as to "preference of assets" in the charter.

g. Requirements are the same as *(f)*, except that the charter *does* provide for a preference to assets for the preferred stock.

8–8. **(1)** It has been said that the use of the LIFO inventory method during an extended period of rising prices and the expensing of all human resource costs are among the accepted accounting practices which help create "secret reserves."

Required:
a. What is a "secret reserve"? How can "secret reserves" be created or enlarged?
b. What is the basis for saying that the two specific practices cited above tend to create "secret reserves"?
c. Is it possible to create a "secret reserve" in connection with accounting for a liability? If so, explain or give an example.
d. What are the objections to the creation of "secret reserves"?

(2) It has also been said that "watered stock" is the opposite of a "secret reserve." reserve."

Required:
a. What is "watered stock"?
b. Describe the general circumstances in which "watered stock" can arise.
c. What steps can be taken to eliminate "water" from a capital structure?

(AICPA)

Chapter 9

9–1. Please refer to the financial statements of Alfa, Inc., in Appendix 4B.

Required:
I. For the asset "Nonconsolidated finance subsidiaries":
   a. Explain all changes during 19x6.
   b. Identify all effects in the SCFP that relate to this asset.
II. Note 13 presents condensed financial statements of Alfa's nonconsolidated finance subsidiaries. The questions that follow relate to 19x6.
   a. What items (and amounts) in these condensed financial statements correspond to items in Alfa's consolidated financial statements?
   b. Have the nonconsolidated finance subsidiaries paid any dividends to Alfa in 19x6? How would you go about determining the amount, if any, of such dividends?
III. The balance sheet shows an investment of $32,443 (in 19x6) in nonconsolidated finance subsidiaries. As a credit analyst, what questions would you ask management about this investment? Consider only the four or five most important questions.
IV. Note 4 describes the April 1, 19x2, acquisition of Commonwealth, Inc. Identify the effect of this acquisition on the consolidated balance sheet at date of acquisition.

V.   Note 5, under "Other Assets," shows "Excess of Cost Over Equity of Subsidiary Companies at Dates of Acquisition." Why is this asset not being amortized?

VI. The stockholder's equity section shows "Excess of Equity Over Cost of Subsidiary Companies at Dates of Acquisition."
   a.   Why is this credit not being amortized?
   b.   Is Alfa's presentation of this credit generally followed?

9–2.   The diagram below portrays Company X (the parent or investor company), its two subsidiaries C1 and C2, and its "50 percent or less owned" affiliate C3.

Each of the companies has only one type of stock outstanding, and there are no other significant stockholders in either Corporation C2 or Corporation C3. All four companies are engaged in commercial and industrial activities.

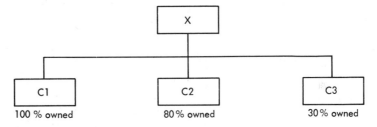

Required:

The following questions require short answers:

1.   Will each of the above companies maintain separate accounting records?

2.   What type of financial statements will each company present for public reporting purposes?

3.   Assuming that the analyst has the ability to enforce his requests, what type of financial statements and other information of these companies, separate or consolidating, can he request?

4.   What will Company X show in its assets for C1 Corporation?

5.   If C1 Corporation were legally dissolved into Company X, how would Company X's balance sheet be changed?

6.   If C1 Corporation were legally dissolved into Company X, how would the consolidated balance sheet be changed?

7.   In the consolidated balance sheet, how is the 20 percent of C2 Corporation not owned by Company X shown?

8.   What transaction would be required before C3 Corporation could be included line by line in the consolidated statements?

9.   If "combined" statements were presented for C1 Corporation and C2 Corporation, would there be any elimination entries?

10. Suppose that Company X sold its entire investment in C2 Corporation to C1 Corporation (C2 Corporation would be 80 percent owned by C1 Corporation). How would the consolidated balance sheet be changed?

11. If C1 Corporation sold additional common stock to Company X for cash, how would the consolidated balance sheet be changed?

9-3. On July 1, 19x1, P Company purchased 80 percent of the outstanding common stock of S Company for $360,000 payable in cash. On that date, each of the assets and liabilities of S Company had book value approximately equal to their respective fair market values. Balance sheets of the companies on July 1, 19x1, are as follows:

	P Company	S Company
Cash	$ 600,000	$100,000
Accounts receivable	400,000	50,000
Inventory	300,000	80,000
Land	80,000	—
Equipment (net of accumulated depreciation)	200,000	120,000
Investment in S Company	360,000	
Totals	$1,940,000	$350,000
Accounts payable	$ 400,000	$ 50,000
Common stock—P Company	200,000	
Common stock—S Company		100,000
Additional paid-in capital—P Company	100,000	
Retained earnings—P Company	1,240,000	
Retained earnings—S Company		200,000
Totals	$1,940,000	$350,000

On July 1, 19x1, the equipment of S Company had a fair market value of $200,000.

Required:
a. Prepare an allocation schedule to compute goodwill.
b. Prepare a consolidated working paper.

9-4. The following are condensed balance sheets of Nut Company and Bolt Company as of December 31, 19x0.

Balance Sheets
As of December 31, 19x0

	Nut Company	Bolt Company
Assets		
Cash and receivables	$200,000	$ 50,000
Other assets	400,000	150,000
Total assets	$600,000	$200,000
Liabilities and Equity		
Liabilities	$100,000	$ 60,000
Capital stock, $100 par value	300,000	100,000
Paid-in capital	50,000	—
Retained earnings................	150,000	40,000
Total liabilities and equity	$600,000	$200,000

Nut Company acquired an 80 percent interest in Bolt Company on January 1, 19x1, for $120,000, by paying $60,000 in cash and the balance in notes payable to Bolt Company's shareholders.

Required:

Prepare a consolidated financial statement.

9–5. Data on two companies planning a combination are as follows:

	ABC Company	*XYZ Company*
Book value of common stock	$200 million	$30 million
Common shares outstanding	4 million	1 million
Net earnings for common	$ 20 million	$ 3 million
Market price of common	$75 per share	$30 per share

Assume this is all the information available. Assume a 50 percent tax rate. *APB Opinions Nos. 16* and *17* on "Business Combinations" and "Intangible Assets" apply.

Required:

a. In the combination, .5 shares of ABC Company are to be exchanged for each XYZ Company share.
   (1) Is this (i) a pooling; (ii) a purchase; (iii) part pooling, part purchase; or (iv) either, depending on intent?
   (2) What are the total dollar earnings of the new entity?
   (3) How much goodwill is created in the consolidation?
   (4) Calculate earnings per share of the new entity—show calculations.
b. In the combination, .2 shares of ABC Company plus $25 worth of 6 percent debt is to be exchanged for each share of XYZ Company.
   (1) Is this (i) a pooling; (ii) a purchase; (iii) part pooling, part purchase; or (iv) either, depending on intent?
   (2) How much goodwill is created in the consolidation?
   (3) What is the yearly write-off of goodwill assuming the maximum life allowed for goodwill?
   (4) On a pro forma basis, assuming the combination had taken place a year ago, calculate the net earnings and per share earnings of the new entity. Show calculations.

(CFA)

9–6. Axel Company acquired 100 percent of the stock of Wheal Company on December 31, 19x4. The following information pertains to Wheal Company on that date:

	Book value	*Fair value*
Cash	$ 40,000	$ 40,000
Accounts receivable	60,000	55,000
Inventory	50,000	75,000
Property, plant, and equipment (net)	100,000	200,000
Secret formula		30,000
	$250,000	$400,000

	Book value	Fair value
Accounts payable	30,000	30,000
Accrued employee pensions	20,000	22,000
Long-term debt..........................	40,000	38,000
Capital stock............................	100,000	—
Other contributed capital	25,000	—
Retained earnings	35,000	—
	$250,000	$ 90,000

Axel Company issued $110,000 par value (market value on December 31, 19x4 — $350,000) of its own stock to the stockholders of Wheal to consummate the transaction, and Wheal became a wholly owned, consolidated subsidiary of Axel Company.

Required:
a. Entries to record the acquisition of Wheal Company stock.
b. Entries to eliminate in working papers the investment in Wheal Company stock for a consolidated balance sheet at December 31, 19x4.
c. A calculation of consolidated retained earnings at December 31, 19x4—Axel's retained earnings at that date are $150,000—if:
   (1) Axel uses the pooling of interests method for the business combination.
   (2) Axel uses the purchase method for acquisition of Wheal.

9–7. Problems 9–7 and 9–8 are based on the following financial statements for Companies B and S:

Balance Sheet
As of December 31, 19x0

	Company B	Company S
Assets		
Current assets	$200,000	$150,000
Depreciable assets	100,000	50,000
Total assets	$300,000	$200,000
Liabilities and Equity		
Liabilities	$100,000	$ 70,000
Common stock	100,000	70,000
Paid-in capital	25,000	—
Retained earnings	75,000	60,000
Total liabilities and equity	$300,000	$200,000

Income Statement
For Year 19x1

	Company B	Company S
Net sales	$500,000	$300,000
Cost of goods sold*	350,000	240,000
Gross profit	150,000	60,000
Selling, administrative, and general expenses	50,000	12,000
Depreciation	20,000	5,000
All other expenses	30,000	18,000
Net income	$ 50,000	$ 25,000

* Does not include depreciation or amortization.

On January 1, 19x1, Company B acquired all the outstanding common shares of Company S by issuing 10,000 shares of its $10 par value common stock. Separate books were kept during 19x1, and there were no business transactions between the two companies. Assets of Company S include depreciable assets with a book value of $50,000. There were no additions to fixed assets during 19x1.

Required:
a. Prepare a consolidated balance sheet as of January 1, 19x1, on a pooling of interests basis.
b. Prepare a consolidated income statement for year 19x1.
c. Compute the following ratios for Company B alone and Companies B and S consolidated. Compare and comment on the results.
   (1) Net income to sales.
   (2) Gross profit ratio.
   (3) Selling, administrative, and general expenses to sales.

9-8. On January 1, 19x1, Company B purchased 100 percent interest of Company S by paying $100,000 in cash and $50,000 in a long-term note payable. Assets of Company S include depreciable assets with a book value of $50,000; however, their fair market value on the date of acquisition was $60,000. The current value of liabilities was computed to be $75,000. There were no business transactions between the two companies, and there were no additions to fixed assets during 19x1. It was determined that the rate of depreciation is proper.

Required:
a. Prepare a consolidated balance sheet as of January 1, 19x1, on the purchase basis.
b. Prepare a consolidated income statement for 19x1. Goodwill is to be amortized over five years.
c. Compute the following ratios for Company B alone and Companies B and S consolidated:
   (1) Net income to sales.
   (2) Gross profit ratio.
   (3) Selling, administrative, and general expenses to sales.
d. Compare and comment on the consolidated results of operations of Companies B and S in Problem 9–7 *(c)* with those of *(c)* above.

e. Compare the balance sheets in Problem 9–7 *(a)* and Problem 9–8 *(a)* and comment on the differences.

9–9. Five years ago Bard Corporation acquired 20 percent of the outstanding common stock of Stratford Company at a cost of $16,000,000, which represented book value at that time. Stratford's total earnings and the total cash dividends for the past five years were:

STRATFORD COMPANY

Year	Total earnings	Cash dividends paid
1	$10,200,000	$ 6,200,000
2	11,400,000	6,200,000
3	5,200,000	6,200,000
4	11,700,000	6,700,000
5	12,000,000	6,700,000
Total	$50,500,000	$32,000,000

Required:
a. Calculate the total income to be reported by Bard on the investment for the five-year period assuming (1) the cost method of valuation and (2) the equity method of valuation.
b. Calculate the carrying value of the investment in Stratford Company on Bard's balance sheet at the end of the five years, assuming (1) the cost method of valuation and (2) the equity method of valuation.

(CFA)

9–10. The Tiger Corporation, a retail fuel oil distributor, has increased its annual sales volume to a level three times greater than the annual sales of a dealer it purchased in 19x8 in order to begin operations.

The board of directors of Tiger Corporation recently received an offer to negotiate the sale of Tiger Corporation to a large competitor. As a result, the majority of the board wants to increase the stated value of goodwill on the balance sheet to reflect the larger sales volume developed through intensive promotion and the current market price of sales gallonage. However, a few of the board members would prefer to eliminate goodwill altogether from the balance sheet in order to prevent "possible misinterpretations." Goodwill was recorded properly in 19x8.

Required:
a. (1) Discuss the meaning of the term *goodwill.* Do *not* discuss goodwill arising from consolidated statements or the conditions under which goodwill is recorded.
   (2) List the techniques used to calculate the tentative value of goodwill in negotiations to purchase a going concern.
b. Why are the book and market values of the goodwill of Tiger Corporation different?
c. Discuss the propriety of—
   (1) Increasing the stated value of goodwill prior to the negotiations.
   (2) Eliminating goodwill completely from the balance sheet prior to negotiations.

(AICPA)

9–11. On January 1, 19x6, Lincoln Corporation exchanged 10,000 shares of its own $20 par value common stock for 90 percent of the capital stock of the Juilliard Company.

Required:

a. The principal limitation of consolidated financial statements is their lack of separate information about the assets, liabilities, revenues, and expenses of the individual companies included in the consolidation. List the problems that the reader of consolidated financial statements encounters as a result of the limitation.

b. Depending upon the examination of the accompanying circumstances, the combination of Lincoln Corporation and Juilliard Company may be accounted for as a purchase or as pooling of interests. Discuss the differences between (1) a consolidated balance sheet prepared for a purchase and (2) a consolidated balance sheet prepared for a pooling of interests.

c. The minority interest in Juilliard Company can be presented several ways on the consolidated balance sheet. Discuss the propriety of reporting the minority interest on the consolidated balance sheet—

(1) As a liability.

(2) As a part of stockholders' equity.

(3) In a separate classification between liabilities and the equity of the Lincoln Corporation.

(AICPA adapted)

9–12. AVC Company shows goodwill of $3,378,000 and elaborates on it in Note 5 below. The auditor's report is qualified with respect to the realizability of the carrying amount of goodwill.

Note 5–Goodwill: Goodwill is attributable to the assets of the Philadelphia television station. Although this station has incurred substantial operating losses since acquisition through December 31, 19x4, management believes that the current outlook indicates no diminution in value has occurred.

At December 31, 19x4, the tax basis of AVC's investment in the television station exceeds the financial basis, including goodwill, by $4,800,000. Should the television operations be excluded from the consolidated federal income tax return, such excess may result in additional tax operating loss or capital loss carry-forwards aggregating $8,200,000.

Required:

(1) How would you treat this goodwill for analytical purposes?

(2) As a credit analyst, would you raise any questions concerning the goodwill?

9–13. Part a. The Whit Company and the Berry Company, a manufacturer and retailer, respectively, entered into a business combination whereby the Whit Company acquired for cash all of the outstanding voting common stock of the Berry Company.

Required:

(1) The Whit Company is preparing consolidated financial statements immediately after the consummation of the above-stated business combination. How should the Whit Company determine in general the amounts to be reported for the assets and liabilities of Berry Company? Assuming that the business combination resulted in goodwill, indicate how the amount of goodwill is determined.

(2) Why and under what circumstances should Berry Company be included in the entity's consolidated financial statements?

Part b. The Bert Company and the Lyle Company entered into a business combination accounted for as a pooling of interests.

Required:
(1) How should the expenses related to effecting the business combination be handled, and why?
(2) How should the results of operations for the year in which the business combination occurred be reported? Why is this reporting appropriate?

9–14. An accounting controversy concerns the widespread use of pooling in mergers. Opponents of the use of pooling believe that the surviving company often uses pooling (rather than purchase) to hide the "true" effects of the merger.

Required:
What may be "hidden" and how is the analysis of a company's securities affected by pooling practices?

(CFA)

9–15. Wales Company is a foreign subsidiary (in the U.K.) of Amerco Corporation (a U.S. Corporation) and has been since its incorporation in 19x3.

The following are the financial statements of Wales Company for the year ended December 31, 19x6:

WALES COMPANY
Income Statement
For Year Ending December 31, 19x6
(in thousands of £)

Sales		80,000
Less cost of sales:		
Inventory, January 1, 19x6	20,000	
Purchases	40,000	
	60,000	
Inventory, December 31, 19x6	25,000	35,000
Gross profit		45,000
Selling and administrative expenses	15,000	
Depreciation	10,000	25,000
Pretax income		20,000
Income tax (50%)		10,000
Net income		10,000

WALES COMPANY
Balance Sheet
As of December 31, 19x6
(in thousands of £)

Assets

Current assets:

Cash	5,000	
Accounts receivable	15,000	
Inventories (at cost)	25,000	
Prepaid expenses	2,000	
Total current assets		47,000
Long-term note receivable		23,000
Property, plant, and equipment	75,000	
Less accumulated depreciation	25,000	50,000
		120,000

Liabilities and Stockholders' Equity

Current liabilities:

Accounts payable	15,000	
Notes payable	10,000	
Accrued liabilities	5,000	
Total current liabilities		30,000
Long-term debt		35,000
Stockholders' equity:		
Capital stock	45,000	
Retained earnings	10,000	
Total stockholders' equity		55,000
Total liabilities and stockholders' equity		120,000

Additional information:

1. On January 1, 19x3, the date of incorporation of Wales Company, the exchange rate was £ = $2.10. On this date, all the presently outstanding stock was issued.
2. On January 1, 19x6, the exchange rate was £ = $2.30.
3. The average exchange rate for 19x6 was £ = $2.40.
4. Property, plant, and equipment were purchased on January 1, 19x4, when the exchange rate was 2.35.
5. The long-term note receivable was executed on January 1, 19x6.
6. Prepaid expenses represent unexpired insurance premiums that were paid on June 1, 19x6, when the exchange rate was $2.23.
7. Long-term debt was incurred on January 1, 19x6.
8. All accounts receivable, accounts payable, and long-term debt amounts are denominated in pounds sterling.
9. Sales, purchases, expenses (including taxes), and depreciation were incurred evenly during the year.
10. Exchange rate on December 31, 19x6, was £ = $2.45.
11. The balance of retained earnings on January 1, 19x6, was zero.
12. Management determined that the functional currency of Wales Company is the pound sterling.

Required:
Translate the financial statements of Wales Company into U.S. dollars.

9–16. In its first quarter report dated January 7, 1983, Walgreen Company commented: "Equity income for the quarter reflects the dollar-translated performance of our Mexican affiliate, Sanborns. The Mexican government fixed the value of the peso at 70 to the dollar on September 1, 1982, the second major devaluation in 1982. This quarter's equity income was aided by a translation gain of $1,727,000 or 11¢ per share due to a favorable monetary position. Equity income, however, was *negatively* affected by a $629,000 (4¢ per share) writedown of Walgreen Company's receivables from Sanborns.

"It will be another year before the difficult income comparisons we currently face from Sanborns will be behind us. We do expect continued growth in Sanborns' LIFO-adjusted *peso* earnings, which were up 159 percent this quarter."

Required:
a. How did "a favorable monetary position" result in a translation gain?
b. How would such a translation gain be shown if—
    (1) Sanborns' functional currency were considered to be the peso?
    (2) Sanborns' functional currency were considered to be the dollar, or if the Mexican peso were considered affected by cumulative inflation of 100 percent or more?
c. How would Walgreen's equity in Sanborns' income have been negatively affected?
d. Why does Walgreen believe that "it will be a year before the difficult income comparisons we currently face from Sanborns' will be behind us"?

9–17. The trial balance of Swisco Corporation, a Swiss corporation at December 31, 19x8, is shown below (in Swiss francs).

	Debit	Credit
Cash	50,000	
Accounts receivable	100,000	
Property, plant, and equipment, net	800,000	
Depreciation expense	100,000	
Other expenses (including taxes)	200,000	
Inventory, January 1, 19x8	150,000	
Sales		2,000,000
Allowance for doubtful accounts		10,000
Accounts payable		80,000
Notes payable		20,000
Capital stock		100,000
Retained earnings, January 1, 19x8		190,000
Purchases	1,000,000	
	2,400,000	2,400,000

Additional information:
1. Swisco uses the periodical inventory system as well as the FIFO method for measuring inventory and cost of good sold. On December 31, 19x8, inventory on hand was SFr120,000. It is carried at cost.

2. The capital stock was issued six years ago when the company was established, at which time the exchange rate was SFr1 = 30 cents. Plant and equipment was purchased five years ago when the exchange rate was SFr1 = 35 cents; the note payable was made out to a local bank at the same time.

3. Revenue and expense items were realized or incurred uniformly throughout 19x8. However, inventory on hand on December 31, 19x8, was purchased throughout the second half of 19x8.

4. The retained earnings balance in the December 31, 19x7, balance sheets (in dollars) of Swisco Corporation was $61,000, and the inventory balance was $47,000.

5. The spot rates for SFr in 19x8 were as follows:

January 1, 19x8	32 cents
Average for 19x8	37
Average for second half of 19x8	36
December 31, 19x8	38

6. Management determined that the functional currency of Swisco is the Swiss franc.

Required:

a. Prepare a trial balance in dollars for Swisco Corporation at December 31, 19x8.

b. Prepare the income statement for the year ending December 31, 19x8, and the balance sheet at that date (in dollars) for Swisco Corporation.

c. Assuming that Unisco Corporation, a U.S. firm, purchased a 75 percent ownership interest in Swisco Corporation at book value on January 1, 19x8, prepare the entry that Unisco would make at December 31, 19x8, to record its equity in Swisco's 19x8 earnings (Unisco uses the complete equity method, to account for its investments in Swisco).

Chapter 10

10–1. Please refer to the financial statements of Alfa, Inc., in Appendix 4B. (See Note 1 "Sugar Revenues," and Note 2 (a), "Deferral of Sugar Profits.")

Required:

I. From the analyst's point of view, which method of revenue recognition (the *old or the new*) better reflects the economic performance of the company? Why?

II. (See Note 5.) Explain the nature of the receivables from C and H of $17,648 (19x6) and $13,875 (19x5). Consider the parenthetical figures of $3,375 and $6,622 in your explanation.

III.* For trend analysis purposes, compute net income for 19x3 through 19x6 under the *old* method and under the *new* method. (Support your figures and list any assumptions you make.)

10–2. On May 5, 19x7, Sterling Corporation signed a contract with Stony Associates under which Stony agreed (1) to construct an office building on land owned by Sterling, (2) to accept responsibility for procuring financing for the project and finding tenants, and (3) to manage the property for 50 years. The annual profit from the project, after debt service, was to be divided equally between Sterling Corporation and Stony Associates. Stony was to accept its share of future profits as full payment

---

* Designates problems of a more advanced or more challenging nature.

for its services in construction, obtaining finances and tenants, and management of the project.

By April 30, 19x8, the project was nearly completed and tenants had signed leases to occupy 90 percent of the available space at annual rentals aggregating $2,600,000. It is estimated that after operating expenses and debt services, the annual profit will amount to $850,000. The management of Stony Associates believed that the economic benefit derived from the contract with Sterling should be reflected on its financial statements for the fiscal year ended April 30, 19x8, and directed that revenue be accrued in an amount equal to the commerical value of the services Stony had rendered during the year, that this amount be carried in contracts receivable, and that all related expenditures be charged against the revenue.

Required:
a. Explain the main difference between the economic concept of business income as reflected by Stony's management and the measurement of income under generally accepted accounting principles.
b. Discuss the factors to be considered in determining when revenue has been realized for the purpose of accounting measurement of periodic income.
c. Is the belief of Stony's management in accord with generally accepted accounting principles for the measurement of revenue and expense for the year ended April 30, 19x8? Support your opinion by discussing the application to this case of the factors to be considered for asset measurement and revenue and expense recognition.

(AICPA)

10–3. In its 1971 annual report, ITT comments as follows regarding the accounting of its Hartford Insurance Group:

"Realized investment gains. Hartford invests in common and preferred stocks to produce earnings from a combination of dividends and appreciation. The Corporation feels that shareholders are entitled to participate currently in the earnings generated by appreciation. However, present accounting rules require the sale of securities in order to record these earnings. Hartford, therefore, sells securities to realize investment gains each year which are equivalent to the appropriate historical rate of return on its portfolio of stocks."

Required:
a. Is the sale of the securities the only way the company's shareholders can participate currently in the appreciation of its securities portfolio?
b. Are the present rules governing the recognition of income from investments useful from the point of view of the financial analyst?

10–4. In your discussion of the financial statements of the Savage Publishing Company, you find that one of the new directors says he is surprised the income statement assumes that an equal proportion of the revenue is earned with the publication of every issue of the company's magazine. He feels that the "crucial event" in the process of earning revenue in the magazine business is the cash sale of the subscription. He says that he does not understand why—other than for the smoothing of income—most of the revenue cannot be "realized" in the period of the sale.

Required:

a. List the various accepted methods for recognizing revenue in the accounts and explain when the methods are appropriate. Do not limit your listing to the methods for the recognition of revenue in magazine publishing.

b. Discuss the propriety of timing the recognition of revenue in the Savage Publishing Company's accounts with—

    (1) The cash sale of the magazine subscription.

    (2) The publication of the magazine every month.

    (3) Both events, by recognizing a portion of the revenue with cash sale of the magazine subscription and a portion of the revenue with the publication of the magazine every month.

(AICPA adapted)

10–5. Square Corporation's financial statements show the following items related to the company's sales and receivables (in thousands):

	19x6	*19x5*
Balance sheet:		
Current assets—notes and accounts receivable less allowance for doubtful accounts	$11,150	$11,910
Noncurrent assets—notes from customers due to 19x9	3,900	2,530
Income statement:		
Sales	65,600	63,900
Statement of changes in financial position:		
Sources:		
Net income	2,200	1,700
Depreciation	1,150	1,010
Working capital from operations	3,350	2,710
Long-term borrowing	4,300	2,200
Decrease in noncurrent receivables	—	340
	7,650	5,250
Uses:		
Additions to plant and equipment	4,580	3,030
Dividends	950	950
Increase in noncurrent receivables	1,370	—
Other	210	140
	7,110	4,120
Increase in net working capital	$ 540	$ 1,130

Required:

1. How much cash was collected from customers during 19x6?

2. How much working capital was provided during 19x6 by the company's operations (consider only *inflows* of working capital provided)?

3. Explain how the increase in noncurrent receivables of $1,370 during 19x6 is a use of working capital.

10–6. Crime Control Company accounts for a substantial part of its alarm systems sales under the sales-type (capitalized) leases method. Simply stated, under this method, the company computes the present value of the total receipts it expects to get (over periods as long as eight years) from a lease and takes that present value amount into sales in the first year of the lease. Justification for this accounting is that the 8-year lease represents more than 75 percent of the 10-year useful life of the equipment.

While the above accounting is done for book purposes, for tax purposes the company reports revenues only as they are received. Since first-year expenses of a lease are particularly heavy, the company reports substantial tax losses on these leases.

Required:

a. Critics maintain that this accounting "front loads" income and that the reported earnings may not be received in cash for years. Comment on this criticism.
b. Will the company's tax accounting benefit reported income?
c. The company asserts that it could achieve earnings results similar to those achieved by its present sales-type lease accounting by selling the lease receivables to third-party lessors or financial institutions. Comment on this assertion.

10–7. Trinket Company started with $3,000 cash in a business to produce trinkets using a simple assembly process. During the first month of business, the company signed sales contracts for 1,300 units (sales price of $9 per unit), produced 1,200 units (production cost of $7 per unit), shipped 1,100 units, and collected in full for 900 units.

Production costs are paid at the time of production. The company has only two other costs: *(a)* sales commissions of 10 percent of sales price are paid at the same time that the company collects from the customer and *(b)* shipping costs of $.20 per unit are paid at time of shipment.

The sales price and all costs have been constant per unit and are likely to remain the same.

Required:

A. Prepare comparative (side-by-side) balance sheets and income statements for the first month of Trinket Company for *each* of the following *three* alternatives:
   (a) Profit is recognized at the time of shipment.
   (b) Profit is recognized at the time of collection.
   (c) Profit is recognized at the time of production.

Note: Net income for each of the three alternatives should be *(a)* $990, *(b)* $810, and *(c)* $1,080.

B. (a) The method whereby profit is recognized only at time of collection, known as the "installment method" is acceptable for financial reporting only in rare and specialized cases. Why would Trinket Company be likely to prefer this method for tax purposes?
   (b) Comment on the usefulness of the "installment method" to a credit analyst.

10–8. Income determination for long-term construction contracts presents special problems because the construction work often extends over two or more accounting periods. The two methods commonly followed are the percentage-of-completion method and the completed-contract method.

Required:

Evaluate the use of the percentage-of-completion method for income determination purposes for long-term construction contracts. Discuss only theoretical arguments.

10–9. A summary of a large contract signed by Builder Construction Company is as follows:

Builder Construction Company uses the percentage-of-completion method when accounting for long-term contracts for financial reporting and the completed-contract method for tax reporting.

Builder signed a large contract on January 2, 19x5. A summary of the contract information shows:

For 19x5:

Contract price	$1,000,000
Estimated total construction costs	800,000
Estimated completion date	December 19x7

Billing schedule:

    June 30, 19x5—20%; December 31, 19x5—15%

    June 30, 19x6—15%; December 31, 19x6—10%

    June 30, 19x7—15%; December 31, 19x7—15%

    After final test—10%

Actual costs incurred during 19x5 = $400,000

Collection of $200,000 for the June 30, 19x5, billing (the December 31, 19x5, billing had not been collected at the end of the year)

For 19x6:

Revised estimated total construction costs	$ 840,000
Actual costs incurred during 19x6	200,000

Collection of $300,000 (for December 31, 19x5, and June 30, 19x6, billings)

For 19x7:

Actual costs incurred during 19x7 (construction completed)	$ 240,000

Collection of $250,000 (for December 31, 19x6, and June 30, 19x7, billings)

Required (ignore income taxes):

1. Prepare comparative income statements for 19x5, 19x6, and 19x7 for financial reporting (stop at the figure "income before taxes"). Assume that the only profit-directed activities occurring during 19x5, 19x6, and 19x7 are described in the summary. Show calculations.†

2. Prepare comparative tax return information showing taxable income for 19x5, 19x6, and 19x7.

---

† A common method of calculating revenue for a long-term contract is:

$$\begin{array}{c}\text{Current year's} \\ \text{revenue}\end{array} = \left[\frac{\text{Total costs incurred to date}}{\text{Estimated total costs}} \times \begin{array}{c}\text{Contract} \\ \text{price}\end{array}\right] \text{less} \left[\begin{array}{c}\text{Revenue recognized} \\ \text{in all prior years}\end{array}\right]$$

3. Balance sheets must be presented for tax reporting also. How will the balance sheet shown for tax reporting differ from the balance sheet in the financial reports at the end of 19x5? (Suggestion: Reconstruct journal entries for both methods and locate differences.)
4. The completed-contract method is not considered preferable for financial reporting. Why do you think that Builder has chosen this method for tax reporting?
5. Which of the two methods of reporting long-term contracts would be most useful to a credit analyst?

10–10. You were requested to personally deliver your report to the board of directors of Sebal Manufacturing Corporation and answer questions posed about the financial statements. While reading the statements, one director asked, "What are the precise meanings of the terms *cost, expense,* and *loss?* These terms sometimes seem to identify similar items and other times seem to identify dissimilar items."

Required:
a. Explain the meanings of the terms (1) *cost,* (2) *expense,* and (3) *loss* as used for financial reporting in conformity with generally accepted accounting principles. In your explanation discuss the distinguishing characteristics of the terms and their similarities and interrelationships.
b. Classify each of the following items as a cost, expense, loss, or other category and explain how the classification of each item may change:
   (1) Cost of goods sold.
   (2) Bad debts expense.
   (3) Depreciation expense for plant machinery.
   (4) Organization costs.
   (5) Spoiled goods.
c. The terms *period cost* and *product cost* are sometimes used to describe certain items in financial statements. Define these terms and distinguish between them. To what types of items do each apply?

10–11. The Smith Company, just starting business, builds a new plant costing $1,000,000. The plant will be fully depreciated over a 10-year period. The company has 100,000 shares of common stock outstanding and no debt. Operating earnings are $400,000 each year before depreciation and income taxes. The tax rate is 50 percent.

Required:
a. Calculate the provision for depreciation on the new plant in year 1 and year 10 using:
   (1) Straight-line method.
   (2) Sum-of-the-years'-digits method.
b. Construct condensed income statements, as reported to stockholders, for year 1 and year 10 if:
   (1) Straight-line depreciation method is used for both tax and reporting purposes.
   (2) Sum-of-the-years'-digits depreciation method is used for both tax and reporting purposes.
   (3) Sum-of-the-years'-digits depreciation method is used for tax purposes and the report to stockholders presented on a "normalized" basis.

c. Show the earnings per share for each of the situations, in *(b)* above, for year 1 and year 10. Explain briefly how you account for the different earnings per share figures. (Figures may be rounded to thousands.)

(CFA)

10–12. Recognition Equipment, Inc., is a specialist in optical character recognition (OCR) systems. Optical character recognition is a system that reads printed forms and feeds the information into computers. Essentially, it is a process used to bypass keypunching. The following footnote describes the noncurrent asset "systems available for lease to customers."

"*Note:* Systems for lease to customers comprise the following:

Systems on lease to customers	$ 9,971,297
Systems available for lease	8,934,132
Systems in process, to be leased	954,048
	$19,859,477

"Systems available for lease include systems that have been completed and which are awaiting shipment or have been shipped, but not yet accepted by customers and systems that have been returned from lease. . . . Provision for depreciation of the various system components is computed on a double-declining balance method over the estimated useful life, ranging from four to eight years. The Company does not depreciate components during the periods that they are not on lease."

Required:
How can Recognition Equipment, Inc., possibly justify not recording any depreciation on components which clearly have a limited useful life?

10–13. Depreciation continues to be one of the most controversial, difficult, and important problem areas in accounting.

Required:
a. (1) Explain the conventional accounting concept of depreciation accounting; and
   (2) Discuss its conceptual merit with respect to *(a)* the value of the asset, *(b)* the charge(s) to expense, and *(c)* the discretion of management in selecting the method.
b. (1) Explain the factors that should be considered when applying the conventional concept of depreciation to the determination of how the value of a newly acquired computer system should be assigned to expense for financial reporting purposes. (Income tax considerations should be ignored.)
   (2) What depreciation methods might be used for the computer system?

(AICPA)

Chapter 11

11–1. Please refer to the financial statements of Alfa, Inc., in Appendix 4B.

Required (dollars in thousands):
a. Estimate the amount of depreciation expense shown on Alfa's 19x6, 19x5, and 19x4 tax return. Use a tax rate of 48 percent and assume that the entire depreciation expense is as shown in the income statement.

b. Identify the amounts for 19x6, 19x5, and 19x4 of the following (combine federal, foreign and state taxes) and show your source.
   (1) Earnings before income taxes.
   (2) Expected income tax at 48 percent.
   (3) Total income tax expense.
   (4) Total income tax due to governments.
   (5) Total income tax due and not yet paid at December 31, 19x6, 19x5, and 19x4 (ignore deferred taxes).

c. (1) Why does the effective tax rate for 19x6, 19x5, and 19x4 differ from 48 percent of income before tax? (Hint: See Note 7.)
   (2) Is it likely that the effective tax rate will continue to be low in the future?

d. Was the company's effective tax rate in 19x5 different from that in 19x4? And if it was, what were the main reason(s)?

e. (1) What was the increase or decrease in deferred tax (current) during 19x6, 19x5, and 19x4?
   (2) What was the increase (decrease) in deferred tax (noncurrent) during 19x6, 19x5, and 19x4?

f. What effect did the investment tax credit have on the 19x6 and 19x5 financial statements?

g. How much was the gain on sale of assets in 19x6? (Hint: Use information in Note 7 and assume a capital gains tax rate of 28 percent.)

h. The company used to recognize revenue at time of shipment until it changed its accounting for revenue recognition in 19x5 (see Note 2). Why then did it show deferred taxes of $29,642 for uncollected sugar revenue in 19x4 (as per Note 7)?

11–2.   Please refer to the financial statements of Alfa, Inc., in Appendix 4B.

Required:

I. The income statement for 19x6 shows a negative expense for "interest capitalized" of $64 while Note 6 indicates a decrease of $47 in net income resulting from capitalized interest. How can you explain that? How much was the amortization, in 19x6, of previously capitalized interest (assuming a tax rate of 48 percent)?

II. (See Note 3, first paragraph.) In connection with the discontinuance of Wilhelm Foods Division, the following four loss figures are mentioned: 19x5—$2,083; 19x4—$1,700; 19x6—$427; and 19x5—$2,713.

   Describe the effects of *each* of these four figures on the balance sheet accounts.

11–3.   Many companies have pension plans for their employees. Accounting for the cost of pension plans is a complex subject in which many technical terms are encountered.

Required:

a. Describe normal cost.

b. Describe vested benefits. Include in your discussion what the actuarially computed value of vested benefits represents.

c. How should actuarial gains and losses directly related to the operation of a pension plan be accounted for?

d. What disclosures concerning pension plans should be made in the company's financial statements or notes?

(AICPA)

11–4. The note excerpt below describes Esmark's accounting for "oil and gas exploration and development activities."

Principal Accounting Policies:

Property and operating facilities: The field cost method of accounting is used for oil and gas exploration and development activities. Under this method, costs of acquisition, exploration and development, other than exploratory dry holes, are capitalized as oil and gas properties. Costs associated with a producing field are depleted on the unit-of-production method over the remaining proven developed reserves of the field as estimated by the Company. Capitalized costs in excess of the estimated economic value of a field's estimated reserves and capitalized costs applicable to fields which prove to be nonproductive are charged against operations by additional depletion provisions when such determinations are made.

Required:

a. Describe any acceptable accounting methods and indicate whether you prefer Esmark's method or an alternative, and why.
b. From the point of view of the financial statement analyst and user, what is the major weakness of all accounting methods for natural resources in present use?

11–5. The following footnote is from the financial statements of Maust Coal and Coke Corporation (the company had net income of $1,912,595 and sales of $42,949,034):

Note 1—Mine Development: During the fiscal year, the company was engaged in a major mine development program in both new and existing coal mines. At the same time substantial coal tonnage was produced from mines considered to be wholly or partly in the development stage. It was not practicable to make a definite allocation of costs and expenditures for these mines between development and production. For this reason, costs and expenditures aggregating $13,447,804 (including $1,230,051 of depreciation and $603,370 of interest on long-term debt but excluding selling, general, and administrative expense) reduced by sales revenues aggregating $9,800,950 have been capitalized as net mine development expense of $3,646,854 to be amortized over future years on the basis of production. In recent years, mine development expenditures were immaterial and being incidental to production activities, were absorbed in current operations.

Required:

(1) What major problem of accounting measurement did Maust face?
(2) How did Maust solve the measurement problem?
(3) Do you agree with Maust's solution? Why or why not?
(4) How can Maust possibly justify capitalizing depreciation and interest as an asset?
(5) What is the main significance of the footnote to an analyst?

11–6. Effective January 1, 1975, Ford Motor Company changed from the deferred method to the flow-through method of accounting for the investment tax credit. A note in the annual report explaining this change reads in part as follows:

"The flow-through method recognizes the increased emphasis the federal government has placed on the investment credit as an economic stimulus and it reflects more accurately the effect of investment decisions on the company's earnings. The change improved earnings . . . in 1975 by $95 million or $1.02 per share.

The Ford Motor Company Annual Report contained the following information:

	Income per share data				
	1975	*1974*	*1973*	*1972*	*1971*
Income before cumulative effect of an accounting change	$2.44	$3.50	$9.13	$8.52	$6.18
Cumulative effect of an accounting change	1.02	—	—	—	—
Net income (historical)	$3.46	$3.50	$9.13	$8.52	$6.18
Net income (pro forma)*		$3.90	$9.46	$8.68	$6.27

* These pro forma amounts assume that the investment tax credits accrued after 1970 flowed through to income in the year the assets were placed in service. Investment tax credits for years prior to 1971 continue to be amortized.

Required:

a. In light of the data provided above, comment on the reasons given by Ford for the change in its accounting treatment of the investment tax credit.
b. Appraise the statement: ". . . (the flow-through method) reflects more accurately the effect of investment decisions on the company's earnings. . . ."
c. Discuss the effect of this accounting change on Ford's cash flow in 1975.

(CFA)

11–7. Aetna Life & Casualty Company, the large property and casualty company, has large amounts of municipal bond interest as well as dividend income most of which escapes taxation. During a period of highly competitive conditions and of adverse results from the property and casualty business, the company was still able to report operating profits to its shareholders while reporting large losses for tax purposes.

The tax losses can now be carried forward for 15 years. At the end of 1981, these unutilized tax loss carry-forward benefits amounted to $736 million. Aetna and its auditors concluded that realization of these tax loss carry-forward benefits from the shielding of future taxable income was assured "beyond any reasonable doubt" and consequently credited the expected tax savings to income currently. Instead of booking the future tax benefits as an asset, Aetna chose to show the item in the liability section in brackets—a sort of "negative liability." The company justifies this unusual balance sheet treatment by claiming that the $144 million item on June 30, 1982, would be more visible on the liability side rather than among the large asset categories into which it would have to be merged on the left-hand side of the balance sheet.

Among the justifications the company seemingly advances for concluding that the benefits are realizable "beyond any reasonable doubt" are the now longer 15-year carry-forward period, the option to consolidate profitable life insurance business results, and the ability to increase taxable income by shifting its portfolio from tax exempt to higher yielding taxable securities, as well as hopes for a reversal of unfavorable property and casualty insurance results.

Required:

Evaluate Aetna's tax loss carry-forward accounting practices.

11–8. Big Deal Construction Company specializes in building dams. During the years 19x3, 19x4, and 19x5, three dams were completed. The first dam was started in 19x1 and completed in 19x3 at a profit before income taxes of $120,000.

The second and third dams were started in 19x2. The second dam was completed in 19x4 at a profit before income taxes of $126,000, and the third dam was completed in 19x5 at a profit before income taxes of $150,000.

The company uses the percentage-of-completion method of accounting in its books and the completed-contract method of accounting for income tax purposes.

Data relating to the progress toward completion of work on each dam as reported by the company's engineers are set forth below:

Dam	19x1	19x2	19x3	19x4	19x5
1	20%	60%	20%		
2		30	60	10%	
3		10	30	50	10%

Required:

Assuming that the applicable income tax rate is 50 percent, for each of the five years 19x1 through 19x5 show *(a)* the book income, *(b)* the taxable income, and *(c)* the change in deferred income taxes.

11–9. Steady Corporation was formed in 19x4 to take over the operations of a small business. This business proved to be very stable for Steady as can be seen below (dollars in thousands):

	19x4	19x5	19x6
Sales	$10,000	$10,000	$10,000
Expenses (except income tax)	9,000	9,000	9,000
Income before taxes	1,000	1,000	1,000

In addition, Steady expended $1,400,000 on preoperating costs for a new product during 19x4. These costs were deferred for financial reporting purposes but were deducted in calculating 19x4 taxable income. During 19x5, the new product line was delayed; and in 19x6, Steady abandoned the new product and charged the deferred cost of $1,400,000 to the 19x6 income statement.

Required:

a. Prepare comparative income statements in good form for the three years. Be certain to identify all tax amounts as either "current" or "deferred."
b. List each tax item on the balance sheets at the end of each year (assume all tax payments and refunds occur in the year following the reporting year and that the tax rate is 50 percent in each year).

11–10. Schoolyards, Inc., was granted a distribution franchise by Delorean Products in 19x1. Operations were profitable until 19x4 when certain of the company's inventories were confiscated and large legal expenses were incurred. Schoolyards' tax rate was 50 percent each year (assume the 19x4 expenses to be deductible; in thousands).

	19x1	19x2	19x3	19x4	19x5	19x6	19x7	19x8
Sales	$50	$80	$120	$100	$200	$400	$500	$600
Cost of sales	20	30	50	300	50	120	200	250
General and administrative	10	35	20	100	20	30	40	50
Net before tax	20	35	50	(300)	130	250	260	300

Required:

Prepare journal entries to record tax expense for each of these years and present the comparative income statements.

11–11. The following quotation from an article written by Leopold Bernstein highlights the issue concerning the use of reserves to recognize future costs and losses— are they valid or merely a means of further clouding reports?

"The growing use of reserves for future costs and losses impairs the significance of periodically reported income and should be viewed with skepticism by the analyst of financial statements. That is especially true when the reserves are established in years of heavy losses, when they are established in an arbitrary amount designed to offset an extraordinary gain, or when they otherwise appear to have as their main purpose the relieving of future income of expenses properly chargeable to it.

"The basic justification in accounting for the recognition of future losses stems from the doctrine of conservatism which, according to one popular application, means that one should anticipate no gains, but take all the losses one can clearly see as already incurred."

Required:

a.   Discuss the merits of Bernstein's arguments and apprehensions.

b.   Explain how such information may be factored into your review of past trends, the estimates of future earnings, and valuation of the common stock.

(CFA)

11–12. The preliminary condensed income statements of Disposo Corporation is shown below.

	19x8	19x7
Sales	$1,100	$900
Costs and expenses	990	860
Loss on asset disposal	10	—
Income before taxes	100	40
Tax expense	50	20
Net income	$ 50	$ 20

Note: On August 15, 19x8, the company decided to discontinue its Metals Division. The business was sold on December 31, 19x8, at book value except for a factory building with a book value of $25 which was sold for $15.

Operations of the Metals Division were:

	Sales	Income (loss)
19x7	$300	$ 8
Jan. 1 to Aug. 15, 19x8	250	(3)
Aug. 16 to Dec. 31, 19x8	75	(1)

Required:

a.   Correct the statements to reflect the proper presentation of the discontinued operations.

b.   *Assume* that the actual disposal had not occurred until January 20, 19x9. The loss on sale of asset is still $10 before tax, and operations for the 20 days of January are sales, $25; and net loss, $2. How would the 19x8 corrected income statement have been different?

11–13.   It is important in accounting theory to be able to distinguish the types of accounting changes.

Required:
a.   If a public company desires to change from the sum-of-the-years'-digits depreciation method to the straight-line method for its fixed assets, what type of accounting change would this be? Discuss the permissibility of this change.
b.   When pro forma disclosure is required for an accounting change, how are these pro forma amounts determined?
c.   If a public company obtained additional information about the service lives of some of its fixed assets which showed that the service lives previously used should be shortened, what type of accounting change would this be? Include in your discussion how the change should be reported in the income statement of the year of the change, and what disclosures should be made in the financial statements or notes.
d.   Changing specific subsidiaries comprising the group of companies for which consolidated financial statements are presented is an example of what type of accounting change, and what effect does it have on the consolidated income statements?

(AICPA)

11–14.   Part a.   The various types of accounting changes may significantly affect the presentation of both financial position and results of operations for an accounting period and the trends shown in comparative financial statements and historical summaries.

Required:
1.   Describe a change in accounting principle and how it should be reported in the income statement of the period of the change.
2.   Describe a change in accounting estimate and how it should be reported in the income statement of the period of the change.
3.   Describe a change in reporting entity and how it should be reported. Give an appropriate example of a change in reporting entity.

Part b.   A corporation has a noncompensatory stock purchase plan for all of its employees and a compensatory stock option plan for some of its corporate officers.

Required:
1.   Compare and contrast the accounting at the date the stock is issued for the noncompensatory stock purchase plan and the compensatory stock option plan.
2.   What entry should be made for the compensatory stock option plan at the date of the grant?

(AICPA)

11–15.   In January 1980, Union Carbide announced a series of accounting changes that in the aggregate are expected to increase the company's reported calendar 1980 earnings by more than $5 per share. Prior to this announcement, most analysts were estimating that Union Carbide would report 1980 earnings of about $7 a share but with the accounting changes, their estimates have been raised to around $12 per share.

The accounting changes and their estimated contribution to reported 1980 earnings are as follows:

Inclusion of all deferred investment tax credits in reported
    earnings .... $3.20 per share
Adoption of the flow-through method of reporting investment
    tax credits .... 0.25 per share
Extending the depreciable life of certain physical assets for book
    purposes .... 1.35 per share
Application of FASB statement providing for capitalizing interest
    on construction, for book purposes .... 0.30 per share
        Total .... $5.10 per share

Required:

a. Indicate which, if any, of these accounting changes will affect Union Carbide's calendar 1980 cash flow.
b. Indicate which, if any, of the four changes in accounting will be considered nonrecurring and so identified in the 1980 annual report.
c. Briefly discuss how these accounting changes in total might influence the board of directors in their determination of the common dividend payout policy.

(CFA)

11–16. With reference to the following note to the financial statements of U.S. Industries, answer the questions below:

Change in accounting for membership revenues. The Corporation has two subsidiaries, one of which is 80 percent owned, which operate health spas. These companies sell health club memberships that have specific terms, which presently range up to 30 months. In prior years, revenue from sale of memberships, less a deferred portion, was taken into income at the time of sale. The deferred portion was taken into revenue on a straight-line basis over the membership terms and was equivalent to the estimated future cost of providing facilities and services. These costs consisted of a pro rata share of estimated future operating expenses. In December 1974, Touche Ross & Company, independent accountants for the corporation's health spa subsidiaries, informed the corporation that they had taken a position as a firm, which they suggested should be effective for fiscal years ended after December 31, 1974, to recognize membership fee revenue and associated costs over the period of membership.

The subsidiaries have concluded that, even though the change has not been required by an authoritative accounting body, there is sufficient authoritative support within similar industries and they have accepted the change suggested by their independent accountants.

Accounting Principles Board (APB) Opinion No. 20, "Accounting Changes," provides that such a change be made by including, as an element of net earnings during the year of change, the cumulative effect of the change on prior years. Had *APB Opinion No. 20* been followed literally, the cumulative effect of the accounting change would have been included as a charge, net of tax benefits, in the 1975 consolidated statement of income and would have resulted in reporting a consolidated net loss of $3,398,000 ($.24 per common share) in 1975 and a consolidated net income of

$18,171,000 ($.44 per common share) in 1974. Because of the magnitude and pervasiveness of this change, the corporation believes a literal application of *APB Opinion No. 20* would result in a misleading presentation, and that this change should, therefore, be made on a retroactive basis. The corporation's and the subsidiaries' independent accountants concur in this treatment.

As a result of retroactive treatment of the change in the method of accounting for membership revenues, the consolidated financial statements for prior years have been restated. The effect of the change was to reduce consolidated net income for 1975 by $90,000 and to increase consolidated net income previously reported for 1974 by $5,160,000 ($.16 per share). The increase in deferred revenue at January 1, 1974, net of related tax benefits, resulted in an adjustment to opening retained earnings of $19,037,000.

Required:
a. Do you prefer the old method or the new method of accounting for membership revenues as a measurement of *economic* performance? Support your conclusion.
b. Given the decision to change accounting methods, do you agree or disagree with the company's decision to restate prior years and thereby *NOT* follow generally accepted accounting principles? Explain why!
c. Identify the effects of the change in accounting upon both the 1974 *and* 1975 (1) balance sheets and (2) income statements. Identify specific accounts and amounts (assume none of the effects relates to minority interest) and list any assumptions and explain any unidentified accounts or amounts.

11–17. *The Hot Tub Company* started business on January 1, 19x5, and requires its customers to make a 20 percent cash deposit with each sales order. Such deposits are credited to sales when received. The remaining 80 percent is collected and credited to sales when delivery is made to the customer.

Deposits on sales orders for which goods had not yet been produced and shipped amounted to $8,000 at the end of 19x5, $11,000 at the end of 19x6, and $10,000 at the end of 19x7.

You believe that the company's accounting for deposits is not generally accepted and you propose to revise (for analytical purposes) the company's financial statements to record sales revenue only at time of shipment. Customer deposits received will be shown as liabilities until earned.

Required:
How would your analytical adjustment *change* Hot Tub's 19x5, 19x6, and 19x7 balance sheets and income statements? *(Ignore tax consequences.)*

11–18. *UPS Company* determined that $1 million of inventory purchased during 19x5 was obsolete and worthless at December 31, 19x5. During 19x7, the management discovered that this inventory has been included in error in the total inventories reported at December 31, 19x5, and December 31, 19x6. What effect did these errors have on the income *before* taxes in the most recent year 19x6?

11–19. The Century Company, a diversified manufacturing company, had four separate operating divisions engaged in the manufacture of products in each of the following areas: food products, health aids, textiles, and office equipment.

Financial data for the two years ended December 31, 1975, and 1974 are presented below:

| | Net sales | | Cost of sales | | Operating expenses | |
	1975	1974	1975	1974	1975	1974
Food products....	$3,500,000	$3,000,000	$2,400,000	$1,800,000	$ 550,000	$ 275,000
Health aids....	2,000,000	1,270,000	1,100,000	700,000	300,000	125,000
Textiles ..	1,580,000	1,400,000	500,000	900,000	200,000	150,000
Office equipment ...	920,000	1,330,000	800,000	1,000,000	650,000	750,000
	$8,000,000	$7,000,000	$4,800,000	$4,400,000	$1,700,000	$1,300,000

On January 1, 1975, Century adopted a plan to sell the assets and product line of the office equipment division and expected to realize a gain on this disposal. On September 1, 1975, the division's assets and product line were sold for $2,100,000 cash resulting in a gain of $640,000 (exclusive of operations during the phase-out period).

The company's textiles division had six manufacturing plants that produced a variety of textile products. In April 1975, the company sold one of these plants and realized a gain of $130,000. After the sale, the operations at the plant that was sold were transferred to the remaining five textile plants that the company continued to operate.

In August 1975, the main warehouse of the food products division, located on the banks of the Bayer River, was flooded when the river overflowed. The resulting damage of $420,000 is not included in the financial data given above. Historical records indicate that the Bayer River normally overflows every four to five years causing flood damage to adjacent property.

For the two years ended December 31, 1975, and 1974, the company had interest revenue earned on investments of $70,000 and $40,000, respectively.

For the two years ended December 31, 1975, and 1974, the company's net income was $960,000 and $670,000, respectively.

The provision for income tax expense for each of the two years should be computed at a rate of 50 percent.

Required:
Prepare in proper form a comparative statement of income of the Century Company for the two years ended December 31, 1975, and December 31, 1974. Footnotes are *not* required.

(AICPA)

11–20. Corporate management has considerable freedom of action in selecting from generally acceptable accounting procedures that have a material effect on reported results. List five such procedures relating to different areas of accounting, and explain in a sentence or two how each might be used to report higher current earnings per share.

(CFA)

Chapter 12

12–1. Earnings per share (EPS) is the most featured single financial statistic about modern corporations. Daily published quotations of stock prices have recently been expanded to include a "times earnings" figure for many securities which is based on EPS. Often the focus of analysts' discussions will be on the EPS of the corporations receiving their attention.

Required:

a. Explain how dividends or dividend requirements on any class of preferred stock that may be outstanding affect the computation of EPS.

b. One of the technical procedures applicable in EPS computations is the "treasury stock method."

   (1) Briefly describe the circumstances under which it might be appropriate to apply the treasury stock method.

   (2) There is a limit to the extent to which the treasury stock method is applicable. Indicate what this limit is and give a succinct indication of the procedures that should be followed beyond the treasury stock limits.

c. Under some circumstances, convertible debentures would be considered "common stock equivalents," while under other circumstances, they would not.

   (1) When is it proper to treat convertible debentures as common stock equivalents? What is the effect on computation of EPS in such cases?

   (2) In case convertible debentures are not considered as common stock equivalents, explain how they are handled for purposes of EPS computations

(AICPA)

12–2. Generally accepted accounting principles require the presentation of corporate earnings per share data on the face of the income statement.

Required:

(1) Explain the meaning of "primary earnings per share."

(2) Explain how "fully diluted earnings per share" differs from primary earnings per share."

12–3. a. At December 31, 19x6, the Front Company had 400,000 shares of common stock outstanding. On October 1, 19x7, an additional 100,000 shares of common stock were issued. In addition, Front had $10,000,000 of 8 percent convertible bonds outstanding at December 31, 19x6, which are convertible into 225,000 shares of common stock. The bonds were considered common stock equivalents at the time of their issuance, and no bonds were converted into common stock in 19x7. The net income for the year ended December 31, 19x7, was $3,500,000. Assuming the income tax rate was 50 percent, what should the primary earnings per share for the year ended December 31, 19x7, be?

b. At December 31, 19x4, the Back Company had 350,000 shares of common stock outstanding. On September 1, 19x5, an additional 150,000 shares of common stock were issued. In addition, Back had $10,000,000 of 8 percent convertible bonds outstanding at December 31, 19x4, which are convertible into 200,000 shares of common stock. The bonds were not considered common stock equivalents at the time

of their issuance and no bonds were converted into common stock in 19x5. The net
income for the year ended December 31, 19x5, was $3,000,000. Assuming the income
tax rate was 50 percent, what should be the fully diluted earnings per share for the
year ended December 31, 19x5?

(AICPA adapted)

12–4. **a.** Weaver Company had 100,000 shares of common stock issued and
outstanding at December 31, 19x8. On July 1, 19x9, Weaver issued a 10 percent
stock dividend. Unexercised stock options to purchase 20,000 shares of common
stock (adjusted for the 19x9 stock dividend) at $20 per share were outstanding at
the beginning and end of 19x9. The average market price of Weaver's common stock
(which was not affected by the stock dividend) was $25 per share during 19x9. Net
income for the year ended December 31, 19x9, was $550,000. What should be Weaver's
19x9 primary earnings per common share, rounded to the nearest penny?

b. During 19x2, Hoffman Company had a net income of $50,000 (no extraordinary
items) and 50,000 shares of common stock and 10,000 shares of preferred stock
outstanding. Hoffman declared and paid dividends of $.50 per share to common
and $6 per share to preferred. Although the preferred stock is convertible into common
stock on a share-for-share basis, it is not classified as a common stock equivalent.
For 19x2, Hoffman Company should report fully diluted earnings (loss) per share
of?

c. A company has net income of $900,000 for computation of primary earnings
per share (EPS) and net income of $960,000 for computation of fully diluted EPS.
Its capital structure consists only of common stock and $2,000,000 of bonds convertible
into common stock, all outstanding all year. The bonds were issued at face value
and are not common stock equivalents. Assuming an effective income tax rate of
40 percent, what is the stated interest rate on these bonds?

(AICPA adapted)

12–5. Foster, Inc., showed the following for 19x6:

Income before extraordinary item	$600,000
Extraordinary item—casualty loss	
(net after taxes)	100,000
Net income for period	$500,000

1. At January 1, 19x6, there were 190,00 shares of common stock outstanding.
   On October 1, 19x6, an additional 40,000 shares were sold for cash.
2. In 19x4, 6 percent bonds were issued at par, $1,000,000. These are convertible
   into 20,000 shares of common stock. None have been converted. At date of
   issue, the bank prime rate was 8 percent.
3. In 19x2, 25,000 shares of $3 cumulative preferred stock were issued at $90 per
   share. Each preferred share is convertible into two shares of common stock.
   None have been converted. At date of issue, the bank prime rate was 9 percent.
4. In 19x3, 40,000 options were granted to purchase common stock (one option
   for each share) at $48 per share. None have been exercised. During 19x6, the
   average market price per share of common stock was $50 and on December
   31, 19x6, the market price was $60. Assume an income tax rate of 40 percent.

Required:

a. Calculate primary earnings per share.

b. Calculate fully diluted earnings per share.

12–6. The Arctic Corporation had net income of $5,000,000. The company had (for the entire year) 3,000,000 common shares outstanding. The year-end price of the shares was $45 per share. Average market price for the year was $40 per share. The company has options and warrants outstanding to purchase at $30 per share, 1,000,000 common shares. Assume that all borrowings are at 10 percent interest and that a 50 percent tax rate is in effect.

Required:

Calculate primary and fully diluted earnings per share.

12–7. Mason Corporation's capital structure is as follows:

	December 31	
	1980	*1979*
Outstanding shares of:		
Common stock	336,000	300,000
Nonconvertible preferred stock	10,000	10,000
8% convertible bonds	$1,000,000	$1,000,000

The following additional information is available:

1. On September 1, 1980, Mason sold 36,000 additional shares of common stock.
2. Net income for the year ended December 31, 1980, was $750,000.
3. During 1980, Mason paid dividends of $3 per share on its nonconvertible preferred stock.
4. The 8 percent convertible bonds are convertible into 40 shares of common stock for each $1,000 bond, and were not considered common stock equivalents at the date of issuance.
5. Unexercised stock options to purchase 30,000 shares of common stock at $22.50 per share were outstanding at the beginning and end of 1980. The average market price of Mason's common stock was $36 per share during 1980. The market price was $33 per share at December 31, 1980.
6. Warrants to purchase 20,000 shares of common stock at $38 per share were attached to the preferred stock at the time of issuance. The warrants, which expire on December 31, 1985, were outstanding at December 31, 1980.
7. Mason's effective income tax rate was 40% for 1979 and 1980.

Required (show supporting computations in good form, and round earnings per share to the nearest penny):

1. Compute the number of shares which should be used for the computation of primary earnings per common share for the year ended December 31, 1980.
2. Compute the primary earnings per common share for the year ended December 31, 1980.
3. Compute the number of shares which should be used for the computation of fully diluted earnings per common share for the year ended December 31, 1980.

4. Compute the fully diluted earnings per common share for the year ended December 31, 1980.

12–8. According to a brokerage firm report in your files, the major reason for the $.76 net per share increase in Masonite's 1979 earnings to $3.49 was the decline in the number of shares outstanding. Referring to the following statements, calculate the change in 1979 per share earnings (a) due to the decline in shares and (b) due to any other major factors. On the basis of your calculations, indicate whether you agree with the brokerage report.

MASONITE CORPORATION AND SUBSIDIARY COMPANIES
Consolidated Statements of Income (Extracts)

	Year ended August 31	
	1979	*1978*
Net sales	$542,467,000	$529,024,000
Cost of sales	421,430,000	406,224,000
Selling, administrative, and research expenses	53,881,000	49,295,000
Income from operations.....................	67,156,000	73,505,000
Other income (expense):		
Income from sale of timber..................	3,717,000	4,703,000
Income from oil operations, net	1,617,000	1,692,000
Income from foreign affiliates	1,250,000	879,000
Interest net	1,844,000	1,443,000
Other, net	3,516,000	(1,333,000)
Income before income taxes	79,100,000	80,889,000
Total income taxes	27,600,000	36,400,000
Net income	$ 51,500,000	$ 44,489,000
Per share	$3.49	$2.73

(CFA adapted)

12–9. Although numerous rulings by the Accounting Principles Board and the Financial Accounting Standards Board have limited the flexibility of corporate accounting, management still has opportunities to "manage" earnings. Listed below are six actions company managements may take to influence earnings per share.
A. Management writes down goodwill because it is no longer supported by high earning power of the related assets.
B. A nondividend paying company repurchases some of its shares at 50 percent of book value.
C. A company shifts from the cost method to the equity method of accounting for a profitable, nondividend paying affiliate.
D. A company liquidates an unprofitable division.
E. Management records a major loss contingency when a new revolutionary government in a foreign country nationalizes all foreign-owned businesses including the company's subsidiary.
F. A consolidated foreign subsidiary sells an undeveloped mining lease at a 50 percent profit after all taxes. The dollar has appreciated 100 percent against the local currency since the lease was acquired. Cash from the sale is invested by the subsidiary in a bank time deposit in that country.

Required:

For each action *(a–f)*, separately *indicate* whether the effect would be an "increase," a "decrease," or "unchanged" on the following four items:

1. Net income per share in the year of the action.
2. Net income per share in the following year.
3. Total cash flow in the year of the action.
4. Total cash flow in the following year.

Any assumptions you feel necessary should be stated with your answer.

(CFA)

12–10. On July 1, 19x8, the board of directors of Movie Company decided to acquire the Camera and Projector Corporations. Following is some additional information on this purchase transaction:

	Movie Company	Camera Company	Projector Company
Net income from January 1 to June 30, 19x8 ..	$300,000	$200,000	$100,000
Common shares outstanding on July 1, 19x8 ..	100,000	50,000	200,000
Shares issued after January 1, 19x8:			
Shares issued on April 1, 19x8		30,000	
Shares issued on May 1, 19x8			100,000
Shares issued on July 1, 19x8 for acquisition of:			
Camera (3 for 1)	150,000		
Projector (1 for 2)	100,000		
Net income from July 1 to December 31, 19x8	$750,000		

Required:

Calculate EPS for Movie Company for the year ending December 31, 19x8.

12–11. On October 1, 19x5, the management of the Morning Corporation decided to merge with the Afternoon and Evening Corporations. Following is some additional information (the merger was accounted for as a pooling):

	Afternoon Corporation	Evening Corporation	Morning Corporation
Net income from January 1 to September 30, 19x5..............	$200,000	$300,000	–0–
Common shares outstanding on October 1, 19x5	100,000	80,000	300,000
Shares issued on July 1, 19x5	50,000		
Shares issued on September 1, 19x5		20,000	
Net income from October 1 to December 31, 19x5			$500,000
Number of shares issued for acquisition of:			
Afternoon Corp. (2 for 1)			200,000
Evening Corp. (5 for 1)			400,000

Required:
Compute earnings per share for the Consolidated Company on December 31, 19x5.

12–12. The Splitting Company, in its annual reports for the years ending December 31, reported per share earnings as shown below:

19x0	$3.00
19x1	2.00
19x2	1.50
19x3	3.00
19x4	1.80
19x5	2.50
19x6	2.50

The following changes in capitalization took place in December of each of the years shown:

19x1 ..... 50% stock dividend paid
19x2 ..... 400,000 shares of common stock issued for cash
19x3 ..... 2-for-1 split effective
19x5 ..... 300,000 shares issued on conversion of an outstanding debenture issue
19x6 ..... 80% stock dividend paid

The head of the research department has asked you to make the necessary adjustments to the reported figures so that a better comparison of changes in earnings on the common stock can be made.

(CFA adapted)

Chapter 13

13–1. Please refer to the financial statements of Alfa, Inc., in Appendix 4B.

Required:
I.   How much cash was collected from customers during 19x5? (Hint: Use SCFP to derive beginning balance of receivables.)
II. How much was *paid* in cash dividends on common stock during 19x6?
III. How much was the total cost of goods and services produced and otherwise generated in 19x6? Consider *all* inventories (including real estate and other).
IV. What does the $3,409 amount of "Property sales and retirements—other" for 19x6 represent (see item 49)?
V.   Is the item "Issuance of capital stock for business acquired $2,494" (item 48) a source of working capital? If not, how can it appear as a "source" in a tabulation that ends with an increase in working capital (item 60)? Explain.
VI. How much was the deferred tax provision for 19x6? What effect did it have on current liabilities?
VII. What effect did the 19x6 depreciation expense have on working capital (i.e., on current assets and/or current liabilities)? Discuss as fully as you can.

13–2. Please refer to the financial statements of Alfa, Inc., in Appendix 4B.

Required:
Determine the net cash flow from operation for 19x4 and 19x5.
(a) The inflow-outflow approach.
(b) The net approach.
(Assume that noncurrent receivables relate to operations.)

13–3.* Please refer to the financial statements of Alfa, Inc., in Appendix 4B.
   The comparison of "Cash from operations" over a period can be affected by items such as accounting changes and discontinued operations. To put both inflows and outflows of cash on a comparable basis, such comparative statements of sources and uses of cash must be appropriately adjusted.

Required:
(A) Prepare comparative (side-by-side) complete cash statements for 19x4 and 19x5 (exclude 19x6). Use inflow-outflow approach and the best presentation, even for insignificant amounts. Round to millions of dollars. Consider the effect of the change in accounting method by showing four columns as follows:

---

* Designates problems of a more advanced or more challenging nature.

	As reported		Restated
19x5	*19x5*	*19x4*	*19x4*
Unadjusted	*(New method)*	*(Old method)*	*(New method)*

Explain all necessary adjustments and restatements clearly. Your statement should end with the increase (decrease) in cash and marketable securities combined. (Hint: Use pro forma amounts to obtain effect of accounting change on each year and footnote information to determine both revenues and expenses of discontinued operations.)

(B) Comment on the most important information provided by your statements in (A) above, with respect to the company's *trend* of performance from 19x4 to 19x5.

13–4. a. There have been considerable discussion and research in recent years concerning the reporting of changes in financial position (sources and applications of funds). *APB Opinion 19* concluded

". . . that the statement summarizing changes in financial position should be based on a broad concept embracing all changes in financial position and that the title of the statement should reflect this broad concept. The Board therefore recommends that the title be Statement of Changes in Financial Position."

Required:

(1) What are the two common meanings of "funds" as used when preparing the statement of changes in financial position? Explain.

(2) What is meant by ". . . a broad concept embracing all changes in financial position . . ." as used by the Accounting Principles Board in its *Opinion 19?* Explain.

b. Chen Engineering Company is a young and growing producer of electronic measuring instruments and technical equipment. You have been retained by Chen to advise it in the preparation of a statement of changes in financial position. For the fiscal year ended October 31, 1975, you have obtained the following information concerning certain events and transactions of Chen.

1. The amount of reported earnings for the fiscal year was $800,000, which included a deduction for an extraordinary loss of $93,000 (see item 5 below).
2. Depreciation expense of $240,000 was included in the earnings statement.
3. Uncollectible accounts receivable of $30,000 were written off against the allowance for uncollectible accounts. Also, $37,000 of bad debts expense was included in determining earnings for the fiscal year, and the same amount was added to the allowance for uncollectible accounts.
4. A gain of $4,700 was realized on the sale of a machine; it originally cost $75,000 of which $25,000 was undepreciated on the date of sale.

5. On April 1, 1975, a freak lightning storm caused an uninsured inventory loss of $93,000 ($180,000 loss, less reduction in income taxes of $87,000). This extraordinary loss was included in determining earnings as indicated in 1 above.

6. On July 3, 1975, building and land were purchased for $600,000; Chen gave in payment $100,000 cash, $200,000 market value of its unissued common stock, and a $300,000 purchase-money mortgage.

7. On August 3, 1975, $700,000 face value of Chen's 6 percent convertible debentures were converted into $140,000 par value of its common stock. The bonds were originally issued at face value.

8. The board of directors declared a $320,000 cash dividend on October 20, 1975, payable on November 15, 1975, to stockholders of record on November 5, 1975.

Required:

For each of the eight (8) numbered items above, explain whether each item is a source or use of working capital and explain how it should be disclosed in Chen's statement of changes in financial position for the fiscal year ended October 31, 1975. If any item is neither a source nor a use of working capital, explain why it is *not* and indicate the disclosure, if any, that should be made of the item in Chen's statement of changes in financial position for the fiscal year ended October 31, 1975.

(AICPA)

13–5. The following data were taken from the accounting records of McClure Corporation and subsidiaries for 19x6:

	Millions
Income before extraordinary items	$33.3
Extraordinary items (net gain after tax)	6.7
Deferred income taxes for 19x6	5.0
Major disposals of property, plant and equipment (book value)	10.2
Depreciation, depletion, and amortization	15.0
Amortization of deferred investment tax credit	3.5
Undistributed earnings of unconsolidated subsidiary and affiliates	7.7
Net proceeds from sale of new debentures	24.3
Amortization of discount on bonds payable	2.5
Decrease in noncurrent assets	3.9
Proceeds from exercise of stock options	3.6

Required:

Prepare a step-by-step determination of the amount of working capital provided by operations.

(CFA adapted)

13–6. The following is the income statement of NYC Corporation for the year ended December 31, 19x0.

NYC CORPORATION

Income Statement

For the Year Ended December 31, 19x0

(in thousands)

Revenues:		
Sales..	$2,690	
Equity in earnings of 30 percent owned affiliate*............	50	
Gain on sale of machinery	20	
Gain on bond retirement...............................	65	
Total revenues		$2,825
Costs and expenses:		
Cost of goods sold	1,350	
Selling and administrative expenses	750	
Depreciation expense	45	
Interest expense†	33	
Equity in loss of a 40 percent owned affiliate	30	
Goodwill amortization.................................	25	
Minority stockholder's share of net income	7	2,240
Income before taxes...................................		585
Income taxes:		
Current	165	
Deferred	115	280
Net income	$ 305	

* Dividends received from the 30 percent owned affiliate during 19x0 were $30,000.

† Interest expense includes bond discount amortization, $8,000.

‡ In preparing its SCFP, NYC Corporation shows *total* proceeds from sales of fixed assets as sources of funds.

Required:

Compute working capital provided by operations during 19x0.

13–7. The ability to visualize quickly the effect of a given transaction on the working capital (or cash) resources of an enterprise is a valuable analytical skill. Such visualization requires an understanding of the reality behind the transaction as well as how it is accounted for. Expressing such accounting in journal entry form is the most helpful approach.

Required:

A simplified schematic statement of changes in financial position of a company for the year is shown below. The company closes its books once each year, on December 31.

Nine of the lines in the schematic shown below are given labels (letters). For each of the activities listed, identify which of these nine lines is affected and by *how much.* Use the labels (letters) shown below. Do not indicate the effect on any line not given a label. If a transaction has no effect, write *none.* In indicating effects for lines Y and WC use a + to indicate an increase and a − to indicate a decrease. Be sure to show the amount!

Note: Every item, with an effect, affects at least two lines. (Debits must equal credits.)

Schematic Statement of Changes in Financial Position of the Company for the Year

Sources of working capital:

(Y)	Net income	_____(Y)
(YA)	Additions or addbacks for expenses, losses etc., not using working capital	_____(YA)
(YS)	Subtractions for revenues, gains, etc., not producing working capital	_____(YS)
	Total sources from operations = Y + YA − YS...........................	_____
(DE)	Proceeds of debt and equity issues	_____(DE)
(AD)	Proceeds of long-term asset dispositions	_____(AD)
	Total sources	_____

Uses of working capital:

(ID)	Income distributions	_____(ID)
(R)	Retirements of debt and equity	_____(R)
(AA)	Long-term assets acquisitions	_____(AA)
	Total uses	_____
(WC)	Increase (decrease) in working capital for year.....................................	_____(WC)

Illustration:
   0.   Sales of $10,000 are made on account.
  00.   Dividends of $4,000 are declared.

   Answers:
   0.   +WC   10,000   +Y   10,000
  00.   ID   4,000   −WC   4,000

1. Inventories that cost originally $10,000 have been used by production departments in producing finished goods that have been sold for $15,000 in cash and $5,000 in accounts receivable.
2. Accounts receivable of $8,000 are written off. There is an allowance for doubtful accounts balance of $5,000 only.
3. The company acquired a long-lived asset for $100,000 in cash. Of that amount, the company decided to expense $20,000 this year and to amortize $10,000 in the following eight consecutive years.
4. A machine that costs $15,000 and had an accumulated depreciation of $10,000 is sold for $8,000 in cash.
5. Treasury stock with a cost of $7,000 is retired and canceled.

6. The company has outstanding 50,000 shares of common stock with par value of $1. The company declared a 20 percent stock dividend at the end of the year when the stock was selling for $16 a share.

7. Inventory costing $12,000 has been destroyed by fire. The insurance company paid only $10,000 for that loss, although the market value of the inventory was $15,000.

8. The company bought a patent for $25,000 in cash. This amount will be amortized over five years—beginning next year.

9. Depreciation of $16,000 was charged to cost of goods sold.

10. A building was acquired by issuance of a long-term mortgage note for $100,000, the first payment of $10,000 being due 10 months from now.

13–8. Selected business activities for XYZ Company are listed below. Each item is unrelated to any other item. Use the simplified schematic statement of changes in financial position shown in the preceding problem. Identify which of the labeled lines is affected and by *how much.* When indicating effects for line Y and WC, use a + to indicate an increase and a − to indicate a decrease.

Part A

1. The annual installment of $100,000 due on the long-term debt was paid on its due date.

2. Equipment that originally cost $12,000 and with $7,000 of accumulated depreciation is sold for $4,000 cash.

3. Obsolete inventory that cost $75,000 is written down to zero.

4. Treasury stock that cost $30,000 is sold for $28,000 cash.

5. A plant is acquired by the issuance of a $400,000 mortgage payable due in equal installments over 10 years.

6. The company's 30 percent owned unconsolidated company earned $100,000 and paid total dividends of $30,000. The company recorded its 30 percent share of these items using the cost plus equity method.

7. Cash of $400,000 is given to acquire 100 percent of ZXY Manufacturing Company. At date of acquisition, ZXY had current assets of $300,000; plant and equipment, $600,000; goodwill, $70,000; current liabilities, $160,000; and long-term debt, $410,000.

8. A provision for bad debt expense of $60,000 is made (calculated as a percentage of sales for the period).

Part B

a. Investment in 30 percent owned company for $120,000 cash.

b. The 30 percent owned company earned $25,000 (in total) and paid no dividends.

c. Assume instead that the 30 percent owned company earned $30,000 (in total) and paid dividends of $10,000 (in total).

d. Equipment with an original cost of $15,000 and accumulated depreciation of $12,000 was sold for $4,000 cash.

e. The company borrowed $60,000 from its banks on November 30 payable on June 30 of next year.

f. Convertible bonds with a face value of $9,000 are converted into 1,000 shares of common stock with a part value of $2 per share.

g. Treasury stock with a cost of $4,000 is sold for $6,000 cash.

h. Common stock (par value $2) with a fair market value of $100,000 plus $100,000 cash are given to acquire 100 percent of ZYX Manufacturing Company. At date of acquisition, ZYX had current assets of $120,000; plant and equipment, $150,000; goodwill, $30,000; current liabilities, $60,000; and long-term debt, $40,000. Goodwill arose from acquisition.

    (1) Effect on *parent's* statement.

    (2) Effect on *consolidated* statement.

i. The minority's share of income was $4,000.

j. Inventory with a cost of $80,000 was written down to its market value of $30,000.

k. The account receivable of Worman for $1,200 is written off. The company uses an allowance for doubtful accounts.

l. A noncancelable lease of equipment for 10 years at $4,000 per year is capitalized.

m. A 15 percent stock dividend is declared. The 60,000 shares of common stock issued as the dividend have a par value of $2 per share and a fair market value of $3 per share.

n. A provision of $27,000 for uncollectible accounts is made (calculated as a percentage of sales for the period).

o. Dividends of $40,000 are declared on December 20 and are payable on January 20 of *next* year. (Consider only the effect for this year.)

13–9. Condensed balance sheets for the St. Estephe Corporation are shown below (in millions):

	December 31, 19x8		December 31, 19x7	
Assets				
Cash	$100		$ 90	
Receivables (net)	150		140	
Inventories	250	$ 500	230	$460
Gross plant	990		960	
Less: Accumulated Depreciation	(490)	500	(480)	480
Total assets		$1,000		$940
Liabilities and Stockholders' Equity				
Current liabilities		$ 250		$240
Long-term debt		250		230
Stockholders' equity		500		470
Total liabilities and stockholders' equity		$1,000		$940

No fixed assets were sold in 19x8.

Required:

(a) Prepare a Reconciliation of Working Capital Statement for 19x8 by reproducing and completing the following schedule:

Reconciliation of Working Capital
December 31, 19x8
(in millions)

Net income for 1978	$50
Depreciation	
Other	
Working capital from operations	
Capital expenditures	
Common stock dividends	
Other	
Increase (decrease) in working capital	

(b) List four financial items normally expected to be found in a statement of changes in financial position that do not affect working capital and would consequently go undetected by the sole use of the reconciliation of *working capital* statement such as the one used in (a) above.

(CFA adapted)

13–10. An investor concerned by the decline in both the cash and the working capital of the Fluid Corporation hands you the following data:

FLUID CORPORATION
Comparative Balance Sheets
As of December 31, 19x3, and 19x2
(in thousands)

	19x3	*19x2*
Assets		
Current assets:		
Cash	$ 50	$ 450
Accounts receivable	1,000	750
Inventories	500	450
Prepaid expenses	300	350
Total current assets	1,850	2,000
Property, plant, and equipment	4,000	3,250
Accumulated depreciation	(850)	(550)
Patents	200	300
Total assets	$5,200	$ 5,000

Liabilities and Stockholders' Equity

Current liabilities:		
Accounts payable	$ 500	$ 400
Notes payable	250	250
Accrued expenses	400	350
Total current liabilities	1,150	1,000
Bonds payable	1,000	1,400
Common stock	2,700	2,300
Retained earnings	350	300
Total liabilities and stockholders' equity	$5,200	$ 5,000

FLUID CORPORATION
Income Statement
For the Year Ended December 31, 19x3

Sales		$20,000
Cost of goods sold		15,000
Gross profit		5,000
Depreciation ($400) and patent amortization ($100)	$ 500	
Selling and administrative expenses	2,650	
Other expenses	1,700	4,850
Income from operations		150
Add: Gain on sale of equipment ($200) net of loss on land		100
		250
Interest expense		150
Pretax income		100
Income taxes (50%)		50
Net income		$ 50

Additional Information:
1. Equipment originally costing $500,000 was sold for $600,000.
2. Land with an original cost of $250,000 was sold for $150,000.
3. Convertible bonds in the amount of 400,000 were converted into $400,000 of common stock.

Required:
(a) Prepare a statement of changes in financial position (working capital focus) using the T-account method. Show full proceeds from sales of property as "other" sources.
(b) Prepare a statement of changes in financial position (cash focus) using the T-account method and on the same basis as the SCFP in (a) above.
(c) Prepare a statement of cash from operations under:
   (1) Inflow-outflow approach.
   (2) Net approach.

13–11. A fellow analyst who became aware of your understanding of financial statements asks your help in understanding the composition as well as the significance of the variety of flows that measure performance. She is interested in the Fluid Motion Company for which the data below are provided:

FLUID MOTION COMPANY
Comparative Balance Sheets
As of December 31, 19x6 and 19x5
(dollars in millions)

	19x6	19x5	Change
Assets			
Cash	$ 6.3	$ 1.5	4.8
Receivables (net)	19.8	17.2	2.6
Inventories	36.0	29.5	6.5
Prepaid expenses	.4	.2	.2
Fixed assets (net)	29.2	24.0	5.2
Total assets	$91.7	$72.4	19.3
Liabilities and Capital			
Notes payable (banks)	$11.9	$ 3.9	8.0
Accounts payable	4.7	2.8	1.9
Accrued expenses	7.0	6.8	.2
Dividends payable...............................	.5	.3	.2
Federal income tax payable	1.9	1.8	.1
Long-term debt (including convertible bonds)	7.3	10.9	(3.6)
Deferred income tax	2.4	1.9	.5
Capital stock (common and preferred)	28.0	24.0	4.0
Retained earnings	28.0	20.0	8.0
Total liabilities and capital......................	$91.7	$72.4	19.3

FLUID MOTION COMPANY
Income Statement Data
For the Year Ended December 31, 19x6
(in millions)

Sales		$110.0
Cost of goods sold*		57.7
Gross profit		52.3
Selling, administrative and general expenses*	$30.7	
Research and development costs	5.6	
Interest expenses	1.1	37.4
Income before taxes		14.9
Income taxes:		
Current.....................................	4.0	
Deferred	.5	4.5
Net income		$ 10.4

* Depreciation included in above, $3.3.

Additional information:

1. During 19x6, $3.0 of convertible bonds were exchanged for $3.0 of common stock. The long-term debt is reduced by annual payments. $2.5 of preferred stock was retired.

2. $3.5 of fixed assets were acquired by exchange for the company's common stock.
3. Dividends declared:

    Preferred stock 8
    Common stock 1.6   2.4

Required:

(A) Prepare a statement of changes in financial position (working capital focus) using the T-account method of preparation.
(B) Compute cash from operations using the—
     (1) Inflow-outflow approach.
     (2) Net approach.
(C) Prepare a statement of changes in financial position (cash focus) using the T-account method of preparation.
(D) As an aid to an understanding of the three different measures of performance, prepare a side-by-side comparative statement comparing three bases of reporting (1) net income, (2) WCFO, and (3) CFO.

13–12. The following financial statements are provided for the Doit Corporation for the calendar years 1979 and 1980 (dollars in millions):

	1980	1979	Year-to-year change
Balance sheet at December 31:			
Cash	$ 27.5	$ 19.4	$ 8.1
Accounts receivable	23.0	20.0	3.0
Merchandise inventory . .	27.0	22.0	5.0
Prepaid insurance	.3	.6	(.3)
Investments, long term			
(ABC Corp. stock) . . .	12.0	—	12.0
Fixed assets (net)	220.0	134.0	86.0
Patent (net)	16.0	—	16.0
	$325.8	$196.0	$129.8
Accounts payable	$ 18.0	$ 12.0	$ 6.0
Notes payable, short			
term (nontrade)	10.0	18.0	(8.0)
Accrued wages payable .	.8	1.0	(.2)
Income taxes payable . . .	7.0	5.0	2.0
Notes payable, long term	10.0	30.0	(20.0)
Bonds payable	100.0	—	100.0
Capital stock (par $10) . .	140.0	100.0	40.0
Contributed capital			
in excess of par	6.0	5.0	1.0
Retained earnings	34.0	25.0	9.0
	$325.8	$196.0	$129.8

Income statement:

Sales	$200.0	100.0%	$150.0	100.0%
Cost of goods sold	126.0	63.0	100.0	66.7
Gross margin on sales ..	74.0	37.0	50.0	33.3
General and				
administrative	39.0	19.5	22.0	14.7
Depreciation expenses ...	14.0	7.0	14.0	9.3
Amortization of patent ..	1.0	.5	—	—
Income tax expense	7.0		5.0	
Net income	$ 13.0		$ 9.0	

Other information:
(1) Doit Corporation declared and paid a total cash dividend of $4.0 during 1980.
(2) Fixed assets were acquired in exchange for bonds issued.

Required:
Based on the information above, prepare statements of changes in financial position (with "funds" defined as all financial resources) for the year ended December 31, 1980, *using* the T-account method:

a. On a "working capital focus" basis.
b. On a "cash focus" basis.

(CFA adapted)

13–13. Your banker friend confides to you that after looking at a number of financial statements she is confused about the difference between three operating flow concepts, i.e., income, WCFO, and CFO.

Required:
a. Clarify the purpose and significance of these three operating flow concepts.
b. Several financial events are listed below. For each event, indicate whether it resulted in an increase (+), decrease (−), or no change (NC) for each of the three concepts. If you have any difficulty, try illustrating the appropriate T-account "in words" to help.

	Effect of the financial event upon		
	Income	*Working capital from operations*	*Cash from operations*
1. Sale of merchandise on 90-day credit terms.			
2. Provision for uncollectible accounts receivable.			
3. Write-off of a specific uncollectible receivable (i.e., "name" an account as uncollectible).			

Effect of the financial event upon

	Income	Working capital from operations	Cash from operations
4. Collection of an account receivable.			
5. Recording the cost of goods sold.			
6. Purchase of inventories on account (credit terms).			
7. Accrual of sales commissions (to be paid at a later date).			
8. Payment of accounts payable (which resulted from purchase of inventory).			
9. Provision for depreciation on a sales office.			
10. Provision for income tax expense (to be paid the following month).			
11. Provision for deferred income taxes (set up because depreciation for tax reporting exceeded depreciation for financial reporting).			
12. Purchase of a machine (fixed asset) for cash.			
13. Borrowing cash from a bank on a 90-day note payable.			
14. Accrual of interest on the bank loan.			
15. Sale of partially depreciated equipment for cash at less than its book value.			
16. Flood damage to merchandise inventories (no insurance coverage).			
17. Declaration and payment of a cash dividend on preferred stock.			
18. Sale of marketable securities for cash at more than their original cost.			
19. Sale of merchandise to be paid during the following two years (one half within one year and one half after one year).			
20. Movement of noncurrent receivable to current receivables.			
21. Payment of current portion of long-term debt.			

13–14. A popular analytical tool employed by financial analysts and other readers of financial statements is the computation of the amount of cash flow. To provide more meaningful cash flow information that cannot readily be obtained from the balance sheet and the statement of income and retained earnings, it has been suggested that a funds statement be provided along with the other financial statements. The title of the funds statement should be descriptive, such as "statement of source and application of funds" or "summary of changes in financial position."

Required:
a. Define the term *cash flow* from an accounting standpoint.
b. Discuss each of the following statements:
   (1) Cash flow provides a more significant indication of the results of a company's operations than does net income.
   (2) A large cash flow permits steady expansion and the regular payment of cash dividends.
c. Discuss the uses to which funds statements may be put by the readers of the statements.

(AICPA)

13–15. A well-known text on economics contained the following statement:
"For the business firm there are, typically, three major sources of funds. Two of these, depreciation reserves and retained earnings, are internal. The third is external, consisting of funds obtained either by borrowing, or by the sale of new equities."

Required:
(a) Is depreciation a source of funds? (Exclude all considerations pertaining to depreciation expense tax-book differences.)
(b) If not, what has led to the widespread belief that depreciation *is* a source of funds?
(c) If yes, in what sense is depreciation a source of funds?

13–16. In a September 1980 speech, H. Williams, then chairman of the SEC, addressed the importance of "cash flow from operations":
"Because of the limitations of such information, the effective director must recognize that corporate earnings reports communicate, at best, only part of the story. And, their most critical omission—in recognition that insufficient cash resources are a major cause of corporate problems, particularly in inflationary times—is their failure to speak to a corporation's cash position. Indeed, in my view, cash flow from operations is a better measure of performance than earnings-per-share.
"Directors should, therefore, also consider the more revealing analytical concepts of cash flow or cash-flow-per-share, which reflect the total cash earnings available to management—that is, earnings *before* expenses such as depreciation and amortization are deducted. An even more sophisticated—and, in my opinion, more informative—analytical tool is free cash flow, which considers cash flow *after* deducting such spiralling corporate costs as capital expenditures. . . .
"There is, in fact, evidence that the market multiple reflects net free cash flow more closely than earnings. And institutional investors are clearly devoting increased attention in an effort to assess "distributable" income and project the likelihood of dividend increases."

Required:
(a) What is Williams' concept of "cash flow from operations"?
(b) What is his definition of "free cash flow"?
(c) Evaluate the statement that "cash flow from operations" is a better measure of performance than "earnings per share."
(d) What is the significance of "free cash flow" as defined by Williams?

13–17. While on an urgent assignment you discover to your dismay that you have left behind the balance sheet of Zeta Corporation as of January 1, 19x0. You realize that you do have the following data on that company:

ZETA CORPORATION
Post-closing Trial Balance
December 31, 19x0

Debit balances:

Current assets	$ 350,000
Property, plant, and equipment	550,000
Other noncurrent investments	200,000
	$1,100,000

Credit balances:

Current liabilities	$ 180,000
Accumulated depreciation	270,000
Long-term debt	200,000
Common stock	300,000
Retained earnings	150,000
	$1,100,000

ZETA CORPORATION
Statement of Changes in Financial Position
For the Year Ended December 31, 19x0

Sources of working capital:

A. From operations:

Net income		$150,000
Add: Expenses and losses not using working capital:		
Depreciation	$85,000	
Loss on sale of equipment	5,000	90,000
		240,000
Deduct: Revenues and gains not producing working capital:		
Gains on sale of noncurrent investments		50,000
Working capital provided by operations		190,000

B. Other sources:

From issuance of common stock	10,000
From issuance of long-term debt	15,000
From sale of equipment	10,000
From sale of investments	95,000
Total sources of working capital	320,000

Uses of working capital:

Cash dividends on common stocks	80,000
Purchase of plant and equipment	150,000
Total uses of working capital	230,000
Increase in working capital for the year	$ 90,000

Additional information:

(a) The equipment which has been sold had accumulated depreciation of $50,000.

(b) On January 1, 19x0, total current assets were $250,000.

Required:

Reconstruct the T-accounts of Zeta Corporation by use of the above data and information. Use the T-accounts to prepare the balance sheet of Zeta Corporation as of January 1, 19x0, which you so urgently need.

13–18.* Please refer to the financial statements of Alfa, Inc., in Appendix 4B.

Required:

Using a conversion worksheet, prepare a cash inflow and outflow statement for Alfa for 19x5. Assume that noncurrent receivables relate to operations.

13–19.* Please refer to the financial statements of Alfa, Inc., in Appendix 4B. Having been unable to obtain a balance sheet for Alfa, Inc., as at December 31, 19x4, you decided to reconstruct one from all available data.

Required:

(a) Reconstruct Alfa's December 31, 19x4, balance sheet as far as possible. Leave a clear trail and explanations of your work. Wherever you lack information necessary to compute a certain balance, clearly indicate so.

(b) Prove that the changes in the company's balance sheets (19x4 to 19x5) are explained in the 19x5 statement of changes in financial position. Draw T-accounts for the balance sheet items showing the beginning and ending balances and one T-account for *all* working capital accounts. Post the items shown in the 19x5 statement of changes in financial position to these T-accounts. "Key" each figure to an explanation. Summarize unexplained differences. (Hint: Combine asset accounts to the extent that you have insufficient information to establish individual opening balances of individual accounts. Use information developed in requirement *(a)* above to arrive at opening balances and use any other data available elsewhere in Alfa's financial statements.)

13–20.* Please refer to the financial statements of Alfa, Inc., in Appendix 4B. An analyst has prepared a conversion worksheet (see page 419) to be used to prepare an inflow-outflow cash statement for 19x6. Review the analyst's conversion worksheet as an aid in answering the questions that follow (all dollars in thousands).

Required:

I.   In general, how is it possible for this company to have a net income of $19,139 but only generate $9,365 in cash from operations? (Describe in general using selected figures—do not merely repeat the calculation shown by the analyst.)

II. It is not evident whether the noncurrent notes receivables relate to operating or nonoperating events. How should the change in noncurrent notes receivables be shown by the analyst when presenting a—

(1) Working capital statement?

(2) Cash statement?

III. The provision for uncollectible accounts is "buried" in selling and administrative expenses. How has this affected the analyst's presentation of working capital and cash statements?

IV. Note 3 discloses that Alfa decided to discontinue operations of its Wilhelm Foods division on November 15, 19x4, and since that date has been in the process of disposing of the division's assets. In 19x5, Alfa made a $2,083 provision before tax for anticipated loss on sale of assets and from operations during phase-out periods. Some of this provision did, most likely, not require an expenditure of cash during 19x5. Did most of this provision use working capital in 19x5? How would the analyst have handled this "noncash" expense in his conversion of the 19x5 SCFP to a cash statement?

V. Assume that Alfa had to write down $1,000 in inventory from cost to market. Since this requires no cash outlays, how would that be handled on a working capital to cash conversion sheet?

13–21. Refer to the financial statements of Gama Corporation in Problem 23–7.

Required:

*a. Prepare a "cash statement" for 19x6 for Gama Corporation. Include a conversion worksheet to support your work.

Your explanation of "cash from operations" should show at least the following subtotals:

> Cash receipts from customers
> Cash receipts from other (if any)
> Cash disbursements for usual operations
> Cash disbursements for unusual operations (if any)
> Income taxes paid
> Net cash from operations

Include a list of important *assumptions* and *weaknesses* as a footnote to your 19x6 cash statement.

(Hint: Discontinued operations cannot be separated from continuing operations, but unadjusted income and expense of discontinued operations can be segregated.)

b. Does the increase of $6,000 in "accounts payable and accruals" during 19x6 reflect a source or use of cash?

c. What problems will the acquisition of ACR Company create for an analyst who is trying to calculate *cash receipts* from operations for 19x6?

13–22. Please refer to the financial statements of Tandy Corporation in Problem 17–9.

Required:

I. Prepare a worksheet to convert from working capital to cash (assume that the increase in long-term receivables is not related to operations):
  (1) For 1982.
  (2) For 1981.

II. Prove that the changes in Tandy's balance sheets (1981 to 1982) are explained in the 1982 SCFP. Draw T-accounts for the balance sheet items showing the beginning and ending balances and one T-account for all working capital accounts. Post the items shown in the 1982 SCFP to these T-accounts. "Key" each figure to an explanation. Summarize unexplained differences.

Chapter 14

14–1. Financial reporting should provide information to help investors, creditors, and other users of financial statements. *SFAS 33* requires large public enterprises to disclose certain supplementary information.

Required:
a. Describe the historical-cost/constant-dollar (HC/CD) method of accounting. Include in your discussion how historical-cost amounts are used to make HC/CD measurements.
b. Describe the principal advantage of the HC/CD method of accounting over the historical-cost method of accounting.
c. Describe the current-cost method of accounting.
d. Why would depreciation expense for a given year differ using the current-cost method of accounting instead of the historical-cost method of accounting? Include in your discussion whether depreciation expense is likely to be higher or lower using the current-cost method of accounting instead of the historical-cost method of accounting in a period of rising prices, and why.

(AICPA)

14–2. You have deposited $20,000 in a savings account at a local bank on January 2, 19x1. The balance on December 31, 19x1, is $21,200. You made no withdrawals during the year. The general price-level index on January 1, 19x1, was 110, but it increased to 121 by December 31, 19x1. Inflation progressed evenly throughout the year.

Required:
a. Compute the interest rate and amount of interest earned.
b. Compute the loss due to inflation on principal, if any.
c. Compute the net increase or decrease in your wealth caused by the savings account, inclusive of interest earned.

14–3. On January 1, 19x0, Brill Company, sole proprietorship, was formed. Mr. Brill contributed $200,000 cash. On the same day, land and a building were purchased for $50,000 and $200,000, respectively, paid for by $150,000 cash and $100,000 mortgage. No payments were made on the mortgage, and no other transactions occurred during the year. The consumer price index was 150 on January 1, 19x0, and 165 on December 31, 19x0. Depreciation is computed at 4 percent, straight line (no salvage value).

Required:
Prepare the balance sheet, restated for general price-level changes, at December 31, 19x0, and any necessary schedules to accompany it.

14–4. The following data summarize three years of operations of a single-product company:

	19x5	19x6	19x7
Sales	$50,000	$66,000	$90,000
Units sold	1,000	1,200	1,500
Units purchased	1,100	1,400	1,200
Cost per unit purchased	$30	$34	$40
Expenses other than cost of goods sold	$12,000	$15,000	$20,000

The company accounts for its inventory on the LIFO basis. Expenses other than cost of goods sold are the same on a current-cost basis as on the historical-cost basis. Assume that the cost per unit purchased in a given year does not change throughout that year. The balance of inventory at January 1, 19x5, was 300 units at $27 per unit.

Required:
a. Prepare an income statement for each of the three years using the historical-cost basis.
b. Prepare the current-cost income statement for each of the three years. Recognize holding gains in income as they are realized.
c. Assume that the company is using the FIFO basis to account for its inventory. Prepare an income statement for each of the three years using the historical-cost basis. Then, compare the income figures under LIFO, FIFO, and CC. What conclusion can you reach from this comparison?

14–5. Following are the conventional financial statements of Edwards & Bell Corporation for 19x8:

EDWARDS & BELL CORPORATION
Income Statement
For the Year Ended December 31, 19x8
(in thousands)

Sales		$100,000
Cost of goods sold:		
Beginning inventory	$ 10,000	
Purchases	60,000	
	70,000	
Less: Ending inventory	15,000	
Cost of goods sold		55,000
Gross profit		45,000
Depreciation	5,000	
Other expenses (including taxes)	20,000	
		25,000
Net income		$ 20,000

EDWARDS & BELL CORPORATION
Balance Sheet
As at December 31, 19x8, and 19x7

	19x8	19x7
Assets		
Current assets:		
Cash	$ 7,000	$ 5,000
Accounts receivable	18,000	15,000
Marketable securities (common stocks)	20,000	12,000
Inventory	15,000	10,000
Total current assets	60,000	42,000
Land	40,000	40,000
Equipment	50,000	50,000
Less: Accumulated depreciation	(5,000)	—
Total assets	$145,000	$132,000
Liabilities and Equity		
Accounts payable	$ 15,000	$ 12,000
Long-term notes payable	10,000	30,000
Equity:		
Capital stock	60,000	50,000
Retained earnings	60,000	40,000
Total equity	120,000	90,000
Total liabilities and equity	$145,000	$132,000

The following are the current costs estimates that were provided by management for certain of the company's assets:

	19x8	19x7
At December 31:		
Inventory..	$19,000	$12,000
Land	45,000	42,000
Equipment.......................................	60,000	50,000
Marketable securities	22,000	13,000
For year ended December 31:		
Depreciation	6,000	
Cost of goods sold	60,000	

The following CPI-U readings prevailed on the following dates:

Dates	Index
January 1, 19x5 (date of issuance of original capital stock)	105
January 1, 19x6 (date of land acquisition)	115
October 31, 19x6 (date the December 2 19x7, inventory was acquired)	132
December 31, 19x7 (date equipment was acquired)	135
November 30, 19x6 (date marketable securities were acquired)	133
April 1, 19x8 (date additional marketable securities were purchased and additional capital stock was issued)	140
Average for 19x8	145
December 31, 19x8	150

Note: The December 31, 19x8, inventory was purchased when the CPI-U was 148.

Required:

(A) Prepare HC/CD financial statements for Edwards & Bell Corporation using December 31, 19x8, CD.

(B) Develop a worksheet to prepare CC/ND financial statements for Edwards & Bell Corporation.

*(C) Prepare a statement of income from continuing operations adjusted for changing prices as required by *FASB 33* using *average* of 19x8 dollars.

14–6. Following are the conventional financial statements of Value King Company for 19x2:

VALUE KING COMPANY
Income Statement
For the Year Ended December 31, 19x2
(in thousands)

Sales		$300,000
Cost of goods sold:		
Beginning inventory	$ 35,000	
Purchases	135,000	
	170,000	
Less: Ending inventory	65,000	
Cost of goods sold		105,000
Gross profit		195,000
Selling and administrative expenses	55,000	
Depreciation expense	25,000	
Interest expense	25,000	105,000
Pretax income		90,000
Income tax expense		42,000
Net income		$ 48,000

VALUE KING COMPANY
Comparative Balance Sheets
As of December 31, 19x2, and 19x1
(in thousands)

	19x2	19x1
Assets		
Current assets:		
Cash	$ 10,000	$ 8,000
Accounts receivable	30,000	25,000
Inventories	65,000	35,000
Total current assets	105,000	68,000
Property, plant, and equipment	270,000	270,000
Less: Accumulated depreciation	(75,000)	(50,000)
Total assets	$300,000	$288,000
Liabilities and Equity		
Liabilities:		
Current liabilities	$ 47,000	$ 46,000
Long-term debt	60,000	60,000
Deferred income taxes	8,000	6,000
Total liabilities	115,000	112,000
Equity:		
Capital stock	165,000	165,000
Retained earnings	20,000	11,000
Total equity	185,000	176,000
Total liabilities and equity	$300,000	$288,000

Additional information:

1. The CPI-U was as follows on the respective dates:

Dates	*Index*
January 1, 19x0 (date of issuance of $160,000 of capital stock and acquisition of all property, plant, and equipment)	120
November 30, 19x1 (date of acquisition of December 31, 19x1 inventory)	123
December 31, 19x1 (date when additional $5,000 capital stock was issued)	125
October 31, 19x2 (date of acquisition of December 31, 19x2 inventory)	128
December 31, 19x2	129
Average for 19x2	126

2. Property, plant, and equipment have been acquired for $270,000 and are being depreciated over 10 years on straight-line basis with $20,000 salvage value assumed.

3. The retained earnings balance at December 31, 19x1 in December 31, 19x1 dollars was $14,069.

4. $39,000 in dividends were paid in cash during the year.
5. The following are current-cost estimates provided by management at December 31:

	19x2	19x1
Inventories	$ 75,000	$ 41,000
Property, plant, and equipment	300,000	290,000
Accumulated depreciation	(84,000)	(55,000)
For year ending December 31:		
Cost of goods sold at dates of sale	120,000	
Depreciation expense	30,000	

6. Sales, purchases, expenses (except depreciation), taxes, and dividends are assumed to have occurred evenly throughout the year.

Required:
A. Prepare end-of-year HC/CD financial statements for Value King Company for 19x2.
B. Develop a worksheet to prepare CC/ND financial statements for Value King Company for 19x2.
*C. Prepare a statement of income adjusted for changing prices, as required by *SFAS 33* using average 19x2 dollars for 19x2.
*D. Prepare a reconciliation of stockholders' equity from January 1, 19x2, to December 31, 19x2, for the three bases of reporting shown in the statement compiled for requirement (c) above.

14–7. Following are the conventional financial statements of Toyland Corporation for the year ended December 31, 19x9:

TOYLAND CORPORATION
Income Statement
For the Year Ended December 31, 19x9

Sales	$500,000	
Cost of goods sold	300,000	
Gross profit		$200,000
Selling and administrative expenses	70,000	
Depreciation expense	25,000	
Interest expense	5,000	100,000
Pretax income		100,000
Income tax expense		40,000
Net income		60,000
Retained earnings, January 1, 19x9		15,000
		75,000
Less dividends		30,000
Retained earnings, December 31, 19x9		$ 45,000

TOYLAND CORPORATION
Comparative Balance Sheets
As of December 31, 19x9, and 19x8

	19x9		19x8	
Assets				
Current assets:				
Cash	$ 10,400		$ 10,000	
Accounts receivable	69,600		65,000	
Inventories	120,000		100,000	
Total current assets		$200,000		$175,000
Land		150,000		100,000
Building	110,000		110,000	
Less: Accumulated depreciation	15,000	95,000	10,000	100,000
Equipment	250,000		250,000	
Less: Accumulated depreciation	55,000		35,000	
		195,000		215,000
Total assets		640,000		$590,000
Liabilities and Shareholders' Equity				
Current liabilities:				
Accounts payable	90,000		85,000	
Income tax payable	20,000		15,000	
Total current liabilities		$110,000		$100,000
Bonds payable		150,000		150,000
Deferred income taxes		20,000		10,000
Total liabilities		280,000		260,000
Shareholders' equity:				
Common stock ($10 par)	300,000		300,000	
Additional paid-in capital	15,000		15,000	
Retained earnings	45,000		15,000	
Total shareholders' equity		360,000		330,000
Total liabilities and shareholders' equity		$640,000		$590,000

Additional information:
1. CPI-U prevailed:

Dates	Index
January 1, 19x7 (when the corporation was formed and the buildings were acquired)	100
March 1, 19x7 (when a parcel of land was acquired for $100,000)	102
April 1, 19x7 (when the equipment was acquired for $250,000)	105
December 31, 19x7	106
Average for 19x7	104
December 31, 19x8	112
Average for 19x8	108
Average for last quarter of 19x8	110
March 1, 19x9 (at which date additional parcel of land was acquired for $50,000 in cash)	114
Note: For purposes of requirement (D) of this problem the March 1, 19x9, purchase of land is assumed to have occurred at midyear.	
December 31, 19x9	120
Average for 19x9	116
Average for last quarter of 19x9	118

2. Sales, purchases, expenses (except depreciation), dividends, and taxes are assumed to have occurred evenly throughout the year.
3. Inventory is accounted for on a FIFO basis and turns over four times a year.
4. Buildings have been acquired on January 1, 19x7 for $110,000 and are being depreciated over 20 years on a straight-line basis with $10,000 salvage value.
5. Equipment has been acquired on April 1, 19x7 for $250,000 and is being depreciated over 10 years on a straight-line basis, with an assumed $50,000 salvage value.
6. Retained earnings balance at December 31, 19x8, in December 31, 19x8, dollars was $15,155.
7. The following are the current-cost estimates as provided by management:

At December 31	19x9	19x8
Inventories	$130,000	$105,000
Land	195,000	130,000
Buildings	160,000	140,000
Buildings—accumulated depreciation	20,000	13,000
Equipment	320,000	300,000
Equipment—accumulated depreciation	85,000	60,000
Cost of goods sold	310,000	—
Depreciation expense	32,000	

Required:
(A) Prepare HC/end-of-year CD financial statements for 19x9.
(B) Develop a worksheet to prepare CC/ND financial statements for 19x9.
*(C) Prepare a statement of income adjusted for changing prices (as required by *SFAS 33*, using average 19x9 dollars) for 19x9.
*(D) Prepare a reconciliation of stockholder's equity from January 1, 19x9, to December 31, 19x9, in order to validate the computations in Requirement *(c)* above. (The reconciliation will be for the HC/ND, HC/CD, and CC/CD bases.)

14–8. Following are the comparative conventional financial statements of Honey-moon Corporation for 19x8 and 19x9.

HONEY-MOON CORPORATION
Comparative Income Statements
For the Years Ended December 31

	19x9		19x8	
Sales		$775,000		$600,000
Cost of goods sold:				
Beginning inventory	$120,000		$ 90,000	
Purchases	510,000		430,000	
	630,000		520,000	
Less: Ending inventory	95,000	535,000	120,000	400,000
Gross profit		240,000		200,000
Selling and administrative expenses	175,500		163,500	
Depreciation	6,500	182,000	6,500	170,000
Pretax income		58,000		30,000
Income tax		23,200		12,000
Net income		$ 34,800		$ 18,000

HONEY-MOON CORPORATION
Comparative Balance Sheets
As of December 31

	19x9	19x8	19x7
Assets			
Current assets:			
Cash	$ 16,250	$ 6,500	$ 8,200
Accounts receivable	107,360	75,945	74,135
Inventory	95,000	120,000	90,000
Total current assets	218,610	202,445	172,335
Property, plant, and equipment	130,000	130,000	130,000
Accumulated depreciation	(45,500)	(39,000)	(32,500)
Total assets	$303,110	$293,445	$269,835

Liabilities and Equity	19x9	19x8	19x7
Liabilities:			
Current liabilities	$ 34,885	$ 36,020	$ 24,160
Long-term liabilities	50,000	50,000	35,000
Total liabilities	84,885	86,020	59,160
Equity:			
Capital stock	140,000	140,000	140,000
Retained earnings	78,225	67,425	70,675
Total equity	218,225	207,425	210,675
Total liabilities and equity	$303,110	$293,445	$269,835

Additional information:

1. The CPI-U was as follows on the respective dates:

Dates	Index
January 1, 19x3 (date of issuance of capital stock and of acquisition of property, plant, and equipment)........................	100
October 1, 19x6................................	110
December 31, 19x6	111
November 1, 19x7 (date of acquisition of December 31, 19x7, inventory)	114
December 31, 19x7	115
Average for 19x7	113
September 1, 19x8 (date of acquisition of December 31, 19x8, inventory)	117
December 31, 19x8	118
Average for 19x8	116
October 1, 19x9 (date of acquisition of December 31, 19x9, inventory)	121
December 31, 19x9	123
Average for 19x9	120

2. Property, plant, and equipment are being depreciated over 20 years on a straight-line basis with no salvage value assumed.
3. Cash dividends of $24,000 and $21,250 were paid in 19x9 and 19x8, respectively.
4. Sales, purchases, expenses (except depreciation), taxes, and dividend payments are assumed to have occurred evenly throughout the respective years.
5. The December 31, 19x8, retained earnings expressed in December 31, 19x8, dollars are $59,631.
6. The following are the year-end current cost estimates provided by management:

	19x9	19x8
Inventory	$110,000	$130,000
Property, plant, and equipment	170,000	165,000
Accumulated depreciation	65,000	57,000
For the year ending December 31:		
Cost of goods sold	560,000	—
Depreciation expense	8,500	

Required:
(A) Prepare HC/end-of-19x9 CD financial statements for Honey-moon Corporation.
(B) Prepare HC/end-of-19x8 CD financial statements for Honey-moon Corporation.
(C) Roll forward the HC/end-of-19x8 CD financial statements to end of 19x9 CD basis so that the financial statements of 19x8 are comparable to those of 19x9 which should be placed alongside.
(D) Develop a worksheet to prepare CC/ND financial statements for Honey-moon Corporation for the year ended December 31, 19x9.
*(E) Prepare a statement of income adjusted for changing prices (as required by *SFAS 33* using average 19x9 dollars).
*(F) Prepare a reconciliation of stockholders' equity from January 1, 19x9, to December 31, 19x9, for the three bases of reporting shown in the statement compiled in (E) above.

14–9. Some companies and industries show comparatively small differences between earnings per share, as reported in their annual reports, and "current-cost earnings" disclosed pursuant to *SFAS 33*.

Required:
List and briefly explain *seven* financial characteristics of companies that would tend to *reduce* the differences between earnings per share, as reported in their annual reports, and "current-cost earnings."

(CFA adapted)

14–10. The Financial Accounting Standards Board now requires that supplementary disclosures on the effects of inflation be included in annual reports. The following data appear in the *General Electric 1979 Annual Report:*

	Traditional statements (in millions)	Adjusted for general inflation (in millions)	Adjusted for current costs (in millions)
Sales	$22,461	$22,461	$22,461
Cost of goods sold	15,991	16,093	16,074
Selling and other expenses	3,716	3,716	3,716
Depreciation	624	880	980
Interest and other income (net)	(261)	(261)	(261)
Pretax income	2,391	2,033	1,952
Income taxes	953	953	953
Minority interest	29	16	13
Net income	$ 1,409	$ 1,064	$ 986
Shareholders' equity— year-end	$ 7,362	$10,436	$11,153

Required:
(a) Explain how depreciation is calculated under the general inflation method.
(b) Explain how depreciation is calculated under the current-costs method.

(c) Describe the adjustments that are made in calculating the cost of goods sold under the general inflation method <u>and</u> the current-costs method.

(d) General Electric had net monetary assets of nearly $2 billion in 1979. Assuming the inflation rate in 1979 was 10 percent, describe the supplemental disclosure required in General Electric's annual report.

(CFA)

14–11.   Financial policies that are advantageous in an extended inflationary period can lead to liquidity problems for a corporation in a business slowdown.

Required:
a.   Illustrate this point by discussing appropriate balance sheet items.
b.   How can inflation result in overstating net income?
c.   How can inflation result in overstating a company's return on net worth?

(CFA)

Chapter 16

16–1.   The questions that follow are based on the financial statements of Alfa, Inc., in Appendix 4B.

Required:
I.   Will the company have to borrow in 19x7? (Hint: Prepare a projected income statement and cash flow statement for 19x7.)

Management projects for 19x7 a 15 percent growth in sales, purchases, and expenses except depreciation which is expected to increase by only 10 percent. There are no book-tax differences, but the equity in income of nonconsolidated subsidiaries is not currently taxed. The average inventory turnover for 19x7 is expected to be 6. To achieve these operating goals, management will lengthen the receivable collection period to 90 days, based on year-end accounts receivable. Ending accounts payable turnover will be 6. Notes payable of $15 million will be due in 19x7. Management desires to maintain a minimum cash balance of 20 million. Effective income tax rate for 19x7 is expected to be 40 percent and 10 percent of tax expense is expected to be deferred. Dividends on preferred stock will be the same as in 19x6 and on common stock will be 12.3 million.

II.   (a)   Construct a table containing the following short-term liquidity ratios for the five-year period 19x2–x6*:

Current ratio
Acid-test ratio
Cash and cash equivalents to total current assets
Cash and cash equivalents to total current liabilities
Average accounts receivable turnover
Average collection period
Average inventory turnover
Average number of days to sell inventory

* Hint: Use statements of changes in financial position to derive any missing figures for years 19x1 to 19x4.

Average number of days to pay accounts payable†
Average conversion period
Net trade cycle†
Liquidity index‡
Funds provided by operations to current liabilities
Net nonfund items in income to net income

† Assume that the percentage of trade accounts payable to total accounts payable and accrued expenses in 19x2 to 19x5 was equal to the average of the same ratio as prevailed in 19x5 and 19x6 (see Note 8).
‡ Assume prepaid expenses will expire in 90 days.

(b) Based on your table in (a) above, present your best possible analysis and evaluation of short-term liquidity of the company.

16–2. The management of Fire Corporation wants to improve the appearance of their current position, i.e., current and quick ratios, on their financial statements.

Required:
a. List and briefly describe four ways in which they might accomplish this goal.
b. For each, state the procedures, if any, that an analyst can use to detect these window-dressing devices.

16–3. Give the effect of each of the following transactions or events on working capital, current ratio, and the quick ratio (acid test). Assume a current ratio of 3 to 1 and a quick ratio of 1.4 to 1 before any of the transactions that follow. (Effects: I for increase, D for decrease, and N for no effect.)

	Working capital	*Current ratio*	*Quick ratio*
1. Company pays $5,000 short-term notes payable in cash.			
2. Company sells equipment for $3,000 cash.			
3. Company purchases short-term marketable securities for $4,000.			
4. Company purchases building by issuing common stock, valued at (par value $20) $40,000.			
5. Company purchases equipment for cash $2,000.			
6. Company pays long-term bond payable, $5,000.			
7. Company collects $2,000 on a long-term note receivable.			
8. Company purchases inventory of $5,000 for cash $2,000 plus long-term note payable $3,000.			
9. Company issues short-term note payable and receives cash $5,000.			

	Working capital	Current ratio	Quick ratio
10. Fire destroys $4,000 of inventory (no insurance).	_____	_____	_____
11. Obsolete inventory of $3,000 was found and written off.	_____	_____	_____
12. Accounts payable of $10,000 were paid in cash.	_____	_____	_____
13. Land with a book value of $20,000 was sold for $15,000.	_____	_____	_____
14. Merchandise inventory of $2,000 bought on open trade credit.	_____	↓	⇃
15. Automobile sold for $2,000 at loss of $6,000.	_____	_____	_____

16–4. State the effect of the events or transactions that follow on the following ratios. Consider each transaction or event independently.

(A) Accounts receivable turnover ratio. (3 before the event)
(B) Collection period.
(C) Inventory turnover ratio. (3 before the event)

The three columns to the right of the transactions that follow are identified as *(a)*, *(b)*, and *(c)* and compare to the three measures above. For each transaction or event, indicate the effect in each of the three columns as follows: I for increase, D for decrease, and N for no effect.

	(a)	*(b)*	*(c)*
1. Sales on account were under recorded by $10,000.	I	d	N
2. $10,000 of accounts receivable were written off by charge to the allowance for doubtful accounts.	I	d	N
3. $10,000 accounts receivable were written off using the direct write-off method.	I	d	N
4. Under the lower-of-cost-or-market method inventory was reduced to market by $1,000.	N	N	I
5. Beginning inventory overstatement of $500 is now being corrected.	N	N	I
6. Beginning inventory understatement of $500 is now being corrected.	N	N	D

16–5. State the effect of the transactions that follow on the following ratios or measures. Each transaction should be considered independently.

(A)   Dollar amount of working capital.

(B) $\dfrac{\text{Funds provided by operation}}{\text{Current liabilities}} \cdot\dagger$

(C) $\dfrac{\text{Current liabilities}}{\text{Cash from operations}} \cdot\dagger$

   † These exceed I *before* the transaction.

The three columns to the right of the transactions that follow are identified as *(a)*, *(b)*, and *(c)* and compare to the three measures above. For each transaction or event, indicate the effect in each of the three columns as follows: I for increase, D for decrease, and N for no effect.

Note: The company shows full proceeds from sales of assets as "other," nonoperating, sources of funds or cash.

		(a)	*(b)*	*(c)*
1.	Uncollectibles are estimated at 2 percent of sales. Sales = $100,000; the "allowance method" is used.	_____	_____	_____
2.	$10,000 of accounts receivable are collected.	_____	_____	_____
3.	The specific account receivable from Mr. Smith is written off for $500 against the allowance for uncollectible accounts.	_____	_____	_____
4.	A previously declared cash dividend of $20,000 is paid.	_____	_____	_____
5.	Purchase of $1,000 of inventory on account.	_____	_____	_____
6.	Uninsured fire loss of $5,000 of merchandise inventory.	_____	_____	_____
7.	The company has a capital gain of $3,000 from sale of building with with a book value of $10,000.	_____	_____	_____
8.	Prepaid insurance in the amount of $1,000 expired this year.	_____	_____	_____
9.	Issuance of bonds for cash.	_____	_____	_____
10.	Company exchanges old equipment for new modern equipment and pays for the difference in common stock.	_____	_____	_____
11.	Company pays off $10,000 in long-term debt by issuing common stock.	_____	_____	_____
12.	A firm owns marketable securities; interest of $30,000 is received.	_____	_____	_____

16–6. IFSO Corporation has estimated its activity for December 19x6. Sales are expected to increase by $70,000 beyond those achieved in November 19x6 to $350,000. Selected data from IFSO's estimates of its activity are as follows:

Gross profit (based on sales) 30%
Increase in trade accounts receivable during month .. $10,000
Change in accounts payable during month .... –0–
Increase in inventory during month 5,000

Selling, general, and administrative (S, G&A) expenses are paid as incurred. Variable S, G&A (including a charge for uncollectible accounts of 1 percent of sales) are expected to amount in total to 15 percent of sales. Fixed S, G&A expenses of $35,500 per month include depreciation expense of $20,000.

Required

A. On the basis of the above data, estimate the cash receipts from operations for December.

B. On the basis of the above data, estimate the cash disbursements for operations for December.

C. Assume *instead* that at the end of November accounts receivable were $20,000 and that trade accounts receivable at end of December are going to amount proportionately the same as they were at end of November relative to sales. Estimate December cash recepits.

D. Assume *instead* a collection period of 18 days of sales in month-end accounts receivable for December. Estimate cash receipts, assuming that the accounts receivable at end of November amounted to $20,000.

16–7. Following are selected accounts of the Baxter Company at the end of 19x0:

Cash	$100,000	
Accounts receivable ...	150,000	
Inventory	200,000	
Purchases	500,000	
Depreciation	100,000	
Accounts payable		$ 200,000
Other liabilities		400,000
Capital stock		1,200,000
Sales		600,000
Net income		100,000

During 19x0, cost of goods sold including depreciation was $200,000. All 19x0 costs are expected to double for 19x1.

Baxter Company has decided to change the ending inventory turnover ratio to 4, effective during 19x1. A cash balance of $100,000 must be maintained. Sales and cash from sales will both increase to $1,200,000. Assume the 19x1 accounts payable to purchases ratio will be the same as in 19x0.

Required:

How much excess cash, if any, will be available to replace assets and for other purposes?

16–8. Zeta Corporation presents the following income statement and balance sheet for the year ended December 31, 19x1:

ZETA CORPORATION
Income Statement
For the Year Ended December 31, 19x1

Net sales		$800,000
Cost of goods sold		320,000
Gross margin		480,000
Depreciation	$ 30,000	
Selling and administrative expenses	200,000	230,000
Income before taxes		250,000
Income taxes (48%)		120,000
Net income		$130,000

ZETA CORPORATION
Balance Sheet
As of December 31, 19x1

Assets				*Liabilities and Equity*			
Current assets:				Current liabilities:			
Cash	$ 20,000			Accounts payable .	$ 44,000		
Marketable				Notes payable	21,000		
securities	2,000			Total current			
Accounts re-				liabilities . . .			$ 65,000
ceivable	45,000			Long-term debt			95,000
Inventories	60,000			Equities:			
Total current				Capital stock	230,000		
assets		$127,000		Retained earnings .	137,000		367,000
Plant and equipment .	580,000			Total liabilities and			
Less: Accumulated				equity			$527,000
depreciation	180,000	400,000					
Total assets		$527,000					

Additional information:
1. Purchases in 19x1 were $220,000.
2. In 19x2, management expects 12 percent growth in sales and a 10 percent increase in all expenses except for depreciation which will increase only by 5 percent.
3. Average inventory turnover for 19x1 was 5, and management expects an average inventory turnover ratio of 6 for 19x2.
4. A receivable collection period of 90 days, based on year-end accounts receivable, is planned for 19x2.
5. Income taxes at the same rate on pretax income as in 19x1 will be paid in cash.
6. Notes payable of $15,000 will be paid during 19x2.
7. Long-term debts of $25,000 will be repaid in cash in 19x2.
8. Zeta desires a minimum cash balance of $40,000 in 19x2.

Required:
A. Prepare a statement of expected cash inflows and outflows.
B. Will Zeta Corporation have to borrow in 19x2?

16–9. Below are some of the accounts of Sineb Corporation as of December 31, 19x5:

Account	Debit	Credit
Cash	$ 60,000	
Accounts receivable	120,000	
Inventory	150,000	
Accounts payable		$150,000
Notes payable—bank		50,000
Accrued taxes		20,000
Fixed assets (estimated life 10 years)	400,000	
Accumulated depreciation		75,000

The following additional information is available for 19x5:

Sales	$800,000
Cost of sales	600,000
Depreciation	40,000
Net income	30,000

For 19x6, the company anticipates the following:

1. A growth of 10 percent in sales.
2. An increase of 20 percent in all expenses except cost of sales and depreciation.
3. All expenses will be paid in cash as they are incurred during the year.
4. The gross profit percentage will remain the same.
5. Notes payable—bank at December 31, 19x6, will be $75,000.
6. At December 31, 19x6, there will be no balance in the accrued taxes account.
7. On January 1, 19x6, the company will buy a new machine at a cost of $100,000, an estimated life of 10 years and no salvage value. The company depreciates all fixed assets by the straight-line method.
8. The new machine will be paid for as follows:
   a. $25,000 at time of purchase.
   b. Note payable to vendor payable at the rate of $1,000 a month, starting in February (ignore interest).
9. The company intends to maintain a cash balance of $150,000 at all times.

Required
Under each of the following separate and independent circumstances, how much, if anything, will the company have to borrow during 19x6?
a. The company will have an inventory turnover of 4, an accounts payable turnover of 3, and the same credit policy as in 19x5.
b. The company will have an inventory turnover of 4, an accounts payable turnover of 4, and an accounts receivable turnover of 8.
(Turnover figures are based on the average of opening and closing account balances.)

16–10. After completing your "Financial Statements Analysis" course in the spring of 19x5, you decided to use your knowledge of tools of analysis to make some money during the summer. You offered your services to a CPA firm on a part-time basis. During your interview with the senior partner, you convinced him that you will be able to help him spot audit problem areas through financial statement analysis techniques, and he decided to hire you.

On your first day, he presented you with the following condensed financial statements of Pam Stores, Inc., a retail organization, which include audited financial statements for 19x3 and 19x4 as well as preliminary 19x5 figures taken from the books before the audit.

PAM STORES, INC.
Comparative Condensed Balance Sheets
As of June 30

Assets	19x5	19x4	19x3
Cash	$ 12,000	$ 15,000	$ 16,000
Accounts receivable, net	183,000	80,000	60,000
Inventory	142,000	127,000	52,000
Other current assets	5,000	6,000	4,000
Plant and equipment (net)	60,000	80,000	70,000
Total assets	$402,000	$308,000	$202,000

Liabilities and Equity	19x5	19x4	19x3
Accounts payable	$ 38,000	$ 51,000	$ 32,000
Federal income tax payable	30,000	14,400	28,000
Long-term liabilities	120,000	73,000	42,400
Common stock	110,000	110,000	80,000
Retained earnings	104,000	59,600	19,600
Total liabilities and equity	$402,000	$308,000	$202,000

PAM STORES, INC.
Condensed Income Statements
For the Years Ended June 30

	19x5	19x4	19x3
Net sales	$1,684,000	$1,250,000	$1,050,000
Cost of goods sold	927,000	810,000	512,000
Gross margin on sales	757,000	440,000	538,000
Selling and administrative expenses	682,000	404,000	470,000
Income before federal income tax	75,000	36,000	68,000
Income tax expense	30,000	14,400	28,000
Net income	$ 45,000	$ 21,600	$ 40,000

Additional information:
1. The company has only an insignificant amount of cash sales.
2. Cost of goods sold consist primarily of purchases of merchandise.
3. Inventory at July 1, 19x2, was $64,000.

You were requested by the senior partner to apply your knowledge of financial statement analysis and compute those ratios that could be helpful in forming a judgment about areas where audit risks, and consequent audit emphasis, should be the greatest. (Hint: Investigate, as a minimum, conclusions that can be derived from days sales in receivables, inventory turnover, and days of purchases in accounts payable.)

Required:

Write a concise report evaluating the significance of the ratios and other measures that you computed.

16–11. As the CPA responsible for an "opinion" audit engagement, you are requested by the client to organize the work to provide him at the earliest possible date with some key ratios based on the final figures appearing on the comparative financial statements. This information is to be used to convince creditors that the client business is solvent and to support the use of going-concern valuation procedures in the financial statements. The client wishes to save time by concentrating on only these key data.

The data requested and the computations taken from the financial statements follow:

	Last year	This year
Current ratio	2.0:1	2.5:1
Quick (acid-test) ratio	1.2:1	.7:1
Property, plant, and equipment to owners' equity	2.3:1	2.6:1
Sales to owners' equity	2.8:1	2.5:1
Net income	Down 10%	Up 30%
Earnings per common share	$2.40	$3.12
Book value per common share	Up 8%	Up 5%

Required:

a. The client asks that you prepare a list of brief comments stating how each of these items supports the solvency and going-concern potential of his business. He wishes to use these comments to support his presentation of data to his creditors. You are to prepare the comments as requested, giving the implications and the limitations of each item separately and then the collective inference one may draw from them about the client's solvency and going-concern potential.

b. Having done as the client requested in Requirement *(a),* prepare a brief listing of additional ratio-analysis-type data for this client that you think his creditors are going to ask for to supplement the data provided in Requirement *(a).* Explain why you think the additional data will be helpful to these creditors in evaluating this client's solvency.

c. What warnings should you offer these creditors about the limitations of ratio analysis for the purpose stated here?

(AICPA)

16–12. As a lending officer for the Prudent Bank you were handed the financial statements of Gama Corporation (see Problem 23–7) which has applied for a loan. Your superior wants you to evaluate Gama's short-term liquidity based on the limited two-year information supplied. (All dollar amounts in thousands.)

The following additional information applies to this problem only:

Inventory at January 1, 19x5 ..... $32,000
Accruals:
    19x5 3,000
    19x6 4,000

Required:
I. Compute the following for 19x5 and 19x6:
  (a) Current ratio.
  (b) Collection period (use ending accounts receivable).
  (c) Inventory turnover.
  (d) Days to sell inventory (use ending inventory).
  (e) Days' purchases in accounts payable (simplifying assumption: all cost of sales items are purchased).
  (f) Funds provided by operations to current liabilities.
  (g) The liquidity index (base number of days to sell inventory on cost of goods sold; assume prepaid expenses are 90 days removed from cash).
II. Comment on the significance of the year-to-year change.

16–13. Please refer to the financial statements of Tandy Corporation in Problem 17–9.

Required:
I. Compute for 1978 to 1982:
  (a) Current ratio.
  (b) Collection period.
  (c) Inventory turnover.
  (d) Days to sell inventory.
  (e) Funds provided by operations to accounts payable.
  (f) The liquidity index (ignore "Other assets").
II. Comment on the level as well as the year-to-year trend of these measures.
    The following industry and comparable company ratios are available for 1981:

	Retail	Manufacturing	Apple Computer
Current ratio	1.4	2.3	3.23
Collection period (days) ...	11	68	46
Inventory turnover	3.3	2.6	1.7
Days to sell inventory	111	140	210
Liquidity index	N.A.	N.A.	105

    Source of industry composite figures: "1981 Annual Statement Studies," Robert Morris Associates.

17–1. Please refer to the financial statements of Alfa, Inc., in Appendix 4B.

Required:
I. Prepare a projected income statement for 19x7 given the following assumptions (dollar amounts in thousands):
  (1) It is estimated that revenues will be $1,350,000 in 19x7.
  (2) Cost of sales is estimated to be at a level representing the average percentage

of cost of sales to sales as prevailed in the five-year period ending December 31, 19x6.

(3) Selling, general, and administrative expenses in 19x7 are expected to increase by the same percentage as these expenses increased from 19x5 to 19x6.

(4) Depreciation and amortization is expected to be 10 percent higher in 19x7 than in 19x6.

(5) There will be no income or loss from discontinued operations in 19x7, and net income of nonconsolidated finance subsidiaries is estimated to be $1,500 in that year.

(6) The interest expense net of interest capitalized is expected to be 15 percent higher than in 19x6 because of expected financing at somewhat higher rates.

(7) The effective tax rate in 19x7 will equal that of 19x6 *before* the investment tax credit. The latter is expected to be only 40 percent of the 19x6 amount.

II. Explain the meaning of the following ratios:
   (a) The funds flow adequacy ratio.
   (b) The funds reinvestment ratio.
   (c) Compute the funds reinvestment ratio for 19x5.

17–2. The Sterling Corporation is a merchandising concern. The following data have been gathered for the month of February. Prepare a *cash budget* for the month (amounts are in thousands).

Cash on hand, February 1, 19x6	$ 10
Accounts receivable, February 1, 19x6	20
Sales for February (forecasted)	100
Expected accounts receivable, February 28, 19x6	18
Gross profit, 25% of cost of goods sold	
Inventory, February 1, 19x6	20
Desired inventory, February 28, 19x6	10
Depreciation expense	2
Miscellaneous outlays	15
Minimum cash balance desired	4
Accounts payable, February 1, 19x6	22

Other information:

(1) All inventory is bought on the first day of the month and received the following week.

(2) Sterling Corporation ordinarily pays 60 percent within the month of purchase and the balance in the following month.

(3) All other expenses are paid in cash.

17–3. The following information was available from Montero Corporation's books:

1982	Purchases	Sales
January	$42,000	$72,000
February	48,000	66,000
March	36,000	60,000
April	54,000	78,000

Collections from customers are normally 70 percent in the month of sale, 20 percent in the month following the sale, and 9 percent in the second month following the sale. The balance is expected to be uncollectible. Montero takes full advantage of the 2 percent discount allowed on purchases paid for by the 10th of the following month. Purchases for May are budgeted at $60,000, while sales for May are forecasted at $66,000. Cash disbursements for expenses are expected to be $14,400 for the month of May. Montero's cash balance at May 1 was $22,000.

Required:
Prepare the following schedules:
1. Expected cash collections during May.
2. Expected cash disbursements during May.
3. Expected cash balance at May 31.

(AICPA)

17–4. Prepare a cash forecast for the Foresight Corporation for the period of July 1 through December 31. Show your result in a monthly and total summary. The opening cash balance is $34,000. The company's policy is to maintain a minimum cash balance of $30,000.

a. Sales:

	June	July	August	September	October	November	December
Cash sales ...	$12,000	$10,000	$ 8,000	$ 8,000	$13,000	$ 18,000	$ 40,000
Credit sales ..	30,000	60,000	52,000	52,000	78,000	96,000	130,000
Total ..	$42,000	$70,000	$60,000	$60,000	$91,000	$114,000	$170,000

Assume that one half of the accounts receivable are collected in the month of sale and the balance in the following month.

b. Purchases:

June	July	August	September	October	November	December
$30,000	$34,000	$34,000	$42,000	$68,000	$100,000	$20,000

The company pays 10 percent down, and the balance is paid in the following month.
c. Wages and salaries are $5,000 plus $1,000 for each $10,000 or any fraction thereof of sales of more than $50,000.
d. Operating expenses are 10 percent of sales.
e. Dividends on preferred of $15,000 are payable on September 30; dividends of $18,000 on common are payable on December 31.
f. Selling, administrative, and other fixed costs in the amount of $2,000 are paid in July, September, and November.
g. The estimated quarterly tax payable September 15 is $8,000.
h. Mortgage payments are $2,000 monthly.
i. Dividends from a subsidiary totaling $4,000 are due September 15.
j. Notes payable of $23,000 are due August 15.

17–5. In December 19x2, Magic Electronic Company was planning its cash needs during the first quarter of 19x3. The following data were available:

A. *Projected sales and accounts receivable:*

January 19x3	$150,000
February 19x3	180,000
March 19x3	200,000

Collections on sales are expected to be as follows:

60% in month of sale.
30% in month following sale.
8% in second month following sale.
2% uncollectible.

The company gives a 2 percent cash discount for payments made by customers during the month of sale.
Sales for the last quarter of 19x2 were as follows:

October 19x2	$100,000
November 19x2	120,000
December 19x2	140,000

B. *Projected purchases and accounts payable:*

January 19x3	$ 80,000
February 19x3	100,000
March 19x3	120,000

All purchases are 3/20 and net/45.
Payments on purchases are expected to be 40 percent in the month of purchase and 60 percent in the following month. Purchases during the last quarter of 19x2 were as follows:

October 19x2	$50,000
November 19x2	70,000
December 19x2	80,000

C. *Other projected financial data:*

Cash balance on January 1, 19x3	$25,000
Mortgage payments (monthly)	30,000
Operating expenses (monthly)	40,000
Taxes to be paid on March 1, 19x3	15,000
Minimum cash balance required	20,000

D.   To achieve its minimum cash balance, the company can borrow at 10 percent in $5,000 multiples to be repaid with interest after two months.

Required:

Develop a monthly cash budget for the first quarter of 19x3. (Assume that all cash transactions take place in the last day of each month.)

17–6.   Deer Corporation, a newly formed corporation, will begin its operation on January 1, 19x3. The following information is available for the development of its six months' estimated performance covering the period January 1 to June 30, 19x3:

1.	Expected monthly sales	$500,000
2.	Monthly operating expenses:	
	a. Manufacturing labor	65,000
	b. Rent for building	20,000
	c. Overhead costs	50,000
	d. Depreciation	70,000
	e. Amortization of patents.......................	1,000
	f. Selling and administrative expenses	95,000
	g. Purchase of materials.........................	200,000
3.	Other information:	
	a. Terms of sale	n/30
	b. Collection period expected to be................	45 days
	c. Purchase terms	n/30
	d. Ending raw material inventory level	$ 70,000
	e. Ending finished goods inventory level	180,000
	f. Accrued taxes (50% effective rate)..............	As incurred
	g. Beginning cash balance was $75,000 and minimum cash balance required is $50,000.	
	h. Prepaid expenses on June 30, 19x2, are expected to be $6,000.	
	i. Stockholder's equity is $1,535,000; equipment, $1,-400,000; and patents, $60,000.	

Required:

Develop a pro forma operating statement and balance sheet in order to portray the expected financial position of Deer at the end of the six-month period.

17–7.   You are given the following details about The Appliance Business to be formed:

Estimated sales in terms of units by months:

January	100
February	160
March..........	180
April...........	220
May	380
June	360

Each appliance will be sold for $200. It is anticipated that 25 percent will be sold for cash and the balance on an installment contract. The installment contract requires a down payment of 10 percent and monthly payments of $20 each which include the finance charge. The finance charge is assumed to be earned in proportion to the collections on installment contracts.

The appliances cost $125 each. Their purchase can be financed by paying 20 percent down with a noninterest-bearing floor-plan note for the balance. This balance must be paid at the end of the month in which the appliance is sold. An average inventory of 200 units should be maintained. The same purchase terms will be available for all replacements.

The installment contracts will be pledged as collateral for loans of 60 percent of the unpaid balance. These loans will be reduced, monthly, by 60 percent of all installment collections received. The client agrees to maintain a minimum bank balance of $15,000.

Salesmen will be allowed a commission of $22 per unit to be paid the month of the sale. Other variable expenses will be approximately $28 per unit sold. Other fixed expenses are estimated at $1,000 per month. Interest expense on bank loans will be 6 percent per annum on loans outstanding at the end of the previous month.

Assume that payments to the manufacturer and monthly advances from the bank will be consummated on the last day of each month. Bank interest will be payable monthly following the date the loan is received. For budgeting purposes all computations should be to the nearest $10.

From the foregoing information you are to prepare a cash buget by months, with appropriate supporting schedules, which will summarize cash receipts, cash disbursements, and additional cash investments required to comply with the terms of the bank loans.

(AICPA adapted)

17–8. Ruidoso Ski Lodge operates a ski shop, restaurant, and lodge during the 120-day ski season from November 15 to March 15. The proprietor is considering changing his operations and keeping the lodge open all year.

Results of the operations for the year ended March 15, 1969, were as follows:

	Ski Shop		Restaurant		Lodge	
	Amount	Percent	Amount	Percent	Amount	Percent
Revenue	$27,000	100	$40,000	100	$108,000	100
Costs:						
Cost of goods						
sold	14,850	55	24,000	60		
Supplies	1,350	5	4,000	10	7,560	7
Utilities	270	1	1,200	3	2,160	2
Salaries	1,620	6	12,000	30	32,400	30
Insurance	810	3	800	2	9,720	9
Property taxes						
on building . .	540	2	1,600	4	6,480	6
Depreciation . . .	1,080	4	2,000	5	28,080	26
Total costs .	20,520	76	45,600	114	86,000	80
Net income or						
(loss)	$ 6,480	24	$(5,600)	(14)	$ 21,600	20

1. The lodge has 100 rooms, and the rate from November 15 to March 15 is $10 per day for one or two persons. The occupancy rate from November 15 to March 15 is 90 percent.
2. Ski shop and restaurant sales vary in direct proportion to room occupancy.
3. For the ski shop and restaurant, cost of goods sold, supplies, and utilities vary in direct proportion to sales. For the lodge, supplies and utilities vary in direct proportion to room occupancy.
4. The ski shop, restaurant, and lodge are located in the same building. Depreciation on the building is charged to the lodge. The ski shop and restaurant are charged with depreciation only on equipment. The full cost of the restaurant equipment became fully depreciated on March 15, 1969, but the equipment has a remaining useful life of three years. The equipment can be sold for $1,200, but will be worthless in three years. All depreciation is computed by the straight-line method.
5. Insurance premiums are for annual coverage for public liability and fire insurance on the building and equipment. All building insurance is charged to the lodge.
6. Salaries are the minimum necessary to keep each facility open and are for the ski season only except for the lodge security guard who is paid $5,400 per year.

Two alternatives are being considered for the future operation of Ruidoso Ski Lodge:

1. The proprietor believes that during the ski season the restaurant should be closed because "it does not have enough revenue to cover its out-of-pocket costs." It is estimated that lodge occupancy would drop to 80 percent of capacity if the restaurant were closed during the ski season. The space utilized by the restaurant would be used as a lounge for lodge guests.
2. The proprietor is considering keeping the lodge open from March 15 to November 15. The ski shop would be converted into a gift shop if the lodge should be operated during this period with conversion costs of $1,000 in March and $1,000 in November each year. It is estimated that revenues from the gift shop would be the same per room occupied as revenues from the ski shop, that variable

costs would be in the same ratio to revenues, and that all other costs would be the same for the gift shop as for the ski shop. The occupancy rate of the lodge at a room rate of $7 per day is estimated at 50 percent during the period from March 15 to November 15 whether or not the restaurant is operated.

Required:
(Ignore income taxes and use 30 days per month for computational purposes.)
a. Prepare a projected income statement for the ski shop and lodge from November 15, 1969, to March 15, 1970, assuming the restaurant is closed during this period and all facilities are closed during the remainder of the year.
b. Assume that all facilities will continue to be operated during the four-month period of November 15 to March 15 of each year.
   (1) Assume that the lodge is operated during the eight months from March 15 to November 15. Prepare an analysis which indicates the projected marginal income or loss of operating the gift shop and lodge during this eight-month period.
   (2) Compute the minimum room rate that should be charged to allow the lodge to break even during the eight months from March 15 to November 15 assuming the gift shop and restuarant are not operated during this period.
                                                                                            (AICPA)

17–9. The following are the consolidated income statements, balance sheets, and statements of changes in financial position of Tandy Corporation for the years 1977 to 1982. Tandy, through 5,500 company-owned and 3000 franchised outlets, distributes electronic equipment, microcomputers and other products—40 percent of which are manufactured by the company.

Required (all dollar amounts are thousands):
I. Analyze and evaluate the SCFP of Tandy for the period 1978–82.
II. Recast analytically the SCFP of Tandy for the period 1981–82. (Hint: Use at least the type of adjustments found in Exhibit 17–9 of the text.) Assume that based on an analysis of *SFAS 33* disclosures and other data you conclude that depreciation and amortization that represent the best estimate of the current (replacement) cost of long-term assets used up by operations are $40,915 and $32,370 for the years 1982 and 1981, respectively.
   Evaluate the most significant conclusions that can be derived from the analytically recast statements.
III. Compute for 1981 and 1982:
   a. The funds flow adequacy ratio.
   b. The funds reinvestment ratio.
   Evaluate the level of these two ratios and the conclusions that can be derived therefrom.
IV. Based on the financial statements of Tandy and on the basis of the assumptions stated below prepare a forecasted SCFP for Tandy for 1983.
   (1) Net income in 1983 will be at a level representing the ratio of net income to revenues as prevailed in 1982.
   (2) Depreciation and amortization in 1983 will bear the same relationship to net income as have the average depreciation and amortization over the five-year period 1978–82 borne to the average net income over the same period.
   (3) The company has no immediate plans for any long-term debt financing.

(4) There will be no issuance, conversion, or decrease in subordinated debentures in 1983.

(5) Other expense items not affecting working capital will bear the same relationship to net income as has the average over the five-year period borne to the average net income over the same period.

(6) Revenues are estimated to be $2,400,000 in 1983 (an approximate 16 percent increase).

(7) Sale of treasury stock to Tandy Corporation Employee Stock Purchase Program will be $41,000 in 1983 (an approximate 40 percent increase).

(8) Additions to property, plant, and equipment will be 90,000 (an approximate 33 percent increase).

(9) Foreign currency translation adjustments will be $12,000 in 1983.

(10) Reductions to long-term debt will be $2,500 in 1983.

(11) Increase in long-term receivables related to computer leasing will be $7,850 in 1983 (an approximate 5 percent increase).

TANDY CORPORATION
Consolidated Income Statements
For the Years Ended June 30, 1977–1982
(in thousands except per share amounts)

Per share amounts restated for two-for-one stock splits in May 1981, December 1980, and June 1978
Fiscal 1982 amounts reflect the adoption of *FAS No. 52.* Foreign Currency Translation

	1977	1978	1979	1980	1981	1982
Net sales	$949,267	$1,059,324	$1,215,483	$1,384,637	$1,691,373	$2,032,555
Other income	3,763	5,629	11,403	11,360	15,697	28,657
	953,030	1,064,953	1,226,886	1,395,997	1,707,070	2,061,212
Costs and expenses:						
Cost of products sold	434,031	491,509	535,549	594,841	701,777	826,842
Selling, general, and administrative	350,878	403,173	484,249	546,325	645,934	780,378
Depreciation and amortization	11,140	13,879	17,121	19,110	23,288	29,437
Interest expense,* net of interest income	15,192	30,260	28,466	25,063	15,454	1,168
	811,241	938,821	1,065,385	1,185,339	1,386,453	1,637,825
Income from continuing operations before income taxes	141,789	126,132	161,501	210,658	320,617	423,387
Provision for income taxes†	69,970	59,986	78,272	98,423	151,015	199,302
Income from continuing operations	71,819	66,146	83,229	112,235	169,602	224,085
Loss from discontinued operations, net of income taxes	(2,777)	—	—	—	—	—
Net income	69,042	66,146	83,229	112,235	169,602	224,085
Income (loss) per average common share and common share equivalent:						
Continuing operations	$ .54	$ .69	$ .81	$ 1.12	$ 1.65	$ 2.17

Discontinued operations	(.02)	—	—	—	—	—
Net income	$ .52	$ .69	$ .81	$ 1.12	$ 1.65	$ 2.17
Average common shares and common share equivalents outstanding	132,336	96,136	106,004	103,644	102,578	103,395
* Interest expense	$16,415	$ 31,278	$ 29,700	$ 27,397	$ 22,633	$ 22,114

† Income tax expense:

Current:					
Federal		48,477	64,858	84,992	122,678	159,007
State		3,959	5,147	6,552	10,568	15,981
Foreign		4,667	5,515	9,996	15,882	21,604
		57,103	75,520	101,540	149,128	196,592
Deferred:					
Federal		1,874	1,649	(1,223)	2,318	3,879
Foreign		1,009	1,103	(1,894)	(431)	(1,169)
Total income tax expense		$ 59,986	$ 78,272	$ 98,423	$151,015	$199,302

Statutory versus effective tax:

Components of pretax income:					
United States		$109,153	$146,827	$183,342	$285,089	$367,970
Foreign		16,979	14,674	27,316	35,528	55,417
Income before income taxes		126,132	161,501	210,658	320,617	423,387
Statutory tax rate		×48%	×47%	×46%	×46%	×46%
Federal income tax at statutory rate		60,543	75,905	96,903	147,484	194,758
Investment tax credit		(1,479)	(695)	(1,499)	(2,992)	(5,310)
State and provincial income taxes, less federal income tax benefit		2,657	3,430	4,418	6,970	10,177
Other, net		(1,735)	(368)	(1,399)	(447)	(323)
Total income tax expense		$ 59,986	$ 78,272	$ 98,423	$151,015	$199,302
Effective tax rate		47.6%	48.5%	46.7%	47.1%	47.1%

TANDY CORPORATION
Consolidated Balance Sheets
As of June 30 for Years 1977–1982
(in thousands)

	1977	1978	1979	1980	1981	1982
Assets						
Current assets:						
Cash and equivalents	$ 20,930	$ 35,778	$ 37,621	56,365	$141,994	$ 167,547
Accounts and notes receivable	7,082	10,635	15,841	25,725	42,088	83,616
Inventories	300,279	333,065	381,649	435,160	513,709	670,568
Net asset of disposed division	5,157	—	—	—	—	—
Other assets	11,395	14,152	12,590	13,809	11,416[a]	27,000[a]
Total current assets	344,843	393,630	447,701	$531,059	709,207	948,731
Property and equipment	147,082	195,348	216,648	239,825	284,594	339,355
Accumulated depreciation	(36,911)	(48,273)	(59,978)	(74,685)	(94,165)	(114,360)
Net plant and equipment	110,171	147,075	156,670	165,140	190,429	224,995
Net assets of discontinued operations	8,220	—	—	—	—	—
Other assets	11,441	12,750	5,218	14,099	36,909	53,918
Total assets	$474,675	$553,455	$609,589	$710,298	$936,545	$1,227,644

[a] Includes deferred taxes of | | | | | 4,927 | 10,441

Liabilities and Capital

	1977	1978	1979	1980	1981	1982
Current liabilities:						
Notes payable	$ 60,462	$ 52,964	$ 37,189	$ 25,918	$ 34,862	$ 24,942
Current portion of long-term debt	2,208	—	—	—	—	—
Accounts payable	47,968	49,933	34,390	58,926	54,560	63,641
Accrued expenses	39,936	42,385	52,343	59,170	67,206	92,125
Income taxes payable	2,833	839	13,931	24,703	47,152	52,160
Total current liabilities	153,407	146,121	137,853	168,717	203,780	232,868
Notes payable	8,565	5,357	8,688	6,523	3,903	20,642
Revolving credit agreement	—	110,000	—	—	—	—
Debentures	121,721	121,858	222,045	222,175	122,428	122,666
Store managers' deposits	17,434	18,168	16,718	14,045	11,972	9,306
Deferred income taxes	7,442	9,458	10,978	8,902	12,069	18,886
Other noncurrent liabilities	1,769	3,497	4,954	6,811	10,530	10,599
Total liabilities	310,338	414,459	401,236	427,173	364,682	414,967
Net worth*	164,337	138,996	208,353	283,125	571,863	812,677
Total liabilities and capital	$474,675	$553,455	$609,589	$710,298	$936,545	$1,227,644
Stockholders' equity composition:						
Common stock—$1 par, 105,645,000 shares issued					$105,645	$105,645
Additional paid-in capital					16,523	39,627
Retained earnings					467,020	691,105
Foreign currency translation effects					(17,325)	(12,317)
Common stock in treasury, at cost						(11,383)
					$571,863	$812,677

TANDY CORPORATION
Consolidated Statements of Changes in Financial Position
For the Years Ended June 30, 1977–1982
(dollars in thousands)

	1977	1978	1979	1980	1981	1982	Total Amount	Total Percent
Sources:								
From operations:								
Income from continuing operations	$ 71,819	$ 66,146	$ 83,229	$112,235	$169,602	$224,085	$ 727,116	51.6
Items not affecting working capital:								
Depreciation and amortization	11,140	13,879	17,121	19,110	23,288	29,437	113,975	8.1
Other	3,572	3,437	3,772	(536)	7,637	7,318	25,200	1.8
Total from operations	86,531	83,462	104,122	130,809	200,527	260,840	866,291	61.5
Conversion of convertible debentures into common stock	—	—	—	—	98,552	—	98,552	7.0
Issuance of convertible debentures	—	—	98,875	—	—	—	98,875	7.0
Additions to long-term borrowings	—	110,000	5,081	—	903	18,209	134,193	9.5
Sale of securities	—	8,558	7,808	—	—	—	16,366	1.2
Issuance of debentures in exchange for common stock	98,039	—	—	—	—	—	98,039	6.9
Sale of treasury stock to the employee stock purchase program	8,362	10,000	12,954	15,833	21,077	29,048	97,544	6.9
Total sources	193,202	212,020	228,840	146,642	321,059	308,097	1,409,860	100.0

							Total	
	1977	*1978*	*1979*	*1980*	*1981*	*1982*	*Amount*	*Percent*
Applications:								
Additions to property and equipment	41,518	50,357	26,579	31,063	48,494	67,678	265,689	18.8
Foreign currency translation adjustments	—	—	—	—	—	10,688	10,688	0.8
Reductions of long-term debt	4,130	3,208	111,750	2,165	3,523	1,470	126,246	9.0
Decrease in convertible debentures	—	—	—	—	99,954	—	99,954	7.1
Purchase of common stock	—	101,487	—	—	—	—	101,487	7.2
Purchase of treasury stock	21,180	—	27,396	53,342	—	—	101,918	7.2
Retirement of common stock in exchange for debentures	98,039	—	—	—	—	—	98,039	6.9
Increase in long-term receivables related to computer leasing	—	—	—	3,070	7,253	7,494	17,817	1.3
Other, net	(5,114)	895	776	4,508	18,750	10,331	30,146	2.1
Total applications	159,753	155,947	166,501	94,148	177,974	97,661	851,984	60.4
Working capital increase (decrease)	$ 33,449	$ 56,073	$ 62,339	$ 52,494	$143,085	$210,436	$ 557,876	39.6

Note: Analysis of changes in working capital omitted.

Chapter 18

18–1. Part A. Please refer to the financial statements of Alfa, Inc., in Appendix 4B.

Required:

Compute the following ratios for 19x4–x6. Use the statutory income tax rate in all ratios except the fixed-charge coverage ratios for which you are to use the effective tax rate:

a. Financial leverage index—compute the return on total owners' equity rather than common equity since the amount of the 19x4 common equity is unavailable.

b. Total long-term debt to equity capital—assume that the present value of minimum financing lease payments was $167,210 on December 31, 19x6, $173,000 on December 31, 19x5, and $178,000 on December 31, 19x4. Assume for purposes of computing this ratio that all other leases are operating.

c. Total liabilities to total liabilities and equity capital.

d. Total liabilities to equity capital.

e. Preferred stock to total owners' equity—use stated value of preferred stock for all years. Assume no change in preferred stock in 19x4 as compared to 19x5.

f. The analytically adjusted ratio of debt to equity for 19x5 and 19x6 only.

g. Earnings coverage of fixed charges—assume that total financing leases include those designated as "other" in Note 11 and that at December 31, 19x5 they were $252,880 and at December 31, 19x4 were $257,860 and that the applicable implicit interest rate for all years was 8 percent.

h. Funds flow coverage of fixed charges.

i. Working capital from operations to total debt and preferred stock.

j. Earnings coverage of preferred dividends.

k. Equity capital to net fixed assets.

l. Net tangible assets to long-term debt.

Part B. Comment on the significance of the level as well as the trend of the above measures and ratios.

18–2. Susan Corporation needs additional funds for plant expansion. The board of directors is considering obtaining the funds by issuing additional short-term notes, long-term bonds, preferred stock, or common stock.

Required:

a. What primary factors should the board of directors consider in selecting the best method of financing plant expansion?

b. One member of the board of directors suggests that the corporation should maximize trading on equity, that is, using stockholders' equity as a basis for borrowing additional funds at a lower rate of interest than the expected earnings from the use of the borrowed funds.
   (1) Explain how trading on equity affects earnings per share of common stock.
   (2) Explain how a change in income tax rates affects trading on equity.
   (3) Under what circumstances should a corporation seek to trade on equity to a substantial degree?

c. Two specific proposals under consideration by the board of directors are the issue of 7 percent subordinated income bonds or 7 percent cumulative, nonparticipating, nonvoting preferred stock, callable at par. In discussing the impact of

the two alternatives on the debt to stockholders' equity ratio, one member of
the board of directors stated that he felt the resulting debt-to-equity ratio would
be the same under either alternative because the income bonds and preferred
stock should be reported in the same balance sheet classification. What are the
arguments (1) for and (2) against using the same balance sheet classification in
reporting the income bonds and preferred stock?

(AICPA)

18–3. The following information is available for Companies A, B, and C.

	A	B	C
Total assets....................	$1,000,000	$2,000,000	$3,000,000
Total liabilities	300,000	—	1,500,000
Interest rate on total liabilities	10%	—	5%
Operating income	80,000	200,000	270,000
Percentage of operating income to			
total assets	8%	10%	9%

Required:
Compute the financial leverage indexes for Companies A, B, and C. Assume a
tax rate of 48 percent. What do the respective levels of the leverage indexes for
these companies mean?

18–4. The analytical thrust of bond selection normally focuses on earning power,
liquidity, financial position, and other factors that are indicative of a change in the
level of protection for bond interest and principal.

Required:
Financial statement ratio tests have been developed to assist in assessing the level
of protection for principal and interest. Explain how each of the following is treated
in one or more tests of earning power, liquidity, and/or financial position:
(a) Market value of common stock.
(b) Short-term debt.
(c) Depreciation.
(d) Financial leases.

(CFA)

18–5. The Expo Company is planning to invest $10,000,000 in an expansion
program that is expected to increase earnings before interest and taxes by $2,500,000.
The company currently is earning $5 per share on 1,000,000 shares of common out-
standing. The capital structure prior to the investment is:

Debt	$10,000,000
Equity	30,000,000
	$40,000,000

The expansion can be financed by sale of 200,000 shares at $50 net each, or by
issuing long-term debt at a 6 percent interest cost. The firm's recent income statement
was as follows:

Sales	$101,000,000
Variable cost	60,000,000
Fixed cost	30,500,000
	90,500,000
Earnings before interest and taxes	10,500,000
Interest	500,000
Earnings before taxes	10,000,000
Taxes (50%)	5,000,000
Earnings after taxes	$ 5,000,000

Required:

a. Assuming the firm maintains its current earnings and achieves the anticipated earnings from the expansion, what will be the earnings per share—
   (1) If the expansion is financed by debt?
   (2) If the expansion is financed by equity?
b. At what level of earnings before interest and taxes will the earnings per share under either alternative be the same amount?
c. The choice of financing alternatives influences the earnings per share. The choice might also influence the earnings multiple used by the "market." Discuss the factors inherent in choice between the debt and equity alternatives that might influence the earnings multiple. Be sure to indicate the direction in which these factors might influence the earnings multiple.

18–6. Based on the data presented below, answer the questions that follow.

Required:

a. Compute the earnings per share of common stock based on the 19x5 results to indicate the earnings power attributable to the common stock as of April 19x6. *Show your calculations.*
b. Compute the coverage ratio or ratios which indicate the financial risk bearing on the bonds assuming they were being analyzed as of April 19x6. *Explain briefly your reasoning.*
c. Show an itemized breakdown of the capital structure of Golden-Gate Company as it existed after the sale of the common stock and retirement of the debentures in February 19x6.

GOLDEN-GATE COMPANY
Balance Sheet Data, December 31, 19x5
(in thousands)

Cash	$ 10,000
Net current assets	50,000
Net fixed assets—plant, etc.	80,000
First mortgage 4s of 19y0...................	10,000
Debentures 4 ½s of 19z0	40,000
6% preferred stock	20,000
Common stock—$1 par	600
Retained earnings and capital surplus	70,000

GOLDEN-GATE COMPANY
Income Statement Data
For the Year Ended December 31, 19x5
(in thousands)

Gross revenues	$100,000
Cost of goods sold, etc.	77,000
Amortization and depreciation	10,000
Lease rentals*	2,000
Interest expense	2,200
Net operating income	8,800
Profit on sale of property—after taxes	1,200
Total net income before taxes	10,000
Income taxes—50% rate	4,400
Net to stockholders	5,600
Preferred dividends	1,200
Common dividends	2,000
Transfer to retained earnings	2,400

* All property taxes, insurance, and maintenance paid by company.

Additional information:

In February 19x6, the company sold 300,000 new common shares for cash of $19,000,000 and the proceeds were used to retire $20,000,000 par value of the debenture 4 1/2s at an average price on the market of 95.

(CFA adapted)

18–7. Two measures of debt service protection of corporate bonds are as follows:

$$\text{Times debt service earned} = \frac{\text{Pretax earnings} + \text{Interest expense} + \frac{1}{3}\text{ Rental expense}}{\text{Interest expense} + \frac{1}{3}\text{ Rental expense} + \dfrac{\text{Annual debt repayment}}{1 - \text{Tax rate}}}$$

$$\text{Time cash flow earned} = \frac{\text{Pretax earnings} + \text{Depreciation expense} + \text{Interest expense} + \frac{1}{3}\text{ Rental expense}}{\text{Interest expense} + \frac{1}{3}\text{ Rental expense} + \text{Annual debt repayment*}}$$

Required:

Evaluate and compare the usefulness of these two ratios in appraising the quality of corporate bonds.

(CFA adapted)

18–8. Following is the income statement of Boro Corporation for the year ended December 31, 19x1:

---

* If debt repayment exceeds depreciation, it is customary to add to the denominator an amount equal to the excess divided by (1 − income tax rate).

BORO CORPORATION
Consolidated Income Statement
For the Year Ended December 31, 19x1
(in thousands)

Sales		$13,700
Undistributed income of less than 50%		
owned affiliates		300
		14,000
Less: Cost of goods sold		7,000
Gross profit		7,000
Selling and administrative expenses	$1,800	
Depreciation [a]	600	
Rental expense [b]	700	
Share of minority interests in consoli-		
dated income [c]	300	
Interest expense—[d]	600	4,000
Pretax income		3,000
Income taxes:		
Current	$1,000	
Deferred.....................................	500	1,500
Net income		1,500
Dividends:		
Preferred stock	$ 200	
On common stock	500	700
Earnings retained for the year		$ 800

[a] Represents depreciation excluded from all other expenses categories and includes $40 of amortization of previously capitalized interest.

[b] Includes $200 of interest implicit in operating lease rental payments that should be considered as having financing characteristics.

[c] These subsidiaries have fixed charges.

[d] Interest expense includes:

Interest incurred (except items below)	$440
Amortization of bond discount	50
Interest portion of capitalized leases	170
Interest capitalized	(60)
	$600

[e] Use a 50 percent tax rate.

Required:
Compute the following coverage ratios:
   I. Ratio of earnings to fixed charges.
  II. Funds flow coverage of fixed charges.
 III. Earnings coverage of preferred dividends.

18–9. In December 1978, Mr. Karl Vogt, senior investment officer of the Bedrock Life Insurance Company, was deciding whether his company should sell $500,000 of Union Carbide debenture 8½s of 2005, and purchase an equal amount of Dow

Chemical debenture 8½s of 2005. Union Carbide debentures currently outstanding totaled $300 million, and the Dow Chemical debentures $225 million. Mr. Vogt noted that both Moody's and Standard & Poor's had reviewed their ratings on the bonds of both companies earlier in 1978.

Significant data as of December 8, 1978, follow:

						Bond quality rating	
			Current call	Closing Price	Yield to		
Issuer	Description	Maturity	price*	12/8/78	maturity	Moody's	S&P
Dow Chem.	Deb. 8½s	2/1/2005	107.48	91⅜	9.39%	Aa	A+
Union Carb.	Deb. 8½s	1/15/2005	107.48	95¾	8.92%	Aa	AA-

* Neither bond was refundable at an interest cost of less than 8½ percent over the next six years.

Dow Chemical Company ranks third in worldwide sales and second in net income among U.S. chemical companies. Products and services include organic and inorganic chemicals, magnesium, plastic molding resins, coatings, and monomers. In 1977, foreign sales were 45 percent of sales, and research and development expenditures were 3.3 percent of sales.

Union Carbide Corporation ranks second in sales and third in net income among U.S. chemical companies. Chemicals and plastics include ethylene glycol, urethane intermediates, and polyethylene; gases and metals include oxygen, ferroalloys, tungsten, vandium, and graphite electrodes. Consumer products include batteries, antifreeze, plastic wraps and bags, waxes, and polishes. In 1977, foreign sales accounted for 32 percent of sales, and research and development expenditures were 2.2 percent of sales.

Mr. Vogt was uncertain whether he should approve the switch in view of the difference of opinion regarding the credit quality of the two companies as expressed in the S&P bond rating. Therefore, he had an assistant prepare a comparative company analysis shown in the accompanying table. Ratios 2 through 5 assume that the debt service burden anticipated as of December 1978 had been serviced in each of the years 1968 to 1977. The 1978 companywide sinking fund requirements of $100.3 million for Dow Chemical and $75.3 million for Union Carbide would remain at those approximate annual requirements for the next two or three years.

Required:
(a) In receiving the data prepared by Mr. Vogt's assistant, identify and explain which of the ratios have greater significance in appraising the debt-service ability of the two companies.
(b) Based *solely* on the data presented in the accompany table plus the introductory material, select the company that appears to have better prospects for servicing its indebtedness. Explain your selection.
(c) Assuming similar marketability for each of the two issues, discuss whether Mr. Vogt should make the contemplated switch.

(CFA adapted)

DOW CHEMICAL COMPANY versus UNION CARBIDE CORPORATION
Comparative Analysis of Debt Service Capacity

Ratio number	Description of ratio	Ten-year average 1968–77	Five-year average 1973–77	1977	Nine months 1978*	Poorest year 1968–77
1	Times actual interest expense earned (before income taxes):					
	Dow Chemical	5.43x	6.78x	4.59x	5.08x	3.41x (1971)
	Union Carbide	7.91x	8.89x	5.00x	4.71x	5.00x (1977)
2	Times anticipated 1978 interest expense earned (before income taxes):					
	Dow Chemical	2.66x	4.05x	4.28x	5.08x	1.11x (1968)
	Union Carbide	3.80x	5.21x	4.83x	4.71x	1.98x (1968)
3	Times anticipated 1978 interest expense and sinking fund requirements earned (before income taxes):					
	Dow Chemical	1.58x	2.37x	2.60x	2.91x	.67x (1968)
	Union Carbide	2.31x	3.16x	3.09x	2.97x	1.23x (1968)
4	Earnings before depreciation, interest expense and income tax (EBDIT) divided by 1978 interest and sinking fund requirements†					
	Dow Chemical	3.22x	3.93x	4.41x	5.19x	1.24x (1968)
	Union Carbide	3.95x	5.07x	5.13x	5.31x	2.50x (1968)

5	Excess of EBDIT over anticipated interest expense and sinking fund requirements as a percent of net sales†					
	Dow Chemical	14.6%	20.8%	19.7%	20.3%	5.1% (1968)
	Union Carbide	14.4%	15.7%	12.6%	12.0%	12.0% (1968)
6	Net tangible assets per $1,000 bond:					
	Dow Chemical	$2,296	$2,378	$2,282	n.a.	$2,060 (1970)
	Union Carbide	3,108	3,236	3,069	n.a.	2,907 (1969)
7	Net current assets per $1,000 bond:					
	Dow Chemical	$ 353	$ 439	$ 373	n.a.	$212 (1971)
	Union Carbide	1,094	1,233	1,028	n.a.	858 (1970)
8	Book value equity as percent of total invested capital:					
	Dow Chemical	57.3%	58.8%	56.8%	n.a.	53.2% (1970)
	Union Carbide	67.8%	69.9%	68.0%	n.a.	65.4% (1970)
9	Market value equity as percent of total invested capital (‡):					
	Dow Chemical	76.4%	78.3%	65.4%	n.a.	65.4% (1977)
	Union Carbide	72.5%	71.2%	67.0%	n.a.	67.0% (1977)

† Based on actual interest expense and three fourths of long-term debt repayment requirement for 1978 where appropriate.

† Depreciation expense substantially exceeded 1978 sinking fund requirement on long-term debt in all years.

‡ Total invested capital equal to the sum of equity at market plus long-term debt at face value.

n.a. = not available.

18–10. You are considering the bonds of Gama Company (see Problem 23–7) for long-term investment. Incident to your decision-making process, you decide to compute pertinent ratios for the years 19x5 and 19x6.

The following are additional data and information to be considered only for purposes of this problem (in thousands):

		19x6	19x5
a)	Interest expense is composed of:		
	Interest incurred (except items below)	$9,200	$5,000
	Amortization of bond discount	2,500	2,000
	Interest portion of capitalized leases	80	—
	Interest capitalized	(1,780)	(1,000)
		$10,000	$6,000

b) Depreciation includes amortization of previously capitalized interest of $1,200 for 19x6 and $1,000 for 19x5.
c) Interest portion of operating rental expense that should be considered a fixed charge: $20 in 19x6 and $16 in 19x5.
d) The associated company is less thant 50 percent owned.
e) You have concluded that deferred taxes constitute a long-term liability.
f) Present value of noncapitalized financing leases is $200 for both years.
g) The excess of vested pension benefits over market value of pension fund assets is $2,800 for both years.
h) Year-end 19x4 total assets and equity capital are $94,500 and $42,000, respectively.
i) Average market price for 19x6 and 19x5 per share of Gama's common stock was $40 and $45, respectively.

Required:
I. Compute for 19x6 and 19x5:
    A. Financial leverage index.
    B. Total liabilities to total liabilities and equity capital.
    C. Total liabilities to total liabilities and equity capital (based on market value of common equity).
    D. Total liabilities to equity capital.
    E. Long-term debt to equity capital.
    F. Ratio of earnings to fixed charges.
    G. Funds flow coverage of fixed charges.
II. Comment on the level as well as on the year-to-year trend of these measures.
III. Compute the analytically adjusted long-term debt to long-term debt and equity ratio for 19x6 and 19x5 and comment on the conclusion one can derive from it. (For purposes of this ratio assume that only 60% of deferred taxes constitute a long-term liability.)

18–11. Please refer to the financial statements of Tandy Corporation in Problem 17–9. The following data and information should be considered only for purposes of this problem:
(a) You have concluded that 50 percent of deferred taxes constitute a long-term liability and you decide to adjust all ratios accordingly.

	1982	1981	1980	1979	1978
(b) Market prices of common shares (to be used in computing market value of common equity	28	21	10	5	6
(c) Number of common shares outstanding (in thousands)	103,400	102,600	103,600	106,000	96,100

(d) There are only common shares outstanding.

Required:
I. Compute for 1978 to 1982:
   A. Total liabilities to total liabilities and equity capital.
   B. Total liabilities to total liabilities and equity capital (based on market value of common equity).
   C. Total liabilities to equity capital.
   D. Long-term debt to equity capital.
   E. Ratio of earnings to fixed charges.
   F. Funds flow coverage of fixed charges.
II. Comment on the level as well as on the year-to-year trend of these measures.

Chapter 19

19–1. Please refer to the financial statements of Alfa, Inc., in Appendix 4B.

Required:
I. Compute the following for Alfa, Inc., for 19x5 and 19x6:
   (1) Return on total assets.
   (2) Return on long-term liabilities plus equity.†
   (3) Return on common equity.
   (4) Return on total equity.
   (5) Equity growth rate.
   (6) Disaggregate the return on common stockholders equity.
II. Compute all asset utilization ratios for Alfa, Inc., for 19x5 and 19x6.
III. Based on your answer to *I* and *II* above, analyze and evaluate the return on investment and asset utilization of Alfa, Inc., for 19x5 and 19x6.
IV. Analyze the composition of the return on common stockholders' equity for Alfa, Inc., for 19x6.

   (Hint: Construct a table showing the net amounts accruing to [or detracting from] return on common equity from various sources of financing including current liabilities and then comment on the table. List any assumptions you make).
V. Compute return on investment for 19x6 under the following investment bases:
   a) Gross productive assets, assuming that property includes gross idle facilities of $50 million in 19x6 and $40 million in 19x5 and that 20 percent of total "other assets" are not productive.

---

† See item 81 for interest on long-term debt.

b) Year-end market value of common stock assuming that the market value at year-end was equal to the average of the price given for the fourth quarter in 19x6 (item ⌐70¬).

19–2. Telco Corporation supplied you with the following condensed balance sheet for 19x2:

Assets

Current assets	$ 250,000
Noncurrent assets	1,500,000
Total assets	$1,750,000

Liabilities and Equity

Current liabilities	$ 120,000
Noncurrent liabilities (8% bonds)	630,000
Stockholders' equity	1,000,000
Total liabilities and equity	$1,750,000

Additional information:
1. Net income for the year is $150,000.
2. Income tax rate is 50 percent.

Required:
a) Based on the above information, determine whether financial leverage (long-term debt) benefits Telco's stockholders.
b) If Telco Corporation achieved a 20 percent return on total assets, determine what its return on equity would be and the level of the financial leverage index.
c) What can you conclude from the level of its financial leverage index that you have computed in *(b)* above?

19–3. IBM's balance sheet and income statement for the year ended December 31, 1976, are summarized below (in millions):

Income Account

Gross income	$16,304
Costs and expenses	10,517
Depreciation	1,717
Net operating income	4,070
Other income	494
Total income	4,564
Interest expense	45
Pretax earnings	4,519
Income taxes	2,121
Net income	2,398

Balance Sheet

Assets		*Liabilities and Net Worth*	
Current assets:			
Cash	$ 209	Current liabilities	$ 4,082
Marketable securities	5,947	Reserves	617
Receivables	2,626	Long-term debt	275
Inventories	770		
Prepayments	368	Common equity	12,749
Current assets	9,920		
Gross property and			
rental machines	16,055		
Less: Depreciation	8,714		
Net plant	7,341		
Investment, etc.	462	Total liabilities	
Total assets	$17,723	and net worth	$17,723

Required:
(a) Based on the above data, calculate IBM's return on assets.
(b) Explain why you included or excluded marketable securities in your calculation.
(c) Explain why you used *gross* or *net* fixed assets in your calculation.
(d) Discuss the limitations inherent in any such return on assets calculation for a major industrial corporation in 1976.

(CFA)

19–4. TOTO Corporation's total capital structure of $20,000,000 consists of 30 percent bonds and 70 percent common equity. The bonds have a 5 percent coupon. The tax rate is 50 percent. Retained earnings amount to $4,000,000. The operating margin (before deduction of interest and taxes) is 15 percent.

Required:
a. What level of net operating income has to be attained in order to earn 15 percent on stockholders' equity?
b. If the corporation had net operating income of $1,000,000 for the year, was financial leverage (trading on equity) beneficial, detrimental, or neither? Prove it.
Show all computations.

(CFA adapted)

19–5. The statements of financial position of two similar companies in the same industry, as of December 31, 19x1, are as follows:

Assets		*Company L*	*Company M*
Cash		$ 150,000	$ 500,000
Accounts receivable		225,000	750,000
Inventories........................		450,000	750,000
Land		300,000	
Plant and equipment	$3,000,000		
Less: Depreciation	900,000	2,100,000	
Prepaid expenses		15,000	40,000
Total assets		$3,240,000	$2,040,000

Equities

Accounts payable	$ 180,000	$ 270,000
Six percent notes payable	60,000	300,000
30-year, 6%, first-mortgage bonds	2,250,000	
Owners' investment	300,000	300,000
Retained income	450,000	1,170,000
Total equities	$3,240,000	$2,040,000

The annual sales for each company are approximately the same. The income of each, before deducting interest and income taxes, was 20 percent of sales in 19x1.

Required:

a. Explain in detail in what way you would expect the fixed expenses of the two to differ.

b. In what way would their net incomes as a percentage of revenues probably differ?

c. Assuming that the net income of each before income tax and interest was $400,000:
   (1) Compute the rate of return before interest and tax on total assets.
   (2) Compute the number of asset turnovers.
   (3) Assuming an average income tax rate of 40 percent of net income before income tax, compute the rate of return of each company to its owners.

d. What differences in the policies of the two companies can you detect from the illustrated statements?

19–6. Air Products and Chemicals, Inc. (APD), and Big Three Industries, Inc. (BIG), are two of the leading North American producers of industrial gases, primarily those separated from air—oxygen, nitrogen, and argon. These gases are used in a wide variety of industrial applications with newer uses contributing to increased productivity, energy savings, and a cleaner environment.

Both companies are diversified, with APD engaged in the production of industrial and medical gases together with related equipment and services; the manufacture of industrial chemicals, fertilizers, plastics, and catalysts; and the engineering, construction, and maintenance of process and power plants. BIG produces and sells industrial gases, welding equipment and supplies, and industrial and oil field equipment. Both companies have significant sales and operations outside the U.S.A., APD primarily in Europe and BIG primarily in Canada.

A breakdown of 1978 sales is shown below, together with growth rates since 1974:

	Air Products and Chemicals (APD)			Big Three Industries (BIG)		
	Sales (millions)	Percent of total	Compound annual increase: 1974–78	Sales (millions)	Percent of total	Compound annual increase: 1974–78
Industrial gases	$ 544.1	49%	20.2%	$142.5	33%	34.4%
Equipment and services	165.2	15	12.9	—	—	—
Chemicals	373.3	34	14.6	—	—	—
Engineering and construction	17.6	2	3.2	—	—	—
Energy operations	—	—	—	181.0	42	30.1
Welding equipment	—	—	—	105.4	25	17.9
Total	$1,100.2	100%	16.6%	$428.9	100%	27.7%
Foreign...........	$ 217.6	20%		$102.9	24%	
Domestic	882.6	80		326.0	76	
Total	$1,100.2	100%		$428.9	100%	

As to the industry, shipments of industrial gases remained strong throughout 1979 with dollar sales up 16 percent and earnings up 13 percent over 1978. At year-end 1979, *The Value Line Investment Survey* reported that competition was increasing, making it somewhat more difficult to pass on higher costs to customers. Capacity was considered ample, with several new plants due to come on-stream during 1980. Producers do have downside protection through their long-term contracts. Growth of specialized new uses of industrial gases was projected to offset any downturn in traditional applications, resulting in estimated compound annual increases of 13 percent in sales and 12 percent in earnings between 1979 and 1983. For the longer run, technology in industrial gas manufacturing is likely to attract potentially large government funding for synthetic fuel projects.

Required:
(A) *Base your answer to both questions solely on the data in the two tables below and the background information.*

Compare each company in terms of return on equity during the period 1969–78. Discuss the impact of operating profit margin, effective tax rates, asset turnover, and total assets to common equity. Comment on the probable reasons for the differences and trends.

(B) Using 1978 data, calculate the estimated internal growth rate for each company. Comment on whether these growth rates are supported by historical company and industry data and the forecast for the industrial gas-chemical industry.

Earnings and Financial Position

Year	Pretax interest coverage		Asset turnover		Acid-test ratio		After-tax return on common equity	
	APD	BIG	APD	BIG	APD	BIG	APD	BIG
1978	8.0X	9.0X	.95X	.77X	.84X	1.24X	17.0%	16.9%
1977	6.6	8.6	.99	.71	1.12	1.34	17.6	16.9
1976	7.2	8.4	.99	.75	.94	2.20	19.7	16.1
1975	6.6	9.7	.99	.85	.85	1.71	20.5	18.4
1974	6.0	10.4	.97	.86	1.01	1.36	18.0	17.5
1973	4.7	11.2	.83	.79	1.01	1.49	12.6	13.7
1972	3.9	8.5	.78	.74	1.12	1.57	10.9	14.3
1971	3.6	4.3	.73	.62	1.09	.95	11.2	15.1
1970	3.7	4.1	.69	.64	1.14	1.48	11.9	16.5
1969	4.2	4.9	.67	.79	1.06	1.30	11.9	14.6
Averages								
1973–78	6.5X	9.6X	.95X	.79X	.96X	1.56X	17.6%	16.6%
1969–73	4.0	6.6	.74	.72	1.08	1.36	11.7	14.8
1969–78	5.5	7.9	.86	.75	1.02	1.46	15.1	16.0

Taxes, Profit Margins, Financial Position, and Dividends

Year	Income tax rate		Operating profit margin*		Total assets to common equity		Dividend payout ratio	
	APD	BIG	APD	BIG	APD	BIG	APD	BIG
1978	50%	37%	14.8%	23.6%	2.49X	1.69X	19%	24%
1977	46	28	15.2	22.6	2.48	1.64	10	16
1976	47	38	16.2	23.2	2.55	1.65	5	19
1975	46	38	16.3	22.8	2.66	1.57	5	15
1974	46	39	14.6	20.7	2.76	1.81	7	16
1973	43	43	12.7	20.9	2.56	1.65	8	22
1972	43	41	12.1	19.7	2.60	1.51	7	25
1971	42	39	11.8	19.8	2.89	2.38	7	28
1970	42	37	12.9	20.0	3.38	2.57	7	28
1969	47	46	13.8	18.1	3.23	2.21	8	41
							Average payout	
Averages								
1973–78	46%	37%	15.0%	22.3%	2.58X	1.67X	9.0%	18.7%
1969–73	43	41	12.7	19.7	2.93	2.06	7.4	28.5
1969–78	45	39	14.0	21.2	2.76	1.87	8.3	23.4

* Income before interest and taxes.

(CFA adapted)

19–7. Zear Manufacturing Company is a major producer of faucets that it sells on a wholesale basis to the plumbing trade at $10 per unit. In its 19x8 fiscal year, just ended, it sold 500,000 units. Fixed costs last year to total $1,500,000 which included interest charges on its 7½ percent debentures. Variable costs are $4 per unit for materials. There are 100 hourly paid plant employees each earning $7,000 in the year 19x8.

Labor negotiations are now underway, with the union demanding substantial increases in the hourly rated plant workers. Zear Manufacturing is budgeting for a 6 percent increase in overall fixed costs and foresees no change in unit price or unit costs for materials. A 10 percent growth in sales volume is forecast for the current year, and to obtain the necessary increase in production 10 more hourly rated plant employees have been hired.

A condensed balance sheet for Zear Manufacturing at the end of the 19x8 fiscal year is shown as follows:

Current assets:			
Cash	$ 700,000	Current liabilities	$2,000,000
Receivables	1,000,000	Long-term debt 7½%	
Other	800,000	debenture.............	2,000,000
		6% preferred stock	
Total current		10,000 shares, $100	
assets	2,500,000	par value	1,000,000
Fixed assets (net of		Common stock and	
depreciation)	5,500,000	retained earnings.......	3,000,000
	$8,000,000		$8,000,000

Required:

a. Assuming an income tax rate of 50 percent, calculate the percentage return for 19x8 on (1) total invested capital and (2) common equity.

b. Calculate the maximum annual wage increase Zear Manufacturing can afford to pay each plant employee and show a 10 percent return on total invested capital. (Total invested capital can be based on that shown at the end of the 19x8 fiscal year.)

(CFA adapted)

19–8. As a financial analyst at a debt-rating agency you were asked to analyze the return on investment and the asset utilization measures of Gama Corporation based on the limited information contained in its two year financial statements (see Problem 23–7).

The additional information that follows pertains to this problem only:

Balances at December 31, 19x4 (in thousands):

Total assets	$94,500
Long-term debt	11,200
Deferred income taxes (assume to be long-term liability)	1,000
Minority interest	800
Stockholders' equity..............................	42,000

Interest expense on long-term debt is $4,000 for 19x6 and $3,000 for 19x5. Use a 50 percent tax rate.

Required:
I. Compute the following for 19x5 and 19x6:
    (a) Return on total assets.
    (b) Return on long-term liabilities plus equity capital.
    (c) Return on common stockholders' equity (ROCSE).
    (d) Disaggregate the ratio in (c) above and comment on the usefulness of such disaggregation.
    (e) Equity growth rate.
    (f) Analysis of composition of return on stockholders' equity for 19x6 only.
II. Comment on the year-to-year changes in the above measures. What is the significance of the analysis in I (f) above?

19–9. Please refer to the financial statements of Tandy Corporation in Problem 17–9.
The following data pertains to this problem only:

	1982	1981	1980	1979	1978
Market prices per common share	$28	$21	$10	$5	$6
Number of common shares outstanding (in thousands)	103,400	102,600	103,600	106,000	96,100

Assume that the entire interest expense is on long-term debt and that there are only common shares outstanding.

Required:
I. Compute the following for 1978 to 1982:
    (a) Return on total assets.
    (b) Return on long-term liabilities and equity capital.
    (c) Return on stockholders' equity:
        (1) Conventional basis.
        (2) On the basis of market value of equity capital (use price and share data given above).
    (d) Equity growth rate.
II. Page 617 presents Tandy's analysis of the composition of its return on equity for 1978–82. Give your supporting computations to the figures used by Tandy.
III. Comment on the level and the trend of the measures in I and II above.
IV. Tandy discloses that in 1982, when adopting *SFAS 52,* it made two charges to the Foreign Currency Translation Effects account in the equity section (in thousands):

        Effect of restating asset and liability balances as of
            July 1, 1981, for adoption of *SFAS 52* $5,482
        Foreign currency translation adjustments for the period $6,835

What effect will these entries have on Tandy's return on equity? Discuss.

Chapter 20

20–1. Please refer to the financial statements of Alfa, Inc., in Appendix 4B.

Required:
I. Prepare a five-year summary and common-size analysis of costs by operating groups. (See five-year summary of revenues and contributions of operating groups—items 106 and 107.)
II. Prepare three separate tables showing five-year trend analysis of revenues, costs, and contributions by operating groups using 19x2 as a base year.
III. What conclusions can you draw from I and II above about the results of operations and their trend over the last five years for Alfa, Inc.?
IV. Alfa had a $9,624 loss in the agriculture operating group in 19x6. Using the figures derived above and assuming that 30 percent of total costs were fixed costs, compute Alfa's agriculture group contribution margin (both in dollars and percent) for 19x6. What would the dollar revenue level have to be for Alfa's agriculture operations to break even? For Alfa to earn a pretax profit of $5,000 from agriculture operations?

20–2. The comparative income statements of the Essex Manufacturing Company for 19x9 and 19x8 are as follows:

	19x9	19x8
Net sales	$600,000	$500,000
Cost of goods sold	490,000	430,000
Gross margin on sales	110,000	70,000
Operating expenses	101,000	51,000
Income before taxes	9,000	19,000
Federal income taxes	2,400	5,000
Net income after taxes	$ 6,600	$ 14,000

Required:
a. Prepare common-size statements that show the percentage of each item to sales for the two years. Include a column for percent of increase or decrease of 19x9 amounts from 19x8. Round to the nearest tenth of 1 percent.
b. Is a good trend indicated by your percentage calculations? What areas should be a matter of managerial concern?

20–3. The most recently published statement of consolidated income of Standard Industries, Inc., appears as follows:

STANDARD INDUSTRIES, INC.
Statement of Consolidated Income
For the Year Ended March 31, 19x8

Revenue:	
Net sales	$38,040,000
Other revenue	408,600
Total revenue	38,448,600
Cost and expenses:	
Cost of products sold	27,173,300
Selling and administrative expenses	8,687,500
Interest expense	296,900
Total cost and expenses	36,157,700
Income before income taxes	2,290,900
Provision for income taxes	1,005,000
Net income	$ 1,285,900

Charles Norton, a representative of a firm of security analysts, visited the central headquarters of Standard Industries for the purpose of obtaining more information about the company's operations.

In the annual report, Standard's president stated that Standard was engaged in the pharmaceutical, food processing, toy manufacturing, and metal-working industries. Mr. Norton complained that the published income statement was of limited utility in his analysis of the firm's operations. He said Standard should have disclosed separately the profit earned in each of its component industries. Further, he maintained that several items appearing on the statement of consolidated retained earnings should have been included on the income statement, namely, a gain of $633,400 on the sale of the furniture division in early March of the current year and an assessment of additional income taxes of $164,900 resulting from an examination of the returns covering the years ended March 31, 19x5 and 19x6.

Required:
a. Explain what is meant by the term *conglomerate* company.
b. (1) Discuss the accounting problems involved in measuring net profit by industry segments within a company.
   (2) With reference to Standard Industries' statement of consolidated income identify the specific items where difficulty might be encountered in measuring profit by each of its industry segments and explain the nature of the difficulty.
c. (1) What criteria should be applied in determining whether a gain or loss should be excluded from the determination of net income?
   (2) What criteria should be applied in determining whether a gain or loss that is properly includable in the determination of net income should be included in the results of ordinary operations or shown separately as an extraordinary item after all other items of revenue and expense?
   (3) How should the gain on the sale of the furniture division and the assessment of additional taxes each be presented in Standard's financial statements?

(AICPA adapted)

20–4. Super Corporation is a diversified company that discloses supplemental financial information as to industry segments of its business. Summary information for its segments is as follows:

	Segment		
	A	B	C
Information for segments:			
Sales to unaffiliated customers	$12,200	$ 800	$300
Sales to affiliated customers	200	500	200
Operating profit	700	(50)	30
Identifiable assets	11,500	1,360	420
Depreciation and depletion	1,200	140	110
Capital expenditures	1,600	80	230
Other information:			
Total operating profit			$680
Less:			
General expenses		$ 20	
Interest expense		35	
Minority interest income		15	
Income taxes		300	370
Net income			$310

Required:

a. Which of the Super Corporation segments are reportable segments? (Support your answer computationally.)

b. Is the A segment a dominant segment?

20–5. The following is a summary of Turner–Burn Corporation's revenue and income (contribution):

Line of business	19x0	19x1	19x2	19x3
Revenue:				
Manufactured and engineered products:				
Engineered equipment	$ 30,341	$ 29,807	$ 32,702	$ 43,870
Other equipment	5,906	5,996	6,824	7,424
Parts, supplies, and services	29,801	29,878	33,623	44,223
Total	66,048	65,681	73,149	95,517
Engineering and erection services	—	—	12,261	36,758
Total environmental				
systems group......................	66,048	65,681	85,410	132,275
Frye Copysystems	25,597	28,099	31,214	39,270
Sinclair & Valentine	—	53,763	57,288	60,973
A. L. Garber	16,615	15,223	20,445	24,808
Total graphics group	42,212	97,085	108,947	125,051
Total consolidated revenue	$108,260	$162,766	$194,357	$257,326

Income:

Manufactured and engineered products ..	$ 3,785	$ 3,943	$ 9,209	$ 10,762
Engineering and erection services	—	—	1,224	3,189
International operations	2,265	2,269	2,030	2,323
Total environmental systems group......................	6,050	6,212	12,463	16,274
Frye Copysystems	1,459	2,011	2,799	3,597
Sinclair & Valentine	—	3,723	4,628	5,142
A. L. Garber	(295)	926	1,304	1,457
Total graphics group	1,164	6,660	8,731	10,196
Total divisional income	7,214	12,872	21,194	26,470
Unallocated expenses and taxes	(5,047)	(8,146)	(13,179)	(16,449)
Total income from continuing operations	$ 2,167	$ 4,726	$ 8,015	$ 10,021

Required:

A. Analyze by means of common size statements each division's (1) contribution to total consolidated revenue and (2) contribution to total divisional income. Also compute each division's ratio of income to revenue.

B. Comment on the trends revealed by your computations.

20–6. Within the last three or four years, several requirements for fuller disclosure in the footnotes to corporate financial statements have been imposed by the Accounting Principles Board, the Financial Accounting Standards Board, and the Securities and Exchange Commission.

Required:

a. List at least five of these requirements, indicating their nature.

b. For each of the requirements that you have listed, discuss how the additional information aids financial analysis.

(CFA)

Chapter 21

21–1. Please refer to the financial statements of Alfa, Inc., in Appendix 4B.

Required:

A. Reconstruct all entries related to income taxes for 19x4. Post these to all T-accounts that are affected by taxes and reconstruct them to the best of your ability. State clearly any assumptions you make. Determine the amount of income taxes paid.

B. Explain how a company with income before tax of $69,167 (in 19x5) could report as much as $42,658 (62 percent) of current federal income tax (per Note 7) while the federal statutory tax rate is 48 percent?

21–2. Please refer to the financial statements of Alfa, Inc., in Appendix 4B.

Required:

I. Compute the following for 19x5 and 19x6:

(1) Ratio of depreciation expense to assets subject to depreciation.

(2) Effective interest rate on long-term debt (use ending balances for simplicity).
(3) Ratio of tax expense to income before tax (effective tax rate).
(4) Ratio of cost of goods sold plus other operating expenses to net sales.
(5) Ratio of net income to total revenues.

II. Comment on the trend of the ratios in I above from 19x5 to 19x6.

21–3. The following is a comparative income statement of Day & Sons, Inc.:

DAY & SONS, INC.
Comparative Income Statement
For the Years Ended December 31, 19y1, and 19y2

	19y2	19y1
Net sales	$162,000	$160,600
Cost of goods sold	102,000	104,500
Gross profit	60,000	56,100
Expenses:		
Selling expenses	15,630	16,802
General and administrative expenses	7,215	7,560
Other expenses	1,205	1,095
Total expenses ..	24,050	25,457
Income before income taxes	35,950	30,643
Income taxes	18,089	14,472
Net income	$ 17,861	$ 16,171
Units of merchandise sold	10,000	11,000

Required:
a. Prepare an analysis of the variation in gross margin.
b. Prepare an analysis of the variation in net income.

21–4. The Moon Mining Company mines selum, a commonly used mineral. Following is the company's report of operations:

THE MOON MINING COMPANY
Report of Operations
For the Years Ended December 31, 19x4, and 19x3

	19x4	19x3	Increase (Decrease)
Net sales	$880,000	$ 840,000	$ 40,000
Cost of goods sold	680,000	945,000	(265,000)
Gross profit (loss)	$200,000	$(105,000)	$ 305,000

The following information pertains to the company's operations:

1. The sales price of selum was increased from $8 per ton to $11 per ton on January 1, 19x4.

2. New mining machinery was placed in operation on January 1, 19x4, which reduced the cost of mining from $9 per ton to $8.50 per ton.
3. There was no change in ending inventories which were valued on the LIFO basis.

Required:

Prepare an analysis accounting for the change in the gross profit of The Moon Mining Company. The analysis should account for the effects of the changes in price, volume, and volume-price factors upon *(a)* sales and *(b)* cost of goods sold.

(AICPA adapted)

21–5. The following statistics are available for the Disco Company for 19x1 and 19x2:

	19x2	19x1
Gross profit percentage	40%	35%
Ending accounts receivable	$150,000	$90,000
Number of days sales in accounts receivable	60	45
Income tax rate	50%	40%
Net income as a percentage of sales	6%	9%

Required:

a. Prepare income statements in comparative form for the two years.
b. Comment on the trend in sales volume, gross profit percentage, and net income percentage.

21–6. Part 1. After reading an article on cost behavior which you recommended, your client asks you to explain the following excerpts from it:

1. "Fixed costs are variable per unit of output and variable costs are fixed per unit of output (though in the long run all costs are variable)."
2. "Depreciation may be either a fixed cost or a variable cost, depending on the method used to compute it."

Required:

For each excerpt:
a. Define the underlined terms. Give examples where appropriate.
b. Explain the meaning of the excerpt to your client.

Part 2. A break-even chart, as illustrated below, is a useful technique for showing relationships between costs, volume, and profits.

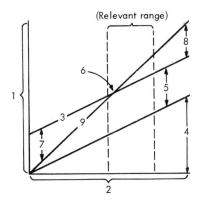

(Relevant range)

Required:

a. Identify the numbered components of the break-even chart.
b. Discuss the significance of the concept of the "relevant range" to break-even analyses.

(AICPA)

21–7. The income statement of an unincorporated retail store for 19x7 was as follows:

Sales (5,000 identical units)		$100,000
Expenses:		
Store rent	$12,500	
Salesmen's commissions	25,000	
Cost of goods sold	60,000	97,500
		$ 2,500

Salesmen's commissions are a constant percentage of sales price. The store lease has five more years to run at the present annual rental.

Required:

a. Compute the sales volume below which the company would operate at a net loss (the break-even volume).
b. Compute the volume of sales that would be needed under present conditions to double the amount of net income.
c. Compute the break-even sales volume for 19x8 if the company rented additional space for $6,500 a year and other operating conditions remained unchanged.
d. Prepare an income statement for 19x8 if the number of units is expected to remain unchanged but the sales price per unit is expected to decline $1.50. No other changes in operating conditions are anticipated.
e. If the number of units sold in 19x8 doubles and all other factors behave as in 19x7 prepare the resulting income statement.

21–8. Voss Company has an operating capacity of 100,000 units per year. Fixed factory overhead is $350,000 per year. Variable manufacturing costs are $20 per unit, and variable selling expenses are $4 per unit. Fixed selling and administrative expenses amount to $226,000 annually. The unit sales price is $36.

Required:

a. Compute the break-even point in units and dollars for Voss Company.
b. The company is proposing an addition to the plant that would increase capacity to 250,000 units and increase fixed factory overhead to $452,000 per year. The plant addition will cost $138,000. What increase in unit and dollar sales must the company obtain in order to earn a 10 percent return on the additional investment?

(CFA adapted)

21–9. *The Wall Street Journal* of January 18, 1983, had the following news item:

"General Motors, Ford and Chrysler are expected to post losses on fourth-quarter operations despite sales gains. Auto makers' revenues are based on factory output rather than retail sales by dealers, and last quarter's sales increases were from the bulging inventories at the end of the third quarter, rather than from models produced in the fourth quarter."

Required:
Describe the most likely specific reason for the auto makers' fourth-quarter losses.

21–10. The following are the cost structures of Companies A and B:

	Company A	Company B
Fixed costs	$12,000	$10,000
Variable costs (% of sales)	40%	60%

Required:
a. What are the break-even points in sales dollars for Companies A and B?
b. What will be the net income at sales of $18,000?
c. What will be the net income at sales of $27,000?
d. (1) Assume that sales can be increased to $30,000. What percentage of accounts receivable does each company have to collect to break even? (All sales are made on credit.)
   (2) How much additional cost outlays beyond the break-even point are required by each company to increase sales to $30,000? (Assume all sales on credit are fully collectible.)
   (3) What is the rate of incremental profits on additional cost outlays at a sales level of $30,000 in (1) above?
e. (1) Past experience has been that bad debts amounted to 10 percent of accounts receivable. What are the sales required if the company wants to net a profit of $10,000?
   (2) Assume that the present sales are $30,000 and that a maximum sales level of $40,000 can be achieved with an additional incurrence in fixed costs of $4,000 while variable costs per unit remain the same. The bad debt ratio is 10 percent. What is the net income for each company?
f. (1) Is a lower fixed cost always advantageous?
   (2) Which company is in a better position to take marginal risk in Requirement e (2) above?

21–11. Sher Sales Corporation's management is concerned over the corporation's current financial position and return on investment. They request your assistance in analyzing their financial statements and furnish the following statements:

SHER SALES CORPORATION
Statement of Working Capital Deficit
December 31, 19x8

Current liabilities		$223,050
Less current assets:		
Cash	$ 6,990	
Accounts receivable, net	70,560	
Inventory	112,500	190,050
Working capital deficit		$ 33,000

SHER SALES CORPORATION
Income Statement
For the Year Ended December 31, 19x8

Sales (90,000 units)	$756,000
Cost of goods sold	450,000
Gross profit	306,000
Selling and general expenses, including $22,980 depreciation	153,960
	152,040
Income taxes	76,020
Net income	$ 76,020

Additional data:

Assets other than current assets consist of land, building, and equipment with a book value of $352,950 on December 31, 19x8.

Required:

a. Assuming Sher Sales Corporation operates 300 days per year, compute the following (show your computations):
    (1) Number of days' sales uncollected.
    (2) Inventory turnover.
    (3) Number of days' operations to cover the working capital deficit.
    (4) Return on total assets as a product of asset turnover and the net income ratio (sometimes called profit margin).

b. Sales of 100,000 units are forecasted for 19x9. Within this relevant range of activity costs are estimated as follows (excluding income taxes):

	Fixed costs	Variable costs per unit
Cost of goods sold		$4.90
Selling and general expenses, including		
$15,450 depreciation	$129,720	1.10
Totals	$129,720	$6.00

The income tax rate is expected to be 50 percent. Past experience indicates that current assets vary in direct proportion to sales.

1. Management feels that in 19x9 the market will support a sales price of $8.30 at a sales volume of 100,000 units. Compute the rate of return on book value of total assets after income taxes assuming management's expectations are realized.
2. Assuming sales of 100,000 units at a price of $8.30 per unit in 19x9 prepare an analysis of the variation in gross profit between 19x8 and 19x9. Your analysis should show the effects of changes in 19x9 in sales volume, sales prices, and unit costs on gross profit.

(AICPA adapted)

21–12. The following information pertains to Woodbine Circle Corporation:

Adjusted Trial Balance
December 31, 1981

	Debit	Credit
Cash	$ 500,000	
Accounts receivable, net	1,500,000	
Inventory	2,500,000	
Property, plant, and equipment	15,100,000	
Accumulated depreciation		$ 4,900,000
Accounts payable		1,400,000
Income taxes payable		100,000
Notes payable		1,000,000
Common stock ($1 par value)		1,100,000
Additional paid-in capital		6,100,000
Retained earnings, January 1, 1981		3,000,000
Sales—regular		10,000,000
Sales—AL Division		2,000,000
Interest on municipal bonds		100,000
Cost of sales—regular	6,200,000	
Cost of sales—AL Division	900,000	
Administrative expenses—regular	2,000,000	
Administrative expenses—AL Division	300,000	
Interest expense—regular	210,000	
Interest expense—AL Division	140,000	
Loss on disposal of AL Division	250,000	
Gain on repurchase of bonds payable		300,000
Income tax expense	400,000	
	$30,000,000	$30,000,000

Other financial data for the year ended December 31, 1981:

Federal income taxes:

Paid on Federal Tax Deposit Forms 503	$ 300,000
Accrued	100,000
Total charged to income tax expense (estimated)	$ 400,000*

* Does not properly reflect current or deferred income tax expense or intraperiod income tax allocation for income statement purposes.

Income per tax return	$2,150,000
Tax rate on all types of taxable income	40%
Timing difference:	
Depreciation, per financial statements	$ 600,000
Depreciation, per tax return	750,000
Permanent difference:	
Interest on municipal bonds	100,000

Discontinued operations:

On September 30, 1981, Woodbine sold its Auto Leasing (AL) Division for $4,000,000. Book value of this business segment was $4,250,000 at that date. For financial statement purposes, this sale was considered as discontinued operations of a segment of a business. Since there was no phase-out period, the measurement date was September 30, 1981.

Liabilities:

On June 30, 1981, Woodbine repurchased $1,000,000 carrying value of its long-term bonds for $700,000. All other liabilities mature in 1982.

Capital structure:

Common stock, par value $1 per share, traded on the New York Stock Exchange:

Number of shares outstanding at January 1, 1981	900,000
Number of shares sold for $8 per share on June 30, 1981	200,000
Number of shares outstanding at December 31, 1981	1,100,000

Required:

Using the multiple-step format, prepare a formal income statement for Woodbine for the year ended December 31, 1981, together with the appropriate supporting schedules. Recurring and nonrecurring items in the income statement should be properly separated. All income taxes should be appropriately shown.

(CPA adapted)

21–13. Please refer to the financial statements of Gama Corporation in Problem 23–7.

Required:
A. Reconstruct all entries related to income taxes for 19x6 and show the amount of income tax paid.
B. What effect did the investment tax credit have on the 19x6 balance sheet?
C. Estimate the amount of depreciation expense shown for *tax return* reporting.

21–14. At a meeting of your institution's Investment Policy Committee, at which Gama Corporation (see Problem 23–7) was considered for investment, a member wondered about which were the major factors that accounted for the 19x5 to 19x6 change in the net income of that company.

Required:
Prepare a statement accounting for the variation in Gama's net income for the period in question.

21–15. Please refer to the financial statements of Tandy Corporation in Problem 17–9.

Required (dollar amounts in thousands):
I. By means of a T-account analysis reconcile as best you can the 1982 tax accounts and determine the amount of income taxes paid in fiscal 1982.

Needed additional information:

"Other assets" include deferred taxes—current of $4,927 at fiscal year-end 1981 and $10,441 at fiscal year-end 1982.

II. Prepare a statement accounting for variations in net income comparing the 1977 to 1979 period with the 1980–82 period (in millions of dollars).

Chapter 22

22–1. Please refer to the financial statements of Alfa, Inc., in Appendix 4B.

Required:
I. Construct an index of seasonal variability (between quarters) of sales and net income for 19x6.
II. Compute the percentage of net earnings to sales for each quarter and comment on the changes.
III. Analyze the discretionary expenses for 19x6. (Hint: Prepare a table showing the percentages of maintenance and repairs; advertising expenses; and research and development expenses to revenues as well as the percentage of maintenance and repairs to net property, plant, and equipment for 19x6. Compare these percentages for 19x6 to a four-year (19x2–x5) average of the same percentages to see whether management has attempted to "save" in 19x6 on any of these three discretionary items.)

22–2. The financial statements of the Bicentennial Company are given below:

BICENTENNIAL COMPANY
Balance Sheet
As of December 31, 19x3, and 19x2

	19x3	*19x2*
Current assets	$ 300,000	$ 250,000
Plant, property, and equipment	500,000	350,000
Accumulated depreciation	(150,000)	(100,000)
All other assets	150,000	100,000
Total assets	800,000	600,000
Liabilities and capital	$ 800,000	$ 600,000

BICENTENNIAL COMPANY
Income Statement
For the Years Ended December 31, 19x3 and 19x2

	19x3	19x2
Sales	$1,500,000	$1,000,000
Cost of goods sold	1,050,000	700,000
Gross profit	450,000	300,000
All other expenses	85,000	50,000
Repairs and maintenance	50,000	50,000
Research and development	25,000	30,000
Advertising	60,000	50,000
Other selling expenses	90,000	50,000
Net income	$ 140,000	$ 70,000

The economy has recovered strongly in 19x3 after a long depression, and business has been good in 19x2. Research and development outlays are expensed in accordance with *SFAS 2.*

Required:
a. What significant changes do you notice in the company's operational policies in 19x3? (Limit your analysis to repair and maintenance, advertising, and research and development expenses.)
b. Do you think the changes may have an effect on future earnings?

22–3. Robert G. Wingerter, president, Libbey-Owens-Ford Company, said, among others, in an address to analysts:

"While on the subject of management attitudes, I would like to comment that LOF has resisted joining a seemingly increasing number of companies who along with earnings announcements also make extraordinary or non-recurring loss announcements. Many of these situations read like regular operating problems when you get into the detail. When we closed plants and the like, we have charged earnings for the costs involved or reserved as we approached the event. Such costs in my judgment are quite usually a normal operating expense and something that good management should expect or anticipate. That, of course, brings up the question as to what earnings figure should be regarded by your profession in assigning a P/E ratio and what is the quality of the reported earnings figure."

Required:
a) Comment on Mr. Wingerter's statement.
b) What factors determine whether an item of gain or loss is extraordinary or not?
c) Which of the following would you classify as extraordinary and why? All amounts are material.
   (1) Loss suffered by foreign subsidiaries because of a change in the foreign exchange rate.
   (2) Write-down of inventory from cost to market.
   (3) Loss attributable to the appearance of improved product developed by a competitor.
   (4) Decrease in net profit as a result of next taxation.

(5)   Increase in net profit as a result of the liquidation of low-cost LIFO inventories because of long strikes.

(6)   Expenses incurred in relocating plant.

(7)   Expenses incurred in liquidating unprofitable product lines.

(8)   Research and development expenses written off as a result of product failure (nonmarketed).

(9)   Research and development expenses written off because demand for a product proved to be weaker than anticipated.

(10) Failure of a major customer resulting in a substantial bad debt provision.

(11) Loss on the sale of rental cars by a car rental company.

(12) Gains on sales of fixed assets.

(13) Rentals received from employees who rented company-owned houses.

(14) Uninsured casualty losses.

(15) The expropriation by a foreign government of an entire operation owned by the enterprise.

(16) The seizure or destruction of property as a result of an act of war.

22–4.   An article entitled "A Sea of Red Ink" appearing in *Forbes* of January 1, 1973, comments:

"For management, write-offs serve a useful function. They are a way of clearing the books of the mistakes of the past and preparing the way for a better future. For investors, however, they raise some real questions.

"So big have write-offs been—$3.4 billion in the last seven years, with most of it in the last two—that the editors of *Forbes* decided we must somehow reflect them in our five-year Yardsticks of Growth and Profitability. We have, in effect, deducted the full amount of the major write-offs from earnings for the last seven years. The result, in many cases, is a dramatic drop in profitability and in earnings growth. Without the write-offs Celanese Corp., for example, showed a five-year return of 7.3% on stockholders' equity. After deducting the write-offs, Celanese had a deficit return.

"So drastic were some write-offs that 31 companies on our list ended the year with a negative return on equity. Among them: Allis-Chalmers, Boise Cascade, Anaconda, American-Standard and L-T-V.

"Our reasoning was very simple. The write-offs occurred either because costs had been understated or income overstated in the past. Therefore, the earnings as reported were not real.

"In so adjusting the write-off long-term figures, we make no judgment as to the future. In some cases, the write-off may indeed usher in better days. RCA, for example, rid of its computer incubus, should report even better earnings in the future than it did in the past. But in other cases, write-offs may serve merely to cover mistakes made in the ordinary line of business. . . ."

Required:

Do you agree with *Forbes'* treatment of write-offs in computing longer-term growth and profitability? How should financial analysts treat them?

22–5.   The owner of a small manufacturing firm came to you, a loan officer of a local bank, for a short-term loan of $20,000. You told him that your bank did not approve a loan for any business with a gross profit ratio of 25 percent or less.

The client said, "I think we qualify under your criteria. I will ask my bookkeeper to prepare an analysis."

A few days later he came back with an analysis that showed a gross profit ratio of 30 percent. The following additional information for the period is available:

1. Cost of goods sold is $70,000.
2. The bookkeeper included the following items in the cost of goods sold:
   (a) Freight-out of $1,000.
   (b) The salary of $10,000 of plant supervisor (who spends one half of his time as sales manager) is charged to production.
   (c) The entire electricity bill of $1,000 was charged to production (plant using 85 percent of electricity).
   (d) Sales taxes of $5,000 on sales of goods.
   (e) Plant employees' salary of $30,000.
   (f) Automobile expenses of $4,000 (two fifths of the time used by the owner for private use, three fifths by plant supervisor mentioned in (b) above.
3. The following items were excluded from cost of goods sold:
   (a) Freight-in costs of $1,500 incurred for the purchase of material for production.
   (b) Advertising expenses of $8,000.
   (c) Federal excise taxes of $2,000, and custom duties of $500.
   (d) Vacation salary for plant mechanics of $1,500.
   (e) Depreciation of plant of $10,000, and depreciation of office of $2,000.
   (f) Ordinary repair and maintenance cost of machines of $600.
   (g) Payroll taxes for plant employees of $3,000 and office employees of $2,000.
   (h) Installation costs of $10,000 of new machines which are to be depreciated over 10 years.
4. Beginning inventory, $15,000.
   Ending inventory, $15,000.
5. The company used the FIFO method of inventory accounting.

Required:
Does the company meet the bank's cutoff point of a 25 percent gross profit?

22–6.   Fashion Styles Corporation, a manufacturer of molded plastic containers, determined in October 19x8 that it needed cash to continue operations. The corporation began negotiating for a one-month bank loan of $100,000 that would be discounted at 6 percent per annum on November 1. In considering the loan, the bank requested a projected income statement and a cash budget for the month of November.

The following information is available:

1. Sales were budgeted at 120,000 units per month in October 19x8, December 19x8, and January 19x9, and at 90,000 units in November 19x8.

   The selling price is $2 per unit. Sales are billed on the 15th and last day of each month on terms of 2/10 net 30. Past experience indicates sales are even throughout the month, and 50 percent of the customers pay the billed amount within the discount period. The remainder pay at the end of 30 days, except for bad debts which average ½ percent of gross sales. On its income statement the corporation deducts from sales the estimated amounts for cash discounts on sales and losses on bad debts.

2. The inventory of finished goods on October 1 was 24,000 units. The finished goods inventory at the end of each month is to be maintained at 20 percent of sales anticipated for the following month. There is no work in process.

3. The inventory of raw materials on October 1 was 22,800 pounds. At the end of each month the raw materials inventory is to be maintained at not less than 40 percent of production requirements for the following month. Materials are purchased as needed in minimum quantities of 25,000 pounds per shipment. Raw material purchases of each month are paid in the next succeeding month on terms of net 30 days.

4. All salaries and wages are paid on the 15th and last day of each month for the period ending on the date of payment.

5. All manufacturing overhead and selling and administrative expenses are paid on the 10th of the month following the month in which incurred. Selling expenses are 10 percent of gross sales. Administrative expenses, which include depreciation of $500 per month on office furniture and fixtures total $33,000 per month.

6. The standard cost of a molded plastic container, based on "normal" production of 100,000 units per month, is as follows:

Materials—½ pound	$ .50
Labor	.40
Variable overhead	.20
Fixed overhead	.10
Total	$1.20

Fixed overhead includes depreciation on factory equipment of $4,000 per month. Over- or underabsorbed overhead is included in cost of sales.

7. The cash balance on November 1 is expected to be $10,000.

Required:

Prepare the following for Fashion Styles Corporation assuming the bank loan is granted. (Do not consider income taxes.)

a. Schedules computing inventory budgets by months for—
   (1) Finished goods production in units for October, November, and December.
   (2) Raw material purchases in pounds for October and November.

b. A projected income statement for the month of November.

c. A cash forecast for the month of November showing the opening balance, receipts (itemized by dates of collection), disbursements, and balance at end of month.

(AICPA adapted)

22–7. Interim financial reporting has become an important topic in accounting. There has been considerable discussion as to the proper method of reflecting results of operations at interim dates. Accordingly, the Accounting Principles Board issued an *Opinion* clarifying some aspects of interim financial reporting.

Required:

a. Discuss generally how revenue should be recognized at interim dates and specifically how revenue should be recognized for industries subject to large seasonal fluctuations in revenue and for long-term contracts using the percentage-of-completion method at annual reporting dates.

b. Discuss generally how product and period costs should be recognized at interim dates. Also discuss how inventory and cost of goods sold may be afforded special accounting treatment at interim dates.

c. Discuss how the provision for income taxes is computed and reflected in interim financial statements.

(AICPA)

22–8. In the 19x1 annual report of Spiral Metal Company the newly elected chairman of the board explained the company's recently incurred substantial losses as follows:

"The substantial losses incurred last year were primarily attributable to the refining operations in South Amboy, New Jersey. In order to arrest these continuing losses, we decided in September 19x1 to suspend refining operations in South Amboy. Sales of the continuing operations for the fiscal year ended March 31, 19x1, were approximately $31 million.

"Because the refinery did not maintain a perpetual inventory system, the magnitude of the losses incurred during fiscal 19x1 became clear only after the close of the year, when the physical inventory was taken.

"Although your new management is continuing to study the various causes for the loss, we still do not know all the detailed reasons for the operating losses and inventory differences. Part of the cause for the inventory difference is believed to be process losses—literally up the smokestack—but just how significant these were we do not know.

"Basically, what happened, in broad terms, was that Spiral expanded its refinery operations too rapidly, installed new equipment with which Company personnel had too little experience, and tried to integrate its various acquisitions simultaneously. Also contributing to the Company's difficulties was an almost complete change in top echelon refinery management."

Required:
How can analysts foresee the possibility of such a loss of control by the management of an enterprise? What are possible symptoms to watch for?

22–9. What factors *(a)* within the company and *(b)* within the economy have and are likely to affect the degree of variability in the earnings per share, dividends per share, and market price per share, of common stock?

(CFA)

22–10. Hereunder are the income statements of Ferro Corporation and Note 7 on income taxes:

Consolidated Statements of Income and Earnings Retained in the Business
Years Ended December 31, 1976, and 1975
(in thousands)

	1976	1975
Net sales	$376,485	$328,005
Cost of sales	266,846	237,333
Selling and administrative expenses ...	58,216	54,140
Research and development	9,972	8,205
	335,034	299,678
Operating income	41,451	28,327

Other income:

Equity in net earnings of affiliated companies	1,394	504
Royalties	710	854
Interest earned	1,346	1,086
Miscellaneous	1,490	1,761
	4,940	4,205

Other charges:

Interest expense	4,055	4,474
Unrealized foreign currency translation loss	4,037	1,851
Miscellaneous	1,480	1,448
	9,572	7,773
Income before taxes	36,819	24,759

United States and foreign income taxes, including deferred
taxes of $493,000 in 1976 and $64,000 in 1975

(Note 7)	16,765	11,133
Net income	$ 20,054	$ 13,626

Notes to the financial statements:

7. Income Tax Expense: Income tax expense is comprised of the following components (dollars in thousands):

	United States federal	Foreign	Total
1976:			
Current	$5,147	11,125	16,272
Deferred	353	140	493
Total	$5,500	11,265	16,765
1975:			
Current	$2,974	8,095	11,069
Deferred	180	(116)	64
Total	$3,154	7,979	11,133

Deferred income taxes were mainly the result of using accelerated depreciation for income tax purposes and straight-line depreciation in the consolidated financial statements.

State and local income taxes totaling approximately $750,000 and $698,000 in 1976 and 1975, respectively are included in other expense categories.

A reconciliation between the United States federal income tax rate and the effective tax rate for 1976 and 1975 follows:

	1976	1975
United States Federal income tax rate	48.0%	48.0%
Earnings of consolidated subsidiaries taxed at rates less than the United States federal income tax rate	(5.3)	(5.3)
Equity in after-tax earnings of affiliated companies	(1.4)	(0.8)
Unrealized foreign exchange translation loss	5.3	3.6
Additional U.S. taxes on dividends from subsidiaries and affiliates	.8	1.0
Investment tax credit	(1.5)	(.9)
Miscellaneous	(.4)	(.6)
Effective tax rate	45.5%	45.0%

In addition, you were able to obtain the following information from Form 10-K filed with the SEC:

1. Cost of sales includes the following items (in thousands):

	1976	1975
Repairs and maintenance	$15,000	$20,000
Loss on disposal of chemicals division	—	7,000

2. Selling and administrative expenses include (in thousands):

	1976	1975
Advertising	$ 6,000	$ 7,000
Employee training program	4,000	5,000

Required:
a. Identify erratic and unstable factors, as well as the factors that caused income tax expense to differ from 48 percent of pretax income, and present analytically recast income statements for 1975 and 1976.
b. What significant changes, if any, do you notice in the company's operational policies in 1976? (Limit your analysis to outlays for repairs and maintenance, advertising, and employee training program expense.)

22–11. Please refer to the financial statements of Tandy Corporation in Problem 17–9.

The following data and information should be considered only for purposes of this problem.

In its financial statements Tandy discloses the following (in thousands):

	1978	1979	1980	1981	1982
Manufacturing employees payroll (included in cost of products sold)	$ 24,022	$ 28,344	$ 32,958	$ 42,128	$ 53,105
Included in selling, general, and administrative expenses:					
Nonmanufacturing employee's payroll	170,962	206,507	232,569	286,494	339,559
Advertising expense	95,386	114,238	124,138	137,722	160,905
Rent expense	48,758	54,606	61,491	73,857	89,732
Foreign currency translation (gains), losses	1,034	3,230	1,722	(5,295)	—
Other selling, general, and administrative expenses	87,033	105,668	126,405	153,156	190,182

	1978	1979	1980	1981	1982
Included in "Other Income"					
Sale of Tandy's interest in an airplane*		504			
Disposal of Dillard Department Store, Inc., common stock*		1,060			
Settlement of a dispute*		530			
Gain on sale of Canadian warehouse*			662		

* Net of tax at the statutory rate shown on the income statement.

Required:
Prepare analytically recast income statements for 1978 to 1982.

Chapter 23

23–1. Please refer to the financial statements of Alfa, Inc., in Appendix 4B.

Required:
Using such measures and such analytical techniques as you deem appropriate, evaluate the following:

I. Short-term liquidity.
II. Capital structure and long-term solvency.
III. Return an investment and asset utilization.
IV. Operating performance.

23–2. Discuss the factors that would determine the relative price-earnings ratios to be applied to each of these two makers of industrial machinery for which the following financial data are available:

	A	B
Capital structure:		
5% 20-year notes	$10,000,000	$ None
Common and surplus	20,000,000	30,000,000
Number of common shares	500,000	750,000
Earnings per share:		
1966	$4.25	$3.00
1965	3.50	2.50
1964	2.25	1.67
1963	2.75	2.00
1962	1.70	1.95
Sales (1966)	$30,000,000	$30,000,000
Net income	2,125,000	2,250,000

	A	B
Balance sheet data at December 31, 1966:		
Current assets:		
Cash	3,000,000	5,850,000
Receivables	5,000,000	3,750,000
Inventories	12,000,000	10,000,000
Total current assets	20,000,000	19,600,000
Current liabilities:		
Accounts payable	4,000,000	3,500,000
Accruals	2,000,000	2,000,000
Taxes	1,000,000	1,100,000
Total current liabilities	7,000,000	6,600,000
Net plant	13,000,000	15,900,00
Patents, etc.	4,000,000	100,000

(CFA)

23–3. Please refer to the financial statements of Doit Corporation in Problem 13–12.

Required:

As a member of the staff of Doit Corporation, you have been asked to assist in the preparation of an analysis of the profitability and financial position of the company. Provide answers and relevant calculations to the following questions:

(1) Were accounts receivable being collected faster in 1980 than accounts payable were being paid? Explain.

Assume:

250 working days during the year.

100 percent of purchases made on credit and 50 percent of sales are for credit.

The average of beginning and ending balances for receivables and pay-ables, respectively, are regarded as reasonable estimates of the average balance throughout 1980.

Use cost of goods sold and change in inventories to compute purchases.

(2) Has inventory turnover improved or worsened in 1980 compared with 1979? Explain.

Assume that merchandise inventory at December 31, 1978, was $18.0 and that the average inventory balance during any given year is the average of begin-ning and ending balances.

(3) Compute the pretax and after-tax profit margins in 1979 and 1980 and explain the reasons underlying the changes in these margins.

(4) (a) Compute the return on average total capital and on average stockholders' equity (net worth) for 1979 and 1980.

Assume that on December 31, 1978, total capital was $120.0 and stock-holders' equity was $70.0.

(b) A director of the company asks, "If our net margin has improved, why has return on investment (ROI) declined?" Provide a general response to this question. Indicate what additional information you would like to have in order to give management a more detailed and specific answer.

(5) (a) Identify evidence in the financial statements that indicates when, in 1980, Doit Corporation purchased the additional fixed assets.

(b) Based on this evidence, is the return on investment computed in Requirement (4) (a) either overstated or understated?

(CFA adapted)

23–4. Based on the data for Jos. Schlitz Company (S) and Heileman Company (H) below, compare the progress of the two companies from 1960 to 1971 and their respective positions in 1971.

The major brand of Jos. Schlitz Company is Schlitz beer, which is sold nationally at premium prices and accounts for most of the company's sales. Eight breweries are located in important marketing territories throughout the United States. Most facilities are modern.

Heileman sells beer in 40 states under a variety of names and in 1969 purchased the Blatz label, a prominent brand name, and certain other assets (but not the brewing facility) from Pabst Brewing Company for $10,750,000. The Heileman's three breweries are not modern but have been considerably upgraded. In 1970, the company added capacity to handle the added Blatz volume but had to purchase 300,000 barrels from Pabst. Heileman has had to establish an aggressive distributor organization in certain sections of Blatz's market territory.

Year	Earned on net worth		Operating profit margin		Assets turnover		Total debt: Net worth		Current ratio		Acid-test ratio	
	S Per-cent	H Per-cent	S Per-cent	H Per-cent	S Per-cent	H Per-cent	S Per-cent	H Per-cent	S x	H x	S x	H x
1972*	—	—	—	—	—	—	—	—	—	—	—	—
1971	15.5	20.0	15.0	12.1	n.a.		n.a.		n.a.		n.a.	
1970	14.4	23.3	14.5	10.5	1.4	2.3	.62	1.11	1.8	1.3	1.0	.8
1969	10.9	21.8	13.8	10.1	1.4	2.2	.49	1.16	1.7	1.4	1.2	.9
1968	9.1	21.1	14.6	9.5	1.5	2.9	.27	.62	2.0	1.6	1.4	1.1
1967	11.0	18.4	12.4	9.0	1.3	1.9	.27	.92	2.6	2.0	1.7	1.3
1966	10.4	16.5	11.4	9.4	1.3	2.2	.25	.50	2.4	1.9	1.0	1.5
1965	8.9	15.2	11.6	11.5	1.2	2.4	.24	.41	1.5	1.9	1.2	1.6
1964	9.3	15.5	11.1	9.7	1.3	2.3	.94	.42	1.8	1.4	n.a.	1.1
1963	8.8	11.7	11.5	8.9	1.3	2.1	.23	.47	3.3	1.4	2.2	.8
1962	6.9	8.2	10.5	6.4	1.1	2.1	.19	.30	3.3	1.5	2.3	1.0
1961	5.0	8.5	7.6	5.3	.9	2.0	.17	.32	3.3	2.0	2.4	1.3
1960	6.4	9.2	10.0	6.1	1.0	2.1	.17	.40	3.4	1.6	2.4	1.1

* 1972 figures are estimates where given.

n.a. = not available.

Year	Sales per share S $	Sales per share H $	Earnings per share S $	Earnings per share H $	Dividends per share S $	Dividends per share H $	Price-earnings ratio* S x	Price-earnings ratio* H x	Div. yield on com.* S Per-cent	Div. yield on com.* H Per-cent
1972	—	—	4.20	1.60	—	—	—	—	—	1.9
1971	54.00	27.35	3.60	1.40	1.55	.40	24.2	15.0	1.6	1.5
1970	48.09	28.49	3.14	1.37	1.40	.35	21.5	17.5	2.1	1.5
1969	43.41	23.21	2.58	1.05	1.35	.26	24.8	17.6	2.1	1.4
1968	37.08	16.55	2.20	.70	1.15	.21	22.8	15.3	2.3	1.9
1967	31.62	12.13	2.02	.55	.98	.18	15.5	7.8	3.1	4.1
1966	28.65	9.30	1.80	.44	.88	.16	11.9	7.1	4.1	4.9
1965	26.11	8.44	1.68	.38	.78	.16	16.1	8.9	2.9	4.7
1964	24.93	7.71	1.47	.35	.70	.16	16.2	8.6	3.0	5.3
1963	22.37	6.55	1.35	.26	.73	.14	13.9	9.6	3.9	5.6
1962	18.84	5.61	1.00	.17	.60	.13	14.1	11.7	4.3	6.5
1961	15.86	5.22	.71	.17	.60	.13	n.a.	14.1	n.a.	5.2
1960	15.88	5.22	.90	.20	.60	.13	n.a.	10.0	n.a.	6.5

* Price based on midpoint of range for year.
n.a. = not available.

Compound Growth Rates

Year	Sales per share S	Sales per share H	Earnings per share S	Earnings per share H	Dividends per share S	Dividends per share H
1960–71	12.1%	18.9%	14.0%	23.0%	11.0%	10.5%
1966–71	14.0	26.7	15.2	29.0	11.2	12.0

	Schlitz (NYSE)	Heileman (Midwest Exchange)
Market close:		
January 3, 1972	124	18⅜
Range of market:		
Year 1971	111–67	28–14

(CFA)

23–5. In 1977, Seymour Cleerly, an investment officer of Paramutual Life Insurance Company, negotiated a $1.5 million private placement loan to Bee-Tee-U Corporation, a manufacturer of industrial heating equipment. The purpose of the 10.25 percent Senior Notes, due 1987, was to reduce borrowings incurred under bank lines of credit. Although not rated by a bond rating agency, Paramutual's "in house" quality rating was a solid "medium."

Seymour and his staff had focused their credit analysis on Bee-Tee-U's growth, average profitability, and fixed charge coverage for the past five years. From 1972 through 1976, sales had more than tripled, earnings more than doubled, return on total assets averaged 14.0 percent, and pretax fixed charge coverage averaged 7.5 times. Seymour regarded the capital structure as satisfactory, with long-term debt equal to 42 percent of total capital (pro forma). Lastly, net working capital had increased by 50 percent and would be strengthened (as would the current ratio) by proceeds of the new note issue. The economic outlook for capital goods and the company's products, in particular, appeared to be favorable, and Seymour felt very comfortable with his investment decision.

Accordingly, he was shocked and dismayed upon receiving a call in mid-1979 from the company's treasurer who advised him that due to Bee-Tee-U's strained financial position, regular interest and sinking fund payments could not be made. Aside from some general comments about inflation and rising costs, the treasurer did not offer a complete explanation. Seymour was puzzled by this news because he recalled from the company's 1977 and 1978 annual reports that sales and earnings had continued their vigorous growth.

Therefore, he quickly ordered a complete review of the original Bee-Tee-U analysis for the years 1972–76, updated to include the post-loan years 1977 and 1978. This financial data have been assembled for your analysis and are shown below.

Required:
Based on this financial data:
(a) Calculate the pretax fixed charge coverage ratios for the two years 1972 and 1976. Show all calculations.
(b) Showing all calculations, calculate for 1977 the turnover rate for:
   (1) Receivables.
   (2) Inventories.
   (3) Trade payables.
(c) Identify and briefly describe those relationships and trends which Seymour Cleerly overlooked or misinterpreted. Organize your answer under the headings:
   (1) Revenue and Profitability Characteristics.
   (2) Fixed Charge Coverages.
   (3) Capital Structure.
   (4) Liquidity.

(CFA adapted)

BEE-TEE-U CORPORATION
Selected Financial Data
(dollars in thousands)

	Pre-loan period					Post-loan period	
	1972	1973	1974	1975	1976	1977	1978
Net Sales	$2,530	$3,642	$6,162	$8,327	$9,637	$10,285	$14,303
Cost of goods sold	1,701	2,419	3,899	5,213	5,951	6,774	9,036
Debt interest expense	24	33	51	139	234	281	379
Interest component of leases (no plants owned)	6	9	36	36	36	37	53
Pretax income	283	365	647	728	702	375	970
Pretax margin (%)	11.2%	10.0%	10.5%	8.7%	7.3%	3.6%	6.8%
Net income	$ 186	$ 256	$ 448	$ 450	$ 407	$ 248	$ 629
Net margin (%)	7.4%	7.0%	7.3%	5.4%	4.2%	2.4%	4.4%
Fixed charge coverage		9.7X	8.4X	5.2X		2.2X	3.2X
Return on total assets	15.2%	16.2%	17.7%	12.2%	8.7%	4.0%	7.7%
Long-term debt:							
5.00% subordinated debentures	$ 442	$ 315	$ 227	$ 147	$ 50	$ 50	$ —
10.25% senior notes	—	—	—	—	—	$ 1,500	$ 1,350
Common stock and surplus	$ 501	757	1,205	1,448	1,855	2,103	2,732
Total capital	943	$1,072	$1,432	$1,595	$1,905	$ 3,653	$ 4,082
Total assets	1,350	$1,819	$3,254	$4,097	$5,224	$ 7,192	$ 9,137
Receivables	631	$ 813	$1,320	$1,208	$1,598	$ 2,788	$ 3,528
Inventories (FIFO method)	545	$ 809	$1,461	$2,130	$2,670	$ 3,137	$ 3,824
Notes payable to banks	-0-	$ 166	700	911	1,625	1,290	$ 1,916
Trade payables	88	$ 200	$ 233	$ 257	$ 499	$ 706	$ 1,347
Net working capital	825	$ 954	$1,234	$1,230	$1,262	$ 2,978	$ 3,517
Current ratio	3.1	2.3	1.7	1.5	1.4	1.9	1.7
Receivables turnover*	4.8X	5.0X	5.8X	6.6X	6.9X		4.5X
Inventory turnover	3.4X	3.6X	3.4X	2.9X	2.5X		2.6X
Trade payables turnover	28.8X	16.8X	18.0X	21.3X	15.7X		8.8X

* Customary industry credit terms are net 60 days.

23–6. As the CPA responsible for an "opinion" audit engagement, you are requested by the client to organize the work to provide him at the earliest possible date with some key ratios based on the final figures appearing on the comparative financial statements. This information is to be used to convince creditors that the client business is solvent and to support the use of going-concern valuation procedures in the financial statements. The client wishes to save time by concentrating on only these key data.

The data requested and the computations taken from the financial statements follow:

	Last year	This year
Current ratio	2.0:1	2.5:1
Quick (acid-test) ratio	1.2:1	.7:1
Property, plant, and equipment to owners' equity	2.3:1	2.6:1
Sales to owners' equity	2.8:1	2.5:1
Net income	Down 10%	Up 30%
Earnings per common share	$2.40	$3.12
Book value per common share	Up 8%	Up 5%

Required:

a. The client asks that you prepare a list of brief comments stating how each of these items supports the solvency and going-concern potential of his business. He wishes to use these comments to support his presentation of data to his creditors. You are to prepare the comments as requested, giving the implications and the limitations of each item separately and then the collective inference one may draw from them about the client's solvency and going-concern potential.

b. Having done as the client requested in part *(a),* prepare a brief listing of additional ratio-analysis-type data for this client which you think his creditors are going to ask for to supplement the data provided in part *(a).* Explain why you think the additional data will be helpful to these creditors in evaluating this client's solvency.

c. What warnings should you offer these creditors about the limitations of ratio analysis for the purpose stated here?

(AICPA)

23–7.   REVIEW PROBLEM
The following are the financial statements of Gama Corporation:

GAMA CORPORATION
Consolidated Balance Sheets
as of December 31, 19x6, and 19x5
(in thousands)

	19x6	19x5
Assets		
Current assets:		
Cash	$ 2,000	$ 2,000
Receivables	25,000	20,000
Inventories (Notes 1 and 2)	56,000	38,000
Prepaid expenses	1,000	1,000
Total current assets	84,000	61,000
Investment in associated company	14,000	11,000
Property, plant, and equipment	61,000	52,000
Less: Accumulated depreciation	23,000	19,000
Net property, plant, and equipment	38,000	33,000
Goodwill	2,000	—
Total assets	$138,000	$105,000
Liabilities and Stockholders' Equity		
Current liabilities:		
Notes payable to banks	$ 16,000	$ 14,000
Accounts payable and accruals	29,000	23,000
Income taxes payable	7,000	2,000
Current portion of long-term debt (Note 6)	2,000	1,000
Total current liabilities	54,000	40,000
Long-term debt due after one year (Note 6)	25,000	15,200
Deferred income taxes (Note 5)	3,600	2,000
Minority interest	1,400	800
Stockholders' equity (Note 7):		
Common stock, $5 par value	5,500	5,000
Paid-in capital	24,500	15,000
Retained earnings	24,000	27,000
Total stockholders' equity	54,000	47,000
Total liabilities and stockholders' equity	$138,000	$105,000

GAMA CORPORATION
Consolidated Statement of Income
For the Years Ended December 31, 19x6, and 19x5
(in thousands)

	19x6	*19x5*
Net sales	$186,000	$155,000
Equity in income (loss of associated companies)	2,000	(1,000)
Expenses:		
Cost of sales	120,000	99,000
Selling and administration	37,000	33,000
Interest expense	10,000	6,000
Total expenses	167,000	138,000
	21,000	16,000
Income tax expense (Note 5)	10,000	7,800
	11,000	8,200
Minority interest	200	—
Income from continuing operations	10,800	8,200
Discontinued operations (Note 4):		
Operations, net of tax	(1,100)	(1,200)
Loss on disposal, net of tax	(700)	—
Total	(1,800)	(1,200)
	9,000	7,000
Cumulative effect of change in accounting,		
net of tax (Note 1)	1,000	—
Net income	$ 10,000	$ 7,000
Pro forma income (assuming the effect of change in		
accounting is applied retroactively):		
Income from continuing operations	$ 10,800	$ 8,500
Discontinued operations	(1,800)	(1,200)
Total	$ 9,000	$ 7,300

Earnings per share (information omitted).

GAMA CORPORATION
Consolidated Statement of Changes in Financial Position
For the Years Ended December 31, 19x6 and 19x5
(in thousands)

	19x6	19x5
Sources:		
Operations:		
Net income	$10,000	$ 7,000
Items not affecting working capital:		
Depreciation	6,000	4,000
Deferred income taxes	1,600	1,000
Minority interest	200	—
Undistributed income of associated		
companies	(1,400)	1,300
Loss on discontinued operations	1,000	—
From operations	17,400	13,300
Issuance of long-term debt	7,500	5,000
Proceeds from disposal of equipment	500	—
	25,400	18,300
Uses:		
Acquisition of ACR Company (exluding		
working capital of $4,200 acquired)		
(Note 3):		
Property, plant, and equipment	6,000	
Goodwill	2,000	
Long-term debt	(4,800)	
Minority interest	(400)	
	2,800	—
Additions to property, plant, and equipment	6,500	5,800
Investment in associated companies	1,600	—
Reduction in long-term debt	2,500	1,000
Dividends paid	3,000	2,000
	16,400	8,800
Increase in working capital	$ 9,000	$ 9,500
Increase (decrease) in working capital:		
Cash	$ —	$ 400
Receivables	5,000	2,400
Inventories	18,000	6,000
Prepaid expenses	—	200
Notes payable to bank	(2,000)	3,500
Accounts payable and accruals	(6,000)	(2,000)
Income taxes payable	(5,000)	(1,000)
Current portion of long-term debt	(1,000)	—
Increase in working capital	$ 9,000	$ 9,500

GAMA CORPORATION
Notes to Consolidated Financial Statements
For the Years Ended December 31, 19x6, and 19x5
(all amounts in thousands)

Note 1: Change in accounting principle

During 19x6, the company broadened its definition of overhead costs to be included in the determination of inventories to more properly match costs with revenues. The effect of the change in 19x6 was to increase income from continuing operations by $400. The adjustment of $1,000 (after reduction for income taxes of $1,000) for the cumulative effect for prior years is shown in the net income for 19x6.

The pro forma amounts show the effect of retroactive application of the revised inventory costing assuming that the new method had been in effect for all prior years.

Note 2: Inventories

Inventories are priced at cost (principally last-in, first-out [LIFO] method of determination) not in excess of replacement market. If the first-in, first-out (FIFO) method of inventory accounting had been used, inventories would have been $6,000 and $4,500 higher than reported at December 31, 19x6, and December 31, 19x5, respectively.

Note 3: Acquisition of ACR Company

Effective December 31, 19x6, the company purchased most of the outstanding common stock of ACR Company for $7,000 in cash. The excess of the acquisition cost over fair value of the net assets acquired, $2,000, will be amortized on a straight-line basis over a 40-year period.

The following unaudited supplemental pro forma information shows the condensed results of operations as though ACR Company had been acquired as of January 1, 19x5.

	19x6	*19x5*
Revenues	$205,000	$172,000
Net income	10,700	7,400

Note 4: Discontinued operations

As of October 31, 19x6, the board of directors adopted a plan authorizing the disposition of the assets and business of its wholly owned subsidiary, Shortlife Corporation. The "Loss on Disposal" is $700 (net of income tax credits of $700) and is based upon the estimated realizable value of the assets to be sold plus a provision for costs of $300 for operating the business until its expected disposition in early 19x7.

Property, plant, and equipment has been reduced by $1,000 and inventories were reduced by $100 to net realizable value. The provision for costs of $300 was included in "Accounts payable and accruals" and has been reduced to $200 at year-end.

Net sales of the operations to be discontinued were $18,000 in 19x6 and $23,000 in 19x5.

Note 5: Income taxes

The income tax expense consists of the following:

	19x6	19x5
Current	$ 8,400	$6,800
Deferred	1,600	1,000
Total	$10,000	$7,800

The effective tax rates of 47.6 percent and 48.8 percent for 19x6 and 19x5, respectively, differ from the statutory federal income tax rate of 50 percent* due to investment tax credits of $500 in 19x6 and $200 in 19x5.

Deferred taxes result from the use of accelerated depreciation methods for income tax reporting and the straight-line method for financial reporting.

Note 6: Long-term debt

	19x6	19x5
10% promissory notes to institutional investors payable in annual installments of $900 through 1990	$13,000	$13,900
Unsecured notes to banks—interest 1% over prime	4,000	—
Capitalized lease obligations—payable to 19x7 with an average interest rate of 8%	1,000	—
11% subordinated note payable in annual installments of $500 from 19x7 through 19x6	5,000	—
Other mortgages, notes, etc.	4,000	2,300
	27,000	16,200
Less current maturities	2,000	1,000
Total	$25,000	$15,200

The various loan agreements place certain restrictions on the corporation including the payment of cash dividends on common stock and require the maintenance of working capital, as defined, of not less than $18,000. Approximately $10,000 of retained earnings was available for payment of cash dividends on common stock at December 31, 19x6.

The corporation entered into several long-term noncancelable leases of equipment during 19x6 which have been capitalized for financial reporting. There are no other significant lease arrangements.

Note 7: Stockholders' equity

The corporation has 5 million shares of authorized common stock, par value $5. There were 1 million shares outstanding at December 31, 19x5, and this was increased by a 10 percent dividend payable in common stock during 19x6.

The changes in retained earnings are as follows:

* A 50 percent tax rate has been used throughout these financial statements for calculation convenience—the actual statutory rate was slightly lower.

	19x6	19x5
Beginning balance	$27,000	$22,000
Add net income	10,000	7,000
Less cash dividends	(3,000)	(2,000)
Less 10% stock dividend	(10,000)	—
Ending balance	$24,000	$27,000

Required (in thousands):
Support all conclusions! Identify specific accounts and amounts!

A. What caused the $7,000 increase during 19x6 in stockholders' equity?
B. Note 6 shows "capitalized lease obligations" of $1,000. What journal entry was made in 19x6 to record these leases *and* how are these leases reflected in the working capital statement?
C. How much long-term debt was paid during 19x6?
D. Note 1 describes a change in accounting principle.
    (1) What effect did this change in accounting have on the December 31, 19x6, balance sheet *and* the 19x6 income statement?
    (2) Describe how the 19x5 balance sheet *and* 19x5 income statement should be changed for *analytical* purposes to make 19x5 comparable to 19x6.
    (3) How would the $1,000 "cumulative effect" for 19x6 be shown in a statement of changes in financial position using the *cash* format with an "inflow-outflow" explanation of cash from operations? Your description must be clear enough that someone else could prepare a cash statement using your description. (You will need to show some figures.) *Hint:* Remember to start by reconstructing the journal entry to record the $1,000.
E. Note 3 describes the acquisition of ACR Company.
    (1) Is ACR a separate legal entity at December 31, 19x6, or has it been dissolved into Gama Corporation?
    (2) What effect did the acquisition of ACR Company have at December 31, 19x6 (date of acquisition) on:
        (i) Gama Corporation balance sheet?
        (ii) Consolidated balance sheet?
    (3) What were ACR's revenues for 19x6?
F. For the asset "investment in associated company":
    (1) Explain all changes during 19x6.
    (2) Identify all effects in the working capital statement which relate to this investment.
    (3) How much cash dividends were received by Gama during 19x6 from the associated company?
G. For the minority interest shown on the balance sheet:
    (1) Explain all changes during 19x6.
    (2) Show how this account relates to the asset "investment in associated company."
H. If the Fifo method of inventory valuation had been used (instead of Lifo), how much would 19x6 net income have been increased or decreased?
I. Note 4 describes "discontinued operations":
    (1) What journal entries were made on October 31, 19x6, to record the loss on disposal?

(2) What effect did the loss on disposal of $700 have on the working capital statement? (Identify specific items and amounts.)

(3) How should the discontinued operation of $(1,100) loss be shown in a statement of changes using the *cash* format with an "inflow-outflow" explanation of cash from operations?

J. How will "goodwill" be reflected in the 19x7 *(next year)* working capital statement?

K. Explain all changes during 19x6 in the *net* property, plant, and equipment account.

Note: For additional problems based on the financial statements of Gama, see Problems 13–21, 16–12, 18–10, 19–8, 21–12, and 21–13.

23–8.   Based on the financial statements of a company selected by your instructor, answer, as applicable, questions specified by him or her such as found in the preceding problem as well as in Problems 13–21, 16–12, 18–10, 19–8, 21–12 and 21–13.

23–9.   Select a company from a nonregulated industry for which you can obtain adequately informative financial statements for at least six years.

Required:

Based on the financial statements, background information on the company and its industry, as well as financial measures of other companies in the industry, prepare a *comprehensive analysis and report* covering the following specific points:

a. General (brief) description of the company and its industry.

b. An evaluation of the following areas:

(1) Short-term liquidity (current debt paying ability).

(2) Capital structure and long term solvency.

(3) Return on investment.

(4) Operating performance.

(5) Capital utilization.

c. Comment on the degree of informative disclosure, useful to the analyst, which was found in the financial statements examined.

d. In what way did alternative principles of accounting used in the financial statements affect the analytical measures used in this report?

You are expected to use a broad variety of financial analysis tools in your analysis and evaluation leading to a conclusion regarding the five areas detailed above.

Index

This book has been set VideoComp, in 10 and 9 point Times Roman, leaded 2 points. Part and chapter numbers are 96 point Onyx, chapter titles are 18/24 Bauer Classic Roman, and part titles are 24/26 Bauer Classic Roman. The size of the type page is 30 by 47½ picas.